W9-BGQ-999

THE CONCORD
DESK
ENCYCLOPEDIA

PRESENTED BY

Concord Reference Books, Inc.
New York 1982

The Concord Desk Encyclopedia

Copyright © 1982 by Concord Reference Books, Inc. No portion of this book may be reproduced in any form or by any means in whole or in part without written permission of the publisher. Reproduction for use in electronic data bases is also prohibited. Address all inquiries to the Rights and Permissions Department, Concord Reference Books, Inc., 135 W. 50th St., New York, N.Y. 10020.

Portions of this book were based on the University Desk Encyclopedia, Copyright © 1977 by Elsevier Publishing Projects S.A., Lausanne.

ISBN 0-940994-01-1

Library of Congress Catalog Card 81-71378

Manufactured in the U.S.A.

The Concord Desk Encyclopedia is published by Concord Reference Books, Inc., a subsidiary of Whitney Communications Corporation, 135 W. 50th St., New York, N.Y. 10020. (212) 307-1491. Kristin S. Loomis, President; Steven E. Spaeth, Vice President & General Manager.

The CONCORD——
A New and Different Encyclopedia

For the contemporary researcher, the CONCORD DESK ENCYCLOPEDIA offers a unique combination of strengths: first, basic coverage of all fields of knowledge appropriate for the student and the intelligent reader; second, up-to-date coverage of the contemporary world scene—politics, literature, science, art, film, sports—to an extent impossible for larger, more costly encyclopedias.

In no major encyclopedia, for example, is the reader likely to find articles on Bill Tilden *and* John McEnroe, Anwar Sadat *and* Hosni Mubarak, Space Exploration *and* Voyagers I and II, Computers *and* Electronic Games, Baseball *and* Baseball Strike, Economics *and* Supply-Side Economics, Fundamentalism *and* Moral Majority, Iran *and* Hostage Crisis.

The CONCORD DESK ENCYCLOPEDIA—concise, compact, up to date—contains over 18,000 articles and one million words. Location maps accompany the articles on 175 countries and 50 US states. Two 32-page color portfolios provide a world atlas and a series of instructive picture essays on the human body, the earth, and astronomy.

Entries and How They Are Listed

All entries are listed in alphabetical order. To find the entry you want, just look up its keyword, the word that appears in **bold type** at the beginning of each entry. The overall order is determined by everything that forms the main part of the keyword, whether one word or more; this part is—with a few exceptions—in bold capitals. **ALEXANDER NEVSKY,** therefore, comes before **ALEXANDER THE GREAT.**

Sometimes the main part of the keyword is the same in two or more entries. In this case the entries are usually distinguished by a subsidiary part (not in capitals) after a comma: the initial letters *after* the comma will decide the order in which they come.

Where entries have no subsidiary keyword part to distinguish them, places—countries, states and cities, in that order—come before everything else. Places of the same name but in different countries appear in the alphabetical order of the country.

People come after places. Saints come before popes, followed by emperors and then kings. Kings with the same name are placed in the alphabetical order of their countries.

Keywords appear in the form most familiar to the majority of readers. Well-known people are given the commonest form of their names; the full name is repeated in the following parentheses with birth and death dates. Where the keyword is a pseudonym the real name will appear either in this way or in the text if less well known.

Common abbreviations are rarely used as keywords. Instead, the full name is given, with the abbreviation following in parentheses. For instance, you won't find **CIA** listed. Rather, you'll find **CENTRAL INTELLIGENCE AGENCY (CIA).**

Subheadings and Cross-References

Bold type is used not only for keywords but also for subheadings. These normally indicate the divisions of longer entries, breaking them up to make the information easier to find. They also give alternative names for the keywords, or titles of subsidiary entries.

Sometimes, so you can spot them at a glance, subheadings are used for important people, members of a family forming the subject of an entry, or concepts within entries—that is, subjects that might otherwise appear as entries in their own right in a larger encyclopedia.

A sophisticated system of cross-references has been used, so that each entry (like a building block) combines with others to enable you to follow up lines of interest and to gain a vision of the true dimensions of any particular subject. These cross-references, indicated by SMALL CAPITALS, reduce the amount of overlapping in different entries so that we have been able to give as much information as possible in the space.

Cross-references indicate entries that provide further relevant information, or that explain an unfamiliar term. They have been used selectively to enable the reader who follows them to glean the maximum information, thus making an index unnecessary. One-line cross-references guide you to where the information has been placed. Those at the end of an article (after "see" or "see also") lead on to related topics.

Abbreviations

A – ampere
A – mass number
Å – angstrom unit
AC – alternating current
AD – *anno domini* (in the year of our Lord)
AF – audio frequency
AFL-CIO – American Federation of Labor–Congress of Industrial Organizations
Ala. – Alabama
AM – amplitude modulation
ANZAC – Australian and New Zealand Army Corps
AP – Associated Press
ARC – American Red Cross
Ariz. – Arizona
Ark. – Arkansas
atm – atmosphere
AU – astronomical unit
AW – atomic weight

b. – born
BC – before Christ
Btu – British thermal unit

C – coulomb
c – circa, centi-
C° – centigrade degree
°C – degrees Celsius
Cal. – California
cal – calorie
CENTO – Central Treaty Organization
CIA – Central Intelligence Agency
Col. – Colorado
Conn. – Connecticut
cos – cosine
cot – cotangent
CSA – Confederate States of America
csc – cosecant
cu ft – cubic foot
cwt – hundredweight

d. – died
dB – decibel
DC – direct current
Del. – Delaware
DST – Daylight Saving Time

e – electron charge, base of natural logarithms

EEC – European Economic Community
EEG – electro-encephalogram
EHF – extremely high frequency
°F – degrees Fahrenheit
FAO – Food and Agriculture Organization
FBI – Federal Bureau of Investigation
Fla. – Florida
FM – frequency modulation
ft – foot
G – universal constant of gravitation, giga-
g – gram
g – acceleration due to gravity
Ga. – Georgia
gal – gallon
GATT – General Agreement on Tariffs and Trade
GNP – gross national product
gr – grain
Gs – gauss

H – henry
h – Planck constant
HF – high frequency
HMS – His/Her Majesty's Ship
hp – horse power
Hz – hertz

Ia. – Iowa
Ida. – Idaho
i.e. – *id est* (that is)
Ill. – Illinois
IMF – International Monetary Fund
in – inch
Ind. – Indiana
IQ – intelligence quotient
IRA – Irish Republican Army

J – joule

K – kelvin
k – kilo-
Kan. – Kansas
kg – kilogram
KGB – *Komitet Gosudarstvennoye Bezopastnosti* (Committee for State Security)
kn – knot
Ky. – Kentucky

l – litre
La. – Louisiana
lb – pound
LF – low frequency
log – common logarithm

M – mega-
m – metre, milli-
Mass. – Massachusetts
mbar – millibar
Md. – Maryland
Me. – Maine
MF – medium frequency
mi – mile
Mich. – Michigan
min – minute (time)
Minn. – Minnesota
MIT – Massachusetts Institute of Technology

Mo. – Missouri
Mont. – Montana
mph – miles per hour
Mx – maxwell

N – newton
N – Avogadro number, neutron number
NAACP – National Association for the Advancement of Colored People
NASA – National Aeronautics and Space Administration
NATO – North Atlantic Treaty Organization
N.C. – North Carolina
N.D. – North Dakota
Neb. – Nebraska
Nev. – Nevada
N.H. – New Hampshire
N.J. – New Jersey
N.M. – New Mexico
N.Y. – New York

OECD – Organization for Economic Cooperation and Development
Okla. – Oklahoma
Ore. – Oregon

Pa. – Pennsylvania
pH – hydrogen ion concentration
pop – population
ppm – parts per million

R – röntgen
RAF – Royal Air Force
RCAF – Royal Canadian Air Force
R.I. – Rhode Island
rpm – revolutions per minute
RSFSR – Russian Soviet Federated Socialist Republic
RSV – Revised Standard Version (Bible)

s – second
sb – stilb

S.C. – South Carolina
S.D. – South Dakota
SEATO – Southeast Asia Treaty Organization
sec – secant
SHF – superhigh frequency
sin – sine
sq mi – square mile
SSR – Soviet Socialist Republic
St. – Saint

tan – tangent
Tenn. – Tennessee
Tex. – Texas

U. – University
UHF – ultrahigh frequency
UK – United Kingdom
UN – United Nations
UNESCO – United Nations Educational, Scientific and Cultural Organization
UNICEF – United Nations Children's Fund
US – United States
USAF – United States Air Force
USCG – United States Coast Guard
USN – United States Navy
USS – United States Ship
USSR – Union of Soviet Socialist Republics
Ut. – Utah

V – volt
v. – *versus* (against)
Va. – Virginia
VHF – very high frequency
Vt. – Vermont

W – watt
Wash. – Washington
Wb – weber
WHO – World Health Organization
Wis. – Wisconsin
W.Va. – West Virginia
WWI – World War I
WWII – World War II
Wyo. – Wyoming

Staff

Editor in Chief	Robert A. Rosenbaum
Executive Editors	Eleanor M. Gates
	Wesley F. Strombeck
Senior Editors	Walter Fox
Francis Bloch	Robert J. Quinlan
William B. Cummings	Patricia A. Rodriguez

Contributing Editors — Margaret Miner

Diane Barnard	Steven Moll
Arthur Biderman	Kelly Monaghan
Eugene Brown	Barbara H. Nelson
Mariana A. Fitzpatrick	Thomas D. O'Sullivan
Richard Foerster	Hugh Rawson
Sarah I. Fusfeld	Edwin E. Rosenblum
Murray Greene	Irina Rybacek
A. Tom Grunfeld	Diane Tasca
Ernest Hildebrande	Heidi Thaens
Joyce Kovalesk	Carol Ueland
Henry I. Kurtz	Edward J. Vernoff
Frank B. Latham	Kenneth D. Whitehead
Alan Lazar	Gerald M. Williams
Cynthia Lechan	Dan Woog
Carol Mankin	Donald Young

Managing Editor	John Berseth

Publisher	Kristin S. Loomis
Associate Publisher	Steven E. Spaeth
Production Manager	Frank Behrendt
Assistant Production Manager	Patricia B. Werner

THE
CONCORD
DESK ENCYCLOPEDIA

VOLUME ONE: A-E

A 1st letter of the English and of many other alphabets, derived from the Latin, Etruscan and Greek alphabets. The capital letter "A" is from the Greek *alpha*, which in turn came from an ancient North Semitic symbol. The small letter "a" came from the Roman. (See also ALPHABET.)

AACHEN (French: Aix-la-Chapelle), important West German industrial city in a coal region near the Belgian and Dutch borders. A spa since Roman times, it was the capital of the Frankish Emperor CHARLEMAGNE, who was founder of its famous cathedral which holds his tomb. Aachen was the coronation seat of the German Emperors until 1531, and site of two major European peace conferences (see AIX-LA-CHAPELLE, TREATIES OF). Pop 243,000.

AALTO, Alvar (1898–1976), Finnish architect and designer. His early buildings were functionalist (e.g., Toppila Mill at Oulu, 1930), as was his famous plywood furniture. But his later work, such as the dormitory at MASSACHUSETTS INSTITUTE OF TECHNOLOGY (MIT), Cambridge, Mass., 1947, emphasized natural materials and free forms.

AARDVARK (Afrikaans: earth pig), southern African burrowing mammal (*Orycteropus afer*) of the family Orycteropidae. A nocturnal animal, up to 2m (6ft) in length and weighing up to 70kg (150lb), the aardvark has a stout body with a plump, ratlike tail, elongated piglike snout, large ears and powerful limbs. It feeds on TERMITES, picking them out of their nests with its long, sticky tongue.

AARHUS, second-largest and second-oldest city in Denmark, a seaport and industrial center on Aarhus Bay on the E coast of Jutland. Pop 245,000.

AARON, Henry ("Hank," 1934–   ), US baseball player who broke Babe Ruth's record in 1974 with his 715th career home run. He retired in 1976 with 755 homers. Aaron, an outfielder with the Milwaukee and Atlanta Braves, also set a National League record with 2,297 runs batted in.

ABACUS, or counting frame, a simple calculating instrument still widely used in Asia. It comprises a wooden frame containing a series of parallel rods divided into upper and lower portions. The rods represent the powers of 10, with each of the five beads on their lower portion counting 1 and the two on their upper portion each counting 5. In the hands of a skilled operator it allows addition, subtraction, multiplication and division problems to be solved with great rapidity.

ABADAN, port in SW Iran, on Abadan Island in the Shatt-al-Arab delta, at the head of the Persian Gulf. An important oil-refining center and a petroleum pipeline terminus since 1909, despite damage sustained during the Iran-Iraq war of the early 1980s. Pop 296,081.

ABALONE, or earshell, any large saltwater mollusk of the genus *Haliotis*, native to warm seas throughout the world. The fleshy "body" of the abalone is edible and the MOTHER-OF-PEARL on the inside of the single flattened oval shell is commercially important. Family: Fissurellidae.

ABALONE ALLIANCE, antinuclear-power organization, based in Cal. In 1981 it targeted the Pacific Gas & Electric Co.'s Diablo Canyon nuclear plant near San Luis Obispo, Cal.

ABBASIDS, dynasty of Arab caliphs descended from Abbas, uncle of the Prophet MOHAMMED. They ruled the Islamic Arab empire, following the OMAYYADS, from 750 until overthrown by the Mongol HULAGU KHAN (grandson of Genghis Khan) in 1258. The Abbasids founded Baghdad (c762) as their capital and made it a center for the arts and sciences. The dynasty was at its most magnificent during the reigns of HARUN AL-RASHID (786–809) and his son al-Ma'mun (813–833).

ABBEVILLIAN, term for prehistoric cultural stage characterized by crude stone handaxes made c540,000–480,000 BC in the Pleistocene Ice Age and discovered near Abbeville in the Somme Valley, France. The term is rarely used today.

ABBEY, monastic community of 12 or more, led by an abbot or abbess. The first abbey in Western Europe was built in France c360 AD, but most later abbeys were inspired by the example of St. BENEDICT OF NURSIA, who founded Monte Cassino Abbey in S Italy in the 6th century and laid down the monastic rules of celibacy, poverty, obedience, work and prayer. The typical Benedictine abbey was built in a quadrangle with the church on the northern side, and with workshops, dormitories, kitchens and library opening onto it. Later abbeys, such as those of the CISTERCIANS, became more elaborate.

Abbeys were important centers of learning in medieval Europe. (See also MONASTERY.)

ABBEY THEATRE, Irish repertory theater founded by W. B. YEATS and Lady GREGORY in 1904, during the Irish literary revival. It fostered playwrights and actors such as J. M. SYNGE, Sean O'CASEY, Barry Fitzgerald and Siobhan McKenna. In 1924 it became the first state-subsidized, English-speaking theater.

ABBOTT, Berenice (1898–   ), US photographer who served an apprenticeship under Man RAY in Paris, 1921–29. There she collected the photographs of Eugène Atget. Her subject became New York City after her return to the US. Her books include *Changing New York* (1939) and *Greenwich Village Today and Yesterday* (1949).

ABBOTT, George (1887–   ), US playwright and director of comedies and musicals including *The Boys from Syracuse, Room Service, Pal Joey, Damn Yankees* and *Pajama Game*. He won a Pulitzer Prize (1960) for his musical *Fiorello!*

ABBOTT, Grace (1878–1939), US social worker who administered the first federal Child Labor Act (1917) and US Children's Bureau (1921–34).

ABBOTT AND COSTELLO, US comedians Bud Abbott (1895–1974) and Lou Costello (1906–1954), who formed a team (1931) and became the kings of slapstick comedy in vaudeville and on Broadway. Best known for their baseball routine, "Who's on First," they made a series of successful films in the 1940s.

A.B.C. POWERS, a loose entente between Argentina, Brazil and Chile, initiated in 1906 and taking its name from the countries' initials. The entente's mediation averted a US–Mexican war in 1915. Its aims were cooperation and mutual nonaggression, though a treaty signed by the three countries in May 1915 had little real effect.

ABD-EL-KRIM (1882–1963), Rif leader of Moroccan resistance to the Franco-Spanish protectorates. In 1921, after routing a Spanish army, he set up his own state. He surrendered to the French in 1926.

ABDUL HAMID, name of two Turkish sultans. **Abdul Hamid I** (1725–1789), succeeded in 1774. Turkey was weakened by the Treaty of Kuchuk Kainarji (1774) with Russia, by the forced cession of Bukovina to Austria (1775), and by continued foreign wars and internal revolt. **Abdul Hamid II** (1842–1918), succeeded in 1876. His war with Russia in 1877 resulted in Turkey's loss of many of her European territories. He was notorious for the bloody massacres of Armenians in 1894–96. In 1908, the Young Turks forced him to restore a parliamentary constitution, and he was deposed in 1909.

ABDUL-JABBAR, Kareem (born Lew Alcindor; 1947–   ), US basketball player. A 7ft, 2in center, he was six times the NBA's most valuable player and led the Milwaukee Bucks and Los Angeles Lakers to NBA championships. His UCLA teams completely dominated college basketball during his playing career (1967–69).

ABDULLAH IBN HUSSEIN (1882–1951), emir of Transjordan from 1921; king of Jordan from its independence in 1946. After the creation of Israel in 1948, he annexed most of the remainder of Palestine. He was assassinated by Arab extremists in 1951.

ABELARD, Peter (1079–1142), leading French Scholastic philosopher and teacher noted for his discussion of UNIVERSALS. His career was marked by controversy and by a famous love affair with Héloïse, one of his pupils. Following the birth of a child, Héloïse and Abelard married secretly, and in revenge Héloïse's uncle had Abelard castrated. After separating to take up monastic life, the couple exchanged a series of moving love letters. The church condemned Abelard's original teachings as heretical.

ABERDEEN AND TEMAIR, John Campbell Gordon, 1st Marquis of (1847–1934), lord lieutenant of Ireland (1886; 1906–15) and governor general of Canada (1893–98). During his term in Canada he governed an unsettled political scene, marked by sectional disputes, with considerable skill.

ABERHART, William (1878–1943), political leader and founder of the Canadian Social Credit Party. He was premier of Alberta from 1935 to 1943. His radical monetary policies were drastically modified by the federal government.

ABERNATHY, Rev. Ralph David (1926–   ), U.S. black civil rights leader and Baptist minister. In 1968 he succeeded the murdered Martin Luther KING as president of the Southern Christian Leadership Conference and led the "Poor People's March" on Washington, D.C., that year.

ABERRATION, Optical, the failure of a lens to form a perfect image of an object. The commonest types are chromatic aberration, where DISPERSION causes colored fringes to appear around the image; and spherical aberration, where blurring occurs because light from the outer parts of the lens is brought to a focus at a shorter distance from the lens than that passing through the center. Chromatic aberration can be reduced by using an ACHROMATIC LENS and spherical aberration by separating the elements of a compound lens.

ABERRATION OF LIGHT, in astronomy, a displacement between a star's observed and true position caused by the earth's motion about the sun and the finite nature of the velocity of light. The effect is similar to that observed by a man walking in the rain: though the rain is in fact falling vertically, because of his motion it appears to be falling at an angle. The maximum aberrational displacement is 20.5″ of arc; stars on the ECLIPTIC appear to move to and fro along a line of 41″; stars 90° from the ecliptic appear to trace out a circle of radius 20.5; and stars in intermediate positions ellipses of major axis 41″.

ABIDJAN, capital and chief port of Ivory Coast, W Africa. A major communications center, it also has such industries as canning, shipping, and the export of coffee, timber, pineapples and cocoa. Pop 900,000.

ABIOGENESIS. See SPONTANEOUS GENERATION.

ABOLITIONISM, movement in the US and other countries which aimed at the abolition of slavery. The *Liberator*, an antislavery paper edited by William Lloyd GARRISON, began publication in 1831, and in 1833 the American Anti-Slavery Society was founded in Philadelphia. Some abolitionists used their homes as "stations" for fugitive slaves on the UNDERGROUND RAILROAD, and the movement produced much literature, such as Harriet Beecher STOWE's novel *Uncle Tom's Cabin*. In 1840 the abolitionists split over the formation of a political party, and John BROWN's single-handed effort to free the slaves in 1859 was a failure. Increasingly a crucial political issue, abolitionism was a major factor in the outbreak of the Civil War. Lincoln's Emancipation Proclamation (1863) and the 13th Amendment (1865) completed the abolition of slavery in the US. William Wilberforce and others led the movement in Britain to abolish the slave trade (1807) and slavery (1833).

ABOMINABLE SNOWMAN, See YETI.

ABORTION, ending of PREGNANCY before the fetus is able to survive outside the womb. It can occur spontaneously (in which case it is often termed **miscarriage**) or it can be artificially induced. Spontaneous abortion may occur as a result of maternal or fetal disease and faulty implantation in the WOMB. Induction may be mechanical, chemical or using HORMONES, the maternal risk varying with fetal age, the method used

and the skill of the physician. In most countries, and until recently throughout the US, the practice was considered criminal unless the mother's life was at risk. In recent years, despite continuing moral controversy, abortion has become widely regarded as a means of BIRTH CONTROL.

ABORTION CONTROVERSY. Whether or not medically induced abortion is morally acceptable and/or should be legally permitted has been a subject of bitter controversy in many Western countries since at least the 1960s. In the US, legalization of abortion, backed especially by women's reform groups, made headway at the state level from 1967 and was legitimized by the US Supreme Court's decision in *Roe vs. Wade* in 1973 (see ROE VS. WADE). Nevertheless, various groups continued to oppose abortion, notably at first the Roman Catholic Church. By 1980, the antiabortion right-to-life movement in association with leaders of the New Right had become extremely powerful, claiming reasonably to have helped to elect 11 senators and President Ronald Reagan (see NEOCONSERVATISM). With 1.5 million women (including about 400,000 teenagers) annually seeking abortions, antiabortionists, numbering more than 10 million, succeeded in virtually eliminating public funding of abortion, and by 1981 they had rallied behind a proposed Constitutional amendment designed to override the Court's 1973 ruling (see EQUAL RIGHTS AMENDMENT).

ABOUKIR (also Abukir), Egyptian village on the Mediterranean coast between Alexandria and the Rosetta mouth of the Nile, on the site of ancient Canopus. The Battle of Aboukir Bay in 1798 saw the defeat of Napoleon's fleet by Nelson and marked the beginning of an Anglo-French rivalry in Egypt lasting until 1904.

ABRAHAM, biblical father of the Hebrew people, first of the patriarchs and regarded as the founder of JUDAISM. The Book of Genesis describes him as a descendant of Shem, and son of Terah, being born in UR of the Chaldees. He vowed to worship God and was promised that his people should inherit Canaan through his son ISAAC. However, as a test of faith and obedience, God commanded Abraham to slay Isaac. Abraham unquestioningly obeyed, and Isaac was spared. Through Abraham's faith a covenant of plenty and fecundity was established between God and the Israelites.

ABRAHAM, Karl (1877–1925), German psychoanalyst whose most important work concerned the development of the LIBIDO, particularly in infancy. He suggested that various PSYCHOSES should be interpreted in terms of the interruption of this development.

ABRAMOVITZ, Max (1908–   ), US architect who designed the interfaith chapel group (1955) at Brandeis U., the law school (1962) at Columbia U. and is best known as the architect of New York City's Philharmonic Hall at Lincoln Center (1962).

ABRAMS, General Creighton Williams (1914–1974), commander of US troops in Vietnam (1968–72) and US Army chief of staff (1972–74).

ABRASIVE, any material used to cut, grind or polish a softer material by ABRASION. Mild abrasives such as CHALK are incorporated in toothpaste, and others, SILICA, PUMICE or ALUMINUM oxide, are used in household cleansers; but various industrial applications demand even harder abrasives (see HARDNESS) such as CARBORUNDUM, BORAZON or DIAMOND. Some abrasives are used in solid blocks (as with knife-grinding stones), but **coated abrasives** such as sandpaper in which abrasive granules are stuck onto a carrier make more economic use of the material. **Sandblasting** exemplifies a third technique in which abrasive particles are thrown against the workpiece in a stream of compressed air or steam. Sandblasting is used for cleaning buildings and engraving glass.

ABREACTION. See CATHARSIS.

ABSCAM, short for "Abdul-scam," in turn referring to Abdul Enterprises, Ltd., a fake company used by undercover FBI agents in a 1979–80 investigation of political corruption that resulted in the convictions of one US senator, six US representatives and assorted local officials. Posing as wealthy Arabs or their representatives, the FBI agents secretly videotaped meetings at which they paid tens of thousands of dollars to the politicians in return for promises of special immigration legislation, government contracts and other favors. Federal officials convicted of the charges were Sen. Harrison Williams, Jr. (D., N.J.), Rep. John Murphy (D., N.Y.), Rep. John W. Jenrette, Jr. (D., S.C.), Rep. Frank Thompson, Jr. (D., N.J.), Rep. Michael Myers (D., Pa.), Rep. Raymond Lederer (D., Pa.) and Rep. Richard Kelly (R., Fla.).

ABSCISSION, in botany, the process whereby plants shed leaves, flowers and fruits. Controlled by plant HORMONES (abscisins) such as ABSCISIC ACID, leaf drop occurs in many plants through the formation of an intermediate **abscission layer** of cells which constricts sap flow to the leaf and is then broken.

ABSOLUTE, In philosophy the term refers to what is unconditional, noncontingent, self-existent or even arbitrary. In 19th-century IDEALISM, the Absolute (Idea) came to refer to the ultimate cosmic totality.

ABSOLUTE ZERO, the TEMPERATURE at which all substances have zero thermal ENERGY and thus, it is believed, the lowest possible temperature. Although many substances retain some nonthermal ZERO-POINT ENERGY at absolute zero, this cannot be eliminated and so the temperature cannot be reduced further. Originally conceived as the temperature at which an ideal GAS at constant pressure would contract to zero volume, absolute zero is of great significance in THERMODYNAMICS, and is used as the fixed point for the absolute or Kelvin (k) temperature scale. In practice the absolute zero temperature is unattainable, although temperatures within a few millionths of a KELVIN of it have been achieved in CRYOGENICS laboratories.

$$0°K = -273.16°C = -459.69°F$$

ABSOLUTION, theological term for the act of setting free from guilt, sin or ecclesiastical penalty. In Roman Catholic usage the priest, acting as Christ's intermediary, grants this remission through the oral confession of the penitent. Two of the acknowledged conditions for absolution are sincere contrition and a firm intention of personal amendment.

ABSOLUTISM, form of government in which all power is held by an unchecked ruler. Monarchies in the ancient world were usually absolute, but with the rise of FEUDALISM, the nobility often limited royal power. With the destruction of feudal rights opportunities for absolutism reappeared. In England the STUART attempt to rule by DIVINE RIGHT failed but in Europe, and especially France, absolutism flourished until the early 19th century. More sophisticated 20th-century forms such as NAZISM and COMMUNISM are better termed TOTALITARIANISM.

ABSTRACT ART, term applied to 20th-century paintings and sculptures which have no representational function. The precursors were CÉZANNE, SEURAT and GAUGUIN who believed that the formal elements of painting—color, line and composition—could be used expressively. FAUVISM and CUBISM developed these ideas. The first completely abstract works were painted by KANDINSKY and MONDRIAN in 1912. By 1914 Kandinsky's pictures were composed of regular non-representational forms, and color was used freely. In Paris, DELAUNAY, Kupka, and Morgan Russell developed the Orphist movement which influenced the German painter MARC. Mondrian and Van DOESBURG launched DE STIJL in Holland in 1917, which applied abstract theories to architecture and design, and affected British art. In Russia MALEVICH led the movement of SUPREMATISM and El LISSITZKY and Tatlin were involved in CONSTRUCTIVISM. Many abstract artists went to the US before WWII, where they developed the tradition.

ABSTRACT EXPRESSIONISM, American movement of ABSTRACT ART which explored the emotional, expressive power of non-figurative painting. The "action painter" Jackson POLLOCK stressed the creative act and dripped and spattered paint on the canvas. KLINE and DE KOONING are also considered abstract expressionists.

ABU BAKR (c573–634), the first Muslim caliph of Arabia in 632, following MOHAMMED'S death. He ordered incursions into Syria and Iraq, thus beginning the Muslim conquests. He was Mohammed's closest companion and adviser.

ABU DHABI, largest (25,000sq mi) sheikhdom of the UNITED ARAB EMIRATES, located on the southern side of the Persian Gulf; mostly desert, it has extensive oil deposits. Pop 235,662.

ABUJA, new city and future capital of Nigeria under construction in the centrally located Federal Capital Territory. It is scheduled to replace Lagos as the nation's capital in the early 1980s.

ABU SIMBEL, archaeological site of two temples commissioned by RAMSES II (13th century BC) on the west bank of the Nile 762mi south of Cairo. The Aswan High Dam construction threatened to submerge the site, but a UNESCO project, supported internationally, saved the temples by removing them and reconstructing them above the future waterline.

ABYDOS, Greek name for a religious center in Middle Egypt inhabited since the early dynastic period (3100–2686 BC) and connected with the god OSIRIS. It is noted for its tombs of early dynastic kings and its 19th-dynasty temple (c1300 BC).

ABYSSAL PLAIN, a large flat area of the OCEAN floor, lying usually between 4km and 6km below the surface. These plains, which together cover some 40% of the earth's surface, are formed of thick layers of mud and other sediments.

ABYSSINIA. See ETHIOPIA.

ABYSSINIAN CAT, slender breed of "foreign" type with long tail, almond-shaped eyes and pointed ears. Recognized in two colors: ruddy and red, both having a lighter belly. The Ruddy has a brick-red nose and black paw pads, in the Red both are pink. Each hair of the Abyssinian's coat has two or three distinct bands of black or dark brown on the ground color (known as "agouti" ricking). It has been claimed that the breed descends from cats of ancient Egypt but this has no basis in fact. The breed is intelligent and affectionate but may be unhappy if confined to an apartment.

ABZUG, Bella (1920–   ), US feminist and political leader. While serving as a Democratic congresswoman from New York City 1971–76, she became a prominent spokeswoman for the feminist and anti-Vietnam War movements. She was defeated in races for the US Senate 1976, the New York mayoralty 1977 and the US House 1978. Known for her flamboyant and abrasive style, she served as cochairwoman of the President's National Advisory Committee on Women 1977–79 until a disagreement with President CARTER forced her from the post.

ACACIA, a genus comprising about 800 species of mainly tropical and subtropical trees and shrubs. Feathery foliage and a mass of fragrant, golden-yellow flowers make many acacias popular garden plants. Other species yield gum arabic, TANNIN and wood. Family: Leguminosae.

ACADEMIC FREEDOM, the right of members of the academic community to freedom of thought and expression. Historically, it dates back to the Greek philosopher Socrates' attempt in 399 BC to have taught his pupils "to follow the argument wherever it may lead." In this century in the US the American Association of University Professors' code of conduct proposes complete freedom of research, but restricts classroom freedom to open discussion of the teacher's own subject. Despite this stand, scholastic immunity has been affected by Boards of Trustees, government agencies which fund some university projects, and student rebels who object to the politics or theories of certain professors.

ACADÉMIE FRANÇAISE (French Academy), a literary, linguistic society officially recognized in 1635. Membership is limited to 40, the so-called "Immortals," and includes prominent public men as well as literary figures. It has been criticized for electing individuals with personal influence, while often ignoring those with real merit. MOLIÈRE and ZOLA were never elected. Over the centuries, the Academy has produced the *Dictionnaire*, considered the official arbiter of the French language.

ACADEMY AWARDS, the annual awards ("Oscars") given by the Academy of

Motion Picture Arts and Sciences for outstanding achievement in various branches of film-making. The major awards are for best leading and supporting actor and actress, best direction, best screenplay and best film.

ACADIA, the name given to Nova Scotia and neighboring regions of New Brunswick, Prince Edward Island and parts of Quebec and Maine, by the French colonists who settled there starting in 1604. All but Prince Edward Island and Cape Breton passed under British control by the TREATY OF UTRECHT (1713). The French colonists, dispersed by the British in 1755, are the subject of LONGFELLOW's poem *Evangeline*. Those who went to Louisiana are the ancestors of the present-day CAJUNS.

ACCELERATORS, Particle, research tools used to accelerate electrically charged SUBATOMIC PARTICLES to high velocities. The resulting particle beams can be focused to interact with other particles or break up atomic nuclei in order to learn more about the fundamental nature of matter. Accelerators use electromagnetic fields to accelerate the particles in a straight line or in a circular or spiral path. The devices are rated according to the kinetic ENERGY they impart, which is measured in ELECTRON VOLTS (eV).

The first accelerator was designed by J. D. Cockcroft and E. T. S. Walton in 1932. It used a transformer, a hydrogen-gas discharge ion source and a simple evacuated tube to accelerate PROTONS to energies of 700 keV. At about the same time, R. J. Van de Graaff designed an advanced electrostatic generator that could achieve voltages as high as 3 MeV. The first **linear accelerator,** or linac, was built in 1928 by R. Wideröe. The largest linear accelerator yet in operation is a device 3.2km long at STANFORD UNIVERSITY, which can accelerate ELECTRONS to energies of 20 GeV. In linear accelerators, the particles pass through a series of electrodes that impart greater and greater velocities.

The first circular accelerator, the CYCLOTRON, was built by E. O. LAWRENCE in 1931. The particles—mainly protons or deuterons—were accelerated twice in each revolution, spiraling outward and eventually shot out toward a target. The relativistic (see RELATIVITY) gain in MASS of the particles tended to throw them out of PHASE with the acceleration pulses, however; the solution was the **synchrocyclotron,** or frequency-modulated cyclotron, which varies the acceleration frequencies to keep them in phase with the particles. The device was first suggested separately in 1945 by E.

M. MCMILLAN and V. I. Veksler; the largest synchrocyclotron today achieves energies of more than 700 MeV.

As still higher energies continued to be sought, the massive magnets needed to cover the whole spiral path of the particles became impractical. This problem was solved by the **synchrotron,** which guides the particles around a ring of magnets through a thin evacuated tube. As the particles continue to accelerate, the strengths of the magnetic fields are slowly increased in such a way that the size of the orbits remains constant. The first such devices used electrons, but most large synchrotrons today are proton accelerators. The first to pass the 1-GeV mark was the so-called Cosmotron of BROOKHAVEN NATIONAL LABORATORY, which began operating in 1952; the largest now operating is at the Fermi National Accelerator Laboratory in Batavia, Ill., which achieves energies in excess of 500 GeV. The latest accelerators are **colliding-beam** machines, in which positive and negative particles circle in opposite directions. The resulting head-on collisions yield much higher effective energies than collisions with stationary targets.

ACCLIMATIZATION, the process of adjustment that allows an individual organism to survive under changed conditions. In a hot, sunny climate man acclimatizes by eating less, drinking more and wearing lighter clothes; furthermore, his skin may darken. At higher altitudes he can adjust to the diminished oxygen by increased production of red blood corpuscles. (See also ADAPTATION.)

ACCORDION, small portable reed organ, used for jazz as well as folk music. Tuned metal reeds are set in vibration by air directed at them from the central bellows through valves operated by pianotype keys on the instrument's right. Buttons on the left produce chords. Although they were known in ancient China, the first modern accordions were built in the 1820s.

ACCOUNTING, the recording and analysis of financial transactions in order to reveal the financial position of an individual or firm. While the bookkeeper merely records transactions and makes no attempt at analysis, it is the accountant who analyses the data thus collected and produces balance sheets and income (or profit-and-loss) statements. On a balance sheet assets must balance liabilities. An income statement balances income against expenditure over a given period, recording any difference between them as a profit or loss, and is used to assess the performance of a firm. All such financial statements are audited, that is, checked for accuracy and fairness by independent accountants. The US professional body for accountants is the American Institute of Accountants, founded in 1916.

ACCRA, W African seaport on the Gulf of Guinea, capital of Ghana. The center of a rich cacao-producing district, it is now a major export harbor. Originally the capital of a Ga kingdom, the city grew up around several 17th century European forts and later became the terminus of a railroad into the interior. Pop 636,067.

ACE, Goodman (1899–) and **Jane Sherwood** (1904–1974), US husband and wife team who starred in the popular radio program "The Easy Aces" (1930–45); he played the role of the aggravated husband, she his malaprop-prone wife.

ACETYLENE, or ethyne (CHCH), the simplest ALKYNE; a colorless, flammable gas prepared by reaction of water and calcium carbide (or acetylide; see CARBON); it is a very weak ACID. Acetylene may explode when under pressure, so is stored dissolved in acetone. It is used in the oxyacetylene torch for cutting and WELDING metals, in lamps, and in the synthesis of ACETALDEHYDE, VINYL compounds, neoprene rubbers and various solvents and insecticides. MW 26.04 subl –84°C.

ACHAEANS, one of the four main ethnic groups of ancient Greece and traditionally victors in the TROJAN WAR (in HOMER synonymous with all Greeks). They may have entered northern Greece about 2000 BC and, moving south, created the Bronze Age civilization of MYCENAE. Other authorities believe they came to Greece only shortly before the DORIANS in the 12th century BC, dominating Mycenae only briefly before being displaced by the Dorians.

ACHESON, Dean Gooderham (1893–1971), US statesman who helped rebuild Europe's economic and military strength after WWII. He served Roosevelt and Truman in the State Department (1941–53), becoming secretary of state in 1949. After the war he promoted the recovery of Europe and worked to curb Soviet expansion by helping to formulate the TRUMAN DOCTRINE, MARSHALL PLAN and NATO.

ACHEULIAN, a lower Paleolithic (see STONE AGE) culture, prevalent about 430,000–130,000 years ago, whose remains were first discovered near St. Acheul (France). The type-tool is a flint hand ax.

ACHILLES, legendary Greek warrior of the TROJAN WAR, celebrated by HOMER. He was dipped in the STYX by his mother Thetis and made invulnerable except at the point on his heel by which she had held him. Joining in the Greek attack on Troy, he killed many men including the Trojan hero HECTOR (in revenge for the death of Achilles' friend Patroclus). Achilles was himself killed when the god APOLLO guided an arrow from the Trojan prince PARIS into his heel.

ACID, a substance capable of providing HYDROGEN ions (H+) for chemical reaction. In an important class of chemical reactions (acid-base reactions) a hydrogen ION (identical to the physicist's PROTON) is transferred from an acid to a BASE, this being defined as any substance which can accept hydrogen ions. The strength of an acid is a function of the availability of its acid protons (see pH). Free hydrogen ions are available only in SOLUTION where the minute proton is stabilized by association with a solvent molecule. In aqueous solution it exists as the hydronium ion (H_3O+).

Chemists use several different definitions of acids and bases simultaneously. In the Lewis theory, an alternative to the Brönsted-Lowr theory outlined above, species which can accept ELECTRON pairs from bases are defined as acids.

Many chemical reactions are speeded up in acid solution, giving rise to important industrial applications (acid-base CATALYSIS). Mineral acids including SULFURIC ACID, NITRIC ACID and HYDROCHLORIC ACID find widespread use in industry. Organic acids, which occur widely in nature, tend to be weaker. CARBOXYLIC ACIDS (including ACETIC ACID and OXALIC ACID) contain the acidic group –COOH; aromatic systems with attached hydroxyl group (PHENOLS) are often also acidic. AMINO ACIDS, constitutive of proteins, are essential components of all living systems.

ACIDOSIS, medical condition in which the acid-base balance in the blood PLASMA is disturbed in the direction of excess acidity, the pH falling below 7.35. It may cause deep-sighing breathing and drowsiness or coma. Respiratory acidosis, associated with lung disease, heart failure and central respiratory depression, results from underbreathing and a consequent buildup of plasma CARBON dioxide. Alternative metabolic causes include the ingestion of excess acids (as in ASPIRIN overdose), KETOSIS (resulting from malnutrition or diabetes), heavy alkali loss (as from a FISTULA) and the inability to excrete acid which occurs in some KIDNEY disorders. (See also ALKALOSIS.)

ACID RAIN, the popular name for the acidity from the atmosphere that is polluting lakes and streams near heavily populated areas, particularly in the northeastern US and southeastern Canada. It is also damaging to forests and farm lands. The acid comes from oxides of sulfur and nitrogen created by burning fossil fuels. Some Adirondack Mountain lakes are now so acid that fish cannot spawn. A great deal of acid pollution crosses the US–Canadian border, and the two countries have agreed to enforce antipollution regulations more vigorously and to form work groups to study air quality.

ACNE, a common pustular SKIN disease of the face and upper trunk, most prominent in ADOLESCENCE. BLACKHEADS become secondarily inflamed due either to local production of irritant FATTY ACIDS by BACTERIA or to bacterial infection itself. In severe cases, with secondary infection and picking of spots, scarring may occur. Acne may be aggravated by diet (chocolate and nuts being worst offenders), by HORMONE imbalance, by greasy skin or by poor hygiene. Methods of treatment include degreasing the skin, removing the blackheads, controlling diet or hormones, and exposure to ULTRAVIOLET RADIATION. TETRACYCLINES may be used to decrease fatty acid formation.

ACONCAGUA, snowcapped peak in the ANDES (22,834ft), the highest in the W Hemisphere. The summit is in NW Argentina, the W slopes in Chile. It was first climbed by E. A. Fitzgerald's expedition in 1897.

ACOUSTICS, the science of SOUND, dealing with its production, transmission and effects. Engineering acoustics deals with the design of sound-systems and their components, such as MICROPHONES, headphones and LOUDSPEAKERS; musical acoustics is concerned with the construction of musical instruments, and ULTRASONICS studies sounds having frequencies too high for men to hear them. Architectural acoustics gives design principles of rooms and buildings having optimum acoustic properties. This is particularly important for auditoriums, where the whole audience must be able to hear the speaker or performers clearly and without ECHOES. Also, the **reverberation time** (the time taken for the sound to decay to one millionth of its original intensity) must be matched to the intended uses of the hall; for speech it should be less than 1s; for chamber music between 1s and 2s; for larger scale works, from 2s to 3.5s. All this is achieved by attending to the geometry and furnishings of the hall and incorporating the appropriate sound-absorbing, diffusing and reflecting surfaces. **Anechoic chambers,** used for testing acoustic equipment, are completely surfaced with diffusing and absorbing materials so that reverberation is eliminated. **Noise insulation engineering** is a further increasingly important branch of acoustics.

ACROPOLIS (Greek: high city), the fortified hilltop site of an ancient Greek city. Such places eventually became sanctuaries for city gods and centers of religious ceremonies. Remains of their defenses and temples are known from the sites of many ancient Greek cities. The most famous is the Acropolis of ATHENS, with its Parthenon.

ACROSTIC, written composition where the initial or final letters (sometimes both) in successive lines spell a word or phrase. A popular verse form among the rhetoricians of antiquity, it appears now in literary puzzles.

ACRYLIC PAINTS (or polymer colors), ground pigments polymerized (combined) with an acrylic resin emulsion. They are easily mixed with water, dry rapidly, and are at least as permanent as OIL PAINTS, though generally flatter and less versatile. First developed in a somewhat different form by automobile manufacturers, they have become popular especially among "Sunday painters," who find them easier to handle than oils.

ACTH (Adrenocorticotrophic Hormone), or corticotropin, a HORMONE secreted by the PITUITARY GLAND which stimulates the secretion of various STEROID hormones from the cortex of the ADRENAL GLANDS. ACTH has been used in the treatment of a number of diseases including MULTIPLE SCLEROSIS.

ACTING. See MIME; MOTION PICTURES; STANISLAVSKY, CONSTANTIN; THEATER.

ACTION FRANÇAISE, French nationalist and anti-republican movement, formed in 1898 and led by Charles MAURRAS. Its newspaper *Action Française* (1908–44) advocated extreme rightwing monarchism. Although banned in 1936, the movement revived to make a pro-VICHY stand in WWII.

ACTION PAINTING. See ABSTRACT EXPRESSIONISM.

ACTIUM (now Akra Nikolaos), promontory on the W coast of Greece. A great sea battle was fought near it in 31 BC when Octavian's naval forces crushed those of Mark ANTONY and CLEOPATRA. Victory gave mastery of the Roman world to Octavian, later the first Roman emperor AUGUSTUS.

ACT OF SETTLEMENT, British parliamentary act of 1701 securing the succession of the Hanoverian line. It increased parliamentary control over the monarch, who was also required to belong to the Protestant CHURCH OF ENGLAND.

ACT OF UNION, four acts of the British parliament uniting England with Wales (1536), Scotland (1707) and Ireland (1801), and uniting Upper and Lower Canada (1840).

ACTON, John Emerich Edward Dalberg-Acton, 1st Baron (1834–1902), English Catholic historian and moralist, proponent of the Christian liberal ethic. He attacked nationalism, racism and authoritarianism and made the famous remark: "All power tends to corrupt, and absolute power corrupts absolutely." Lord Acton introduced German research methods into English history and launched the monumental *Cambridge Modern History*.

ACTORS STUDIO, the professional workshop for actors, established in New York City in 1947; Lee STRASBERG became director in 1948. The school's training, often called "the Method," is based on the teachings of Constantin STANISLAVSKI and stresses an actor's psychological interpretation of his role and emotional identification with the personality of the character he plays.

ACTS OF THE APOSTLES, fifth book of the New Testament, a unique history of the early Christian Church. Probably written between 60 and 90 AD by the Evangelist Luke, it is a continuation of St. Luke's Gospel and deals mainly with the deeds of the apostles, Peter and Paul. Events described include the descent of the Holy Spirit at PENTECOST, St. Stephen's martyrdom, and St. Paul's conversion, journeys and missionary work.

ACTUARY, a person who calculates insurance risks and premiums. Actuaries working for insurance organizations use statistics and mathematical probability to calculate policyholders' premiums and the cash reserves needed by insurers to meet possible claims.

ACUFF, Roy Claxton (1903–   ), US country music star. A founding member of the Smokey Mountain Boys (1939), he won enormous popularity by his earnest, emotional delivery of thousands of songs.

ACUPUNCTURE, an ancient Chinese medical practice in which fine needles are inserted into the body at specified points, used for relieving pain and in treating a variety of conditions including MALARIA and RHEUMATISM. It was formerly believed that this would correct the imbalance between the opposing forces of YIN AND YANG in the body which lay behind the symptoms of sickness. Although it is not yet understood how acupuncture works, it is still widely practiced in China and increasingly in the West, mainly as a form of ANESTHESIA.

ACUTE BRONCHITIS, often due to VIRUS infections, is accompanied by COUGH and FEVER and is short-lived; ANTIBIOTICS are only needed if there is bacterial infection. **Chronic bronchitis** is a more serious, often disabling and finally fatal disease. The main cause is SMOKING which irritates the LUNGS and causes overproduction of MUCUS. The CILIA fail, and sputum has to be coughed up. Bronchi thus become liable to recurrent bacterial infection, sometimes progressing to PNEUMONIA. Areas of lung become non-functional, and ultimately CYANOSIS and HEART failure may result. Treatment includes PHYSIOTHERAPY, antibiotics and bronchial dilator drugs. Stopping smoking limits damage and may improve early cases.

ADAM, first man and father of the human race, according to the Old Testament Book of Genesis. This tells how God made Adam (Hebrew for "man") from *adamah* (Hebrew for "dust") and Adam's wife Eve from one of his ribs. The tale of their temptation, fall and expulsion from Paradise is the basis of such Judaic and Christian concepts as grace, sin and divine retribution.

ADAM, Adolphe-Charles (1803–1856), French composer, best remembered for his ballet *Giselle* (1841). He also wrote operatic, religious and choral works.

ADAM, Robert (1728–1792) and **James** (1730–1794), Scottish architect brothers who developed the neoclassical "Adam style" in England. Robert's studies of ancient Roman architecture in Italy helped to inspire their joint designs of graceful and sumptuous buildings, interiors and furnishings which brought a new elegance to many town and country houses in Britain, the Continent and America.

ADAMOV, Arthur (1908–1970), French-Russian writer and leading figure in the avant-garde theater since the mid-1940s. He is best known for his plays *Ping-Pong* (1955) and *Paolo Paoli* (1957).

ADAMS, Abigail (1744–1818), wife of President John ADAMS and mother of President John Quincy ADAMS. Largely self-educated but highly intelligent, she wrote letters giving a lively account of contemporary American life.

ADAMS, Ansel (1902–   ), US photographer. One of the foremost nature photographers of the 20th century, Adams is known for his dramatic black and white photos celebrating the natural beauty of California's Sierra Nevada range and the

American Southwest. He pioneered in folio reproduction and wrote several instructional books.

ADAMS, Brooks (1848–1927), US historian, son of Charles Francis ADAMS, who saw economic history as a series of growth cycles. In 1900 he predicted that the US and Russia would be the only world powers in 1950, but that America's wealth would decline and her democratic tradition would be destroyed by uncontrolled private business.

ADAMS, Charles Francis (1807–1886), US diplomat and son of John Quincy ADAMS. He supported the new Republican Party after 1856 and, as minister to Britain (1861–68), helped to keep Britain neutral during the American Civil War. In 1871–72 he represented the US in the ALABAMA CLAIMS settlement.

ADAMS, Franklin Pierce (1881–1960), US newspaper columnist and radio commentator. A social critic and humorist, F.P.A. published his views in a witty, irreverent column ("The Conning Tower") that appeared successively, 1914–1941, in four New York papers. He also appeared on the popular radio show "Information Please" (1938–48).

ADAMS, Henry (Brooks) (1838–1918), major US historian, brother of Brooks ADAMS, whose history of the Jefferson and Madison administrations is a classic work. His other works include *Mont-Saint-Michel and Chartres* (1913), on the social and religious background of medieval culture, and his autobiography, *The Education of Henry Adams*, in which he attempted to show how ill-prepared his generation was for the technological society of the 20th century.

ADAMS, John (1735–1826), one of the leaders in America's struggle for independence and second president of the US (1797–1801).

Born at Braintree (now Quincy), Mass., he gained political prominence as one of the chief protesters against the STAMP ACT (1765). At the First Continental Congress called to protest against the INTOLERABLE ACTS of 1774 he helped draft a declaration of rights and a petition to the king. By then a major figure in colonial politics, at the Second Continental Congress he urged the creation of a Continental Army headed by George Washington, and later helped draft the DECLARATION OF INDEPENDENCE. In and after the REVOLUTIONARY WAR he served abroad as a diplomat (1777–88), gaining American support from France and Holland and helping to negotiate a peace treaty with Britain, to which he became the first American minister (1785–88).

Adams then began an active political career at home. As runner-up to Washington in the first two presidential elections he automatically became the nation's first vice-president (1789–96). When Washington retired, Adams was elected president in 1796, heading the new FEDERALIST PARTY favoring strong central government in opposition to the Republicans (later renamed Democrats) under Thomas Jefferson, who defeated his bid for re-election in 1800.

Adams soon faced major problems. His moderate federalism antagonized extreme Federalists including Alexander HAMILTON, who intrigued against him, especially when Adams refused to fight France over French seizures of American shipping in the Anglo-French conflict following the French Revolution. Instead, Adams sought peace with France, and (after the fiasco of the XYZ AFFAIR) secured a Franco-US treaty (1800)—but alienated Federalist supporters by not consulting Congress. He had already angered the pro-French Republicans by a seemingly autocratic distrust of popular democracy, and his (reluctant) involvement in the ALIEN AND SEDITION ACTS (1798) curbing criticism of Congress's military preparations against France.

Unpopularity lost Adams the election of 1800, but his policy of non-involvement had saved the country from what could have been a costly war. Adams was the first president to live in the White House in Washington.

ADAMS, John Quincy (1767–1848), sixth president of the US (1825–29) and sole example of a son following his father (John ADAMS) to the presidency. However, his main achievement, promoting national expansion, came while he was secretary of state.

Trained in law and educated in international affairs by his father, he held diplomatic posts abroad under George Washington, John Adams and James Monroe, becoming the first American ambassador to Russia (1809–14) and helped to negotiate the Treaty of GHENT (1814).

As Monroe's secretary of state (1817–25), he helped formulate the MONROE DOCTRINE, declaring US opposition to European involvement in the Americas (a cornerstone of future US foreign policy), and urged recognition of the emergent Latin American states. He negotiated the ADAMS-ONÍS TREATY with Spain (1819) for the purchase of Florida and fixed a border with Mexico to the Pacific Ocean, prerequisites for national expansion. He also helped to restrict British influence to N of the 49th parallel as far W as the Rockies.

Elected president in 1824, Adams had been an unpopular compromise choice and faced a hostile congressional coalition headed by Andrew JACKSON. Congressional opposition largely blocked Adams' ambitious schemes for national improvements including a national bank and university, new roads and canals, and protective tariffs. His main presidential achievement, completion of the ERIE CANAL, was offset by the passing of the unpopular "Tariff of Abominations" (1828).

Adams lost the 1828 election but went on (1831–48) to be the only ex-president to sit in the House of Representatives.

ADAMS, Maude (1872–1953), US actress famous around the turn of the century. She is best remembered for her leading roles in plays by James BARRIE, Edmond ROSTAND and SHAKESPEARE.

ADAMS, Samuel (1722–1803), American revolutionary leader and signer of the Declaration of Independence. His forceful oratory and inflammatory writings increased colonial discontent with British rule. Adams opposed the sugar and stamp acts, helped organize the BOSTON TEA PARTY, pioneered the COMMITTEES OF CORRESPONDENCE and urged independence at the First Continental Congress (1774). He served as governor of Mass. (1794–97).

ADAMS, Sherman (1899–   ), US politician, President Eisenhower's assistant 1953–58. He resigned on being widely criticized for taking gifts from an industrialist whose affairs were under government investigation.

ADAMS BRIDGE, line of shoals between Sri Lanka (Ceylon) and SE India; the reputed remains of a causeway by which the legendary hero RĀMA reached Ceylon to rescue his wife SĪTĀ.

ADAMS-ONÍS TREATY, also called the **Transcontinental Treaty**, US–Spanish agreement (1819) defining the western boundary of the US, negotiated by J. Q. ADAMS and the Spanish minister Onís. Spain ceded Florida to the US in return for the abandonment of US claims to Texas.

ADAPTATION, the process of modification of the form or functions of a part of an organism, to fit it for its environment and so to achieve efficiency in life and reproduction. Adaptation of individual organisms is called ACCLIMATIZATION, and is temporary since it involves ACQUIRED CHARACTERISTICS; the permanent adaptation of species arises from transmitted genetic variations preserved by NATURAL SELECTION (see also EVOLUTION). Successful and versatile adaptation in an organism usually leads to widespread distribution and long-term survival. Examples include the development of lungs in amphibians, and of wings in birds and insects. The term is sometimes also used for the modified forms of the organism.

ADAPTIVE RADIATION, a sequence of EVOLUTION in which an unspecialized group of organisms gives rise to various differentiated types adapted to specific modes of life. Early placental mammals, for example, gave rise to modern burrowing, climbing, flying, running and swimming forms.

ADDAMS, Charles (1912–   ), US cartoonist whose work features an endearing community of ghouls, vampires and goblins living in a dilapidated Victorian mansion. His macabre humor appeares regularly in the *New Yorker* (from 1935) and his characters came to life in a popular 1960s TV series, *The Addams Family*.

ADDAMS, Jane (1860–1935), American social reformer who pioneered the settlement house movement in the US. (See SOCIAL SETTLEMENTS.) With Ellen Gates Starr she founded Chicago's Hull House (1889) which provided social and cultural activities for poor European immigrants. She was its resident head until her death. An ardent pacifist, she became first president of the Women's International League for Peace and Freedom, and was co-winner, with Nicholas Murray BUTLER, of the 1931 Nobel Peace Prize.

ADDER, the European or Northern VIPER (*Vipera berus*), with a short, thick, brownish body and a dark zigzag pattern along its back. Its venom is dangerously toxic. Family: Viperidae.

ADDICTION. See DRUG ADDICTION.

ADDIS ABABA, capital of Ethiopia (since 1889) and of Shoa province, stands on an 8,000ft central plateau. It has the former imperial palace and government buildings; new hospitals, theaters and factories have been built since the 1950s. The city is the headquarters of the Organization of African Unity. Pop 1,125,340.

ADDISON, Joseph (1672–1719), English man of letters and public servant, whose witty, elegant style had a lasting effect on English prose. He wrote plays, poems, and, above all, essays dealing with the literature, life and manners of the day in *The Tatler* and *The Spectator* (which he founded with Sir Richard STEELE). He was secretary of state 1717–18.

ADDISON'S DISEASE, failure of STEROID

production by the ADRENAL GLAND cortex, first described by English physician **Thomas Addison** (1793–1860). Its features include brownish skin pigmentation, loss of appetite, nausea and vomiting, weakness, and malaise and faintness on standing. The stress associated with an infection or an operation can lead to sudden collapse. Autoimmune disease (see IMMUNITY), TUBERCULOSIS and disseminated CANCER may damage the adrenals and long-term steroid therapy may suppress normal production. Treatment is normally by steroid replacement.

ADE, George (1866–1944), American newspaper humorist and playwright whose *Fables in Slang* (1899) used colloquialisms and down-to-earth characters to poke fun at society.

ADELAIDE, capital of South Australia state, founded in 1836 and named for Queen Adelaide of Great Britain. A manufacturing and marketing center with about two-thirds of South Australia's population, Adelaide is known for its new (1977) Festival Center and biannual Festival of the Arts. Nearby Port Adelaide is the state's main shipping center. Met pop 933,500.

ADEN, seaport of the People's Democratic Republic of Yemen (Southern Yemen), on the Gulf of Aden. Under British rule (1839–1967) it became a coaling station for ships sailing between Europe and India via the Suez Canal. Although the city's importance as a port has declined, it is the country's industrial center, with an oil refinery. Pop 264,326.

ADEN, Gulf of, 550mi-long W arm of the Arabian Sea between Somalia and Southern Yemen, linked to the Red Sea by the narrow BAB EL-MANDEB. It is part of the Suez Canal–Indian Ocean sea route. The strategically important port of Aden commands traffic through the gulf.

ADENA CULTURE, Amerindian culture (c1000 BC–800 AD) which flourished in the middle Ohio R valley. Adena Indians grew corn, built circular houses and earthen burial mounds, made pottery, shaped stone and copper ornaments and traded widely.

ADENAUER, Konrad (1876–1967), first chancellor of West Germany (1949–63), who headed its spectacular postwar economic and financial recovery. A politician since before WWI, he was twice imprisoned by the Nazis. He became leader of the Christian Democratic Union party in 1947, and as chancellor made West Germany an integral part of W Europe, taking it into NATO and the European Common Market.

ADENOIDS, lymphoid tissue (see LYMPH)

draining the nose, situated at the back of the throat. They are normally largest in the first five years and by adult life have undergone ATROPHY. Excessive size resulting from repeated nasal infection may lead to mouthbreathing, middle-ear diseases, sinusitis and chest infection. If these are prominent or persistent complications, surgical removal of the adenoids may be needed.

ADHESION, the force of attraction between contacting surfaces of unlike substances, such as glue and wood or water and glass. Adhesion is due to intermolecular forces of the same kind as those causing COHESION. Thus the force depends on the nature of the materials, temperature and the pressure between the surfaces. A liquid in contact with a solid surface will "wet" it if the adhesive force is greater than the cohesive force within the liquid. (See also ADHESIVES; SOLDERING; SOLUTION.)

ADHESIVES, substances that bond surfaces to each other by mechanical ADHESION (the adhesive filling the pores of the substrate) and in some cases by chemical reaction. Thermoplastic adhesives (including most animal and vegetable glues) set on cooling or evaporation of the solvent. Thermosetting adhesives (including the epoxy resins) set on heating or when mixed with a catalyst. There are now many strong, long-lasting adhesives designed for use in such varied fields as electronics, medicine, house-building and bookbinding, and for bonding plastics, wood and rubber. (See also CEMENT, GLUE, SOLDERING.)

ADIGE, river in N Italy, the most important after the Po. Rising in the Alps and flowing through Trent and Verona, it enters the Adriatic Sea N of the Po delta. About 255mi long, it is navigable for 170mi.

ADIPOSE TISSUE, specialized fat-containing connective TISSUE, mainly lying under the skin and within the ABDOMEN, whose functions include FAT storage, energy release and insulation. In individuals its distribution varies with age, sex and OBESITY.

ADIRONDACK MOUNTAINS, range in NE N.Y., in Hamilton, Essex, Franklin and Clinton Counties, source of the Hudson R. Although often taken as part of the Appalachians, they are in fact structurally related to the Laurentian (Canadian) Shield. Mt Marcy (5,344ft) is the highest peak. Many scenic lakes and millions of acres of woodland (largely included in the Adirondack Forest Preserve) make the region a tourist and sportsman's paradise. Important resources include lumber, iron ore and graphite.

ADLER, Cyrus (1863–1940), US educator and Semitics scholar who founded the American Jewish Historical Society and wrote and edited several books on Jewish history and comparative religion. He was a founder of the American Jewish Committee (1906) and president of Dropsie College (1908–40) and of the Jewish Theological Seminary (1924–40) in New York City.

ADLER, Dankmar (1844–1900), German-born US architect and engineer, whose partnership with Louis SULLIVAN from 1881 helped to create the famous Chicago School of architecture. His first important work was the Chicago Central Music Hall (1879).

ADLER, Kurt Herbert (1905–   ), Austrian-US conductor and opera director. As general director of the San Francisco Opera from 1956 to 1981, he introduced numerous modern operas and outstanding foreign singers to the US.

ADLER, Mortimer (1902–   ), US philosopher and educator who spent his career popularizing the "great ideas" of Western civilization. At the U. of Chicago from 1930, he reorganized the curriculum to emphasize the classics and, with president Robert M. HUTCHINS, edited the 54-volume *Great Books of the Western World* (1952). He also was editorial consultant for the 20-volume *Annals of America* (1969) and planned the 15th edition of the *Encyclopedia Britannica* (1974).

ADMIRALTY ISLANDS, group of volcanic and coral islands in the W Pacific, in the W Bismarck Archipelago, part of Papua New Guinea. Discovered in 1616 by the Dutch navigator Schouten, they were claimed by Germany in 1884 and were under Australian administration 1914–75. Principal export is copra.

ADOLESCENCE, in humans, the transitional period between childhood and adulthood. The term has no precise biological meaning, but adolescence is generally considered to start with the onset of PUBERTY and to end at the age of about 20. In primitive societies the period is marked by RITES OF PASSAGE such as those at puberty and at MARRIAGE. These rites are less specifically defined in more sophisticated cultures. Adolescence is both a biological and social concept. In industrialized societies, where the economic dependence of youth is prolonged, it lasts longer and is generally characterized by behavioral patterns and stresses unknown or rare elsewhere.

ADONIS, in Greek myth, a beautiful youth fought over by APHRODITE and PERSEPHONE.

ZEUS decreed that he should spend the summer on earth with Aphrodite and the winter in the underworld with Persephone, thus symbolizing the cycle of the seasons. He is identified with the Middle Eastern vegetation god Tammuz.

ADRENAL GLANDS, or Suprarenal Glands, two ENDOCRINE GLANDS, one above each kidney. The inner portion (medulla) produces the hormones ADRENALINE and noradrenaline and is part of the autonomic NERVOUS SYSTEM. The outer portion (cortex), which is regulated by ACTH, produces a number of STEROID HORMONES which control sexual development and function, glucose metabolism and electrolyte balance. Adrenal cortex damage causes ADDISON'S DISEASE.

ADRENALINE, or Epinephrine, a HORMONE secreted by the ADRENAL GLANDS, together with smaller quantities of **Noradrenaline.** The nerve endings of the sympathetic NERVOUS SYSTEM also secrete both hormones, noradrenaline in greater quantities. They are similar chemically and in their pharmacological effects. These constitute the "fight or flight" response to stress situations: blood pressure is raised, smaller blood-vessels are constricted, heart rate is increased, METABOLISM is accelerated, and levels of blood glucose and FATTY ACIDS are raised. Adrenaline is used as a heart stimulant, and to treat serious acute ALLERGIES.

ADRIAN, name of six popes. **Adrian I** (d.795) was pope 772–95. He enlisted Charlemagne's help in crushing the Lombards and enlarging papal territories, condemned ADOPTIONISM and, through his legates at the second Council of NICAEA (787), joined in the condemnation of Iconoclasm. **Adrian IV** (c1100–1159), born Nicholas Breakspear, was the only English pope (1154–59). He died while preparing to lead a coalition of Italian forces against the Holy Roman Emperor Frederick I. **Adrian VI** (1459–1523) was the only Dutch pope. After his election in 1522 he attempted to correct abuses within the Church, but during his 20-month reign failed to check the advance of the Reformation.

ADRIAN (Gilbert Adrian Greenburgh; 1903–1959), US fashion and costume designer who helped to create Hollywood's glamor image in the 1930s and 1940s with his designs for Greta Garbo, Joan Crawford and Katharine Hepburn. The Adrian suit with padded shoulders became a fashion essential.

ADRIAN, Edgar Douglas. 1st Baron Adrian of Cambridge (1889–1977), English physiologist who shared the 1932 Nobel

Prize for Physiology or Medicine with Charles SHERRINGTON for work elucidating the functioning of the neurons of the NERVOUS SYSTEM.

ADRIANOPLE, Battle of, decisive victory of the VISIGOTHS and their allies, led by FRITIGERN, over the Romans in 378 AD. The Emperor VALENS and two-thirds of his army perished. THEODOSIUS I had to allow the Visigoth army to settle within the empire, opening the way for future barbarian inroads.

ADRIATIC SEA, arm of the Mediterranean, between Italy, and Yugoslavia and Albania. Along the Italian coast, which is straight and flat with shallow lagoons and marshes in the N, the chief ports include Venice, Ancona and Brindisi. At the head of the Adriatic on the Italian-Yugoslav border lies the port of Trieste. The indented Yugoslav coast is lined by the steep limestone cliffs and numerous islands of Dalmatia. Among the major ports are Rijeka, Split and Dubrovnik. On the marshy Albanian coast the main port is Durrës. The Adriatic coast extends for about 500mi with an average width of 110mi. The Straits of Otranto link it to the Ionian Sea to the S.

ADULT EDUCATION, learning undertaken by adults. It was at first an attempt to give people opportunities missed in youth. While this remains a major aim, adult education is now seen more as part of a continuing process. With improvements in formal education, the demand for adult education has increased. In America it started with the LYCEUM MOVEMENT, early in the 19th century. After the Civil War important advances were made by the CHAUTAUQUA MOVEMENT and in various federal AGRICULTURAL EDUCATION acts. During the Depression the WORKS PROJECTS ADMINISTRATION provided education programs for 2,000,000 adults, and after WWII came the G.I. BILL OF RIGHTS. In the 1960s federal funds provided for basic literacy programs under the Economic Opportunity Act.

ADVENT (from Latin *adventus*, coming or arrival), in the CHURCH YEAR, the season before Christmas. It includes four Sundays, starting from the Sunday nearest St. Andrew's Day (Nov. 30), and marks the beginning of the church year. Advent has been observed since the 6th century as a season of meditative preparation for Christmas and Christ's birth and second coming.

ADVENTISTS, Christian sects, mainly in the US, who believe in the imminent advent (SECOND COMING) of Christ. Adventism grew from the teachings of William MILLER, who announced the end of the world would come in 1843. After the failure of Miller's predictions new Adventist churches arose. The largest is the Seventh-day Adventists, formally organized in 1863. Its members observe Saturday as the Sabbath and support an extensive missionary program.

ADVERTISING, paid publicity designed to persuade people to buy a product or service or to adopt a viewpoint. Advertising started with storekeepers' signs, but modern advertisers include manufacturers, as well as political candidates and governments—using media ranging .from billboards to magazines, newspapers, radio and television. In the US advertising provides these media with most of their income and is very big business, accounting for no less than $20 billion a year, involving some 5,000 advertising offices and employing some 100,000 specialists backed by as many clerical and administrative personnel.

Most advertising material comes from advertising agencies which formulate advertising campaigns, buy the necessary time or space in the media chosen, and produce the actual advertisements. Large agencies also offer specialized market research and other facilities. Most agency earnings come from commissions deducted from the payments that clients make for the space or time bought.

Key agency staff include: the agency chief in overall charge; account executives providing liaison between the agency and its clients; copywriters writing the texts of advertisements and working with artists and layout men handling illustrations and typography; the space-buyer; the research department assessing market potential; and the traffic department supervising work flow.

AEGEAN CIVILIZATION, a collective term for the BRONZE AGE civilizations surrounding the Aegean Sea, usually extended to include the preceding STONE AGE cultures there. Early archaeological work in the area was performed in the 1870s–80s by Heinrich SCHLIEMANN, whose successes included the location of Troy, and early in this century by Sir Arthur EVANS. The Bronze Age cultures of the Aegean have been identified as follows: **Helladic,** the cultures of the Greek mainland, including subdivisions such as Macedonian; **Cycladic,** the cultures not only of the Cyclades but of all the Aegean Islands except Crete; and **Minoan,** the cultures of Crete, so named by Evans for MINOS, in legend the most powerful of Cretan kings. The Late Helladic cultures are often termed

Mycenaean.

Around 3000 BC the region was invaded by Chalcolithic (i.e. bronze- and stone-using) peoples, displacing the previous Neolithic inhabitants. This population appears to have remained static until around 2000 BC, when the Greek tribes arrived on the mainland, overpowering and submerging the previous cultures. Around the same time Crete established a powerful seafaring empire, and throughout the area there were rapid and substantial advances in the arts, technology and social organization. Around 1550 BC it would appear that the Mycenaeans occupied Crete, and certainly by this time the Greeks were established as the dominant culture in the area. The Cretan civilization seems to have been eclipsed about 1400 BC. During the 17th century BC there emerged on the mainland a wealthy and powerful aristocracy, whose riches have been discovered in many of their tombs. It would appear that for several hundred years there was a period of stability, since fortifications were not added to the aristocrats' palaces until the 13th century BC. The artistry of this era is exquisite, as evidenced by archaeological discoveries in the tombs: gold cups superbly wrought, small sculptures, jewelry, dagger blades inlaid with precious metals, and delicate frescoes. During the 13th century BC there probably was a war with Troy, ending with the destruction of that city around 1260 BC and a general decline of the civilizations as a whole into the so-called Dark Ages.

AEGEAN SEA, arm of the Mediterranean Sea between mainland Greece and Turkey. It is about 400mi long and 200mi wide and has numerous islands: among them the N and S SPORADES (including the DODECANESE) and CYCLADES groups; EUBOEA, LESBOS and SAMOTHRACE. Many of the islands are the peaks of submerged mountains. Almost all are Greek. Islanders live by farming, fishing and tourism. The Aegean civilization was the first in Europe, and the area became the heart of the Classical Greek world.

AEHRENTHAL, Count Alois Lexa von (1854–1912), Austro-Hungarian foreign minister (1906–12) who formally annexed BOSNIA AND HERZEGOVINA in 1908. This inflamed Slav opinion, eventually leading to WWI.

AENEAS, in Greek and Roman myth, a Trojan hero, son of APHRODITE and ANCHISES. He escaped from the fall of Troy to Carthage, where he lived with DIDO. At the gods' command he deserted her and went to Italy, where he founded Lavinium, legendary parent city of Rome. VERGIL'S *Aeneid* tells Aeneas' story to glorify the Emperor AUGUSTUS, reputedly his descendant.

AENEID. See AENEAS; VERGIL.

AEOLIAN HARP, stringed musical instrument played by the wind. Named for Aeolus, Greek god of the winds, it usually comprises 8–15 catgut strings stretched above a long, narrow wooden sound box and tuned in unison.

AERIAL PHOTOGRAPHY. See PHOTOGRAMMETRY.

AERODYNAMICS, the branch of physics dealing with the flow of air or other gas around a body in motion relative to it. Aerodynamic forces depend on the body's size, shape and velocity; and on the density, compressibility, VISCOSITY, temperature and pressure of the gas. At low velocities, flow around the body is streamlined or laminar, and causes low drag; at higher velocities TURBULENCE occurs, with fluctuating eddies, and drag is much greater. "Streamlined" objects, such as AIRFOILS, are designed to maintain laminar flow even at relatively high velocities. Pressure impulses radiate at the speed of SOUND ahead of the moving body; at SUPERSONIC velocities these impulses pile up, producing a shock wave—the "sonic boom" (see DOPPLER EFFECT). In AIRPLANE design all of these factors must be considered. In normal cruising flight all the forces acting on an airplane must balance. The lift provided by the wings must equal the aircraft's weight; the forward thrust of the engine must balance the forces of drag. Lift occurs because the wing's upper surface is more convex, and therefore longer, than the lower surface. Air must therefore travel faster past the upper surface than past the lower, which leads to reduced pressure above the wing. (See also WIND TUNNEL.)

AERONAUTICS, the technology of aircraft design, manufacture and performance. See AERODYNAMICS; AIR-CUSHION VEHICLE; AIRPLANE; AIRSHIP; BALLOON; FLIGHT, HISTORY OF; GLIDER; HELICOPTER.

AEROSOL, a suspension of small liquid or solid particles (0.1–100m diameter) in a gas. Examples include smoke (solid particles in air), FOG and CLOUDS. Aerosol particles can remain in suspension for hours, or even indefinitely. Commercial aerosol sprays are widely used for insecticides, air fresheners, paints, cosmetics, etc. (See also COLLOID; ATMOSPHERE.)

AEROSPACE MEDICINE. See SPACE MEDICINE.

AERTSEN, Pieter (c1508–1575), Dutch painter of finely-detailed still lifes and domestic interiors. He is regarded as one of the founders of GENRE painting in the Netherlands.

AESCHYLUS (c525–456 BC), earliest of the three great dramatists of ancient Greece, regarded as the "father of tragedy." Only 7 of at least 80 plays survive, including *The Persians*, *Prometheus Bound* and the *Oresteia*. The latter is a trilogy based on the murder of Agamemnon by his wife Clytemnestra, and the subsequent revenge by their son Orestes. Aeschylus elaborated Greek dramatic form by adding a second actor and exploiting the dramatic possibilities of dialogue. His tragedies develop a belief that worldly success may lead to pride, incurring the punishment of providence. His style is marked by a unique grandeur and richness.

AESCULAPIUS, the Roman god of healing and medicine. In Greek myth he was known as Asclepius (or Asklepios), the son of APOLLO and Coronis, and learned the art of healing from CHIRON the centaur. His symbol was a snake entwined around a staff.

AESOP, traditional Greek author of animal fables, said to have been a slave on 6th-century BC Samos. He may be a wholly legendary figure. Rooted in folklore, Aesop's fables acquired literary additions and influenced writers such as LA FONTAINE.

AESTHETICS, the study of the nature of art and beauty. The term, from the Greek *aisthesis* ("sense perception"), was coined in the 18th century, though philosophers have discussed art and beauty since PLATO and ARISTOTLE. Modern aesthetics, however, recognizes that not all art is necessarily beautiful in the classic sense.

Philosophers have differed as to whether there are objective formal criteria of artistic value, or whether these criteria are entirely subjective. KANT tried to reconcile the two approaches by arguing that subjective aesthetic judgments involve universal attributes of imagination and understanding. Particularly influential in modern times have been CROCE, who saw aesthetics as a matter of intuitive knowledge, and SANTAYANA, who argued that beauty lay in the pleasure experienced by the observer.

AFFIRMATIVE ACTION, any program or policy designed to increase the numbers of minority group members or of women in jobs or schools from which they were previously wholly or partly excluded. Affirmative action flourished in the 1960s under the leadership of Presidents Johnson and Kennedy, but under subsequent Republican administrations the program waned rapidly. Affirmative action was dealt a sharp blow in 1978, when the Supreme Court, in the BAKKE CASE, ruled against the use of strict racial quotas in affirmative-action programs.

AFGHAN HOUND, ancient breed of dog, introduced into the US in 1926. It is tall (25–27in; weight 50–60lb), has a long-haired silky coat, curved tail, and great speed and endurance. It was originally used for hunting.

Official name: Democratic Republic of Afghanistan
Capital: Kabul
Area: 250,000sq mi
Population: 22,000,000
Languages: Pushtu: Dari Persian
Religions: Muslim (Sunni)
Monetary unit(s): 1 Afghani = 100 puls

AFGHANISTAN, republic in Central Asia. It is a mountainous and rugged country, bisected by the mountains of the Hindu Kush, which form a major watershed. The main rivers are the Amu Darya (Oxus), Hari Rud, Kabul, Farah Rud and Helmand. Temperatures can range from 0°F in winter to 113°F in summer.

Economy and People. The economy is mainly pastoral and agricultural, and the chief exports are agricultural products. Though industrialization may be facilitated by further exploitation of natural gas deposits, the emphasis is still on craft industries. Manufactured goods, including machinery and petroleum products, are imported. There are no railways and few good roads. Strategically placed between the USSR, China, Kashmir, Pakistan and Iran, Afghanistan has received substantial development aid from the US and USSR.

The main cities are Kabul (the capital), Kandahar, Jalalabad and Herat. Most Afghans live a traditional, rural life; about 2.5 million are nomadic. Though elementary education is compulsory, 90% of the people are illiterate.

History. Conquered by Alexander the Great in 330 BC, Afghanistan retained elements of Greek culture as the kingdom of BACTRIA (c250–150 BC). After a brief period of Buddhist culture, the country fell to the Arabs in the 7th century AD, and

Islam became the dominant culture. Afghanistan was subsequently overwhelmed by Genghis Khán and Tamerlane, and from his base in Kabul, Babur (1483–1530) established the MOGUL EMPIRE in India.

Afghanistan became a united state in 1747 under AHMED SHAH, founder of the Durani dynasty. During the 19th century Britain and Russia contested influence over the country, but later Amanullah (ruled 1919–29) succeeded in wresting control of foreign policy from the British. He began modernizing Afghanistan, and proclaimed a monarchy in 1926. The last king, Mohammed Zahir Shah, ruled from 1933 to 1973, when he was overthrown in a coup led by Lt. Gen. Sardar Mohammed Daud Khan. The latter became president and prime minister of the new republic. Daud was overthrown in 1978 and a pro-Russian government installed under Noor Mohammed Taraki. A year later Hafizullah Amin overthrew Taraki only to be ousted himself three months later by Babrak Karmal. In Dec. 1979 100,000 Russian troops invaded and the country was swept by a raging civil war.

AFRICA, the world's second-largest continent 11,677,239sq mi in area, including offshore islands, or about 10% of the world's land area—a land of tropical forests, grasslands and deserts, famous for big game. It was perhaps man's first home, and was the cradle of the Negro peoples. Since the 1950s the new nations of Africa have seen great social and political change and have formed a new force in world politics while struggling to develop their often rich resources.

Land. Africa is a vast landmass straddling the equator and extending almost 5,000mi from N to S and 4,600mi from E to W. Only at the Suez isthmus does it touch another landmass (Asia). Except for the Atlas Mts which are structurally related to the mountains of Europe most of Africa is an ancient plateau that has been tilted and warped to form a number of basins (e.g. Congo Basin) in the N and W and highlands in the S and E. Africa's highest peak, Mt Kilimanjaro (19,340ft) is in Tanzania and the lowest point (436ft below sea level) is in Egypt. E Africa's GREAT RIFT VALLEY contains the world's second largest area of lakes. The Nile, Niger, Congo and Zambezi are major rivers. Coasts are smooth, lacking natural harbors.

Climate and Vegetation. W equatorial Africa is generally hot and rainy and supports dense rainforests, the home of gorillas, chimpanzees, monkeys and okapis.

N, S and E of these forests are tropical areas with alternating dry and rainy seasons. Their savanna grasslands are roamed by lions, giraffes, antelopes and zebras. N of the northern savannas and SW of the southern savannas lie great deserts including the SAHARA and KALAHARI. Extreme N and S Africa have Mediterranean-type climates with mild wet winters and warm dry summers. Tough-leaved olives, cork oaks, etc. survive the summer drought, and animals include porcupines in the N and the Cape buffalo in the S. Grasslands cover Africa's high mountain slopes, scoured by birds of prey. Crocodiles and hippopotamus live in lakes and rivers, where water birds include storks and flamingoes.

People. Some 70% of Africa's 424 million people are Negroes, but whites predominate N of the Sahara and include Berbers and Arabs. Whites and Negroes intermingle in Ethiopia and the Sahara. S of the Sahara live various Negro groups, Congo Forest pygmies, and (in the SW) the dwindling HOTTENTOTS and BUSHMEN. The S and SE also have large populations of European (mainly of Dutch and British) and Asian origins. Africa has around 50 major languages (spoken by more than 1 million) and as many as 2,000 lesser languages, excluding those established by Europeans. Islam, Christianity and animism are major religious forces. The population is fragmented by more than 50 national and numerous regional divisions. It is also changing rapidly as urbanization and modern ways disrupt traditional tribal life.

Economy. Outside the economically developed S and parts of the N, most African nations are part of the technologically developing Third World. Their agriculture mainly involves subsistence raising of millet, sorghum, maize (corn), cassava, etc., or nomadic cattle herding, and there are commercial tea, coffee, cocoa and citrus plantations geared to world markets. Africa provides one-twentieth of the world's minerals. These include gold and diamonds from South Africa, chrome and copper from Zimbabwe, uranium and copper from Zaire, oil from Nigeria, Libya and Algeria. Except in South Africa and the Mediterranean states, industrialization lags—mainly through insufficient capital, skilled labor and home markets, lack of a comprehensive rail or surfaced road network and other transportation problems. The continent mainly exports tropical crops and minerals, importing machinery and manufactured goods.

History. Fossil finds suggest that early man

may have evolved in E Africa. By 3,000 BC Egypt had one of the world's first civilizations and from the 9th century BC Phoenicians founded coastal colonies, later seized by Rome. In the 7th century AD Arabs overran N Africa and established trading contacts in the E. Powerful states developed S of the Sahara in the 8–15th centuries, but southern Africa remained unknown to Europe until the 1400s when Portugal explored and colonized its coasts. European trading posts and colonies were subsequently established along the coast, and in the 19th century European explorers probed interior Africa. By 1900 almost all Africa lay divided among colonial European powers (Great Britain, France, Belgium, Portugal, Spain, Italy, and Germany). Since 1960 most former colonies have become independent states.

AFRICAN LANGUAGES. More than 1,000 languages are spoken in Africa, many of them as different from one another as English is from Japanese. Systems of classifying these languages vary, however. In N Africa is the Hamito-Semitic, or Afroasiatic, family of languages; in the S are the Khoisan languages (which are click languages); and between them are at least two other language families: Nilo-Saharan and Congo-Kordofanian (including the Niger-Congo and Kordofanian groups). In the latter family is the important subfamily of Bantu languages. SWAHILI is a LINGUA FRANCA.

AFRICAN METHODIST EPISCOPAL CHURCH, Negro Protestant denomination akin to but separate from white Methodist denominations. Founded in Philadelphia (1816) by the Rev. Richard Allen, it is the largest Negro Methodist body, with 6,105 churches and 1,166,000 members.

AFRICAN METHODIST EPISCOPAL ZION CHURCH (The AME Zion Church), independent Negro Methodist denomination founded in New York City by blacks disaffected by white prejudices. They built a church in 1800 and formed the denomination in 1821. It has 940,000 members.

AFRIKAANS, an official language of South Africa. It evolved from the South Holland form of Dutch spoken by 17th-century BOER settlers, but incorporated Bantu, Hottentot, Malayo-Portuguese and English words.

AGA KHAN, spiritual leader of the Ismaili sect of SHI'ITE Muslims, an hereditary title. His millions of followers are dispersed through the Near East, India, Pakistan and parts of Africa, and are descended from 14th-century Hindus converted by Persian Ismailis. **Aga Khan I** (1800–1881), a Persian provincial governor who emigrated to India in 1840, was invested as leader of the sect in 1866. **Aga Khan II,** Ali Shah, held the title from 1881 until his death in 1885. **Aga Khan III,** Sultan Sir Mohammed Shah (1877–1957), spent much time in Europe and took an active part in international affairs. He represented British India at numerous conferences and as first president of the All-Indian Muslim League worked for Indian independence. **Aga Khan IV,** Prince Karim (1936–   ), inherited the title in 1957.

AGAMEMNON, in Greek legend, a son of ATREUS and king of Mycenae who organized the expedition against Troy recounted in Homer's ILIAD. Before setting sail he was forced to sacrifice his daughter IPHIGENIA, and was murdered on his return by his wife CLYTEMNESTRA and her lover, his cousin Aegisthus. His death was avenged by his son ORESTES and his daughter ELECTRA. These events are the subject of AESCHYLUS' trilogy, the *Oresteia.*

AGASSIZ, Jean Louis Rodolphe (1807–1873), Swiss-American naturalist, geologist and educator, who first proposed (1840) that large areas of the northern continents had been covered by ice sheets (see ICE AGE) in the geologically recent past. He is also noted for his studies of fishes. Becoming natural history professor at Harvard in 1848, he founded the Museum of Comparative Zoology there in 1859. On his death he was succeeded as its curator by his son, **Alexander Agassiz** (1835–1910).

AGASSIZ, Lake, a large prehistoric lake which covered parts of N.D., Minn., Manitoba, Ontario and Saskatchewan in the PLEISTOCENE epoch, named for Louis AGASSIZ. It was formed by the melting ice sheet as it retreated (see ICE AGE). When all the ice had melted, the lake drained northward, leaving fertile silt.

AGEE, James (1909–1955), US writer remarkable for his sensitive character studies and polished prose style. *Let Us Now Praise Famous Men* (1941) portrayed the life of the Alabama sharecropper. From 1943 to 1948 Agee was film critic of *The Nation,* after which he wrote several screenplays, including *The Quiet One* (1949) and *The African Queen* (1951). His partly autobiographical novel, *A Death in the Family* (1957), won a Pulitzer Prize in 1958.

AGENCY FOR INTERNATIONAL DEVELOPMENT (AID), US government agency formed in 1962 to administer foreign economic aid. It promotes long-range economic programs in developing countries by securing loans from private industry, guaranteeing investment abroad, and supporting certain international organizations. Its best-known program is the ALLIANCE FOR PROGRESS.

AGENT ORANGE, herbicide used by the US in the Vietnam War to defoliate the jungle. Agent Orange was contaminated with dioxin, a lethal poison, and its use had to be abandoned after Vietnamese women reported an extraordinary rise in birth defects. In postwar years, 60,000 veterans complained to the Veterans Administration that they had suffered lasting damage from Agent Orange poisoning, but they were refused compensation. In 1981, the Reagan administration revealed that on some 90 occasions Agent Orange had been dumped over or near US bases by US planes.

AGE OF REASON. See ENLIGHTENMENT, THE.

AGGLUTINATIVE LANGUAGES (from Latin *gluten*, glue), LANGUAGES (e.g. Turkish) in which words are formed by joining together groups of MORPHEMES (individual meaning elements), so that a single word may convey the sense of a complete English clause. Their words do not undergo INFLECTION.

AGINCOURT, village in NW France, scene of a decisive battle in the HUNDRED YEARS' WAR. On Oct. 25, 1415, English forces under HENRY V routed the French under Claude d'Albret, demonstrating the power of the English longbow over a heavily armored enemy. The French lost over 7,000 men, the English only a few hundred.

AGNEW, Spiro Theodore (1918–   ), U.S. political leader, who served as vice president (1969–73). Born in Baltimore, Md., the son of a Greek immigrant, Agnew received a law degree from Baltimore U. He was elected county executive of Baltimore (1962), and governor of Maryland (1966), and gained a reputation as a moderate liberal, though he later took a conservative stand towards civil rights demonstrations and urban unrest. As vice-president, he was regarded as the Nixon administration's conservative spokesman on domestic issues. Agnew resigned in 1973 and pleaded no contest to a charge that he had failed to report income from payoffs by Maryland businessmen. He was fined $10,000.

AGNON, Shmuel Yosef (1888–1970), Israeli writer remembered for his penetrating and often introspective novels and stories of Jewish life in his native Galicia and in Palestine. In 1966 he shared the Nobel Prize for Literature for works which include *Bridal Canopy* (1937), *A Guest for the Night* (1938) and his greatest novel *The Day Before Yesterday* (1945).

AGNOSTICISM, doctrine that man cannot know about things beyond the realm of his experience, in particular about God. It is a skeptical reservation of judgment in the absence of proof rather than an explicit rejection of any divine order.

AGORA, the public square and marketplace of ancient Greek towns where civic and commercial meetings were held. Surrounded by colonnades and public buildings, it sometimes contained temples and statues of heroes. The famed Agora of Athens has been extensively excavated and reconstructed.

AGOSTINO DI DUCCIO (1418–1481?), Florentine sculptor famed for his subtle and delicate handling of marble. His finest works are the reliefs in ALBERTI's Tempio Malatestiano in Rimini and on the façade of S. Bernardino in Perugia.

AGRA, historic city in NE India, on the Jumna (Yamuna) R 110mi SE of New Delhi. It is the capital of the district of Agra in Uttar Pradesh state and an important military and commercial center. During the late 16th and early 17th centuries, Agra was the capital of the MOGUL EMPIRE; it still has several magnificent Mogul buildings, including the world-famous tomb, the TAJ MAHAL. Pop 594,858.

AGRARIAN REVOLUTION, advances in farming methods in 18th-century England and Western Europe in which three English agriculturists played an important part. Robert BAKEWELL sponsored scientific breeding of animals. Jethro TULL invented new agricultural machinery and imported root crops and clover from Europe. Charles, Viscount TOWNSHEND used these crops and another new arrival, artificial grasses, in his new "four-course" system of crop rotation. This eliminated the fallow year and supplied more fodder for the animals, which no longer had to be slaughtered in quantity before winter, leaving more meat and more manure for cereal crops. Higher profits motivated renewed enclosure of land, thus encouraging the urban drift of peasant farmers.

AGRIBUSINESS, agriculture developed with big-business techniques, including heavy capitalization, specialization of production and a company's control of several stages of the entire operation. Increasing involvement in agriculture by large US corporations, now a significant factor in the food economy worldwide, dates from the post-WWII era.

AGRICOLA, Georgius, Georg Bauer (1494–1555), German physician and scholar, "the father of mineralogy." His pioneering studies in geology, metallurgy and mining feature in his *De natura fossilium* (1546) and *De re metallica* (1556).

AGRICULTURAL ADJUSTMENT ADMINISTRATION (AAA), US NEW DEAL agency established in 1933 to reduce the output of staple crops and so raise prices. In 1936 the Supreme Court ruled as unconstitutional the AAA processing tax for regulating production as an infringement on the power of the states. A second Agricultural Adjustment Act (1938) virtually reestablished, with improvements, the old AAA program, and formulated the principle of the "ever-normal granary." (See also PARITY.)

AGRICULTURE, the science and practice of farming in the widest sense, including the production of crops of all types, the rearing of livestock and the care of the soil. Man's settled agricultural activities probably date back about 10,000 years. But the essential characteristic of true agriculture, the storing and sowing of seeds, did not develop until the Neolithic period (see STONE AGE). The practice probably originated in the highlands of the Near East and spread to the river valleys of Mesopotamia, Egypt and China. By the 4th or 5th millennium BC men were growing grain and keeping livestock, and using stone tools for chopping and digging the ground. Much of the agriculture was practiced by nomadic tribes, who moved from one place to another as soon as they had exhausted the fertility of the soil. As the density of population grew, and nomadic life became more difficult, more clearly defined agricultural systems arose. On these were based the great civilizations of antiquity.

Ancient Egypt possessed a highly productive agriculture owing to the fertility of the Nile valley, whose soil was perpetually replenished by the annual flooding of the river. The Egyptians were familiar with the principles of irrigation, crop rotation and livestock breeding. The Romans too were good farmers and several of their agricultural treatises make interesting reading. The medieval European farm economy rested on the MANORIAL SYSTEM. The usual method adopted was a three-field crop rotation, one field being sown with wheat or rye, the second with a combination of barley, oats, beans and peas, and the third being left fallow to recover its fertility. With the coming of the industrial revolution, farming underwent radical changes. The AGRARIAN REVOLUTION of the 18th and 19th centuries replaced the old village communities with individual farms and estates. Farming therefore became concentrated in fewer hands, and its output was geared to supplying food for the urban population and raw materials for the manufacturers.

The Indians of North America were agriculturalists long before the Europeans arrived. The first colonists inherited methods already established for growing corn, beans, pumpkins, tobacco and many other crops. The great expansion of farming to the west of the Appalachians began after the Revolution. A new type of agriculture developed, combining large tracts of land with relatively small amounts of labor and capital. During the 19th century America led the world in agricultural development. Many factors played a part in this: the transportation revolution, the invention of such new machines as MCCORMICK'S reaper, which opened up the prairies to wheat farmers, the introduction of artificial FERTILIZERS and the increase of specialization were all instrumental in raising the productivity of the farms.

Agriculture in most advanced countries is today marked by increasing specialization, with farmers tending to concentrate more and more on a particular line of production. This factor, together with the fall in the number of farm laborers, has led to a high degree of mechanization and produced great sophistication in agricultural techniques. Milking machinery, automated poultry farms, harvesting by combines, grain drying, and automatic potato planting and manure spreading are almost universal. Artificial insemination is commonly used as a means of improving cattle stock. Crops are selectively bred to improve yields and increase resistance to disease. Livestock are fattened in feedlots, weeds and pests are controlled by chemicals, and antibiotics are fed to farm animals to speed their growth.

AGRICULTURE, US Department of, executive department of the US government concerned with the promotion and regulation of agriculture. Established in 1862, the department today operates through research, credit extension, conservation, crop control, distribution and other programs.

AGRONOMY, the branch of agricultural science dealing with production of field crops and management of the SOIL. The agronomist studies crop diseases, selective breeding, crop rotation and climatic factors. He also tests and analyzes the soil, investigates SOIL EROSION and designs LAND RECLAMATION and IRRIGATION schemes.

AGUINALDO, Emilio (1869–1964), leader of the Philippine independence movement against both Spain (1896–99) and the US

(1899–1901). Used by the US to help capture the Philippines during the Spanish–American War (1898), he later led Filipino guerrilla warfare against US occupation and was finally captured in 1901. He withdrew from public life until WWII when, in 1942, he supported the Japanese occupation of the Philippines. Imprisoned by the US in 1945, he was granted an amnesty at the end of the war.

AHAD HA'AM (1856–1927), Hebrew pen name, meaning "one of the people," of Asher Ginzberg, Russian Hebrew writer and proponent of "spiritual Zionism." Opposed to political Zionism, he believed that a Jewish nation in Palestine was to be achieved through spiritual rebirth.

AHIDJO, Ahmadou (1924–   ), President of the Republic of Cameroun, which achieved independence from France under his leadership in 1960. He was elected to a fifth term in 1980.

AHMADABAD, city in NW India, capital of Gujarat state, on the Sabarmati R about 290mi N of Bombay. It is a railroad junction and a major trade center, particularly for cotton textiles. It is the site of many mosques and Jain temples. Founded in 1411, it flourished in the 16th century as a major city of Mogul India. Pop 1,588,378.

AHMED SHAH (c1723–1773), Afghan ruler who founded the Durani dynasty. Through several successful invasions of India he acquired a huge empire. Although unable to hold his empire together, he succeeded in strengthening and uniting Afghanistan, and is thus often thought of as founder of the modern nation.

AIDA, opera by Giuseppe VERDI, one of his most popular works ever since its first performance in Cairo, Egypt, in 1871. The famous aria "Celeste Aida" comes early in the opera, imposing special demands on the tenor who sings it.

AID TO DEPENDENT CHILDREN (ADC), program of federal and state aid to needy children and the families on which they are dependent. Aid varies from state to state, but the federal government contributes well over half the amount. Some 10,200,000 recipients were given a monthly average of about $93 each in 1979.

AIKEN, Conrad Potter (1889–1973), US writer, whose *Selected Poems* (1929) won a Pulitzer Prize. His often incisive critiques and essays on poetry were published in *A Reviewer's ABC* (1958). Other prose works include the novel *Great Circle* (1933) and his sensitive autobiography *Ushant* (1952).

AIKEN, Howard Hathaway (1900–1973), US mathematician and inventor whose team at IBM developed (1944) the 35-ton Mark I, the first large-scale computer and the forerunner of the modern-day digital computer. It was used by the US Navy during WWII.

AILEY, Alvin (1931–   ), US dancer and choreographer, pupil of Lester HORTON, with whom he made his debut in 1950. He began choreographing in 1953 and in 1958 formed his own company. *Blues Suite* (1958) and *Revelations* (1960) are among his most noted works.

AINU, the primitive hunting and fishing AUSTRALOID Japanese ABORIGINES. They are distinguished by stockiness, pale skins and profuse body hair, hence their frequent description as "the Hairy Ainu." Ainu speech, little used now, bears no relation to any other language. They are now few in number, many having been absorbed into ordinary Japanese society.

AIRBORNE WARNING AND CONTROL SYSTEM (AWACS), a modified Boeing 707 used for electronic surveillance within the US early warning screen. An AWACS, costing over $130 million, is equipped with a Westinghouse doppler-pulse radar system with a range of 250 miles at low altitude and 350 miles at high altitude. The position of all targets whether flying high or low and all or part of a battle area beneath the aircraft is displayed on nine onboard consoles. The AWACS' highly sophisticated IBM computers can track 400 aircraft simultaneously. After detecting and tracking enemy bombers and cruise missiles, an AWACS is designed to direct defensive actions. Fast-reaction computers, reliable communications and good low-level coverage are featured. AWACS can fly 11 hours unrefueled and 22 hours if refueled in flight by a tanker plane.

The Reagan's sale of three fully equipped AWACS to Saudi Arabia in 1981 to be used without US supervision sparked considerable controversy. Potential leakage of advanced technology techniques was measured against political and economic gain. The British Nimrod Airborne Early Warning Mark-3 plane, a converted Hawker Siddeley four-engine Comet airliner, is considered a competitive aircraft.

AIR CONDITIONING, the regulation of the temperature, humidity, circulation and composition of the air in a building, room or vehicle. In warm weather an air-conditioning plant, working like a refrigerator (see REFRIGERATION), cools, dehumidifies (see also DEHYDRATION) and filters the air. In colder weather it may be reversed to run as a HEAT PUMP.

The first commercial air-conditioning installation dates from 1902, when W. H. CARRIER designed a cooling and humidifying system for a New York printing plant. During the 1920s, motion-picture theaters and then office buildings, department stores and hospitals began to install air-conditioning equipment. After WWII, home units became available, resulting in the rapid growth of the industry manufacturing the equipment. Room air conditioners (window units) are the most widely used domestic equipment, though the installation of the more versatile central air-conditioning equipment (unitary equipment) is becoming more widespread.

AIRCRAFT CARRIER, the largest type of warship in the world. While early carriers had straight flight decks, modern vessels use angled decks for simultaneous takeoffs and landings. Planes are launched by steam catapults, and arresting cables are used to bring landing aircraft to a halt. Each carrier is equipped with anti-aircraft guns and missiles, and is protected by its own planes and sister ships. The US Navy's Forrestal class carriers are over 1,000ft long, weigh 75,000 tons when loaded, and can carry approximately 70 airplanes. The largest built so far is the US nuclear-powered carrier *Enterprise* (1,102ft), displacing almost 90,000 tons full load and able to run five years without refueling.

The first successful takeoff from a ship's deck was made in 1910, and aircraft carriers played a limited role in WWI. They emerged fully in WWII as a decisive factor in the Pacific campaign. Despite the development of long-range aircraft and vulnerability to nuclear attack, they remain a vital part of the US fleet.

AIR-CUSHION VEHICLE (ACV), or **Hovercraft,** a versatile marine, land or amphibious vehicle which supports its weight on a high-pressure air cushion maintained by a system of fans. Because this minimizes the friction between the craft and the ground, the auxiliary propulsion equipment can maintain speeds up to 100 knots, even over difficult surfaces. Although the air-cushion principle was rediscovered by the UK engineer Christopher Cockerell in the early 1950s, technical difficulties have so far limited the use of ACVs to military applications and ferry services on a few short sea crossings. **Ground-effect machines** (GEMs) are sometimes distinguished from ACVs as, like AIRPLANES, they derive most of their lift from their aerodynamic design and forward motion.

AIR DEFENSE, the means of detecting and intercepting enemy aircraft or missiles entering a country's airspace. The US Air Defense Command (ADC) relies on a chain of radar systems around the world including the Ballistic Missile Early Warning Systems (BMEWS), Distant Early Warning Line (DEW), Semi-Automatic Ground Environment (SAGE) and Over-the-Horizon radar (OTH). Their range has been significantly expanded by the Airborne Warning and Control System (AWACS) and the newly developed Over-the-Horizon Backscatter radar (OTHB). The Space Defense Center, located in the North American Air Defense Command (NORAD) in Cheyenne, Wyo., coordinates optical and electronic information about man-made satellites. But at present the only defense against an attack launched from space is a viable deterrent.

AIREDALE TERRIER, variety of dog originally bred for otter hunting in the Aire valley, Yorkshire, England. Airedales are large terriers, weighing 40–50lb, with short black and tan coats.

AIR FORCE, United States, a highly complex and sophisticated branch of the Department of Defense, which controls one of the largest accumulations of destructive power ever known. The United States Air Force employs about 560,000 units on active duty, flies some 115,000 aircraft, has total assets and equipment worth about 100 billion dollars and an annual budget of from 25 to 30 billion dollars. It deploys some of the most advanced aircraft in the world including the AWACS, an aircraft mounted radar system which provides ultramodern surveillance. Many of its more than 2,000 fighter attack planes, including the F-4 Phantoms, are capable of supersonic speeds. Its fleet of B-52 bombers can be armed with missiles and nuclear bombs. Reconnaissance craft like the SR-71 can reach speeds three times the speed of sound at 80,000 ft. The huge C-5A transport plane can carry 700 men, 16 trucks, or two battle tanks 5,000 mi without refueling. But the most powerful items of equipment, at least in terms of pure destructive potential, are nuclear missiles.

Air force personnel are organized into several different "commands." Among those responsible for the actual fighting are the Strategic Air Command (SAC), which is the long range bombardment and reconnaissance force, the Tactical Air Command (TAC), which supports land and sea forces in action, and the Military Airlift Command (MAC) which transports combat resources for mission requirements. Aerospace Defense Command (ADCOM) warns against attacks from a hostile force and provides the first line of defense. Other commands are devoted to communications and intelligence. There are also several training commands, such as the AIR FORCE ACADEMY, which ensure a steady flow of trained recruits.

AIR FORCE ACADEMY, US, national center which trains men to become officers in the US Air Force. Established in 1954, it is located at Colorado Springs, Col. Studies include basic and military sciences, aeronautic theory and airmanship, in addition to liberal arts. Graduates are awarded a BS degree and are commissioned as second-lieutenants in the Air Force.

AIR GUN, a weapon using compressed air to fire a dart or pellet with a maximum range of about 90m. The charge of air released on pressing the trigger is produced either by prior compression or instantaneously by releasing a spring-loaded piston. In the similar **gas gun,** a replaceable carbon dioxide reservoir provides several hundred charges.

AIR LAW, the law governing the use and status of air space. A body of international rules was first formulated at the Paris Convention of 1919 which established that all nations have the right to control their air space. The Chicago Convention of 1944 (Convention on International Civil Aviation) recognized the right of civil aircraft of the signatory states to fly across or land in each other's territories for non-commercial purposes (subject to certain limitations). Commercial scheduled air services are arranged bilaterally. The Convention established the International Civil Aviation Organization (ICAO), which formulates technical standards and codifies the law with respect to liability, property rights and criminal acts, including HIJACKING.

AIR NATIONAL GUARD, reserve force of the US Air Force including men in all the states and territories. Enlistment is voluntary, and the men are given short periods of paid training throughout the year, under the supervision of the Continental Air Command. Normally under state command, the guard may be activated by the federal government.

AIRPLANE, a powered heavier-than-air craft which obtains lift from the aerodynamic effect of the air rushing over its wings (see AERODYNAMICS). The typical airplane has a cigar-shaped fuselage which carries the pilot and payload; wings to provide lift; a power unit to provide forward thrust; stabilizers and a tail fin for controlling the plane in flight, and landing gear for supporting it on the ground. The plane is piloted using the throttle and the three basic control surfaces: the ELEVATORS on the stabilizers which determine "pitch" (whether the plane is climbing, diving or flying horizontally); the rudder on the tail fin which governs "yaw" (the rotation of the plane about a vertical axis), and the AILERONS on the wings which control "roll" (the rotation of the plane about the long axis through the fuselage). In turning the plane, both the rudder and the ailerons must be used to "bank" the plane into the turn. The airplane's control surfaces are operated by moving a control stick or steering column (elevators and ailerons) in conjunction with a pair of footpedals (rudder).

The pilot has many instruments to guide him. Chief among these are the air-speed indicator, altimeter, compass, fuel gauge and engine-monitoring instruments. Large modern aircraft also have flight directors, artificial horizons, course indicators, slip and turn indicators, instruments which interact with ground-based navigation systems and radar. In case any individual instrument fails, most are duplicated. (See also AIR TRANSPORTATION; FLIGHT, HISTORY OF.)

AIR POLLUTION, the contamination of the atmosphere by harmful vapors, AEROSOLS and dust particles, resulting principally from the activities of man but to a lesser extent from natural processes. Natural pollutants include pollen particles, saltwater spray, wind-blown dust and fine debris from volcanic eruptions. Most man-made pollution involves the products of COMBUSTION—smoke (from burning wood, coal, and oil in municipal, industrial and domestic furnaces); carbon monoxide and lead (from automobiles), and oxides of nitrogen and sulfur dioxide (mainly from burning coal)—though other industrial processes, crop-spraying and atmospheric nuclear explosions also contribute. Most air pollution arises in the urban environment, with a large portion of that coming from the AUTOMOBILE. **Pollution control** involves identifying the sources of contamination; developing improved or alternative technologies and sources of raw materials, and persuading industries and individuals to adopt these, if need be under the sanction of legislation. Automobile emission control is a key area for current research, exploring avenues such as the RECYCLING and thorough OXIDATION of exhaust gases; the production of lead-free GASOLINE, and the development of alternatives to the conventional INTERNAL COMBUSTION ENGINE. On the industrial front, flue-gas cleansing using catalytic conversion (see CATALYSIS) or centrifugal, water-spray or electrostatic precipitators is becoming increasingly widespread. The matching of smokestack design to local meteorological and topographic conditions is important for the efficient dispersal of remaining pollutants. Domestic pollution can be reduced by restricting the use of high-pollution fuels as in the UK's "smokeless zones." In the short term, the community must be prepared to pay the often high prices of such pollution-control measures, but bearing in mind the continuing economic rewards ensuing and the vital necessity of preserving the purity of the air we breathe, the sacrifice must be worthwhile. (See also POLLUTION).

AIR POWER, the military potential of aircraft and airborne weapons. The reality of air power has changed the basic concepts of strategy. In the past, armies were obliged to base their tactics not only on the time it took them to move forward against the enemy, but on the limitations imposed by natural barriers such as rivers, canals and mountain chains. Vulnerable points were bound to be strongly protected. Air power, operating almost unrestricted in three dimensions, with little concern for natural barriers, has made defense much more difficult. Between the two world wars, theorists such as the Italian Giulio Douhet and the US General William ("Billy") MITCHELL postulated that victory in a future war would be achieved only by using strategic bombing to destroy an enemy's industries, and possibly morale, before he had a chance to strike back. This strategy was employed too late in WWII to provide a real test of its effectiveness. Fear of escalation limited the use of air power in the Korean War, but the Vietnam War showed that bombing alone could not defeat unconventional forces operating in dense cover.

The aircraft used in these engagements were nonetheless terrifying weapons, even when compared with the already sophisticated planes of WWII. Some bombers can now fly 11,000mi from a base on one continent, bomb a target on another, and return to base. Modern fighters fly at supersonic speeds, have tremendous maneuverability and can carry missiles, either of an air-to-ground or air-to-air type. New laser-guided "smart" bombs have proved deadly accurate for strategic bombing. Reconnaissance aircraft equipped with high-resolution cameras are able to distinguish objects one foot apart from a height of 50,000ft. Helicopters have proved essential for transporting troops over dangerous or rugged terrain as well as for combat missions as evidenced in the Vietnam War. The Cruise missile, a pilotless aircraft, is slated for launching from B52s in 1982.

While manned aircraft still form the basis of air power, it is the intercontinental ballistic missile (ICBM) that now provides the principal means of carrying on strategic nuclear war. Orbiting weapons are technically possible and some are on the drawing boards. They could be developed in the absence of an arms-limitation agreement and assembled in and launched from space shuttles. Thus air power has now become aerospace power. (See also MISSILE.)

AIR PRESSURE. See ATMOSPHERE.

AIR-RAID SHELTER. See FALLOUT SHELTER.

AIR RIGHTS, rights to use of building space, especially over railroad tracks, highways, bridge and tunnel approaches and so on. Air rights were used in New York City over the New York Central track as early as 1910. As urban land grew scarcer in all big cities, such rights became increasingly valuable for housing developments and office construction.

AIRSHIP, or dirigible, a lighter-than-air, self-propelled aircraft whose buoyancy is provided by gasbags containing hydrogen or helium. The first successful airship was designed by Henri Giffard, a French engineer, and flew over Paris in 1852, though it was only with the development of the INTERNAL COMBUSTION ENGINE that the airship became truly practical. From 1900 Germany led the world in airship design, as Count Ferdinand von ZEPPELIN began to construct his famous "Zeppelins." Most of the large airships built during the next 40 years were of the "rigid" type, with a metal-lattice frame, and used hydrogen as the lifting gas. Their vulnerability in storms and a series of spectacular fire disasters brought an abrupt end to their use in about 1937. During WWII much use was made of small "nonrigid" patrol airships ("blimps") in which the gasbag formed the outer skin and altitude was controlled by inflating and venting air "ballonets" inside the main gas-bag. Most existing craft are of this type, with engines slung beneath the gasbag either on the cabin or in separate "nacelles." "Semi-rigid" airships are similar to blimps but, being larger, usually have a longitudinal metal keel. Airship enthusiasts envisage a great future for airships filled with nonflammable helium, noiselessly transporting freight right into the heart of large cities.

AIRSICKNESS. See MOTION SICKNESS.

AIR TRAFFIC CONTROLLERS ORGANIZATION, Professional (PATCO), 17,000-

member union of air traffic controllers, headed by Robert E. Poli, which went on strike Aug. 3, 1981. This was illegal since they were federal employees and, after a warning, President Ronald Reagan terminated the approximately 11,000 men who had stayed off the job. Thereafter, the Federal Labor Relations Authority stripped the union of its bargaining rights. Substitute controllers were found, and the airlines industry continued to function, although with fewer flights, some 5,000 fewer employees, and many flight delays.

AIR TURBULENCE, irregular eddying in the ATMOSPHERE, such as that encountered in gusts of wind. Turbulence disperses water vapor, dust, smoke and other pollutants through the atmosphere, and is important in transferring heat energy upward from the ground. There is little turbulence in the upper atmosphere except in developing thunderclouds. **Clear-air turbulence** (CAT), which is often found around the margins of JET STREAMS, can be hazardous to high-flying jet aircraft.

AISE, French nationalist and anti-republican movement, formed in 1898 and led by Charles MAURRAS. Its newspaper *Action Française* (1908–44) advocated extreme rightwing monarchism. Although banned in 1936, the movement revived to make a pro-VICHY stand in WWII.

AIX-LA-CHAPELLE, Congress of (1818), meeting at Aachen (Aix-la-Chapelle) at which the victors in the Napoleonic Wars—Great Britain, Austria, Prussia and Russia—agreed to preserve the political arrangements they had established for Europe at the Congress of Vienna (1815). It also confirmed the withdrawal of occupying troops from France, which was to be restored to the status of an independent major power and was to join the other powers in the Quintuple Alliance.

AIX-LA-CHAPELLE, Treaties of, name of two agreements. The first treaty (1668) ended the War of DEVOLUTION between France and the TRIPLE ALLIANCE of England, Holland and Sweden over France's claim to the Spanish Netherlands. It allowed France to retain most of the Flanders towns captured the previous year. The second treaty (1748) concluded the War of the AUSTRIAN SUCCESSION, in which several nations, led by France and Prussia, had tried to annex the vast territories held by the Empress Maria Theresa of Austria. By the terms of the treaty the empress's right to the Hapsburg throne was recognized, and Prussia gained the important region of Silesia.

AJACCIO, capital of the French island of Corsica in the Mediterranean, a port on the W coast. Celebrated as the birthplace of Napoleon, it is today a commercial center and popular resort. Industries include fishing and shipbuilding. Pop 50,700.

AKBAR (1542–1605), greatest of the MOGUL emperors, who extended Mogul power over most of Afghanistan and India. An excellent administrator, he pursued a policy of religious toleration and took an active interest in the study of religious sects. He also improved social laws, commerce and transportation.

AKELEY, Carl Ethan (1864–1926), American naturalist and sculptor of animals who pioneered large-scale museum displays of stuffed animals, especially African big game, in their natural habitats.

AKHENATON (or Ikhnaton), title taken by Amenhotep IV, king of Egypt c1379–1362 BC. Married to NEFERTITI, he started the cult of the sungod ATON, despite the opposition of the priesthood of Amon-Ra. Changing his name to Akhenaton ("he who serves Aton"), he moved the capital from Thebes, city of Amon, to Akhetaton (now Tell el-Amarna), where he fostered a naturalistic school of art and literature. After his death the old religion was reestablished and Akhenaton's name was erased from his monuments.

AKHMATOVA, Anna, pseudonym of Anna Andreyevna Gorenko (1888–1966), Russian poet who joined the reaction against Symbolist vagueness and obscurity. Her own poems, often confessional lyrics, are notable for clarity and formal precision.

AKIBA BEN JOSEPH (c40–135), famous Jewish rabbi, one of the greatest compilers of Hebrew law, whose work later formed the basis of the MISHNAH. After supporting a revolt against the Romans, he was executed as a rebel.

AKIHITO (1933–   ), crown prince of Japan, elder son of Emperor Hirohito and Empress Nagako Kuni. His marriage to a commoner, Michiko Shodo, in 1959 was followed in 1960 by the birth of a son and heir.

AKRON, industrial city in NE Ohio on the Cuyahoga R, seat of Summit Co., 36mi S of Cleveland. Akron is famed as the rubber and tire manufacturing capital of the world: B. F. Goodrich founded his pioneer rubber factory here in 1871. Other industries produce transportation equipment, metal products and plastics. Pop 237,177.

AKSAKOV, Sergei Timofeyevich (1791–1859), Russian writer, whose *Family Chronicle* (1846–56) and *Years of Childhood* (1858) combine the novel and memoir forms. He was a prominent member of the Slavophile movement, as were his writer sons Konstantin (1817–1860) and Ivan (1823–1886).

AKSUM (or Axum), town in Tigre province, N Ethiopia, capital of the Aksumite Empire, which included much of present-day Ethiopia and Sudan, from about the 1st to the 7th centuries AD. Aksum is the most sacred city of Ethiopia's Coptic Christians: the biblical Ark of the Covenant is said to be kept in the Church of St. Mary Zion. Gigantic carved stelae, as large as the obelisks of Egypt, stand as the most impressive achievements of Aksumite art. The city is now an agricultural market center.

AKUTAGAWA RYUNOSUKE (1892–1927), Japanese writer of short stories, poetry and plays. From medieval themes he turned to autobiographical subjects. His work's fantastic and morbid nature reveals susceptibilities which led to his suicide. His most famous story is *Rashomon* (1915).

Name of state: Alabama
Capital: Montgomery
Statehood: Dec. 14, 1819 (22nd state)
Familiar names: Cotton State, Yellowhammer State, the Heart of Dixie
Area: 51,609sq mi
Population: 3,890,061
Elevation: Highest—2,407ft, Cheaha Mountain. Lowest—sea level, Gulf of Mexico
Motto: Audemus jura nostra defendere ("We dare defend our rights.")
State flower: Camellia
State bird: Yellowhammer
State tree: Southern pine
State song: "Alabama"

ALABAMA, state, SE US, bounded to the E by Ga., to the S by Fla. and the Gulf of Mexico, to the W by Miss. and to the N by Tenn.

Land. NE Alabama runs into the SW end of the Appalachians. It includes the Cumberland Plateau, a series of forested mineral-rich ridges, and a section of the Piedmont region. The Black Belt, a narrow strip of prairie land, crosses the East Gulf Coastal Plain (drained by the Alabama,

Tombigbee and other rivers), which occupies most of the S two-thirds of the state. Climate is mild and moist.

People. About half the people now live in six urban areas, including the steel center of Birmingham in the N central part of the state, and Alabama's only Gulf port, Mobile.

Economy. Alabama's traditional agricultural economy, once based on cotton, has greatly changed since the 1930s. Economic diversification, aided by the exploitation of hydroelectricity, has led to marked industrial growth, particularly in iron and steel production. Coal, iron ore, limestone, bauxite, timber, petroleum and natural gas provide raw materials for the state's industries, which are now the chief source of income. Major manufactures include clothes, textiles, metal and wood products, processed foods and chemicals. In the N, Tennessee Valley Authority dams provide low-cost hydroelectricity.

History. Choctaws, Creeks and other members of the FIVE CIVILIZED TRIBES originally peopled Alabama (the state is named for a Choctaw tribe). Spain's Hernando DE SOTO explored the region in 1540, and France's Sieur de BIENVILLE founded the first permanent European settlement in the Mobile area in 1702. France ceded the region to Britain (1763), which lost it to the US (1783), but Spain held the Mobile area until 1813. The defeat of the Creeks at the Battle of HORSESHOE BEND (1814) opened S Alabama to settlers, who developed a slave-based plantation economy. At the outbreak of the Civil War Montgomery became the first Confederate capital. The state suffered greatly during the war and then afterward during Reconstruction. Industry began to develop towards the end of the century, but one-crop farming and the sharecropping system brought widespread agricultural depression and poverty, accentuated from 1915 by the infestation of the boll weevil. TVA projects and WWII boosted industry, and despite racial tension in the 1950s and 1960s, Alabama has become a leader in the S in basing its economy firmly on manufacturing. Still, with a population increase of 12.9% from 1970 to 1980, Alabama is growing more slowly than neighboring states, and only two other states in the nation had lower per capita incomes than Alabama's of $6,962 in 1979. In 1980, retired Admiral Jeremiah Denton, a former Vietnam prisoner of war, became the first Republican elected to the US Senate from Alabama in the 20th century.

ALABAMA CLAIMS, compensation

claimed by the US from Britain for property seized and destroyed by the *Alabama* and other Confederate vessels during the Civil War. Britain was charged with violating its neutrality by allowing the Confederate warships to be built or equipped in its shipyards. In 1871 the dispute was submitted to an international tribunal, which found Britain liable and awarded the US $15,500,000 in gold.

ALABAMA RIVER, formed by the junction of the Tallapoosa and Coosa rivers near Montgomery, Ala., flows W and SW 315mi to join the Tombigbee about 40mi N of Mobile, forming the Mobile and Tensaw rivers. Navigable throughout its course, its headwaters are harnessed to produce hydroelectricity.

ALAIN-FOURNIER, pseudonym of Henri Alban Fournier (1886–1914), French writer whose one novel, *Le Grand Meaulnes* (1913), is the haunting tale of a boy's attempt to rediscover the dreamlike setting of his meeting with a beautiful girl.

ALAMO, Spanish mission-fortress in San Antonio, Texas, the site of a heroic defense in 1836 by less than 200 Texans in the struggle for independence from Mexico. All the defenders, including such heroes as Davy CROCKETT and Jim BOWIE, died in a lengthy siege by 4,000 Mexicans under General SANTA ANNA.

ALAMOGORDO, town in S central N.M., seat of Otero Co. and the center of an agricultural, timber and recreation area which includes White Sands National Monument. The first atomic bomb was exploded near Alamogordo in a test on July 16, 1945. Pop 23,035.

ALANBROOKE, Alan Francis Brooke, 1st Viscount (1883–1963), British field marshal, one of the leading military strategists of WWII. Chief of the Imperial General Staff 1941–46, he participated in important wartime conferences of the Allies.

ALAND ISLANDS, archipelago in the Baltic Sea between Sweden and Finland. Originally Swedish, they today form the Finnish province of Ahvenanmaa, though some 96% of the population speaks Swedish. Fishing, shipping, tourism and farming are principal occupations. Pop 20,608.

ALANI, a warlike tribe of Asia Minor who resembled the Mongols and spoke an Iranian language. Around the 1st century AD they made several attacks on the eastern Roman Empire. The Alani eventually migrated westward across S Europe and were absorbed by the Huns and Vandals.

ALARCÓN, Pedro Antonio de (1833–1891), Spanish regional writer best known for his novel *The Three-Cornered Hat* (1874). His work is distinguished by sharp realistic observation and picturesque effects.

ALARCÓN Y MENDOZA, Juan Ruiz de (c1580–1639), Spanish playwright of the Golden Age who wrote brilliant moralizing comedies. The best-known, *The Suspicious Truth,* influenced the great French dramatist, CORNEILLE.

ALARIC, name of two Visigoth kings. **Alaric I** (c370–410) was commander of the Visigoth auxiliaries under the Roman Emperor Theodosius until the latter's death, when Alaric was proclaimed king by his countrymen. After invading Greece and N Italy, he captured and sacked Rome in 410. **Alaric II** (d. 507), ruled Spain and S Gaul from 484, and issued the Breviary of Alaric, a Visigoth code of Roman law, in 506. His army was defeated and he was slain by Clovis I, king of the Franks.

Name of state: Alaska
Capital: Juneau
Statehood: Jan. 3, 1959 (49th state)
Familiar names: Last frontier; Land of the Midnight Sun; Great Fun Land
Area: 586,400sq mi
Population: 400,481
Elevation: Highest—20,320ft, Mt. McKinley. Lowest—sea level, Pacific coast
Motto: North to the future
State flower: Forget-me-not
State bird: Willow ptarmigan
State tree: Sitka spruce
State song: "Alaska's Flag"

ALASKA, largest of the 50 states, and potentially one of the richest, America's "Last Frontier." It occupies the extreme NW corner of North America, bounded N by the Arctic Ocean, W by the Bering Sea, S by the Pacific Ocean, and E by the Yukon and British Columbia. Alaska lies only 51mi E of the Siberian mainland across the Bering Strait.

Land. Including the coasts of thousands of offshore islands (notably the 1,200mi long Aleutian Islands, the Alexander Archipelago and the Pribilof Islands), Alaska's coastline exceeds those of all the other states combined. Major mountain chains are the Brooks Range in the N and the Alaska Range in the S (with Mt McKinley reaching 20,320ft), separated by the Central Plateau through which the Yukon R flows. In the far N, the lowland North Slope faces the Arctic Ocean. The climate is cold in the N and the interior, but during the long daylight hours of the brief interior summer temperatures can be extremely high. Warm ocean currents and sheltering mountains make the climate of the S mild and moist.

People. Alaska is still the least populated of the 50 states, though its population grew by a third in the 1970s. Most people live in Anchorage (the largest city), Fairbanks and smaller centers in the Panhandle.

Economy. Minerals (especially oil from Prudhoe Bay and the Kenai Peninsula; also gravel, coal and copper) are the state's chief source of income. Hunting fur seals is also important, and Alaska has the largest commercial fisheries of any state. Processing of the fish catch and production of pulp and lumber are the largest industries. Tourism is a relatively new and fast-growing industry. Farms are few and most food must be imported, which adds to the high cost of living. Transportation is difficult in this remote, rugged state where long winters hamper road construction and maintenance. The ALASKA HIGHWAY links Fairbanks with Canada and the US, and roads and a railroad join some S centers, but much travel is by sea or air.

History. Russia claimed Alaska after Vitus BERING and Alexander CHIRIKOV sighted it (1741). Grigori SHELEKHOV founded the first permanent settlement, on Kodiak Island (1784). Secretary of State William H. SEWARD bought Alaska for the US in 1867 for $7.2 million (about 2 cents an acre), which some referred to as "Seward's Folly." Economic growth remained slow until the 1896 Klondike gold rush in the Yukon and after subsequent deposits were discovered in Nome (1899) and Fairbanks (1902). Crude oil began flowing along the Trans-Alaska pipeline to the port of Valdez in 1977, with more than 1¼ billion barrels being transmitted in the first three years of operation. Construction of a gas line from Prudhoe Bay also began. Alaska's revenues from oil and gas have been so large that the state income tax was repealed in 1980. A commission also was appointed that year to review Alaska's role within the federal union. Perceived by some as a cover for secessionist sentiments, the commission is mandated to study the statehood act and propose such lawful changes as may seem

warranted. Debate continues on environmental issues, too. In a major compromise that left neither environmentalists nor development interests entirely happy, a US Senate act in 1980 set aside more than 104 million acres for wilderness areas, wildlife refuges and national parks and preserves, while allocating other lands for mining and logging.

ALASKA BOUNDARY DISPUTE, disagreement concerning the demarcation of the border between the Alaska Panhandle and Canada, which arose in 1898 during the Klondike gold rush. Skagway and the head of the LYNN CANAL, through which supplies reached the Yukon, were claimed to be in Canadian territory. The question was settled in favor of the US by a joint US–British commission in 1903.

ALASKA HIGHWAY, road extending 1,523mi from Fairbanks, Alaska, through Whitehorse, Yukon, to Dawson Creek, British Columbia. It was built by the US as a strategic all-weather military route in 1942, and in 1946 Canada took over control of the 1,221mi passing through its territory. Formerly known as the Alaskan International Highway and Alcan Highway, the road is kept open throughout the year.

ALASKAN MALAMUTE, wolflike Arctic sled dog, developed by the Mahlemut Eskimos of NW Alaska. It has a heavy coat, gray or white and black, and a great bushy tail, and possesses great strength and endurance. Average height, 24in at the shoulder; weight, 75–85lb.

ALASKAN PIPELINE, oil pipeline with a flow potential of one million barrels daily, running 789mi from Alaska's North Slope to the port of Valdez. Constructed by a consortium of oil companies and finished in 1977, it has been bitterly opposed by environmentalists for adversely affecting the ecology.

ALBA (or ALVA), Fernando Álvarez de Toledo, Due of 1507–1582), Spanish general who tyrannized the Netherlands. During his brutal campaign against rebellious Dutch Protestants (1567–73), he executed some 18,000 people, including the counts of Horn and EGMONT. Hated for his atrocities and harsh taxes, and harassed by WILLIAM THE SILENT'S liberating army, Alva was recalled to Spain in 1573. In 1580 he conquered Portugal for Spain.

ALBANIA, communist nation in SE Europe, the smallest Balkan State. Albania is bounded on the N and NE by Yugoslavia, S and SE by Greece, W by the Adriatic Sea. Barren mountains (reaching 9,026ft in the North Albanian Alps), with wooded lower slopes, dominate all inland Albania. They are pierced by the Drin, Vijosé and other rivers flowing W to the narrow fertile plain which flanks the N and central coast. Summers are hot and dry; winters mild and moist.

Albanians (mainly descendants of ancient Balkan hill tribes) are officially atheists; but traditionally Muslims outnumber Christians. Two Albanian dialects are spoken: Gheg in the N, Tosk in the S. Most people live on the coast or in the fertile mountain basins linked by poor roads. Agricultural products include corn, wheat, sugar beets, potatoes, fruit, tobacco and cotton. Industries are small but under rapid development. Copper, chromium, nickel, coal, naphtha and oil are being exploited, and Chinese aid helped hydroelectric schemes and farm mechanization. But agriculture remains the basis of the economy.

About 300 BC Albania was part of the region known as ILLYRIA, which came under Greek, Roman and then Byzantine influence and control. Between 300 AD and 1100 AD it was successively invaded by Goths, Bulgars, Slavs and Normans. Later, the national hero SCANDERBEG (d. 1468) delayed, but failed to stop, Ottoman Turkish conquest. Turkish rule Islamized Albania and suppressed nationalist aspirations until the First Balkan War (1912). Occupied in WWI, ruled by self-proclaimed King Zog I (1928–39), then annexed by Italy and occupied in WWII, Albania regained independence under Enver HOXHA'S communist regime in 1945. Stalinist Albania broke with Russia in 1961 and allied with Communist China, but in the late 1970s it attacked the more moderate policies of China's post-Mao leadership. Albania remains probably Europe's poorest and most isolated country.

Official name: The People's Republic of Albania
Capital: Tiranë
Area: 11,101sq mi
Population: 2,730,000
Languages: Albanian
Religions: No official religion

Monetary unit(s): 1 Lek = 100 qintars
ALBANIAN, Indo-European language developed from ancient Albanian. It is a separate branch of the Indo-European family. Though spoken in an area nearer to Greece than to Rome, it shows the influence of Latin rather than Greek.

ALBANY, commercial and industrial city of SW Ga., seat of Dougherty Co., 170mi S of Atlanta on the Flint R. Founded in 1836, Albany is a transportation hub and center of a rich agricultural region. Pop 72,623.

ALBANY, capital of N.Y. State and seat of Albany Co. on the W bank of the Hudson R about 145mi N of New York City. An important industrial and shipping center, Albany can be reached by oceangoing vessels sailing up the Hudson and is also a major railroad junction. Its industries produce chemicals, paper, felt and textiles. Established in 1614 as Fort Nassau, a Dutch fur-trading post, it was renamed Albany in honor of the Duke of York and Albany when the British assumed control of New Netherlands in 1664. The site of the ALBANY CONGRESS of 1754, the city became the capital of N.Y. State in 1797. The opening of the Erie and Champlain canals in the 1820s and the first railroad connection with Schenectady in 1831 established Albany's position as a commercial and shipping center. Pop 115,781.

ALBANY CONGRESS (1754), a meeting of 25 representatives from seven British colonies at Albany, N.Y., aimed at conciliating the Iroquois and improving the common defense of the colonies against the French. The congress adopted a plan, chiefly designed by Benjamin FRANKLIN, providing for greater colonial unity, one of the first significant attempts at colonial cooperation. The colonial governments later rejected the plan.

ALBATENIUS (c858–929), Arab mathematician and astronomer who improved on the results of Claudius PTOLEMY by applying TRIGONOMETRY to astronomical computations. He had a powerful influence on medieval European ASTRONOMY.

ALBATROSSES, the 14 species of large, long-winged, gliding, hook-billed seabirds forming the family Diomedeidae in the tubenose order, Procellariiformes. Two species form the genus *Phoebetria* (sooty albatrosses), the other 12 the *Diomedea*. Most albatrosses are white with darker markings on the back, wings and tail. The wandering albatross (*D. exulans*) has the broadest wingspan of any living bird—up to 3.5m (11.5ft). Living mainly over the southern oceans, albatrosses have wings uniquely adapted for gliding flight.

ALBEE, Edward Franklin (1928–   ), US playwright who gained international fame with his play *Who's Afraid of Virginia Woolf?* (1962), a penetrating commentary on contemporary American marriage. His other plays include *The Zoo Story* (1958) and *The American Dream* (1961), both one-act plays, *Tiny Alice* (1964) and *A Delicate Balance* (1966), which won a Pulitzer Prize.

ALBENIZ, Isaac (1860–1909), Spanish composer and pianist. A child prodigy, he wrote operas and songs, but is best remembered for his later piano works, including the suite *Iberia* (1906–9), based on Spanish folk themes and popular music forms.

ALBERS, Josef (1888–1976), German-American painter, graphic artist and art teacher, whose style of geometrical abstraction and theories of art have influenced many modern artists. A teacher at the BAUHAUS in Germany (1923–33), he emigrated to the US (1933) and headed the department of design at Yale (1950–58).

ALBERT, Lake, 2,064sq mi lake between Uganda and Zaire, also known as Albert Nyanza, now Lake Mobuto Seso. The source of the Albert Nile, it is fed by the Semliki R, draining Lake Edward (or Lake Idi Amin Dada) and by the Victoria Nile. It was discovered 1864 by Sir Samuel Baker.

ALBERT, Prince (Francis Charles Augustus Albert Emmanuel; 1819–1861), Prince Consort of England, husband of Queen Victoria. German-born son of the Duke of Saxe-Coburg-Gotha, he married Victoria in 1840, and as her trusted adviser worked to establish the nonpartisan influence of the crown in government. He was active in promoting science and art. A man of irreproachable character, he was deeply mourned by Victoria after his early death.

Name of province: Alberta
Joined Confederation: Sept. 1, 1905
Capital: Edmonton
Area: 255,285sq mi
Population: 2,079,000

ALBERTA, Canada's westernmost prairie province, the country's leading petroleum producer and a rich agricultural region.
Land. The S and E was originally covered by prairie grasslands, fertile but dry and rising towards the Rocky Mountains in the SW. The rugged Rockies (containing BANFF, JASPER and other national parks) dominate the W; dense forests and swamp cover the N. The Peace, Athabasca and other rivers drain the province, and the Athabasca and Lesser Slave are the largest of many lakes. Long cold winters alternate with hot, sunny summers.

People. About 45% of all Albertans are of British origin; others are of German, Ukrainian, Scandinavian and French descent. Most of the 30,000 Indians live on reserves. Nearly half the rapidly growing population lives in the Edmonton and Calgary metropolitan areas, and the rural population has declined to less than a third of the total.

Economy. Since the 1950s Alberta's mineral wealth and manufacturing have become the chief source of income. The province produces 86% of Canada's crude oil and 80% of its natural gas, as well as coal from Canada's largest deposits. Two recovery plants are in operation N of Fort McMurray, but full exploitation of the immensely rich Athabasca oil sands still remains in the future. Oil refining and petrochemical production are major industries. Agriculture remains important with wheat and livestock the principal products.

History. In 1670 unexplored Alberta became part of RUPERT'S LAND, granted to the Hudson's Bay Company. Anthony Henday was its earliest European visitor (1754), and Fort Chipewyan (1788) was among the first of the settlements by fur traders and missionaries. But few white settlers arrived until after 1869, when the Canadian Government bought Rupert's Land. The arrival of the Mounties (1874), completion of the Canadian Pacific Railway (1885) and peace treaties handing most Indian lands to the Canadian government by 1899, encouraged immigrants. Alberta became a province in 1905. Depressed farm income during the 1920s and 1930s led to the victory of the SOCIAL CREDIT PARTY (1935), which stayed in power until 1971. Discovery of oil and natural gas at Leduc, near Edmonton, in 1947 opened a new era in the province's history. Petroleum, natural gas, and coal have made Alberta one of Canada's richest provinces.

ALBERT I (1875–1934), King of Belgium (1909–34). Nephew and successor of LEOPOLD II, he did much to improve conditions in the Belgian Congo. In Belgium he strengthened national defense and the merchant fleet, and introduced various social reforms. During WWI he personally commanded the armed forces.

ALBERTI, Domenico (c1710–1740), Venetian composer who gave his name to a style of accompaniment where the left hand plays broken chords, the "Alberti Bass."

ALBERTI, Leon Battista (1404–1472), Florentine Renaissance scholar, architect and art theorist whose contributions in the arts and sciences make him typical of the Renaissance "Universal Man." Architectural works include the Palazzo Rucellai in Florence and the Tempio Malatestiano (S. Francesco) in Rimini.

ALBERT NYANZA. See ALBERT, LAKE.

ALBERTUS MAGNUS, Saint (c1200–1280), German scholastic philosopher and scientist; the teacher of St. Thomas AQUINAS. Albert's main significance was in promoting the study of ARISTOTLE and in helping to establish Aristotelianism and the study of the natural sciences within Christian thought. In science he did important work in botany and was possibly the first to isolate ARSENIC.

ALBIGENSES, members of the heretical (actually non-Christian) CATHARI sect, active in the 12th and 13th centuries, who took their name from the city of ALBI in S France. Believing that worldly things represented the forces of evil and that the human spirit alone was good, they attacked the Church. Pope Innocent III attempted to break the power of the Albegensian Crusade (1208–29), but it flourished for another century. See also DUALISM and MANICHAEISM.

ALBINO, an organism lacking the pigmentation normal to its kind. The skin and hair of albino animals (including man) is uncolored while the irises of their eyes appear pink. Albinism, which may be total or only partial, is generally inherited. Albino plants contain no CHLOROPHYLL and thus, being unable to perform PHOTOSYNTHESIS, rapidly die.

ALBINONI, Tomaso (1671–1750), Italian composer. A famous violinist, he also wrote over 50 operas. BACH, his contemporary, made use of several of Albinoni's themes in his own compositions.

ALBITE, common mineral occurring in igneous rocks, consisting of sodium aluminum silicate; often forms VITREOUS crystals of various colors. It is one of the three end members (pure compounds) of the FELDSPAR group.

ALBRIGHT, Ivan Le Lorraine (1897–   ), US painter of microscopically detailed canvases whose mood and symbolism focus on decay and human dissolution. His works include *That Which I Should Have Done I Did Not Do* (1941), which took ten years to complete, and a series of paintings for the film *The Picture of Dorian Gray* (1944).

ALBUMIN, group of PROTEINS soluble in water and in 50% saturated sulfate solution; present in animals and plants. Ovalbumin is the chief protein in egg white; serum albumin occurs in blood PLASMA, where it controls osmotic pressure.

ALBUQUERQUE, largest city in N.M.,

seat of Bernalillo Co., on the Rio Grande R. Founded in 1706 on the old Chihuahua Trail, it is today an important commercial and industrial city with defense and atomic energy installations, as well as a transportation and tourist center. Pop 331,767.

ALCAEUS, Greek lyric poet of c600 BC. Like his contemporary, Sappho, he came from the island of Lesbos and wrote in the Aeolic dialect. He is best remembered for poetry about his fondness for wine. The four-line Alcaic stanza, named for him, was widely used in Greek lyric poetry, and was adopted by the Latin poet Horace and by English poets such as Tennyson.

ALCAMENES (460–400 BC), Greek sculptor, somewhat younger than PHIDIAS. After Phidias' death he became the leading sculptor in Athens. Apart from a famous Roman copy of his statue of Hermes, few examples of his work survive.

ALCAN HIGHWAY. See ALASKA HIGHWAY.

ALCATRAZ, rocky island in San Francisco Bay, famous as the site (1933–63) of a federal prison for dangerous criminals, nicknamed "the Rock." In 1970 the island was occupied for a time by a group of American Indians. It is now part of the Golden Gate National Recreation Area.

ALCAZAR, name for the massive fortified palaces built in Spain under Muslim rule. The ALHAMBRA in Granada is a well-known and beautiful example. The Alcazar of Toledo withstood a famous siege in 1936 during the Spanish Civil War.

ALCESTIS, in Greek legend, wife of Admetus, king of Pherae in Thessaly, who made a pact with Apollo to die in her husband's place. A classic example of love and fidelity, she is the subject of a tragedy by EURIPIDES and an opera by GLUCK.

ALCHEMY, a blend of philosophy, mysticism and chemical technology, originating before the Christian era, seeking variously the conversion of base metals into gold, the prolongation of life and the secret of immortality. In the Classical world alchemy began in Hellenistic Egypt and passed through the writings of the great Arab alchemists such as Al-Razi (RHAZES) to the Latin West. The late medieval period saw the discovery of NITRIC, SULFURIC and HYDROCHLORIC acids and ETHANOL (*aqua vitae*, the water of life) in the alchemists' pursuit of the "philosopher's stone" or *elixir* which would transmute base metals into gold.

In the early 16th century PARACELSUS set alchemy on a new course, towards a chemical pharmacy (IATROCHEMISTRY), although other alchemists—including John

Dee and even Isaac NEWTON—continued to work along mystical, quasireligious lines. Having strong ties with ASTROLOGY, interest in alchemy, particularly in the Hermetic writings (see HERMES TRISMEGISTUS), has never quite died out, though without any further benefit to medical or chemical science. (See also CHEMISTRY.)

ALCIBIADES (c450–404 BC), Athenian statesman and general, nephew of PERICLES and a favorite student of SOCRATES. Always a disturbing influence, during the Peloponnesian War he temporarily fell out of favor. Escaping to Sparta, he betrayed Athens, but later rejoined his fleet, which he led successfully against Sparta. Once more out of favor, he was assassinated in exile.

ALCOHOLIC BEVERAGES, drinks containing ETHANOL, the only variety of ALCOHOL that may be consumed in moderation without damaging effects. Popular alcoholic beverages include BEER, WINE, WHISKEY, BRANDY, RUM and compounded liquors such as liqueurs and GIN. They vary widely in alcoholic content, ranging from 2% or 3% in light beers to more than 60% in some VODKAS and distilled fruit brandy. (See also DISTILLED LIQUOR.)

Intoxicating beverages were known to the ancient Egyptians and Babylonians, and in the past many people used them instead of impure water. Today their use is general for conviviality; excessive drinking may be due to ALCOHOLISM. (See also INTOXICATION.) Many governments strictly control the sale of alcoholic beverages, and they are an important source of revenue.

ALCOHOLICS ANONYMOUS (A.A.), world-wide organization numbering over 1,000,000 anonymous members, in which former alcoholics aid those suffering from ALCOHOLISM. It stresses self-help, and all involved pool their experiences for mutual encouragement.

ALCOHOLISM, compulsive drinking of alcohol in excess, one of the most serious problems in modern society. Many people drink for relaxation and can stop drinking without ill effects; the alcoholic cannot give up drinking without great discomfort: he is dependent on alcohol, physically and psychologically.

Alcohol is a DEPRESSANT that acts initially by reducing activity in the higher centers of the BRAIN. The drinker loses judgment and inhibitions; he feels free of his responsibilities and anxieties. This is the basis for initial psychological dependence. With further alcohol intake, thought and body control are impaired (see also INTOXICATION). The alcoholic starts by drinking more and longer than his fellows. He then finds that the unpleasant symptoms of withdrawal—"hangover," tremor, weakness. and hallucinations—are relieved by alcohol. In this way his drinking extends through the greater part of the day and physical dependence is established. The alcoholic often has a reduced tolerance to the effects of alcohol and may suffer from AMNESIA after a few drinks. Social pressures soon lead to secretive drinking, work is neglected and financial difficulties add to the disintegration of personality; denial and pathological jealousy hasten social isolation. Alcohol depresses the appetite and the alcoholic may stop or reduce eating. Many of the diseases associated with alcoholism are in part due to MALNUTRITION and VITAMIN deficiency: CIRRHOSIS, NEURITIS, dementia, and KORSAKOV'S PSYCHOSIS. Prolonged alcohol withdrawal leads to DELIRIUM TREMENS. Treatment of alcoholism is very difficult. SEDATIVES and ANTABUSE may help to counteract dependence. Reconciliation of the patient to society is crucial; he must understand the reasons for his drinking and learn to approach his problems and fears realistically. Psychotherapy and ALCOHOLICS ANONYMOUS are valuable in this. Total abstinence is essential to avoid relapse.

ALCOHOLS, class of ALIPHATIC COMPOUNDS, of general formula ROH, containing a hydroxyl group bonded to a carbon atom. They are classified as monohydric, dihydric, etc., according to the number of hydroxyl groups; and as primary, secondary or tertiary according to the number of hydrogen atoms adjacent to the hydroxyl group. Alcohols occur widely in nature, and are used as solvents and antifreezes and in chemical manufacture. They are obtained by fermentation, oxidation or hydration of ALKENES from petroleum and natural gas, and by reduction of fats and oils

Alcohols of lower molecular weight are colorless, flammable liquids, miscible with water. The simplest alcohols are METHANOL and ETHANOL (the intoxicating constituent of ALCOHOLIC BEVERAGES); others include BENZYL ALCOHOL, DIHYDRIC, ETHYLENE GLYCOL and GLYCEROL. (See also CARBOHYDRATES.)

ALCOTT, (Amos) Bronson (1799–1888), US educator, philosopher and author. As a teacher in several Conn. schools, his progressive methods were too advanced to be popular. In 1840 he retired to Concord, Mass., where he was closely associated with the TRANSCENDENTALISM of Emerson, Hawthorne, Thoreau and Channing. His writings include *Concord Days* (1872) and *Table Talk* (1877).

ALCOTT, Louisa May (1832–1888), US author of *Little Women* (1869) and other autobiographical books for children. Daughter of Amos Bronson ALCOTT, she began by publishing stories in magazines like the *Atlantic Monthly*. *Hospital Sketches* (1863) was based on her experiences as a Union nurse in the Civil War.

ALCUIN (735–804 AD), English prelate and scholar whose classical and humanist scholarship influenced medieval teaching of the liberal arts. In 781 he became master of the palace school of CHARLEMAGNE and supervised Charlemagne's program of ecclesiastical and educational reform among the Franks in the Carolingian empire.

ALDEGREVER, Heinrich (1502–c1555), German painter and engraver. One of the "little masters," his work was influenced by DÜRER'S assimilation of Italian Renaissance discoveries in classical art.

ALDEHYDES, class of organic compounds of general formula RCHO, containing a carbonyl group (see also KETONES). They are highly reactive, and find many uses in industry in the preparation of solvents, dyes, resins, and other compounds. Many aldehydes occur in nature and are often responsible for the flavor and scent of animals and plants. The simplest aldehydes are FORMALDEHYDE and acetaldehyde. Aromatic aldehydes, such as benzaldehyde and vanillin, are used in dyes and as perfumes and food flavorings. Aldehydes can be prepared by dehydrogenation or oxidation of primary ALCOHOLS, or by reduction of acid chlorides.

ALDEN, John (c1599–1687), a MAYFLOWER Pilgrim Father, an able assistant to the governor of Plymouth Colony. He is best known through LONGFELLOW'S poem *The Courtship of Miles Standish*, based on the legend that he courted Priscilla Mullens on behalf of Miles Standish, but married her himself.

ALDINGTON, Richard (1892–1962), English novelist, critic, biographer and pre-WWI IMAGIST poet, who wrote controversial biography of T. E. LAWRENCE.

ALDRICH, Thomas Bailey (1836–1907). US editor and writer of poems, stories, novels and essays. He was editor of the *Atlantic Monthly* (1881–90). *The Story of a Bad Boy* (1870), his best-known book, tells of his youth in Portsmouth, N.H.

ALDRIDGE, Ira Frederick (1805–1867), first US black to achieve fame as an actor. Known in Britain and on the Continent for his bold interpretations of such Shakespearean roles as Lear, Othello and Macbeth, he eventually became a British citizen.

ALDUS MANUTIUS (1450–1515), Venetian founder of the *Aldine Press* whose scrupulous editions of Greek and Roman classics (including Aristotle) advanced Renaissance scholarship. He was the first man to use italic type (1501) especially cut in order to produce cheap, pocket-sized editions of the Latin classics.

ALE, in the US, a light-colored, top-fermented beer with an alcohol content of about 5%. It excludes bottom-fermented or continental-type beers. Malt liquors such as ale are generally called beer in England.

ALEATORY MUSIC (from Latin *alea*, dice), music dependent on chance applied to the post-1950 tendency of composers to leave some elements in their work to be settled by the performer's decision or by random chance. John CAGE'S work is perhaps the best-known example.

ALEICHEM, Sholem. See SHOLEM ALEICHEM.

ALEKSANDROV, Aleksandr Vassilievich (1883–1946), Russian composer who wrote operas, orchestral works and popular songs and choruses, including the Soviet national anthem. He also founded (1928) and directed the Red Army Chorus.

ALEMÁN, Mateo (1547–1614), Spanish writer of picaresque novels reflecting his own colorful life. *Guzman de Alfarache* (1599) was widely translated.

ALEMÁN VALDÉS, Miguel (1902–   ), President of Mexico (1946–1952), a successful lawyer, son of a revolutionary general. He initiated a vigorous program of economic development. After his presidency, he directed promotion of tourism, including development of Acapulco and bringing the 1968 Olympics to Mexico City.

ALEMBERT, Jean Le Rond d' (1717–1783), French philosopher, physicist and mathematician, a leading figure in the French ENLIGHTENMENT and coeditor with DIDEROT of the renowned *Encyclopedia*. His early fame rested on his formulation of D'ALEMBERT'S PRINCIPLE in mechanics (1743). His other works treat calculus, music, philosophy and astronomy.

ALEPPO (Halab), second-largest city of Syria, located in the N, at the junction of ancient caravan routes. An important city since Hittite times more than 3,000 years ago, it was long one of the greatest emporiums of the Middle East. Today Aleppo is a leading manufacturing center, with a population including many Armenian and Syrian Christians. Pop 878,000.

ALEUTIAN ISLANDS, chain of some 150 Alaska islands Bering Sea from the Pacific.

These treeless, rugged and the Alaska Peninsula in a wide arc, and separating the Bering Sea from the Pacific. These treeless, rugged and foggy islands support a population of approximately 8,000; fishing is the chief occupation. In 1942 the Japanese occupied Agattu, Attu and Kiska, the westernmost islands of this strategic chain, and bombed the naval base at Dutch Harbor.

ALEWIFE, or branch herring (*Alosa*—or *Pomolobus*—*pseudoharengus*), a fish of the HERRING and SHAD family (Clupeidae) caught in large numbers along the Atlantic coast of North America. Growing up to 300mm (12in) long, adult fish return to coastal rivers to spawn, though one variety spends its whole life in the fresh water of the Great Lakes.

ALEXANDER, name of eight popes. **Alexander II** (Anselm of Lucca; d. 1073), pope 1061–73, laid the foundations of the reform movement that reached fruition under GREGORY VII. His deposition of the bishop of Milan for simony led to the INVESTITURE CONTROVERSY. **Alexander III** (Orlando Bandinelli; d. 1181), pope 1159–81, continued the long battle against the Emperor FREDERICK I Barbarossa. Opposed by three antipopes, he was victor over Frederick at the Battle of Legano (1176). He convened the Third Lateran Council (1179) and forced King Henry II of England to recognize papal supremacy. He canonized Thomas à BECKET. **Alexander VI** (Rodrigo Borgia; 1431–1503), pope from 1492, was the most notorious of the Renaissance popes. Born in Valencia, Spain, he was deeply involved in the political turmoil of the Italy of his day. His efforts were directed at increasing the temporal power of the papacy and creating great hereditary domains for his children, among them Cesare and Lucrezia BORGIA. He was a keen patron of the great artists of his day. **Alexander VII** (Fabio Chigi; 1599–1667), pope from 1655, ruled at a time when the papacy was losing temporal power, and was worsted in controversy with Louis XIV of France.

ALEXANDER, Franz Gabriel (1891–1964), German-born US psychoanalyst who identified emotional factors based on human relationships as the cause of psychosomatic illness. He founded and directed (1932–56) the Chicago Institute for Psychoanalysis and wrote *Fundamentals of Psychoanalysis* (1948).

ALEXANDER, Grover Cleveland (1887–1950), one of the greatest right-handed pitchers of all times, playing with the Phillies, Cubs and Cardinals from 1911 to 1930. He gained the major league record for shutouts in a season (16) and the National League career record in complete games and shutouts.

ALEXANDER, Samuel (1859–1938), Australian-born British philosopher. A professor at Victoria University, Manchester (1893–1924), he was concerned with metaphysics, ethics, and the mind-body relationship. His best-known works were *Space, Time, and Deity* (1920) and *Beauty and Other Forms of Value* (1933).

ALEXANDER, name of three Russian Tsars. **Alexander I** (1777–1825) succeeded his father, Paul I, in 1801, with a reform program which he later abandoned. In 1805 he joined England and Austria against Napoleon. After French victories at Austerlitz and Friedland, however, Napoleon proposed joint Franco-Russian domination of Europe. But mutual mistrust came to a head when Alexander encouraged British, not French, trade. Napoleon invaded Russia in 1812. Almost the whole French army was destroyed in the freezing Russian winter, and in 1814 Alexander entered Paris. In 1815 he formed a coalition with Austria and Prussia, the HOLY ALLIANCE. At his death, internal repression was abetted by a corrupt Church and enforced by the secret police, and the country itself faced economic ruin and rebellion. **Alexander II** (1818–1881), succeeded his father, Nicholas I, in 1855. Russian defeat in the CRIMEAN WAR and peasant unrest forced on him limited reforms, most importantly the emancipation of the serfs in 1861. But this did not satisfy revolutionary groups, and fear of their activities inspired him at first to more reactionary policies. He finally relented, but on the very day he signed a decree for moderate reform he was killed by nihilist bombs. In foreign policies he was a moderate, making peace in the Crimea and keeping out of the FRANCO-PRUSSIAN WAR (1870–71), though extending Russian power in the Far East as well as in Central Asia. **Alexander III** (1845–1894) succeeded his father Alexander II in 1881. He discarded the latter's proposals for moderate reform in favor of rigid repression and persecution of minorities. But industrial development prospered and construction of the TRANS-SIBERIAN RAILROAD began. In Europe his policies were peaceful.

ALEXANDER I, (1888–1934), king of Yugoslavia from 1921 until his assassination by a Croatian terrorist at Marseille. He became prince-regent of Serbia in 1914 and commanded the Serbian forces in WWI. An autocratic ruler, he earned the enmity of separatist minorities.

ALEXANDER NEVSKY (1220–1263), Russian national hero and saint. His victories over the Swedes at the Neva R (1240) and over the Teutonic Knights on the ice of Lake Peipus (1242) made him preeminent among Russian princes.

ALEXANDER OF TUNIS, Harold (Rupert Leofric George), 1st Earl (1891–1969), British field marshal and statesman, in charge of the evacuation from DUNKERQUE (1940), later commander of British forces in the Middle East (under whom MONTGOMERY won the victory of EL ALAMEIN), and eventually Supreme Allied Commander in the Mediterranean and Italy. He was Governor-General of Canada (1946–52) and British minister of defense (1952–54).

ALEXANDER THE GREAT (356–323 BC), king of Macedonia (336–323 BC) and conqueror of the Persian Empire. The son of PHILIP II of Macedonia, he was born in Pella and educated by ARISTOTLE, the great philosopher. In 338 Philip's defeat of the Thebans and Athenians at CHAERONEA brought all the Greek city-states but Sparta under Macedonian rule. At the age of 20 Alexander succeeded his father and went on to execute Philip's plans for freeing the Greeks of Asia Minor from Persian rule. He invaded the Persian Empire with 30,000 infantry and 5,000 cavalry, but military victory was not his only concern; he also took with him a team of scholars, with the aim of bringing the blessings of Greek culture to Asia. After his defeat of the Persian King DARIUS III at ISSUS in 333, he pressed on to subdue Phoenicia and Egypt, founding Alexandria. As his dominions in the East spread, he thought of himself more and more as an Eastern prince, thus alienating much of his Macedonian army. In 331 Alexander again defeated Darius in the decisive battle of GAUGAMELA, after which the principal cities of the Persian Empire, Babylon, Susa and Persepolis, fell easily to his attack. He was proclaimed king of Asia, and then moved on eastward through Bactria and along the Indus Valley

to the Indian Ocean. He had intended to go on to conquer India, but his men refused. On his return to Babylon he began planning further conquests, but did not have time to realize in detail his plans for consolidating the union he had achieved between the East and the West. With no legitimate succession, the empire was pulled apart after his death by rival generals, known collectively as the DIADOCHI. But though he lived to be only 33, he had conquered the greatest empire civilization had yet known, and he prepared the way for the penetration of HELLENISTIC CULTURE into all parts of the known world.

ALEXANDRIA, historic city in Va., on the Potomac R 6mi S of Washington, D.C., settled late 17th century by Scottish merchants, laid out 1749 and part of D.C. from 1791 to 1847. A residential town rich in colonial architecture and historic associations, it was once the home of George WASHINGTON and Robert E. LEE. Pop 103,217.

ALEXANDRIA, chief port and second-largest city of Egypt, at the NW corner of the Nile delta, 110mi NW of Cairo. Alexandria was founded by Alexander the Great c332 BC; it was the capital of Ptolemaic Egypt and a great center of trade and learning in the Hellenistic and Roman world. Among its ancient landmarks were the greatest library of antiquity, a renowned museum and school, and the famous PHAROS. The city entered a long period of decline after the Arab conquest of 642, but since the time of MEHMET ALI it has grown into Egypt's principal channel for foreign trade, a cosmopolitan city with many of the country's industries. Pop 2,318,655.

ALEXANDRIAN SCHOOL, or *Museum* (place dedicated to the MUSES), founded c300 BC, the foremost center of learning in the ancient world during the HELLENISTIC AGE, and which housed the ALEXANDRIAN LIBRARY. The school was renowned from the first, its teachers including the mathematicians APOLLONIUS OF PERGA, EUCLID and HERO; the physicians ERASISTRATUS, EUDEMUS and HEROPHILUS; the geographer ERATOSTHENES and the astronomer HIPPARCHUS. The last great Alexandrian scientist was Claudius PTOLEMY, who worked in the city between 127 AD and 151 AD. With the decline of Hellenistic cluture, activity in the school turned away from original research towards compilation and criticism, the study of mystical philosophy and theology assuming an increasingly significant role.

ALEXEYEV, Vasili (1942–   ), Russian weight-lifting champion. He broke 80 official world records in less than eight years. He won gold medals at the 1972 and 1976 Olympics in the super-heavyweight division.

ALEXIA, a disorder of language, the complete inability to comprehend the written word. (See SPEECH AND SPEECH DISORDERS; DYSLEXIA.)

ALFALFA, or **lucerne**, important forage plant, *Medicago sativa*, widely grown for pasture, hay and silage. The high protein content of this PERENNIAL makes it an excellent food for livestock, and the nitrogen-fixing BACTERIA in the nodules on its roots are important in enriching depleted soil. Alfalfa is of particular value in arid countries as its extremely long taproot enables it to survive severe drought. Alfalfa has trifoliate leaves and dense clusters of small purple, blue or yellow flowers. Family: Leguminosae.

ALFIÉRI, Count Vittorio (1749–1803), Italian dramatist and poet, founder of modern Italian tragic drama. Among his works are *Saul*, *Maria Stuarda* and *Oreste* (1787–89). Hatred of tyranny and a passionate republicanism marked his impetuous and stormy life.

ALFONSO XIII (1886–1941), king of Spain, posthumous son of Alfonso XII, became king at birth and began personal rule in 1902. His intervention in politics brought instability and unpopularity and he associated himself with the dictatorship of PRIMO DE RIVERA. After a republican landslide in municipal elections he was forced to leave the country in 1931, though he refused to abdicate. His grandson JUAN CARLOS became king on General Franco's death.

ALFRED THE GREAT (c848–899), king of the West Saxons from 871. He halted the Danish invasions, making his kingdom of Wessex the nucleus of a unified England. Already a noted general, he came to the throne in the middle of a Danish invasion which he had to buy off despite spirited resistance. He used the truce period to consolidate his army and navy, and won a conclusive victory at Edington (878). He occuped London in 886 and was recognized as overlord of all England not in the extensive DANELAW. A pious ruler, he had many writers, such as BOETHIUS and BEDE, translated for his subjects' benefit, and introduced educational and legal reforms.

ALFVÉN, Hannes Olof Gösta (1908–), Swedish physicist who shared the 1970 Nobel Prize for Physics with Louis NÉEL for contributing to the development of PLASMA physics. Alfvén himself introduced the study of MAGNETOHYDRODYNAMICS.

ALGAE, a large and extremely diverse group of plants, including some of the simplest organisms known to man. They are mostly aquatic, and range in size from microscopic single-celled organisms living on trees, in snow, ponds and the surface waters of oceans to strands of seaweed several meters long in the deep oceans. Some algae are free-floating, some are motile and some grow attached to a substrate.

Algae are separated into seven major divisions, primarily on the basis of pigmentation. Blue-green algae have also been grouped in the algae by some authorities but differ from other algae in that they are prokaryotic organisms. Green algae (division Chlorophyta) are found mainly in freshwater and may be single-celled, form long filaments (like *Spirogyra*) or a flat leaf-like mass of cells called a thallus (like the sea lettuce, *Ulva lactuca*). Golden-brown algae (division Chrysophyta) also include the DIATOMS. Brown algae (division Phaeophyta) include the familiar seaweeds found on rocky shores. The largest, the KELPS, can grow to enormous lengths. Red algae (division Rhodophyta) are found mostly in warmer seas and include several species of economic importance. Desmids and dinoflagellates (both in division Pyrrophyta) are single-celled algae and are important constituents of marine PLANKTON. Yellow-green algae and chloromonads (division Xanthophyta) are mainly freshwater forms, mostly unicellular and nonmotile. Motile unicellular algae such as *Euglena* (division Euglenophyta) are classified by some biologists as PROTOZOA, but most contain CHLOROPHYLL and can synthesize their own food.

Algae in both marine and freshwater plankton are important as the basis of food chains (see ECOLOGY). Many of the larger algae are important to man; for example, the red algae *Porphyra* and *Chondrus crispus* are used as foodstuffs. *Gelidium*, another red algae, is a source of AGAR, and the kelps (such as the giant kelp *Macrocystis*) produce alginates, one use of which is in the manufacture of ice cream. Other uses of algae are in medicine and as manure. (See also PLANT KINGDOM.)

ALGARDI, Alessandro (1595–1654), Italian baroque sculptor, pupil of Lodovico CARRACCI, contemporary and more conservative rival of BERNINI. His masterpieces include the tomb of Pope Leo XI (1642) and a great relief of St. Leo and Attila the Hun (1646–50), both in St. Peter's, Rome.

ALGEBRA, that part of mathematics

dealing with the relationships and properties of numbers by use of general symbols (such as a, b, x, y) to represent mathematical quantities. These are combined by addition $(x+y)$, subtraction $(x-y)$, multiplication $(x \times y, x \cdot y$ or most usually xy) and division $(x \div y$, or most usually x/y). The relationship between them are expressed by symbols such as $=$ ("is equal to"), $\neq$ ("is not equal to") $\simeq$ ("is approximately equal to"), $>$ ("is greater than"), and $<$ ("is less than"). These symbols are also used in ARITHMETIC. Should a number be multiplied by itself one or more times it is said to be raised to a POWER:

$$x \cdot x = x^2,$$
$$x \cdot x \cdot x = x^3, \text{ etc.}$$

x^2 is termed "x to the power of two" or more usually "x squared"; x^3 is termed "x to the power of three" or more often "x cubed." From this emerges the concept of the ROOT: if $x^2 = y$ then x is the square root of y or $\sqrt{y}$ (or $\sqrt{y}$); if $x^3 = y$ then x is the cube root of y, written $\sqrt[3]{y}$.

Expressions containing two or more terms, such as $x+y+z$, or x^2+2x+5, are called polynomials. A special case is an expression containing two terms, such $x+y$, which is termed a binomial. Algebraic operations obey the Associative, Commutative and Distributive Laws.

Addition and multiplication of numbers are said to be *commutative*:

$$a+b=b+a \text{ and } a \cdot b=b \cdot a$$

Addition and multiplication are also *associative*:

$$a+(b+c)=(a+b)+c$$
$$\text{and } a \cdot (b \cdot c)=(a \cdot b) \cdot c$$

Addition and multiplication are together *distributive*:

$$a \cdot (b+c)=a \cdot b+a \cdot c.$$

See also EQUATION.

ALGEBRA, Abstract, a branch of mathematics that deals with sets (see SET THEORY) of abstract symbols on which certain formal operations are defined. The basic algebraic system is the GROUP, in which there is one operation, which may be written as multiplication: $a \cdot b = c$, in which a, b and c all belong to the group. **Rings** and **fields** have both multiplication and addition and more closely resemble ordinary NUMBER systems; the real and complex number systems are fields. A **vector space** is an abstract system with formal properties similar to those used in ordinary VECTOR algebra. Functions, or mappings, from one algebraic system to another that preserve the operations of the system play an essential role in abstract algebra (see FUNCTION). Mappings of vector spaces can be represented by MATRICES, the study of

which has been an important part of abstract algebra.

ALGER, Horatio (1834–1899), US author of more than 100 boys' books, in which the heroes rise from rags to riches through virtue and hard work. Among his books were *Ragged Dick* (1867), *Luck and Pluck* (1869) and *Sink or Swim* (1870).

Official name: Democratic and Popular Republic of Algeria
Capital: Algiers
Area: 919,590sq mi
Population: 18,707,000
Languages: Arabic, Berber, French
Religions: Muslim
Monetary unit(s): 1 Algerian dinar=100 centimes

ALGERIA, socialist republic in North Africa extending from the Mediterranean deep into the Sahara Desert. The Atlas Mountains, running E-W, divide the country into three regions: the rugged coastal zone in the N, clothed with evergreen trees; the steppe, covered with scrub and grass, pocked by salt lakes and flanked by the Atlas ranges; and the stony and sandy Sahara Desert in the S, with the sharply fretted Ahaggar Mountains reaching 9,852ft in the SE. Apart from the Tafna and Chéliff (in the NW), most rivers are intermittent and useless for irrigation or hydroelectricity. The climate is marked by mild winters and warm, dry summers in the N, and by greater extremes on the steppe; the Sahara varies between roasting days and frosty nights.

People. Some 75% of Algerians (chiefly Muslim Arabs and Berbers, but still including some Christian Europeans) live in the fertile coastal area. The ports of Algiers, Oran and Annaga, and northern trading centers (Constantine, Sidi-bel-Abbes, Blida) provide urban employment, but most Algerians still live on their land; their distribution reflects the mainly agricultural economy.

Economy. Northern farms produce citrus fruits, grapes, grain and vegetables. Nomads tend sheep, goats and cattle on the steppe; and desert oases yield dates. Algeria is one of the world's most important oil-producing countries and a primary exporter of liquefied natural gas. Oil and gas provide 90% of total export earnings and have buoyed the country's economic growth in the last decade. Industrial growth is assisted by extensive road and rail systems.

History. Phoenicians settled N Algeria c1200 BC. It became part of Carthage but after the victory of Rome in 201 BC became the Roman province of Numidia. Vandals (by 440 AD), Byzantines (in 534) and Arabs (in the 17th century) all conquered the area. Moors expelled from Spain became the Algerian-based BARBARY PIRATES (from 1518 under nominal Ottoman Turkish control). They ravaged Mediterranean shipping until defeated by US warships. The French then absorbed all Algeria (1830–1909), and French colonists largely governed it until a nationalist revolt (1954–62) forced France to grant Algeria independence. An exodus of skilled French followed. In recent years, Algeria has given material and moral support to the Polisario Front—a group fighting for the independence of W Sahara from Morocco—which has placed it at odds with its neighbors, Mauritania and Morocco.

ALGIERS, capital, major port and largest city of Algeria. Founded by Berbers in 935 on the site of the Roman settlement of Icosium, it was taken by the French in 1830. The modern city lies at the base of a hill overlooking the Bay of Algiers; higher up the slope is the old Moorish city, dominated by the Casbah, a citadel built by the Turks. Pop 1,503,720.

ALGOL (*Algo*rithmic *L*anguage), sometimes given as *Alge*braic *O*riented *L*anguage), universal COMPUTER language devised 1958, adapted 1960. Similar to FORTRAN, but with several important advantages, it is used more in Europe than in the US.

ALGONQUIAN (or Algonkian), largest North American Indian linguistic family, including languages spoken from Newfoundland to the Great Plains and from the Churchill R to Cape Hatteras. In parts of New York occupied by the Iroquois, and elsewhere, there were breaks in this continuity, but isolated Algonquian tribes were also found in California and the Gulf states. (See INDIANS, NORTH AMERICAN.)

ALGONQUIN (or ALGONKIN) INDIANS, North American Indian tribe. ~~a~~ French made an alliance, they were driven out of their territory along the St. Lawrence and Ottawa rivers by the Iroquois in the 17th and 18th centuries. Some united with the

Ottawa Indians; a few remain in Ontario and Quebec. Originally the name "Algonquin" was applied only to the Weskarini of the Gatineau valley, but its application was widened to include other closely related tribes such as the Nipissing and Abitibi. The tribe gave its name to the ALGONQUIAN linguistic division.

ALGORITHM, a set of simple mathematical operations which together, in the right order, constitute a complex mathematical operation. Algorithms are used extensively in COMPUTER science (see ALGOL).

ALGREN, Nelson (1909–1981), US naturalistic novelist, best known for his fiction describing Chicago slum life; author of *The Man with the Golden Arm* (1949) and *A Walk on the Wild Side* (1956).

ALHAMBRA, 13th-century citadel and palace dominating the city of Granada, the finest large-scale example of Moorish architecture in Spain. The name is Arabic for "the red castle." It is decorated in an elaborate but delicate style.

ALI, Muhammad (1942–   ), US heavyweight boxer. Born Cassius Marcellus Clay in Louisville, Ky., he fought his way to the world heavyweight championship, dethroning Sonny LISTON in 1964. Ali was stripped of his title in 1967 by the World Boxing Association while he was appealing against conviction for draft evasion, later overturned. He returned to the ring in 1971 only to be defeated by Joe FRAZIER, but beat him in a return match in 1974. He defeated George FORMAN for the title in 1974 and held it until beaten in 1978 by Leon Spinks.

ALIEN AND SEDITION ACTS, four unpopular laws passed by the US Congress in 1798. Two empowered the president to expel or imprison aliens; one made naturalization more difficult; another, the Sedition Act, punished those who wrote or spoke "with intent to defame" the government. Enacted by the Federalists to prepare for a possible war with France (see XYZ AFFAIR), and to silence Jeffersonian criticism, the Alien Acts were not put into force. But several Jeffersonian newspaper editors were convicted under the Sedition Act. This led to the KENTUCKY AND VIRGINIA RESOLUTIONS.

ALIENATION, man's estrangement from society and from himself as an individual. The idea appears in ROUSSEAU, was first used as a term by HEGEL, and is now often associated with MARX. According to Marx, the sale of labor power as a commodity and the general conditions of production and exchange under capitalism deprive the individual of his essential humanity.

ALI KHAN, Liaquat (1895–1951), prime

minister of Pakistan from independence in 1947 until his assassination by an Afghan fanatic. Chief aide of Muhammad Ali JINNAH, he became secretary of the MUSLIM LEAGUE in 1937.

ALIMENTARY CANAL. See GASTRO-INTESTINAL TRACT.

ALINSKY, Saul (1909–1972), US pioneer in community organization, known for his early community action work in the Chicago stockyards area (1939). Creator of the Woodlawn Organization on Chicago's South Side (1960), he founded a school for community organization there in 1969.

ALKALI, a water-soluble compound of the ALKALI METALS (or ammonia) which acts as a strong BASE producing a high concentration of hydroxyl ions in aqueous solution. Alkalis neutralize acids to form salts and turn red litmus paper blue. Common alkalis are sodium hydroxide (NaOH), ammonia (NH₃), sodium carbonate (Na₂CO₃) and potassium carbonate (K₂CO₃). They have important industrial applications in the manufacture of glass, soap, paper and textiles. Caustic alkalis are corrosive and can cause severe burns.

ALKALI METALS, highly reactive metals in Group IA of the PERIODIC TABLE, comprising LITHIUM, SODIUM, POTASSIUM, RUBIDIUM, CESIUM and FRANCIUM. They are soft and silvery-white with low melting points. Alkali metals react with water to give off hydrogen, and so much heat is generated (except by lithium and sodium) that spontaneous combustion may occur. Because of this extreme reactivity they never occur naturally as the metals, but are always found as monovalent ionic salts.

ALKALINE-EARTH METALS, gray-white metals in Group IIA of the PERIODIC TABLE, comprising BERYLLIUM, MAGNESIUM, CALCIUM, STRONTIUM, BARIUM and RADIUM. They never occur in an uncombined state, but are usually found as carbonates or sulfates. Except for beryllium, they are highly reactive and inflammable, readily dissolving in acids to form divalent ionic salts. The hydroxides of the four heaviest elements are alkalis.

ALKALOIDS, narcotic poisons found in certain plants and fungi. They have complex molecular structures and are usually heterocyclic nitrogen-containing BASES. Many, such as coniine (from hemlock) or atropine (deadly nightshade), are extremely poisonous. Others, such as morphine, nicotine and cocaine, can be highly addictive, and some, such as mescaline, are psychedelics. But in small doses alkaloids are often powerful medicines, and are used as analgesics,

tranquilizers, and cardiac and respiratory stimulants. Other examples are quinine, reserpine and ephedrine. Caffeine (found in coffee and tea) is a stimulant. Although alkaloids may be found in any part of the plant, they are usually contained in the seeds, seed capsules, bark or roots. One plant, the opium poppy, contains about 30 alkaloids. Alkaloids are extracted from plants and separated by chromatography; synthetic alkaloids are seldom economically competitive.

ALLAH, Arabic name (*al-ilah*) for the supreme being, used by the prophet Mohammed to designate the God of ISLAM.

ALL-AMERICAN CANAL, completed 1940, brings water 80mi from the Imperial Reservoir on the Colorado R to irrigate 500,000 acres of the Imperial Valley, Cal., and also supplies water to San Diego. A branch delivering an equal amount of water to the Coachella Valley was opened in 1958.

ALLEGHENY MOUNTAINS, range of the central Appalachians extending from SW Va. through Md. into N central Pa. The Alleghenies run parallel to and W of the Blue Ridge Mountains, with average heights of 2,000ft in the N and more than 4,500ft in the S. The steep E slope is called the Allegheny Front. The upland region between the Cumberland Plateau and Mohawk Valley is known as the Allegheny Plateau.

ALLEGHENY RIVER, important head-stream of the Ohio R. Rising in Potter Co., N central Pa., it crosses the SW corner of N.Y., then flows S through Pa. to Pittsburgh, where it joins the Monongahela to form the Ohio R.

ALLEGORY, term applicable in any of the arts where the literal content of the work is subsidiary to its symbolic meaning. Concrete and material images are used to represent more abstract notions; thus death might be personified as a reaper. BUNYAN's *Pilgrim's Progress* is a classic example of allegory in literature; many modern writers also use allegory. It is common in the visual arts, perhaps most notably those of the Renaissance and Baroque periods, as for example in BOTTICELLI's *Primavera*.

ALLEN, Ethan (1738–1789), American revolutionary hero, leader of the GREEN MOUNTAIN BOYS of Vermont. In May 1775 he seized the British fort at TICONDEROGA, together with its valuable cannon, but in Sept. was captured in a reckless attack on Montreal. Released after almost three years, he was unsuccessful in petitioning Congress for Vt.'s statehood; he then attempted to negotiate the annexation of

Vt. by British Canada.

ALLEN, Fred (stage name of John Florence Sullivan, 1894–1956), US comedian who achieved enormous success with his radio show, broadcast 1932–50. The wry humor and nasal delivery of his *Allen's Alley* sketches won him national popularity.

ALLEN, Frederick Lewis (1890–1954), US journalist and social historian. After teaching at Harvard he entered journalism, becoming chief editor of *Harper's Magazine* (1941–54). His historical works, including *Only Yesterday* (1932), were readable and popular.

ALLEN, Hervey (1889–1949), US novelist and poet, co-founder of the Poetry Society of S.C. His best-known work is a long historical novel set in Napoleonic times, *Anthony Adverse* (1933), which was an international success.

ALLEN, Steve (1921–   ), US comedian, songwriter and television talk show personality who hosted the original "Tonight Show," 1954–57. His comedy was showcased in the "Steve Allen Show" in which Jayne Meadows, his wife, also appeared.

ALLEN, Woody (1935–   ), US comedian, author and film director. An unprepossessing stature and self-effacing wit established him as one of the major comedic talents of the 1960s and 1970s. Following a nightclub career he broke into films (1965) and wrote, directed and starred in such favorites as *Bananas* (1971) and the Academy Award-winning *Annie Hall* (1977). His comic short stories and parodies were published in *Getting Even* (1971) and *Side Effects* (1980).

ALLENBY, Edmund Henry Hynman, 1st Viscount (1861–1936), British field marshal who directed the brilliant campaign that won Palestine and Syria from the Turks in WWI. From 1919–25 he was British High Commissioner in Egypt.

ALLENDE, Salvador (1908–1973), Marxist founder of the Chilean Socialist Party, elected president of Chile in 1970, having won the largest minority vote. He subsequently failed to win a majority in the 1972 elections. His radical reform program disrupted the economy; strikes and widespread famine led to a military coup and to his death, reportedly by suicide.

ALLERGY, a state of abnormal sensitivity to foreign material (allergen) in susceptible individuals. It is essentially the inappropriate reaction of ANTIBODY AND ANTIGEN defense responses to environmental substances. Susceptibility is often inherited but manifestations vary with age. Exposure to allergen induces the formation of an-

tibodies; when, at a later date, the material is again encountered, it reacts with the antibodies causing release of HISTAMINE from mast cells in the tissues. INFLAMMATION follows, with local irritation, redness and swelling, which in skin appear as ECZEMA or urticaria (see HIVES). In the nose and eyes HAY FEVER results, and in the GASTROINTESTINAL tract diarrhea may occur. In the LUNGS a specific effect leads to spasm of bronchi, which gives rise to the wheeze and breathlessnness of ASTHMA. In most cases, the route of entry determines the site of the response; but skin rashes may occur regardless of route and asthma may follow eating allergenic material. If the allergen is injected, ANAPHYLAXIS may occur. Localized allergic reactions in skin following chronic exposure to chemicals (e.g., nickel, poison ivy) are the basis of contact dermatitis. Common allergens include drugs (PENICILLIN, ASPIRIN), foods (shellfish), plant pollens, animal furs or feathers, insect stings and the house dust mite. Treatment includes ANTIHISTAMINES, cromoglycate, STEROIDS and desensitizing INJECTIONS; ADRENALINE may be life-saving in severe allergic reactions. (See also IMMUNITY.)

ALLIANCE FOR PROGRESS, program designed to aid the economic and social development of Latin America, instituted by President John F. Kennedy in 1961 and brought into being when 22 nations and the US signed the Charter of Punta del Este. The Latin American countries draw up development plans and guarantee the larger part of capital costs, the US meeting the remainder. Most US funds are administered by the AGENCY FOR INTERNATIONAL DEVELOPMENT, and since 1970 the ORGANIZATION OF AMERICAN STATES has also reviewed and coordinated programs.

ALLIES, two or more nations bound by treaty or alliance to act together against a common enemy in case of war. In WWI the "Allies" were the members of the TRIPLE ENTENTE, together with Serbia, Belgium, Japan, Italy and, as an "associated power," the US. In WWII "Allies" was the popular term for some 25 nations that opposed the Axis powers. The major nations among the Allies were the US, Britain, Russia, China and, later, the Free French. These five became the permanent members of the UN Security Council, established in 1945.

ALLIGATORS, two species of large aquatic, carnivorous lizard-like REPTILES comprising the genus *Alligator*. With the CAIMANS, they form the family Alligatoridae of the order Crocodilia. The American alligator (A. mississippiensis), now largely restricted to Fla. and La., has been known to attain 6m (20ft) in length, but the rare Chinese alligator (*A. sinensis*), which inhabits the upper Yangtze valley, rarely exceeds 1.8m (6ft). Alligators can live up to 75 years.

ALLITERATION, device in poetry of repeating a sound, usually a consonant, at the beginning of neighboring words; in the line from TENNYSON's *Lotos Eaters,* "Surely, surely, slumber is more sweet than toil," the "s" and "l" sounds are alliterative. Early Germanic, Old Norse and Old English verse is characterized by subtle accented alliterative measures, and it is often found in Gaelic and Welsh poetry. LANGLAND's *Piers Plowman* exemplifies a school of alliterative verse which survived in W England until the late 14th century.

ALLON, Yigal (1918–1980), Israeli political leader, a commander of the Hagana in the 1947–48 Arab-Israeli War. He first entered the cabinet as minister of labor (1961), and became deputy prime minister (1968) and foreign minister in 1974.

ALLOTROPY, the occurrence of some elements in more than one form (known as allotropes) which differ in their crystalline or molecular structure. Allotropes may have strikingly different physical or chemical properties. Allotropy in which the various forms are stable under different conditions and are reversibly interconvertible at certain temperatures and pressures, is called enantiotropy. Notable examples of allotropy include DIAMOND and GRAPHITE, OXYGEN and OZONE, and SULFUR.

ALLOY, a combination of metals with each other or with nonmetals such as carbon or phosphorus. They are useful because their properties can be adjusted as desired by varying the proportions of the constituents. Very few metals are used today in a pure state. Alloys are formed by mixing their molten components. The structures of alloys consisting mainly of one component may be substitutional or interstitial, depending on the relative sizes of the atoms. The study of alloy structures in general is complex.

The commonest alloys are the different forms of STEEL, which all contain a large proportion of iron and small amounts of carbon and other elements. BRASS and BRONZE, two well-known and ancient metals, are alloys of copper, while PEWTER is an alloy of tin and lead. The very light but strong alloys used in aircraft construction are frequently alloys of aluminum with magnesium, copper or silicon. SOLDERS contain tin with lead and bismuth; type metal is an alloy of lead, tin and antimony. Among familiar alloys are those used in

coins: modern "silver" coinage in most countries is an alloy of nickel and copper. Special alloys are used for such purposes as die-casting, dentistry, high-temperature use, and for making thermocouples, magnets and low-expansion materials. (See also AMALGAM; BABBITT METAL; GERMAN SILVER; GUN METAL; INVAR; MONEL METAL.)

ALLPORT, Gordon Willard (1897–1967). US psychologist, important figure in the study of personality, who stressed the "functional autonomy of motives." Among his many works, *The Nature of Prejudice* (1954) has become a classic in its field.

ALL SAINTS' DAY, religious feast day celebrating all Christian saints, observed by most Christian churches on Nov. 1. Its present form dates from the reign of Pope Gregory III (731–741).

ALL SAVERS CERTIFICATE, a one-year US bank certificate with a tax exemption on up to $1,000 of its interest for individuals. This tax-free feature attracts savers back to banks, which in the early 1980s had lost deposit funds because interest rates increased well above the rates banks were allowed to pay on savings deposits.

ALLSTON, Washington (1779–1843), first major US landscape painter. He painted large dramatic canvases of biblical and Classical scenes, but this early Italianate style gave way to romanticism influenced by TURNER.

ALMA-ATA, capital of Kazakh SSR, USSR, and administrative center of Alma-Ata oblast in foothills of Trans-Alay Alatau Mts at junction of Bolshaya and Malaya Almaatinka R. Noted for its agricultural products and heavy machinery, Alma-Ata is also a major cultural and educational center with an opera house, museums, theaters and 12 institutions of higher learning. Pop 932,000.

ALMAGRO, Diego de (1475–1538), Spanish conquistador who helped to capture Peru. He joined Francisco PIZARRO in the conquest (1533), then fruitlessly sought gold in Chile. Returning to Peru, he claimed and seized Cuzco, then was defeated and executed by Pizarro's brother.

ALMANACH DE GOTHA, handbook of the genealogies of Europe's royal and noble families, founded in Germany (1763) and later annually produced at Gotha. Publication stopped in 1944 but was resumed in 1959.

ALMEIDA, Francisco de (c1450–1510), first viceroy of Portuguese India (1505–09). His conquests, forts and trading posts strengthened Portuguese influence in coastal India and E Africa and spread it E to Sumatra.

ALONSO, Alicia (1917–   ), Cuban dancer, born Alicia Martinez. She was a leading ballerina of the American Ballet Theatre (1941–60), where she and Igor YOUSKEVITCH formed one of the most famous teams in ballet history, notably in *Giselle*. In 1948 she formed her own company in Cuba, which became Ballet de Cuba in 1955.

ALPACA, S American herbivore (*Lama pacos*) closely related to the LLAMA. It has a long body and neck, and is about 1m (3ft) high at the shoulder. Its long thick coat of black, brown or yellowish hair provides valuable wool. All alpacas are now domesticated, living mainly in the Andes above 13,000ft. Family: Camelidae.

ALPHABET (from Greek *alpha* and *beta*), a set of characters intended to represent the sounds of spoken language. Because of this intention (which in practice is never realized) written languages employing alphabets are quite distinct from those using characters which represent whole words (see IDEOGRAM; HIEROGLYPHICS). The word alphabet is, however, usually extended to describe syllabaries, languages in which characters represent syllables. The chief alphabets of the world are Roman (Latin), Greek, Hebrew, Cyrillic (Slavic), Arabic and Devanagari.

Alphabets probably originated around 2000 BC. Hebrew, Arabic and other written languages sprang from a linear alphabet which had appeared c1500 BC. From the Phoenician alphabet, which appeared around 1700 BC, was derived the Greek. Roman letters were derived from Greek and from the rather similar Etruscan, also a descendant of the Greek. Most of the letters we now use are from the Latin alphabet, U and W being distinguished from V, and J from I in the early Middle Ages. The Cyrillic alphabet, used with the Slavic languages, derives from the Greek. It is thought that Devanagari was possibly invented to represent Sanskrit.

Chinese and Japanese are the only major languages that function without alphabets, although Japanese has syllabary elements. (See also CUNEIFORM and WRITING, HISTORY OF; and, for the evolution of the letters of our alphabet, the headings to each alphabetical section.)

ALPHA PARTICLES. See RADIOACTIVITY.

ALPHONSUS LIGUORI, Saint (1696–1787), Italian priest who founded the Congregation of the Most Holy Redeemer (Redemptorist Order), a society of missionary preachers working with the rural poor. He was canonized in 1839.

ALPS, Europe's largest mountain system, 650mi long and 30–180mi wide. Its fold mountains result from earth movements in Tertiary times. The Western Alps, with the highest peak, Mont Blanc (15,771ft), run along the French-Italian border. The Central Alps run NE and E through Switzerland. The Eastern Alps extend through S Germany, Austria and NE Italy into Yugoslavia. Peaks are snowy and etched by ice action. The Alps are known for their magnificent mountain scenery, glacially deepened valleys and many glaciers.

ALSACE-LORRAINE, region in NE France occupying 5,608sq mi W of the Rhine. It produces grains and grapes; timber, coal, potash and salt (from the Vosges Mts); iron ore and textiles. Metz, Nancy, Strasbourg and Verdun are the chief cities.

The people are part French, part German in origin. France and Germany have long disputed control of the area. In medieval times it was in the Holy Roman Empire. France took Alsace after 1648 and Lorraine in 1766. Germany seized most of both in 1871, lost them to France after WWI, regained control in WWII, then lost it again.

ALSOP, Joseph Wright, Jr. (1910–   ), US journalist who was an influential Washington pundit for decades. He wrote a political column with his brother **Stewart** for the *New York Herald Tribune* syndicate (1945–58) and was sole author of a widely-read column in the *Washington Post* (1958–74).

ALTACHIERO (active 1369–90), Italian painter, founder of the Verona school. His few surviving works are mainly in Padua, in the form of frescoes showing the influence of GIOTTO.

ALTAIC LANGUAGES, group of languages comprising three subgroups: Mongol, Manchu-Tungus and principally the TURKIC LANGUAGES. The Altaic languages are spoken in the USSR, Turkey, Iran, Afghanistan, China and the Mongolian People's Republic.

ALTAMIRA, cave near Santander, N Spain, inhabited during the Aurignacian, upper Solutrean and Magdalenian periods. In 1879 the daughter of an amateur archaeologist discovered the striking cave paintings, believed to date from the Magdalenian period. They depict such animals as bison, boars, horses.

ALTAMONT FESTIVAL, concert of the ROLLING STONES rock group on Dec. 6, 1969, at Altamont Speedway in Livermore, Cal., at which 3 people died—one apparently trampled to death, another of a drug overdose, and the third stabbed by a member of the HELL'S ANGELS motorcycle gang when he approached the stage with a revolver in hand. The Angels, who had been hired to keep order, also staged a mini-riot, reportedly after a concert-goer had kicked their leader's cycle.

ALTDORFER, Albrecht (1480–1538), German painter and engraver. Most of his paintings had religious subjects, but because of the prominence of forest and mountain settings he is often held to be the first German landscape painter.

ALTGELD, John Peter (1847–1902), US political leader and jurist who sought to defend the individual against abuses of governmental power and vested interests. As a Cook Co., Ill. superior court judge he argued that legal practice was weighted against the poor. Elected Democratic governor of Illinois (1892), he backed labor and championed reform, arousing controversy by freeing three anarchists imprisoned for Chicago's HAYMARKET AFFAIR riot (1886) and by opposing President Cleveland's use of troops to crush the PULLMAN STRIKE of 1894.

ALTHUSSER, Louis (1918–   ), French philosopher, leading figure in the influential Marxist-structuralist school. He wrote *For Marx* (1965; tr. 1969) and *Reading Capital* (1965; tr. 1970).

ALTIMETER, an instrument used for estimating the height of an aircraft above sea level. Most are modified aneroid BAROMETERS and work on the principle that air pressure decreases with increased altitude, but these must be constantly recalibrated throughout the flight to take account of changing meteorological conditions (local ground temperature and air pressure reduced to sea level). **Radar altimeters,** which compute ABSOLUTE altitudes (the height of the aircraft above the ground surface immediately below) from the time taken for RADAR waves to be reflected to the aircraft from the ground, although essential for blind landings, are as yet too expensive for general installation.

ALTIPLANO, a high plateau region in S America between the W and E cordilleras of the Andes. Its bleak grasslands lie between 10,000 and 12,000ft and run S from Peru through Bolivia and into Argentina. It contains lakes Titicaca and Poopó.

ALTITUDE SICKNESS, a condition of OXYGEN lack in blood and tissues due to low atmospheric PRESSURE. Night vision is impaired, followed by breathlessness, headache, and faintness. At 5,000m mental changes include indifference, euphoria and

faulty judgment but complete ACCLIMATIZATION is possible up to those heights. At very high altitude (6,000m to 7,000m), CYANOSIS, COMA and death rapidly supervene. Treatment is by oxygen and descent. The use of pressurized cabins prevents the occurrence of the condition.

ALTMAN, Robert (1925–   ), US film producer and director whose first big hit was *M*A*S*H* (1970). His other cinematic explorations of American myths included *McCabe and Mrs. Miller* (1971) and *Nashville* (1975).

ALTO ADIGE. See TRENTINO–ALTO ADIGE.

ALUMINUM (Al), silvery-white metal in Group IIIA of the PERIODIC TABLE, the most abundant metal, comprising 8% of the earth's crust. It occurs naturally as BAUXITE, CRYOLITE, FELDSPAR, clay and many other minerals, and is smelted by the HALL-HÉROULT PROCESS, chiefly in the US, USSR and Canada. It is a reactive metal, but in air is covered with a protective layer of the oxide. Aluminum is light and strong when alloyed, so that aluminum ALLOYS are used very widely in the construction of machinery and domestic appliances. It is also a good conductor of electricity and is often used in overhead transmission cables where lightness is crucial. AW 27.0, mp 660°C, bp 2467°C, sg 2.6989 (20°C).

Aluminum compounds are trivalent and mainly cationic (see CATION), though with strong bases aluminates are formed. (See also ALUM.) **Aluminum Oxide** (Al$_2$O$_3$), or **Alumina,** is a colorless or white solid occurring in several crystalline forms, and is found naturally as CORUNDUM, EMERY and BAUXITE. Solubility in acid and alkali increases with hydration. mp 2045°C, bp 2980°C. **Aluminum Chloride** (AlCl$_3$) is a colorless crystalline solid, used as a catalyst. The hexahydrate is used in deodorants and as an astringent.

ALVARADO, Pedro de (c1485–1541), Spanish colonizer of Guatemala. He was CORTES's chief lieutenant in the conquest of Mexico (1519–21), then (1523–24) led the force that seized what are now Guatemala and El Salvador. As governor of Guatemala he instituted forced Indian labor and founded many cities.

ALVAREZ, Luis Walter (1911–   ), US physicist awarded the 1968 Nobel Prize for Physics for work on SUBATOMIC PARTICLES, including the discovery of the transient resonance particles. He helped develop much of the hardware of NUCLEAR PHYSICS.

AMADO, Jorge (1912–   ), Brazilian novelist, author of *The Violent Land* (1942) and *Gabriela, Clove and Cinnamon* (1958). His books are particularly concerned with the plight of the poor.

AMANITA, genus of mainly poisonous MUSHROOMS found in woods and forests. They have white spores and gills, a ring of tissue (annulus) surrounding the stem just below the cap, and a sac or cup (volva) around the swollen base of the stalk. The volva is the remains of the membrane that completely enclosed the young mushroom. The commonest species, the fly agaric (*A. muscaria*), is poisonous but not usually fatal; it has a distinctive scarlet cap. Family: Agaricaceae.

AMARYLLIS, genus containing a single species, *A. belladonna*, native to S Africa but widely grown as an ornamental. Also called belladonna lily, it has a long stem bearing a terminal cluster of showy, lilylike flowers. Straplike leaves develop after the flowers. The name amaryllis is often applied to any member of the family Amaryllidaceae. Amaryllis is a popular house plant requiring a light position in a sunny east, south or west window and a temperature between 17°C and 24°C (62°F and 75°F). After blooming the stem should be cut off at soil level. Propagation is by means of offsets.

AMATI, Italian family of violin makers in Cremona (16th–17th centuries). Noted members were **Andrea** (c1520–c1578), his sons Antonio and Girolamo, and Girolamo's son **Nicolò** (1596–1684), the most famous of all. His superb instruments became models for those of Andrea GUARNERI and Antonio STRADIVARI.

AMAZON RIVER, world's largest river in volume and drainage area, and second-longest, at 3,900mi. Its basin drains 40% of South America. The Amazon rises in Andean Peru near the Pacific Ocean and flows E through the world's largest equatorial forest to the Atlantic Ocean. It is a broad sluggish stream up to 30mi wide in flood, with hundreds of tributaries, 17 of which are more than 1,000mi long.

Fed by annual runoff from 70–120in of rain, the river pours an estimated one-fifth of all water falling on earth into the Atlantic Ocean, where its current extends 200mi out to sea. Tides are felt 600mi upstream and oceangoing vessels can travel 2,300mi to Iquitos in Peru. Other ports are Belém and Manaus, handling river commerce in hardwoods and other river products of sparsely peopled Amazonia. Spain's Vicente Pinzón discovered the river mouth in 1500; Francisco de ORELLANA was the first to travel downriver from the Andes to the Atlantic (1541).

AMBEDKAR, Bhimrao Ramji (1893–1956), Indian politician who championed his fellow "untouchables," members of the lowest Hindu caste in India. He helped ensure that India's constitution of 1949 banned discrimination against them but failed to eliminate the untouchable castes from Hinduism.

AMBER, fossilized RESIN from prehistoric EVERGREENS. Brownish-yellow and translucent, it is highly valued and can be easily cut and polished for ornamental purposes. Its chief importance is that FOSSIL insects up to 20 million years old have been found embedded in it.

AMBERGRIS, waxy solid formed in the intestines of SPERM WHALES, perhaps to protect them from the bony parts of their squid diet. When obtained from dead whales, it is soft, black and evil-smelling, but on weathering (as when found as flotsam) it becomes hard, gray and fragrant, and is used as a perfume fixative and in the East as a spice.

AMBLER, Eric (1909–   ), English suspense writer, noted especially for stories in which ordinary, unheroic characters are caught up in international intrigue and danger. His numerous works include *Epitaph for a Spy* (1938) and *A Coffin for Dimitrios* (1939).

AMBO, early Christian form of church pulpit comprising a stand raised on steps, from which the Epistle and the Gospel were read.

AMBROSE, Saint (c340–397), an important Father of the Latin Church. A Roman governor who became the influential bishop of Milan, he attacked imperial moral standards and strengthened the position of the Church amid the ruins of the Roman Empire by his preaching and writing. St. AUGUSTINE was one of his converts.

AMERICA, the two major continents of the Western Hemisphere, North and South America, or only the United States. The term was coined in 1507 by the German geographer Martin Waldseemüller in honor of the Italian navigator Amerigo Vespucci, who supposedly discovered much of South America—the area to which the term was originally confined.

AMERICAN ACADEMY IN ROME, institute for US students engaged in advanced studies in fine arts and Classical subjects in Rome, Italy. Annual fellowships offer a fixed stipend, travel allowances and residence facilities.

AMERICAN ASSOCIATION OF RETIRED PERSONS (AARP), organization which provides services and sponsors programs aimed at improving all aspects of life for persons 55 years of age or older, whether or not retired. Founded 1958, it has about 11,500,000 members.

AMERICAN AUTOMOBILE ASSOCIATION (AAA), US federation of automobile clubs providing domestic and foreign travel services, emergency road services, and auto insurance. Founded 1902, the AAA has a membership of about 21 million.

AMERICAN CIVIL LIBERTIES UNION (ACLU), organization founded 1920 and dedicated to defending constitutional freedoms in the US. Its work centers on providing legal aid in cases of violated civil liberties especially those of political, religious and racial minorities. From its founding the ACLU has participated in the nation's most important civil rights cases: the Scopes Trial (1925), which challenged a Tennessee law barring the right to teach Darwin's theory of evolution in schools; the federal court test (1933) that ended censorship of James Joyce's *Ulysses*; and the landmark *Brown v. Board of Education* (1954) case, which successfully challenged the constitutionality of racially segregated public schooling. Frequently attacked by right-wingers, the organization again generated controversy in 1978 by upholding the American Nazi Party's right to march in Skokie, Ill., and to display swastika symbols. ACLU membership totals some 200,000.

AMERICAN COLONIZATION SOCIETY, US organization formed in 1822 to found an overseas home for free Negroes. Some abolitionists thought it secretly pro-slavery. Its West African colony, established in 1816, became Africa's first black republic, LIBERIA, in 1847.

AMERICAN CONSERVATIVE UNION, organization formed in 1964 to mobilize conservative opinion throughout the country. Headquartered in Washington, D.C., it has 300,000 members in 42 state groups. It conducts forums on such topics as "prejudice in the press," maintains an information service on conservative publications and rates members of Congress according to their votes on key pieces of legislation.

AMERICAN FEDERATION OF LABOR AND CONGRESS OF INDUSTRIAL ORGANIZATIONS (AFL-CIO), powerful US federation of labor unions created in 1955 by the merger of the AFL and CIO. Some 125 constituent unions represent over 13 million members. A national president, secretary-treasurer and 27 vice-presidents make up the executive council. This enforces policy decisions made at biennial conventions attended by several thousand delegates.

The organization's main objectives are more pay, fewer working hours and better working conditions for employees, obtained by union–management agreements that preserve industrial harmony and prosperity. Each affiliated union conducts its own collective bargaining and determines much of its own policy. The AFL-CIO takes influential stands on such issues as social welfare, conservation, education and international problems. It has recently backed Democratic presidential candidates.

The AFL originated in 1886 in the reorganized Federation of Organized Trade and Labor Unions. Initially led by Samuel GOMPERS, it comprised only craft unions, excluding unskilled and semiskilled workers, whose numbers multiplied as mass production increased in the early 1900s. To cater to these workers, AFL dissidents in 1935 formed the Committee for Industrial Organization, later the CIO, led by John L. LEWIS. In the 1950s laws hostile to organized labor encouraged union cooperation and in 1955 the AFL and CIO merged, with George MEANY (head of AFL) as president. Meany retired in 1979 and was replaced by his hand-picked successor, Lane KIRKLAND. Although nearly 40% of all union workers are women, it was not until 1980 that a woman labor leader was named to the AFL-CIO executive council: Joyce Miller, vice-president of the Amalgamated Clothing & Textile Workers.

AMERICAN FUR COMPANY, the earliest US trading monopoly, founded 1808 by John Jacob Astor. With his Pacific Fur Co., it controlled the fur trade from the Great Lakes W to the Pacific and monopolized trade in the Mississippi valley.

AMERICAN INDEPENDENT PARTY, US political party with a strongly conservative position on social issues. Created 1968 as the vehicle for the presidential candidacy of George C. WALLACE, who polled 9,906,473 votes, or 13.5% of the total, it declined sharply after Wallace left the party, winning only 41,268 votes in the 1980 presidential election.

AMERICAN JEWISH COMMITTEE, organization founded in 1906 by a group of Jewish Americans, led by Jacob Schiff, to protect the civil and religious liberties of Jews throughout the world. It publishes a journal and yearbook.

AMERICAN LABOR PARTY, N.Y. State left-wing political party (1936–56). Founded by labor leaders, it helped elect its member Fiorello LA GUARDIA mayor of New York in 1937 and 1941 and Herbert LEHMAN governor in 1938. In WWII it split over attitudes to Russia: the right under

David DUBINSKY accused Sidney HILLMAN'S left of being communist-controlled. The party disbanded in 1956.

AMERICAN LEGION, organization of US war veterans, founded in 1919. Its 2,700,000 members are survivors of WWI and WWII and the Korean and Vietnam wars. The legion publicizes national defense needs, cares for needy veterans and their families and influences legislation.

AMERICAN LITERATURE began with accounts of the hopes, discoveries and disasters experienced by the explorers of the New World. The writings of established settlers followed in the 1600s, reflecting the Puritan and Colonial concerns of the time, and including Anne BRADSTREET's devotional poetry and Cotton MATHER's pious New England history, *Magnalia Christi Americana* (1702). The late 1700s heralded the eloquent prose of the American Revolutionaries, such as Thomas PAINE's *Common Sense* (1776) and Benjamin FRANKLIN's *Autobiography* (1790). After the Revolutionary War, the satirist Washington IRVING became the first American fiction writer to gain an international reputation with *Sketchbook* (1820), and James Fenimore COOPER became the first eminent American novelist with his rough-hewn historical romances such as *The Last of the Mohicans* (1826).

With the gradual development of the vast country during the 1800s, a distinctively American individualism began to assert itself in writings such as *Walden* (1854) by Henry David THOREAU and the essays of Ralph Waldo EMERSON (1803–1882), which championed independent thought and spiritual rejuvenation. There also arose a cluster of major works that established a body of serious American fiction. Nathaniel HAWTHORNE's *The Scarlet Letter* (1850) and Herman MELVILLE's masterpiece *Moby Dick* (1851) displayed profound insight into the dilemmas of man's isolation, his place in nature and his capacity for evil. Edgar Allan POE, a pioneer of the short story and of the detective fiction genre, was also in the vanguard of the French Symbolist movement with such feverish works as the poem *The Raven* (1845) and the story *The Tell-Tale Heart* (1843). Walt WHITMAN's epic collection of poems, *Leaves of Grass* (1855–1892), celebrated the American experience with a vivid evocation of love and concern for the people and their democracy. With his innovative rhythms, Whitman influenced the free-verse poetry of the 20th century. Meanwhile, Emily DICKINSON (1830–1886) wrote the compressed, idiosyncratic verse which has since established her as one of the most original of American poets. Henry Wadsworth LONGFELLOW (1807–1882), though his melodious narrative verse was not enduring, was the most popular poet of his day.

In the late 19th century, two men implanted a new realism in American literature: the expatriate Henry JAMES effected new psychological action in novels such as *Portrait of a Lady* (1881), and the humorist Mark TWAIN legitimatized the colloquial voice and the regional setting in his masterpiece *Huckleberry Finn* (1885). Meanwhile, the novelist and poet Stephen CRANE (1871–1900) became the first American naturalist writer. These three influenced the work of such contemporaries as William Dean HOWELLS, Edith WHARTON and Theodore DREISER, and laid the foundations for a generation of early 20th century writers concerned with the effects of industrialized society on the individual, the focus of such works as Sinclair LEWIS's *Main Street* (1920), John DOS PASSOS' *U.S.A.* (1934) and John STEINBECK's *The Grapes of Wrath* (1939).

In the post WWI period, three important American writers emerged. F. Scott FITZGERALD precisely rendered the glamour and tragedy of the 1920s in novels such as *The Great Gatsby* (1925). William FAULKNER expanded the boundaries of the novel, taking it far beyond naturalism with works such as *The Sound and The Fury* (1929). And Ernest HEMINGWAY established a distinctively direct, spare and vivid prose style in short stories and his first novel, *The Sun Also Rises* (1926). Post WWII novelists of note include Saul BELLOW, Eudora WELTY, J.D. SALINGER, Norman MAILER, John CHEEVER, and John UPDIKE.

Not until the 20th century did America produce a major dramatist—Eugene O'NEILL. In such powerful masterpieces as *Desire Under the Elms* (1924), *The Iceman Cometh* (1946) and *Long Day's Journey Into Night* (1957), O'Neill developed a realistic theatrical form that subsumed his own early experiments in expressionism and stream-of-consciousness. He stood alone among US playwrights until the appearance after WWII of such major talents as Tennessee WILLIAMS, Arthur MILLER, Edward ALBEE, and Sam SHEPARD.

Early 20th-century heirs of the free-form poetry of Whitman and the verse of Dickinson included Amy LOWELL (1874–1925), Carl SANDBURG (1878–1967) and Robert FROST (1874–1963). Between the world wars a New Poetry movement formed, influenced by Whitman, Dickinson, the French Symbolists and even the

Chinese ideogram. It included such poets as Ezra POUND (1885–1972), and Wallace STEVENS (1879–1955). Eliot, whose poem *The Waste Land* (1922) was perhaps the most influential written in the 20th century, introduced the term "objective correlative" to describe the singular situation or image which a poet uses to convey a particular emotion. Wallace Stevens advanced a new "romantic" notion of the now-transcending imagination. After WWII, major names in US poetry have included LOWELL, Sylvia PLATH, and Allen GINSBERG.

AMERICAN MEDICAL ASSOCIATION (AMA), organization of US physicians mainly from state medical associations. It was founded in 1847 to advance medical knowledge, raise medical standards, improve public health and support the medical profession. It holds conferences, issues periodicals and investigates standards in pharmacy, foods, medical education and hospitals, and has influenced national and state legislation.

AMERICAN MUSEUM OF NATURAL HISTORY, an institution in New York City founded in 1869 and dedicated to research and popular education in anthropology, astronomy, mineralogy and natural history. It is noted for its mounted specimens of birds and other animals from all over the world, fossil collections which include a 47-foot-long skeleton of a Tyrannosaurus rex, its gem collection with the Star of India sapphire, and the Hayden Planetarium.

AMERICAN NAZI PARTY, US political party espousing anti-Semitism and other tenets of German Nazism. The party was founded in 1959 by Harold N. Arrowsmith, Jr. and George Lincoln Rockwell. Its total membership has not exceeded a few dozen young men.

AMERICAN PHILOSOPHICAL SOCIETY, the oldest surviving US learned society, based in Philadelphia where it was founded by Benjamin FRANKLIN in 1743. The US counterpart of the ROYAL SOCIETY OF LONDON (1660), it currently has nearly 600 US and foreign members. It has an extensive library, much relating to early American science. Its publications commenced in 1769 with *Transactions*.

AMERICAN PROTECTIVE ASSOCIATION (APA), anti-Roman Catholic secret society founded in 1887. Its members blamed Catholic immigrants for unemployment during the depression of the 1890s. It collapsed after 1896, split by national election issues.

AMERICANS FOR DEMOCRATIC ACTION (ADA), organization founded 1947 to create and promote liberal political and social policies in the US. It has remained prestigious and influential, and its ratings of members of Congress are widely publicized. The ADA's membership is about 40,000.

AMERICAN SHORTHAIR, breed of cat developed in US, also known as Domestic Shorthair. A well-built cat with medium to large body, it has a longer nose than the European type from which it descends and a squarer muzzle and firm chin. Its thick coat has an even, hard texture and may be a wide range of solid, tabby or shaded colors.

AMERICAN STOCK EXCHANGE (AMEX), second largest securities market in the US (after the New York Stock Exchange). Located in the financial district of New York City, the Amex has 650 regular members and trades more than 1,000 issues of stocks and bonds. Founded as the New York Curb Exchange in 1849, it received its present name in 1953.

AMERICAN SYSTEM, Senator Henry Clay's name for his national economic plan to establish protective tariffs to help industry, reestablish a national bank, finance new roads and canals to open the West and broaden agricultural markets. Under President Monroe tariffs were indeed raised and a national bank reestablished. But the more extreme schemes of President John Quincy Adams alienated sectional interests, and after 1829 Andrew Jackson let American System provisions lapse.

AMERICAN TELEPHONE AND TELEGRAPH COMPANY (AT&T), the world's largest corporation with assets at the end of 1980 of $125.5 billion, revenues for the year of $50.2 billion and a net income of $6 billion. Employees number more than one million. Established in 1885 as a subsidiary of American Bell Telephone Co., AT&T took over Bell in a corporate reorganization in 1900. It provides most of the nation's telephone services through 23 regional companies; other key units include Bell Laboratories, which does research for the system; Western Electric Co., which manufactures equipment; and AT&T International, Inc. In 1980, following a decision by the Federal Communications Commission to deregulate portions of the telephone industry, AT&T decided to divide itself into two independently managed subsidiaries. The first provides the traditional telephone services of Ma Bell, while the other, Baby Bell, enters unregulated fields such as data processing and telecommunications, which had been previously barred to AT&T under the terms of a 1956 antitrust consent order.

AMERICA'S CUP, the most famous

international yachting trophy, held continuously by the US since 1851, when the New York Yacht Club's *America* outraced 14 British sailing craft. Yacht clubs of any country may challenge the US holders in US waters, 12-meter yachts competing for the best four out of seven races. Since the series began, challenges have been mounted about once every six years, on an average. Dennis Conner's *Freedom* captured the 1980 series from the Australians, 4-1. In the two previous series, held in 1977 and 1974, Ted Turner's *Courageous* beat back Australian challenges without losing a race.

AMERICA THE BEAUTIFUL, popular patriotic song, with words written in 1893 by Katherine Lee Bates and music by Samuel A. Ward.

AMETHYST, transparent violet or purple variety of QUARTZ, colored by iron or manganese impurities. The color changes to yellow on heating. A semiprecious GEM, the best amethysts come from Brazil, Uruguay, Ariz. and the USSR.

AMHARIC, official language of Ethiopia, spoken by some six million people. It is a Semitic tongue evolved mostly from ancient Ge'ez or Ethiopic. Its alphabet has 33 characters, each with seven forms that represent a consonant and different vowels.

AMHERST COLLEGE, Amherst, Mass., small liberal arts college founded in 1821 by Congregationalists dissatisfied with the teaching at Harvard, and named for Lord Jeffrey AMHERST. Originally for men, it is now coeducational.

AMIENS, Peace of (1802), short-lived Franco-British truce ending the FRENCH REVOLUTIONARY WARS. Britain returned to France or its allies all conquests except Trinidad and Ceylon. France recognized the Republic of the Seven Ionian Islands and Malta was to return to the Knights of Malta.

AMIN DADA, Idi (c1925–   ), Ugandan soldier who became president in 1971, deposing Milton Obote. A flamboyant and dictatorial ruler, he expelled Uganda's Asian middle class in 1972 and purged many opponents. In 1975–76 he was president of the ORGANIZATION OF AFRICAN UNITY. Insurrectionists, aided by Tanzanian forces, drove Amin into exile in 1979. In 1981 he was discovered to be living in Saudi Arabia.

AMINO ACIDS, an important class of CARBOXYLIC ACIDS containing one or more amino (-NH$_2$) groups (see AMINES). Twenty or so α-amino acids (RCH[NH$_2$]COOH) are the building blocks of the PROTEINS found in all living matter. They are also found and synthesized in cells. Amino acids are white, crystalline solids, soluble in water; they can act as ACIDS or BASES depending on the chemical environment (see pH). In neutral solution they exist as ZWITTERIONS. An amino acid mixture may be analyzed by CHROMATOGRAPHY. All α-amino acids (except glycine) contain at least one asymmetric carbon atom to which are attached the carboxyl group, the amino group, a hydrogen atom and a fourth group (R) that differs for each amino acid and determines its character. Thus amino acids can exist in two mirror-image forms (see STEREOISOMERS). Generally only L-isomers occur in nature, but a few bacteria contain D-isomers. Humans synthesize most of the amino acids needed for NUTRITION, but depend on protein foods for eight "essential amino acids" which they cannot produce. Inside the body, amino acids derived from food are metabolized (see METABOLISM) in various ways. As each amino acid contains both an acid and an amino group, they can form a long chain of amino acids bridged by AMIDE links and called PEPTIDES. Peptide synthesis from constituent amino acids is a stage in PROTEIN SYNTHESIS. Thus some are converted into HORMONES, ENZYMES and NUCLEIC ACIDS. Proteins may be broken down again by HYDROLYSIS into their constituent amino acids, as in DIGESTION. When amino acids are deaminated (the amino group removed), the nitrogen passes out as UREA. The remainder of the molecule enters the CITRIC ACID CYCLE, being broken down to provide energy.

Scientists have produced amino acids and simple peptide chains by combining carbon dioxide, ammonia and water vapor under the sort of conditions (including electric discharges) thought to exist on earth millions of years ago. This may provide a clue to the origin of LIFE.

AMIS, Kingsley (1922–   ), English novelist, poet and critic. He emerged as one of the ANGRY YOUNG MEN in *Lucky Jim* (1954), an amusing attack on social and academic pretensions. Among his later works are *New Maps of Hell* (1960), *One Fat Englishman* (1963), and *The Green Man* (1969).

AMISH, conservative group of the MENNONITE sect, founded by Jakob AMMANN in Switzerland in the 1690s. In the 18th century members settled in what are now Ind., Ohio and Pa., and today they live in 23 states. Literal interpretation of the Bible leads their farm communities to reject modern life (including electricity and cars). Amish wear old-style clothes, plow with horses and observe the Sabbath strictly. (See also PENNSYLVANIA DUTCH.)

AMISTAD CASE, US legal case of 1841, involving Negro slaves who mutinied aboard the Spanish slaveship *Amistad* and sought asylum as free men in the US. John Quincy ADAMS successfully defended them in the Supreme Court against the Van Buren administration's decision to return the Negroes to their Spanish masters.

AMMAN, capital and largest city of Jordan, 25mi NE of the Dead Sea. Jordan's main industrial and trading center, it has food and tobacco processing and produces textiles, leatherware and cement. Some historic buildings predate the Hellenistic period. Much damage was caused by the fighting between government troops and Palestinian guerrillas in 1970. Pop 648,587.

AMMANN, Othmar Hermann (1897–1965), American engineer. He designed the George Washington Bridge in New York City (1931), the San Francisco Golden Gate Bridge (1935) and the Verrazano-Narrows Bridge in New York (1964).

AMMONIA (NH₃), colorless acrid gas, made by the HABER PROCESS; a covalent HYDRIDE. The pyramidal molecule turns inside out very rapidly, which is the basis of the ammonia clock (see ATOMIC CLOCK). Ammonia's properties have typical anomalies due to HYDROGEN BONDING; liquid ammonia is a good solvent. Ammonia is a BASE; its aqueous solution contains ammonium hydroxide, and is used as a household cleaning fluid. Ammonia is used as a fertilizer, a refrigerant, and to make ammonium salts, UREA, and many drugs, dyes and plastics. mp −78°C, bp −33°C.

On reaction with acids, ammonia gives ammonium salts, containing the NH₄⁺ ion, which resemble ALKALI METAL salts. They are mainly used as fertilizers. **Ammonium Chloride** (NH₄Cl), or **Sal Ammoniac,** a colorless crystalline solid used in dry cells and as a flux. **Ammonium Nitrate** (NH₄NO₃), a colorless crystalline solid, used as a fertilizer and in explosives. mp 170°C. (See also HYDRAZINE.)

AMMUNITION, any material designed to be used with destructive effect against a target or an enemy. It includes mines, self-propelled missiles, BOMBS, TORPEDOES and grenades, together with gun ammunition. Sufficient materials to operate a weapon a single time constitute a round of ammunition. **Gun ammunition** usually comprises a bullet, shell or shot, a propellant charge and a primer which fires the propellant. High-explosive shells also include a fuse which detonates the charge either upon impact or a fixed time after firing. Ingredients are usually supplied as a single unit (fixed ammunition) although large artillery often uses separate-loading ammunition for ease of handling. The propellant is usually a mixture of relatively slow burning explosives which liberates a large volume of gas on firing, thus propelling the projectile up the gun barrel. The size of ammunition depends on the **caliber,** or barrel diameter, of the gun used. Caliber is usually expressed in mm or in decimal fractions of an inch. (See also BALLISTICS.)

AMNESIA, the total loss of MEMORY for a period of time or for events. In cases of CONCUSSION, **retrograde amnesia** is the permanent loss of memory for events just preceding a head injury while **post-traumatic** amnesia applies to a period after injury during which the patient may be conscious but incapable of recall, both at the time and later. Similar behavior to the latter, termed **fugue,** occurs as a psychiatric phenomenon.

AMNESTY INTERNATIONAL, founded 1961 to aid political prisoners and others detained for reasons of conscience throughout the world. With 200,000 members in 35 countries, including 12,000 in the US, it has advisory status with the UN and other international organizations. Amnesty International received the Nobel Prize for Peace in 1977.

AMNIOCENTESIS, the procedure of obtaining a sample of the amniotic fluid surrounding a fetus by puncturing the abdomen of the pregnant woman with a very fine, hollow needle. Cells and other substances shed into the amniotic fluid by the fetus are used for diagnosing the presence of such disorders as DOWN'S SYNDROME, TAY-SACHS DISEASE and spinal malformations. Amniocentesis also can be used to determine the sex of an unborn child with 95% accuracy.

AMNION, a tough membrane surrounding the EMBRYO of reptiles, birds and mammals and containing the amniotic fluid, which provides a moist, aquatic environment for the EMBRYO. All land-laid EGGS contain amnions; those of fishes and amphibians do not, and thus must be laid in moist surroundings or water.

AMNIOTIC FLUID. See AMNION.

AMOEBAS, a large order (Amoebida) of the class Sarcodina (Rhizopodea) of PROTOZOA. They are unicellular (see CELL), a relatively rigid outer layer of ectoplasm surrounding a more fluid mass of endoplasm, in which lie one or more nuclei. They move by extending PSEUDOPODIA, into which they flow; and feed by surrounding and absorbing organic particles. REPRODUCTION is almost always asexual, generally by binary FISSION, though sometimes by multiple fission of the nucleus; a tough wall of CYTOPLASM forms about each of these small nuclei to create cysts. These can survive considerable rigors, returning to normal amoeboid form when circumstances are more clement. (Some species of amoeba may form a single cyst to survive adversity.) Certain amoebas can reproduce sexually. Amoebas are found wherever there is moisture, some parasitic (see PARASITE) forms living within other animals: *Entamoeba histolytica*, for example, causes amoebic DYSENTERY in man. The type-species is *Amoeba proteus*, which has a single nucleus and can form only one pseudopodium at a time.

AMORSOLO, Fernando (1892–   ), Philippine genre painter whose *Afternoon Meal of the Workers* won first prize at the 1939 New York World's Fair. Influenced by VELASQUEZ, he frequently painted portraits and country landscapes that featured tropical backlighting.

AMOS (8th century BC), Hebrew prophet, the first to proclaim clearly that there was one God for all peoples. A shepherd from Judah, he preached in neighboring Israel, denouncing its corruption until expelled by the king. The probably posthumous biblical Book of Amos is the earliest record of a prophet's sayings and life.

AMOS AND ANDY (Freeman Gosden, 1899–   , and Charles Correll, 1890–1972), US comedy team who originated and starred in the "Amos and Andy" radio show (1929–54). These white vaudevillians affected black dialects to create this tremendously popular program, which also appeared on TV in the 1950s.

AMOY (Hsia-men), seaport in Fukien province, SE China, on Amoy Island. It produces food and paper products, wine and chemicals. Its fine natural harbor has good dock facilities and trades in sugar, timber and tobacco. Amoy was the first Chinese port to trade with the English and the Dutch (17th century). Pop 400,000.

AMPÈRE, André Marie (1775–1836), French mathematician, physicist and philosopher best remembered for many discoveries in electrodynamics and electromagnetism. In the early 1820s he developed OERSTED's experiments on the interaction between magnets and electric currents and investigated the forces set up between current-carrying conductors.

AMPHETAMINES, a group of STIMULANT drugs, including **benzedrine** and **methedrine**, now in medical disfavor following widespread abuse and addiction. They counteract fatigue, suppress appetite, speed up performance (hence **"Speed"**) and give confidence, but pronounced DEPRESSION often follows; thus psychological and then physical addiction are encouraged. A paranoid PSYCHOSIS (resembling SCHIZOPHRENIA) may result from prolonged use, although it may be that amphetamine abuse is rather an early symptom of the psychosis. While no longer acceptable in treatment of OBESITY, they are useful in **narcolepsy**, a rare condition of abnormal sleepiness.

AMPHIBIA, a class of vertebrates, including FROGS, TOADS, NEWTS, SALAMANDERS and CAECILIANS. Typically they spend part of their life in water, part on land. They are distinct from REPTILES in that their EGGS lack AMNIONS, and must hence be laid in moist conditions, and that their soft, moist skins have no scales. They are of the subphylum VERTEBRATA, of the phylum CHORDATA. It is thought that amphibia were the first vertebrates to venture from the aquatic environment on to the land, and that they were the ancestors of all other vertebrates (see EVOLUTION). They are cold-blooded, and therefore many species hibernate (see HIBERNATION) during winter. Their development is in two stages: the egg develops into a larval form (see LARVA), which is usually solely aquatic, then the larva into an adult. All adult amphibia are carnivorous.

AMPHIBIOUS WARFARE, coordinated use of naval, air and landing forces to seize a beachhead. Such warfare reached full development in WWII in N Africa, W Europe and the Pacific. Naval and air bombardment softened up defenses, then special landing craft moved inshore to land the infantry and artillery.

AMPLIFIER, any device which increases the strength of an input signal. Amplifiers play a vital role in most electronic devices: RADIO and TELEVISION receivers, PHONOGRAPHS, TAPE-RECORDERS and COMPUTERS: but nonelectronic devices such as the horn of a windup phonograph or the PANTOGRAPH used for enlarging drawings are also amplifiers of a kind. Electronic amplifiers, usually based on TRANSISTORS or ELECTRON TUBES, can be thought of as a sort of variable switch in which the output from a power source is controlled (modulated) by a weak input signal. An important factor is the fidelity (see HIGH-FIDELITY) with which the waveform of the output signal reproduces that of the input over the desired BANDWIDTH.

AMPUTATION, the surgical or traumatic removal of a part or the whole of a limb or other structure. It is necessary for severe limb damage, infective GANGRENE, loss of BLOOD supply and certain types of CANCER. Healthy tissue is molded to form a stump as a base for artificial limb prosthesis. (See PROSTHETICS.)

AMRAM, David Werner (1930–   ), US composer for TV, film and theater; music director of the New York Shakespeare Festival 1956–67. His colorful compositions are influenced by jazz rhythms.

AMRITSAR, largest city in Punjab state, N India. It has important chemical and textile industries and rolling mills, and also produces electrical equipment, bicycles and carpets. The city is the center of the Sikh faith and has the Sikhs' main place of worship, the Golden Temple or Darbar Sahib ("court divine"). There are several colleges. The city was founded in the 1570s and in the 1800s was the center of a Sikh confederacy. Pop 432,663.

AMSTERDAM, capital and largest city of the Netherlands, and one of Europe's great commercial, financial and cultural centers. It stands in N Holland at the S of man-made Lake IJssel. This "Venice of the North" is centered on a series of concentric semicircular canals. Other canals linked to the Rhine and North Sea make Amsterdam one of Europe's major transshipment ports. It is also a major rail center and has an international airport.

Amsterdam is world-famous for diamond cutting and polishing and produces chemicals, machinery, bicycles, beer and textiles. It has an important stock exchange, two universities and about 40 museums. Amsterdam grew from a medieval fishing village, and had become a major city by the 17th century. Pop 716,900.

AMTRAK, official nickname of the National Railroad Passenger Corp., established by Congress in an effort to halt the post-WWII deterioration of railroad passenger service. Amtrak began operations on May 1, 1971, with 150 intercity trains. It improved service and increased ridership but, like the private carriers it replaced, accumulated large deficits ($906 million in 1981) that had to be funded by Congress. President Ronald Reagan reduced Amtrak's budget by nearly 20% for 1982, and service was curtailed accordingly.

AMU DARYA (ancient Oxus), the major river of Soviet Central Asia. Rising in the Pamir Mts, it flows 1,578mi, NW between the USSR and Afghanistan, then W and NW to enter the Aral Sea through a delta. The lower 900mi are navigable, and this stretch also irrigates large arid areas.

AMUNDSEN, Roald (1872–1928), Norwegian polar explorer who was the first man to reach the S Pole (Dec 14, 1911). His party beat the ill-fated Robert F. SCOTT expedition by one month. In the Arctic he was the first to navigate the Northwest Passage (1903–06), later crossing the N Pole in the dirigible *Norge* (1926). He was lost over the Barents Sea in an air search for the Italian explorer Umberto NOBILE.

AMUR RIVER, river in NE Asia. Rising in Mongolia, it flows 2,700mi NE through the USSR, then SE, dividing the USSR from China, then NE through the USSR into the Tatar Strait. Navigable for the six months it is not frozen, it carries oil, grain and lumber. The Amur has fisheries and hydroelectric installations.

ANABAPTISTS ("rebaptizers"), radical Protestant sects of the REFORMATION that sought a return to primitive Christianity. The first group was formed in 1523 at Zurich by dissatisfied followers of Ulrich ZWINGLI. Denying the validity of infant baptism, they rebaptized adult converts. Most stressed the dictates of individual conscience, and urged nonviolence and separation of church and state. Despite widespread persecution (notably at Münster) their doctrines spread, inspiring the MENNONITES in the Netherlands and the HUTTERITES in Moravia.

ANACLETUS, name of a pope and an antipope. **Saint Anacletus** (or Cletus), the third pope (76–88 or 79–91), was probably martyred. **Anacletus II** (d. 1138) was antipope (1130–38) in rivalry to INNOCENT II, and held Rome until his death.

ANACONDA, city in SW Mont., seat of Deer Lodge Co., ranking among the world's biggest producers of nonferrous metal. It produces copper, zinc and phosphates, and was founded in 1883. Pop 12,518.

ANACONDAS, two species, subfamily Boinac, of South American BOA. *Eunectes notaeus* is found in Paraguay and *E. murinus,* probably the largest SNAKE in the world with a length up to about 15m (50ft) though more usually 3–6m (10–20ft), throughout Brazil. Anacondas do not have a poisonous bite, killing prey by constriction. In general they shun human beings.

ANACREON (c582–c485BC), Greek lyric poet who celebrated wine and love in mellow, simple verses. These were later copied in the so-called Anacreontics; fashionable in 18th-century Europe. His main patrons were the "tyrants" of Samos and Athens.

ANALGESICS, drugs used for relief of pain. They mainly impair preception of, or emotional response to pain by action on the higher BRAIN centers. ASPIRIN and paracetamol are mild but effective. Phenylbutazone, indomethacin and ibuprofen are, like aspirin, useful in treating RHEUMATOID ARTHRITIS by reducing INFLAMMATION as well as revlieving pain. NARCOTIC analgesics derived from OPIUM ALKALOIDS range from the milder CODEINE and dextroprop-oxyphene, suitable for general use, to the highly effective euphoriants and addictive MORPHINE and HEROIN. These are reserved for severe acute pain and terminal disease, where addiction is either unlikely or unimportant. Pethidine (demerol) is an intermediate narcotic.

ANALYSIS, the branch of MATHEMATICS concerned particularly with the concepts of FUNCTION and LIMIT. Its important divisions are CALCULUS, ANALYTIC GEOMETRY and the study of differential equations.

ANALYSIS, chemical, determination of the compounds or elements comprising a chemical substance. Qualitative analysis deals with what a sample contains; quantitative analysis finds the amounts. The methods available depend on the size of the sample: macro (>100mg), semimicro ($1–100$mg), micro (1μg–mg), or submicro ($<1\mu$g) Chemical analysis is valuable in chemical research, industry, archaeology, medicine and many other fields. A representative sample must first be taken and prepared for analysis. Preliminary separation is often carried out by CHROMATOGRAPHY. ION-EXCHANGE, DISTILLATION or precipitation.

In qualitative analysis, classical methods involve characteristic reactions of substances. After preliminary tests— inspection, heating, and FLAME TESTS—systematic schemes are followed which separate the various IONS into groups according to their reactions with standard reagents, and which then identify them individually. Cations and anions are analyzed separately. For organic compounds, carbon and hydrogen are identified by heating with copper (II) oxide, carbon dioxide and water being formed; nitrogen, halogens and sulfur are identified by heating with molten sodium and testing the residue for CYANIDE, HALIDES and SULFIDE respectively. Classical quantitative analysis is performed by gravimetric analysis (separation and weighing) and volumetric analysis (measurements of volume).

Modern chemical analysis employs instrumental methods to give faster, more accurate assessments than do classical methods. Many modern methods have the additional advantage of being nondestructive. They include colorimetry, spectro-photometry, POLAROGRAPHY. MASS SPECTROSCOPY, differential thermal analy-sis, potentiometric titration and methods for determining MOLECULAR WEIGHT. Neutron activation analysis subjects a sample to NEUTRON irradiation and measures the strength of induced radioactivity and its rate of decay. In X-ray analysis, a sample is irradiated with X RAYS and emits X rays of different, characteristic wavelengths.

ANALYSIS, in psychology, determination of the individual components of a complex experience or mental process: often also used for PSYCHOANALYSIS.

ANALYTIC GEOMETRY, that branch of GEOMETRY based on the idea that a POINT may be defined relative to another point or to AXES by a set of numbers. In plane geometry, there are usually two axes, commonly designated the x- and y-axes, at right angles. The position of a point in the plane of the axes may then be defined by a pair of numbers (x, y), its coordinates, which give its distance in units in the x- and y-direction from the **origin** (the point of INTERSECTION of the two axes). In three dimensions there are three axes, usually at mutual right angles, commonly designated the x-, y- and z-axes.

Equation of a curve. A curve may be defined as a set of points. A relationship may be established between the coordinates of every point of the set, and this relationship is known as the EQUATION of the curve. The simplest form of plane curve is the straight LINE, which in the system we have described has an equation of the form $y=ax+b$, where a and b are CONSTANTS. All points whose coordinates satisfy the relationship $y=ax+$ will lie on this line. Equations of curves may involve higher POWERS of x or y: a parabola (see CONIC SECTIONS) may be expressed as $y=ax^2+b$. Since $x^2=(-x)^2$ for all values of x, the curve is symmetrical (see SYMMETRY) about the y-axis.

These principles may be applied to different coordinate systems, and to figures in more than two dimensions.

Analytic geometry was created by DESCARTES. Bringing algebra and geometry together in this way was a major advance in mathematics.

ANARCHISM, political belief that government should be abolished and the state replaced by the voluntary cooperation of individuals and groups. Like socialists, anarchists believe that existing governments tend to defend injustice, and they would do away with the institution of private property. But, unlike socialists, they believe that government is unnecessary and intrinsically harmful.

Pioneers of modern anarchism included England's William GODWIN (1756–1836),

France's Pierre Joseph PROUDHON (1809–1865) and the Russian propagandist of violence, Mikhail BAKUNIN (1814–1876). Political leaders, such as President William McKinley (1901), have been assassinated by individual anarchists, and the SACCO-VANZETTI CASE strengthened the popular idea that anarchism was linked with crime. Outside SYNDICALISM, once strong in Spain, anarchism has had little political influence, but has recently become linked with student radicalism in Europe and America.

ANASTASIA (1901–1918?), Russian grand duchess. Daughter of the last czar, Nicholas II, she was probably murdered with her family during the Revolution. Several women later claimed to be Anastasia but none could prove her identity.

ANATOLIA, large mountainous plateau in Asian Turkey, now more or less identical with the peninsula of ASIA MINOR.

ANATOMY, the structure and form of biological organisms (see BIOLOGY) and its study (MORPHOLOGY). The subject has three main divisions: gross anatomy, dealing with components visible to the naked eye; microscopic anatomy, dealing with microstructures seen only with the aid of an optical MICROSCOPE, and submicroscopic anatomy, dealing with still smaller ultrastructures. Since structure is closely related to function, anatomy is related to PHYSIOLOGY.

The study of anatomy is as old as that of MEDICINE, though for many centuries physicians' knowledge of anatomy left much to be desired. ANAXAGORAS had studied the anatomy of animals and anatomical observations can be found in the Hippocratic writings (see HIPPOCRATES), but it was ARISTOTLE who was the true father of comparative anatomy, and human dissection (the basic of all systematic human anatomy) was rarely practiced before the era of the ALEXANDRIAN SCHOOL and the work of HEROPHILUS and ERASISTRATUS. The last great experimental anatomist of antiquity was GALEN. His theories, as transmitted through the writings of the Arab scholars RHAZES and AVICENNA, held sway throughout the medieval period. Further progress had to await the revival of the practice of human dissection by SERVETUS and VESALIUS in the 16th century. The latter founded the famous Paduan school of anatomy which also included FALLOPIUS and FABRICIUS, whose pupil William HARVEY reunited the studies of anatomy and physiology in postulating the circulation of the BLOOD in *de Motu Cordis*

(1628). This theory was confirmed some years later when MALPIGHI discovered the capillaries linking the arteries with the veins. Since the 17th century many important anatomical schools have been founded and the study of anatomy has become an essential part of medical training. Important developments in the late 18th century included the foundation of HISTOLOGY by BICHAT and that of modern comparative anatomy by CUVIER.

The rise of microscopic anatomy has of course depended on the development of the microscope; it found its greatest success in the announcement of SCHWANN's cell theory in 1839.

ANAXAGORAS (c500–c428 BC), Greek philosopher of the Ionian school, resident in Athens, who taught that the elements were infinite in number and that everything contained a portion of every other thing. He also discovered the true cause of ECLIPSES and thought of the sun as a blazing rock and showed that air has substance.

ANAXIMANDER (c610–c545 BC), Greek philosopher of the Ionian school who taught that the cosmos was derived from one "indeterminate" primordial substance by a process of the separating out of opposites. He was probably the first Greek to attempt a map of the whole known world and thought of the earth as a stubby cylinder situated at the center of all things.

ANAXIMENES OF MILETUS (6th century BC), Greek philosopher of the Ionian school who held that all things were derived from air; this becoming, for instance, fire on rarifaction, water, and finally earth on condensation.

ANCESTOR WORSHIP, ritual propitiation and veneration of dead kin in the belief that their spirits influence the fortunes of the living. It has figured strongly in Asian faiths, notably Confucianism in China, Shintoism in Japan and Hinduism in India, and also occurs in Africa and Melanesia.

ANCHORAGE, largest city in Alaska and its main commercial and transportation center, located in S Alaska on Cook Inlet. It is a seaport with road and rail communications with the mining and farming interior and with an international airport. Anchorage has a major petroleum industry, canneries, sawmills and railroad shops, and is an important air defense center. Pop 173,017.

ANCHOVIES, family (Engraulidae) of small, shoalforming fishes allied to the HERRING, usually inhabiting salt water. They are most often 100–150mm (4–6in), sometimes up to 300mm (1ft) long. About 100 species are known. They have a pointed snout and a long lower jaw extending behind the eye. (Order: Clupeiformes).

ANCIEN RÉGIME ("old order"), the political and social system of France overthrown by the Revolution of 1789. It was based on an absolute monarchy and on privileged social classes.

ANDALUSIA, populous region of S Spain, extending to the Atlantic and Mediterranean and embracing eight provinces. It includes the Sierra Morena and Sierra Nevada Mts., and the warm fertile Guadalquivir River Valley—"the garden of Spain." There is metal mining, food processing and tourism along the Costa del Sol. Phoenicians first settled the area; later came Greeks, Romans and Vandals. Arabs and Berbers built a rich medieval culture. Today there is much rural poverty.

ANDAMAN AND NICOBAR ISLANDS, two island groups in the Bay of Bengal, forming a territory of India (area 3,200sq mi). The islands produce copra, coconut oil, rubber, coffee, rice, wood and wood products. Port Blair is the capital. Andamanese include the shy primitive Negrito aborigines.

ANDERS, Wladislaw (1892–1970), Polish general whose Polish army-in-exile helped the Allies win Italy in WWII. In England after 1945 he was a leader of exiled anticommunist Poles.

ANDERSEN, Hans Christian (1805–1875), Danish writer, best remembered for his 168 fairy tales. Based on folklore and observation of people and events in Andersen's life, they have a deceptively simple, slyly humorous style and often carry a moral message for adults as well as children. Among his best known stories are *The Ugly Duckling, The Emperor's Clothes,* and *The Red Shoes.*

ANDERSON, (Franklin) Leroy (1908–1975), US composer and conductor. An orchestrator and arranger for the Boston Pops Orchestra (1936–50), he was also guest conductor of other US and Canadian symphony orchestras. His compositions include *The Syncopated Clock* and *Blue Tango.*

ANDERSON, Carl David (1905–   ), US physicist who shared the 1936 Nobel Prize for Physics for his discovery of the positron (1932). Later he was codiscoverer of the first meson (see SUBATOMIC PARTICLES).

ANDERSON, Dame Judith (1898–   ), Australian-born actress who worked in the US. She is best known for her tragic roles in the plays of Eugene O'NEILL and Shakespeare and in Robinson JEFFERS' version of *Medea* (1947).

ANDERSON, Elizabeth Garrett (1836–1917), one of the first Englishwomen to become a doctor (1865). She helped establish the place of women in the professions and founded a women's hospital and a medical school for women.

ANDERSON, Jack (1922–   ), US journalist who was the chief investigative reporter for Drew PEARSON's column "Washington Merry-Go-Round." He took over the nationally syndicated column after Pearson died (1969) and specialized in exposing political scandal and corruption.

ANDERSON, John (1922–   ), US political leader, in the US House of Representatives (Ill.) 1961–81. Always a fiscal conservative, he gradually became a moderate on social issues, serving as chairman of the House Republican Conference from 1969. After losing a bid for the Republican presidential nomination in 1980, he ran for president as an independent and polled 5,719,722 votes, or 6.6% of the total.

ANDERSON, Marian (1902–   ), US black contralto. Overcoming the handicaps of poverty and discrimination, she became an international singing star in the 1930s, and in 1955 was the first Negro to sing a leading role at the Metropolitan Opera—Ulrica in *A Masked Ball.*

ANDERSON, Maxwell (1888–1959), US playwright. After early realistic plays, he concentrated on the revival of verse drama, achieving some success with such plays as *Elizabeth the Queen* (1930), *Winterset* (1935) and *High Tor* (1936).

ANDERSON, Sherwood (1876–1941), US writer. His novels and short stories deal largely with men rebelling against contemporary industrial society. He is best remembered for *Winesburg, Ohio* (1919), stories of the frustrations of small-town Midwestern life and such story collections as *The Triumph of the Egg* (1921) and *Horses and Men* (1923). His best novels are *Poor White* (1920) and *Dark Laughter* (1925).

ANDERSONVILLE, village in W Ga. where some 13,000 Union troops died of disease or wounds in a Confederate prison (1864–65). Its dreadful conditions provoked Union propaganda and reprisals. The site is now a federal park.

ANDES, South America's largest mountain system, 4,500mi long and averaging 200–250mi wide, running close to the entire W coast of the continent. Only the Himalayas exceed its average height of 12,500ft, and ACONCAGUA (22,835ft) is the highest peak in the W Hemisphere.

The Andes rose largely in the Cenozoic era (the last 70 million years), and volcanic eruptions and earthquakes suggest continuing uplift. There are three main sections. The S Andes form a single range (cordillera) dividing Chile and Argentina, with peaks ranging from 20,000ft in the N to 7,000ft in the S. The central Andes form two ranges flanking the high Bolivian plateau (the ALTIPLANO). The N Andes divide in Colombia and form four ranges ending in the Caribbean area. Many high Andean peaks are jagged and snowy, and glaciers fill some southern valleys.

ANDOVER, town in NE Mass., famous for the nation's oldest incorporated school (Phillips Academy, boys' secondary school, founded 1778) and New England's oldest incorporated girls' school (Abbot Academy, founded 1829). Pop 26,370.

ANDRE, John (1750–1780), British army officer, hanged as a spy by the Americans during the Revolutionary War. He secretly met Benedict ARNOLD behind American lines to arrange Arnold's surrender of West Point, but was caught in civilian clothes, with incriminating papers.

ANDREA DEL SARTO (1486–1530), leading 16th-century Florentine painter, influenced by Michelangelo and Dürer and renowned for delicately-colored church frescoes. He rivalled Raphael's classicism but foreshadowed MANNERISM through his pupils PONTORMO, ROSSO and VASARI.

ANDREA DORIA, Italian luxury liner that sank on July 26, 1956, following an inexplicable collision with the *Stockholm*, a Swedish liner, about 45mi S of Nantucket Island; 51 persons died. In 1981 a salvage operation run by Peter Gimbel and his wife, Elga Andersen, raised the ship's safe; further work was abandoned because of dangerous conditions.

ANDRETTI, Mario (1940–   ), Italian race car driver. He is the first man ever to win three different types of races: the Daytona 500 stock car race (1967), the Indianapolis 500 (1969) and a Formula One Grand Prix event (1971). He won the world Grand Prix championship in 1978.

ANDREW, Saint (1st century AD), one of Christ's 12 Apostles, formerly a fisherman and disciple of John the Baptist. He reputedly preached in what is now Russia and was martyred in Patras, Greece, on an X-shaped ("St. Andrew's") cross. He is the patron saint of Russia and of Scotland.

ANDREWS, Charles McLean (1863–1943), US historian. He stressed colonial America's dependence upon Britain in works like *The Colonial Period of American History* (1934–38), the first volume of which won him a Pulitzer Prize.

ANDREWS, Julie (1935–   ), English

actress and singer who came to prominence as Eliza in the stage musical *My Fair Lady* (1956). She won an Academy Award for her film portrayal of *Mary Poppins* (1964) and also starred in the films *The Sound of Music* (1965) and *S.O.B.* (1981).

ANDREWS, Roy Chapman (1884–1960), US naturalist, explorer and author. From 1906 he worked for the AMERICAN MUSEUM OF NATURAL HISTORY (later becoming its director, 1935–41) and made important expeditions to Alaska, the Far East and Central Asia. Among many important discoveries he made in Mongolia were the first known fossil dinosaur eggs.

ANDREWS SISTERS (Laverne, 1913–67; Maxine, 1916–   ; and Patty, 1918–   ), US vocal group whose popularity peaked during WWII. Best known for singing "Bei Mir Bist Du Schoen," "In Apple Blossom Time" and "Rum and Coca-Cola," they sold more than 50 million records.

ANDRIC, Ivo (1892–1975), Yugoslav novelist who won the Nobel Prize for Literature in 1961, largely for the epic quality of *The Bridge on the Drina*. His themes are man's insecurity and isolation in face of change and death.

ANDROGENS, STEROID HORMONES which produce secondary male characteristics such as facial and body hair and a deep voice. They also develop the male reproductive organs. The main androgen is TESTOSTERONE, produced in the TESTES; others are produced in small quantities in the cortex of the ADRENAL GLANDS. Small amounts occur in women in addition to the ESTROGENS and may produce some male characteristics. (See also ENDOCRINE GLANDS; PUBERTY.)

ANDROMEDA, constellation in the N Hemisphere. The Great Andromeda Nebula (M31), seen near the DOUBLE STAR Gamma Andromedae, is the most distant object visible to the naked eye in N skies. It is the nearest external GALAXY to our own, like it a spiral but larger (49kpc across), and about 600kpc from earth.

ANDROS, Sir Edmund (1637–1714), British governor of the Dominion of New England, 1686–89. His attempt to curb the colonists' rights caused a rebellion. Imprisoned and sent to England for trial, he was acquitted and became governor of Virginia 1692–97.

ANEMIA, condition in which the amount of HEMOGLOBIN in the BLOOD is abnormally low, thus reducing the blood's oxygen-carrying capacity. Anemic people may feel weak, tired, faint and breathless, have a rapid pulse and appear pale.

Of the many types of anemia, five groups can be described. In iron-deficiency anemia, the red blood cells are smaller and paler than normal. Usual causes include inadequate diet (especially in PREGNANCY), failure of iron absorption, and chronic blood loss (as from heavy MENSTRUATION HEMORRHAGE or disease of the GASTROINTESTINAL TRACT). Iron replacement is essential and in severe cases blood transfusion may be needed. In megaloblastic anemia, the red cells are larger than normal. This may be due to nutritional lack of VITAMIN B_{12} or folate, but the most important cause is pernicious anemia. B_{12} is needed for red-cell formation and patients with pernicious anemia cannot absorb B_{12} because they lack a factor in the stomach essential for absorbtion. Regular B_{12} injections are needed for life. In aplastic anemia, inadequate numbers of red cells are produced by the bone MARROW owing to damage by certain poisons, drugs or irradiation. Treatment includes transfusions and androgens. In hemolytic anemia, the normal life span of red cells is reduced, either because of ANTIBODY reactions or because they are abnormally fragile. A form of the latter is sickle-cell anemia, a hereditary disease, common among NEGROIDS in which abnormal hemoglobin is made. Finally, many chronic diseases including RHEUMATOID ARTHRITIS, chronic infection and UREMIA suppress red-cell formation and thus cause anemia.

ANEMOMETER, an instrument for measuring wind speed and often direction. The rotation type, which estimates wind speed from the rotation of cups mounted on a vertical shaft, is the most common of mechanical anemometers. The pressure-tube instrument utilizes the PITOT-TUBE effect, while the sonic or acoustic anemometer depends on the velocity of sound in the wind. For laboratory work a hot-wire instrument is used: here air flow is estimated from the change in RESISTANCE it causes by cooling an electrically heated wire.

ANEMONE, genus of mainly N temperate perennial herbs of the buttercup family (Ranunculaceae). Up to 3ft high, anemones have deeply cut, whorled leaves and white, pink, red, blue or, rarely yellow flowers. Many are cultivated but some, such as the wood anemone and PASQUE FLOWER, grow wild.

ANESTHESIA, or absence of sensation, may be of three types: general, local or pathological. **General anesthesia** is a reversible state of drug-induced unconsciousness with muscle relaxation and suppression of REFLEXES; this facilitates many surgical procedures and avoids distress. An anesthesiologist attends to ensure stable anesthesia and to protect vital functions. While ETHANOL and NARCOTICS have been used for their anesthetic properties for centuries, modern anesthesia dates from the use of diethyl ETHER by William MORTON in 1846, and of CHLOROFORM by Sir James SIMPSON in 1847. Nowadays injections of short-acting BARBITURATES, such as SODIUM PENTOTHAL, are frequently used to induce anesthesia rapidly; inhaled agents, including halothane, ether, nitrous oxide, trichlorethylene and cyclopropane, are used for induction and maintenance. **Local and regional anesthesia** are the reversible blocking of pain impulses by chemical action of COCAINE derivatives (e.g., PROCAINE, lignocaine). Nerve trunks are blocked for minor SURGERY and DENTISTRY, and more widespread anesthesia may be achieved by blocking spinal nerve roots, useful in obstetrics and patients unfit for general anesthesia. **Pathological anesthesia** describes loss of sensation following trauma or disease.

ANEURYSM, a pathological enlargement of, or defect in, a blood vessel. These may occur in the HEART after CORONARY THROMBOSIS, or in the AORTA and ARTERIES due to ARTERIOSCLEROSIS, high blood pressure, congenital defect, trauma or infection (specifically syphilis). They may rupture, causing HEMORRHAGE, which in the heart or aorta is rapidly fatal. Again, their enlargement may cause pain, swelling or pressure on nearby organs; these complications are most serious in the arteries of the BRAIN. SURGERY for aneurysm includes tying off and removal; larger vessels may be repaired by synthetic grafts.

ANGEL, supernatural messenger and servant of the deity. Angels figure in Christianity, Judaism, Islam and Zoroastrianism. In Christianity, angels traditionally serve and praise God, but guardian angels may protect the faithful against the evil of the Devil (the fallen angel Lucifer). The hierarchy of angels was said to have nine orders: Cherubim, Seraphim, Thrones; Dominions, Virtues, Powers; Principalities, Archangels, Angels.

ANGEL FALLS, world's highest known waterfall (3,212ft), on the Churún R in SE Venezuela. US aviator Jimmy Angel discovered it in 1935.

ANGELICO, Fra (c1400–1455), Italian painter and Dominican friar, a major figure in Renaissance art. His church frescoes and altarpieces, using religious figures, combined traditionally bright, clear colors with the new use of perspective settings. His Tuscan backgrounds are among the first great Renaissance landscapes.

ANGELOU, Maya (1928–), black US author best known for her autobiographical books *I Know Why the Caged Bird Sings* (1970) and *Gather Together in My Name* (1974), which recount her struggles for identity in a hostile world.

ANGEVIN, name of two medieval royal dynasties originating in the Anjou region of W France. The earliest ruled in parts of France, Jerusalem, and in England after Henry II, son of Geoffrey of Anjou, became England's first Angevin (or Plantagenet) ruler in 1154. His descendants held power in England until 1485. The younger branch began in 1266 when Charles, brother of Louis IX of France, became king of Naples and Sicily. This dynasty ruled in Italy, Hungary and Poland until the end of the 15th century.

ANGINA PECTORIS, severe, short-lasting CHEST pain caused by inadequate blood supply to the myocardium (see HEART), often due to coronary artery disease such as ARTERIOSCLEROSIS. It is precipitated by exertion or other stresses which demand increased heart work. Pain may spread to nearby areas, often the arms; sweating and breathlessness may occur. It is rapidly relieved or prevented by sucking NITROGLYCERIN tablets or inhaling AMYL nitrite.

ANGIOSPERMS, or **flowering plants,** large and very important class of seed-bearing plants, characterized by having seeds that develop completely enclosed in the tissue of the parent plant, rather than unprotected as in the only other seedbearing group, the GYMNOSPERMS. Containing about 250,000 species distributed throughout the world, and ranging in size from tiny herbs to huge trees, angiosperms are the dominant land flora of the present day. They have sophisticated mechanisms to ensure that pollination and fertilization take place and that the resulting seeds are readily dispersed and able to germinate. There are two subclasses: MONOCOTYLEDONS (with one leaf) and DICOTYLEDONS (with two).

ANGKOR, extensive ruins in NW Cambodia the ancient KHMER EMPIRE, noted for the city Angkor Thom and the Angkor Wat temple complex. Covering 40sq mi and dating from the 9th–13th centuries, the remains were found in 1861. Angkor Thom with its temples and palace is intersected by a canal system and has a perimeter wall 8mi long. Angkor Wat is a massive complex of carved Hindu temples with a 2.5mi

perimeter, and is the foremost example of Khmer art and architecture.

ANGLE, in plane GEOMETRY, the figure formed by the intersection of two straight lines. The point of intersection is known as the vertex.

Consider the two lines to be radii of a CIRCLE of unit radius. There is then a direct way of defining the magnitudes of angles in terms of the proportion of the circle's circumference cut off by their two sides: as the length of the circle's circumference is given by $2\pi r$, and $r=1$, the **radian** (rad) is defined as the magnitude of an angle whose two sides cut off $1/2\pi$ of the circumference. A **degree** (°) is defined as an angle whose two sides cut off $1/360$ of the circumference.

An angle of $\pi/2$ rad (90°), whose sides cut off one quarter of the circumference, is a **right angle,** the two lines being said to be PERPENDICULAR. Should the two sides cut off one half of the circumference (πrad or 180°), the angle is a straight angle or straight line. Angles less than $\pi/2$ rad are termed acute; those greater than $\pi/2$ but less than πrad, obtuse; and those greater than πrad but less than 2πrad, reflex. Pairs of angles that add up to $\pi/2$rad are termed complementary; those that add up to πrad, supplementary. Further properties of angles lie in the province of TRIGONOMETRY.

In SPHERICAL GEOMETRY a **spherical angle** is that formed by intersecting arcs of two great circles: its magnitude is equal to that of the angle between the PLANES (see DIHEDRAL ANGLE) of the great circles.

A **solid angle** is formed by a conical surface (see CONE). Considering its vertex to lie at the center of a SPHERE, then a measure of its magnitude may be obtained from the ratio between the area (L^2) of the surface of the sphere cut off by the angle, and the square (R^2) of the sphere's radius. Solid angles are measured in steradians (sr), an angle of one steradian subtending an area of R^2 at distance R.

ANGLES, Germanic tribe from which England derives its name. Coming from the Schleswig-Holstein area of N Germany, the Angles, with the SAXONS and JUTES, invaded England from the 5th century and founded kingdoms including East Anglia, Mercia and Northumbria. (See also ANGLO-SAXONS.)

ANGLICANISM, the body of doctrines originally developed by the CHURCH OF ENGLAND and now broadly followed by the other members of the Anglican Communion. These include the Anglican Church of Canada, the EPISCOPAL CHURCH in the US, and other Episcopal churches in former

British colonies and elsewhere.

ANGLO-SAXON CHRONICLE, historical record of England from early Christian times until after the Norman Conquest. Various versions were made between 890 and 1155, based on monastic annals, genealogies and episcopal records. They constitute the oldest W European history written in the vernacular, and the chief source for Anglo-Saxon history.

ANGLO-SAXONS, collective name for the Germanic peoples who dominated England from the 5th to the 11th centuries. They originated as tribes of ANGLES, SAXONS and JUTES who invaded England after Roman rule collapsed, creating kingdoms that eventually united to form the English nation. In modern usage, Anglo-Saxons are the English or their emigrant descendants in other parts of the world.

Official name: People's Republic of Angola
Capital: Luanda
Area: 481,351sq mi
Population: 6,745,000
Languages: Bantu; Portuguese
Religions: Roman Catholic; Protestant; Animist
Monetary unit(s): 1 Kwanza = 100 Lwei

ANGOLA, independent state in SW Africa, formerly a Portuguese overseas province. Angola is bounded on the N and NE by Zaire; on the SE by Zambia; on the S by Namibia (SW Africa); and on the W by the Atlantic Ocean.

Land. Beyond the coastal plain is a dominant central plateau 5,000ft high. Main rivers include the Congo, Zambezi, Cuanza and Cunene. The warm wet N has tropical rain forest; the cooler, seasonally dry plateau supports savanna. There is abundant savanna wildlife.

People. Over 90% of Angolans are Bantu with a few Bushmen. Bantu tongues and animist beliefs predominate among the largely illiterate majority. The capital, Luanda, and most towns lie in the W.

Economy. Angola has a prosperous oil industry and is expected to become a major oil-producing country. Crude oil is the principal export, followed by coffee, diamonds, iron ore, cotton and corn. There is some light industry.

History. The Bantu Bakongo kingdom held NW Angola when the Portuguese navigator Diogo CAM arrived in 1482. Portugal exerted control over Angola from 1576 onwards, and the export of Negro slaves to Brazil caused severe depopulation. Portuguese colonization and economic development grew in the early 20th century. Nationalist guerrillas were active in the fight for independence from 1961. Upon independence in 1975, conflict erupted among the three movements vying for power. With support from Cuba and the USSR, the Popular Liberation Movement of Angola gained control, but sporadic violence has continued. Angola has been a sympathetic center for several liberation groups from neighboring countries, and has been a focus of attacks by South African troops stationed in Namibia (SW Africa).

ANGORA, term used for long-haired varieties of goats, cats and rabbits. Originally it referred to goats bred in the Angora (now Ankara) region of Turkey. The silky white hair of Angora goats has long been used for fine yarns and fabrics, especially for making mohair cloth.

ANGRY YOUNG MEN, post-WWII generation of British writers whose works reflected a mood scathingly critical of established social values, as in John OSBORNE's play *Look Back in Anger* (1956). Most had lower middle-class or working-class backgrounds and leftist political sympathies. They included Kingsley AMIS, Arnold WESKER, John Braine, John Wain, Alan Sillitoe and Doris Lessing.

ANGST, German word meaning dread or anxiety. It implies modern man's unease, frustration and sense of insignificance in face of an inexplicable universe, and reflects a loss of faith in God and of man's belief in himself. It appears in the literature of EXISTENTIALISM and in works by Franz KAFKA, T. S. ELIOT, W. H. AUDEN and others.

ANGSTRÖM, Anders Jonas (1814–1874), Swedish physicist who was one of the founders of SPECTROSCOPY and was the first to identify hydrogen in the solar spectrum (1862). The ANGSTROM UNIT is named in his honor.

ANGUILLA, small island in the West Indies (area 35sq mi), which reverted to British dependent-territory status when the association of St. Kitts and Nevis with Anguilla was dissolved in 1980. Its mainly Negro people fish and produce salt, boats and livestock. Pop 6,500.

ANIMAL, a living organism which displays most, if not all, of the following characteristics:

(1) it does not contain CHLOROPHYLL;

(2) it has the ability, at least at some time during its life-cycle, to move actively;

(3) its CELLS are limited by a cell membrane, rather than by a CELLULOSE or CHITIN wall;

(4) it is heterotrophic (see AUTOTROPH);

(5) it is limited in the extent of its growth (that is, it does not continue to grow larger and larger with increasing age, but reaches a maximum size at some point in its life-cycle);

(6) it produces male and female GAMETES, and its development includes the formation of an EMBRYO and often a LARVA.

In fact, many animals do not display all of these characteristics. For example, the PROTOZOA generally reproduce asexually by FISSION; and some contain chlorophyll. Again, the SLIME MOLDS show both plant and animal characteristics at different stages of their life cycles. Moreover, some PLANTS display some animal characteristics: FUNGI do not contain chlorophyll; BACTERIA are considered as plants although many types are motile.

Because of these borderline cases, the exact differentiation between plants and animals has long been a subject of dispute. Despite this, there is in general little confusion between the two kingdoms. (See also ANIMAL BEHAVIOR; ANIMAL KINGDOM; ECOLOGY; EVOLUTION; FOSSIL; TAXONOMY; ZOOLOGY.)

ANIMAL BEHAVIOR, the responses of animals to internal and external stimuli. Study of these responses can enable advances to be made in our understanding of human PSYCHOLOGY and behavior. Animal responses may be learned by the animal during its lifetime or may be instinctive or inherited (see HEREDITY; INSTINCT).

Even the simplest animals are capable of learning—to associate a particular stimulus with pain or pleasure, to negotiate mazes, etc. Moreover, there are critical periods in an animal's life when it is capable of learning a great deal in a very short time. Thus baby geese hatched in the absence of the mother will follow the first moving object they see, another animal or a human being. If, later, they must choose between this other animal and the mother, they prefer the other animal. This rapid early learning is called **imprinting.**

Among even the most intelligent animals much behavior is instinctive: the shape of a baby's head, for example, evokes an instinctive parental response in man. The complicated dance of the BEES, by which they inform the hive of the whereabouts of food, each species of bee having its own dance "dialect," is an example of more complex instinctive behavior. Instinctive ritual, too, plays its part (see APPEASEMENT BEHAVIOR; MATING RITUALS). Instinct can determine the behavior of a single animal, or of a whole animal society (see HIBERNATION; MIGRATION). (See also AGGRESSION; ETHOLOGY; TERRITORIALITY.)

ANIMAL HUSBANDRY, branch of agriculture dealing with the care and breeding of livestock, often making profitable use of land unsuitable for arable farming. Though scientific husbandry dates from only the 18th century, many special skills have been evolved to deal with various animals. Man, however, may have first domesticated an animal—the goat—about 8,000 years ago. (See also AGRICULTURE.)

ANIMAL KINGDOM, Animalia, one of the kingdoms into which all living organisms are classified. More than a million distinct species of animals have been identified, and these are divided into various groups, groups within groups, etc. (see TAXONOMY).

The animal kingdom is divided into phyla (singular, phylum). Within these phyla, animals are further divided into classes, based primarily on their bodily structure but also (though the two are usually equivalent) on their evolutionary history (see EVOLUTION); classes may be grouped into subphyla. Thus the phylum CHORDATA has, amongst others, the subphylum VERTEBRATA which includes classes such as AMPHIBIA, Pisces (FISHES), Reptilia (REPTILES),Aves (BIRDS) and Mammalia (MAMMALS). In the same way, classes contain (in descending order of magnitude) orders, families, genera, species and subspecies.

ANIMATION, cinematographic technique creating the illusion of movement by projecting a series of drawings or photographs showing successive views of an action. The first animated cartoons were made by Émile Cohl in France in 1907. Walt DISNEY pioneered sound and color in films such as the *Mickey Mouse* cartoons and the full-length *Fantasia,* which became world famous. In modern cartoon making, drawings on transparent celluloid ("cells") are superimposed to form each picture and only cells showing motion need changing from frame to frame.

ANIMISM, a term first used by E. B. TYLOR to designate a general belief in spiritual beings, which belief he held to be the origin of all religions. A common corruption of Tylor's sense is to interpret as animism the belief that all natural objects possess spirits.

PIAGET has proposed that the growing child characteristically passes through an animistic phase.

ANISE, an E Mediterranean herb (*Pimpinella anisum*) widely cultivated for its licorice-flavored seedlike fruits called anise seed. The fruits yield spice and oil used to flavor foods, candy and liqueurs such as OUZO. Family: Umbelliferae.

ANJOU, former province of W France, now a wine-growing area in the department of Maine-et-Loire. Its name derives from the Celtic Andes tribe, which occupied the area before the Romans. Anjou was a county in the 9th century, later a powerful feudal state, and a duchy in 1360; it became part of the French monarchy in 1480.

ANKARA, capital of Turkey and of Ankara province in Asia Minor. It produces textiles, cement, flour and beer, and trades in local Angora wool and grain. Landmarks: the university, ATATURK'S mausoleum and the old fortress. Ankara (formerly Ancyra or Angora) may be pre-Hittite in origin. It replaced ISTANBUL as Turkey's capital in 1923. Pop 2,203,729.

ANNA COMNENA (1083-d. after c1148), Byzantine princess and historian. Her *Alexiad* dealt mainly with the life of her father, Emperor ALEXIUS I COMNENUS. and gave a Byzantine viewpoint of the confrontation of East and West during the First Crusade.

ANNAM, ancient SE Asian Kingdom (now the republic of VIETNAM). Under Chinese domination from the 2nd century BC, Annam first became independent in 1428. It expanded S, was split in two in the 16th century, but was reunited with French help in 1802. By the later 1800s Annam was divided into French-dominated Tonkin, Annam and CochinChina. From WWII to the division in 1954, the whole region, nominally ruled by Emperor Bao Dai, was known as Vietnam.

ANNAPOLIS, capital city of Md., seat of Anne Arundel Co. on the Severn R near Chesapeake Bay. A historic and beautiful city, it was settled in 1649 by Puritans from Va. and was given its present name in 1694. It was the site of the ANNAPOLIS CONVENTION of 1786. It has many historic buildings, including the statehouse (1772). It is the site of St. John's College (founded 1696) and the US Naval Academy (established 1845). There are a number of local industries, including the processing of seafood. Pop 31,740.

ANNAPOLIS CONVENTION (1786), meeting which foreshadowed the US Constitutional Convention. It was held at ANNAPOLIS, Md., to discuss problems of interstate commerce. Alexander HAMILTON and James MADISON wanted its scope broadened to discuss revision of the ARTICLES OF CONFEDERATION. But only five of the 13 states were represented and thus a full-scale meeting was called for, which led to the Constitutional Convention at Philadelphia.

ANNAPOLIS ROYAL, seat of Annapolis Co. on the W Coast of Nova Scotia, Canada. It is one of North America's oldest settlements N of the Gulf of Mexico. The town originated nearby on Annapolis Basin in the French town of Port Royal (1605), moving to the present site in 1636. After nearly a century of fighting, the British finally captured it in 1710 and renamed it for Queen Anne. It is now a summer resort with national historic parks, and serves a farming area. Pop 738.

ANNAPURNA, Himalayan mountain in Nepal with the world's 11th-highest peak (26,391ft). Its conquest in 1950 by Maurice Herzog's team was the first such success involving any great Himalayan peak.

ANN ARBOR, city of SE Mich. and seat of Washtenaw Co. It is on the Huron R in a farming region 36mi W of Detroit. The city has light precision industries and is the home of the U of Michigan. Pop 107,316.

ANNE (1665–1714), Queen of Great Britain and Ireland 1702–14 and last of the Stuart monarchs. A devout Anglican Protestant of Whig persuasion, she was influenced in political and religious affairs by the Duke of MARLBOROUGH and his wife, Sarah. Her reign was dominated by the War of the SPANISH SUCCESSION (1701–14). It also saw the ACT OF UNION (1707) uniting England and Scotland to form the kingdom of Great Britain.

ANNEALING, the slow heating and cooling of METALS and GLASS to remove stresses which have arisen in CASTING, cold working or machining (see MACHINE TOOLS). The annealed material is tougher and easier to process further. (See also METALLURGY.)

ANNENBERG, Walter (1908–   ), US publisher. He inherited a Philadelphia-based publishing empire which included the *Philadelphia Inquirer*, founded *Seventeen* magazine (1944) and *TV Guide* (1953) and bought the *Philadelphia Daily News* (1957). A heavy contributor to the Republican Party, he was appointed ambassador to Great Britain by President Richard Nixon (1969).

ANNE OF CLEVES (1515–1557), queen consort and fourth wife of England's HENRY VIII. She was the daughter of a powerful German noble, and Henry married her (1540) on Thomas CROMWELL's advice to forge international bonds. But he disliked her and six months later had Parliament annul the marriage.

ANNUAL, plant that completes its life cycle in one growing season and then dies. Annuals propagate themselves only by seeds. They include such garden flowers and food plants as MARIGOLDS, CORNFLOWERS, CEREALS, PEAS and TOMATOES. Preventing seeding may convert an annual, e.g. MIGNONETTE, to a biennial or a perennial.

ANNULMENT, decree to the effect that a marriage was invalid when contracted. Grounds for annulment include fraud, force and close blood links between the parties. The Roman Catholic Church recognizes annulment but not DIVORCE.

ANNUNCIATION, in Christian belief, the archangel GABRIEL's announcement to the Virgin MARY that she would give birth to the Messiah. The Roman Catholic Church celebrates the annunciation as Lady Day, March 25. The annunciation appears in many Christian paintings.

ANODE, the positive ELECTRODE of a BATTERY, electric CELL or ELECTRON TUBE. ELECTRONS, which conventionally carry negative charge, enter the device at the CATHODE and leave by the anode.

ANOPHELES, a genus of MOSQUITOES. The only known MALARIA carrier, it also transmits ENCEPHALITIS and FILARIASIS.

ANOREXIA NERVOSA, pathological loss of appetite with secondary MALNUTRITION and HORMONE changes. It often affects young women with diet obsession and may reflect underlying psychiatric disease.

ANOUILH, Jean (1910–   ), French playwright of polished, highly theatrical dramas which emphasize the dilemma of modern man who must compromise in order to achieve happiness. His works include *Antigone* (1944), *The Lark* (1953) and *Beckett* (1959).

ANSCHLUSS, the union of Austria with Germany, effected (in violation of the VERSAILLES TREATY) when the Nazi army entered Austria on March 12, 1938. It had a logical basis in a common Austro-German language and culture, but was forced by Adolf Hitler for Nazi aggrandizement.

ANSELM, Saint (1033–1109), archbishop of Canterbury (from 1093) who upheld Church authority and became the first scholastic philosopher. He endured repeated exile for challenging the right of English kings to influence Church affairs. Anselm saw reason as the servant of faith and probably invented the ontological "proof" of God's existence: that our idea of a perfect being implies the existence of such a being.

ANSERMET, Ernest (1883–1969), Swiss conductor who directed many premieres of STRAVINSKY ballets. He founded the *Orchestre de la Suisse Romande* in 1918, conducting it until his death.

ANSKY, Shloime (pen name of Solomon Samuel Rapaport, 1863–1920), Russian Yiddish author and playwright, best known for *The Dybbik* (1916), an arresting tragedy of demonic possession. He was active in Russian Jewish socialism, but left Russia after the Revolution, and died in Poland.

ANSON, George Anson, 1st Baron (1697–1762), English admiral, known as "father of the navy" for his Admiralty reforms—which contributed to British naval success in the SEVEN YEARS' WAR (1756–63). He was made a baron after his victory over the French off Cape Finisterre (1747).

ANTABUSE, or disulfiram (tetraethylthiuram disulfide), drug used in the treatment of ALCOHOLISM. Though nontoxic, it prevents the breakdown of ACETALDEHYDE, a highly toxic product of ETHANOL metabolism. Thus if alcohol is drunk after Antabuse has been taken, unpleasant symptoms occur, including palpitations and vomiting.

ANTACIDS, mild ALKALIS or BASES taken by mouth to neutralize excess STOMACH acidity for relief of DYSPEPSIA, including peptic ULCER and HEARTBURN. MILK OF MAGNESIA, aluminum hydroxide and sodium bicarbonate are common antacids.

ANTANANARIVO, formerly Tananarive, capital and largest city of Madagascar, on the central plateau. It is the national commercial, manufacturing (food products, textiles) and educational center. Pop 400,000.

ANTARCTICA, a continental landmass of almost 6,000,000sq mi, covered by an icecap between 6,000 and 14,000ft thick, except where mountain peaks, such as the 16,900ft Vinson Massif, break through the ice. The general shape of the continent is circular, indented by the arc-shaped Weddell Sea (S of the Atlantic Ocean) and the rectangular Ross Sea (S of New Zealand). The Antarctic Peninsula and other areas facing Tierra del Fuego are structurally similar to the adjacent South American coast while the rest of the continent resembles Australia and South Africa. Such facts provide evidence for the theory of CONTINENTAL DRIFT, also supported by recent fossil discoveries.

No warm ocean currents or winds reach the mainland, so the climate is intensely cold. All precipitation falls as snow, and in winter temperatures as low as −80°F and winds up to 100mph occur frequently. Few animals other than mites, microscopic rotifers and tiny wingless insects can survive inland; but the coasts and offshore waters support seabirds, including penguins, skuas, petrels and fulmars, and marine mammals (whales and seals). Vegetation is limited to lichen, mosses and fungi S of the 62nd parallel, though it is richer in the N offshore islands.

Captain James COOK was the first to attempt a scientific exploration of the Antarctic region (1773), but he believed that the whole area was a frozen ocean. The mainland was probably first sighted in 1820 by the American sea captain, Nathaniel PALMER. Expeditions to the area were led by the Englishmen Weddell (1823) and Biscoe (1832) and the American Charles WILKES (1838–40). James Clark ROSS discovered the sea later named for him, and charted much of the Antarctic coast between 1840 and 1842, taking his English team as far as latitude 78°9'S. About the turn of the century a series of Belgian, Norwegian, German, British and French expeditions gathered much valuable data, and on Dec. 14, 1911, the Norwegian Roald AMUNDSEN reached the S Pole, a month before Captain Robert SCOTT. Sir Ernest SHACKLETON had come within 100mi of the Pole in 1909, and later led other expeditions (1914 and 1921). Admiral Richard Evelyn BYRD was responsible for many Antarctic expeditions, including "Operation Highjump" (1946–47).

Since the International Geophysical Year (1957–58), international cooperation in Antarctica has increased. On Dec. 1, 1959, 12 nations signed the 30-year Antarctic Treaty, temporarily setting aside various territorial claims and reserving the area S of 60°S for peaceful scientific investigation. There are now over 30 permanent stations belonging to 10 countries on the continent itself, the largest being McMurdo Station on the Ross Ice Shelf, equipped with Antarctica's first nuclear reactor. Other stations on the nearby islands are used for meteorological and other research.

ANTEATERS, four species of MAMMALS, family Myrmecophagidae, order EDENTATA, including the Giant Anteater (*Myrmecophaga tridactyla*) and the TAMANDUA, among others. They have long snouts, tubular mouths and long, sticky tongues with which they catch their food, chiefly ANTS and TERMITES. Other animals with the same adaptations and feeding habits, and thus also sometimes called anteaters, are the AARDVARK, ECHIDNA, NUMBAT and PANGOLIN.

ANTELOPES, swift-moving hollow-horned RUMINANTS of the family BOVIDAE, order ARTIODACTYLA. The term generally includes the American PRONGHORN, *Antilocapra americana*, the sole living member of the Antilocapridae family and not a true antelope. Common features include a hairy muzzle, narrow cheek teeth and permanent, backward-pointing HORNS. Distribution is throughout Africa and Asia (except for the Pronghorn) in widely varying habitats. They range in size from the Royal Antelope, probably the smallest hoofed mammal, standing about 250mm (10in) high at the shoulders, to the giant ELAND, which may be as tall as 2m (6.6ft) at the shoulders.

ANTENNA, or aerial, a component in an electrical circuit which radiates or receives RADIO waves. In essence a transmitting antenna is a combination of conductors which converts AC electrical ENERGY into ELECTROMAGNETIC RADIATION. The simple **dipole** consists of two straight conductors aligned end on and energized at the small gap which separates them. The length of the dipole determines the frequency for which this configuration is most efficient. It can be made directional by adding electrically isolated director and reflector conductors in front and behind. Other configurations include the folded dipole, the highly-directional loop antenna and the dish type used for MICROWAVE links. Receiving antennas can consist merely of a short DIELECTRIC rod or a length of wire for low-frequency signals. For VHF and microwave signals, complex antenna configurations similar to those used for transmission must be used. (See also RADIO TELESCOPE.)

ANTHEIL, George (1900–1959), US composer. He studied under Ernest BLOCH and brought popular motifs into serious music in works such as *Jazz Symphonietta* (1926) and the opera *Transatlantic* (1928–29). In later work he was more traditional, and after WWII he developed a neoclassical style influenced by STRAVINSKY.

ANTHONY, Susan Brownell (1820–1906), major US leader and organizing genius of the fight for women's rights. She was a N.Y. schoolteacher who backed the temperance and abolitionist movements, but devoted herself to female suffrage after befriending Elizabeth Cady STANTON. She co-founded the National Woman Suffrage Association (1869), and served as president of the National American Woman Suffrage Association (1892–1900). She also helped

to write *The History of Woman Suffrage*.

ANTHONY OF PADUA, Saint (1195–1231), Franciscan friar, theologian and preacher. He was born near Lisbon, but taught and preached in France and Italy. Canonized a year after his death, he is the patron saint of the poor, and his feast day is June 13. He is invoked to aid the discovery of lost objects.

ANTHRAX, a rare BACTERIAL DISEASE causing characteristic SKIN pustules and LUNG disease; it may progress to SEPTICEMIA and death. Anthrax spores, which may survive for years, may be picked up from infected animals (such as sheep or cattle), or bone meal. Treatment is with PENICILLIN and people at risk are VACCINATED; the isolation of animal cases and DISINFECTION of spore-bearing material is essential. It was the first disease in which bacteria were shown (by KOCH) to be causative and it had one of the earliest effective vaccines, developed by PASTEUR.

ANTHROPOID APES, the animals most closely resembling MAN (genus *Homo*) and probably sharing with him a common evolutionary ancestor (see EVOLUTION). Together the genera *Pan* and *Homo* form the family Hominidae in the suborder Anthropoidea (order PRIMATES). The apes concerned are the GORILLA, CHIMPANZEE, and the ORANG-UTAN (family Pongidae), the other members of the superfamily Hominoidea. (See also MONKEYS.)

ANTHROPOLOGICAL LINGUISTICS. See LINGUISTICS.

ANTHROPOLOGY, the study of man from biological, cultural and social viewpoints. HERODOTUS may perhaps be called the father of anthropology, but it was not until the 14th and 15th centuries AD, with the mercantilist expansion of the Old World into new regions, that contact with unknown peoples kindled a scientific interest in the subject. In the modern age there are two main disciplines, physical anthropology and cultural anthropology, the latter embracing social anthropology. **Physical anthropology** is the study of man as a biological species, his past EVOLUTION and his contemporary

physical characteristics. In its study of PREHISTORIC MAN it has many links with ARCHAEOLOGY, the difference being that anthropology is concerned with the remains or fossils of man himself while archaeology is concerned with the remains of his material culture. The physical anthropologist studies also the differences among RACES and groups, relying to a great extent on techniques of ANTHROPOMETRY and, more recently, genetic studies. **Cultural anthropology** is divided into several classes. ETHNOGRAPHY is the study of the culture of a single group, either primitive (see PRIMITIVE MAN) or civilized. Fieldwork is the key to ethnographical studies, which are themselves the key to cultural anthropology. ETHNOLOGY is the comparative study of the cultures of two or more groups. Cultural anthropology is also concerned with cultures of the past, and the borderline in this case between it and archaeology is vague. **Social anthropology** is concerned primarily with social relationships and their significance and consequences in primitive societies. In recent years its field has been extended to cover more civilized societies, though these are still more generally considered the domain of SOCIOLOGY. (See also CEPHALIC INDEX; CLAN; ENDOGAMY AND EXOGAMY; FAMILY; MARRIAGE; TRIBE.)

ANTHROPOSOPHY, a modern spiritual movement developed under Rudolf STEINER, who founded the Anthroposophical Society in 1912. It aims at higher spiritual experience and knowledge, through man's inner powers independent of the senses. Steiner claimed his "spiritual science" had practical applications, especially in education, and some schools are based on his ideas.

ANTIBIOTICS, substances produced by microorganisms that kill or prevent growth of other microorganisms; their properties are made use of in the treatment of bacterial and fungal infection. PASTEUR noted the effect and Alexander FLEMING in 1929 first showed that the mold *Penicillium notatum* produced PENICILLIN, a substance able to destroy certain bacteria. It was not until 1940 that FLOREY and CHAIN were able to manufacture sufficient penicillin for clinical use. The isolation of STREPTOMYCIN by WAKSMAN, of Gramicidin (from tyrothricin) by DUBOS, and of the Cephalosporins were among early discoveries of antibiotics useful in human infection. Numerous varieties of antibiotics now exist and the search continues for new ones. Semi-synthetic antibiotics, in which the basic molecule is chemically modified, have increased the range of naturally occurring substances.

Each antibiotic is effective against a wider or narrower range of bacteria at a given dosage; their mode of action ranges from preventing cell-wall synthesis to interference with PROTEIN and NUCLEIC ACID metabolism. Bacteria resistant to antibiotics either inherently lack susceptibility to their mode of action or have acquired resistance by ADAPTATION (e.g., by learning to make substances which inactivate an antibiotic). Among the more important antibiotics are the penicillins, Cephalosporins, TETRACYCLINES, STREPTOMYCIN, Gentamicin and Rifampicin. Each group has its own particular value and side effect, and antibiotics may induce ALLERGY. Many antibiotics are effective by mouth or INJECTION may be more suitable; topical application can also be used.

ANTIBODIES AND ANTIGENS. As one of the body's defense mechanisms, PROTEINS called antibodies are made by specialized white cells to counter foreign proteins known as antigens. Common antigens are VIRUSES, bacterial products (including TOXINS) and allergens· (see ALLERGY). A specific antibody is made for each antigen. Antibody reacts with antigen in the body, leading to a number of effects including enhanced phagocytosis by white cells, activation of complement (a substance capable of damaging cell membranes) and HISTAMINE release. Antibodies are produced faster and in greater numbers if the body has previously encountered the particular antigen. IMMUNITY to second attacks of diseases such as MEASLES and CHICKENPOX, and VACCINATION against diseases not yet contracted are based on this principle. Antibody detection in blood samples may show AGGLUTININS, precipitins or complement fixation, according to the technique used and the antibody involved.

ANTICHRIST, the opponent of Christ. The name is given to enemies of the Church and to impersonal evil forces. The concept can be traced to Jewish tradition and is mentioned by name in the Epistles of St. John. Christian writers commonly associate the idea of the coming of Antichrist with the approach of the end of the world.

ANTICOAGULANTS, drugs that interfere with blood CLOTTING, used to treat or prevent THROMBOSIS and clot EMBOLISM. The two main types are heparin, which is injected and has an immediate but short-lived effect, and the coumarins (including WARFARIN) which are taken by mouth and are longer-lasting. They affect different parts of the clotting mechanism, coumarins depleting factors made in the LIVER.

ANTI-COMINTERN PACT, an agreement between Germany and Japan (1936), ostensibly to counter the influence of a Russian-inspired anti-capitalist organization, the COMINTERN (Communist International). The pact was later joined by Italy, Spain, Bulgaria, Rumania, Hungary, Denmark and Finland, countries that directly or indirectly aided the German war effort in WWII.

ANTIDEPRESSANTS, drugs used in the treatment of DEPRESSION; they are of two types: tricyclic compounds and monoamine oxidase inhibitors. Although their mode of action is obscure, they have revolutionized the treatment of depression.

ANTIETAM, Battle of, a bloody encounter which repulsed Confederate General Robert E. LEE's first northward thrust during the Civil War. It was fought in Sept. 1862 when 40,000 men under Lee met 70,000 Union troops under McCLELLAN at Antietam Creek, Md. McClellan used only two-thirds of his army and sustained 12,000 casualties, while Lee used his total force, losing almost a quarter of it. Halted before he could reach Washington, Lee was forced to retreat across the Potomac.

ANTIFEDERALISTS, name given in the US to those who opposed the ratification of the Federal Constitution of 1787. They feared that centralized power would become despotic. After the new government's inauguration, the Antifederalist group joined the Republicans to form the DEMOCRATIC-REPUBLICAN PARTY under Jefferson.

ANTIFREEZE, a substance added to water, particularly that in AUTOMOBILE cooling systems, to prevent ice forming in cold weather. The additive most commonly used is ethylene glycol; METHANOL and ETHANOL, although cheaper alternatives, tend to need more frequent replacement, being much more volatile.

ANTIGENS. See ANTIBODIES AND ANTIGENS.

ANTIGONE, in Greek myth, the daughter of OEDIPUS, noted for her fidelity and courage. She followed her father into exile. Later she buried her brother Polynices against the orders of King CREON. Creon imprisoned Antigone who killed herself, provoking the suicide of Creon's son Haemon to whom she was betrothed. Antigone is the heroine of plays by SOPHOCLES, EURIPIDES and ANOUILH.

ANTIGUA, island in the E Caribbean Sea, one of Britain's West Indies Associated States. Britain handles only defense and external affairs. Tourism and the production of sugar, cotton and fruits and vegetables are the major industries. Antigua was discovered by Columbus in 1493. Pop 75,000.

Official name: Antigua and Barbuda
Capital: St. John's
Area: Antigua (108sq mi);
Barbuda (62sq mi)
Population: 74,000
Language: English
Religion: Protestant
Monetary Unit: East Caribbean
dollar=100 cents

ANTIGUA AND BARBUDA, independent nation in the West Indies, largest and most developed of the Leeward Islands.

Land. It includes the islands of Antigua and Barbuda, both low-lying and of volcanic origin. White sandy beaches, the nation's principal resource, fringe the coasts; few places rise to more than 1,000ft above sea level. The climate is tropical with a dry season Jul.–Dec.

People and Economy. The population is predominantly of African and British origins. St. John's is the largest town and chief port. Tourism is the principal economic activity, especially in the winter months. Cotton replaced sugar as the chief crop in the 19th century, and some tropical fruits are also grown. The US maintains a large naval and army base near Parham.

History. Antigua was discovered and named by COLUMBUS in 1493. The island passed briefly to Spanish and French control in the 17th century and to the British in 1666. With Barbuda as a dependency it became a self-governing West Indies Associated State in 1967 and independent in 1981. Leaders on Barbuda seek a separate independence for their island.

ANTIHISTAMINES, drugs that counteract HISTAMINE action; they are useful in HAY FEVER and HIVES (in which ALLERGY causes histamine release) and in some insect bites. They also act as SEDATIVES and may relieve MOTION SICKNESS.

ANTIKNOCK ADDITIVES, substances added to GASOLINE to slow the burning of the fuel and thus prevent "knocking," the premature ignition of the combustion mixture in the cylinder head. Most widely used is LEAD tetraethyl [$Pb(C_2H_5)_4$]. This is usually mixed with 1,2-dibromo- and 1,2-dichloroethane, which prevent the formation of lead deposits in the engine.

ANTI-MASONIC PARTY, US political faction active from 1827 to 1836. It emerged after the disappearance in 1826 of William Morgan, author of a book revealing the secrets of FREEMASONRY. The Masons were accused of murdering him and public outrage was exploited politically against Masons in office, first by Thurlow WEED and William H. SEWARD in New York state against Martin VAN BUREN and the ALBANY REGENCY, then by a national campaign to defeat President Andrew Jackson, himself a Mason, which won a number of congressional seats.

ANTIMATTER, a variety of MATTER differing from the matter which predominates in our part of the UNIVERSE in that it is composed of antiparticles rather than particles. Individual antiparticles, many of which have been found in COSMIC RAY showers or produced using particle ACCELERATORS, differ from their particle counterparts in that they are oppositely charged (as with the antiproton-PROTON pair) or in that their magnetic moment is orientated in the opposite sense with respect to their SPIN (as with the antineutrino and neutrino). In our part of the universe antiparticles are very short-lived, being rapidly annihilated in collisions with their corresponding particles, their mass-energy reappearing as a gamma-ray PHOTON. (The reverse is also true; a high-energy GAMMA RAY sometimes spontaneously forms itself into a positron-ELECTRON pair.) However, it is by no means inconceivable that regions of the universe exist in which all the matter is antimatter, composed of what are to us antiparticles. The first antiparticle, the positron (i.e., the antielectron), was discovered by C. D. ANDERSON in 1932, only four years after DIRAC had theoretically predicted the existence of antiparticles. (See also SUBATOMIC PARTICLES.)

ANTIMONY (Sb), brittle, silver-white metal in Group VA of the PERIODIC TABLE, occurring mainly as STIBNITE, which is roasted to give antimony (III) oxide. Its ALLOTROPY resembles that of ARSENIC. Antimony, though rather unreactive, forms trivalent and pentavalent oxides, halides and oxyanions. It is used in SEMICONDUCTORS and in lead ALLOYS, chiefly BABBITT METAL, PEWTER, type metal and in lead storage batteries. Certain antimony compounds are used in the manufacture of medicines, paints, matches, explosives and fireproofing materials. AW 121.75, mp 631°C, bp 1750°C, sg 6.691 (20°C).

ANTIN, Mary (1881–1949), Russian-born US writer noted for her autobiography *The Promised Land* (1912) and her book on immigrants *They Who Knock at Our Gates* (1914).

ANTINOMIANISM, heretical doctrine that Christians are set free by grace from the obligation to obey the moral law, especially the TEN COMMANDMENTS. In the patristic period it was held by many gnostics (see GNOSTICISM) and the followers of MARCION and MONTANUS. At the Reformation it was revived by Johann AGRICOLA and the ANABAPTISTS, though opposed by the Reformers, and was later held by radical sects during the COMMONWEALTH, Anne HUTCHINSON in New England and many METHODISTS and dispensationalists (see DISPENSATIONALISM). Antinomians have often been accused of licentiousness, in some cases justly.

ANTIOCH (now Antakya), ancient city in Asia Minor on the Orontes R. Founded c300 BC by Seleucus Nicator, it became the capital of the SELEUCID Empire and, in 64 BC, the Asian capital of the Roman Empire. Antioch was an important center of early Christianity. Antakya, the modern commercial city, became part of French-administered Syria after WWI and joined Turkey in 1939. Pop 91,551.

ANTIPARTICLES. See ANTIMATTER; SUBATOMIC PARTICLES.

ANTIPOPE, a pretender to the papal throne, elected by faction in the Roman Catholic Church or by a secular ruler. The first antipope was Hippolytus (3rd century); the last was Felix V (abdicated 1449). In the GREAT SCHISM (1378) Italy elected Urban VI while France set up court for Clement VII in Avignon. Their successors were deposed by the Council of CONSTANCE (1415).

ANTI-SALOON LEAGUE, temperance organization established in 1893 to curb the sale of liquor. It played an important part in the campaign to achieve national PROHIBITION.

ANTI-SEMITISM, hostility towards Jews, ranging from social prejudice to genocide. Common motives for anti-Semitism include religious opposition to Judaism, national resentment of a people who remain in some ways apart from the life of the country they live in and simple jealousy of the Jews' material success. Anti-Semites have often justified their standing by claiming that the Jews' exile and persecution were punishment for their part in Christ's crucifixion.

Segregation, expulsion and massacres have dogged Europe's Jewish communities, notably in the Middle Ages, and later in Tsarist Russia and in Nazi Germany before and during WWII, when some 6,000,000 Jews were put to death in concentration camps at AUSCHWITZ, BELSEN, BUCHENWALD and elsewhere. Despite the decline of avowed anti-Semitism since WWII, anti-Jewish feeling has increased in Arab lands hostile to the young Jewish state of Israel. Jews are still persecuted in the USSR.

ANTISEPTICS, or germicides, substances that kill or prevent the growth of microorganisms (particularly BACTERIA and FUNGI); they are used to avoid SEPSIS from contamination of body surfaces and surgical instruments. Some antiseptics are used as disinfectants to make places or objects GERM-free. VINEGAR and cedar oil have been used from earliest times to treat wounds and for EMBALMING. Modern antisepsis was pioneered by SEMMELWEIS, LISTER and KOCH, and dramatically reduced deaths from childbirth and surgery. Commonly used antiseptics and disinfectants include IODINE, CHLORINE, hypochlorous acid, ETHANOL, isopropanol (see ALCOHOLS), PHENOLS (including hexachlorophene), quaternary ammonium salts (see AMMONIA), FORMALDEHYDE, hydrogen PEROXIDE, potassium permanganate, and acriflavine (an acridine dye). HEAT, ULTRAVIOLET and ionizing radiations also have antiseptic effects. (See also STERILIZATION; ASEPSIS.)

ANTITOXINS, antibodies produced in the body against the TOXINS of some bacteria. They are also formed after INOCULATION of toxoid, chemically inactivated toxin that can still confer IMMUNITY.

ANTOFAGASTA, a major Pacific seaport city in N Chile, capital of Antofagasta province. An important industrial center, it processes and exports copper, nitrates and sulfur mined nearby. Founded c1870, it was ceded to Chile by Bolivia in 1883. Pop 161,226.

ANTONELLO DA MESSINA (c1430–1479), allegedly the first Italian to paint in oils. He was influenced by Dutch and Flemish painters and excelled in spatial composition. The S. Cassiano altarpiece in Venice and a *St. Sebastian* in Dresden are among his major works.

ANTONESCU, Ion (1882–1946), Romanian general and pro-Nazi right-wing leader. Becoming prime minister in 1940, he persuaded King Carol to abdicate and established a military dictatorship favoring the AXIS POWERS. He was executed as a war criminal.

ANTONINUS PIUS (86–161 AD), Roman

emperor (138–161), the last to achieve relative stability in the empire. Chosen consul in 120, he adopted MARCUS AURELIUS and Lucius Verus as successors. He was a prudent and economical ruler, tolerant of Christians.

ANTONIONI, Michelangelo (1912–   ), Italian film director of international renown. His motion pictures include *L'Avventura* (1959), *La Notte* (1961), *Eclipse* (1962), *The Red Desert* (1964), *Blow Up* (1966) and *Zabriskie Point* (1969).

ANTONY, Mark (or Marcus Antonius, c82–30 BC), Roman general who became one of three joint rulers of the Roman state. He fought notably in Gaul and became a tribune in 50 BC and a consul in 44 BC. After Caesar's murder, Antony, his brother-in-law Octavian (see AUGUSTUS) and Lepidus formed a Triumvirate (43 BC), dividing the empire into three. Antony controlled the E from the Adriatic to the Euphrates, but alienated Octavian by falling in love with the Egyptian queen, CLEOPATRA, and combining forces with her. Attacked by Octavian, Antony committed suicide after his naval defeat at ACTIUM.

ANTONY OF THEBES, Saint (c251–356), Egyptian hermit, considered the founder of Christian MONASTICISM. He founded a desert community of ascetics near Fayum, then lived alone in a mountain cave near the Red Sea and died aged over 100. He supported St. ATHANASIUS in the Arian controversy.

ANTS, social INSECTS of the family Formicidae of the order HYMENOPTERA, recognizable through the petiole or "waist" between abdomen and THORAX. There are some 3,500 species of ant, each species containing three distinct castes: male, female and worker. **Males** can be found only at certain times of year: winged, they are not readmitted to the nest after the mating flight. The **queen** is likewise winged, but she rubs her wings off after mating; she may survive for as long as 15 years, still laying eggs fertilized during the original mating flight. The **workers** are sterile females, sometimes falling into two distinct size categories, the larger ones (soldiers) defending the nest and assisting with heavier work. The most primitive ants (*Ponerinae*) may form nests with only a few individuals; nests of wood ants (*Formica rufa*), however, may contain more than 100,000 individuals. *Dorylinae,* the so-called Army Ants, do not build nests at all but are nomadic, traveling in "armies" up to 150,000 strong: like *Ponerinae* (but unlike the more sophisticated species, which are

vegetarian) they are carnivorous. Nesting ants welcome often "farm" APHIDS for honeydew.

ANTWERP, Belgium's second-largest city and leading port, on the Scheldt R 60mi from the North Sea. It is the capital of Antwerp province, the commercial and cultural center of Flemish Belgium (with a large university) and an important manufacturing city, with oil, metal, automobile and diamond industries. Around 1560 it was the leading port of Europe, and the center of the great Flemish school of painting: artists like BREUGHEL, RUBENS and VAN DYCK worked there. Pop 194,000.

ANURADHAPURA, capital of the North-Central province of Sri Lanka, former capital of the Sinhalese kings and site of Buddhist ruins. Its ancient Bo tree reputedly sprang from a branch of the tree under which the Buddha attained enlightenment. Restoration of the ruins has attracted tourists and pilgrims. Pop 30,000.

ANXIETY, an emotional state in which the individual is fearful and distressed because of a perceived threat to his or her well being or EGO integrity. It may trigger DEFENSE MECHANISMS.

ANZIO, Italian fishing port and seaside resort about 30mi S of Rome. As the ancient Roman Antium, the town was the birthplace of the emperors CALIGULA and NERO. Anzio was badly damaged when the Allies landed there in Jan. 1944, and a force of 50,000 men was pinned down at the beachhead by German counteroffensives.

ANZUS PACT, treaty signed on Sept. 1, 1951, by Australia, New Zealand and the US for mutual defense in the Pacific. The name consists of the initials of the participating countries, which meet annually.

AO, largest island (182sq mi) of the Netherlands Antilles, West Indies, 60mi N of NW Venezuela. It is flat and barren. The chief industries are oil-refining and phosphate mining. The liqueur *Curaçao* originated here. The capital is Willemstad.

AORTA, the chief systemic ARTERY, distributing oxygenated blood to the whole body except the LUNGS via its branches. (See also BLOOD CIRCULATION; HEART.)

APACHE INDIANS, North American Indians of the Athabaskan linguistic family. The major tribes were the Jicarilla, Lipan, Mescalero, Airavaipa, Coyotero, Pinaleno, Kiowa and Chiricahua. Apaches lived in SW North America, maintaining a nomadic hunting culture that depended on free movement over a large area. The arrival of white settlers thus threatened their survival, and many Apaches rejected repeated federal government attempts to confine the tribes to reservations. Bloody conflicts followed, and Apache numbers were greatly decimated by 1896, when the last great Apache chief, GERONIMO, was captured. Most present-day Apaches live on federal reservations in Okla., N.M. and Ariz.

APARTHEID, policy of strict racial segregation practiced in the Republic of South Africa in order to maintain the domination of the white minority. Segregation and discrimination against non-white peoples is observed in housing, employment, education and public services, and enforced by legislation punishing dissent or resistance with imprisonment, exile or house arrest. The policy also involves the "separate development" of eight Bantu homelands, where black people have a measure of self-government. Organizations suppressed for opposing apartheid have included the AFRICAN NATIONAL CONGRESS, the Pan-African Congress and Alan PATON's Liberal Party. Apartheid is almost universally condemned outside South Africa.

APENNINES, mountain chain forming the backbone of the Italian peninsula. It is about 800mi long and 25–80mi wide. The highest peak is Monte Corno (9,560ft). The predominant rocks are limestone and dolomite; sulfur and cinnabar (sulfide of mercury) are mined in the volcanic area near Vesuvius. Olives, grapes and grains are widely grown; lack of fertile topsoil prevents intensive agriculture.

APES. See ANTHROPOID APES.

APHASIA, a speech defect resulting from injury to certain areas of the brain and causing inability to use or comprehend words; it may be partial (dysphasia) or total. Common causes are cerebral THROMBOSIS, HEMORRHAGE and brain TUMORS. (See SPEECH DISORDERS AND SPEECH THERAPY.)

APHIDS (or greenflies or plant-lice), some 4,000 species of sap-feeding insects, comprising the family Aphididae of the order HOMOPTERA. They have needle-like mouthparts with which they pierce the plant tissue, the pressure within this forcing the sap into the insect's gut. Because of the damage caused by their feeding and because many species carry harmful VIRUSES, aphids are one of the world's greatest crop pests. The life cycle is a complex one, so that within a species there may at any one time be a diversity of forms; winged and wingless, reproducing sexually or parthenogenetically (see PARTHENOGENESIS; REPRODUCTION; also ALTERNATION OF GENERATIONS). Aphids excrete (see EXCRETION) a substance known as honeydew, an important food source for ANTS and other insects.

APHRODITE, the Greek goddess of love, fertility and beauty. She was supposedly the daughter of ZEUS and Dione, or alternatively rose from the sea near Cyprus. Her intensely sensual beauty aroused jealousy among other goddesses, particularly after PARIS chose her as the most beautiful goddess over HERA and ATHENA. Aphrodite was the wife of HEPHAESTUS (but took divine and mortal lovers). Aeneas and Eros were her sons. The Greeks honored her with major shrines at Athens, Corinth, Sparta, Cos, Cnidus and Cyprus, and the Romans identified her with Venus.

APIA, capital, main port and commercial center of Western Samoa, sited on the N coast of Upolu Island. Robert Louis STEVENSON died there in 1894 and is buried nearby. Pop 32,099.

APICULTURE. See BEEKEEPING.

APOCALYPSE, a prophetic revelation, usually about the end of the world and the ensuing establishment of a heavenly kingdom. Jewish and Christian apocalyptic writings appeared in Palestine between 200 BC and 150 AD and offered hope of liberation to a people under alien rule. (See also MESSIAH; REVELATION, BOOK OF.)

APOCRYPHA, writings not accepted by Jews or all Christians as canonical (that is, as part of Holy Scripture). Protestants use the term mainly for books written in the two centuries before Christ and included in the SEPTUAGINT and the VULGATE, but not in the Hebrew Bible. These include Esdras I and II, Tobit, Judith, additions to Esther, the Wisdom of Solomon, Ecclesiasticus, Baruch, the Song of the Three Children, Susanna and the Elders, Bel and the Dragon, the Prayer of Manasses and Maccabees I and II. (See also BIBLE; PSEUDEPIGRAPHA.)

APOGEE. See ORBIT.

APOLLINAIRE, Guillaume (real name: Wilhelm Apollinaris de Kostrowitzki; 1880–1918), influential French avant-garde poet and critic. The friend of DERAIN, DUFY and PICASSO, he helped to publicize Cubist and primitive art. His poetry, as in the collections *Alcools* (1913) and *Calligrammes* (1918), often anticipated SURREALISM with its use of startling associations and juxtapositions.

APOLLO, major deity in Greek and Roman mythology. In the Greek myths, Apollo was the son of ZEUS and Leto, and twin of ARTEMIS. Second only to Zeus, he had the power of the sun as giver of light and life. He was the god of justice and masculine beauty, and the purifier of those stained by crime. He was the divine patron of the arts, leader of the MUSES, and god of music and poetry. Apollo was a healer, but could also send disease, and from his foreknowledge he spoke through the ORACLE at DELPHI. The Romans adopted Apollo, honoring him as healer and as god of the sun.

APOLLONIUS OF RHODES (b. c295 BC), Greek epic poet who was a pupil of CALLIMACHUS and later head of the ALEXANDRIAN LIBRARY. His best-known work is the epic poem *Argonautica*, the story of JASON and the ARGONAUTS written in a style and meter owing much to Homer.

APOLLO PROGRAM, the $20 billion endeavor that landed 12 Americans on the moon. The program was announced July 29, 1960, and essentially concluded with the return of Apollo 17 on Dec. 19, 1972. Nine Apollo spacecraft traveled to the vicinity of the moon; six of them landed on its surface. The first landing occurred July 20, 1969.

The three-man Apollo spacecraft, consisting of command, service and lunar landing modules, was launched into earth orbit by the huge Saturn 5 rocket (at lift-off, the entire moon rocket stood 363ft high and weighed some six million pounds). After separating from the booster rocket, the spacecraft voyaged to the moon, with two astronauts landing while the third orbited the moon in the command and service modules. On the return flight, the landing and service modules were jettisoned and the command module alone splashed down into the Pacific. The landing missions lasted from eight to 15 days, with stay-times on the lunar surface ranging from about 21 to 75 hours. See also SPACE EXPLORATION.

APOLLO PROJECT. See SPACE EXPLORATION.

APOPLEXY, obsolete term for STROKE due to cerebral HEMORRHAGE.

APOSTLES, the 12 disciples closest to Jesus, whom he chose to proclaim his teaching. They were Andrew, John, Bartholomew, Judas, Jude, the two Jameses, Matthew, Peter, Philip, Simon and Thomas. When Judas died, Matthias replaced him. Paul and Barnabas became known as apostles for their work in spreading the Gospel.

APOSTLES' CREED, a CREED ascribed to Christ's apostles and maintained in its present form since the early Middle Ages. The Roman Catholic Church uses it in the sacraments of baptism and confirmation. It is also used by various Protestant denominations.

APOSTOLIC SUCCESSION, a doctrine held by several Christian churches. They believe that Christ's apostles ordained the first bishops and other priests, that these ordained their successors, and so on, forging an unbroken chain of succession reaching to the present day which thereby guarantees their authority. Many Protestants, excepting Episcopalians, reject the doctrine as unproven and unnecessary.

APOTHECARIES' WEIGHTS, a system of weights formerly used by pharmacists in preparing medicines. (See also PHARMACY, WEIGHTS AND MEASURES.)

APPALACHIA, region of the SE US embracing the economically poor S part of the Appalachian Mts. It includes parts of 13 states, covers 355 counties and has 16 million inhabitants. In 1965 Congress voted $1.2 billion towards rebuilding the region's declining economy and improving social conditions.

APPALACHIAN MOUNTAINS, mountain system of E North America about 1,800mi long and 120–375mi wide, stretching south from Newfoundland to central Ala. The system's ancient sandstone, limestone, slate and other rocks have been folded, eroded, uplifted and again eroded. Major ranges of the N include the Notre Dame, Green, and White Mts. The central area has the Allegheny Mts and part of the Blue Ridge Mts. The S contains the S Blue Ridge, Cumberland, Black and Great Smoky Mts. The highest peak is Mt Mitchell (6,684ft) in N.C.

Appalachian forests yield much timber, and rich deposits of coal and iron have stimulated the growth of such industrial areas as Birmingham and Pittsburgh. The Connecticut, Hudson, Delaware, Susquehanna, Potomac, Kanawha, Tennessee and other rivers have cut deep gaps in the ranges. But in the early years of the US the Appalachians were a barrier to westward expansion.

APPALACHIAN TRAIL, the longest marked hiking trail in the world, stretching over 2,000mi along the crest of the Appalachian Mts from Mt Katahdin in N Me. to Springer Mountain in N Ga.

APPEASEMENT, conciliatory policy adopted by a government to avoid conflict with a potentially hostile body. An example which gave the term a bad name is the Franco-British appeasement of Nazi Germany that resulted in the hollow MUNICH PACT (1938).

APPEL, Karel (1921–), Dutch abstract expressionist painter, a founder of the international experimenobra. His work is marked by colorful yet aggressive sensuality.

APPENDICITIS, inflammation of the APPENDIX, often caused by obstruction to its narrow opening, followed by swelling and bacterial infection. Acute appendicitis may lead to rupture of the organ, formation of an ABSCESS or PERITONITIS. Symptoms include abdominal pain, usually in the right lower ABDOMEN, nausea, vomiting and FEVER. Early surgical removal of the appendix is essential; any abscess requires drainage of PUS and delayed excision.

APPIA, Adolphe (1862–1928), Swiss stage designer whose ideas revolutionized early 20th-century theater. He stressed the use of three-dimensional settings and of mobile lighting with controlled intensity and color.

APPIAN WAY, the oldest and most famous Roman road. Built by Appius Claudius Caecus in 312 BC to link Rome and Capua, it was later extended to Brindisi, covering in all about 350mi. Sections near Rome are still largely intact.

APPLE, popular edible fruit of the apple tree, *Malus sylvestris* (family Rosaceae), widely cultivated in temperate climates. Over 7,000 varieties are known but only about 40 are commercially important, the most popular US variety being Delicious. Some 15%–20% of the world's crop is produced in the US, mostly in the states of Wash., N.Y., Cal., Mich., and Va. There are three main types of apples: cooking, dessert, and those used in making CIDER.

APPLESEED, Johnny (1774–1845), US folk hero, a mild eccentric whose real name was John Chapman. A pioneer in the Ohio river region, he wandered around for some 40 years, planting and tending apple orchards.

APPLIED LINGUISTICS. See LINGUISTICS.

APPOMATTOX COURT HOUSE, US historical site in central Va., where the Civil War was ended with Lee's surrender to Grant on April 9, 1865. The McLean House (where the surrender took place) and other buildings have been reconstructed as part of the 972-acre Appomattox Court House National Historical Park.

APPORTIONMENT, Legislative, the distribution of voters' representation in the lawmaking bodies. Although each state, whatever its size, elects two senators only, members of the US House of Representatives are elected from districts with equal populations, and the federal census results in a reapportionment of seats each decade. Since the 1980 census, each congressman represents about 500,000 voters.

In the past, state legislature district boundaries were often erratically drawn to give voting advantage to one political party (see GERRYMANDER). Also, most counties had equal representation in state senates; thus, one vote in a rural county might be worth 30 times that in a city, due to lower population. But in 1962 the Supreme Court ruled that unfair districting may be brought before federal courts, and later rulings established that one man's vote should be "worth as much as another's," or, "one man, one vote." This principle is slowly shifting political power from rural to urban areas.

APPROXIMATION, the setting of an approximate value V_a in place of a true but imprecisely known value V where $[V—V_a]$ lies within known limits. There are several different ways of expressing approximations and their limits of accuracy.

If we approximate 2.3654202 by 2.365420 we say that this is correct to 6 decimal places, in that the six figures after the decimal point are correct (see also DECIMAL SYSTEM). It is common practice, when approximating to an $(n—1)$ decimal places a number that has n decimal places, to round *up* if the nth figure after the point is 5 or greater, *down* if it is less than 5. Thus 3.65 can be written as 3.7 to 1 decimal place; 3.64 as 3.6.

Similarly, 2.3654202 can be expressed as 2.365420 to 7 significant figures, since the first 7 figures are correct, rounding down.

An alternative way of writing approximations is by use of the sign ± (read "plus or minus"). Thus $2.365420 ± 0.0000004$ is an approximation stating that the correct value lies between 2.3654196 and 2.3654204. This can be expressed as a percentage (see PERCENT): $2.365420 ± 0.0000169\%$.

Approximation is required in almost all computations, due either to inherent inaccuracies in the calculating device or to the technique of calculation, or because greater accuracy is unnecessary. The techniques of approximation to a FUNCTION are of paramount importance in CALCULUS.

APRICOT, orange-colored fruit of the apricot tree, *Prunus armeniaca* (family Rosaceae), native to China but grown throughout temperate regions. Commercial production is mainly in central and SE Asia, Europe and the US; over 90% of the US crop comes from California. Apricots are eaten fresh, or preserved by drying or canning; the kernels are used to make a liqueur. Apricot trees are often grown as ornamentals.

APRIL, fourth month of the year in the Gregorian Calendar; first full spring month in the Northern Hemisphere. The Christian EASTER and Jewish PASSOVER usually fall in

April. The month is probably named from *aperire* (Latin: to open), referring to the opening spring buds. Birthstone: diamond. Astrological signs: Aries and Taurus.

APRIL FOOLS' DAY, or All Fools' Day, April 1, the traditional day for practical jokes. The custom probably began in France in 1564, when New Year's Day was changed from April 1 to Jan. 1. Those continuing to observe April 1 were ridiculed.

A PRIORI AND A POSTERIORI, terms descriptive of knowledge or reasoning reflecting whether or not they result from experience of the real world. Alleged knowledge attained solely through reasoning, as in pure logic, is *a priori* (Latin: from earlier things); that gained empirically, from observation or experience, is *a posteriori* (Latin: from later things). This modern usage of the terms derives from the philosopher KANT.

APRISTA, political movement based in Peru, known fully as the American Popular Revolutionary Alliance. Founded (1924) and guided for decades by Victor Raúl Haya de la Torre, Aprista opposed foreign imperialism and favored integration of Indians into Latin American economic and political life and nationalization of land and industry. Several times close to winning power in Peru, the movement was thwarted by the military and other conservative elements.

APTITUDE TESTS, tests designed to measure a person's potential ability. Although satisfactory in dealing with well-defined skills such as problem-solving, they are less successful in evaluating artistic skills. Widely used in vocational guidance and college entry, they are also used for staff selection by some companies.

APULEIUS, Lucius (c125–185 AD), Roman author of *Metamorphoses* or *The Golden Ass*. The hero of this story is turned into an ass, whose humorous adventures provide a fascinating insight into contemporary Roman society.

APULIA (Italian: *Puglia*), SE region forming the "heel" of the "boot" of Italy. It is composed of the provinces of Bari, Brindisi, Foggia, Lecce and Taranto. Its principal town and main port is Bari; it also contains the important naval base and steel industry of Taranto.

AQABA, Gulf of, NE arm of the Red Sea, between the Sinai Peninsula and Saudi Arabia. Geologically part of the GREAT RIFT VALLEY of Africa and Asia, it is some 110mi long and 5–17mi wide. At the N end of the Gulf stand the ports of Aqaba (Jordan) and Elat (Israel). The Egyptian blockade of

Elat sparked off the 1967 Arab-Israeli Six Days' War.

AQUALUNG or **SCUBA** (*s*elf-*c*ontained *u*nderwater *b*reathing *a*pparatus), a device allowing divers to breathe and move about freely underwater. It comprises a mouthpiece, a connecting tube, a valve and at least one compressed-air cylinder. The key component is the "demand valve" which allows the diver to breathe air at the PRESSURE prevailing in the surrounding water however great the pressure in his supply cylinder. Used air is vented into the water.

AQUARIUS (the Water Bearer), a large but faint constellation on the ECLIPTIC; the 11th sign of the ZODIAC.

AQUATINT, an ENGRAVING process used with particular success by GOYA, in which the plate is repeatedly etched through a porous (usually resin) ground. What are to produce the white areas of the finished print are stopped out with acid-resisting varnish before the first ETCHING, the other areas being stopped out in order of increasing darkness between subsequent etchings. The color-wash effect of aquatint is particularly striking when used in combination with drypoint.

AQUAVIT (or Akvavit), colorless spirits distilled from grain or potatoes and flavored with caraway seeds. It is popular in Scandinavia.

AQUEDUCT, man-made conduit for water. The Babylonians and Egyptians built large-scale underground aqueducts, but the Romans preferred a row of arches supporting the channels along which water flowed downhill from mountains to cities. Rome itself was supplied by nine aqueducts, but the most famous Roman ones are at Segovia and Tarragona, Spain, and near Nîmes France (the *Pont du Gard*).

AQUEOUS HUMOR, the clear, watery fluid between the cornea and the lens of the EYE.

AQUIFER, an underground rock body through which GROUNDWATER can easily percolate and possessing the porosity required to store sufficient quantities of water to supply wells. SANDSTONES, GRAVEL beds and jointed LIMESTONES make good aquifers.

AQUINAS, St Thomas (c1225–1274 AD), known as the "angelic doctor," major Christian theologian and philosopher who attempted to reconcile faith with reason. In his *Summa Theologica* he uses Aristotelian logic to examine the existence of God: he finds God the logical uncaused cause, the prime reason for order in the universe. He sees man as a rational social animal gaining knowledge from sensory experience. His morality is based on the principle of man's harmony with himself, with other men and with God. Thomism, the philosophy of St. Thomas, has been very influential, and his teachings are basic to Roman Catholic theology.

AQUITAINE, historic French region, between the rivers Garonne and Loire, extending to the Pyrenees. Henry II of England's marriage to Eleanor of Aquitaine in 1152 resulted in centuries of Anglo-French territorial conflicts. The French crown regained control of Aquitaine in 1453, at the end of the HUNDRED YEARS' WAR.

ARAB, one whose language is ARABIC and who identifies with Arab culture. Besides the countries of the Arabian Peninsula, the Arab world includes Algeria, Egypt, Iraq, Jordan, Lebanon, Libya, Morocco, Sudan, Syria and Tunisia. Arab culture spread after the coming of MOHAMMED (c570 AD). In the 7th century the Arabs extended their hegemony from NW Africa and Spain to Afghanistan and N India where many non-Arabic peoples were converted to the religion of ISLAM, adopting Arabic language and culture. Although Arab political control crumbled in the 10th and 11th centuries, elements of the culture remained.

The precepts of Islam, as set out in the KORAN, still govern much of Arab life and social institutions. Non-Muslim peoples who are also Arabs include Palestinian, Lebanese and Syrian Christians. In the 20th century the discovery and exploitation of petroleum in Arab lands has resulted in sudden wealth and modernization for many Arab Countries. Arab reaction to the creation of the state of Israel has strengthened Pan-Arab nationalism and led to four ARAB-ISRAELI WARS.

ARABESQUE, elaborate decorative style characterized by curved or intertwining shapes with grotesque, animal, human or symbolic forms and delicate foliage. Arab culture promoted the use of geometric rather than figurative forms.

ARABIA (Arabic: *Jazirat al-Arab*, the "island of the Arabs"), SW Asian peninsula bounded by the Red Sea, Indian Ocean and Persian Gulf. It comprises Saudi Arabia, the Republic of Yemen, the Southern Yemen People's Republic, the Sultanate of Oman and the Persian Gulf States, including Bahrain, Kuwait, Qatar and the United Arab Emirates. The world's richest reserves of petroleum were discovered in the peninsula in the 1930s and have since flooded wealth into an almost feudal seminomadic society, creating large income-differentials within it. In 1973, Saudi Arabia and other Arab countries cut back oil supplies to the West, thus adding an important new economic weapon to the continuing Arab-Israeli conflict.

Between the birth of Christ and the emergence of MOHAMMED (c570 AD), various foreign powers influenced or controlled the area. Mecca, on a busy caravan route, was a prosperous trading center, but other towns remained little more than small oasis farming settlements. When Mohammed first achieved prominence, Arabia was divided between continually warring tribes. His founding of ISLAM resulted in a partial unification of the Arab tribes and rapid political and territorial expansion. By 800 Muslims controlled almost half the civilized world. But this power crumbled by the 11th century, when Turkey began its domination of the area. In the 18th and 19th centuries the Islamic Wahabi movement weakened this power. In the 19th century Britain gained considerable footholds in Aden and on the Persian Gulf. After the Turks joined the Central Powers at the start of WWI, the British successfully encouraged the Arabs to revolt (1916) and by 1932 Saudi Arabia had extended political control over most of the region.

ARABIAN NIGHTS, or *The Thousand and One Nights*, a collection of 8th–16th century Arabic stories, probably of Indian origin with Persian and Arab additions. The stories, which include *Aladdin, Ali Baba* and *Sinbad*, are linked by Scheherazade who, sentenced to die at dawn, tells her husband the king one story per night, leaving the ending till the next day. She is reprieved after 1,001 nights.

ARABIAN SEA, NW Indian Ocean, between India and Arabia. Connected with the Persian Gulf by the Gulf of Oman, and with the Red Sea by the Gulf of Aden. Its ports include Bombay and Karachi.

ARABIC, one of the SEMITIC LANGUAGES. The Arabic ALPHABET comprises 28 letters, all consonants, vowels being expressed either by positioned points or, in some cases, by insertion of the letters *alif, waw* and *ya* in positions where they would not otherwise occur, thereby representing the long *a, u* and *i* respectively. Arabic is written from right to left. Classical Arabic, the language of the Koran, is today used occasionally in writing, rarely in speech; a standardized modern Arabic being used for newspapers, etc. Arabic played a large part in the dissemination of knowledge through medieval Europe as many ancient Greek and Roman texts were available solely in Arabic translation.

ARAB-ISRAELI WARS, the results of persistent conflicts between Israel and the Arabs since the BALFOUR DECLARATION (1917) pronounced British Palestine a Jewish national home. When Britain's mandate ended, the Jews declared an independent state of Israel (May 14, 1948). The next day, Egypt, Iraq, Transjordan (Jordan), Lebanon and Syria attacked, but within a month Israel had occupied the greater part of Palestine. By July 1949, separate ceasefires had been concluded with the Arab states, where hundreds of thousands of Palestinian Arabs now sought refuge.

On Oct. 29, 1956, with the Suez Canal and Gulf of Aqaba closed to her ships, Israel invaded Egypt, which had nationalized the canal in July. British and French supporting troops occupied the canal banks, but were replaced by a UN force after international furor. By March 1957 all Israeli forces had left Egypt in exchange for access to the Gulf of Aqaba.

In 1967 Egypt closed the gulf to Israel and on June 5, at the start of the Six-Day War, Israeli air strikes destroyed Arab air forces on the ground. Israel won the west bank of the Jordan R, the Golan Heights, the Gaza Strip, the Sinai Peninsula and the Old City of Jerusalem. A ceasefire was accepted by June 10. In the following years, worldwide Arab anti-Jewish terrorism became common, reaching a climax in the 1972 Munich Olympic massacre of Israeli athletes.

On Oct. 6, 1973, Yom Kippur (the Jewish Day of Atonement), Egypt and Syria attacked Israel to regain the lost territories. A ceasefire was signed on Nov. 11, 1973. Although Israeli troops penetrated deep into Syria and crossed onto the W bank of the Suez Canal, initial Arab success restored confidence and encouraged Arab states to use economic measures, principally an oil boycott, against Israel's Western sympathizers. (See also MIDDLE EAST.)

Talks between Egypt and Israel led to a peace treaty (1979). But tension ran high elsewhere, especially in Lebanon, used as a guerrilla base by the Palestinians and a target for Israeli attacks.

ARAB LEAGUE, an organization to promote economic, cultural and political cooperation among Arab states, set up on March 22, 1945. Although quite successful in its first two aims, it achieved real political unity of action only in 1956 (Suez Crisis), 1961 (Franco-Tunisian conflict) and 1973 (cutback of oil to the West). Egypt was an original member of the league, but the other 20 members broke with Egypt in 1979 after Egypt signed a peace treaty with Israel, and the league's headquarters were moved from Cairo to Tunis. Member states are Algeria, Bahrain, Djibouti, Iraq, Jordan, Kuwait, Lebanon, Libya, Mauritania, Morocco, Oman, Qatar, Saudi Arabia, Somalia, Sudan, Syria, Tunisia, the United Arab Emirates, Yemen, Southern Yemen, and the government of the Palestine Liberation Organization.

ARAFAT, Yassir (1929–   ), Palestinian leader of the anti-Israel Al Fatah guerrillas, and chairman of the PALESTINE LIBERATION ORGANIZATION since 1968. In 1974 Arafat opened a debate on Palestine at the UN, where he led the first non-governmental delegation to take part in a General Assembly plenary session. An ardent spokesman for an independent Palestinian state, he was associated with hard-line opponents of Israel in the Middle East.

ARAGON, historic region of NE Spain, stretching from the central Pyrenées to S of the Ebro R. The medieval kingdom of Aragon comprised what are now Huesca, Teruel and Saragossa provinces though the influence of the kings of Aragon was more extensive. King Ferdinand II of Aragon's marriage to Isabella of Castile (1469) laid the foundations of a unified Spain. Aragon's sovereignty was ended 1707–09 by Philip V during the war of SPANISH SUCCESSION (1701–14).

ARAGON, Louis (1897–   ), French novelist, poet and journalist, a leading figure in the dadaist and surrealist movements of the 1920s and 1930s, as is reflected in his early poetry. He joined the Communist Party in the 1930s, and thereafter turned to social realism. After WWII he edited the left-wing weekly *Les Lettres Françaises.*

ARAL SEA, inland sea or saltwater lake covering 24,904sq mi in the S USSR. It is the fourth-largest lake in the world and is fed by the AMU DARYA and SYR DARYA rivers. The sea is commercially important for its bass, carp, perch and sturgeon.

ARAMAEANS, nomadic Semites of the N Syrian desert in the 11th to 8th centuries BC. They assimilated features of earlier FERTILE CRESCENT civilizations. Most of the smaller Aramaean tribes were subjugated by the Assyrians 740–720 BC. But the Chaldean tribe, which settled near the Tigris and Euphrates estuary, extended its control over all Mesopotamia, succeeding the Assyrians. (See also BABYLONIA AND ASSYRIA.)

ARAMAIC, the Semitic language of the ARAMAEANS. Its use spread throughout Syria and Mesopotamia from the 8th century BC onwards and it became the official language of the Persian Empire. Aramaic was probably spoken by Jesus and the apostles, being by then the everyday language of Palestine. Parts of the Old Testament are in Aramaic. Aramaic survives only in isolated Lebanese villages and among some NESTORIANS of N Iraq and E Turkey.

ARAPAHO, North American Indian tribe of the ALGONQUIAN family. They lived as nomadic buffalo hunters on the Great Plains in two groups—the N and S Arapaho. Fierce enemies of white settlement, they were forced onto reservations at the end of the 19th century. By the 1970s, only 5,000 remained, mostly on reservations in Okla. and Wyo.

ARARAT, Mount, dormant volcanic mountain in E Turkey with two peaks (16,950ft and 13,000ft) 7mi apart. Genesis 8:4 says that Noah's Ark landed "upon the mountains of Ararat." The Armenians venerate the mountain as the Mother of the World. The last eruption was in 1840.

ARAUCANIAN INDIANS, South American tribes famous for their resistance to the 16th-century Spanish invasion of what is now central Chile. Many Araucanians crossed the Andes into Argentina. During the 19th century the Araucanians were settled on Chilean and Argentinian reservations where they have since maintained much of their traditional culture.

ARAWAK INDIANS, linguistic group of often culturally distinct South American tribes, now living mostly in Brazil, the Guianas and Peru. They also inhabited the Caribbean islands at the time Columbus landed there in 1492, but were later exterminated by the CARIB INDIANS.

ARBELA. See GAUGAMELA.

ARBITRATION, process for settling disputes by submitting the issues involved to the judgment of an impartial third party or arbitrator. In the recent past, most US industrial collective bargaining agreements have allowed for an arbitrator to act in cases where problems of interpretation arise. An arbitration- service, providing panels for commercial and industrial disputes, has been established by the American Arbitration Association. Several state and federal laws ensure the enforcement of agreements to submit disputes to arbitration. The Taft-Hartley Act (1947) provides for emergency fact-finding boards if serious strikes loom but, as their decisions are not binding, they lack the power of arbitrating bodies. (See also FEDERAL MEDIATION AND CONCILIATION SERVICES; INTERNATIONAL COURT OF JUSTICE; INTERNATIONAL LAW.)

ARBOR DAY, annual tree-planting day in some US states. In northern areas it is normally held in the spring and in southern areas in winter. It was first held in Neb. on April 10, 1872.

ARBUS, Diane (1923–1971), US photographer who achieved prominence during the 1960s for her photographs of dwarfs, giants, transvestites and other grotesques.

ARBUTHNOT, John (1667–1735), Scots-born mathematician, physician to Queen Anne and eminent satirist. Arbuthnot belonged to the famous Scriblerus Club, together with Alexander POPE, Jonathan SWIFT, and John GAY. He is noted for *The History of John Bull* (1712) and his contributions to *The Memoirs of Martinus Scriblerus* (1741).

ARBUTUS-HALETHORPE-RELAY, an unincorporated town of three villages. It is a residential and industrial suburb of Baltimore, Md. Pop 22,402.

ARC. See CIRCLE.

ARCARO, Eddie (George Edward Arcaro; 1916–), the only US jockey to have won the triple crown twice (1941 and 1948). Arcaro was also the world's third-greatest race-winner (4,779 wins) and the second-greatest money-winner (more than $30 million).

ARC DE TRIOMPHE, Napoleon I's triumphal arch in the Place Charles de Gaulle at the end of the Champs Elysées, Paris. It was built 1806–36 and is 162ft high and 147ft wide. Inspired by Roman triumphal arches, it bears reliefs celebrating Napoleon's victories. The arch is also the site of the tomb of France's Unknown Soldier.

ARCH, structural device to span openings and support loads. In ARCHITECTURE the simplest form of arch is the round (semicircular): here, as in most arches, wedge-shaped stones (**voussoirs**) are fitted together so that stresses in the arch exert outward forces on them; downward forces from the load combine with these to produce a diagonal resultant termed the THRUST. The voussoirs at each end of the arch are termed **springers**; that in the center, usually the last to be inserted, is the **keystone**. Although the arch was known in Ancient Egypt and Greece, it was not until Roman times that its use became popular.

ARCHAEOLOGY, the study of the past through identification and interpretation of the material remains of human cultures. A comparatively new social science, involving many academic and scientific disciplines such as ANTHROPOLOGY, history, PALEOGRAPHY and PHILOLOGY, it makes use of numerous scientific techniques. Its keystone is fieldwork.

Archaeology was born in the early 18th century. There were some excavations of Roman and other sites, and the famous ROSETTA STONE, which provided the key to Egyptian HIEROGLYPHICS, was discovered in 1799 and deciphered in 1818. In 1832 archaeological time was classified into three divisions—STONE AGE, BRONZE AGE and IRON AGE—though this system is now more commonly used to describe cultures of PRIMITIVE MAN.

However, it was not until the 19th century that archaeology graduated from its amateur status to become a systematized science. SCHLIEMANN, Arthur EVANS, WOOLLEY, CARTER and others adopted an increasingly scientific approach in their researches.

Excavation is a painstaking procedure, as great care must be taken not to damage any object or fragment of an object, and each of the different levels of excavation must be carefully documented and photographed. The location of suitable sites for excavation is assisted by historical accounts, topographical surveys and aerial photography. Any object or fragment of an object that was produced by man is of interest to the archaeologist. These include such obvious items as tools, weapons, utensils and clothing. The discovery of a midden, or refuse pile, is especially welcome. Natural objects, such as seeds of cultivated plants, are also revealing. Each item on discovery is recorded on a map that establishes its physical relationship with other artifacts found, and is numbered and photographed. Once in the laboratory, the archaeologist will examine it more closely, comparing it with similar finds.

Dating is accomplished in several ways. First, of course, is comparison of the relative depths of objects that are discovered. Analysis of the types of pollen in an object can provide an indication of its date. The most widespread dating technique is RADIOCARBON DATING, incorporating the corrections formulated through discoveries in DENDROCHRONOLOGY.

Archaeology contains many divisions and areas of specialty. Some embrace the study of great civilizations, like those of Greece, Rome, Egypt, China and Mexico. Other scholars concentrate on the cultures of peoples of humble achievements. In the US a major field of study is that of the American Indian. Another area concentrates on settlements of colonial America—an example of historic archaeology, which deals with peoples who flourished during a time when written documents were left.

The earth continues to yield a rich harvest of artifacts from the past. In the 1970s, Chinese archaeologists recovered vast collections of priceless art objects in gold and other metals as well as more mundane objects from ancient China. The presentation of these treasures to the world of scholarship and art was especially welcome because of earlier fears that the Chinese Communist regime was unconcerned about the nation's past.

ARCHANGEL, a prince of angels, or chief angel, often entrusted with God's messages and counsel to men. The most prominent are Gabriel (Daniel 8:16; 9:21; Luke 1:19, 26), Michael (Daniel 10:13, 21; 12:1; Jude 9; Revelation 12:7) and Raphael (Tobit). Later writings refer to the archangels Phanuel, Raguel, Remiel, Uriel and Saraquael.

ARCHANGEL. See ARKHANGELSK.

ARCHBISHOP, a metropolitan BISHOP of the Roman Catholic, Anglican and Eastern churches, and the Lutheran churches of Finland and Sweden, having jurisdiction over the bishops of a church province, or archdiocese, within which he consecrates bishops and presides over synods. Archbishops do not form a separate order of MINISTRY. The term may be applied to bishops of distinguished sees, or PATRIARCHS.

ARCHERY, shooting with bow and arrow, used in warfare by primitive peoples in the Americas, Africa and Asia, and in ancient Greece and the Near East. It was vital in medieval European warfare. The English longbow's superiority over the French crossbow won the Battle of AGINCOURT (1415). Between the 14th and 15th centuries, the bow's use in W Europe declined with the development of firearms. But in late 18th-century England archery was revived as a sport. The US National Archery Association was formed in 1879 and, since 1900, archery has been part of the Olympic Games. The sport involves shooting at a standard circular target marked with colored concentric circles.

ARCHES NATIONAL PARK, 82,953 acres in E Utah containing natural rock arches formed by weathering and erosion. The park was established in 1929.

ARCHETYPE, term used by JUNG to refer to the concepts that derive from the historic experience of the human race, which are contained in that part of the mind Jung called the COLLECTIVE UNCONSCIOUS.

ARCHIMEDES (c287–212 BC), Greek mathematician and physicist who spent most of his life at his birthplace, Syracuse

(Sicily). In mathematics he worked on the areas and volumes associated with CONIC SECTIONS, fixed the value of PI (π) between $3^{10}/_{70}$ and $3^{10}/_{71}$ and defined the **Archimedean Spiral** ($r=a\theta$). He founded the science of HYDROSTATICS with his enunciation of **Archimedes' Principle**. This states that the force acting to buoy up a body partially or totally immersed in a fluid is equal to the weight of the fluid displaced. In MECHANICS he studied the properties of the LEVER and applied his experience in the construction of military catapults and grappling irons. He is also said to have invented the **Archimedes Screw**, a machine for raising water still used to irrigate fields in Egypt. This consists of a helical tube or a cylindrical tube containing a close-fitting screw with the lower end dipping in the water. When the tube (or screw) is rotated. water is moved up the tube and is discharged from the top.

ARCHIPENKO, Alexander (1887–1964), Ukrainian-born US sculptor, famous for nude female torsos in which naturalistic forms are reduced to elegant geometric shapes.

ARCHITECTURE has usually been defined as the art of building. The architect today is both an artist and an engineer who must combine a knowledge of design and construction, and of the available resources in labor, techniques and materials, to produce a harmonious, durable and functional whole. His building must be fitted to its environment and must satisfy the social needs for which it is required—whether it is a church, dwelling, factory or office building. In the past all this was accomplished in a traditional manner by largely anonymous builders; today the architect plans both the aesthetics and the construction of his building in a highly conscious manner, often deliberately attempting to communicate artistic concepts and abstract ideas through the structure itself.

The architect designs buildings for human activities; and most such buildings spring directly out of the culture of their time. Hence architecture in any period is one of the most visible and significant expressions of the culture that produced it. The Egyptian pyramid, for instance, as a royal tomb, translated the pharaoh's hope for an eternal afterlife into huge, long-lasting piles of masonry, while the awesome, columned halls of the royal palace at Persepolis were built to display the majesty of the ancient kings of Persia. The Islamic mosque and the Gothic cathedral, one open to sunny skies, the other closed and vaulted against northern weather, provided equally generous spaces for communal worship. Rome and the modern city both produced apartment houses for urban living; the Pueblo Indians built them for agricultural communities. The English stately home expressed the power and aspirations of a remarkable ruling class, while the modern glass skyscraper fulfills the needs of our industrial and business society.

Architecture has always been limited by the materials and techniques at its command; conversely, architectural advances and the development of new styles have been marked by the adoption of new materials or the discovery of new techniques. Traditionally the materials have been stone, earth, brick, wood, glass, concrete, iron and steel—with plastics and new metals added today. With its great compressive strength, stone has been the material of most major buildings in the past. It gave rise to the common post and lintel type of construction, and to the arch, the latter culminating in the soaring lightness of the Gothic cathedrals. The acme of the ancient post and lintel construction was reached in the classic simplicity of the Greek temple, notably in the PARTHENON. To these elements the Romans added daring experiments in vaulting, made possible by the use of concrete, as in the PANTHEON (2nd century AD), carried still further in Byzantine, Romanesque and Islamic architecture. But the tensile strength of stone is poor, while wood and steel have tensile as well compressive strength. This made frame construction possible, as in the wooden buildings of Japan or the steel-framed modern building. Geodesic and stressed-frame methods of construction, with reinforced concrete, have further extended the range of the modern architect.

Not only new materials and techniques, but also developments in social and institutional needs, the exigencies of climate and the need to express new aspirations and ideals in differing cultures have brought about changing styles in architecture. Often new architectures have repeated and elaborated older styles, as in the Renaissance and the Greek and Roman revivals. The use of ornamentation or decoration in architecture—as in the intricate surface decoration of Islamic buildings or the elaborations of the Rococo—has varied in response to changing tastes. Today we are emerging from a period of intense reaction against surface decoration embodied in the plain and functional International style of recent modern architecture. Styles change, but at all times and in all places the architect has attempted to manipulate space, mass, light and color to produce the optimum proportion and scale called for by the human mind. Thus the importance of architecture in civilization is three-fold; it is an art, it is made for people, and it is always a major expression of culture. See also articles on various styles and periods, for example GOTHIC ART AND ARCHITECTURE, ROMAN ART AND ARCHITECTURE; articles on building forms, such as BASILICA, SKYSCRAPER; and articles on architectural elements, such as BUTTRESS, DOME.

ARCHIVES, documents of a public body preserved in an organized fashion. Systematic collection and supervision by a central government agency began in 1789 with the French *Archives Nationales.* The US National Archives and Records Service (originating in 1934) houses records in the National Archives Building, Washington, D.C. It has the originals of the DECLARATION OF INDEPENDENCE and the CONSTITUTION. Corporations, foundations, universities and cities also keep archives, which now include tape recordings and space-saving microfilms.

ARC LAMP, an intensely bright and comparatively efficient form of LIGHTING used for lighthouses, floodlights and spotlights, invented by DAVY in 1809. An arc discharge is set up when two carbon ELECTRODES at a moderate POTENTIAL difference (typically 40V) are "struck" (touched together then drawn apart). The light is emitted from vaporized carbon IONS in the discharge. In modern lamps the arc is enclosed in an atmosphere of high-pressure XENON.

ARCTIC REGIONS, regions N of the Arctic Circle (66°30'N); alternatively regions N of the tree line. The Arctic comprises the Arctic Ocean, Greenland, Spitsbergen and other islands, extreme N Europe, N Siberia, Alaska and N Canada. The central feature is the Arctic Ocean, opening S into the N Atlantic Ocean and joined with the N Pacific Ocean by the Bering Strait. The Arctic Ocean comprises two main basins and has a shallow rim floored by the continental shelves of Eurasia and North America. Much of the ocean surface is always covered by ice.

The Arctic climate is cold. In midwinter the sun never rises and the mean Jan. temperature is −33°F, far lower in interior Canada and Siberia. Snow and ice never melt in high altitudes and latitudes, but elsewhere the short mild summer with 24 hours' sunlight a day thaws the sea and the topsoil. In spring, melting icebergs floating south from the Arctic Ocean endanger N Atlantic shipping. Vegetation is varied but confined mainly to shrubs, flowering herbaceous plants, mosses and lichens. Wild mammals include polar bears, reindeer, musk oxen, moose, wolves, weasels, foxes and lemmings. Geese, ducks, gulls, cranes, falcons, auks and ptarmigan all nest in the Arctic, and its seas harbor whales, seals, cod, salmon and shrimp. Invits (Eskimos), Lapps, Russians and others make up a human population of several million. Eskimos have lived in the Arctic for at least 9,000 years, and total 60,000 or more. Once exclusively hunters and fishermen, Eskimos now work in towns and on oil fields. There are scattered agricultural, mining and fishing industries; and the US, Canada and USSR man air bases and meteorological stations. Oil production began at Prudhoe Bay (Alaska) in 1978, the oil moving S to Valdez through the Trans-Alaska pipeline.

Vikings were the first recorded Arctic explorers: Norwegians visited the Russian Arctic in the 9th century and the Icelander ERIC THE RED established a Greenland settlement c982 AD. In the 16th and 17th centuries search for a "Northwest Passage" and a "Northeast Passage" to the Orient encouraged exploration. In the 16th century Martin FROBISHER reached Baffin Island and Willem BARENTS explored Novaya Zemlya and saw Spitsbergen. Henry HUDSON probed E Greenland and the Hudson Strait in the early 17th century. But the longed-for passages remained undiscovered, and interest in Arctic exploration declined until Canadian and Russian fur traders revived it late in the 18th century. Early in the 19th century the British naval officers John and James ROSS, W. E. PERRY, John RAE and Sir John FRANKLIN traveled to unexplored areas, James Ross discovering the north magnetic pole. N. A. E. Nordenskjöld of Sweden navigated the Northeast Passage (1878–79) and R. AMUNDSEN the Northwest Passage (1906) and in 1909 Robert E. PEARY reached the North Pole. Richard E. BYRD and Floyd BENNETT overflew the Pole in 1926, pioneering polar air exploration and transpolar air travel. In 1958 the US nuclear submarine *Nautilus* reached the Pole under the icecap.

ARDEN, Elizabeth (1884–1966), Canadian-born US cosmetics specialist and entrepreneur. A former nursing student, she modernized the cosmetics field with her emphasis on hygiene and purity.

ARDENNES, forested upland in SE Belgium, N Luxembourg and around the Meuse valley of N France. The area is a sparsely populated plateau with some agriculture and quarrying. It was a battleground in WWI and WWII (see BATTLE OF THE BULGE).

AREA, in plane GEOMETRY, the measure of the extent of an enclosed surface or region in terms of the number of squares with sides of unit length, or fractions of those squares, that could be fitted exactly into it. Areas are usually measured in square metres (m²). The area of an enclosed region on a curved surface is given by the area it would cover if spread out on a PLANE surface.

ARENDT, Hannah (1906–1975), German-born US political philosopher. In 1959 she became the first woman to be appointed a full professor at Princeton U, and she later taught at the U of Chicago and the New School for Social Research in New York. In *The Origins of Totalitarianism* (1951) she traced nazism and communism back to 19th-century anti-Semitism and imperialism. Her controversial *Eichmann in Jerusalem* (1963), with its theory of the "banality of evil," analyzed Nazi war crimes and the 1960 trial of Adolph EICHMANN by the Israeli government.

AREQUIPA, city in S Peru, located at 8,000ft between the Pacific Ocean and the Andes. It is the capital of Arequipa department and Peru's second largest city, producing textiles, shoes and foodstuffs and trading in wool. The Spanish founded Arequipa in 1540 on the site of an Inca city. Pop 304,653.

ARES, the Greek god of war. See MARS.

ARETINO, Pietro (1492–1556), Italian satirist and playwright who wrote coarse, sensual and lively political satires. His works include *I Ragionamenti* (1534–36), dialogues between prostitutes describing the escapades of contemporary notables.

ARGALL, Sir Samuel (d. 1626), daring English navigator and soldier in North America. He pioneered a N sea route to Va. (1609), captured POCOHONTAS (1612), crushed French colonies in Me. and Nova Scotia and became deputy governor of Va. (1617–19).

Official name: Republic of Argentina

Capital: Buenos Aires
Area: 1,072,163sq mi
Population: 27,064,000
Languages: Spanish
Religions: Roman Catholic
Monetary unit(s): 1 Argentine peso = 100 centavos

ARGENTINA, second largest country in Latin America, economically one of its most advanced nations.

Land. Argentina occupies most of South America E of the Andes. There are four main areas: W, N, Central and S. The W comprises the Andes Mts, which exceed 20,000ft in parts of the N but are low in the S. The N consists largely of the forests of the Gran Chaco and the swampy region in the NE Central Argentina comprises great grassy plains or *pampas*, a temperate region and economically the most important area, with two-thirds of the population. In the S lie the barren and cold plateaus of Patagonia.

People. About 90% of the people are descended from S European immigrants. There are only 20-30,000 native Indians. The national language is Spanish and about 90% of the population is Roman Catholic. Over 70% live in urban areas. Argentina has a better educational system and a higher literacy rate (93%) than most Latin American states.

Economy. Grain growing and cattle raising dominate the pampas, and the S is a big sheep raising region. Sugarcane, grapes, citrus fruits, tobacco, rice and cotton grow in the subtropical N. Oil and other minerals come from the N and the S. About 30% of the labor force works in industry, notably in food processing, chemicals, plastics machine tools and automobiles. Much of this industry is located in and around the capital, Buenos Aires.

History. Argentina's first Spanish settlers arrived in the 16th century. After nearly 300 years of Spanish rule, independence followed the war of 1816. The 19th century was a period of increasing European immigration and economic progress. Argentina's development during the 20th century has suffered from political uncertainties and social unrest. The reformist but dictatorial government of Juan PERÓN (1946–55) ended with a military uprising and was followed by several military and civilian governments. Widespread violence broke out in the early 1970s and in 1973 popular demand restored the aging Perón to power. He died in 1974, however, and was succeeded by his wife Isabel PERÓN. She was unable to solve Argentina's problems, and after a brief lull was overthrown in 1976. A military junta under Gen. José Videla took over. Kidnapings and terrorist activities were widespread in the late 1970s and the military introduced stern measures to cope with the increasing instability. Some 20-30,000 people allegedly disappeared. In 1981 Isabel Perón was released from house arrest and allowed to leave the country.

ARGON (Ar), the commonest of the NOBLE GASES, comprising 0.934% of the ATMOSPHERE. It is used as an inert shield for arc welding and for the production of silicon and germanium crystals, to fill electric light bulbs and fluorescent lamps, and in argon–ion LASERS. AW 39.9, mp — 189°C, bp — 186°C.

ARGONAUTS, heroes of Greek mythology who set sail under JASON to find the GOLDEN FLEECE. They reputedly included such illustrious figures as ORPHEUS, HERCULES, CASTOR AND POLLUX and THESEUS. The Argonauts set forth in the ship *Argo* for Colchis E of the Black Sea, where the fleece was guarded by a dragon. After many perils they obtained the fleece and returned to mainland Greece.

ARGONNE FOREST, a wooded hilly region south of the Ardennes, in NE France. In 1792 it was the site of the French victory over the Prussians at Valmy. The Meuse-Argonne offensive of late 1918 was one of the major US actions fought in WWI.

ARGONNE NATIONAL LABORATORY, a nuclear power research center 25mi S of Chicago. The University of Chicago operates it for the US ENERGY RESEARCH AND DEVELOPMENT ADMINISTRATION.

ARGUMENTS FOR THE EXISTENCE OF GOD, rational proofs for God's existence. ARISTOTLE (384–322 BC) asserted the need for a First Cause, or Unmoved Mover. St Thomas AQUINAS (c1225–1274) proposed his classical Five Ways, arguing from 1) motion back to an Unmoved Mover; 2) from causality back to a First Cause; 3) from contingent being to Necessary Being; 4) from the good to a Perfect Being; and 5) from order to an Intelligent Being. Immanuel KANT (1724–1804) rejected these arguments by denying the validity of any principle of causality outside human experience. See ONTOLOGY, TELEOLOGY, COSMOLOGY.

ARIA, formal solo song in opera and oratorio. It was developed in 17th-century opera and given its formalized pattern by SCARLATTI and GLUCK. MOZART turned it from a singer's display piece into an integral part of the drama. WAGNER and most modern composers tend to avoid the aria form.

ARIANISM, 4th-century Christian heresy founed in Alexandria by the priest Arius. He taught that Christ was not coequal and coeternal with God the Father, for the Father had created him. To curb Arianism, the Emperor Constantine called the first Council of NICAEA (325), and the first Nicene Creed declared that God the Father and Christ the Son were of the same substance. Arianism later almost triumphed, but most of the church returned to orthodoxy by the end of the century (see TRINITY).

ARICA, city in N Chile, a Pacific port and terminus of the La Paz railroad. Peru lost it to Chile in the War of the Pacific (1883). A free port since 1954, Arica is used by Peru and Bolivia for the shipment of mineral exports. Pop 116,115.

ARIES (the Ram), second constellation of the ZODIAC. In N skies it is a winter constellation.

ARISTARCHUS OF SAMOS (c310–230 BC), Alexandrian Greek astronomer who realized that the sun is larger than the earth and who is reported by ARCHIMEDES to have taught that the earth orbited a motionless sun.

ARISTOCRACY (from Greek *aristos*, the best, and *kratos*, rule), originally meaning the ruling of a state by its best citizens in the interest of all. It was used by both PLATO and ARISTOTLE in this sense. Gradually the term came to mean a form of government ruled by a small privileged class. Today, the term refers to members of a family which traditionally has hereditary privileges and rank.

ARISTOPHANES (c450–385 BC), comic dramatist of ancient Greece. Political, social and literary satire, witty dialogue, vigorous ribaldry, cleverly contrived comic situations and fine choral lyrics all feature in his works. Eleven of his 40 plays survive, notably *The Frogs* (satirizing Euripides), *The Clouds* (satirizing Socrates), *Lysistrata* (a plea for pacifism) and *The Birds* (a fantasy about a sky city).

ARISTOTLE (384–322 BC), Greek philosopher, one of the most influential thinkers of the ancient world. He was the son of the Macedonian court physician, and studied at PLATO's academy in Athens. In 343 BC he became tutor to the young ALEXANDER THE GREAT. In 335 BC Aristotle set up his own school at the Lyceum in Athens (see PERIPATETIC SCHOOL). Many of Aristotle's teachings survive as lecture notes. His work covered a vast range, including *Physics*, *Metaphysics*, *On the Soul*, *On the Heavens*, and several works on LOGIC and BIOLOGY, in both of which subjects he was a pioneer.

In studying such diverse topics as nature, man or the soul, Aristotle considered how things became what they were and what function they performed. In doing this he introduced his fourfold analysis of causes (formal, material, efficient and final), and such important notions as form and matter, substance and accident, actual and potential—all of which became philosophical commonplaces. In logic he invented the SYLLOGISM. The *Nicomachean Ethics* argues that virtue is a "mean" between extremes. *Politics* considers civic participation an outgrowth of human nature and reason. *Poetics* argues that a tragic drama brings emotional CATHARSIS through "pity and fear" evoked by the stage action. Aristotle's writings reached the West through Latin translations in the 11th and 13th centuries and had a prevailing influence on medieval and later thought.

ARITHMETIC (from Greek *arithmos*, number), the science of NUMBER. Until the 16th century arithmetic was viewed as the study of all the properties and relations of all numbers; in modern times, the term usually denotes the study of the positive REAL NUMBERS and ZERO under the operations of ADDITION, SUBTRACTION, MULTIPLICATION and DIVISION. Arithmetic can therefore be viewed as merely a special case of ALGEBRA, although it is of importance in considerations of the history of MATHEMATICS.

ARIUS. See ARIANISM.

Name of state: Arizona
Capital: Phoenix
Statehood: Feb. 14, 1912 (48th state)
Familiar name: Grand Canyon State
Area: 113,909sq mi
Population: 2,717,866
Elevation: Highest—12,633ft, Humphrey's Peak. Lowest—70ft, Colorado River at the Mexican border
Motto: Didat Deus (God Enriches)
State flower: Saguaro (Giant Cactus)
State bird: Cactus wren
State tree: Paloverde
State song: "Arizona"

ARIZONA, state, SW US, bounded to the E by N.M., to the S by Mexico, to the W by Cal. and Nev., and to the N by Utah. Once a largely worthless desert area, Arizona has developed rapidly and in population is now one of the fastest growing states in the Union.

Land. The Colorado Plateau to the N contains such spectacular features as the Grand Canyon, the Painted Desert, the Petrified Forest and Monument Valley, all of which have helped to make tourism an important part of the economy. A mountain chain, heavily forested and rich in minerals, extends NW to SE, while desert occupies the SW.

People. Arizona's population is predominantly urban, about half being concentrated in the Phoenix metropolitan area. More Indians live in Arizona than in any other state, the majority on the 19 reservations which cover almost 25% of the total land area. The Navaho, Hopi and Apache are the largest of the tribes.

Economy. With the aid of irrigation and of a long growing season, Arizona has developed a varied and intensive agricultural economy. About 60% of farm income is from livestock products. More than 1.1 million cattle and about 500,000 sheep are raised on ranches and grazing land. Cotton is the principal cash crop, while truck farming is so extensive it has earned the state a reputation as the "Salad Bowl of the Nation."

Arizona is also rich in minerals, supplying half the nation's copper as well as mining gold, silver, tungsten, molybdenum, zinc and vanadium. Manufacturing began with the smelting of copper and other ores and the establishment of sawmills.

Since WWII, industrial growth has been rapid and manufacturing now contributes more than agriculture or mining to the state's wealth. The electronics and electrical industry centered in Phoenix employs the largest number of workers engaged in manufacturing. Other industries include food processing, publishing, aircraft construction, and the production of metal goods.

History. Arizona was under Spanish influence from 1539, when it was first explored by Friar Marcos de Niza, until 1821 when it was ceded to Mexico. The Treaty of GUADALUPE HIDALGO (1848) granted most of present-day Arizona to the US, and in 1853–54, the Gadsden Purchase was made, thereby extending the area to the Gila R. Movement for statehood began after the defeat of the Navahos—by Kit CARSON (1863)—and the Apache (1886).

Recently, Arizona has suffered some of the pains of growing too quickly. While its population increased 53.1% in the 1970s, unemployment also rose, reaching 8.1% at the decade's end. A continuing influx of illegal aliens helped aggravate ethnic tensions and the crime rate is high, with Phoenix ranking third among the nation's metropolitan centers in this unenviable category in 1978. Excessive use of water for agriculture has lowered water tables in the southern part of the state; in an effort to halt this, a state code regulating ground-water use was adopted in 1980.

Name of state: Arkansas
Capital: Little Rock
Statehood: June 15, 1836 (25th state)
Familiar name: Land of Opportunity
Area: 53,104sq mi
Population: 2,285,513
Elevation: Highest—2,753ft, Magazine Mountain. Lowest—55ft, Ouachita River at the Louisiana border
Motto: Regnat Populus (The People Rule)
State flower: Apple blossom
State bird: Mockingbird
State tree: Pine
State song: "Arkansas"

ARKANSAS, state, SE central US on the W bank of the Mississippi R. and bounded to the S by La., to the W by Tex. and Okla. and to the N by Mo. Arkansas has suffered in the past from over-dependence on the cotton crop and from low per capita income, but industrial growth has accelerated since the mid-1950s. Now income from manufacturing exceeds that from agriculture.

Land. In addition to the Mississippi, Arkansas has several major rivers, including the Arkansas, Red, Ouachita, White and St. Francis rivers. To the N and W are the rugged Ozark and Ouachita Mts, while the alluvial plain in the E is the chief agricultural region. More than half the state is forested. Three national forests—in the Ozarks, the Ouachitas and the Gulf Coastal Plain—have been established to protect valuable timberlands. Climate is mild and rainy.

People. Arkansas is one of the least urbanized states with only one out of every two inhabitants living in urban areas. Little Rock is the largest city, followed by Fort Smith and Pine Bluff. The General Assembly consists of a 35-member Senate and 100-member House of Representatives.

Economy. Cotton, rice and soybeans are the most important cash crops. Arkansas supplies about 10% of the national cotton total while Mississippi Co. is the country's leading soybean producer. Rice, introduced in the 1920s, is now one of the state's most important crops. In the W, however, livestock and poultry provide the major farm income.

Arkansas has important mineral deposits and produces a large proportion of the bauxite mined in the US. There are also valuable oil and natural gas fields, as well as deposits of barite, manganese, bromine, vanadium and coal. The first diamond field in the US (no longer in industrial use) was established near Murfreesboro in SE Arkansas. Arkansas' forests provide timber and pulp for lumber, paper and other wood products, which account for a major share of the state's industry. Other major manufactures include metal goods, electrical parts, clothes, building materials and petroleum products.

History. First explored by Hernando DE SOTO (1541) Arkansas passed from Spanish to French hands, and then to the US as part of the LOUISIANA PURCHASE (1803). It first entered the Union as a slave state in 1836 and was readmitted after the Civil War in 1868 over President Andrew Johnson's veto. The Reconstruction period was marked by controversy and discontent. Racism brought Arkansas into the headlines in 1957 when federal troops were called to enforce integration at a Little Rock school. In the 1970s, Arkansas was troubled by rising unemployment and business failures, with part of the state losing rail service when the Rock Island RR went bankrupt. At the same time, many cities and counties had to cut programs, lay off workers and reduce salaries because the rate of inflation has risen faster than their tax revenues.

ARKANSAS RIVER, longest tributary of the Mississippi–Missouri R system. It rises in the Rocky Mts of central Col. and flows 1,450mi through Kan., Okla., and Ark. to the Mississippi R. It is the main water source for Ark. state, and is controlled by dams and locks to curb flooding.

ARKHANGELSK (Archangel), city and major port in NW USSR, the administrative center for Arkhangelsk oblast. It stands on the Northern Dvina R and although icebound for six months is of considerable economic importance, specializing in furs, timber, paper-making, fishing, and ship-building. Arkhangelsk was Russia's leading port until the founding of St. Petersburg (1703). Pop 385,000.

ARK OF THE COVENANT, in the Old Testament, the chest containing the tablets bearing the Ten Commandments received by Moses. The most sacred object of ancient Israel, it was carried into battle before it was deposited in the Temple.

ARKWRIGHT, Sir Richard (1732–1792), English industrialist and inventor of cotton carding and SPINNING machinery. In 1769 he patented a spinning frame which was the first machine able to produce cotton thread strong enough to use in the warp. He was a pioneer of the factory system of production, building several water- and later steam-powered mills. (See also CROMPTON, Samuel; HARGREAVES, James.)

ARLINGTON NATIONAL CEMETERY, famous US national cemetery in N Va. It was established in 1864 on land once owned by George Washington CUSTIS and Robert E. LEE. Over 160,000 American war dead and public figures are buried here. Monuments include the Custis-Lee Mansion, the mast of the battleship *Maine*, the Tomb of the Unknown Soldier and the grave of John F. Kennedy with its eternal flame.

ARLISS, George (1868–1946), British actor who became popular in the US while touring with Mrs Patrick Campbell (1901). He won an Academy Award for the title role in the film *Disraeli* (1930).

ARM, the part of the human forelimb between WRIST and SHOULDER. The upper arm bone (humerus) is attached at the shoulder by a ball and socket JOINT and to the lower arm by a hinge joint at the elbow. The lower arm consists of the ulna and the radius, which rotates over the ulna to turn the wrist. The chief arm muscles are the BICEPS and TRICEPS and the strong hand muscles.

ARMADA, fleet of armed ships, in particular Spain's "Invincible Armada," 130 ships carrying 27,000 men sent by PHILIP II in 1588 to seize control of the English Channel for an invasion of England. After a running fight with Howard, DRAKE, HAWKINS and FROBISHER, the Spaniards took refuge in Calais Roads. Driven out by fire-ships, the surviving vessels nearly all perished in storms as they attempted to return to Cadiz via N Scotland and W Ireland.

ARMADILLOS, about 20 species of armored MAMMALS (family Dasypodidae) of the order ENDENTATA, which also contains ANTEATERS and SLOTHS. They range in length from about 120mm (5in) to about 1.5m (5ft). They are usually nocturnal, sometimes diurnal, and live in burrows either excavated by themselves or deserted by other animals. Polyembryony (production of several identical offspring from a single fertilized EGG) is general amongst armadillos.

ARMAGEDDON, biblical site of the world's last great battle, in which the powers of good will destroy the forces of evil (Revelation 16:16). The name may refer to biblical MEGIDDO.

ARMAGNAC, hilly farming area of SW France noted for its brandy. Count Bernard VII of Armagnac was virtual ruler of France in 1413–18. Armagnac passed to the French crown in 1607. The chief city, Auch, is a commercial center.

ARMATURE, the part of an electric MOTOR or GENERATOR which includes the principal current-carrying windings. In small motors it usually comprises several coils of wire wound on a soft iron core and mounted on the drive shaft, though on larger AC motors the armature is often the stationary component. When the current flows in the armature winding of a motor, it interacts with the magnetic field produced by the field windings giving rise to a TORQUE between the rotor and stator. In the generator the armature is rotated in a magnetic field giving rise to an ELECTROMOTIVE FORCE in the windings.

ARMENIA, historic country in SW Asia S of the Caucasus Mts, now mainly divided between the Armenian Soviet Socialist Republic and NE Turkey. Primarily a tableland, the entire region averages some 6,000–7,000ft above sea level. A range of mountains cuts across it from E to W; the highest point being Mt Ararat (16,945ft) in Turkey. The Tigris, Euphrates, Kyros and Araxes rivers all have their source in the highlands.

Armenia's landscape extends from subtropical lowland to snow-covered peaks. Small mountain pastures provide rich grazing for sheep and cattle, while the valleys are fertile when irrigated. The main crops are green vegetables, barley, potatoes, wheat, sugar beets and grapes. Pomegranates, figs, peaches and apricots are also grown.

Mining is the chief industry, the mountains yielding small but useful quantities of copper, iron, manganese, nepheline and molybdenum. Transportation facilities are limited, but industrialization is increasing. Hydroelectric schemes, particularly on Lake Sevan, have been a prime factor in Soviet Armenia's economic growth.

Armenia was conquered in 328 BC by Alexander the Great and in 66 BC by Rome. In 303 AD it became the first country to make Christianity its state religion. Later it was successively under Byzantine, Persian, Arab, Seljuk, Mongol and Ottoman Turkish control. Russian influence grew in the 19th century. A short-lived Armenian republic emerged after WWI but was swiftly absorbed by the USSR and Turkey.

ARMENIA, or Armenian Soviet Socialist Republic, smallest of the 15 constituent republics of the USSR, occupies a mountainous landlocked region on the slopes of the Caucasus Mts., bordered by Turkey and Iran. Of the population 88% is Armenian, an ancient people noted for their cultural achievements, particularly in architecture and painting. Traditionally an agricultural region, Armenia produces many crops including vegetables, fruits, tobacco, meat and wool. Recently it has become more industrialized with fertilizers, fabrics and cement the major products. (See USSR.)

ARMENIAN, an Indo-European language related to Indo-Iranian and Greek. It evolved in the mountainous region of Armenia.

ARMENIAN CHURCH, the national church of Armenia. It evolved as part of the EASTERN CHURCH and adopted a form of MONOPHYSITISM. It was the first Christian church to be established.

ARMOR, protective clothing or covering used in armed combat. The earliest armor consisted of boiled and hardened animal skins but, with the coming of organized military campaigns, armor became more sophisticated. Roman soldiers wore standardized armor made of iron. Later, chain mail, a fabric of interlocking metal rings, was developed. By the end of the 11th century it was the standard form of armor. It provided poor protection against heavy blows, however, and the Middle Ages saw the development of full suits of metal plates with chain mail joints for flexibility. Later, as these suits were used more for tournaments and state occasions, certain cities, notably Milan and Augsburg, became renowned for their armorial artistry. Full armor was used in Europe only until the 16th century. Modern armor employs nylon, fiberglass and other synthetic materials. New advances in tank armor include the British Chobham, consisting of laminated steel, aluminum, fabric and ceramic materials, which is designed to dissipate kinetic energy more effectively than steel alone, and the French appliqué with removable plates.

ARMORY SHOW, officially the International Exhibition of Modern Art, the first show of its kind to be held in the US at the 69th Regiment Armory, New York City, Feb.–March 1913. Comprising over 1,300 works it included a large section of paintings by contemporary Americans, and works by such modern European artists as BRANCUSI, BRAQUE, CÉZANNE, DUCHAMP, MATISSE and PICASSO. The avant-garde paintings caused much controversy but also the acceptance of modern art in the US.

ARMOUR, Philip Danforth (1832–1901), US meatpacking pioneer and philanthropist. He made his fortune supplying pork to Union forces in the Civil War, and in 1870 established Armour & Co. which soon made Chicago the meatpacking center of the US. He founded the Armour Institute of Technology in 1892.

ARMSTRONG, Edwin Howard (1890–1954), US electronics engineer who developed the FEEDBACK concept for AMPLIFIERS (1912), invented the superheterodyne circuit used in radio receivers (1918) and perfected FM RADIO (1925–39).

ARMSTRONG, Henry (1912–   ), US boxer. Nicknamed "Perpetual Motion" for his aggressive style, he was the only fighter to hold three world championships (featherweight, welterweight and lightweight) simultaneously (1938).

ARMSTRONG, Louis Daniel (1900–1971), US jazz musician renowned as a virtuoso trumpeter and singer. A master of improvisation, he is considered perhaps the most influential and important figure in the early history of jazz. "Satchmo" grew up in the back streets of New Orleans, moved to Chicago in 1922 and by the 1930s was internationally famous. In later life he played at concerts around the world as "goodwill ambassador" for the State Department.

ARMSTRONG, Neil Alden (1930–   ), first man to set foot on the moon. Born in Wapakoneta, Ohio, he studied aeronautical engineering at Purdue U. (1947–55) with time out on active service in the Korean War. He joined NASA in 1962, commanding Gemini 8 (1966), and landing the Apollo II module on the moon on July 20, 1969.

ARMSTRONG-JONES, Anthony Charles (1st Earl of Snowdon; 1930–   ), British photographer who was married to Princess Margaret from 1960–78. He was appointed official court photographer (1958), collaborated on *Private View* (1965), about the British art scene, and published a collection of *Assignments* (1972).

ARMY, traditionally the land fighting force of a nation. By a narrower definition an army is also a large unit of ground forces under a single commander (e.g. the US Fifth Army).

The 20th century has shown how far the modern army depends upon technology and industry. Germany was defeated in WWII not by superior military power but by superior machine power. However, the constant development of weapons and detection systems makes any land force extremely vulnerable. Modern armies must, therefore, be highly mobile, a need which has led to a blurring of the traditional distinctions between army, navy and air force. Cooperation among the services is essential for the successful application of advanced technology. Canada, for example, has combined all three branches of her armed forces.

Primitive armies perhaps consisted of raiding parties mainly engaged in individual combat, using rudimentary weapons such as stones and clubs. Later, skills in handling horses and chariots increased the complexity and mobility of armies, while the development of artillery, which had its origins in catapult machines, and the revolutionary invention of gunpowder in China, extended their range of effectiveness. Formation tactics evolved through the Macedonian *phalanx* and Roman *legion*.

It might be said that the modern army has brought all these developments to a very high level of sophistication. Rapid mobility, first made practicable by the construction of rail networks in the 19th century, has been increased in the 20th century by the development of air transportation. Nuclear weaponry has taken the effective range of firepower virtually to its limits and the value of tactical formations has largely been eliminated by radar detection equipment, making unconventional military units (e.g. guerrillas, paratroops) increasingly important in warfare.

ARMY, United States, though not the world's largest army, certainly one of the best equipped and most powerful land forces the world has ever known, organized to fight any war, local or global, conventional or atomic.

The highest ranking officer is the chief of staff, answerable to the secretary of the army, a civilian who in turn is responsible to the secretary of defense and the president. Under the chief of staff come several major commands: the *Continental Army Command*, responsible for US ground defense; the *Air Defense Command*; the *Army Matériel Command*, charged with procuring equipment, weapons, etc. for army units; the *Army Combat Developments Command*, which equips and organizes army units, plus various other commands.

The US Army originated with the colonial forces who fought in the 18th-century FRENCH and INDIAN WARS. Its main role, until well into the 19th century, was the protection of settlers against Indians. However, it fought successfully in the MEXICAN WAR (1846–48) and during the Civil War its strength rose to about 3,000,000 men.

In 1903 the army was radically reorganized, gaining a General Staff Corps and chief of staff. Numbers increased to 4,000,000 by 1918. WWII brought conscription, raising the number of men on active duty from 200,000 in 1939 to over 8,000,000 in 1945. In the Korean War the US Army contingent formed the core of the UN forces. In the Vietnam War the army faced new tactics of infiltration and guerrilla warfare. Conscription ended with US participation in that war in Jan. 1973 and the estimated strength of the army in June 1973 was 825,000, after the major withdrawal from SE Asia. That same year the All Volunteer Force was formed.

In peacetime, the US Army comprises the Regular Army (professional career soldiers), members of the reserves and National Guard (under individual state control) on active duty. The army's peacetime work includes helping to train military forces of friendly powers and performing various civilian assistance tasks and emergency measures.

ARNE, Thomas Augustine (1710–1778), English composer whose settings of Shakespeare's *Blow, Blow, Thou Winter Wind* and *Where The Bee Sucks* became perennial favorites. He also composed the air *Rule, Britannia.*

ARNOLD, Benedict (1741–1801), American general and traitor in the Revolutionary War. He fought outstandingly for the American cause at Ticonderoga (1775) and Saratoga (1777) and in 1778 received command of Philadelphia. In 1780 Arnold was reprimanded for abusing his authority. That year, however, he assumed the important command of West Point and with John ANDRÉ plotted its surrender to the British in revenge for past criticisms. André's capture forced Arnold to flee to the British side, and in 1781 he went into exile in London.

ARNOLD, Eddy (1918–   ), US country and western singer known for his smooth blend of standard country themes and electric guitars. He sang with the Golden West Cowboys at the start of his long career and was a solo performer in later decades.

ARNOLD, Henry Harley (1886–1950), pioneer aviator and US Air Force general who helped build US air power and develop the air force as a unified separate service. "Hap" Arnold held several early flying records, became chief of the Air Corps (1938), headed the Army Air Forces in WWII and was made general of the Army (1944), being later retitled general of the Air Force.

ARNOLD, Matthew (1822–1888), English poet and literary critic. His poetry, perhaps best represented by the collections *Empedocles on Etna, and other Poems* (1852) and *New Poems* (1867), is characteristically introspective, though Arnold could equally achieve a classical impersonality. Both in his poetry and his criticism (*Culture and Anarchy* 1869; *Literature and Dogma* 1873) Arnold showed a keen awareness of the changing cultural climate of his time. He worked as a schools inspector (1851–86) and was Professor of Poetry at Oxford (1857–67).

ARNOLD, Thomas (1795–1842), English headmaster of Rugby School whose approach to teaching, with its stress on character development, radically influenced English public school education. He was the father of Matthew ARNOLD.

ARON, Raymond (1905–   ), French sociologist, political scientist and journalist. A professor at the Sorbonne 1955–68, he was a critic of both the Gaullists and left-wing intellectuals. His books include *Opium of the Intellectuals* (1955), *Main Currents in Sociological Thought* (1961), and *In Defense of Decadent Europe* (1977).

ARONSON, Boris (1899–1980), Russian-born US stage designer who moved from the Yiddish theater to Broadway, where his sets and costumes were continually honored for their originality. He won Tony Awards for *The Rose Tatoo* (1951), *Cabaret* (1966),

Zorba (1968), *Company* (1970), *Follies* (1971) and *Pacific Overtures* (1976).

ARPINO, Gerald Peter (1928–   ), US dancer and choreographer. After dancing in television and Broadway musicals he became associated with Robert JOFFREY in 1953 and in 1956 was one of the six original members of the Robert Joffrey Theater Dancers. Since 1961 he has created such works as *Viva Vivaldi!* and *Olympics* (1966) for the company.

ARRABAL, Fernando (1932–   ), controversial Spanish playwright writing in French. Influenced by BECKETT and IONESCO, as well as the art of DALÍ, MIRÓ, and CALDER, Arrabal's nightmarish, absurdist dramas depict a world riddled with violence and evil. His more than 60 plays have been collected since 1958 in an ongoing series known as *Théâtre*.

ARRAU, Claudio (1903–   ), famous Chilean pianist. A child prodigy, he became noted throughout his long career mainly for his performances of the Romantic composers such as BRAHMS.

ARRHENIUS, Svante August (1859–1927), Swedish physical chemist whose theory concerning the DISSOCIATION OF SALTS in solution (see CONDUCTIVITY) earned him the 1903 Nobel Prize for Chemistry and laid the foundations for the study of ELECTROCHEMISTRY.

ARROWROOT, a form of edible starch obtained from the RHIZOMES of various tropical plants. True arrowroot is the West Indian arrowroot (*Maranta arundinacea*). Easily digestible, it is used in feeding invalids and children, and also as a thickening agent in sauces.

ARSENIC (As), metalloid in Group VA of the PERIODIC TABLE. Its chief ore is ARSENOPYRITE, which is roasted to give arsenic (III) oxide, or white arsenic, used as a poison. Arsenic has two main allotropes (see ALLOTROPY): yellow arsenic, As$_4$, resembling white PHOSPHORUS; and gray (metallic) arsenic. It burns in air and reacts with most other elements, forming trivalent and pentavalent compounds, all highly toxic. It is used as a doping agent in TRANSISTORS; gallium arsenide is used in LASERS. AW 74.9, subl 613°C, sg 1.97 (yellow), 5.73 (gray).

ART. See COMMERCIAL ART; PAINTING; SCULPTURE. Also entries under various styles and periods, for example ABSTRACT ART; BAROQUE; CUBISM; IMPRESSIONISM.

ARTAUD, Antonin (1896–1948), French author, actor and director. His theories of a "Theater of Cruelty," where the elemental forces of the psyche would be spectacularly exposed, have had a strong influence on modern theater.

ART DECO, a style of design popular in the US and Europe from the late 1920s through the 1930s. It emphasized geometrical or modified geometrical shapes and simplified lines, representing a radical reaction to the ornateness of Victorian design and expressing implied admiration of functionalism and machine technology. Receiving impetus at the 1925 Paris Exhibition for Decorative Arts, the style was applied in architecture, interior decoration, furniture-making and the design of a wide range of objects, from locomotives to salt-and-pepper shakers. Prime existing examples of art deco are the Chrysler Building and the interior of the Radio City Music Hall in New York City.

ARTEMIS, in Greek mythology, goddess of chastity and of the hunt, counterpart of the Roman DIANA. Daughter of ZEUS and twin to APOLLO, she was also said to protect childbirth and wild animals and was sometimes linked with the moon. Grain and animals were sacrificed to her at harvest time. One of her most famous temples was at Ephesus in Asia Minor.

ARTERIOSCLEROSIS, disease of arteries in which the wall becomes thickened and rigid, and blood flow is hindered. **Artherosclerosis** is the formation of fatty deposits (containing CHOLESTEROL) in the inner lining of an ARTERY, followed by scarring and calcification. It is commoner in older age groups, but in DIABETES, disorders of fat METABOLISM and high-blood pressure, its appearance may be earlier. Excess saturated fats in the blood may play a role in its formation. A rarer form, **medial sclerosis,** is caused by degeneration and calcification of the middle muscular layer of the artery. Narrowing or obstruction of cerebral arteries may lead to STROKE, while that of coronary arteries causes ANGINA PECTORIS and CORONARY THROMBOSIS. Reduced blood flow to the limbs may cause CRAMP on exertion, ULCERS and GANGRENE. Established arteriosclerosis cannot be reversed, but a low fat diet, exercise and the avoidance of smoking help in prevention. Surgery by artery-replacement or removal of deposits is occasionally indicated.

ARTERY, blood vessel which carries BLOOD from the HEART to the TISSUES (see BLOOD CIRCULATION). The arteries are elastic and expand with each PULSE. In most vertebrates, the two main arteries leaving the heart are the pulmonary artery, which carries blood from the body to the LUNGS to be reoxygenated, and the AORTA which supplies the body with oxygenated blood. Major arteries supply each limb and organ

and within each they divide repeatedly until arterioles and CAPILLARIES are reached. Fish have only one arterial system, which leads from the heart via the GILLS to the body. (See also ARTERIOSCLEROSIS.)

ARTESIAN WELL, a well in which water rises under hydrostatic pressure above the level of the AQUIFER in which it has been confined by overlying impervious strata. Often pumping is necessary to bring the water to the surface, but true artesian wells (named for the French province of Artois where they were first constructed) flow without assistance.

ARTHRITIS, INFLAMMATION, with pain and swelling, of JOINTS. **Osteoarthritis** is most common, though there is no true inflammation; it is a wear-and-tear arthritis, causing pain and limitation of movement. OBESITY, previous trauma and inflammatory arthritis predispose. Bacterial infection (e.g., by STAPHYLOCOCCI or TUBERCULOSIS), with PUS in the joint, and GOUT, due to deposition of crystals in SYNOVIAL FLUID, may lead to serious joint destruction. **Rheumatoid arthritis** is a systemic disease manifested mainly in joints, with inflammation of synovial membranes and secondary destruction. In the hands, tendons may be disrupted and extreme deformity can result. Arthritis also occurs in many other systemic diseases including RHEUMATIC FEVER, LUPUS erythematosus, PSORIASIS and some VENEREAL DISEASES. Treatment of arthritis includes anti-inflammatory ANALGESICS (e.g., ASPIRIN), rest, local heat and PHYSIOTHERAPY. STEROIDS are sometimes helpful but their long-term use is now discouraged. Badly damaged joints may need surgical treatment or replacement.

ARTHUR, Chester Alan (1830–1886), 21st president of the US. Arthur was vice-president under James A. Garfield and became president on the latter's assassination in 1881. Born in Fairfield, Vt., he was the son of a teacher from N Ireland. He entered a New York City law office in 1853 and soon after won a reputation as a progressive attorney in two important civil rights cases. During the Civil War he became quartermaster-general of the N.Y. Militia.

Returning to the law after the war, Arthur became active in city politics as a Republican, and President Grant appointed him customs collector for the port of New York in 1871. In this post, Arthur's name became linked with the "spoils system" and, although his personal integrity was not openly doubted, he was eventually removed from office in 1878 following an inquiry instigated by President Hayes. Arthur attended the Republican National Convention of 1880 and was chosen to make up the ticket under Garfield. On Garfield's death, he supported demands for the reform of the civil service, and the important PENDLETON ACT was passed in 1883. His attempts to cut taxes and tariff duties failed to gain the backing of Congress.

Arthur's stand against narrow party interests won the approval of many of his critics but alienated his own party, and cost him the renomination in 1884. He retired to his law practice.

ARTHURIAN LEGENDS, the literature relating the feats of King ARTHUR and his knights. Arthur himself is mentioned in a 9th-century chronicle, but the basis of the legends is found in GEOFFREY OF MONMOUTH (†137). From then until the 16th century a cycle of romances of chivalry developed, mainly written in French and in both prose and verse, drawing upon Celtic folklore (probably from Brittany) and incorporating the life and death of Arthur himself, the loves of LANCELOT and GUINEVERE and of Tristan and Yseult, the story of Merlin and the quest for the HOLY GRAIL. From them Sir Thomas MALORY distilled his *Morte d'Arthur* (1485), which inspired Lord TENNYSON's *Idylls of the King* (1859) and T. H. White's *The Once and Future King* (1958).

ARTICLES OF CONFEDERATION, the first written framework of government for the US. They were drafted in 1776–77 after the Declaration of Independence, but it was 1781 before all 13 states ratified them. The states were wary of a centralized and remote government because of their experience of the English Parliament, and the national government they set up had limited powers. It was to operate through Congress, in which each state had one vote, and to control foreign affairs, war and peace, coinage, the post office and some other matters. But "sovereignty, freedom and independence" remained with the separate states. Congress had no way of enforcing its decrees, and there were no federal courts. The shortcomings of the Articles were evident, particularly with reference to interstate trade, and the Constitutional Convention of 1787 abandoned them in favor of the present UNITED STATES CONSTITUTION which took effect in 1789.

ARTIFICIAL INSEMINATION, introduction of SPERM into the vagina by means other than copulation. The technique is widely used for breeding livestock as it produces many offspring from one selected male (see HEREDITY). It has a limited use in treating human IMPOTENCE and STERILITY.

ARTIFICIAL LIMBS. See PROSTHETICS.

ARTIFICIAL ORGANS, mechanical devices that can perform the functions of bodily organs. The **heart-lung machine** can maintain BLOOD CIRCULATION and oxygenation and has enabled much new cardiac SURGERY. **Artificial kidneys** clear waste products from the blood (see UREMA) by DIALYSIS and may take over KIDNEY function for life. Both machines require ANTICOAGULANTS during use.

ARTIFICIAL RESPIRATION, the means of inducing RESPIRATION when it has ceased, as after DROWNING, ASPHYXIA, in COMA or respiratory PARALYSIS. It must be continued until natural breathing returns and ensuring a clear airway via the mouth to the lungs is essential. The most common first aid methods are: "mouth-to-mouth", in which air is breathed via the mouth into the lungs and is then allowed to escape, and the less effective Holger Nielsen technique where rhythmic movements of the CHEST force air out and encourage its entry alternately. If prolonged artificial respiration is needed, mechanical pumps are used and these may support respiration for months or even years.

ARTILLERY, once the term for all military machinery, it now refers to guns too heavy to be carried by one or two men. The branch of the army involved is also known as the artillery. Modern artillery may be said to have its origins in the 14th century when weapons that used gunpowder were first developed. The importance of artillery in battle increased as equipment became more mobile, and scientific advances improved its accuracy and effectiveness. WWII saw the development of specialized antitank and antiaircraft guns, and the first really effective use of rockets. Since then the guided MISSILE has been produced, with its long ranges and high accuracy offering a formidable threat.

Many advances have been made in recent years to increase the mobility of US artillery units and to improve the accuracy of their fire. These include the use of lighter tougher alloys for towed pieces, improved ammunition and ultra-modern target acquisition systems drawing on laser and radar technology. Accuracy is further increased by the use of electronic data processing in fire control systems.

ART NOUVEAU, late 19th-century art movement which influenced decorative styles throughout the West. Its themes were exotic or decadent and its characteristic line sinuous and highly ornamental. The movement aimed to reunite art and life, and so to produce everyday objects of beauty. It was of importance in the applied arts, some notable architecture, furniture, jewelry and book designs being produced in this style. Graphic art too was much affected by Art Nouveau, as seen in the work of Aubrey BEARDSLEY. Other notable artists of the movement were the painter Gustav KLIMT and the architects Antonio GAUDI and Victor HORTA, and in the applied arts TIFFANY, Lalique and Charpentier.

ARTS AND CRAFTS MOVEMENT. See INTERIOR DECORATION.

ARTS AND HUMANITIES, National Foundation on the, independent agency of the US government created by the National Foundation on the Arts and Humanities Act of 1965. It aims to encourage and support national progress in the arts and humanities, for which purpose it awards grants.

ARUBA, small island off the Venezuelan coast, 45mi W of Curaçao, part of the NETHERLANDS ANTILLES. It is about 19mi long and 4mi wide, and is inhabited by people of Indian and Negro descent who speak a hybrid language called *Papiamento.* The chief industry is the refining of crude oil imported from Venezuela. Pop 63,049.

ASBESTOS, name of various fibrous minerals, chiefly CHRYSOTILE and AMPHIBOLE. Canada and the USSR are the chief producers. It is a valuable industrial material because it is refractory, alkali- and acid-resistant and an electrical insulator. It can be spun to make fireproof fabrics for protective clothing and safety curtains, or molded to make tiles, bricks and automobile brake linings. Asbestos particles may cause PNEUMOCONIOSIS and lung CANCER if inhaled.

ASBURY, Francis (1745–1816), first Methodist bishop in the US. Born in England, he came to the US in 1771 as a Methodist missionary. With his energetic guidance, and despite his ill-health, Methodism in the US became widely established. Asbury was elected bishop in 1784.

ASCENSION, The, the bodily ascent into heaven of Jesus Christ on the 40th day after his resurrection. The event, described in the New Testament, signifies Christ's entry into glory and thus promises believers a heavenly life. Ascension Day is a major Christian festival.

ASCENSION ISLAND, small volcanic island in the S Atlantic, 750mi NW of the British colony of St. Helena, of which it is a dependency. During WWII US forces built an airstrip there and it now has an important missile and satellite tracking station. Most of the population centers on Georgetown. The island is 34sq mi in area. Pop 1,022.

ASCH, Sholem (1880–1957), leading Yiddish novelist and playwright. Born in Poland, he spent most of his life in the US. His many books deal with Jewish life both in Europe and the US, and with the relationship between Judaism and Christianity, as in *The Nazarene* (1939).

ASCORBIC ACID, or Vitamin C. See VITAMIN.

ASCOT, English town near Windsor. It is the site of the famous June horse race meeting, Royal Ascot, traditionally attended by British royalty.

ASGARD, in Norse mythology, the realm of the gods. It contained many halls and palaces; chief of these was VALHALLA, where ODIN entertained warriors killed in battle. The only entry to Asgard was by the rainbow bridge called BIFROST.

ASHANTI, a region of S Ghana, and the name of the people who live there. From the 17th century to 1902, when Britain annexed the region, the powerful Ashanti Confederacy linked several small kingdoms under one chief. The symbol of their unity was the sacred GOLDEN STOOL which, in their religion of ancestor-worship, represents the departed spirits of the Ashanti. The present-day Ashanti are a thriving agrarian people numbering about one million.

ASHCAN SCHOOL, or "The Eight," name given to a New York City group of painters, formed in 1908. They were so called because they chose to paint everyday aspects of city life. The Eight—Arthur DAVIES, William GLACKENS, Ernest LAWSON, George LUKS, Maurice PRENDERGAST, Everett SHINN, Robert HENRI and John SLOAN—differed in many ways but were united in their dislike of academicism. They were instrumental in bringing the ARMORY SHOW to New York in 1913; it was the first major exhibition in the US of the work of PICASSO and other important European artists.

ASHE, Arthur (1943–   ), US tennis player. In 1975 he became the first Negro to win the Wimbledon men's singles. In 1968 he won the US Men's National Singles title, the first black and first US player since 1955 to do so.

ASHKENAZIM, those Jews whose medieval ancestors lived in Germany. Persecution drove them to spread throughout the central and E Europe, and in the 19th and 20th centuries overseas, notably to the US. Their ritual and Hebrew pronunciation differ from those of the SEPHARDIM (Jews of Oriental countries). Up to the beginning of the 20th century most Ashkenazim spoke Yiddish. Most Jews in the US and the majority of the world's Jews are Ashkenazim. (See also JEWS.)

ASHKENAZY, Vladimir (1937–   ), celebrated Russian pianist, now living in Iceland. In 1955 he won the Chopin Competition in Warsaw, and was joint winner of the Tchaikovsky Competition in Moscow in 1962.

ASHTON, Sir Frederick (1906–   ), British dancer and choreographer. His work, which included such new productions as *Façade* (1931) and *La Fille Mal Gardée* (1960), has had great influence on British ballet. He was director of the Royal Ballet 1963–70.

ASHURBANIPAL, last of the great kings of Assyria, ruled from c669–630 BC over a huge empire which included Babylonia, Syria and Palestine. His reign was prosperous, though troubled by numerous revolts. He established the library of cuneiform tablets in Nineveh, discovered in the 1840s.

ASH WEDNESDAY, first of the 40 days of the Christian fast of LENT. The name derives from the early practice of sprinkling penitents with ashes. Today the ash of burnt palms is used to mark the sign of the cross on the foreheads of believers.

ASIA, the world's largest continent, covers more than 17,139,000sq mi (nearly one-third of the earth's land surface) and has about 2,600,000,000 people (nearly 60% of the total world population. It extends from the Arctic Ocean in the N to the Indian Ocean in the S, and from the Pacific Ocean in the E to the Mediterranean in the W. Its traditional border with Europe is formed by the Black Sea, the Caucasus Mts, the Caspian Sea, the Ural R and the Ural Mts, but the USSR located W of the Urals is often excluded in modern usage. In the SW, Asia is separated from Africa by the Red Sea and the Suez Canal. The combined land mass of Europe and Asia is sometimes treated as a single continent, Eurasia.

Land. Asia is a continent of infinite diversity, with extremes of every kind, the ultimate physical contrast being between Mt Everest (29,028ft), the world's highest mountain, and the Dead Sea (1,294ft below sea level). At its heart is the great system of mountain chains and high plateaus focused on the Pamir Knot. Among these huge mountain chains are the Karakoram Range, Himalayas, Kunlun Shan, Tien Shan, Altai Mountains, Hindu Kush and Sulaiman

Range. Extensions include the lesser ranges of Asia Minor and, in the E, the Arakan Yoma range (Assam and Burma) which reappears in Indonesia. Another system of ranges stretches from E Siberia to Japan and the Philippines. The major plateaus include the plateau of Tibet, the Tarim basin and the great plateau of Mongolia. The triangular lowland region N of the mountains embraces the W Siberian lowlands and the low plateau of central Siberia. Weaknesses in the earth's crust are reflected in the active volcanoes bordering the Pacific Ocean in Indonesia, the Philippines, Japan and the Kamchatka peninsula and also in Turkey and Iran.

The major rivers include the Ob and its tributary, the Irtysh, the Yenisey and Lena, all flowing to the Arctic Ocean; the Indus (Pakistan), Ganges (India and Bangladesh) and Brahmaputra (China and India); and the Yellow and Yangtze rivers in China. Lake Baikal is the largest freshwater lake. Deserts include the Gobi Desert in Mongolia and the Great Sandy Desert of Arabia.

Climate and Vegetation. Asia has every known type of climate, from the polar to the tropical. The heart of the continent has extremes of temperature in winter and summer and low rainfall while much of E and SE Asia is monsoonal and annual rainfall may reach 400in. Vegetation ranges from the tundra of the far north to the taiga (coniferous forest) of Siberia, the treeless grasslands of the steppes and the tropical rain forests of India and SE Asia.

People. The product of thousands of years of migrations, invasions, conquests and intermingling, the people of Asia belong mainly to three ethnic groups: Mongoloid (including Chinese, Japanese and Koreans), Caucasoid (including Arabs, Afghans, Iranians, Pakistanis and most Indian people) and Negroid (in parts of the Philippines and SE Asia). Racial mixtures are frequent in SE Asia, where the Malays are the largest group. The population is unevenly distributed, almost uninhabited areas like "High Asia" (the heart of the continent) and the deserts contrasting with the densely populated Ganges valley and the great cities of Japan and China. About one in every three Asians is urban-dwelling. A multitude of languages and dialects is spoken, derived from Indo-European, Semitic, Sino-Tibetan and other language families. Asia was the birthplace of several religions. Hinduism claims the largest following, but there are also millions of Buddhists and Muslims. Only about 4% of Asians are Christians. Because of this cultural diversity, it is usual to divide the continent into homogeneous cultural regions such as East Asia (China, Korea, Japan), South Asia (India, Pakistan, Sri Lanka), Southeast Asia (Malaysia, Indonesia, etc.) and SW Asia or Middle East.

Economy. About 66% of the population depend on agriculture, vital to a continent whose population is increasing at a rate of about 100,000 every 24 hours. Oil is the chief mineral resource and industrialization has been rapid in Japan, India, China, and the USSR.

History. Man has lived in Asia for about 500,000 years. The earliest-known civilizations—Sumerian, Babylonian and Assyrian—evolved in SW Asia. In S Asia the Indus valley civilization flowered in the 3rd millennium BC, while China's remarkable culture began in the Yellow R valley about 4,000—5,000 years ago. European colonial powers (Britain, France, Portugal, Spain, Netherlands) ruled much of S and SE Asia in the 18th and 19th centuries, but except for a few (e.g. Hong Kong, Macao) most former colonies became independent after WWII.

ASIA MINOR, peninsula in SW Asia comprising most of modern Turkey. Mountainous and surrounded on three sides by sea, it is bounded on the E by the upper Euphrates R. Civilizations such as that of Troy flourished here from the Bronze Age onwards. After the destruction of the Hittite empire in 1200 BC, the land belonged successively to the Medes, Persians, Greeks and Romans. In the 5th century AD it passed to the Byzantine Emperors and remained among their last possessions, constantly eroded as their power declined until in the 15th century it became part of the OTTOMAN EMPIRE and remained so until the Republic of Turkey was founded (1923).

ASIMOV, Isaac (1920–   ), prolific US author and educator, best known for his science fiction books such as the *Foundation* trilogy (1951–53) and *The Gods Themselves* (1972), and for his many science books for laymen. He was associate professor of biochemistry at Boston U. from 1955.

ASKENASE, Stefan (1896–   ), Belgian pianist, born in Poland, who gained a worldwide reputation for his performances of CHOPIN.

ASMARA, second-largest city in Ethiopa, capital of the province of Eritrea, about 40mi from the Red Sea on a plateau 7,500ft above sea level. It is a road and rail link between the inland and coast and a center for light industry. Pop 373,827.

ASOKA (d. 232 BC), third emperor of the Maurya dynasty of India, whose acceptance of BUDDHISM as the official religion of his vast empire had a major effect on that faith's predominance in Asia. He was said to have been so repelled by a particularly bloody victory of his troops over what is now Orissa that he turned to nonviolence and the Buddhist way of righteousness, and sent missionaries into Burma, Ceylon (Sri Lanka), Syria, Greece and Egypt.

ASP, the Egyptian COBRA *Naja haje* (family: Elapidae), an extremely poisonous snake up to 2m (6.6ft) in length. Sacred in ancient Egypt, it was legendarily the cause of Cleopatra's death. The name is also applied to the horned and asp VIPERS.

ASPEN, city in W central Col. on the Roaring Fork R, seat of Pitkin Co. The city was founded by prospectors c1878. After a decline it became a ski resort and cultural center, site of the Aspen Music Festival. Pop 3,678.

ASPHALT, a tough black material used in road paving, roofing and canal and reservoir lining. Now obtained mainly from PETROLEUM refinery residues (although natural deposits are still worked), it consists mainly of heavy HYDROCARBONS.

ASPIRIN, or acetylsalicylic acid, an effective analgesic, which also reduces FEVER and INFLAMMATION and also affects BLOOD platelets. It is useful in HEADACHE, minor feverish illness, MENSTRUATION pain, RHEUMATIC FEVER, inflammatory ARTHRITIS, and may also be used to prevent THROMBOSIS. Aspirin may cause gastrointestinal irritation and HEMORRHAGE, and should be avoided in cases of peptic ULCER.

ASQUITH, Herbert Henry (1852–1928), British prime minister 1908–16, 1st Earl of Oxford and Asquith. His term as head of the LIBERAL PARTY was one of great activity and political reform, but his leadership foundered in Dec. 1916 over his conduct of WWI, coupled with the chaos brought about by the EASTER REBELLION in Ireland. He resigned in favor of the rival Liberal leader David LLOYD GEORGE.

ASSAM, state in the far NE of India, lying around the Brahmaputra R beneath the Himalayas and separated from most of India by Bangladesh. The area, surrounded by Burma, China, Tibet and Bengal, became an Indian state in 1950. Its capital is Shillong. The climate is subtropical. E Himalayas lie along its N border, and the terrain becomes hilly beyond the S Brahmaputra plain. Its principal crop is tea. Textiles and oil are also important.

ASSASSIN, perpetrator of a political murder. The term derives from the name given to members of a fanatical sect of Islam founded by Hasan ibn-al-Sabbah, who refused to recognize the SELJUK regime in Persia at the end of the 11th century. His followers hid in the mountains and made periodic murderous raids on their enemies after smoking HASHISH; hence "hashshasin," which became "assassin."

ASSASSINATION, murder of a prominent person, often for political reasons. Although there has been a modern tendency to assassination by a lone individual, it has usually been practiced by rivals for power or their representatives. In the last 100 years US presidents Garfield, McKinley and Kennedy, Prime Minister Verwoerd of South Africa, President Sadat, Mahatma Gandhi, Martin Luther King and many other public figures have been assassinated.

ASSAYING, a method of chemical ANALYSIS for determining NOBLE METALS in ores or alloys, used since the 2nd millennium BC. The sample is fused with a flux containing LEAD (II) oxide. This produces a lead button containing the noble metals, which is heated in oxygen to oxidize the lead and other impurities, leaving a bead of the noble metals which is weighed and separated chemically.

ASSEMBLIES OF GOD, largest of the Protestant PENTECOSTAL denominations in the US. They were organized as a separate entity in 1914, and later established their headquarters in Springfield, Mo. They now have over 1 million members.

ASSIGNMENT, in law, usually the transfer of rights in tangible or, especially, intangible property or prospects, such as insurance policies, business contracts, certificates of corporate shares, and rights in monies due or to become due.

ASSINIBOIA, once the name of two separate districts of Canada. One was formed by the HUDSON'S BAY COMPANY around the Red River in 1835 and the other was in the NORTHWEST TERRITORY (in present-day S Saskatchewan and Manitoba).

ASSINIBOIN INDIANS, Sioux tribe of the North American plains who left the Yanktonai Sioux to spread out from Canada across the NW US. A nomadic people, they lived primarily by hunting. Like other Sioux, they took quickly to the use of horses and guns. They were easily defeated by the white settlers, because of the extinction of the buffalo, and were placed on reservations in 1884. (See also PLAINS INDIANS.)

ASSISI, town about 15mi SE of Perugia in Italy, situated on Mt Subasio above the plains of Umbria. The birthplace of St.

FRANCIS and St. CLARE, it is also noted for its medieval buildings, particularly the Gothic Basilica of St. Francis and the Church of St. Clare. Pop 23,800.

ASSISI, Saint Francis of. See FRANCIS OF ASSISI, SAINT.

ASSOCIATED PRESS (AP), the oldest and largest US news agency, founded in 1848 by six New York City newspapers, now with offices sending and receiving throughout the world. It is a non-profit organization financed by subscriptions from member newspapers, periodicals and broadcasting stations.

ASSOCIATION, in PSYCHOLOGY, the mental linking of one item with others: e.g., black and white, Tom with Dick and Harry, etc. The connections are described by the principles of association involving similarity, contiguity, frequency, recency and vividness. In **association tests,** subjects are presented with one word and asked to respond either with a specifically related word, such as a rhyme or antonym, or merely with the first word that comes to mind.

ASSOCIATIONISM, a psychological school which held that the sole mechanism of human learning consisted in the permanent association in the intellect of impressions which had been repeatedly presented to the senses. Originating in the philosophy of John LOCKE and developed through the work of John Gay, David HARTLEY, James and John Stuart MILL and Alexander Bain, the "association of ideas" was the dominant thesis in British PSYCHOLOGY for 200 years.

ASSOCIATION OF SOUTHEAST ASIAN NATIONS (ASEAN), a framework for regional cooperation created by the five non-Communist governments of Malaysia, Thailand, Indonesia, Singapore and the Philippines in 1967. Since 1976 the members have elected a secretary general to preside over implementation of decisions on a wide range of issues from tourism and tariff preferences to foreign-policy matters. It has consistently called for a Zone of Peace in the troubled area of Southeast Asia.

ASSUMPTION OF THE VIRGIN, official dogma of the Roman Catholic Church (declared by Pope PIUS XII in 1950) that the Virgin Mary was "assumed into heaven body and soul" at the end of her life. The feast day of the Assumption is August 15.

ASSYRIAN CHURCH. See NESTORIANS.

ASTAIRE, Fred (1899–   ), US dancer, choreographer and actor, born Frederick Austerlitz. First in partnership with his sister Adele on the stage and later with

Ginger ROGERS in such films as *Top Hat* (1935) and *Swingtime* (1938), he became one of the most popular US musical comedy stars as well a dancer whose drive for originality and perfection made him the idol of other dancers. Later films, with other partners, included *Holiday Inn* (1942), *The Band Wagon* (1953) and *Funny Face* (1957).

ASTARTE, Phoenician goddess of fertility, love and war. Her cult was widespread in the Near East. She is mentioned in the Old Testament as Ashtoreth. There were shrines to her at Hierapolis, Tyre and Sidon.

ASTATINE (At), radioactive HALOGEN, occurring naturally in minute quantities, and prepared by bombarding BISMUTH with ALPHA PARTICLES. The most stable isotope, At^{210}, has half-life 8.3h. Tracer studies show that astatine closely resembles IODINE. AW^{210}, mp 302°C, bp 337°C.

ASTEROIDS, the thousands of planetoids, or minor planets, ranging in diameter from a few meters to 760km (CERES), most of whose orbits lie in the asteroid belt between the orbits of Mars and Jupiter. Vesta is the only asteroid visible to the naked eye, although Ceres was the first to be discovered (1801) by PIAZZI). Their total mass is estimated to be 0.001 that of the earth. A few asteroids have highly elliptical, earth-approaching orbits, and the so-called Trojan group of asteroids share the orbit of the planet Jupiter. (See also METEORITE; SOLAR SYSTEM.)

ASTHENOSPHERE, the worldwide "soft layer" underlying the rigid LITHOSPHERE and located some 70 to 250km below the earth's surface. The zone is considered part of the upper MANTLE and is characterized by low seismic velocities, suggesting that it may be partially molten. In plate tectonic theory, rigid slablike plates of the lithosphere move over the asthenosphere. (See also PLATE TECTONICS.)

ASTHMA, chronic respiratory disease marked by recurrent attacks of wheezing and acute breathlessness. It is due to abnormal bronchial sensitivity and is usually associated with ALLERGY to house dust, motes, pollen, FUNGI, furs and other substances which may precipitate an attack. Chest infection, exercise or emotional upset may also provoke an attack. The symptoms are caused by spasm of bronchioles (see BRONCHI) and the accumulation of thick MUCOUS. Cyanosis may occur in severe attacks. Desensitization INJECTIONS, cromoglycate, STEROIDS and drugs that dilate bronchi are used in prevention; acute attacks may require OXYGEN, aminophylline

or ADRENALINE, and steroids.

ASTIGMATISM, a defect of VISION in which the LENS of the EYE exhibits different curvatures in different planes, corrected using cylindrical lenses. Also, an ABERRATION occurring with lenses having spherical surfaces.

ASTOR, Nancy, Viscountess Astor (1879–1964), first woman to sit in the British Parliament. She was born in Greenwood, Va., in the US but lived in England after marriage (her second) to Waldorf Astor in 1906. When her husband was elevated to the House of Lords she won his seat in Commons as a Conservative (1919). Serving until 1945, she supported welfare measures to assist women and children, but opposed socialism. Colorful and witty, she could also be controversial, as when, as hostess of the "Cliveden Set", she was linked with an attitude of appeasement toward Germany before WWII.

ASTRAKHAN, city in the USSR, administrative center of Astrakhan oblast in the Russian SFSR, on the delta of the Volga R about 60mi from the Caspian Sea. Once a TARTAR capital, it is now a major port and rail center near the Baku oil fields and in a rich agricultural region. Pop 461,000.

ASTROLABE, an astronomical instrument dating from the Hellenic Period, used to measure the altitude of celestial bodies and, before the introduction of the SEXTANT, as a navigational aid. It consisted of a vertical disk with an engraved scale across which was mounted a sighting rule or "alidade" pivoted at its center.

ASTROLOGY, system of beliefs and methods of calculation where practitioners attempt to divine the future from the study of the heavens. Originating in ancient Mesopotamia as a means for predicting the fate of states and their rulers, the astrology which found its way into Hellenistic culture applied itself also to the destinies of individuals. Together with the desire to devise accurate CALENDARS, astrology provided a key incentive leading to the earliest systematic ASTRONOMY and was a continuing spur to the development of astronomical techniques until the 17th century. The majority of classical and medieval astronomers, PTOLEMY and KEPLER among them, practiced astrology, often earning their livelihoods thus. Astrology exercised its greatest influence in the Graeco-Roman world and again in renaissance Europe (despite the opposition of the Church) and, although generally abandoned after the 17th century, it has continued to excite a fluctuating interest down to the present. The key datum in

Western astrology is the position of the stars and planets, described relative to the 12 divisions of the ZODIAC, at the moment of an individual's birth.

ASTRONAUT, name given to US test pilots and scientists chosen by the NATIONAL AERONAUTICS AND SPACE ADMINISTRATION to man US space flights. The first seven astronauts were chosen in 1959. The first manned flight was made by Commander Alan B. SHEPARD in 1961. Lt. Col. John GLENN, Jr., became the first American to orbit the earth in 1962, and astronauts Edwin Eugene ALDRIN, Jr., and Neil Alden ARMSTRONG became the first men on the moon in 1969. (See also SPACE EXPLORATION.)

ASTRONOMY, the study of the heavens. Born at the crossroads of agriculture and religion, astronomy, the earliest of the sciences, was of great practical importance in ancient civilization. Before 2000 BC, Babylonians, Chinese and Egyptians all sowed their crops according to calendars computed from the regular motions of the sun and moon.

Although early Greek philosophers were more concerned with the physical nature of the heavens than with precise observation, later Greek scientists (see ARISTARCHUS; HIPPARCHUS) returned to the problems of positional astronomy. The vast achievement of Greek astronomy was epitomized in the writing of Claudius PTOLEMY. His *Almagest*, passing through Arabic translations, was eventually transmitted to medieval Europe and remained the chief authority among astronomers for over 1,400 years.

Throughout this period the main purpose of positional astronomy had been to assist in the casting of accurate horoscopes, the twin sciences of astronomy and ASTROLOGY having not yet parted company. The structure of the universe meanwhile remained the preserve of (Aristotelian) physics. The work of COPERNICUS represented an early attempt to harmonize an improved positional astronomy with a true physical theory of planetary motion. Against the judgment of antiquity that sun, moon and planets circled the earth as lanterns set in a series of concentric transparent shells, in his *de Revolutionibus* (1543) Copernicus argued that the sun lay motionless at the center of the planetary system.

Although the Copernican (or heliocentric) hypothesis proved to be a sound basis for the computation of navigators' tables (the need for which were stimulating renewed interest in astronomy), it did not become unassailably established in astronomical theory until NEWTON published his mathematical derivation of KEPLER'S LAWS in 1687. In the meanwhile KEPLER, working on the superb observational data of Tycho BRAHE, had shown the orbit of Mars to be elliptical and not circular and GALILEO had used the newly invented TELESCOPE to discover SUNSPOTS, the phases of Venus and four moons of Jupiter.

Since the 17th century the development of astronomy has followed on successive improvements in the design of telescopes. In 1781 William HERSCHEL discovered Uranus, the first discovery of a new PLANET to be made in historical times. Measurement of the PARALLAX of a few stars in 1838 first allowed the estimation of interstellar distances. Analysis of the FRAUNHOFER LINES in the spectrum of the sun gave scientists their first indication of the chemical composition of the STARS.

In the present century the scope of observational astronomy has extended as radio and X-ray telescopes (see X-RAY ASTRONOMY) have come into use, leading to the discovery of QUASARS, PULSARS and neutron stars. In their turn these discoveries have enabled cosmologists to develop even more self-consistent models of the UNIVERSE. (See also COSMOLOGY; OBSERVATORY.)

ASTROPHYSICS, deals with the physical and chemical nature of celestial objects and events, using data produced by RADIO ASTRONOMY and SPECTROSCOPY. By investigating the laws of the universe as they currently operate, astronomers can formulate theories of stellar evolution and behavior (see COSMOLOGY).

ASTURIAS, historic region of Spain, now part of the modern province of Oviedo. Originally a Visigothic refuge from the Moorish invasions, it became a powerful and independent Christian kingdom from the 8th to the 10th centuries. From 1388 until 1931 the heir to the Spanish throne was called Prince of Asturias. Today this mountainous region is a major mining center for coal and other minerals.

ASUNCIÓN, capital, main port and industrial center of Paraguay. Founded in 1537 by Spanish explorers, it rivaled Buenos Aires until the 18th century. A large part of the city was destroyed in the War of the Triple Alliance (1865–70), but much colonial architecture remains. Modern industries include sugar refining, meat packing, textiles, distilling and shipbuilding. Pop 481,706.

ASWAN, capital of the Aswan governorate, upper Egypt, on the Nile 555mi S of Cairo. Aswan occupies the site of ancient Syene.

Granite from quarries was used by the pharaohs to build temples and pyramids. Today, hydroelectric power from Aswan and Aswan High dams serves the local iron-mining, fertilizer and quarrying industries. Tourism is also important. Pop 144,654.

ASWAN HIGH DAM, one of the world's largest dams built on the Nile 1960–70, located 4mi above the 1902 Aswan dam. Having created the vast Lake Nasser, stretching some 300mi along the course of the Nile, the dam's waters drive one of the world's largest hydroelectric generating stations and are used to irrigate over 1 million acres of farmland.

ASYLUM, Right of, a nation's right to grant protection to a refugee from another country. Asylum is granted by most countries only to political fugitives; ordinary criminals are not usually given asylum, though political crimes are loosely defined. The right to asylum is recognized by signatories to the UN Universal Declaration of Human Rights (1948).

ATABRINE (quinacrine hydrochloride), a synthetic ALKALOID drug for treating MALARIA and TAPEWORM, introduced in WWII when the Japanese captured natural QUININE supplies, and now rarely used.

ATACAMA DESERT, extremely arid plateau in N Chile, 600mi long with an average width of 90mi. Rich in borax and saline deposits, it is a major source of natural nitrates, copper and other minerals.

ATAHUALPA (c1500–1533), last Inca emperor of Peru. He was the eldest son of Huayna Capac, who died in 1525, leaving the kingdom to his younger son Huascar. Atahualpa inherited the Quito region and a large army. In 1530 he attacked Huascar, deposing him in 1532, just before the arrival of the CONQUISTADORS under PIZARRO. Atahualpa refused to accept Christianity and Spanish suzerainty; the Spaniards kidnapped him, extorted a vast ransom and murdered him after a show trial.

ATATURK, Kemal (originally: Mustafa Kemal; 1881–1938), first president (1923–38) of the modern Turkish state he helped to found. Born in Salonika, he received a military education and, as a member of the Young Turk movement, helped depose the Ottoman Sultan Abdul Hamid II in 1909. After distinguished service in the Second Balkan War (1913) and WWI, he led the Turkish war of independence as the head of a provisional government in Ankara (1919–23), repulsing a Greek invasion of ANATOLIA. Heading the new republic, Kemal reduced the power of Islam, abolishing the caliphate and the DERVISH sects, substituted Roman for Arabic lettering, rid TURKISH of Arabic words and modernized Turkey's economy. In 1934 he passed a law requiring all Turks to use surnames in the Western style and himself took the name Ataturk—"Father of the Turks."

ATAVISM, the inheritance (see HEREDITY) by an individual organism of characteristics not shown by its parental generation. Once thought to be throwbacks to an ancestral form, atavisms are now known to be primarily the result of the random reappearance of recessive traits (see GENETICS), though they may result also from aberrations in the development of the embryo or from disease.

ATAXIA, impaired coordination of body movements resulting in unsteady gait, difficulty in fine movements and speech disorder. Caused by disease of the cerebellum or spinal cord, ataxia occurs with MULTIPLE SCLEROSIS, certain hereditary conditions and in the late stages of syphilis (see VENEREAL DISEASES).

ATHABASCA, river and lake in N Alberta and Saskatchewan, Canada. The river rises in Jasper National Park and flows 765mi to the 3,120sq mi lake. The Athabascan tar sands between Fort McMurray and Fort Chipewyan are rich in crude oil. Uranium mining and fur trapping are the region's main industries.

ATHANASIAN CREED (sometimes called *Quicumque Vult*, from its opening words), Latin CREED expounding chiefly the doctrines of the Trinity and the Incarnation, regarded as authoritative by the Roman Catholic and Anglican churches, and also by some Protestant churches. Modern scholars believe it was composed in the 5th century.

ATHANASIUS, Saint (c293–373), Egyptian ecclesiastical statesman of the early Church. A devout adherent of the orthodox faith and opponent of ARIANISM, he took an active part in the religious and political controversies of his time, suffering many banishments as a result.

ATHENA (Pallas Athene), Greek goddess of wisdom and war who sprang fully-grown from ZEUS's head. She bore a helmet, lance and the AEGIS. The patroness of Athens, she protected legendary heroes such as ODYSSEUS. In peacetime she taught men agriculture, law, shipbuilding and all the crafts of civilization. The Romans identified her with Minerva.

ATHENS, capital of Greece, on the SW side of the Attica peninsula. Athens lies on a plain near the Saronic Gulf, with mountains to the W, N and E. The city was already important by c1500 BC, but reached its political peak after the PERSIAN WARS (490–479BC) when it led the DELIAN LEAGUE. In the 5th century PERICLES used the League's funds to rebuild the ACROPOLIS. Athens became a major center of art, architecture, philosophy and drama, the home of SOPHOCLES, EURIPIDES, SOCRATES and PLATO. Athens lost her supremacy to SPARTA in the PELOPONNESIAN WAR (431–404 BC), and later became a subject of Macedon and Rome.

Greater Athens is today the administrative, political, cultural and economic center of Greece. Tourism is a major source of income, but Athens is also an industrial center. Among its products are carpets, ships, petroleum, chemicals, textiles, electrical goods and canned foods. Exports handled at the city's port, Piraeus, include tobacco, oil, wine, aluminum and marble. Met pop 2,540,200.

ATHEROSCLEROSIS. See ARTERIOSCLEROSIS.

ATHLETE'S FOOT, a common form of RINGWORM, a contagious fungal infection of the feet, causing inflammation and scaling or maceration of the skin, especially between the toes. It may be contracted in swimming pools or from shared towels or footwear. Treatment consists in foot hygiene, dusting powder, certain CARBOXYLIC ACID and antifungal ANTIBIOTICS.

ATHOS, Mount, mountain (6,670ft) in NE Greece, since the Middle Ages the site of the famous monastic community, now including 20 monasteries and 3,000 monks. The mountain and surrounding Athos peninsula constitute the semi-independent theocratic republic of Mount Athos, which proclaimed itself independent in 1913 and was granted autonomy by Greece in 1927. No women or female animals are allowed to enter the region.

ATKINS, Chet (1924–   ), US country music star, influential both as a sophisticated guitarist and fiddler and, after 1947, as a recording company executive.

ATKINSON, Brooks (1894–   ), US theater critic who reviewed Broadway shows for the *New York Times* 1925–42 and 1946–60. The most influential critic of his day, he reputedly had the power to make or break shows.

ATLANTA, capital and largest city of Ga., seat of Fulton Co. Founded 1837 as the terminus of the Western and Atlantic Railroad, Atlanta was a major supply center during the Civil War and was burned to the ground by Union forces in 1864. It was rapidly rebuilt, and is today the major commercial and financial center of the S Atlantic states. The town has more than 20 colleges and universities. Pop 425,022.

ATLANTA CHILD MURDERS, a series of 28 murders of black children and youths in and around Atlanta, Ga., from July 1970 to May 1981, which provoked national sympathy expressed by the wearing of green ribbons. Though evidently committed by more than one person, many of the murders, especially the later ones, seemed to be related. On May 22, 1981, FBI agents and police stopped and questioned Wayne B. Williams, a freelance photographer who was subsequently arrested and indicted for two of the murders. No similar deaths were discovered during the months immediately following his arrest.

ATLANTIC CABLES, the telegraph and telephone cables on the bed of the North Atlantic Ocean linking North America with Europe. The first successful cable was laid by promoter Cyrus West Field (1819–1892) under the direction of William Thomson (later Lord KELVIN) at the third attempt, in 1858, but this soon failed and was replaced by a more permanent one in 1866. The first Atlantic telephone cable was not laid until 1956 and the method is at present suffering strong competition from COMMUNICATIONS SATELLITES.

ATLANTIC CHARTER, declaration of common objectives signed by F.D. Roosevelt and Churchill on Aug. 14, 1941, before the US entered WWII. It affirmed the determination of the American and British governments not to extend their territories and to promote every people's right to independence and self-determination.

ATLANTIC CITY, seaside resort and convention center in SE N.J., home of the Miss America Pageant. The first legal gambling casino opened in 1978, and other hotels with casinos have been operating since then. Its famous Boardwalk (1870) is lined by hotels and restaurants and has the Convention Hall, one of the world's largest auditoriums. Pop 40,199.

ATLANTIC INTRACOASTAL WATERWAY, a shallow sheltered water route extending 1,134mi along the Atlantic seaboard from Norfolk, Va., to Key West, Fla., and serving pleasure craft and light shipping. The Atlantic route and the GULF INTRACOASTAL WATERWAY together make up the INTRACOASTAL WATERWAY.

ATLANTIC OCEAN, ocean separating North and South America from Europe and Africa and creating by its currents the GULF STREAM which moderates the climate of NW Europe. It is the second largest of the world's oceans, the Pacific being the largest. Lying between highly industrialized continents, the N Atlantic carries the greatest proportion of the world's shipping. About half the world's fish comes from the area, 60% from the GRAND BANKS; some Atlantic fish species are verging on extinction due to the rapid development of modern fishing techniques and increasing pollution.

ATLANTIS, a mythical continent from which the Atlantic takes its name. Atlantis, as described by PLATO in the *Timaeus* and *Critias*, is situated just beyond the PILLARS OF HERCULES. He presents it as an advanced civilization that was destroyed by volcanic eruptions and earthquakes, sinking into the sea. The legend has fascinated men since antiquity, and many searches for the lost continent have been made.

ATLAS, Charles (Angelo Siciliano) (1894–1972), US bodybuilder. Once a self-proclaimed "97-pound weakling," he built himself into a powerful man with a 54¾in. chest and 17in. biceps. He was named the World's Perfect Man in 1922. He created a multimillion dollar mail-order muscle-building business.

ATLAS MOUNTAINS, an extension of the Alpine mountain system of Europe into NW Africa, the highest peak being Mt Toubkal (13,660ft) in SW Morocco. Olive and citrus crops are cultivated on some of the moister N slopes; sheep grazing predominates on the Saharan margins. The Atlas Mts are rich in coal, oil, iron ore and phosphates.

ATLAS ROCKET. See SPACE EXPLORATION.

ATMOSPHERE, the roughly spheroidal envelope of GAS, VAPOR and AEROSOL particles surrounding the EARTH, retained by gravity and forming a major constituent in the environment of most forms of terrestrial life, protecting it from the impact of METEORS, COSMIC RAY particles and harmful solar radiation. The composition of the atmosphere and most of its physical properties vary with ALTITUDE, certain key properties being used to divide the whole into several zones, the upper and lower boundaries of which change with LATITUDE, the time of day and the season of the year. About 75% of the total MASS of atmosphere and 90% of its water vapor and aerosols are contained in the TROPOSPHERE, the lowest zone. Excluding water vapor, the **air** of the troposphere contains 78% NITROGEN; 20% OXYGEN; 0.9% ARGON; and 0.03% CARBON dioxide, together with traces of the other NOBLE GASES; and METHANE, HYDROGEN and nitrous oxide. The water vapor content fluctuates within wide margins as water is evaporated from the OCEANS, carried in

CLOUDS and precipitated upon the continents. The air flows in meandering currents, transferring ENERGY from the warm equatorial regions to the colder poles. The troposphere is thus the zone in which weather occurs (see METEOROLOGY), as well as that in which most air-dependent life exists. Apart from occasional INVERSIONS, the TEMPERATURE falls with increasing altitude through the troposphere until at the tropopause (altitude 7km at the poles; 16km on the equator) it becomes constant (about 217K), and then slowly increases again into the STRATOSPHERE (up to about 48km). The upper stratosphere contains the OZONE layer which filters out the dangerous ULTRAVIOLET RADIATION incident from the SUN. Above the stratosphere, the MESOSPHERE merges into the IONOSPHERE, a region containing various layers of charged particles (IONS) of immense importance in the propagation of RADIO waves, being used to reflect signals between distant ground stations. At greater altitudes still, the ionosphere passes into the **exosphere,** a region of rarefied HELIUM and hydrogen gases, in turn merging into the interplanetary medium. In all, the atmosphere has a mass of about 5.2×10^{18}kg its DENSITY being about 1.23kg/m³ at sea level. Its WEIGHT results in its exerting an average **air pressure** of 101.3kPa (1013mbar) near the surface, this fluctuating greatly with the weather and falling off rapidly with height (see also PRESSURE). The other PLANETS of the SOLAR SYSTEM (with the possible exception of PLUTO), all have distinctive atmospheres, though none of these contains as much life-supporting oxygen as does that of the earth.

ATOLL, a typically circular CORAL reef enclosing a LAGOON. Many atolls, often supporting low arcuate islands, are found in the Pacific Ocean.

ATOM, classically, one of the minute, indivisible, homogeneous particles of which physical objects are composed (see ATOMISM); in 20th-century science, the name given to a relatively stable package of MATTER, that is itself made up of at least two SUBATOMIC PARTICLES. Every atom consists of a tiny nucleus (containing positively charged PROTONS and electrically neutral NEUTRONS) with which are associated a number of negatively charged ELECTRONS. These, although individually much smaller than the nucleus, occupy a hierarchy of ORBITALS that represent the atom's electronic ENERGY LEVELS and fill most of the space taken up by the atom. The number of protons in the nucleus of an atom (the atomic number, Z) defines the chemical

ELEMENT of which the atom is an example. In an isolated neutral atom the number of electrons equals the atomic number, but an electrically charged ION of the same atom has either a surfeit or a deficit of electrons. The number of neutrons in the nucleus (the neutron number, N) can vary between different atoms of the same element, the resulting species being called the ISOTOPES of the element. Most stable isotopes have slightly more neutrons than protons. Although the nucleus is very small, it contains nearly all the MASS of the atom—protons and neutrons having very similar masses, and the mass of the electron (about 0.05% of the proton mass) being almost negligible. The mass of an atom is roughly equal to the total number of its protons and neutrons. This number $Z + N$, is known as the mass number of the atom, A, the mass of a proton being counted as one. In equations representing nuclear reactions, the atomic number of an atom is often written as a subscript preceding the chemical symbol for the element, and the mass number as a superscript following it. Thus an atomic nucleus with mass number 16 and containing 8 protons belongs to an atom of "oxygen-16", written $_8O^{16}$. The average of the mass numbers of the various naturally occurring isotopes of an element, weighted according to their relative abundance, gives the chemical ATOMIC WEIGHT of the element. Subatomic particles fired into atomic nuclei can cause nuclear reactions that give rise either to new isotopes of the original element or to atoms of a different element, and that emit ALPHA PARTICLES, or BETA RAYS, sometimes accompanied by GAMMA RAYS.

The earliest atomistic concept, regarding the atom as that which could not be subdivided, was implicit in the first modern, chemical atomic theory, that of John DALTON (1808). Although it survives in the once-common chemical definition of atom—the smallest fragment of a chemical element that retains the properties of the element and can take part in chemical reactions—chemists now recognize that the MOLECULE, not the atom, is the natural chemical unit of matter. The atomic nuclei form the basic structure of the molecules; but the interaction of the VALENCE electrons associated with these nuclei, rather than the properties of the individual component atoms, is responsible for the chemical behavior of matter.

According to the model of atomic structure put forward by Niels BOHR and later refined by the application of QUANTUM MECHANICS, the electrons in an atom exist in certain orbits (see ORBITAL) of fixed ENERGY and angular MOMENTUM. Only one pair of electrons of opposite SPIN can occupy each orbit (see EXCLUSION PRINCIPLE), and one may think of the orbits as being filled up to a certain level. It is the outer, or VALENCE, electrons that are mainly responsible for the chemical properties of the atom (see PERIODIC TABLE). When an electron drops into a vacancy in an orbit of lower energy, the difference in energy is radiated in the form of a PHOTON of energy $h\nu$, where h is the Planck constant and ν is the FREQUENCY of the radiation.

ATOMIC BOMB, a weapon of mass destruction deriving its energy from nuclear FISSION. The first atomic bomb was exploded at Alamogordo, N.M., on July 16, 1945. As in the bomb dropped over Hiroshima, Japan a few weeks later (August 6), the fissionable material was uranium-235, but when Nagasaki was destroyed by another bomb three days after that, plutonium-239 was used. Together the Hiroshima and Nagasaki bombs killed more than 100,000 people. Since the early 1950s, the power of the fission bomb (equivalent to some 20,000 tons of TNT in the case of the Hiroshima bomb) has been vastly exceeded by that of the HYDROGEN BOMB which depends on nuclear FUSION. (See also NUCLEAR WARFARE.)

ATOMIC CLOCK, a device which utilizes the exceptional constancy of the FREQUENCIES associated with certain electron SPIN reversals (as in the CESIUM clock) or the inversion of AMMONIA molecules (the ammonia clock) to define an accurately reproducible TIME scale.

ATOMIC ENERGY. See NUCLEAR ENERGY.

ATOMIC REACTOR. See NUCLEAR REACTOR.

ATOMIC WEIGHT, the MEAN MASS of the ATOMS of an ELEMENT weighted according to the relative abundance of its naturally occurring ISOTOPES and measured relative to some standard. Since 1961 this standard has been provided by the CARBON isotope C^{12} whose atomic mass is defined to be exactly 12. On this scale atomic weights for the naturally occurring elements range from 1.008 (HYDROGEN) to 238.03 (URANIUM).

ATOMISM, the theory that all matter consists of atoms—minute indestructible particles, homogeneous in substance but varied in shape. Developed in the 5th century BC by LEUCIPPUS and DEMOCRITUS and adopted by EPICURUS, it was expounded in detail by the Roman poet LUCRETIUS.

ATOMS-FOR-PEACE, a plan for promoting international cooperation in the development of atomic power for non-military purposes, proposed to the UN by President Eisenhower in 1953. Although not adopted, it led to the establishment in 1957 of the International Atomic Energy Agency (IAEA) to which both Soviet-bloc and Western nations belong.

ATOM SMASHER. See ACCELERATORS. PARTICLE.

ATONALITY, systematic departure in music from established tonal centers. The notion of tonality was increasingly blurred in the 19th century by the fluid chromaticism of WAGNER, Richard STRAUSS and MAHLER, foreshadowing DEBUSSY'S "whole-tone" scale. SCHÖNBERG and his disciples BERG and WEBERN went one stage further, abandoning tonal structure altogether and substituting the TWELVE-TONE system. Schönberg's *Moses and Aaron* and Berg's *Wozzeck* are leading examples of atonal composition.

ATP (adenosine triphosphate). See NUCLEOTIDES.

ATTICA RIOT. On Sept. 9, 1971, approximately 1,000 prisoners in the Attica State Correctional Facility in N.Y. rebelled and took over a large part of the prison. Demanding reforms and amnesty in exchange for the lives of some 30 hostages, the prisoners attracted nationwide attention. Under the ultimate authority of Gov. Nelson A. ROCKEFELLER, police and prison personnel stormed the prison compound on Sept. 13, killing 43 people including 10 hostages (an eleventh had died after being beaten by inmates). This harsh, punitive reaction quickly came to symbolize official indifference to the unbearable conditions in many US prisons.

ATTILA (c406–453), king of the Huns, who claimed dominion from the Alps and the Baltic to the Caspian. From 441–50 he ravaged the Eastern Roman Empire as far as Constantinople and invaded Gaul in 451, this expedition earning him the title of "Scourge of God." The following year he invaded Italy, but retired without attacking Rome. He died of overindulgence at his wedding feast.

ATTLEE, Clement Richard Attlee, 1st Earl (1883–1967), British statesman and prime minister (1945–51). Attlee led the Labour party from 1935 and served in Winston CHURCHILL'S wartime coalition cabinet. During his administration he instituted a broad program of social change and nationalization.

ATTU, westernmost island of the Aleutians, in the N Pacific. Mountainous and rugged, it covers 388sq mi and has no permanent population. The Japanese held Attu briefly during WWII.

ATTUCKS, Crispus (c1723–1770), black and Indian American who was the first of five men to die in the BOSTON MASSACRE.

ATWOOD, Margaret (1939–   ), Canadian poet and novelist. Her spare, terse poems in such collections as *Power Politics* (1971) and *You Are Happy* (1974) have been widely admired. Her novels include *Surfacing* (1972) and *Life before Man* (1979).

AUCHINCLOSS, Louis Stanton (1917–   ), US novelist whose work, noted for its character analysis, often deals with East Coast upper-class life. His best known books include *The Rector of Justin* (1964) and *A World of Profit*(1969).

AUCHINLECK, Sir Claude John Eyre (1884–1981), British field marshal. He served in the Indian army and in the Middle East during WWI. After the war he again served in India. As commander in chief of British armies in the Middle East early in WWII, he at first routed the Germans in North Africa but then had to abandon Tobruk and was dismissed by Churchill. Returning to his old post in India, he turned back the Japanese.

AUCKLAND, largest city, chief port and commercial and manufacturing center of New Zealand, between Waitemata and Manukau harbors of North Island. It has a shipbuilding industry and produces textiles, foodstuffs, vehicles, chemicals and plastics. Founded in 1840, it was New Zealand's capital until replaced by Wellington in 1865. Pop 808,800.

AUCKLAND ISLANDS, six uninhabited volcanic islands covering 234sq mi in the S Pacific. They lie 200mi S of New Zealand, to whom they belong.

AUDEN, W. H. (Wystan Hugh Auden; 1907–1973), English poet and a major influence on modern poetry, particularly during the 1930s when his highly energetic, often witty verse probed and laid bare Europe's ailing culture in the years that were to lead to WWII. Auden went to the US in 1939, becoming an American citizen in 1946. From this point his work reflects his growing religious concern (*The Double Man*, 1941). Some of Auden's best mature writing appeared in *Nones* (1951) and *The Shield of Achilles* (1955). He also collaborated on drama and opera librettos, and wrote literary criticism.

AUDUBON, John James (1785–1851), US artist and naturalist famous for his bird paintings, born in Santo Domingo (Haiti) of French parents and brought up in France. Some years after emigrating to the US in 1803, he embarked on what was to become his major achievement: the painting of all the then-known birds of North America. His *Birds of America* (London: 1827–38), was followed by a US edition (1840–44) and other illustrated works on American natural history.

AUER, Leopold (1845–1930), Hungarian-born violinist, a famous teacher of the instrument. He taught in Russia, Germany and England before emigrating in 1918 to the US, where he taught in New York and Philadelphia.

AUERBACH, Arnold "Red" (1917–), US basketball coach. The most successful coach in the history of professional basketball, he led the Boston Celtics to nine championships in ten years (1957; 1959–66). He retired in 1966 after having won 1,037 professional games.

AUGSBURG, Peace of (1555), agreement between Ferdinand—future Holy Roman Emperor, acting for his brother Emperor Charles V—and the German princes to end the religious wars of the REFORMATION. It legalized the coexistence of Lutheranism (as the sole recognized form of Protestantism) and Roman Catholicism in the empire. Each territory was to adhere to the denomination of its ruling prince.

AUGSBURG, War of the League of (1689–97), war between Louis XIV of France and the Grand Alliance, comprising the League of Augsburg (Emperor Leopold I and Saxony, Bavaria, the Palatinate, Savoy, Sweden and Spain), the Netherlands and England. The immediate cause was French devastation of the Palatinate in 1688. By the Treaty of RYSWICK which ended the war, Louis returned Luxembourg and Lorraine, but kept Strasbourg, and recognized William III as king of England.

AUGSBURG CONFESSION, statement of Lutheran beliefs presented to the Diet of Augsburg on June 25, 1530. The Confession was largely the work of Philip MELANCHTHON, and was an attempt to reconcile LUTHER'S reforms with Roman Catholicism. Emperor Charles V rejected the document, sealing the break between the Lutherans and Rome.

AUGUSTA, capital of Me. and seat of Kennebec Co., at the head of navigation on Kennebec R. The city produces textiles, shoes, paper and foodstuffs. The site was first occupied by a Plymouth Colony trading post in 1628. Pop 21,819.

AUGUSTAN AGE, the high point of Roman culture, marked by the reign of Emperor Augustus (27 BC–14 AD) and the literary works of Livy, Horace, Ovid and Vergil. In the first half of the 18th century, English neoclassicists sought to emulate such writers and the term Augustan

denoted all that was admirable in art and politics, though, in a manner typical of the period's liking for paradox and representative of its political divisions, it was often used ironically.

AUGUSTINE, Saint (354–430), Christian theologian and writer, the most prominent of the Latin Fathers of the Church. During his early years in Carthage, N Africa, he embraced MANICHAEISM, but in Rome (where he arrived in 383) he was much influenced by NEOPLATONISM. Moving to Milan, he met and was greatly impressed by St. Ambrose, bishop of Milan, and became a baptized Christian in 387.

Ordained a priest in 391, he became bishop of Hippo in N Africa in 396. There followed many famous books, including the autobiographical *Confessions* (397–401) and *De Civitate Dei* (413–26), the great Christian philosophy of history.

AUGUSTINE, Saint (d. c604–07), first archbishop of Canterbury (from 601). A Benedictine monk, he was sent to England by Pope Gregory the Great to convert the pagans and bring the Celtic Church under the control of Rome. Arriving in 597, he was given support by King ETHELBERT of Kent.

AUGUSTINIAN FATHERS, common name for the Order of the Hermit Friars of St. Augustine, a Roman Catholic order dedicated to the advancement of learning and to missionary work. It was created in 1256 by Pope Alexander IV from a number of Italian hermit groups and adopted the Rule of St. Augustine of Hippo. The order now has some 4,000 members.

AUKS, 22 species (including the extinct GREAT AUK) of marine diving birds of the family Alcidae (order Charadriiformes), including RAZORBILLS, PUFFINS, GUILLEMOTS and MURRES. Lengths vary between about 150mm (6in) and about 750mm (30in): the smallest is dovekie, or Little Auk (*Plautus alle*), which is about the size of a ROBIN. They usually breed in colonies, sometimes millions of individuals, and nest on high ledges or in burrows.

AULD LANG SYNE, Scottish song traditionally sung on Hogmanay (New Year's Eve). Written by Robert Burns c1788, its title means "old long since," or old times.

AURELIAN, (Lucius Domitius Aurelianus; c212–275), Roman emperor (270–75) who consolidated the imperial territories. He repulsed the barbarians, began construction of a wall—the Aurelian wall—around Rome and recovered the western provinces, Gaul, Spain and Britain. He was murdered by some of his officers.

AURIC, Georges (1899–), French

composer, especially of ballet and film music. The youngest member of the group of composers known as *Les Six*, he was administrator of the two Paris opera houses 1962–68.

AURIOL, Vincent (1884–1966), first president of the Fourth Republic of France (1947–54). An active socialist, he was finance minister in Léon BLUM'S government. He opposed the Vichy regime in 1940 and in 1943 managed to escape to England, where he worked with General DE GAULLE.

AURORA, or **polar lights,** striking display of lights seen in night skies near the earth's geomagnetic poles. The *aurora borealis* (northern lights) is seen in Canada, Alaska and N Scandinavia; the *aurora australis* (southern lights) is seen in Antarctic regions. Auroras are caused by the collision of air molecules in the upper atmosphere with charged particles from the sun that have been accelerated and "funneled" by the earth's magnetic field. Particularly intense auroras are associated with high solar activity. Nighttime AIRGLOW is termed the permanent aurora.

AUSABLE CHASM, spectacular gorge in the Adirondacks, NE N.Y. This popular tourist attraction consists of a 2mi long series of waterfalls and rapids in the Ausable R flowing beneath sheer cliff faces.

AUSCHWITZ, present-day Oświęçim in Poland, site of a notorious Nazi concentration camp in WWII. Some 4 million inmates, mostly Jews, were murdered there. The town is now a transportation center with a chemical industry. Pop 39,600.

AUSTEN, Jane (1775–1817), English novelist. Daughter of a clergyman, in novels like *Sense and Sensibility* (1811), *Pride and Prejudice* (1813) and *Emma* (1815–16), she portrayed the provincial middle-class of her time with great subtlety and ironic insight. Her novels are admired as among the finest in the English language.

AUSTERLITZ, town in what is now S Czechoslovakia where, on Dec. 2, 1805, Napoleon's army defeated the combined forces of Emperor Francis I of Austria and Tsar Alexander I of Russia. This "Battle of the Three Emperors" was among the French emperor's most brilliant campaigns and marked the beginning of his rise to mastery in Europe.

AUSTIN, capital of Tex. and seat of Travis Co. It manufactures machinery, furniture and foodstuffs and it is the home of the U. of Texas and St. Edward's U. Founded in 1838, the city was originally named Waterloo, but on becoming state capital in 1839 it was renamed in honor of Stephen Austin. Pop 345,496.

AUSTIN, John Langshaw (1911–1960), British philosopher who was a leader in the field of linguistic analysis. His important papers appeared in *How to Do Things with Words* (1961) and *Sense and Sensibilia* (1962).

AUSTIN, Moses (1761–1821), US merchant who laid the basis for American colonization of Texas. In 1821 he was given permission to settle 300 families in Texas (then part of Mexico). His son, Stephen AUSTIN, implemented the plan after his death.

AUSTIN, Stephen Fuller (1793–1836), US pioneer statesman who helped create the state of Texas, son of Moses Austin. In 1821 he brought 300 families to Tex. and was made the settlement's administrator. Between 1822 and 1830 he presented Texan demands for autonomy to the Mexican government; the negotiations proved difficult, and the Mexicans went so far as to imprison Austin. On his release in 1835, he joined the Texan rebellion against Mexico. In 1836, Sam HOUSTON appointed Austin secretary of state of the Republic of Tex.

AUSTIN, Tracy (1962–   ), US tennis player. At 17, she became the youngest player ever to earn $1 million in tournaments. She captured the US Open in 1979.

AUSTRALASIA, term sometimes used to indicate an area of the S Pacific that includes Australia, New Zealand, Tasmania and adjacent islands. In a wider sense, it has been used to include OCEANIA. The term's lack of adequate definition has led to a decline in its use and importance.

Official name: Commonwealth of Australia
Capital: Canberra
Area: 2,966,150sq mi
Population: 14,567,000
Languages: English
Religions: No official religion; Protestant
Monetary unit(s): 1 Australian dollar = 100 cents

AUSTRALIA, island continent entirely occupied by a single nation, the Commonwealth of Australia, a federation of six states (NEW SOUTH WALES, VICTORIA, QUEENSLAND, SOUTH AUSTRALIA, WESTERN AUSTRALIA and TASMANIA) and two territories (NORTHERN TERRITORY, and AUSTRALIAN CAPITAL TERRITORY containing Canberra, the federal capital).

Australia led Papua New Guinea, self-governing from 1973, toward full independence (1975) and controls Norfolk Island, the Cocos (Keeling) Islands, Christmas Island (Indian Ocean) and about 5,000,000sq mi of Antarctica.

Land. The flat Western Plateau or Australian Shield extends from the NE coast across nearly half of the continent, sloping eastward with Lake Eyre, 43ft below sea level, as its lowest point. In the desert-like "Red Heart" of the continent are the rugged Macdonnell and Musgrave ranges. Plains stretch from the Gulf of Carpentaria to the S coast. Parallel to the E coast is the Great Dividing Range, running from N Queensland to Tasmania (Mt Kosciusko, 7,310ft/2,228m, is Australia's highest peak). Along the Queensland coast is the Great Barrier Reef, the world's largest coral reef. Major rivers include the Murray (1,600mi) and its tributaries the Darling and Murrumbidgee.

Climate. Australia enjoys a mainly warm, dry and sunny climate. Summer maximum shade temperatures are well above 100°F in most areas. Annual rainfall sometimes exceeds 117in in E Queensland, but only a small part of Australia has plentiful rainfall and evaporation is high. Basically the N is a monsoon zone of dry winters and wet summers, separated by a transitional zone from the S, where summer drought and winter rains prevail.

Gum trees (eucalyptus) and wattles (acacia) are the continent's typical vegetation. The unique wildlife includes the platypus and spiny anteater, the most primitive surviving mammals; the koala bear, kangaroo, wallaby and wombat; the dingo, a wild dog; the emu, kookaburra and other colorful birds; and the deadly tiger-snake and other reptiles.

People and Economy. The people are mainly of British origin but there are some 144,381 Aborigines, now mostly detribalized, and many immigrants from Italy, Yugoslavia, Greece, Germany, the Netherlands and the US. Most of the population is concentrated in the coastal cities, of which the largest is Sydney.

Australia provides about 30% of the world's wool and is a major producer of wheat and meat. The rich mineral resources include iron ore, gold, copper, silver, lead, zinc, bauxite, uranium and some oil and natural gas. Australia is highly industrialized and products range from aircraft, ships and automobiles to textiles, chemicals, electrical equipment and metal goods.

History. Discovered by the Dutch in the early 1600s, Australia was claimed for Britain by Capt James COOK (1770). New South Wales, the first area settled, began as a penal colony (1788). But free settlement began in 1816 and no convicts were sent to Australia after 1840. The gold rushes (1851, 1892) brought more people to Australia, and in 1901 the six self-governing colonies formed the independent Commonwealth of Australia.

AUSTRALIAN ABORIGINES, aboriginal population (see ABORIGINES) of AUSTRALIA. They have dark wavy hair (except in childhood), medium stance, broad noses and narrow heads—typical AUSTRALOID features. Before white encroachment in the 18th and 19th centuries they lived by well-organized nomadic food-gathering and hunting and numbered about 300,000. Since the enfranchisement of the remaining 40,000 full-blooded aborigines in 1962, varyingly successful attempts at integration have been made. (See also TASMANIANS.) Recent researches have suggested that they may be the result of interbreeding between an original population of *Homo erectus* and the earliest members of *Homo sapiens* (see PREHISTORIC MAN).

AUSTRALIAN ALPS, mountain ranges in SE Australia which form the S part of the Great Dividing Range. They include the highest peak in Australia, Mt Kosciusko (7,310ft).

AUSTRALIAN CAPITAL TERRITORY, an enclave surrounded by New South Wales, chosen in 1908 as the seat of the federal government, and ceded by New South Wales in two parts in 1911 and 1915. Known as the Federal Capital Territory until 1938, it contains the Australian capital, CANBERRA. Pop 228,500.

AUSTRIA, a federal republic in central Europe divided into nine provinces: Vienna, Lower Austria, Burgenland, Upper Austria, Salzburg, Styria, Carinthia, Tyrol and Vorarlberg. There are four physical regions: the Austrian Alps to the W, including the highest mountain in Austria, Grossglockner (12,457ft); the N Alpine foreland, a plateau cut by fertile valleys between the Danube and the Alps; the Austrian granite plateau, N of the Danube; and the E lowlands, where the capital, Vienna stands. Most rivers drain north from the mountains into the

Danube and its tributaries. Climate varies widely: in general, summers are warm, winters fairly severe, with moderate rainfall throughout the year.

Economy. Austrian farms are small, and the only crops the country is self-sufficient in are sugar beets and potatoes. Other important crops include grains, grapes, fruits, tobacco, flax and hemp; wines and beers are produced in quantity. Almost 40% of the country is forested: wood and paper are important products. Iron ore is the most important mineral resource, but there are also deposits of lead, magnesium, copper, salt, zinc, aluminum, silver and gypsum. There is oil near Zisterdorf, but production has decreased in favor of natural gas. The areas around Vienna, Graz and Linz are the chief industrial centers. Manufacturing industries provide one third of the GDP. Tourism has also helped to stimulate economic growth in recent years.

History. Inhabited from prehistoric times, settled by the CELTS, and subsequently part of the Roman Empire, from the 3rd century AD Austria was devastated by invading VANDALS, GOTHS, ALAMANNI, HUNS and AVARS. Early in the 9th century CHARLEMAGNE made Austria the East March, which the Babenberg family inherited in 967 and retained as a duchy until their extinction in 1246. In 1247 the HAPSBURGS acquired these lands as Archdukes of Austria. Until their fall in 1918, the history of Austria is the history of the Hapsburg lands. (See AUSTRIA-HUNGARY; AUSTRIAN SUCCESSION, WAR OF; AUSTRO-PRUSSIAN WAR; FRENCH REVOLUTIONARY WARS; HOLY ROMAN EMPIRE; NAPOLEONIC WARS; SEVEN YEARS' WAR; SPANISH SUCCESSION, WAR OF; THIRTY YEARS' WAR.) By the Treaty of VERSAILLES,

Official Name: The Republic of Austria
Capital: Vienna
Area: 32,366sq mi
Population: 7,510,000
Languages: German, Slovenian, Croatian
Religions: Roman Catholic
Monetary unit(s): 1 schilling=100 groschen

independent states (Czechoslovakia, Hungary, Yugoslavia) were created from what had wholly or partially been within the old empire, while Austria herself, the Hapsburg patrimony, became a republic. Following the ANSCHLUSS in 1938, Austria became part of HITLER'S Third Reich, regaining independence following the Allied victory in 1945, although the last Allied occupation forces did not leave the country until 1955.

Austria's contributions to culture, especially in music, have been large: MOZART, HAYDN, SCHUBERT, BRUCKNER and MAHLER were all Austrians, while BEETHOVEN, Johann STRAUSS, and Franz LEHAR spent most of their lives in Vienna. Vienna is also considered the home of Freudian psychoanalysis.

AUSTRIA-HUNGARY, name given to the empire formed by the union of the Kingdom of Hungary and the Austrian Empire in 1867. It ceased to exist at the end of WWI, and its lands were divided among the East European nations.

AUSTRIAN SUCCESSION, War of the (1740–1748), war fought between the Austrian Empire and European powers disputing the right of MARIA THERESA to Austrian territories inherited from her father. It was called KING GEORGE'S WAR by Americans because of the involvement of Britain's George II. The treaty of AIX-LA-CHAPELLE, ending the war, guaranteed Maria Theresa's right to the throne on condition that she ceded Silesia to Prussia.

AUSTRO-PRUSSIAN WAR (or "Seven Weeks' War"), war fought in 1866 by Austria against Prussia and Italy. Count Otto von BISMARCK, the Prussian premier, involved Austria in a dispute over the joint Austro-Prussian rule of SCHLESWIG-HOLSTEIN which forced her to declare war on June 14. By keeping the French neutral, he left Austria politically isolated. Despite the collapse of his Italian allies, the Prussian General MÖLTKE broke the Austrians at the battle of Königgrätz on July 3. The Peace of Prague (signed Aug. 23) excluded Austria from the new German confederation and ceded Venice to Italy, a major step towards Bismarck's dream of German unification under Prussia.

AUTISM, withdrawal from reality and relations with others. Pathological autism occurs in various psychoses, especially SCHIZOPHRENIA. Certain children who fail to establish either normal communication with others or social responses are termed autistic.

AUTOBIOGRAPHY, biography written by the subject himself. St. Augustine's *Confessions* (5th century AD) is generally regarded as the first, and the modern form of autobiography is believed to have grown out of the Christian tendency towards self-examination. Today the influence of psychoanalysis and the need to assert individuality may have a similar influence. Some notable autobiographies include those written by CELLINI, Samuel PEPYS, Jean Jacques ROUSSEAU, Benjamin FRANKLIN, George SAND, Cardinal NEWMAN and HITLER.

AUTOGIRO, a short-takeoff, heavier-than-air flying machine that derives its lift from a rotating wing which turns in response to the aerodynamic forces (see AERODYNAMICS) acting on it as the aircraft is driven forward through the air by a conventional PROPELLER. It is potentially faster and mechanically far simpler than the HELICOPTER, capable of flying more slowly than the AIRPLANE, and impossible to stall.

AUTOGRAPH, original manuscript of words or music in the writer's own hand, or any specimen of a person's handwriting, particularly his signature. The collection of autographs first became popular in the 17th century. The signatures of long-dead statesmen are now among the most valuable autographs in the collectors' market. In the mid-20th century, the pursuit of the autographs of celebrities in the entertainment world became a growing fad.

AUTOMATIC PILOT. See GYROPILOT.

AUTOMATION, the detailed control of a production process without recourse to human decision-making at every point, typically involving a negative-FEEDBACK system. (See MECHANIZATION AND AUTOMATION.)

AUTOMOBILE, or passenger car, a small self-propelled passenger-carrying vehicle designed to operate on ordinary HIGHWAYS and usually supported on four wheels. Power is provided in most modern automobiles by an INTERNAL COMBUSTION ENGINE which uses GASOLINE (vaporized and premixed with a suitable quantity of air in the CARBURETOR) AS FUEL. This is ignited in the (usually 4, 6 or 8) cylinders of the engine by SPARK PLUGS, fired from the DISTRIBUTOR in the appropriate sequence. The gas supply and thus the engine speed is controlled from the accelerator pedal. The driving power is communicated to the road wheels through the TRANSMISSION which includes a clutch (enabling the driver to disengage the engine without stopping it), a gearbox (allowing the most efficient use to be made of the engine power), various drive-shafts (with universal joints), and a DIFFERENTIAL which allows the driving wheels to turn at marginally different rates in cornering. Steering is controlled from a hand wheel which moves a transverse tie rod mounted between the independently-pivoted front wheels. Service BRAKES of various types are mounted on all wheels, an additional parking-brake mechanism being used when stationary. In modern automobiles service brakes and steering may be power-assisted and the transmission automatic rather than manually controlled with a gearshift. Although the first propelled steam vehicles were built by the French army officer Nicholas-Joseph Cugnot in the 1760s, it was not until Karl BENZ and Gottlieb DAIMLER began to build gasoline-powered carriages in the mid-1880s that the day of the modern automobile dawned. The DURYEA brothers built the first US automobile in 1893 and within a few years several automobile manufacturers, including Henry FORD, had started into business. The Ford Motor Company itself was founded in 1903, pioneering the cheap mass-market auto with the Model T of 1908. The AUTOMOBILE INDUSTRY expanded fitfully until the 1960s, improving automobile performance, comfort and styling, but more recently has been forced by economic considerations and the activity of consumer groups (led by Ralph NADER) to pay more attention to safety and environmental factors. (See also AUTOMOBILE EMISSION CONTROL; AUTOMOBILE RACING; DRIVING; HIGHWAY SAFETY.)

AUTOMOBILE EMISSION CONTROL, the reduction of the AIR POLLUTION caused by AUTOMOBILES by modification of the fuel and careful design. The principal pollutants are unburnt HYDROCARBONS, CARBON monoxide, oxides of NITROGEN and LEAD halide particles. The last can be eliminated if alternatives to lead-based ANTIKNOCK ADDITIVES in the GASOLINE are used but the others require redesigned cylinder heads, recycling and afterburning of exhaust gases and better metering of the GASOLINE supply through FUEL INJECTION. An alternative approach investigates alternatives to the conventional INTERNAL COMBUSTION ENGINE—BATTERY- and FUEL-CELL-powered vehicles, GAS-TURBINE and even steam-powered units.

AUTOMOBILE INDUSTRY, US, comprising companies manufacturing cars, buses, trucks and motorcycles, the second largest industry in the US (oil is first). The earliest US firms hand-produced small numbers of electric-, steam-, and gas-powered cars; by the 1890s, pioneers such as the DURYEA brothers, Ransom OLDS, and Henry FORD were custom building gas-powered cars in small but growing numbers. In 1913, Ford successfully introduced new assembly-line techniques for mass-producing his Model T, the first car designed to be made and sold in volume. General Motors was established in 1908 by William C. DURANT, and was soon producing a range of cars in a number of price categories—a marketing strategy Ford refused to adopt until long after his company had lost its leading position to GM. By 1929, annual output of US cars totaled five million, with Ford, GM, and Chrysler forming the Big Three of auto manufacturers. There also were a number of smaller firms including Nash and Hudson, which merged to become American Motors in 1954; and Packard and Studebaker, which ended production in 1964.

American automobiles dominated the world market until the 1960s, when manufacturers in Europe and Japan began to cut into US sales abroad and even penetrated the market at home. By the late 1970s, small foreign cars with their relatively low fuel consumption were being bought by Americans in ever larger numbers. Imports were a major factor in the record losses of the auto industry in 1980—the largest in the history of the industry—and the near-bankruptcy of Chrysler, which was rescued by federal government loan guarantees.

AUTOMOBILE RACING, a variety of forms of competition using specially designed or adapted motor vehicles. The drivers of Formula One cars compete under FIA (Federation Internationale de l'Automobile) rules for the title of world champion, won by scoring the highest points in nine out of 11 Grand Prix events. Sports car competition tends to be as keen between manufacturers as between drivers. Major U.S. races include the INDIANAPOLIS 500 and the Daytona 500, a stock car race. European events of note are the Grand Prix de Monaco and the LE MANS 24-hour race. Attempts on the land speed record are carefully scrutinized by the FIA; following the approval of jet-powered cars the record soared to over 400 mph. Stock car racing is controlled in the US by the National Association for Stock Car Racing.

AUTRY, Gene (1907–   ), US songwriter ("Rudolph, the Red-Nosed Reindeer") who was popular as a singing cowboy in films of the 1930s and 1940s, appearing with his horse Champion. He was later a film and television producer.

AUTUMN. See SEASONS.

AUVERGNE, region of extinct volcanoes and former province of S central France in the Massif Central now divided between three departments. Its principal city is Clermont-Ferrand. It was once the home of the Arverni, whose chief, VERCINGETORIX, rebelled against Julius Caesar.

AVEDON, Richard (1923–   ), US photographer. World famous for his on-location fashion photography for *Vogue* and *Harper's Bazaar*, he also took revealing portraits of celebrities, collected in *Observations* (1959) and *Portraits* (1976).

AVERAGE. See MEAN, MEDIAN AND MODE.

AVERNUS (or Averno), lake in Italy 10mi W of Naples. About 2mi wide and 118ft deep, it has no natural outlet. The sinister sulfurous fumes that rise from the lake led the ancients to regard it as an entrance to the underworld.

AVESTA. See ZEND AVESTA.

AVIATION. See AERODYNAMICS; FLIGHT, HISTORY OF.

AVICENNA, Latin name of abu-Ali al-Husayn **ibn-Sina** (980–1037), the greatest of the Arab scientists of the medieval period. His *Canon of Medicine* remained a standard medical text in Europe until the Renaissance.

AVIGNON, French city on the E bank of the Rhone, capital of the Vaucluse department; its industries include the production of metals and textiles and food processing. It was a Roman outpost, and the home of the popes during the BABYLONIAN CAPTIVITY (1309–1378). Pop 93,000; met pop 162,600.

AVILA CAMACHO, Manuel (1897–1955), Mexican soldier and statesman. As Mexico's president (1940–46) he supported the US and promoted Latin American opposition to the Axis powers.

AVOGADRO, Count Amedeo (1776–1856), Italian physicist who first realized that gaseous ELEMENTS might exist as MOLECULES which contain more than one ATOM, thus distinguishing molecules from atoms. In 1811 he published **Avogardo's hypothesis**—that equal volumes of all GASES under the same conditions of TEMPERATURE and PRESSURE contain the same number of molecules—but his work in this area was ignored by chemists for over 50 years. The **Avogardo Number** (N), the number of molecules in one MOLE of substance, 6.02×10^{23}, is named for him.

AVOIRDUPOIS (corruption of French: property of weight), the system of weights customarily used in the US (and formerly in the UK) for most goods except gems and drugs for which are employed respectively TROY WEIGHTS and APOTHECARIES WEIGHTS. There are 7,000 grains or 16 ounces in the pound avoirdupois (see WEIGHTS AND MEASURES).

AVON, name of several British rivers. The longest, the Warwickshire or "Shakespeare" Avon flows 96mi from near Naseby, through Stratford-on-Avon, to join the Severn at Tewkesbury.

AXELROD, Julius (1912–), US biochemist who shared the 1970 Nobel Prize for Medicine or Physiology with Bernard KATZ and Ulf von EULER for their independent contributions toward elucidating the chemistry of the transmission of nerve impulses (see NERVOUS SYSTEM). Axelrod identified a key ENZYME in this mechanism.

AXES, in mathematics, straight lines used as reference lines. In plane ANALYTIC GEOMETRY (and GRAPHS) two axes, usually at right angles, are most commonly used. In three-dimensional geometry, three axes, usually at mutual right angles, are most common. Their point of INTERSECTION is the **origin.**

AXIS OF SYMMETRY, a LINE drawn through a geometric figure such that the figure is symmetrical (see SYMMETRY) about it. The line may be considered as an axis of rotation: if the figure is rotated about it, there will be two or more positions which are indistinguishable from each other. If the letter Z, for example, is rotated about an axis drawn perpendicularly into the paper through the center of the diagonal stroke, there will be two correspondent positions: the letter has 2-fold rotational symmetry about that axis. In general, if a figure has n correspondent positions on rotation about an axis, it is said to have n-fold symmetry about that axis. (See also PLANE OF SYMMETRY.)

AXIS POWERS, countries that fought against the Allies in WWII. The Rome-Berlin Axis, a diplomatic agreement between Hitler and Mussolini, was reinforced by an Italian-German military pact in 1939. In 1940 Japan joined the pact, then Hungary, Bulgaria, Romania, Slovakia and Croatia.

AXON, the fiber of a nerve cell that conducts impulses away from the cell body. (See NERVOUS SYSTEM.)

AYATOLLAH, honorific title meaning "reflection of God" given to the more important Muslim clergymen in Iran. Many of the ayatollahs joined the movement against the SHAH in the 1970s. After the Iranian revolution they became the dominant political leaders of the new Islamic republic, occupying most important positions of authority. While many of the ayatollahs participated in the excesses of the regime, others, more moderate, remained quiet.

AYER, Sir Alfred Jules (1910–), English philosopher whose *Language, Truth and Logic* (1936) was influential in founding the "Oxford school" of philosophy, with its emphasis on the careful analysis of the use of words. The LOGICAL POSITIVISM of the Vienna Circle was an important formative influence in his philosophy.

AYMARA, Amerindian group numbering some 500,000, in the central Andes, Bolivia and Peru. Mainly herdsmen, they lead a meager existence under harsh climatic conditions.

AYMÉ, Marcel (1902–1967), French author noted for his humorous novels, *The Green Mare* (1933) and *The Conscience of Love* (1960). He also wrote children's stories and several plays, including *Clérambard* (1949).

AYUB KHAN, Mohammad (1907–1974), president of Pakistan 1958–69. He won office by a military coup, introduced land, education and local government reforms and created a new constitution.

AZERBAIJAN (Azerbaidjan), mountainous region E of the Caspian Sea divided between Iran and the USSR by the Araks R. Settled by MEDES as part of the Persian Empire, it was periodically dominated by Romans, Arabs, Mongols and Turks, returning to Persia in the 16th century. The Russian Tsar Alexander I annexed N Azerbaidzhan in 1813. An independent republic was formed there in 1918 but was conquered by the Soviets in 1920. Now a Transcaucasian socialist republic, its subtropical plain produces cotton, wheat and tobacco. It is rich in minerals, especially oil, and its capital Baku is an industrial and refining city. Iranian Azerbaidzhan was made an autonomous republic by a communist revolt in 1945 but Iran regained it in 1946. Its eastern province (capital Tabriz) grows grain, its western (capital Rezaiveh) tobacco and fruit.

AZIMUTH, in navigation and astronomy, the angular distance measured from 0–360° along the horizon eastward from an observer's north point to the point of intersection of the horizon and a great circle (see CELESTIAL SPHERE; SPHERICAL GEOMETRY) passing through the observer's ZENITH and a star or planet.

AZKØY, village in N central Turkey, 125mi E of Ankara, site of Hattusas, capital of the HITTITE Empire. King Labarnas II made it his capital in the 17th century BC. It was destroyed in 1190 BC and reinhabited in the 8th century BC. In 1906–07 excavations uncovered thousands of Hittite cuneiform tablets at Boğazköy.

AZORES, nine mountainous islands in the N Atlantic 800mi W of Portugal. São Miguel to the E is the largest and most populated. Their economy is agricultural, producing fruits and grain. Colonized and under Portuguese rule since the mid-15th century, the islands enjoy considerable autonomy. Pop 259,000.

AZTECS, pre-Columbian Indians of Central Mexico, traditionally thought to have migrated from Aztlán in the N to the Valley of Mexico. A warrior tribe, they took over the cities of the Toltecs, from whom they also derived part of their culture. The Aztec empire consisted of a confederation of three city states, Tenochtitlán (the capital, site of present-day Mexico City), Tlacopan and Texcoco. Religious belief contributed greatly to Aztec political and social structure. The two chief gods were Huitzilopochtli, god of war and the sun, and QUETZALCOATL, god of learning. Thousands of human victims were sacrificed to these and other gods. The Aztecs were superb artisans, working in gold, silver and copper, and creating fine pottery and mosaics. They are famed for their lavishly decorated temples, such as those at Tenochtitlán, Tula, Cuicuilco, Xochicalco and Cholula. The arrival of the conquistador Hernán CORTÉS (1519) heralded the collapse of the Aztec empire. (See also MONTEZUMA.)

AZUELA, Mariano (1873–1952), Mexican novelist who was the pioneer writer of the Mexican revolution. A social realist who was the first Latin American novelist to utilize the masses as protagonist, he is best known for *The Underdogs* (1916), *The Bosses* (1917) and *The Flies* (1918).

AZURITE, blue mineral consisting of basic COPPER carbonate ($Cu_3[OH]_2[CO_3]_2$), occurring with MALACHITE, notably in France, SW Africa and Ariz. It forms monoclinic crystals used as GEMS, and was formerly used as a pigment.

2nd letter of the alphabet. It can be traced back to an ancient Semitic character, the origin of both the Hebrew *beth* ("house")

and Greek *beta* (β). The lower-case "b" developed in late Roman times.

B-1, manned strategic penetrating bomber, originally slated to replace the US Air Force's B-52. In 1977 the B-1 program was cancelled by President Carter in favor of developing the cruise missile. At that time three prototype B-1s had been built and a fourth was under construction.

In late 1981 President Reagan proposed a new B-1 program which raised heated debate. Opponents said that the costly aircraft was already outmoded and that efforts should be focused on Stealth technology; proponents said it was necessary to fill the weapons gap until the Stealth was ready and that an advanced B-1 would force the Soviets to develop new defensive modes, diverting funds from offensive armaments.

The proposed modified B 1s would be 147 feet in length, with a 137-foot wingspan (full), an 87 foot wingspan (swept) and a maximum takeoff weight of 477,000 pounds, manned by a crew of 4 or 5. Designed to fly under Soviet radar at treetop levels, they would be equipped with highly sophisticated radar and electronic countermeasures. Their 125,000-pound maximum payload would include short-range attack missiles. Travelling at speeds of more than Mach 2 they would be one-tenth as "visible" to radar as B-52s.

B-52 BOEING STRATOFORTRESS, long-range manned penetrating bomber, the backbone of the US Strategic Air Command. In the 1970s the B-52 underwent a variety of modifications and improvements particularly in electronic countermeasures. Manned by a crew of 6, the B-52 is 160.9 feet long and has a wingspan of 185 feet. Maximum takeoff weight is 488,000 pounds with a 25,000-pound payload. Top speed is 650 miles per hour. The B-52 can carry four multimegaton bombs as well as additional missiles mounted on underwing pylons. Converted to carry strategic nuclear cruise missiles, it could have 3,418 of these aloft by 1987.

B-52s are viewed as ripe for retirement but deployment as cruise missile carriers could extend their lives. There is a question of whether to fill the gap between their expiration and readiness of the Stealth aircraft with the B-1 bomber.

BAADER-MEINHOF GANG, German terrorist organization. Also known as the Red Army Faction, it flourished in the 1970s in protest against an alleged fascist trend in Germany. Its young, well-educated members included Andreas Baader, imprisoned for life in 1977, and Ulrike Meinhof, who committed suicide in prison in 1976. Its acts were well organized, notably including the kidnapping and murder in 1977 of Hanns Martin Schleyer, a leading businessman. Despite the capture of many members, the group remained active into the 1980s.

BAAL, Semitic word meaning "lord" or "owner," name of an ancient Near East fertility deity. Canaanite tablets dating from c2500 BC represent him combating Mot, god of drought and sterility. There were many local variants: in Babylonia, Baal was known as Bel, and in Phoenicia, as Melkart.

BAATH, socialist party in Syria and Iraq dedicated to pan-Arab nationalism and social reform. The 1963 coup in Iraq was engineered by Baath supporters. In both countries its appeal to the educated officer class has kept it close to power.

BABBITT, Irving (1865–1933), US scholar and noted opponent of Romanticism. He led the New Humanism, a movement in literary criticism which stressed classical reason and restraint. His works include *The New Laokoön* (1910) and *On Being Creative* (1932).

BABBITT, Milton (1916–   ), US composer of complex 12-tone and electronic music whose pioneering work on the synthesizer (1959) led to the establishment of the Electronic Music Center of Columbia and Princeton universities.

BABCOCK, Stephen Moulton (1843–1931), US agricultural chemist who devised the **Babcock test** for determining the butterfat content of milk (1890).

BABEL, Isaac Emanuilovich (1894–1941?), Russian short-story writer. The famous collection of stories *Red Cavalry* (1926) is based on his service with the Red Cossacks. His other works are often about Jewish life in Russia before and after the Revolution. Arrested c1938, he died in a Siberian prison camp.

BABEUF, François Emile (1760–1797), French revolutionary agitator, also known as Gracchus. His "Manifesto of Equals" advocated common ownership of property and the right of all to work. He was executed for plotting to overthrow the DIRECTORY.

BABI YAR, a ravine near Kiev, in the Ukraine. On Sept. 29 and 30, 1941, German SS troops executed by gunshot, and buried, more than 33,000 Soviet Jews. The victims had been assembled and brought to the ravine on a promise of "resettlement." In his poem "Babi Yar" (1962) the Russian poet Yevgeni Yevtushenko indicted the Soviet Union for indifference toward the massacre.

BABOONS, social MONKEYS of the African SAVANNAS, distinguished by their long muzzles (particularly in the males) and large size. They move in troops containing as few as 20 individuals or as many as 150 or more. They are highly aggressive (see AGGRESSION) and dangerous omnivores. There is generally a hierarchical structure within each troop, though the nature of this may change with differing circumstances: females are always subordinate to males, though females with infants are treated with great consideration. Appeasement (see APPEASEMENT BEHAVIOR) is usually by "presentation," the adoption even by males of a subservient sexual posture. Their bodies are covered with unusually long hair except for parts of the face, and the buttocks, which may be brightly colored. They belong to the PRIMATE order and the family Cercopithedidae. (See also DRILL; MANDRILL.)

BABY BOOM, steep increase in the US birthrate following WWII. During 1946–64, 76 million people were born, accounting for nearly one-third of the US population in 1980; in the 1970s, the birthrate then dropped. The resulting uneven age distribution has had a multitude of social effects on educational systems, job markets, urban and suburban economies and so on, including almost every aspect of contemporary life.

BABYLON, capital of the ancient kingdom of Babylonia, between the Tigris and Euphrates rivers 55mi S of modern Baghdad. Prosperous under HAMMURABI (reigned c1729–1686 BC) and his successors, it was later attacked by Hittites, Kassites and Assyrians. The reign (605—561 BC) of NEBUCHADNEZZAR II was marked by the building of its great walls, temples, ZIGGURAT and Hanging Gardens. Cyrus of Persia took Babylon in 539 BC. Alexander the Great died at Babylon in 323 BC, his plans to rebuild part of the city coming to nothing. (See also BABYLONIA AND ASSYRIA.)

BABYLONIA AND ASSYRIA, ancient kingdoms of the Near East. Both lay in MESOPOTAMIA, the fertile area between the rivers Tigris and Euphrates. Around 3200 BC the SUMERIANS migrated westward into S Babylonia and established what is generally considered to be the first major civilization, based on CITY STATES such as UR. Clay tablets from SUMER, inscribed in CUNEIFORM script, have preserved king-lists, historical records and even some literature from this period, including the Epic of

GILGAMESH.

Babylonia. In the 24th century BC N Babylonia was conquered by a Semitic people who established the kingdom of AKKAD. Its founder, SARGON the Great (c2360–2305 BC), conquered Sumer, but after two centuries Akkadian culture was shattered in the north by an invasion of Gutians from Iran. In the south a Sumerian renaissance flowered in the creation of such monuments as the ZIGGURATS.

In the first centuries of the 2nd millennium BC invading Semitic AMORITES established Babylon as the center of power in Mesopotamia. HAMMURABI (c1728–1686 BC), the sixth king of the Amorite dynasty, drew up a remarkable code of laws, but his S Babylonian Empire did not long survive his death. In about 1531 BC Babylon was sacked by a HITTITE army, leaving Babylonia wide open to an invasion of KASSITES, who ruled there until about 1150 BC. Despite flourishing trade and a strong alliance with Egypt, the Kassites were weakened by a series of internal conflicts and sporadic war with neighboring nations.

Assyria. The Assyrians took their name from Ashur, their first capital, on the banks of the Tigris. Conquered by Sargon of Akkad, they later came under Sumerian rule, and around 1475 BC the Hurrian king of MITANNI made Assyria a vassal state. Assyria only became a great military power after the decline of the Hurrian kingdom. King Adadnirari I (1308–1276 BC) captured Carchemish, defeated the Hittites and the Kassites, and reached the Euphrates. Under King TIGLATH-PILESER I (1116–1078 BC) this Middle Assyrian Empire spread across Syria and Phoenicia into Anatolia and overwhelmed Babylon.

After a period of decline, Assyria rose to new power under such warrior kings as Shalmaneser III (859–825 BC), Tiglath-Pileser III (745–727 BC) and Sargon II (722–705 BC). In addition to Babylonia, Syria, Israel, Carchemish and Tyre, even Egypt became subject to Assyrian rule. Sargon's son SENNACHERIB (705–681 BC) made his capital, NINEVEH, into one of the most magnificent cities of its time. It is to ASHURBANIPAL (c669–630 BC) that we owe much of our knowledge of the literature of ancient Mesopotamia: some 25,000 tablets from his library are now in the British Museum, London. The kingdom collapsed after his death, in the face of an alliance of CHALDEA with the SCYTHIANS and MEDES.

Neo-Babylonian Empire. Under the Chaldean King NABOPOLASSAR (626–605 BC) Babylonia recovered its independence. The new empire was consolidated by his son NEBUCHADNEZZAR II (605–562 BC), who continued his father's war with Egypt and put down revolts in Tyre and Judah, destroying Jerusalem in 586 BC. He also built the famous HANGING GARDENS OF BABYLON. The internal power struggle following his death was settled by the accession of the usurper Nabonidus to the throne in 555 BC. Nabonidus' son Belshazzar held power in Babylon when CYRUS THE GREAT, king of the Medes and Persians, captured the city in 539 BC. Babylonia then became a province of the Persian Empire.

BABYLONIAN CAPTIVITY, exile of the Jews to Babylon after the conquest of Jerusalem by NEBUCHADNEZZAR II in 597 BC and 586 BC. In 538 BC CYRUS THE GREAT, who had taken Babylon, allowed them to return to Judea. The term is also used in European history for the period from 1309 to 1377 when, under French domination, the popes resided at Avignon in S France. Pope Gregory XI returned to Rome in 1377, but after his death the papacy was split by the GREAT SCHISM.

BACALL, Lauren (1924–   ), US actress who achieved stardom in her first film, *To Have and Have Not* (1944), opposite Humphrey BOGART, whom she married. Other films include *The Big Sleep* (1946), *Key Largo* (1948) and *Harper* (1966). She also had success in such stage musicals as *Applause* (1969) and *Woman of the Year* (1981).

BACCARAT, card game, probably of French origin, played in casinos. Players bet against the bank, and the winner is the one who, in a two-card deal and optional one-card draw, gains a point total whose last digit is nearest to nine. Picture cards count as nothing.

BACCHUS, Roman god of wine and fertility, counterpart of the Greek DIONYSUS. The *bacchanalia* held in his honor became increasingly licentious, and the Senate banned them in 186 BC.

BACH, name of a family of musicians originating in Thuringia, Germany. **Johann Sebastian Bach** (1685–1750) was one of the greatest composers of all time. His music is a culmination and enrichment of the polyphonic tradition of BAROQUE music, but also reflects the harmonic innovations which were supplanting polyphony. Bach held posts at the courts of the Duke of Weimar and Prince Leopold of Köthen, and was musical director of St. Thomas' School, Leipzig.

Bach first excelled as an organist, and his works include many organ compositions. Other keyboard works include *The*

Well-Tempered Clavier and the *Goldberg Variations*. Among his instrumental masterpieces are the works for solo violin and cello and the six *Brandenburg Concertos*. The bulk of Bach's work is religious in inspiration, as seen particularly in his choral works. In addition to more than 200 cantatas, these include the famous *St. Matthew Passion*, *St. John Passion*, *B Minor Mass* and *Christmas Oratorio*.

Of Bach's 20 children, some became composers in their own right. **Wilhelm Friedemann Bach** (1710–1784) was organist at Dresden and Halle, and left some undistinguished compositions. **Carl Philipp Emanuel Bach** (1714–1788) was an outstanding composer and keyboard musician, whose development of symphonic, concerto and sonata forms influenced Haydn, Mozart and Beethoven. His *Essay on the True Art of Playing Keyboard Instruments* remains an essential manual of 18th-century techniques. He was court musician to Frederick the Great and musical director at Hamburg. **Johann Christoph Friedrich Bach** (1732–1794) was chamber musician and *Konzertmeister* to Count Wilhelm of Bückeburg and a prolific composer. **Johann Christian Bach** (1735–1782) wrote numerous graceful orchestral and chamber works and several operas. He was particularly successful in England, where he spent the last 20 years of his life.

BACHARACH, Burt (1929–   ), US composer who wrote many popular songs during the 1960s and 1970s, including "What the World Needs Now," "The Look of Love," "Raindrops Keep Falling on My Head," and "I'll Never Fall in Love Again."

BACKGAMMON, a board game for two players. Each is equipped with 15 counters, which he must move from position to position and bear off the board, his possible moves being controlled to a degree by the throw of a pair of dice. The player's ability to block an opponent's moves adds strategic complexity to the game. Invented in ancient India and known in ancient Babylonia, Greece and Rome, backgammon is often described as a game that is easy to learn but difficult to play.

BACON, Francis (1909–   ), British painter. A self-taught artist, he developed a unique style which expresses the isolation and horror of the human condition, concentrating on distorted figures which manage to convey both panic and menace.

BACON, Francis; Lord Verulam, Viscount St. Albans (1561–1626), English philosopher and statesman who rose to become Lord Chancellor (1618–21) to JAMES I but is chiefly remembered for the stimulus he gave to scientific research in England. Although his name is indelibly associated with the method of induction and the rejection of A PRIORI reasoning in science, the painstaking collection of miscellaneous facts without any recourse to prior theory which he advocated in the *Novum Organum* (1620) has never been adopted as a practical method of research. The application of the Baconian method was, however, an important object in the foundation of the ROYAL SOCIETY OF LONDON some 40 years later.

BACON, Roger (c1214–1292?), English scholar renowned in his own day for his great knowledge of science and remembered today for allegedly prophesying many of the inventions of later centuries: aircraft; telescopes; steam engines; microscopes. In fact he was a wealthy lecturer in the schools of Oxford and Paris with a passion for alchemical and other experiments, whose later life was overshadowed by disputes with the Franciscan Order, of which he had become a member in 1257. His principal writings (in aid of an encyclopedia of knowledge) were the *Opus Majus*, *Opus Minor* and *Opus Tertium*.

BACON'S REBELLION, a rising in colonial America led by planter Nathaniel Bacon (1647–1676) against the governor of Va., Sir William BERKELEY. When Berkeley failed to defend the frontier against Indians, Bacon claimed the right of frontiersmen to form their own militia and led unauthorized forces against the Indians in 1676. Proclaimed traitor, he marched on Jamestown and briefly controlled the colony, instituting legal reforms. The subsequent civil war against forces raised by Berkeley ended shortly after Bacon's death.

BACTERIA, unicellular microorganisms between 0.3 and 2 μm in diameter. They differ from plant and animal cells in that their nucleus is not a distinct organelle surrounded by a membrane: they are usually placed in a separate kingdom, the Protista.

The majority of bacteria are saprophytic: they exist independently of living hosts and are involved in processes of decomposition of dead animal and plant material. As such they are essential to the natural economy of living things.

Some bacteria are parasitic, and their survival depends on their presence in or on other living cells. They may be commensals which coexist harmlessly with host cells, or pathogens, which damage the host organism by producing toxins, which may cause tissue damage (see BACTERIAL DISEASES). This distinction is not absolute: *Escherichia coli* is a commensal in the human intestine, but may cause infection in the urinary tract.

Bacteria are like plant cells in that they are surrounded by a rigid cell wall. Most species are incapable of movement, but certain types can swim using hairlike flagella (see FLAGELLATES). Bacteria vary in their food requirements: AUTOTROPHS can obtain energy by oxidizing substances which they have built up from simple inorganic matter; heterotrophs need organic substances for nutrition. Aerobic (see AEROBE) bacteria need oxygen to survive, whereas anaerobic (see ANAEROBE) species do not. Included in the latter group are the putrefactive bacteria, which aid decomposition. Bacteria generally reproduce asexually by binary FISSION, but some species reproduce sexually. Some can survive adverse conditions by forming highly resistant spores.

Bacteria are important to man in many ways. Commensal bacteria in the human intestine aid digestion of food; industrially they are used in the manufacture of, for example, acetone, citric acid and butyl alcohol and in many dairy products. Some bacteria, especially the ACTINOMYCETES, produce ANTIBIOTICS, used in destroying pathogenic bacteria.

Classification. There is no standard way of classifying bacteria. The higher bacteria are filamentous and the cells may be interdependent—they include the family ACTINOMYCETES. The lower bacteria are subdivided according to shape: COCCI (round), BACILLI (cylindrical), VIBRIOS (curved), and SPIRILLA (spiral). Cocci live singly, in pairs (DIPLOCOCCI), in clusters (STAPHYLOCOCCI) or in chains (STREPTOCOCCI)—as a group they are of great medical importance. SPIROCHETES form a separate group from the above: although spiral they are able to move. Bacteria are also classified medically in terms of their response to GRAM'S STAIN: those absorbing it are termed Gram-positive, those not, Gram-negative. (See also BACTERIOLOGY; MICROBIOLOGY.)

BACTERIAL DISEASES, diseases caused by BACTERIA or their products. Many bacteria have no effect and some are beneficial, while only a small number lead to disease. This may be a result of bacterial growth, the INFLAMMATION in response to it or of TOXINS (e.g., TETANUS, BOTULISM and CHOLERA). Bacteria may be contracted from the environment, other animals or humans, or from other parts of a single individual.

Infection of SKIN and soft tissues with STAPHYLOCOCCUS or STREPTOCOCCUS leads to BOILS, CARBUNCLES, IMPETIGO, CELLULITIS, SCARLET FEVER and ERYSIPELAS. ABSCESS represents the localization of bacteria, while SEPTICEMIA is infection circulating in the BLOOD. Sometimes a specific bacteria causes a specific disease (e.g., ANTHRAX, DIPHTHERIA, TYPHOID FEVER), but any bacteria in some organs cause a similar disease: in LUNGS, PNEUMONIA occurs; in urinary tract, CYSTITIS or pyelonephritis, and in the BRAIN coverings, MENINGITIS. Many VENEREAL DISEASES are due to bacteria. In some diseases (e.g., TUBERCULOSIS, LEPROSY, RHEUMATIC FEVER), many manifestations are due to hypersensitivity (see IMMUNITY) to the bacteria. While ANTIBIOTICS have greatly reduced death and ill-health from bacteria, and VACCINATION against specific diseases (e.g., WHOOPING COUGH) has limited the number of cases, bacteria remain an important factor in disease.

BACTERIOLOGICAL WARFARE. See CHEMICAL AND BIOLOGICAL WARFARE.

BACTERIOLOGY, the science that deals with BACTERIA, their characteristics and their activities as related to medicine, industry and agriculture. Bacteria were discovered in 1676 by Anton von LEEUWENHOEK. Modern techniques of study originate from about 1870 with the use of stains and the discovery of culture methods using plates of nutrient AGAR media. Much pioneering work was done by Louis PASTEUR and Robert KOCH. (See also BACTERIAL DISEASES; NITROGEN FIXATION; SPONTANEOUS GENERATION.)

BACTERIOPHAGE, or phage, a VIRUS which attacks BACTERIA. They have a thin PROTEIN coat surrounding a central core of DNA (or occasionally RNA), and a small protein tail. The phage attaches itself to the bacterium and injects the NUCLEIC ACID into the cell. This genetic material (see GENETICS) alters the metabolism of the bacterium, and several hundred phages develop inside it: eventually the cell bursts, releasing the new, mature phages. Study of phages has revealed much about PROTEIN SYNTHESIS and nucleic acids.

BACTRIA, ancient country of central Asia between the Amu Darya R and the Hindu Kush Mts. The area is now part of Afghanistan and the Tadzhik and Uzbek soviet socialist republics. From the mid-6th century BC it was successively ruled by the Persian Empire, ALEXANDER THE GREAT and the SELEUCIDS. Bactria played an important part in the dissemination of Hellenistic culture through central Asia.

BADAJOZ, city in SW Spain near the Portuguese border. Formerly the capital of a Moorish kingdom, it is now the capital of Badajoz province and a center for food processing and transit trade with Portugal. Pop 101,710.

BADEN-POWELL, Robert, 1st Baron Baden-Powell of Gilwell (1857–1941), British army officer, founder in 1907 of the BOY SCOUTS and in 1910, with his sister Agnes Baden-Powell, of the Girl Guides. (See also GIRL SCOUTS and GIRL GUIDES.)

BADEN-WÜRTTEMBERG, state in SW West Germany formed in 1952 from three postwar provinces. It is a tourist area, containing the Black Forest, Lake Constance, Swabian Jura Mts, Neckar R and the university city of Heidelberg. Cereals, fruit and cattle are raised but the economy depends largely on the industrial cities of Mannheim, Karlsruhe and the capital, Stuttgart.

BADGERS, medium-sized omnivorous burrowing MAMMALS of the WEASEL family Mustelidae. There are six genera (seven including the RATEL) distributed throughout Eurasia, North America and parts of Indonesia. They have potent anal scent GLANDS especially effective in the Oriental Stink Badgers *Mydaus* and *Suillotaxus.* Three genera, *Meles, Taxidea* (which includes the American Badger, *T. Taxus*) and *Melogale,* have distinctive black and white facial masks. Badgers are almost always nocturnal.

BADLANDS NATIONAL PARK, some 243,302 acres of badlands in SW S.D. It comprises barren ravines and ridges of multicolored shale; its sandstone layers are famous for fossils. Created as a national monument in 1929, the area was renamed a national park in 1978.

BADOGLIO, Pietro (1871–1956), Italian field marshal and statesman, instrumental in Italy's seizure of Ethiopia (1935) and in MUSSOLINI's overthrow (1943). He became prime minister and surrendered Italy to the Allies on Sept. 3, 1943.

BAECK, Leo (1873–1956), German rabbi, a leader of Reform Judaism. He braved Nazi persecution rather than emigrate and was one of the few to survive the Theresienstadt concentration camp. His major work, *Essence of Judaism* (1905), stresses the ethical importance of Judaism.

BAEDEKER, Karl (1801–1859), German publisher who developed the tourist guidebooks which bear his name. "Baedekers" now cover most European and many non-European countries.

BAEKELAND, Leo Hendrik (1863–1944), Belgian-born chemist who, after emigrating to the US in 1889, devised Velox photographic printing paper (selling the process to EASTMAN in 1899) and went on to discover BAKELITE, the first modern synthetic PLASTIC.

BAER, Max (1909–1969), US prizefighter, world heavyweight champion 1934–35. Baer beat Primo Carnera for the world title. He retired in 1941 having won 65 out of 79 fights.

BAEZ, Joan (1941–   ), US folk singer noted for the purity of her voice and simple, direct style. She sings traditional ballads, and pacifist and protest songs, many of which she composes herself.

BAFFIN BAY, branch of the Atlantic Ocean N of Davis Strait, between Baffin Island and Greenland. The bay, which is frozen for most of the year, reaches a depth of some 1500 fathoms. It was named for the explorer William Baffin.

BAFFIN ISLAND, island between Greenland and Canada, part of Canada's Northwest Territories. It is a rugged, glaciated tract of some 183,810sq mi with an impressive 7000ft high mountain range along its E coast. The largely Eskimo population lives by fishing, fur-trading and whaling. There is also some coal mining. Pop 3,387.

BAGEHOT, Walter (1826–1877), English social scientist, editor and literary critic, a man of great originality and influence. Among his most important works are *The English Constitution* (1867), *Physics and Politics* (1872) and *Lombard Street* (1873). Bagehot, who came from a banking family, edited *The Economist* from 1861 until his death.

BAGHDAD, capital of Iraq, situated on the Tigris R, some 330mi inland from the Persian Gulf. It is Iraq's main communications, trading and industrial center, and manufactures petroleum products and textiles. Founded in 762 AD, it was a center of Muslim culture until 1258 when it was sacked and largely destroyed by the Mongols. Baghdad was ruled by Turkey from 1638, captured by Britain in WWI and finally made capital of the new nation of Iraq in 1921. Pop 2,183,760.

BAGLEY, William Chandler (1874–1946), US educator who was an influential critic of pragmatism and progressive education. A professor at Columbia Teachers College 1917–1940, he wrote *Education and Emergent Man* (1934) and collaborated with Charles Beard on *A History of the American People* (1918).

BAGPIPE, wind instrument in which air is blown into a leather bag and forced out through musical pipes. The melody is played on one or two pipes (the chanters) while one or more drone pipes sound bass tones. The bagpipe originated in Asia, but is best known as Scotland's national instrument.

BAHA'I FAITH, religion founded by the Persian Mirza Husain Ali, known as Baha'u'llah ("glory of god"), in the second half of the 19th century. It developed from the teaching of the prophet Bab (1820–1850) who preached in Persia until Islamic leaders had him executed. Mirza Husain Ali (1817–1892) succeeded him and founded Baha'i, proclaiming himself a manifestation of God. The Baha'i faith is based on belief in human brotherhood and promotes peace and racial justice. It has a world-wide following.

Official name: Commonwealth of the Bahamas
Capital: Nassau
Area: 5,382sq mi
Population: 240,000
Language: English
Religions: Protestant, Roman Catholic
Monetary units: 1 Bahamian dollar = 100 cents

BAHAMAS, a nation of some 700 subtropical islands and more than 2,000 islets or *cays* extending about 760mi from the SE coast of Fla. to the N coast of Haiti. The most important island is New Providence, where the capital, Nassau, is situated. Among the largest islands in the chain are Andros, Great Abaco, Grand Bahama and Inagua.

About 85% of the population is Negro. Most people live in Nassau or elsewhere on New Providence. The economy is based on tourism and fishing and on the export of wood products, cement, salt and crayfish.

Columbus probably made his first New World landfall on Watling Island (San Salvador). English settlement began in the 1640s, and British rule was almost unbroken until internal self-government in 1964. Full independence came in 1973.

BAHRAIN, independent Arab emirate, an archipelago, consisting of Bahrain Island and a number of smaller islands, in the

Official name: State of Bahrain
Capital: Manama
Area: 258.5sq mi
Population: 281,750
Languages: Arabic, English
Religions: Muslim
Monetary unit(s): 1 Bahrain dinar = 1000 fils

Persian Gulf between the Saudi Arabian coast and the Qatar peninsula. The country has a desert climate and agriculture is limited. The economy is based on oil drilling and refining, pearl fishing being now relatively unimportant. The main population centers are Manama and Muharraq. A trading center in ancient times, Bahrain has been ruled as an emirate since 1783. Bahrain was a British protectorate 1861–1971.

BAILEY, Mildred (real name Mildred Rinker; 1907–1951), US jazz singer. She joined Paul Whiteman's band in 1929, becoming one of the first female singers to appear regularly with a leading band.

BAILEY, Pearl (1918–   ), US jazz singer and actress. She sang with Count BASIE and Cootie Williams and acted in stage and motion-picture musicals, including *Porgy and Bess* and *Hello Dolly.*

BAILY'S BEADS, named for Francis Baily (1774–1844), the apparent fragmentation of the thin crescent of the sun just before totality in a solar ECLIPSE, caused by sunlight shining through mountains at the edge of the lunar disk.

BAIRD, Bil (1904–   ) and **Cora** (1912–1967), US puppeteers who were instrumental in the revival of puppet theater in the US. They created more than 2,000 puppets, traveled the world for the US State Department and set up a puppet theater in New York. Their creations frequently appeared in films and on TV.

BAJA CALIFORNIA (Lower California), peninsula in NW Mexico W of the Gulf of California. A dry mountainous area, it extends for 760mi and is 25–150mi wide. To the N the state of Baja California forms the boundary with the US, while in the S is the territory of Baja California Sur. The main border cities, Mexicali and Tijuana, benefit from nearby US markets, but the region is generally undeveloped with agriculture limited by poor water supply. The peninsula is of great archaeological interest, settlement there probably dating back to around 21000 BC. The Spanish landed here in 1533.

BAKER, Howard Henry, Jr. (1925–   ), US political leader. A lawyer, he was the first Republican to be elected to the US Senate from Tennessee by popular vote. He was senior Republican on the Senate WATERGATE committee. He was elected minority leader of the Senate (1977), a position once held by his father-in-law, Sen. Dirksen, and became majority leader in 1981.

BAKER, Josephine (1906–1975), US-born, naturalized-French singer and dancer of international fame. Film and stage artist, philanthropist and social campaigner, Miss Baker, a black woman, won a special place in the hearts of the French people.

BAKER, Ray Stannard (1870–1946), US journalist and author, awarded a Pulitzer prize for his *Woodrow Wilson—Life and Letters* (1927–39). At the request of President Wilson, Baker led the American Press Bureau at the Paris Peace Conference (1919). He also wrote homely philosophical essays under the pseudonym David Grayson.

BAKER, Russell (1925–   ), US journalist noted since 1962 for his satirical "Observer" column in *The New York Times*. His books include *An American in Washington* (1961) and *Poor Russell's Almanac* (1972).

BAKKE CASE, a suit brought by Allan Bakke in 1974 against the University of California claiming that as a result of the institution's affirmative-action program he had been wrongfully denied admission to medical school solely because he was white. On June 28, 1978, the US Supreme Court ruled five to four in Bakke's favor, concluding that the use of strict racial quotas in determining university admissions is unconstitutional.

BAKST, Lèon Nikolaevich (Lev Samuilovich Rosenberg; 1866–1924), Russian painter and theater designer. He designed sets and costumes for DIAGHILEV's ballets.

BAKU, capital of the Azerbaijan SSR, USSR, on the Caspian Sea's west coast. It is an important port and one of Russia's major oil-refining centers. There are also electrical, shipbuilding, textile and other industries. Pop 1,550,000.

BAKUNIN, Mikhail Alexandrovich (1814–1876), Russian revolutionary, a founder of political ANARCHISM. He was involved in uprisings in Paris (1848) and Dresden (1849). Exiled to Siberia (1857), he escaped to England (1861). Bakunin founded anarchist groups in W Europe and joined the First INTERNATIONAL, but clashed bitterly with MARX and was expelled from the movement with his followers.

BALAKIREV, Mili Alekseyevich (1837–1910), Russian nationalist composer, leader of "The Five." His works include two symphonies; the symphonic poem *Tamara* (1867–82); piano pieces, notably a sonata and *Islamey* (1869); and many songs.

BALAKLAVA, seaport village in the Crimean region, SW USSR, and site of a CRIMEAN WAR battle (Oct. 25, 1854). Commemorated by Tennyson's *The Charge of the Light Brigade* (1854).

BALALAIKA, plucked, usually three-stringed instrument of ancient Slavic origin used in Russian and E European folk music. It has a triangular body and long fretted neck. Its six sizes may be combined in ensemble playing.

BALANCE OF PAYMENTS, the balance between what a country pays out abroad and what it receives. Factors involved are trade, invisible earnings (as from insurance and banking) and the movement of capital between countries. A country receiving more than it pays out has a balance of payment surplus; a country paying out more than it receives has a balance of payment deficit: A persistent deficit may call for DEVALUATION.

BALANCE OF POWER, situation in which a nation or group of nations match the power of another nation or group of nations. After WWII the concept became global with the confrontation of two superpowers, the US and USSR, and their supporters. But this pattern has been affected by national changes in economic or military power, for instance in China.

BALANCHINE, George (real name: Georgy Melitonovich Balanchivadze; 1904–   ), Russian-born choreographer, founder of an American ballet style. He worked for DIAGHILEV in France and in 1948, with Lincoln KIRSTEIN, established the New York City Ballet, for which he created many brilliant ballets.

BALBO, Italo (1896–1940), Italian aviator, Fascist leader and first air minister (1929–33), who built up Italian air power. Distrusted by Mussolini, he was made governor of Libya, dying there when Italian troops shot down his plane, allegedly in error.

BALBOA, Vasco Nùnez de (c1475–1519),

Spanish conquistador who discovered the Pacific Ocean. In 1510 he cofounded and became leader of the first lasting European settlement on the American mainland, Antigua in Darièn (Panama). Encouraged by Indian tales of a wealthy kingdom on "the other sea," in 1513 Balboa led an expedition across the isthmus, saw the Pacific, and claimed it and all its coasts for Spain. Pedrarias DÁVILA succeeded Balboa in Darièn and jealously had him executed on a false charge of treason.

BALD EAGLE, *Haliaetus leucocephalus,* only North American native EAGLE, the national bird of the US since 1782. About 1m (3.2ft) long with a wingspan around 2m (6.6ft), it is black, with white feathers on neck, tail and head giving it a bald appearance. It preys on fish and is protected in all states. Family: Accipitridae.

BALDER (or Baldur), Norse god of light, called "the beautiful," son of FRIGG and ODIN. Frigg made all earthly things promise not to harm Balder but omitted mistletoe. LOKI, the jealous fire god, tricked the blind god Hödr into throwing a stick of mistletoe at Balder and so killed him.

BALDNESS, or **alopecia,** loss of hair, usually from the scalp, due to disease of hair FOLLICLES. **Male-pattern baldness** is an inherited tendency, often starting in the twenties. **Alopecia areata** is a disease of unknown cause producing patchy baldness, though it may be total. Prolonged FEVER, LUPUS erythematosus and RINGWORM may lead to temporary baldness, as may certain drugs and poisons.

BALDUNG GRIEN, Hans (c1484–1545), German painter and engraver. He was at first influenced by DÜRER. His masterpiece is the Freiburg cathedral altarpiece containing the *Coronation of the Virgin*(1516). His morbid allegorical paintings include a dramatic "Death and the Maiden" series.

BALDWIN, James (1924–   ), black U.S. novelist, essayist and playwright, dealing with racial themes. *Go Tell It On The Mountain* (1953) reflects his Harlem adolescence; *Another Country* (1962) deals with sexual and racial identity. His nonfiction includes *The Fire, Next Time* (1963), on racial oppression.

BALDWIN, Robert (1804–1858), Canadian statesman, leader, with Louis LAFONTAINE, of the first responsible Canadian administration: the "Great Ministry" (1848–51). He later worked for improved relations between English and French Canadians.

BALDWIN, Stanley, Earl Baldwin of Bewdley (1867—1947) British Conserva-

tive statesman, prime minister 1923–24, 1924–29, 1935–37. He maintained stable government, but provoked labor hostility (before and after the General Strike of 1926) and failed to curb unemployment or to rearm against Nazi Germany. He handled the crisis of EDWARD VIII'S abdication. He became Earl Baldwin of Bewdley on his retirement.

BALEARIC ISLANDS, group of Mediterranean islands off E Spain, under Spanish rule since 1349. The largest are Majorca, Minorca and Ibiza. Products include grapes, olives and citrus fruit. Tourism is important.

BALENCIAGA, Cristóbal (1895–1972), Spanish fashion designer. A major fashion influence from the 1930s to the 1960s, his tunic, chemise "sack" dress, and shift became accepted internationally. He was known as a "designer's designer," and numbered among his students GIVENCHY and COURRÉGES.

BALEWA, Sir Abubakar Tafawa (1912–1966), first prime minister of Nigeria (1957–66), murdered in a military coup. He founded and led a major political party, the Northern People's Congress.

BALFOUR, Arthur James Balfour, 1st Earl of (1848–1930), English statesman best known for the BALFOUR DECLARATION. He was an influential Conservative member of parliament 1874–1911; prime minister 1902–05; and foreign secretary 1916–19.

BALFOUR DECLARATION, statement of British policy issued in 1917 by Foreign Secretary Arthur BALFOUR. It guaranteed a Jewish national home in Palestine without prejudice to the rights of non-Jews there, but did not mention a separate Jewish state. In 1922 the League of Nations approved a British mandate in Palestine based on the Balfour Declaration. (See also PALESTINE; WEIZMANN, CHAIM; ZIONISM.)

BALI, volcanic island (2,171sq mi) of the Lesser Sunda group, Indonesia, E of Java. Freed from Japanese occupation after WWII, it became an Indonesian province in 1950. Rice is the main crop. The largely Hindu Balinese are famous for dancing, GAMELAN music and decorative arts.

BALKAN PENINSULA, SE Europe S of the Danube and Sava rivers and abutting the Adriatic, Ionian, Mediterranean, Aegean and Black seas. It comprises Bulgaria, Albania, Greece, European Turkey and most of Yugoslavia. The region is mountainous and limited in natural resources. Its SLAVS, Turks and Greeks live mainly in small communities, raising sheep, goats, vines and cereals. Little industry exists outside big cities like Belgrade,

Athens and Istanbul.

The area was influenced by Greece; ruled by Rome (c148 BC-mid-5th century AD); then partly controlled by the Byzantine Empire. Invading Slavs and others founded ancient Bulgaria and Serbia, and crusaders seized the S early in the 13th century. But by 1500 the Ottoman Turks held almost all the Balkans. New nations emerged through 19th-century nationalist movements, which also sparked off the BALKAN WARS and WORLD WAR I. After WWII Albania, Bulgaria and Yugoslavia became communist; Turkey and Greece joined NATO.

BALKAN WARS, two wars in which the Ottoman Empire lost almost all its European territory. In the First Balkan War (1912–13) Serbia, Bulgaria, Greece and Montenegro conquered all Turkey's European possessions except Constantinople. But Bulgaria, Serbia and Greece disputed control in Macedonia. In the Second Balkan War (1913) Bulgaria attacked Serbia, but was itself attacked by Romania, Greece and Turkey. In the ensuing Treaty of Bucharest (Aug. 1913) Bulgaria lost territory to each of her enemies.

BALL, George Wildman (1909–   ) US diplomat who influenced US foreign policy in the 1960s. He was undersecretary of state under Johnson and Kennedy, and for a brief period US ambassador to the UN.

BALL, Lucille (1911–   ), US actress and comedienne. Following a varied screen acting career during the 1930s and 1940s, she began her TV series, *I Love Lucy*, in 1951. Appearing as the wife of her then real-life husband, Desi Arnaz, her instantly recognizable face and genuine comedic talents made the program one of the most popular to have ever appeared on television.

BALLA, Giacomo (1871–1958), Italian painter, a leading exponent of FUTURISM. His works include attempts to show objects in motion and pioneer abstract paintings.

BALLAD, simple verse narrative, often meant to be sung, originally anonymous and orally transmitted. Many ballads comprise rhymed four-line stanzas each followed by a refrain. Traditionally, ballads celebrated folk heroes or related popular romances, and were developed by European minstrels of the Middle Ages. Romantic writers, such as Sir Walter SCOTT, WORDSWORTH and COLERIDGE, adapted the form. In popular music today, the term is used loosely as a synonym for any kind of sentimental song, but the US has produced many ballads of the traditional type, ranging from the anonymous *Frankie and Johnny* to the work of Bob DYLAN and Joan BAEZ.

BALLARAT, city in SE Australia, in S central Victoria. Founded in the 1851 gold rush, it is now a manufacturing center producing iron and steel and processed agricultural products. Pop 39,606.

BALLET, form of theatrical dance that tells a story or expresses a theme, mood or idea. It originated in Renaissance Italian court entertainments introduced into France in 1581 by Catherine de Médicis. Louis XIV in 1661 established the first ballet school, whose ballet master, Pierre Beauchamp, originated the five basic foot positions of ballet.

Early 18th-century ballet was part of opera, and dancers were hampered by heavy costumes; but by the mid-18th century pantomime ballet, in which all meaning was conveyed by movement, had evolved. The French choreographer Jean-Georges Noverre made ballet an independent art uniting plot, music, decor and movement. The 19th-century emphasized lightness and grace: dancing *sur les pontes* (on the tips of the toes) and the short tutu appeared. Russia became the world center with the appointment of Marius PETIPA to the Imperial Ballet in 1862. He inspired the originals of *Swan Lake, The Nutcracker Suite* and *The Sleeping Beauty.*

Early in the 1900s, in Paris, the Russian Ballet of Sergei DIAGHILEV, with NIJINSKY, PAVLOVA, MASSINE and FOKINE, revitalized dance drama. In 1933 Ninette de Valois formed England's first permanent company, now the Royal Ballet, noted for ASHTON's choreography. BALANCHINE established American ballet in the 1930s, his New York City Ballet fusing classical tradition with modern dance as developed by Isadora DUNCAN, Ruth ST. DENIS, Martha GRAHAM and Jerome ROBBINS. (See also CHOREOGRAPHY; DANCE.)

BALLISTIC MISSILE. See MISSILE.

BALLISTICS, the science concerned with the behavior of projectiles, traditionally divided into three parts. **Interior ballistics** is concerned with the progress of the projectile before it is released from the launching device. In the case of a gun this involves determining the propellant charge, barrel design and firing mechanism needed to give the desired muzzle velocity and stabilizing spin to the projectile. **External ballistics** is concerned with the free flight of the projectile. At the beginning of the 17th century GALILEO determined that the trajectory (flight path) of a projectile should be parabolic (see CONIC SECTIONS), as indeed it would be if the effects of air resistance, the rotation and curvature of the earth, the variation of air density and gravity with height, and the rotational

INERTIA of the projectile could be ignored. The shockwaves accompanying projectiles moving faster than the speed of sound (see SUPERSONICS) are also the concern of this branch.

Terminal or **penetration ballistics** deals with the behavior of projectiles on impacting at the end of their trajectory. The velocity-to-mass ratio of the impact particle is an important factor and results are of equal interest to the designers of AMMUNITION and of ARMORPLATE. A relatively recent development in the science is **forensic ballistics**, which now plays an important role in the investigation of gun crimes.

BALLOON, a nonpowered, nonrigid lighter-than-air craft comprising a bulbous envelope containing the lifting medium and a payload-carrying basket or "gondola" suspended below. Balloons may be captive (secured to the ground by a cable, as in the barrage balloons used during WWII to protect key installations and cities from low-level air bombing) or free-flying (blown along and steered at the mercy of the WIND). Lift may be provided either by GAS (usually HYDROGEN or noninflammable HELIUM) or by heating the air in the envelope. A balloon rises or descends through the air until it reaches a level at which it is in EQUILIBRIUM in accordance with ARCHIMEDES' principle. In this situation the total WEIGHT of the balloon and payload is equal to that of the volume of air which it is displacing.

If the pilot of a gas balloon wishes to ascend, he throws ballast (usually sand) over the side, thus reducing the overall DENSITY of the craft; to descend he releases some of the lifting gas through a small valve in the envelope. The ALTITUDE of a hot-air balloon is controlled using the PROPANE burner which heats the air; increased heat causes the craft to rise; turning off the burner gives a period of level flight followed by a slow descent as the trapped air cools.

The MONTGOLFIER brothers' hot-air balloon became the first manned aircraft in 1783, and in the same year the first gas balloon was flown by Jacques CHARLES. In 1785 Jean BLANCHARD piloted a balloon across the English Channel. In due time the powered balloon, or AIRSHIP, was developed, though free balloons have remained popular for sporting, military and scientific purposes. The upper atmosphere is explored using unmanned gas balloons, and RADIOSONDE balloons are in regular meteorological use. In 1931 Auguste PICCARD pioneered high-altitude manned flights. Many modern sporting balloons are built on the hot-air principle.

BALLROOM DANCING. See DANCE.

BALMAIN, Pierre (1914–   ), French fashion designer. Once a colleague of DIOR, he opened his own house in 1946. His elegant fashions attracted an exclusive following including Gertrude Stein.

BALMORAL CASTLE, private residence of the British monarch, near Braemar, in Grampian, Scotland. It was built 1853–56 by Prince ALBERT, who bequeathed it to Queen Victoria.

BALSA, West Indian and South American tree (*Ochroma lagopus*) producing a very light wood twice as buoyant as cork. Balsa is used for rafts, life preservers, small boats, gliders and model airplanes.

BALSAM, term often used for any aromatic substance from trees or shrubs but strictly confined to resins and oleoresins (such as Peru balsam used in perfume or Tolu balsam used in cough medicines) containing benzoic or cinnamic acid. Also, a garden herb (*Impatiens balsamina*) with pale green lanceolate leaves and pink flowers, although some varieties have white, crimson and purple flowers.

BALTIC LANGUAGES, group of INDO-EUROPEAN LANGUAGES, closely related to the Slavonic languages, spoken in the area SE of the Baltic Sea. They include Lithuanian, Lettish and the now extinct Old Prussian.

BALTIC SEA, an arm of the Atlantic Ocean, bounded by Sweden, Finland, the USSR, Poland, Germany and Denmark. It is linked to the North Sea by the SKAGERRAK, KATTEGAT and ØRESUND. Its 163,000sq mi of weakly saline water freeze over in winter. There is a limited fishing industry based on herring, cod and salmon. Baltic trade flourished in the 14th century through the HANSEATIC LEAGUE, but declined in competition with Atlantic ports. Copenhagen, Stockholm, Helsinki, Leningad and Kiev are the main ports. (See also BOTHNIA, GULF OF; FINLAND, GULF OF.)

BALTIMORE, largest city in Md., on the Patapsco R near Chesapeake Bay. It is the seventh-largest city in the US, one of the nation's busiest ports and an important road, rail and air transportation hub. Since WWI it has become a leading manufacturing center with metallurgical, electronic and food-processing industries. Baltimore is the educational center of Md., with Johns Hopkins U. and many other institutions. Established in 1729 and named for Lord Baltimore, the city grew as a grain-exporting port. It suffered economic disruption as a Civil War "border city," and was largely rebuilt after the great fire of 1904. Pop 905,759.

BALTIMORE FOUR. See HARRISBURG SEVEN.

BALTIMORE ORIOLE, *Icterus galbula*, North American songbird of the family Icteridae (not Oriolidae, as are true ORIOLES). About 200mm (8in) long, it has a wingspan of about 300mm (12in). Males are black and bright orange; females and young are olive, yellow and brownish.

BALUCHISTAN, mountainous, largely barren province of Pakistan (capital: Quetta) with cultural ties to Baluchs in adjacent areas of Iran and Afghanistan. The people are largely pastoral nomads and, increasingly, arable farmers, renowned for their handwoven carpets. Seeking greater self-determination, the Baluchs revolted unsuccessfully in Pakistan in 1972.

BALZAC, Honoré de (1799–1850), French novelist noted for his acute social observation and sweeping vision. In the nearly 100 works forming *La Comédie Humaine*, he attempted to portray all levels of contemporary French society, their interdependence and the influence of the environment upon them. The most famous such novels of this series are *Eugénie Grandet* (1833), *Le Père Goriot* (1834) and *La Cousine Bette* (1846). Balzac had a great capacity for hard work, but was also known for his debts and love affairs.

BAMAKO, capital and largest town of Mali, a trade and transportation center on the Niger R. It exports oil products, cement, livestock and nuts. Pop 201,300.

BAMBOO, woody grasses with hollow stems found in Asia, Africa, Australia and the southern US. Some species grow to 36m (120ft). In Asia the young shoots are a major foodstuff, while mature stems are used in building houses and furniture. Amorphous SILICA from stems is used as a catalyst in some chemical processes.

BANANA, edible fruit of a large (9m–30ft) perennial stooling herb that reaches maturity within 15 months from planting. Cultivated clones evolved in SE Asia from two wild species, *Musa acuminata* and *M. balbisiana*, and spread across the Pacific, Africa and the New World. Main areas of commercial cultivation are in tropical and South America and the West Indies, a major part of the crop being exported to the US and Europe; but bananas are of great importance locally in many tropical diets.

BANCROFT, Anne (1931–   ), US actress. She appeared on Broadway in *Two for the Seesaw* (1958) and as Helen KELLER's teacher in *The Miracle Worker* (1959), winning an Academy Award when she recreated the role on film. Other films include *The Graduate* (1967) and *The Turning Point* (1977).

BANCROFT, George (1800–1891), US historian and statesman whose 10-volume *History of the United States* (1834–74) was the first attempt fully to cover US history. As secretary of the navy (1845–46), he helped develop the US Naval Academy, Annapolis. His *History* became a standard work, though it was later criticized for its strong nationalistic bias.

BANCROFT, Hubert Howe (1832–1918), US historian and publisher. The 39-volume history of western North America, the *West American Historical Series*, which he edited and partly wrote, remains a useful source for the history of the West.

BAND, a musical ensemble generally of wind and percussion instruments, though sometimes devoted to a particular type of instrument. Bands accompany military and civil parades and other ceremonies, and play dance music. Famous US bands have included those founded by John Philip SOUSA and Glenn MILLER.

BANDA, Hastings Kamuzu (1906–   ), African nationalist leader, first prime minister (1964–66) and president of Malawi (from 1966). As leader of the Nyasaland nationalists, and head of the Malawi Congress party from 1960, he sought dissolution of the Federation of Rhodesia and Nyasaland. He later had a moderating influence on African affairs.

BANDARANAIKE, Sirimavo Ratwatte Dias (1916–   ), prime minister of Sri Lanka and the world's first woman premier. After the assassination of her husband, Prime Minister Solomon Bandaranaike, in 1959, she led his Sri Lanka Freedom party to victory in 1960, continuing his pro-Buddhist and pro-Sinhalese policies. She lost office in 1965 but was returned in 1970 with a landslide victory for her left-oriented coalition.

BANDELLO, Matteo (1485–1561), Italian writer, diplomat and monk. His 214 stories or *novelle* greatly influenced European literature, and provided the bases of plots used by SHAKESPEARE (*Romeo and Juliet*) and John WEBSTER (*The Duchess of Malfi*).

BANDICOOTS, several genera of the family Peramelidae. They are roughly rabbit-sized MARSUPIALS, probably most closely related to the DASYURES. They have tapering snouts, varying in length from species to species. There are considerable reproductive differences from other marsupials: though GESTATION is for only 12 days, the newborn young are comparatively large; while in the UTERUS, the EMBRYOS are nourished by a complex PLACENTA quite unlike those of other marsupials. Their FOSSIL history is problematic, so that their relationship to other marsupials is not fully understood.

BANDUNG, capital of West Java province, Indonesia, 75mi SE of Jakarta. It is a cultural, educational, tourist, transportation and manufacturing (textiles and machinery) center. It was founded by the Dutch in 1810. Pop 1,202,000.

BANDUNG CONFERENCE, first major conference on world affairs by 29 independent African and Asian nations, held in Bandung, April 1955. It condemned colonialism and urged world peace and economic and cultural cooperation.

BANFF NATIONAL PARK, Canada's first national park, founded 1885. Situated in SW Alberta, it covers 2,564sq mi of spectacular mountain scenery, and is also noted for sulfur springs and rich wildlife.

BANGALORE, capital of Karnataka State, S India. A major industrial, transportation and educational center with a university and research laboratories. Products include electrical equipment, chemicals and textiles. Pop 1,648,000.

BANGKOK, capital of Thailand, on the Chao Phraya R near the Gulf of Siam. It is Thailand's chief port, manufacturing center and university city, with many picturesque Buddhist temples. Also SEATO headquarters and regional headquarters for the World Health Organization and UNESCO. Pop 2,840,000.

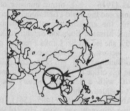

Official name: People's Republic of Bangladesh
Capital: Dacca
Area: 55,598sq mi
Population: 88,677,000
Languages: Bengali, English
Religions: Muslim, Hindu, Buddhist
Monetary unit(s): 1 taka = 100 paisa
BANGLADESH (Bengal Nation), republic in the NE of the Indian subcontinent, on the Bay of Bengal; formerly East PAKISTAN.
Land and People. It is a low-lying land centered on the alluvial Ganges-Brahmaputra Delta. A tropical monsoon climate prevails, and because of the seasonal heavy rains and severe cyclones, most of the country is subject to flooding. Overpopulation accentuates periodic famines and epidemics among the mainly Muslim Bengalis who constitute the great majority of the population.

Economy. Bangladesh produces nearly 90% of the world's jute; tea is the other main cash crop and sugarcane is also grown. Rice and wheat are the major subsistence crops. Natural gas is the only important mineral resource, and manufacturing is largely limited to the processing of raw materials.

History. The region was created as East Pakistan (Pakistan's eastern province) in 1947. The province sought greater independence under Sheikh Mujibur RAHMAN, whose Awami League won a majority in the 1970 Pakistan election. West Pakistan refused large-scale autonomy and troops crushed large-scale opposition in the ensuing civil war (March–Dec. 1971). But guerrilla fighting continued, Bengalis exiled in India proclaimed a Bengali republic, and Indian invasion forces overran the West Pakistani forces. A Bangladesh government was established in Dacca in Dec. 1971, and Mujibur Rahman became prime minister in Jan. 1972. But the war had left the country with severe economic and political problems, and in 1975 Mujibur Rahman established a presidential, one-party regime. In Aug. 1975 he and his family were assassinated in a coup; two military counter-coups and martial law followed in Nov. 1975. Martial law was ended in 1979, when in general elections Ziaur Rahman (Zia) was chosen president. President Zia was assassinated in 1981, and the vice president was sworn in as acting president.

BANJO, stringed musical instrument with a circular skin soundboard and a long fretted neck. Its 4–9 strings are played by plucking. The banjo originated among Negro slaves in North America, and may have derived from W African instruments. It became popular in 19th-century minstrel shows and early jazz bands and for some folk music.

BANK FOR INTERNATIONAL SETTLEMENTS, a European bank founded in 1930 in Switzerland to handle the payments of German war reparations. A major international bank, it is a focal point for the central banks of W Europe—whose presidents sit on its board of governors—and the agent for the European Fund of the European Community.

BANKHEAD, Tallulah Brockman (1903–1968), US actress, famous for her colorful performances in plays such as *The Little Foxes* (1939) and *The Skin of Our Teeth* (1942). Among her films was

Lifeboat (1943).

BANKHEAD, William Brockman (1874–1940), US politician, speaker of the House of Representatives 1936–40. A Democratic Congressman for Ala. from 1917, he was the father of actress Tallulah Bankhead. His brother, **John Hollis Bankhead** (1872–1946), was a Democratic senator from Ala. from 1931.

BANKING, the business dealing with money and credit transactions. It can be traced back beyond 2500 BC, but modern banking originated in medieval Italy (taking its name from *banca*, the money-lender's bench). Banking grew among traders needing to exchange one country's coins for those of another, to buy and sell without handling bulky gold or silver, and to borrow cash to bridge the period between buying goods and selling them. Thus major trading cities such as Venice, Antwerp, Hamburg and London also became great banking centers.

Banking in the US. The first BANK OF THE UNITED STATES (1791–1811) was promoted by Alexander HAMILTON to finance industrial and commercial expansion. But politicians prejudiced against national banks closed the bank and its successor (1816–36). For 30 years, before the Civil War, WILDCAT BANKS incorporated in western border states profited from selling largely worthless notes in east coast cities. The 1863 National Bank Act forced banks to pledge US government bonds with the treasury to back their note issues, but bank insolvencies continued in times of depression.

In 1913 the FEDERAL RESERVE SYSTEM was set up to strengthen the US banking system. Bank failures in 1933 led to a BANK HOLIDAY (after which only solvent banks were allowed to reopen) and to the setting up of the FEDERAL DEPOSIT INSURANCE CORPORATION. Today, some states do not allow banks to maintain branches. There are restrictions, too, on the number and type of subsidiary companies a bank may own.

Banking services. Banks offer four main services: safe storage facilities; interest payments on deposits, which are in effect loans from the customer to the bank; money transfers in the form of checking accounts; and loans for home mortgages, automobile financing, business expansion, etc. In recent years, regulations which narrowly controlled the kinds of loans and the amount of interest banks could offer have been relaxed somewhat. Many banks now provide credit cards to credit-worthy customers, and will advance specified credit amounts to cardholders. Interest-paying checking ac-

counts (NOW, or Negotiable Order of Withdrawal) are available. Certificates of Deposit, which pay high interest rates on specified amounts for a specified time (usually six months or one year) can be bought at most banks. These and other services are intended to attract customer deposits, which form the basis of a bank's ability to maintain its own investments and to loan money at interest. Every bank account is federally insured for the amount of the deposit, up to $100,000.

Banks as creators of money. Banks "create" money by lending sums banked by depositors. For instance, a $5,000 bank deposit may engender a $4,000 bank loan, which raises the money supply from $5,000 to $9,000. (The $1,000 not lent forms "liquid" assets which the bank keeps to cover depositors' claims for immediate repayments.) The money supply deeply affects a nation's economy, for money is the means of measuring the relative value of all commodities. (See also CHECK; CREDIT; ECONOMICS; MINT, UNITED STATES BUREAU OF THE; MONEY.)

BANK OF ENGLAND, central bank of the British government, founded 1694, nationalized 1946. It acts as banker for the government and the country's commercial banks; advises the government on finance; influences the money supply; finances the government deficit; issues banknotes; and administers the foreign exchange reserve.

BANK OF THE UNITED STATES, name of two central banks set up in the early years of the US. In 1791 Alexander HAMILTON created the First Bank of the US, chartered by Congress for 20 years, with a central office in Philadelphia. It held government deposits and was able to extend some control over the issue of paper currency and the extension of credit. However, its constitutionality was questioned, and it was so strongly opposed by agrarian interests and by the state banks that its charter was not renewed.

The nation's chaotic financial system after the War of 1812 led Congress to charter the Second Bank of the US in 1816 for another 20-year period. However, opposition continued, especially in the West, and in 1832 President JACKSON refused to extend the charter. In the "Bank War" which followed, Nicholas BIDDLE, the bank's president, restricted national credit, and Jackson retaliated by withdrawing government deposits from the bank. The bank's charter was allowed to expire in 1836 without renewal. Only with the creation of the FEDERAL RESERVE SYSTEM in 1913 were the first real steps taken towards a central

US banking system.

BANNISTER, Roger Gilbert (1929–   ), British athlete. He was the first man to run a mile in under four minutes, on May 6, 1954, at Oxford. His time was 3 minutes 59.4 seconds.

BANNOCKBURN, battlefield named for a village in Stirlingshire, Scotland. Here, in 1314, Scottish forces under Robert BRUCE routed the numerically superior English army of King EDWARD II assuring the throne of Scotland for Bruce and securing Scottish independence until the 18th century.

BANTING, Sir Frederick Grant (1891–1941), Canadian physiologist who, with C. H. BEST, first isolated the hormone INSULIN from the pancreases of dogs (1922). For this he shared the 1923 Nobel Prize for Physiology or Medicine with J.J.R. MACLEOD who had provided the experimental facilities.

BANTU, outmoded collective term for a group of tribes in central, E and S Africa possessing a common group of languages. The term may also be used in South Africa to denote black Africans as distinct from Afrikaners.

BANTUSTANS. See HOMELANDS.

BAO DAI (1913–   ), Vietnamese emperor during the French colonial period. He was the last emperor of ANNAM (1932–45), until overthrown by the Viet Minh. He was later made head of state of a unified Vietnam (1949–55) created by the French in a final bid to retain Indochina, but was forced into exile.

BAPTISM, Christian sacrament which constitutes an initiation into the Church. The ceremony involves the application of water; by sprinkling, pouring or immersion according to the denomination. Baptism has its origins in pagan and Jewish ceremony, and was commanded by Christ (Matthew 28:19).(See also JOHN THE BAPTIST.)

BAPTISTS, members of the many independent branches of the Baptist Church, one of the most diverse of Protestant denominations. There are more than 31,000,000 Baptists in the world, most of whom live in America. In general, Baptist churches are lay churches having no elaborate priesthood, and are known for their evangelical and revivalist traditions. The strongest unifying principle among all Baptist churches is the method of baptism by total immersion in water when a person who has reached the age of reason professes faith in Christ.

The history of the Baptists can be traced to religious dissension in Europe in the early 17th century, particularly in the Puritan movement. Baptist churches were established in the English colonies after the Restoration (1660), but it was only with America's 18th-century religious revival, the GREAT AWAKENING, that the Baptist tradition spread, notably in the Midwest and the South, where it is still most influential. The Baptists have always had a great interest in higher education and have founded many colleges and universities throughout the US.

BARA, Theda (1890–1955), US film star, born Theodosia Goodman. The word "vamp" (short for vampire) was coined to describe the evil but enticing women she portrayed between 1915 and 1920.

BARABBAS, a murderer released by PILATE in place of Jesus. According to Luke 23:18–25, Pilate asked the mob to choose between the two. The mob chose Barabbas, and Pilate "washed his hands" of the matter.

BARAKA, Imamu Amiri, known formerly as LeRoi Jones, (1934–   ), black US author whose plays, especially *Dutchman* (1964), express the revulsion of a black man at white society. Many of his poems and essays also express outrage at social inequalities.

Official Name: Barbados
Capital: Bridgetown
Area: 166sq mi
Population: 253,100
Languages: English
Religions: Anglican, Methodist, Moravian, Roman Catholic
Monetary unit(s): 1 Barbados dollar = 100 cents

BARBADOS, a densely populated small island in the Caribbean; a parliamentary state, part of the British Commonwealth.
Land. About 21mi long and 14 mi wide, Barbados lies 250mi NE of Venezuela. It is surrounded by coral reefs. The climate is pleasant, with a hot and rainy season from June to December.
People and Economy. The majority of the people are of African descent; about 5% are white. Known as "Little England," Barbados is the most British of the West Indies islands. Literacy rate is 97%. The

fertile land, intensely cultivated, produces sugarcane. Tourism is the second most important source of income, and there is some light industry (food processing, plastic products, electrical components) for local consumption.

History. Barbados was occupied by the British in 1627 and remained a colony for over 300 years. Internal autonomy was attained in 1961 and full independence in 1966. In the late 1970s, reserves of petroleum and natural gas were discovered.

BARBAROSSA, Frederick. See FREDERICK I (Holy Roman Emperor).

BARBARY APE, small tailless MACAQUES of Algeria, Morocco and Gibraltar; the genus *Macaca sylvana* of the Cercopithecidae family. Legend has it that the British will lose the Rock of Gibraltar should its small colony of Barbary apes depart.

BARBARY STATES, countries along the Mediterranean coast of N Africa, the region of present-day ALGERIA, TUNISIA, LIBYA and MOROCCO. Named for the Berber tribes who lived there, the Barbary states were known from the 16th to the 19th centuries as centers of piracy. The area was ruled earlier by Carthage, Rome and Byzantium, then conquered by the Arabs in the 8th century. After centuries of relative autonomy, the states were taken over largely by France, in the 19th century.

BARBARY WARS, two wars waged by the US against the BARBARY STATES of N Africa. By the late 18th century brigandage by the Barbary states had become a highly organized and lucrative trade. The first Barbary War, or Tripolitan War, broke out in May 1801. For 15 years the US had been forced to pay tribute to protect its shipping. The war was sparked by new, exorbitant demands by the pasha of Tripoli. The US blockaded Tripoli, and subjected it to naval bombardment. But the war was not won until 1805, when Capt. William Eaton marched his forces 500mi across the desert from Alexandria to take Derna and threaten Tripoli itself. The second Barbary War was fought in 1815 with Algiers. Commodore Stephen DECATUR was dispatched to suppress an upsurge of piracy. Forcing his way into the harbor of Algiers, he compelled the dey of Algiers to sign a treaty ending piracy and freeing all US captives. Decatur went on to exact similar treaties from Tunis and Tripoli.

BARBER, Samuel (1910–1981), US composer. His works include *Adagio for Strings* (1936); the ballet *Medea* (1946); *Knoxville: Summer of 1915* (1947), for soprano and orchestra; and the operas *Vanessa* (1958) and *Antony and Cleopatra*

(1966). He was awarded Pulitzer prizes in 1958 and 1963.

BARBER OF SEVILLE, The, lively and melodious comic opera by Gioacchino ROSSINI, first produced in Rome in 1816. During the long stage history of the opera many sopranos have introduced into the lesson scene songs of their own choice, including "Home, Sweet Home."

BARBIROLLI, Sir John (1899–1970), English conductor, famous for his interpretations of SIBELIUS and other late classics. After conducting the New York Philharmonic Orchestra (1937–42), he began a lifelong association with the Hallé Orchestra in Manchester, and conducted the Houston Symphony Orchestra (1961–67).

BARBITURATES, a class of drugs acting on the central NERVOUS SYSTEM which may be SEDATIVES, anesthetics or anticonvulsants. They depress nerve cell activity, the degree of depression and thus clinical effect varying in different members of the class. Although widely used in the past for insomnia, their use is now discouraged in view of high rates of addiction and their danger in over-dosage; safer alternatives are now available. Short-acting barbiturates are useful in ANESTHESIA; phenobarbitone is used in treatment of CONVULSIONS, often in combination with other drugs.

BARBIZON SCHOOL, group of French painters of natural and rural subjects, active 1830–70, who frequented the village of Barbizon, near Paris. It included Théodore ROUSSEAU, Diaz de la Peña, COROT, MILLET, Dupré, Troyon, Daubigny and Jacque.

BARBUSSE, Henri (1873–1935), French author best known for his bitter WWI novel, *Le Feu* (*Under Fire*, 1916). *Clarté* (*Light*, 1919), his next novel, expressed Barbusse's ideas for the achievement of world peace. It inspired a short-lived international movement.

BARCAROLE, musical composition in the style of the songs of Venetian *barcaiuoli* or gondoliers. Typified by a gently rocking rhythm in $\frac{6}{8}$ or $\frac{12}{8}$ time, barcaroles were written by many composers, including Chopin, Mendelssohn and Offenbach.

BARCELONA, Spain's second-largest city and chief port, and its greatest industrial and commercial center. Located in NE Spain on the Mediterranean, it is the historic capital of Catalonia. Barcelona was reputedly founded by Hamilcar Barca c230 BC. The countship of Barcelona was united with Aragon in 1137, and during the Middle Ages Barcelona became one of the Mediterranean's great maritime and commercial cities. The center of Catalan nationalism in modern times, it was the stronghold of left-wing politics and Republican allegiance in the Spanish Civil War. Pop 1,745,000.

BAR COCHBA, Simon (d. 135 AD), leader of the last Jewish revolt against Roman rule in Palestine (132–35 AD), during the reign of Hadrian. Hailed as the Messiah by Rabbi AKIBA, he was at first successful and captured Jerusalem, but the revolt was finally put down and Bar Cochba slain.

BARD, Celtic poet-musician of ancient and medieval times, most notably in Ireland and Wales. The bards were highly esteemed figures, and bardic poetry reached a high level of sophistication. In Wales the tradition has been revived in the EISTEDDFODS.

BARDEEN, John (1908–   ), US physicist who shared the 1956 Nobel Prize for Physics with SHOCKLEY and BRATTAIN for their development of the TRANSISTOR. In 1972 he became the first person to win the physics prize a second time, sharing the award with COOPER and SCHRIEFFER for their development of a comprehensive theory of SUPERCONDUCTIVITY.

BARDOT, Brigitte (1934–   ), French film actress who first rose to fame in *And God Created Woman* (1956), and became a leading sex-symbol of the 1950s and 1960s.

BAREA, Arturo (1897–1957), Spanish novelist best known for his autobiographical trilogy *The Forging of a Rebel* (*The Forge*, 1941; *The Track*, 1943; *The Clash*, 1946), which described the agony of the Spanish Civil War (1936–39).

BARGELLO, national museum of art in Florence, Italy, housed in a 13th–14th-century palace which was once an official residence and later a prison. It houses a world-famous collection of Renaissance sculpture.

BARKLEY, Alben William (1877–1956), 35th vice-president of the US (1949–53), under Truman. A Democrat from Ky., Barkley served in the US House of Representatives (1913–27) and the Senate (1927–49), including 10 years (beginning 1937) as majority leader. He returned to the Senate in 1954.

BARLACH, Ernst (1870–1938), German Expressionist sculptor, graphic artist and playwright, whose powerful figures in bronze or wood owe much to a very personal combination of Gothic and cubist influences. Barlach also produced many woodcuts and lithographs, some of them to illustrate his own dramas.

BARLEY, *Hordeum vulgare* and *H. distichon*, remarkably adaptable and hardy cereal, cultivated since ancient times. The USSR is the world's largest producer, with Canada and the US following. Over half of the world crop is used for animal feed and 10% (more in the US and W Europe) is turned into MALT. For human consumption barley is ground into a flour used to make porridge or flatbread, or, in the US and elsewhere, polished to produce "pearl barley" commonly used in soup. Six-rowed and two-rowed barleys are the commonest varieties.

BARLOW, Joel (1754–1812), American man of letters and diplomat, one of the HARTFORD WITS. Barlow was author of the mock-pastoral *The Hasty Pudding* (1796) and a long epic about the promise of the New World, *The Vision of Columbus* (1787), revised as *The Columbiad* (1807). A friend of liberals in France and Britain, he was US consul to Algiers (1795–96) and an envoy to France (1811–12).

BAR MITZVAH (Hebrew: son of the commandment), Jewish religious ceremony marking a boy's coming of age at his 13th birthday. The event is usually celebrated in the synagogue by calling on the boy to read the weekly portion of the Law (Torah) or the Prophets. Some congregations have a ceremony for girls, the "Bas Mitzvah." Reform Judaism often has a joint confirmation ceremony at 15 or 16.

BARN (b), unit of nuclear CROSS-SECTION (area) equal to 10^{-28} m².

BARNABAS, Saint (1st century AD), early Christian apostle, a Jew from a Cypriot family who joined the early church in Jerusalem. He introduced PAUL to the other apostles and apparently accompanied him on his first missionary journey.

BARNACLES, marine CRUSTACEA of the subclass Cirripedia, whose free-swimming LARVAE are an important part of the PLANKTON. Most adults are HERMAPHRODITE. Their SHELLS consist primarily of CALCIUM carbonate (see also LIMESTONE). Adults attach themselves to solid surfaces (even the bodies of other sea animals) and trap plankton by means of feathery organs known as cirri. There are some 1000 species.

BARNARD, Christiaan Neethling (1922–   ), South African surgeon who performed the first successful human heart TRANSPLANT operation in 1967.

BARNARD COLLEGE, liberal arts college for women founded in New York City in 1889. It is part of Columbia University whose facilities it shares.

BARNAY, Robert (1876–1936), Austrian-born physiologist who received the 1914 Nobel Prize for Physiology or Medicine for research on the functioning of the organs of the inner EAR. From 1916 he continued his research in Sweden.

BARNBURNERS, radical, antislavery faction of the N.Y. State Democratic Party in the 1840s, opponents of the HUNKERS. Breaking away from the party in 1847–48, they joined the FREE-SOIL PARTY in supporting Martin Van Buren for the presidency. This threw the state's electoral votes, and victory, to the Whig candidate Zachary Taylor. The Barnburners disbanded, but many later joined the new Republican Party.

BARNES, Djuna (1892–   ), US poet, playwright and novelist. Her works include a collection of stories and poems entitled *A Book* (1923), and the novels *Ryder* (1928) and *Nightwood* (1936).

BARNUM, Phineas Taylor (1810–1891), US impresario, showman and publicist. The hoaxes, freaks and curiosities exhibited in his American Museum (founded 1841) in New York included the original Siamese twins and General Tom Thumb. He toured Europe, and in 1850 engaged soprano Jenny LIND for a US tour. In 1871 he opened his famous traveling circus show, which merged in 1881 with James A. BAILEY's show to become the Barnum and Bailey "Greatest Show on Earth."

BAROMETER, an instrument for measuring air pressure (see ATMOSPHERE), used in WEATHER FORECASTING and for determining ALTITUDE. Most commonly encountered is the **aneroid barometer** in which the effect of the air in compressing an evacuated thin cylindrical corrugated metal box is amplified mechanically and read off on a scale or, in the **barograph**, used to draw a trace on a slowly rotating drum, thus giving a continuous record of the barometric pressure. The aneroid instrument is that used for aircraft ALTIMETERS. The earliest barometers, as invented by TORRICELLI in 1643, consisted simply of a glass tube about 800mm long closed at one end and filled with MERCURY before being inverted over a pool of mercury. Air pressure acting on the surface of the pool held up a column of mercury about 760mm tall in the tube, a "Torricellian" vacuum appearing in the closed end of the tube. The height of the column was read as a measure of the pressure. In the **Fortin barometer**, devised by Jean Fortin (1750–1831) and still used for accurate scientific work, the lower mercury level can be finely adjusted and the column height is read off with the aid of a Vernier scale.

BARON, Salo Wittmayer, (1895–   ), Austrian-born US scholar who earned doctorates in philosophy, political science and law from the U. of Vienna (1917–23) before emigrating to the US, where he became the first professor of Jewish history in a US university (Columbia, 1930–63). He also helped establish Columbia's Center of Jewish Studies (1950) and wrote the monumental multivolume *A Social and Religious History of the Jews.*

BARONS' WAR (1263–67), English civil war between a baronial faction led by Simon de MONTFORT, Earl of Leicester, and the supporters of King HENRY III. The war was the result of Henry's refusal to abide by the reforms of the Provisions of Oxford (1258). Henry was defeated at the Battle of Lewes (1264) and taken prisoner; de Montfort consolidated his own power and summoned a parliament. In 1265 Henry's son, the future EDWARD I, killed de Montfort at the Battle of Evesham and restored the monarchy.

BAROQUE, dynamic and expressive style that dominated European art c1600–1750. The term has been used to describe not only the painting, sculpture and architecture of the period, but also, by analogy, its music. Baroque was born in a rejection of the balance of Renaissance Classicism and the uncertainty of Mannerism. Much Baroque art is characterized by its emotional appeal, and by the energy and fluidity of its forms. From the works of CARAVAGGIO and, above all, BERNINI in Rome, the dramatic and illusionistic style of the High Baroque spread throughout Europe, glorifying faith in the Counter-Reformation Church and the absolutist state. In N Europe as well as in Italy, through painters as diverse as RUBENS and REMBRANDT, the Baroque created a new vocabulary of artistic expression.

BAROQUE MUSIC, that period of music c1600–1750 which began with the development of OPERA, CANTATA, ORATORIO and RECITATIVE, and ended with the death of its two greatest composers, HANDEL and J. S. BACH. Baroque music shared with the visual arts of its time dynamism, exuberance and forceful emotional expression. Musically, this was shown by ornamented melodies and by a striking use of harmonies and strong rhythms. The idea of stylistic contrast between instruments developed the CONCERTO form. In addition, both the SONATA and FUGUE forms developed, because of the increased attention paid to counterpoint.

BARR, Alfred Hamilton, Jr. (1902–1981), US art historian. Called the most influential museum man of the 20th century, Barr directed New York's Museum of Modern Art, 1929–43 (where he remained until

1967) and organized some of the most important shows in the history of modern art. He also wrote three contemporary classics: *Cubism and Abstract Art* (1936), *Picasso* (1946) and *Matisse* (1951).

BARRACUDAS, the family Sphyraenidae (order Perciformes), tropical marine fishes renowned for their ferocity. The smallest is *Sphyraena borealis,* about 0.5m (20in) long; the largest the Great Barracuda, *S. barracuda,* which attains lengths around 2.5m (8.2ft).

BARRAS, Paul François Jean Nicolas, Vicomte de (1755–1829), French revolutionary. At first a JACOBIN, in favor of Louis XVI's execution, he turned against ROBESPIERRE and commanded the troops that arrested him (1794). Barras became the most powerful member of the DIRECTORY, and aided Napoleon's rise to power. But after Napoleon's coup d'etat of 18 Brumaire (1799), Barras was exiled.

BARRAULT, Jean-Louis (1910–   ), French actor, director, producer and mime. A member of the Comédie Française 1940–46, he directed the Théâtre de France 1959–68. His most famous film role was that of mime in *Les Enfants du Paradis* (1944).

BARRÈS, (Auguste) Maurice (1862–1923), French man of letters and political figure, best known for his intransigent nationalism and emphasis on regional ties. Among his many influential novels, *The Uprooted* (1897) stands preeminent.

BARRIE, Sir James Matthew (1860–1937), Scottish playwright and novelist. His plays— including *The Admirable Crichton* (1902), *Peter Pan* (1904) and *Dear Brutus* (1917)—are marked by charm and ingenuity, and range in tone from whimsy and sentimentality to satire and pathos.

BARRIOS, Eduardo (1884–1963), Chilean novelist, known for the psychological insight of such powerful novels as *The Love-Crazed Boy* (1915) and *Brother Ass* (1922).

BARRON, James (1769–1851), US naval commodore, who was commander of the frigate *Chesapeake* in its disastrous engagement with the British warship *Leopard* in 1807. He surrendered and allowed the removal of four sailors the British claimed as deserters. Barron was court-martialed and temporarily suspended from duty. Blaming Commodore DECATUR for being refused a further sea command, he killed him in a duel in 1820.

BARROW, Isaac (1630–1677), English mathematician and theologian. The first Lucasian professor of mathematics in the University of Cambridge (1663), Barrow resigned in favor of his pupil Isaac NEWTON

in 1669. His work on tangents and areas was influential in Newton's development of the CALCULUS.

BARROW, Point, northernmost point on the North American continent (71°23′N), at the tip of Point Barrow Peninsula on the Arctic coast of Alaska. Named for Sir John Barrow, the city of Barrow (pop 2,104) lies some 12mi S.

BARRY, Sir Charles (1795–1860), English architect who, with his assistant A.W.N. Pugin, designed the Houses of Parliament in London (1840–65), a masterpiece of the GOTHIC REVIVAL. Among his other buildings was the Reform Club in London (1837).

BARRY, John (1745–1803), Irish-born naval hero famed for many brilliant exploits in the Revolutionary War, often called the "Father of the American navy." As ranking captain of the navy (from 1794) he commanded the frigate *United States* and saw action in the undeclared naval war with France (1798–1800).

BARRY, Philip (1896–1949), US playwright, best known for popular drawing-room comedies such as *Holiday* (1928) and *The Philadelphia Story* (1939).

BARRYMORE, name of a noted American theatrical family. The father was the British actor Herbert Blythe (1847–1905), who adopted the stage name **Maurice Barrymore**. He came to the US in 1875 and married actress Georgina Drew. **Lionel Barrymore** (1878–1954), their eldest child, became an outstanding character actor on stage and radio and in many films— continuing to act even after arthritis had confined him to a wheelchair. **Ethel Barrymore** (1879–1959), famous for her beauty, style and wit, gave many distinctive performances on stage and screen. She won an Academy Award for her supporting role in *None But the Lonely Heart* (1944). **John Barrymore** (1882–1942) was a distinguished interpreter of Shakespearean roles, particularly *Richard III* (1920) and *Hamlet* (1922). Later he became a popular and flamboyant film actor, nicknamed "the great profile." His children, **Diana Barrymore** (1921–1960) and **John Barrymore, Jr** (1932–   ), also became actors.

BARTH, John (1930–   ), US novelist known for his ironic style and use of comic and elaborate allegory. His best-known works include *The Sot-Weed Factor* (1960) and *Giles Goat-Boy* (1966).

BARTH, Karl (1886–1968), Swiss theologian, one of the most influential voices of 20th-century Protestantism. He taught in Germany 1921–35, was expelled by the Nazis and spent the rest of his life in Basel. In his "crisis theology," Barth stressed revelation and grace and reemphasized the principles of the Reformation, initiating a movement away from theological "liberalism" (see NEO-ORTHODOXY.)

BARTHELME, Donald (1931–   ), US short-story writer and novelist noted for his innovative techniques and surrealistic style. His works include the novels *Snow White* (1967) and *The Dead Father* (1975); the children's book *The Slightly Irregular Fire Engine or the Hithering Thithering Djinn* (1971), for which he won a National Book Award; and *Sixty Stories* (1981).

BARTHES, Roland (1915–1980), French philosopher and social critic. His works include *Writing Degree Zero* (1968), *Mythologies* (1972), *A Lover's Discourse* (1978) and his autobiography, *Roland Barthes* (1975).

BARTHOLDI, Frédéric Auguste (1834–1904), French sculptor, creator of the Statue of Liberty (see LIBERTY, STATUE OF). His other monumental works include the *Lion of Belfort* at Belfort, France.

BARTHOLOMEW, Saint, one of the 12 Apostles, sometimes identified with NATHANAEL. He was said to have preached in the Middle East, Asia Minor and India, and to have been martyred in Armenia by being flayed alive. His feast day in the West is Aug 24.

BARTLETT, John (1820–1905), US editor and publisher, best known for his famous *Familiar Quotations*, which has gone through more than a dozen editions since its first appearance in 1855.

BARTLETT, Josiah (1729–1795), American patriot and physician, delegate to the Continental Congress (1775–76, 1778–79) and signer of the Declaration of Independence. He was chief executive (1790–92) and first governor (1793–94) of N.H.

BARTÓK, Béla (1881–1945), Hungarian composer, one of the major figures of 20th-century music. He was also a virtuoso concert pianist, and taught piano at the Budapest Academy of Music (1907–34). In 1940 he emigrated to the US. His work owes much to the rhythmic and melodic vitality of E European folk music, on which he was an authority. Bartók's works include such masterpieces as his six string quartets (1908–39), *Music for Strings, Percussion and Celesta* (1936) and *Concerto for Orchestra* (1943).

BARTOLOMMEO, Fra (c1472–1517), Florentine painter of the High Renaissance, born Baccio della Porta. A Dominican monk, he painted religious subjects (largely altarpieces) with telling grandeur and simplicity.

BARTON, Clara (1821–1912), founder of the American Red Cross (1881) and its first president. She began a lifetime of relief work by organizing care and supplies for the wounded in the Civil War. On a trip to Europe (1869–73) she became involved in the activities of the International Red Cross and was later influential in extending the range of its relief work.

BARUCH, Bernard Mannes (1870–1965), US financier and public official, who made a fortune on Wall Street and became an influential adviser to US presidents. He served Woodrow Wilson as chairman of the War Industries Board in WWI and at the Versailles peace talks; was adviser to F. D. Roosevelt in WWII; and under Truman was US delegate to the UN Atomic Energy Commission, where he proposed the "Baruch Plan" for the international control of atomic energy.

BARUCH, Book of, a biblical work attributed to Baruch, the prophet Jeremiah's secretary. Relegated to the APOCRYPHA by Protestants, it is included in the Old Testament by Roman Catholics. The book survives in a Greek version, and is probably the work of several authors of Hellenistic times.

BARYSHNIKOV, Mikhail (1948–   ), Soviet dancer and choreographer who defected to the West in 1974. He was a soloist with the Kirov Ballet, Leningrad, from 1966. In the West he joined the American Ballet Theatre, appearing there and with other companies in modern and classical ballets. He became director of the American Ballet Theatre in 1980.

BASAL METABOLIC RATE (BMR), a measure of the rate at which an animal at rest uses energy. Human BMR is a measure of the heat output per unit time from a given area of body surface, the subject being at rest under certain standard conditions. It is usually estimated from the amounts of oxygen and carbon dioxide exchanged in a certain time. (See METABOLISM.)

BASALT, a dense igneous rock, mainly plagioclase feldspar, fine-grained and dark gray to black in color; volcanic in origin, it is widespread as lava flows or intrusions. Basalt can assume a striking columnar structure, as exhibited in the Palisades along the Hudson R, or in Devils Postpile in Cal., and it can also form vast plateaus, such as the 200,000sq mi Deccan of India. Most oceanic islands of volcanic origin, such as Hawaii, are basaltic.

BASE, in chemistry, the complement of an acid. Bases used to be defined as substances which react with acids to form SALTS, or as substances which give rise to hydroxyl ions in aqueous solution. Some such inorganic strong bases are known as ALKALIS. In modern terms, bases are species which can accept a HYDROGEN ion from an acid, or which can donate an electron-pair to a Lewis ACID.

BASEBALL, America's national sport, had its beginnings more than a century ago. Its true origins are obscure, and the supposed role of Abner DOUBLEDAY has been hotly disputed. It is generally thought that the sport is a hybrid, loosely developed from the English games of cricket and rounders. Many of its rules were first set down by Alexander CARTWRIGHT of the New York Knickerbocker Baseball Club, founded in 1845. The National Association of Baseball Players was organized in 1858; the game became popular among Union troops in the Civil War, and in 1865 a convention of 91 amateur clubs met in New York. **The major leagues.** In 1869 the Cincinnati Red Stockings became the first fully professional baseball team. The National Association of Professional Baseball Players was formed in 1871; it was replaced by a new National League of Professional Baseball Clubs in 1876. Attempts at creating a rival league failed until the turn of the century, when the American League had become sufficiently established to match the National League.

The first World Series between the leading teams in each league was played in 1903. In 1933 the first "All-Star" exhibition game was played, followed in 1939 by the establishment of a Baseball Hall of Fame in Cooperstown, N.Y. In 1953 the major leagues started shifting franchises to new cities and a great expansion began. By 1969, each league had grown to 12 clubs, and by the 1980s, the American League had 14. Each league was divided into two divisions, with the division winners meeting in three-out-of-five game playoffs to determine the league champions. This arrangement was altered once, in 1981, when a BASEBALL STRIKE interrupted play at mid-season.

BASEBALL STRIKE, a 50-day, mid-season strike by major league baseball players that began June 12, 1981, and stemmed in part from earlier modifications of baseball's RESERVE CLAUSE. At issue was the team owners' insistence that when a free-agent ball player moved from one club to another, the club that lost him should be compensated by getting a player from the club that signed him up. The complex compromise settlement involved creating a pool of players that could be drawn on for compensation.

BASEL, second-largest city in Switzerland, capital of (and virtually coextensive with) the half-canton of Basel-Stadt. A port on the Rhine near the junction of the French and German borders, it is a major center of industry, commerce and international finance. It joined the Swiss confederation in 1501 and figured prominently in the Reformation. Pop 180,900; met pop 363,700.

BASEL, Council of, general Church council opened in Basel, Switzerland, in 1431, concerned with the heresy of Jan HUS and the continuing struggle over papal supremacy. Pope Eugene IV tried to dissolve the council, but it denied his right to do so, claiming that as an ecumenical council it, rather than the pope, held ultimate authority. Eugene relented, but in 1437 ordered it to move to Ferrara, Italy, to consider reunion with the Eastern Church. Most bishops complied, but a small number remained in Basel, deposing Eugene and electing the antipope Felix V in 1439, and continuing to meet until 1449.

BASIC (beginner's all-purpose symbolic instruction code), COMPUTER language similar to FORTRAN. It was developed in the mid-1960s as an interactive language—one in which a response to the programmer's input can be immediately obtained. Meant to be used by beginners who would soon convert to other languages, it has gained wide appeal for many beyond the beginning stage and is used in many personal computers for the home.

BASIC ENGLISH, selected vocabulary of 850 English words, meant for use as an auxiliary or international language. Developed by English scholar C. K. Ogden between 1926 and 1930, it was the first attempt to create a usable, simpler language system out of an existing one.

BASIE, William "Count" (1904–   ), US jazz pianist, composer and bandleader. Count Basie's big band, which included some of the outstanding jazz musicians of the time, brought the ragged rhythm and improvisational verve of jazz into the smooth swing era of the late 1930s and 1940s.

BASIL, *Ocimum basilicum,* aromatic annual herb of the mint family, native to Asia. The leaves are used fresh or dried in cooking and in the preparation of Chartreuse liqueur.

BASILICA, in its earliest usage, a type of large public building of ancient Rome. The term came to refer to a building of characteristic rectangular layout, with a central area (nave) separated by rows of columns from two flanking side aisles with high windows. At one or both ends was a semicircular or polygonal apse. This design was adopted as a basic pattern for Christian churches from the time of Constantine. The term "basilica" is also a canonical title for certain important Roman Catholic churches.

BASILISKS, the genus *Basiliscus* (family Iguanidae), LIZARDS of Central America. Their chief means of catching prey and evading enemies is speed, and they are well known for their ability to dash across the surface of still water: this they can do only until their speed begins to slacken, at which point they must start to swim. The name is also applied to the cockatrice, born of a cockerel and a serpent, a legendary beast whose glance was fatal.

BASIL THE GREAT, Saint (c330–379), one of the great Fathers of the Eastern Church, a founder of Greek monasticism and author of the *Longer* and *Shorter Rules* for monastic life. As Bishop of Caesarea, he also played a role in subduing ARIANISM. His brother was St. GREGORY OF NYSSA.

BASIN AND RANGE PROVINCE, geological region of the SW US extending into NW Mexico, bounded by the Columbia Plateau, the Sierra Nevada, the Wasatch Mts and the Colorado Plateau. It is a semidesert region with parallel mountain ranges and valley basins running N to S. Many sections have no outlet to the sea; the Great Salt Lake is one remnant of much larger lakes that once existed.

BASKERVILLE, John (1706–1775), English printer and type designer, whose elegant Baskerville type was the ancestor and inspiration of the "modern" group of typefaces. He took great care in all aspects of his craft and produced many handsome editions.

BASKETBALL, the most popular indoor sport in the US. Its object is to score points by propelling a ball through a hoop and net construction, the "basket," 18in in diameter and 10ft from the floor. It is played on a court with maximum dimensions of 94×50ft by two teams, each consisting of 12 players and a coach, with five players on the court at any one time. The ball may be moved by "passing" from one player to another, or by "dribbling," in which case the ball must not be kicked, or held for more than one pace. Rules vary in detail between organizations.

Conceived by Dr. James A. NAISMITH in 1891, the game quickly became popular. In 1898, teams from New York, Brooklyn, Philadelphia and southern New Jersey formed the first professional league, but these early leagues lasted only a few seasons. International interest was fostered by an exhibition game played at the 1904 Olympics in St. Louis, Mo. and the game subsequently became an Olympic sport and a popular scholastic and collegiate sport. The first National Invitation Tournament, featuring the nation's best college teams, was held in Madison Square Garden in NYC in 1938. The union of the National Basketball League, the Basketball Association of America and the American Basketball Association created a strong professional league whose popular following was still growing in the 1980s.

BASKIN, Leonard (1922–   ), American graphic artist and sculptor. He studied art at New York and Yale universities, and in Paris and Florence. After winning a Guggenheim Fellowship for graphics in 1953, he taught at Smith College, Mass., where he founded the Gehenna Press.

BASKING SHARK, *Cetorhinus maximus*, second largest of the SHARKS, attaining lengths of up to 15m (50ft) and weights of over 4 tons. Found chiefly in temperate waters, it is not carnivorous but feeds on PLANKTON.

BASQUES, a people of unknown origin living mainly in the vicinity of the Pyrenees Mts (about 100,000 in France and 600,000 in NE Spain). Ethnically they seem to belong to the Caucasoid group, but research into their blood groups indicates a long separation from other Europeans; their language is remarkably conservative and quite unlike the Indo-European tongues. Basques were living along the Ebro valley in N Spain in the 3rd century BC, and have preserved many features of their ancient culture despite incursions by Romans, Visigoths, Moors and Franks, and eventual Spanish rule. After the Spanish Civil War, in which many Basques fought against General Franco, an effort was made to subdue the region. A surge of Basque nationalism in recent years was marked by the assassination of Admiral Luis Blanco by the Basque resistance movement ETA in Dec. 1973 and the execution of five terrorists shortly before Franco's death.

BASRA, city in Iraq, major port situated on the Shatt-el-Arab about 75mi from the Persian Gulf. Main products include petroleum and dates. Basra was a noted center of Arab culture from the 8th to the 13th centuries. Pop 311,000.

BASS, or double bass, largest instrument of the violin family. Usually it stands about 6ft high, and has four, or sometimes five, 42.5in strings of copper or steel. It is played with a bow, or the strings may be plucked.

BASS, term used for two species,

Dicentrarchus labrax and *D. punctatus*, of the Serranidae family (order Perciformes). Coastal fish, they usually weigh 1–3kg (2–7lb) though sometimes up to 8kg (18lb). In America the term Black Bass is applied to the freshwater fishes (genus *Micropterus* and family Centrarchidae) *M. salmoides* and *M. dolomieu*. They are nest-builders and predatory, occasionally playing with their prey rather as a cat does with a mouse.

BASS, Sam (1851–1878), US outlaw. He rode the West, first with the Joel Collins gang and then with one of his own. Called the "Robin Hood of Texas," he died of gunshot wounds.

BASSANO, Jacopo (Jacopo da Ponte; c1510–92),leading member of a family of Italian painters. Arriving in Venice c1534, he was at first influenced by TITIAN. TINTORETTO and others. With its use of everyday scenes in religious subjects, his work tended towards GENRE painting, a tradition continued by his three sons.

BASSET HOUND, a hunting dog 11–15in high at the shoulder, weighing 25–45lb. It has a long, bulky body, with a large head, a long nose and long ears. It is used to hunt foxes, rabbits and pheasants and is also popular as a pet.

BASSOON, the bass of the woodwind family, an 8ft conical tube bent double, with a double reed mouthpiece, 8 holes, and 20–22 keys. It has a range of 3.5 octaves (B-flat bass to E-flat alto) but irrational key placing and an unstable pitch make it difficult to play. The contrabassoon is 6ft long and sounds an octave lower.

BASTILLE, fortress in Paris built in 1370, destroyed during the French Revolution. It was first used to house political prisoners by Cardinal Richelieu, in the 17th century, but was almost empty by the time of the Revolution. It remained a symbol of oppression, however, and its capture on July 14, 1789, was the first act of the Revolution. Today, July 14 is the French national holiday.

BASTOGNE, small town on the Ardennes plateau in SE Belgium. During the German counter-offensive of 1944, the BATTLE OF THE BULGE, an American division under Gen. Anthony McAuliffe was surrounded here for some weeks before the Germans were driven back.

BATES, Katharine Lee (1859–1929), US author, best known for writing the lyrics of AMERICA THE BEAUTIFUL. She was professor of English at Wellesley College and wrote much children's literature.

BATESON, Gregory (1904–1980), British-born US anthropologist, best known for his study of New Guinea, *Naven* (1936; rev.

1958), and *Ecology of Mind* (1972). He wrote *Balinese Character* (1943) with his wife, Margaret MEAD.

BATH, famous resort city in the county of Avon, England, on the Avon R about 12mi from Bristol. Noted for its mineral springs since Roman times, it is distinguished for its elegant Georgian architecture. Its industries include bookbinding, printing and weaving. Pop 84,760.

BATH, Order of the, British honor, established by George I in 1725 (supposedly based on an order founded in 1399). There are two divisions, military and civil, with three classes in each: knight grand cross (G.C.B.), knight commander (K.C.B.) and companion (C.B.).

BATH MITZVAH. See BAR MITZVAH.

BATHS AND BATHING. In the past baths have served a primarily religious, social or pleasurable function far more often than a hygienic one. The Egyptians, Assyrians and Greeks all used baths, but the Romans developed bathing as a central social habit, constructing elaborate public buildings, often ornately decorated and of enormous size, with several rooms for disrobing, exercise, and entertainment, as well as bathing. Men and women bathed at separate times, except for one brief period in the 1st century AD. The baths were tended by slaves. After the fall of the Roman Empire bathing declined in popularity in Europe, though it did survive as a part of monastic routine and in Muslim countries. In Russia and Turkey the steam bath became popular. The crusaders brought steam bathing back with them from the Middle East, but an association with immorality caused it to fall into disrepute.

In the 18th century, it became fashionable to spend a season at a watering-place, such as BATH in England, but only 19th-century research into hygiene made a virtue of bathing, often with primitive and usually portable cold baths at schools and institutions. Only after WWI did plumbing and bathtub production allow the bath to become a permanent installation in the home.

BATHYSCAPHE, submersible deep-sea research vessel, invented by Auguste PICCARD in the late 1940s, comprising a small, spherical, pressurized passenger cabin suspended beneath a cigar-shaped flotation hull. On the surface most of the flotation tanks in the hull are filled with GASOLINE, the rest, sufficient to float the vessel, with air. To dive the air is vented and seawater takes its place. During descent, sea water is allowed to enter the gasoline-filled tanks from the bottom, compressing the gasoline and thus increasing the DENSITY of the vessel. The rate of descent is checked by releasing iron ballast. To begin ascent, the remaining ballast is jettisoned. As the vessel rises, the gasoline expands, expelling water from the flotation tanks, thus lightening the vessel further and accelerating the ascent. Battery-powered motors provide the vessel with a degree of submarine mobility.

BATIK, a dyeing technique. Before the fabric is dipped into the dye the portions which are to remain uncolored are covered with wax. When the dye is dry, the wax is removed by boiling. The technique was introduced into Europe from Indonesia by Dutch traders.

BATISTA Y ZALDÍVAR, Fulgencio (1901–1973), Cuban military dictator. Becoming army chief of staff after the overthrow of the Machado government in 1933, he appointed and deposed presidents at will. He was himself president 1940–44, and took the title permanently in 1952. After his overthrow by CASTRO in 1959 he lived in exile in Spain.

BATON ROUGE, capital of La. since 1849, situated on the Mississippi R W of New Orleans. It is an important trade and communications center producing oil, chemicals and aluminum. Pop 219,486.

BATS, the order Chiroptera, the flying MAMMALS. Since they are all nocturnal, and many tropical, it is not generally realized that bats account for about one-seventh of mammalian species. There are two suborders: the Megachiroptera ("big bats"), with weights from 25g (0.9oz) to 1kg (2.2lb) and wingspans of about 250–1500mm (10in–5ft); and the Microchiroptera ("little bats"), weights of about 3–200g (0.1–7oz) and wingspans of 150–900mm (6–35in). The former usually have large eyes adapted for night vision, but the latter navigate by use of echolocation (see SONAR). Most are insectivorous, but some are vegetarian and yet others carnivorous—the three species of the family Desmodontidae (the VAMPIRE BATS) are blood suckers, preying on birds and mammals.

BATTANI, abu-Abdullah Muhammad ibn-Jabir, al-, or Latin **Albategnius** or **Albatenius** (c858–929), Arab mathematician and astronomer who improved on the results of Claudius PTOLEMY by applying TRIGONOMETRY to astronomical computations. He had a powerful influence on medieval European ASTRONOMY.

BATTERY, a device for converting internally-stored chemical ENERGY into direct-current ELECTRICITY. The term is also applied to various other electricity sources, including the SOLAR CELL and the nuclear cell, but is usually taken to exclude the FUEL CELL, which requires the continuous input of a chemical fuel for its operation. Chemical batteries consist of one or more electrochemical (voltaic) cells (comprising two ELECTRODES immersed in a conducting electrolyte) in which a chemical reaction occurs when an external circuit is completed between the electrodes. Most of the energy liberated in this reaction can be tapped if a suitable load is placed in the external circuit, impeding the flow of ELECTRONS from CATHODE to ANODE. (The conventional current, of course, flows in the opposite sense.) Batteries are classified in two main divisions. In **primary cells,** the chemical reaction is ordinarily irreversible and the battery can yield only a finite quantity of electricity. Single primary-cell batteries are used in flashlights, shavers, LIGHT METERS, etc. The most common type is the dry **Leclanché cell,** which has a ZINC cathode, a CARBON anode, and uses a zinc chloride and ammonium chloride paste as electrolyte. MANGANESE dioxide "depolarizer" is distributed around the anode (mixed with powdered GRAPHITE) to prevent the accumulation of the HYDROGEN gas which would otherwise stop the operation of the cell. The dry Leclanché cell gives a nominal 1.54V. For the higher voltages necessary to power transistor radios, batteries containing several thin laminar cells are used. In **alkaline cells,** potassium hydroxide is used in place of ammonium chloride; this permits higher currents to be drawn. The **mercury cell,** with a mercury and graphite cathode, is smaller than other cells of the same power.

Secondary cells, known also as storage batteries or accumulators, can be recharged and reused at will, provided too much electricity has not been abstracted from them. The most common type, as used in AUTOMOBILES, is the lead-acid types in which both electrodes are made of LEAD (the positive covered with lead (IV) oxide when charged) and the electrolyte is dilute SULFURIC ACID. Its voltage is about 2V, depending on the state of charge. The robust yet light nickel-iron battery (having a POTASSIUM hydroxide solution electrolyte) is widely used in telephone exchanges and other heavy-duty situations. In spacecraft, however, where the batteries must be airtight, nickel-cadmium batteries are used instead. Nickel oxide serves as the cathode, and potassium hydroxide is the electrolyte. Such batteries provide about 1.3V and can last about 25 years.

The first battery was the voltaic pile

invented c1800 by VOLTA. This comprised a stack of pairs of silver and zinc disks, each pair separated by a brine-soaked board. For many years from 1836 the standard form of battery was the **Daniell cell**, with a zinc cathode, a copper cathode and a porous-pot barrier separating the anode electrolyte (copper(II) sulfate) from the cathode electrolyte (sulfuric acid). The lead-acid storage battery was invented by Gaston Planté in 1859 and the wet Leclanché cell, the prototype for the modern dry cell, by Georges Leclanché in 1865.

BATTLE HYMN OF THE REPUBLIC, American patriotic song, unofficial hymn of Union troops in the Civil War. Written in 1861 by Julia Ward HOWE and sung to the tune of *John Brown's Body*, it later became a Protestant hymn and a protest marching song.

BATTLE OF BRITAIN, air battle in WWII from Aug. 8 to Oct. 31, 1940, between the British Royal Air Force (RAF) and the German Luftwaffe. The Germans intended to weaken British defenses and morale before invading the country. The Luftwaffe forces were much greater than those of the RAF, but the latter proved to be technically and tactically superior. The Germans first bombed shipping and ports, then airfields and Midland industries and, finally, in Sept., London. Daylight raids proving too costly, the Germans turned to night attacks. At the end the RAF had lost some 900 planes, the Germans over 2,300, and Hitler had postponed his projected invasion indefinitely, thus tacitly admitting failure.

BATTLE OF THE ATLANTIC, the WWII air and sea effort of the Axis powers to stop US supplies coming to Britain and the USSR. Allied convoys, guarded by British, Canadian and later US destroyers and escort carriers, ran the gauntlet of German U-boats and surface raiders. Through antisubmarine devices, air patrols and bombing of submarine pens and factories the Allies gradually overcame the Axis threat at sea.

BATTLE OF THE BULGE, last major western counteroffensive by the Germans in WWII. They planned to capture Liège and Antwerp, thus dividing the Allied armies. The German assault in the Ardennes began on Dec. 16, 1944, and created a huge "bulge" into the Allied lines. Although suffering about 77,000 casualties, the Allies stopped the German advance by Jan. 16, 1945.

BATTLESHIP, historically the largest of conventionally-armed warships. Though some battleships are still kept in reserve, aircraft carriers superseded them during WWII as the largest fighting ships afloat. The first US battleships were the *Indiana, Massachusetts* and *Oregon,* completed in 1895–96. Since 1946 no more have been built. (See also DREADNOUGHT; NAVY.)

BAUCIS AND PHILEMON, in Greek mythology, an old man and his wife who gave hospitality to ZEUS and HERMES. The two gods, disguised as travelers, had been refused hospitality by all others in Phrygia. In reward, the aged couple were spared from a flood, their house became a temple and after death they were turned into trees. Their names are associated with faithful marriage.

BAUDELAIRE, Charles Pierre (1821–1867), French poet and critic, forerunner of SYMBOLISM. The poems in *Les Fleurs du Mal* (1857), with their sensitive probing of even the most bizarre sensations, outraged public opinion and led to the poet's being tried for obscenity. His later prose poems were posthumously published in *Le Spleen de Paris* (1869). He was also a brilliant critic of music and fine art, and was renowned for his translations of Edgar Allan POE.

BAUDOUIN I (1930–   ), fifth king of the Belgians. He spent WWII with his family in Nazi internment, and succeeded his father, King Leopold III, who abdicated in 1951. In 1960 Baudouin proclaimed Congolese independence. He married a Spanish noblewoman, now Queen Fabiola.

BAUGH, Sammy (1914–   ), the first prominent passing football quarterback. He starred at Texas Christian University (1934–36), then for 16 years with the Boston and Washington Redskins. When he retired he held nearly every passing record.

BAUHAUS, the most influential school of design and architecture in the 20th century. Walter GROPIUS founded it in 1919 at Weimar, Germany, and its teachers included some of the leading artists of the time. Gropius' ideal of uniting form with function is now a universal canon of design, and the dictum "less is more" has influenced much US design. The Bauhaus left Weimar in 1925 and was installed in new premises designed by Gropius in Dessau in 1927. The school was closed by the Nazis in 1933. Bauhaus teachers Gropius, FEININGER and MIES VAN DER ROHE later moved to the US.

BAUM, Lyman Frank (1856–1919), US childrens' writer, author of the famous *Wonderful Wizard of Oz* (1900), a tale of a girl carried by a cyclone to a land of adventure. The 1939 film adaptation became a motion-picture classic.

BAUMEISTER, Willi (1889–1955), German artist who was, in turn, a constructivist, abstract and ideographic painter. His important canvases of the 1950s utilized brightly colored geometric forms.

BAUXITE, the main ore of ALUMINUM, consisting of hydrated aluminum oxide, usually with iron oxide impurity. It is a claylike, amorphous material formed by the weathering of silicate rocks, especially under tropical conditions. High-grade bauxite, being highly refractory, is used as a lining for furnaces. Synthetic corundum is made from it, and it is an ingredient in some quick-setting cements. Leading bauxite-producing countries include Jamaica, Australia, the USSR, Suriname, Guyana, France, Guinea and the US (especially Ark.).

BAX, Sir Arnold Edward (1883–1953), British composer best known for his romantic and richly orchestrated symphonic poems and symphonies. He was appointed master of the king's music in 1941.

BAY, popular name for the LAUREL tree (*Laurus nobilis*), also known as the sweet bay or bay laurel, native to the Mediterranean countries. Dried leaves are used to season foods. Bay trees are planted as ornamentals and their leaves were used in classical Greece to crown heroes.

BAYAR, Mahmud Cêlal (1883–   ), president of Turkey 1950–60. He was prominent in ATATURK'S nationalist movement after WWI, and later became economics minister (1932–37) and prime minister (1937–38) of the Turkish republic. He founded the opposition Democratic Party in 1946.

BAYARD, Pierre Terrail, Seigneur de (c1473–1524), French commander famous for his bravery, who became the epitome of French chivalry. He first distinguished himself in French campaigns in Italy. Later at Mézières in 1521, with only 1,000 men against 35,000, he held off an invasion of central France by the emperor Charles V.

BAYEUX TAPESTRY, embroidered linen wallhanging of the early Middle Ages, depicting the Norman Conquest of England in 1066. It is 231ft long and 19.5in wide, and contains over 70 scenes. It is believed to have been commissioned by Bishop Odo, half-brother of WILLIAM the Conqueror, for Bayeux Cathedral in NW France.

BAYLE, Pierre (1647–1706), French philosopher, whose great *Historical and Critical Dictionary* (1697) embodied his skeptical critique of Christian orthodoxy. His rationalistic approach to belief strongly influenced 18th-century thinkers.

BAY OF PIGS, English name for Bahia de Cochinos, SW Cuba, scene of an abortive invasion of Cuba on April 17, 1961. The invaders were Cubans who had fled to the US after Fidel CASTRO seized power. Although Americans were not directly involved, the CIA had helped plan the invasion.

BAY PSALM BOOK, name commonly given to the first book printed in Colonial America. *The Whole Booke of Psalmes Faithfully Translated into English Metre* was published in Cambridge, Mass., in 1640 as a hymnal for the Massachusetts Bay Colony. It was the work of Richard MATHER, John Eliot and Thomas Weld and was printed by Stephen DAY.

BAYREUTH, industrial city in NE Bavaria, in W Germany. It is famous as the last home of Richard WAGNER and as the site of his opera house, the *Festspielhaus*, where the annual Wagnerian festival (begun in 1876) is now run by Wagner's grandson Wolfgang. Pop 63,530.

BEACH, Amy (1867–1944), US composer whose *Gaelic Symphony* (1896) was the first symphony known to have been composed by an American woman. She wrote over 150 works, including a piano concerto (1900), string quartet (1929), and a one-act opera, *Cabildo* (1932).

BEACH, Sylvia (1887–1962), US bookstore owner whose shop, Shakespeare & Co., was the center of expatriate literary life in Paris during the interwar period. She also published James JOYCE'S Ulysses (1922).

BEACH BOYS, a California-based rock group popular in the 1960s. Much of their music was written by group member Brian Wilson (b. 1942) in praise of such teen-age pleasures as hot-rodding and surfing, as in the 1963 hit song "Surfin' USA".

BEACON HILL, most famous of three hills in Boston, Mass. A beacon stood there in the Colonial period. The state capitol was constructed on it in 1795, and its streets are lined with elegant, early red-brick houses.

BEAGLE, the smallest trailing hound, often used for hare hunts. Its short coat shows black, white and brown coloring. It stands 13in–15in high at the shoulder.

BEAMON, Bob (1946–   ), US long jumper. At the 1968 Olympics in Mexico City, he jumped 29ft, 2 1/2in shattering the previous world record by a phenomenal 16in.

BEAN, common name given to a number of species of the family Leguminosae, cultivated for the food value of their seeds, immature pods and shoots. Important species include: the SOYBEAN (*Glycine max*), the fruit of which has a high protein content and is a dietary staple in Asia and is now grown in the US; the common garden bean or French bean (*Phaseolus vulgaris*), grown extensively in Europe and the US; the Scarlet Runner bean (*P. multiflorus*), which may be grown as an ornamental plant as well as for its pods; the Lima bean (*P. lunatus*), originating from South America; the Broad bean (*Vicia fabo*) grown mainly in Europe; and the Mung bean, the source of bean sprouts popular in Chinese cuisine and staple in Asia. Bean plants in general are of great value in replenishing nitrogen-deficient soils, using, in association with BACTERIA, a process known as NITROGEN FIXATION. (See LEGUMINOUS PLANTS.)

BEAN, Judge Roy (c1825–1903), US justice of the peace who called himself "the only law west of the Pecos." After an adventurous early life which included arrest, jail break and proprietorship of tent saloons, he settled at what later became Langtry in W Tex. He built a combination store, saloon and pool hall, and held court as justice and coroner. His decisions were more notable for six-gun drama and humor than legal sagacity.

BEARD, growth of hair on a man's chin, cheeks and neck, regarded by many races as a symbol of strength and virility. Among the ancient Egyptians, Assyrians and Chinese the beard had a ritual significance. The religious cult of the beard is still prevalent in Eastern cultures. Indian Sikhs are forbidden to remove a hair from their bodies; Hindus are usually clean-shaven. The Western habit of shaving became common with the Romans.

BEARD, Charles Austin (1874–1948), controversial American historian, author of *An Economic Interpretation of the Constitution* (1913), and co-author, with his wife **Mary Ritter Beard** (1876–1958), of *The Rise of American Civilization* (1927), a popular survey. Beard's iconoclastic analysis of the origins of the Constitution in terms of the economic self-interest of its authors was a landmark in US historiography. He later became a bitter critic of the ROOSEVELT administration and the circumstances of US entry into WWII.

BEARD, Daniel Carter (1850–1941), organizer of the BOY SCOUTS of America. As National Scout Commissioner (1910–41), he gave the movement its distinctly American character, based on Indian and pioneer lore.

BEARDSLEY, Aubrey Vincent (1872–1898), English illustrator and author. By 1894 Beardsley had become art editor of the *Yellow Book* magazine and a prolific artist. His graphic style was one of sharp black-and-white contrasts, with flowing lines and detailed patterning; his subject matter tended towards the decadent or erotic, for instance, Oscar WILDE's *Salomé*, or ARISTOPHANES' *Lysistrata*.

BEAR FLAG REPUBLIC, republic declared in 1846 by a group of American settlers in Sacramento Valley, Cal., who rejected Mexican rule. Their flag, with a grizzly bear, a single star and the words "California Republic," was raised at Sonoma in June 1846. The explorer John C. FREMONT aided the insurgents, but the Republic collapsed after the outbreak of the Mexican War in May 1846; this ended in Feb. 1848 with Cal. ceded to the US. The Cal. state flag is modeled on the "Bear Flag."

BEARS, the world's largest extant terrestrial carnivores, characterized by their heavy build, thick limbs, diminutive tail and small ears and included in a single mammalian family, Ursidae. The differences between the seven species are small and are mainly limited to details of the skeleton. All have coarse thick hair which is, with the exception of the POLAR BEAR, dark in color. The varieties of the BROWN BEAR have the widest distribution. Other species are the North American Black Bear, the SPECTACLED BEAR, the ASIATIC BLACK BEAR, the SUN BEAR and the SLOTH BEAR.

BEAT GENERATION, literary movement of the 1950s, which burst onto the American scene in 1956 with Jack KEROUAC's *On the Road* (the adventures of the original social dropout), Allen GINSBERG's *Howl and Other Poems* and work by such poets as Lawrence Ferlinghetti and Gregory Corso, and later by the novelist William S. BURROUGHS. The movement was a protest against complacent middle-class values and, though shortlived, influenced artistic experiments for the next 15 years.

BEATITUDES, eight blessings pronounced by Christ as a prologue to the Sermon on the Mount (Matthew 5:3–10). Jesus calls "Blessed" those who are poor in spirit, the meek, those who mourn, those who seek after holiness, the merciful, the pure in heart, the peacemakers and those who suffer persecution for righteousness' sake.

BEATLES, The, English rock-music group that dominated popular music in the 1960s. Guitarists and composers **Paul McCartney** (1942–   ), **John Lennon** (1940–1980), and **George Harrison** (1943–   ), and drummer **Ringo Starr** (1940–   ) won fame in Britain with their recording "Please Please Me" (1963). The 1964 song "I Want To Hold Your Hand" introduced them to the US, where their concerts became scenes of mass adulation. *Revolver* (1966) and *Sgt.*

Pepper's Lonely Hearts Club Band (1967) are ranked among their finest albums, and their first film, *A Hard Day's Night* (1964) is highly regarded. The group disbanded in 1970. Paul McCartney later formed the successful group Wings. John Lennon's murder by a demented fan in New York City caused mourning around the world.

BEATON, Sir Cecil Walter Hardy (1904–1980), English photographer and designer, well known for his royal portraits, collections such as *Cecil Beaton's Scrapbook* (1937) and for set and costume designs for shows and films such as *My Fair Lady* (stage, 1956; motion picture, 1964). He was knighted in 1972.

BEATRICE, name given by the Italian poet DANTE ALIGHIERI to his ideal woman, signifying "bearer of blessings." She was based on the real Beatrice Portinari (d. 1290). Her main function in the *Divine Comedy* is as the intercessor who sends VIRGIL to Dante's aid, meets him in Purgatory and guides him through Paradise.

BEATTY, David, 1st Earl Beatty of the North Sea and of Brooksby (1871–1936), British admiral famous for his part in the Battle of JUTLAND (1916). He served in Egypt and Sudan and in China during the BOXER REBELLION. A rear admiral in 1910, he was made first sea lord and given an earldom in 1919.

BEATTY, Warren (1937–   ), US film actor who produced some of his own best acting vehicles, including *Bonnie and Clyde* (1968), *Shampoo* (1975) and *Heaven Can Wait* (1978).

BEAUHARNAIS, Joséphine de (1763–1814), first wife of NAPOLEON I and empress of the French. Before her marriage to Napoleon in 1796 (annulled in 1809) she had been the wife of Alexandre, Vicomte de Beauharnais (1760–94). Their son, Eugène **de Beauharnais** (1781–1824), was made viceroy of Italy by Napoleon. He distinguished himself in campaigns against Austria and Russia.

BEAUMARCHAIS, Pierre Augustin Caron de (1732–1799), French dramatist and variously an artist, litigant and political agent. His best-known plays, *The Barber of Seville* (1775) and *The Marriage of Figaro* (1784; the basis of MOZART'S opera) ridiculed the established order and the nobility. He was instrumental in furnishing the Americans with arms and money at the outbreak of the Revolution.

BEAUMONT, Francis (c1584–1616), and **FLETCHER, John** (1579–1625), English Jacobean playwrights. Their many plays, both as individuals and in collaboration, strongly influenced English drama. Their best-known collaborations are *Philaster* (c1608), *The Maid's Tragedy* (c1609) and *A King and No King* (1611).

BEAUREGARD, Pierre Gustave Toutant de (1818–1893), Confederate general during the American Civil War. In 1861 Beauregard commanded the attack on FORT SUMTER, S.C., which opened the war. He distinguished himself at the First Battle of BULL RUN, shared command at SHILOH and held off Union naval attacks on Charleston. Joining General Joseph E. JOHNSTON, he fell back to the Carolinas in the face of Sherman's Georgia campaign, and remained there until the end of the war.

BEAUVOIR, Simone de (1908–   ), French writer, friend of Jean-Paul SARTRE and a leading exponent of EXISTENTIALISM and the role of women in politics and intellectual life. Her best-known works are *The Second Sex* (1953) and *The Mandarins* (1956). She has also written an autobiographical trilogy, and a moving account of her mother's death, *A Very Easy Death* (1966).

BEAVERBROOK, William Maxwell Aitken, 1st Baron (1879–1964), Canadianborn British newspaper owner and Conservative cabinet minister. His government posts included minister of aircraft production 1940–42, and lord privy seal 1943–45. Among his mass-circulation newspapers are the *Daily Express, Sunday Express* and *Evening Standard*.

BEAVERS, large RODENTS (family Castoridae), weighing up to 40kg (90lb) or over, of northern lands. They have thick, furry waterproof coats, powerful, webfooted hindlegs and small forelimbs with dexterous, sensitive paws. They are lissencephalic (smooth-brained), but nevertheless by far the most intelligent rodents: their technical constructive skill, exemplified by their building, from logs and mud, dams and lodges (domes up to 7m (23ft) in diameter in which they live), is surpassed only by that of man. The dominant features of their SKULLS are the powerful incisors (see TEETH), with which they fell trees and gnaw logs into shape. Their large, heavy tails are used on land for balance and in the water as rudders. Their respiratory system (see RESPIRATION) enables them to remain underwater for up to 15 minutes.

BECCARIA, Cesare Bonesana, Marchese di (1738–1794), Italian criminologist and economist, instrumental in many major reforms in the treatment of criminals. His *Essay on Crimes and Punishments* (1764) recommended the abolition of capital punishment and torture.

BECHET, Sidney (1897–1959), US jazz clarinet and soprano saxophone player, who performed with such leading jazz artists as Bunk Johnson, King Oliver and Clarence Williams. After many tours in Europe, he settled in France in 1947.

BECK, Dave (1894–   ), US labor leader; president of the Teamsters Union 1952–1957. Expelled as a vice-president of the AFL-CIO in 1957 for misuse of union funds, he was convicted of that charge and of income-tax evasion, and was imprisoned 1962–64.

BECK, Jozef (1894–1944), Polish foreign minister 1932–39. His friendly relations with the German Nazi party enabled Poland to gain border territory from Czechoslovakia. However, when Hitler threatened Poland, Beck was forced to take refuge in Romania, where he remained until his death.

BECK, Ludwig (1880–1944), German general and chief of general staff, 1935. He resigned in protest from the Nazi party in 1938, and was then involved in the attempt to assassinate Hitler in 1944. When the plot failed, he was shot.

BECK, Martin (1867–1940), Hungarian-born US theatrical producer. He managed the 60-theater Orpheum Circuit (established 1903), west of Chicago. In New York he built vaudeville's Palace Theater (1913) and his legitimate Broadway theater, the Martin Beck (1924).

BECKENBAUER, Franz (1945–   ), West German soccer player who invented the position of "libero," or offensive sweeperback. He participated in three World Cups, and was captain of the 1974 championship team.

BECKER, Carl Lotus (1873–1945), US historian of Cornell University, Ithaca, N.Y., who brought an elegant style and original insights to such subjects as *The Declaration of Independence* (1922) and *The Heavenly City of the Eighteenth-Century Philosophers* (1932).

BECKET, Thomas à, Saint (1118–1170), martyr and archbishop of Canterbury. He first served as chancellor under Henry II, becoming a close friend, but in 1162 was appointed archbishop of Canterbury. Thereafter he supported the Church against the monarchy, and soon he and the king were at odds. The rift culminated in Becket's refusal to approve the royal "Constitutions of Clarendon," which sought to limit Church authority. A threatened papal interdict brought a temporary reconciliation, but in 1170 the intransigent Becket was murdered in the cathedral at Canterbury by four knights inspired by some rash words of the king's. Becket was canonized in 1173.

BECKETT, Samuel Barclay (1906–   ), Irish dramatist and novelist, resident in France since 1937. His work, much of it written in French, deals with habit, boredom and suffering, and is deeply pessimistic. His novels include *Murphy* (1938) and the trilogy, *Molloy, Malone Dies,* and *The Unnamable* (1951–53). Among his plays are *Waiting for Godot* (1952) and *Happy Days* (1961). Beckett won the 1969 Nobel Prize for Literature.

BECKMANN, Max (1884–1950), German painter and graphic artist. An expressionist until c1917, he then fell under the influence of George GROSZ, developing a more individual and strongly symbolic style. In 1933 his work was declared degenerate by the Nazis. He took refuge in Holland (1937–47) and later the US.

BECQUEREL, Antoine Henri (1852–1908), French physicist who, having discovered natural RADIOACTIVITY in a URANIUM salt in 1896, shared the 1903 Nobel physics prize with Pierre and Marie CURIE.

BEDBUGS, a number of BUGS of the family Cimicidae, order HEMIPTERA, bloodsuckers parasitic (see PARASITES) on man and other animals. The common bed-bug, *Cimex lectularius,* found throughout most of the world, is about 5mm (0.2in) long and 3mm (0.12in) broad, and colored usually mahogany brown, though it may appear reddish if it has recently fed or purplish if an older meal is still in its gut. Adults may survive for up to a year without feeding. Very occasionally they may transmit dangerous diseases.

BEDE, Saint (c673–735), known as "The Venerable," an Anglo-Saxon monk and scholar whose work embraced most of contemporary learning. His *Ecclesiastical History of the English Nation* is indispensable for the early history of England.

BEDLAM, familiar name for London's oldest insane asylum. It is a corruption of the name St. Mary of Bethlehem, founded in 1247 as a priory and made a hospital for the insane (1547). The term is now used for a madhouse or any uproar or chaos.

BEDOUIN, nomadic herdsmen of the Syrian, Arabian and Sahara deserts. Although Muslim, Bedouin society retains pre-Islamic beliefs. It is comprised of rigidly hierarchical tribal groups, some of which still practice slavery. Such values as obedience, generosity, honor, cunning, vengefulness and forgiveness are emphasized. (See ARAB; NOMAD.)

BEDSORES, sores and ULCERS occurring in bedridden patients when pressure and friction restrict skin blood supply. They may be prevented by frequent change of position and bathing; treatment includes ASTRINGENTS, SILICONE creams and ultraviolet light.

BEE, superfamily (Apoidea) of insects which convert nectar into HONEY for use as food. There are about 20,000 species. Bees and flowering plants are largely interdependent; plants are pollinated as the bees gather their pollen. Many farmers keep bees specially for this purpose.

Most bees are solitary and each female builds her own nest, although many bees may occupy a single site. Eggs are laid in cells provided with enough pollen-nectar paste to feed the larva until it becomes a flying, adult bee. Social bees (honeybees and bumblebees) live in a complex society of 10,000–50,000 members. Headed by the queen, whose function is to lay eggs (up to 2,000 a day), the community comprises female workers which collect pollen and build cells, and male bees, or drones, which fertilize the few young queens that appear each fall. Parasitic bees, not equipped to build hives, develop in the cells of the host working bees.

BEEBE, Charles William (1877–1962), US naturalist remembered for the descents into the ocean depths he made with Otis Barton in their BATHYSPHERE. Diving off Bermuda in 1934 they reached a then-record depth of 3,028ft (923m).

BEECHAM, Sir Thomas (1879–1961), English conductor. He introduced many operas to England, notably Richard STRAUSS' *Der Rosenkavalier*, and was an eloquent advocate of the music of his friend DELIUS. Beecham founded two orchestras, the London Philharmonic and the Royal Philharmonic.

BEECHER, Henry Ward (1813–1887), US clergyman, lecturer and author; preacher of Plymouth Congregational Church (1847–87), who was the subject of a notorious and sensational lawsuit for adultery. Like his father, Lyman BEECHER, he was renowned as an orator. He was a staunch advocate of ABOLITIONISM.

BEECHER, Lyman (1775–1863), US clergyman and liberal theologian who helped found the American Bible Society (1816). Beecher's sermons against slavery and intemperance made him one of the most influential orators of his time. His daughter was Harriet Beecher STOWE.

BEEF, the flesh of CATTLE. Beef cattle, bred to produce high quality meat, are heavily built with short necks and legs. They are usually slaughtered at the age of about three years, although modern techniques can fatten animals up within a year. About 12 cuts (e.g. brisket, sirloin, rump) are taken from a carcass. For the best flavor and texture, beef must be cooled and matured under controlled conditions.

BEEFEATER, obscure nickname given to the costumed warders of the Tower of London and sometimes to the YEOMEN OF THE GUARD. A great tourist attraction, Beefeaters' costumes date back to Tudor times.

BEE GEES, a British-Australian ROCK MUSIC group founded in 1963 by three brothers, Barry Gibb (b. 1947) and twins Robin and Maurice (b. 1949). Highly successful during the late 1960s, the Bee Gees reclaimed hit status with their 1977 score for the movie *Saturday Night Fever*.

BEEKEEPING, or **apiculture,** the husbandry (see ANIMAL HUSBANDRY) of BEES. The chief purpose of apiculture is the POLLINATION of crops, but commercial products of the hive include BEESWAX and of course HONEY: some 120,000 tons of honey are produced annually both in the USA and in the USSR.

BEELZEBUB, or Baalsebub ("Lord of flies"), god worshiped by the Philistines of Palestine. Being a pagan deity, he appears in the New Testament as the chief demon (Matthew 12:24). He is among the fallen angels in MILTON's *Paradise Lost*.

BEENE, Geoffrey (1927–   ), award-winning American fashion designer of women's and men's fashions and accessories. Some of Beene's designs are included in the costume collection of the Metropolitan Museum of Art.

BEER, an ALCOHOLIC BEVERAGE made by fermenting cereals (see BREWING). Known since ancient times, beer became common where the climate was unsuited to WINE production. Beer includes all the malt liquors variously called ale, stout, porter (drunk in the UK and Ireland) and lager. The alcohol content is 3–7%.

BEERBOHM, Sir Max (1872–1956), English satirical writer and caricaturist, educated at Merton College, Oxford. He is best known for the caustic yet benign wit of his caricatures of eminent Victorian and Edwardian figures, and for his satirical novel about Oxford, *Zuleika Dobson* (1911).

BEERSHEBA, chief city in southern Israel (the Negev), about 45mi SW of Jerusalem. Home of the Biblical patriarchs ISAAC and ABRAHAM and once the southernmost town of JUDAH, it is now a major industrial and trading center. Pop 77,400.

BEESON, Jack Hamilton (1921–   ), US

composer who wrote his first opera at the age of 12, and studied composition with Béla Bartók. Known best for his operas, which include *Jonah* (1950) and *Lizzie Borden* (1965), he also composed a symphony and choral works.

BEET, *Beta vulgaris,* biennial plant with a fleshy taproot. The most extensively grown variety is SUGAR BEET, which provides 33% of the world's SUGAR. Also cultivated are the garden (or red) beet, eaten, either boiled or pickled, the MANGELWURZEL, used as forage, and the leaf beet (SWISS CHARD), used as a potherb.

BEETHOVEN, Ludwig van (1770–1827), German composer, born in Bonn. His prodigious talent was soon recognized: HAYDN singled him out and offered to take the young musician on as a pupil in Vienna. There Beethoven's remarkable piano playing attracted attention, as did his eccentric behavior. Beethoven's deafness began when he was about 30 and was total by the time he was in his late 40s. This did not interfere with his creativity, but he never heard much of his mature work.

Beethoven's musical life is commonly divided into three periods. The *Pathétique* piano sonata and the First Symphony belong to the first period, ending about 1802, when he was still influenced by Haydn and MOZART. To the middle period, ending about 1816, belong works in his own individual style, such as the Third (*Eroica*) and Fifth Symphonies, Fifth Piano Concerto (*Emperor*), the *Kreutzer* Violin Sonata and the opera *Fidelio*. His later, more intense, highly individual works include the Ninth (Choral) Symphony, the *Missa Solemnis* (Mass in D) and the innovating late string quartets, including the *Grosse Fuge.*

BEETLES, common name for all insects of the order Coleoptera, the largest in the animal kingdom. Beetles occur in diverse forms, colors and habitats and range from 0.4mm to over 150mm in length. They are distinguished by hard protective wing cases which enclose a more fragile pair of wings. Some, however, such as the ground beetles and weevils, are flightless. All beetles develop from eggs into LARVAE and then pupate (see PUPA) before becoming adults. The life cycle can range from the usual three larval stages to as many as 12 or more and may last for as little as 2–3 weeks or as much as 5 years. Beetles and their larvae eat animal, vegetable and even inorganic matter; some eat carrion, others live off dung and a number prey on other beetles. Among the economically harmful beetles are the potato-destroying COLORADO BEETLE, and the woodworm and DEATHWATCH BEETLES which attack and destroy furniture and woodwork.

BEGIN, Menachem (1913–   ), Israeli prime minister. From boyhood in Poland he was active in the movement to establish a Jewish state in Palestine. After Israel won independence, he entered the Knesset (1948) and was an opposition leader for most of the next 30 years. He became the leader of the new Likud Party (1973) and won the prime ministership in 1977. He pressed Israel's claim to the West Bank of the Jordan and refused to consider sovereignty for the Palestinians. He signed a peace treaty with Egypt (1979) and was reelected in 1981. In 1978 he shared the Nobel Peace Prize with Egyptian President Anwar Sadat.

BEGONIA, a genus of perennial plants with about 900 species. Mostly succulent herbs, native to tropical regions, they are cultivated in house and garden for their colorful foliage, for example *Begonia diadema,* *B. rex* (silver leaf) and *B. masoniana* (iron cross), or for their attractive large flowers, for example *B.tuberhybrida* and the Reiger begonias. They have tuberous, rhizomatous or fibrous roots. Indoors, begonias grow best in a sunny east or west window during the winter, but the degree of direct summer sunlight that individual varieties can tolerate varies. They grow best within the temperature range 16°C to 21°C (60°F to 70°F) and hot dry air must be avoided. The soil should be kept evenly moist, avoiding extreme dryness or wetness. They can be propagated from seed, tuber and rhizome cuttings, leaf cuttings or division of the tubers. Family: Begoniaceae.

BEGUINES, religious communities of women established in Europe in the 12th century. Devoted to charitable works, Beguines were not, however, bound by any religious oath. From 1200 the movement spread from Belgium across W Europe. After a decline, it revived in the 1700s and a few communities still exist in Belgium and the Netherlands.

BEHAN, Brendan (1923–1964), Irish playwright and author, noted for his vivid ribaldry and satire. His best-known works, *The Quare Fellow* (1956), *The Hostage* (1959) and the autobiographical *Borstal Boy* (1958), deal largely with his experiences in the Irish Republican Army and subsequent imprisonment.

BEHAVIORAL SCIENCES, those sciences dealing with human behavior, individually or socially. The term, which is sometimes considered synonymous with SOCIAL SCIENCES, embraces such fields as PSYCHOLOGY, SOCIOLOGY and ANTHROPOLOGY.

BEHAVIORISM, school of PSYCHOLOGY based on the proposal that behavior should be studied empirically—by objective observations of reactions— (see EMPIRICISM) rather than speculatively. It had its roots in ANIMAL BEHAVIOR studies, defining behavior as the actions and reactions of a living organism (and, by extension, man) in its environment; and more specifically in the work of PAVLOV in such fields as conditioned REFLEXES. Behaviorism developed as an effective factor in US psychology following the work of J. B. WATSON just before WWI; and since then it has influenced most schools of psychological thought.

BEHN, Aphra (1640–1689), English dramatist, novelist and poet, the first professional English woman writer. Her many works, including the novel *Oroonoko* (1678) and the plays *The Forced Marriage* and *The Rover* (1681) show technical ingenuity, wit and vivacity.

BEHRENS, Peter (1868–1940), German architect who pioneered a mode of functional design suited to industrial technology. His most influential work was the AEG turbine factory in Berlin (1908–09). He influenced LE CORBUSIER and GROPIUS.

BEHRMAN, Samuel Nathaniel (1893–1973), US dramatist noted for his comedies of manners (*Biography*, 1932; *No Time for Comedy*, 1939). He has also written film scripts and a biography of satirist Max BEERBOHM (1960).

BEIDERBECKE, Leon Bismarck "Bix" (1903–1931), US jazz musician. An accomplished pianist and brilliant trumpet player, he joined the renowned Paul WHITEMAN band in 1928. Despite his early death through alcoholism and general ill health, he greatly influenced the development of jazz.

BEIRUT, capital and chief port of Lebanon on the E Mediterranean coast. It stands on a triangular peninsula at the foot of the Lebanon Mts. Beirut is an important commercial center and a major hub for international airways and railroads. The city was long a major Middle Eastern commercial and transportation center. Since the Lebanese civil war (1975–76), however, continued sporadic fighting in Beirut has destroyed much of the city and reduced its economic role. Pop 800,000.

BÉJART, Maurice (1927–   ), French dancer and choreographer. He danced with various companies in Europe and organized his own company in 1954. As director of the Ballet of the 20th Century in Brussels, Belgium, from 1959 he gave the company an international reputation.

BELAFONTE, Harry (1927–   ), US singer and actor, born in New York City. Famous originally for his West Indian calypso music, he has since worked as a film, TV and theater producer. Belafonte has also been active in civil rights.

BELASCO, David (1853–1931), US playwright and theatrical producer. In New York after 1880 he became famous for mounting spectacular productions, with lavishly detailed sets, to promote newly-discovered stars.

Official name: Republic of Belau
Capital: Koror
Area: 178sq mi
Population: 14,800
Languages: Palauan, English
Religions: Christian, traditional
Monetary unit(s): 1 US dollar = 100 cents
BELAU (formerly Palau), self-governing Micronesian island group in the W Pacific.
Land and People. The westernmost of the Caroline Island chain, Belau consists of about 200 volcanic and coral islands extending over an area 125mi long and 25mi wide. Babelthuap, the largest island, covers 156sq mi. On the larger islands the terrain consists of gently rolling, fertile, forested hills reaching 641ft on Babelthuap. Only eight of the islands are inhabited, with most people living on Koror, the administrative center and major port. With the exception of some Americans, the inhabitants are Micronesian.

Economy. Much of the labor force is engaged in small-scale agriculture, raising coconuts, breadfruit, bananas, taro and yams. Commercial fishing, especially for tuna, has become increasingly important. There is little industry except for a large mill that processes copra for export.

History. Belau was a Spanish possession from 1710 to 1898, when control passed to Germany. Commercial exploitation of Belau's resources begun under the Germans intensified after Japan captured the islands in 1914. With the Japanese defeat at the end of World War II, Belau and the rest of the Carolines passed to the US, and in 1947 were included in the US Trust Territory of the Pacific Islands. Self-government was instituted in 1981 after voters approved a constitution and the trusteeship was scheduled to terminate in the early 1980s.

BELAÚNDE TERRY, Fernando (1912–   ), Peruvian political leader who organized the reformist Popular Action Party (1956) and was elected president in 1963. He was overthrown in a military coup 1968 but was reelected when political democracy was restored 1980.

BEL CANTO, style of singing in 19th-century Italian opera, characterized by the singer's extravagant ornamentation of the music in order to heighten the emotional content and display versatility. Two great modern exponents are Maria CALLAS and Joan SUTHERLAND.

BELÉM, capital of Pará state, N Brazil, and chief port on the Amazon R basin, about 90mi from the Atlantic. Founded in 1616 by the Portuguese, Belém now handles rubber, Brazil nuts and timber exports. Pop 642,514.

BELFAST, seaport and capital of N Ireland (Ulster). Despite major shipbuilding and other industries, the area remains the most depressed in Britain. Since 1969 Belfast has seen violent clashes between the dominant Protestants and the Catholic minority. Pop 360,150.

Official name: Belgium
Capital: Brussels
Area: 11,778sq mi

Population: 9,860,000
Languages: French, Flemish, German
Religions: Roman Catholic
Monetary unit(s): 1 Belgian franc = 100 centimes

BELGIUM, kingdom of NW Europe, bordered to the W by France, to the E by Luxembourg and West Germany and to the N by the Netherlands. It has a short North Sea coastline. Belgium is one of Europe's most densely populated countries. There are nine regions: Antwerp, Brabant, E Flanders, W Flanders, Hainault, Liège, Limburg, Namur and Luxembourg.

Land. Flanders borders the sea and is mostly flat plain with sandy beaches; further inland, the region is intensively cultivated and drained by the Leie, Scheldt and Dender rivers. Central Belgium consists of a low plateau (300–600ft), which is also a rich agricultural area. The southern edge of this plateau is bounded by the Sambre-Meuse valley, the main industrial and coal-mining region of Belgium. About 25% of all Belgians live in this area of only 800sq mi. In SE Belgium lies the ARDENNES plateau, a mainly uncultivated area of peat bogs and woodlands, about 1000–1,500ft high. The country has a generally temperate climate.

People.   Belgium is politically and culturally divided because it has never been linguistically united. A line running East-West, just S of Brussels, divides the Flemish-speaking Flemings in the north and the French-speaking Walloons in the south. Both languages are in official use. The predominant religion in Belgium as a whole is Roman Catholicism.

History. The kingdom emerged only in the 1830s, when it seceded from the Netherlands. A revolutionary government proclaimed independence in 1830, and in 1839 Belgium was recognized as a perpetually neutral sovereign state. The country was led to prosperity under Kings LEOPOLD I and II.

Belgian neutrality was violated by Germany in 1914 and 1940, and massive destruction was caused before its liberation by Allied and resistance forces in 1944. Belgium recovered rapidly, economically and industrially, under King BAUDOUIN, and is now a prosperous member of the European COMMON MARKET, thanks to successful manufacturing industries and transportation systems.

BELGRADE, capital of Yugoslavia, a busy port and industrial center at the junction of the Danube and Sava rivers. Important products include machine tools, tractors, furniture and foodstuffs. Pop 1,209,000.

BELINSKY, Vissarion Grigoryevich (1811– 1848), Russian literary critic who founded the socially conscious school of criticism dominant in Russia until the end of the 19th century. He championed what he saw as the social realism of GOGOL, LERMONTOV and PUSHKIN.

Official name: Belize
Capital: Belmopan
Area: 8,866sq mi
Population: 152,000
Languages: English, Spanish, Indian dialects
Religion: Roman Catholic, Protestant
Monetary unit(s): 1 Belizean dollar = 100 cents

BELIZE (known as British Honduras until 1973), an independent nation since 1981.

Land. Situated on the subtropical Caribbean coast of Central America, Belize is bordered by Mexico on the N and by Guatemala on the SW. The country, which is densely forested, is about the size of New Hampshire.

People and economy. The population consists of Creoles (of mixed African and European origin), descendants of Carib Indians, Maya Indians, and a small minority of Europeans. Most people live on the coast. Timber used to be the mainstay of the export-oriented economy, but it has been supplanted by citrus fruits, bananas and sugarcane. Fishing and livestock industries are being developed.

History. European settlement began in the 17th century and in the 18th century African slaves were brought in to cut mahogany. The country became a British colony in 1862 and achieved internal self-government in 1964. Disputes with Guatemala concerning the latter's claim that Belize is an inheritance from Spain delayed the proclamation of independence until 1981.

BELL, residential city in Cal., 5mi S of Los Angeles. It manufactures automobile parts and paint products. Pop 21,836.

BELL, Alexander Graham (1847–1922), Scottish-born US scientist and educator who invented the TELEPHONE (1876), founded the Bell Telephone Company and devised the wax-cylinder PHONOGRAPH and various aids for teaching the deaf. In later life he helped perfect the AILERON for airplanes.

BELL, Clive (1881–1964), English art and literary critic and member of the BLOOMSBURY GROUP. He married Virginia WOOLF'S sister, Vanessa Stephen (1907). Some of his best criticism is to be found in his books *Art* (1914) and *Since Cézanne* (1922).

BELL, Daniel (1919–), US sociologist, author of the controversial *The End of Ideology* (1960) and *The Coming of Post-Industrial Society* (1973). He co-founded, with Irving Kristol, the quarterly *Public Opinion* (1965), and has taught at Harvard since 1969.

BELL, John (1797–1869), "Tennessee Bell," presidential candidate of the CONSTITUTIONAL UNION PARTY (1860) who lost to Lincoln on the eve of the American Civil War. As congressman 1827–41 and senator 1847–59, he was leader of a conservative group of anti-secessionist southerners. He held Tenn. in the Union until President Lincoln's call to arms, when he openly, but not actively, espoused the rebel cause.

BELLADONNA, or **deadly nightshade,** *Atropa belladonna,* poisonous bushy herb, native to Europe and parts of Asia. Its dried leaves and roots provide the belladonna drug from which medicinal ALKALOIDS such as ATROPINE are produced. Modern synthetic drugs are more reliable and are superseding belladonna alkaloids. (See also BITTERSWEET.)

BELLAMY, Edward (1850–1898), US author. His Utopian *Looking Backward: 2000–1877* (1888) pictured a benevolent state socialism with worker-ownership. Following its success, "Bellamy Clubs" and a "Nationalist" movement to promote his ideas attracted a nationwide following.

BELLINI, family of Early Renaissance Venetian artists. **Jacopo** (c1400–c1470) evolved a much-imitated compositional technique of depicting small figures in vast, precisely detailed architectural settings. Few of his paintings survive, but he influenced others directly and through his sons and son-in-law, Andrea MANTEGNA. **Gentile** (c1429–1507), his elder son, is noted for his strong, realistic portraits as well as for his use of PERSPECTIVE to give a sense of true spatial depth. **Giovanni** (c1430–1516), the younger son, was the greatest Early Renaissance Venetian painter. His early works were influenced by Mantegna, but he later developed the poetic use of light and color for which he is famous. His pupils, TITIAN and GIORGIONE, continued and developed his style.

BELLINI, Vincenzo (1801–1835), Italian opera composer of the BEL CANTO school. His most popular works today are his last three: *La Sonnambula* (1831), *Norma* (1831) and *I Puritani* (1835).

BELLOC, (Joseph Pierre) Hilaire (1870–1953), French-born English poet, essayist and historian. An ardent Roman Catholic polemicist and close friend of G. K. CHESTERTON, his first well-known work was *The Bad Child's Book of Beasts* (1896).

BELLOW, Saul (1915–   ), Canadian-born American novelist noted for his narrative skill and for his studies of Jewish-American life. His best-known books are *Herzog* (1964) and *The Adventures of Augie March* (1953). Other novels include *Dangling Man* (1944), *Henderson the Rain King* (1959), *Mr. Sammler's Planet* (1970) and *Humboldt's Gift* (1975).

BELLOWS, George Wesley (1882–1925), US painter and lithographer. One of the best and most interesting early 20th-century "realists," he often succeeded in capturing the raw human energy of his countrymen. Bellows, who remained aloof from modern European influences, was also influential in reviving US lithography.

BELL TELEPHONE LABORATORIES, research organization set up in 1925 by the American Telephone and Telegraph Company. The Bell Laboratories have been responsible for many important developments in telecommunications technology, notably the TRANSISTOR.

BELMONDO, Jean Paul (1933–   ), French film actor who achieved international prominence with his performance in *Breathless* (1959) and became France's movie superstar. His films include *That Man From Rio* (1964), *Pierrot le Fou* (1965) and *Stavisky* (1974).

BELMONTE, Juan (1892–1962), matador who revolutionized bullfighting (1913–34). He developed the practice of deviating the bull, rather than sidestepping it, a style that was copied for years. In 1919 he appeared in a record-breaking 109 corridas (programs).

BELSEN, German village in Lower Saxony, former site of the infamous Nazi concentration camp where over 115,000 people, mostly Jews, were killed.

BELUGA, *Huso huso*, the largest STURGEON, found in seas and rivers of the USSR, and achieving lengths of nearly 9m (30ft); also, *Delphinapterus leucas*, a small whale, also known as the White Whale, related to the NARWHAL and found in

northern seas at lengths up to 5.5m (18ft).

BELY, Andrei (pseudonym of Boris Bugaev, 1880–1934), Russian poet and novelist, a leading theoretician of the Russian Symbolist movement. In addition to several collections of verse, Bely wrote modernist novels, including *The Silver Dove* (1909), *Kotik Letaev* (1916) and his masterpiece, *Petersburg*, a novel of the 1905 Revolution set in the tsarist capital.

BEMBO, Pietro (1470–1547), Italian humanist, scholar, writer and cardinal. He played an important part in the Renaissance language debate, writing one of the first Italian grammars, and advocating a literary language modelled on the examples of BOCCACCIO and PETRARCH.

BEMELMANS, Ludwig (1898–1962), Austrian–American writer and illustrator of *Hansi* (1934), *Madeline* (1939), *My War with the United States* (1937) and other satiric and children's stories.

BEMIS, Samuel Flagg (1891–1973), US historian. A Yale professor (1935–60), he was an expert on US diplomatic history. His books included *A Diplomatic History of the United States* (1936) and two Pulitzer Prize winning works, *Pinckney's Treaty* (1926) and *John Quincy Adams and the Foundations of American Foreign Policy* (1950).

BENARES. See VARANASI.

BENAVENTE Y MARTÍNEZ, Jacinto (1866–1954), Spanish playwright who wrote and staged 172 comedies and helped establish the modern theater in Spain. He was awarded the 1922 Nobel Prize for Literature for such popular plays as *Bonds of Interest* (1907) and *La Malquerida* (1913).

BEN BELLA, Ahmed (1918–   ), Algerian revolutionary who helped plan the 1954 anti-French revolt. After the post-independence power struggle of 1963, Ben Bella became president but was ousted by Col. BOUMEDIENNE's coup of June 19, 1965.

BENCHLEY, Robert Charles (1889–1945), US writer, drama critic of *Life,* 1920–29, and the *New Yorker,* 1929–40. He is best known for his short humorous pieces, published in several collections, and his satirical short films. His grandson, **Peter Benchley** (1928–   ) wrote the best-selling novel *Jaws* (1975).

BENDA, Julien (1867–1956), French novelist and philosopher. A leading rationalist, he was best known for his influential work *The Treason of the Intellectuals* (1927), which decried the contemporary decline of reason and the growth of political and racial ideologies.

BENEDICT, Ruth (née Fulton;

1887–1948), US cultural anthropologist, whose extensive fieldwork helped illustrate the theory of cultural relativism— that what is deemed deviant in one culture may be normal in another. (See ANTHROPOLOGY.)

BENEDICTINE ORDERS, the "Black Monks," order of monks and nuns following the rule of St. Benedict of Nursia. Their motto is "Pray and work." Stress is laid on a combination of prayer, choral office, study and manual labor under an abbot's supervision. There has been a great revival of the Benedictine rule since 1830 in Europe and the US.

BENEDICT OF NURSIA, Saint (c480–547), father of Western monasticism, whose "rule" set the pattern of monastic life from the mid-7th century. For three years he lived as a hermit near Subiaco, Italy. His piety attracted many followers, some of whom he later grouped in 12 monasteries. Benedict also founded the monastery of MONTE CASSINO.

BENELUX, a custom union between Belgium, the Netherlands and Luxembourg, established in 1944 and revised by the Hague protocol of 1947. Benelux is often used collectively for the countries themselves.

BENES, Eduard (1884–1948), cofounder, with Tomáš MASARYK, of the Czechoslovak Republic. He was foreign minister 1918–35, prime minister 1921–22, president 1935–38 and 1946–48, and head of government-in-exile 1939–45. His appeals to Britain and France in 1938 failed to prevent Hitler's occupation of the Sudetenland. He died after the 1948 communist coup.

BENÉT, Stephen Vincent (1898–1943), US poet, novelist and short story writer, whose works center on US history and tradition. His epic poems *John Brown's Body* (1928) and *Western Star* (1943) won Pulitzer prizes. Among his most famous short stories is *The Devil and Daniel Webster* (1937).

BENGAL, region including Bangladesh and NE India on the Bay of Bengal. Its chief city, Calcutta, was capital of British India 1833–1912, and it was an autonomous province from 1935 until the partition of India in 1947. The W became West Bengal State and the E was included in Pakistan until Bangladesh's 1971 declaration of independence. Most of the S is occupied by the Ganges-Brahmaputra delta.

BENGALI, Indo-Aryan language, related to Assamese, Bihari and Oriya. One of the principal languages of the Indian subcontinent, it has a rich literary heritage and is spoken by some 90 million people in Bangladesh and 50 million in West Bengal.

BENGHAZI, second-largest city of Libya. It is a port on the Gulf of Sidra and the marketing center for a rich agricultural region. It was the scene of heavy fighting in WWII. Pop 337,423.

BEN-GURION, David (1886–1973), Polish-born founder and first prime minister of Israel. After WWI he cofounded the *Haganah* underground Jewish army and the *Histadrut*, the General Federation of Jewish Labor (1920). He became leader of the *Mapai* labor party (1930) and the World Zionist Organization (1935). As prime minister and defense minister, 1949–53 and 1955–63, he, more than any other leader, molded modern Israel.

BENIN, historic W African kingdom, on the Guinea Coast. It flourished between the 14th and 17th centuries, later enjoying a lively trade in pepper and ivory. Its culture was highly sophisticated: Benin bronze sculpture is now world-famous. By the 19th century the slave trade had decimated its male population. It became part of British Nigeria in 1897.

Official name: People's Republic of Benin
Capital: Porto Novo
Area: 43,480sq mi
Population: 3,567,000
Languages: French; Fon, Mina, Yoruba, Dendi
Religions: Animist; Muslim, Roman Catholic, Protestant
Monetary uni(s): 1 CFA franc = 100 centimes

BENIN, a republic in W Africa, bounded by Togo, Upper Volta, Niger, Nigeria and the Atlantic, until 1975 known as Dahomey.

Land. Benin is long and narrow, extending inland some 450mi from the Gulf of Guinea to the Niger R. Beyond the lagoons that lie behind the coastal strip, the country is flat and forested. In the N, streams flow to the Volta and Niger rivers. In the NW are the Atacora Mts, Benin's highest elevation, about 2,000ft. S Benin has an equatorial climate, with two rainy and two dry seasons. There is only one rainy season in the N, where the climate is tropical.

People. The population is concentrated in the S coastal region, where Cotonou, a major port city and commerce city, and Porto Novo, the capital, are located. There are four major tribes: the Fon, Adja and Yoruba in the S and the Bariba in the NE and central regions. There is a small European community, mostly French. There are some technical schools and one university, but illiteracy is high.

Economy. Benin is one of the world's poorer countries. Its economy is based on agriculture; the major cash crop is the oil palm. Other exports include hides and skins, cotton, peanuts and coffee. Excessive dependence on one commodity and on foreign aid have hampered economic growth; however, Benin's position as a transit point for Nigeria and landlocked Niger has provided the impetus for an expanding transport sector. Industry, on the whole, is presently small-scale.

History. Benin or Dahomey came under French influence in 1851, after taking a profitable part in the slave trading which earned the region the title of the Slave Coast. It became part of French West Africa in 1904 but gained independence in 1960 and joined the UN. Since then it has suffered from political turmoil, including a series of coups in the 1960s. A three-man Presidential Council was established in 1970. The council was overthrown by the army in 1972. Power was transferred to a civilian government in 1979–80, although a military leader remains as president.

BENIOFF ZONE, an inclined zone of progressively deeper EARTHQUAKE foci, usually extending from a deep-sea trench into the earth's upper MANTLE to a position underlying an adjacent continent. In plate tectonic theory, Benioff Zones are characteristic of convergent (destructive) plate margins where the leading edge of a plate is subducted into the upper mantle and is destroyed by melting. (See also PLATE TECTONICS; SUBDUCTION ZONE.)

BENJAMIN, Judah Philip (1811–1884), West Indian-born US politician and lawyer, called the "brains of the Confederacy." As US senator from La. (1853–61), he proved an able advocate of the Southern cause. After secession, Jefferson DAVIS, his personal friend, appointed him successively attorney general, secretary of war, and finally secretary of state (1862–65) in the Confederate government. On the collapse of the Confederacy Benjamin fled to England, where he became a highly successful barrister.

BENN, Anthony Wedgwood (1925–), British political leader. Elected to Parliament (1950), he renounced his family's peerage (1963) in order to remain in the House of Commons. An important Labour Party figure thereafter, associated with its left wing, he lost a contest for deputy leader in 1981.

BENNETT, (Enoch) Arnold (1867–1931), English novelist, journalist and playwright. He is famous for his novels set in the potteries of Staffordshire: *Anna of the Five Towns* (1902), *The Old Wives' Tale* (1908), *Clayhanger* (1910), *Hilda Lessways* (1911) and *These Twain* (1916).

BENNETT, Floyd (1890–1928), US aviator who piloted Richard BYRD on the first flight over the N Pole (May 9, 1926). He was awarded the Congressional Medal of Honor.

BENNETT, James Gordon (1795–1872), Scottish-born US newspaper publisher and editor, pioneer of modern news reporting. In 1835 he launched the popular, sensationalist *New York Herald*, becoming the first to print stock market items and use the telegraph as a news source. His son, **James Gordon Bennett** (1841–1918), sent H. M. STANLEY to find David LIVINGSTONE (1869), and founded the *New York Evening Telegram* (1869) and the *Paris Herald* (1887).

BENNETT, Richard Bedford, Viscount (1870–1947), Canadian premier 1930–35. He presided over the 1932 Ottawa Conference which created preferential tariffs within the British Commonwealth. He was leader of the Conservative party (1927–38) and was created a viscount in 1941.

BENNETT, Richard Rodney (1936–), English composer known primarily for the strong dramatic sense with which he imbued his works. His opera *Mines of Sulphur* displays this dramatic gift above all in the emotional intensity of its orchestration.

BENNINGTON, town in SW Vt., seat of Bennington Co. On Aug. 16, 1777, during the Revolutionary War, the GREEN MOUNTAIN BOYS defeated a British raiding force nearby. The present small manufacturing town includes the first Vt. schoolhouse, several colonial buildings and W. L. GARRISON'S printing shop. Pop 15,815.

BENNY, Jack (1894–1974), US radio and television comedian, considered a master of comic timing. Both in his radio program (1932–55) and throughout his television career (1955–65), he portrayed a vain skinflint who refused to age beyond his 39th birthday. His show, which made good use of a stock company of regulars, was one of the most consistently popular on the air.

BENTHAM, Jeremy (1748–1832), English philosopher, economist and jurist. He propounded UTILITARIANISM, the aim of which was to achieve "the greatest happiness of the greatest number," and argued that legislation should be governed by that aim. These ideas were expressed in *An Introduction to the Principles of Morals and Legislation* (1789). He had a major influence on prison and law reform in the 19th century, and on the thinking of J. S. MILL and D. RICARDO. His head and skeleton, dressed in his own suit, sit in University College, London.

BENTLEY, Eric (1916–   ), British-born US drama critic and university teacher. Through his translations and theater work he was instrumental in introducing the plays and ideas of BRECHT to the English-speaking world.

BENTON, Thomas Hart (1782–1858), US statesman. He represented Mo. in the US Senate for 30 years (1821–51), championing the development of the West and the interests of the common man. Benton was a leader in the fight against the Second Bank of the United States, earning the nickname "Old Bullion Benton" for his advocacy of hard money. His principles led him to oppose the Mexican War, and his opposition to the spread of slavery lost him his Senate seat and brought his brief career in the House (1853–55) to an end.

BENTON, Thomas Hart (1889–1975), US painter, grandnephew of Senator T. H. Benton. He was a leader of the influential 1930s regionalist school of painting, devoted to depicting the life of rural America. He was particularly known for his vivid murals of the midwestern scene.

BENZ, Karl (1844–1929), German engineer who built the first commercially successful AUTOMOBILE (1885). His earliest autos were tricycle carriages powered by a small INTERNAL-COMBUSTION ENGINE.

BENZENE (C_6H_6), colorless toxic liquid HYDROCARBON produced from PETROLEUM by refining, and from COAL GAS and COAL TAR. It is the prototypical aromatic HYDRO-CARBON compound; its molecular structure, first proposed by KEKULÉ, is based on a regular planar hexagon of carbon atoms. Stable and not very reactive, benzene forms many substitution products, and also reacts with the HALOGENS to give addition products—including γ-benzene hexachloride, a powerful insecticide. It is used as a solvent, in motor fuel, and as the starting material for the manufacture of a vast variety of other aromatic compounds, especially PHENOL, STYRENE, ANILINE and

maleic anhydride, mp 5°C, bp 80°C.

BEN-ZVI, Itzhak (1884–1963), Russian-born second president of Israel (1952–63). He was active in Jewish pioneer and self-defense groups in Palestine from 1907, and in 1929 was a founder of the VAAD LEUMI (National Council of Palestine Jews).

BEOWULF, anonymous heroic epic poem, c8th century, the greatest extant poem in Old English. The poem uses elements of Germanic legend and is set in Scandinavia. It tells of the hero Beowulf's victories over the monster Grendel and Grendel's mother, his battle with a dragon, and his death and burial. The only manuscript (c1000) is in the British Museum.

BERBERS, several culturally separate N African tribes who speak the Hamitic Berber language or any of its many dialects. Almost all the tribes are Muslim. They live mainly in Algeria, Libya, Morocco and Tunisia. Most are farmers or nomadic herders, but some are oasis-dwellers. They include the Jerbans, Kabyles, Mzabites, Riffians, Beraber, Shluh, Shawia and TUAREGS.

BERCEUSE (French: lullaby), a musical composition, often in 6/8 time, with a rocking bass line similar to a lullaby. The German term is *Wiegenlied*.

BERCHTESGADEN, small SE Bavarian resort town in the Bavarian Alps, West Germany. Nearby, Hitler built the Berghof, his fortified chalet retreat, with its deep mountainside bunkers. Pop 4,500.

BERCHTOLD, Count Leopold von (1863–1942), Austro-Hungarian foreign minister 1912–15. His ultimatum to Serbia (July 23, 1914), following the assassination of Archduke FRANZ FERDINAND, was the spark that ignited WORLD WAR I.

BERDYAEV, Nikolai Aleksandrovich (1874–1948), Russian religious philosopher. A Marxist in his youth, he later turned to Christianity and created a highly individual Christian existentialism. Expelled from the USSR in 1922, he settled in Paris.

BERENSON, Bernard (1865–1959), Lithuanian-born US art historian. An expert on Italian Renaissance painting, he wrote the definitive study *Italian Painters of the Renaissance* (1894–1907). Berenson bequeathed his Italian villa, art collection and library to Harvard.

BERG, Alban (1885–1935), Austrian composer of expressive TWELVE-TONE MUSIC. A pupil of SCHOENBERG, he adopted his technique in such works as his violin concerto (1935) and two operas, *Wozzeck* (1925) and the unfinished *Lulu* (1935).

(See also ATONALITY.)

BERG, Gertrude (1899–1966), US radio and television performer. She created "Molly Goldberg," one of the great radio characters of the 1930's. Her long-running program, *The Goldbergs*, depicted the daily life of a Jewish family in New York City.

BERG, Paul (1926–   ), US biochemist who developed recombinant DNA technology (or "gene splicing") which made it possible for scientists to manipulate and reproduce genetic material of CELLS from any species. He shared the 1980 Nobel Prize in Chemistry with Frederick SANGER and Walter GILBERT.

BERGEN, seaport city in SW Norway, on the By Fjord, Norway's second-largest city and second most important port, a major manufacturing center. It was a member of the medieval HANSEATIC LEAGUE. Pop 208,900.

BERGEN, Edgar (1903–1978), US comedian and ventriloquist. Inseparable in the public mind from his wisecracking dummy, Charley McCarthy, he appeared (1937–47) on radio and later in films and on television. Bergen, who also worked with the dummy Mortimer Snerd, was one of the few ventriloquists to introduce true wit and character comedy into his act.

BERGER, Thomas (1924–   ), US writer. He traced the life of his favorite protagonist, Carlo Reinhart, from youth to middle age in four exuberant, insightful novels, including *Reinhart's Women* (1981). Another novel, *Little Big Man* (1967), related the improbable adventures of the lone survivor of Custer's Last Stand.

BERGER, Victor Louis (1860–1929), the first US Socialist congressman (1911–13, 1918, 1919, 1923–29). Born in Austria, Berger was a founder and leader of the American Socialist party. In WWI he was sentenced to 20 years' imprisonment for aiding the enemy, but was freed on appeal.

BERGMAN, (Ernst) Ingmar (1918–   ), Swedish film and stage director, producer and writer. He combines realism with imaginative symbolism to explore themes such as good and evil, love, old age and death. Famous motion pictures include *The Seventh Seal* (1956), *Wild Strawberries* (1957), *Persona* (1966) and *Cries and Whispers* (1971).

BERGMAN, Ingrid (1915–   ), Swedish stage and screen actress. She went to Hollywood in 1939 and became an internationally admired film star, winning Academy Awards for *Gaslight* (1944), *Anastasia* (1956) and *Murder on the Orient Express* (1974). She has made several notable stage appearances in Paris, London and New York.

BERGSON, Henri Louis (1859–1941), French philosopher, the first exponent of PROCESS PHILOSOPHY. Reacting against the physicists' definition of TIME and substituting a notion of experienced duration; rejecting the psychophysical parallelism of the day and asserting the independence of mind, and viewing EVOLUTION not as a mechanistic but as a creative process energized by an *élan vital* (vital impulse), Bergson was perhaps the most original philosopher of the early 20th century. He was awarded the Nobel Prize for Literature in 1927.

BERIA, Lavrenti Pavlovich (1899–1953), head of the Soviet secret police (1938–53). As commissar for internal affairs he was responsible for thousands of political executions. Shortly after Stalin's death he was secretly executed for treason.

BERIBERI, deficiency disease caused by lack of VITAMIN B_1 (thiamine); it may occur in MALNUTRITION, ALCOHOLISM or as an isolated deficiency. NEURITIS leading to sensory changes, and foot or wrist drop, palpitations, EDEMA and HEART failure are features; there may be associated dementia. Onset may be insidious or acute. Treatment is thiamine replacement; thiamine enrichment of common foods prevents beriberi.

BERING SEA, the extreme N arm of the N Pacific Ocean, 885,000sq mi in area, bounded by E Siberia, Alaska and the Aleutian Islands. It contains Nunivak Island, St. Lawrence Island, the Pribilof Islands (all US) and the Komandorskiye Islands (USSR). The international dateline crosses it diagonally.

BERING SEA CONTROVERSY, Anglo-American dispute in the late 19th century. When indiscriminate slaughter by various nations threatened the valuable seal herds of the US-owned Pribilof Islands in the Bering Sea, the US seized three Canadian ships (1886) and claimed dominion over the Bering Sea (1889). Britain objected, and in 1893 an arbitration tribunal declared the Bering Sea international.

BERING STRAIT, linking the Arctic and Pacific oceans and separating Asia (the USSR) from America (Alaska). It contains the Diomede Islands and is icebound from Nov. to June.

BERKELEY, city in W Cal., on San Francisco Bay, opposite the Golden Gate bridge. A residential suburb of San Francisco, it has the main campus of the U. of Cal. and research laboratories. Pop 103,328.

BERKELEY, Busby (1895–1976), US

choreographer and film director who revolutionized the staging of musical-production numbers in Hollywood films. He introduced lavish settings, revolving platforms and giant staircases upon which hundreds of extras performed in such extravaganzas as *Forty-Second Street* (1933) and *Gold Diggers of 1933*.

BERKELEY, George (1685–1753), Irish philosopher and bishop who, rejecting the views of LOCKE as to the nature of material substance, substituted the *esse-percipi* principle: to be is to be perceived (or to be capable of perception). Thus for Berkeley there is no material reality but only ideas belonging to minds and deriving from God. Berkeley's acute analysis of experience and his cogent argumentation rendered his "subjective idealism" an important influence on subsequent views of knowledge.

BERKELEY, Sir William (1606–1677), royal governor of Virginia (1642–52 and 1660–77). His autocratic rule in his second term and an inability or unwillingness to deal with Indian frontier attacks caused BACON'S REBELLION (1676). Berkeley's harsh treatment of the rebels led to his recall to England.

BERLE, Adolf Augustus, Jr. (1895–1971), US economist, member of President Franklin D. Roosevelt's "brain trust" and assistant secretary of state 1938–44. He cowrote *The Modern Corporation* (1932), a study of economic concentration in the US.

BERLE, Milton (1908–), US comedian who became known as "Mr. Television" for his pioneering comedy work in that medium. Originally a vaudevillian and radio performer, he developed extravagant comedy routines which are believed to have played a major role in spreading the sale of television sets to lower-income households during the late 1940s and early 1950s. He also appeared in over a dozen films.

BERLIN, major city located in the E central part of East Germany, with a corridor to West Germany. It covers 341sq mi and stands on a sandy plain at the center of a network of roads, railroads and waterways.

Berlin was the capital of Germany, 1871–1945. Since WWII it has been divided into East Berlin (formerly the Russian zone, now capital of communist East Germany) and West Berlin (a state of West Germany, though not constitutionally part of it). West Berlin contains 12 districts of the original city and is divided into British, French and US zones. East Berlin contains 8 districts of the old city. The BERLIN WALL separates both halves of the city; East Germany and the USSR have restricted movement between them and at times between West Berlin and West Germany (see BERLIN AIRLIFT). The Four Power Agreement of June 1972 guaranteed freer access to West Berlin and allowed its citizens to visit the East.

Berlin emerged in the Middle Ages, became the capital of Prussia in 1701 and grew into one of Europe's greatest political, commercial and cultural centers. The city was shattered in WWII, but has been rebuilt and revitalized. Pop:. East Berlin 1,085,400; West Berlin 2,131,900.

BERLIN, Conference of, held in Berlin (1884–85) by 14 countries to discuss colonial rivalries in Africa. It established the principle that occupation of African territory had to be effective to be legal, recognized the Congo Free State set up by Leopold of Belgium and discussed the control of the Congo and Niger rivers.

BERLIN, Congress of, international meeting held in June–July 1878 to settle problems created by the 1877–78 Russo-Turkish war, notably Russian claims to Balkan territory. The resultant Treaty of Berlin was signed on Aug. 24. Romania, Bulgaria, Serbia and Montenegro became independent; Romania gained N Dobrudja and ceded Bessarabia to Russia; Russian possession of the Caucasus was confirmed; the UK gained Cyprus, and Austria-Hungary was to administer Bosnia-Hercegovina. The congress was chaired by BISMARCK, acting as "honest broker."

BERLIN, Irving (1888–), US song writer, born in Russia as Israel Baline. He wrote over 900 popular songs, including *Alexander's Ragtime Band* (1911) and *God Bless America* and *White Christmas* (1942); film scores, including *Top Hat* (1935); and musicals such as *Annie Get Your Gun* (1946) and *Call Me Madam* (1950). He won a Congressional gold medal (1954) for his patriotic songs.

BERLIN, Sir Isaiah (1909–), Latvian-born British philosopher and historian of ideas. He is best known for a biography of Karl Marx (1939), his study of Tolstoy *The Hedgehog and the Fox* (1953), and *Historical Inevitability* (1955). He also wrote *Russian Thinkers* (1978) and *Against the Current* (1980).

BERLIN AIRLIFT, operation by the UK and US to fly essential supplies into West Berlin during the Russian blockade of Allied land and water routes to the city (June 28, 1948–May 12, 1949). It continued until Sept. 30, 1949, involving 250,000 flights, 2 million tons of supplies and a cost of $224 million.

BERLIN WALL, 27mi-long wall built in

Aug. 1961 by the East Germans to separate East and West Berlin. Made of concrete, steel and barbed wire, it is floodlit and constantly patrolled by armed guards. There are 12 official crossing points.

BERLIOZ, Louis Hector (1803–1869), French Romantic composer of dramatic, descriptive works, some for immense orchestras. Major works include his *Symphonie Fantastique* (1830), *Requiem* (1837), the choral symphony *Romeo and Juliet* (1838–39), the oratorio *The Childhood of Christ* (1850–54) and the operas *Benvenuto Cellini* (1838) and *The Trojans* (1856–59). Berlioz also wrote music criticism, a valuable treatise on instrumentation (1844), and his memoirs (1870).

BERMAN, Shelley (1926–   ), US comedian whose album *Inside Shelley Berman* (1959) sparked off a new trend in low-key "stand-up" comedy. He later turned to straight acting.

BERMUDA, British colony comprising about 150 coral islands of which 20 are inhabited. It lies in the N Atlantic Ocean, 580mi E of N.C. The main island is Bermuda Island, with the capital, Hamilton. The climate is warm and the vegetation lush and tropical. Bermuda's first British colonists arrived in 1609. Some 60% of present inhabitants are descendants of Negro slaves, and the rest are mainly British. The economy depends on tourism and two US bases. Pop 55,000.

BERMUDA TRIANGLE, an area roughly bounded by Bermuda, Puerto Rico, and Miami, in which many ships and planes are said to have vanished. Natural and supernatural causes, ranging from storms to space-time warps, have been proposed to explain the allegedly mysterious disappearances.

BERN (Berne), capital city of Switzerland and of Bern canton. It lies on the Aare R in the German-speaking area. It is an important commercial, industrial and cultural center and the headquarters of some major international communications organizations. Bern was founded in 1191 and retains many old buildings. Pop 141,300.

BERNADETTE, Saint (1844–1879), born Marie-Bernarde Soubirous. French peasant girl who claimed to have had 18 visions of the Virgin Mary in a LOURDES grotto in 1858. The grotto became a shrine, and she was beatified (1925) and canonized (1933). Her feast day is Feb. 18 in France, April 16 elsewhere.

BERNADOTTE, Count Folke (1895–1948), Swedish UN mediator in the 1948 Arab–Israeli war. In spring 1945 he was the go-between for HIMMLER'S offer to the Allies of a conditional Nazi surrender. It was rejected. On Sept. 17, 1948, he was assassinated in Jerusalem by the Zionist Stern gang.

BERNADOTTE, Jean Baptiste Jules (1763–1844), French general who founded Sweden's present royal dynasty. He became one of Napoleon's marshals (1804), and was elected Swedish crown prince in 1810. He fought Napoleon at Leipzig (1813) and ruled Sweden and Norway as Charles XIV (1818–44).

BERNAL, John Desmond (1901–1971), Irish-born British physicist who was a pioneer in the fields of x-ray crystallography and molecular biology. An avowed Marxist, he wrote books, including *The Social Function of Science* (1939) and *Science in History* (1954), that reflected his analysis of science as a social phenomenon.

BERNANOS, Georges (1888–1948), French novelist whose theme was the struggle of good and evil forces for man's soul. His masterpiece was *Journal d'un Curé de Campagne* (Diary of a Country Priest, 1936).

BERNARD, Claude (1813–1887), French physiologist regarded as the father of experimental medicine. Following the work of BEAUMONT he opened artificial FISTULAS in animals to study their DIGESTIVE SYSTEMS. He demonstrated the role of the PANCREAS in digestion, discussed the presence and function of GLYCOGEN in the LIVER (1856) and in 1851 reported the existence of the vasomotor nerves (see VASOMOTION).

BERNARD OF CLAIRVAUX, Saint (1090–1153), French theologian and mystic who reinvigorated the CISTERCIANS and inspired the Second Crusade. The founder abbot of Clairvaux Abbey (1115–53), he established 68 religious houses. He was adviser to popes, kings and bishops and was instrumental in ABELARD'S condemnation (1140). Bernard was canonized in 1174. His feast day is Aug. 20. (See also CRUSADES.)

BERNAYS, Edward L. (1891–   ), Austrian-born US originator of professional public relations. He opened the first US public relations firm (1919) and later lectured on public relations. He was a nephew of Sigmund Freud.

BERNBACH, William (1911–   ), US advertising executive who in 1949 cofounded Doyle, Dane, Bernbach, the ad agency that revolutionized Madison Avenue with its intelligent, entertaining copy.

BERNE CONVENTION, international copyright protection agreement signed in 1886 by over 40 countries and periodically revised. It now has 59 members. It covers literary publications, drama, motion pictures, artwork, music, records and photographs. The US did not sign but subscribed to the similar Universal Copyright Convention (1952).

BERNHARDT, Sarah (1844–1923), French actress of great emotional power, born Henriette Rosine Bernard. She achieved great successes in classic French plays, created many roles for Victorien Sardou and ROSTAND, and made several triumphant worldwide tours.

BERNINI, Giovanni Lorenzo (1598–1680), Italian sculptor and architect who gave Rome many of its characteristic BAROQUE features. He designed the tomb of Urban VIII, the canopy over the high altar in St. Peter's, the Piazza S. Pietro, the *Four Rivers* fountain in the Piazza Navona and the statue *St. Teresa in Ecstasy.*

BERNOULLI, family of Swiss mathematicians important in establishing CALCULUS as a mathematical tool of widespread application. **Jacques (Jakob) Bernoulli** (1654–1705), who applied calculus to many geometrical problems, is best remembered in the Bernoulli numbers and the Theorem of Bernoulli that appeared in a posthumous work on PROBABILITY. **Jean (Johann) Bernoulli** (1667–1748), brother of Jacques, also a propagandist on behalf of the Leibnitzian calculus, assisted his brother in founding the calculus of variations. **Daniel Bernoulli** (1700–1782), son of Jean, anatomist, botanist and mathematician—perhaps the family's most famous member—published his *Hydrodynamics* in 1738, applying calculus to that science. In it he proposed **Bernoulli's principle,** which states that in any small volume of space through which a fluid is flowing steadily, the total ENERGY, comprising the pressure, potential and kinetic energies, is constant. This means that the PRESSURE is inversely related to the VELOCITY. This principle is applied in the design of the AIRFOIL, the key component in making possible all heavier-than-air craft, where the faster flow of air over the longer upper surface results in reduction of pressure there and hence a lifting force acting on the airfoil (see also AERODYNAMICS).

BERNSTEIN, Leonard (1918–   ), US conductor–composer, best known for his score for the musical film *West Side Story* (1957). He rose to fame as conductor of the New York Philharmonic Orchestra (1958–69). His varied works include the symphony *The Age of Anxiety* and the scores for the musical *On the Town* (1944) and the film *On the Waterfront* (1954).

BERRA, Lawrence Peter "Yogi" (1925–   ), US baseball player for the New York Yankees, 1946–63. He gained the record for world series games played (75) and the greatest number of series hits (71). He won the American League's "Most Valuable Player Award" in 1951, 1954 and 1955.

BERRIGAN, Daniel (1922–   ) and **Philip** (1924–   ), Roman Catholic priests in the pacifist "Catonsville Nine" group. In 1969, as a Vietnam War protest, the nine broke into the Selective Service Office at Catonsville, Md., and poured ox-blood over records and files. The Berrigans were convicted and given three years; in 1972 Philip was tried on conspiracy charges but acquitted. In 1981 the Berrigans were convicted of burglary and conspiracy after they broke into a General Electric plant and damaged two nuclear-missile nose cones.

BERRY, Charles Edward "Chuck" (1926–   ), US singer. His 1955 hit "Maybelline" made him one of rock 'n' roll's first big stars and launched him on a long career as a performer and songwriter. Other hits included the rock classics, "Johnny B. Goode" and "Sweet Little Sixteen."

BERRYMAN, John (1914–1972), US poet, active from the 1930s. His reputation was confirmed by the long poem *Homage to Mistress Bradstreet* (1956). Berryman's later work, distinguished by its black ironies and linguistic innovation, includes *His Toy, His Dream, His Rest* (1968) and *Dream Songs* (1969). He committed suicide, throwing himself off a bridge in Minneapolis.

BERTHELOT, Pierre Eugène Marcellin (1827–1907), French chemist and statesman, who pioneered the synthesis of organic compounds not found in nature and later introduced the terms exothermic and endothermic (descriptive of chemical reactions) to THERMOCHEMISTRY. His public career was crowned in 1895 when he became foreign secretary.

BERTILLON, Alphonse (1853–1914), French criminologist who devised a system (*Bertillonage*) for identifying criminals based on anthropometric measurements (see ANTHROPOMETRY), adopted by the French police in 1888 and used until the adoption of fingerprinting (see FINGERPRINTS).

BERTOIA, Harry (1915–1978) Italian-born US sculptor. His large metallic screens show the geometric influence of industrial design. He also was well-known as a furniture designer.

BERTOLUCCI, Bernardo (1940–   ), Italian film director whose controversial productions reflect his radical politics and psychological orientation. His best-known works are *Before the Revolution* (1964), *The Conformist* (1970), *Last Tango in Paris* (1972) and *1900* (1976), an epic covering 70 years of social conflict in Italy.

BERZELIUS, Jöns Jakob, Baron (1779–1848), Swedish chemist who determined the ATOMIC WEIGHTS of nearly 40 elements before 1818, discovered CERIUM (1803), SELENIUM (1818) and THORIUM (1829), introduced the terms PROTEIN, ISOMERISM and CATALYSIS and devised the modern method of writing empirical formulas (1813).

BESANT, Annie (1847–1933), British theosophist and social reformer, born Annie Wood. Mrs. Besant joined the FABIAN SOCIETY and was an early advocate of birth control. Madame BLAVATSKY's writings converted her to THEOSOPHY and she joined the Theosophical Society (1889) and became international president (1907–33). She also championed independence for India, becoming president of the Indian National Congress (1917).

BESSARABIA, historic region of SE Europe, NW of the Black Sea, between the Dniester and Danube rivers. After various Russo–Turkish conflicts it was ceded to Russia in 1812. After the CRIMEAN WAR it passed to Moldavia (1856) but was regained by Russia (1878). Romania controlled it almost continuously from 1918 to 1944, when it joined the USSR as part of the Moldavian and Ukrainian SSR.

BESSARION, John (c1410–1472), Byzantine humanist scholar and churchman. As a Byzantine archbishop at the councils of Ferrara and Florence he tried to reunite the divided Greek and Latin churches. He stayed in Italy, becoming a cardinal and helping to spread Greek classical learning.

BESSEMER, Sir Henry (1813–1898), British inventor of the BESSEMER PROCESS for the manufacture of steel, patented in 1856.

BETANCOURT, Rómulo (1908–   ), Venezuelan politician and founder of the left-wing Acción Democràtica party (1941). Provisional president 1945–47 and president 1958–63, he spent 1948–58 in exile after a military coup, and survived an assassination attempt in 1960.

BETA RAYS. See RADIOACTIVITY.

BETEL NUT, fruit of the betel palm (*Areca catechu*), native to tropical Asia. It is boiled, sliced, dried and chewed as a stimulant with betel pepper vine leaves (*Piper betle*) and coral lime. Chewing produces red saliva which may temporarily stain the mouth orange–brown.

BETHE, Hans Albrecht (1906–   ), German-born US theoretical physicist who proposed the nuclear CARBON CYCLE to account for the sun's energy output (1938). During WWII he worked on the Manhattan Project. He was awarded the 1967 Nobel physics prize for his work on the source of stellar energy.

BETHLEHEM (Hebrew: Bayt Lahm), town in Israeli-occupied WEST BANK, 6mi S of Jerusalem, and sacred to Jews, Christians, and Muslims. It was the Biblical city of David where he was annointed by Samuel; the traditional tomb of Rachel is outside the town, which was the birthplace of Christ. A basilica built by the Emperor CONSTANTINE over the Grotto of the Nativity (326–33) and rebuilt by JUSTINIAN I now forms the Church of the Nativity, a major attraction for tourists and pilgrims. Long contested by Christians and Muslims, it was taken by Israel during the 1967 Six-Day War. Pop 25,000.

BETHMANN-HOLLWEG, Theobald von (1856–1921), German chancellor (1909–17) who was opposed to WWI but defended Germany's role during it. His calling the international guarantee of Belgian neutrality "a scrap of paper" was considered typical German cynicism.

BETHUNE, Mary McLeod (1875–1955), black American educator and civil rights activist. She founded the Daytona Normal and Industrial School for Negro Girls (1904), now Bethune–Cookman College, and was Director of Negro Affairs in the National Youth Administration (1936–44) and President F. D. ROOSEVELT's adviser on minority problems.

BETJEMAN, Sir John (1906–   ), English poet laureate and architectural conservationist, often called a lyrical satirist. His books include *New Bats in Old Belfries* (1945), *Selected Poems* (1948), *Collected Poems* (1958), *Victorian and Edwardian Architecture in London* (1969).

BETTELHEIM, Bruno (1903–   ), Austrian-born US psychologist who drew on his prewar experience as an inmate of Nazi concentration camps to describe men's behavior in extreme situations (1943). His subsequent work has mainly concerned the treatment of autistic (see AUTISM) and disturbed children.

BETTER BUSINESS BUREAU, a US non-profit-making corporation designed to protect consumers from unfair or illegal business practices. It handles offending businesses by persuasion or referral to a government agency. The bureau has over 100,000 members and annually handles some 4 million inquiries.

BETTI, Ugo (1892–1953), Italian playwright and poet, once a judge. His plays, deeply concerned with guilt and evil, are often shaped as judicial enquiries. His works include *La Padrona* (1927) and *Il Giocatore* (1951).

BETTING. See GAMBLING.

BEVAN, Aneurin "Nye" (1897–1960), British labor leader and major left-wing socialist politician. As Minister of Health (1945–50) under ATLEE, he introduced and administered the 1946 National Health Act which established a vast national health program.

BEVERIDGE, William Henry, 1st Baron of Tuggal (1879–1963), British economist and social planner whose report on social insurance (1942) revolutionized the British welfare system. It became law under the 1945–51 Labor government. Beveridge became a knight in 1919 and a baron in 1946.

BEVIN, Ernest (1881–1951), British labor leader and statesman. He formed the Transport and General Workers' Union (1922), the nation's largest union. He was minister of labor in WWII and as foreign minister in 1945–51 took a tough pro-European, anti-Soviet stand.

BEZA, Theodore, or de Bèze (1519–1605), French Calvinist theologian, CALVIN'S successor in Geneva (1564). His Latin translation of the New Testament was a source for the King James version.

BHAGAVAD-GITA (song of the Lord), anonymous SANSKRIT poem of about 200 BC, embedded in the Mahābhārata epic, a world-famous religious discourse. It consists of a dialogue (700 verses), covering many aspects of Hindu religious thought, between Prince Arjuna and the god KRISHNA on a field of battle.

BHUMIBOL, Adulyadej (1927–), US-born constitutional monarch of Thailand from 1946, after the assassination of his brother Ananda Mahidol. He was formally crowned in 1950.

Official name: Bhutan
Capital: Thimbu

Area: 18,000sq mi
Population: 1,326,000
Languages: Dzongkha
Religions: Buddhist, Hindu
Monetary unit(s): 1 Indian rupee = 2 tikchung = 100 paise

BHUTAN (or Drukyul), kingdom in the E Himalayas between Tibet and India. It is a mountainous land with fertile subtropical valleys. Rice, tea and other farm products dominate its mainly subsistence economy. Poor communications have hampered development. Some 65% of the people are Bhutias of Tibetan–Himalayan origin. There are also many Nepalese. Dzongkha is the official language and LAMAISM the major faith.

Bhutan's early history is a mystery. The British East India Company made a treaty with the king in 1774, and in 1910 the British took over Bhutan's foreign relations, a responsibility India assumed in 1947. Bhutan is ruled by the hereditary king (Druk Gyalpo) Jigme Singye Wangchuck with a council of ministers and national assembly. China has claimed Bhutanese territory since the 1950s.

BHUTTO, Zulfikar Ali (1928–1979), president and prime minister of Pakistan. Educated in the US and in England, he returned to Pakistan and served in several cabinet positions. He became president (1971) and then prime minister (1973), gaining power after the secession of Bangladesh. Ousted by a military coup in 1977, Bhutto was convicted and executed on a charge of having ordered the murder of a political opponent.

BIAFRA, name assumed by Nigeria's Eastern Region during its attempted secession (1967–70). Under the leadership of Colonel Ojukwu, the IBO people of the Eastern Region declared their independence in May, 1967, and the civil war, for which both sides had been preparing for some time, broke out. Outnumbered and outgunned, the Biafrans suffered heavy losses, with large numbers dying from starvation, before their final surrender. The former breakaway region was divided to form the East-Central rivers and South-Eastern states.

BIALIK, Haim Nahman (1873–1934), one of the greatest of modern Hebrew poets. Born in the Ukraine, he settled in Palestine in 1924. Firmly rooted in tradition, his poetry gave fiery expression to Jewish national aspirations, making Bialik his people's national poet.

BIARRITZ, famous resort in SW France. It stands on the Bay of Biscay near Bayonne, in the department of Basses Pyrenees. Pop

26,750.

BIBLE, collection of sacred books of JUDAISM and CHRISTIANITY, often called the Holy Scriptures. Being inspired (that is, given by God), they form the basis for belief and practice (see CANON). Modern theologians generally regard the Bible as the record and vehicle of divine revelation: equally the word of God and the word of man. Major biblical themes center in God, his creation and care of the world, his righteousness, love, and saving activity (see COVENANT; JESUS CHRIST; CHURCH). The Bible has had an incalculable influence on the thought, attitudes, beliefs, art, science and politics of Western society.

The Christian Bible comprises the OLD TESTAMENT and the NEW TESTAMENT. The Hebrew Bible is essentially the Old Testament. Its 39 books, plus the 27 of the New Testament, make up the Protestant Bible. Most of the books of disputed authority, known as the APOCRYPHA, are included in the Old Testament by the Eastern and Roman Catholic Churches while in Protestant editions they are excluded or placed between the two Testaments.

There have been many versions and many translations of the Bible. The original Old Testament, written almost entirely in Hebrew, was translated into Aramaic (the TARGUMS) and later into Greek (see SEPTUAGINT) and Latin. The VULGATE is still the standard Latin version in the Roman Catholic Church. It was the basis of the first major English version, named for John WYCLIFFE, and completed in 1388. The REFORMATION aimed to give the Bible to the common people, and Martin LUTHER's German version pioneered much translation work. Several scholarly English translations, including those by William TYNDALE and Miles COVERDALE, appeared in the 16th century. A significant Roman Catholic translation by the English colleges in exile in Rheims and Douai appeared in 1582 and 1610. Still supreme among English versions is the King James or Authorized Version (1611), a major work of English literature. This remains perhaps the most popular translation, although outmoded by later, more accurate versions, notably the Revised Version (1881 and 1885) and the Revised Standard Version (1952). The Roman Catholic Church has produced the Jerusalem Bible (1966), and Ronald Knox's version (1945 and 1949). The New English Bible (1962 and 1970), produced by an interdenominational committee, is another major modern translation.

The Bible has now been translated into more than 1400 languages, and millions of copies are sold annually throughout the world.

BIBLIOTHÈQUE NATIONALE, the French national library in Paris. Developed from early royal collections, some of which date back to the 14th century, it now has over 6 million books, and the legal right to receive any book published in France.

BICHAT, Marie François Xavier (1771–1802), French anatomist and pathologist, the founder of HISTOLOGY. Although working without the MICROSCOPE, Bichat distinguished 21 types of elementary TISSUES from which the organs of the body are composed.

BIDAULT, Georges (1899–), French statesman who opposed France's decolonization policies. He was provisional president (1946), prime minister (1946; 1949–50) and foreign secretary (1944; 1947–48; 1953–54). In 1962 he was exiled by President de Gaulle for backing militant opposition to Algerian independence, and went to Brazil. He returned to France in 1968.

BIDDLE, James (1783–1848), US naval officer. In an adventurous life, he was shipwrecked, imprisoned by Barbary pirates and captured by the British during the War of 1812. He later claimed the Oregon territory for the US (1817) and negotiated the first treaty between the US and China (1846).

BIDDLE, Nicholas (1786–1844), president of the second BANK OF THE UNITED STATES (1823–36). He made it the nation's first authoritative central bank. Renewal of the bank's charter was vetoed by President Jackson after Biddle had unwisely made rechartering a major presidential election issue.

BIEDERMEIER, utilitarian bourgeois style of furniture prevailing in Germany between about 1810 and 1850. The term derived from the caricature bourgeois figure "Papa Biedermeier" who featured in a popular magazine of the 1850s, and came to apply disparagingly to German bourgeois taste of the period.

BIENVILLE, Jean Baptiste le Moyne, Sieur de (1680–1768), French naval officer who founded New Orleans. Born in Canada, he helped to colonize French Louisiana, which he governed at various periods between 1701 and 1743.

BIERCE, Ambrose (Gwinett) (1842–1914?), US short-story writer and satirical journalist. His works include the gloomy tales of *Can Such Things Be?* (1893) and the cynical definitions of *The Devil's Dictionary* (1906). He disappeared without trace during the Mexican Revolution of 1913–14.

BIERSTADT, Albert (1830–1902), German-born American landscape painter. He is famous for his massive, realistic Western scenes.

BIG BEN, the clock in the tower of the Houses of Parliament, London. It is named for Sir Benjamin Hall, commissioner of works in 1856 when the bell was installed. The name originally referred only to the 13-ton bell.

BIG BEND NATIONAL PARK, vast tract of mountains and desert on the Texan border with Mexico, in the Big Bend of the Rio Grande. The park, which covers some 708,221 acres, was established in 1944 and is the last great expanse of truly wild land left in Tex.

BIG BROTHERS OF AMERICA, a social welfare organization in the US and Canada. Its professionally supervised male volunteers help boys who are either fatherless or in need of parental care.

BIG DIPPER. See GREAT BEAR.

BIGELOW, John (1817–1911), US journalist, author and diplomat. As US consul in Paris (1861–64), he prevented the Confederate states from gaining French-built warships. Bigelow also served as minister to France (1865–66). He was co-editor of the New York *Evening Post* (1848–61).

BIGGS, E(dward) Power (1906–1977), English-born US concert organist. He was a master of old and modern music, and has edited various organ works.

BIKINI, an atoll in the Marshall Islands in the central Pacific Ocean. It was the site of US nuclear bomb tests in the 1940s and 1950s. Inhabitants evacuated during the tests began to return in the early 1970s, but the island was again declared uninhabitable because of dangerously high radiation levels in 1978.

BILBAO, a major seaport in N Spain, capital of Vizcaya province. It is important for heavy industry, including shipbuilding and metallurgy, and for its fishing fleet. Pop 410,500.

BILE, a yellow-brown fluid secreted by the liver and containing salts derived from CHOLESTEROL. Stored and concentrated in the GALL BLADDER and released into the DUODENUM after a meal, the bile emulsifies fats and aids absorption of fat-soluble vitamins A, D, E and K. Other constituents of bile are in fact waste products. Yellow bile and black bile were two of the HUMORS of Hippocratic medicine.

BILLIARDS, name for several indoor games in which balls set on a felt-covered rectangular table are struck by the end of a long tapering stick (the cue). Obscure in origin, billiards was popular in France and England as early as the 14th century. The name came from the French *billard* which meant "a cue." Until the 19th century billiard balls were made of ivory, but now compressed plastic composition balls are most common. The cue has a rubber cushion tip. The table usually has a slate bed in a wooden frame and must be plumb level. In most forms of the game, the table has six pockets: one in each corner and one midway along each of the longer sides. The object is to sink balls into the pockets by playing one ball off another or, in games played without pockets, to hit the balls against each other successively. **Carom billiards** and **English billiards** feature two white cue balls and one red ball. **Snooker** has one white cue ball, 15 red balls and six balls of other colors. **Pool,** as played in the US, or **pocket billiards,** has one white cue ball and 15 numbered colored balls and is the billiard game most popular in the U.S.

BILL OF ATTAINDER, a legislative act that inflicts punishment without due process. It is prohibited in the US Constitution, but in 1943 Congress passed an appropriations act denying salaries to three employees because Congress disliked their political views. In 1946 the US Supreme Court overturned this act as an unconstitutional bill of attainder.

BILL OF RIGHTS, a constitutional document which defines the rights of a people, safeguarding them against undue governmental interference. In the US these rights and safeguards are embodied in the first 10 amendments to the constitution. After the Revolutionary War there was great popular demand for constitutionally defined rights to limit the power of the new government. Bills of rights were drafted in eight states between 1776 and 1781, but when the constitution was drawn up in 1787 no such bill was included, and ratification by the states lagged until promises were made that a bill of rights would be added to the Constitution. When the first Congress met in 1789, James Madison presented a bill of rights. Twelve amendments to the constitution were proposed in the debate on Madison's bill, 10 of which were accepted, and on Dec. 15, 1791, Secretary of State Thomas Jefferson proclaimed the Federal Bill of Rights in full force. The bill guarantees freedom of speech, of the press and of religion. It protects against arbitrary searches and self-incrimination. It sets out proper procedures for trials, giving to all the right to trial by jury and to cross-examine witnesses. In addition to these rights, the 5th Amendment provides that no person shall "be deprived of life, liberty, or property, without due process of law."

The Bill of Rights sought to protect the people against arbitrary acts by the federal government, not the states. In 1868 the states ratified the 14th Amendment, which granted citizenship to the newly freed Negroes and directed the federal government to protect the citizens of a state against arbitrary state actions. Over the years the US Supreme Court increasingly has used the "due process" clause of the 14th Amendment to apply the Federal Bill of Rights against the states.

BILL OF RIGHTS, English, an act passed by the English parliament in 1689 to consolidate constitutional government after the GLORIOUS REVOLUTION. It abolished the royal power to suspend laws, established free parliamentary elections and defined citizens' rights.

BILLY THE KID (1859–1881), nickname of a US outlaw born William H. Bonney. Notorious in the Southwest as a cattle thief and murderer, he was eventually captured and sentenced to hang. He escaped from jail by killing two guards but was soon tracked down and killed by Sheriff Pat Garrett.

BINARY NUMBER SYSTEM, a number system which uses the POWERS of 2. Thus the number which in our everyday system, the DECIMAL SYSTEM, would be represented as 25 ($=(2 \times 10^1) + (5 \times 10^0)$) is in binary notation 11001 ($=(1 \times 2^4) + (1 \times 2^3) + (0 \times 2^2) + (0 \times 2^1) + (1 \times 2^0)$), which is equivalent to $(1 \times 16) + (1 \times 8) + (1 \times 1)$ or $(16 + 8 + 1)$. The system is of particular note since digital COMPUTERS use binary numbers for calculation.

BINET, Alfred (1857–1911), French psychologist who pioneered methods of mental testing. He collaborated with Théodor Simon in devising the Binet-Simon tests, widely used to estimate INTELLIGENCE.

BING, Sir Rudolf (1902–   ), Austrian-born British opera impresario. An opera administrator in Germany, he emigrated to Britain when the Nazis came to power, headed the Glyndebourne Opera (1935–49) and helped organize the Edinburgh Festival (1947). He achieved his greatest fame as general manager of New York's Metropolitan Opera (1950–72), where he introduced black singers and presided over the company's move to Lincoln Center.

BINGHAM, George Caleb (1811–1879), US genre painter noted for his Midwestern river scenes, for example *The Jolly Flatboatmen* (1846). He also treated political subjects with warmth, humor and

vigor, as in *Canvassing for a Vote* (1851), and was, in fact, a politician himself in his home state of Missouri.

BINGO, a lottery game which, in its present form, originated c1880, though it can be traced to a 17th-century Italian game called *tumbule*. Bingo is now conducted both by gambling professionals for profit and by churches and other groups as a means of raising money for charitable enterprises.

BINOMIAL THEOREM, the theorem that a binomial (see POLYNOMIAL) $(a + b)$ may be raised to the POWER n by application of the formula

$$(a+b)^n = a^n + na^{(n-1)}b + \frac{(n-1)\,n}{2}$$
$$\dots a^{(n-2)}b^2 + an.b^{(n-1)} + b^n$$

(for evaluation of COEFFICIENTS see PASCAL'S TRIANGLE). Thus, for example,

$$(a+b)^4 = a^4 + 4a^3b + 6a^2b^2 + 4ab^3 + b^4.$$

Expansion of $((a - b)^n$ is equivalent to expansion of $(a + (- b))^n$. Thus, for example,

$(a-b)^4 = a^4 + 4a^3(-b) + 6a^2(-b)^2 + 4a(-b)^3 + (-b)^4$

$= a^4 - 4a^3b + 6a^2b^2 - 4ab^3 + b^4.$

Note that the expansion of $(a+b)^n$ has $(n+1)$ terms.

BIOCHEMISTRY, study of the substances occurring in living organisms and the reactions in which they are involved. It is a science on the border between BIOLOGY and ORGANIC CHEMISTRY. The main constituents of living matter are water, CARBOHYDRATES, LIPIDS and PROTEINS. The total chemical activity of the organism is known as its METABOLISM. Plants use sunlight as an energy source to produce carbohydrates from carbon dioxide and water (see PHOTOSYNTHESIS). The carbohydrates are then stored as starch; used for structural purposes, as in the CELLULOSE of plant cell walls; or oxidized through a series of reactions including the CITRIC ACID CYCLE, the energy released being stored as adenosine triphosphate (see NUCLEOTIDES). In animals energy is stored mainly as lipids, which as well as forming fat deposits are components of all cell membranes. Proteins have many functions, of which metabolic regulation is perhaps the most important. ENZYMES, which control almost all biochemical reactions, and some HORMONES are proteins. Plants synthesize proteins using simpler nitrogenous compounds from the soil. Animals obtain proteins from food and break them down by HYDROLYSIS to AMINO ACIDS. New proteins are made according to the pattern determined by the sequence of NUCLEIC ACIDS in the GENES. Many reactions occur in all CELLS and may be studied in simple systems. Methods used by biochemists and chemists are similar and include labelling with radioactive ISOTOPES and separation techniques such as CHROMATOGRAPHY, used to analyze very small amounts of substances, and the high-speed CENTRIFUGE. Molecular structures may be determined by X-RAY DIFFRACTION. Landmarks in biochemistry include the synthesis of urea by WÖHLER (1828), the pioneering research of von LIEBIG, PASTEUR and BERNARD, and more recently the elucidation of the structure of DNA by James WATSON and Francis CRICK in 1953.

BIOFEEDBACK, electronically-produced signals indicating the occurrence of a specific kind of biological event, such as a rise in blood pressure, especially as used to help a person control otherwise unconscious physiological processes. Biofeedback techniques have been used with some success in the treatment of hypertension, chronic headaches, epilepsy and other disorders.

BIOGENESIS, theory that all living organisms are derived from other living organisms. It is the opposite of the theory of SPONTANEOUS GENERATION. (See also LIFE.)

BIOLOGICAL CLOCKS, the mechanisms which control the rhythm of various activities of plants and animals. Some activities, such as mating, migration and hibernation, have a yearly cycle; others, chiefly reproductive functions (including human menstruation), follow the lunar month. The majority, however, have a period of roughly 24 hours, called a **circadian rhythm.** As well as obvious rhythms such as the patterns of leaf movement in plants and the activity/sleep cycle in animals, many other features such as body temperature and cell growth oscillate daily. Although related to the day/night cycle, circadian rhythms are not directly controlled by it. Organisms in unvarying environments will continue to show 24-hr rhythms, but the pattern can be changed—the clock reset. Scientists in the Arctic, with 6 months of daylight, used watches which kept a 21-hr day, and gradually their body rhythms changed to a 21-hr period. The delay in adjustment is important in modern travel. After moving from one time zone to another, it takes some time for the body to adjust to the newly imposed cycle. Biological clocks are important in animal navigation. Many animals, such as migrating birds or bees returning to the hive, navigate using the sun. They can only do this if they have some

means of knowing what time of day it is. (See also MIGRATION.) Biological clocks are apparently inborn, not learned, but need to be triggered. An animal kept in the light from birth shows no circadian rhythms, but if placed in the dark for an hour or so immediately starts rhythms based on a 24-hr cycle. Once started, the cycles are almost independent of external changes, indicating that they cannot be based on a simple rhythm of chemical reactions, which would be affected by temperature. The biological clock may be somehow linked to external rhythms in geophysical forces, or may be an independent and slightly adjustable biochemical oscillator. In either case the mechanism is unknown. Not all biological rhythms are controlled by a "clock": in many cases they are determined simply by the time taken to complete a certain sequence of actions. For example, the heart rate depends on the time taken for the heart muscles to contract and relax. Unlike those controlled by biological clocks, such rhythms are easily influenced by drugs and temperature. (See also BIORHYTHMS.)

BIOLOGICAL CONTROL, the control of pests by the introduction of natural predators, parasites or disease, or by modifying the environment so as to encourage those already present. This first took place in Cal. in 1888, when Australian Ladybird beetles were introduced to eliminate the damage to citrus trees by the cottony-cushion scale insect. Another example is the introduction of MYXOMATOSIS to combat crop damage by rabbits. The "sterile male" technique is used to control many insect pests. Large numbers of males are bred, sterilized with X-rays and released. Since the females mate only once, many of them with the sterile males, the population rapidly decreases.

BIOLOGY, the study of living things, i.e. the science of plants and animals, including humans. Broadly speaking there are two main branches of biology, the study of ANIMALS (ZOOLOGY) and the study of PLANTS (BOTANY). Within each of these main branches are a number of traditional divisions dealing with structure (ANATOMY, CYTOLOGY), development and function (PHYSIOLOGY, EMBRYOLOGY), inheritance (GENETICS, EVOLUTION), classification (TAXONOMY) and interrelations of organisms with each other and with their environment (ECOLOGY). These branches are also split into a number of specialist fields, such as MYCOLOGY, ENTOMOLOGY, HERPETOLOGY.

However, the traditional division into zoology and botany no longer applies since groups of biosciences have developed which span their limits, e.g. MICROBIOLOGY, BACTERIOLOGY, VIROLOGY, OCEANOGRAPHY, MARINE BIOLOGY, LIMNOLOGY. There are also biosciences that bridge the gap between the physical sciences of CHEMISTRY, PHYSICS and GEOLOGY, e.g. BIOCHEMISTRY, BIOPHYSICS and PALEONTOLOGY. Similarly there are those that relate to areas of human behavior, e.g. PSYCHOLOGY and SOCIOLOGY.

Disciplines such as MEDICINE, VETERINARY MEDICINE, AGRONOMY and HORTICULTURE also have a strong basis in biology.

To a large extent the history of biology is the history of its constituent sciences. Since the impetus to investigate the living world generally arose in a desire to improve the techniques of medicine or of agriculture, most early biologists were in the first instance physicians or landowners. An exception is provided by ARISTOTLE, the earliest systematist of biological knowledge and himself an outstanding biologist—he founded the science of comparative anatomy—but most other classical authors, as GALEN, CELSUS and the members of the Hippocratic school, were primarily physicians. In the medieval period much biological knowledge became entangled in legend and allegory. The classical texts continued to be the principal sources of knowledge although new compilations, such as AVICENNA's *Canon* of medicine, were produced by Muslim philosophers. In 16th-century Europe interest revived in descriptive natural history, the work of GESNER being notable; physicians such as PARACELSUS began to develop a chemical pharmacology (see IATROCHEMISTRY) and experimental anatomy revived in the work of VESALIUS, FABRICIUS and FALLOPIUS. The discoveries of SERVETUS, HARVEY and MALPIGHI followed. Quantitative plant physiology began with the work of van HELMONT and was taken to spectacular ends in the work of Stephen HALES. In the 17th century, microscopic investigations began with the work of HOOKE and van LEEUWENHOEK; GREW advanced the study of plant organs and RAY laid the foundation for LINNAEUS' classic 18th-century formulation of the classification of plants. This same era saw BUFFON devise a systematic classification of animals and von HALLER lay the groundwork for the modern study of physiology.

The 17th century had seen controversies over the role of mechanism in biological explanation—LA METTRIE had even developed the theories of DESCARTES to embrace the mind of man; the 19th century saw similar disputes, now couched in the form of the mechanist-vitalist controversy concerning the possible chemical nature of life (see BICHAT; MAGENDIE; Claude BERNARD). Development biology, foreshadowed by LAMARCK, was thoroughly established following the work of DARWIN; in anatomy, SCHWANN and others developed the cell concept; in histology Bichat's pioneering work was continued; in physiology, organic and even physical chemists began to play a greater role, and medical theory was revolutionized by the advent of bacteriology (see PASTEUR; KOCH). The impact of MENDEL's discoveries in genetics was not felt until the early 1900s. Possibly the high point of 20th-century biology came with the proposal of the double-helix model for DNA (see NUCLEIC ACIDS), the chemical carrier of genetic information, by CRICK and WATSON in 1953.

BIOLUMINESCENCE, the production of nonthermal light by living organisms such as fireflies, many marine animals, bacteria and fungi. The effect is an example of CHEMILUMINESCENCE. In some cases its utility to the organism is not apparent, though in others its use is clear. Thus, in the firefly, the ABDOMEN of the female glows, enabling the male to find her. Similarly, LUMINESCENCE enables many deep-sea fish to locate each other or to attract their prey. The glow in a ship's wake at night is due to luminescent microorganisms.

BIOMEDICAL ENGINEERING, development and application of mechanical, electrical, electronic and nuclear devices in medicine. The many recent advances in biomedical engineering have occurred in four main areas: ARTIFICIAL ORGANS; new surgical techniques involving the use of LASERS, cryosurgery and ULTRASONICS; diagnosis and monitoring using thermography and computers; and PROSTHETICS.

BIONICS, the science of designing artificial systems which have the desirable characteristics of living organisms. These may be simply imitations of nature, such as military vehicles with jointed legs, or, more profitably, systems which embody a principle learned from nature. Examples of the latter include RADAR, inspired by the echolocation system of bats, or the development of associative memories in COMPUTERS as in the human brain.

BIOPHYSICS, a branch of BIOLOGY in which the methods and principles of PHYSICS are applied to the study of living things. It has grown up in the 20th century alongside the development of ELECTRONICS. Its tools include the ELECTROENCEPHALOGRAPH and the ELECTRON MICROSCOPE, its techniques those of SPECTROSCOPY and X-RAY

DIFFRACTION and its problems the study of nerve transmission, BIOLUMINESCENCE and materials transfer in RESPIRATION and secretion.

BIORHYTHMS, cyclical patterns of biological activity. Although such patterns are the subject of serious scientific research, this term usually refers to cyclical patterns postulated in various popular works that purport to relate a person's psychological state on a given day to his or her date of birth. In this sense, biorhythms were invented in Vienna at the turn of the century by Drs. Wilhelm Fliess and Hermann Swoboda; in 1964, George Thummen's *Is This Your Day?* sparked contemporary interest in biorhythms.

BIRD, type of animal adapted for flight and unique in its body covering of feathers. Birds are the largest group of VERTEBRATES, with over 8,500 extant species. They are descended from the group of prehistoric reptiles which took to living in trees (see ARCHAEOPTERYX). Their most striking anatomical features are those associated with flight. The forelimbs are modified as wings and are associated with enormous breast muscles which make powered flight possible. Even in FLIGHTLESS BIRDS such as the PENGUIN and OSTRICH it is clear that the forelimbs were once used as wings. The rest of the skeleton is constructed of thin, light bones. A further weight reduction resulted from the replacement of the teeth by a horny beak or bill early in the evolutionary history of birds. Feathers, developed from scales (still present on the legs), streamline the body, and provide flight surfaces.

Flightless birds are mainly adapted for running or swimming. Runners such as the ostrich have strong legs and swimmers may have their wings modified as flippers as in the penguin. Birds have been able to adapt to diverse ways of life, ranging from that of the Emperor penguin of the Antarctic to Egyptian plovers of equatorial desert regions, because, being warm-blooded, they can function independently of the surrounding temperature. Different groups of birds have evolved a variety of shapes and sizes of bill to take advantage of different food sources. The majority of birds are active by day. Owls, the prominent nocturnal group, have highly developed night vision estimated to be up to 100 times more sensitive than that of man. All birds lay eggs, sometimes in quite elaborate nests. Incubation is by one or both parents, dependent on species.

BIRDSEYE, Clarence (1886–1956), US inventor and industrialist who, having observed during furtrading expeditions to Labrador (1912–16) that many foods keep indefinitely if frozen, developed a process for the rapid commercial freezing of foodstuffs. In 1924 he organized the company later known as General Foods to market frozen produce.

BIRDS OF PARADISE, members of the family Paradisaeidae, found in forests of Australia and New Guinea. The males have colorful and elaborately-shaped tail feathers designed to attract females and used in courtship displays. There are 43 species, many of which are rare due to their slaughter by collectors, a practice made illegal in 1924.

BIRDSONG, the pattern of notes, often musical and complex, with which birds attract a mate and proclaim their territory. Ornithologists call all such sounds songs, though those that are harsh and unmusical are often referred to simply as the "voice."

BIRMINGHAM, second-largest city in Britain, about 110mi NW of London. A source of metal products since medieval times, it is now an industrial city of world status making vehicles, machine tools, armaments, electrical equipment and toys. It has two universities. Pop 1,033,900.

BIRMINGHAM, city of N central Ala., seat of Jefferson Co. The largest city in Ala., it is the South's chief iron and steel producer and a major rail and air terminus with a port linked to the Gulf of Mexico. It is also an educational center. Pop 284,413.

BIRMINGHAM RIOTS, important milestone in the US civil rights movement. In the spring of 1963 thousands of blacks, led by the Rev. Martin Luther KING, Jr., and others, conducted a series of marches in Birmingham, Ala., protesting segregation and discrimination in hiring. White authorities attacked them with fire hoses and police dogs. Rioting erupted. Blacks won limited concessions, but full vindication came with adoption of the US Civil Rights Act of 1964.

BIRNEY, James Gillespie (1792–1857), leading US abolitionist. Birney, who came from an old slave-owning family, freed his slaves in 1834. He launched the abolitionist newspaper the *Philanthropist* in 1836, became executive secretary of the AMERICAN ANTI-SLAVERY SOCIETY in 1837 and founded the LIBERTY PARTY, standing as its presidential candidate in 1840 and 1844.

BIRTH, emergence from the mother's WOMB, or, in the case of most lower animals, from the EGG, marking the beginning of an independent life. The birth process is triggered by HORMONE changes in the mother's bloodstream. Birth may be induced, if required, by oxytocin. Mild labor pains (contractions of the womb) are the first sign that a woman is about to give birth. Initially occurring about every 20 minutes, in a few hours they become stronger and occur every few minutes. This is the first stage of labor, usually lasting about 14 hours. The contractions push the baby downward, usually head first, which breaks the membranes surrounding the baby, and the AMNIOTIC FLUID escapes.

In the second stage of labor, stronger contractions push the baby through the cervix and vagina. This is the most painful part and lasts less than 2 hours. Anesthetics (see ANESTHESIA) or ANALGESICS are usually given, and delivery aided by hand or obstetric forceps. A CESARIAN SECTION may be performed if great difficulty occurs. Some women choose "natural childbirth," in which no anesthetic is used, but pain is minimized by prior relaxation exercises.

As soon as the baby is born, its nose and mouth are cleared of fluid and breathing starts, whereupon the UMBILICAL CORD is cut and tied. In the third stage of labor the PLACENTA is expelled from the womb and bleeding is stopped by further contractions. Birth normally occurs 38 weeks after conception. Premature births are those occurring after less than 35 weeks. Most premature babies develop normally with medical care, but if born before 28 weeks the chances of survival are poor. (See also EMBRYO; GESTATION; OBSTETRICS; PREGNANCY.)

BIRTH CONTROL, prevention of unwanted births, by means of CONTRACEPTION, ABORTION, STERILIZATION, and formerly infanticide. Many believe abortion to be medically advisable if the child is likely to be defective. By limiting the size of families, birth control can help prevent poverty, while globally it could help prevent mass starvation.

Certain forms of birth control have been used from ancient times, but modern methods have been available only since the late 19th century. Arising out of the early WOMEN'S RIGHTS movement, the first birth control clinics were opened in 1916 in the US by Margaret SANGER, and in 1921 in Britain by Marie STOPES. The need for worldwide birth control intensified from the 1920s onwards as the world population "exploded," with modern medicine cutting the death rate while the BIRTH RATE stayed high. In 1952 international groups formed the International Planned Parenthood Federation. In the 1960s the UN urged the universal adoption of voluntary birth control. Organizations promoting ZERO POPULATION GROWTH have become active.

Birth rates have fallen in many developed countries and in some developing countries such as India and China, whose governments have instituted public birth-control practices. The chief hindrances are apathy, ignorance and social pressure for large families. Ethical and religious objections to artificial forms of birth control derive from the view that procreation is the primary purpose of marriage and of coitus, and (in the case of abortion) from the sanctity of life. The most influential proponent of this view is the Roman Catholic Church. (See also ABORTION CONTROVERSY; PLANNED PARENTHOOD; WORLD POPULATION.)

BIRTHMARKS, skin blemishes, usually congenital. There are two main types: pigmented nevuses, or moles, which are usually brown or black and may be raised or flat; and vascular nevuses, local growths of small blood vessels, such as the "strawberry mark" and the "port-wine stain." Although harmless, they are sometimes removed for cosmetic reasons or if they show malignant tendencies. (See also TUMOR.)

BIRTH RATE, ratio of the annual number of births in a population to the total midyear population, usually expressed in births per 1000 persons. Being uncorrected for sex and age distribution, it is a crude measure of fertility. Birth rates range from around 50 per 1000 in some developing countries to under 20 per 1000 in advanced nations. (See also DEMOGRAPHY.)

BISCAY, Bay of, part of the Atlantic Ocean bordering W France and N Spain, renowned for sudden and violent storms. Principal ports are Nantes, Bordeaux (France,) Bilbao and Santander (Spain.)

BISHOP, highest order in the ministry of the Roman Catholic, Anglican, Eastern and some Lutheran Churches. As head of his diocese, a bishop administers its affairs, supervises its clergy and administers CONFIRMATION and ORDINATION. Roman Catholic bishops are appointed by the pope, Anglican bishops by the sovereign. In the US, Protestant Episcopal bishops are elected by both clergy and laity. (See also APOSTOLIC SUCCESSION; ARCHBISHOP; MINISTRY.)

BISHOP, Elizabeth (1911–1979), US poet and translator of Brazilian poetry, widely acclaimed for her succinct and lyrical style. Her books include the Pulitzer prizewinning *North & South–A Cold Spring* (1955), *Questions of Travel* (1965) and *Geography III* (1977).

BISMARCK, capital of N.D., seat of Burleigh Co. The city, which overlooks the Missouri R, was a busy river port in the 19th century. It is now a grain and livestock-trading center. There are rich lignite and petroleum deposits nearby. Pop 44,485.

BISMARCK, Prince Otto von (1815–1898), the "Iron Chancellor," who was largely responsible for creating a unified Germany. Born of Prussian gentry, he entered politics in 1847. From the first he was intent on increasing German power. He served as ambassador to Russia and France, then as chancellor (prime minister). He defeated Austria in the AUSTRO-PRUSSIAN WAR and annexed or coerced neighboring states into the North German Federation. Following his defeat of Napoleon III in the FRANCO-PRUSSIAN WAR, the German Empire was created and Bismarck made imperial chancellor and prince in 1871. He was forced to resign in 1890 after the accession of Kaiser William II.

BISMUTH (Bi), metal in Group VA of the PERIODIC TABLE, brittle and silvery-gray with a red tinge. It occurs naturally as the metal, and as the sulfide and oxide from which it is obtained by roasting and reduction with carbon. In the US it is obtained as a byproduct of the refining of copper and lead ores. Bismuth is rather unreactive; it forms trivalent and some pentavalent compounds. Physically and chemically it is similar to LEAD and ANTIMONY. Bismuth is used in low-melting-point alloys in fire-detection safety devices. Since bismuth expands on solidification, it is used in alloys for casting dies and type metal. Bismuth (III) oxide is used in GLASS and CERAMICS; various bismuth salts are used in medicine. AW 209.0, mp 271°C, bp 1560°C, sg 9.747 (20°C).

BISON, ox-like animals, of the family Bovidae, which may weigh half a ton and stand 1.8m (6ft) tall. Their forequarters are covered by a shaggy mane. The American bison, often miscalled the buffalo, once grazed the plains and valleys from Mexico to W Canada in herds of millions and was economically vital to the Plains Indians. Hunted ruthlessly by the white man, it was almost extinct by 1900. There are still a few herds in US and Canadian national parks.

BIT. See INFORMATION THEORY.

BITTERNS, wading birds, related to the HERONS, which live in marshes. Bitterns have plumage usually streaked with brown, which provides camouflage when the bird stands motionless with neck and bill turned upward against a background of reeds. Bitterns are well known for the distinctive mating calls produced by the males.

BIVALVE, name for some 7,000 species of shellfish, including the OYSTER, CLAM and MUSSEL, that have two shells (valves) joined together by a muscular hinge. Most live in the sea, though there are some freshwater species. They range in size from the Giant clam (almost 1.2m (4ft) long) to the Turton clam (only 1mm (0.01in) long). The valves, open except when the animal is disturbed, contain the fleshy body. This consists of a foot, by which the animal moves, and the viscera. There is no head, only a mouth towards which food is directed by moving hairs known as cilia. Most bivalves feed on PLANKTON, though the "boring" bivalve feeds on wood. Bivalves are prey to whelks, birds, fish and aquatic mammals. They are also commercially important. (See also MOLLUSK.)

BIZET, Georges (1838–1875), French composer. The works for which he is now famous—the piano suite *Jeux d'Enfants* (1871), the incidental music for DAUDET'S *L'Arlésienne* (1872), the *Symphony in C* and the operas *Les Pêcheurs de Perles* (1863) and *Carmen* (1875)—were mostly ignored or vilified when first performed. The failure of *Carmen*, now one of the most popular of all operas, affected Bizet's health and may have contributed to his death.

BJÖRLING, Jussi (1911–1960), internationally famous Swedish operatic tenor. He specialized in Italian opera, especially works by VERDI and PUCCINI.

BJØRNSON, Bjørnstjerne Martinius (1832–1910), major Norwegian poet, critic, novelist, dramatist and politician; winner of the Nobel Prize for Literature (1903). Concerned at first with Norwegian history, he later wrote about modern social problems.

BLACK, Hugo Lafayette (1886–1971), US politician and jurist, Supreme Court associate justice 1937–71, senator from Ala. 1927–37. He backed NEW DEAL legislation and, although an ex-Ku Klux Klan member, was a noted campaigner for civil rights.

BLACK, Joseph (1728–1799), Scottish physician and chemist who investigated the properties of CARBON DIOXIDE, discovered the phenomena of LATENT and SPECIFIC HEATS, distinguished HEAT from TEMPERATURE and pioneered the techniques used in the quantitative study of CHEMISTRY.

BLACK AND TANS, name for recruits to the Royal Irish constabulary and also to the "Auxis" or Auxiliary Division, made up of demobilized British officers, introduced into Ireland in 1920 to maintain order during the struggle for Home Rule. They wore black berets and khaki or tan uniforms. Their repressive measures earned "the Tans" lasting hatred in Ireland and did much to discredit British rule there.

BLACKBEARD (d. 1718), nickname of Edward Teach, an English pirate proverbial for his extreme savagery. A privateer in the War of the Spanish Succession, he turned to piracy in the West Indies and along the Atlantic coast. Blackbeard was killed when his ship was taken by a British force.

BLACKBELT, name once commonly used for a broad belt of rich black soil across S.C., Ga., Ala. and Miss., used for cotton planting. The black belt is also the highest JUDO award.

BLACKBIRD, name for several dark-colored birds, including the Red-winged blackbird, Yellow-headed blackbird and the GRACKLE. Their song is loud and monotonous; they eat fruit, insects and worms. The European blackbird is a member of the THRUSH family Turdidae; the New World blackbird a member of the ORIOLE family Icteridae.

BLACK BODY, in theoretical physics, an object which absorbs all the ELECTROMAGNETIC RADIATION which falls on it. In practice, no object acts as a perfect black body, though a closed box admitting radiation only through a small hole is a good approximation. Black bodies are also ideal thermal radiators.

BLACK CANYON OF THE GUNNISON, a national monument in Col., established in 1933. It centers on a 10mi section of the Black Canyon, a deep 50mi-long gorge of the Gunnison R. In places it reaches a depth of 3,000ft.

BLACK CAUCUS, CONGRESSIONAL, was formed in 1970 following President Richard M. Nixon's refusal to meet with nine black representatives. The caucus has a permanent staff and provides a forum for blacks to map political and legislative strategy. At the start of 1982 the membership stood at 18.

BLACK CODES, laws enacted by the Southern states after the Civil War. Allegedly intended to facilitate the transition from slavery to freedom, they were in fact a veiled device to deny real equality to newly-freed blacks. In 1866 the Civil Rights Act provided full rights to Negroes and further amendments were made during the next four years. However, some codes persisted into the 20th century.

BLACK DEATH, name for an epidemic of bubonic PLAGUE which swept through Asia and Europe in the mid-14th century, annihilating whole communities and perhaps halving the population of Europe. Originating in China, it was carried by flea-infested rats on vessels trading to the West. Its economic effects were far-reaching. It also fanned the flames of superstition and religious prejudice. European Jews, accused of poisoning wells, were massacred, and the idea that the plague was punishment for sin led to a wave of fanatical penance. (See also PLAGUE.)

BLACKETT, Patrick Maynard Stuart, Baron (1897–1974), British physicist who, having developed the Wilson CLOUD CHAMBER into an instrument for observing COSMIC RAYS, won the 1948 Nobel physics prize for the results he obtained using it.

BLACKFOOT INDIANS, tribes of the ALGONQUIAN linguistic family, chiefly the Siksika, Piegan and Blood. Originally hunters and trappers, they adopted firearms and kept vast herds of horses, giving them power in Mont., Alberta and Saskatchewan. The disappearance of the bison, a smallpox epidemic and "incidents" with the white man led to a great reduction in their numbers. There are now under 8,000 Blackfoot on reservations in Mont. and Alberta.

BLACK FOREST, wooded mountain range in the province of Baden-Württemberg, SW West Germany An area of great scenic beauty, it is an important tourist attraction, with lumbering, clock and toy industries.

BLACK FRIDAY, term referring to disasters, particularly financial, occurring on Fridays. The most famous American Black Friday was Sept. 24, 1869, when the speculators Jay GOULD and James FISK tried to corner the gold market with the connivance of government officials. Government gold sales were stopped and prices rose rapidly until the plot was discovered and sales resumed. The market collapsed, and many were ruined.

BLACK HAWK WAR, revolt by Sauk and Fox Indians (1832), following their removal in 1831 from fertile lands owned by the Indians in the Illinois country. Refusing to recognize government claims to the lands, a group of Sauk and Fox Indians, led by Black Hawk, returned to plant corn the following spring but were once more driven out, pursued, and finally almost completely annihilated at the Massacre of Bad Axe River.

BLACK HILLS, mountain range in S.D. and Wyo., famous for the Mt Rushmore Memorial. Here, the heads of four past US presidents are carved out of the mountainside. The Black Hills are rich in minerals, including gold. Highest point is Harney Peak (7,242ft).

BLACK HOLE, according to current physical theory, the final stage of evolution for very massive stars following total gravitational collapse. At the center of a black hole are the densely packed remains of the star, perhaps only a few km across; the condition of matter under such circumstances is not yet understood. The gravitational field of a black hole is so intense that nothing, not even ELECTROMAGNETIC RADIATION (including light), can escape. Black holes, if they exist, can be detected through their gravitational effects on other bodies and through the emission of X- and gamma rays by matter falling into them. Also, according to QUANTUM MECHANICS small black holes would produce pairs (particle and antiparticle) of SUBATOMIC PARTICLES in their immediate vicinity; one of each pair would escape, and the black hole would thus in effect radiate matter. It has been suggested that the end of the universe will be its becoming a single black hole. Astronomers have identified a number of possible black holes, but none as yet has been fully confirmed.

BLACK HOLE OF CALCUTTA, prison cell where 146 British captives were incarcerated on the night of June 20, 1756, during which all but 23 were suffocated. They were held by the Nawab of Bengal, who opposed the monopoly of the EAST INDIA COMPANY.

BLACKJACK, also called **Twenty-one,** a popular card game, the object of which is to obtain a score higher than the dealer (banker) without exceeding 21. Ace counts as 1 or 11, and a picture card is 10. The best hand is ace and picture card. The game is featured at most gambling casinos.

BLACK LIBERATION ARMY, covert, violent organization, an offshoot of the BLACK PANTHER PARTY. Although small in numbers, it has functioned since the late 1960s and is believed responsible for various robberies and the murder of several policeman. There is evidence that it is linked with the WEATHERMEN.

BLACK LUNG DISEASE, a lay term for PNEUMOCONIOSIS, which affects coal miners.

BLACKMORE, Richard Doddridge (1825–1900), English author of 14 novels, notably *Lorna Doone* (1869), a romance set in the English west country during the 17th century.

BLACKMUN, Harry (1908–   ), US lawyer, elevated to the US Court of Appeals in 1959, and in 1970 appointed Supreme Court justice by President Nixon.

BLACKMUR, Richard Palmer (1904–1965), US critic, editor and poet. His criticism, for which he is best known, is closely analytical. Among his books are *The Expense of Greatness* (1940) and *Language as Gesture* (1952). He taught at Princeton

U. (1940–43; 1946–65).

BLACK MUSLIMS, the chief US black nationalist movement, founded in 1930 by Wali Farad. He rejected racial integration, taught thrift, hard work and cleanliness, and foretold an Armageddon where Black would crush White. Under Elijah MUHAMMAD, the Muslims proclaimed black supremacy and demanded a nation within the US.

BLACKOUTS, incidents of widespread loss of electric power. In the most famous blackout, on Nov. 9, 1965, the power failure extended from Canada down the East Coast of the US into N.J. and Penn. A large part of France was struck by a blackout on Dec. 19, 1978. Blackouts are usually the result of a failure of one component of a power-supply network, or grid, which causes a "chain reaction" that spreads through the complex system.

BLACK PANTHER PARTY, US black revolutionary party, founded in 1966, advocating "armed self-defense" by black people. Though small in numbers, it enjoyed considerable influence until weakened by disputes in the early 1970s. Under the leadership of Eldridge CLEAVER and Huey P. Newton, the party opened community centers and bookshops and fought legal battles with the authorities, frequently securing the release of members held on violence charges.

BLACK SEA, tideless inland sea between Europe and Asia, bordered by Turkey, Bulgaria, Romania and the USSR, and linked to the Sea of Azov and (via the Bosporus) to the Mediterranean. It covers 180,000sq mi and is up to 7,250ft deep. The Danube, Dniester, Bug, Don and Dnieper rivers all flow into the sea, which is vital to Soviet shipping. The chief ports are Odessa, Sevastopol, Batumi, Constanta and Varna. Russia's Black Sea coast is an important resort area.

BLACK SEPTEMBER, terrorist group affiliated with Al Fatah, the Palestinian guerrilla organization. Created in 1971, Black September was named for the crackdown in 1970 by Jordan's King Hussein on Arab terrorist groups operating out of Jordan. Black September, using Lebanon as its base, claimed responsibility for, or was implicated in, many assassinations, airline hijackings and other violent acts. Members of the group killed 11 Israeli athletes at the 1972 Olympic Games in Munich.

BLACKSNAKE, *Constrictor constrictor,* one of the largest nonvenomous North American SNAKES, varying in length from 1.2m to 2.1m (4–6.9ft) and slate black in color as an adult. Very agile, known as the "racer," it can move as fast as a running man.

BLACK SOX SCANDAL, ironic term for the scandal which shook the world of baseball 1919–20 and led to radical reorganization in the administration of the sport. It involved members of the Chicago White Sox and broke out when Edward Cicotte confessed to accepting a bribe to influence the outcome of the 1919 World Series. He named seven other players allegedly involved. All eight were suspended for a season but were cleared of fraud.

BLACKSTONE, Harry (1885–1965), US magician and illusionist who dazzled audiences around the world for more than 50 years (1907–59). Called the last of the great magicians, he sawed women in half, made handkerchiefs dance and gave away more than 80,000 rabbits.

BLACKSTONE, Sir William (1723–1780), English jurist whose *Commentaries on the Laws of England* (1765–69) deeply influenced jurisprudence and the growth of COMMON LAW. He was the first professor of English Law at Oxford 1758–63, became a member of parliament 1761 and was a judge in the Court of Common Pleas 1770–80.

BLACKWELL, Elizabeth (1821–1910), English-born first woman doctor of medicine. Rebuffed at first by the authorities and later ostracized by her fellow students, she went on to gain her degree, with the highest grades for her year, at Geneva, N.Y., in 1849. After study in Europe, she returned to the US in 1857 and opened a hospital run by women (later also a medical school for women) in New York City.

BLACK WIDOW, *Latroclectas matans,* a common US name for a SPIDER whose bite is dangerous to man. The female has a rounded shiny abdomen and a scarlet hourglass-shaped mark on the underside; the male is smaller and harmless.

BLADDER, a hollow muscular sac; especially the urinary bladder (see also AIR BLADDER; GALL BLADDER), found in most vertebrates except birds. In humans it lies in the front of the PELVIS. URINE trickles continually into the bladder from the KIDNEYS through two tubes called ureters, and the bladder stretches until it contains about 500ml, causing desire to urinate. The bladder empties through the urethra, a tube which issues from its base, being normally closed by the external sphincter muscle. The female urethra is about 30mm long: the male urethra, which runs through the PROSTATE GLAND and the PENIS, is about

200mm long. The bladder is liable to CYSTITIS and to the formation of CALCULI.

BLAINE, James Gillespie (1830–1893), US statesman and post-Civil War Republican leader. His career was marked by an intense rivalry with fellow Republican Roscoe CONKLING and also by allegations of corruption. Blaine served as congressman 1863–76 (speaker 1869–75) and US senator 1876–81; he was secretary of state 1881, 1889–92, and presidential candidate 1884. He backed RECONSTRUCTION and protective tariffs but fostered PAN AMERICANISM as an extension of the MONROE DOCTRINE.

BLAIR, US family influential in 19th-century politics. **Francis Preston Blair** (1791–1876), politician and journalist, a member of Andrew Jackson's "kitchen cabinet." Blair played an important part in forming the new Republican party and also in organizing the unsuccessful HAMPTON ROADS PEACE CONFERENCE. He lived at the famous BLAIR HOUSE. His eldest son, **Montgomery Blair** (1813–1883), an eminent lawyer, defended Scott in the DRED SCOTT CASE, and served as postmaster general under Lincoln 1861–64. After the Civil War he backed Andrew Johnson's moderate policies and became a Democrat. His brother, **Francis Preston Blair, Jr.** (1821–1875), was a soldier and an ardent abolitionist. As a Republican congressman he helped keep Mo. in the Union during the Civil War. He was Democratic vice-presidential candidate in 1868.

BLAKE, Eubie (1883–   ), US ragtime pianist and composer best known for his Broadway musical *Shuffle Along* (1921) and his songs "I'm Just Wild About Harry" and "Memories of You." Associated with the RAGTIME revival of the 1970s, he was still performing publicly in his 90s.

BLAKE, Eugene Carson (1906–   ), US Protestant clergyman. A controversial liberal, he was president of the National Council of Churches (1954–57) and chief executive of the Presbyterian church during the 1950s and 1960s. He was a leader of the ecumenical movement and served as president of the WORLD COUNCIL OF CHURCHES (1966–72).

BLAKE, William (1757–1827), English poet, painter and prophet. He was apprenticed to an engraver 1772–79 and developed his own technique of engraving plates with both text and illustrations which were then colored by hand. In this manner he reproduced his *Songs of Innocence* (1789) and *Songs of Experience* (1794), collections of lyrics that contrast natural beauty and energy with the ugliness of man's material world. Blake was a revolutionary in both politics and religion and this is reflected in his art, particularly in the powerful though often opaque "Prophetic Books" which form the bulk of his work. Among perhaps the most impressive of these are *The Marriage of Heaven and Hell* (1793) and the epic *Jerusalem* (begun c1804). Blake's work was little understood by his contemporaries.

BLAKEY, Art (1919–   ), US jazz drummer who joined the Fletcher Henderson band in 1939 and has played with most of the big names in modern jazz. He formed the Jazz Messengers in 1955.

BLANC, (Jean Joseph Charles) Louis (1811–1882), French politician whose egalitarian ideas influenced modern socialism. He was a member of the provisional government in the 1848 Revolution, after which he was driven into exile in England. On his return to France (1871) he reentered politics but followed a less radical line.

BLANC, Mont, highest peak (15,771ft) in the European Alps, in SE France on the border with Italy. One of the world's longest vehicular tunnels (7.5mi), exceeded in Europe only by the 10.2mi St. Gotthard (1980), was constructed through Mont Blanc's base in 1965.

BLANCHARD, Jean Pierre François, (1753–1809), French balloonist and inventor who made the first aeronautical crossing of the English Channel (1785) and the first BALLOON ascent in America (1793). He also invented the PARACHUTE (1785).

BLAND, James A. (1854–1911), US Negro songwriter and banjo player in Negro minstrel shows. His *Carry Me Back to Old Virginny* is the Va. state song.

BLANDA, George (1927–   ), US football player. A quarterback and field-goal and extra-point kicker, he played 26 years for three pro teams: Chicago Bears, 1949–59, Houston, 1960–66 and Oakland, 1967–75, setting a career record for total points scored in 1971.

BLANK VERSE, unrhymed verse in iambic lines of five stresses. It is basically 10-syllabled but not rigidly so. The form originated in Italy. It was introduced to England by the Earl of SURREY, used to great effect by MARLOWE and by SHAKESPEARE, whose innovations made it a vehicle for natural speech rhythms. MILTON's *Paradise Lost* is written in highly distinctive and flexible blank verse.

BLANQUI, (Louis) Auguste (1805–1881), French revolutionary thinker and activist, an advocate of class struggle as a means to achieving COMMUNISM. He was involved in the revolutions of 1830, 1848 and 1870, and spent some 40 years in prison or exile. The Blanquist party became part of the French Socialist party in 1905.

BLASCO IBÁÑEZ, Vicente (1867–1928), Spanish politician and novelist. He is best known for *Blood and Sand* (1909) and *The Four Horsemen of the Apocalypse* (1916), but his true literary worth is to be found in his earlier naturalistic novels, such as *The Cabin* (1899) and *Reeds and Mud* (1902).

BLASS, Bill (1922–   ), US fashion designer whose sophisticated styles invigorated the ready-made fashion industry. He was one of the first to design for men as well as women.

BLAST FURNACE, furnace in which a blast of hot, high-pressure air is used to force combustion; used mainly to reduce IRON ore to pig iron, and also for lead, tin and copper. It consists of a vertical, cylindrical stack surmounting the bosh (the combustion zone) and the hearth from which the molten iron and slag are tapped off. Modern blast furnaces are about 30m high and 10m in diameter, and can produce more than 1800 tons per day. Layers of iron oxide ore, COKE and LIMESTONE are loaded alternately into the top of the stack. The burning coke heats the mass and produces CARBON monoxide, which reduces the ore to iron; the limestone decomposes and combines with ash and impurities to form a slag, which floats on the molten iron. The hot gases from the top of the stack are burned to preheat the air blast.

BLAUE REITER (Blue Rider), group of Expressionist painters formed by KANDINSKY and MARC in Germany 1911–14. They issued an almanac, *Der Blaue Reiter*, containing the artists' essays and pictures, and essays by SCHOENBERG, BERG and WEBERN. KLEE and ARP were invited to show at the exhibitions they organized in Germany. (See EXPRESSIONISM.)

BLAVATSKY, Helena Petrovna (1831–1891), Russian occultist, founder of the Theosophical Society (1875). She expounded her theory of human and religious evolution in *Isis Unveiled* (1877). (See also THEOSOPHY.)

BLENHEIM, Battle of, battle in the War of the SPANISH SUCCESSION. On Aug. 13, 1704, an English army under the Duke of Marlborough, with Austrian troops under Eugene of Savoy, defeated a superior French–Bavarian force near Blenheim, Bavaria. The battle ended Louis XIV's hopes of mastering Europe.

BLÉRIOT, Louis (1872–1936), French pioneer aviator and airplane manufacturer. In 1909 he became the first person to fly a heavier-than-air machine across the English Channel.

BLIGH, William (1754–1817), English admiral, captain of HMS BOUNTY at the time of the famous mutiny (1789). Master of the *Resolution* on COOK's last voyage to the Pacific, he later fought at Camperdown and Copenhagen. In 1805 he became governor of New South Wales, where his overbearing behavior caused another revolt.

BLINDNESS, severe loss or absence of VISION, caused by injury to the EYES, congenital defects, or diseases including CATARACT, DIABETES, GLAUCOMA, LEPROSY, TRACHOMA and VASCULAR disease. MALNUTRITION (especially VITAMIN A deficiency) may cause blindness in children. Infant blindness can result if the mother had GERMAN MEASLES early in PREGNANCY; it was also formerly caused by gonorrheal infection of eyes at birth, but routine use of silver nitrate reduced this risk. Transient blindness may occur if one is exposed to a vertical ACCELERATION of more than 5g. Cortical blindness is a disease of the higher perceptive centers in the BRAIN concerned with vision: the patient may even deny blindness despite severe disability. Blindness due to cataract may be relieved by removal of the eye lens and the use of GLASSES. Prevention or early recognition and treatment of predisposing conditions is essential to save sight, as established blindness is rarely recoverable.

Many special books (using BRAILLE), instruments, utensils and games have been designed for the blind. With the help of guide dogs or long canes, many blind persons can move about freely. They can detect obstacles around them by the change of pitch of high-frequency sound from the feet or a cane, a skill acquired by training, and by using other senses.

BLISS, Sir Arthur (1891–1975), English composer and Master of the Queen's Music. He is best known for his ballet *Checkmate* (1937), his *Colour Symphony* (1922), cinema scores such as *The Shape of Things to Come* (1935), and the less successful opera, *The Olympians* (1949).

BLITZKRIEG, a German word meaning "lightning war." Originally used to describe German tactics in WWII, it is now applied to any fast military advance, such as the 1944 sweep through France by the US 3rd Army under PATTON.

BLITZSTEIN, Marc (1905–1964), US composer and librettist. He wrote the texts and music for the operas *The Cradle Will Rock* (1937) and *Regina* (1949) and the American text for the 1954 production of *The Three-Penny Opera*.

BLIXEN, Karen. See DINESEN, ISAK.

BLOCH, Ernest (1880–1959), Swiss-American composer. He made great use of traditional Jewish music, particularly in his *Israel: Symphony* (1916) and *Sacred Service* (1930–33) and *Three Jewish Poems* (1913).

BLOCK, Herbert L. (1909–), US political cartoonist. His dry and witty cartoons have been appearing under the signature *Herblock* in the *Washington Post* since 1943. He was awarded Pulitzer prizes in 1942 and 1954.

BLOCKADE, a war maneuver designed to cut an enemy's supply routes by obstructing outside access to his territory. Napoleon introduced the CONTINENTAL SYSTEM in order to strangle British trade; in the CIVIL WAR, the Federal navy's command of waterways weakened the Confederates. In WWI the British navy blockaded Germany; in WWII German U-boats cut off much of Britain's food supply. In 1948 a Soviet blockade of West Berlin was broken by the BERLIN AIRLIFT.

BLOCK GRANTS, in the US, a form of financial aid to the states from the federal government. Under this program, states receive money for use in very broad subject areas, such as health, community development or transportation.

BLOCK ISLAND, a small island off R.I., part of Washington Co., and coextensive with New Shoreham, a resort town. On the coasts there are important lighthouses.

BLOEMBERGEN, Nicolaas (1920–), Dutch-born US physicist. A professor at Harvard (from 1949), he shared the 1981 Nobel Prize in Physics for his work in LASER spectroscopy.

BLOK, Alexander Alexandrovich (1880–1921), Russian dramatist and poet. He rose to fame as a symbolist poet before the 1917 Revolution, which he used as the backdrop in his great long poem *The Twelve* (1918).

BLOOD, the body fluid pumped by the heart through the vessels of those animals (all vertebrates and many invertebrates) in which diffusion alone is not adequate for transport of materials, and which therefore require BLOOD CIRCULATION systems. Blood plays a part in every major bodily activity. As the body's main transport medium it carries a variety of materials: oxygen and nutrients (such as glucose) to the tissues for growth and repair (see METABOLISM); carbon dioxide and wastes from the tissues for excretion; HORMONES to various tissues and organs for chemical signaling; digested food from the gut to the LIVER; immune bodies for prevention of infection and clotting factors to help stop bleeding to all parts of the body. Blood also plays a major role in HOMEOSTASIS, as it contains BUFFERS which keep the acidity (pH) of the body fluids constant and, by carrying heat from one part of the body to another, it tends to equalize body temperature.

The adult human has about 5 litres of blood, half PLASMA and half blood cells (erythrocytes or red cells, leukocytes or white cells, and thrombocytes or platelets). The formation of blood cells (hemopoiesis) occurs in bone MARROW, lymphoid tissue and the RETICULOENDOTHELIAL SYSTEM. Red cells (about 5 million per mm^3) are produced at a rate of over 100 million per minute and live only about 120 days. They have no nucleus, but contain a large amount of the red pigment HEMOGLOBIN, responsible for oxygen transfer from lungs to tissues and carbon dioxide transfer from tissues to lungs. (Some lower animals employ copper-based HEMOCYANINS instead of hemoglobin. Others, e.g., cockroaches, have no respiratory pigments.) White cells (about 6,000 per mm^3) are concerned with defense against infection and poisons. There are three types of white cells: granulocytes (about 70%), which digest bacteria and greatly increase in number during acute infection; lymphocytes (20–25%), which participate in immune reactions (see IMMUNITY; ANTIBODIES); and monocytes (3–8%), which digest nonbacterial particles, usually during chronic infection. (See also HODGKIN'S DISEASE; LEUKEMIA.) Platelets, which live for about 8 days and which are much smaller than white cells and about 40 times as numerous, assist in the initial stages of blood CLOTTING together with at least 12 plasma clotting factors and fibrinogen. This occurs when blood vessels are damaged, causing THROMBOSIS, and when HEMORRHAGE occurs (see also HEMOPHILIA.)

Blood from different individuals may differ in the type of antigen on the surface of its red cells and the type of ANTIBODY in its plasma. Consequently, in a blood TRANSFUSION, if the blood groups of the donor and recipient are incompatible with respect to antigens and antibodies present, a dangerous reaction occurs, involving aggregation or clumping of the red cells of the donor in the recipient's circulation. Many blood group systems have been discovered, the first and most important being the ABO system by Karl LANDSTEINER in 1900. In this system, blood is classified by whether the red cells have antigens A (blood group A), B (group B), A and B (group AB), or neither A nor B antigens (group O).

Another important antigen is the Rhesus antigen (or Rh factor). People who have the Rh factor (84%) are designated Rh+, those who do not, Rh−. Rhesus antibodies do not occur naturally but may develop in unusual circumstances. In a few cases, where Rh− women are pregnant with Rh+ babies, blood leakage from baby to mother causes production of antibodies by the mother which may progressively destroy the blood of any subsequent baby. (See also EDEMA; SEPTICEMIA; SERUM; TOXEMIA.)

BLOOD CIRCULATION, the movement of BLOOD from the HEART through the ARTERIES, CAPILLARIES and VEINS and back to the heart. The circulatory system has two distinct parts in animals with lungs: the pulmonary circulation, in which blood is pumped from the right ventricle to the left atrium via the blood vessels of the lungs (where the blood is oxygenated and carbon dioxide is eliminated); and the systemic circulation, in which the oxygenated blood is pumped from the left ventricle to the right atrium via the blood vessels of the body tissues (where—in the capillaries— the blood is deoxygenated and carbon dioxide is taken up). As it leaves the heart, the blood is under considerable pressure—about 120mmHg maximum (systolic pressure) and 80mmHg minimum (diastolic pressure). Sustained high blood pressure, or **hypertension**, occurs in kidney and hormone diseases and in old age, but generally its cause is unknown. It may lead to ARTERIOSCLEROSIS and heart, brain and kidney damage. Low blood pressure occurs in SHOCK, TRAUMA and ADDISON'S DISEASE.

BLOODHOUND, a breed of dog famous for its ability to track by scent. Its coat is generally either tan or black, or both, and when fully grown it reaches from 23in to 27in in height. It has a characteristically heavy-jowled face.

BLOOD POISONING. See SEPTICEMIA.

BLOOMER, Amelia Jenks (1818–1894), US feminist reformer. A famous lecturer, she also edited *The Lily*, a journal which campaigned for temperance and women's rights. In a search for more practical clothes for women she unsuccessfully tried to introduce the baggy pantaloons which were derisively nicknamed "bloomers."

BLOOMSBURY GROUP, name applied to a coterie of writers and artists who met in Bloomsbury, London, in the early 20th century. Influenced by G. E. MOORE, they gathered about Virginia and Leonard WOOLF, and Virginia's sister, Vanessa Bell. The group included Clive BELL, E. M. FORSTER, Roger FRY, Duncan GRANT, J. M. KEYNES and Lytton STRACHEY.

BLOOR, Mother (Ella Reeve Bloor;

1862–1951), US radical activist. She participated in the temperance and women's suffrage movements and was a Socialist Party organizer (1902–19) before becoming a cofounder of the US Communist Party (1919). Called the "Matron Saint" of the party, she served on its national committee from 1932 to 1948.

BLOWFLY, also known as the bluebottle or greenbottle. It is a large fly of the family Calliphoridae, that lays eggs in carrion, excrement or open wounds. It attacks livestock and because of its breeding habits spreads dysentery and perhaps jaundice and anthrax.

BLÜCHER, Gebhard Leberecht von (1742–1819), Prussian commander, a fierce opponent of Napoleon. After distinguished service at Jena (1806), he was made a field marshal for his part in the Battle of Leipzig (1813). He led Prussian troops into Paris a year later. In 1815 the timely intervention of the Prussian army under Blücher made conclusive victory at Waterloo possible.

BLUE BABY, infant born with a HEART defect (a hole between the right and left sides, or malformation of the arteries) that permits much of the BLOOD to bypass the LUNGS. The resulting lack of oxygen causes CYANOSIS. These conditions used to be fatal but can now often be corrected by surgery.

BLUEBEARD, villain of a traditional tale in which a rich man, who has had several wives, marries a young girl. He forbids her to enter a particular room in his castle; she disobeys him, and finds there the bodies of former wives he has murdered. In some versions he threatens to kill her also, but she is saved by her brothers. MAETERLINCK based a play on the legend. BARTÓK's opera *Duke Bluebeard's Castle* (1911) is a more modern symbolic treatment of the story.

BLUEBIRD, songbird which visits the US as a summer bird of passage. A member of the family Turdidae, it often nests near human habitations. Its upper part is sky-blue in color and its breast is chestnut. Its song is mellow and sweet. The female lays four or five eggs.

BLUEBOTTLE. See BLOWFLY.

BLUEFISH, voracious fish of the family Pomatomidae found in the Atlantic Ocean. It can grow to a length of about 1.2m (4ft) and attain a weight of 5.5–9kg (12–20lb). Large shoals of bluefish pursue and kill enormous numbers of small fish. They are caught commercially and are a popular game fish.

BLUEGRASS, a traditional country-music instrumental style, streamlined by an intense hard-driving pace. The style was developed in the late 1930s by Bill MONROE and his Bluegrass Boys, and by the famous banjo player Earl SCRUGGS.

BLUEJAY. See JAY.

BLUE NILE, a river in Sudan which joins the White Nile at Khartoum to form the NILE. The Blue Nile has its headwaters in Ethiopia and is the source of Egypt's historically important seasonal floods.

BLUE RIDGE MOUNTAINS, a range lying E of the Appalachians and stretching through Md., W. Va., Va., N.C. and Ga. for 615mi. Shenandoah National Park is sited here and part of the Appalachian Trail follows the crest of the range.

BLUES, type of US Negro music, often sad and slow, characterized by the use of flattened "blue notes." Derived from the work songs, spirituals and "field hollers" of the Negroes of the South and became a principal basis of the JAZZ idiom. The characteristic pattern of the blues is a 12-bar structure with certain distinctive harmonies, but the form is flexible and has undergone many adaptations. At first a song, usually with guitar, harmonica or piano accompaniment, the blues have since also become an instrumental form, and their influence has pervaded many types of modern music. They were first popularized by W. C. HANDY's *Memphis Blues* and *St. Louis Blues*.

BLUE WHALE, *Balaenoptera musculus*, the largest species of whale and the largest known animal. It may reach 30m (100ft) in length and weigh 130 tons. A member of the RORQUAL group, it has a small dorsal fin on its blue-colored back and a series of ridges running down its chest. It feeds on PLANKTON, straining its food through the BALEEN which hangs from its upper jaw. The Blue whale lives mainly in the Antarctic Ocean, moving to warmer waters to breed. Like other whales it is a mammal (family Balaenopteridae), being warm-blooded and suckling its young. In the 20th century the number of Blue whales has been severely reduced by whaling, and it is now a protected species.

BLUM, Léon (1872–1950), creator of the modern French Socialist party, and the first socialist and the first Jew to become premier of France. As premier 1936–37 he led the Popular Front, a coalition of Socialists and Radicals opposed to fascism. He carried out major domestic reforms and was greatly concerned with defense against the Rome-Berlin axis.

BLUMENBACH, Johann Friedrich (1752–1840), German physiologist generally regarded as the father of physical ANTHROPOLOGY. As a result of careful measurement of a large collection of skulls, he divided mankind into five racial groups: Caucasian, Mongolian, Malayan, Ethiopian and American.

BLY, Nellie, pen name of Elizabeth Cochrane (1867–1922), US woman reporter. Her most famous exploit was her successful attempt in 1889 to beat the record of Jules Verne's Phileas Fogg (*Around the World in Eighty Days*): it took her 72 days, 6 hours, 11 minutes and 14 seconds.

B'NAI B'RITH (Hebrew: Sons of the Covenant), Jewish service and cultural organization. Founded in New York City in 1843, B'nai B'rith was first concerned with social work and the establishment of community centers for Jewish students. It has greatly expanded and now has branches in 33 countries.

BOADICEA (BOUDICCA), queen of the Iceni in Norfolk. In 60 AD she led a revolt against Roman ill-treatment, and sacked Camulodunum (Colchester), Londinium (London) and Verulamium (St. Albans) before being defeated in 61. She reportedly took poison to avoid capture.

BOAR, the wild pig, *Sus scrofa*, smaller than the domestic pig, dark gray or brown in color with large upward-pointing tusks. It inhabits many parts of Europe, N Africa and Asia. Its favorite habitat is marshy ground and deciduous woods, where it feeds on roots and grain and sometimes small animals. Boars have long been hunted for sport. The male domestic pig is also called a boar.

BOAS, nonpoisonous snakes that kill their prey by squeezing and suffocating it. Boas range from 2.5m to 9m (8–30ft) in length and feed on birds and mammals. They are found mostly in tropical America and the West Indies, and live on the ground or in trees. Boas give birth to live young and have vestigial hind limbs and a rudimentary pelvis. There are 35 species, including the ANACONDA.

BOAS, Franz (1858–1942), German-born US anthropologist who played a leading part in the establishment of the cultural-relativist school of ANTHROPOLOGY in the English-speaking world. The first professor of anthropology at Columbia U. (1899–1936), he wrote more than 30 books, including *The Mind of Primitive Man* (1911) and *Anthropology and Modern Life* (1928).

BOAT PEOPLE, thousands of people from Indochina who attempted to flee Communist rule in the aftermath of the Vietnam War. Most of them left in small boats, bribing guards and officials to let them try the perilous journey on the high seas, where they were easy prey for bandits and bad weather. Those who reached other shores were often placed indefinitely in poorly supplied camps and denied permanent homes. The US admitted thousands of these boat people after 1975. (See REFUGEE.)

BOATS AND BOATING. Boats are nautical craft, smaller in size than a SHIP. They may be propelled by sail, motor, paddle, oars or pole. The first boats were rafts and dugout CANOES. Many early boats were made from skins stretched over a framework. They were used for fishing and transport, and similar craft are still built. Today boats are used in LIFESAVING, as auxiliary craft, for pleasure or in sports such as sailing, ROWING, WATER SKIING or SKIN DIVING, all of which are widely popular in the US. Small-boat sailing, with numerous organized classes of boat and national and international competition, is now a popular sport all over the world. (See also CATAMARAN; HYDROFOIL; MOTORBOATING; YACHTS AND YACHTING.)

BOB AND RAY (Robert Elliot 1923– ; and Ray Goulding, 1922–), US satirical comedy team. Their subtle, low-key parodies (frequently ad-libbed) earned them an enthusiastic radio following (from 1951). They performed their routines on Broadway in *The Two and Only* (1968).

BOBCAT, a wild cat, *Lynx rufus*, closely related to the LYNX, named for its short (150mm—6in) tail. It grows to a length of about 0.9m (3ft) and has a brown and white coat with black spots and stripes. It is nocturnal, feeding on rodents and occasionally on livestock. The bobcat is found in most parts of North and Central America.

BOBOLINK, *Dolichonyx oryzivorus*, a North American migratory songbird named for its distinctive song. Also called ricebird or redbird, it is 150–200mm (6–8in) long with a dull plumage—except in spring, when the male is black and yellow. The bobolink breeds in the US and S Canada, migrating to South America for the winter.

BOBSLED, a heavy sled used on packed snow or ice runs, having four runners and carrying two or four people. The bobsled derived from the toboggan in Switzerland and became popular in the early 20th century. Bobsledding has been included in the winter Olympic Games since 1928, but with its steep runs and speeds up to 100mph it is very dangerous and is not widely practiced.

BOBWHITE, *Colinus virginiarus*, North American gamebird related to the QUAIL and PARTRIDGE. It is about 250mm (10in) long and reddish-brown in color. Bobwhites feed on insects and seeds and keep within a group or covey.

BOCCACCIO, Giovanni (1313–1375), great Italian writer and humanist of the early Renaissance whose work had a lasting influence on European literature. A classical scholar and a friend and admirer of PETRARCH, his works include *Filostrato, Teseida* and the famous DECAMERON tales—the first literary expression of Renaissance humanist realism.

BOCCHERINI, Luigi (1743–1805), Italian composer and cellist, noted for his chamber music. His numerous charming and elegant works have been compared to those of HAYDN, his contemporary.

BOCCIE, Italian bowling game. One player tosses a "jack" ball from one end of a level court to the other. Each team then tries to roll its eight balls closest to the jack ball, alternating shots. Points are awarded for the closest balls. Twelve points constitutes a game, with most matches consisting of two-out-of-three games.

BOCCIONI, Umberto (1882–1916), Italian painter and sculptor. A pioneer of Italian FUTURISM, he was a signer of the "Manifesto of Futurist Painters" (1910). He tried to capture movement and the speed and sensations of modern life by using dynamic forms.

BOCHUM, industrial city in the Ruhr area of West Germany. Once an important mining center, the city has a unique mining museum. It was badly bombed during WWII. Pop 346,010.

BÖCKLIN, Arnold (1827–1901), major Swiss painter who lived mainly in Italy and drew inspiration from that country's classical heritage. Primarily a landscape painter, he often used mythological subjects and strongly influenced German Romantic painting.

BODHISATTVA, in Mahayana (a form of BUDDHISM) he is a gentle spiritual being, a potential Buddha who, through generosity and compassion, postpones his entry into NIRVANA to help mankind. Buddhist legend has many instances of the lives and good works of bodhisattvas.

BODIN, Jean (c1530–1596), French political philosopher who argued that stable government lay in a moderate absolutism founded on divine right, but subject to divine and natural law. Tolerant in religion, he also tried to show that religious differences could be settled by adherence to the Ten Commandments.

BODLEIAN LIBRARY, the library of Oxford University. Originally established in the 14th century, it was restored 1598–1602 by the English diplomat Sir Thomas Bodley (1545–1613). Its collection

has grown from 2,000 to 2.5 million books, including many oriental and other MSS.

BODONI, Giambattista (1740–1813), Italian printer and type-designer. The Bodoni typeface, with its sharp contrast between thick and thin strokes, has been widely used in modern printing.

BODYBUILDING, an activity that usually involves the development of musculature by weight-lifting. It is also a sport in which competitors display their muscular development in posing routines, being rated by judges on muscle size, definition (absence of fat), symmetry, shape and general appearance. Several international competitions are held annually.

BOERS (Dutch: farmers), in South Africa, term once used for people of Dutch, German and Huguenot descent who settled in the Cape of Good Hope from 1652. The British annexed the Cape in 1806, and in 1835–43 the Boers left on the Great Trek to found the new republics of the Transvaal and the Orange Free State. Now called Afrikaners, they speak their own language (AFRIKAANS) and belong to the Dutch Reformed Church. Their racial attitudes resulted in the APARTHEID policy.

BOER WAR, or South African War, fought between the British and the Boers from 1899 to 1902. The Boers resented British territorial expansion, while the British aimed at a united South Africa and complained of the harsh treatment of the Boers, under Paul KRUGER, gave to immigrant gold prospectors. In 1895 tension was increased by the Jameson Raid, aimed at supporting an anti-Boer rebellion in the Transvaal. Well-equipped by Germany, the more numerous Boer forces took the offensive in 1899. In the early part of the war the Boers besieged Ladysmith and Mafeking, but the arrival of British reinforcements turned the tide and by late 1900 the Boers had to resort to guerrilla tactics. Their resistance steadily weakened and the war ended with the treaty of Vereeniging in 1902. The British victory did not, however, end the conflict between Boers and British, which moved into the political arena.

BOETHIUS, Anicius Manlius Severinus (c480–525), Roman philosopher, statesman and Christian theologian whose works were a major source of Classical thought for medieval Scholastic philosophers. A high official under Theodoric The Great, he was accused of treason and executed. While in prison, he wrote his influential work *On the Consolation of Philosophy.*

BOGART, Humphrey DeForest (1899–1957), US film actor, famous for his screen image as the cool, tough anti-hero. Some of his most notable films were *The Maltese Falcon* (1942), *Casablanca* (1942) and *The African Queen* (1951)—for which he won an Academy Award.

BOGDANOVICH, Peter (1939–   ), US film critic turned director whose early work was praised for its elegant visual style. His films include *The Last Picture Show* (1971) and *Paper Moon* (1973).

BOGOMILS, religious sect founded in Bulgaria in the 10th century by the priest Bogomil. Its members held that all material things were created by the devil and that therefore all close contact with matter, even the Eucharist, must be rejected. The sect flourished in the Balkans until the 14th century. (See also CATHARI.)

BOGOTA, capital and largest city of Colombia. Founded by the Spanish in 1538 on the site of Chibcha settlement, commercial and cultural center with several universities (the oldest from 1573). Its climate is mild because of its altitude of over 8,500ft, at the edge of an Andean plateau. Pop 4,055,909.

BOHÈME, La, opera by Giacomo PUCCINI, a staple of the repertory since its first performance in Turin, Italy, in 1896 under Arturo TOSCANINI. Puccini's expressive melodies and powerful orchestration give warmth and life to this story of young love in the artists' quarter of Paris in the mid-19th century.

BOHEMIA, historic region in central Europe. It was once part of the Austro-Hungarian Empire. In 1918, after a war-torn history, it became a province in the republic of Czechoslovakia, of which its chief city, Prague, became the capital. In 1949 it lost its separate provincial status. The area is rich in minerals and in fine agricultural land.

BOHLEN, Charles Eustis (1904–1974), US diplomat and adviser on Soviet affairs. He served as adviser and interpreter at Russian conferences for presidents Roosevelt and Truman, and was US ambassador to the USSR (1953–57), the Philippines (1957–59) and France (1962–68).

BÖHME, Jakob (1575–1624), German mystic and religious philosopher. Claiming divine revelation, he argued that all opposites, including good and evil, are reconciled in God. His ideas influenced many late philosophers and theologians.

BOHR, Niels Henrik David (1885–1962), Danish physicist who proposed the Bohr model of the ATOM while working with RUTHERFORD in Manchester, England, in 1913. Bohr suggested that a HYDROGEN atom consisted of a single electron performing a circular orbit around a central PROTON (the nucleus), the energy of the ELECTRON being quantized (i.e., the electron could only carry certain well-defined quantities of energy—see QUANTUM THEORY). At one stroke this accounted both for the properties of the atom and for the nature of its characteristic radiation (a SPECTRUM comprising several series of discrete sharp lines). In 1927 Bohr proposed the COMPLEMENTARITY PRINCIPLE to account for the apparent paradoxes which arose on comparing the wave and particle approaches to describing SUBATOMIC PARTICLES. After escaping from Copenhagen in 1943 he went to the UK and then to the USA, where he helped develop the ATOMIC BOMB, but he was always deeply concerned about the graver implications for humanity of this development. In 1922 he received the Nobel Prize for Physics in recognition of his contributions to atomic theory. His son, **Aage Niels Bohr** (1922–   ), shared the 1975 Nobel Prize for Physics with B. Mottelson and J. Rainwater for contributions made to the physics of the atomic nucleus. Niels Bohr's brother, **Harald August Bohr** (1887–1951), was a distinguished mathematician.

BOILEAU (-DESPRÉAUX), Nicolas (1636–1711), French poet, satirist and literary critic. His insistence on classical standards, notably in the didactic poem *L'Art poétique* (1674), greatly influenced literary taste both in France and England in the 18th century.

BOISE, capital city of Ida., founded in 1863. It is a center for wool and agricultural products and manufactures steel, furniture and electrical goods. Pop 102,451.

BOITO, Arrigo (1842–1918), Italian poet and composer. His own operas include *Mefistofele* (1868; revised 1875) and *Nerone* (1918), though he is best known as the librettist of VERDI's *Otello* and *Falstaff* and of PONCHELLI's *La Gioconda*.

BOK, Edward William (1863–1930), Dutch-born US editor, writer and philanthropist. In 1889 he became editor of *The Ladies' Home Journal* and used the magazine to campaign for good causes. In his retirement he wrote the Pulitzer prize-winning *The Americanization of Edward Bok* (1920).

BOKASSA I (1921–   ), deposed emperor of the Central African Republic. As army chief of staff he staged a coup in 1966 to become president of the country that was once part of French Equatorial Africa. In 1977 he had himself crowned the "world's first socialist emperor." His lavish spending and autocratic and bizarre behavior led to his overthrow and exile in Sept. 1979.

BOLERO, a Spanish national dance for one or two people. The steps are intricate and are performed to a clear rhythm usually marked by castanets. Many composers, such as RAVEL in *Bolero,* employ this rhythm.

BOLEYN, Anne (c1507–1536), second wife of HENRY VIII and mother of Elizabeth I. When he met her, Henry was already tiring of his first queen, who had failed to produce a son, and he married Anne in 1533 as soon as he was divorced. Their daughter Elizabeth was born later that year, but Anne too bore no living son. She was beheaded, having been convicted, on dubious evidence, of adultery and incest.

BOLGER, Ray (1904–), US comedian, dancer and actor. He appeared on stage in musical comedy, in films and on television. His successes include *On Your Toes* (1936), *The Wizard of Oz* (1939) and *Where's Charley?* (1948).

BOLINGBROKE, Henry St. John, 1st Viscount (1678–1751), English statesman. A member of the Tory party, as secretary of state he successfully handled the negotiations for the treaty of UTRECHT (1713). He lost office on the death of Queen Anne, and in 1715 was forced to seek exile in France, where he remained for the next 10 years. Out of the mainstream of affairs, Bolingbroke devoted his time to political journalism and the study of history.

BOLÍVAR, Simón (1783–1830), South American soldier, statesman and liberator. Born of a wealthy Venezuelan family, he studied in Europe, where he was influenced by the work of the 18th-century rationalists, particularly by ROUSSEAU. Bolívar returned to South America in 1807, convinced that the Spanish colonies were ready to fight for independence. After two abortive attempts, he successfully liberated Venezuela in 1821. His country united with New Granada and Quito to form the state of Gran Colombia, with Bolívar as president. He went on to liberate Peru (1824) and to form, from Upper Peru, the republic of Bolivia (1825). Bolíva envisaged a united South America, but Peru and Bolivia turned against him in 1826. Venezuela seceded from Gran Colombia in 1829, and in the following year Bolíva resigned as president. He died of tuberculosis.

BOLIVIÁ, landlocked South American republic, bordered by Brazil to the N and E, Paraguay to the SE, Argentina to the S, and in the W by Peru and Chile.

Land. There are three main regions: the Oriente lowlands in the E, consisting largely of tropical rainforest and swamps; the Montanas, a central zone of mountains and fertile valleys; and in the W, the Altiplano, a bleak Andean plain of coarse grassland, the home of most of the people. At its northern end, shared with Peru, is Lake Titicaca, South America's largest lake and at 12,500ft the world's highest navigable stretch of water.

People. About 75% of the population is concentrated within Andean Bolivia. The Oriente, in contrast, averages less than 2 persons per sq mi. The population consists of about 30% Quechua Indians, 25% Aymará ndians, 30% mestizos and 15% whites. The illiteracy rate is about 40%.

Economy. Bolivia is one of the poorest countries in South America. Minerals, particularly tin, but also, increasingly, petroleum and natural gas, dominate the country's economy and form more than 75% of its exports. Antimony, lead, tungsten, bismuth and zinc are also important, while there are also large, but as yet unexploited, deposits of iron and manganese. Inadequate transportation has considerably hampered Bolivia's growth. Some two-thirds of the population still depend on the land for a livelihood. On the Altiplano the main crops are sugar, potatoes, barley and beans. Sheep, llamas and alpacas are the chief livestock. Corn, wheat, barley, tobacco, dairy cattle and a wide variety of fruits and vegetables are raised in the Montana region.

History. Before Spanish conquest an advanced Aymará civilization around Lake Titicaca was subjugated by the INCAS. During colonial times the region was known as Upper Peru and was famous for its mineral wealth. Freed from the Spanish rule by Simon BOLÍVAR in 1825, Bolivia later lost more than its present territory in armed conflicts with Brazil, Chile and Paraguay. In the 20th century the country had an unhappy history of recurring military coups.

Official Name: Republic of Bolivia
Capital: La Paz
Area: 424,160sq mi

Population: 5,150,000
Languages: Spanish
Religions: Roman Catholic
Monetary Unit(s): 1 Peso Bolivian = 100 centavos

BÖLL, Heinrich (1917–   ), German author and winner of the Nobel Prize for Literature in 1972. His books are bitterly satiric, exploring themes of despair and love in post-WWII Europe. Important among his works are *Billiards at Half Past Nine* (1961) and *The Clown* (1965).

BOLLINGEN PRIZE, a prize of $5,000 awarded to US poets by the Yale University Library. The prize was originally given by the Library of Congress and was first awarded, amid great controversy, to Ezra POUND (1949) who, at the time, stood accused of treason during WWII. Other winners have been E. E. CUMMINGS and ROBERT FROST.

BOLL WEEVIL, *Anthonomus grandis,* the most damaging cotton pest in the US. The beetle, which is 6mm (0.24in) long, lays eggs in cotton buds and fruit and feeds on the bolls and blossoms, causing an estimated loss of $203,000,000 every year. It first appeared in the US in the 1890s from Central America. Modern methods of combating it include soil improvement, cleansing its hibernating places and the use of insecticides.

BOLOGNA, Italian city 51mi N of Florence at the foot of the Apennines. It is an ancient Etruscan and Roman city, with a university founded c1088, many medieval buildings and some fine Renaissance paintings and sculptures. Capital of the Emilia Romagna region, it is an agricultural and industrial center, producing farm machinery and chemicals. Pop 476,500.

BOLSHEVISM, name given to the policy of the majority group (Russian *bolsheviki*) at the 1903 congress of the Russian Social Democratic Workers' party, as opposed to the minority or *mensheviki*. The bolsheviks, under the leadership of LENIN, formed a radical left-wing group in 1917 and took over the leadership of the Russian Revolution. Their doctrines derived from the work of MARX and ENGELS and upheld a revolution led by workers and peasants. (See COMMUNISM.)

BOLSHOI THEATER, Russian theater, ballet and opera house. The Bolshoi, which possesses one of the largest stages in the world, is the home of the famous ballet school. Its classical ballet and opera productions have a worldwide reputation.

BOLT, Robert (Oxton) (1924–   ), English dramatist best known for the play and movie about Thomas More, *A Man for*

All Seasons (1962). Bolt also wrote the screenplays for *Lawrence of Arabia* (1962) and *Doctor Zhivago* (1966).

BOLTZMANN, Ludwig (1844–1906), Austrian physicist who made fundamental contributions to THERMODYNAMICS, classical STATISTICAL MECHANICS and KINETIC THEORY. The **Boltzmann constant** (k), the quotient of the universal gas constant R and the AVOGADRO number (N), is used in statistical mechanics.

BOMB, device designed to explode, with the aim of destroying property or killing and maiming human beings. A bomb may be dropped from an aircraft, incorporated in a warhead, or "planted" in position. Essential to all bombs is a fuze (see AMMUNITION), in effect a miniature bomb whose explosion precipitates the explosion of the bomb proper. In particular, fuzes of **timebombs** incorporate devices such that the fuze, and hence the bomb, may be set to explode after a determined elapse of time. Types of conventional bombs include **fragmentation bombs,** with cases designed to disintegrate into shrapnel; **fire bombs** and **incendiary bombs,** whose purpose is to destroy by fire; **gas bombs,** whose explosion distributes poisonous gas (see CHEMICAL AND BIOLOGICAL WARFARE); **smoke bombs,** which create a smokescreen; and **photoflash bombs,** used in night photography. Underwater bombs, designed to explode at a specific depth, are usually termed **depth charges.** (See also ATOMIC BOMB; EXPLOSIVES; HYDROGEN BOMB.)

BOMBAY, large seaport in W India, capital of Maharashtra State, on the Arabian Sea. Bombay was built on several small islands, now joined to each other and to the mainland, forming an area of 25sq mi. Its large harbor deals with the bulk of India's imports, notably wheat and machinery, and many exports such as cotton, rice and manganese. Local industries include textiles, leather goods and printing. Bombay is an important cultural center, with a university founded in 1857. The city is overcrowded, with a fast growing, mainly Hindu, population. The site was ceded to the Portuguese in 1534 and passed to Great Britain in 1661. The city was a headquarters of the British East India Company (1668–1858). Pop 5,700,358.

BOMBECK, Erma (1927–   ), US author known for her humorous newspaper column "At Wits End," widely syndicated since 1965, and for witty essays on middle-class life delivered twice weekly on a morning TV program, 1979–81. Her popular books include *The Grass Is Always Greener over the Septic Tank* (1976).

BONAVENTURE, Saint (1221–1274), Italian medieval scholastic philosopher and theologian. He taught principally at Paris and later became Master General of the Franciscan order. Called the "Seraphic Doctor," he distinguished between PHILOSOPHY, based on man's natural knowledge, and THEOLOGY, which attempts to understand the Christian mysteries.

BOND, Chemical, the links which hold ATOMS together in compounds. In the 19th century it was found that many substances, known as **covalent compounds**, could be represented by structural FORMULAS in which lines represented bonds. By using double and triple bonds, most organic compounds could be formulated with constant VALENCES of the constituent atoms. STEREOISOMERISM showed that the bonds must be localized in fixed directions in space. **Electrovalent compounds** (see ELECTROCHEMISTRY) consist of oppositely charged IONS arranged in a lattice; here the bonds are nondirectional electrostatic interactions. The theory that atoms consist of electrons orbiting in shells around the nucleus (see PERIODIC TABLE) led to a simple explanation of both kinds of bonding: atoms combine to achieve highly-stable filled outer shells containing 2, 8 or 18 electrons, either by transfer of electrons from one atom to the other (**ionic bond**), or by the sharing of one electron from each atom so that both electrons orbit around both nuclei (**covalent bond**). In the **coordinate bond**, a variant of the covalent bond, both shared electrons are provided by one atom. QUANTUM MECHANICS has now shown that electrons occupy ORBITALS having certain shapes and energies, and that, when atoms combine, the outer atomic orbitals are mixed to form molecular orbitals. The energy difference constitutes the bond energy—the energy required to break the bond by separating the atoms. Molecular orbitals are classified as σ if symmetric when rotated through 180° about the line joining the nuclei, or π if antisymmetric. The energy and length of chemical bonds, and the angles between them, may be investigated by SPECTROSCOPY and X-RAY DIFFRACTION. (See also HYDROGEN BONDING.)

BONDI, Sir Hermann (1919–), Austrian-born British cosmologist who with T. GOLD in 1948 formulated the steady-state theory (see COSMOLOGY).

BONE, the hard tissue that forms the SKELETON of vertebrates. Bones support the body, protect its organs, act as anchors for MUSCLES and as levers for the movement of limbs, and are the main reserve of calcium and phosphate in the body. Bone consists of living cells (osteocytes) embedded in a matrix of COLLAGEN fibers with calcium salts similar in composition to hydroxyapatite (see APATITE) deposited between them. Some carbonates are also present. All bones have a shell of compact bone in concentric layers (lamellae) around the blood vessels, which run in small channels (Haversian canals). Within this shell is porous or spongy bone, and in the case of "long" bones (see below) there is a hollow cavity containing MARROW. The bone is enveloped by a fibrous membrane, the periosteum, which is sensitive to pain, unlike the bone itself, and which has a network of nerves and blood vessels which penetrate the bone surface. After primary growth has ended, bone formation (ossification) occurs where the periosteum joins the bone, where there are many bone-forming cells (osteoblasts). Ossification begins in the embryo at the end of the second month, mostly by transformation of CARTILAGE: some cartilage cells become osteoblasts and secrete collagen and a hormone which causes calcium salts to be deposited. Vitamin D makes calcium available from the food to the blood, and its deficiency leads to RICKETS. The two ends of a "long" bone (the epiphyses) ossify separately from the shaft, and are attached to it by cartilaginous plates, at which lengthwise growth takes place. Radical growth is controlled by the periosteum, and at the same time the core of the bone is eroded by osteoclast cells to make it hollow. Primary growth is stimulated by the PITUITARY and SEX HORMONES; it is completed in adolescence, when the epiphyses fuse to the shaft. Bones are classified anatomically as "long," cylindrical and usually hollow, with a knob at each end; "short," spongy blocks with a thin shell; and "flat" two parallel layers of compact bone with a spongy layer in between. Some hand and foot bones are short; the ribs, sternum, skull and shoulder-blades are flat; and most other bones are long. The shape and structure of bones are quickly modified if the forces on them alter. Disorders of bone include OSTEOMYELITIS and various TUMORS and CANCER. Dead bone is not readily absorbed and can be a focus of infection. In old age thinning and weakening of the bones by loss of calcium (osteoporosis) is common.

BONHEUR, Rosa (1822–1899), French artist famous for her animal paintings. She made her reputation with *The Horse Fair* (1853), a scene full of vigor and grace, representative of her most accomplished work.

BONHOEFFER, Dietrich (1906–1945), German Lutheran pastor and theologian. He was the author of many radical books on ecumenism and Christianity in a secular world. A prominent anti-Nazi, he was arrested in 1943 and executed at Flossenbür concentration camp two years later.

BONIFACE, Saint (c672–754), English missionary, the apostle of Germany. Backed by CHARLES MARTEL and later by PEPIN THE SHORT, he organized the German Church, reformed the Frankish clergy and advanced the conversion of the Saxons. He was martyred by the Frisians.

BONINGTON, Richard Parkes (1801–1828), English artist noted for his watercolor landscapes and GENRE subjects. He spent most of his brief career in France; among those he influenced there were DELACROIX and COROT.

BONIN ISLANDS, group of volcanic islands about 500mi SE of Japan. In all there are 27 islands with some 200 inhabitants. They were administered by the US 1945–68, when they were returned to Japan.

BONN, capital of West Germany since the partition of the country after WWII (1949). This historic city is situated on the Rhine, in North Rhine-Westphalia. The birthplace of Beethoven, it has a museum and hall devoted to the composer. Much of the city has been rebuilt since WWII. It is now West Germany's administrative center and has attracted many modern industries. Pop 274,518.

BONNARD, Pierre (1867–1947), French artist whose almost impressionist style gives sparkling life and color to the sunny interiors he favored. These made him known as a leader of the intimist school. While at the Acadèmie Julian he met Maurice Denis and Jean VUILLARD, with whom he formed the group known as the NABIS.

BONNEVILLE DAM, large hydroelectric dam spanning the Columbia R in NW Ore., about 40mi E of Portland. It is 170ft high and 1,250ft wide and was built 1933–43 as part of the New Deal program.

BONNEVILLE FLATS, an extremely level stretch of arid salt desert W of the Great Salt Lake in Ut. It is a favorite location for land speed trials and one where many world records have been established.

BONSAI, the ancient oriental art of growing trees in dwarf form. The modern enthusiast may spend three years cultivating the "miniature" trees, mainly by root pruning and shoot trimming. Plants that can be "dwarfed" include the cedars, myrtles, junipers, oaks, cypresses, pyracanthas and pines. Bonsai has spread throughout the world, and is a fast-growing hobby in North America, where there are many "bonsai" clubs.

BONUS MARCH, a demonstration, in 1932, in Washington, D.C. by some 15,000 jobless veterans of WWI. They hoped to persuade Congress to enable them to cash bonus certificates issued in 1924 in recognition of their war service. President Hoover worsened his reputation by ordering the military to drive the "Bonus Army" from the city. In 1936 Congress finally passed a law, against a presidential veto, allowing the exchange of the certificates.

BOOKBINDING, the craft of joining up leaves or folios into a volume with a protective cover. It began, as we know it, after rolls of PAPYRUS gave way to sheets of PARCHMENT as the commonly used writing material. Leather bindings, often richly tooled, were used for many centuries but are now reserved for special editions. Today the entire process, from folding the paper into sections to fitting the cover or case, can be mechanized. Cover materials include cloth, heavy paper, molded plastic paper and imitation leather.

BOOKKEEPING, the systematic recording of financial transactions. The single-entry system consists of a single account which shows the debts owed to and by the firm in question. The double-entry system is more detailed; the debit and credit items are entered in a journal; they are then classified in a ledger. From this information a comprehensive balance sheet can be drawn up. The monthly system was developed to meet the needs of a complex commercial society. There are a number of separate daybooks, and the monthly totals are posted to the ledger accounts. ACCOUNTING differs in that it also includes the analysis of financial data.

BOOK OF COMMON PRAYER, the official LITURGY of the CHURCH OF ENGLAND, including (among others) the services of Morning and Evening Prayer and Holy COMMUNION, and the Psalter, Gospels and Epistles. The first Prayer Book was written by CRANMER (1549); a more reformed version (see ANGLICANISM; REFORMATION) was published in 1552 and, with minor revisions, 1559 and 1662. The 1662 Prayer Book has been used ever since, and has been a major formative influence on the English language. Since 1966, various modern experimental services have also legally been in use.

BOOK OF HOURS, books of prayers to be said at the canonical hours, widely used by laymen during the late Middle Ages. These were often masterpieces of the miniaturist's art; among the most famous are the Rohan and the de Berry Hours.

BOOK OF KELLS, a copy of the Gospels from the late 8th century, completed by the monks of Kells in County Meath, Ireland. Its richly elaborate decoration makes it one of the finest examples of medieval illuminated manuscripts. It is now in the library of Trinity College, Dublin.

BOOK OF MORMON. See MORMONS.

BOOLE, George (1815–1864), British mathematician and logician, chiefly remembered for devising **Boolean algebra**, which allowed mathematical methods to be applied to non-quantifiable entities such as logical propositions.

BOOLEAN ALGEBRA, an algebraic system obeying certain rules that resemble, but are distinct from, those of ordinary numerical algebra. The most important examples of Boolean algebras are the algebra of sets and that of logical propositions. (See SET THEORY; LOGIC.) The rules were formulated by G. BOOLE in the 19th century in order to apply mathematical methods to logic. Using the notation of the article SET THEORY, the rules are:

$$A \cup A = A, \quad A \cup A = A$$
$$A \cup B = B \cup A, \quad A \cap B = B \cap A$$
$$A \cup (B \cup C) = (A \cap B) \cap C,$$
$$O \cup A = A, \quad I \cup A = I$$
$$O \cap A = O, \quad I \cap A = A$$
$$A \cap A' = I, \quad A \cap A' = O$$
$$(A')' = A$$

When Boolean algebra is applied to logic, A, B and C are any propositions, $\cup$ is interpreted as *or*, $\cap$ as *and*, ' as *not*, I as a proposition that is necessarily true, and O as a proposition that cannot be true. Boolean algebra is important today in the design of telecommunications systems and electronic logic circuits, and hence in computer technology.

BOOMERANG, a primitive weapon developed uniquely in Australia. Deceptively simple in shape, this angular throwing club is precisely bent and balanced. When thrown, it follows a curved path, spinning end for end, and can strike a vicious blow. It can be thrown in such a way that it comes back to the thrower.

BOONE, Daniel (1734–1820), American pioneer and hunter. Beginning in 1767 he made a series of trips into what is now Ky. and in 1775 built a fort there, called Boonesboro. In 1778 he was captured by the Shawnee, who were allied with the British against the American revolutionaries. Boone escaped to warn settlers at Boonesboro of a planned attack, which they

successfully resisted. Traditionally, he is hailed as the founder of Ky., which he was not, and more justly as a great frontiersman.

BOORSTIN, Daniel Joseph (1914–   ), US historian. A professor at the University of Chicago (1944–69), Boorstin wrote several notable works in American history including *The Americans* (3 vols., 1958–73). He served as the Librarian of Congress from 1974.

BOOTH, an English family, founders and leaders of the SALVATION ARMY. **William Booth** (1829–1912) started his career as a Methodist minister but left the church in 1861 to work among the poor in the slums of London. In 1878 he founded the Salvation Army, assisted by his wife **Catherine Booth** (1829–1890), a noted orator who did valuable work for women's rights. **William Bramwell Booth** (1856–1929), the eldest son of William Booth, served as second general of the Salvation Army. **Ballington Booth** (1859–1940), second son, brought the Salvation Army to the US in 1887. With his wife Maud, he instituted the VOLUNTEERS OF AMERICA, a similar organization. **Catherine Booth-Clibborn** (1859–1905), the eldest daughter of William Booth, founded the Salvation Army in France and Switzerland. **Emma Moss Booth-Tucker** (1860–1903) helped to establish the Salvation Army in India in 1881. **Herbert Henry Booth** (1862–1926), the youngest son of William Booth, founded the Salvation Army in Australia and New Zealand. **Evangeline Cory Booth** (1865–1950), daughter of William Booth, was the Salvation Army's first woman general, with international command of the organization (1934–39). She also commanded the US Salvation Army (1904–34) and wrote popular evangelical songs.

BOOTH, Charles (1840–1916), British merchant and sociologist, who applied statistical research methods to sociology. The 17-volume *Life and Labour of the People in London* (1903) is his major work. A member of the royal commission on the poor law (1905–09), Booth also wrote *Poor Law Reform* (1910).

BOOTH, Edwin Thomas (1833–1892), US actor, famous on both the New York and London stages. His Shakespearean roles, particularly Hamlet, were considered theatrical landmarks. The son of Junius Brutus BOOTH, he was the brother of Lincoln's assassin, John Wilkes BOOTH.

BOOTH, John Wilkes (1838–1865), US actor who assassinated Abraham Lincoln, a son of the actor Junius Brutus BOOTH. He was a Confederate sympathizer; eager to avenge the South's defeat, he shot President Lincoln during a performance at Ford's Theater, Washington, D.C., on April 14th, 1865. Booth, breaking a leg, escaped but was finally trapped in a barn near Bowling Green, Va., where he was either shot or shot himself.

BOOTH, Junius Brutus (1796–1852), English-born actor, founder of a famous American family of actors. Emigrating to the US in 1821, he achieved great success, particularly in Shakespeare. He was the father of Edwin and John Wilkes BOOTH.

BOP, or Bebop, seminal style of modern JAZZ, named for its basic rhythmic feature. Inspired by musicians like Dizzy GILLESPIE and Charlie PARKER, Bop emerged in the 1940s to break with the Blues tradition and explore new harmonic and rhythmic fields. It added greater sophistication and complexity to jazz, deepening and reinvigorating it.

BORAH, William Edgar (1865–1940), Republican senator from Ida. 1907–40, a vigorous and independent champion of progressive reforms. He opposed US membership in the League of Nations and was a prominent isolationist on the eve of WWII, but was also an able chairman of the Senate Foreign Relations Committee (1924–33).

BORDEAUX, city in SW France and capital of Gironde department, on the Garonne R. It is France's third-largest port and chief center for the French wine trade. Bordeaux also has canning and shipbuilding industries. The city dates from Roman times. Pop 226,000; met pop 612,000.

BORDEN, Gail (1801–1874), US inventor of the first process for making condensed milk by evaporation. He also influenced the development of Tex.: he helped to write its first state constitution, prepared the first topographical map of Tex. and laid out the city of Houston.

BORDEN, Lizzie Andrew (1860–1927), US woman accused of murdering her father and stepmother with an ax on Aug. 4, 1892. She was acquitted but remained popularly condemned. The murder became part of American folklore.

BORDEN, Sir Robert Laird (1854–1937), Canadian prime minister (1911–20) who gave his country a new and more independent voice in world affairs. Borden became Conservative leader in 1901. He was a vigorous WWI prime minister, forming a Union party government with pro-conscription Liberals in 1917, and securing separate representation for Canada at the peace conference and in the League of Nations.

BORDER WAR (1854–59), conflict on the Kan.-Mo. border in the area known as "Bleeding Kansas." After the KANSAS-NEBRASKA ACT, proslavery "Border Ruffians" from Mo. infiltrated Kan. and, by fraud and intimidation in the 1855 elections, made Kan. a slave state. This led to four years of skirmishing, murder and pillage by opposing proslavery and antislavery Free-State bands. Violence was intensified by the proslavery attack on Lawrence, Kan., and John BROWN'S antislavery raid on Pottawatomie in 1856.

BORGES, Jorge Luis (1899–), Argentinian poet and prose writer. At first influenced by the metaphorical style of Spanish *Ultraísmo*, he later developed a unique form between short story and essay, the "fiction." Some of the best examples are in his *Ficciones* (1944) and *El Aleph* (1949).

BORGHESE, aristocratic Roman family, originally from Siena. Camillo Borghese (1552–1621) became Pope PAUL V. The many Borghese cardinals included the noted art collector, **Scipione Borghese** (1576–1633), patron of Giovanni Lorenzo BERNINI. He commissioned the Borghese Palace and Villa Borghese, two of Rome's finest Baroque buildings. **Prince Camillo Filippo Ludovico Borghese** (1775–1832) married Napoleon's sister Marie Pauline and became duke of Guastalla. Borghese family power declined with falling land values in the 1890s.

BORGIA, powerful Italian family descended from the Borjas of Valencia in Spain. **Alfonso de Borja** (1378–1458) became Pope CALIXTUS III. By bribery, his nephew **Rodrigo Borgia** (1431–1503) became Pope ALEXANDER VI in 1492 and worked to enrich his family by crushing the Italian princes. His son, **Cesare Borgia** (c1476–1507), used war, duplicity and murder to seize much of central Italy. Alexander's notorious daughter, **Lucrezia Borgia** (1480–1519), was probably a pawn in her family's schemes. As duchess of Ferrara (from 1505), she generously patronized the arts and learning.

BORGLUM, Gutzon (1867–1941), US sculptor best remembered for Mt Rushmore S.D. National Memorial, with its enormous portrait heads of Washington, Jefferson, Lincoln and Theodore Roosevelt. After Borglum's death the project was completed by his son. (See RUSHMORE, MOUNT.)

BORIC ACID (H_3BO_3), or boracic acid, colorless crystalline solid, a weak inorganic acid. It gives boric oxide (B_2O_3) when strongly heated; SODIUM borate typifies its salts. Boric acid is used as an external antiseptic, in the production of glass and as a welding flux. Powdered boric acid is an effective agent against cockroaches.

BORIS GODUNOV, opera by Modest MUSSORGSKY, first performed in St. Petersburg (now Leningrad), Russia, in 1874. Initially successful, the opera lost popularity and Nicholas RIMSKY-KORSAKOV revised the score, hoping to revive interest in it. In recent years Mussorgsky's original version has regained its place in the repertory.

BORMANN, Martin Ludwig (1900–1945), German Nazi politician who wielded brutal power as Hitler's deputy from 1941. Though he vanished in 1945, he was sentenced to death for war crimes at the NUREMBERG TRIALS in 1946. It is now thought he was probably killed as Berlin fell.

BORN, Max (1872–1970), German theoretical physicist active in the development of quantum physics, whose particular contribution was the probabilistic interpretation of the SCHRÖDINGER wave equation, thus providing a link between WAVE MECHANICS and the QUANTUM THEORY. Sharing the Nobel physics prize with W. Bothe in 1954, he devoted his later years to the philosophy of physics.

BORN-AGAIN CHRISTIANS, term applied predominantly to Fundamentalist Christians who feel themselves regenerated through the experience of being "born again" (John 3:3). Related to the Calvinist doctrine of election, the experience today assumes a revivalist character. President Jimmy Carter proudly claimed the experience. In the late 1970s, citing a decline in morality, Born-again Christians became active in US politics through such organizations as the MORAL MAJORITY and such evangelists as the Rev. Jerry FALWELL. See FUNDAMENTALISM.

BORNEO, largest island of the Malay Archipelago and third largest in the world (280,100sq mi). It contains the Indonesian provinces of Central, E, W, and S KALIMANTAN, with the sultanate of BRUNEI and the Malaysian states of SABAH and SARAWAK to the N and NW. Borneo is a mountainous equatorial island largely clad in tropical rain forest, and drained by several major rivers. Its highest point is Mt Kinabalu (13,455ft). Its peoples include Dayak, Malays, Arabs and Chinese. Products include copra, rubber, rice, timber, oil, bauxite and coal. The Portuguese reached Borneo in the 1500s, followed by the Dutch and the British, who had most influence in the 19th century.

BORODIN, Alexander Porfirevich (1833–1887), Russian composer and chemist, one of the group known as the FIVE. Though music came second to his scientific work in St. Petersburg, he wrote some notable works, including the opera *Prince Igor*; completed after his death by GLAZUNOV and RIMSKY-KORSAKOV.

BORROMEO, Saint Charles (1538–1584), Italian Roman Catholic religious reformer. As secretary of state to Pope Pius IV he influenced the Council of TRENT. As archbishop of Milan he developed popular children's "Sunday Schools" and priests' seminaries, and set a high personal standard of clerical selflessness.

BORROMINI, Francesco (1599–1677), major Italian BAROQUE architect, renowned for his dramatic use of space and light. Among his best-known works are the Roman churches of Sant'Ivo della Sapienza and San Carlo alle Quattro Fontane.

BORZOI, or Russian wolfhound, breed of tall, lean, longhaired dogs developed in Russia for hunting wolves. Borzois may be white or dark, with black, gray or tan spots. Similar to greyhounds, they are swift runners.

BOSANQUET, Bernard (1848–1923), British idealist philosopher whose best-known works were *The Philosophical Theory of the State* (1899) and *The Value and Destiny of the Individual* (1913). A controversial public figure, he was a champion of social reform and progressive education.

BOSCH, Hieronymous (c1450–1516), Dutch painter, from Hertogenbosch in North Brabant, whose work is unique in its grotesque fantasy. In paintings like the *Haywain* (c1485) and *The Garden of Earthly Delights* (1500) he uses an array of part-human, part-animal, part-vegetable forms to express symbolically, his obsessive vision of worldly sin and its eternal damnation.

BOSCH, Juan (1909–   ), Dominican writer and political leader. He founded the *Las Cuevas* literary group and, in exile (1937–61), the Dominican Revolutionary Party. He was elected president of the Dominican Republic in 1963, but was deposed the same year. The US, fearing supposed communist influence on Bosch, intervened militarily to prevent his restoration in 1965. In 1966 he lost an election for president.

BOSNIA AND HERZEGOVINA, a constituent republic of Yugoslavia. Most of its 19,741sq mi are mountainous, with barren limestone in the SW (the Dinaric Alps), forests in the E and arable land in the N. The population of over 3,700,000 consists of

Serbs (Orthodox), Croats (Roman Catholics) and Muslims. The capital is Sarajevo. Once independent states, they were held by the Ottoman Empire from the late 15th century until occupied (1878) and annexed (1908) by Austria–Hungary. Serbian terrorists, hostile to Austrian rule, assassinated the Austrian Archduke Francis Ferdinand in Sarajevo in 1914, precipitating WWI. After the war, Bosnia and Herzegovina became part of the new state of Yugoslavia.

BOSPORUS, Turkish strait 19mi long and about 0.5mi to 2.25mi wide connecting the Black Sea and Sea of Marmara. Historically important as the sole sea link between the Black Sea and the Mediterranean, it was bridged in 1973.

BOSSUET, Jacques Bénigne (1627–1704), French prelate and historian who was renowned for his eloquence as an orator, especially in his funeral orations. He was bishop of Condom (1669–71) and of Meaux (from 1681). He wrote the famous *Discourse on Universal History* (1681).

BOSTON, capital and largest city of Mass., a seaport on Massachusetts Bay. It is the most populous state capital, New England's leading city and the nearest major US seaport to Europe. It is also a major commercial, financial, manufacturing, cultural and educational center. Boston's industries include shipbuilding, electronics, chemicals, plastics, rubber products and printing. The city's wool market is the nation's largest. Historic buildings include the Old State House, Paul Revere House, Christ Church and Faneuil Hall. Boston itself has many notable educational institutions, and nearby Cambridge has Harvard University and the Massachusetts Institute of Technology. Settled by English Puritans in 1630, Boston became the capital of Massachusetts Bay Colony and—in the BOSTON MASSACRE and BOSTON TEA PARTY—led colonial unrest that erupted into the REVOLUTIONARY WAR. Modern Boston shares the acute urban problems of most large US cities. Pop 641,017.

BOSTON MARATHON, annual marathon race held since 1897 from Hopkinton, Mass. to Boston.

BOSTON MASSACRE, an incident which strengthened anti-British feeling in America preceding the REVOLUTIONARY WAR. On March 5, 1770, some 60 Bostonians, enraged by the presence of British soldiers in Boston, harassed a British sentry. Troops came to his aid and fired on the mob, killing three and wounding eight (two died later).

BOSTON POLICE STRIKE, stoppage called on Sept. 9, 1919, when Mass. authorities had failed to recognize a police labor union or to offer better working conditions. Gangs terrorized Boston for two nights until Governor Calvin Coolidge's firm action in calling out the state militia and ending the strike catapulted him to the vice-presidency in 1920.

BOSTON STRANGLER, name given by the media to the rapist-murderer who terrorized the Boston area in 1962–64, killing 13 women. Albert Henry DeSalvo, arrested in 1964 for armed robbery, assault and sex offenses, confessed to the murders, but the state lacked concrete evidence against him and he was never brought to trial. However, DeSalvo was sentenced in 1967 to life imprisonment for armed robbery.

BOSTON TEA PARTY, American revolutionary incident at Boston on Dec. 16, 1773. In protest against the tea tax and British import restrictions, a party of colonial patriots disguised in Indian dress boarded three British East India Company ships and dumped their cargo of tea into the harbor.

BOSTON TERRIER, US breed of dog, developed in Boston after 1870. It is small, with a square head, short muzzle and dark, smooth coat with white markings. The Boston terrier is a popular pet and show dog.

BOSWELL, James (1740–1795), Scottish writer and advocate, most famous for his *Life of Johnson* (1791), one of the greatest of English biographies. In his private journals he recorded his life and times with great zest. From them he culled the accounts of his travels in Corsica and elsewhere, and the brilliant conversations which distinguish the portrait of his friend Samuel JOHNSON.

BOSWORTH FIELD, site of a battle near Leicester, England. There, on Aug. 22, 1485, Yorkist Richard III was defeated and killed by Lancastrians under Henry Tudor (Henry VII)—who thus ended the Wars of the ROSES and founded the Tudor dynasty.

BOTANY, the study of plant life. Botany and ZOOLOGY are the major divisions of BIOLOGY. There are many specialized disciplines within botany, the classical ones being morphology, physiology, GENETICS, ECOLOGY and TAXONOMY. Although the present day botanist often specializes in a single discipline, he frequently draws upon techniques and information obtained from others.

The plant morphologist studies the form and structure of plants, particularly the whole plant and its major components, while the plant anatomist concentrates upon the cellular and subcellular structure, perhaps using the ELECTRON MICROSCOPE. The behavior and functioning of plants is studied by the plant physiologist, though since he frequently uses biochemical techniques, he is often called a plant biochemist. A plant geneticist uses biochemical and biophysical techniques to study the mechanism of inheritance and may relate this to the EVOLUTION of an individual. An important practical branch of genetics is plant BREEDING. The plant ecologist relates the form (morphology and anatomy), function (physiology) and evolution of plants to their environment. The plant taxonomist or systematic botanist specializes in the science of classification, which involves cataloging, identifying and naming plants using their morphological, physiological and genetic characters. CYTOLOGY, the study of the individual cell, necessarily involves techniques used in morphology, physiology and genetics.

Within these broad divisions there are many specialist fields of research. The plant physiologist may, for instance, be particularly interested in PHOTOSYNTHESIS or RESPIRATION. Similarly, the systematic botanist may specialize in the study of ALGAE (algology), FUNGI (mycology) or MOSSES (bryology). Other specialists study the plant in relation to its uses (economic botany), PLANT DISEASES (plant pathology) or the agricultural importance of plants (agricultural botany). BACTERIOLOGY is often considered to be a division of botany since bacteria are often classified as plants. (See also AGRONOMY; BIOCHEMISTRY; BIOPHYSICS; HORTICULTURE; PLANT; PLANT KINGDOM.)

The forerunners of the botanists were men who collected herbs for medical use long before philosophers turned to the scientific study of nature. However, the title of "father of botany" goes to THEOPHRASTUS, a pupil of ARISTOTLE, whose *Inquiry into Plants* sought to classify the types, parts and uses of the members of the plant kingdom. Passing over the work of the elder Pliny and that of his contemporary, Dioscorides, botany received few further lasting contributions until the Renaissance, the intervening period making do with the more or less fabulous "herbals" of the medical herbalists. The most famous pre-Darwinian classification of the plant kingdom was that of LINNAEUS, in which modern binomial names first appeared (1753). While Nehemiah GREW and John RAY had laid the foundations for plant anatomy and physiology in the 17th and 18th centuries, and HOOKE had even identified the cell (1665) with the aid of the MICROSCOPE, these subjects were not actively pursued until the 19th century when R. BROWN identified the nucleus and SCHWANN proposed his comprehensive cell theory. The work of DARWIN revolutionized the theory of classification, while that of MENDEL pointed the way to a true science of plant breeding.

BOTERO, Fernando (1932–), Colombian-born painter known for his cartoonlike satirical renderings of Latin American cultural archetypes, including generals, politicians and religious and historical figures.

BOTHA, Louis (1862–1919), Boer politician and general, first prime minister of the Union of South Africa (1910–19). He led guerrilla fighting in the BOER WARS (1899–1902), but as premier worked to reconcile Boers and British.

BOTHA, Pieter (1916–), prime minister of South Africa (1978–) who earlier served in a number of government posts including that of minister of defense. Although his Afrikaner government was beset by scandals concerning misuse of funds and foreign bribes, he remained in office, a staunch defender of his country's apartheid policies.

BOTHNIA, Gulf of, N arm of the Baltic Sea, E of Sweden and W of Finland, about 400mi long and 50–150mi wide. It has low salinity and is frozen for 3–7 months of the year.

BOTHWELL, James Hepburn, 4th Earl of (c1536–1578), powerful Scottish noble who married MARY QUEEN OF SCOTS in May 1567, after helping to murder her husband, Lord Darnley. In June he fled Scotland, and later died in a Danish prison.

Official name: Botswana
Capital: Gaborone
Area: 231,804sq mi
Population: 763,000
Languages: English, Tswana, Khoisan
Religions: Christian; and tribal religions
Monetary unit(s): 1 Pula = 100 Thebe
BOTSWANA (formerly Bechuanaland Protectorate), landlocked republic bounded by South Africa, NAMIBIA (SW Africa) and

ZIMBABWE.

Land. It is mainly plateau (at 3,300ft), with the Okavango Swamp in the N, the Kalahari Desert in the S and SW, and mountains in the E. Rivers include the Limpopo and Zambezi. The climate is generally subtropical, with one rainy season (averaging 18in of rain), supporting savanna vegetation except in the Kalahari Desert.

People and Economy. A few Bushmen survive in the desert and elsewhere, but Bantu-speaking Negroes form the majority. They live chiefly in the SE around Gaborone, the capital. Cattle raising and export dominate the economy. Products include corn, peanuts, sorghum, asbestos and manganese. Diamonds, beef and copper fueled Botswana's growth in the 1970s. South Africa is the principal trade partner and the primary market for Botswana's beef.

History. Immigrant Negro tribes largely ousted the aboriginal Bushmen after 1600. In 1885 the area was placed under British supervision and became known as the Bechuanaland Protectorate. As Botswana, it became an independent member of the Commonwealth of Nations in 1966. Sir Seretse M. Khama was president from 1965 until his death in 1980. He was succeeded by his vice-president.

BOTTICELLI, Sandro (c1444–1510), one of the greatest painters of the Italian Renaissance, born Alessandro di Mariano Filipepi in Florence. His work is noted for superb draftsmanship, a use of sharp yet graceful and rhythmic line, and exquisite coloring. Among his most famous works are the allegorical tableaux on mythological subjects, *Primavera* and *The Birth of Venus.*

BOTTLED GAS, liquefied PETROLEUM gas (LPG) kept under pressure in steel cylinders and used for fuel by campers etc., and for tractors and buses. It is PROPANE, BUTANE or a mixture of the two.

BOTTLE-NOSED WHALE, two species of whales, *Hyperoodon rostratus* and *H. planifrons,* with a projecting snout, like a bottle-neck or beak, and a domed forehead containing an oil reservoir. They feed mainly on cuttlefish and are quite widespread. Individuals may reach 9m (30ft) in length.

BOTULISM, usually fatal type of FOOD POISONING caused by a toxin produced by the anaerobic bacteria *Clostridium botulinum* and *C. parabotulinum,* which normally live in soil but may infect badly canned food. The toxin paralyzes the nervous system. Thorough cooking destroys both bacteria and toxin.

BOUCHER, François (1703–1770), French painter whose work epitomizes the ROCOCO taste of 18th-century France. Influenced by TIEPOLO, he painted airy, delicately-colored portraits and mythological scenes. He also designed Gobelin tapestries and decorated interiors.

BOUCICAULT, Dion (c1822–1890), Irish-born actor and playwright active in London and New York. The 150 plays that he wrote or adapted, such as *London Assurance* (1841) and *The Shaughraun* (1874), ranged from light social drama to melodrama.

BOUGAINVILLE, largest of the Solomon Islands (3,880sq mi) and site of copper deposits found in 1964. Previously agricultural and part of a UN Trust Territory administered by Australia from 1947, it unsuccessfully attempted secession from Papua New Guinea upon independence (1975).

BOUGAINVILLEA, genus of tropical South American shrubs, including climbers which have large gaudy purple or red bracts (modified leaves) enclosing tiny flowers. It is a popular decorative plant in Fla., S Cal. and along the coast of the Gulf of Mexico.

BOULANGER, Georges Ernest Jean Marie (1837–1891), French general, leader of an antirepublican movement which threatened the government in the late 1880s. War minister 1886–87 and a member of the Chamber of Deputies 1888 and 1889, he was convicted of treason in 1889, but had by then fled to Brussels. He later committed suicide.

BOULANGER, Nadia (1887–1979), enormously influential French teacher of musical composition. Her pupils included US composers Aaron Copland, Roy Harris and Virgil Thomson, as well as Darius Milhaud. She is also renowned as an instrumentalist and conductor.

BOULDER DAM. See HOOVER DAM.

BOULEZ, Pierre (1925–   ), versatile French composer and conductor, noted for his extension of 12-tone techniques in *Le Marteau sans maître* (1951) and *Pli selon Pli* (1960). He has conducted many of the world's leading orchestras.

BOULLE, Pierre (1912–   ), French novelist, best known for *The Bridge on the River Kwai* (1952) and *Planet of the Apes* (1963).

BOULT, Sir Adrian Cedric (1889–   ), English conductor. He was founder and first director of the BBC Symphony Orchestra (1930–49) and became noted for his interpretations of English composers, especially ELGAR and VAUGHAN WILLIAMS.

BOULTON, Matthew (1728–1809), English industrial innovator and a founder member of the Lunar Society of Birmingham. In 1775 he went into partnership with James WATT to manufacture the latter's improved STEAM ENGINE. Boulton became England's foremost manufacturer and it is often said that his engines powered the INDUSTRIAL REVOLUTION.

BOUMÉDIENNE, Houari (real name: Mohammed Boukharouba; 1927–1978), president of Algeria. A teacher, he became active in the rebellion against France. After independence (1962), he was defense minister and vice-premier. In 1965 he overthrew President BEN BELLA and assumed power. He promoted nationalization and industrialization and was a radical spokesman for the Third World. He was president from 1976 until his death.

BOUNDARY LAYER, the portion of a FLUID near to a surface in motion relative to it: specifically, the layers of air nearest to the wing of an aircraft in flight (see AERODYNAMICS). Because of the air's VISCOSITY, these layers are subject to SHEARING, which reduces their velocity relative to the wing; thus lift is reduced and drag increased. Turbulence may also occur. (See also REYNOLDS NUMBER.)

BOUNTY, Mutiny on the, uprising on *H.M.S. Bounty* in the S Pacific Ocean in 1789. Mutineers under master's mate Fletcher Christian cast their overbearing commander, Lt. William BLIGH, and 18 others adrift in a longboat. Bligh brought his party 3,618mi to Timor. Some of the mutineers founded a colony on Pitcairn Island.

BOURASSA, Henri (1868–1952), French Canadian journalist and politician who championed French Canadians. He was several times a member of the Canadian House of Commons, and was founder and editor of the Montreal daily *Le Devoir* (1910–32).

BOURBAKI, Nicolas, pen-name adopted by a group of French mathematicians under which (since 1939) they have published a momentous survey of mathematics along original but strictly formal lines. The work of the Bourbaki authors has been of considerable importance in the development of 20th-century mathematics.

BOURBON, whiskey produced from corn mash, and especially from at least 51% mashed corn mixed with malt and rye and aged in containers of newly charred oak. First made in the 1780s, it is named for Bourbon Co., Ky.

BOURBONS, powerful French family which for generations ruled France, Naples and Sicily (the Two Sicilies), Parma and Spain, named for the castle of Bourbon NW of Moulins. The family is popularly remembered for its love of luxury and its obdurate resistance to political progress.

Bourbons became part of the French ruling house when a Bourbon heiress married Duke Robert, Louis IX's sixth son, in 1272. In 1589 their descendant, Henry of Navarre, founded France's Bourbon dynasty (as HENRY IV). Bourbon rule in France was interrupted with Louis XVI's execution in 1793, was restored in 1814 under Louis XVIII, and finally ended with Louis Philippe's overthrow in 1848.

Meanwhile, Louis XIV's grandson came to the Spanish throne in 1700 as Philip V. In Italy, cadet branches of his family ruled Parma 1748–1860 and Naples and Sicily (the TWO SICILIES) 1759–1861. Bourbons ruled Spain to 1931, when Alfonso XIII abdicated. In 1947 Spain was again declared a monarchy, and in 1975 Prince Juan Carlos of Bourbon succeeded the head of state, General Franco.

BOURGUIBA, Habib Ben Ali (1903–   ), Tunisian nationalist politician who became Tunisia's first president in 1957. He led the campaign for independence from the 1930s onwards and was imprisoned by the French several times. He was made president for life in 1976.

BOURKE-WHITE, Margaret (1906–1971), US photographer and war correspondent who covered WWII and the Korean War for Time-Life Inc.

BOUTS, Dirk (also Dierick or Thierry; c1420– 1475), Netherlands painter whose sober work conveys intense emotion. His backgrounds (especially landscapes) are vivid and lifelike, his figures dignified. His masterpiece is the Louvain altarpiece, *The Last Supper*.

BOW, Clara (1905–1965), US silent-screen actress famous in the 1920s (notably in *It* and *Wings*) as the "It" girl, personifying the post-WWI era of "flaming youth" and flappers.

BOWDITCH, Nathaniel (1773–1838), self-taught US mathematician and astronomer remembered for his *New American Practical Navigator* (1802), "the seaman's bible," later made standard in the US navy. He was the first to describe the LISSAJOUS' FIGURES (Bowditch curves), later studied in detail by Lissajous.

BOWDLER, Thomas (1754–1825), Scottish editor and doctor, whose popular *Family Shakespeare* expunged all supposedly blasphemous or indecent passages from Shakespeare's plays. The term "bowdlerize" came to mean any such misguided attempt to "clean up" a text.

BOWDOIN, James (1726–1790), American revolutionary leader and scientist. Bowdoin served in the Mass. legislature (1753–76) and supported the patriots' cause. As governor of Mass. (1785–87), he suppressed SHAYS' REBELLION. He was first president of the American Academy of Arts and Sciences.

BOWEN, Elizabeth (1899–1973), English-Irish novelist, born in Dublin, whose works are distinguished by their meticulous style and fine emotional sensitivity. They include *The Death of the Heart* (1938), *The Heat of the Day* (1949) and *Eva Trout* (1969).

BOWERS, Claude Gernade (1878–1958), US journalist, historian and diplomat whose popular historical accounts of the Jeffersonian era praised the early leaders of the Democratic Party. An editorial writer for the New York *World* (1923–31), he was active in Democratic party politics and served as ambassador to Spain (1933–39) and Chile (1939–53).

BOWIE, James (c1796–1836), Texan frontier hero who reputedly invented the Bowie hunting knife. He grew rich by land speculation and slave trading, moving W from Ga. to Ala., Miss., La., and eventually Tex. Bowie joined the Texan fight for independence from Mexico and was one of the leaders at the ALAMO, where he died.

BOWLES, Chester (1901–), US advertising man, politician and diplomat. He cofounded 1929 the advertising firm of Benton and Bowles, served on the War Production Board during WWII and was Democratic governor of Connecticut 1948–50. An internationalist, he served as ambassador to India 1951–53 and 1963–69, under secretary of state 1961 and special adviser to President John F. Kennedy 1961–63.

BOWLES, Paul (1910–), US author and composer living in Morocco, known for his exotic novels and short stories of alienation, despair and psychological horror. His works include *The Sheltering Sky* (1949) and *Collected Stories: 1939–1976* (1979).

BOWLES, Samuel (1826–1878), US newspaper editor who transformed the Mass. *Springfield Republican* (founded by his father) into one of the nation's most influential papers. He became an opponent of slavery, and his paper's concise hardhitting prose set a new standard of journalism.

BOWLING, popular indoor sport which involves rolling a ball to knock down wooden pins. In tenpin bowling, the most popular form in the US, players aim a large heavy ball down a long wooden lane at 10 pins set in a triangle. The number of pins felled determines the score. Bowling became popular in 14th-century Europe, and was brought to America by the Dutch in the 17th century. Tenpin bowling was standardized by the American Bowling Congress, founded in 1895.

BOXER, breed of medium-sized dog with broad chest, square head with a black mask, and short brownish coat. Boxers do sometimes playfully hit out with their forelegs.

BOXER REBELLION, violent uprising in China in 1900 directed against foreigners and instigated by the secret society "Harmonious Fists" (called Boxers by the Europeans). Encouraged by the Dowager Empress TZ'U HSI, the Boxers showed their dislike of growing European influence and commercial exploitation in China, attacking missionaries and Chinese converts to Christianity. When the European powers sent troops to protect their nationals at Peking they were repulsed (June 10–26, 1900). The German minister in Peking was murdered and foreign legations were besieged for nearly two months until relieved by an international force. Boxer violence was the pretext for Russian occupation of S Manchuria. On Sept 7, 1901, China was forced to sign the humiliating Boxer Protocol, in which it promised to pay a huge indemnity to the US and the European powers concerned.

BOXING, the sport of skilled fist-fighting. Two contestants wearing padded gloves attack each other by punching prescribed parts of the body, and defend themselves by avoiding or blocking their opponent's punches. Boxing contests are arranged between opponents in the same weight division or class: there are 10 classes ranging from flyweight to heavyweight. Fights take place in a square roped-off ring and consist of a number of two- or three-minute rounds separated by rests. Scoring is usually made by a referee and two judges.

If a contest goes its full length, the contestant awarded the most points or rounds wins by a *decision*. But a win can occur earlier by a *knockout*, if a boxer legitimately knocks down his opponent and the man cannot regain his feet in 10 seconds. A fight may also end in a *technical knockout* if the referee decides that a boxer is physically unfit to go on fighting. Boxing rules are slightly different for amateurs and professionals, and interstate and international practices vary in some respects.

Boxing can be traced back to the Olympic

Games of ancient Greece, and to Roman gladiatorial contests where fighters' hands were encased in an iron-studded guard called a *cestus*. Modern boxing has its roots in 18th-century English fairground fights between bareknuckled pugilists, who battered each other for bets until one could no longer continue. James Figg (1696–1734) opened one of the first boxing arenas in London in 1719, and champion fighter John Broughton (1704–1789) designed the first boxing gloves and in 1743 introduced some rules of fair play.

Modern rules date from those introduced for glove fighting by the Marquis of Queensberry in 1867. Glove fighting became firmly established after 1892, when James J. CORBETT beat John L. SULLIVAN in New Orleans in the first acknowledged gloved heavyweight world championship contest. The National Sporting Club in England laid down weight ratings that helped to internationalize boxing. World heavyweight contests promoted by men like Tex Rickard (who set up the first million-dollar gate) continue to dominate public interest. Since 1900, the US has often held the heavyweight title, through holders like Jack Dempsey, 1919–26, Gene Tunney, 1926–28, Joe Louis, 1937–49, Rocky Marciano, 1952–56, Cassius Clay (MUHAMMED ALI), 1964–67 and from 1973 and Joe Frazier, 1970–73. (See also the names listed.)

BOYAR, member of the Russian aristocracy that dominated government and army from the 10th century. In the 15th and 16th centuries the boyars (through the tsar's boyar council) virtually ran Russia. Their power later declined, until the title was abolished by Peter the Great in 1711.

BOYCOTT, the refusal to deal with a person or organization as a sign of disapproval or as a means of forcing them to meet certain demands. The word comes from **Captain Charles Boycott** (1832–1897), an English estate manager in Ireland who refused demands to lower rents and was isolated by the tenants who worked for him.

BOYD, Belle (1843–1900), Confederate spy in the American Civil War. An actress, she lived in Va., and passed military information to the South. Caught in 1862, she was released for lack of evidence in 1863.

BOYD, William (1898–1972), US film actor who starred as cowboy hero Hopalong Cassidy in 26 Hollywood movies from 1935 to 1940. He won new popularity in the 1950s and 1960s when the films were telecast.

BOYER, Charles (1899–1978), French-born US screen actor known as "the great lover" for the romantic polish he displayed in such films as *Mayerling* (1937) and *Algiers* (1938). He later showed skill in character roles.

BOYLE, Robert (1627–1691), British natural philosopher often called the father of modern CHEMISTRY for his rejection of the theories of the alchemists and his espousal of ATOMISM. A founder member of the ROYAL SOCIETY OF LONDON, he was noted for his pneumatic experiments.

BOYLE'S LAW, or Mariotte's Law, an empirical relation reported by BOYLE (1662) and MARIOTTE (1676) but actually discovered by Boyle's assistant R. Towneley, which states that given a fixed MASS of GAS at constant TEMPERATURE, its VOLUME is inversely proportional to its PRESSURE. Real gases deviate considerably from this law.

BOYNE, Battle of the, battle on the R Boyne in E Ireland on July 1, 1690, which ended JAMES II's attempt to regain the English throne. WILLIAM III's 35,000 troops decisively defeated the Catholic JACOBITES' 21,000. Northern Ireland's Protestants celebrate (July 12) the victory to this day.

BOYS' CLUBS OF AMERICA, national federation of boys' clubs chartered by Congress, with headquarters in New York City. It presides over 600 clubs devoted to recreation and social, mental and vocational development for more than 600,000 boys aged 7–18.

BOY SCOUTS, international boys' organization founded in 1907 by Sir Robert BADEN-POWELL to develop character, initiative and good citizenship. It stresses outdoor skills in woodcraft and nature lore. There are some 8 million scouts in about 100 countries. Members of the Boy Scouts of America include Cubs (aged 8–10), Scouts (11–17) and Explorers (14 plus). Senior scouts include Sea Scouts and Air Scouts.

BOYS TOWN, village in E Nebr., near Omaha. It was founded in 1917 as a community for homeless and abandoned boys by Father Edward J. Flanagan and is governed by the boys. Pop c9,000.

BRACTON, Henry de (d. 1268), English judge whose *Laws and Customs of England* was the first systematic work on English law. His *Note Book* of important legal decisions embodied the trend towards case law, which still deeply influences English common law today.

BRADBURY, Ray (1920–   ) US science-fiction writer. A master of the short-story form, his characteristic tales deal with moral dilemmas. Among his best-known science-fiction works are *The

Martian Chronicles (1950) and *Fahrenheit 451* (1953).

BRADDOCK, Edward (1695–1755), commander-in-chief of British forces in North America, who was disastrously defeated in the FRENCH AND INDIAN WARS. Unused to frontier conditions, in 1755 he led a cumbersome expedition against Fort Duquesne (on the site of present-day Pittsburgh), which ran into a French and Indian ambush. Braddock was fatally wounded and his men were routed. Among the survivors was a Virginian officer, George Washington.

BRADFORD, William (1590–1657), Pilgrim Father who helped to establish PLYMOUTH COLONY and governed it most of his life (reelected 30 times from 1621). He described the *Mayflower*'s voyage and the colony's first years in his *History of Plymouth Plantation*.

BRADLAUGH, Charles (1833–1891), English radical who was the first professed atheist to enter parliament.

BRADLEY, James (1693–1762), English astronomer who discovered the ABERRATION OF LIGHT (1728) and the earth's nutation.

BRADLEY, Omar Nelson (1893–1981), US general. In 1944–45 he led the 12th Army Group (1,000,000 men in four armies) in Europe. He was chief of staff of the US Army (1948–49) and first chairman of the joint chiefs of staff (1949–53).

BRADSTREET, Anne Dudley (c1612–1672), English-American colonial poet. She began writing after her emigration to Mass. in 1630. Her poems deal with personal reflections on the Puritan ethic and her coming to spiritual terms with it. Her collection, *The Tenth Muse Lately Sprung Up in America*, was published in England in 1650.

BRADSTREET, John (1711–1774), British colonel in the FRENCH AND INDIAN WARS. By astute use of waterways, he moved his forces up to take Fort Frontenac (1758), thus badly damaging French communications in Canada. Later, during PONTIAC's Rebellion, he commanded the forces at Detroit (1764).

BRADY, James Buchanan ("Diamond Jim"; 1856–1917), US railroad tycoon and philanthropist. He acquired his fortune through the selling of railroad equipment and the establishing of two steel railroad car manufacturing firms. He is noted as a legendary spender on both entertainments and charities.

BRADY, Mathew B. (c1823–1896), US photographer of eminent people and historic events. He photographed 18 US presidents and spent his fortune in hiring 20 teams of photographers to take over 3,500 shots covering almost every big battle of the Civil War. The project bankrupted him. His most famous photographs are those of Lincoln and of the battles at Bull Run and Gettysburg.

BRAGG, Braxton (1817–1876), US Confederate general. He led the Army of Tennessee which defeated William S. ROSECRANS at Chickamauga (1863) but soon afterwards lost to Ulysses S. GRANT at Chattanooga and forfeited his command.

BRAHE, Tycho (1546–1601), Danish astronomer, the greatest exponent of naked-eye positional ASTRONOMY. KEPLER became his assistant in 1601 and was driven to postulate an elliptical orbit for MARS only because of his absolute confidence in the accuracy of Tycho's data. Brahe is also remembered for the "Tychonic system," in which the planets circled the sun, which in turn orbited a stationary earth, this being the principal 17th-century rival of the Copernican hypothesis.

BRAHMANISM, Indian religion based on belief in BRAHMA. It developed c500 BC from old Dravidian and Aryan beliefs. Its ritual, symbolism and theosophy came from the *Brahmanas*, sacred writings of the priestly caste, and from the UPANISHADS. It developed the "divinely ordered" caste system and gave rise to modern HINDUISM.

BRAHMAPUTRA RIVER, rises in the Himalayas and flows about 1800mi through Tibet, NE India, Bangladesh and S to the Ganges, forming the Ganges-Brahmaputra delta on the Bay of Bengal. A holy river to the Indians, its name means "son of Brahma."

BRAHMS, Johannes (1833–1897), major German Romantic composer. Though strongly influenced by Beethoven and the Romantic movement, he developed his own rhythmic originality and emotional intensity, while using classical forms. He lived largely in Vienna from 1863. His major works include four symphonies, two piano concertos, a violin concerto, a double concerto for violin and cello, piano and chamber works, songs, part-songs and choral works—notably *A German Requiem* (1868) and the *Alto Rhapsody* (1869).

BRAILLE, system of writing devised for the blind by Louis BRAILLE. It employs patterns of raised dots that can be read by touch. Braille typewriters and printing presses have been devised for the mass-production of books for the blind.

BRAILLE, Louis (1809–1852), French inventor of BRAILLE. Accidentally blinded at the age of three, he conceived his raised-dot system at 15, while at the National Institute for the Blind in Paris. In 1829 he published a book explaining how his system could be used, not only for reading but also for writing and musical notation.

BRAIN, complex organ which, together with the SPINAL CORD, comprises the central NERVOUS SYSTEM and coordinates all nerve-cell activity. In INVERTEBRATES the brain is no more than a GANGLION; in VERTEBRATES it is more developed—tubular in lower vertebrates and larger, more differentiated and more rounded in higher ones. In higher MAMMALS, including man, the brain is dominated by the highly developed cerebral cortex. The brain is composed of many billions of interconnecting nerve cells (see NEURONS) and supporting cells (neuroglia). The BLOOD CIRCULATION, in particular the regulation of blood pressure, is designed to ensure an adequate supply of oxygen to these cells: if this supply is cut off, neurons die in only a few minutes. The brain is well protected inside the SKULL and is surrounded, like the spinal cord, by three membranes, the meninges. Between the two inner meninges lies the CEREBROSPINAL FLUID (CSF), an aqueous solution of salts and GLUCOSE. CSF also fills the four ventricles (cavities) of the brain and the central canal of the spinal cord. If the circulation of CSF between ventricles and meninges becomes blocked, HYDROCEPHALUS results. Relief of this may involve draining CSF to the atrium of the heart.

The human brain may be divided structurally into three parts: (1) the hindbrain consisting of the *medulla oblongata*, which contains vital centers to control heartbeat and breathing; the *pons* which, like the *medulla oblongata*, contains certain cranial nerve nuclei and numerous fibers passing between the higher brain centers and the spinal cord; and the *cerebellum*, which regulates balance, posture and coordination. (2) The *midbrain*, a small but important center for REFLEXES in the brain stem, also containing nuclei of the cranial nerves and the *reticular formation*, a diffuse network of neurons involved in regulating arousal: SLEEP and alertness. (3) The forebrain, consisting of *thalamus*, which relays sensory impulses to the cortex; the *hypothalamus*, which controls the autonomic nervous system, food and water intake and temperature regulation, and to which the PITUITARY GLAND is closely related (see also PINEAL BODY); and the *cerebrum*. The cerebrum makes up two-thirds of the entire brain and has a deeply convoluted surface; it is divided into two interconnected halves or hemispheres. The main functional zones of the cerebrum are the surface layers

of gray matter, the cortex, below which is a broad white layer of nerve fiber connections, and the *basal ganglia*, concerned with muscle control. (Disease of the basal ganglia causes PARKINSON'S DISEASE.) Each hemisphere has a motor cortex, controlling voluntary movement, and a sensory cortex, receiving cutaneous sensation, both relating to the opposite side of the body. Other areas of cortex are concerned with language (see APHASIA, SPEECH AND SPEECH DISORDERS), memory, and perception of the special senses (sight, smell, sound); higher functions such as abstract thought may also be a cortical function (see also INTELLIGENCE, LEARNING). Diseases of the brain include infections—specifically MENINGITIS, ENCEPHALITIS, syphilis (see VENEREAL DISEASES) and ABSCESSES; also trauma, TUMORS, STROKES, MULTIPLE SCLEROSIS, and degenerative diseases with early ATROPHY, either generalized or localized. Investigation of brain diseases includes X RAYS, using various contrast methods, SPINAL TAP (lumbar puncture)—to study CSF abnormalities—and the use of the ELECTROENCEPHALOGRAM. Treatments range from a variety of drugs, including ANTIBIOTICS and STEROIDS, to SURGERY.

BRAINE, John (1922–   ), English novelist best known for his first novel *Room at the Top* (1957), about the rise of a young, ambitious working-class man. Braine's other works include *The Queen of a Distant Country* (1972) and *J.B. Priestley* (1979).

BRAKES, devices for slowing or halting motion, usually by conversion of kinetic ENERGY into HEAT energy via the medium of FRICTION. Perhaps most common are drum brakes, where a stationary member is brought into contact with the wheel or a drum that rotates with it. They may be either *band brakes*, where a band of suitable material encircling the drum is pulled tightly against its circumference; or *shoe brakes*, where one or more shoes (shaped blocks of suitable material) are applied to the inner or outer circumference of the drum. Similar in principle are disk brakes, where the frictional force is applied to the sides of the wheel or a disk that rotates with it. The simplest form is the *caliper brake*, as used on bicycles, in which rubber blocks are pressed against the rim of the wheel. Almost all AIRCRAFT, AUTOMOBILE and RAILROAD brakes are of drum or disk type.

Mechanically operated brakes cannot always be used; as when a single control must operate on a number of wheels, thus involving problems in simultaneity and equality of braking action. In such cases, pressure is applied to a HYDRAULIC system (usually oil-filled), and hence equally to the brakes. Similar in principle are vacuum brakes, where creation of a partial VACUUM operates a PISTON which applies the braking action; and AIR BRAKES. **Fluid brakes**, used mainly in trucks to restrict speed in downhill travel, must be used in combination with mechanical brakes if it is desired to halt the vehicle. They consist of a rotating and a stationary element, between which a liquid (usually water) is introduced. Here it is FLUID rather than mechanical friction that converts the kinetic energy. (Cooling is usually performed by circulation through the radiator.) **Electric brakes**, similarly, may only restrict motion. The most common, used on electric trains on downhill runs, consists merely of a GENERATOR driven by the axle (the electricity generated may be used by the train).

BRAMANTE, Donato (1444–1514), leading Italian architect who developed the classical principles of High Renaissance architecture. In 1499, he moved from Milan to Rome, where his major designs included the Tempietto of S. Pietro in Montorio (1502) and the Belvedere Court at the Vatican (c1505). His greatest project, the reconstruction of St. Peter's, was not realized.

BRANCUSI, Constantin (1876–1957), Romanian sculptor famous for his simple, elemental, polished forms. Living in Paris from 1904, he rejected Rodin's influence, turning to abstract forms and the example of primitive art. Among his best-known works are *The Kiss* (1908) and *Bird in Space* (1919).

BRANDEIS, Louis Dembitz (1856–1941), US jurist, influential in securing social, political and economic reforms, especially while an associate justice of the Supreme Court (1916–39). As a lawyer he crusaded for organized labor against big business interests.

BRANDES, Georg Morris Cohen (1842–1927), Danish literary critic who deeply influenced the course of Scandinavian literature in the late 19th and early 20th centuries. Particularly important was his series of lectures published as *Main Currents in 19th-Century Literature* (1871–87).

BRANDO, Marlon (1924–   ), US actor. His first major film role was in *A Streetcar Named Desire* (1952), and international acclaim came with *On the Waterfront* (1954), for which he won an Academy Award. Later successes include *The Godfather* (1971) and *Last Tango in Paris*

(1972).

BRANDT, Willy (1913–   ), Social Democratic chancellor of West Germany 1969–74, whose *Ostpolitik* (Eastern policy) marked a major step towards East-West detente in Europe. Born Karl Herbert Frahm, he was mayor of West Berlin 1957–66. As chancellor, he secured friendship treaties with Poland and the USSR (1970), with East Germany (1972) and with Czechoslovakia (1974). Brandt's initiative won him the 1971 Nobel Peace Prize. Forced to resign in 1974 over a spy scandal in his own administration, he returned to political life in 1975.

BRANDY, alcoholic drink of distilled grape or other wine, usually matured in wood. Brandies include cognac, from French wines of the Cognac area, kirsch (made from cherries) and slivovitz (made from plums). (See also ALCOHOLIC BEVERAGES.)

BRANT, Joseph (1742–1807), Mohawk Indian chief, Episcopal missionary and British army colonel. His tribal name was Thayendanegea. He served with the British forces in the FRENCH AND INDIAN WARS and in the REVOLUTIONARY WAR.

BRANT, Sebastian (c1458–1521), German poet, renowned for his satirical allegory, *The Ship of Fools* (1494), telling of 111 fools led by other fools to a fools' paradise.

BRAQUE, Georges (1882–1963), French painter and sculptor, a seminal figure in modern art. From FAUVISM he went on, together with PICASSO, to evolve CUBISM and to be among the first to use COLLAGE. Among his many major works are *Woman with a Mandolin* (1937) and the *Birds* series (1955–63).

BRASÍLIA, federal capital of Brazil since 1960, located on the Paraná R, 600mi NW of the old coastal capital, Rio de Janeiro. It was built to help open up the immense Brazilian interior. Its cross-shaped plan was designed by Lúcio Costa, while such major buildings as the presidential palace and the cathedral are the work of Oscar NIEMEYER. Pop 978,600.

BRASS, an ALLOY of COPPER and ZINC, known since Roman times, and widely used in industry and for ornament and decoration. Up to 36% zinc forms α-brass, which can be worked cold; with more zinc a mixture of α- and β-brass is formed, which is less ductile but stronger. Brasses containing more than 45% zinc (white brasses) are unworkable and have few uses. Some brasses also contain other metals: lead to improve machinability, aluminum or tin for greater corrosion-resistance, and nickel, manganese or iron for higher strength.

BRASS, Ornamental, finely worked brassware such as the famous centuries-old Benares ware of India. Islamic countries produced engraved and inlaid brassware in the 7th–15th centuries, an example being the Resulid brazier now at New York's Metropolitan Museum of Art. In 11th-century Belgium, the town of Dinant gave its name to *dinanderie* brassware. During the 16th and 17th centuries BENIN and IFE, in what is now Nigeria, produced some of the best examples of the craft.

BRASS INSTRUMENTS. See WIND INSTRUMENTS.

BRATISLAVA (formerly Pressburg), important industrial center on the Danube R in Czechoslovakia, capital of Slovakia. Manufactures include textiles, timber, processed foods and oil products. The city's historic interest (it was capital of Hungary 1526–1784) and scenic beauty attract many tourists. Pop 368,000.

BRAUN, Wernher Magnus Maximillian von (1912–   ), German ROCKET engineer who designed the first self-contained missile, the V-2, which was used against the UK in 1944. In 1945 he went to America, where he led the team that put the first US artificial SATELLITE in ORBIT (1958).

Official name: Federative Republic of Brazil
Capital: Brasília
Area: 3,286,000sq mi
Population: 119,670,000
Languages: Portuguese
Religions: Roman Catholic
Monetary unit(s): 1 Cruzeiro = 100 centavos

BRAZIL, fifth-largest country in the world, covering nearly half of South America. It derives its name from its vast dyewood (*pau-brasil*) forests. Brazil shares borders with all the S American countries except Ecuador and Chile.
Land. There are two major geographical regions: the lowlands of the Amazon R basin, mostly tropical rain forests (*selvas*); and the Brazilian highlands, an extensive mountainous tableland in the S and E making up two-thirds of the country's land area. Brazil has over 4,600mi of coastline.

People. Brazil differs from its Spanish-speaking neighbors in having a racially integrated population. This consists of a three-fold mixture: the Portuguese inter-married both with the native Indians and with the Negro slaves imported from W Africa. About 200,000 Indians of several tribes live in the Amazon basin. The majority of Brazilians belong to the Roman Catholic Church, which also runs most state schools. About two-thirds of the people live in cities. As a result of a literacy drive in the 1970s, the illiteracy rate declined to about 14%.

Economy. Although Brazil is rich in natural resources, few of these have been developed. Iron ore deposits may be the largest in the world; and there is also manganese, chromium, tin, gold, nickel, coal, tungsten and bauxite. No big reserves of oil have been discovered. But Brazil is best known as South America's biggest producer of cattle, coffee and cocoa. In 1977 the country was the world's largest exporter of agricultural products. Manufactures include textiles, chemicals, plastic, appliances, and machinery. An impressive economic growth in the 1970s made Brazil the leading industrial power in Latin America and led to improvements in transport, energy, and social welfare.

History. Brazil was explored by the Spanish navigator Vicente Yáñez Pinzón early in 1500, and later in the same year, independently, by Portugal's Pedro Alvares Cabral, but colonization did not begin until after 1532. Slaves were used extensively by the plantation owners, until Jesuit missionaries intervened in the 17th century. The country gained independence in 1822 under its governor, Dom Pedro, who then ruled Brazil as emperor for the next nine years. Largely under military rule after 1889 when it became a republic, Brazil made rapid technological progress under President Juscelino KUBITSCHEK, who replaced the previous capital, Rio de Janeiro, by BRASÍLIA in 1960. The left-wing civilian government of João Goulart was overthrown by the military in 1964. The successive military governments were often accused of torture and other human-rights violations. A gradual democratization took place in the late 1970s.

BRAZING, technique in METALLURGY whereby two pieces of metal are joined using a nonferrous ALLOY (usually of COPPER) of lower MELTING POINT. The process is akin to SOLDERING but is performed at higher temperatures (about 1,000 K).

BRAZZAVILLE, river port and capital of

the Congo, formerly capital of French Equatorial Africa (1910–58). It is mainly an administrative and educational center, with light industries. Pop 310,000.

BREAD, one of humanity's earliest and most important foods, basically comprising baked "dough"—a mixture of FLOUR and water. In developed western societies, WHEAT flour is most commonly used and the dough is "leavened" (i.e., increased in volume by introducing small bubbles of CARBON dioxide throughout) using YEAST. In making bread, the chosen blend of flours is mixed with water, yeast, shortening and salt (and sometimes sugar and milk) to form the dough. This is then kneaded to distribute the GLUTEN throughout the mix, left to rise, kneaded again, molded into shape and left to rise a second time before baking. Bread is generally high in CARBOHYDRATES though low in PROTEIN. The vitamin and mineral content depends on the ingredients and additives used.

BREADFRUIT, the staple food of the East Indian and Pacific islands, it is the fruit of the bread-fruit tree (*Artocarpus altilis*). The melon-like fruit is eaten cooked or dried and ground to a flour that is used in puddings and bread. Some seedless varieties have been bred. Cloth can be made from the inner bark and the wood is used for canoes and furniture.

BREAM, *Abramis brama*, European freshwater fish of the carp family, weighing up to 7.5kg (16.5lb). In the US freshwater sunfish are known as bream, and the marine porgies and wrasses as sea bream.

BREAM, Julian (1933–), British guitarist and musicologist who rediscovered compositions from the Elizabethan era and transcribed classical piano compositions for the guitar.

BREASTED, James Henry (1865–1935), US archaeologist and historian, who advanced archaeological research in Egypt and W Asia. He specialized in Egyptology, and in 1919 organized the Oriental Institute at the U. of Chicago, subsequently sponsoring expeditions at Megiddo and Persepolis.

BREASTS, or mammary glands, the milk-secreting glands in MAMMALS. The breasts develop alike in both sexes, about 20 ducts being formed leading to the nipples, till puberty when the female breasts develop in response to SEX HORMONES. In PREGNANCY the breasts enlarge and milk-forming tissue grows around multiplied ducts; later milk secretion and release in response to suckling occur under the control of specific pituitary hormones. Disorders of the breast include mastitis, breast CANCER (see also

MASTECTOMY) and adenosis. In humans, the breasts are erogenous zones in both males and females.

BREATHING. See RESPIRATION.

BRECCIA. See CONGLOMERATE; TALUS.

BRECHT, Bertolt (originally, Eugen Berthold Friedrich Brecht; 1898–1956), German Marxist playwright and poet, who revolutionized modern theater with his production techniques and concept of EPIC THEATER. He left Nazi Germany in 1933, returning to East Berlin in 1948 to found the Berliner Ensemble. His plays include *The Threepenny Opera* (1928), *The Life of Galileo* (1938), *Mother Courage* (1939) and *The Caucasian Chalk Circle* (1949).

BRECKINRIDGE, John Cabell (1821–1875), US politician, vice-president of the US 1857–61. He became a congressman from Ky. in 1851, and was elected to the Senate while still vice-president. He was Democratic presidential candidate in 1860, but lost to Lincoln. He joined the Confederate government in the Civil War, becoming a major general and, in 1865, secretary of war.

BREEDER REACTOR, a NUCLEAR REACTOR that produces more nuclear fuel than it consumes, used to convert material that does not readily undergo FISSION into material that does. Commonly, nonfissile URANIUM-238 is converted into PLUTONIUM-239. (See also NUCLEAR ENERGY.)

BREEDING, the development of new strains of plants and animals with more desirable characteristics, such as higher yields or greater resistance to disease and suitability to the climate. Breeding has been practiced since prehistoric times— producing our modern domestic animals—but without firm scientific basis until MENDEL's theory of GENETICS. The breeder first decides which traits he wishes to develop, and observes the range of PHENOTYPES in the breeding population. Discounting variants due to environmental differences, he selects those individuals of superior GENOTYPE. This genetic variation may occur naturally, or may be produced by HYBRIDIZATION or MUTATIONS induced by radiation or certain chemicals. The selected individuals are used as parent stock for INBREEDING to purify the strain. (See also ANIMAL HUSBANDRY.)

BREMEN, second-largest port in West Germany, situated on both banks of the Weser R. Established as an episcopal see by Charlemagne in 787, it is now capital of Bremen State, and known for shipbuilding and for import and export shipping. Pop 606,500.

BREMERHAVEN, North Sea port in the

state of Bremen, West Germany, located at the estuary of the Weser R. Home of West Germany's largest trawler fleet and seafood center. Pop 139,000.

BRENNAN, William Joseph, Jr. (1906–   ), US Supreme Court associate justice appointed by Eisenhower in 1956. He championed civil rights and labor relations.

BRENNER PASS, important pass across the Alps, in the Tyrol, linking Innsbruck in Austria with Bolzano in Italy. The first good road along this ancient route was completed in 1772, and the railroad was built 1864–67.

BRENTANO, Clemens (1778–1842), German Romantic poet, novelist and dramatist. Together with Ludwig Joachim von ARNIM he edited the famous *Des Knaben Wunderhorn* (1805–08), a collection of folksongs which greatly influenced later German lyric poetry.

BRENTANO, Franz (1838–1917), German philosopher and psychologist, a Roman Catholic priest from 1864 to 1873, who founded the school of intentionalism and taught both FREUD and HUSSERL.

BRESSON, Robert (1901–   ), French film director, noted for the austere, penetrating quality of his work. His films include *The Diary of a Country Priest* (1950) and *The Trial of Joan of Arc* (1962).

BREST (formerly Brest-Litovsk), river port in the Belorussian SSR, on the Bug R. It is a rail center with light industry. Pop 122,000.

BREST-LITOVSK, Treaty of, the separate peace imposed on Soviet Russia by Germany and her allies during WWI, signed March 3, 1918, at Brest-Litovsk (now Brest) in Belorussia. By it Russia lost the Ukraine, Finland, and its Polish and Baltic possessions. The treaty was nullified on Nov. 11, 1918.

BRETON, André (1896–1966), French poet and critic, a founder of SURREALISM. Associated at first with DADA, he broke with it and in 1924 issued the first of three Surrealist manifestos, becoming the new movement's chief spokesman. Among his works is the poetic novel, *Nadja* (1928).

BRETTON WOODS CONFERENCE, international gathering at Bretton Woods, N.H., in July 1944, at which 44 members of the United Nations planned to stabilize the international economy and national currencies after WWII. They also established the INTERNATIONAL MONETARY FUND and the WORLD BANK.

BREUER, Josef (1842–1925), Austrian physician who pioneered the methods of PSYCHOANALYSIS and collaborated with FREUD in writing *Studies in Hysteria* (1895). He also discovered the role of the semicircular canals of the inner EAR in maintaining balance (1873).

BREUER, Marcel (Lajos) (1902–   ), Hungarian-born US architect. A student and teacher at the BAUHAUS 1920–28, he moved in 1937 to Harvard and continued working with GROPIUS. A pioneer of the International Style, he collaborated in the design of the UNESCO headquarters, Paris (1953–58).

BREUGHEL. See BRUEGEL.

BREWING, the process of making ALCOHOLIC BEVERAGES—generally BEER, but also SAKE and PULQUE—from starchy cereal grains. Brewing has been practiced for more than five millennia. The cereal (generally barley) is malted (steeped in moisture and germinated). The malt is then dried, cured at 100°C and mashed—ground and infused with hot water; in mashing, the ENZYMES produced during malting break down the starch to fermentable SUGARS. The wort (aqueous solution) is filtered and boiled with hops, and then fermented in large vessels with YEAST (see FERMENTATION). When this has almost ceased, the beer is run off and stored to mature; finally, it is filtered, carbon dioxide is added, and the beer is packaged.

BREWSTER, William (1567–1644), a leader of the Plymouth Colony, New England. He led the Puritan congregation formed in England in 1606, and sailed with the Pilgrims on the MAYFLOWER in 1620. He played a major part in regulating the civil and religious affairs of the Plymouth Colony.

BREZHNEV, Leonid Ilyich (1906–   ), USSR political leader, who became first secretary of the Communist party in 1964 and, as such, effective head of the Soviet government. He first became a member of the party central committee in 1952, and was chairman of the presidium of the supreme soviet 1960–64. Brezhnev, KOSYGIN and PODGORNY took control when KHRUSHCHEV was ousted in 1964. Brezhnev assumed the additional office of chief of state in 1977. He pursued a policy of détente with the West while overseeing a massive buildup of Soviet military might. He was only partially successful in overcoming shortcomings in industry and agriculture.

BRIAN BORU (941–1014), king of Ireland from 1002. His reign marked the end of Norse domination but unified rule died with him. He was murdered after his victory against the Danes at Clontarf.

BRIAND, Aristide (1862–1932), French statesman, lawyer and socialist leader who was 11 times premier of France. As foreign minister (1925–32), he was the author of the KELLOG-BRIAND PACT. He was awarded the Nobel Peace Prize in 1926.

BRIARD, French sheepdog breed dating back to the 12th century, now often used as a guard or police dog as well as with sheep. Strongly built, it stands 23–27in high. The coat may be any solid color except white (darker shades preferred), and is long and harsh. This lively and intelligent breed is easily offended.

BRICE, Fanny (1891–1951), US singer and comedienne who was a star of the ZIEGFELD FOLLIES from 1910. She created the character Baby Snooks, playing it on radio, 1938–51. *Funny Girl* (play, 1964; film, 1968) was based on her life.

BRIDGE, a card game developed from WHIST. Contract bridge, the form now universally adopted, was perfected by Harold S. Vanderbilt in 1925–26. It is played by two pairs of partners, who before starting play must make bids according to how many tricks they calculate they can win. Demanding great skill, bridge has become immensely popular as a social and competitive game, with international championships controlled by the World Bridge Federation.

BRIDGE, any device that spans an obstacle and permits traffic of some kind (usually vehicular, bridges that carry canals being more generally termed aqueducts) across it.

The most primitive form is the **beam** (or **girder**) **bridge,** consisting of a rigid beam resting at either end on piers. The span may be increased by use of intermediate piers, possibly bearing more than one beam. A development of this is the **truss bridge,** a truss being a metal framework specifically designed for greatest strength at those point where the load has greatest MOMENT about the piers. Where piers are impracticable, **cantilever bridges** may be built: from each side extends a beam (cantilever), firmly anchored at its inshore end. The gap between the two outer ends may be closed by a third beam. Another form of bridge is

the **arch bridge,** essentially an ARCH built across the gap: a succession of arches supported by intermediate piers may be used for wider gaps. A **suspension bridge** comprises two towers that carry one or more flexible cables that are firmly anchored at each end. From these is suspended the roadway by means of vertical cables. **Movable bridges** take many forms, the most common being the **swing bridge,** pivoted on a central pier; the **bascule** (a descendant of the medieval drawbridge), whose cantilevers are pivoted inshore so that they may be swung upward; the **vertical-lift bridge,** comprising a pair of towers between which runs a beam that may be winched vertically upward; and the less common **retractable bridge,** whose cantilevers may be run inshore on wheels. The most common temporary bridges are the **pontoon,** or floating bridge, comprising a number of floating members that support a continuous roadway; and the BAILEY BRIDGE.

BRIDGER, James (1804–1881), US trader, explorer and army scout. He traded in the unexplored American West and Southwest. He discovered Great Salt Lake (1824), and founded Fort Bridger, Wyo.

BRIDGES, Harry (Alfred Bryant Renton Bridges; 1901–), US labor leader, born in Australia. He helped form the International Longshoremen's and Warehousemen's Union (ILWU) in 1937, and as its president fought to improve dockworking conditions. Until 1955 there were many government attempts to deport him as a communist.

BRIDGES, Robert Seymour (1844–1930), English poet laureate, noted for the technical mastery of his verse and his editing of the poetry of Gerard Manley HOPKINS (1916). His works include the philosophical poem, *The Testament of Beauty* (1929).

BRIDGET OF SWEDEN, Saint (c1303–1373), also called Birgitta, patron saint of Sweden and founder of the Brigittine Order (1346). A mystic who also engaged in work among the community, she worked to bring the papacy back from Avignon to Rome.

BRIGHT, John (1811–1889), British politician and orator, of Quaker descent. He entered parliament in 1843, and held office under Gladstone. A champion of free trade and of electoral reform, he was a cofounder of the Anti-Corn-Law League and opposed British participation in the Crimean War.

BRIGHT'S DISEASE, a form of acute NEPHRITIS that may follow infections with certain STREPTOCOCCUS types. Blood and protein are lost in the urine; there may be

EDEMA and raised blood pressure. Recovery is usually complete but a few patients progress to chronic KIDNEY disease.

BRILL, Abraham Arden (1874–1948), Austrian-born US psychiatrist, the "father of American PSYCHOANALYSIS," who introduced the Freudian method to the US and translated many of FREUD'S works into English.

BRINKLEY, David. See HUNTLEY, Chet.

BRISBANE, industrial seaport in E Australia, capital of Queensland. Situated on the Brisbane R, about 15mi from the Pacific Ocean, it was founded as a penal settlement in 1824. Met pop 1,015,200.

BRISBANE, Albert (1809–1890), US Utopian philosopher and socialist. A disciple of FOURIER, he wrote the influential *Social Destiny of Man* (1840).

BRITAIN, modern form of the ancient name for the island now comprising England, Scotland and Wales. The Romans referred to the 1st-century BC Celtic inhabitants as *Pritani*, hence their own name for the island, *Britannia*. (See GREAT BRITAIN.)

BRITISH ANTARCTIC TERRITORY, British colony in Antarctica, covering 652,000sq mi and including the South Shetlands and the South Orkney Islands. It is administered from the Falkland Islands.

Name of province: British Columbia
Joined Confederation: July 20, 1871
Capital: Victoria
Area: 366,255 sq mi
Population: 2,637,000

BRITISH COLUMBIA, province on the W coast of Canada, bounded on the W by the Pacific Ocean and S Alaska and on the E by the province of Alberta.

Land. About 500mi from E to W and about 770mi from N to S, it is the most rugged of Canada's provinces. There are two main mountain chains, the Coast Mts in the W and the Canadian Rocky Mts in the E. In the remarkable Rocky Mountain Trench the upper courses of many rivers can be found, notably the Columbia, the Fraser and the Kootenay. The 700mi coastline is broken by fjords, among the offshore chains of islands Vancouver Island and the Queen Charlotte Islands are the most important. Temperatures and rainfall differ greatly in various parts of the province, with a mild climate near the coast, but temperatures vary between 100°F and −35°F in the interior.

People and Economy. About 75% of the population, predominantly of British origin, live in the milder southwest of the province, where Vancouver is the largest city. There

are also considerable Chinese, Japanese and East Indian minorities. Forestry now generates about 50 cents of every dollar earned in the province, and many of the world's major newspapers are printed on paper produced there. Copper, molybdenum, zinc and lead are major minerals; oil and natural gas are produced in the NE. Dairy farming and the production of livestock and related products dominate the agricultural sector of the economy. A 200mi fishing zone was adopted in 1977 and has boosted the fishing industry. Manufacturing, with transportation equipment, chemicals, machinery and fabricated metals the chief producers, has expanded in recent years and is concentrated in the Vancouver/New Westminster area.

History. The area was first visited by the Spanish explorer Juan Pérez in 1774, and in 1778 Captain Cook anchored in Nootka Sound. Britain commissioned George VANCOUVER to survey the coast in 1792. Other early explorers were Alexander MACKENZIE, David THOMPSON and Simon FRASER. For a time, the region was called New Caledonia, and its trade was controlled by the Hudson's Bay Company after 1821. Settlement increased following the discovery of gold in 1858, when the colony of British Columbia was established. It became a province of Canada in 1871. A new era began in 1885, when the railroad reached Vancouver, which grew to become the capital. The Social Credit Party was led into power by W. A. C. Bennett in 1952, and retained control for 20 years. He built extensive road and rail networks, two of the largest hydroelectric projects in North America, introduced hospital insurance and began operation of the province's power-distribution system, railway and ferry fleet. The New Democratic Party government, led by Dave Barrett, in power 1972–75, introduced social policies in the areas of health care, old age security, auto insurance and housing and instituted the Land Commission Act to encourage family farming and conservation. The present Social Credit government, concerned with financial management, showed a 34.2% growth in 1979 over 1978.

BRITISH INDIAN OCEAN TERRITORY, British colony, covering about 20sq mi in land area and over 20,000sq mi of ocean, established in 1965 to provide defense facilities for Britain and the US. It consists of the Chagos archipelago, which includes DIEGO GARCIA military base. Aldabra, Farquhar and Desroches islands were part of the territory until 1976 when they were transferred to newly independent SEYCHELLES.

BRITISH LIBRARY, national library of Britain, established in London in 1753 as part of the BRITISH MUSEUM. It houses some 8.5 million printed books and 150,000 MSS. By law, the library must be sent a copy of every book published in the UK. It became a separate entity in 1973, with several divisions.

BRITISH MUSEUM, national museum of antiquities and ethnography in London. Founded in 1753, when the British government acquired the art collection and library of Sir Hans Sloane, it opened to the public in 1759. Its present neoclassical premises were built 1823–47 and its natural history section was separated 1881–83. The museum has one of the world's foremost collections, including the ELGIN MARBLES.

BRITISH NORTH AMERICA ACT, an act passed by the British parliament in 1867 to create the Dominion of Canada, uniting Canada (Quebec and Ontario), New Brunswick and Nova Scotia under a federal government. The act serves as Canada's constitution. In the early 1980s, Prime Minister Trudeau led efforts aimed at patriation of the act from Britain, which would eliminate the need, onerous to many Canadians, to secure the approval of the British Parliament for any amendments. Canada, however, was unable to present a united front on this issue because of efforts by some provinces to achieve greater autonomy under the act, and of Trudeau to have the British insert a bill of rights.

BRITTANY (French: Bretagne), historic peninsular region of NW France. The Romans conquered the area in 56 BC and named it Armorica. It was settled c500 AD by Celtic Britons fleeing the Anglo-Saxon invasion. After struggles for independence from the Franks and from Normandy, Anjou, England and France in turn, it became a French province in 1532. The Bretons retain their own cultural traditions and language.

BRITTEN, (Edward) Benjamin, 1st Baron Britten of Aldeburgh (1913–   ), outstanding British composer. His works include several important operas, among them *Peter Grimes* (1945), *Billy Budd* (1951), *The Turn of the Screw* (1954) and *Death in Venice* (1973). Among his many notable instrumental and choral works are the *Variations on a Theme by Frank Bridge* (1937) and *War Requiem* (1962).

BROAD, Charlie Dunbar (1887–1971), British philosopher who contributed to the philosophy of science, ethics, perception and the theory of knowledge. His works include *Scientific Thought* (1923) and *Ethics and the History of Philosophy* (1952).

BROADCASTING NETWORKS, US, American companies which produce programs for broadcasting to the public over a network or affiliated group of radio or television stations, interlinked by wire or radio relay. The four prime US networks (all commercial) are NBC (National Broadcasting Company), which organized the first radio network (1926), introduced regular TV service in 1939 and began coast-to-coast TV broadcasting in 1951; CBS (Columbia Broadcasting System, Inc.), organized in 1927, which broadcasts radio and TV programs, manufactures electronic equipment and operates hundreds of stations through the US; ABC (American Broadcasting Companies, Inc.), founded 1943; and the Mutual Broadcasting System (MBS), with close to 500 affiliated independently-owned radio outlets, which became a coast-to-coast network in 1936. The Public Broadcasting System (PBS) was established in 1969 for educational, noncommercial public TV; it is funded by the federal government and private foundations.

BROCK, Lou (1939–   ), US baseball player. In 1974 he stole a record-breaking 118 bases in one season. He also holds the career base-stealing record of 938, set 1961–79 with the Chicago Cubs and St. Louis Cardinals.

BROD, Max (1884–1968), Czech author, best known as editor of the works of his friend Franz KAFKA, which he saved from destruction. His own works include the novel, *The Redemption of Tycho Brahe* (1916) and a biography of Kafka (1937). He emigrated to Palestine in 1939.

BRODSKY, Joseph (1940–   ), Russian poet and critic. Born in Leningrad, he emigrated to the US in 1972, having served a five-year sentence at hard labor in the 1960s as a "social parasite." He published several collections of verse, including *A Part of Speech* (1978).

BROMFIELD, Louis (1896–1956), US novelist, winner of a 1926 Pulitzer Prize for his novel, *Early Autumn*. His other works include *The Rains Came* (1937) and *Pleasant Valley* (1945).

BRONCHI, tubes through which air passes from the TRACHEA to the LUNGS. The trachea divides into the two primary bronchi, one to each lung, which divide into smaller branches and finally into the narrow bronchioles connecting with the alveolar sacs. The bronchi are lined with a mucus membrane which has motile CILIA to remove dust, etc.

BRONCHITIS, inflammation of BRONCHI. **Acute bronchitis,** often due to VIRUS infection, is accompanied by COUGH and FEVER and is short-lived; ANTIBIOTICS are only useful if there is bacterial infection. **Chronic bronchitis** is a more serious, often disabling and finally fatal disease. The main cause is SMOKING which irritates the LUNGS and causes overproduction of MUCUS. The CILIA fail, and sputum has to be coughed up. Bronchi thus become liable to recurrent bacterial infection, sometimes progressing to PNEUMONIA. Areas of lung become non-functional, and ultimately CYANOSIS and HEART failure may result. Treatment includes PHYSIOTHERAPY, antibiotics and bronchial dilator drugs. Stopping smoking limits damage and may improve early cases.

BRONK, Detlev Wulf (1897–1975), US biologist who was a pioneer in the application of physics to biological processes. He influenced the growth of medical research in the US as president of Johns Hopkins University (1949–53) and Rockefeller Institute for Medical Research (1953–68).

BRONTË, name of three English novelists, daughters of an Irish-born Anglican clergyman. They lived chiefly in the isolated moorland town of Haworth, Yorkshire. Their lives, marred by the early death of their mother and the dissipations of their brother, Branwell, were closely bound together, and this domestic intensity informed much of their work. **Charlotte Brontë** (1816–1855) published the partly autobiographical *Jane Eyre* (1847) under the name Currer Bell, and met with immediate success. Together with *Shirley* (1849) and *Villette* (1853), it represents an important advance in the treatment of women in English fiction. **Emily Brontë** (1818–1848), using the name Ellis Bell, published a single novel, *Wuthering Heights* (1847), a masterpiece of visionary power. **Anne Brontë** (1820–1849) published two novels, *Agnes Grey* (1847) and *The Tenant of Wildfell Hall* (1848), under the name Acton Bell.

BRONTOSAURUS, a vegetarian DINOSAUR whose fossilized skeleton has been found in the western US. About 20m (66ft) long and calculated to be 35 tonnes in weight, it had a long neck and tail, small head and brain, ponderous body and thick legs.

BRONZE, an ALLOY of COPPER and TIN, known since the 4th millennium BC (see BRONZE AGE), and used then for tools and weapons, now for machine parts and marine hardware. Statues are often cast in bronze. It is a hard, strong alloy with good corrosion-resistance (the patina formed in air is protective). Various other components are added to bronze to improve hardness or machinability, such as aluminum, iron, lead, zinc and phosphorus. Aluminum bronzes, and some others, contain no tin. (See also BELL METAL; GUN METAL.)

BRONZE AGE, the phase of man's material cultural development following the STONE AGE, and the first phase in which metal was used. The start of the bronze age varies from region to region, but certainly the use of copper was known as early as 6,500 BC in Asia Minor, and its use was widespread shortly thereafter. By about 3,000 BC BRONZE was widely used, to be replaced around 1000 BC by iron.

BROOK, Peter (1925–   ), English theatrical director noted for his inventive, unconventional productions of such classics as Shakespeare's *King Lear* and *A Midsummer Night's Dream.* A proponent of the avant garde, Brook directed highly acclaimed English performances of DÜRRENMATT's *The Visit* (1958) and Peter WEISS' *Marat/Sade* (1964).

BROOKE, Edward William (1919–   ), US senator from Mass., who in 1966 became the first Negro senator since Reconstruction. As attorney general of Mass. (1962–66), he fought corruption.

BROOKE, Rupert (1887–1915), English war poet whose patriotic sonnets were widely popular during the early days of WWI. His *Collected Poems* were published in 1918.

BROOKE, Sir James (1803–1868), English adventurer who became the ruler of Sarawak, Borneo. Appointed raja in 1841, he founded a dynasty which ruled Sarawak until 1946, when the region was ceded to Britain.

BROOK FARM, US Utopian community, founded at West Roxbury, Mass., by George RIPLEY in 1841. The aim was to create an egalitarian community of workers and thinkers. The community contained a noted progressive school and attracted many leading intellectuals, but lasted only until 1847.

BROOKHAVEN NATIONAL LABORATORY, center for nuclear research at Camp Upton, Long Island, N.Y. Under the aegis of the US Atomic Energy Commission, it has facilities for medical and agricultural research.

BROOKINGS INSTITUTION, nonprofit-making, public service corporation founded in 1927 in Washington, D.C., for research and information on government and economic problems. It was named for the St. Louis merchant, Robert S. Brookings.

BROOKLYN BRIDGE, famous suspension bridge in New York City between the borough of Brooklyn and Manhattan Island. It was built in 1869–83 by A. J. Roebling and his son, pioneers in the use of steel-wire support cables, which give the bridge its characteristic spider-web appearance. Its two huge masonry towers are supported by pneumatic caissons, another pioneering feat of the Roeblings.

BROOKS, Cleanth (1906–), US literary critic and editor, one of the New Critics. In such works as *The Well Wrought Urn* (1947), he argued that the essential core of poetry is metaphor and meter. With Robert Penn WARREN he wrote or edited several texts, including *Modern Rhetoric* (1949), *Understanding Poetry* (1938) and *Understanding Fiction* (1943).

BROOKS, Gwendolyn Elizabeth (1917–), black US poet. Born in Chicago, Ill., she was the first Negro poet to win the Pulitzer Prize, with her semiautobiographical *Annie Allen* (1948).

BROOKS, Mel (1928–), US writer and comedian turned film producer and director. He was a writer for Sid Caesar's popular TV show in the 1950s and became known for his recorded impersonation of a 2,000-year-old man. His screenplay for *The Producers* (1968), which he also directed, won the Academy Award. His films include *Blazing Saddles* (1974), *Young Frankenstein* (1975) and the HITCHCOCK spoof *High Anxiety* (1978), in which he starred.

BROOKS, Phillips (1835–1893), US Episcopal clergyman, the most famous preacher of his day, with a wide intellectual influence. Many of his sermons were published 1881–1902. He was minister at Trinity Church, Boston, 1869–91, and bishop of Mass. He is known for his hymn, *O Little Town of Bethlehem* (1868).

BROOKS, Preston Smith (1819–1857), US politician, congressman from S.C. from 1852. Enraged by Charles SUMNER's denunciation of Brooks' uncle in an antislavery speech, he beat Sumner senseless with a cane in the Senate, rather than duel with a social inferior. Forced to resign, he was at once reelected. The incident revealed pre-Civil War tensions.

BROOKS, van Wyck (1886–1963), US critic who examined American writers in the context of their contemporary society. In *America's Coming of Age* (1915), he saw the 19th-century US as torn between the idealistic and the materialistic. In biographies of Mark TWAIN, Henry JAMES,

EMERSON and others he traced their development in this society.

BROUGHAM AND VAUX, Henry Peter Brougham, 1st Baron (1778–1868), influential Scottish lawyer, social reformer and politician. Cofounder of the *Edinburgh Review* (1802), he was a member of parliament 1810–12 and 1816–30. As lord chancellor 1830–34, he forced both legal reforms and the 1832 REFORM BILL through the House of Lords.

BROUN, Heywood Campbell (1888–1939), US journalist. In his *It Seems To Me* column in the *New York Tribune* and later in the *New York World*, he expounded and defended liberal ideas and causes, such as the SACCO-VANZETTI CASE. He established and headed the American Newspaper Guild.

BROUWER, Adriaen (1605–1638), Flemish painter of humorous peasant scenes such as *The Smokers* (1626), *Drinkers at a Table, Peasant Interior* and *Tavern Brawl*. He was influenced by Pieter BRUEGEL and Frans HALS.

BROUWER, Luitzen Egbertus Jan (1881–1966), Dutch mathematician who developed the doctrine of intuitionism, which rejected the idea that formal logic was the foundation of mathematics. He was a pioneer in the study of TOPOLOGY and contributed to the theory of functions and the theory of sets.

BROWDER, Earl Russell (1891–1973), US Communist party secretary-general 1930–44, and president of the communist political association, 1944–45. Claiming "Communism is 20th-century Americanism" he won great support for the party. Although communist presidential candidate in 1936 and 1940, he was expelled as a deviationist in 1946.

BROWN, "Capability" (Lancelot Brown; 1715–1783), English garden and landscape designer. In his work for English estate owners, he made frequent references to the "capabilities" of a given landscape—thus his nickname.

BROWN, Charles Brockden (1771–1810), one of the first US professional writers. Influenced by William GODWIN, his *Alcuin: A Dialogue* (1798) and novel *Edgar Huntly* (1799) plead for social reform. *Wieland*, (1799) is an outstanding Gothic novel.

BROWN, Dee (1908–), US Native American author. A librarian by profession, he turned to the writing of novels and nonfiction with Western themes. Of his more than 20 books, the best-known is *Bury My Heart at Wounded Knee* (1971), a pro-Indian account of the Indians' losing military struggle against the whites in the late 19th century.

BROWN, Edmund G. ("Jerry"), Jr. (1938–   ), US political leader. The son of a governor, he served as California secretary of state (1971–75) and as governor (1975–   ). An economic conservative who spoke about an era of lower expectations, he was also a liberal on social issues and had a strong pro-environment record. He was an unsuccessful candidate for the Democratic presidential nomination in 1976 and 1980.

BROWN, Ford Madox (1821–1893), English literary, religious and historical painter, a precursor of the PRE-RAPHAELITE BROTHERHOOD. He is famous for *Work*, (1852–63), and *Pretty Baa-Lambs*, (1851).

BROWN, Harold (1927–   ), US physicist and public official. Secretary of the Air Force (1965–69) and president of California Institute of Technology (1969–77), he served as secretary of defense (1977–81), revising US defense strategy and stressing the need to prepare for a limited nuclear war.

BROWN, James (1928–   ), US singer. He emphasized moaning vocals and strong rhythms in his ballads, which became increasingly popular as rock developed into a distinct musical style in the 1960s.

BROWN, Jim (1936–   ), US football player, the all-time leading rusher in National Football League history, with 12,312yds gained, 1957–65. The Cleveland Browns star also set NFL records for most career touchdowns (126) and highest lifetime rushing average (5.2yds). After retiring from football, he became a film actor.

BROWN, John (1800–1859), US abolitionist whose exploits helped bring on the Civil War. He was involved in the slave UNDERGROUND RAILROAD in Pa. and then with his five sons moved to Kan. to help the antislavery settlers in 1855. After proslavery men burned down the town of Lawrence, Brown retaliated by murdering five proslavery men at Pottawatamie Creek. During 1857–58 Brown planned to establish a new state in the Va. mountains as a refuge for fugitive slaves and a base for antislavery activity. In October 1859 he seized the government arsenal at Harper's Ferry, Va., and awaited a massive slave insurrection. Instead, the arsenal was stormed; Brown was tried for treason and hanged.

BROWN, Norman O. (1913–   ), US social critic whose Freudian reappraisal of history, *Life Against Death* (1959), made him a hero in the emerging counterculture. His other books, *Love's Body* (1966) and *Closing Time* (1973), further enhanced his

status.

BROWN, Robert (1773–1858), Scottish botanist who first observed BROWNIAN MOTION (1827) and who identified and named the plant nucleus CELL (1831).

BROWN BEAR, *Ursus arctos,* formerly the most widespread species of bear, found in N Europe and Asia and North America. It is now present in small numbers in montane regions of Europe and in the USSR. It is also found with the subspecies, GRIZZLY BEAR and ALASKAN BROWN BEAR, in North America. It has a short neck and a large dog-like head.

BROWNE, Robert (c1550–1633), English Puritan clergyman, leader of a separatist group, the Brownists. He taught independence of the Church from secular government and duty to conscience rather than to outward regulation. His writings are considered the first expression of CONGREGATIONALISM.

BROWNE, Sir Thomas (1605–1682), English physician and author. He is most famous for his book, *Religio Medici* (1643), a fine example of ornate English prose which displays religious toleration in an age of intolerance. His other major work is *Urne-Buriall* (1658), a meditation on death and immortality.

BROWNIAN MOTION, frequent, random fluctuation, of the motion of particles suspended in a fluid; first described by Robert BROWN (1827) after observation of a SUSPENSION of pollen grains in water. It is a result of the bombardment of the particles by the MOLECULES of the fluid (see KINETIC THEORY): a chance greater number of impacts in one direction changes the direction of motion of a particle. The first theoretical analysis of Brownian motion was given by EINSTEIN in 1905 and helped to convince the scientific world of the reality of molecules.

BROWNING, Elizabeth Barrett (1806–1861), English poet. In her own day she was second in reputation only to Tennyson. She is now best known for *Sonnets from the Portuguese* (1850), inspired by her romance with Robert BROWNING, who "rescued" her from illness and family tyranny in 1846.

BROWNING, John Moses (1855–1926), US inventor of the Browning automatic guns used by the Allies in WWI and WWII. His 1917 .30 caliber machine gun was recoil-operated and water-cooled. The later .50 caliber version was used in WWII aircraft.

BROWNING, Robert (1812–1889), English poet. He perfected the dramatic monologue in such poems as "Andrea del

Sarto" and "Bishop Blougram's Apology" (*Men and Women*; 1855). He also used it in what is considered his masterpiece, *The Ring and the Book* (1868–69), a 17th-century Roman murder story told from several different viewpoints. His psychological insight and use of colloquial language profoundly influenced 20th-century poets.

BROWNSVILLE AFFAIR, an incident in 1906, in which Negro soldiers from Fort Brown, Tex. allegedly entered nearby Brownsville and fired on houses · and townspeople. President Theodore Roosevelt ordered the dishonorable discharge of 167 soldiers, a decision reversed by the army in 1972.

BROWN VS. BOARD OF EDUCATION OF TOPEKA, the historic case in which the US Supreme Court unanimously held on May 17, 1954, that "in the field of public education the doctrine of 'separate but equal' has no place." Thus the Court reversed *Plessy vs. Ferguson,* an 1896 case in which a majority had held that "separate but equal accommodations" on railways did not necessarily stamp "the colored race with a badge of inferiority." That ruling had provided the constitutional umbrella for a host of state and local laws requiring segregation in practically every walk of life. Thus, *Brown vs. Board of Education* was the first in a series of court decisions striking down those laws.

BRUBECK, David Warren (1920–   ), US jazz pianist and composer. After classical training, in 1951 he formed his own jazz quartet, which became one of the most popular "progressive" groups.

BRUCE, David Kirkpatrick (1898–1977), US diplomat. The son-in-law of industrialist Andrew Mellon, he headed the Office of Strategic Services in Europe during WWII and served as ambassador to France (1949–52), West Germany (1957–59) and Britain (1961–69). He later participated in the Vietnam peace negotiations (1970), headed the US liaison office in Peking (1973) and was chief delegate to the North Atlantic Treaty Organization (1974–76).

BRUCE, Robert the (1274–1329), King Robert I of Scotland. His family's claim to the throne was disputed by John de Baliol, the English nominee. Bruce was crowned in 1306 in defiance of EDWARD I of England, who favored de Baliol. Pursued as a rebel, he defeated Edward II at BANNOCKBURN (1314). English recognition of Scottish independence was eventually granted in 1328.

BRUCELLOSIS, or **Bang's disease,** a BACTERIAL DISEASE of cattle, goats and swine, caused by *Brucella.* It causes ABORTION and affected animals have to be slaughtered to prevent spread. The disease in man (once known as **undulant fever**) is contracted from milk or by contact with infected animals; it is a variable illness, often causing FEVER, malaise and DEPRESSION, and may be treated with ANTIBIOTICS.

BRÜCKE, Die ("The Bridge"), name adopted by a group of German expressionists who worked together between 1905 and 1913. Leading members of Die Brücke were Ernst Ludwig KIRCHNER, Karl Schmidt-Rottluff, Erich Heckel, Emil NOLDE, Max Pechstein, and Otto Mueller. Like the FAUVES in France, these painters used bold colors and crude forms to convey violent emotion.

BRUCKNER, (Josef) Anton (1824–1896), Austrian composer, noted for his nine massive symphonies and his choral music. His deep Catholic piety permeated all his works. A major influence was Richard WAGNER, whom he greatly admired. Bruckner was a professor at the Vienna Conservatory from 1868. A simple and good-natured man, he ranks with MAHLER among the great late Romantic symphonists.

BRUEGEL, family of Flemish artists flourishing from the 16th to the 18th centuries. **Pieter Bruegel the Elder** (c1525–1569) was a great painter of landscapes and peasant scenes. Influenced at first by BOSCH, he was much impressed by the scenery of Italy, which he visited in 1552. His works, some on religious subjects, are often allegorical or satirical, profoundly affected by his view of the human condition. **Pieter Bruegel the Younger** (1564–1638), also called Hell Bruegel, worked in his father's manner, often with an emphasis on the grotesque. **Jan Bruegel** (1568–1625), also called Velvet Bruegel, the second son, painted landscapes and still lifes with great subtlety and delicacy. He often collaborated with RUBENS.

BRUGGE, or Bruges, well-preserved medieval city in NW Belgium. Once a center for wool trade, and in the 15th century home of a school of painting led by the VAN EYCKS and Hans MEMLING, its commercial interest revived in the 19th century when the Zeebrugge Canal to the North Sea was opened. It manufactures lace and textiles. Pop 118,200.

BRUHN, Erik (1928–   ), Danish dancer. He made his debut with the Royal Danish Ballet in 1947, becoming its leading male dancer in 1949. He is considered one of the greatest classical dancers of his time.

BRUISE, or contusion, a lesion of the SKIN, usually caused by a blow, in which CAPILLARY damage allows blood to leak into the dermis where it is slowly broken down and absorbed. A **hematoma**, a larger blood-filled cavity, may require draining. Bruising without injury may indicate BLOOD disease.

BRUMMELL, George Bryan "Beau" (1778–1840), English man of fashion. He was a friend of the Prince of Wales (later George IV) and an arbiter of fashion in REGENCY society. He fled to France in 1816 to escape his creditors.

Official Name: State of Brunei
Capital: Bandar Seri Begawan
Area: 2,226sq mi
Population: 212,840
Languages: Malay, Chinese, English
Religions: Muslim, Buddhist
Monetary Unit(s): 1 Brunei dollar=100 cents.

BRUNEI, sultanate on the N coast of the island of Borneo, on the South China Sea. It has a humid tropical climate that supports dense forests. The population is 56% Malay and 25% Chinese, the latter running many small businesses. Malay is the chief language, Islam the official religion. Rubber and timber were superseded as main products after petroleum was found in 1929. Petroleum and natural gas are now extracted both on and off shore. A local sultanate was established here in the 15th century and during the 16th century it controlled all of Borneo. It became a British protectorate in 1888, and a 1959 constitution gave it domestic autonomy. Brunei is due to receive full independence in 1984.

BRUNEL, Sir Marc Isambard (1769–1849), French-born British engineer and inventor who built the world's first underwater tunnel (under the River Thames) and devised machines for the mass production of pulley blocks and army boots. His son, **Isambard Kingdom Brunel** (1806–1859), pioneered many important construction techniques, designing the Clifton suspension bridge at Bristol, England, laying the Great Western Railway with a controversial 7ft (2.13m) gauge and building ironhulled steamships, including the giant *Great Eastern*.

BRUNELLESCHI, Filippo (1377–1446), first great Italian Renaissance architect. He was one of the first practitioners of linear perspective. Influenced by classical Roman and 11th-century Tuscan Romanesque architecture, his masterpiece is the dome of Florence cathedral (1420–36).

BRUNHILD, in Germanic mythology, a warrior maiden, heroine of the Old Norse EDDAS and VOLSUNGA SAGA (in which she is portrayed as a VALKYRIE) and prominent in the German NIBELUNGENLIED. The legends, on which WAGNER based his operas, *The Ring of the Nibelungs*, tell of the love between her and Sigurd (or SIEGFRIED) and their tragic deaths.

BRUNING, Heinrich (1885–1970), German statesman. Chancellor of the Weimar Republic 1930–32, his measures to restore the German economy aroused opposition, and his dismissal from office by President VON HINDENBURG led eventually to HITLER'S chancellorship.

BRUNO, Giordano (1548–1600), Italian pantheist philosopher, poet and cosmologist, an apostate Dominican, who taught the plurality of inhabited worlds, the infinity of the universe and the truth of the Copernican hypothesis. Burned at the stake for heresy, he became renowned as a martyr to science—except among scientists.

BRUSSELS, Belgian capital city, headquarters of the European Common Market, NATO and the Atomic Energy Commission. First commercially important in the 12th century, it was granted a ducal charter in 1312. From the 16th to the 19th centuries it was subject successively to Spain, Austria and France. It manufactures textiles, lace and furniture and is a transport center. Pop 161,089.

BRUTUS, name of an ancient Roman family. **Lucius Junius Brutus** (6th century BC) founded the Roman Republic by expelling King Lucius Tarquinius Superbus in 509 BC. **Decimus Junius Brutus** (d. 43 BC) served with Julius Caesar in Gaul and was one of his assassins. **Marcus Junius Brutus** (85–42 BC) was a highly respected statesman who helped lead the assassination plot against Caesar. He committed suicide after his defeat by Antony and Octavian at Philippi.

BRYAN, William Jennings (1860–1925), US political leader, orator and lawyer. Elected to Congress in 1890, he was an unsuccessful Democratic presidential candidate in 1896, 1900 and 1908 and secretary of state in 1913–15. His famous "cross-of-gold" speech at the 1896 Democratic convention led to his first nomination. A fundamentalist, he prosecuted at the SCOPES TRIAL in 1925, winning the case against teaching evolution in schools over defense attorney Clarence DARROW.

BRYANT, Paul "Bear" (1913–   ), US college football coach with the best winning average ever, more than eight victories per season. In over 35 seasons, his teams won or shared six national championships. In 1981 the Alabama U. coach succeeded in breaking Amos Alonzo STAGG's record of 314 career wins.

BRYANT, William Cullen (1794–1878), US poet and journalist. Editor of the New York *Evening Post* from 1829, he campaigned against slavery and for free speech. He wrote pastoral odes, the most famous being *Thanatopsis* (1817), and translated the *Iliad* and *Odyssey* (1870–72).

BRYCE, James Bryce, 1st Viscount (1838–1922), British statesman and historian. He wrote *The Holy Roman Empire* (1864) and *The American Commonwealth* (1888). He was British ambassador to the US 1907–13.

BRYCE CANYON NATIONAL PARK, an area of 36,010 acres in S Ut., created as a park in 1928. It contains extraordinary formations in colorful limestone and sandstone, the result of erosion.

BRYN MAWR, top-ranking liberal arts college for women founded by the Society of Friends in 1885 in Bryn Mawr, Pa. It was one of the first US women's colleges to grant graduate degrees.

BRZEZINSKI, Zbigniew (1928–   ), US political scientist and national security adviser (1977–81). Born in Poland, he became a professor and expert on Communist affairs at Harvard and Columbia universities. While director of the Trilateral Commission (1973–77) he was consultant to another commission member, Jimmy CARTER. As president, Carter named him to the national security post, where he gained a reputation as an anti-Communist "hard-liner".

BUBBLE CHAMBER, device invented by Glaser (1952) to observe the paths of SUBATOMIC PARTICLES with energies too high for a CLOUD CHAMBER to be used. A liquid (e.g., liquid HYDROGEN or OXYGEN) is held under PRESSURE just below its BOILING POINT. Sudden reduction in pressure lowers this boiling point: boiling starts along the paths of energetic subatomic particles, whose passage creates local heating. At the instant of reduction, their paths may thus be photographed as a chain of bubbles.

BUBER, Martin (1878–1965), Jewish philosopher, born in Austria. Editor of a major German–Jewish journal, *Der Jude*, 1916–24, he was a leading educator and scholar of HASIDISM. An ardent Zionist, he moved to Palestine in 1938. His central philosophical concept is that of the direct "I-Thou" relationship between man and God and man and man.

BUBONIC PLAGUE. See BLACK DEATH; PLAGUE.

BUCHAN, John, 1st Baron Tweedsmuir (1875–1940), Scottish author and politician. He wrote historical works, biographies and such classic adventure stories as *The Thirty-Nine Steps* (1915). From 1935 he was governor-general of Canada.

BUCHANAN, Franklin (1800–1874), US Confederate naval officer. He commanded the ironclad *Virginia*, which destroyed two Union ships at the Hampton Roads blockade. Promoted to admiral, he was captured in a heroic fight against Union Admiral David G. FARRAGUT in 1864.

BUCHANAN, James (1791–1868), 15th president of the US. A Pennsylvania lawyer, he was first a Federalist, later a Democrat. He was a US congressman 1821–31, minister to Russia 1831–33, and a US senator 1834–45. While he was secretary of state under President Polk (1845–49), the dispute with Britain over Oregon was settled and the Mexican War broke out, following the annexation of Tex. Under President Pierce he was minister to Britain 1853–56, and with J. Y. Mason and Pierre Soule worked out the controversial OSTEND MANIFESTO, stating that the US must protect its security by acquiring Cuba through purchase or force.

Though morally opposed to slavery, he believed the constitution gave individual states the right to decide the issue, and on this compromise platform won the presidency, serving 1857–61. He attempted to settle Kansas' admission to statehood by "popular sovereignty," allowing popular vote to decide the slavery issue in the territory. His proposal passed the Senate but failed in the House. His upholding of the DRED SCOTT DECISION aroused opposition in both houses. With the Democratic party divided, Abraham Lincoln won the 1860 election. When secession began, Buchanan tried desperately to maintain peace. He disapproved of secession but knew no constitutional authority to prevent it. Believing that federal troops should be used only to protect federal property, he eventually sent troops to Fort Sumter. After Lincoln took office, Buchanan supported the Union.

BUCHAREST, capital of Romania, on the Dämbovit R. A medieval fortress, it became the residence of the princess of Walachia in 1459 and the capital when the new Romania was formed in 1861. It produces pharmaceutical and electrical goods, machinery and automobiles. Pop

1,525,291.

BUCHENWALD, Nazi concentration camp set up near Weimar in 1937 to hold political and "non–Aryan" prisoners. More than 100,000 (chiefly Jews) died there through starvation, extermination and medical experimentation.

BÜCHNER, Georg (1813–1837), German dramatist, forerunner of EXPRESSIONISM. His *Danton's Death* (1835) and *Woyzeck* (1837), use colloquial language and sometimes sordid settings. With psychological insight, they trace the powerlessness of isolated individuals, whether against historical forces or society. Woyzeck, for example, is a soldier pressured into murdering his unfaithful mistress. *Lenz*, unfinished, is about a dramatist on the verge of madness.

BUCHWALD, Art (1925–   ), US humorist whose syndicated column, emanating from Washington, brilliantly satirizes the US political scene. His collected columns appeared in *Getting High in Government Circles* (1971), *I am Not a Crook* (1974) and *The Buchwald Stops Here* (1978).

BUCK, Pearl Sydenstricker (1892–1973), US author. Most of her novels are set in China, where she lived up to 1934. She won the Pulitzer Prize in 1932 for *The Good Earth* (1931), and the 1938 Nobel Prize for Literature.

BUCKINGHAM, George Villiers, 1st Duke of (1592–1628), English nobleman whose influence over JAMES I and CHARLES I imflamed anti–monarchical feeling. He promoted costly and unsuccessful military ventures, notably the expedition to relieve the Huguenots of LA ROCHELLE. Charles, however, shielded him from impeachment. He was eventually assassinated.

BUCKINGHAM PALACE, London residence of the British royal family, built in 1703 and bought by George III from the Duke of Buckingham in 1761. Queen Victoria, in 1837, was the first monarch to use it as an official residence.

BUCKLE, Henry Thomas (1821–1862), English historian. With the influential *History of Civilization in England* (1857–61), he broke from the tradition of treating only individuals, wars and politics and considered peoples, cultures and environments.

BUCKLEY, William Frank, Jr. (1925–   ), US author, editor and lecturer. He founded the weekly *National Review* (1955) to voice often controversially conservative views.

BUDAPEST, capital of Hungary, on the Danube R. Two settlements, Buda on the right bank and Pest on the left, date from Roman times but were destroyed by Mongol invaders in 1241. Buda became Hungary's capital in 1361. They declined under the Turks but revived under the Hapsburgs and were united in 1873. Textiles are the main industry. The city was virtually destroyed in WWII. It was the center of the Hungarian uprising in 1956. Pop 2,060,000.

BUDAPEST STRING QUARTET, musical group organized in Hungary in 1917. It soon became known for performances of Mozart and Bartok. Moving to the US in 1938, it was "quartet in residence" at the Library of Congress (1938–62). The group played all over the world and was famed for its Beethoven performances before it disbanded in 1968.

BUDDHA, Gautama (c563–483 BC), founder of BUDDHISM. Son of the raja of Kapilavastu near Nepal, his name was Siddhartha Gautama. At the age of 29, confronting human misery for the first time, he at once set out to find the path to peace and serenity. For six years he studied under Brahman teachers, living as a hermit. Enlightenment came to him while seated under a *bodhi* or pipal tree; he remained there in contemplation of truth some six or seven weeks. Thereafter he preached and gathered disciples as Buddha ("the Enlightened One").

BUDDHISM, religion and philosophy developed from HINDUISM in the 6th century BC by Siddhartha Gautama, the BUDDHA. His monastic disciples shaved their heads, dressed in rags and devoted themselves to the philosophy of Enlightenment.

The Pali canon is the scriptural basis of Buddhism, transcribing from oral tradition Buddha's teaching and monastic rules. It was set down by the first Buddhist council at Rajagaha in the 5th century BC. The next council, at Vesali in the 4th century BC, saw Buddhism divided into two schools because of debate over the stringency of monastic regulations. The third, called by Emperor ASHOKA in the 3rd century BC, sent missionaries throughout India and into Syria, N Africa and Ceylon. Spreading to Tibet in the 7th century AD, Buddhism combined with existing beliefs to form LAMAISM, and in China an Indian Buddhist, Bodhidarma, introduced spontaneous enlightenment, Ch'an (ZEN in Japanese). In the 6th century AD Buddhism reached Japan, where for the first time it became involved with politics.

Buddhist teaching advocates a middle course between mortification and the pursuit of ambition. Buddha's Four Noble

Truths are: life involves suffering; the cause of suffering is desire; elimination of desire leads to cessation of suffering; the elimination of desire is the result of a method or path that must be followed. The Noble Eightfold Path (right mode of seeing things, right thought, right speech, right action, right way of living, right effort, right mindedness, right meditation) leads to the cessation of pain. Through these steps Nirvana is achieved, a state beyond thought which frees one from the perpetual cycle of birth, suffering, death and rebirth. Buddhism has no service, ritual or church. The stricter *Theravada* school is followed in Ceylon, Burma, Thailand and Cambodia (Kampuchea), the more lenient *Mahayana* school in Nepal, Korea, Indonesia, Japan and China. The religion numbers 300–500 million followers; many others in the East and West practice Buddhist teaching to achieve self-awareness.

BUDGE, Donald (1915–), US tennis player. His team won the Davis Cup in 1937, and in 1938 he was the first player to win four top world championships (US, British, Australian and French). He turned professional in 1938.

BUENOS AIRES, capital of Argentina. On the Río de la Plata, it is a port for Argentine agricultural products, meat, hides, wool and cereals. It has several universities, an opera house (Teatro Colón) and is the world's leading Spanish language publishing center. Industries include food processing and textiles, automobiles and chemical manufactures. Founded in 1536, Buenos Aires became the capital of Río de la Plata viceroyalty in 1776. An impressive economic growth after 1850 has attracted many immigrants. Pop 2,985,000.

BUFFALO, second-largest city in N.Y., on Lake Erie near Niagara Falls. In the 19th century it gained importance as a junction for road, rail and lake transport from its location between the eastern cities and Chicago. Major industries are flour milling and steel production. Pop 462,768.

BUFFALO, name of several species of wild ox, incorrectly applied to the American BISON. They are members of the mammalian family Bovidae. The domesticated Indian water buffalo or CARABAO is a draft animal and gives milk. It weighs about a ton, is 1.5m (5ft) high and has large curved horns. Other types of Asiatic buffalo are the Philippine Tamarau and the small ANOA of the Celebes. These are shy, but Cape buffaloes are dangerous big-game animals living in herds. Their populations have been reduced in the past by RINDERPEST, a cattle disease.

BUFFALO BILL, nickname of William Frederick Cody (1846–1917), US scout and showman. He claimed to have killed 4,280 buffalo to feed the builders of the Kansas Pacific Railway. He rode with the PONY EXPRESS in 1860 and during the Civil War was a scout in Tenn. and Mo. for the Union army. From 1872 he toured the US and Europe with his Wild West Show.

BUFFET, Bernard (1928–), French artist, book illustrator and stage designer. His austere, angular naturalistic style won him international fame in his youth, and his work has since been much sought after.

BUFFON, Georges Louis Leclerc, Comte de (1707–1788), French naturalist who was the first modern taxonomist of the ANIMAL KINGDOM and who led the team which produced the 44-volume *Histoire Naturelle* (1749–1804).

BUGLE, brass WIND INSTRUMENT. It has a cup-shaped mouthpiece, a conical tube and a five-to-eight note range. It is used mostly for military calls.

BUGS, common name for the insect order Hemiptera. They have beaks for piercing and sucking. Some, like the stinkbug, emit unpleasant odors, others secretions: aphids secrete honeydew; larvae of froghoppers (spittle bugs) secrete protective foam; scale insects secrete a waxy substance used in shellac. Most are plant-feeders and many are pests, attacking crops and transmitting diseases (e.g., squash bugs, lace bugs and whitefly). Some are blood-suckers (e.g., bedbugs and assassin bugs) which transmit disease. Others live on ponds (e.g., water skaters) or underwater (e.g., water scorpions). In America the word "bug" often colloquially refers to any insect.

BUKHARIN, Nikolai Ivanovich (1888–1938), an early Bolshevik theoretician and friend of Lenin, editor of *Pravda*. A party leader in the 1920s, he was ousted by Stalin in 1929, but was reinstated to edit *Izvestia* in 1934. He wrote several works on political science and economics. He was liquidated in the Great Purge in 1938.

BULB, a short, underground storage stem composed of many fleshy scale leaves that are swollen with stored food and an outer layer of protective scale leaves. Bulbs are a means of overwintering; in the spring, flowers and foliage leaves are rapidly produced when growing conditions are suitable. Examples of plants producing bulbs are DAFFODIL, tulip, SNOWDROP and onion.

BULFINCH, Charles (1763–1844), US architect, designer of the Mass. statehouse, Boston (1800), University Hall, Harvard U. (1815) and the E portico of the Capitol,

Washington, D.C. (1818). He emphasized the dignified neoclassical style in American civic architecture.

BULFINCH, Thomas (1796–1867), US mythologist. His classic, *The Age of Fable* (1855; "Bulfinch's Mythology"), popularized Greek, Roman, Nordic and oriental mythologies.

BULGAKOV, Mikhail Afanasievich (1891–1940), Russian author and playwright. His work, mostly suppressed until the 1960s, blends realism and fantasy with great humor, as in his most brilliant novel, *The Master and Margarita*, which describes the antics of the devil in modern Moscow.

BULGANIN, Nikolai Alexandrovich (1895–1975), Soviet leader. With the support of Nikita KHRUSHCHEV, he succeeded MALENKOV as premier in 1955. He was expelled from the central committee when Khrushchev became premier in 1958.

Official Name: The People's Republic of Bulgaria
Capital: Sofia
Area: 42,823sq mi
Population: 8,860,000
Languages: Bulgarian, Turkish
Religions: Bulgarian Orthodox
Monetary Unit(s): 1 Lev = 100 stotinki

BULGARIA, republic located on the Balkan Peninsula, bordered by the Black Sea, the Danube and Yugoslavia. The country is traversed by the Balkan and Rhodope Mts; its climate is continental in the N and Mediterranean in the S. Until the 1940s most Bulgarians lived in peasant farming villages, but industrialization has greatly progressed since WWII. Industry produces machinery, textiles and chemicals; and lead, zinc, iron ore, copper and coal are mined. Wheat, corn, sugar beets and barley are the principal crops. Exports include tobacco, foodstuffs, minerals and machinery. The Black Sea resorts and the country's mineral springs are important tourist attractions.

The Bulgars, a Turkic people, conquered the Slavic population in the 7th century, adopting their language and customs. The Bulgar Empire was a major Balkan force until the 14th century, but from 1396 to 1878 Bulgaria was under rigid Ottoman rule. At the Congress of Berlin (1878), Turkish hegemony was restricted, and in 1908 Bulgaria proclaimed its independence under Ferdinand I. Bulgaria supported Germany in WWI and II, though not against the USSR. In 1944 the USSR occupied the country and the communist Fatherland Front seized power. In 1947 Bulgaria became a People's Republic. A new constitution was adopted in 1971, with Communist party chief Todor Zhivkov as president. Bulgaria has remained a faithful Soviet satellite.

BULLDOG, breed of dog native to Britain, used in bullbaiting until the 19th century. A heavybodied breed, it has a large head with a flat drooping face, and is renowned for the great strength of its jaws.

BULLFIGHTING, Spanish national sport and spectacle, also popular in Latin America. Probably developed by the Moors, it was taken over by aristocratic professionals in the 18th century. The modern bullfight stresses the grace, skill and daring of the *matador*. (The most famous matadors have been Juan Belmonte, Joselito, Manolete and El Cordobes.) After a procession, the bull is released. Two mounted *picadors* jab the bull's neck with lances to lower its head for the matador's capework. Then three *banderilleros* thrust decorated wooden goads into the bull's back. The matador, after using his cape to make daring and graceful passes at the bull, kills it with a swordthrust between the shoulders.

BULLINGER, Heinrich (1504–1575), Swiss Protestant reformer. He played an important part in composing the First Helvetic Confession (1536), formulated the *Consensus Tigurinus* with CALVIN (1549) and composed the Second Helvetic Confession (1566), a popular CREED of the Reformation.

BULLITT, William Christian (1891–1967), US diplomat. He was a member of the US peace delegation at the end of WWI, and in 1933 was the first US ambassador to the USSR.

BULL RUN, Battles of, two clashes in the American Civil War around Manassas Junction near Bull Run Creek, 25mi SW of Washington, D.C. In the First Battle of Bull Run, July 1861, Union General McDowell was sent against Confederates led by P.G.T. BEAUREGARD, but was repulsed by them. Gen. "Stonewall" JACKSON was so nicknamed for his tenacity in this battle. In the Second Battle of Bull Run, Aug. 1862, Jackson attacked Union general John Pope and forced his retreat. (See also CIVIL WAR, AMERICAN.)

BULL SNAKE, large nonpoisonous North American snake of the genus *Pituophis*, found in S and W states. It reaches a length of 2.5m (8ft) and has a loud whirring hiss. It feeds on rodents but is harmless to humans.

BULL TERRIER, small dog bred from a cross between the English terrier and the bulldog. It weighs 20–60lb, has short hair and may be either white or colored (generally brindle).

BÜLOW, Bernhard Heinrich Martin von (1849–1929), German chancellor. He capped a distinguished diplomatic and political career by serving as chancellor 1900–09. Anxious to achieve imperial glory for Germany, he was responsible for causing Britain, France and Russia to draw closely together. His poor judgments on foreign policy helped bring on WWI.

BÜLOW, Hans Guido von (1830–1894), German pianist and noted virtuoso conductor. A pupil of LISZT and WAGNER, he championed their music and that of BRAHMS and Richard STRAUSS. He married Liszt's daughter, Cosima, who later left him for Wagner.

BULTMANN, Rudolf (1884–1976), German theologian who advocated "demythologizing" the New Testament and reinterpreting it in existentialist terms. He developed a critical approach to the Gospels, studying the oral tradition behind them. His books include *History of the Synoptic Tradition* (1921; tr. 1963) and the five-volume *Kerygma and Myth: A Theological Debate* (1948–55; tr. 1953–62).

BULWER-LYTTON, Edward George Earle Lytton, 1st Baron Lytton (1803–1873), English author and politician. His best-known works include the historical novels, *The Last Days of Pompeii* (1834) and *Rienzi* (1835), and the Utopian *The Coming Race* (1871).

BUNAU-VARILLA, Philippe Jean (1859–1940), French engineer who organized the Panama Canal Project. He was instrumental in arranging for the canal to go through Panama and then in planning the revolution which led to Panamanian independence. As Panama's minister to the US, he negotiated the HAY-BUNAU-VARILLA TREATY (1903), giving the US control of the canal zone.

BUNCHE, Ralph Johnson (1904–1971), US diplomat. He entered the UN in 1946, and was undersecretary for political affairs in 1958. Having supervised the 1949 Arab-Israeli armistice, he became the first Negro to win the Nobel Peace Prize (1950).

BUNDY, McGeorge (1919–   ), US political aide. He influenced foreign policy as adviser on national security affairs under presidents Eisenhower, Kennedy and Johnson. He resigned in 1966 to become president of the Ford Foundation.

BUNIN, Ivan Alekseyevich (1870–1953), Russian novelist, short-story writer and poet. He is best known for his short stories such as *The Gentleman from San Francisco* (1916). He emigrated to France in 1919, and won the Nobel Prize for Literature in 1933.

BUNKER HILL, Battle of, important early encounter of the American Revolutionary War, on June 17, 1775. As part of the encirclement of Boston, American militia under Col. William Prescott occupied Breed's Hill—although the original objective had been Bunker's Hill nearby. The first two British attempts to dislodge them, led by Maj. Gen. William Howe, resulted in heavy losses from close American fire. On the third assault the Americans ran out of ammunition and had to retreat. Though a British victory, the battle damaged British confidence and was a vital boost to American morale.

BUNSEN BURNER, burner promoted by Robert Bunsen, used widely in laboratories and sometimes in metal heat-treatment (see METALLURGY). Through a nozzle at the base is introduced slightly pressurized fuel GAS (usually COAL GAS) which is mixed with air (primary air) which the flow induces through adjustable inlets: the usual gas:air ratio is 1:2. The mixture proceeds up a short metal tube and is ignited at the top, giving a flame temperature of the order of 2,000K. Outer portions of the flame mix with further air (secondary air) to give a cooler, more luminous flame, where the gas:air ratio is about 1:4.

BUNTINGS, several varieties of small birds of the finch family (Fringillidae), found in Europe and North America. In North America the name is applied to relatives of the cardinal, the indigo bunting and the painted bunting; while counterparts of the European buntings are called sparrows and finches. They eat seeds and live in woods and grasslands.

BUNUEL, Luis (1900–   ), Spanish-Mexican director of many outstanding films, often marked by their fierce realism, social criticism and wry humor. Surrealist fantasy has been another recurrent element in his work, ever since his first film, *Un Chien Andalou* (made with Salvador DALI in 1929).

BUNYAN, John (1628–1688), English author. A tinker by trade, he became a Baptist preacher in 1657. While imprisoned for unlicensed preaching (1660–72; 1675) he wrote his most famous work, *The Pilgrim's Progress* (1678), an allegory in simple prose describing Christian's journey to the Celestial City.

BUNYAN, Paul, in US frontier myth a lumberjack, a genial giant who worked with his huge blue ox Babe. By the time the first tall stories about this frontier hero were published in 1910, oral tradition had spread them across the country.

BUONARROTI, Michelangelo. See MICHELANGELO.

BURBAGE, Richard (c1567–1619), first great English actor. He played many of Shakespeare's leading roles, including Richard III, Hamlet, Othello and Lear. From his father, **James Burbage** (c1530–1597), builder of the first English theater (The Theatre, 1576), he and his brother Cuthbert inherited the Blackfriars Theatre in London. In 1599 they built the famous Globe Theatre.

BURBANK, Luther (1849–1926), US horticulturalist who developed more than 800 varieties of plants, including the Burbank potato.

BURBIDGE, Margaret (1919–　), British-born astronomer who specialized in the study of quasars, radio galaxies and stellar formation. She directed the Royal Greenwich Observatory (1971–73), headed the Center for Astrophysics and Space Science at the University of California at San Diego (from 1979) and was elected president of the American Association for the Advancement of Science (1980).

BURCHFIELD, Charles Ephraim (1893–1967), US watercolorist known for his midwestern landscapes and small town scenes. A leader of the realistic movement in American painting, he liked to depict architectural relics of the late 1800s and was sensitive to lighting and atmospheric effects.

BURGER, Warren Earl (1907–　), chief justice of the US, appointed in 1969 by President Nixon. He was previously assistant attorney general of the US and chief judge of the US Court of Appeals. Burger led the Supreme Court away from the judicial activism of his predecessor, Earl Warren, and toward a more conservative philosophy.

BURGESS, Anthony (1917–　), English writer, mostly of satirical novels, best known for *A Clockwork Orange* (1962), about a violent gang leader in a corrupt, equally violent society of the near future. His other works include *Enderby* (1961), *Earthly Powers* (1980) and the critical study *Re Joyce* (1965).

BURGOYNE, John (1722–1792), British general in the American Revolutionary War. He fought in the Seven Years' War (1756–63), and became a fashionable playwright, socialite and politician. Posted to America, he attempted to put into effect his plan to split off the New England colonies but was eventually forced to surrender by Gen. Horatio GATES at Saratoga (1777).

BURGUNDY (French: Bourgogne), historic region of E France, occupying what are now the departments of Côte-d'Or, Saône-et-Lori and Yonne. It was named for the Burgundians, a Germanic tribe. In 843 the area was divided into the E county of Franche-Comté and the W Duchy of Burgundy, which became virtually an independent state. From 1477 until the Revolution the duchy was a French province. A rich agricultural region, Burgundy is famous for its wines.

BURKE, Edmund (1729–1797), Irish-born British statesman, political philosopher and outstanding orator. He entered parliament in 1765, and advocated more just policies towards the American colonies, opposing the STAMP ACT and (in 1775) arguing for conciliation. Concerned for justice in India, he promoted the impeachment of Warren HASTINGS (1786–87). His famous *Reflections on the Revolution in France* (1790) presented his rational case against violent change.

BURLEIGH, Harry T. (1866–1949), US singer and composer. He made concert arrangements of more than 100 Negro spirituals (including "Deep River," "Swing Low, Sweet Chariot" and "Sometimes I Feel Like a Motherless Child") and introduced them to the concert halls of the US and Europe before WWI.

BURLESQUE, form of literary or stage humor characterized by exaggeration or distortion of its subject matter. Aristophanes' comedies are early examples. In mid-19th-century America the term was applied to a low-comedy, sometimes bawdy, entertainment, which developed into a form of variety show. After 1920 striptease acts became the main burlesque attraction, and the Minsky chain, with theaters in several US cities, became the leading provider of such entertainment.

BURMA, country in SE Asia on the Bay of Bengal, bounded by Bangladesh, India, China, Laos and Thailand. It comprises five federated states.

Land. The country is fringed by high mountain ranges to the E, W and N, which enclose a fertile central plain watered chiefly by the Irrawaddy R and its great delta. Central and N Burma are thickly forested, and much of Burma has a tropical monsoon climate.

People. The Burmans, a Mongoloid people, form 75% of the population, the Karens and Shans being the other major groups; Indians and Chinese constitute significant minorities. Some 80% of the population live in rural areas. Rangoon, the capital and chief port, is by far the largest city. Other centers include Mandalay and Moulmein.

Economy. Agriculture is the country's economic mainstay. Rice (grown particularly in the Irrawaddy basin and delta) is the main crop, followed by sugarcane and groundnuts. Forestry provides hardwoods for export. Industry is confined mainly to rice-milling, oil-refining and textiles. The country is rich in minerals, including oil, lead, tin and tungsten, but deposits are poorly exploited.

History. Burma was settled by the Burmans in the 9th century, establishing a kingdom which reached its height under Buddhist King Anawratha in the 11th century. In 1287 the kingdom fell to KUBLAI KHAN and was later divided among Shan and other rulers, though it was again unified in the 16th century. In the 1750s a new dynasty was established by King Alaungpaya, who made his capital at Rangoon. After a series of wars (1826–85), Britain annexed Burma as part of its Indian empire, and in 1937 granted the country separate dominion status. During World War II, Burma was occupied by the Japanese who set up a puppet government. The independent Union of Burma was established in 1948. Its democratic constitution was suspended in 1962 by General Ne Win and a new socialist constitution was announced in Dec. 1973.

Official Name: The Socialist Republic of the Union of Burma
Capital: Rangoon
Area: 261,218
Population: 33,310,000
Languages: Burmese
Religions: Buddhist
Monetary Unit(s): 1 kyat = 100 pyas
BURMESE CAT, an elegant breed of

"foreign" type similar to the Siamese but more solid in conformation and with round eyes which should be an intense yellow. The short, satin-like coat may shade almost imperceptibly lighter on the underparts and be slightly darker on face and ears but should otherwise be an even color. Brown, blue, chocolate (champagne) and lilac are recognized in the US but a wider range is known in the UK.

BURNE-JONES, Sir Edward Coley (1833–1898), English artist, a member of the PRE-RAPHAELITE BROTHERHOOD. His paintings (e.g., *King Cophetua and the Beggar Maid*) evince a romantic, dreamy medievalism. In 1858 he worked with ROSSETTI on the Oxford Union frescoes. He also designed many stained-glass windows for William MORRIS.

BURNET, Sir Frank Macfarlane (1899–), Australian physician and virologist who shared the 1970 Nobel Prize for Physiology or Medicine with P. B. MEDAWAR for his suggestion that the ability of organisms to form ANTIBODIES in response to foreign tissues was acquired and not inborn. Medawar followed up the suggestion and performed successful skin transplants in mice.

BURNETT, Carol (1936–), US actress and comedienne. She hosted *The Carol Burnett Show* (1967–78), a highly popular comedy-variety series which won five Emmy Awards. She made Broadway appearances in *Once Upon a Mattress* (1959) and *Plaza Suite* (1970) and excelled on the screen in both comedic and dramatic roles.

BURNETT, Frances (Eliza) Hodgson (1849– 1924), English-born US author. She is particularly famous for her children's stories, *Little Lord Fauntleroy* (1885–86) and *The Secret Garden* (1910).

BURNEY, Fanny (Frances) (1752–1840), English novelist and diarist. Her first novel, *Evelina* (1778), won her the respect of Samuel JOHNSON. She spent five years from 1786 as a member of Queen Charlotte's household. Her *Early Diary: 1768–78* (1889) and *Diary and Letters: 1778–1840* (1842–46) provide interesting background to the period.

BURNHAM, Daniel Hudson (1846–1912), US architect, a pioneer of city planning. He built some of America's early skyscrapers, including the Masonic Temple Building, Chicago (1892), and the Flatiron Building, New York City (1902). He also designed the plan for the Columbian Exposition in Chicago (1893). Much of his improvement plan for Chicago (1907–09) was subsequently put into effect.

BURNS, Arthur Frank (1904–), Austrianborn US economist. An expert on the BUSINESS CYCLE, he served as presidential adviser on economics 1953–56 and on labor management 1961–66. Among his many books, the most influential was *Measuring Business Cycles* (1946), written with Wesley Clair MITCHELL.

BURNS, Robert (1759–1796), famous Scottish poet. The son of a poor farmer, he himself farmed for a living and later worked as a customs official. In 1786 he published *Poems, Chiefly in the Scottish Dialect* (enlarged 1787). His poetry, in Scots-English idiom, deals with rural human experience and feeling. He also wrote satires and radical poems, such as *The Twa Dogs* and *The Jolly Beggars*. Influenced by Scottish folk tradition, he was a master at writing songs to traditional airs—for example, *Auld Lang Syne*. At first taken up by fashionable society, he died neglected and in debt. Among his best-known poems are *Tam O'Shanter*, *To a Mouse* and *The Cotter's Saturday Night*.

BURNS AND ALLEN, US husband and wife comedy team of **Nathan Birnbaum ("George Burns"; 1896–),** and **Grace Ethel ("Gracie") Allen** (1906–1964). They started out in vaudeville in the 1920s and went on to be immensely successful on radio and television. They also made a number of movies. In old age, George Burns, who had been the "straight man" in the team, blossomed as a comedian in his own right, starring in such films as *The Sunshine Boys* (1977) and *Oh God* (1979).

BURNS AND SCALDS, injuries caused by heat, electricity, radiation or caustic substances, in which protein denaturation causes death of tissues. (Scalds are burns due to boiling water or steam.) Burns cause PLASMA to leak from blood vessels into the tissues and in severe burns substantial leakage leads to SHOCK. In **first-degree burns**, such as mild SUNBURN, damage is superficial. **Second-degree burns** destroy only the epidermis so that regeneration is possible. **Third-degree burns** destroy all layers of SKIN, which cannot then regenerate, so skin-grafting is required. Infection, ulceration, hemolysis, KIDNEY failure and severe scarring may complicate burns. Treatment includes ANALGESICS, dressings and ANTISEPTICS and fluids for shock. Immediate FIRST AID measures include cold water cooling to minimize continuing damage.

BURNSIDE, Ambrose Everett (1824–1881), Union general in the American Civil War. Succeeding McClellan as general of the Army of the Potomac,

he resigned after the Union defeat at FREDERICKSBURG in 1862. He was later governor of R.I. (1866–69) and US senator (1875–81). His whiskers gave rise to the term "sideburns."

BURR, Aaron (1756–1836), brilliant and controversial US vice-president, who killed Alexander HAMILTON in a duel (1804). Hamilton had blocked Burr's election as president in a tie vote with Jefferson in 1800, and (as Burr believed) his election as governor of N.Y. in 1804. Burr was admitted to the New York bar in 1782, was attorney general (1789–91) and US senator (1791–97) while helping to organize the new Republican party. After his term as vice-president (1800–05) he was involved in conspiracies to form an empire in the West, and was tried but acquitted of treason. After 1812 he returned to the law in N.Y.

BURROUGHS, Edgar Rice (1875–1950), US writer of adventure novels. He is most famous for *Tarzan of the Apes* (1914), whose characters have passed into comic strips, films and television.

BURROUGHS, John (1837–1921), US naturalist and author who made his reputation with philosophical nature essays. His *Notes on Walt Whitman* (1867) was the first biographical study of the poet, who was his friend.

BURROUGHS, William Seward (1914–), US novelist associated with the beat and hippie movements; his principal subject matter is drug addiction. He is best known for *Naked Lunch* (1959), *Soft Machine* (1961) and *Nova Express* (1964).

BURROWS, Abe (1910–), US librettist, theatrical director and humorist, who, with Joe Swerling, adapted several Damon Runyon stories into the hit musical *Guys and Dolls* (1950). He also wrote the books for *Can-Can* (1953) and *Silk Stockings* (1955) and was a celebrated play "doctor," stepping in to turn ailing Broadway shows into successes.

BURSA, fibrous sac containing SYNOVIAL FLUID which reduces friction where TENDONS move over bones. Extra bursae may develop where there is abnormal pressure or friction.

BURSITIS, inflammation of a BURSA, commonly caused by excessive wear and tear (as in housemaid's knee) or by rheumatoid ARTHRITIS, GOUT or various bacteria. It causes pain and stiffness of the affected part, and may require CORTISONE injections and, if infected, surgical drainage.

BURSTYN, Ellen (1932–), US actress noted for her portrayals of normal women under abnormal stress. She won the Tony Award for her performance in the play *Same Time, Next Year* (1975). Her films include *The Exorcist* (1973), *Alice Doesn't Live Here Anymore* (1974), for which she won the Academy Award, and a 1981 TV film in which she sympathetically portrayed convicted murderess Jean Harris.

BURTON, Sir Richard Francis (1821–1890), English explorer, linguist and author, famous for his translation of the ARABIAN NIGHTS. Burton was fluent in several Middle Eastern languages. In 1853, disguised as a Muslim, he visited Mecca, an event recorded in his book, *Pilgrimage to Al-Medina and Meccah* (1855). Together with John SPEKE, he discovered Lake Tanganyika (1858).

BURTON, Richard (1925–), British actor. Starting as a promising Shakespearean at the Old Vic, London, in the 1950s, he appeared on Broadway in *Camelot* (1960) and *Hamlet* (1964) and has made numerous films, including *Look Back in Anger* (1959), *Becket* (1964) and, with his then wife, Elizabeth TAYLOR, *Who's Afraid of Virginia Woolf?* (1966).

BURTON, Robert (1577–1640), English clergyman, author of the *Anatomy of Melancholy* (1621), a compendious study of the causes and symptoms of melancholy, which, from the frankness and perception of its section "On Love Melancholy," has led to his being regarded as a precursor of FREUD.

Official Name: Republic of Burundi
Capital: Bujumbura
Area: 10,747sq mi
Population: 4,287,000
Languages: Kirundi, French, Swahili
Religions: Roman Catholic, Animist, Muslim
Monetary Unit(s)s: 1 Burundi franc = 100 centimes

BURUNDI, a small African state on the NE shore of Lake Tanganyika, originally part of Ruanda-Urundi.
Land. It consists mostly of high plateau, and is bordered to the N by Rwanda, to the E and S by Tanzania and to the W by Zaire.

Burundi has a tropical climate with equable temperatures and irregular rainfall.
People. Although exceptionally small in area, Burundi is Africa's second most-densely populated state, after Rwanda, its neighbor. The population is about 84% Hutu (Bahutu), 15% Tutsi (Watutsi or Watusi) and 1% pygmy Twa. The Hutu are mainly farmers; the Tutsi, cattle raisers, and the Twa, hunters. Although a small minority, the Tutsi dominate politically and socially.
Economy. A poor country, Burundi depends almost exclusively upon coffee for its income. Reliance upon this one commodity and the poor transport infrastructure of this land-locked country are major obstacles to development.
History. The earliest inhabitants, the Twa hunters, were conquered by the Hutu, who in turn were reduced to serfdom by the Tutsi. In 1899, Germany claimed the Ruanda–Urundi territory; after WWI it was administered by Belgium as a trust territory under the League of Nations and, after WWII, under the UN. The two states separated in 1962; Burundi was granted independence that same year. In 1966 long-standing rivalry between the Hutu and Tutsi peoples erupted, and the monarchy was replaced by a military government. In 1973 a short war with Rwanda ended amicably.

BUSH, George (1924–), Texas businessman, political leader and vice-president of the US (1981–). He first ran for the Senate as a Texas Republican in 1964 and was narrowly defeated. In 1966 he was elected to Congress and reelected in 1968. Defeated for the Senate in 1970, he was appointed ambassador to the UN in 1971 by President Nixon. The next year he became Republican national chairman and in 1974 head of the US liaison office in China. He served President FORD as head of the CIA in 1976–77. After unsuccessfully seeking the Republican nomination for the presidency in 1980, he was chosen as Ronald REAGAN's running mate.

BUSH, Vannevar (1890–1974), US electrical engineer, director of the Office of Scientific Research and Development in WWII. In the 1930s he developed a "differential analyzer"—in effect the first analog COMPUTER.

BUSHIDO, code of honor among the SAMURAI (warrior) class of Japan, influenced by ZEN and CONFUCIANISM, which stressed military virtues, feudal loyalty and filial piety. It was formulated in the 12th–14th centuries, but the term itself was first used in the 16th century. After the abolition of the samurai class in 1868, it formed a basis for emperor-worship and nationalism.

BUSHMEN, a people of South Africa related to the pygmies, living around the Kalahari Desert. They average about 5ft in height and have yellowish-brown skin, broad noses and closely curled hair. They are nomadic hunters, living in bands of 25–60. Their language, related to Hottentot and belonging to the Khoisan group, employs a series of "clicks." Bushmen are a musical people, and are also noted for their vivid painting.

BUSINESS CYCLE, periodic fluctuation in the economy of an industrialized nation, between prosperity and recession or depression, with marked variations in growth rate and employment levels. Recession may be caused by overproduction, declining demand, changes in money supply and generally by a loss of confidence. Government interventions to strengthen the economy have become common in recent years.

BUSINESS SCHOOLS, Graduate, institutions that train business professionals and grant the M.B.A. (Master of Business Administration) degree. Such institutions, many of them associated with larger universities, have grown significantly in number in the US from the 1970s (there are now almost 500), as more college graduates chose business as a career. Top-ranked business schools include Harvard, Stanford, U of Chicago, the Wharton School of the U of Pa. and Yale.

BUSING, SCHOOL, the most common means of desegregating US public schools on an area or citywide basis. In 1971, in *Swann vs. Charlotte-Mecklenburg,* the US Supreme Court upheld the constitutionality of busing students to achieve racial balance. This decision applied to cases of *de jure* segregation (where segregation is due to official actions) but not to *de facto* segregation (the result of residential patterns). The issue continues to be extremely controversial in both the N and S. Many parents, blacks as well as whites, who otherwise agree with the principle of desegregation as enunciated by the Supreme Court in BROWN VS. BOARD OF EDUCATION OF TOPEKA, nevertheless have grave reservations about busing their children away from neighborhood schools—particularly when the distant schools are perceived as being inferior.

BUSONI, Ferruccio Benvenuto (1866–1924), Italian pianist and composer. His works include a lengthy piano concerto with chorus (1904) and the opera, *Doctor*

Faust (1916–24). He also made many piano transcriptions of works by J. S. Bach and others.

BUSSOTTI, Sylvano (1931–   ), Italian avant-garde composer who devoted himself to applying the principles of abstract expressionism to music. He abandoned traditional notation and used instead drawings that the performer was required to duplicate in sound, as in his *Five Pieces for David Tudor* and *Frammento.*

BUSTARDS, large game birds of the family Otidae, native to Europe, Asia and Africa. Plumage on the back and tail is gray and brown. During courtship the male displays the white feathers of his throat and chest. They are turkey-sized and feed on grains, leaves and small animals.

BUTE, John Stuart, 3rd Earl of (1713–1792), favorite of King GEORGE III. Though unpopular, he dominated the King until 1765. As prime minister 1762–63, he ended the SEVEN YEARS' WAR.

BUTLER, Benjamin Franklin (1818–1893), US politician and Union general in the Civil War. Because of his harsh autocratic rule as military governor of New Orleans (1862), he was known as "Beast," and he was recalled by President Lincoln. As congressman (1867–75, 1877–79), he supported RECONSTRUCTION and the impeachment of President JOHNSON. A Populist party candidate, he was governor of Mass. (1882) and ran for president (1884).

BUTLER, John (1920–   ), US dancer and choreographer. He was a member of the Martha GRAHAM company 1945–55 and thereafter devoted most of his time to choreography, combining traditional and modern styles in a strongly theatrical mixture. His *Carmina Burana* (1959) became a mainstay of the Netherlands Dance Theater repertory.

BUTLER, Nicholas Murray (1862–1947), US educator. He was president of Columbia College (1902–45), and developed it into Columbia U. He was president of the Carnegie Endowment for International Peace (1925–45) and, in 1931, shared the Nobel Peace Prize. He was also active in Republican politics and was president of the AMERICAN ACADEMY OF ARTS AND LETTERS (1928–41).

BUTLER, Richard Austen (1902–   ), British political leader. He held a number of important cabinet posts in Conservative governments, including chancellor of the exchequer 1951–55, home secretary 1957–62 and foreign secretary 1963–64. Twice a favorite to be named prime minister, he was passed over twice.

BUTLER, Samuel (1612–1680), English poet, author of *Hudibras* (1663–78), a mock-heroic, anti-Puritan satire. He attacked the hypocrisy and pedantry of the Puritans of the Commonwealth.

BUTLER, Samuel (1835–1902), English novelist. He considered Darwinism too mechanistic and satirized it in *Erewhon* (1872), his version of Utopia. His major work is *The Way of All Flesh* (1903), an autobiographical novel satirizing Victorian morality.

BUTTE, mining city in SW Mont., seat of Silver Bow Co., founded in 1864. A mining camp, then a silver-mining center, it gained importance in 1880 with the discovery of copper. Pop 37,205.

BUTTE, small, flat-topped hill formed when EROSION dissects a MESA.

BUTTER, a dairy product (see DAIRY FARMING) made by churning MILK or CREAM, containing fat, protein and water. Made in some countries from the milk of goats, sheep or yaks, it is made in the US from cows' milk only. Continuous mechanized production has been general since the 1940s. After skimming, the cream is ripened with a bacterial culture, pasteurized (see PASTEURIZATION), cooled to 4°C and then churned causing the butterfat to separate from the liquid residue, buttermilk. The butter is then washed, worked, colored and salted. World butter production in 1971 was 5.28 million tons, of which the US accounted for 10%.

BUTTERFLIES, a large group of INSECTS characterized by wide, brightly colored wings. With MOTHS, they comprise the order LEPIDOPTERA. The life history of the butterfly is composed of several stages, each divided by a METAMORPHOSIS. The EGG grows into a LARVA called a CATERPILLAR, which feeds on vegetation. The next stage, the PUPA, does not feed and eventually produces the adult butterfly.

BUTTON, Dick (1929–   ), US figure skater. At 16 he was the youngest man ever to win the US senior title, and in 1948 was the first man to win the Grand Slam. He captured seven national, two Olympic and five world medals.

BUTTRESS, in architecture, a masonry or brickwork element built against a wall to support it or to take the thrust of a vault or dome. The principle was much developed in the Gothic style. As vaults became higher and walls were pierced by increasingly large windows, the **flying buttress** was evolved. This is a half arch which transfers the thrust to a freestanding masonry member. (See GOTHIC ART AND ARCHITECTURE.)

BUXTEHUDE, Dietrich (c1637–1707), Danish-born German composer and organist. His cantatas and organ toccatas and chorale preludes influenced J. S. Bach. The evening music concerts he held at Lübeck were famous.

BUZZARDS, a group of medium-sized hawks of the family Accipitridae, easily identifiable by their soaring flight, widespread wings and broad tail. They prey on small mammals by swooping from the air or from a perch. In North America they are called hawks, "buzzard" being applied to VULTURES.

BYNG, Julian Hedworth George Byng, 1st Viscount (1862–1935), British field marshal and distinguished WWI commander. In 1917 he took Vimy Ridge with the Canadian Corps in France, and later commanded the first-ever large-scale tank offensive. He was governor-general of Canada 1921–26.

BYRD, Harry Flood (1887–1966), US legislator and Democratic governor of Va. 1926–30. During his 32 years in the Senate (1933–65), he advocated stricter government economy and opposed most NEW DEAL programs, foreign aid and integration policies.

BYRD, Richard Evelyn (1888–1957), US aviator, explorer and pioneer of US exploration and research in Antarctica. He led the air unit with D. B. MacMillan's 1925 Arctic expedition and, with Floyd BENNETT, overflew the North Pole (1926); in 1929 he flew over the South Pole. He made five important expeditions to Antarctica (1928–56), established the base camp Little America there, and worked an whole winter of 1933–34 alone at an advance camp. He headed the US Antarctic program from 1955.

BYRD, Robert Carlyle (1917–   ), US legislator. After service in the US House (1953–59), he entered the Senate, 1959. A moderate who rose to power in the Senate through hard work and knowledge of parliamentary procedure, he served as majority whip for the Democrats and then as majority leader (1977–1980). He became minority leader in 1981.

BYRD, William (1543–1623), English composer, one of Europe's greatest masters of POLYPHONY. His choral music includes the "Great Service" for the Anglican Church, three fine Roman Catholic mass settings, some superb motets, *Cantiones Sacrae* (1589; 1591) and many anthems. He also wrote important keyboard music and madrigals. He was closely associated with TALLIS, and in 1575 they were granted a joint monopoly for the printing and sale of music.

BYRD, William (1674–1744), colonial American planter at Westover, Va., active in political and cultural life. He laid out the city of Richmond on part of his family's vast estates. His delightful books and diaries are important records of his times.

BYRNE, Jane (1934–   ), mayor of Chicago. In her first bid for elected office she defeated the remnants of the Democratic machine of her old patron, Mayor Richard DALEY, to become (1979) the first woman mayor in Chicago's history.

BYRNES, James Francis (1879–1972), US statesman. He was director of WWII mobilization 1943–45, and as secretary of state 1945–47 he worked to lessen tensions with the USSR. He was Democratic governor of S.C. 1951–55.

BYRON, George Gordon Byron, 6th Baron (1788–1824), English poet, a leading figure of European ROMANTICISM. Lameness and an unhappy childhood bred morbidity, a scorn for authority and hatred of oppression. A disastrous marriage and the strictures of English society drove him to exile in Italy (1816). He later joined the Greek revolt against the Turks, dying of fever at Missolonghi, Greece. *English Bards and Scotch Reviewers* (1809), a savage riposte to his critics, brought overnight fame, and the first two cantos of *Childe Harold's Pilgrimage* (1812), a European reputation. The moody, defiant "Byronic" hero of the poetic drama, *Manfred* (1817), became a great Romantic theme. Major works include the incomplete satiric epic, *Don Juan* (1819–24), and *The Vision of Judgement* (1822), satirizing the poet laureate SOUTHEY and King George III.

BYZANTINE ART AND ARCHITECTURE, work created in the cultural area of the BYZANTINE EMPIRE in the 4th to early 15th centuries. In architecture, the great church of HAGIA SOPHIA (532–37) in Constantinople (now Istanbul), dominated by its great dome, was a model for later Christian work and for Turkish architects. Other superb Byzantine churches can be seen at S. Vitale in Ravenna, Italy, and Daphne near Athens, while St. Mark's, Venice, is Byzantine-inspired. The interiors of such churches were covered with glowing glass MOSAICS, the supreme Byzantine medium. From dome to floor a strictly ordered scheme of images depicted themes of faith and theology.

Enamels, ivory carving and the art of the goldsmith and silversmith were used to beautify reliquaries that were the envy of Christendom; many came to Western churches after the Latin sack of Constantinople in 1204. Manuscript illumination, which reached remarkable heights, was a means of diffusing Byzantine styles, and the mystical serenity of the Byzantine masters clearly influenced Italian artists of the medieval Sienese school. The conservative imagery of Byzantine religious art survived for centuries after the fall of Constantinople (1453) in the work of Russian, Greek and Balkan icon painters. Little secular art survives, though Byzantine luxury goods, notably silk, were much sought after in the West. The massive walls of Theodosius at Istanbul are among the monuments to Byzantine military architecture.

BYZANTINE EMPIRE, historical term for the successor state to the Roman Empire in the East. Its capital was Constantinople (see ISTANBUL), founded by CONSTANTINE I in 330 AD at the ancient Greek BYZANTIUM. Its heartlands were Asia Minor and the Balkans; at its height it ruled S Spain, Italy, Sicily, N Africa, Egypt, Syria, Palestine, the Crimean coast, Cyprus and the Aegean islands. Its religion was Eastern Orthodox Christianity; Byzantine missionaries took Christianity to Russia and Byzantine theologians are among the chief Church Fathers. Its literature was based on the ancient Greek classics. BYZANTINE ART AND ARCHITECTURE influenced W Europe and Turkey, and Byzantine scholars contributed to Western Humanism.

The Roman Empire was divided after the death of Theodosius I in 395. By c500 the Western Empire had fallen, and Germanic invaders occupied Italy, Spain and N Africa. In the East, Roman institutions continued; JUSTINIAN I (527–565) reconquered Italy, S Spain and N Africa and made a great codification of Roman law. However, after c600 fundamental changes displaced Roman with typically Byzantine (Greek) institutions. By 700, S Spain, N Africa, Egypt and Syria were lost to the VISIGOTHS and ARABS, and the LOMBARDS were conquering Italy. Later, Bulgars occupied much of the Balkans and, after the disastrous Byzantine defeat at the Battle of Manzikert in 1071, the SELJUKS pushed deep into Asia Minor. A 12th-century recovery ended when, in 1204, Venice and the Fourth Crusade sacked Constantinople. In 1261 Michael VIII regained the city, but the Turkish threat grew. Western Europe, considering the Eastern Church in schism since a break (1054) between the patriarch of Constantinople and the pope, refused to help. In 1453, the one great Eastern Christian empire fell when the Turks captured Constantinople.

On the rich trade routes from Asia and N

Africa to Europe and Russia, Constantinople was the greatest city of the Christian world; its empire rested on a money economy, while feudalism and the Church dominated Western society and government. Byzantine emperors ruled through paid professional administrators, commanded paid professional armies and were supreme in religion as in politics, though affairs were often marked by court intrigues. They controlled early Church Councils and, during the 8th-century ICONOCLASTIC CONTROVERSY, ordered images to be destroyed as idolatrous. Theological debate was a passion with all classes. Military success was expected of emperors and military coups were frequent. Foreign diplomacy was subtle and usually successful. The Byzantines considered themselves to be the heirs to Rome; their high and ancient civilization justified their claim.

C 3rd letter of the English alphabet, a rounded form of the Greek *gamma*, used by the Romans instead of *k*. In some languages *c* retains both the *k* and *c* sounds (cat, certain, cycle, etc.). C is the chemical symbol for carbon and in Roman numerals equals 100.

CABAL, clandestine group or organization engaged in intrigues; also applied to the intrigues themselves. The term was already used in the 17th century for any secret council of the king. The conduct of English King Charles II's ministers Clifford, Arlington, Buckingham, Ashley and Lauderdale, whose initials spelled "cabal," gave it a sinister sense.

CABALA, or Kabbalah (Hebrew: tradition), a body of esoteric Jewish mystical doctrines dealing with the manifestations of God and his revelation. The Cabala attaches mystical significance to every detail in the TORAH. Its chief books are the *Sefer Yezirah* (Book of Creation; 3rd–6th centuries) and the *Sefer HaZohar* (Book of Splendor; 13th century). The Cabala arose in S France and Spain in the Middle Ages and was later a major influence on HASIDISM.

CABALETTA, short operatic song with a

regular rhythm, also the final section of an operatic aria. A fine example is Violetta's "Sempre libera degg'io" in Verdi's *La Traviata.*

CABALLÉ, Montserrat (1933–), Spanish soprano. She made her operatic debut at Basel, Switzerland, in 1957 as Mimi in LA BOHÈME and in 1955 began appearing in the US, first in concert versions of Donizetti operas. Her pianissimo singing is particularly notable.

CABBAGE, *Brassica olearacea,* a biennial vegetable from which other BRASSICAS, such as KALE, CAULIFLOWER and BROCCOLI have been developed. The cabbage originated many centuries ago from the European wild cabbage. It has a characteristic tight "head" of leaves. Cabbages can be boiled or pickled, or fermented in salt to give Sauerkraut. They are also used as an animal feed.

CABELL, James Branch (1879–1958), US novelist, who combined an ironic, often anti-romantic style with a strong element of fantasy in plots and settings. His best-known novel is *Jurgen* (1919).

CABET, Étienne (1788–1856), French Utopian socialist, whose novel of an ideal communistic society, *Voyage en Icarie* (1840), gained wide readership. An unsuccessful attempt in 1848 to found an "Icarian" community in Texas was followed by other short-lived colonies, notably one led by Cabet himself (1849–56) at Nauvoo, Ill.

CABEZA DE VACA, Álvar Núñez (c1490-1557), Spanish explorer. Shipwrecked in 1528 after an expedition to Florida, he reached Mexico City after several years among the Indians. His account of the present-day SW US, including descriptions of "Seven Cities of Cíbola' supposedly laden with riches, stirred Spanish interest in the area. He was made governor of the Río de la Plata region in 1540, but after a rebellion against him was recalled to Spain. He was tried and exiled to Africa, but in 1552 he was pardoned by the king.

CABEZÓN, Antonio de (c1510–1566), Spanish composer of keyboard music. Blind from infancy, he served at the Spanish court, writing for the organ, harpsichord and vihuela. His theme-and-variations compositions were notable early examples of the form.

CABINDA, or Kabinda, coastal territory belonging to Angola where there is a separatist movement. It covers 2,800sq mi; its economy is traditionally agricultural, based on timber, palm oil, cocoa and coffee but now increasingly on oil. Pop 81,625.

CABINET, in the US, top-level advisory council to the president, composed of the heads of the major executive departments. Though not mentioned in the US constitution, the cabinet has been accepted as a consultative body to the executive since George Washington. Normally the cabinet meets weekly with the president, though procedure varies.

Members of the cabinet are appointed by the president and are responsible as individuals to him: they are not members of either house of Congress and may not address them, though they are often called to testify before committees. In Great Britain and most of the Commonwealth the cabinet is a policy-making body of ministers chosen by the prime minister from the political party in power, and collectively responsible to parliament. (See also US Departments of AGRICULTURE; COMMERCE; DEFENSE; HEALTH, EDUCATION AND WELFARE; HOUSING AND URBAN DEVELOPMENT; INTERIOR; JUSTICE; LABOR; STATE; TRANSPORTATION; TREASURY.)

CABINETMAKING, the art of precise and delicate woodworking, exemplified by Thomas CHIPPENDALE in England and Duncan PHYFE in America. Cabinetmaking involves dovetailing, using mortises and tenons, and glue rather than screws or nails, but 20th-century MASS PRODUCTION has led to its steady decline. (See also FURNITURE.)

CABLE, George Washington (1844–1925), US author noted for his depiction of New Orleans and Creole life in works such as *Old Creole Days* (1879) and *The Grandissimes* (1880).

CABLE TELEVISION, or **CATV** (community antenna television), system used originally in areas where mountains or tall buildings made TELEVISION reception poor or impossible, but now expanding throughout the US because of the multiplicity of channels and programs it makes available. Normally, subscribers' sets are connected by coaxial CABLE to a single ANTENNA erected in a suitably exposed position. Many signals are now fed to cable systems via satellite.

CABOT, John (Giovanni Caboto; c1450–1499), Italian navigator and explorer, probably the first European to reach the North American mainland. In 1497, after receiving letters patent from Henry VII of England authorizing his voyage, Cabot sailed in search of a western route to Asia and reached the coasts of Nova Scotia and Newfoundland. He made a landing and set up the English and Venetian flags. On a second voyage (1498) Cabot may have reached America again, but it is not clear

what happened to the expedition. Cabot himself was not mentioned again, though he drew his English annuity for 1499.

CABRAL, Pedro Álvares (c1467–1520), Portuguese navigator credited with the discovery of Brazil, where he landed in 1500 on a voyage from Lisbon to India. The expedition succeeded in establishing trading posts in India, but after his return in 1501 Cabral was given no other position of authority.

CABRILLO, Juan Rodríguez (d. c1543), Portuguese explorer in the service of Spain, best known for his discovery of California. In 1542 he explored the coastline from Lower California northwards to San Diego Bay, and may have succeeded in landing on some of the islands.

CABRINI, Saint Frances Xavier (1850–1917), Italian–American nun, first US citizen to be canonized (1946). She founded the Missionary Sisters of the Sacred Heart in 1880, and established 67 houses of the order throughout the world. In 1889 she immigrated to New York from Italy.

CACAO, *Theobroma cacao*, the tree that produces cacao or cocoa beans. The raw material for CHOCOLATE is prepared by roasting, grinding and pressing the dried seeds (or beans) from the woody cacao fruits. Pressing squeezes out cocoa butter and leaves a solid mass that is reground to make cocoa powder. Eating chocolate is made from a blend of ground beans, sugar and cocoa butter, with milk added for milk chocolate. The cacao tree grows in Africa and Middle America and has been cultivated since the time of the Aztecs, who used it for beverages and currency. Christopher Columbus introduced cocoa beans into Europe in 1502 and by the 1700s the hot chocolate drink was popular.

CACTI, family of prickly plants (Cactaceae) comprising over 1,500 species, almost all of which are native to America. The succulent cactus is a XEROPHYTE and well adapted to life in the driest desert conditions. It has no leaves, the main source of water loss in other plants, and PHOTOSYNTHESIS takes place in the stem or trunk, which also stores a great deal of water. A network of roots radiating from the stem makes maximum use of brief desert showers. The characteristic spines have two functions: they prevent the stem from being eaten by animals; and where the spines form a dense covering, they help to retain water without obstructing light. Cacti bear beautiful flowers which are shortlived and often open only at night. Cacti are prized as ornamental plants. They are also the source of the drug MESCALINE and some species are edible. As house plants they should be kept in sunny south-facing windows. They tolerate normal house temperatures, although some species require a cold period in winter to set buds. They should be well watered whenever the surface of the soil dries out. They can be propagated by means of seeds, cuttings or by dividing the plants. (See also PEYOTE.)

CADE, Jack (d. 1450), leader of the Kentish rebellion against Henry VI of England in 1450. His army occupied London for three days, but disbanded after the promise of concessions and pardons. Cade was captured and mortally wounded, and the concessions were revoked.

CADENCE, used in music to describe the notes or chords which close a phrase or movement. It is a melodic or harmonic formula which brings a phrase or passage to a rest.

CADENZA, musical passage at the close of a movement in which a soloist displays his instrumental or vocal skill. In the 18th and 19th centuries, composers would often leave an opening for improvisation by the performer. Eventually cadenzas were written out, whether by the composer or by a famous performer, and became an integral part of the CONCERTO.

CADILLAC, Antoine Laumet de la Mothe (c1658–1730), French colonial governor and founder of Detroit (1701). Governor of Mackinac in 1694, he felt the site of Detroit would be a better strategic position. In 1710 he was appointed governor of Louisiana, but was recalled in 1717.

CÁDIZ, ancient city and port in SW Spain, on the Atlantic coast NW of Gibraltar. Founded by the Phoenicians in c1100 BC as Gadir, the city became prosperous under Roman rule. After the discovery of America it became important as the headquarters of the Spanish fleets. It is now a commercial port noted for sherry exports. Pop 135,700.

CAEDMON (7th century), early English Christian poet. After a dream commanding him to "sing the beginning of created things," he spent the rest of his life rendering biblical stories into verse. Only nine lines of his hymn to God survive.

CAESAR, family name of the Julian clan of Rome. The success of Julius CAESAR made it charismatic, and it was retained as a family name by the first five Roman emperors. The title was kept by later emperors for their heirs designate, and the German *kaiser* and Russian *tsar* were derived from it.

CAESAR, Gaius Julius (100–44 BC), Roman general, politician and writer, one of the most famous of the ancient Romans. Although a member of the ancient patrician Julian clan, he supported the antisenatorial party. His early career through various public offices won him popularity, and in 60 BC he formed the First Triumvirate with POMPEY, who supplied the army, and CRASSUS, who provided the money. With Caesar as consul in 59 BC they succeeded in controlling Roman politics, and in 58 BC he chose Gaul as his proconsular command.

Caesar's successful GALLIC WARS (58–51 BC) gained him great esteem and a loyal and well-trained army. Pompey was given extraordinary powers in Rome and tried to force Caesar to lay down his command, but in 49 BC Caesar crossed the Rubicon R (the boundary between his province and Rome) and civil war began. Pompey was finally defeated at Pharsalus in 48 BC, and by 45 BC Caesar had secured the defeat of all the Pompeian forces. In 44 BC he was made dictator for life, but on the IDES OF MARCH he was murdered by a group of senators. An outstanding writer (*Commentaries*) and orator, he introduced the Julian calendar.

CAESAR, Sid (1922–), US comedian who starred, with Imogene Coca, Carl Reiner and Howard Morris, in *Your Show of Shows* (1950–54), the most memorable and creative of the early TV variety programs. He later was the star of TVs *Caesar's Hour* (1954–57).

CAESARIAN SECTION. See CESARIAN SECTION.

CAETANO, Marcello (1906–1980), Portuguese political leader, who succeeded Antonio SALAZAR as premier in 1968. In April 1974 Caetano was deposed and exiled after a military coup.

CAFFEINE, or trimethylxanthine ($C_8H_{10}N_4O_2$), an ALKALOID extracted from coffee, and also found in tea, cocoa and cola. Caffeine stimulates the central NERVOUS SYSTEM and HEART, and is a DIURETIC. It increases alertness, in excess causing insomnia (see SLEEP), and is mildly addictive. mp 238°C.

CAGE, John (1912–), US experimental composer and musical theoretician. He composed for "prepared piano," attaching objects to the strings to alter tone and pitch and get percussive effects. Later work included prolonged silences, improvisation, ALEATORY MUSIC and ELECTRONIC MUSIC.

CAGNEY, James (1904–), US film actor who played cocky, aggressive tough guys in such classic gangster movies as *The Public Enemy* (1931) and *The Roaring Twenties* (1939). He won an Academy Award for his portrayal of George M. COHAN in *Yankee Doodle Dandy* (1942).

CAHAN, Abraham (1860–1951), Russian-born US journalist and novelist, cofounder in 1897 of the Social Democratic party and the influential newspaper, the *Jewish Daily Forward*.

CAHOKIA MOUNDS, a group of prehistoric MOUNDS, mostly in the form of truncated pyramids, near East St. Louis, Ill. The largest of these, Monks Mound, is about 350m by 200m at base and some 30m high, and is the largest mound in the US. More than 300 of the mounds have in recent years been bulldozed to make way for agricultural and municipal expansion, but the 18 largest remain.

CAICOS ISLANDS. See TURKS AND CAICOS ISLANDS.

CAIN, James M(allahan) (1892–1977), US writer of crime novels admired for their accuracy of dialogue and characterization. His best-known works are *The Postman Always Rings Twice* (1934), *Serenade* (1937), *Mildred Pierce* (1941) and *Double Indemnity* (1943), all of which were made into films.

CAIRO, or Al-Qāhirah, capital of Egypt. It lies at the head of the Nile delta and is the largest African city. Founded in 969 by the Fatimids, it became and has remained the intellectual center of the Islamic world with the foundation of al-Azhar University (970–78). An allied base during WWII and site of the CAIRO CONFERENCE, it became capital of republican Egypt (1952), and remains a major Arab political, economic and nationalist center. The nearby pyramids, sphinx and Memphis ruins make it a tourist center. Metro pop 8,539,000.

CAIRO, city in SW Ill., seat of Alexander Co., at the confluence of the Mississippi and Ohio rivers. An important Civil War Union base. Now a trading and shipping center for the surrounding area. Pop 6,277.

CAIRO CONFERENCE, WWII meeting of CHURCHILL, F. D. ROOSEVELT and CHIANG KAI-SHEK in Cairo, Egypt, Nov. 22–26, 1943. The Cairo Declaration (Dec. 1, 1943) asserted that on Japan's defeat her boundaries would revert to what they were before the late-19th–century conquests of Chinese territory.

CAISSON DISEASE, or **bends.** See AEROEMBOLISM.

CAJUNS, descendants of expatriate French–Canadians, living in S La. They were deported from Acadia (Nova Scotia) by the British in 1755. They have a distinctive patois: a combination of archaic French forms with English, Spanish, German, Indian and Negro idioms.

CAKEWALK, dance originated by Negro slaves in the southern US before the Civil War. It became a popular dance craze around 1900. Couples walked in a square formation, men on the inside, taking exaggerated high steps. Its music influenced the growth of RAGTIME.

CALABRIA, autonomous Italian region; the "toe" of Italy's "boot." Its capital is Catanzaro and other chief cities are Cosenza and Reggio Calabria. It suffered disastrous earthquakes 1783–87, 1905 and 1908. Area: 5,822sq mi.

CALAMINE, former name of two ZINC minerals, SMITHSONITE and HEMIMORPHITE. In medicine, calamine lotion (zinc carbonate) is a mild ASTRINGENT used to treat ECZEMA and other itchy skin diseases.

CALAMITY JANE, nickname of Martha Jane Burke (c1852–1903), frontier-town prostitute and campfollower who roamed the West in male garb. Famous in Deadwood, S.D., during the 1870s gold boom, she claimed she had been an army scout, pony express rider, Custer's aide and Wild Bill Hickok's mistress.

CALCIUM (Ca), a fairly soft, silvery-white ALKALINE-EARTH METAL, the fifth most abundant element. It occurs naturally as CALCITE, GYPSUM and FLUORITE. The metal is prepared by ELECTROLYSIS of fused calcium chloride. Calcium is very reactive, reacting with water to give a surface layer of calcium hydroxide, and burning in air to give the nitride and oxide. Calcium metal is used as a reducing agent to prepare other metals, as a getter in vacuum tubes, and in alloys. A W 40.1, mp 839°C, bp 1484°C, sg 1.55 (20°C).

Calcium compounds are important constituents of animal skeletons: calcium phosphate forms the bones and teeth of vertebrates, and many seashells are made of the carbonate. **Calcium Carbonate** ($CaCO_3$), colorless crystalline solid, occurring naturally as CALCITE and aragonite, which loses carbon dioxide on heating above 900°C. It is an insoluble BASE. **Calcium Chloride** ($CaCl_2$), colorless crystalline solid, a by-product of the Solvay process. Being very deliquescent, it is used as an industrial drying agent. mp 782°C. **Calcium Fluoride** (CaF_2), or FLUORITE, colorless phosphorescent crystalline solid, used as windows in ultraviolet and infrared SPECTROSCOPY. mp 1423°C, bp c2500°C. **Calcium Hydroxide** ($Ca(OH)_2$), or **Slaked Lime,** colorless crystalline solid, slightly soluble in water, prepared by hydrating calcium oxide and used in industry and agriculture as an ALKALI, in mortar and in glass manufacture. **Calcium Oxide** (CaO), or **Quicklime,** white crystalline powder, made by calcination of calcium carbonate minerals, which reacts violently with water to give calcium hydroxide and is used in arc lights and as an industrial dehydrating agent. mp 2580°C, bp 2850°C. **Calcium Sulfate** ($CaSO_4$), colorless crystalline. When the dihydrate is heated to 128°C, it loses water, forming the hemihydrate, **plaster of paris**. This re-forms the dihydrate as a hard mass when mixed with water, and is used for casts.

CALCULATING MACHINE, device that performs simple ARITHMETIC operations (see also ALGEBRA). There are two main classes: **adding machines**, for addition, and subtraction only; and **calculators**, able also to perform MULTIPLICATION and DIVISION. They may be mechanical, electromechanical, or electronic.

The forerunner of the calculating machine was perhaps the ABACUS. The first adding machine, invented by PASCAL (1642), was able to add and carry. A few decades later (1671), LEIBNIZ designed a device that multiplied by repeated addition (the device was built in 1694). BABBAGE built a small adding machine (1822): in 1833 he conceived his Difference Engine, a predecessor of the digital COMPUTER, but his device was never completed. (See also SLIDE RULE.)

CALCULI, or stones, solid concretions of calcium salts or organic compounds, formed in the KIDNEY, BLADDER or GALL BLADDER. They are often associated with infection. There may be no symptoms but they may pass down or block tubes, causing COLIC, or obstruction in an organ. They may pass on unaided with antispasm drugs and ANALGESICS, but may require surgical removal to prevent damage to kidney or liver.

CALCULUS, the branch of MATHEMATICS dealing with continuously varying quantities. It can be seen as an extension of ANALYTIC GEOMETRY, much of whose terminology it shares. It was invented by NEWTON and independently by LEIBNIZ.

Differential Calculus. Suppose a continuous FUNCTION $f(t)$ represents the position, x, along a road of a moving vehicle at any time t. In the interval between two times t and $t+\Delta t$, the vehicle travels a distance $\Delta x = f(t+\Delta t) - f(t)$ and its average velocity, which is defined as the distance traveled divided by the time taken to travel it, is

$$\frac{\Delta x}{\Delta t} = \frac{f(t+\Delta t)}{\Delta t}$$

Suppose we wish (as Newton did) to define the velocity of an instant t, i.e. the rate of change of x at the time t. We can approximate it as closely as we wish by taking a sufficiently short time interval Δt at t; the LIMIT of the average velocity $\Delta x/\Delta t$ as Δt approaches 0 is the instantaneous velocity, written

$$\frac{dx}{dt} \text{ or } f'(t)$$

and called the **derivative** of x (or of the function $f(t)$ with respect to t. If x is plotted as a GRAPH against t, the derivative gives the slope of the TANGENT to the curve at t. One can take the derivative of the derivative of $f(t)$ and obtain the second derivative

$$\frac{d^2x}{dt^2} \text{ or } f''(x).$$

This is the rate of change of velocity, or ACCELERATION.

There are simple rules for determining the derivatives of the elementary functions. For example (now calling the independent variable x instead of t), if $f(x)=x^2$, then $f'(x)=2x$; and in general, if $f(x)=x^n$, then $f'(x)=nx^{n-1}$. Equations that include derivatives are called differential equations and are widely used in science.

Integral calculus. In order to find the area under the curve representing a function $f(x)$, another limiting process is used. The area is divided into narrow vertical strips and their areas are added; the limit of the sum as the width of the strips approaches 0 is the area under the curve, called the integral of $f(x)$ and written $\int f(x)dx$. This is a function of x, called the indefinite integral, because we have not specified which part of the curve we want the area under; the value of the area from $x=a$ to $x=b$ (a definite integral) is the value of the indefinite integral or $x=b$ minus its value for $x=a$.

The **fundamental theorem of calculus** states that differentiation (finding the derivative of a function) is the reverse of integration (finding the integral). In other words, the derivative of the (indefinite) integral of $f(x)$ is $f(x)$. It follows that the rules for integration are the reverse of those for differentiation, e.g.

$$x^n dx = \frac{x^{n+1}}{n+1}$$

CALCUTTA, capital of W Bengal and largest city of India, near the E border with Bangladesh. It lies in the Ganges delta on the Hooghly R. The principal port and industrial center of E India, it has manufactures that include jute products, chemicals, textiles and glass. It was founded by the British East India Company (1690) and Fort William was built on the site (1696). It was captured by Siruj-ud-Daula, Nawab of Bengal, in 1756; he imprisoned the British in what is known as the BLACK HOLE OF CALCUTTA. Calcutta was retaken by

CLIVE (1757) and was capital of British India 1774–1912. In the 1947 Indian partition, it lost its valuable jute-producing hinterland and received thousands of religious refugees, causing severe overcrowding. Pop 3,141,180.

CALDECOTT, Randolph (1846–1886), British painter and illustrator, particularly of children's books. Among his best-known illustrations are those for Irving's *Old Christmas* (1876) and Cowper's *John Gilpin* (1878). In 1938 the Caldecott Medal was established as an annual award for the best US children's picture book.

CALDER, Alexander (1898–1976), US abstract sculptor and creator of the "mobile." His mobiles consist of flat metal shapes connected by rods, wire or string, which are hung or balanced and moved by motors or by air currents.

CALDERÓN DE LA BARCA, Pedro (1600–1681), Spanish playwright and poet. He and Lope de VEGA were the leading dramatists of Spain's Golden Age. He wrote over 200 plays, distinguished by their heightened style and poetic symbolism, many on religious themes. Among his most famous works are *The Constant Prince* (1629), *Life is a Dream* (1635) and *The Surgeon of His Honor* (1635).

CALDWELL, Erskine Preston (1903–), US author noted for his portrayal of poor Southern whites in short stories and novels such as *Tobacco Road* (1932), *God's Little Acre* (1933) and *Trouble in July* (1940).

CALDWELL, Sarah (1928–), US conductor and opera producer. She was director (1953–57) of the Boston U Opera Workshop and, in 1957, founded the Opera Company of Boston. As its artistic director she staged more than 50 productions noted for their originality. She was the first woman to conduct at the NY Metropolitan Opera, 1975.

CALEDONIA, Roman name for Britain N of the Antonine Wall, between the firths of Clyde and Forth, roughly corresponding to modern Scotland. The name is now used as a poetic synonym for all Scotland.

CALENDAR, a system for reckoning the passing of time. The principal problem in drawing up calendars arises from the fact that the solar DAY, the lunar MONTH and the tropical YEAR—the most immediate natural time units—are not simple multiples of each other. In practice a solution is found in basing the system either on the phases of the moon (lunar calendar) or on the changing of the SEASONS (solar calendar). The difficulty that the days eventually get out of step with the moon or the seasons is got over by

adding in (intercalating) one or more extra days or months at regular intervals in an extended cycle of months or years. The earliest Egyptian calendar had a year of 12 months with 30 days each, though later 5 extra days were added at the end of each year so that it approximated the tropical year of 365¼ days. In classical times, the Greeks came to use a lunar calendar in which three extra months were intercalated every eight years (the octennial cycle), though, about 432 BC, the astronomer Meton discovered that 235 lunar months fitted exactly into 19 years (the Metonic cycle), this becoming the basis of the modern Jewish and ecclesiastical calendars. The Roman calendar was reformed under Julius CAESAR in 46 BC, fixing the year at 365 days but intercalating an additional day every fourth year (thus giving an average 365¼-day year). The 366-day year is known as a leap year. This Julian calendar continued in use until the 16th century when it had become about 10 days out of step with the seasons, the tropical year in fact being a little less than 365¼ days. In 1582, therefore, Pope GREGORY XIII ordered that 10 days be omitted from that year. Furthermore, century years would no longer be leap years unless divisible by 400, so that there would be no recurrence of any discrepancy. This Gregorian calendar was only slowly adopted, particularly in non-Catholic countries—the reform waiting until 1752 in England and its American colonies, by which time 11 days had to be dropped. But today it is in civil use throughout the world. Various proposals for further reform have come to nothing.

Years are commonly numbered in Western societies from the birth of Christ—as computed by a 6th-century monk. Years since that epoch are labeled AD, years before, BC. There is no year 0, 1 AD following directly from 1 BC. Astronomers, on the other hand, figure years BC as negative numbers one less than the date BC and include a year 0 (=1 BC). The astronomers' year −10 is thus the same as 11 BC. (See also CHRONOLOGY.)

CALGARY, city on the Bow and Elbow rivers in S Alberta, Canada. Famous for the annual 10-day "Calgary Stampede" rodeo, it is a grain and livestock trading center for a rich farming and ranching region. Nearby coal, gas and oil deposits have led to rapid expansion. Pop 403,319.

CALHOUN, John Caldwell (1782–1850), prominent US statesman and lifelong defender of Southern interests. He was a member of the House of Representatives 1811–17; secretary of war to Monroe

1817–25 and a member of the 1812 War Hawks. He was twice vice-president, under Adams (1825–29) and under Jackson (1829–32). Following Congress' 1828 "Tariff of Abominations," seen as an attack on the South, he wrote his *South Carolina Exposition* (1828), expounding the "doctrine of nullification": when a federal law violates the Constitution, a state can consider the law void. In 1832 he resigned the vice-presidency and became a senator for S.C. (1833–43; 1845–50) and secretary of state under Tyler (1844-45). He was fiercely proslavery, calling slavery the "perfect good." He argued against the 1846 WILMOT PROVISO, saying that slaves were property and property could be moved at will. The last 20 years of his life were spent in fighting ABOLITIONISM.

CALIFANO, Joseph (1931–), US public official. As assistant to President Johnson (1965–69) he developed and helped win passage for many liberal "Great Society" programs. As President Carter's secretary of health, education and welfare (1977–79) he administered many of the same programs.

Name of state: California
Capital: Sacramento
Statehood: Sept. 9, 1850 (31st state)
Familiar name: Golden State
Area: 158,693sq mi
Population: 23,668,562
Elevation: Highest—14,494ft, Mt. Whitney, Lowest—282ft below sea level, Death Valley
Motto: Eureka (I have found it)
State flower: Golden poppy
State bird: California valley quail
State tree: California redwood
State song: "I Love You, California"

CALIFORNIA, state SW US, on the Pacific, bounded to the N by Ore., to the W by Nev. and Ariz., and to the S by Mexico. It has the largest state population, and is third largest in area. Its capital is Sacramento, but the most important cities are LOS ANGELES and SAN FRANCISCO. Well over 50% of California's population lives in the Los Angeles-Long Beach and San Francisco-Oakland metropolitan areas. This high percentage of urban population, its sheer size and one of the highest per capita incomes in the US make California an increasingly influential power in national politics.

Land. California's land features are varied, including the Sierra Nevada Mts to the W, the coastal ranges to the E, and the Mojave Desert to the SW. There are occasional earth tremors in California, some caused by the San Andreas fault, which runs two-thirds of the state's length.

People. California has a diverse ethnic population. Before 1849 it was comprised of Indians, Mexicans and Spaniards. The Gold Rush brought an influx of US citizens of European descent, and by 1850 they were the vast majority. Extensive railway and road construction in the 1870s and 1880s brought a large number of Chinese immigrants. By 1900 the Japanese also began to emigrate to California as a labor force. From WWII onwards large numbers of S and E blacks moved to the state. Other significant groups are the Italians, Russians, Filipinos, and Scandinavians and most recently Vietnamese.

The state's system of higher education is constantly expanding. The University of California, founded 1868, moved from Oakland to Berkeley in 1873. Its campuses are located at Berkeley, Los Angeles, Davis, Santa Cruz, Irvine, Riverside, San Diego, Santa Barbara and San Francisco. California has a large number of state and private colleges and universities and a comprehensive system of community and junior colleges.

Economy. Although under 5% of California's population lives on farms, and under 9% of the area is cultivated, intensive irrigation gives California one of the highest state farm incomes. It produces every major US crop except tobacco, has the largest fishing industry, and produces nearly 85% of US wine and 15% of US petroleum. Major manufactures include processed foods, metal goods, machinery, electric and electronic equipment and chemicals. Tourism is also a large industry with primary attractions outside the cities including Sequoia and Yosemite national parks and Disneyland.

History. The Spanish explorer CABRILLO is usually credited with California's discovery. In 1542 he named the present state's area Alta (Upper) California. In 1579 DRAKE ineffectively claimed the area for England, calling it New Albion. The first European settlement was the Spanish San Diego

Franciscan mission and fort (1769). In 1822 the Californians changed their allegiance from Spain to the new Mexican Congress; and later US presidents Jackson (1835) and Polk (1845) unsuccessfully attempted to buy the area. On June 14, 1846, a group of Californian settlers declared the independent Republic of California in the "Bear Flag" revolt against Mexico. A few weeks later, the Mexican-US War broke out, and California was occupied by US forces. In 1848, the postwar Treaty of GUADALUPE HIDALGO ceded the area to the US. It was admitted to the Union as a free state under the COMPROMISE OF 1850 on Sept. 9, 1850. Before that, on Jan. 24, 1848, gold had been discovered on the American R. This caused the 1849 GOLD RUSH and within seven years the state's population leaped from 15,000 to 300,000. The present constitution was adopted in 1879. There have been over 420 amendments: since 1911 these can be proposed by petition and approved by popular vote. Voters can also propose measures through the power of initiative and challenge a new law by calling a referendum.

In recent years, the strong growth of the state's economy and population has continued. Supplying water to the densely populated S part of the state has been a problem for decades, and in 1980 a major and controversial extension of the monumental California Water Project (dating from 1960) was initiated at an estimated cost of $5.1 billion. In 1981, the state, although basically wealthy, faced a fiscal crisis brought on by the reduction of taxes required by Proposition 13, passed in 1978.

CALIFORNIA, UNIVERSITY OF, the largest American state university system, founded 1868. It is housed on nine campuses, the principal one being at Berkeley. One of the world's foremost universities, it boasts a library of more than 10 million items, the Lawrence Radiation Laboratory, the Scripps Institute of Oceanography at La Jolla and the Lick Observatory at Mt Hamilton. More than 130,000 students were enrolled in 1980.

CALIFORNIA TRAIL, trade and travel routes to the early 1850s Cal. goldfield. In particular, the 800mi route from the Oregon Trail near Fort Bridger to Sutter's Fort near Sacramento. Now part of highways 26, 30, 40 and 50.

CALIGULA (12–41 AD), nickname (meaning "little boots") of Roman Emperor Gaius Caesar, 37–41 AD. He was insanely cruel and despotic and believed he was a god. He reputedly planned to make his horse a consul. His demands that his statue be erected in Jerusalem's temple almost precipitated a revolt in Palestine. He was assassinated by a tribune of his guard.

CALIPHATE (Arabic: *khalifa*, successor), highest office in ISLAM. Early caliphs were the successors of MOHAMMED. They were the rulers of the Muslim community throughout the world and guardians of Islamic law. In 632 AD the Muslims of Medina elected Abu Bakr as first caliph. He was succeeded by Omar (634–44), the first caliph to adopt the title "commander of the faithful." Omar was murdered, as were Othman (644–56) and Ali (656–61). The OMAYYAD dynasty of caliphs then ruled from Damascus until 750, when the Shiite Muslims, descendants of Ali who had always claimed their right to the caliphate, massacred the Omayyad family. However, Abd-al-Rahman escaped, fled to Spain, and established an independent emirate at Cordoba which lasted from 750 to 1031. Meanwhile, the Shiite Muslims established the ABBASID family in the caliphate. They ruled from Baghdad until it was sacked by the Mongols in 1258. A puppet Abbasid caliphate also continued in Egypt from 909 until 1520. Until the fall of the Ottoman Empire the Turkish sultans used the title. The caliphate was abolished in 1924 by ATATURK.

CALLAGHAN, (Leonard) James (1912–   ), Prime Minister of the UK 1976–79. He was elected Labour party leader on the resignation of Harold WILSON and became prime minister immediately. Labour lost the 1979 general election to Margaret Thatcher's Conservatives.

CALLAGHAN, Morley Edward (1903–   ), Canadian novelist and short story writer, with a powerful, precise style influenced by HEMINGWAY. His books include the novel *They Shall Inherit the Earth* (1935) and a memoir, *That Summer in Paris* (1963).

CALLAO, city and seaport capital of Callao province, W Peru, near Lima. Founded in 1537 by Francisco PIZARRO, it is the country's main port, handling over 50% of its foreign trade. Pop 296,220.

CALLAS, Maria (1923–1977), leading Greek–American operatic soprano, born Maria Kalogeropoulos. She was famous for her expressive phrasing and acting ability in a wide variety of roles in over 40 operas.

CALLICRATES, Greek architect of the 5th century BC who collaborated with Ictinus and Phidias on the PARTHENON. He is credited with the temple of Athena Nike, which is also on the Athenian acropolis.

CALLIGRAPHY, the art of penmanship. Combining beauty with legibility, it evolved in the Far East, where it was a recognized art form as early as 250 BC. In early medieval Europe calligraphy was practiced in monastic communities, which developed the Carolingian and Insular scripts. A high point was reached with the BOOK OF KELLS and the LINDISFARNE gospels. The superb Italian Renaissance manuscripts provided models for the first printed books and roman and italic types. The Englishman Edward Johnston (1872–1944) and his pupil Graily Hewitt (1864–1952) began the remarkable modern revival of calligraphy in the early 1900s.

CALLIMACHUS (c310–240 BC), Greek poet, grammarian and critic, leading member of the Alexandrian school. Only six hymns and 64 epigrams of his poetry survive. He also produced the *Pinakes*, the earliest work of systematic bibliography, now lost.

CALLIOPE, keyboard instrument dating from 1855 and much used in circuses and amusement parks. The original version was operated by steam forced through whistles controlled by a keyboard, but later models used compressed air.

CALLISTHENES (c360–328 BC), Greek historian, nephew of Aristotle. The official chronicler of ALEXANDER THE GREAT'S Asian expedition, he criticized Alexander's adoption of Oriental customs and was thrown into prison, where he died. None of his works have survived.

CALLOT, Jacques (c1592–1635), French graphic artist, whose 1,500 etchings and engravings are among the greatest of their kind. The two series called *Miseries of War* (1633) are considered his greatest achievement; they were inspired by the Thirty Years' War and seek to depict its horrors. He also produced numerous light, playful works during his residence at the Florentine Medici Court. REMBRANDT and WATTEAU, among others, benefited from Callot's example, and his technical innovations greatly refined engraving techniques.

CALLOWAY, Cabell ("Cab") (1907–), US singer and bandleader. Known as the "King of Hi De Ho," he was famous for *Minnie the Moocher*, and for his versions of *St. James Infirmary Blues* and *Ain't Misbehavin'*. He also starred in the 1930s in George Gershwin's *Porgy and Bess*.

CALLUS, or Callosity. See CORNS AND CALLUSES.

CALMETTE, Albert Léon Charles (1863–1933), French bacteriologist who with C. GUÉRIN discovered the BCG

(bacillus Calmette-Guérin) vaccine, which has greatly reduced the incidence of TUBERCULOSIS.

CALORIC THEORY OF HEAT, the view, formalized by LAVOISIER toward the end of the 18th century, that heat consists of particles of a weightless, invisible fluid, caloric, which resides between the atoms of material substances. The theory fell from favor as physicists began to appreciate the equivalence of WORK and HEAT.

CALORIE, the name of various units of HEAT. The calorie or gram calorie (c or cal), originally defined as the quantity of heat required to raise 1g of water through $1C°$ at 1 atm pressure, is still widely used in chemical THERMODYNAMICS. The large calorie, kilogram calorie or kilocalorie (Cal or kcal), 1000 times as large, is the "calorie" of dietitians. The $15°$ calorie (defined in terms of the $1C°$ difference between $14.5°C$ and $15.5°C$) is 4.184 joules; the International Steam Table calorie (cal_{IT}) of 1929, originally defined as 1/860 watt-hour, is now set equal to 1.1868J in SI UNITS.

CALOTYPE METHOD, in photography. See TALBOT, WILLIAM HENRY FOX.

CALVARY, or Golgotha, Jerusalem hill site of the crucifixion of Jesus. Although archaeologists are not agreed, it is traditionally accepted to be the hill on which Constantine founded the Church of the Holy Sepulcher in the 4th century.

CALVERT, English Roman Catholic family which founded and owned colonial Maryland. **George, 1st Baron Baltimore** (c1580–1632), occupied various public offices until 1625. He founded Ferryland, Newfoundland, in 1621, and lived there 1627–29. Seeking a warmer climate, he petitioned for a grant in N Virginia (present-day Md.), for which King Charles I granted a charter to his son Cecil in 1632. **Cecil (or Cecilius), 2nd Baron Baltimore** (c1605–1675), never visited Md., and left its administration to his younger brother **Leonard Calvert** (1606–1647). In 1649, the colony's Act of Toleration was the first practical expression of the principle of freedom of conscience in the New World. **Charles, 3rd Baron Baltimore** (1637–1715), son of Cecil, was governor of Md. from 1661, governed the colony in person 1679–84 and then returned to England. In 1689 his Md. administration was overthrown by a Protestant rebellion, and in 1691 the Crown withdrew his authority to govern.

CALVIN, John (1509–1564), French theologian and reformer. He studied in Paris, and was converted to Reformation doctrines c1533, becoming prominent in the reforming party. He was forced to flee to Basel, where he published his *Institutes of the Christian Religion* (1536). Guillaume FAREL persuaded him to help establish the Reformation in Geneva. They enforced subscription to a confession of faith, but were expelled from the city in 1538. Calvin joined Martin BUCER at Strassburg. Geneva recalled him in 1541, and, despite controversy, he set up a church polity which became the paradigm for PRESBYTERIANISM and the REFORMED CHURCHES. Despite fragile health, Calvin worked unceasingly in preaching, lecturing and advising in the city councils, and aided foreign Protestant refugees. On his death, his work was continued by Theodore BEZA. (See also CALVINISM; REFORMATION.)

CALVINISM, the theological system of John CALVIN. Its key principle is that God, not man, is central and supreme. Hence scripture is the source of doctrine. Calvin's *Institutes of the Christian Religion* is a systematic account of biblical teaching, with much in common with early LUTHERANISM, including JUSTIFICATION BY FAITH, PREDESTINATION, assurance of SALVATION, and denial of FREE WILL since the Fall. One distinguishing feature is the view that in Holy COMMUNION the believer participates in Christ in heaven by faith. Calvinism became the doctrine of the REFORMED CHURCHES, which developed Calvin's theology in a scholastic fashion, elevating PRESBYTERIANISM to a major principle, and emphasizing the divine decrees and COVENANTS. Calvinism has been influential in the CHURCH OF ENGLAND (see THIRTY-NINE ARTICLES), among the PURITANS and nonconformists, and in the EVANGELICAL REVIVAL. Recently Karl BARTH has popularized a modified Calvinism. (See also ARMINIANS; DORT, SYNOD OF; HUGUENOTS; REFORMATION.)

CALVINO, Italo (1923–), Italian writer notable for his use of fantasy. Calvino has written in several genres, including science fiction and historical allegory, but received his greatest acclaim for *Italian Folktales* (1956; repr. 1980) and the experimental *If on a Winter's Night a Traveler* (1979; trans. 1981).

CALYPSO, a West Indies musical style notable for its lyrics, which are usually improvised and often humorous or ironic. The music is typically played on steel drums, which carry the tune as well as provide the beat. Calypso was first popularized in the US by Harry BELAFONTE.

CAMBODIA. See KAMPUCHEA.

CAMBODIAN "INCURSION." On April 30, 1970, President NIXON announced that 70,000 US and South Vietnamese troops had begun an attack on North Vietnamese "sanctuaries" in Cambodia; he said that this was "not an invasion" since the areas were already under North Vietnamese control. This widening of a war that the president had previously said he was ending inspired many demonstrations in the US, and led to the tragic KENT STATE SHOOTING on May 4. In the Senate, on June 30, the same day that the return of the troops was announced, an amendment was passed barring the use of funds to support future military action in Cambodia without the express approval of Congress. This was the first such curtailment of a president's wartime powers. The next year, the US supplied only air and artillery support for a similar operation in Laos (official objections were made when broadcasters called the 44-day operation an "invasion").

CAMBRAI, Battle of, first major British WWI tank offensive (Nov. 20, 1917) and successful German counterattack (Nov. 30) at Cambrai, N France. The battle emphasized the tank's striking power, but also the necessity to consolidate territorial gains.

CAMBRIAN, the earliest period of the PALEOZOIC Era (see GEOLOGY), dated roughly 570–500 million years ago, and immediately preceding the ORDOVICIAN. Cambrian rocks contain the oldest FOSSILS that can be used for dating (see PRECAMBRIAN).

CAMBRIDGE, county town of Cambridgeshire, England, home of a famous university (see CAMBRIDGE, UNIVERSITY OF). On the Cam R 48mi NNE of London, it is a center for British scientific research as well as being a commercial center. The city has many fine medieval buildings. Pop 98,519.

CAMBRIDGE, city in Mass., on the Charles R opposite Boston, seat of HARVARD UNIVERSITY (founded 1636), Radcliffe College and the Massachusetts Institute of Technology. It became the site of America's first printing plant in 1639 and was the place where Washington took command of the Continental Army in 1775. Pop 195,322.

CAMBRIDGE, University of, one of the world's leading universities, at Cambridge, England. Its history dates from c1209, and its first college, Peterhouse, was established in 1284. Today, the university is coeducational, and has about 9,000 students. It has a total of 29 colleges and approved societies, and is a self-governing body, with authority vested in its senior members.

CAMBRIDGE PLATONISTS, an influential group of philosophers centered on the U. of Cambridge in the mid-17th century, founded by Benjamin Whichcote and including Henry More and Ralph Cudworth. Their philosophy was Platonist, their outlook was tolerant and one of their chief aims was the reconciliation of faith with scientific knowledge and rational philosophy.

CAMELOT, court of King ARTHUR and the Knights of the Round Table in ARTHURIAN LEGENDS. It has been identified variously with Caerleon (Wales), Camelford (Cornwall) and South Cadbury (Somerset), where excavations have taken place.

CAMELS, two species of haired, cud-chewing animals with humped backs, long necks and callosities on knee joints. The one-humped or Arabian camel, or dromedary, *Camelus dromedarius*, of N Africa and the Near East is a widely-kept domestic animal which has even been introduced into desert regions of Australia. The two-humped or Bactrian camel, *C. bactrianus* is found from Asia Minor to Manchuria, and there are still a few living wild in the Gobi Desert. Recorded as being domesticated in Babylonia from about 1100 BC, the animals are invaluable in the desert since they can carry enormous loads and are able to withstand the loss of about one-third of their body fluid without danger (not, however, exclusively from their humps, which are fatty tissue, not water storage vessels).

CAMERA, device for forming an optical image of a subject and recording it on a photographic film or plate or (in TELEVISION CAMERAS) on a photoelectric mosaic. The design of modern cameras derives from the ancient camera obscura, represented in recent times by the pinhole camera. This consists of a light-tight box with a small hole in one side and a ground-glass screen for the opposite wall. A faint image of the objects facing the hole is formed on the screen and this can be exposed on a photographic plate substituted for the screen.

Although the image produced in the pinhole camera is distortion-free and perfectly focused for objects at any distance, the sensitive materials used when photography was born in the 1830s required such long exposure times that the earliest experimentalists turned to the already available technology of the LENS as a means of allowing more light to strike the plate. From the start cameras were built with compound lenses to overcome the effects of chromatic aberration (see ABERRATION,

OPTICAL) and the subsequent history of camera design has seen constant improvement in lens performance.

Today's simple camera consists of a light-tight box, a fixed achromatic lens, a simple shutter, a view finder and a film support and winding mechanism. The lens will focus all subjects more than a few feet distant and the shutter (usually giving an exposure of $\frac{1}{30}$ or $\frac{1}{50}$) admits sufficient light to expose negative materials on a sunny day. If exposures are to be made for reversal processing (see PHOTOGRAPHY) or of close-by or rapidly moving subjects, or in poor light, a more complex camera is required. This may include a movable lens perhaps coupled to a RANGE FINDER (allowing the precise focusing of objects at different distances), a variable diaphragm (aperture) and shutter-speed mechanism (allowing adjustment to meet a wide range of light conditions) perhaps coupled to an exposure meter (LIGHT METER), a flash synchronization unit (allowing use of a flash gun) or a facility for interchangeable lenses (allowing the photographer to alter the width of the camera's field of view). With the advent of the MICROPROCESSOR, some cameras for amateurs have come to include refinements that leave little adjusting for the user to do.

Special types of camera include those that produce a finished print within seconds; the earliest of these was the Polaroid Land camera, first marketed by its inventor, E. H. LAND, in 1948. Another special camera is the stereo camera, which takes two pictures from slightly different points to create an illusion of depth when one picture is seen with each eye. Motion picture cameras take 24 successive photographs per second on a long reel of film (see MOTION PICTURES).

CAMERA LUCIDA AND CAMERA OBSCURA, simple optical devices which assist artists in drawing faithful reproductions of distant scenes, plans and diagrams or microscopic specimens. The principle of the **camera obscura** was known to ARISTOTLE; light admitted through a small hole into a darkened chamber projects a real image of the scene outside on the opposite wall. Later versions have used LENSES and MIRRORS to give an evenly-illuminated horizontal image. The **camera lucida,** invented in 1807 by WOLLASTON, employs a four-sided prism to allow the artist to see a virtual image of an object in the plane of the paper on which he copies the image. It is of particular use in enlarging or reducing artwork and in drawing from the MICROSCOPE.

CAMERON, Simon (1799–1889), US

politician. He built a powerful political machine in Pa., was a US senator (1845–49; 1857–61; 1867–77) and served as secretary of war under Lincoln (1861–62). His career was marked by considerable scandal and corruption.

CAMEROON, republic adjoining Nigeria and five other countries, stretching from the Gulf of Guinea to Lake Chad in W Africa.
Land. The coastal plain is about 10–50mi wide, dominated by Cameroon Mountain. The S region is a densely forested 1,000ft plateau. Fertile grasslands lie in the central region, which rises to the N, where the vegetation changes from forest to savanna. The arid far north slopes down to Lake Chad. The entire country is tropical. In the S region, average annual temperatures are 70°F–82°F. The S has two rainy seasons; rainfall in some parts of the coastal plains can be excessive, while in the N, scant.
People. The population is ethnically diverse. In the S are aboriginal pygmies and Bantu farmers, settled in villages; in the N are various Bantu, Sudanese, Hamite and Arab nomads. Some 11% of the population is urban, the main towns being Douala and Yaoundé. Illiteracy is high (85%), though 65% of primary-school-age children attend school; the Federal University at Yaoundé has 2,400 students.
Economy. The economy is based mainly on agriculture and forestry. Manioc, millet, sorghum and rice are grown for home consumption, and cattle and sheep are raised. Coffee, cocoa and timber are the main exports. Industry has been developed since independence, and includes textiles, food processing and aluminum smelting. Trade is mainly with France. Cameroon's road network is growing but not yet well-developed. Douala is the major seaport.
History. The Sao people, who produced a distinctive kind of art and cast objects in bronze, settled near Lake Chad about 900s AD. The Portuguese came in the 1400s. In 1884 Germany established a protectorate in the Cameroon area. British and French troops occupied the area during WWI, after

which the League of Nations mandated the larger part to France (Cameroun) and the remainder to Britain (Southern and Northern Cameroons). In 1946 the territories became UN trust territories. In 1960 Cameroun became an independent republic. After plebiscites in 1961 N Cameroons joined Nigeria, and S Cameroons joined Cameroun to form the Federal Republic of Cameroon. In 1972 the federal system was abandoned in favor of a unitary republic. In 1980 Ahmadou Ahidjo, president since independence, was reelected.

CAMÕES (CAMOËNS), Luís Vaz de (1524–1580), Portugal's greatest poet. His epic poem, *The Lusiads* (1572), is a celebration of Portuguese historical glory. Inspired by the AENEID, it centers around the voyages of Vasco da GAMA. Much of the rest of his poetry was published posthumously, in 1595.

CAMORRA, Italian secret society started in the Kingdom of Naples c1830. Although it specialized in extortion, smuggling, robbery and assassination, it was often used by the authorities, and it became very powerful. After unification with Italy in 1861 attempts were made to suppress it, but it survived until 1911.

CAMP, Walter Chauncey (1859–1925), the father of American FOOTBALL. As a player and coach at Yale U. (1876–92) and Stanford U. (1894–95), Camp helped initiate, implement and develop many of the changes that turned European RUGBY into American football.

CAMPANELLA, Roy (1921–   ), US baseball player. He caught for the Brooklyn Dodgers 1948–57 and was the National League's Most Valuable Player in 1951–53 and 1955. An automobile accident in 1958 left him paralyzed.

CAMPBELL, Alexander (1788–1866), US clergyman, founder of the DISCIPLES OF CHRIST (Campbellites). The Disciples were formed after a split between Campbell's congregation and the Baptist Church in 1830. He also founded Bethany College in Bethany, W. Va., in 1840.

CAMPBELL, Mrs. Patrick (1865–1940), English actress. Popular on stage for over 40 years, she created many classic roles, including Eliza Doolittle in Shaw's *Pygmalion* (1914), a part written for her. She is also remembered for her famous correspondence with Shaw.

CAMPBELL, Sir Malcolm (1885–1949), British racing driver, the first racer to average more than 300mph (Bonneville Salt Flats, Ut. 1935). He set three successive water-speed records, finally attaining

141.74mph in 1939. His son, **Donald Malcolm Campbell** (1921–1967), set a water-speed record of 276.33mph in 1964, but was killed trying to establish a new record. All the vehicles of both father and son were called *Bluebird*.

CAMPBELL-BANNERMAN, Sir Henry (1836–1908), British prime minister 1905–08 and leader of the LIBERAL party from 1899. A member of the House of Commons from 1868 until his death, he held offices under Gladstone. He pursued a progressive policy: established old-age pensions, granted self-government to the Transvaal and the Orange Free State and attempted to end the veto power of the House of Lords.

CAMP DAVID, the woodland camp in the Catoctin mountains in Maryland near Washington, D.C., that has been used by presidents ever since F. D. ROOSEVELT as a retreat, workplace and environment to receive foreign dignitaries. It was called Shangri-La until EISENHOWER renamed it after his grandson, David. Composed of a number of log cabin-like structures snuggled in the mountain scenery, it nevertheless has all the communications and transportation facilities necessary for the work of the president.

CAMP DAVID AGREEMENT, a peace treaty worked out at CAMP DAVID by Egyptian President Anwar SADAT and Israeli Prime Minister Menachem BEGIN with the assistance of President Jimmy CARTER and signed in 1979. Some of the treaty's provisions were: a timetable for a phased withdrawal from the Egyptian Sinai by Israel to be concluded by 1982, mutual diplomatic recognition and setting up a framework for attempting to solve the Palestinian question. The peace process began with Sadat's historic trip to Jerusalem in 1977.

CAMP FIRE GIRLS, recreational and educational organization for girls from 7 to 18. Founded in 1912 and active in more than 20 countries, it aims to perpetuate the spiritual ideals of the home through homemaking, community projects, sports, study programs and outdoor activities.

CAMPHOR, a white crystalline compound distilled from the wood and young shoots of the camphor tree (*Cinnamomum camphora*). Camphor has a strong characteristic odor which repels insects. It is also used medicinally—internally as an anodyne and antispasmodic and externally in linaments. In large doses it is a narcotic poison.

CAMPIN, Robert (1378–1444), Flemish painter best known for his religious paintings. His art reflects the influence of manuscript illumination, though with a keener sense of plasticity in rendering the forms. One of his major works is the triptych of the Annunciation (c1428) known as the *Mérode Altarpiece*. Eager to depict in realistic detail the daily life of the rising bourgeoisie, Campin became a founder of the Netherlandish school, influencing Jan VAN EYCK and Roger Van der WEYDEN, among others.

CAMPION, Saint Edmund (c1540–1581), martyred English JESUIT. After a conversion to Roman Catholicism he entered the Society of Jesus in 1573. In 1580 he joined the first mission of Jesuits to England. He was arrested as a spy in 1581, tortured and executed. He was canonized in 1970.

CAMPION, Thomas (1567–1620), English poet, composer and physician. He is best known for his four books of *Ayres*, his lyric poetry and the controversial "attack" on rhyme, *Observations in the Art of English Poesie* (1602).

CAMPO FORMIO, Treaty of, agreement made between France and Austria on Oct. 17, 1797, giving France domination over N Italy and Austria's Belgian provinces; and Austria, Venice and its territories. A secret clause also pledged Austria to cede the left bank of the Rhine to France.

CAMUS, Albert (1913–1960), French novelist, essayist, dramatist and philosopher. Through fiction and reflective essays he communicated his vision of man in an absurd universe. He felt that the only true possibility for freedom and dignity lay in the awareness of this absurdity. His major works include the essay *The Myth of Sisyphus* (1942), which elucidated the philosophical basis of his novel *The Stranger* (1942). Other important works are the novels *The Plague* (1947) and *The Fall* (1956), the essay *The Rebel* (1951) and the play *Caligula* (1944). He won the Nobel Prize for Literature in 1957.

CANAAN, early name for PALESTINE, probably meaning Land of the Purple—from the purple dye made in the area. The region was inhabited from the second millennium by Semitic peoples, mainly AMORITES, whose script provides the earliest known alphabet. Their culture was a mixture of Egyptian, Mesopotamian and many other influences. During the 13th century BC Canaan was occupied by the Israelites (see JEWS), though in the next century its coasts were taken by the PHILISTINES. The latter were subdued by King David (1000–961 BC), who extended Israelite rule over all Canaan.

CANADA, country in North America, largest in the W hemisphere and second-largest in the world after the USSR. Ironically it derives its name from *Kanata*, a Huron-Iroquois word meaning a small village. It is bounded on the E by the Atlantic Ocean, on the N by the Arctic Ocean, on the W by the Pacific Ocean and Alaska, and on the S by its 3987mi border with the US.

Canada comprises 10 provinces (Newfoundland, Prince Edward Island, Nova Scotia, New Brunswick, Quebec, Ontario, Manitoba, Saskatchewan, Alberta and British Columbia) and the Yukon and Northwest Territories. It is a Commonwealth country in which the British Crown is represented by a governor-general. The federal capital is Ottawa.

Land. Canada is basically a vast, stepped plain bordered on the W by the Rocky Mts, on the SE by the Appalachians and on the NE by the U-shaped CANADIAN SHIELD formation of old and worn rocks, covering about half Canada. In the S, bordering the Great Lakes, is the Ontario Peninsula, and farther E are the fertile St. Lawrence lowlands and the rolling valleys and uplands of Appalachian Canada. Around the center of the Shield are the lakes and muskegs of the Hudson Bay lowlands.

The Canadian Rockies have at least 30 peaks above 10,000ft, but Canada's highest mountain, Mt Logan (19,850ft) is in the St. Elias Mts in the Yukon. There are three major drainage systems, the Great Lakes-St. Lawrence, the Saskatchewan-Red-Nelson rivers system and the Mackenzie, Canada's longest river (2,635mi). Climate is mainly influenced by distance from the sea and distance north; it runs to extremes. Winters are usually long and cold, though milder on the W and SW coasts. Southern summers are usually warm. Rainfall is heaviest in the W and snowfall heaviest in the E. Vegetation ranges from the tundra of the N to mainly coniferous forest, mixed woodlands and prairie grasslands.

People. Canada's population is predominantly of British or French stock, though it includes many of German, Italian, Ukrainian, Dutch and other origins. Indians number about 288,000 and Inuit (Eskimos) about 17,000. Of the total population, 67% speak only English, 18% speak only French, 13.5% are bilingual and 1.5% speak neither. Both French and English are official languages, but the majority of new immigrants prefer to learn English. Population is concentrated in the S part of the country, the most populous provinces being Ontario, Quebec and British Columbia. About 76% of Canadians are

urban, with Ontario the most urbanized of the provinces and Prince Edward Island the least. The largest urban areas are Toronto, Montreal, Vancouver, Ottawa, Winnipeg, Edmonton, Quebec and Hamilton.

Government. Canada has a parliamentary system of government, with executive power vested in a prime minister and cabinet. The federal legislature comprises a Senate of 104 appointed members and a House of Commons whose 282 members are elected for a 5-year term. Each of the 10 provinces has its own premier and elected legislature. The Yukon and Northwest Territories are governed by federally appointed commissioners and elected councils, and each sends one representative to the federal parliament.

Economy. During the present century Canada has emerged as a major manufacturing country and in the early 1980s was far more urban and industrial than rural and agricultural. Two-thirds of all manufacturing plants are located in Ontario and Quebec. Agriculture, however, remains important, ranking first in terms of employment and providing about 11% of Canada's total exports. Canada is one of the world's chief wheat producers, but also grows other grains, oilseeds, fruit (especially apples), vegetables and tobacco. Beef and dairy cattle, hogs, sheep and poultry are reared. Forestry and fisheries are major industries, and Canada remains a leading source of furs, both farmed and trapped. Mineral resources are rich and include petroleum and natural gas, molybdenum, platinum, copper, nickel, iron ore, zinc, lead, silver, gold, asbestos, elemental sulfur and coal. Oil and natural gas are produced mainly in Alberta and Saskatchewan, and are actively being sought in the MacKenzie delta. Abundant energy is provided by hydroelectric and thermal power plants, and several nuclear power plants are operating. Major hydroelectric installations are located on Niagara, St. Lawrence, Ottawa, St. Maurice, Saguenay, Bersimis, Manicouagan, Churchill, Peace and Columbia Rs; and there is great potential for further development in the N as the technology for long-distance transmission is improved.

In 1979 manufacturing accounted for about 20% of all employment. In terms of manufacturers' shipments the leading products were automobiles. Other important products include nonferrous metals, machinery, chemicals, plastics, electrical equipment and textiles. Among Canada's chief trading partners are the US, Britain, Japan, West Germany, Netherlands,

China, Venezuela and the USSR.

History. Visited by 11th-century Vikings, Canada was later penetrated by explorers such as John CABOT, Jacques CARTIER and Samuel de CHAMPLAIN. The French founded Quebec in 1608 and made Canada the royal colony of New France (1663). Anglo-French rivalry culminated in the cession of New France to Britain (Treaty of PARIS, 1763). French rights were guaranteed by the QUEBEC ACT (1774). Only one serious revolt against British rule took place (1837–38), consisting of separate uprisings led by W. L. MACKENZIE in Upper (English-speaking) Canada and Louis PAPINEAU in Lower (French-speaking) Canada. The British North America Act (1867) established Canada as a dominion, the four founding provinces being Quebec; Ontario, Nova Scotia, and New Brunswick. The others entered later: Manitoba (1870), British Columbia (1871), Prince Edward Island (1873), Saskatchewan (1905), Alberta (1905) and Newfoundland (1949). The Northwest Territories, formerly administered by the Hudson's Bay Company, became a federal territory in 1870, and the Yukon was made a separate territory in 1898. Separatist tensions, centering on Quebec, developed particularly during the 1960s and continued into the 1980s. Efforts began in 1978 to amend the British North America Act in order to "repatriate" the Canadian constitution.

Official Name: Canada
Capital: Ottawa
Area: 3,560,238sq mi
Population: 23,914,000
Languages: English, French
Religions: Roman Catholic, United Church of Canada, Anglican
Monetary Unit(s): 1 Canadian dollar = 100 cents

CANADA ACT, British parliamentary act of 1791, also known as the Constitutional Act, which divided the country into Upper and Lower Canada—thus providing a rough territorial separation of French- and English-speaking settlers, each with their own elected legislature.

CANADA GOOSE, *Branta canadensis,* a large migratory bird common to North America, Greenland and parts of Asia. It is recognizable by its long black head and neck and distinctive white cheek bars and is known for its habit of flying in group formations.

CANADIAN BROADCASTING COR-PORATION (CBC), public corporation created in 1936 by the Canadian Broadcasting Act, distributing national network programs through publicly and privately owned radio and television stations throughout Canada.

CANADIAN FOOTBALL, game resembling US FOOTBALL, but differing in the following ways: There are 12 men on a team, not 11; the extra player is a flanker on offense, a halfback on defense. Each team has three, rather than four, downs to gain 10 yds. There is no fair catch when receiving a kick. One point is scored by the punting team if the receivers are unable to move the ball out of the end zone, which is 25 yds deep, as against 10 in US football. The field size is 110 by 65 yds. as against 100 by 53 1/3 in the US game. All backs may be in motion, and no time-outs are allowed.

CANADIAN SHIELD, or **Laurentian Shield,** that area of North America (including the E half of Canada and small portions of the US) which has remained more or less stable since PRECAMBRIAN times. Its surface rocks, which are igneous and metamorphic (see IGNEOUS ROCK; METAMORPHIC ROCK), are amongst the oldest in the world, younger structures having disappeared through EROSION, in some areas by the PLEISTOCENE Epoch.

CANALETTO (1697–1768), born Antonio Canal, 18th-century Venetian painter preeminent in the depiction of architectural vistas. His best-known works, such as *View of the Grand Canal,* are scenes of Venice notable for their sense of spaciousness and light combined with very fine detail. He lived in London 1746–56, and painted many English views of similar quality. His very numerous drawings and etchings are also highly esteemed.

CANALS, man-made waterways used for transportation, drainage and IRRIGATION. They represent one of mankind's earliest attempts to change the environment to suit his convenience. As early as 521 BC a precursor of the Suez Canal joined the Nile to the Red Sea. In China, the Ling Ch'u Canal was completed during the 3rd century BC and the Grand Canal, joining the Paiho, Yellow and Yangtze rivers, had sections in use by the 7th century AD. The Romans built many canals to supply their cities with water and canalized a number of European rivers to create an empire-wide transportation system. AQUEDUCTS were widely used long before Roman times to carry water across roads and valleys, but it was the development of the lock which allowed canals to cross other terrain. By the 15th century this simple device for raising boats from one land level to another was already in use, and one of its inventors, LEONARDO DA VINCI, built several canals with locks near the city of Milan.

Although one of the great engineering projects of the 19th century, the SUEZ CANAL to the Red Sea, was built entirely without locks, the other great international waterway, the PANAMA CANAL, would not have been possible without them. Locks allowed a canal transport system to be built across England and Europe from the 16th century onwards. In North America, the canal system included the ERIE CANAL, completed in 1825 to link the Hudson R to Lake Erie and, more significantly, to provide an opening to the Middle West. The Welland Canal, opened in 1828 between Lake Erie and Lake Ontario, was the next step in an inland waterway transportation network completed by the opening of the ST. LAWRENCE SEAWAY, of which it is now a part, in 1959.

CANARIS, Wilhelm (1887–1945), German admiral, head of military intelligence under the Nazi regime. Involved in conspiracies against Hitler for years, he was arrested after the assassination attempt of July 1944 and executed in April 1945.

CANARY, name of several small song birds, particularly a finch native to the Canary Islands. The wild canary is usually gray or green in color, but tame birds have been bred to produce the characteristic "canary yellow." The birds have been kept and bred in Europe since the 16th century and are valued for their lovely song.

CANARY ISLANDS, group of volcanic islands in the Atlantic, about 65mi off the NW coast of Africa. Comprising two Spanish provinces, the main islands are Tenerife, Palma, Gomera, Hierro, Grand Canary, Fuerteventura and Lanzarote; their land area is nearly 3,000sq mi. Main industries are fishing, farming and tourism; Las Palmas and Santa Cruz are the principal ports. They were called "insulae canariae," or "islands of the dogs," by the Romans. The name passed on to the native wild finch, or CANARY. Pop 1,170,224.

CANASTA, a variation of RUMMY for two to six players. It originated in Argentina, and became very popular in the US in the 1950s.

CANAVERAL, Cape, promontory on the E coast of Fla., site of the John F. Kennedy Space Center, named Cape Kennedy 1963–73. It became famous with the launching of the first US satellite, Explorer I, in 1958; and first manned lunar exploration in 1969. The cape was established as a national seashore in 1975.

CANBERRA, federal capital city of the Commonwealth of Australia, built from 1913 onwards in the Australian Capital Territory. Australia's largest inland city, it is located on a plain about 1,900ft above sea level. There are various light industries, but the economy rests mainly on the public service and governmental departments. Pop 241,300.

CANBY, Henry Seidel (1878–1961), US editor, author and literary critic. Canby founded the *Saturday Review of Literature* in 1924 and was its editor until 1936. He also wrote biographies of *Thoreau* (1939) and *Walt Whitman* (1945) and an autobiography, *American Memoir* (1947).

CANCER, a group of diseases in which some body cells change their nature, start to divide uncontrollably and may revert to an undifferentiated type. They form a malignant TUMOR which enlarges and may spread to adjacent tissues; in many cases cancer cells enter the BLOOD or LYMPH systems and are carried to distant parts of the body. There they form secondary "colonies" called **metastases**. Such advanced cancer is often rapidly fatal, causing gross emaciation. Cancer may present in very many ways—as a lump, some change in body function, bleeding, ANEMIA or weight loss—occasionally the first symptoms being from a metastasis. Less often tumors produce substances mimicking the action of HORMONES or producing remote effects such as NEURITIS.

Cancers are classified according to the type of tissue in which they originate. The commonest type, **carcinoma**, occurs in glandular tissue, SKIN, or visceral linings. **Sarcoma** occurs in connective tissue, MUSCLE, BONE and CARTILAGE. **Glioma** is a sarcoma of BRAIN neuroglia, unusual in that it does not spread elsewhere. **Lymphoma**, including HODGKIN'S DISEASE, is a tumor of the lymphatic system (see LYMPH); LEUKEMIA can be regarded as a cancer of white blood cells or their precursors. The cause of cancer remains unknown, but substantial evidence points to damage to or alteration in the DNA of CHROMOSOMES. Certain agents are known to predispose to cancer including RADIOACTIVITY, high doses of X RAYS and ULTRAVIOLET RADIATION and certain chemicals, known as **carcinogens**.

These include tars, oils, dyes, ASBESTOS and tobacco smoke (see SMOKING). A number of cancers are suspected of being caused by a VIRUS and there appear to be hereditary factors in some cases.

Prevention of cancer is mainly by avoiding known causes, including smoking, excess radiation and industrial carcinogens. People suffering from conditions known to predispose to cancer need regular surveillance. Treatments include surgical excision, RADIATION THERAPY, CHEMOTHERAPY, or some combination of these. The latter two methods destroy cancer cells or slow their growth; the difficulty is to do so without also damaging normal tissue. They have greatly improved the outlook in lymphoma and certain types of leukemia. Treatment can be curative if carried out in the early stages, but if the cancer has metastasized, therapy is less likely to succeed; all that may be possible is the relief of symptoms. Thus, if cure is sought, early recognition is essential.

CANCER (the Crab), a spring constellation in the N Hemisphere, the fourth sign of the ZODIAC. At the time the zodiacal system was adopted, Cancer marked the northernmost limit of the ECLIPTIC. A hazy object near the center of Cancer is a cluster of stars named Praesepe, the Beehive.

CANDLEMAS, feast of the Purification of the Virgin Mary and the presentation of Jesus in the Temple, on Feb. 2. It takes its name from the consecration of church candles before the mass of the day. Groundhog Day falls on the same date.

CANETTI, Elias (1905–   ), Bulgarian-born author of prose and plays in the German language. Major works include the novel *Auto da Fé* (1935) and the political study *Crowds and Power* (1960). He received the 1981 Nobel Prize for Literature.

CANIFF, Milton (1907–   ), US cartoonist who created two of the most popular action-adventure comic strips: *Terry and the Pirates*, set in China, and *Steve Canyon*, about an Air Force captain who fought in Korea and later Vietnam.

CANNABIS. See HEMP; MARIJUANA.

CANNES, French resort and seaport on the Mediterranean coast, in the Alpes Maritime department. Its superb climate makes it a center for tourism and festivals, notably the annual International Film Festival. Pop 71,100; met pop 258,500.

CANNIBALISM, or **anthropophagy**, consumption by humans of human flesh, common throughout the world at various times in the past and still occasionally practiced, though now generally TABOO. Among PRIMITIVE MAN the motive appears to be belief that eating an enemy or a respected elder transfers to the eater the strength, courage or wisdom of the dead.

CANNING, the process of preserving foods in sealed metal containers, developed by the French chef Nicolas Appert in 1809 and first patented in the US by Ezra Daggett in 1815. The fragile glass jars originally used were replaced by tin-coated iron cans after 1810. Today, a production line process is used. The food may reach the cannery a few hours after picking; it is first cleaned, and then prepared by removing inedible matter. After it has been peeled, sliced or diced as necessary, the food is blanched: hot water and steam are used to deactivate enzymes that might later spoil the flavor and color, and to shrink the product to the desired size and weight. The cans are then filled and heated to drive out dissolved gases in the food and to expand the contents, thus creating a partial vacuum when they are cooled after sealing. Finally, the cans are sterilized, usually by steam under pressure. (See also FOOD PRESERVATION.)

CANNING, George (1770–1827), British statesman. As foreign secretary 1822–27 (following an earlier tenure, 1807–09), he opposed the HOLY ALLIANCE, pledged support for the independence of the Spanish American colonies (thus making possible the MONROE DOCTRINE) and secured Greek independence. He became prime minister in 1827, but died shortly afterwards.

CANNON, term used loosely of early ARTILLERY, though some modern devices are still described as cannon. Cannon were present at the Battle of Crécy (1346) but not until the 15th century did artillery power become of note. Early cannon were muzzle-loaded, GUNPOWDER being pushed down the barrel, followed by a pad of material (often cloth), then the stone or metal ball. Flame applied to a touchhole at the rear of the barrel set off the gunpowder. Important developments were increasing maneuverability; the invention of breech-loading; rifling (see RIFLE) of the barrel; and use of explosive AMMUNITION. (See EXPLOSIVES; GUN.)

CANNON, Annie Jump (1863–1941), US astronomer who classified and catalogued more than 225,000 stars during her career at the Harvard College Observatory (1897–1940).

CANNON, Joseph Gurney (1836–1926), US legislator and speaker of the US House of Representatives 1903–11. Elected to the House by Ill. in 1872, he served for 46 years. As speaker, his arbitrary partisan rules became known as "Cannonism," and he had a dictatorial control of the House which was only finally curtailed when he was excluded from the rules committee in 1910.

CANO, Juan Sebastiàn del (1476–1526), Basque seaman who commanded the first ship to circumnavigate the globe (1521), after MAGELLAN's death.

CANOE, long, narrow lightweight boat used on lakes and rivers, today mainly for recreation. The first canoes were made from hollowed-out logs; now they are made from canvas, thin wood, fiberglass and aluminum, often weighing no more than 50 pounds. They are 11ft to 20ft long with a beam of about 3ft, drawing about 1ft of water.

CANON, form of musical composition based on the repeated imitation of the initial theme at specified time intervals. Rounds (such as *Three Blind Mice*) are the commonest form. The oldest known canon, composed during the 13th century, is *Sumer is icumen in* (Summer is coming).

CANON, Biblical, books accepted as part of the Bible and usually considered to have divine authority. The Jewish Old Testament canon was completed by the 1st century AD, and St. ATHANASIUS compiled the oldest canonical list of the New Testament in the 4th century.

CANONIZATION, the process by which a Christian church declares a deceased person to be a saint. In the Roman Catholic Church the process involves a long and careful investigation of the individual's life and reputation for sanctity, heroic virtue and orthodoxy. There is also a scrutiny of miracles reputedly effected by the candidate when alive or after death.

CANON LAW, the body of ecclesiastical laws (canons) governing the organization, administration and discipline of a church, most fully developed in the Roman Catholic Church. In the 12th century GRATIAN, a Benedictine monk, compiled the first systematic collection of canon law, based on papal decrees and the proclamations of SYNODS. It was reinforced by further compilations under Pope PIUS X in 1904 and completed under Pope BENEDICT XV in 1917. It contains 2,414 canons.

CANONSBURG, industrial borough in Pa., 20mi SW of Pittsburgh, producing electrical transformers, metal products and pottery. Pop 11,439.

CANOPIC JARS, covered vessels in which, in ancient Egypt, the embalmed viscera removed during mummification (see MUMMY) were placed for burial. After c1000 BC the embalmed viscera were more generally replaced in the mummy and these jars rarely used.

CANOVA, Antonio (1757–1822), Italian sculptor, a leading exponent of Neoclas-

sicism. His works include *Cupid and Psyche* (1787–92), several statues of his patron Napoleon, and a famous statue of Pauline Bonaparte Borghese as the reclining *Venus Victrix* (1808).

CAN PHUMO. See LOURENÇO MARQUES.

CANSO, Strait of, strait between Cape Breton Island and the Canadian mainland, 1mi wide at its narrowest point.

CANTABRIAN MOUNTAINS, Spanish mountain chain running 300mi from the Pyrenees along the N coast. The highest peak is Torre de Cerredo (8,787ft). There are rich iron and coal deposits.

CANTATA (from Italian *cantare*, to sing), originally a piece of music sung, as opposed to one played instrumentally; now, any work for voices and instruments. Beginning in Italy (1620) the form also developed in France and Germany. One of the earliest composers in this form was Giacomo CARISSIMI, but more famous exponents were Alessandro SCARLATTI, who wrote nearly 700 cantatas, and J. S. BACH, who wrote over 300.

CANTERBURY, city and county borough of Kent, on the Stour R 55mi SE of London. It was England's ecclesiastical capital from 597AD and the archbishop of Canterbury is Primate of All England. Canterbury has many notable buildings, including the cathedral (where Thomas à BECKET was murdered in 1170), a Norman castle and Kent U. Pop 118,600.

CANTERBURY BELL, *Campanula medium,* a cultivated biennial plant, which produces white, blue, pink or violet, bell-shaped flowers from May to July. (See also BELLFLOWER.)

CANTERBURY TALES, the best-known work of the English poet Geoffrey CHAUCER, written between 1387 and his death in 1400. In 17,000 lines (mostly heroic couplets) it describes a party of 30 pilgrims going to the shrine of St. Thomas à Becket, and their plan to tell four tales each on the journey. Only 24 tales were written, 4 of them unfinished, but the work presents a vivid cross-section of medieval society and the tales cover most medieval literary genres.

CANTICLE, a liturgical song similar to a psalm but based on a passage from elsewhere in the Bible. More recently the name has been given to any short choral work with a religious content.

CANTICLE OF CANTICLES. See SONG OF SOLOMON.

CANTINFLAS (Mario Moreno; 1911-   ), Mexican comic actor whose films were box-office hits throughout the Spanish-speaking world. His US films include *Around the World in 80 Days*

(1956) and *Pepe* (1960).

CANTON (Kuang-chou or Guangzhou), largest city in S China, capital of Kuang-tung (Guangdong) province, on the Pearl R about 75mi from Hong Kong. It is the chief seaport and the commercial and industrial center of the area, producing newsprint, textiles, machinery, chemicals, rubber and matches, and also processing many agricultural products. It has been a trading center since the 2nd century AD and was the first to trade with Europeans, in the 16th century. Pop 3,100,000.

CANTOR, a singer or chanter in a church or synagogue. The Jewish cantor of *hazan* chants the prayers, but early Christian cantors not only led the singing but soon took charge of all music used in the services, a duty now performed in Anglican cathedrals by the *precentor.*

CANTOR, Eddie (1892–1964), US comedian and song-and-dance man, born Edward Israel Iskowitz. He began his stage career in 1907, and created a character familiar in radio, television and films for several decades.

CANTOR, Georg Ferdinand Ludwig Philip (1845–1918), German mathematician who pioneered the theory of infinite sets (see SET THEORY).

CANUTE II THE GREAT (Cnut or Knut; c995–1035), king of England, Denmark and Norway, son of King Sweyn of Denmark. His victory at Ashingdon (1016) won him all England N of the Thames R. Edmund II Ironside's death gave him the south. He succeeded his brother Harold in Denmark (1019), seized the throne of Norway (1028) and was recognized as Scotland's overlord. His attempt to hold back the sea is apocryphal.

CANVAS, heavy woven cloth (see TEXTILES) usually made of cotton or linen fibers, used for centuries as sailcloth, and now also for tents, bags, shoes, hammocks, outdoor chairs, coverings, etc. It can be water-proofed (see WATERPROOFING). Artists' canvas is made of finer material specially treated to take paint.

CANVASBACK, *Aythya vallisneria,* a diving duck found in coastal and inland waters of North America, about 600mm (2ft) long and 1.4kg (3.1lb) in weight. It feeds on aquatic plants, shrimps and small fish.

CANYON DE CHELLY NATIONAL MONUMENT, in the Navaho Reservation, NE Ariz., established in 1931 to preserve the ruins of ancient Indian cliff-dwellings. It was an Indian stronghold against first the Spanish, and then the US army.

CANYONLANDS NATIONAL PARK, in

E Ut., established in 1964. It covers an area of 337,258 acres and contains much remarkable scenery, including red rock canyons, stone needles, arches and rapids, and also rock carvings.

CAPA, Robert (born Andrei Friedmann, 1913–1954). Hungarian-born US photographer, a pioneer of journalistic photography, notably in the Spanish Civil War and the WWII Normandy landings.

CAPACITOR, or **condenser,** an electrical component used to store electric charge (see ELECTRICITY) and to provide REACTANCE in alternating-current circuits. In essence, a capacitor consists of two conducting plates separated by a thin layer of insulator. When the plates are connected to the terminals of a BATTERY, a current flows until the capacitor is "charged," having one plate positive and the other negative. The ability of a capacitor to hold charge, its capacitance C, is the ratio of quantity of electricity on its plates, Q, to the potential difference between the plates, V. The electric energy stored in a capacitor is given by $\frac{1}{2}CV^2$. The capacitance of a capacitor depends on the area of its plates, their separation and the DIELECTRIC constant of the insulator. Small fixed capacitors are commonly made with metal-foil plates and paraffin-paper insulation; to save space the plates and paper are rolled up into a tight cylinder. Some small capacitors have a MICA dielectric. Variable capacitors used in RADIO tuners consist of movable intermeshing metal vanes separated by an air gap. In electrolytic capacitors, the dielectric is an oxide film formed on the plates by the action of a solid ELECTROLYTE. They must be connected with the correct polarity.

CAPE BRETON ISLAND, in NE Nova Scotia, 110mi long, up to 75mi wide, separated from the Canadian mainland by the Strait of Canso (since 1955 joined by a causeway). Local industries include tourism, lumbering, fishing and the mining of coal and gypsum.

CAPE COD, peninsula in Barnstable Co., SE Mass., 65mi long, up to 20mi in width, site of the first Pilgrim landing in 1620. Shipping, whaling, fishing and salt production were early industries; today the cape is famous for its cranberries, and its summer resorts such as Provincetown and Hyannis.

CAPE COD CANAL, a 17½mi long channel across CAPE COD (Mass.), privately built (1909–14) and bought by the US Government in 1927. One of the most heavily used toll-free waterways, it shortens the New York City–Boston route by 75mi.

CAPE HATTERAS, a promontory lying

30mi off the N.C. coast and long known as "the graveyard of the Atlantic" because of its rocky shoals.

CAPE HORN, lower tip of South America, known for its cold, stormy climate. Part of Chile, the cape's bare headland lies well S of the Strait of Magellan on Horn Island.

CAPEK, Karel (1890–1938), Czech writer whose works, known for their humor and anti-authoritarian stand, include the plays *R.U.R.* (*Rossum's Universal Robots*, 1920) and *The Insect Play* (1921) and the novel *War with the Newts* (1936).

CAPE LOOKOUT NATIONAL SEASHORE, area of 28,400 acres in SE N.C., the oustanding headland S of Cape Hatteras, established as a national seashore in 1966. Noted for its lighthouse, beaches and bird life.

CAPE OF GOOD HOPE, rocky promontory near the S tip of Africa, 30mi S of CAPE TOWN, chief navigational hazard in rounding Africa. It was discovered by Bartholomew DIAZ in 1488, who named it Cape of Storms. Vasco da GAMA first sailed around it in 1497 into the Indian Ocean.

CAPETIANS, ruling house of France (987–1328) which, by consolidating and extending its power, laid the basis for the French state. HUGH CAPET, founder of the dynasty, was elected king in 987. Though his rule and territory were limited, his successors gradually increased their land and control. Under the Capetian dynasty many basic administration characteristics of the French monarchy were established, including Parliament and the States General.

CAPE TOWN, (Kaapstad), legislative capital of South Africa and capital of Cape of Good Hope province. Founded by the Dutch East India Company in 1652, it has a pleasant climate, excellent beaches and attractive scenery, and the country's largest harbor. Among its major exports are gold, diamonds, fruits, wines, skins, wool, mohair and corn. Pop 691,296.

Official name: Republic of Cape Verde
Capital: Praia, on the island of São Tiago
Area: 1,557sq mi

Population: 315,000
Languages: Portuguese, Creole
Religion: Roman Catholic

CAPE VERDE, independent nation in Africa, lies in the Atlantic Ocean some 400m W of Senegal.

Land. Cape Verde consists of 10 islands and 5 islets, forming a 1500sq mi horseshoe. The islands are volcanic and only about 20% of the land is cultivable. The climate is tropical, with a rainy season, although recently there has been severe cyclical drought.

People and Economy. Over half of the population is of Portuguese and African extraction. Living standards and the rate of literacy are low. Despite a paucity of fertile land, the country is primarily agricultural. However, most food must be imported. The fishing industry provides the major source of exports. Canned fish, salt, bananas and frozen fish are the primary exports, most going to Portugal.

History. The Portuguese discovered the islands in the 15th century. Cape Verde became a supply station for ships and a transit point during the Atlantic slave trade. Blacks from Guinea were taken to the islands to work on Portuguese plantations. Portugal ruled the islands until 1975, when the islands became independent. Cape Verde and GUINEA-BISSAU are politically and culturally close.

CAPILLARIES, minute BLOOD vessels concerned with supplying OXYGEN and nutrients to and removing waste products from the tissues. In the LUNGS capillaries pick up oxygen from the alveoli and release carbon dioxide. These processes occur by DIFFUSION. The capillaries are supplied with blood by ARTERIES and drained by VEINS.

CAPILLARITY, the name given to various SURFACE-TENSION phenomena in which the surface of a liquid confined in a narrow-bore tube rises above or is depressed below the level it would have if it were unconfined. When the attraction between the molecules of the liquid and those of the tube exceeds the combined effects of gravity and the attractive forces within the liquid, the liquid rises in the tube until Equilibrium is restored. Capillarity is of immense importance in nature, particularly in the transport of fluids in plants and through the soil.

CAPITAL, in economics, those goods which are used in production—such as plant and equipment (*fixed capital*) and raw materials, components and semifinished goods (*circulating capital*)—as opposed to goods intended for immediate consumption. To classical economists, capital was one of three main factors of production, the others being labor and land. Modern economists include "management skill" and "human capital," i.e. education and training. The problem being to find the most profitable combination of resources in the manufacture of goods, the decision to invest in capital is determined by the cost and availability of labor and natural resources, and the cost of capital (e.g. interest on the money used to buy equipment). Other factors, such as the state of the market, are also important. Modern industrial countries are highly capitalized, but, among the less developed countries, the lack of capital is often acute.

CAPITALISM, the economic system in which goods and services are provided by the efforts of private individuals and groups who own and control the means of production, compete with one another and aim to make a profit. Historically, first merchants, then factory owners and finally bankers have been dominant in the system, though, as defined by Lenin, the predominance of the state within the system is possible. Capitalism is defended by the argument that private ownership and FREE ENTERPRISE, with a minimum of state interference, is the most efficient method of operating the economy; its critics argue that the system produces luxuries for the rich rather than necessities for all.

CAPITAL PUNISHMENT, (from Latin *caput*, or head), referring originally to death by decapitation and now to execution in general. Historically, there has been a wide variety of death penalties, but in the US electrocution is the most common, followed by lethal gas and hanging. Capital punishment has long been a center of debate as to whether it deters serious crime or is only a form of revenge. Its use has been declining recently as belief in rehabilitation has grown. In most civilized countries, capital punishment has been discontinued. But those who believe that capital punishment is necessary as a deterrent see their argument supported by recent statistics showing that violent crime has been increasing.

CAPITOL, The, federal government building in Washington, D.C. which houses the US Congress. The Capitol, in classical style, was built on 3½ acres of high ground known as Capitol Hill in Washington's center. Designed by William Thornton in 1792, its construction began the next year when President Washington laid the cornerstone. The Senate occupies the N wing (completed 1800), and the House of Representatives the S wing (completed 1807). The building was severely damaged by the British in 1814. After its reconstruction (completed 1863) no significant alterations were made until 1958–62, when the E facade was extended 32½ feet.

CAPONE, Al (1899–1947), US gangster, born in Naples, became head of a lucrative Chicago crime syndicate, and was involved in many gang murders, including the St. Valentine's Day Massacre. Because of the difficulty in securing evidence against him he was eventually convicted only of income tax evasion.

CAPORETTO, Battle of (Oct.–Dec. 1917), major defeat of Italian military forces during WWI in NW Yugoslavia. The 600,000 Italian troops, weary after a 2½ year stalemate, either deserted or surrendered to the Austrian-German forces. The defeat caused Italy's allies to send reinforcements and eventually establish a unified Allied command.

CAPOTE, Truman (1924–   ), US writer known especially for *Breakfast at Tiffany's* (1958) and the "non-fiction" crime novel *In Cold Blood* (1965). His earlier works include *Other Voices, Other Rooms* (1948) and *The Grass Harp* (1951).

CAPP, Al (1909–1979), US cartoonist who created the immensely popular comic strip *Li'l Abner* (1934), which featured Abner Yokum, his buxom girlfriend Daisy Mae and their Dogpatch, Kentucky, relatives and neighbors. Li'l Abner was featured in a movie (1940) and Broadway musical (1956; film 1959).

CAPPADOCIA, a mountainous region of central Anatolia, Turkey, watered by the Halys R. A satrapy of the Persian Empire, it became a semi-independent kingdom under Ariarathes III. Caesarea Mazaca was its chief city.

CAPPADOCIAN FATHERS, term applied to three theologians from Cappadocia (BASIL THE GREAT, GREGORY OF NYSSA and GREGORY OF NAZIANZUS) who had great influence in shaping theological doctrine in the second half of the 4th century.

CAPRA, Frank (1897–   ), US film director and three-time Academy Award winner. With a gift for gentle satire and comic improvisation, he directed, among other films, *Mr. Deeds Goes To Town* (1936), *You Can't Take It With You* (1938) and *Lost Horizon* (1937).

CAPRI, Italian island resort in the Bay of Naples, site of the Villa Iovis of Roman Emperor TIBERIUS. Capri produces olive oil and wine, but its main industry is tourism. Anacapri, at the island's W end, is approachable from the sea by hundreds of steps, called the "Phoenician Stairs."

CAPRICORNUS (the Sea Goat), a fairly inconspicuous constellation of the S Hemisphere, lacking any bright stars, and the tenth sign of the ZODIAC. Lying between AQUARIUS and SAGITTARIUS, Capricornus in ancient times lay at the southernmost limit of the ECLIPTIC.

CAPRIVI STRIP, strip of land 40mi wide in Namibia or South West Africa, running E some 300mi between Angola and Zambia on the N and Botswana on the S. Formerly part of German South West Africa (1890–1919).

CAPUCHINS, Roman Catholic order of friars and an independent branch of the Franciscans. Founded (1525) by Matteo di Basico, a Franciscan who sought a return to the simplicity of St. Francis' life, the order is distinguished by the pointed hood, or *capuccino*.

CAPYBARAS, two species of the world's largest RODENT, living in South America. Like a large guinea pig, it can weigh up to 54kg (119lb) and be as high as 540mm (21.3in) at the shoulder.

CARACALLA (188–217 AD), or Marcus Aurelius Antoninus, son of Septimius SEVERUS, tyrannical Roman emperor (211–217) notable for his edict (212) granting Roman citizenship to all freemen of the Empire. He left the magnificent baths in Rome that bear his name.

CARACAS, Venezuelan capital, near the Caribbean Sea at an altitude of 3,020ft, founded in 1567 by Diego de Losada, and the birthplace of Simón BOLÍVAR in 1783. Independence from Spain was achieved in 1821, as part of the Republic of Gran Colombia. In 1829 Caracas became the capital of independent Venezuela.

After WWII and the discovery of oil in Maracaibo, Caracas greatly expanded. Industries include textiles, cement, steel products, paper, leatherwork and furniture. Pop 2,576,000.

CARAMANLIS, Constantine (1907–), Greek premier (1955–63, 1974–80) and president (1980–). Following a dispute with then King Paul, he resigned as premier and went into exile in Paris (1963). He returned eleven years later when the military junta ruling Greece fell because of the Cyprus crisis. He helped restore constitutional government and his party, New Democracy, won a big victory in 1975. The republican form of government he advocated was also approved and in 1980 he was elected president.

CARAT, a unit of MASS used for weighing precious stones. Since 1913 the internationally accepted carat has been the metric

carat (CM) of 200mg. The purity of GOLD is also expressed in carats (usually spelled "karat" in the US). Here one karat is a 24th part; thus, pure gold is 24-karat; "18-karat gold" contains 75% gold and 25% other NOBLE METALS, and so on.

CARAVAGGIO, Michelangelo Merisi da (1573–1610), Italian Baroque painter who achieved startling and dramatic effects with an interesting technique of shadow and light, called CHIAROSCURO. Among his finest works are the *Death of the Virgin* and *Supper at Emmaus*.

CARBOHYDRATES, a large and important class of ALIPHATIC COMPOUNDS, widespread and abundant in nature, where they serve as an immediate energy source; cellulose is the chief structural material for plants. Most carbohydrates have chemical formulas $(CH_2O)_n$ and so were named as hydrates of carbon—which, however, they are not. Systematic names of carbohydrates end in –ose. They are generally divided into four groups, the simplest being the **monosaccharides** or simple SUGARS and the **disaccharides** or double sugars. The **oligosaccharides** (uncommon in nature) consist of three to six monosaccharide molecules linked together. The **polysaccharides** are POLYMERS, usually homogeneous, of monosaccharide units, into which they are broken down again when used for energy. The main plant polysaccharides are CELLULOSE and STARCH; in animals a compound resembling starch, GLYCOGEN, is formed in the muscles and liver. Other polysaccharides include AGAR, ALGIN, CHITIN, DEXTRIN, GUM acacia, INSULIN and PECTIN. Carbohydrates play an important role in food chains (see ECOLOGY): they are formed in plants by PHOTOSYNTHESIS, and are converted by ruminant animals into PROTEIN. They also form one of the major classes of human FOOD (see NUTRITION). In Europe and the US they provide a third to a half of the calories in the diet, of which starch and the various sugars supply about half each. In less developed countries carbohydrates, especially starch, are even more important.

CARBON (C), nonmetal in Group IVA of the PERIODIC TABLE. It is unique among elements in that a whole branch of chemistry (ORGANIC CHEMISTRY) is devoted to it, because of the vast number of compounds in its forms. The simple carbon compounds described below are usually regarded as inorganic.

Carbon occurs in nature both uncombined (COAL) and as CARBONATES, carbon dioxide in the atmosphere, and PETROLEUM. It exhibits ALLOTROPY, occurring in three

contrasting forms: DIAMOND, GRAPHITE and "white" carbon, a transparent allotrope discovered in 1969 by subliming graphite. So-called amorphous carbon is actually microcrystalline graphite; it occurs naturally, and is found as COKE, CHARCOAL and **carbon black** (obtained from the incomplete burning of petroleum, and used in pigments and printer's ink, and to reinforce rubber). Amorphous carbon is widely used for ADSORPTION, because of its large surface area. A new synthetic form is carbon fiber, which is very strong and is used to reinforce plastics to make electrically-conducting fabrics.

Carbon has several ISOTOPES: C^{12} (used as a standard for ATOMIC WEIGHTS) is much the most common, but C^{13} makes up 1.11% of natural carbon. C^{10}, C^{11}, C^{14}, C^{15} and C^{16} are all radioactive. C^{14} has the relatively long half-life of 5730yr, and is continuously formed in the atmosphere by COSMIC RAY bombardment; it is used in RADIOCARBON DATING.

The element (especially as diamond) is rather inert, but all forms will burn in air at a high temperature to give carbon monoxide in a poor supply of oxygen, and carbon dioxide in excess oxygen. Fluorine will attack carbon at room temperature to give carbon tetrafluoride, and strong oxidizing agents will attack graphite. Carbon will combine with many metals at high temperatures, forming carbides. Carbon shows a covalency of four, the bonds pointing toward the vertices of a tetrahedron, unless multiple bonding occurs. AW 12.011.

Carbides, binary compounds of carbon with a metal, prepared by heating the metal or its oxide with carbon. Ionic carbides are mainly acetylides (C_2^{2-}) which react with water to give ACETYLENE, or methanides (C^{4-}) which give METHANE. There are also metallic interstitial carbides, and the covalent boron carbide (B_4C) and silicon carbide (see CARBORUNDUM). **Carbon Dioxide** (CO^2), colorless, odorless gas. It is nontoxic, but can cause suffocation. The air contains 0.03% carbon dioxide, which is exhaled by animals and absorbed by plants (see RESPIRATION; PHOTOSYNTHESIS; CARBON CYCLE). Carbon dioxide is prepared in the laboratory by reacting a CARBONATE with acid; industrially it is obtained by calcining LIMESTONE, burning coke in excess air, or from FERMENTATION. At atmospheric pressure, it solidifies at $-78.5°C$ to form "dry ice" (used for refrigeration and CLOUD seeding) which sublimes above that temperature; liquid carbon dioxide, formed under pressure, is used in fire extinguishers.

Carbon dioxide is also used to make carbonated drinks. When dissolved in water an equilibrium is set up, with CARBONATE, BICARBONATE and HYDROGEN ions formed, and a low concentration of **Carbonic Acid** (H_2CO_3). **Carbon Disulfide** (CS_2), colorless liquid, of nauseous odor due to impurities; highly toxic and flammable. Used as a solvent and in the manufacture of rayon and CELLOPHANE. mp$-111°C$, bp 46°C, sg 1.261 (22°C). **Carbon Monoxide** (CO), colorless, odorless gas. It is produced by burning carbon or organic compounds in a restricted supply of oxygen, for example, in poorly ventilated stoves, or the incomplete combustion of gasoline in AUTOMOBILE engines. It is manufactured as a component of WATER GAS. It reacts with the halogens and sulfur, and with many metals, to give carbonyls. Carbon monoxide is an excellent reducing agent at high temperatures, and is used for smelting metal ores (see BLAST FURNACE; IRON). It is also used for the manufacture of METHANOL and other organic compounds. It is a component of manufactured gas, but not of natural gas. Carbon monoxide is toxic because it combines with hemoglobin, the red BLOOD pigment, to form pink carboxyhemoglobin, which is stable, and will not perform the function of transporting oxygen to the tissues. mp$-199°C$. **Carbon Tetrachloride** (CCl_4), colorless liquid, nonflammable but toxic, made by chlorinating carbon disulfide. Used as a fire extinguisher, a solvent (especially for dry-cleaning) and in the manufacture of FREON. mp $-23°C$. bp 77°C. (See also CYANIDES; CYANOGEN.)

CARBONARI (Italian: charcoal burners), members of a revolutionary secret society in 19th-century Italy. Although originally formed to restore the Bourbons to Naples, the Carbonari later instigated many revolts against conservative regimes in Italy. The name was also used by French, Spanish and Portuguese revolutionaries.

CARBON BLACK. See CARBON.

CARBON CYCLE, in biology, a very important cycle by which carbon, obtained from the atmosphere as carbon dioxide, is absorbed by green plants, synthesized into organic compounds and then returned to the atmosphere as carbon dioxide. The organic compounds, particularly CARBOHYDRATES, are synthesized in plants from carbon dioxide and water in the presence of CHLOROPHYLL and light by a process known as PHOTOSYNTHESIS. The carbohydrates are then broken down to carbon dioxide and water either by the plant during RESPIRATION or after death by putrefying BACTERIA and FUNGI. (See also PLANT.)

CARBON CYCLE, or carbon-nitrogen cycle, in physics, the chain of nuclear FUSION reactions, catalyzed by CARBON nuclei (see CATALYSIS), which is the main source of ENERGY in the hotter STARS, though of minor importance in the SUN and cooler stars where proton–proton fusion is the chief reaction. Overall, four PROTONS are converted to one ALPHA PARTICLE, with destruction of some matter and consequent evolution of energy (see RELATIVITY). Most of the gamma-radiation produced is absorbed within the star, and energy is released as heat and light. The carbon cycle was first described by Hans BETHE.

$$_6C^{12} + {}_1H^1 \rightarrow {}_7N^{13} + \gamma$$
$$_7N^{13} \rightarrow {}_6C^{13} + e^+ + \nu$$
$$_6C^{13} + {}_1H^1 \rightarrow {}_7N^{14} + \gamma$$
$$_7N^{14} + {}_1H^1 \rightarrow {}_8O^{15} + \gamma$$
$$O^{15} \rightarrow {}_7N^{15} + e^+ + \nu$$
$$N^{15} + H^1 \rightarrow {}_2He^4 + {}_6C^{12}$$

CARBONIFEROUS, collective term used mainly in Europe for the combined MISSISSIPPIAN and PENNSYLVANIAN periods of the geologic time scale.

CARBORUNDUM, or silicon carbide (SiC), black, cubic crystalline solid, made by heating COKE with SILICA in an electric furnace. It is almost as hard as DIAMOND (whose structure it resembles), and hence it is used as an abrasive. It is inert, refractory and a good heat conductor, so is used in making high–temperature bricks; at high temperatures it is a SEMICONDUCTOR. subl 2700°C (with decomposition).

CARBURETOR, an important element in most automobile engines, the carburetor mixes air and GASOLINE in the correct ratio for most efficient combustion (usually about 15:1, air:gasoline, by weight). Most simply, a carburetor has a tube constricted at one point into a narrow throat, or VENTURI. The speed of air flowing through the venturi increases and hence its pressure decreases: fuel from a reservoir (the float chamber) is therefore sucked in through a hole, or jet, at this point. The fuel mixture then passes through a throttle valve, which controls the rate at which the mixture enters the engine and hence the engine speed. A CHOKE in the air-intake regulates the air supply and thus the richness of the mixture. In practice, carburetors incorporate various means of ensuring constancy of mixture strength during running. High-performance engines may use more than one carburetor or a FUEL INJECTION system. (See also INTERNAL-COMBUSTION ENGINE.)

CARCINOGENS. See CANCER.

CARCINOMA. See CANCER.

CARDANO, Girolamo (1501–1576), Italian physician and astrologer, chiefly remembered for his contributions to mathematics. He was responsible for the first systematic theory of possibilities.

CÁRDENAS, Lázaro (1895–1970), Mexican soldier and politician. He joined the Mexican revolutionary forces in 1913, rising to the rank of general. President 1934–40, he initiated many radical reforms, including the expropriation of land and nationalization of foreign-owned oil companies.

CARDIGAN, James Thomas Brudenell, 7th Earl of (1797–1868), British general in the CRIMEAN WAR, who led the charge against the Russians at Balaklava in which the Light Brigade was destroyed. A vain and quarrelsome man, he is remembered as an incompetent commanding officer.

CARDIN, Pierre (1922–   ), French fashion designer. The first to offer collections for both men and women, he is known for his use of synthetic fabrics. His designs influenced the "unisex" and "space age" trends in fashion.

CARDINAL, hierarchically high-ranking official of the Roman Catholic Church, whose principal duties include the election of the pope, counseling the papacy and administrating Church government. Cardinals are chosen by the pope, and have the title of Eminence. Their insignia consists of scarlet cassock, sash, biretta (skullcap) and hat, and a ring.

There are three orders: *cardinal bishops* of the sees near Rome; *cardinal priests* (cardinal archbishops) with responsibilities outside the district of Rome; and *cardinal deacons*, who have been titular bishops since 1962. Cardinal bishops and cardinal deacons are members of the CURIA, the central administrative body of the Church. They head the *tribunals*, the courts of the Church. Together, the cardinals form the Sacred College, which elects the pope. The cardinalate originated in early 6th-century Rome. The term cardinal is derived from Latin *cardo*, meaning hinge, reflecting the essential working relationship between this institution and the papacy.

CARDINAL NUMBER, one that describes the number of elements in a SET. For example, in the phrase "my 3 oranges," 3 is a cardinal number. (See also ORDINAL NUMBER; **TRANSFINITE** CARDINAL NUMBER.)

CARDOZO, Benjamin Nathan (1870–1938), US jurist and Supreme Court justice (1932–38) after an impressive career at the bar and in the N.Y. courts. He believed that the courts should not merely interpret the law but help create it, particularly in adapting it to changing social conditions.

His many significant decisions reflect this view.

CARDS. See PLAYING CARDS.

CARDUCCI, Giosuè (1835–1907), Italian scholar and patriotic poet. His *Hymn to Satan* (1863) is an anticlerical, political satire; the *Barbarian Odes* (1877–89) are perhaps his best work. He won the 1906 Nobel Prize for Literature.

CARE (Cooperative for American Relief to Everywhere, Inc.), a charity founded in 1945, initially for aid to Europe but now operating worldwide. MEDICO (Medical International Cooperation Organization), a medical relief agency, became part of CARE in 1962.

CAREW, Thomas (c1594–1640), English poet and lyricist, in later life a courtier of CHARLES I. His verse, influenced by DONNE, combines a light "cavalier" style with metaphysical elements. He remains best known for his long amatory poem *The Rapture.*

CAREY, Hugh (1919–   ), US political leader. A lawyer, he served in the US House of Representatives 1961–75. As Democratic governor of New York (1975–   ), he supported economic austerity in the wake of lavish public-works spending by his predecessors.

CAREY, James Barron (1911–1973), US labor leader, past president of the United Electrical, Radio and Machine Workers (UEW) (1936–41) and founder and president of the International Union of Electrical, Radio and Machine Workers (IUE) from 1950 to 1965.

CARGO CULTS, religious movements common among the natives of New Guinea and Melanesia, who believe that, by aping in ritual the European society they do not understand, they can persuade supernatural powers to give them European material wealth—"cargo." Often worshiping John Frum, a messianic figure, the cults have even involved building airstrips to receive the "cargo."

CARIBBEAN SEA, a warm oceanic basin bordered by Central America to the E, South America to the S, and the West Indies to the N and E. The GULF STREAM originates here. The construction of the Panama Canal from 1881 increased trade and traffic in the area.

CARIB INDIANS, inhabitants of the Caribbean before the Spanish conquest, living in the Lesser Antilles and parts of South America. They were farmers and formed villages presided over by headmen. Persistent raiders of other tribes, they ate their captives. The Caribs were practically exterminated after the Spanish settlement,

apart from a few on the island of Aruba. Some descendants survive among the area's population today.

CARIBOU, *Rangifer tarandess,* the only member of the DEER family (Cervidae) in which both sexes bear antlers. They were at one time essential food animals for the Canadian Indians. They live wild in Canada and Siberia, while the semi-domesticated reindeer of the same family live in Greenland and Scandinavia. They can travel over boggy or snow-covered ground and they live on lichen, dry grass and twigs.

CARICATURE AND CARTOON. A caricature is a sketch exaggerating or distorting characteristics of its subject for satirical purposes; generally used of pictures, the term may also describe literary works. Caricature became an established form by the 18th century, in the hands of GOYA in Spain and HOGARTH in England, followed by ROWLANDSON, CRUIKSHANK and TENNIEL, and the savagely witty DAUMIER in France. It occasionally proved a powerful means of communication. NAST'S political caricatures helped topple the Tweed Ring and TAMMANY HALL in New York after the Civil War. Today, artists such as David LEVINE and Albert HIRSCHFELD continue the tradition in the US.

Cartoons are related to, and often contain, caricature. Originally meaning a preparatory sketch, the term derives from a series of architectural 'cartoons' parodied by *Punch* magazine in 1843. Today it also includes the COMIC STRIP, the political cartoon and cartoon ANIMATION. The cartoon has been increasingly adopted as an art form by POP ART. Prominent US cartoonists have included Charles ADDAMS, Al CAPP, Charles SCHULTZ, Walt KELLY and HERBLOCK.

CARIES, decay or softening of hard tissues, usually TEETH, but also used for BONE, especially spinal TUBERCULOSIS. Dental caries is bacterial decay of dentine and enamel (see TEETH), hastened by sugary diet and poor oral hygiene. Fluoride in small quantities protects against caries.

CARILLON, musical instrument, usually permanently set in a bell-tower, consisting of an accurately-tuned series of bells on which tunes can be played from a keyboard and pedal console. It originated in the Netherlands and is very popular in the US today. Electronic carillons create bell tones artificially.

CARLETON, Sir Guy (1724–1808), British soldier and governor-general of Quebec. He was responsible for the QUEBEC ACT of 1774 which guaranteed the French the right to speak French and to practice their religion.

During the American Revolution, he led the defense of Quebec against Bénedict ARNOLD and later captured Crown Point, N.Y. In 1782 he was appointed commander-in-chief of the British army in North America; he was several times governor-general of Canada.

CARLISTS, Spanish supporters of the claim of Don Carlos (1788–1855) and his successors to the Spanish throne. They were part of the Falange during the Spanish Civil War. The present pretender is Prince Carlos Hugo de Bourbon-Parma.

CARLOTA (1840–1927), empress of Mexico, wife of Archduke MAXIMILIAN of Austria. When NAPOLEON III stopped supporting Maximilian as emperor, she returned to Europe to seek other assistance, but failed. Not long before Maximilian's execution she went mad and spent the rest of her life in seclusion in Belgium.

CARLSBAD CAVERNS, a series of underground caves in SE N.M. The caverns consist of a three-level chain of limestone chambers studded with magnificent stalactites and stalagmites. They were discovered in 1901 and are millions of years old. The main chamber is 4,000ft long and in places 300ft high; there are over 40mi of explored passages.

CARLYLE, Thomas (1795–1881), Scottish historian and philosopher. His famous *French Revolution* (1837) is a vivid but idiosyncratic presentation of the event rather than a factual account. Believing that man's progress was due to individual "heroes," he scorned egalitarianism, always extolling the right of the stronger. Many of his books, such as *Sartor Resartus* (1833–39), *On Heroes* (1841) and *Past and Present* (1843), are still read, but as literature rather than history.

CARMEL, Mount, mountain ridge extending into the sea in N Israel. The city of Haifa is at its foot. Carmel is often mentioned in the Old Testament, especially in connection with Elijah. Early Christian hermits lived in caves in the area.

CARMELITES, Friars of Our Lady of Mount Carmel, a religious order of the Roman Catholic Church. It is named for Mount Carmel, in Israel, where it originated about 1150. The Carmelites' strict rule was based on silence and solitude but it was slightly relaxed by the English prior, Saint Simon Stock (d. 1265). Saint THERESA OF ÁVILA and Saint JOHN OF THE CROSS were members, and in 1593 founded a separate branch, the Discalced (Barefoot) Carmelites. The order's typical clothing consists of a brown habit and scapular, with a white mantle and black hood.

CARMEN, opera by Georges BIZET, first produced in Paris in 1875. The story of the cigarette factory girl Carmen and her soldier lover Don José has a background of smugglers, gypsies and bullfighters. These elements and the highly melodic music have won great popularity for the opera.

CARMICHAEL, Hoagland ("Hoagy") (1889–1970), songwriter, best known for his song *Stardust* (1930). He received an Academy Award for *In the Cool, Cool, Cool of the Evening* (1951). Many of his tunes became jazz standards. Also a singer and piano player, he played many cameo roles in films.

CARMICHAEL, Stokeley (1941–   ), US BLACK POWER leader. Prominent in the Civil Rights movement in the 1960s, he then advocated violent revolution and spent some time in exile in Algeria. He later argued for the use of political and economic power to attain black demands.

CARMINA BURANA, a collection of about 300 songs by the Goliards, medieval wandering scholars who begged and sang their way from university to university in the 13th century. (See also ORFF, Carl).

CARMONA, António Óscar de Fragoso (1869–1951), Portuguese general and politician who took power in 1926. He outlawed the party system and remained president until his death. He was virtually a dictator but established internal stability.

CARNAP, Rudolf (1891–1970), German-US logician and philosopher of science, a leading figure in the Vienna Circle (see LOGICAL POSITIVISM), who later turned to studying problems of linguistic philosophy and the role of probability in inductive reasoning.

CARNARVON, George Edward Stanhope Molyneux Herbert, 5th Earl of (1866–1923), English Egyptologist. His excavations with Howard Carter in the Valley of Kings area revealed tombs of the 12th and 18th dynasties and, in Nov. 1922, the tomb of TUTANKHAMEN.

CARNÉ, Marcel (1903–   ), French motion-picture maker noted especially for *Quai des Brumes* (1938) and *Les Portes de la Nuit* (1946).

CARNEGIE, Andrew (1835–1919), US steel magnate and philanthropist. Born in Dunfermline, Scotland, he emigrated with his family and acquired his fortune entirely through his own efforts, rising from bobbin-boy in a cotton factory to railroad manager and then steel producer at a time of great demand. In an essay, *The Gospel of Wealth* (1889), he formulated his belief that the duty of the rich is to distribute their surplus wealth, and in 1900 he began to set up the vast number of charitable and educational institutions for which he is remembered, including libraries, pension funds, educational trusts, grants to universities in Scotland and the US, patriotic funds, a Temple of Peace at The Hague and the CARNEGIE FOUNDATIONS.

CARNEGIE, Dale (1888–1955) US author and lecturer whose book *How to Win Friends and Influence People* (1936) became the best-selling nonfiction work of modern times, second only to the Bible. He offered courses in effective speaking and human relations in more than 750 US cities and 15 foreign countries.

CARNEGIE, Hattie (1889-1956), Austrian-born US fashion designer who rose to prominence in 1928 when she began to produce ready-made versions of her own designs. The "little Carnegie suit," with its variations on Parisian fashions, was the suit of the stylish woman of the 1930s and 1940s.

CARNEGIE FOUNDATIONS, philanthropic organizations established by Andrew CARNEGIE to advance education, research and world peace. The Carnegie Institution of Washington, D.C., supports research in physical and biological sciences. The Carnegie Foundation for the Advancement of Teaching works to improve higher education, and the Carnegie Corporation of New York endows projects in preschool education and education for the disadvantaged. The Carnegie Endowment for International Peace promotes peace through studies of international law and diplomacy. These and other organizations set a pattern for other major institutions such as the Ford and Rockefeller foundations.

CARNEGIE HALL, concert hall in New York City, named for Andrew CARNEGIE. It was opened in 1891 with a concert conducted by Tchaikovsky, and was the home of the New York Philharmonic Orchestra until 1959. A citizens' group saved the building from demolition in 1960.

CARNERA, Primo (1906–67), Italian boxer. He was a 6-foot, 6-inch, 260 lb. circus strongman and wrestler before he was persuaded to box by US promoters. He won the heavyweight title from Jack Sharkey in 1933 but lost it in 1934 to Max Baer.

CARNIVORA, order of flesh-eating MAMMALS. Daggerlike canine teeth, cutting cheek teeth (*carnassials*) and sharp claws are distinctive features.

CARNIVOROUS PLANT. See INSECTIVOROUS PLANTS.

CARNOT, Lazare Nicolas Marguerite (1753–1823), French soldier and politician; "Organizer of Victory" for the Revolutionary armies. Disapproving of Napoleon he resigned as minister for war in 1800 and was exiled as a regicide by Louis XVIII in 1816.

CARNOT, Nicholas Léonard Sadi (1796–1832), French physicist who, seeking to improve the EFFICIENCY of the STEAM ENGINE, devised the **Carnot cycle** (1824) on the basis of which Lord KELVIN and R. J. E. CLAUSIUS formulated the second law of THERMODYNAMICS. The Carnot cycle, which postulates a heat engine working at maximum thermal efficiency, demonstrates that the efficiency of such an engine does not depend on its mode of operation but only the TEMPERATURES at which it accepts and discards heat ENERGY.

CARO, Joseph ben Ephraim (1488–1575), Jewish talmudist and philosopher whose codification of Jewish law, the *Shulhan 'Arukh* (1565), became the standard authority. Caro's family were Spanish Jews who settled in Constantinople; in later life he became a leader of the Jewish community in Palestine.

CAROL, two kings of Romania. **Carol I** (1839–1914), elected prince 1866, became Romania's first king in 1881 when it became independent of the Ottoman Empire. His reign brought economic development but no solution to pressing rural and political problems. **Carol II** (1893–1953) became king in 1930. He established a royal dictatorship to counter the growing Fascist movement, but after losing territory to the Axis powers in WWII, he abdicated in 1940 and went into exile.

CAROLINE AFFAIR, incident in 1837 in which the US ship *Caroline* was sunk by loyal Canadians, killing a US sailor. The *Caroline* was running supplies to the Canadian rebel leader MACKENZIE. The affair strained relations between Britain and the US, but the affair was settled in 1842 after the Webster-Ashburton treaty.

CAROLINE ISLANDS, archipelago in the W Pacific, with over 900 islands, the largest being Ponape, Babelthuap, Yap and Truk, now part of the federated states of MICRONESIA. In WWII they were the scene of bitter fighting between US and Japanese forces and were part of the US Trust Territory of the Pacific Islands.

CAROLINGIANS, Frankish dynasty named for the Emperor CHARLEMAGNE. Its first members ruled under puppet MEROVINGIAN kings as mayors of the palace, but in 751 Pepin III the Short deposed Childeric III and ruled as king with the blessing of Pope Stephen III. Pepin III's son, Charlemagne, was crowned emperor of the West in 800. His reign was the golden age when the empire had its frontiers on the Elbe, the Danube and the Ebro, and included north and central Italy. However in 843 it was partitioned among his three grandsons, the first of many divisions. The reigns of Charlemagne and his successors are sometimes called "the Carolingian Renaissance" because of their artistic achievements. The superb palatine chapel at Aachen reflects the Carolingian merging of ancient Roman and Byzantine influences; Carolingian manuscripts are among the masterpieces of manuscript illumination, and from the Carolingian minuscule the present small letters are derived. The Carolingians encouraged close church-state relations and fostered feudal ideas which reached their full development in the Middle Ages.

CAROTHERS, Wallace Hume (1896-1937), US chemist who developed NYLON, the first synthetic fiber, and neoprene, a synthetic rubber, while serving as director of research at the Du Pont Company (1928-37).

CARP, fish of the carp family (Cyprinidae), particularly one species native to Asia and introduced to Europe and America which grows to 1m (40in), weighs up to 27kg (60lb) and has four BARBELS around the mouth. The wild form is yellowish green and lives in shallow, muddy freshwater. Reared for the table, there are also ornamental varieties such as the golden carp.

CARPACCIO, Vittore (c1460-1526), Venetian Renaissance narrative painter. A major work is the cycle of paintings of the *Legend of St. Ursula* (1490-95), typical of his work in atmospheric use of color and meticulous detail to create fantasy settings. He was an accurate observer and delighted in presenting pageantry.

CARPATHIANS, European mountain range, about 900mi long, running from Czechoslovakia through Poland, the USSR and Romania. Though an extension of the Alps, they are much lower. The N Carpathians are densely forested, with isolated valleys inhabited by Slav and Magyar peoples. The S Carpathians (or Transylvanian Alps) are more accessible and have important oil fields.

CARPENTER, Alejo (1904-1980), Cuban novelist and music historian best-known for his novels *The Lost Steps* (1953) and *Explosion in a Cathedral* (1962) and for his encouragement of the Afro-Cuban movement in literature and the arts.

CARPENTERS' HALL, historic meeting place in Philadelphia, Pa., now within Independence National Historical Park. Seat of the Continental Congress in 1774, it served as a hospital in the Revolutionary War and in the 1790s was occupied by the First Bank of the United States. It has been restored and run by the Carpenters' Company since 1857.

CARPENTIER, Georges (1894-1975), French light-heavyweight boxer. He beat Battling Levinsky for the world lightweight title in 1920, but in 1921 he lost a challenge to Dempsey for the world heavyweight title.

CARPET. See RUGS AND CARPETS.

CARPETBAGGERS, name give to Northern opportunists who moved into the South after the Civil War to make their fortunes out of postwar chaos and political spoils grabbed from disenfranchised Southerners. They secured many local and state political posts, mobilizing a politically unsophisticated Negro vote, and earned a reputation for graft, wasteful spending and influence-peddling.

CARPET BEETLES, beetles whose larvae feed on clothing, rugs and upholstery. Moth crystals are generally a successful repellent. Most familiar is the common carpet beetle *Anthrenus scrophulariae.*

CARR, Edward Hallett (1892-   ), British political scientist and historian best known for his 10-vol. *History of Soviet Russia* (1950-78). A specialist in international relations, he also wrote *The Twenty Years' Crisis* (1939) and the controversial *What Is History?* (1961).

CARRACCI, family of Bolognese painters. **Lodovico Carracci** (1555-1619), a painter of the Mannerist school, founded an academy of art in Bologna. **Agostino Carracci** (1557-1602) is famous primarily for his prints and *Communion of St. Jerome* (c1590). **Annibale Carracci** (1560-1609) is considered the greatest painter of the family. Much influenced by CORREGGIO, his work, particularly the vast decorations for the Farnese palace (1597-1604), introduced a strong classical element into a basically Mannerist style.

CARRANZA, Venustiano (1859-1920), Mexican political leader. He became governor of Coahuila state in 1910, and Mexican president in 1917, the first to be elected under Mexico's new constitution, which he had supported. It established basic reforms in land ownership and national control of natural resources. His restrictions on foreign acquisitions of Mexican property made for uneasy foreign relations. He fled an uprising led by General OBREGÓN, but was assassinated.

CARREL, Alexis (1873-1944), French surgeon who won the 1912 Nobel Prize for

Medicine or Physiology for developing a technique for suturing (sewing together) blood vessels, thus paving the way for organ TRANSPLANTS and blood TRANSFUSION.

CARRIER, Willis Haviland (1876–1950), US industrialist and mechanical engineer, pioneer designer of AIR-CONDITIONING equipment. He invented an automatic humidity-control device first used in a New York printing plant in 1902—arguably the first commercial air-conditioning installation.

CARRIER PIGEON, breed of show pigeon derived from the rock pigeon, not used for message-bearing despite its name. (See also PIGEON.)

CARROLL, Charles (1737–1832), US statesman from Md. A delegate to the Continental Congress (1776–79), he signed the Declaration of Independence and later served in the first US Senate (1789–92). At his death he was considered the richest man in the country.

CARROLL, Daniel (1730–1796), US politician from Md. A delegate to the Continental Congress (1781–83) and the 1787 Constitutional Convention, he signed the Articles of Confederation and the Constitution. He also served in the first US Congress (1789–91).

CARROLL, John (1735–1815), first US Roman Catholic bishop. A strong patriot, he helped establish the Catholic hierarchy in the US. In 1790 he was consecrated bishop of Baltimore, and was made archbishop in 1808. He founded a seminary which became Georgetown U.

CARROLL, Lewis (pseudonym of Charles Lutwidge Dodgson; 1832–1898), English mathematician best known for his children's books *Alice in Wonderland* (1865) and *Alice Through the Looking Glass* (1872). Lecturer in mathematics at Christ Church, Oxford, from 1854, he was ordained a deacon in 1861 but did not take further orders. The *Alice* books and poems such as *The Hunting of the Snark* (1876) are built on mathematical illogic and paradox. He was also a noted portrait photographer.

CARSON, Christopher "Kit" (1809–1868), US frontiersman, Indian agent, army officer and folk hero. He worked as a hunter and guide in the 1840s and explored Ore. and Cal. with FRÉMONT. He served in the Mexican War, and fought for the Union in the Southwest during the Civil War, finally becoming a brevet brigadier general.

CARSON, Johnny (1925–   ), US television personality, host of *The Tonight Show* (from 1962). His topical comic monologues, spontaneous wit and disarming interviewing style have made the show one of the most popular, long-lasting and lucrative programs in TV history.

CARSON, Rachel Louise (1907–1964), US marine biologist and science writer whose *Silent Spring* (1962) first alerted the US public to the dangers of environmental POLLUTION.

CARSON CITY, state capital of Nev. and seat of Ormsby Co., named for Kit CARSON. Originally a trading post, it became an important mining center with the discovery of the Comstock Lode in 1859. Pop 32,022.

CARTAGENA, Caribbean seaport on the Bay of Cartagena in N Colombia, capital of Bolíva department. An important gold port of the Spanish Empire, dating from 1533, it suffered a decline until it became a major oil port in the 20th century. Manufactures include sugar, tobacco and textiles. Pop 435,361.

CARTAN, Élie Joseph (1869–1951), French mathematician who developed methods of DIFFERENTIAL GEOMETRY that played an important role in the development of general RELATIVITY. He was a professor at the Sorbonne from 1912 to 1940.

CARTE, Richard d'Oyly. See D'OYLY CARTE, RICHARD.

CARTEL, an association, often illegal, of individuals or firms who agree not to compete with each other in the open, domestic or international markets. The price and volume of goods can therefore be fixed and cartel members' profits increased.

CARTER, Billy (1937–   ), younger brother of President Jimmy CARTER. For a time he cashed in on his relationship to the president, traveling around the country, selling a beer named after himself and projecting a "good ol' boy" image. Public infatuation with him began to sour when it was learned that he had accepted loans from the terrorist Libyan regime and was suspected of attempting to influence arms sales on its behalf. Beset by problems of alcoholism and income-tax evasion, he ultimately became a political liability for his brother.

CARTER, Don (1930–   ), US bowling champion. From 1950–64 he won every major title and tournament, and was the top money winner. He won six Professional Bowling Association championships and five world titles. He was the first president of the PBA.

CARTER, Elliott Cook (1908–   ), a major 20th-century US composer. Marked by unusual instrumentation and structure, his work is often complex and experimental. Among his best-known works are the ballet *The Minotaur* (1947), and the *Double*

Concerto (1961) and *Concerto for Piano and Orchestra* (1965). Carter was awarded Pulitzer prizes in 1960 and 1973.

CARTER, Howard (1873–1939), English Egyptologist, famous for the Valley of the Kings' excavations with Lord CARNARVON that led to the discovery of the tomb of TUTANKHAMEN in 1922. Carter spent ten years in careful excavation and exploration of the tomb.

CARTER, James Earl "Jimmy," Jr (1924–   ), 39th US president 1977–81. A Baptist, Carter grew up on a Georgia farm and graduated from the US Naval Academy in 1946. While in the navy he studied nuclear physics and worked under Admiral Rickover on the atomic submarine program. He then ran his family's farm and entered politics. Elected as a Democrat to the State Senate (1962) he built up a reputation as a liberal on race relations. As governor of Georgia 1971–75 he simplified the complex system of government of the state and instigated electoral and social reforms. He won the Democratic presidential nomination in 1976 and defeated Republican incumbent Gerald FORD. The US Senate refused to ratify Carter's arms-limitation agreement with the USSR but it did approve treaties yielding US control over the Panama Canal. Carter gave full recognition to Communist China and was effective in securing a peace treaty between Egypt and Israel. His last year as president was plagued by Iran's seizure of more than 50 US hostages, who were released on Carter's last day in office. At home, he struggled with record interest and inflation rates and the threat of an energy shortage. He was defeated for reelection in 1980 by Republican Ronald Reagan.

CARTERET, Sir George (c1610–1680), English politician, admiral and lieutenant-governor of Jersey from 1643. A staunch Royalist, he was rewarded after the RESTORATION with proprietorships in New Jersey and Carolina.

CARTER FAMILY (A. P. Carter, 1891–   ; **Sara Dougherty Carter,** 1898–   ; **Maybelle Addington Carter,**

1909–78), US country singers. Their enormous popularity was achieved largely through recordings made during the Depression years of the 1930s. They greatly influenced subsequent generations of country singers.

CARTESIAN PHILOSOPHY. See DESCARTES, RENÉ.

CARTHAGE, ancient N African city which once stood on the Mediterranean coast near the site of modern Tunis. Established around 800 BC by Phoenician traders as an anchorage, by the 5th century BC it had become the capital of a sizeable empire, comprising African colonies, Corsica, Sardinia and much of Sicily and Spain. Greek opposition checked Carthaginian expansion from 480 BC until the 3rd century BC, when the famous rivalry with Rome began. (See PUNIC WARS.)

Although the fortunes of Carthage reached their zenith at this time under HAMILCAR BARCA and his son, HANNIBAL, in 201 BC the city forfeited all but its African possessions, and in 146 BC a Roman army razed it to the ground. Archaeologists have found very few traces of Phoenician Carthage. Julius CEASAR removed the 1st century BC colony to a different site. Roman Carthage had a checkered history passing, after the decline of Rome, through Vandal and Byzantine hands before its final destruction in 698 AD by the forces of Islam.

CARTHUSIANS, contemplative and austere Roman Catholic monastic order founded in France in 1084 by St. Bruno. Each monk spends most of his life in solitude in his private cell and garden. Lay brothers prepare the Chartreuse liqueur which has made the order famous.

CARTIER, Sir George Étienne (1814–1873), Canadian statesman and leading French-Canadian advocate of confederation. Elected to the Canadian parliament in 1848, he was from 1857 to 1862 joint prime minister with Sir John MACDONALD, under whom he later served as minister of defense in the first dominion government.

CARTIER, Jacques (1491–1557), French explorer who, in search of a NORTHWEST PASSAGE, made two important voyages to Canada. In 1534 he explored the Gulf of St. Lawrence and claimed the Gaspé Peninsula for France. In 1535 he explored the St. Lawrence R as far as Mont Royal, which he named. His pessimistic reports on North America deterred many potential colonists.

CARTIER-BRESSON, Henri (1908–   ), internationally famous French documentary photographer who rose to fame with his coverage of the Spanish Civil War. He has published many books and has also made films, some with Jean RENOIR.

CARTILAGE, tough, flexible connective tissue found in all vertebrates, consisting of cartilage cells (chondrocytes) in a matrix of COLLAGEN fibers and a firm protein gel. The skeleton of the vertebrate embryo is formed wholly of cartilage, but in most species much of this is replaced by BONE during growth. There are three main types of cartilage: hyaline, translucent and glossy, found in the joints, nose, trachea and bronchi; elastic, found in the external ear, Eustachian tube and larynx; and fibrocartilage, which attaches tendons to bone and forms the disks between the vertebrae.

CARTLAND, Barbara (1904–), British author, known for her prolific output of best-selling romantic novels, among which are *Debt of Honour* (1970) and *Love in Hiding* (1977).

CARTOON. See ANIMATION; CARICATURE AND CARTOON; COMIC STRIP.

CARTWRIGHT, Alexander (d. 1892), New York surveyor who formulated baseball's first set of rules in 1845. Cartwright drew up plans for baseball's current "diamond," and standardized innings, balls and outs. He also popularized the sport during a transcontinental trip in 1849.

CARTWRIGHT, Edmund (1743–1823), British inventor of a mechanical loom (c1787) that was the ancestor of the modern power loom. He also invented a wool-combing machine (c1790). (See also WEAVING.)

CARUSO, Enrico (1873–1921), Italian operatic tenor famous both for his voice and his artistry. He was the first leading singer to recognize the possibilities of the phonograph, and his recordings brought him worldwide fame.

CARVER, George Washington (c1860–1943), US chemurgist, botanist and educator, born of slave parents in Mo. As director of agricultural research at TUSKEGEE INSTITUTE, Ala., from 1896, he fostered soil improvement by crop rotation, urging an end to the dependence of Southern agriculture on cotton alone. With this in mind he developed hundreds of industrial uses for peanuts and sweet potatoes.

CARVER, John (c1576–1621), leader of the Pilgrim Fathers and first governor of Plymouth Colony (1620–21). He was largely responsible (1617–20) for getting a charter and financial aid, and for chartering the *Mayflower*. He died during the colonists' disastrous first winter.

CARY, (Arthur) Joyce (Lunel) (1888–1957), British novelist whose primary theme is the individual's struggle against society. His best-known works are *The Horse's Mouth* (1944) and *Prisoner of Grace* (1952) both parts of trilogies, and *Mister Johnson* (1939), a novel set in Africa.

CASABLANCA, largest city in Morocco and a major port. Founded by the Portuguese in 1515 and occupied by the French 1907–56, it is a transportation and tourist center with a mixed population of Europeans, Asians and Africans. Its main industries are food, timber and metal processing. Pop 1,506,373.

CASABLANCA CONFERENCE, WWII meeting of Winston Churchill and F. D. Roosevelt (Jan. 1943). It determined Allied strategy in Europe, and established that only unconditional surrender by Germany and Japan would be acceptable.

CASADESUS, Robert (1899–1972), distinguished French pianist and composer, noted for his interpretations of Mozart and Debussy, and also for the two- and three-piano concertos he composed and performed with his wife and eldest son.

CASALS, Pablo (1876–1973), virtuoso Spanish cellist and conductor. In 1919 he founded an orchestra in Barcelona to bring music to the working classes, but left Spain after the Civil War and never returned. He settled in Prades, SW France, and then (1956) in Puerto Rico, organizing annual music festivals in both places. A great interpreter of Bach, he was a model to a whole generation of cellists.

CASANOVA (DE SEINGALT), Giovanni Giacomo (1725–1798), Venetian author and adventurer whose name became a synonym for seducer. His memoirs, both sensual and sensitive, show him as a freethinking libertine; they also give an excellent picture of his times.

CASAS, Bartolomé de Las. See LAS CASAS, BARTOLOMÉ DE.

CASCADE RANGE, mountain range extending from N Cal. to British Columbia in Canada. Its highest peak is Mt Rainier (14,410ft). There are 14 dormant volcanoes and the recently active (1980) MOUNT SAINT HELENS. The range is named for the ferocious rapids in the Columbia R where it crosses the mountains.

CASEIN, the chief milk PROTEIN, found there as its calcium salt. It is precipitated from skim MILK with acid or RENNET, washed and dried. Highly nutritious, it is used in the food industry. In alkaline solution casein forms a COLLOID used as a glue, a binder for paint pigments and paper coatings, and to dress leather. Casein is also used to make PLASTICS.

CASEMENT, Sir Roger David (1864–1918), Irish politician, knighted for his humanitarian work in the Congo and South America. In WWI he was hanged for an attempt to arrange German support for the 1916 Irish Rising.

CASHMERE, very fine natural fiber, the soft underhair of the Kashmir goat, bred in India, Iran, China and Mongolia. Cashmere is finer than the best wools, although the name may be applied to some soft wool fabrics.

CASLON, William (1692–1766), English typefounder, inventor of Caslon type, for many years the basic typeface. Although superseded by the "newstyle" faces of John BASKERVILLE and others, versions of it are much in use today.

CASPIAN SEA, the world's largest inland sea (143,000sq mi), in the SW USSR and Iran. Tideless, it is 92ft below sea level. Although fed by several rivers, including the Volga, the level fluctuates because evaporation losses often exceed inflow. Astrakhan and Baku are the main ports. The northern part of the sea is a major sturgeon-fishing area.

CASS, Lewis (1782–1866), US soldier and political leader. Born in Exeter, N.H., he rose to the rank of brigadier general in the War of 1812, was governor of Michigan Territory (1813–31), and then became secretary of war under Andrew Jackson. Minister to France 1836–42, he was elected a senator for Mich. in 1844 and ran as Democratic presidential candidate in 1848. He lost to Zachary TAYLOR, due largely to the defection of the BARNBURNERS to the FREE SOIL PARTY. Later he returned to the Senate 1849–57 and served as secretary of state.

CASSANDRA, in Greek mythology, a Trojan prophetess who was cursed by Apollo, who decreed that she was never to be believed. Daughter of King Priam, she was enslaved by AGAMEMNON at the fall of Troy and was later murdered with him.

CASSATT, Mary (1845–1926), American Impressionist painter, strongly influenced by her friend DEGAS. She studied, exhibited and lived mainly in Paris. Most of her paintings are of domestic scenes, especially mother-and-child studies.

CASSETTE. See TAPE RECORDER.

CASSIOPEIA, in Greek mythology, the mother of ANDROMEDA. In astronomy, a northern circumpolar constellation (see CIRCUMPOLAR STARS) whose five principal stars form a prominent "W."

CASSIRER, Ernst (1874–1945), German-born philosopher. Based on the ideas of KANT, his work examines the ways in which man's symbols and concepts structure his world. He fled Nazi Germany in 1933, and taught at Oxford, in Sweden and from 1941 in the US.

CASSIUS LONGINUS, Gaius (d. 42 BC), Roman general and politician, one of the conspirators against Julius Caesar in 44 BC. After the assassination, he fled to Syria and with his army joined Brutus to fight Octavian and Mark Antony at Philippi in 42 BC. Despairing of victory, he killed himself during the battle.

CASTAGNO, Andrea del (c1423–1457), outstanding Florentine painter of church frescoes, portraits and murals. Best known for his *Last Supper* (1445–50) and his *Crucifixion*, (1449–50), he stressed perspective and a stark, dramatic illumination. He is notable for the vigor and strength of his figure rendering.

CASTEL GANDOLFO, town in Italy, on Lake Albano near Rome. Its palace, built by Urban VIII in the 17th century, is now the pope's summer residence. Pop 4,814.

CASTELNUOVO-TEDESCO, Mario (1895–1968), Jewish–Italian composer. Forced to leave Italy in 1939, he emigrated to the US. Besides his operas *All's Well That Ends Well* (1957) and *The Merchant of Venice* (1956), he wrote many Shakespeare settings, and also concertos and film music.

CASTENADA, Carlos (1931–   ), Brazilian-born US anthropologist whose accounts of the wisdom and culture of the Yaqui Indians, including *The Teachings of Don Juan* (1968) and *Journey to Ixtlan* (1972), established him as a cult figure.

CASTE SYSTEM, the division of society into closed groups, primarily by birth, but usually also involving religion and occupation. The most caste-bound society today is probably that of Hindu India; caste divisions are mentioned in the RIGVEDA, dating from 3,000 BC, and have not been discouraged until recently. The hierarchy consists of four Varnas (graded classes) with various subdivisions: Brahman (priestly), Kshatriyas (warrior), Vaisyas (merchants and farmers) and Sudras (menials and laborers). There was also a classless element, the outvarnas or untouchables, who performed the lowest tasks. The system solidified social structures by fixing from birth social contacts, thought, diet, ritual, occupation and marriage. Western influences weakened the Indian system in the 19th century; reform was hastened by GANDHI in the 1930s. In India today caste has been drastically modified but not destroyed, despite corrective legislation in the 1950s.

CASTIGLIONE, Baldassare (1478–1529), Italian courtier, diplomat and author famed for his *Libro del cortegiano* (1528), a portrait of the ideal courtier and his relationship with the prince he serves. The book greatly influenced Renaissance mores and inspired such writers as Spenser, Sidney and Cervantes.

CASTILE, traditional name for the central region of Spain, formerly the kingdom of Castile. First united in the 10th century, by the 12th century the kingdom was the dominant power in Spain. A royal union between Castile and Aragon (1479) created the core of modern Spain. Madrid, the capital, is in Castile, and the official language is Castilian. A wide plain bounded by mountains, its 54,463sq mi area is largely arid, but some areas support sheep. Wheat is also grown in some parts.

CASTING, the production of objects of a desired form by pouring the raw material (e.g., ALLOYS; FIBERGLASS; PLASTICS; STEEL) in liquid form into a suitably shaped mold. Both the mold and the pattern from which it is made may be either permanent or expendable. Permanent-mold techniques include **die casting,** where the molten material is forced under pressure into a DIE; **centrifugal casting,** used primarily for pipes, the molten material being poured into a rapidly rotating mold (see CENTRIFUGE); and **continuous casting,** for bars and slabs, where the material is poured into water-cooled, open-ended molds. Most important of the expendable-mold process is **sand casting (founding);** here fine SAND is packed tightly around each half of a permanent pattern, which is removed and the two halves of the mold placed together. The material is poured in through a channel **(sprue);** after setting, the sand is dispersed. In some processes, the mold is baked before use to remove excess water. (See also CAST IRON; METALLURGY.)

CASTLE, Vernon (1887–1918), and **Irene** (1893–1969), who revolutionized ballroom dancing. The couple introduced the one-step and the Castle walk and popularized the hesitation waltz and tango during a meteoric career that began in 1912 and ended with Vernon's death in an air crash, 1918.

CASTLEREAGH, Robert Stewart, Viscount (1769–1822), British statesman, creator of the Grand Alliance which defeated Napolean. As secretary for Ireland, he suppressed the 1788 rebellion and forced the Act of Union through the Irish Parliament (1800). He was war minister 1805–06 and 1807–09 and then, as foreign secretary 1812–22, played a major role in the organization of Europe at the Congress of Vienna (1814). Much maligned in his time, he committed suicide.

CASTOR AND POLLUX, twin heroes of classical mythology, also called the *Dioscuri.* Sons of LEDA, brothers of Helen and Clytemnestra, they were inseparable even after Castor's death, when Pollux asked his father Zeus to let him rejoin his brother by releasing him from immortality. (See also GEMINI.)

CASTOR OIL, a vegetable oil extracted from the purple-streaked seeds of the castor oil plant (*Ricinus communis*). Once widely used as a laxative, castor oil is now mainly used as a lubricant and in the manufacture of oil and varnish.

CASTRATION COMPLEX, the nexus of fears (see COMPLEX) concerned with possible or threatened loss of the reproductive organs, especially the penis. The term is used analogously to describe fears of loss of sexuality or the capacity for erotic pleasure in either males or females. (See OEDIPUS COMPLEX.)

CASTRATO, a male singer who was castrated to retain his high-pitched prepubescent vocal range. Such male sopranos flourished in Europe in the 17th and 18th centuries. Many major operatic roles were written for them. (See also CASTRATION.)

CASTRO (RUZ), Fidel (1926–   ), Cuban premier and revolutionary leader. After his law studies he led an abortive revolution in 1953 against the Cuban dictator Fulgencio BATISTA, and was imprisoned and exiled. On Dec. 2, 1956, he landed again in Cuba, with 81 men, and, after a guerrilla struggle against overwhelming odds, overthrew the regime and established himself as premier in 1959. He brought about many far-reaching social and economic changes, becoming increasingly dependent on the USSR for financial support. His efforts to become a leader of developing "third world" nations were undercut by his reliance on the USSR.

CATACOMBS, the name given to underground cemeteries, particularly those of the early Christians. The best known and most extensive are at Rome. The oldest of the catacombs, those of Saint Sebastian and Saint Priscilla, date from the 1st century AD. They also served as a refuge from the religious persecutions of the Roman emperors. Construction was freely permitted provided they were situated outside the city walls. The catacombs extend through rocky soil at depths between 20ft and 65ft, sometimes at several levels, the oldest catacombs usually being uppermost. They form a labyrinthine network of narrow passages, the sides of which are lined with tiers of recesses (loculi) and frequently decorated with pictorial and written symbols. After a body had been placed in its recess, the opening was sealed with an inscribed slab of marble or terracotta.

CATALAN, one of the nine Romance languages, and native language of Catalonia in Spain. Also spoken in the French Pyrenees.

CATALONIA, autonomous region in NE Spain, comprising the provinces of Lérida, Gerona, Barcelona and Tarragona. Densely populated, it was occupied by the Romans and Goths, who called it Gothalonia. It maintained its own customs and language even after its union with Aragon in 1137. It is now the chief industrial area of Spain, and is dependent on the interior for grain and protected markets. In 1980 the Spanish government handed over certain limited functions to a Catalan regional government with its own parliament and premier.

CATALYSIS, the changing of the rate of a chemical reaction by the addition of a small amount of a substance which is unchanged at the end of the reaction. Such a substance is called a catalyst, though this term is usually reserved for those which speed up reactions; additives which slow down reactions are called inhibitors. Catalysts are specific for particular reactions. In a reversible reaction, the forward and back reactions are catalyzed equally, and the EQUILIBRIUM position is not altered. Catalysis is either homogeneous (the catalyst and reactants being in the same phase, usually gas or liquid), in which case the catalyst usually forms a reactive intermediate which then breaks down; or heterogeneous, in which ADSORPTION of the reactants occurs on the catalytic surface. Heterogeneous catalysis is often blocked by impurities called poisons. Catalysts are widely used in industry, as in the CONTACT PROCESS, the HYDROGENATION of oils, and the cracking of PETROLEUM. All living organisms are dependent on the complex catalysts called ENZYMES which regulate biochemical reactions.

CATANIA, chief seaport and second-largest city of Sicily. After an earthquake in 1693, the city was rebuilt on a regular plan, with five squares and the largest Baroque church in Sicily. It is mainly a commercial city and has oil-pressing, fish-canning, engineering, chemical and cement industries. Pop 400,100.

CATAPULT, ancient military weapon used for hurling missiles. Some catapults were large crossbows, with a lethal range of over 400yd, while others (ballistas) used giant levers to hurl boulders. In the Middle Ages, catapults were an important part of siege artillery, but were made obsolete by the cannon. A modern steam-powered version of the catapult launches jets from aircraft carriers.

CATARACT, disease of the EYE lens, regardless of cause: the normally clear lens becomes opaque and light transmission and perception are reduced. Congenital cataracts occur especially in children born to mothers who have had GERMAN MEASLES in early PREGNANCY, and in a number of inherited disorders. Certain disturbances of METABOLISM or HORMONE production can cause cataracts, especially DIABETES. Eye trauma and INFLAMMATION are other causes in adults. Some degree of cataract formation is common in old age. Once a cataract is formed, vision cannot be improved until the lens is removed surgically. After this, GLASSES are required to correct loss of focusing power. It is among the commonest causes of BLINDNESS in developed countries.

CATASTROPHISM, in geology, the early 19th century theory that major changes in the geological structure of the earth occurred only during short periods of violent upheaval (catastrophes) which were separated by long periods of comparative stability. The theory fell from prominence after LYELL'S enunciation of the rival doctrine of UNIFORMITARIANISM.

CATBIRDS, garden songbirds related to the MOCKING BIRD, named for the mewing notes in their song. They live in the US and in S Canada, migrating in winter to Middle America or to the West Indies.

CATEGORICAL IMPERATIVE, in the ethics of KANT, an absolute moral law, one which is not dependent on ulterior considerations. It was formulated thus: "So act that you could will the maxim of your action to be a universal law."

CATERPILLAR, the larva of a moth or a butterfly, with 13 segments, 3 pairs of true legs and up to 5 pairs of soft false legs. (See also INSECTS, LEPIDOPTERA.)

CATFISH, members of 31 families found throughout the world, chiefly in freshwater. Catfish have BARBELS sometimes resembling cat's whiskers around the mouth, and the bones of the upper jaw are reduced or absent. There are many bizarre forms such as the Upside-down catfish and the transparent Glass catfish.

CATGUT, a strong, thin cord used to string musical instruments and rackets, and to sew up wounds in surgery, made from the intestines of herbivorous animals. In surgery, it has the advantage of being eventually absorbed by the body.

CATHARI, a heretical (actually non-Christian) sect widespread in Europe in the 12th and 13th centuries; called ALBIGENSES in S France. Their philosophy, akin to that of the BOGOMILS, was derived from GNOSTICISM and MANICHAEISM. They saw two principles in the world: good (the spirit) and evil (matter and the body). There were two classes of Cathari, the Believers and the Perfect, the latter practicing extreme asceticism.

CATHARSIS (from Greek *katharsis*, purging), in PSYCHOANALYSIS (where it is also generally termed **abreaction**), the bringing into the open of a previously repressed (see REPRESSION) MEMORY or EMOTION, thus, hopefully, relieving unconscious emotional stress. In medicine, the term is used for the artificial induction of vomiting (see EMETIC). Play, which can be viewed as working off atavistic impulses, is sometimes described as cathartic.

CATHEDRAL, the principal church of a diocese, in which the bishop has his *cathedra*, his official seat or throne. A cathedral need not be particularly large or imposing, though its importance as a major center led to the magnificent structures of the Gothic and Renaissance periods. By its prominent position and size, a cathedral often dominated a city and served as the focus of its life. In Europe, most of the older cathedral cities were already important centers in Roman and early Christian times.

CATHER, Willa Sibert (1873–1947), US novelist noted for her psychologically astute portrayals of the people of Nebraska and the southwest. Her works include *O Pioneers!* (1913), *My Antonia* (1918) and *Death Comes for the Archbishop* (1927). She was also a brilliant writer of short stories, the most famous being *Paul's Case.*

CATHERINE, name of two Russian empresses. **Catharine I** (1684–1727), of Lithuanian peasant origin, became the mistress and later the wife of Peter I. On his death in 1725 she succeeded him to the throne. **Catherine II, the Great** (1729–1796), daughter of a minor German prince, became the wife of the heir to the Russian throne, the future Peter III, in 1745. After his deposition and murder in 1762, she became empress and proposed sweeping reforms, but her apparent liberalism was quenched by the PUGACHEV rebellion and the French Revolution. She greatly extended Russian territory, annexing the Crimea (1783) and partitioning Poland (1772–95).

She was also a great patron of the arts.
CATHERINE OF ALEXANDRIA, Saint (early 4th century), Christian martyr, probably legendary, who may have died in Alexandria in Egypt. Because of her learned defense against the Emperor Maxentius' priests, she was tortured and then beheaded. She is the patron saint of scholars and philosophers.

CATHERINE OF ARAGON (1485–1536), first wife of HENRY VIII of England. The daughter of Ferdinand and Isabella of Spain, she first married Prince Arthur (1501) and then, after his death, his brother, Henry VIII (1509). Henry's annulment of the marriage in 1533 without papal consent led to the English Reformation. She was the mother of Mary I of England.

CATHERINE OF BRAGANZA (1638–1705), Portuguese wife of King CHARLES II of England. The marriage (1662) was intended to promote the Anglo-Portuguese alliance; but she produced no heir. After Charles' death, she returned to Portugal in 1692, serving a⁓ regent (1704–05).

CATHERINE OF SIENA, Saint (1347–1380), Italian religious and mystic renowned for her visions, charity and diplomatic skills. Her influence over Pope Gregory XI (1331–1378) led him to leave Avignon in 1377 and return the papacy to Rome, thus ending the BABYLONIAN CAPTIVITY. Although formally unlettered, she was declared a Doctor of the Church by Paul VI in 1970 for her amazing knowledge. Her feast day is April 30.

CATHETER, hollow tube passed into body organs for investigation or treatment. **Urinary catheters** are used for relief of BLADDER outflow obstruction and sometimes for loss of nervous control of bladder; they also allow measurement of bladder function and special X-RAY techniques. **Cardiac catheters** are passed through ARTERIES or VEINS into chambers of the HEART to study its functioning and ANATOMY.

CATHODE, a negatively charged ELECTRODE, found particularly in ELECTRON TUBES, CATHODE RAY TUBES, and electrochemical CELLS, and used in combination with its positive counterpart, an ANODE, as a source of ELECTRONS or to produce an electric field.

CATHODE RAYS, ELECTRONS emitted by a CATHODE when heated. First studied by Julius Plücker (1801–1868) in 1858, they can be drawn off in vacuo by the attraction of an ANODE to form a beam which causes fluorescence (see LUMINESCENCE) in appropriately coated screens or X-RAY emission from metal targets.

CATHODE RAY TUBE, the principal component of OSCILLOSCOPES and TELEVISION sets. It consists of an evacuated glass tube containing at one end a heated CATHODE and an ANODE, and widened at the other end to form a flat screen, the inside of which is coated with a fluorescent material. ELECTRONS emitted from the cathode are accelerated toward the anode, and pass through a hole in its center to form a fine beam which causes a bright spot where it strikes the screen. Because of the electric charge carried by the electrons, the beam can be deflected by transverse electric or magnetic fields produced by electrodes or coils between the anode and screen: one set allows horizontal deflection, and another vertical. The number of electrons reaching the screen can be controlled by the voltage applied to a third electrode, placed near the cathode, which varies the electric field of the cathode. It is thus possible to move the spot about the screen and vary its brightness by the application of appropriately timed electrical signals, and sustained images may be produced by causing the spot to traverse the same pattern many times a second. In the oscilloscope, the form of a given electrical signal, or any physical effect capable of conversion into one, is investigated by allowing it to control the vertical deflection while the horizontal deflection is scanned steadily from left to right, while in television sets pictures can be built up by varying the spot brightness while the spot scans out the entire screen in a series of close horizontal lines.

CATHOLIC EMANCIPATION ACT, British law enacted on April 13, 1829, removing most of the civil disabilities imposed on British Roman Catholics. A controversial measure, it was introduced by Sir Robert PEEL, after considerable pressure from Irish campaigners headed by Daniel O'CONNELL.

CATHOLIC REFORMATION. See COUNTER REFORMATION.

CATILINE (c108–62 BC), Roman aristocrat, who tried to seize power in 63 BC. He was trapped and killed in battle at Pistoia. CICERO attacked him in a series of four celebrated orations.

CATLIN, George (1796–1872), US artist, noted for his paintings of American Indian life. His books include *Notes on the Manners, Customs, and Conditions of the North American Indians* (1841).

CATNIP, or catmint, *Nepeta cataria*, a Eurasian mint naturalized in North America, so-named because of its strange attraction for cats. Family: Labiatae.

CATO, name of two Roman statesmen. **Marcus Porcius Cato** (234–149 BC), called the Elder, was an orator and prose writer. He became consul in 195 BC and censor in 184 BC. His only surviving work is a treatise on agriculture. **Marcus Porcius Cato** (95–46 BC), called the Younger (great-grandson of Cato the Elder), was a model Stoic and defender of Roman republicanism. He supported POMPEY against Gaius Julius CAESAR in the Civil War, but after the final defeat of the republican army at Thapsus (46 BC), he killed himself at Utica.

CATONSVILLE NINE. See HARRISBURG SEVEN.

CATS, members of the family Felidae, all of which are hunting carnivores. They vary in size from the small domestic cat to the large LION and TIGER.

CATS, Domestic, popular household pets, thought to be descended from the African kaffir (or Bush) cat, mixed with strains from the European wildcat. They were fully domesticated by the time of the ancient Egyptians, who venerated them. Mummies of cats have been found in Egyptian tombs.

The most common type of cat is the tabby (both striped and blotched). Though seemingly derogatory, the term alley or gutter cat (meaning mixed breed) applies to about 90% of cats in the world. Pedigree cats are divided primarily into two groups: shorthaired (including Siamese, Burmese, Russian blue, Manx and Abyssinian) and long-haired (including Persian and Angora).

CAT SCANNER, or CT scanner, advanced X-RAY instrument for medical diagnosis, the letters CAT standing for **computerized axial tomography**. A tomograph is an X-ray image that reveals a thin layer of the body, as opposed to the ordinary radiograph, which superimposes shadows of tissues at various depths. Tomography was developed in the 1930s to obtain more precise images of selected cross sections of the body by rotating the X-ray beam around the body in the plane of the desired section, with the receiving detector rotating in synchronization on the opposite side of the body. The CAT scanner further improved on this by linking the detector to a computer that reconstitutes a two-dimensional image of the cross section and displays it on a television screen. The computer can add false color for a vivid depiction of different tissue densities, and can build up a three-dimensional image with a series of cross sections. The CAT scanner first entered operation in 1973 and is now in widespread use in many medical centers.

The same principle is now also being applied to scanning by means of NUCLEAR MAGNETIC RESONANCE (NMR) and positron emission.

CATSKILL MOUNTAINS, group of low mountains W of the Hudson R in SE N.Y., part of the Appalachian system. Geologically unique, with flat-topped plateaus divided by narrow valleys, they are a popular recreation area. The highest point is Slide Mountain (4,180ft).

CATT, Carrie Lane Chapman (1859–1947), US feminist, suffragette and founder of the LEAGUE OF WOMEN VOTERS. She was also an active advocate of international disarmament. (See also WOMEN'S LIBERATION MOVEMENT.)

CATTLE, large ruminant mammals of the family Bovidae, most of which have been domesticated, including BISON, BUFFALO, YAK, ZEBU or Brahman cattle and European cattle. The last two are fully domesticated. Western cattle are derived from the now extinct AUROCHS. By 2500 BC the Egyptians had several breeds of cattle, which may have been used as draft animals, still an important function in many places, and for leather. Their dung served as fuel and manure.

Today, beef cattle (like Aberdeen Angus or Hereford) are square, heavily built animals commonly kept on poor grazing land, whereas dairy breeds (like Holstein or Guernsey) are kept on good grazing. Recent breeds are mixed beef and dairy animals. A dairy cow can give as much as 14 tons of milk in one year.

CATTON, Bruce (1899–1978), US journalist and Civil War historian. He is best known for his trilogy on the Army of the Potomac: *Mr. Lincoln's Army* (1951), *Glory Road* (1952) and *A Stillness at Appomattox* (1953). He won the Pulitzer Prize in 1954.

CATULLUS, Gaius Valerius (c84–54 BC), Roman lyric poet, born in Verona, Italy. Influenced by Hellenistic Greek poetry, he wrote passionate lyrics, epigrams, elegies, idylls and vicious satires, of which only 116 survive. He influenced the later Roman poets HORACE and MARTIAL.

CAUCASIAN LANGUAGES, group of 40 Indo-European languages spoken by some 5 million people in the region of the Caucasus Mountains, of which Georgian is the only important modern language.

CAUCASOID, a racial division of man. Caucasoids have straight or curly fine hair, generally mesocephalic (see CEPHALIC INDEX) heads, thin lips, straight faces and well-developed chins. The RACE may have originated in W Asia.

CAUCASUS, mountain range in the USSR between the Caspian and Black seas, 700mi long and up to 120mi wide, including the highest mountain in Europe, Mt Elbrus (18,481ft). Its northern parts belong to Europe, but its southern regions (Transcaucasia), bordering on Turkey and Iran, are part of Asia.

CAUSALITY. See ARISTOTLE; HUME; KANT.

CAUTERIZATION, application of heat or caustic substances. Used for minor SKIN or mucous-membrane lesions (especially of the NOSE and cervix uteri) to remove abnormal tissue and encourage normal healing. Before antiseptics, it was used to sterilize wounds.

CAUTHEN, Steve (1960–   ), first jockey ever to win $5 million in purses in a single year. He had nearly 300 wins during his year-long apprenticeship (1976–77). He rode the Triple Crown winner *Affirmed* in 1978.

CAVALIER POETS, group of English poets of the 17th century at the court of Charles I. They include Thomas CAREW, Robert HERRICK, Richard LOVELACE and Sir John SUCKLING.

CAVALRY, military force that fights on horseback. It played a key role in warfare from about the 6th century BC to the end of the 19th century when the development of rapid fire rifles began to reduce its effectiveness. The advent of the tank during WWI and subsequent improvements in military hardware have rendered traditional cavalry redundant. The term is retained in the names of some modern armored units.

CAVE, any chamber formed naturally in rock and, usually, open to the surface via a passage. Caves are found most often in LIMESTONE, where rainwater, rendered slightly ACID by dissolved CARBON dioxide from the ATMOSPHERE, drains through joints in the stone, slowly dissolving it. Enlargement is caused by further passage of water and by bits of rock that fall from the roof and are dragged along by the water. Such caves form often in connected series; they may display STALACTITES AND STALAGMITES and their collapse may form a sinkhole. Caves are also formed by selective EROSION by the sea of cliff bases. Very occasionally they occur in LAVA, either where lava has solidified over a mass of ice that has later melted, or where the surface of a mass of lava has solidified, molten lava beneath bursting through and flowing on.

CAVELIER, Robert. See LA SALLE, RENÉ ROBERT, SIEUR DE.

CAVELL, Edith Louisa (1865–1915), British nurse who became a WWI heroine. As matron of the Berkendael hospital in

Brussels, she was executed by the Germans for helping some 200 Allied soldiers to escape.

CAVEMEN, a term commonly applied to all STONE AGE men, although many of them did not live in caves. (See PREHISTORIC MAN.)

CAVENDISH, Henry (1731–1810), English chemist and physicist who showed HYDROGEN (inflammable air) to be a distinct GAS, water to be a compound and not an elementary substance and the composition of the ATMOSPHERE to be constant. He also used a torsion BALANCE to measure the DENSITY of the earth (1798).

CAVETT, Dick (1936–   ), US television personality, actor and author. After writing comedy material for Johnny Carson and others, he hosted *The Dick Cavett Show,* an interview program that gained a reputation during the 1960s and 1970s for its candor and its willingness to address controversial topics.

CAVIAR, the salted roe of certain STURGEON, a delicacy because of its scarcity. The best caviar comes from the Beluga sturgeon of the Caspian Sea.

CAVOUR, Count Camillo Benso di (1810–1861), Italian statesman largely responsible for the creation of a united Italy. Cavour, a native of Turin, founded the liberal newspaper *Il Risorgimento* in 1847 and, under VICTOR EMMANUEL II, became premier of Piedmont in 1852. Cavour sought to unite the country by making piecemeal additions to Piedmont. A subtle diplomat, he exploited NAPOLEON III'S ambitions to engineer the defeat of Austria in 1859, through which he secured the central Italian states. He then invaded the Papal States and entered Neapolitan territory. GARIBALDI, who had taken Sicily and Naples, was left with little option but to cede these gains to Cavour. The unification was completed, except for Venice and the Province of Rome, in 1861, only a few months before Cavour's death.

CAWNPORE. See KANPUR.

CAXTON, William (c1422–1491), English printer, trained in Cologne. He produced *The Recuyell of the Histories of Troye* (Bruges, c1475), the first book printed in English, and *The Dictes and Sayenges of the Phylosophers* (1477), the first book printed in England.

CAYENNE, capital of French Guiana, on Cayenne island. Founded in 1643, it was the center of French penal settlements during 1852–1945. Its port handles gold, rum, cocoa and cayenne pepper. Pop 35,000.

CAYLEY, Sir George (1773–1857), British inventor who pioneered the science of AERODYNAMICS. He built the first man-carrying GLIDER (1853) and formulated the design principles later used in AIRPLANE construction, although he recognized that in his day there was no propulsion unit which was sufficiently powerful and yet light enough to power an airplane.

CAYMAN ISLANDS, British colony in the Caribbean, formerly a Jamaican dependency, now with its own administration in George Town on Grand Cayman, the largest of the islands. Tourism and sea produce are principal industries. Pop 16,677.

CAYUGA LAKE, in W central N.Y., forms the boundary between Cayuga and Seneca counties and is the longest of the FINGER LAKES (about 66.5mi). Its average width is 2mi and greatest depth is 435ft.

CB RADIO. See RADIO, AMATEUR.

CEAUŞECU, Nicolae (1918–   ), president of Romania from 1967. First elected a full member of the Romanian Communist Party central committee in 1948, he became head of the committee in 1965. As president, he instigated a policy of independence within the Soviet bloc.

CECIL, Lord (Edgar Algernon) Robert, 1st Viscount Cecil of Chelwood (1864–1958), British statesman, awarded the Nobel Peace Prize in 1937 for his part in the formation of the League of Nations.

CECIL, William, 1st Baron Burghley (1520–1598), English statesman who rose to power late in Henry VIII's reign. He was appointed chief secretary of state on the accession of Elizabeth I and remained her chief adviser for 40 years, becoming Lord High Treasurer in 1572. He was responsible for the execution of Mary Queen of Scots and for the defensive measures against the Spanish Armada.

CELESTA, musical instrument resembling a piano, produced during the 19th century as an improvement on the GLOCKENSPIEL. The keys activate hammers which strike metal bars in acoustic chambers, producing a light, bell-like sound.

CELESTIAL SPHERE, in ancient times, the sphere which it was believed all the stars were attached. In modern times, an imaginary sphere of indefinite but very large radius upon which, for purposes of angular computation, celestial bodies are considered to be situated. The **celestial poles** are defined as those points on the sphere vertically above the terrestrial poles, and the **celestial equator** by the projection of the terrestrial EQUATOR onto the sphere. (See also ECLIPTIC.) Astronomical coordinate systems are based on these great circles (circles whose centers are also the center of the sphere) and, in some cases, on the observer's celestial HORIZON. In the most frequently used, the equatorial system, terrestrial latitude corresponds to declination—a star directly overhead in New York City will have a declination of +41° (S Hemisphere declinations are preceded by a minus sign), New York City having a latitude of 41°N—and terrestrial longitude to right ascension, which is measured eastward from the First Point of ARIES. Right ascension is measured in hours, one hour corresponding to 15° of longitude. (See also SPHERICAL TRIGONOMETRY.)

CELIAC DISEASE, a disease of the small intestine (see GASTROINTESTINAL TRACT), among the commonest causes of food malabsorption. In celiac disease, ALLERGY to part of gluten, a component of wheat, causes severe loss of absorptive surface. In children, failure to thrive and DIARRHEA are common signs, while in adults weight loss, ANEMIA, diarrhea, TETANY and VITAMIN deficiency may bring it to attention. Complete exclusion of dietary gluten leads to full recovery.

CELIBACY, voluntary abstinence from marriage and sexual intercourse. Celibacy of the clergy in the Roman Catholic Church was instituted by Pope Siricius (386), but abandoned by Protestants during the Reformation. In the Eastern Church, married men can be ordained as priests, though bishops must be celibates or widowers. Recently there has been opposition to celibacy among some Catholics.

CÉLINE, Louis-Ferdinand (1894–1961), pseudonym of Louis-Ferdinand Destouches, French novelist. His first novels, *Journey to the End of Night* (1932) and *Death on the Installment Plan* (1936), made his vivid, hallucinatory style famous.

CELL, the basic unit of living matter from which all plants and animals are built. A living cell can carry out all the functions necessary for life. BACTERIA, AMOEBA and PARAMECIUM are examples of single-celled organisms. In multicellular organisms cells become differentiated to perform specific functions. All cells have certain basic similarities.

Nearly all cells can be divided into three parts: an outer membrane or wall, a **nucleus** and a clear fluid called CYTOPLASM.

Animal cells are surrounded by a plasma membrane. This is living, thin and flexible. It allows substances to diffuse in and out and is also able to select some substances and exclude others. The membrane plays a vital role in deciding what enters a cell. Plant cells are surrounded by a thick, rigid, non-living CELLULOSE cell wall.

Other types of membrane are found in a cell. Around the nucleus is the nuclear membrane, which has in it tiny pores to allow molecules to pass between the cytoplasm and the nucleus. Another type of membrane is the much-folded endoplasmic reticulum which seems to be a continuation of the cell or nuclear membrane. The endoplasmic reticulum is always associated with the RIBOSOMES where PROTEIN SYNTHESIS takes place, controlled by the CHROMOSOMES which are sited in the nucleus and are mainly made of DNA (see NUCLEIC ACIDS).

The cytoplasm contains many organelles. Among the most important are the rod-shaped **mitochondria**, containing the enzymes necessary for the release of energy from food by the process of RESPIRATION (see also CITRIC ACID CYCLE). Other organelles whose function is still uncertain are the Golgi bodies, which may be involved in the synthesis of cell wall material; and the lysosomes, which may contain enzymes involved in autolysis and controlled destruction of tissues. The cytoplasm of green plants also contains CHLOROPLASTS, where PHOTOSYNTHESIS occurs.

New cells are formed by a process of division called MITOSIS. Each chromosome duplicates and mitosis involves the transfer of this new set of chromosomes to the new daughter cell. Gamete (reproductive) cells are formed by MEIOSIS, which is a division that halves the number of chromosomes; thus a human cell that contains 46 chromosomes will produce gamete cells with 23.

Cells differentiate in a multi-cellular organism to produce cells as different as a nerve cell and a muscle cell. Cells of similar types are grouped together into TISSUES.

There are two broad types of cells. Firstly, **prokaryotic cells,** which have the genetic material in the form of loose filaments of DNA not separated from the cytoplasm by a membrane. Secondly, **eukaryotic cells,** which have the genetic material borne on chromosomes made up of DNA and protein that are separated from the cytoplasm by a nuclear membrane. Eukaryotic cells are the unit of basic structure in all organisms except bacteria and blue green algae, which comprise single prokaryotic cells.

CELLINI, Benvenuto (1500–1571), Italian goldsmith and sculptor. Of his work in precious metals little survives except the gold saltcellar made for Francis I of France in 1543. His most famous work of sculpture is *Perseus with the Head of Medusa* (1545–54). His celebrated *Autobiography*

(1558–62) is colorful and vigorous, though somewhat exaggerated.

CELLO, or *violoncello,* the second-largest instrument of the violin family, with four strings and a range of three octaves starting two octaves below middle C. It is the deepest-toned instrument in the string quartet (see CHAMBER MUSIC). It dates from the 16th century, but did not become a popular solo instrument until the 17th and 18th centuries. Among the finest music for solo cello are J. S. Bach's six cello suites. Many composers, including Elgar, Dvořák and Shostakovich, have written cello concertos.

CELLOPHANE, transparent, impermeable film of CELLULOSE used in packaging, first developed by J. E. Brandenburger (1911). Wood pulp is soaked in sodium hydroxide, shredded, aged and reacted with CARBON disulfide to form a solution of viscose (sodium cellulose xanthate). This is extruded through a slit into an acid bath, where the cellulose is regenerated as a film. It is dried and given a waterproof coating. If the viscose is extruded through a minute hole, rayon is produced (see SYNTHETIC FIBERS).

CELLULOID, the first commercial synthetic PLASTIC, developed by J. W. Hyatt (1869). It is a colloidal dispersion of NITROCELLULOSE and CAMPHOR. It is tough, strong, resistant to water, oils and dilute acids, and thermoplastic. Used in dental plates, combs, billiard balls, lacquers, spectacle frames and (formerly) photographic films and toys, celluloid is highly inflammable, and has been largely replaced by other plastics.

CELLULOSE, the main constituent of the CELL walls of higher plants, many algae and some fungi; cotton is 90% cellulose. Cellulose is a CARBOHYDRATE with a similar structure to starch. In its pure form it is a white solid which absorbs water until completely saturated, but dissolves only in a few solvents, notably strong alkalis and some acids. It can be broken down by heat and by the digestive tracts of some animals, but it passes through the human digestive tract unchanged and is helpful only in stimulating movement of the intestines. Industrially, it is used in manufacturing textile fibers, CELLOPHANE, CELLULOID, and the cellulose PLASTICS, notably NITROCELLULOSE (used also in explosives), cellulose acetate for toys and plastic boxes and cellulose acetate butyrate for typewriter keys.

CELTIC CHURCH, churches organized along monastic lines in areas of Celtic settlement (Scotland, Ireland, Wales and Brittany) between about the 5th century and the Norman Conquest. They differed from Rome only in superficial matters, and were responsible for converting large areas of Europe.

CELTIC LANGUAGES, a major division of the INDO-EUROPEAN LANGUAGES, spoken widely over Europe from pre-Roman times though now confined chiefly to the UK and Brittany. There are two main branches: the now extinct Gaulish, about which little is known, and Insular, to which belong all the modern Celtic tongues. The latter branch is itself split into two: Gaelic, or Goidelic (Irish Gaelic, Scottish Gaelic and Manx), and Brythonic (Breton, Welsh and Cornish). Recent years have seen a revival in certain of these.

CELTIC RENAISSANCE, literary revival of the Gaelic tongues, particularly in Ireland and Wales, in the 19th and 20th centuries. Linked to the rise of nationalism, it resulted in a large and still growing body of literature and scholarship.

CELTS, a prehistoric people whose numerous tribes occupied much of Europe between c2000 and c100 BC, the peak of their power being around 500–100 BC. No European Celtic literature survives, but the later Irish and Welsh sources tell much about Celtic society and way of life. Primarily an agricultural people, though in local areas crafts and iron smelting developed, they grouped together in small settlements. Their social unit, based on kinship, was divided into a warrior nobility and a farming class, from the former being recruited the priests or DRUIDS, who ranked highest of all. Celtic art mixes stylized heads with abstract designs of scrolls and spirals. Remnants of CELTIC LANGUAGES are to be found in the forms of Gaelic, Erse, Manx and Welsh. The Celtic sphere of influence declined during the 1st century BC owing to the simultaneous expansion of the Roman Empire and the incursions of the Germanic races.

CEMENT, common name for Portland cement, the most important modern construction material, notably as a constituent of CONCRETE. In the manufacturing process, limestone is ground into small pieces (about 2cm). To provide the silica (25%) and alumina (10%) content required, various clays and crushed rocks are added, including iron ore (about 1%). This material is ground and finally burned in a rotary kiln at up to 1500°C, thus converting the mixture into clinker pellets. About 5% GYPSUM is then added to slow the hardening process, and the ground mixture is added to sand (for MORTAR) or to sand, gravel and crushed rock (for concrete). When water is added it solidifies gradually, undergoing many complex chemical reactions. The name "Portland" cement arises from a resemblance to stone quarried at Portland, England.

CENOBITES, monks who founded the first monastic communities in the 4th century. They differed from their hermit predecessors in that they formed communities rather than living in solitude. Western cenobitic monasticism was introduced by St. Benedict, and was the basis of the Benedictine Order.

CENSORSHIP, supervision or control exercised by anybody in authority over public communication, conduct or morals. The official responsible is known as the censor. Early censorship in the Greek city-states curbed conduct insulting to the gods or dangerous to public order. In Rome the censor dictated public morality.

Censorship of books was not widespread (although some books were publicly burned) until the invention of printing in the 15th century. The first *Index of Prohibited Books* was drawn up by the Catholic Church in 1559 in an effort to stop the spread of subversive literature. Similar tactics were employed by Protestants and secular authorities. Milton's *Areopagitica* (1644) presented a strong case for freedom of the press, which was won in W Europe during the 18th and 19th centuries. In the US, freedom of the press is protected from federal interference by the First Amendment to the Consititution, but it was not applied to the states through the 14th Amendment until 1931 (see NEAR v. MINNESOTA). In ROTH v. UNITED STATES (1957) the US Supreme Court extended First Amendment protection to material "having even the slightest redeeming social importance" and defined obscenity as "material which deals with sex in a manner appealing to prurient interest." But in 1973 the Court changed the requirement to one of "serious" social purpose. It has upheld film censorship as being within the police power of the states, but has struck down several censorship statutes for being too vague. (See also PORNOGRAPHY.).

CENSUS, enumeration of persons, property or other items at a given time. Today most countries conduct a regular count of population but these vary greatly in reliability, especially in underdeveloped countries. India, for example, conducts only sample censuses; this is cheaper and allows more detailed examination of the chosen sample. Early censuses, such as those mentioned in the Old Testament, were primarily military inventories. Babylonia, China, Egypt and Rome all conducted a census for fiscal purposes. The modern concept dates from the 17th and 18th centuries when regular censuses were taken in some New World colonies. Among the first national censuses was that in the newly founded US in 1790, to determine each state's representation in Congress; since then, as required by the Constitution, a census has been conducted every 10 years. The British census began in 1801. Beyond merely determining the size and content of a country's population, the modern census may seek information on economic development and social issues, and is therefore an essential tool in government planning.

The 1980 US census became ensnarled in lawsuits when some jurisdictions charged that they had been undercounted in some ghetto areas or other areas with large numbers of illegal aliens. An undercount could affect a state's representation in Congress and the amount of disbursement of federal funds for some purposes. Census recounts were ordered by the courts in some instances.

CENTENNIAL EXPOSITION, International, world's fair held in Philadelphia, Pa., from May to Nov. 1876, celebrating the 100th anniversary of the Declaration of Independence. Exhibits from the arts and sciences were displayed by 49 nations. Mass production techniques, then being pioneered in the US, were also put on show. The fair attracted almost 10 million visitors.

CENTER OF GRAVITY, the point about which gravitational FORCES on an object exert no net turning effect, and at which the mass of the object can for many purposes be regarded as concentrated. A freely suspended object hangs with its center of gravity vertically below the point of suspension, and an object will balance, though it may be unstable, if supported at a point vertically below the center of gravity. In free flight, an object spins about its center of gravity, which moves steadily in a straight line; the application of forces causes the center of gravity to accelerate in the direction of the net force, and the rate of spin to change according to the resultant turning effect.

CENTIPEDES, long-bodied members of the phylum ARTHROPODA with two legs to each of their 15–100 segments. They are usually 25–50mm (1–2in) long, though in the tropics some reach 0.3m (1ft). Normally insectivorous they paralyze their food by injecting poison through a pair of pincers located near the head. Centipedes live in moist places under stones or in soil.

Official name: Central African Republic
Capital: Bangui
Area: 240,534sq mi
Population: 1,794,000
Languages: French, Sango
Religions: Christian, Animist, Muslim
Monetary unit(s): 1 CFA Franc = 100 centimes

CENTRAL AFRICAN REPUBLIC, landlocked independent republic in Africa. It lies just N of the equator, bounded by Chad to the N and Sudan to the S, on a well-watered plateau 2,500ft above sea level. The country is mostly savanna, with dense tropical rain forest to the S. The chief river, the Ubangi, is the main link with the outside world. There are no railroads and only 50mi of paved road.

People and Economy. The population is composed of various ethnic groups, with mainly Bantu and Nilotic cultures. The *lingua franca* is Sangho. There are various religious groups, but about 70% of the population are tribal animists. There are few towns, and education and living standards are poor.

History. Various tribes migrated into the area, most fleeing the slave trade in the 19th century. The French established outposts 1886–87, and the area was incorporated into French Equatorial Africa in 1910. It achieved independence on Aug. 13, 1960, under President David Dacko; he was overthrown in 1966 by Colonel Jean-Bedel Bokassa, who in 1972 was appointed president for life. In 1979 Dacko regained control with support from the French and was elected to a six-year term in 1981. Bokassa went into exile.

CENTRAL AMERICA, narrow land bridge between Mexico and South America. With Mexico and the Caribbean islands (West Indies), it forms the vast region known as MIDDLE AMERICA. Central America includes seven independent republics: Belize, Costa Rica, El Salvador, Guatemala, Honduras, Nicaragua, and Panama.

People. Originally the land of MAYA Indians, Central America is now inhabited by Indians, Europeans, Negroes, and people of mixed ancestry. There are great differences between countries: in Costa Rica most of the people are white, while in Guatemala almost half the population are pure Indians. Spanish is the most widely spoken language, except in Belize where English is the official language. Tribal dialects are used by many Indians. Although elementary education is free, Central America—with the exception of Costa Rica—has high illiteracy rates. Ancient customs still prevail in many Indian villages.

Economy. About two thirds of the population work in agriculture, either on plantations owned by US and European companies or on small farms. Export crops include bananas, coffee, cacao and coconuts, and the main subsistence crops are corn and beans. Central America has very little manufacturing and processed goods must be imported. The economic development of the region is hampered by transportation problems, caused partly by the rugged terrain. Most of the roads are unpaved and the railroad network is not dense enough. Many communities can be reached only on foot.

History. The Maya civilization, one of the earliest in the Western Hemisphere, flourished in Central America AD 300–800. Following the Spanish conquest in the early 16th century, the region north of Panama became the Spanish colony of Guatemala. Panama belonged to the viceroyalty of New Granada (Colombia). After the independence proclamation in 1821, the former colony of Guatemala was for a short time the Central American Federation, but in 1838 independent republics were established. In the early 20th century, Central America came under US influence: the Panama Canal was opened in 1914, US marines intervened in Honduras (1903 and 1923) and Nicaragua (1912 and 1924), and US companies became the chief foreign investors. Costa Rica is politically the most stable country; the others have suffered from external conflicts (Guatemala against Belize, Honduras against El Salvador), dictatorships and revolutions.

CENTRALIA MINE DISASTER, an explosion on Mar. 25, 1947, that killed 115 miners at the Centralia (Ill.) Coal Company's Mine Number 5. The operator had a long record of safety violations, but the disaster, the worst such in 19 years, came when the nation's coal mines were under government control and John L. Lewis, head of the United Mine Workers, defied the Supreme Court when he called his men out on a memorial strike. Four years later an even worse disaster occurred at another Illinois coal mine, in West Frankfort, where 119 died. The two tragedies spurred Congress to pass the Mine Safety Act of 1952.

CENTRAL INTELLIGENCE AGENCY (CIA), established in 1947 by the National Security Act to coordinate, evaluate and disseminate intelligence from other US agencies and to advise the president and the National Security Council on security matters. Though its field of operations widened considerably under Allen Dulles (Director 1953–61), its estimated 15,000 employees spend most of their time in research and analysis at CIA headquarters in Langley, Va. The CIA has done much to further the interests of the US and its allies, but such fiascos as the BAY OF PIGS invasion of Cuba and the capture of the U2 spy-plane over Russia, in which it was involved, have not helped international relations. Concern over possible misuse of its considerable independence in the wake of "Watergate" led to a major investigation and internal reorganization in 1975. Especially disturbing to critics was the revelation of domestic spying and the CIA's implication in plots to kill foreign leaders. Persistent rumors that the Soviet Union had planted a "mole," or double agent, within the CIA became the grist for many speculative articles and spy novels.

CENTRAL POWERS, coalition of Germany, Austria–Hungary, Ottoman Turkey and Bulgaria in WWI. (See also ALLIES; TRIPLE ALLIANCE.)

CENTRAL TREATY ORGANIZATION (CENTO), mutual security alliance between Pakistan, Iran, Turkey, Iraq and Britain, with the US an associate member. It was established by the Baghdad Pact (1955). Iraq withdrew its membership in 1959. After Iran and Pakistan withdrew (1979), CENTO became virtually defunct.

CENTRIFUGAL FORCE. See CENTRIPETAL FORCE.

CENTRIFUGE, a machine for separating mixtures of solid particles and immiscible liquids of different DENSITIES and for extracting liquids from wet solids by rotating them in a container at high speed. The separation occurs because the centrifugal force experienced in a rotating frame increases with particle density. Centrifuges are used in drying clothes and slurries, in chemical ANALYSIS, in separating cream and in atomic ISOTOPE separation. Giant ones are used to accustom pilots and astronauts to large ACCELERATIONS. The **ultracentrifuges** invented by Theodor Svedberg (1884–1971), uses very high speeds to measure (optically) sedimentation rates of macromolecular solutes and so determine molecular weights.

CENTRIPETAL FORCE, the FORCE applied to a body to maintain it moving in a circular path. To maintain a body of MASS m, traveling with instantaneous VELOCITY v, in a circular path of radius r, a centripetal force F, acting toward the center of the circle, given by $F = mv^2/r$ must be applied to it. The equal and opposite force of reaction of the mass on its constraint is the **centrifugal force.**

CENTURY OF PROGRESS EXPOSITION, international exhibition celebrating Chicago's centenary, held on the shores of Lake Michigan 1933–34. Primarily concerned with science and technology, it also stimulated design and architecture.

CEPHALIC INDEX, in ANTHROPOMETRY, an index used originally in attempts to classify RACE, now used mainly to indicate possible relationships between small groups. The index is given by

$$\frac{\text{maximum head breadth} \times 100}{\text{maximum head length}}$$

CEPHALOPODA, class of predatory MOLLUSKS including the CUTTLEFISH, OCTOPUS and SQUID. They swim by forcing a jet of water through a narrow funnel near the mouth. Cephalopods have suckerbearing arms and a horny beak. The shell, typical of most mollusks, is absent or reduced.

CEPHEID VARIABLES, stars whose brightness varies regularly with a period of 1–50 days, possibly, but improbably, due to a fluctuation in size. The length of their cycle is directly proportional to their absolute magnitude, making them useful "mileposts" for computing large astronomical distances. (See VARIABLE STARS.)

CERAMICS, materials produced by treating nonmetallic inorganic materials (originally clay) at high temperatures. Modern ceramics include such diverse products as porcelain and china, furnace bricks, electric insulators, ferrite magnets (see SPINEL), rocket nosecones and abrasives. In general, ceramics are hard, chemically inert under most conditions, and can withstand high temperatures in industrial applications. Many are refractory metal OXIDES. Primitive ceramics in the form of pottery date from the 5th millennium BC, and improved steadily in quality and design. By the 10th century AD porcelain had been developed in China. (See also BRICK; CERMETS; CONCRETE; GLASS; POTTERY AND PORCELAIN.)

CEREAL CROPS, annual plants of the

grass family, including WHEAT, RICE, CORN, BARLEY, SORGHUM, millet, oats and RYE. Their grain forms the staple diet for most of the world. Though lacking in calcium and vitamin A, they have more CARBOHYDRATES than any other food, as well as PROTEIN and other VITAMINS. Cereal crops are relatively easy to cultivate and can cope with a wide range of climates. About 1,757 million acres of the world's arable land are sown with cereal crops each year. The US leads in production of corn, oats and sorghum.

CEREALS, Breakfast, popular foods made from cereal grains. They were first developed in the 19th century as part of the health food movement; W. H. KELLOGG and C. W. Post were the first to make them into massive industries. Some cereals, such as oatmeal, must be cooked before eating; more popular are the ready-to-eat cereals such as cornflakes and puffed wheat, on which milk is usually poured.

CEREBELLUM. See BRAIN.

CEREBRAL PALSY, a diverse group of conditions caused by BRAIN damage around the time of BIRTH and resulting in a variable degree of nonprogressive physical and mental handicap. While abnormalities of MUSCLE control are the most obvious, loss of sensation and some degree of DEAFNESS are common accompaniments. Speech and intellectual development can also be impaired but may be entirely normal. SPASTIC PARALYSIS of both legs with mild arm weakness (diplegia), or of one half of the body (hemiplegia), are common forms. A number of cases have abnormal movements (athetosis) or ATAXIA. Common causes include birth trauma, ANOXIA, prematurity, Rhesus incompatibility and cerebral HEMORRHAGE. PHYSIOTHERAPY and training allow the child to overcome many deficits; deformity must be avoided by ensuring full range of movements at all joints, but surgical correction may be necessary. Sometimes transposition of TENDONS improves the balance of strength around important joints. It is crucial that the child is not deprived of normal sensory and emotional experiences. Improved antenatal care, OBSTETRIC skill and care of premature infants have reduced the incidence.

CEREBROSPINAL FLUID, watery fluid circulating in the chambers (ventricles) of the BRAIN and between layers of the meninges covering the brain and SPINAL CORD. It is a filtrate of BLOOD and is normally clear, containing salts, GLUCOSE and some PROTEIN. It may be sampled and analyzed by SPINAL TAP.

CEREBRUM. See BRAIN.

CERENKOV RADIATION, ELECTRO-MAGNETIC RADIATION emitted when a high-energy particle passes through a dense medium at a velocity greater than the velocity of light in that medium. It was first detected in 1934 by P. A. Cherenkov.

CERES, in Roman mythology, goddess of food plants and harvest; according to legend her cult was introduced to stem a famine in 496 BC. Cereals are probably named for her. Her Greek counterpart is DEMETER.

CERES, largest of the ASTEROIDS (470mi in diameter) and the one first discovered (by PIAZZI, 1801). Its orbit was first computed by K. F. GAUSS and found to satisfy BODE's Law. Its "year" is 1,681 days and its maximum apparent magnitude is +7.

CERF, Bennett (1898–1971), US publisher. The president of Modern Library (1925–71) and founder (1927), president (1927–65) and chairman (1965–70) of Random House, Cerf published such authors as JOYCE, PROUST, KAFKA, O'NEILL and FAULKNER. He compiled several humor anthologies and appeared on the weekly television panel show *What's My Line?* (1952–66).

CERMETS, or **ceramels,** composite materials made from mixed METALS and CERAMICS. The TRANSITION ELEMENTS are most often used. Powdered and compacted with an oxide, carbide or boride, etc., they are heated to just below their melting point, when bonding occurs. Cermets combine the hardness and strength of metals with a high resistance to corrosion, wear and heat. This makes them invaluable in jet engines, cutting tools, brake linings and nuclear reactors.

CERVANTES (SAAVEDRA), Miguel de (1547–1616), Spanish novelist and playwright, a major figure of Spanish literature. He left his studies in 1570 to join the army; his left hand was crippled at the sea battle of Lepanto (1571). Captured by pirates in 1575, he was enslaved in Algiers until ransomed in 1580. In 1585 he wrote *La Galatea*, a pastoral novel in verse and prose; after this he entered government service. In 1605 he published the first part of *Don Quixote de la Mancha,* his masterpiece. Not only a masterly debunking of pseudo-chivalric romance but a rich tragi-comic novel, it was an immediate success. He also wrote about 30 plays, of which 16 survive, a volume of short stories and the second part of *Don Quixote* (1615). His last work was *Persilas and Sigismunda* (1617).

CERVERA Y TOPETE, Pascual (1839–1909), Spanish admiral. Minister of marine in 1892, he commanded the Atlantic fleet during the SPANISH-AMERICAN WAR (1898). It was blockaded and sunk at Santiago de Cuba; Cervera was honorably acquitted at his court-martial.

CESARIAN SECTION, BIRTH of a child from the WOMB by abdominal operation. The mother is given an anesthetic and an incision is made in the ABDOMEN and lower part of the uterus; the child is delivered and attended to; the PLACENTA is removed and incisions are sewn up. Cesarian section may be necessary if the baby is too large to pass through the PELVIS, if it shows delay or signs of ANOXIA during labor, or in cases where maternal disease does not allow normal labor. It may be performed effectively before labor has started. With modern ANESTHESIA and BLOOD TRANSFUSION, the risks of Cesarian section are not substantially greater than those of normal delivery. It is believed that Julius Caesar was born in this way.

CETA (COMPREHENSIVE TRAINING AND EMPLOYMENT ACT), of 1973, created a federally funded system for training unemployed people and providing them with jobs and job-related services. Federal grants to states and other governmental units supported the Neighborhood Youth Corps, the JOB CORPS, the Young Adult Conservation Corps and similar programs. Businesses also received tax credits for hiring and training certain disadvantaged workers. The federal government stopped funding CETA programs on Oct. 1, 1981, when the first of President Ronald Reagan's reduced budgets went into effect.

CETEWAYO, or Cetshwayo (c1826–1884), fourth and last Zulu king (1873–79). In 1879 he declared war on British and Boer settlers in the Transvaal, but was finally captured and deposed.

CEZANNE, Paul (1839–1906), French painter, among the most influential of modern times. During his studies in Paris he met and was influenced by Pissarro and other Impressionists. His early work is Impressionist in style, but he later abandoned this to develop an approach of his own, lyrical and vibrantly colorful, as in the *Grande Baigneuses* (1905). He sought to suggest depth through the use of color and to give his paintings a new structural strength and formal integrity. In his efforts "to treat nature in terms of the cylinder, sphere and cone . . . ," and to make his paintings autonomous objects, he became the prime innovator of modern art, anticipating Cubism and other movements.

CGS UNITS, a metric system of units based on the CENTIMETER (length), GRAM (mass)

and SECOND (time), generally used among scientists until superseded by SI UNITS. Several variants are used for electrical and magnetic problems, including electrostatic units (esu or stat-units—see STATAMPERE), electromagnetic units (emu or ab-units—see ABAMPERE) and the Gaussian system. In this last, ab-units are used for quantities arising primarily in an electromagnetic context, stat-units for electrostatic quantities and both the permeability and the permittivity of free space are set equal to unity. As a result, the speed of light (c) tends to occur in equations in which electrostatic and magnetic quantities are mixed.

CHABRIER, Alexis Emmanuel (1841–1894), French composer best remembered for orchestral works such as *España* (1883) and various piano pieces. His work influenced DEBUSSY; RAVEL and SATIE.

CHACONNE, spirited Spanish dance, possibly of Mexican origin, dating from the 17th century, which gave its name to a musical form similar to PASSACAGLIA. Both are usually in triple time and consist of variations on a ground bass.

CHACO WAR, war fought between Paraguay and Bolivia during 1932–35 over possession of part of the Chaco region. It caused significant damage to both countries, with over 200,000 casualties. It was settled by arbitration, largely in favor of Paraguay, the military victor.

Official name: Republic of Chad
Capital: N'djamena
Area: 495,752sq mi
Population: 4,502,000
Languages: French, Arabic, Bantu
Religions: Muslim, Animist, Christian
Monetary unit(s): 1 CFA Franc = 100 centimes

CHAD, landlocked state in N central Africa bordered by six states, including Libya to the N and the Central African Republic to the S.

Land. Its N part extends into the Sahara desert, where the Tibesti highlands rise to 11,000ft. The S part consists largely of semiarid steppe with wooded grasslands (savannas) near Lake CHAD, watered by the Shari and Logone rivers. In the S rainfall reaches 47in during the rainy season.

People. The N part of the country is inhabited by nomadic Muslim tribes such as the Fulani, the Wadai and the Toubou. In the more densely populated S, Negroid tribes predominate, the largest being the Sara. Most live in rural areas, are animists, and speak tribal languages. The rate of illiteracy is high. There are less than 5,000 Europeans, mainly French; French is the official language.

Economy. Agriculture and cattle support the economy. Manufacturing is limited mostly to the processing of cotton, the chief export. Cattle, meat, fish, hides, cotton and groundnut oils and gum arabic are also exported. Trade is primarily with Europe, chiefly France, which has been a major investor and provider of aid.

History. The French had conquered Chad by 1900, and it became the northernmost of the four territories of Ubanga-Shari-Chad when French Equatorial Africa was formed in 1910. It became an independent republic in Aug. 1960, with François (Ngarta) Tombalbaye as president. He was killed during a military takeover in April 1975. Tension between the North and South is strong. In recent years internal fighting among several factions (one of which is supported by Libya) and repeated major governmental changes have strained Chad's already frail economy. At the invitation of the government, France maintains a military presence.

CHAD, Lake, in W central Africa, is bounded by Cameroon, Chad, Niger and Nigeria and fed by the Shari and Logone rivers. The area of the shallow lake varies from 4,000 to 10,000sq mi at low and high water respectively.

CHADWICK, Sir James (1891–1974), English physicist who was awarded the 1935 Nobel physics prize for his discovery of the NEUTRON (1932).

CHADWICK, Florence (1918–   ), US distance swimmer who was the first woman to swim the English Channel in both directions (1950–51), and the first woman to swim the 21-mi Catalina Channel, off Long Beach, Calif. (1952). She also swam the Strait of Gibraltar and the Bosporus.

CHAGALL, Marc (1887–   ), Russian-Jewish painter. Influenced at first by his teacher BAKST, his work developed further in Paris 1910–14. His style is characterized by dreamlike, lyrical fantasy and bright but never harsh colors. His subjects are often derived from the traditions of folklore and pre-WWI Jewish life in Russia. Chagall,

who left Russia in 1922 and later settled in France, also illustrated a number of books and created memorable works in stained glass.

CHAIN, Sir Ernst Boris (1906–1979), German-born UK Biochemist who helped develop PENICILLIN for clinical use. For this he shared with FLOREY and FLEMING the 1945 Nobel Prize for Physiology or Medicine.

CHAIN REACTION. See NUCLEAR ENERGY.

CHALCEDON, Council of, the fourth ECUMENICAL COUNCIL, held Oct. 8–31, 451. It defined Christ as one Person in two natures (divine and human) united 'unconfusedly, unchangeably, indivisibly, inseparably'; the council thus opposed Eutyches, the father of MONOPHYSITISM, and the NESTORIANS.

CHALDEA, name for S Babylonia, after its occupation by the Chaldeans in the 10th century BC. The Chaldeans were accomplished astronomers and astrologers, and ancient writers often used their name as a synonym for "magician." In 626 BC NABOPALASSAR founded the Chaldean Neo-Babylonian Empire, which held sway over the area until the death of NEBUCHADNEZZAR in 561 BC. (See also BABYLONIA and ASSYRIA.)

CHALDEAN RITE. See NESTORIANS.

CHALIAPIN, Fyodor Ivanovich (1873–1938), Russian operatic bass. Famous for his acting as well as for his voice, he settled in France after the Russian Revolution. His main successes were as MUSSORGSKY's *Boris Godunov* and Boito's *Mefistofele.*

CHALK, soft, white rock composed of calcium carbonate, $CaCo_3$; a type of fine-grained, porous LIMESTONE containing calcareous remains of minute marine animals. There are large deposits in Tex., Kan. and Ark. Chalk is widely used in lime and cement manufacture and as a fertilizer. It is also used in cosmetics, plastics, crayons and oil paints; school chalk is today usually made from chemically-produced calcium carbonate.

CHAMBERLAIN, family name of three prominent British statesmen. **Joseph Chamberlain** (1836–1914), entered Parliament in 1876 as a Liberal. He held office under Gladstone, but split with him, opposing home rule for Ireland (1886). As colonial secretary 1895–1903, he failed to prevent the Boer Wars. Until his paralysis by a stroke in 1906, he fought for integration of the Empire through preferential tariffs for Empire trade. His son, **Sir Joseph Austen Chamberlain** (1863–1937), entered parliament as a

Conservative in 1892, and held various government offices from 1902. As foreign secretary 1924–29 under Baldwin, he helped secure the LOCARNO TREATIES, and shared the 1925 Nobel Peace Prize. Austen's half-brother, **Arthur Neville Chamberlain** (1869–1940), was a Conservative member of parliament from 1918. He held office under Baldwin, and succeeded him as prime minister in 1937. In his efforts to avert war with Germany, he followed a policy of appeasement and signed the MUNICH AGREEMENT, finally abandoning the policy when Hitler seized the rest of Czechoslovakia in March 1939. He resigned on May 10, 1940, during WWII, after the failure of an expedition to help Norway.

CHAMBERLAIN, Wilt (1936–   ), US basketball player. A center, he was professional basketball's all-time leading scorer. Combining great height (7ft, 1 1/8in) with great strength, he holds records for most points scored in a career (31,419), in a season (4,029) and in a game (100), and most rebounds per season (2,149).

CHAMBER MUSIC, term applied to a musical composition intended for a small ensemble. Originally it meant domestic music, that is music written by a house composer for his patron. It became established as a special genre during the 17th and 18th centuries. The instrumental combinations are varied, though they do not often exceed a total of 15 instruments. Chamber music is characterized by an intimacy of communication between the performers. The principal form of composition is the string quartet (2 violins, viola and cello), which was developed by HAYDN and MOZART, and expanded to new dimensions by BEETHOVEN.

CHAMBER OF COMMERCE, an association of businessmen set up to improve business conditions and practices, and to protect business interests. The first in the US was the New York Chamber of Commerce (1768) and now most sizeable US cities have one. Activities are coordinated through the US Chamber of Commerce, founded 1912. The International Chamber of Commerce, based in Paris, is mainly concerned with trade problems.

CHAMBERS, (Jay David) Whittaker (1901–1961), US journalist, who exposed Alger HISS as a spy in 1948. Chambers had been a fellow member of the Communist Party 1924–38.

CHAMELEONS, LIZARDS of the family Chamaeleonidae living in Africa and Madagascar with extraordinary adaptability to arboreal life. Their five toes are webbed into two groups of two and three between which they are able to grip branches. Their tails are prehensile, and their eyes can turn independently in all directions. They feed on insects which they catch with their long, sticky tongues, and the color of their skin undergoes swift alteration in response to changes of emotion or temperature. There are over 80 species, some viviparous, ranging in length from 50mm (2in) to 0.6m(2ft).

CHAMOIS, *Rupicapra rupicapra,* a goat-like mammal of the family Bovidae found in the mountain forests of Europe and Asia Minor. Chamois are famous for their agility, being capable of leaps of over 6m (20ft). They have thick brown coats and stand about 0.75m (2.5ft) at the shoulder. Their hides were once used for making "chammy" leather.

CHAMPA, Kingdom of, ancient Indochinese kingdom on the E coast of Vietnam. Originally a Chinese province, it first became prominent under King Bhadravarman c400 AD. In 446 it was subjugated by China. It won independence in the 6th century, and became increasingly powerful until in the 9th century it was threatening Chinese territory and the neighboring Khmer Empire. The Khmers overran it in the 12th century; it then came under Cambodian and later Annamese rule, and by the 17th century it had been absorbed into Annam completely.

CHAMPAGNE, historic province in NE France, famous for the effervescent champagne wines from vineyards between Reims and Épernay. The ruling counts of Champagne were especially powerful during the 12th and 13th centuries, and the region had a central role in French history.

CHAMPLAIN, Lake, narrow lake forming the border between Vt. and N.Y. and jutting partly into Canada. Its area is 435sq mi, excluding 55sq mi of islands. Lake Champlain is drained N by the Richelieu R, a tributary of the St. Lawrence R; though icebound for four months of the year, it is deep enough for commercial navigation. It is a leisure center and a site for many refining industries and was in the past the scene of several battles between American and British forces.

CHAMPLAIN, Samuel de (1567–1635), French explorer, first governor of French Canada. After voyages to the Canary Isles and Central America, he explored the St. Lawrence area in 1603 as far as the Lachine Rapids. In 1604–07 he explored much of what is now Nova Scotia. He founded Quebec in 1608 and discovered Lake Champlain in 1609. Virtual governor, when

Quebec surrendered to the English in 1629, Champlain was imprisoned in England; on his release in 1633 he returned to Canada as governor.

CHAMPS-ÉLYSÉES, avenue in Paris, France, famous for its spacious elegance. Lined with shops and cafés, it runs for over a mile W from the Place de la Concorde to the Arc de Triomphe.

CHANCELLORSVILLE, Battle of, fought during the US Civil War, May 1–5, 1863. Gen. Joseph Hooker's Union forces crossed the Rappahannock R to Chancellorsville, W of Fredericksburg, Va., in a bid to encircle Gen. Robert E. Lee's Confederate forces protecting Fredericksburg. The ploy failed; Lee's counteroffensive led to an indecisive battle claiming 30,000 lives, including that of Gen. "Stonewall" Jackson.

CHANDLER, Raymond Thornton (1888–1959), US detective novelist whose seven novels have received critical acclaim. They combine wit and pace with strong characterization, particularly of their hero Philip Marlowe, a tough but honest private detective. Among his best-known works are *The Big Sleep* (1939) and *The Long Goodbye* (1954).

CHANDLER, Zachariah (1813–1879), US politician, a founder of the Republican Party. He made his fortune as a dry-goods merchant in Detroit and was elected to the Senate in 1857, becoming a firm opponent of slavery and of the Confederade cause. He was secretary of the interior 1875–77.

CHANDRAGUPTA (4th century BC), Indian emperor c321–297 BC, founder of the MAURYA dynasty. He rose to power after Alexander the Great's withdrawal from India, and won territory from the Seleucids, extending his realm into Afghanistan. His grandson was the famous Emperor ASHOKA.

CHANDRAGUPTA, name of two emperors of N India. **Chandragupta I** (reigned c320–330 AD) rose from a local chieftainship to rule a prosperous realm covering what is now Bihar, Bengal and Uttar Pradesh. **Chandragupta II** (reigned c380–415), his grandson, took the foreign-controlled Gujarat area, opening the way for extensive trade with Rome. His reign was benevolent and saw a great cultural flowering in India.

CHANDRASEKHAR, Subrahmanyan (1910–), Indian-born US astrophysicist, a major figure in the theoretical study of stellar evolution, particularly that of dwarf stars.

CHANEL, Gabrielle ("Coco") (1883–1971), French fashion designer who rose to fame in Paris in the 1920s. She created the "Chanel Look" and the celebrated perfume *Chanel No. 5.*

CHANEY, Lon (1883–1930), US film actor who specialized in playing misshapen individuals and monsters. His skill in characterization and makeup won him the title of "Man with a Thousand Faces." His best-known films were *The Hunchback of Notre Dame* (1923) and *The Phantom of the Opera* (1925). His son, **Lon Chaney, Jr.** (1907–1973), also became famous as an actor, portraying the "Wolfman" in a series of horror movies.

CHANG HSUEH-LIANG (1898–), Chinese war lord, called "the Young Marshall". He became military ruler of Manchuria in 1928 after the Japanese assassinated his father. Japan conquered Manchuria in 1932, and Chang urged a common front with the Communists against the Japanese. He seized Chiang Kai-shek briefly in 1936 and held him for two weeks. Chang in turn was seized when Chiang was freed, and held in custody thereafter.

CHANNEL ISLANDS, archipelago totalling 75sq mi in area, in the English Channel off NW France. Dependencies of the British crown since 1066, they are administered according to their own local constitutions. The two main bailiwicks are Jersey, including Les Minquiers and Ecrehou Rocks, and Guernsey, including Sark, Alderney, Herm, Jethou, Lihou and Brechou. The two main towns are St. Helier on Jersey and St. Peter Port on Guernsey. Pop 128,560.

CHANNEL ISLANDS NATIONAL MONUMENT, consisting of the islands of Santa Barbara and Anacapa, off S Cal. A sea-lion colony and wildlife sanctuary, it has rich fossil beds. Only 2sq mi of the monument's 28sq mi area is land.

CHANNEL ISLANDS NATIONAL PARK, consisting of eight islands, off S Cal. extends over 150mi over the Pacific Ocean. The park was established in 1980 and includes Santa Barbara and Anacapa Islands, formerly part of the Channel Islands National Monument, and the islands of San Miguel, Santa Rosa, and Santa Cruz. The islands are known for sea mammals, including the California sea lion, and have rich fossil beds.

CHANNING, William Ellery (1780–1842), US theologian, writer and philanthropist, leader of the Unitarian movement in New England. He led the Unitarian withdrawal from Congregationalism in 1820–25. Active in antislavery, temperance and pacifist causes, he believed that moral improvement was man's prime concern.

CHANSON DE ROLAND (Song of

Roland), most famous and probably the earliest of the CHANSONS DE GESTE. Written in the 11th century, probably by the Norman poet Turold, it tells of the death of Roland at the battle of Roncevaux (Roncesvalles) in 778. It was a formative influence on Spanish, Italian and even Icelandic epic poetry.

CHANSONS DE GESTE, medieval French epic poems. Around 80 have survived, and the form and style have given rise to hundreds of other poems in various languages. Most of them deal with the legendary exploits of the Emperor CHARLEMAGNE and his knights, the Paladins.

CHANT. See PLAINSONG.

CHANUKAH. See HANUKKAH.

CHAPARRAL, a dense thicket of dwarf EVERGREEN trees, usually less than 3m (10ft) high; a locality characterized by such thickets, especially common in the Cal. region.

CHAPLIN, Sir Charles Spencer (1889–1977), British film actor and director, great comedian of the silent cinema. A vaudeville player, he rose to fame in Hollywood 1913–19 in a series of short comedies, in which he established his "little tramp" character. After 1918 he produced his own feature-length films such as *The Gold Rush* (1925) and, with sound, *Modern Times* (1936) and *The Great Dictator* (1940). Accused of communist sympathies, he left America in 1952 to settle in Switzerland. He was awarded a special Academy Award in 1973 and knighted in 1975.

CHAPPAQUIDDICK, small island off Martha's Vineyard, Mass., that achieved notoriety when, after a party on the evening of July 18, 1969, a car driven by Sen. Edward M. KENNEDY (D., Mass.), went off a bridge and his passenger, 28-year-old Mary Jo Kopechne, drowned. The senator did not report the accident to the police until the next morning, a delay he later termed "indefensible" and for which he received a two-month suspended sentence.

CHAPULTEPEC, historic hill near Mexico City. Site of an Aztec royal residence and religious center in the 14th century, it is 200ft high. In 1847 the fort on the hill, built by the Spanish in 1783, was stormed by American forces in the MEXICAN WAR, two days before the occupation of Mexico City. It is now a museum and state residence.

CHARCOAL, form of amorphous CARBON produced when wood, peat, bones, cellulose or other carbonaceous substances are heated with little or no air present. A highly porous residue of microcrystalline GRAPHITE remains. Charcoal is a fuel and was used in BLAST FURNACES until the advent of COKE. A highly porous form, activated charcoal, is made by heating charcoal in steam; it is used for ADSORPTION in refining processes and in gas masks. Charcoal is also used as a thermal insulator and by artists for drawing.

CHARCOT, Jean Martin (1825–1893), French physician and founder of modern NEUROLOGY, whose many researches advanced knowledge of HYSTERIA, MULTIPLE SCLEROSIS, locomotor ATAXIA, ASTHMA and aging. FREUD was one of his many pupils.

CHARDIN, Jean-Baptiste-Siméon (1699–1779), French painter best known for his still lifes and for his middle-period genre paintings, affectionate depictions of the everyday life of the bourgeoisie. All his work is characterized by a straightforward realism, with atmospheric use of light and color.

CHARIOT, light, open, horse-drawn vehicle, usually two-wheeled, used as a weapon of war by many primitive peoples because of its speed. Mesopotamia used chariots c3000 BC, and by c1500 BC Egypt and China made extensive use of them.

CHARISMA, New Testament term from the Greek for the gifts of the Holy Spirit, imparted to apostles, prophets and healers to promote God's kingdom. The term has come to mean those magnetic qualities in certain individuals, especially political leaders such as Napoleon, Lenin or John F. Kennedy, that enable them to win mass support or enthusiastic response from their followers.

CHARLEMAGNE (Charles the Great; c742–814), king of the FRANKS, founder of the HOLY ROMAN EMPIRE and, in legend, hero of the CHANSONS DE GESTE. In 771, on the death of his co-ruler, his brother Carloman, Charlemagne became sole ruler of the Franks and began to extend the kingdom. In response to an appeal by Pope Adrian I, he waged a successful campaign against Lombardy in 773–74. Bavaria was annexed in 788, and the Saxons and Avars (on the Danube) were subjugated and Christianized after some 30 years of war. In 800 Charlemagne was crowned emperor by Pope Leo III. From his court at AACHEN he not only controlled an efficient administrative system, but also fostered the Carolingian cultural renaissance, which spread through much of present-day France, Germany, Austria, Switzerland, Holland and Belgium.

CHARLES, name of seven Holy Roman Emperors. **Charles I** (see CHARLEMAGNE). **Charles II the Bald** (see CHARLES, kings of France). **Charles III the Fat** (839–888), was emperor 881–87. After his overthrow Charlemagne's empire disintegrated. **Charles IV** (1316–1378), was emperor from 1355. He was also king of Bohemia, in whose welfare he was most interested. Making Prague his capital, he founded the Charles University there and promulgated the GOLDEN BULL of 1356, which determined the form of elections for the Holy Roman Emperor. **Charles V** (1500–1558), was emperor 1519–56, and ruler of more territory than any of his predecessors (Spain, with its American colonies, the Netherlands, Naples, Sicily and Austria). His reign was marked by struggles with Pope Clement VII and Francis I of France, by attempts to check the Turks and by the REFORMATION. Exhausted and disillusioned, he abdicated in 1556, and retired to Spain. **Charles VI** (1685–1740), was emperor from 1711. With no male heir, he arranged for the succession of his daughter MARIA THERESA by the PRAGMATIC SANCTION. (See AUSTRIAN SUCCESSION, WAR OF THE.) **Charles VII**, or Charles Albert (1697–1745), also known as Charles of Bavaria, was emperor from 1742. He disputed Maria Theresa's succession.

CHARLES, name of 10 kings of France. **Charles I** (see CHARLEMAGNE). **Charles II the Bald** (823–877), reigned as king of the Franks from 843 and as Holy Roman Emperor from 875. Numerous revolts and invasions troubled his reign. It was the last great reign of his dynasty and culturally the last flowering of the Carolingian renaissance. **Charles III the Simple** (879–929), grandson of Charles II, reigned 893–923. **Charles IV the Fair** (1294–1328), reigned from 1322. **Charles V the Wise** (1337–1380), reigned as regent 1356–64 and as king from 1364. Frail and poor in health, he nevertheless put down the JACQUERIE uprising and various plots by his nobles. He regularized taxation and used the increased revenues to build up his armies. He declared war upon England in 1369, and before his death his armies, under the great commander du Guesclin, had regained most French territory occupied by the English. **Charles VI the Mad** (1368–1422), reigned from 1380. He began a disastrous reign at the age of 12. Subject to frequent and severe fits of madness, he allowed corrupt advisors to reign in his stead. England overran most of N France once more, and Charles was forced to name Henry V of England his heir (1420). **Charles VII** (1403–1461), reigned from 1422. The early part of his reign was marked by his unwillingness to challenge the English occupation of France, even to

the extent of allowing Joan of Arc to be burned as a heretic. With the influence of new advisers and the end of the Burgundian alliance with England, Charles introduced tax reforms, rebuilt his army and regained all occupied territory except Calais. **Charles VIII** (1470–1498), reigned from 1483. **Charles IX** (1550–1574), who reigned 1560–74, was dominated by his mother, Catherine de Médicis, who instigated the ST. BARTHOLOMEW'S DAY massacre. **Charles X** (1757–1836), reigned 1824–30. He returned to France from exile after the restoration of the monarchy, becoming king on the death of his brother Louis XVIII. He was exiled again after the 1830 revolution, largely provoked by his autocratic rule.

CHARLES, name of two Stuart kings of Scotland, England and Ireland. **Charles I** (1600–1649), came to the throne in 1625. His absolutist beliefs and Roman Catholic sympathies alienated the Puritandominated parliaments. Forced to dissolve parliaments in 1625, 1626 and 1629, he ruled without one until 1640, when increasing fiscal problems made him call the LONG PARLIAMENT, which sought to curtail his powers. This precipitated the Civil War in 1642. Charles was defeated, and captured in 1647. His continual duplicity in dealing with his captors led to his trial and execution. (See CIVIL WAR, ENGLISH.) **Charles II** (1630–1685), returned from exile to succeed his father in 1660 after the death of Cromwell. His pro-Roman Catholic foreign policy, reflecting his own sympathies, made him distrusted, but he was much more tolerant in religious matters than his parliaments. A shrewder man than Charles I, he exhibited political expertise and cynicism that kept him much of his power. In the end he retained the country's affection, if only for his flamboyant private life.

CHARLES, name of four kings of Spain. **Charles I** (see CHARLES V, Holy Roman Emperor). **Charles II** (1661–1700), last of the Spanish Hapsburgs, reigned from 1665. Feeble and degenerate, he could not produce an heir, and named Philip of Anjou, grandson of Louis XIV, his successor, causing the War of the SPANISH SUCCESSION. **Charles III** (1716–1788), reigned from 1759. A strongly absolutist monarch, his attempts to expand Spanish interests in South America met with defeat at British hands. His enlightened domestic policy, reducing the power of the Church and Inquisition and introducing administrative reforms, was considerably more successful. **Charles IV** (1748–1819), reigned 1788–1808. Spain was largely ruled by his wife, Maria Luisa of Parma, and her lover, Chief Minister Manuel de Godoy. Defeated by France in 1795, Charles allowed Spain to become a satellite of Napoleonic France, and was forced to abdicate in 1808.

CHARLES, Ray (1932–   ), US singer and pianist. Blind from childhood, he achieved fame in the 1950s with a broad repertoire of gospel, soul, jazz, country and standard songs. Among his greatest hits were "Ruby" and "Georgia on My Mind."

CHARLES EDWARD STUART (1720–1788), pretender to the throne of England, the grandson of JAMES II, known also as the Young Pretender and, in Scotland, as Bonnie Prince Charlie. After the French refused to support his cause, he rallied the Highland clans to invade England, but was defeated at Culloden in 1746 and spent the rest of his life in exile.

CHARLES MARTEL (c688–741), Frankish ruler, who as mayor of the palace (chief minister) from 714, ruled in place of the weak MEROVINGIAN kings. The son of PEPIN II, he received his surname Martel (the hammer) after his famous victory at Tours against the Muslim invaders in 732. His policies assured the Frankish preeminence in N Europe which culminated in his grandson CHARLEMAGNE's coronation as emperor (800).

CHARLES PHILIP ARTHUR GEORGE (1948–   ), PRINCE OF WALES and Duke of Cornwall, heir apparent to the British throne. The first child of Queen Elizabeth II and Prince Philip, he was educated at Cheam, Gordonstoun and Cambridge. In 1981 he married Lady Diana Spencer.

CHARLES THE BOLD (1433–1477), last duke of Burgundy (from 1467). Having failed to defeat him in open war, LOUIS XI of France trapped him in conflicts with other powers, leading ultimately to his death in battle at Nancy.

CHARLESTON, city in S.C., seat of Charleston Co., on a peninsula between the Cooper and Ashley rivers, 3mi from the Atlantic Ocean. A major seaport, it produces fertilizer, cigars, asbestos, pulp, chemicals, paper, textiles and steel. Among Charleston's many attractions are colonial buildings, gardens and annual azalea and performing-arts festivals. Pop 66,945.

CHARLESTON, capital of W. Va., seat of Kanawha Co., in W central W. Va. at the confluence of the Kanawha and Elk rivers. A distributing point for coal, gas and oil. Pop 63,968.

CHARLOTTE, largest city in N.C., seat of Mecklenburg Co., 15mi N of the S.C. border. Settled in 1750, chartered in 1768, it is a flourishing commercial, industrial and railroad center. Pop 314,447.

CHARLOTTE (1896–   ), grand duchess of Luxembourg, elected as ruler by popular vote in 1919, abdicated in 1964 in favor of her son, Jean.

CHARLOTTE AMALIE, capital and only city of the US Virgin Islands, on St. Thomas Island. Founded by Danish colonists 1673, it was bought by the US 1917. Pop 15,041.

CHARLOTTETOWN, capital of Prince Edward Island, Canada, a fishing and shipbuilding center founded 1720 by French colonists. Pop 18,631.

CHARLOTTETOWN CONFERENCE, convened Sept. 1, 1864, at Charlottetown, Prince Edward Island, Canada, first of a series of meetings which led to the formation of the Dominion of Canada.

CHARON, in Greek mythology, the ferryman of dead souls across the rivers ACHERON and STYX to HADES, the underworld. As Charos or Charontas, he is the angel of death in later Greek folklore.

CHARPENTIER, Gustave (1860–1956), French composer, noted for his opera *Louise* (1900), a lyrical work evoking the spirit of Paris.

CHARTER OAK, celebrated oak tree, formerly in Hartford, Conn., in which the Conn. colonial charter was hidden in 1687, to prevent its surrender to the royal governor of New England. In 1856 the Charter Oak was uprooted in a storm. Its age was estimated at 1000 years, and its trunk size was nearly 7ft in diameter.

CHARTISM, a radical and unsuccessful attempt by voteless British laborers to gain economic and social equality. It was one of the first working-class political movements in Britain. The Chartists took their name from the "People's Charter," drafted in 1838 by William Lovett of the London Workingmen's Association. The demands made were universal male suffrage, equal district representation, vote by ballot, abolition of property qualifications for officeholders, parliamentary salaries and an annual parliament.

CHARTRES, historic city in NW France, capital of the Eure-et-Loire department and commercial center of the Beauce region. It is famous for its Gothic cathedral of Notre Dame. Pop 34,128.

CHARYBDIS. See SCYLLA AND CHARYBDIS.

CHASE, Mary Ellen (1887–1973), US author of children's literature, novels, and books about the Bible. Among her more than 40 books are *The Silver Shell* (1930), *The Lovely Ambition* (1960) and *The Psalms for the Common Reader* (1962).

CHASE, Salmon Portland (1808–1873), US senator 1849–55, 1860–61, governor of

Ohio 1855–59, secretary of the treasury 1861–64 and chief justice of the US Supreme Court 1864–73. Active in the antislavery movement, he helped to form the FREE SOIL PARTY. As Lincoln's secretary of the treasury, he instituted a national banking system and issued paper money. Though occasionally a political antagonist of Lincoln, as chief justice he supported the moderate republican view towards RECONSTRUCTION.

CHASE, Samuel (1741–1811), US Supreme Court justice 1796–1811. A signer of the Declaration of Independence, he was a member of the Maryland legislature and the Continental Congress. In 1804 an unsuccessful attempt to impeach him was made by President Jefferson, who believed Chase conducted his circuit court in a partisan pro-Federalist manner.

CHATEAU, the French term for castle, often applied to any stately mansion; originally a well-fortified medieval castle with moat (a *château fort*), used for defense rather than residence. By the 17th century the château became a refined and elegant home for royalty and nobility, often distinguished by intricate gardens.

CHATEAUBRIAND, Francois René, (Vicomte de (1768–1848), French writer and diplomat, sometimes considered a founder of the Romantic movement in 19th-century French literature. His works include the North American romance *Atala* (1801), *René* (1802), and *Mémoires d'outre-tombe* (*Memoirs from Beyond the Tomb*; 1849–50).

CHATTANOOGA, city in S Tenn., on the Tennessee R adjoining Ga. One of the South's major transportation and industrial centers. Aided by cheap hydroelectric power, it produces textiles, chemicals, and steel and iron products. It was an important military objective in the Civil War. Pop 169,565.

CHAUCER, Geoffrey (c1340–1400), one of the first great English poets, who established English as a literary language. His early writing, including an incomplete translation of *Le Roman de la Rose*, shows strong French influence. However, c1370 a new force, due to growing familiarity with BOCCACCIO and DANTE, began to exert itself. This is shown in *The Parliament of Fowls.* His two major works are *Troilus and Criseyde* and the CANTERBURY TALES.

CHAUDIÈRE RIVER, S Quebec, Canada, approximately 120mi long; it rises in Lake Megantic, flowing N to the St. Lawrence R immediately above Quebec. The largest of the rapids along its course are the Chaudièr Falls.

CHAUSSON, Ernest Amédée (1855–1899), French composer, a major figure in the post–Romantic movement, strongly influenced by FRANCK. Among his best-known works is the *Symphony in B Flat Major* (c1890).

CHAUTAUQUA MOVEMENT, US adult education movement which began at Lake Chautauqua, N.Y., in 1874, as a course for Sunday school teachers. The founders, John H. Vincent, a Methodist minister, and Lewis Miller, a businessman, organized lectures, concerts and recreation activities. (See ADULT EDUCATION; LYCEUM MOVEMENT.)

CHAUVINISM, excessive and blind patriotism, a term derived from Nicholas Chauvin, a soldier blindly devoted to a Napoleon who came to represent the militaristic cult of his time. Gradually the term was applied to extreme nationalism of any kind.

CHÁVEZ, Carlos (1899–1978), Mexican composer who founded the Orquesta Sinfónic de México (1928). His compositions are strongly influenced by the rhythms and patterns of Mexican-Indian folk music.

CHÁVEZ, Cesar Estrada (1927–   ), revolutionary Mexican–American labor leader who, as head of the United Union of Farmworkers, was instrumental in organizing Cal.'s CHICANO migrant workers. The early history of his union was filled with strikes, picketing and violent clashes with both farmers and the International Brotherhood of TEAMSTERS.

CHAYEFSKY, Paddy (1923–1981), US TV, film and stage dramatist who became known in the 1950s for his naturalistic depiction of ordinary people in TV plays such as *Marty* (source of an Award-winning film, 1953) and *Middle of the Night* (1954). Outstanding films that he later scripted were *Hospital* (1974) and *Network* (1976).

CHECKERS, called draughts in Britain, a popular game of skill played on a board of 64 alternating light and dark squares. Each of the two players begins with 12 black or white pieces (always identified as such despite the colors used) placed on the 12 dark squares nearest him. It is an ancient game, with roots in Egypt and Greece.

CHECKS AND BALANCES, term used to describe the separation and balance of three branches of government: the legislature which makes the law, the executive which enforces it and the judiciary which interprets it. The idea is based on the theory of SEPARATION OF POWERS advocated by MONTESQUIEU in 1748, which greatly influenced the men who drew up the US

Constitution. The SENATE and the HOUSE OF REPRESENTATIVES, as separate organs of the legislature, were to act as checks upon each other in the national Congress.

In practice, however, the powers are not absolutely separated in the working of today's government. Tensions between the branches of government, usually between the president and Congress, often hold up the passage of essential legislation. Some modern critics have pointed out that delay and inefficiency are all too frequently the price that must be paid for a system of checks and balances. In recent years, however, much more criticism has been raised against abuses of power committed by individual branches of government against the spirit of the checks and balances system. (See also WATERGATE.)

CHEESE, nutritious food made from the milk of various animals, with a high protein, calcium and vitamin content. Cheesemaking was already common by 2000 BC. It involves first the curdling of milk by adding an acid or RENNET, so that the fat and protein (mostly CASEIN) coagulate to form the solid curds. After excess liquid whey has been drained off, the curds are compressed and enough moisture is removed to give the cheese the desired degree of hardness. Most cheeses (but not cottage cheese) are then subjected to a period of FERMENTATION, from two weeks to two years, called ripening or curing, during which they are salted and perhaps flavored. The consistency and flavor of the cheese depend on the time, temperature and humidity of storage and on the microorganisms present. Camembert, for instance, is ripened with two molds, *Penicillium candidum* and *P. camemberti*, which make it soft. Process cheese is a blend of several types of cheese melted together.

CHEETAH, *Acinonyx jubatus*, a member of the cat family FELIDAE. It is the fastest land animal, with a speed of up to 110km/hr (68mph). The tawny coat covered with closely set spots makes the cheetah easily recognizable. Once common in Africa and SW Asia the cheetah is fast disappearing through hunting and the reduction in numbers of small deer and antelope, its main prey.

CHEEVER, John (1912–   ), US author. His witty novels about the conflicts of suburban life have won major prizes: the National Book Award for *The Wapshot Chronicle* (1957) and the Howells Medal for *The Wapshot Scandal* (1964). His collected short stories, *The Stories of John Cheever* (1978), were awarded a Pulitzer prize.

CHEKHOV, Anton Pavlovich (1860–1904), Russian dramatist and short story writer. Between 1898 and 1904 his four major plays were produced by the MOSCOW ART THEATER: *The Seagull, Uncle Vanya, The Three Sisters* and *The Cherry Orchard*. These plays realistically explore the frustrations and unhappiness of life, particularly among the Russian rural upper and middle classes of the time. His work (both plays and short stories) has exerted an immense influence on modern literature.

CHEMICAL AND BIOLOGICAL WARFARE, the use of poisons and diseases against an enemy, either to kill or disable personnel or to diminish food supply, natural ground cover, etc. According to legend, SOLON defeated a Megaran army c600 BC by poisoning their drinking water. THUCYDIDES records that the Spartans in the 5th century BC used in attack the fumes produced by burning wood, sulfur and pitch. Julius CAESAR mentions with disapproval the use of poisons in warfare. GREEK FIRE was in use from about the middle of the 7th century AD. In the US during the FRENCH AND INDIAN WAR, infected blankets were given to the Indians to spread SMALLPOX among them. During the CIVIL WAR, John Doughty proposed the use of an artillery shell containing the choking, corrosive gas CHLORINE. Chemical warfare on a large scale was first waged by the Germans in WWI at YPRES (1915), using chlorine against the Allies. Gas warfare on both sides escalated throughout the remainder of WWI; despite the use of the GAS MASK, around 100,000 may have died as a result of chlorine, PHOSGENE and MUSTARD GAS attacks. During WWII the Germans developed nerve gases, which attack the NERVOUS SYSTEM, but these (Sarin, Soman and Tabun) were not used. More deadly nerve gases have since been developed in the US: some may linger for months and kill in seconds. Binary nerve gas, which consists of two non-lethal substances packed separately which do not mingle into a toxic whole until airborne is considered of special interest. The binaries, which would be packaged in artillery shells and bombs, are perceived as avoiding problems due to lethal leakage and death through improper handling. In the VIETNAM WAR, TEAR GASES were used in combat as distinct from their more normal role in riot control. Also in Vietnam, defoliants known as Agent Orange were sprayed from aircraft on enemy crops and on vegetation to deprive guerrillas of cover (see also NAPALM). As the 1980's began, the Soviets were accused of using chemicals including "yellow rain" against the people of Laos, Cambodia and

Afghanistan.

Waging of biological warfare has been rare, mainly because its effects are hard to control. Nevertheless, most developed countries have encouraged military research in this field. Available preparations could, if used, unleash pneumonic PLAGUE, pulmonary ANTHRAX, and BOTULISM, among other fatal diseases; it has been estimated that 1oz (about 30g) of these would, if well distributed, be sufficient to kill the entire population of North America. Less fatal diseases, such as TULAREMIA, and certain HALLUCINOGENIC DRUGS are also available for such use. In 1979 the death of hundreds of Soviets from anthrax in the Russian town of Sverdlovsk led to suspicion that an explosion in a germ warfare station had caused a lethal cloud of anthrax spores to mix with the town's air. The incident at Sverdlovsk has never been convincingly resolved.

Of the international agreements outlawing the use of chemical and biological warfare, the oldest is the 1925 Geneva Protocol; the UK accepted its strictures only in part, reserving the right to retaliate; and the US, although they signed the agreement in 1925, did not ratify until 1975. The Protocol was contravened by Italy against Ethiopia (1936) and by Japan against China (1943). Most countries have signed the Biological Weapons Convention (1972), agreeing to cease production of biological weapons and destroy existing stockpiles. Bilateral negotiations between the US and the Soviets concerning chemical warfare have been underway in Geneva since 1976.

CHEMISTRY, the science of the nature, composition and properties of material substances, and their transformations and interconversions. In modern terms, chemistry deals with ELEMENTS and compounds, with the ATOMS and MOLECULES of which they are composed, and with the reactions between them. It is thus basic to natural phenomena and modern technology alike. Chemistry may be divided into five major parts: ORGANIC CHEMISTRY, the study of carbon compounds (which form an idiosyncratic group); INORGANIC CHEMISTRY, dealing with all the elements, except carbon, and their compounds; chemical ANALYSIS, the determination of what a sample contains and how much of each constituent is present; BIOCHEMISTRY, the study of the complex organic compounds in biological systems; and PHYSICAL CHEMISTRY, which underlies all the other branches, encompassing the study of the physical properties of substances and the theoretical tools for investigating them.

Related sciences include GEOCHEMISTRY and METALLURGY.

Practical chemistry originated with the art of the metallurgists and artisans of the ancient Middle East. Their products included not only refined and alloyed metals but also dyes and glasses, and their methods were and remain shrouded in professional secrecy. Their chemical theory, expressed in terms of the prevailing theology, involved notions such as the opposition of contraries and the mediation of a mediating third. Classical Greek science generally expressed itself in the theoretical rather than the practical, as the conflicting physical theories of THALES and ANAXAGORAS, ANAXIMENES and ARISTOTLE bear witness. An important concept, that matter exists as atoms—tiny individual material particles—emerged about this time (see ATOMISM) though it did not become dominant for another 2,000 years. During the HELLENISTIC AGE a new practical chemistry arose in the study of ALCHEMY. These early alchemists sought to apply Aristotelian physical theory to their practical experiments. Alchemy was the dominant guise of chemical science throughout the medieval period. Like the other sciences, it passed through Arab hands after the collapse of the Roman world, though, unlike the case with some other sciences, great practical advances were made during this time with the discovery of alcohol DISTILLATION and methods for preparing NITRIC and SULFURIC ACIDS. Chemical theory, however, remained primitive and practitioners sought to guard their secret recipes by employing obscure and even mystical phraseology. The 16th century saw new clarity brought to the description of metallurgical processes in the writings of Georgius AGRICOLA and the foundation by PARACELSUS of the new practical science of IATROCHEMISTRY with its emphasis on chemical medicines. Jan Baptist van HELMONT, the greatest of his successors, began to use quantitative experiments. In the 17th century mechanist atomism enjoyed a revival, with Robert BOYLE leading a campaign to banish obscurantism from chemical description. The 18th century saw the rise and fall of the PHLOGISTON theory of combustion, promoted by STAHL and adopted by all the great chemists of the age: BLACK, SCHEELE and PRIESTLEY (all of whom found their greatest successes in the study of GASES). The phlogiston theory fell before the oxygen theory of LAVOISIER and his associated binomial nomenclature, and the new century (the 19th) saw the proposal of DALTON's atomic theory, AVOGADRO's hypothesis (neglected for 50 years until revived by CANNIZZARO) and the foundation of ELECTROCHEMISTRY which, in the hands of DAVY, rapidly yielded two new elements, SODIUM and POTASSIUM. During the 19th century chemistry gradually assumed its present form, the most notable innovations being the periodic table of MENDELEYEV, the BENZENE ring-structure of KEKULÉ, the systematic chemical THERMODYNAMICS of GIBBS and BUNSEN'S chemical SPECTROSCOPY. In the opening years of the present century the new atomic theory revolutionized chemical theory and the interrelation of the elements was deciphered. Since then successive improvements in experimental techniques (e.g., CHROMATOGRAPHY; isotopic labeling; MICROCHEMISTRY) and the introduction of new instruments (infrared, nuclear-magnetic-resonance and mass spectroscopes) have led to continuing advances in chemical theory. These developments have also had a considerable impact on industrial chemistry and biochemistry. Perhaps the most significant recent change in the chemist's outlook has been that his interest has moved away from the nature of chemical substance itself towards questions of molecular structure, the energetics of chemical processes and REACTION MECHANISMS.

CHEMOTHERAPY, the use of chemical substances to treat disease. More specifically, the term refers to the use of nonantibiotic antimicrobials and agents for treating CANCER. The drug must interfere with the growth of bacterial, parasitic or TUMOR cells, without significantly affecting host cells. In antimicrobial chemotherapy, the work of P. EHRLICH on aniline dyes and arsenicals (SALVARSAN) and of G. DOMAGK on Prontosil led to the development of sulfonamides (see SULFA DRUGS). Many useful synthetic compounds are now available for BACTERIAL and PARASITIC DISEASE, although ANTIBIOTICS are often preferred for bacteria. Cancer chemotherapy is especially successful in LEUKEMIA and lymphoma; in carcinoma it is usually reserved for disseminated tumor. Nitrogen mustard, ALKALOIDS derived from the periwinkle, certain antibiotics and agents interfering with DNA METABOLISM are used, often in combinations and usually with STEROIDS.

CH'ENG-TU, city in S central China. A former imperial capital, it is capital of Szechwan province and a major port, trade and industrial center for the surrounding Ch'eng-tu plains. Pop 2,000,000.

CHÉNIER, André Marie de (1762–1794), French poet who renewed the classical tradition in French poetry. His work forms a bridge between CLASSICISM and ROMANTICISM, with many of the best characteristics of both. He was guillotined during the French Revolution.

CHENNAULT, Claire Lee (1890–1958), US pilot, founder of the WWII *Flying Tigers.* In 1937 he went to China to organize CHIANG KAI-SHEK'S air force in the war against Japan. He reentered US service in 1942 as commander of the US air forces in China.

CH'EN TU-HSIU (1879–1942), founder of the Chinese Communist Party. He was a professor at Peking University, but resigned and founded the party in 1920. In his last years he denounced Soviet communism and outlined China's need for true socialist democracy.

CHERBOURG, French seaport and naval station 190mi NW of Paris. It is a base for French fishing fleets and a port of call for oceangoing vessels. Pop 38,243.

CHEROKEE INDIANS, North American tribe of the IROQUOIS linguistic group. Once numerous in Ga., N.C., S.C. and Tenn., they were decimated by smallpox and conflicts with settlers in the 18th century. Deprived of their land, thousands died on a march west in 1838. Today about 40,000 Cherokee live in the West and another 3,000 in the East.

CHEROKEE NATION v GEORGIA, legal battle fought in 1831, when the Cherokee, claiming to be a foreign nation with treaty rights, appealed to the US Supreme Court to prevent Georgia from taking their lands. The court held that it had no jurisdiction in the case because the Cherokee were not, in fact, a foreign nation.

CHERUBINI, Maria Luigi (1760–1842), Italian composer who spent most of his life in France. Now remembered mainly for his opera *Medea* (1797), and the *Requiem in D major* (1836).

CHESAPEAKE AND OHIO CANAL, waterway running along the Potomac R between Washington, D.C., and Cumberland, Md. It was planned as a route to the Midwest, but went bankrupt because of competition with the railroads. The canal was taken over by the government in 1938 and established as a historical park in 1961.

CHESAPEAKE BAY, large inlet on the E coast of the US in both S Md. and N Va., an important trade route for oceangoing vessels. Baltimore, Norfolk and Newport, important shipping and industrial towns, are on its shores. The bay, formed by the submergence of the lower Susquehanna R, separates the Md.–Del. peninsula from mainland Md. and Va. The area is famous for its waterfowl and seafood.

CHESAPEAKE BAY BRIDGE-TUNNEL, complex of highways, bridges and tunnels stretching 17.65 mi across Chesapeake Bay. The world's largest bridge–tunnel system, it links the E shore of Va. with mainland Va. without obstructing shipping. The project cost 200 million dollars, was built in 42 months, and opened to traffic in 1964..

CHESS, game for two players, each with 16 pieces, played on a board of 64 squares, colored light and dark alternately. Each chessman moves in a certain way. Chess is thought to have originated in India c500 AD, and to have spread to Europe by 1300, perhaps through Byzantium and the Moors; many piece names are of Eastern origin. Chroniclers in N Europe often used the name chess for any board game. Chess as we know it dates from 15th-century Italy and Spain. In the 18th century France was the game's chief center. The USSR gained ascendency in chess after the 1920's. Chess today has been given popularity by publicized international contests including world championship competitions such as those between FISCHER and SPASSKY in 1972 and KARPOV and KORCHNOI in 1981.

CHESSMAN, Caryl (1912–1960), US convict and author. Only two months following his release from prison on robbery charges in 1948, he was arrested for the kidnapping and rape of two women. Proclaiming himself innocent, he began a 12-year legal battle financed by the sale of his bestseller, *Cell 2455, Death Row* (1954). His case drew international attention and intensified debate on the issue of CAPITAL PUNISHMENT. Despite eight stays of execution, he died in the gas chamber.

CHESTERFIELD, Philip Dormer Stanhope, 4th Earl of (1694–1773), English statesman and wit. He is chiefly remembered for his *Letters to His Son*, which give a vivid and often amusing insight into the morality of the age.

CHESTERTON, Gilbert Keith (1874–1936), English author and critic, noted for his lyrical style and delight in paradox. He wrote many poems, short stories and novels; his essays condemn the moral and political evils of his day. He is best known for his Father Brown detective stories.

CHETNIKS, name given to members of WWII Yugoslav resistance group. Led by Draž MIHAJLOVIĆ, they opposed both the Nazis and communist partisans. After loss of Allied support, they were crushed by the partisans.

CHEVALIER, Maurice (1888–1972), popular French singer and film star. He gained international fame in the 1920s and 1930s as the embodiment of French charm and light–heartedness. His films include *The Love Parade* (1930), *Gigi* (1958) and *Can-Can* (1959).

CHEVROLET, Louis (1879–1941), Swissborn US automobile racer and designer; in 1911 he designed and built (with William C. DURANT) the first "Chevrolet," a 6-cylinder car produced to compete with the Ford. He later designed the racers that won the 1920 and 1921 Indianapolis 500-mile race.

CHEWING GUM, confection made from sweetened and flavored sap. For centuries Indian tribes chewed CHICLE (gum from the juice of the sapodilla tree) or spruce resin. Early settlers adopted the habit, and chewing gum has been made commercially in the US since the 1860s. Modern gum contains chicle, other resins and waxes, sugar and corn syrup. US annual consumption is now about 200 sticks per person.

CHEYENNE, capital of Wyo., seat of Laramie Co., in the SE corner of the state. It processes agricultural produce and has large oil refineries. The district is a key site for US intercontinental ballistic missiles. Pop 40,419.

CHEYENNE INDIANS, North American tribe of the ALGONQUIAN linguistic group. By the mid-19th century they had become nomadic hunters on the Great Plains and fierce fighters against neighboring tribes and, after 1860, the encroaching whites. A history of Cheyenne raids and punitive actions by the government (see SAND CREEK MASSACRE), of broken promises and starvation culminated in the defeat of General CUSTER in 1876 by the Sioux and Northern Cheyenne. Eventually all the Cheyenne were resettled in Okla. and Mont.

CHIANG CH'ING (1913–   ), Chinese communist leader, wife of MAO TSE-TUNG. Originally an actress, she fought in the Revolution and thereafter held various offices. She was an active supporter of Mao's policies, particularly during the Cultural Revolution, (1966–69). After Mao died she was arrested with some other Maoists and charged with crimes committed during the Cultural Revolution. In 1981 she was given a death sentence subject to suspension if she repented.

CHIANG KAI-SHEK (1887–1975), Chinese soldier and political leader. He fought in support of SUN YAT-SEN during the Revolution of 1911. After the success of the revolution, Chiang joined the Kuomintang, the governing party, organized the nationalist army and rose rapidly in power.

After Sun's death (1925), Chiang consolidated his position, in part through an association with the communists. By the time he had become president (1928) he had turned on them, but he then forged a new alliance when Japan invaded China in 1937. As generalissimo, Chiang commanded Chinese and later (1942) Allied forces in the China war theater against Japan. After WWII, conflict between Chiang and the communists resumed. US mediation failed, the civil war went badly and Chiang fled the mainland for Taiwan 1949, where he continued as president until he died. With US support he built Taiwan into an economic and military power in its own right.

CHIANTI, a mountainous district in central Italy, part of the Appenines. Its slopes produce the famous red and white Chianti wines.

CHIBCHA or MUYSCA INDIANS, the inhabitants of the plateau of Bogota in central Colombia. Their society was based on farming and the worship of the Sun God. The Spaniards destroyed their culture in the 16th century. Over a million of their descendants survive in the area today.

CHICAGO, city situated on Lake Michigan in Ill. Two branches of the Chicago R divide it into three parts, known as the North, South and West sides. Chicago is the hub of the US road, rail and air systems; the city's wholesale outlets handle more goods than any city except New York. Industry is diverse and immense, including the famous meatpacking plants, grain elevators and chemical, metal and printing industries. Chicago has large public libraries and many museums and art galleries. It is the home of the U. of Chicago, the Chicago Symphony Orchestra and was the major center of "Urban Blues" music.

Chicago grew as a French trading post in the 1700s, but it was not until after the BLACK HAWK WAR (1832) that the Indian threat was ended and a city developed. The arrival of the railroads in the mid-19th century placed Chicago in the path of the nation's economic expansion as the commercial hub of the vast northern plains. Even the Great Fire of 1871, which destroyed 2,000 acres of property, could not end the vitality of Chicago's growth. With sudden economic growth came a tradition of violence, culminating in the 1920s and 1930s in open gang warfare. A large influx of blacks during WWI and WWII has created serious problems, resulting in severe rioting. Unemployment is high and Chicago's West and South sides have some of the worst slums in the US. Pop 6,979,000.

CHICAGO, University of, a private, nondenominational, coeducational institution of Chicago, Ill., incorporated in 1890. The university has about 7,500 students and employs well over 1000 teaching staff. It is famous for research in most subjects.

CHICAGO EIGHT, group of anti-Vietnam War demonstrators accused of inciting riots that surrounded the 1968 Democratic national convention. They included David Dellinger, editor of *Liberation* magazine; Rennie Davis and Tom HAYDEN, founding members of STUDENTS FOR A DEMOCRATIC SOCIETY (SDS); Abbie HOFFMAN and Jerry RUBIN, founders of the YOUTH INTERNATIONAL PARTY (Yippies); John Froines, university chemistry instructor; Lee Weiner, graduate student; and Bobby SEALE, chairman of the BLACK PANTHER PARTY. Their trial, starting Sept. 24, 1969, was marred by hysterical, inappropriate behavior by almost everyone involved, including Judge Julius J. Hoffman, who ordered Seale bound and gagged in the courtroom. Seale's case was then severed from the others, who were acquitted of conspiracy, although five were convicted on a lesser charge. These convictions were later reversed because of the judge's blatant prejudice, and charges against Seale were eventually dismissed.

CHICAGO SCHOOL refers to the conservative, monetarist approach to economic policy advocated at the University of Chicago after WWII by Milton FRIEDMAN and other economists (see ECONOMICS, MONETARISM).

CHICAGO STYLE, in jazz, referred originally to the music recorded by black New Orleans artists in Chicago during the early 1920s. The jazz played by white Chicago musicians in the 1920s was called "Dixieland." More recently, the two terms have been used interchangeably to connote a style closely related to, but smoother and more sophisticated than, that of the New Orleans jazz pioneers.

CHICANO, originally a pejorative nickname for an American of Mexican descent, derived from the common name "Chico." Like the word "black," it has now been accepted as a proud acknowledgement of racial identity. In the 19th century persons of Mexican descent were a majority in the US states bordering on Mexico, and they still constitute significant minorities in the W. In addition, according to 1980 census estimates, another 3-6 million illegal migrants from Mexico live in the US. These "undocumented" persons pose a variety of legal and economic issues; for example, should their children be allowed to attend public schools? Many Mexicans are expected to continue to emigrate as long as greater work opportunities exist north of the border. With their increasing numbers, Chicanos have begun to exercise more political power in some border states. A Chicano labor leader, Cesar CHAVEZ, organized the National Farm Workers Association, and achieved bargaining power for Chicano field workers after years of bitter struggle.

CHICHÉN-ITZÁ, important archaeological remains of a Maya city, in Yucatan state, Mexico. The ruins indicate two periods of prosperity. The first was around 1000 AD when Chichén-Itzá was a modest Maya city and a member of the League of Mayapan. A second period (with strong Toltec-Mexican influences) saw the construction of an astronomical observatory and the huge pyramid temples for the worship of the god QUETZALCOATL, or Kukulcan.

CHICHERIN, Georgi Vasilievich (1872–1936), Russian diplomat, foreign minister 1918–30. He served under the Czars but left Russia in 1904 to help revolutionary activity in Europe. He returned in 1918 and joined the Bolsheviks.

CHICHESTER, Sir Francis Charles (1901–1972), British yachtsman and aviator. In 1931 he became the first to fly solo across the Tasman Sea. His most famous achievement was his solo circumnavigation of the world in 1966–67.

CHICKADEES, common garden birds, of the family Paridae, with dark caps and bibs and white faces, noted for their tameness and agility. Their simple song can be heard throughout most of the year. They nest in tree cavities or nest boxes.

CHICKAMAUGA, Battle of, Confederate victory in the American Civil War, fought in N Ga. in Sept. 1863. After the victories of GETTYSBURG and Vicksburg in July, Union troops under General ROSECRANS drove on Chattanooga, Tenn., a key railway hub. The Confederates under General Braxton BRAGG retreated south of the city, regrouped, and in the ensuing battle along Chickamauga Creek routed the Federals, despite the firm stand of Union General G. H. THOMAS. Both sides lost heavily.

CHICKASAW INDIANS, one of the FIVE CIVILIZED TRIBES of North American Indians of the Muskogean linguistic group. They were moved from N Miss. to Okla. with the Choctaws. Both tribes fought for the Confederacy in the Civil War and lost one third of their territory as a punishment.

CHICKENPOX, or **varicella,** a VIRUS disease due to *Varicella zoster,* affecting mainly children, usually in EPIDEMICS. It is contracted from other cases or from cases of SHINGLES and is contagious. It causes malaise, FEVER and a characteristic vesicular rash—mainly on trunk and face—and cropping occurs. Infrequently it becomes hemorrhagic or LUNG involvement occurs. Chickenpox is rarely serious in the absence of underlying disease but it is important to distinguish it from SMALLPOX.

CHICKENS, domestic birds derived from the Red jungle fowl, *Gallus gallus,* raised for their flesh and eggs. They were first domesticated in India by 2,000 BC. Champion layers like the White Leghorn produce over 300 eggs a year. Chickens raised for meat are sold as broilers and fryers at under three months old and as roasters at 4–8 months.

CHICORY, *Cichorium intybus,* a hardy perennial plant with sky-blue flowers, native to Europe and naturalized in the US. It is cultivated for its leaves, which grow in a firm conical shape and are used in winter and spring salads, and for its roots, which are dried, roasted and added to coffee to increase its color, and body and decrease bitterness.

CHIGGER, the name of two American parasites. The chigger mite, chigoe or red mite is found in central and southern US. It penetrates the skin of birds and mammals to suck lymph, causing irritation and spreading disease. The female sand flea (also called the chigger) which has spread to many tropical countries, burrows into the flesh to lay her eggs. This causes pain and sores and may cause severe infection.

CHIHUAHUA, world's smallest breed of dog, standing about 5in tall and weighing up to 6lb. Descended from a Toltec breed, it is named for the Mexican state.

CHILBLAIN, itchy or painful red swelling of extremities, particularly toes and fingers, in predisposed subjects. A tendency to cold feet and exposure to extremes of temperature appear to be factors in causation. Treatment is symptomatic.

CHILD, Julia (1912–   ), US cookery expert. Her first book, *Mastering the Art of French Cooking* (1961; with Louisette Bertholle and Simone Beck), was the basis of "The French Chef," her first popular cooking series on public TV. Her subsequent books and TV series firmly established the ebullient Child as a star personality in the world of cuisine.

CHILDREN'S CRUSADE, (1212), a sad attempt by 30,000 children to conquer the Holy Land after their elders had failed. Defying king, priests and parents, they set out from France and Germany, led by the youths Stephen of Vendôme and Nicholas of Cologne. Those who survived disease, starvation and the grueling journey over the Alps were mostly sold into slavery by unscrupulous sea captains when they reached the Mediterranean ports.

Official Name: Republic of Chile
Capital: Santiago
Area: 286,397sq mi
Population: 11,104,293
Languages: Spanish
Religions: Roman Catholic
Monetary Unit(s): 1 Chilean peso = 100 centavos

CHILE, South American republic on the Pacific coast.

Land. Chile is a long narrow country, which measures over 2,500mi from N to S, but only 250mi at its widest point. The Andes Mts run the whole length of the country. The N, Central and S parts form three distinct natural regions: the N is dominated by desert and has rich mineral deposits in its dry saline basins. Central Chile is made up of well-watered valleys and has a Mediterranean climate. The S is wetter and cooler, containing dense forests and rolling grasslands in the Southeast.

People. Nine out of ten Chileans live in the Central area, many in Santiago, the capital, and Valparaiso, the chief port. 70% of the population is of mixed Spanish-Indian blood, the other 30% being mainly of Spanish or other European origin. Spanish is spoken by the great majority.

Economy. Chile is one of the world's leading exporters of copper; other minerals include iron ore, nitrates, lead, zinc, iodine, gold, silver and manganese. In the late 1970's the government encouraged diversification of exports in order to lessen the country's vulnerability to fluctuations of world copper prices. After copper, timber is the second most important export. The main crops are grain, rice, beans and potatoes, but Chile is not agriculturally self-supporting. Manufacturing includes textiles, steel, cement and chemicals. After a severe overall crisis (with inflation of 506%

in 1974) a gradual economic recovery took place in the late 1970s.

History. The original inhabitants of the region were the Araucanian Indians. Settled by the Spanish, Chile was dominated by Spain until 1818 when Bernardo O'HIGGINS and José de SAN MARTÍN led a successful war of independence. The addition of the valuable northern area to Chile after the WAR OF THE PACIFIC (1879–83) heralded a period of industrial expansion. Following a revolution in 1891, Chile embarked on a long period of parliamentary rule. In the 20th century it was one of the most democratic and politically stable countries in Latin America, but the 1970 election of Salvador Allende, a Marxist, to the presidency led to political polarization and economic collapse. A military take-over in 1973, one of the bloodiest coups in Latin America history, initiated a right-wing dictatorship intent on 'eradicating' Marxism. Allende allegedly committed suicide during the coup. The military junta headed by Augusto Pinochet remains in control.

CHILLON, a castle on Lake Geneva in Switzerland, built in the 13th century for the dukes of Savoy. It was the prison of Françoi de Bonnivard, inspiring BYRON's poem *The Prisoner of Chillon.*

CHILTERN HILLS, range of chalk hills in the S Midlands of England. They extend for about 50mi and are noted for their fine beech woods. The highest point is Coombe Hill (850ft).

CHIMPANZEE, *Pan troglodytes,* an intelligent African ape. Chimpanzees inhabit woodland or grassy savanna, and feed mostly on vegetable matter. They live in large societies of as many as 60 or 80 individuals.

CH'IN, Chinese dynasty (221–207 BC) whose first emperor, SHIH-HUANG-TI, unified China, completed the GREAT WALL OF CHINA and built new canals and roads. The Ch'in standardized Chinese script, abolished feudalism and initiated local government.

CHINA, republic in E Asia, the world's most populous country.

Land. China is surrounded by natural barriers; sea to the E, and mountains and deserts to the SW and N. Within this framework are three natural regions: the W, an area of high plateaus and desert, the N, fertile plains, and the S, mostly hills and valleys. The two main rivers, the Yangtze R and the Yellow R, flow from the Tibetan plateau, and are of great economic importance. The climate and vegetation are varied, with monsoons and subtropical rain forest in the SE, areas of grassland and desert in the NW, and the Himalayan Plateau in the SW.

People. The Chinese belong to the Mongoloid race, and 95% are Chinese-speaking, though there are sizeable minorities of Mongols and Tibetans, who speak their own languages. The principal dialect is now MANDARIN, taught in all schools. (See also CHINESE.)

The traditional religions are TAOISM, based on the teachings of LAO-TSE (6th century BC), BUDDHISM, introduced in the 3rd century AD, and CONFUCIANISM, based on the teachings of CONFUCIUS (551–479 BC); of these, Confucianism was most responsible for building the very strong family ties, based on patriarchal dominance, that characterized Chinese society. These ties have been replaced under communism by loyalty to the commune and state; and the status of women in society has greatly improved.

Although China is still an agriculturally-based nation, with only one in five living in cities, there are many large cities; in the N, Peking, the capital (pop 8,490,000) and Tientsin (pop 7,000,000); and in S, Shanghai (pop 13,000,000) and Canton (pop 3,100,000).

Economy. The communist government is trying to raise the economy from subsistence to prosperity by a combination of industrialization and improved agriculture, despite the problems of the vast population, which is increasing by 20 million a year.

Although China is the third-largest food producer in the world, raising sheep and growing rice, corn, wheat, vegetables, tea and cotton, it has barely enough to feed the population; but increasing production is difficult as all available land is under cultivation.

Fishing, sea and fresh water, is an important food source. Timber resources have fallen, though reforestation is under way.

Surveys have shown that mineral resources are very rich, and production of coal and iron ore has dramatically increased. More heavy machinery is being built, giving China a sound basis for industrial expansion. Power sources are largely coal and hydroelectricity. While China has become an oil exporter much heavy work is still done by hand. In the late 1970s China embarked on an ambitious program to develop agricultural mechanization and light industry ("Four Modernizations") rapidly.

Transport is largely by canal and river and rail, as the road network is poor. Nearly all trade is by sea, main exports being raw materials and textiles, and imports being machinery and wheat.

History. PEKING MAN and Lan-t'ien man lived in China well over 500,000 years ago, but the earliest farming settlements date from c4,000 BC.

The SHANG dynasty (c1523–1028 BC), ruling near the Yellow R, marks the beginning of the historical period and the Bronze Age; it was succeeded by the CHOU dynasty (1027–256 BC), who were powerful war lords. A period of local wars followed, which only ended when the powerful CH'IN dynasty (221–207 BC) united China. Under the subsequent HAN dynasty (202 BC–220 AD), China expanded S to Vietnam and W to central Asia.

The arts and sciences flourished for two centuries, but army revolts and barbarian invasions brought chaos, and not until the TANG dynasty (618–906 AD) reinstated strong government did trade and civilization thrive again. Prosperity continued through the SUNG dynasty (960–1279), but an invasion by mounted Mongol archers made China part of the great MONGOL EMPIRE. Soon, however, the Mongol Empire broke up and a Chinese ruling house, the MING dynasty (1368–1644), drove the Mongols deep into Asia, and China resumed power in her own right.

The rich empire was again invaded by northern barbarians, this time the MANCHUS, who set up the CH'ING dynasty (1644–1911), the last in Chinese history. Prosperity continued until the mid-19th century, when European expansion led to unfavorable competition. China lost wars against Britain, Russia and Japan, and nationalist revolts against the Manchus caused the fall of the empire.

A new republic was declared in 1912, led first by SUN YAT-SEN and then by YUAN SHIH-KAI. However it was not until 1927 that the nationalists under CHIANG KAI-SHEK, with the help of the communists led by MAO TSE-TUNG, gained control from the Chinese war lords. Though Chiang turned on the communists in 1927, they rejoined forces to fight the Japanese invasion in 1937, and fought together during WWII.

After WWII the communists gained control and drove the nationalists off the mainland to TAIWAN (then Formosa) in 1949. They then consolidated their position, and under the strong leadership of Chairman MAO TSE-TUNG (Mao Zedong), Vice-Chairman LIU SHAOCH'I (Liu Shaoqi), and Premier CHOU EN-LAI (Zhou Enlai) have kept control. In that time they reorganized

Official name: The People's Republic of China
Capital: Peking
Area: 3,704,400sq mi
Population: 1,042,000,000
Languages: Mandarin, local dialects
Religions: No official religion
Monetary unit(s): 1 Yuan = 100 cents

land and factory ownership on a communal basis and made improvements in domestic conditions, although sharply restricting individual liberties. Abroad they encouraged communist movements in Asia, Africa and South America, and notably in Vietnam. However, an easing of relations between China and the West led to her entry into the UN (1971), and an exchange of visits between Chinese and Western political leaders. President Nixon visited China in 1972, President Ford in 1974. Diplomatic relations were formally established between China and the US on Jan. 1, 1979.

Government. Since October 1949 the Chinese Communist Party has ruled China. During the 1950s the government patterned itself after the USSR. This ended in 1959 due to Sino-Soviet ideological split. From 1966–76 China was governed by a radical faction headed by MAO TSE-TUNG and his wife CHIANG CHING (Jiang Qing). In 1976 Mao and Chou En-Lai died and Chiang Ching was jailed as one of the heads of a group of radicals known as the GANG OF FOUR. Since then moderates headed by Teng Hsiao-Ping (Deng Xiaoping), Hu Yao-Bang (Hu Yaobang) and Chao Tsi-Yang (Zhao Ziyang) have ruled China. This group has emphasized economic development and an easing of social and political ferment.

CHINA, Republic of, also Taiwan or Formosa, an island off SE mainland China, the Formosa Strait (about 120mi wide) intervening. It is the only province of China controlled by the (Nationalist) Republic of CHINA and includes the PESCADORES, QUEMOY and Lan Hsü islands.

Land. Forested and mountainous (Yü Shan, 13,113ft), with extensive plains in the W, Taiwan has a monsoon climate, tropical in the S, subtropical in the N, which permits two rice harvests.

People. Most people are of Chinese, largely Fukien province, origin. Taiwan is densely populated. In the late 1940s 1,000,000 mainland Chinese fled to Taiwan increasing density even more. Most Taiwanese are Buddhists or Taoists. The 200,000 Malay-Polynesian aborigines live mainly in the E.

Economy. Taiwan's well-developed economy is no longer largely agricultural but highly industrialized into chiefly an export economy. Irrigation is vital in growing rice, sweet potatoes, soybeans, sugar, 'oolong' tea, fruits and cotton. There are rich fisheries and abundant timber. Minerals include coal, natural gas and some oil, gold, copper and silver. Industry includes steel, aluminum, textiles, petrochemicals, wood and food-processing, and a wide range of manufactured goods. Exports include textiles, metals, machinery, chemicals, sugar and tea.

History. Named Formosa ('beautiful') by the Portuguese, and from 1624 under Dutch control, Taiwan fell to a Ming general in 1662 and then to the Manchus (1683). Ceded to Japan in 1895, it was taken over by CHIANG KAI-SHEK in 1949 when Mao Tse-tung (Mao Zedong) ousted the Nationalists from mainland China. From 1951 to 1965 the US gave $1.5 billion economic aid and $2.5 billion military aid. Though Taiwan (Republic of China) was expelled from the UN in 1971, it continued to enjoy US protection under the Mutual Defense Treaty of 1954, until the treaty ended in 1980. Since then, despite diplomatic isolation (only 20 countries recognize Taiwan) trade continues but the economy is vulnerable to world economic dislocations. The government, led by Chiang Kai-Shek's son, Chiang Ching-Kuo, continues to maintain the now 2,000,000 mainlanders in control of the government, military and economy to the exclusion of the 15,000,000 increasingly restive native Taiwanese.

Official name: Republic of China
Capital: Taipei

Area: 13,892sq mi
Population: 17,805,000
Languages: Mandarin Chinese; Amoy, Hakka dialects
Religions: Buddhist, Taoist, Christian, Muslim
Monetary unit(s): 1 New Taiwan dollar = 100 cents

CHINAGLIA, Giorgio (1947–), the greatest goal scorer in North American Soccer League history. Italian-born, Welsh-bred, he was Italy's highest paid player before the NY Cosmos acquired him for $1 million (1976). He scored seven goals in one playoff game (1980).

CHINAWARE. See CERAMICS; POTTERY AND PORCELAIN.

CHINCH BUG, highly destructive insects of North America whose young, hatched in the spring, feed on wheat. When that becomes too tough for them, they migrate to young corn, where a second generation will feed.

CHINCHILLA, *Chinchilla laniger*, a South American RODENT once common in the Andes, but now decimated for its soft fur. Chinchillas are reared now on fur farms, 100 skins being needed for one coat. Females bear 5 or 6 fully furred young at a time.

CHINESE, a group of languages of the Sino-Tibetan family. MANDARIN, China's official language, is the most commonly used in the world, being spoken by nearly 700 million people. Other dialects include Cantonese, Hakka and Wu. Except for borrowing European technical terms, Chinese is self-sufficient; Japanese and Korean use a version of its writing system. There is evidence of its existence from c2,000 BC. The earliest examples date from c1,400 BC. The written Chinese of CONFUCIUS' time is still used in literature and scholarship, but the spoken word has developed differently, and is the basis for the new literary form, introduced in 1911. The writing system developed from pictorial representation into conventionalized designs, one character being composed of between one and 32 strokes. In the 20th century attempts have been made to simplify the script. Chinese literature spans 3,000 years, and is written in two styles: the classical and, since 1911, the vernacular.

CHINESE ART, one of the major cultural heritages of the world, spanning 3,000 years. In the SHANG dynasty (c1523–1028 BC) artists decorated pottery, cast bronze and carved wood and ivory. Most painting was done on silk in ink and watercolor, until the invention of paper in the 2nd century AD. Three characteristic forms in painting were the wall scroll, the horizontal hand scroll and the album. No examples of painting survive from the HAN dynasty (202 BC to 220 AD), but tomb and pottery decorations indicate that the human form and portrayals of gods were major subjects. In the T'ANG dynasty (618–906 AD) BUDDHISM flourished and temples were lavishly decorated. In the SUNG dynasty (960–1279) landscape painting emerged. The art of the MING dynasty (1368–1644) was scholarly, with court artists returning to earlier traditions, and writing books on technique. Sculpture, which had developed with painting, declined by the end of the Ming dynasty. Art in China since 1949 has gone through several periods of control and is regulated by the state for the purpose of political, social and economic indoctrination. The scope of the artist has thus been greatly narrowed.

CHINESE EXCLUSION ACTS, name of two acts to limit immigration of Orientals to the US. The first, passed in 1879, stemmed from anti-Chinese agitation on the W coast of the US. President HAYES vetoed the act on the grounds that it abrogated the BURLINGAME TREATY. But in 1882 the second act suspended immigration for 10 years, and in 1902 the suspension was made indefinite.

CH'ING, MANCHU dynasty that ruled CHINA after seizing Peking in 1644. It was overthrown by Chinese nationalists in 1911.

CHINOISERIE, European art style using Chinese designs in architecture, ceramics, furniture and decorating, usually in conjunction with BAROQUE and ROCOCO styles. It reached its peak in the mid-18th century, and thereafter waned except for a brief revival in the 1930s.

CHI Pai-shih (1863–1957), Chinese artist and poet who was one of the last great painters in the traditional 17th- and 18th-century Chinese style. A calligrapher as well, he drew finely detailed landscapes, flowers and insects.

CHIPMUNKS, small striped ground-living SQUIRRELS. There are 16 species in North America, and one in Asia. They feed on fruits and nuts which they carry to a store in their cheek pouches; they may also eat small animals. Without hibernating, they sleep for long periods in winter.

CHIPPENDALE, Thomas (c1718–1779), famous English cabinetmaker whose elegant, individual style blended aspects of GOTHIC, ROCOCO and CHINOISERIE. He also worked from designs by Robert ADAM.

CHIPPEWA, common name for the OJIBWA Indians.

CHIRAC, Jacques (1932–), French

political leader. A Gaullist, he was in the cabinets of four premiers before serving as premier (1974–76). He resigned over differences with President Giscard d'Estaing, formed his own party, was elected mayor of Paris (1977) and unsuccessfully sought the presidency in 1981.

CHIRICO, Giorgio de (1888–1978), Greek-born Italian painter who as a founder of the *scuola metafisica*, was a forerunner of SURREALISM. His most characteristic works depict desolate, harshly hued cityscapes that might have been seen in a nightmare.

CHIROPODY. See PODIATRY.

CHIROPRACTIC, a health discipline based on a theory that disease results from misalignment of VERTEBRAE. Manipulation, massage, dietary and general advice are the principal methods used. It was founded by Daniel D. Palmer in Davenport, Ia., in 1895 and has a substantial following in the US.

CHISHOLM TRAIL, 19th-century route for cattle drives and wagon trains between Tex. and Kan., named after the scout and trader Jesse Chisholm. It was superseded by the spread of the railroads.

CHI-SQUARED TEST, in STATISTICS, a test of the closeness of an observed result to an expected result, and hence how closely a model corresponds to a particular sample of n members of a population. x^2 is given by

$$X^2 = \frac{(n-1)s^2}{\sigma^2},$$

where s^2 is the observed sample VARIANCE and σ is the STANDARD DEVIATION of the model. Values of X^2 have been tabulated for a range of values of n, and their distributions (chi-square distributions with $(n-1)$ DEGREES OF FREEDOM) derived in each case.

CHIVALRY, knightly code of conduct in medieval Europe combining Christian and military ideals of bravery, piety, honor, loyalty and sacrifice. These virtues were particularly valued by the crusaders, who founded the earliest chivalric orders. Chivalry was also associated with ideals of courtly love, and it was this, together with changing methods of warfare, that led to its degeneration and decline during the late Middle Ages.

CHLORINE (Cl), greenish-yellow gas with a pungent odor, a typical member of the HALOGENS, occurring naturally as chlorides (see HALIDES) in seawater and minerals. It is made by electrolysis of SALT solution, and is used in large quantities as a bleach, as a disinfectant for drinking water and

swimming pools, and in the manufacture of plastics, solvents and other compounds. Being toxic and corrosive, chlorine and its compound PHOSGENE have been used as poison gases (see CHEMICAL AND BIOLOGICAL WARFARE). Chlorine reacts with most organic compounds, replacing hydrogen atoms and adding to double and triple bonds. AW 35.5, mp $-101°C$, bp $-35°C$.

Chlorides, the commonest chlorine compounds, are typical HALIDES except for carbon tetrachloride (see CARBON), which is inert (see STEREOCHEMISTRY). Other chlorine compounds include a series of oxides, unstable and highly oxidizing, and a series of oxyanions—HYPOCHLORITE, chlorite, chlorate and perchlorate—with the corresponding OXY-ACIDS, all powerful oxidizing agents. Calcium hypochlorite and sodium chlorite are used as bleaches; chlorates are used as weedkillers and to make matches and fireworks; perchlorates are used as explosives and rocket fuels. (See also HYDROGEN CHLORIDE.)

CHLOROFORM, or trichloromethane ($CHCl_3$), dense, colorless volatile liquid made by chlorination of ETHANOL or ACETONE. One of the first anesthetics (see ANESTHESIA) in modern use (by Sir James SIMPSON, 1847), it is now seldom used except in tropical countries, despite its potency, since it has a narrow safety margin and is highly toxic in excess. It is also used in cough medicines and as an organic solvent; it is nonflammable. MW 119.4, mp $-64°C$, bp61°C.

CHLOROPHYLL, various green pigments found in plant CHLOROPLASTS. They absorb light and convert it into chemical energy, thus playing a basic role in PHOTOSYNTHESIS. Chlorophylls are CHELATE compounds in which a magnesium ion is surrounded by a PORPHYRIN system.

CHOCOLATE, popular confectionary made from CACAO beans. Fermented beans are roasted and the outer husks removed by a process that breaks the kernels into fragments called nibs. Chocolate is made from ground nibs, cocoa butter (the fat released when the nibs are subjected to hydraulic pressure), sugar and sometimes milk. It is a high energy food that contains a small amount of the stimulant CAFFEINE. Chocolate may be molded into bars or used as a beverage and in some liqueurs.

CHOLERA, a BACTERIAL DISEASE causing profuse watery DIARRHEA, due to *Vibrio cholerae*. It is endemic in many parts of the East and EPIDEMICS occur elsewhere. A water-borne infection, it was the subject of a classic epidemiological study by John Snow in 1854. Abdominal pain and diarrhea, which rapidly becomes severe and watery, are main features, with rapidly developing dehydration and SHOCK. Without rapid and adequate fluid replacement, death ensues rapidly; ANTIBIOTICS may shorten the diarrheal phase. It is a disease due to a specific TOXIN; a similar but milder disease occurs due to the El Tor Vibrio. VACCINATION gives limited protection for six months.

CHOLESTEROL ($C_{27}H_{46}O$), STEROL found in nearly all animal tissue, especially in the NERVOUS SYSTEM, where it is a component of MYELIN. Cholesterol is a precursor of BILE salts and of adrenal and SEX HORMONES. Large amounts are synthesized in the liver, intestines and skin. Cholesterol in the diet supplements this. Since abnormal deposition of cholesterol in the arteries is associated with ARTERIOSCLEROSIS, some doctors advise avoiding high-cholesterol foods and substituting unsaturated for saturated FATS (the latter increase production and deposition of cholesterol). It is a major constituent of gallstones (see CALCULI).

CHOMSKY, Noam (1928–   ), US linguist. A professor at MIT from 1955, he revolutionized the study of language structure with his theory of generative grammar, first outlined in *Syntactic Structures* (1957). He was also an influential left-wing critic of US foreign policy both during and after the Vietnam War and wrote *American Power and the New Mandarins* (1969), *At War With Asia* (1970) and *The Political Economy of Human Rights* (with E. Herman; 2 vols., 1979).

CHOPIN, Frédéric François (1810–1849), Polish composer and pianist who wrote chiefly for the solo piano. His music is Romantic, inspired by introspection and concern for the fate of his native Poland. Chopin gave his first public performance at the age of eight, in Warsaw. In 1831 he moved to Paris (his father was French) where he began serious composition. His chief works include two piano concertos, 24 preludes, 19 nocturnes, three impromptus, four scherzos, four ballades and many waltzes, mazurkas and polonaises. They display an often startling technical virtuosity. In 1837 he began his famous friendship with the novelist George SAND. Their relationship ended unhappily in 1847 and Chopin, already ill with tuberculosis, died in Paris two years later.

CHORALE, metrical hymn set to a simple tune, associated with the Reformation in Germany. Designed for congregational singing, chorales were often derived from earlier PLAINSONG melodies. LUTHER is credited with having written chorales. Later composers, notably J. S. BACH, reharmonized existing ones.

CHORAL MUSIC, music sung by a choir or chorus. The unaccompanied choral music sung in monasteries and abbeys during the early Christian era is known as PLAINSONG. Choral music continued to be performed without accompaniment through the 16th century. Some of the finest works of this period were written by the Italian PALESTRINA. The development of instrumental accompaniment in the 17th and 18th centuries culminated in J. S. BACH's orchestrated CANTATAS and PASSIONS and the ORATORIOS of HANDEL. Choral music lost some popularity with the development of secular and orchestral music but choral works continued to be written. BEETHOVEN's innovatory inclusion of a choir in the finale of his *Ninth Symphony* (1817–23) marks a turning point in the history of music. Notable among 20th-century choral works are ELGAR's *Dream of Gerontius* (1900) and STRAVINSKY's *Symphony of Psalms* (1930).

CHORD. See HARMONY.

CHOREA, abnormal, nonrepetitive involuntary movements of the limbs, body and face. It may start with clumsiness, but later uncontrollable and bizarre movements occur. It is a disease of basal ganglia (see BRAIN). **Sydenham's chorea,** or **Saint Vitus' dance,** is a childhood illness associated with STREPTOCOCCUS infection and RHEUMATIC FEVER; recovery is usually full. **Huntington's chorea** is a rare hereditary disease, usually coming on in middle age and associated with progressive dementia.

CHOREOGRAPHY, composition of steps and movements for dancing, especially BALLET. The most influential choreographers of the early decades of the 20th century created ballets for DIAGHILEV and include, Michel FOKINE, NIJINSKY and George BALANCHINE. Pioneers in modern dance, such as Martha GRAHAM and Jerome ROBBINS, helped to free the dance theater from the restrictions of classical steps. Teaching is traditionally by demonstration and written records of early dance steps are scant. A notation system was published 1699 by Raoul Feuillet (c1670–c1730) and, in the 20th century, Rudolf von Laban developed his *Labanotation.*

CHOU, Chinese dynasty that ruled from Hao, near present-day Sian, (c1122–770 BC) and then from Loyang (770–256 BC). The two periods, known respectively as the Western and Eastern Chou, were, despite political turmoil, a time of fundamental cultural growth. Irrigation projects were established, great advances were made in iron-casting techniques, and a money economy was evolved. Literature and philosophy flourished, particularly during the Eastern Chou which became the classical age of Chinese philosophy. (See CONFUCIUS; CHUANG-TZU; LAO-TSE; MENCIUS.)

CHOU EN-LAI (1898–1976), first prime minister of the People's Republic of China. Born into the gentry, he became a Marxist after studying in China, Japan and Paris. In 1924 he became political director of the Whampoa Military Academy while CHIANG KAI-SHEK was commandant. In 1926 he organized the Shanghai Strike for Chiang and escaped when Chiang betrayed the communists. He became a Comintern liaison man organizing the proletariat and eventually director of military affairs for MAO TSE-TUNG'S guerrilla forces. After commanding the first stages of the LONG MARCH (1934–35), he became Mao's champion and thereafter always deferred to his authority. As foreign minister (as well as prime minister) until 1958, he won support for China in the Third World. He was a moderating influence during Mao's Cultural Revolution in the 1960s and a major force in taking China into the UN (1971). Seeking to balance worsening Sino-Soviet relations, he was responsible for the rapprochement with the US, symbolized by President Nixon's visit to China in 1972.

CHOU SHU-JEN (Pinyin form: Lu Xun; 1881–1936), Chinese writer who exposed many of the evils of China's traditional society. One of the most prominent of 20th century authors, Chou Shu-jen was especially admired for his short stories *A Madman's Diary* (1918) and *The Story of Ah Q* (1921).

CHOW (or Chow-Chow), a medium-sized red or black dog with a rough coat, lion-like mane and paws, and a plumed tail curling over its back.

CHRÉTIEN DE TROYES, (c1135–1183) French poet who wrote romances rooted in ARTHURIAN LEGEND. His five romances, *Erec*, *Cligés Lancelot, Yvain* and the unfinished *Perceval*, were seminal, greatly influencing French and English literature through the next two centuries.

CHRIST (Greek *Christos*, anointed one), translation from the Hebrew *Mashiah* or Messiah. (See JESUS CHRIST; MESSIAH.)

CHRISTCHURCH, city in New Zealand on the E coast of South Island. It is the island's largest city and the third largest in New Zealand. Founded in 1850, it developed as a grain, meat and wool center but is now also a major manufacturing city. Pop 326,200.

CHRISTIAN BROTHERS, Roman Catholic teaching order founded in 1802 by Edmund Ignatius Rice at Waterford, Ireland, to care for poor Catholic boys. The order now has schools and colleges in many countries.

CHRISTIANITY, a major world religion; arising out of JUDAISM, and founded on the life, death and resurrection of JESUS CHRIST. Christians total some 28% of the world's population. Half of all Christians are in Europe, most of the rest in North and South America. The central Christian proclamation is that by the grace of God men are saved (see SALVATION) through faith in Christ, their sins are forgiven, and they receive new and eternal life in the fellowship of the CHURCH. Arising out of this are the various aspects of Christian life and teaching, broadly divided into worship, THEOLOGY, MISSION and personal and social obedience to God's will—that is, the practice of righteousness, love and mercy. The whole Church regards the BIBLE as authoritative, but the place given to tradition and reason varies.

After Jesus' resurrection and ascension (c30 AD), his APOSTLES and other followers traveled widely, spreading and developing Christian beliefs and worship. Christian communities emerged throughout the Roman Empire, meeting weekly for prayer and Holy COMMUNION. Soon an ecclesiastical structure began to evolve. Meetings were led by bishops, assisted by elders (see PRESBYTERS). Later the elders presided over local congregations and bishops had wider authority (see MINISTRY). Regions were organized into dioceses and provinces.

Christians suffered persecution until the Emperor CONSTANTINE proclaimed freedom of worship throughout the Roman Empire (313 AD). He made Christianity Rome's official religion in 324 AD, and in 325 called the first ECUMENICAL COUNCIL at Nicaea to settle major doctrinal disputes. In the 4th century MONASTICISM spread from Egypt to the West.

Almost from the beginning the Church had been divided into the Greek-speaking East and the Latin-speaking West, with divergent traditions. The WESTERN CHURCH came to recognize the preeminence of the pope, the bishop of Rome, as the direct successor of St. Peter. But the EASTERN CHURCH looked to the patriarch of Constantinople as its head. This division finally led to the GREAT SCHISM of 1054. The MONOPHYSITE CHURCHES had previously separated from the eastern ORTHODOX CHURCHES in the 6th century. The advance of ISLAM was an increasing threat to all the Eastern Churches.

In medieval Western Europe the increasing secular power and corruption of the Roman Church helped to spark off the 16th-century REFORMATION, from which PROTESTANTISM emerged as various national churches separated from the ROMAN CATHOLIC CHURCH, which responded by its own COUNTER-REFORMATION. The LUTHERAN and REFORMED CHURCHES came to dominate northern Europe. The Roman Catholic Church and (two centuries later) Protestant churches embarked on a vigorous missionary program to the Americas, Africa and Asia, often closely connected with colonial expansion.

Today, Christian churches, though still divided by differences of doctrine and practice, work together and share a concern for worldwide social justice, and the ECUMENICAL MOVEMENT offers hope of eventual reunion.

CHRISTIAN SCIENCE, a religious movement which believes in the power of Christian faith to heal sickness. It was founded by Mary Baker EDDY, who organized the first "Church of Christ, Scientist" at Boston, Mass., in 1879. There are now many affiliated churches throughout the world. The *Christian Science Monitor* is a widely respected international daily newspaper.

CHRISTIE, Agatha (1891–1976), British writer of popular detective novels and plays. Her two central characters are the egotistical Hercule Poirot and the elderly Miss Jane Marple. Her play *The Mousetrap* opened in London in 1952 and was still being performed in 1976, the world's longest continuous run.

CHRISTINA (1626–1689), queen of Sweden 1632–54, successor to Gustavus Adolphus. She was a lavish patron of the arts and attracted many scholars to her court, among them Descartes. Christina refused to marry and in 1654 she abdicated, leaving the country in male disguise. She was received into the Roman Catholic Church at Innsbruck in the following year and settled in Rome. She failed in two attempts to regain her throne (1660 and 1667).

CHRISTMAS (Christ's Mass), annual Christian festival observed on Dec. 25 in the Western Churches to commemorate the birth of Jesus Christ. It is a public holiday in Christian countries, usually marked by the exchange of gifts—tokens of the gifts of the three wise men to the infant Jesus. Christmastide lasts from Dec. 25 to Jan. 6 (EPIPHANY).

CHRISTOPHE, Henri (1767–1820), king of N Haiti. He became president of Haiti in 1806, after the murder of DESSALINES. Opposed by Alexandre Pétion, after 1811 he ruled only N Haiti, as King Henri I, building the mountain fortress of La Ferrière. Faced with a revolt, he shot himself.

CHRISTUS, Petrus (d. 1473?), leading Flemish painter, early Netherlandish school. His work, strongly influenced by Jan VAN EYCK, was important in the 15th-century development of realistic perspective.

CHRISTY, Edwin P. (1815–1862), US actor who organized the highly successful Christy Minstrels troupe at Buffalo, N.Y., in 1842. He established the basic format of the MINSTREL SHOW, popular in the 19th century.

CHROMATIC SCALE, musical scale consisting of all 12 semitones within an octave. It contains every tone commonly used in Western music. (See also SCHOENBERG, ARNOLD: TWELVE TONE MUSIC.)

CHROMATOGRAPHY, a versatile technique of chemical separation and ANALYSIS, capable of dealing with many-component mixtures, and large or small amounts. The sample is injected into the moving phase, a gas or liquid stream which flows over the stationary phase, a porous solid or a solid support coated with a liquid. The various components of the sample are adsorbed by the stationary phase at different rates, and separation occurs. Each component has a characteristic velocity relative to that of the solvent, and so can be identified. In **liquid-solid chromatography** the solid is packed into a tube, the sample is added at the top, and a liquid eluant is allowed to flow through; the different fractions of effluent are collected. A variation of this method is ion-exchange chromatography, in which the solid is an ION-EXCHANGE resin from which the ions in the sample are displaced at various rates by the acid eluant. Other related techniques are paper chromatography (with an adsorbent paper stationary phase) and thin-layer chromatography (using a layer of solid adsorbent on a glass plate). The other main type of chromatography—the most sensitive and reliable—is **gas-liquid chromatography (glc)**, in which a small vaporized sample is injected into a stream of inert eluant gas (usually nitrogen) flowing through a column containing nonvolatile liquid adsorbed on a powdered solid. The components are detected by such means as measuring the change in thermal conductivity of the effluent gas.

CHROMIUM (Cr), silvery-white, hard metal in Group VIB of the PERIODIC TABLE; a TRANSITION ELEMENT. It is widespread, the most important ore being CHROMITE. This is reduced to a ferrochromium alloy by carbon or silicon; pure chromium is produced by reducing chromium (III) oxide with aluminum. It is used to make hard and corrosion-resistant ALLOYS and for chromium ELECTROPLATING. Chromium is unreactive. It forms compounds in oxidation states +2 and +3 (basic) and +6 (acidic). Chromium (III) oxide is used as a green pigment, and lead chromate (VI) as a yellow pigment. Other compounds are used for tanning leather and as mordants in dyeing. AW 52.0, mp 1890°C, bp 2482°C, sg 7.20 (20°C).

CHROMOSOMES, threadlike bodies in cell nuclei, composed of GENES, linearly arranged, which carry genetic information responsible for the inherited characteristics of the organism (see HEREDITY). Chromosomes consist of the NUCLEIC ACID DNA (and sometimes RNA) attached to a protein core. All normal cells contain a certain number of chromosomes characteristic of the species (46 in man), in homologous pairs (DIPLOID). GAMETES, however, are haploid, having only half this number, one of each pair, so that they unite to form a ZYGOTE with the correct number of chromosomes. In man there is one pair of sex chromosomes, females having two X chromosomes, males an X and a Y; thus each EGG cell must have an X chromosome, but each spermatozoon (see SPERM) has either an X or a Y, and determines the sex of the offspring. In cell division, the chromosomes replicate and separate (see MEIOSIS; MITOSIS). Defective or supernumerary chromosomes cause various abnormalities, including MONGOLISM. (See also MUTATION; PROTEIN SYNTHESIS.)

CHRONICLES, two Old Testament books summarizing Jewish history from Adam through the Babylonian Captivity. The first consists mainly of genealogies up to Saul, and the second is largely a history of the Kingdom of Judah.

CHRONOLOGY, the science of dating involving the accurate placing of events in time and the definition of suitable timescales. In Christian societies, events are dated in years before (BC) or after (AD—*Anno Domini*) the traditional birth date of Christ. In scientific use, dates are often given BP (Before Present). In ARCHAEOLOGY, dating techniques include DENDROCHRONOLOGY and RADIOCARBON DATING. In GEOLOGY, rock strata are related to the geological time scale by examination of the FOSSILS they contain (see also POTASSIUM).

CHRONOMETER, an extremely accurate clock, especially one used in connection with celestial NAVIGATION at sea (see also CELESTIAL SPHERE). It differs from the normal clock in that it has a **fusee,** by means of which the power transmission of the mainspring is regulated so that it remains approximately uniform at all times; and a balance made of metals of different coefficients of expansion to minimize the effects of temperature changes. The device is maintained in gimbals to reduce the effects of rolling and pitching. A chronometer's accuracy is checked daily and its error noted; the daily change in error is termed the **daily rate.** Chronometers are always set to GREENWICH MEAN TIME. The first chronometer was invented by John HARRISON (1735). (See also ATOMIC CLOCK; CLOCKS AND WATCHES.)

CHRYSLER, Walter Percy (1875–1940), US industrialist who produced the first Chrysler car (1924) and established the Chrysler Corporation (1925), which eventually became the third-largest auto producer in the US.

CHRYSOSTOM, Saint John (c347–407 AD), one of the CHURCH DOCTORS, called Chrysostom ("golden mouthed") for his powers of oratory. He was patriarch of Constantinople (398–404) and became its patron saint.

CHUB, any of several kinds of freshwater fish of the family Cyprinidae, related to the MINNOW. Species include the common or creek chub of E North America which may weigh 1kg (2.2lb) and the European chub which reaches 5.5kg (12lb).

CHUNGKING, (Ch'ung-ch'ing, Chongquing) city in S China, in SE Szechwan (Sichuan) province at the confluence of the Yangtze and Chia-ling rivers. A major trading center with well-developed heavy industry, it was the political capital of China 1938–45. Pop 6,000,000.

CHURCH, the community of Christian believers, a society founded as such by Jesus Christ (though springing from the Jewish community). The term is used both for the universal Church and for its national and local expressions. Governed and served by its MINISTRY, the Church is established by the Holy Spirit through the Scriptures and the SACRAMENTS. Its life, ideally characterized by holiness, is expressed in WORSHIP, teaching, MISSION and good works. The Church consists not only of its present members (the "Church Militant") but also of those departed, the "Church Triumphant" in heaven and (disputedly) the "Church Expectant" in purgatory. The traditional marks of the Church, as in the Nicene Creed, are that it is one, holy, Catholic and apostolic; the first is challenged by schism and the last by heresy. Protestant churches, while generally accepting the visible organization of the Church, have stressed more its spiritual nature, attempting to distinguish true Christians from nominal. (See also CHRISTIANITY; EASTERN CHURCH; WESTERN CHURCH.)

CHURCH, Frederick Edwin (1826–1900), US romantic landscape painter. He was a student of Thomas COLE and the most famous member of the HUDSON RIVER SCHOOL.

CHURCH DOCTORS, saints whose writings on Christian doctrine have special authority. The four great doctors of the E Church are saints ATHANASIUS of Alexandria, BASIL THE GREAT of Caesarea, GREGORY OF NAZIANZUS, and John CHRYSOSTOM. The four great doctors of the W Church are saints AMBROSE, AUGUSTINE, Gregory the Great (Pope GREGORY) and JEROME. The W has 20 other doctors, including saints Thomas AQUINAS, BONAVENTURA, CATHERINE OF SIENA and TERESA OF AVILA. The last two were declared doctors in 1970 by papal decree.

CHURCHES OF CHRIST, US religious denomination based on the primitive Church. It holds that the Church of Christ was founded at PENTECOST and refounded by Thomas CAMPBELL (1763–1854). There are over 17,000 independent churches and 2,290,000 members.

CHURCH FATHERS, eminent early Christian bishops and teachers whose writings deeply influenced Church doctrine. They include the eight great CHURCH DOCTORS and the APOSTOLIC FATHERS.

CHURCHILL, Lord Randolph Henry Spencer (1849–1895), British politician, father of Sir Winston Churchill, famous in the 1880s for advocating a more democratic and reformist Conservative party. Entering the House of Commons in 1874, he led a group called the Fourth Party (1880–85) and was creator of Tory democracy. A brilliant orator, he became chancellor of the exchequer in 1886, but resigned the same year and never again held office.

CHURCHILL, Sir Winston Spencer Leonard (1874–1965), greatest modern British statesman, as a war leader the architect of victory in WWII. He was the son of Lord Randolph Churchill. After an early career as an army officer and war correspondent he became a Conservative member of Parliament, in 1901, changing to the Liberals in 1905. He was home secretary

1910–11, a dynamic first lord of the admiralty 1911–15 and held various government posts 1917–22. He was Conservative chancellor of the exchequer 1924–29 but in the 1930s his unpopular demands for war preparedness kept him from power. In WWII he was first lord of the admiralty 1939–40 and prime minister 1940–45. As such he became one of the greatest-ever war leaders; his oratory maintained Britain's morale, and he was one of the main shapers of Allied strategy working closely with President ROOSEVELT. A postwar reaction cost his party the 1945 election, but he was again prime minister 1951–55, remaining a nationally loved and revered figure for the rest of his life.

CHURCH OF CHRIST, SCIENTIST. See CHRISTIAN SCIENCE.

CHURCH OF ENGLAND, the English national church. Its doctrine is basically Protestant and its hierarchy and ceremony are rooted in Catholic tradition. The Church broke with Rome in 1534 (see REFORMATION) when HENRY VIII assumed the title of head of the Church. In the 16th and 17th centuries the Church was troubled by PURITAN agitation and later by nonconformity. But it remains the established state church with a nominal membership of 25–30 million (active members perhaps total only 10% of this figure). The 26 senior bishops (lords spiritual) sit in the House of Lords, and are led by the archbishop of Canterbury. (See also ANGLICANISM; MINISTRY.)

CHURCH OF SCOTLAND, the Scottish national church, based on PRESBYTERIANISM. It is governed by the General Assembly, which is elected from the presbyteries. Parishes are presided over by kirk sessions elected by the congregation. Membership totals some 1,300,000. (See also KNOX, JOHN; COVENANTERS; CHALMERS, THOMAS.)

CHURCH OF THE NAZARENE, Protestant evangelical denomination created in its present form in Tex. in 1908 when three groups merged. Its headquarters is in Kansas City, Mo.

CHURRIGUERA, José Benito (1665–

1725), Spanish architect who gave his name to the Spanish Baroque style, better known as Churrigueresque (1650–1740). Churriguera designed grandiosely theatrical altars and the entire town of Nuevo Baztán, Madrid.

CHU TEH (1886–1976), Chinese Communist leader. He studied in Germany, became a Communist, helped form the Chinese Red Army, and joined Mao Tse-tung. As commander in chief, he led the Long March (1934–35) and defeated the Nationalists (1949). He held various high posts in the Communist government.

CIANO, Count Galeazzo (1903–44), Italian Fascist statesman. He married Mussolini's daughter (1930) and became propaganda minister (1933). As foreign minister (1936–43), he was overshadowed by Mussolini. Dismissed, he voted against Mussolini at the 1943 Fascist Grand Council. He was caught by the Nazis, handed over to the Fascists in N Italy and shot.

CIARDI, John (1916–   ), US poet, translator and teacher. He made notable translations of Dante's *Inferno* (1954), *Purgatorio* (1961) and *Paradiso* (1970).

CIBBER, Colley (1671–1757), English actor-manager and dramatist who introduced sentimental comedy to the theater in *Love's Last Shift* (1696). His moral comedies were a reaction against Restoration drama. Cibber was made poet laureate in 1730.

CIBOLA, Seven Cities of, golden cities reported in the Southwest of North America in the 16th century. The legend attracted Spanish exploration, notably by Coronado with 300 Spanish cavalry and 1000 Indian allies (1540). In fact the cities were five or six Zuñi pueblos.

CICERO, Marcus Tullius (106–43 BC), Roman orator, statesman and philosopher. As consul (63 BC) he championed POMPEY and saved Rome from civil war by crushing the CATILINE conspiracy. His refusal to submit to the First Triumvirate ruined his political career in 58 BC. Cicero's tacit approval of Caesar's murder and his defense of the Republic in his *First and Second Philippics* led Mark ANTONY to have him killed.

CID, El ("the Lord"), title given to Rodrigo Día de Vivar (c1043–1099), a Castilian Spanish national hero. He led the forces of Sancho II of Castile and Alfonso VI of León Banished by Alfonso in 1081, he fought for the Moorish king of Saragossa and captured Valencia (1094), which he ruled until his death. His romanticized exploits appear in much literature, notably

in *The Song of the Cid* (c1140) and CORNEILLE's *Le Cid* (1637).

CIMABUE, Giovanni (d1302?), Italian fresco painter of the 13th-century Florentine school. His work links Italian Byzantine and early Renaissance art. He possibly taught GIOTTO. He supervised the construction of mosaics in Pisa cathedral, whose *St. John* is said to be his.

CIMAROSA, Domenico (1749–1801), prolific Italian composer famous for his comic operas, notably *Il Matrimonio Segreto* ("The Secret Marriage") of 1792. He was court composer to Catherine the Great of Russia, 1787–91.

CIMBALOM. See DULCIMER.

CINCHONA, or chinchona, genus of tropical evergreen trees and shrubs that are native to the Amazonian slopes of the Andes from Colombia to Bolivia. The main importance of these trees lies in the bark, which yields medicinal ALKALOIDS, notably QUININE, used as a cure for malaria. Cinchona seeds from Bolivia formed the basis of major plantations established in Java by the Dutch. Java is the chief source of cinchona bark today.

CINCINNATI, third-largest city in Ohio, and seat of Hamilton Co. It stands in SW Ohio on the Ohio R. Founded 1788, the city was named for the Society of the Cincinnati (see CINCINNATI, SOCIETY OF THE). By the mid-19th century it was the nation's largest pork packing center, nicknamed "Porkopolis." Cincinnati is now a commercial, manufacturing and railroad center, site of the University of Cincinnati and home of the Cincinnati Symphony Orchestra. Pop 385,457.

CINCINNATI, Society of the, hereditary patriotic association of officers formed by members of the Continental Army in 1783, at the end of the Revolutionary War. Many Americans saw it as an attempt to establish a military aristocracy. There are societies in each of the original 13 states and one in France. George Washington was the first president-general.

CINCINNATUS, Lucius Quinctius (c519–439? BC), early Roman hero renowned for selfless patriotism. He was twice appointed dictator (458 and 439 BC) to save Rome from disaster. Both times he reputedly defeated Rome's enemies and then resigned, rejected all rewards and returned to his farm.

CINEMA. See MOTION PICTURES.

CINÉMA VÉRITÉ, style of documentary filmmaking, characterized by the use of hand-held sound cameras to record scenes and events, ideally with maximum spontaneity and objectivity and minimal staging and direction. The approach dates back to the work of Dziga Vertov, and the term (literally "cinema truth") is a translation of his *Kino-Pravda*, a series of newsreels made in the USSR in the 1920s. Modern cinéma-vérité techniques have been especially popular in France and the US, a pioneer film being Jean Rouch's and Edgar Morin's *Chronique d'un Été* (1961).

CINQUE PORTS, originally five but ultimately thirty-two towns along the S coast of England which from the 11th-17th centuries enjoyed certain privileges in return for providing the crown with ships and men. England had no royal navy at this time.

CIPHERS. See CODES AND CIPHERS.

CIRCADIAN RHYTHM. See BIOLOGICAL CLOCKS.

CIRCASSIANS, a pastoral and fruit-growing mountain people living in the NW Caucasus E of the Black Sea. Today they number over 350,000: 80% live in the Soviet Union, the rest live in Turkey and are descended from Muslims who fled there when Russia annexed Circassia in 1829.

CIRCE, in Greek mythology, the enchantress daughter of Helios and the nymph Perse. She lived on the island of Aeaea, and changed the companions of ODYSSEUS into swine before he outwitted her.

CIRCUIT BREAKER, device now often used in place of a FUSE to protect electrical equipment from damage when the current exceeds a desired value, as in short-circuiting. The circuit breaker opens the CIRCUIT automatically, usually by means of a coil that separates contacts when the current reaches a certain value (see ELECTROMAGNETISM). One advantage of the circuit breaker is that the contacts may be reset (by hand or automatically) whereas a fuse has to be replaced. Small circuit breakers are used in the home (as in many TELEVISION sets), larger ones in industry.

CIRCUS, in the modern sense, an entertainment involving equestrian, acrobatic, animal, trapeze and clown acts. The modern circus first appeared in London in 1768, when Philip Astley launched an equestrian show to which other acts were added. The first US circus was opened by an Englishman, J. W. Ricketts, in Philadelphia in 1793. Its imitators often formed traveling shows, performing under an enormous tent, the "Big Top." The most famous American circuses, later combined, were those of BARNUM AND BAILEY and the RINGLING BROTHERS, which became "three-ring" circuses as they expanded and added additional staging areas for their numerous acts.

CIRRHOSIS, chronic disease of the LIVER, with disorganization of normal structure and replacement by fibrous scars and regenerating nodules. It is the end result of many liver diseases, all of which cause liver-cell death; most common are those associated with ALCOHOLISM and following some cases of hepatitis, while certain poisons and hereditary diseases are rare causes. All liver functions are impaired, but symptoms often do not occur until early liver failure develops with EDEMA, ascites, JAUNDICE, COMA, emaciation, or gastrointestinal-tract HEMORRHAGE; BLOOD clotting is often abnormal and PLASMA proteins are low. The liver damage is not reversible, but if recognized early in the alcoholic, abstention can minimize progression. Treatment consists of measures to protect the liver from excess protein, DIURETICS and the prevention and treatment of hemorrhage.

CISTERCIANS, or White Monks, Roman Catholic religious order founded at Cîteaux France, in 1098 by St. Robert of Molesme and at its height in the 12th and 13th centuries. Cistercians eat and work in silence and abstain from meat, fish and eggs.

CITIZENSHIP, a legal relationship between an individual and the country of his nationality, usually acquired by birth or naturalization. The terms for acquiring citizenship vary in different countries, but usually depend on a person's place of birth and the nationalities of the parents. In the US, anyone born on American soil is an American citizen, unless born of foreign parents having diplomatic status. If born outside the US, the child can acquire US citizenship through either parent, by birth if at least one parent maintains residence in the US, or by residing in the US for at least five years between ages 13 and 21 if only one parent is an American citizen. A person may become a naturalized citizen of the US by residing there for five years under permanent status. The citizen is given a passport, government protection and constitutional rights, and must pay taxes and be ready to serve in the armed forces.

CITIZENS' PARTY, US political party, founded in 1979. It favors public control of energy industries, an end to nuclear power, institution of price controls and a cut in defense spending. The environmentalist and author Barry Commoner, its 1980 presidential candidate, polled 234,279 votes, or 0.3% of the total.

CITRIC ACID ($C_6H_8O_7$), colorless crystalline solid, a CARBOXYLATE ACID widespread in plant and animal tissue, especially citrus fruits. It is made commercially by FERMENTATION of crude sugar with the fungus *Aspergillus niger*, and is used in the food, pharmaceutical and textile industries, and for cleaning metals. It is vital in cell METABOLISM (see CITRIC ACID CYCLE). MW 192.1, mp 153°C.

CITY, any large center of population, often distinguished from a town or village by the diversity of economic and cultural activities within it; or a center officially designated as a city for purposes of local government. Cities first developed in the Middle East, notably in Mesopotamia. One of the earliest true cities was UR in Sumer, dating back to at least 3,500 BC. Thereafter cities proliferated throughout the Middle East and in any parts of the world where civilization developed, either as religious or governmental centers, or as centers of trade, transportation, markets and manufacturing. Few early cities had more than 20,000 inhabitants and even Rome, the largest in the Empire, had no more than 800,000. Urban life decayed in Western Europe during the Dark Ages, but proliferated elsewhere. Around the 6th to 8th centuries AD Ch'ang-an, the T'ang capital in China, was the largest and most cosmopolitan city in the world; Teotihuacan in Mexico had possibly 200,000 inhabitants, and somewhat later Chan-Chan in Peru had possibly 250,000. In Europe the RENAISSANCE was ushered in by the revival of the cities as centers of trade and culture, but the giant cities of today were strictly a product of the INDUSTRIAL REVOLUTION.

In the US, city government originated in the colonial settlements, granted borough or city charters by the state legislatures after the Revolution, and governed usually by a mayor, a city council or similar body and a city judiciary (on the pattern of national government). In the 19th century the Industrial Revolution caused a tremendous population movement into the cities which is still continuing on a worldwide basis. In the US in 1800 only 5% of the population lived in cities, then defined as settlements with more than 8,000 inhabitants; by 1970, 73.5% of the population was urban. Following WWII, there was a massive shift of the middle classes and many corporations to the suburbs, and in the 1970s a slight shift away from the cities toward country living. But the earlier influx of millions of immigrants from Europe, blacks from the S, and small town people seeking greater opportunities—a process that continues—has created cities characterized by pollution, overcrowding, insufficient recreation areas, deteriorating schools and a lack

of funds for essential services, which tend to offset the many advantages of urban living.

CITY PLANNING, planning for the growth of a city or town to take into consideration the physical, social and economic aspects of its environment. Most Roman cities, and many earlier ones in the ancient world, were built on a gridiron pattern, with the public buildings centrally and strategically placed. The cities of the Middle Ages, however, were rarely planned unless powerful monied interests made this possible. The Renaissance, especially in Italy, saw a revival of grandiose city planning, usually intended to glorify a ruler or to strengthen his military position. The Industrial Revolution and the enormous population movements it generated caused rapid piecemeal development, and the situation had become critical before any attempt was made to deal with it.

In the US various civic reform movements were already active before the Civil War, leading to legislation to enforce slum clearance and provide better educational and recreational facilities, while designers such as Frederick L. OLMSTED and Daniel BURNHAM (planner of the Chicago World's Exposition of 1893) stimulated their fellows to more imaginative efforts. Unfortunately the teams responsible for such work tended to impose their own class and moral values on other social classes. More recently efforts have been made to avoid such mistakes; large federal subsidies have been made available, notably for low-cost housing and city center renewal projects, and planning has begun to take human as well as physical factors into account. Local government has become increasingly professional in planning ahead, and over 30 US universities now offer courses in city planning.

CITY-STATES, politically independent communities controlling the lives of their own citizens and dominating the surrounding countryside. They flourished in three major areas of Western culture: among the ancient civilizations of the Middle East, notably in Sumeria (ancient Babylonia), and Phoenicia; in the classical period of Greece (emerging about 700 BC); and in Europe from the 11th to the 16th centuries, notably in Italy and Germany.

CIUDAD JUAREZ. See JUAREZ.

CIVETS, weasel-like carnivorous mammals of the family Viverridae, found in Africa and S Asia. The African civet, *Civettictis civetta*, is reared for the musky-smelling oily substance used as a base for perfumes that is produced by glands under the tail.

CIVIL AERONAUTICS BOARD (CAB), an independent US federal agency which regulates civil aviation, established as the Civil Aeronautics Authority in 1938. The five board members, appointed by the president and confirmed by the Senate, have supervised air safety, airline rates and practices and domestic air routes, and have negotiated international air agreements. Under the Airline Deregulation Act of 1978, however, the CAB is scheduled to lose its authority over domestic air routes and fares by the end of 1982, and the board itself is to be phased out by Jan. 1, 1985.

CIVIL DEFENSE, measures taken to protect the civilian population and its resources from enemy attack. Civil defense programs were launched in several countries just before WWII, when the potential danger of air strikes was first realized. In the US civil defense is directed by the Office of Civil Defense, under the Department of Defense. Measures include nuclear shelter construction, a national attack warning system of 400 stations, an Emergency Broadcast System (EBS) to transmit information and instructions, a radiation monitoring network to determine when it is safe to leave the shelters, and inexpensive gas masks to help deal with CHEMICAL AND BIOLOGICAL WARFARE.

CIVIL DISOBEDIENCE, a form of political action involving intentional violation of the law in order to draw attention to alleged injustices. The aim is to enlist public sympathy, and the idea probably dates back to the essay *On Civil Disobedience* by the 19th-century American writer Henry David THOREAU. It was successfully used by the Indian leader GANDHI to help gain independence for India, and has been employed by movements as diverse as the Suffragettes and the Vietnam-War protesters, not always accompanied by Gandhi's technique of "passive resistance." In the US the civil rights movement has made the most widespread and striking use of civil disobedience.

CIVIL ENGINEERING, that branch of engineering concerned with the design, construction and maintenance of stationary structures such as buildings, bridges, highways, dams, etc. The term "civil engineer" was first used c1750 by John Smeaton, who built the Eddystone Lighthouse. Nowadays, civil engineering incorporates modern technological advances in the structures required by industrial society. The branches of the field include: SURVEYING, concerned with the selection of sites; hydraulic and sanitary engineering, dealing with public WATER SUPPLY and SEWAGE disposal, etc.; TRANSPORTATION engineering, which deals with highways, airports and so on; structural engineering, which is concerned with the actual planning and construction of permanent installations; and environmental, town or city planning, which improves existing urban environments and plans the development of new areas.

CIVILETTI, Benjamin R. (1935–   ), US lawyer. He served President Carter as assistant US attorney general in charge of the criminal division (1977–79) and as attorney general (1979–81).

CIVILIAN CONSERVATION CORPS (CCC), federal agency initiated in 1933 by President F. D. Roosevelt to combat unemployment during the Great Depression by providing jobs in forestry and conservation schemes. Projects included pest control, flood prevention and reforestation. The CCC was abolished in 1942.

CIVIL LAW, law dealing with private rights of individual citizens in contrast to branches of law, such as CRIMINAL LAW, which regulate relationships between individuals and the state. Thus civil law includes mortgages, marriage, inheritance, citizenship and property (COMMERCIAL LAW is often separate). The term civil law is also used for codified legal systems derived from Roman Law, not from the COMMON LAW.

The Romans distinguished civil law (*jus civile*) from international or public law (*jus gentium*). Codified by JUSTINIAN but replaced by customary laws in the Dark Ages, Roman law was rediscovered in the 12th century. It influenced France's CODE NAPOLÉON (1804), soon copied by other West European nations. Today, Western countries comprise civil law nations (most of Europe and Latin America) and common law countries (notably Great Britain, Canada and the US). In civil law countries, courts base judgments on codified principles rather than on precedents, and they do not feature trial by jury or the law of evidence.

CIVIL LIBERTIES UNION. See AMERICAN CIVIL LIBERTIES UNION.

CIVIL RIGHTS ACT OF 1965. See VOTING RIGHTS ACT OF 1965.

CIVIL RIGHTS AND LIBERTIES, rights and privileges held by citizens of a nation, whether deemed natural and inviolable or part of what is legally owed to them.

Civil Rights in the United States. The basis for civil rights in the US is the Constitution and its first 10 amendments, the BILL OF RIGHTS. This deals, for example, with freedom of speech, press, religion and assembly; freedom from unreasonable seizure and searches; right to a speedy, public trial; and prohibition of double jeopardy and self-incrimination.

Attempts to extend the civil rights of blacks were embodied in the 13th Amendment abolishing slavery, the 14th Amendment granting Negro citizenship, and the 15th Amendment giving blacks the vote. But US Supreme Court decisions soon blunted the force of these amendments, and the black became a voteless, second-class citizen, segregated by JIM CROW laws. Finally, in 1954, the US Supreme Court used the "equal protection of the laws" clause of the 14th Amendment to ban segregation in public schools. Passage by Congress of the Civil Rights Acts of 1964 and 1968 and the Voting Rights Act of 1965 banned racial discrimination in employment, public accommodations and voting. The Supreme Court also used the "due process" clause of the 14th Amendment to extend the Bill of Rights guarantees of a fair trial to defendants in state courts, and employed the "equal protection of the laws" clause to force laggard states to reapportion congressional districts and achieve the principle of "one man, one vote." The 1970s witnessed successful efforts to extend the civil rights of women, though the EQUAL RIGHTS AMENDMENT remained unratified by the states at the end of 1981.

Origins of Civil Rights. England's MAGNA CARTA, 1215, and BILL OF RIGHTS, 1698, established a basis in common law for the inviolable liberties of citizens. NATURAL LAW theorists of the 17th and 18th centuries (notably John LOCKE and Jean-Jacques ROSSEAU) reinforced such concepts, which became enshrined in the US DECLARATION OF INDEPENDENCE.

Civil Rights in Canada are based on acts, common law tradition and court decisions. A Bill of Rights (1960) largely parallels that of the US.

International Civil Rights Movement. The UN's Universal Declaration of Human Rights (1948) lists civil rights that should be available to all people. Organizations include UNESCO, the INTERNATIONAL LABOR ORGANIZATION, International Commission of Jurists and International League for the Rights of Man.

CIVIL SERVICE, the permanent body of civilian employees of a government, usually excluding elected officials, judges and military personnel. Appointment and promotion are generally based on merit, to secure efficiency and freedom from political influence. Civil services date from ancient China and Rome, and a civil service bureaucracy has become increasingly important as the functions of national governments have increased in scope and complexity.

In the US the civil service's integrity and continuity suffered from the SPOILS SYSTEM (gifts of government jobs as political rewards), firmly established from 1828 under President Andrew Jackson. Attempts to establish a merit system failed until the PENDLETON ACT (1883) set up the Civil Service Commission to administer a merit system of federal employment. The HATCH ACTS of 1939 and 1940 forbade federal employees to play any active part in politics beyond voting. Since the 1880s many states, cities and countries have set up civil service systems for public employees.

CIVIL WAR, American (1861–1865), conflict between 11 Southern states, known as the CONFEDERATE STATES OF AMERICA, and the US Federal government. Because the 11 states had attempted to secede from the Union, the conflict was officially called the "War of Rebellion" in the North. Since it was a sectional struggle, it is also known, particularly in the South, as the "War between the States."

Significance. The Civil War was one of the most crucial events in American history. It was fought for total aims: restoration of the Union or independence for the South. The conflict destroyed slavery and the agrarian society of the South which depended on it, stimulated northern industry and ensured the supremacy of the Federal government over the states. Military historians often see the struggle as the first modern, or "total" war. More than 4 million men took part, over 600,000 died and new weapons and military tactics made their appearance. The American Civil War was probably the greatest sustained combat in history before WWI.

Origins. The immediate cause of the war was the North's refusal to recognize the right of states to secede from the Union. The war's underlying cause lay in the socio-economic division between North and South. The economy of the South, based on the plantation system of agriculture, depended on slave labor, which became increasingly distasteful to the more industrialized non-slave-owning North. Political differences between the two sides came to a head over the question of westward expansion—whether slavery should be permitted in the new states and territories or remain confined to the South. Attempts to settle this question produced the MISSOURI COMPROMISE (1820) and the COMPROMISE of 1850 which was nullified by the KANSAS-NEBRASKA ACT (1854). The DRED

SCOTT DECISION (1857) and Lincoln's election as president (1860) inflamed the situation. Fearing that a Republican president would enforce abolition, S.C. seceded from the Union on Dec. 20, 1860 and was soon followed by six other states. The CONFEDERATE STATES elected Jefferson Davis provisional president, and after Lincoln ordered supplies to Federal-held Fort Sumter, in Charleston (S.C.) Harbor, Confederate guns opened fire on the fort on April 12. The fort surrendered, and four more states (N.C., Va., Ark. and Tenn.) joined the Confederacy. So began what Senator James M. Mason of Va. aptly called "a war of sentiment and opinion by one form of society against another form of society."

The war. The determination of both sides led to over 2,400 named battles. The war involved 1,600,000 Federal troops and nearly 1,000,000 Confederates. There were over 600,000 dead, Union armies suffering more than 600,000 casualties, the Confederates nearly half as many. The North outnumbered the South by 22,000,000 to 9,000,000 and was constantly reinforced by immigration from Europe. The North also had superior manufacturing, transportation and other facilities. The South had a poor railroad system, few good harbors and little industry. The North set out to crush the South by naval blockade and offensive war—waged both in the East and the West.

Congress gave Lincoln authority to recruit 500,000 men. When volunteers failed to come forward in sufficient numbers, the first national conscription act in American history was passed in March 1863. The South, too, enacted conscription. As the world's major cotton exporter, the South expected financial and diplomatic support from abroad, and what it lacked in numbers and equipment it largely made up for in the quality of its soldiers and their leaders.

The campaigns. The war, which opened in the East with the Federal disaster at BULL RUN, was won by the superior numbers and hard fighting of the Federals against the brilliant tactics of the South, and by the crippling naval blockade (see MONITOR AND MERRIMACK). Britain and France stayed neutral (though British aid to the South provoked the TRENT AFFAIR and ALABAMA CLAIMS). The war really began with the PENINSULA CAMPAIGN (1862) of G. B. MCCLELLAN which bogged down close to Richmond. The great southern commander, Robert E. LEE, harrassed McClellan in the SEVEN DAYS' BATTLES, then blunted a Federal thrust, again at BULL RUN; but his own

northward drive was stopped at ANTIETAM. (The victory gave LINCOLN the occasion to issue the preliminary EMANCIPATION PROCLAMATION.) Undaunted, Lee defeated Federal troops at FREDERICKSBURG and CHANCELLORSVILLE (where he lost his brilliant commander, "Stonewall" JACKSON) and moved north again. In the war's climactic battle, Lee was turned back at GETTYSBURG, Pa. (July 1863). Meanwhile in the West Ulysses S. GRANT moved down into W. Tenn. to win the battle of SHILOH (1862), and W. S. ROSECRANS pushed Braxton BRAGG through Tenn. E. into Ga. at MURFREESBORO and CHICKAMAUGA. New Orleans fell to David FARRAGUT. Grant's objective was VICKSBURG on the Mississippi R. When it fell, a day after Gettysburg, Grant became Supreme Commander and began relentlessly pounding at Lee in the East. From the West W. T. SHERMAN moved on Atlanta, marched to the sea, laying waste the countryside, then turned to join Grant. Caught in a pincers, Lee surrendered at APPOMATTOX COURT HOUSE, April 9, 1865.

The South was devasted, its economy in ruins, but the North emerged stronger than before. Slavery was abolished, but the balance of power between the states and the Federal government remained a problem. (See also CIVIL RIGHTS AND LIBERTIES; RECONSTRUCTION.)

CIVIL WAR, English (1642–51), the conflict between Royalists and Parliamentarians that led to the defeat and execution of CHARLES I, and the establishment of the Commonwealth under Oliver CROMWELL. It is also called the Puritan Revolution, because the king's opponents were mainly Puritan, and his supporters chiefly Episcopalian and Catholic. But the constitutional issue at stake was whether England should be effectively ruled by parliament or by a monarch claiming supreme authority by virtue of the DIVINE RIGHT OF KINGS. War between parliament's ROUNDHEADS and Charles' CAVALIERS began after Charles opposed the LONG PARLIAMENT's efforts to curb his powers. No clear-cut social or geographical boundaries divided the forces.

In the first major battle, Charles' army held back Parliamentarian troops under Robert Devereux, Earl of Essex, at EDGEHILL near Warwick (1642). This enabled Charles to establish headquarters at Oxford. But Prince RUPERT lost to Cromwell's "Ironsides" at Marston Moor (1644). On June 14, 1645, FAIRFAX and Cromwell destroyed the Royalist army at Naseby, and by autumn 1646 parliament held most of England. Fighting flared up again after Charles' capture (1646), but Cromwell routed Scottish invaders at Preston. After Charles' execution (1649) fighting recurred. Cromwell brutally subdued Ireland (1649–50), crushed Scottish troops at Dunbar (1650) and defeated CHARLES II's Scottish forces at Worcester (1651). This was the last battle of the war.

CLAIBORNE, William Charles Coles (1775–1817), first and only governor of the Territory of Orleans (1804–12) and first governor of La. (1812–16). Elected to the US Senate, he died before taking his seat. (See also LOUISIANA PURCHASE.)

CLAIMS, Court of. See COURT OF CLAIMS.

CLAIR, René (René Chomette, 1898–1981), French film director, producer and writer, especially of screen comedies. Born in Paris, he worked on both silent and "talkie" films, including *Sous les toits de Paris* (1930).

CLAM, the general name given to many two-shelled BIVALVE mollusks. Giant clams on coral reefs may reach a diameter of 1.2m (4ft) and weigh 0.25 ton.

CLAMSHELL ALLIANCE, a US antinuclear-power group that began conducting a series of large, nonviolent demonstrations in 1976 in an effort to halt construction of a nuclear power plant in Seabrook, N.H.

CLAPHAM SECT, evangelical Christian group, active 1790–1830, responsible for abolishing slavery and pioneering other social reforms. Founded in Clapham, London, by the banker H. Thornton, and led by William WILBERFORCE, the group included many members of parliament.

CLARE, Saint (or Clara; 1194–1253), Italian founder of the POOR CLARES and patron saint of television. She was born at Assisi, and was influenced by St. FRANCIS OF ASSISI. Canonized 1255.

CLARENDON, Edward Hyde, 1st Earl of (1609–1674), English statesman and historian, author of the *History of the Rebellion*, a personal account of the English Civil War. As lord chancellor 1660–67, he was a chief adviser and minister of Charles II, but lost favor and fled to France.

CLARENDON CODE, penal laws against nonconformists, enacted in England 1661–65 during the RESTORATION to strengthen the Anglican Church. The code was named for Charles II's lord chancellor, the 1st Earl of CLARENDON (who opposed much of it).

CLARINET, woodwind instrument comprising a tube (usually wooden) with a flared bell and tapered mouthpiece with a single reed. Different tones are produced by the fingers opening and closing holes (some covered by keys) in the tube. Clarinets feature in dance bands, military bands, woodwind groups, symphony orchestras and as solo instruments. The clarinet was invented in Germany by Johann Christoph Denner early in the 18th century.

CLARK, (Charles) Joseph (1939–   ), Canadian prime minister (1979–80). He was elected leader of the Progressive Conservative party in 1976. His proposals for higher taxes on gasoline and reductions in spending helped bring down his government.

CLARK, Dick (1929–   ), TV personality and producer who first gained fame in 1958 as host of the pop-music and dance program, *American Bandstand*.

CLARK, George Rogers (1752–1818), US frontiersman and Revolutionary War officer who led the campaign against the British in the Northwest Territory. With about 175 volunteers, he succeeded in capturing key British forts north of the Ohio R, principally Kaskaskia (1778) and Vincennes (1779).

CLARK, James Beauchamp (1850–1921), US Congressman, Democratic Party leader and speaker of the House of Representatives. Born in Ky. but representing Mo. (1893–1921), "Champ" Clark helped to oust dictatorial House Speaker J. G. CANNON, whom he succeeded (1911–19).

CLARK, Kenneth Bancroft (1914–   ), US psychologist whose 1950 report on school segregation was cited in the Supreme Court's 1954 ruling against segregation. A professor at CCNY 1942–1975, he was active in many civil rights and educational organizations and was the first black member of the New York State Board of Regents (1966). His books include *Prejudice and Your Child* (1955), *Dark Ghetto* (1965) and *The Pathos of Power* (1974).

CLARK, Kenneth MacKenzie, Baron Clark of Saltwood (1903–   ), British art critic, director of the National Gallery 1934–45 and chairman of the Arts Council 1953–60. He has held many other important posts, but became most widely known through his television series *Civilisation*, first broadcast in Britain in 1969 and in the US in the late 1970s.

CLARK, Mark Wayne (1896–   ), US general, commander of Allied ground forces in Italy in WWII and commander of UN operations in the Korean War (1952–53). He led the invasion of Italy in 1943.

CLARK, Tom Campbell (1899–1977), US lawyer from Dallas, Tex., who was attorney general 1945–49 and an associate justice of the US Supreme Court (1949–67).

CLARK, William (1770–1838), US explorer, a leader of the LEWIS AND CLARK EXPEDITION 1804–06, and brother of George Rogers CLARK. Previously a frontier soldier (1791–96), he was subsequently superintendant of Indian affairs and governor of Missouri Territory (1813–21).

CLARKE, Arthur Charles (1917–   ), British science fiction and science writer, best known as the author of the film *2001: A Space Odyssey* (1968) and for his detailed design for communications satellites in 1945. His best-known novel is *Childhood's End* (1953).

CLASS ACTION SUIT, a lawsuit brought by one or more members of a large group on behalf of all members who share a common interest in the issues of law and fact, and have suffered a similar wrong for which they seek relief from the court. If the trial court agrees to hear the suit, all members of the group must be informed and be given the opportunity, if they so desire, to exclude themselves from the group. If a member does not exclude himself, he must accept the judgment of the court. One or more stockholders, for instance, may bring a class action suit on behalf of other stockholders who object to the policies of the corporation. Class action suits have been successfully brought against companies which, over a period of years, systematically discriminated against women or minorities in their pay and promotion policies.

CLASSICAL ORDERS, in architecture, the names given to various styles of COLUMN and adjoining parts, notably the ENTABLATURE. They are: **Doric** (the oldest, without base, used in the PARTHENON), **Ionic** (developed in Asia Minor around the 6th century BC, then taken to Greece), **Corinthian** (the most ornate, appearing in Greece in the 4th century BC, but fully developed by the Romans and revived in the RENAISSANCE), **Tuscan** (the simplest, supposedly derived from the Etruscans) and **Composite** (a late-Roman blend of Ionic and Corinthian). As outlined by VITRUVIUS (1st century BC) and described by SERLIO (16th century AD), the classical orders deeply influenced architectural design in and after the Renaissance.

CLASSICISM, art forms and cultural periods characterized by the conscious emulation of classical antiquity, particularly the art and literature of ancient Greece and Rome. Emphasizing order, clarity, restraint and harmony of form, the most notable epoch of classicism was the Renaissance, the "rebirth" of classical civilization. After the Mannerist and Baroque periods, classicism reappeared in the 18th–19th-century movement known as NEOCLASSICISM. Influenced by Johann WINCKELMANN, principal exponents of the movement included Antonio CANOVA, J. L. DAVID and Robert ADAM.

CLASSIFICATION OF LIVING THINGS. See TAXONOMY.

CLAUDEL, Paul (1868–1955), French Roman Catholic dramatist, poet and diplomat. Influenced by RIMBAUD and intensely religious, he drew inspiration for his sensuous, lyrical verse from nature and Oriental thought.

CLAUDE LORRAIN (real name, Claude Gelé or Gellée 1600–1682), a founder of French romantic landscape painting, lived and worked mostly in Rome. His canvases usually show a biblical or classical scene dominated by an idyllically lit landscape. His later works are almost visionary in their intensity and inspired such painters as TURNER.

CLAUDIUS, name of two Roman emperors. **Claudius I** (Tiberius Claudius Nero Germanicus; 10 BC–54 AD), reigned 41–54 AD. A sickly nephew of TIBERIUS, he was a scholar and writer. He invaded Britain (43 AD), annexed Mauretania, Lycia and Thrace (41–46 AD), improved Rome's legal system and encouraged colonization. He was poisoned by his second wife, Agrippina. **Claudius II, Gothicus** (Marcus Aurelius Claudius; 214–270 AD), reigned 268–70. An army officer, he succeeded Gallienus.

CLAUSEWITZ, Karl von (1780–1831), Prussian general, strategist and military historian, known mainly as the author of *On War* (1833), which revolutionized military thinking after his death. He defined war as an extension of diplomacy and urged the destruction of enemy forces, morale and resources. He has thus been called the prophet of total war (although he favored defensive fighting).

CLAUSIUS, Rudolf Julius Emanuel (1822–1888), German theoretical physicist who first stated the second law of THERMODYNAMICS (1850) and proposed the term ENTROPY (1865). He also contributed to KINETIC THEORY and the theory of ELECTROLYSIS.

CLAVELL, James (1924–   ), British-born US author. His popular novels span centuries of history in the Far East and include *King Rat* (1962), *Shogun* (1975) and *Noble House* (1981).

CLAVICHORD, a stringed keyboard instrument used primarily between the 15th and 18th centuries. Its sound is produced by brass blades (tangents) hitting against pairs of strings. Although small-toned, it is especially sensitive and responsive. It was the usual household musical instrument in 16th–18th-century Germany.

CLAVICLE. See COLLAR BONE.

CLAY, Cassius. See MUHAMMAD ALI.

CLAY, Cassius Marcellus (1810–1903), US abolitionist, politician and statesman, founder of the antislavery journal *True American*, in Lexington, Ky., 1845. He was a founder of the Republican Party, 1854, and US ambassador to Russia (1861–62 and 1863–69).

CLAY, Henry (1777–1852), US statesman, famous for his attempts to reconcile North and South in the pre-Civil War period. Born near Richmond, Va., Clay served as both US representative and senator from Ky. 1806–1852, and secretary of state 1825–29. He helped produce the MISSOURI COMPROMISE on slavery (1820). In 1844 he was Whig presidential candidate but lost the election by alienating New York abolitionists on the issue of the annexation of Tex. as a slave state. His career culminated in the COMPROMISE OF 1850, a complex package of "slave" and "free" provisions. Known as "the great compromiser," Clay lost support as the nation became more bitterly divided. He is also remembered as one of the WAR HAWKS of 1812 and for his controversial AMERICAN SYSTEM, a series of radical economic proposals.

CLAY, Lucius Dubignon (1897–1978), US general assigned to govern the American zone of West Germany 1947–49. He supervised the BERLIN AIRLIFT.

CLAYTON ANTITRUST ACT, a law passed by Congress in 1914 to supplement the SHERMAN ANTITRUST ACT of 1890. The Clayton act specified illegal monopolistic practices, among them certain forms of interlocking directorates and holding companies. It also legalized peaceful strikes, picketing and boycotting. In 1921, however, the Supreme Court interpreted the act as doing no more than legalize labor unions and not their practices. (See MONOPOLY AND UNFAIR COMPETITION.)

CLAYTON-BULWER TREATY, an AngloAmerican agreement of 1850 concerning a proposed canal across the Isthmus of Panama. Both sides agreed to control, finance and maintain the canal jointly, and "not to occupy, or fortify, or colonize . . . any part of Central America." But differing interpretations of the treaty produced friction and, after the second HAYPAUNCEFOTE TREATY (1901), the US built the PANAMA CANAL alone.

CLEAN AIR ACT, first passed in 1963 and updated in subsequent years, this law empowered the federal government to give grants, conduct studies, and create and enforce regulations designed to combat air pollution. In particular, under this act, standards were set for limiting pollutants in auto emissions and restricting industrial air pollution in regions in which the atmosphere had become foul. In 1981, when the act came up for reconsideration, the Reagan administration called for major revisions to relax the act's stringent regulations.

CLEARINGHOUSE, name of the type of institution through which banks and other corporations that do extensive business with each other settle their accounts. Clearinghouses operate by offsetting transactions, thus minimizing payment settlements. America's first bank clearinghouse was set up in New York in 1853. The Federal Reserve bank of New York is the major bank clearinghouse in the US.

CLEAVAGE, physical property of a MINERAL, the tendency to split along certain preferred PLANES parallel to an actual or possible CRYSTAL face: e.g., GALENA, whose crystals are cubic, cleaves along three mutually PERPENDICULAR planes (parallel to 100, 010, 001). Such cleavage is useful in identifying minerals. Rock cleavage generally takes place along certain planes defined by the preferred orientation of minerals, or may represent numerous closely spaced cracks (joints) in the rock. Rock cleavage is usually inclined to the bedding of sedimentary rocks.

CLEAVELAND, Moses (1754–1806), US soldier and frontiersman who founded the city of Cleveland, Ohio. Cleaveland led the initial exploring party to "New Connecticut" in 1796, and planned the site at the mouth of the Cuyahoga R. The settlement's name was spelled as Cleaveland until the 1830s.

CLEAVER, (Leroy) Eldridge (1935–   ), US black militant, a leader of the BLACK PANTHER PARTY. His autobiographical *Soul on Ice* (1968) deals with his own experience of racial hatred and of the US penal system. It was to avoid further experience of the latter that Cleaver jumped bail in 1968 and fled first to Cuba and then to Algeria where, until 1972, he organized an international wing of the Black Panthers. In 1975 he returned voluntarily to the US and in 1980 he was placed on probation after pleading guilty to three charges of assault dating from a 1968 shoot-out with police.

CLEFT PALATE, a common developmental deformity of the PALATE in which the two halves do not meet in the midline; it is often associated with HARELIP. It can be familial or follow disease in early PREGNANCY, but may appear spontaneously. It causes a characteristic nasal quality in the cry and voice. Plastic SURGERY can close the defect and allow more normal development of the voice and TEETH.

CLEMENCEAU, Georges (1841–1929), French statesman and journalist, a founder of the Third Republic and twice French premier, 1906–09 and 1917–20. Clemenceau was a committed republican. He worked with GAMBETTA (1870) for the overthrow of the Second Empire and supported ZOLA in the DREYFUS AFFAIR. During his second premiership he made a major contribution to the Allied victory in WWI and to the drafting of the Treaty of VERSAILLES.

CLEMENS, Samuel Langhorne. See TWAIN, MARK.

CLEMENT, René (1913–   ), French film director whose early work, like *Forbidden Games* (1954), was noted for its realism and social consciousness.

CLEMENTE, Roberto (1934–1972), Puerto Rican-born US baseball player. A star outfielder for the Pittsburgh Pirates (1954–72), he amassed 3,000 hits, compiled a .317 lifetime batting average and was a five-time National League batting champion. He was elected to the Baseball Hall of Fame in 1973, soon after his death in an airplane crash.

CLEMENTI, Muzio (1752–1832), Italian composer and pianist, known as "the father of the piano." He enjoyed a successful concert career throughout Europe. John FIELD was among his pupils. In 1799, in London, he became a partner in one of the first firms ever to manufacture pianos.

CLEMENT OF ALEXANDRIA (c150–c215 AD), theologian of the early Christian Church. His most important work is the trilogy *Exhortation to the Greeks*, the *Tutor* and *Miscellanies*. Born in Athens, Clement spent most of his life as a teacher in Alexandria.

CLEOPATRA, name of several queens of the Ptolemaic dynasty, the most famous being the Egyptian Queen Cleopatra VII (69–30 BC) who, as mistress of Julius CAESAR and later wife to Mark ANTONY, had a profound influence on Roman politics. Her marriage to Mark Antony contributed to Egypt's defeat by Rome, which in turn led to the couple's tragic suicide. A celebrated *femme fatale*, she is the subject of dramatic works by Shakespeare and G. B. Shaw.

CLEOPATRA'S NEEDLES, two large stone obelisks erected by Thutmose III at Heliopolis in Egypt, c1500 BC. One now stands on the Thames Embankment in London; the other is in Central Park, New York City.

CLERMONT, Council of, Church reform assembly held at Clermont-Ferrand, France, in 1095. It was at this assembly that Pope Urban II urged the undertaking of the First Crusade.

CLEVELAND, (Stephen) Grover (1837–1908), twice Democratic president of the US, remembered for his unswerving honesty in government. Grover Cleveland was born in Caldwell, N.J. In 1855 he moved to Buffalo and entered the legal profession. In 1881 he was elected mayor of Buffalo, and little more than a year later was catapulted into the job of governor of N.Y. state. There his opposition to graft and opportunism earned him a countrywide following and, in 1884, despite the efforts of TAMMANY HALL, the Democratic presidential nomination.

First Term (1885–89). Cleveland's adherence to principle often cost him political support. He implemented the Pendleton Civil Service Act (1883), cutting by almost 12,000 the number of posts previously controlled by political patronage, and this cost him much of his own party's backing. Cleveland also angered Western timber companies, cattle ranchers and railroaders by exposing illicit land deals. And by trying to reduce tariffs, he antagonized Eastern bankers and industrialists. After losing the presidential election of 1888, Cleveland was renominated by the Democratic Party, once more in spite of Tammany Hall, in 1892.

Second Term (1893–97). Cleveland took office just as the US was beginning to experience severe economic depression. He saw the SHERMAN SILVER PURCHASE ACT (1890) as a major factor in causing the depression and forced its repeal in 1893, but this measure had little impact. Cleveland then attempted to replenish the treasury by buying gold from private financiers. Again, this proved to be no remedy. The situation deteriorated for Cleveland with the outbreak of labor troubles. He lost support by turning away Jacob COXEY and his "army" of unemployed citizens, and by using troops to break the PULLMAN STRIKE (1894). In 1896, with the president's popularity at its lowest ebb, FREE SILVER supporters gained control of the Democratic Party, nominating William Jennings Bryan for the presidency. Cleveland retired to Princeton, where he died.

CLEVELAND, city in NE Ohio, seat of Cuyahoga Co., on Lake Erie at the mouth of the Cuyahoga R. It was founded by Moses

CLEAVELAND in 1796 but developed only with the completion of the Ohio and Erie Canal (1832), and the coming of the railroad in the 1840s. During the Civil War the city's iron and petroleum industries mushroomed. Later Cleveland became the home of the Standard Oil Company. Today the city produces steel, automobile parts, chemicals, precision machinery, petroleum products and electrical goods. In recent years much effort has been expended on urban renewal. In 1967 Cleveland became the first major American city to elect a black mayor, Democrat Carl B. STOKES. Pop 573,822.

CLIBURN, Van (Harvey Lavan, Jr.; 1934–), US concert pianist. He became world famous after winning the International Tchaikovsky Piano Competition in Moscow in 1958. An international event of the same kind is now held annually in his name in the US.

CLIFFORD, Clark McAdams (1906–), US lawyer who served as a special adviser to Presidents Truman and Kennedy, and was secretary of defense in the cabinet of President Johnson (1968–69).

CLIMATE, the sum of the weather conditions prevalent in an area over a period of time. Weather conditions include temperature, rainfall, sunshine, wind, humidity and cloudiness. Climates may be classified into groups. The system most used today is that of Vladimir Köppen, with five categories (A, B, C, D, E), broadly defined as follows:

A   Equatorial and tropical rainy climates;

B   Arid climates;

C   Warmer forested (temperate) climates;

D   Colder forested (temperate) climates; and

E   Treeless polar climates.

These categories correspond to a great extent to zoning by LATITUDE; this is because the closer to the EQUATOR an area is, the more direct the sunlight it receives and the less the amount of ATMOSPHERE through which that sunlight must pass. Other factors are the rotation of the earth on its axis (diurnal differences) and the revolution of the earth about the sun (seasonal differences).

PALEOCLIMATOLOGY, the study of climates of the past, has shown that there have been considerable long-term climatic changes in many areas: this is seen as strong evidence for CONTINENTAL DRIFT (see also PLATE TECTONICS). Other theories include variation in the solar radiation (see SUN) and change in the EARTH's axial tilt. Man's influence has caused localized, short-term climatic changes. (See CLOUDS; METEOROLOGY; TROPIC; WEATHER FORECASTING; WIND.)

CLINTON, De Witt (1769–1828), US politician who promoted the building of the ERIE CANAL and the Champlain–Hudson Canal. As mayor of New York for most of 1803–15 and N.Y. governor, 1817–23 and 1825–28, he set up important civic and political reforms and social relief for the Roman Catholics, slaves and the poor. He had Federalist and Republican support for his presidential candidacy in 1812, but lost to James Madison.

CLINTON, George (1739–1812), US vice president, statesman and revolutionary soldier, often called the "father of New York state." He built up N.Y.'s economy during seven terms as governor (1777–95; 1801–04). He was a leading opponent of the Federal Constitution. He was vice president for 1804–12 and a presidential candidate in 1804.

CLINTON, Sir Henry (c1738–1795), English general appointed (in 1778) commander-in-chief of British forces during the American Revolution after distinguishing himself at BUNKER HILL. He captured Charleston in 1780 but resigned in 1781. He was blamed for the British surrender at YORKTOWN in that year.

CLIPPER SHIPS, 19th-century sailing ships, the fastest ever built. They evolved from the Baltimore clippers and were built in the US and later in Britain. They had a very large area of sail, relied on a good crew, and traded with China and Australia where speed paid off. Two famous ships were Donald McKay's Lightning and the British Cutty Sark (now at Greenwich, England).

CLIVE OF PLASSEY, Robert Clive, 1st Baron (1725–1774), British soldier and administrator, twice governor of Bengal, who established British power in India. He defeated both the French at Arcot (1751) and the Bengal nawab, Siraj-ud-Daula, at Plassey, thus securing all Bengal for the EAST INDIA COMPANY. He reformed administrative corruption in Bengal. Although acquitted by parliament in a long and notorious trial of the charge of dishonesty when in office, he afterwards committed suicide.

CLOCKS AND WATCHES, devices to indicate or record the passage of time; essential features of modern life. In prehistory, time could be gauged solely from the positions of celestial bodies; a natural development was the SUNDIAL, initially no more than a vertical post whose SHADOW was cast by the sun directly onto the ground. Other devices depended on the flow of water from a pierced container (see CLEPSYDRA); the rates at which marked candles, knotted ropes and oil in calibrated vessels burned down; and the flow of sand through a constriction from one bulb of an HOURGLASS to the other. Mechanical clocks were probably known in Ancient China, but first appeared in Europe in the 13th century AD. Power was supplied by a weight suspended from a rope, later by a coiled spring; in both cases an escapement being employed to control the energy release. Around 1657–58 HUYGENS applied the PENDULUM principle to clocks; later, around 1675, his hairspring and balance-wheel mechanism made possible the first portable clocks—resulting eventually in watches. Jeweled bearings, which reduced wear at critical points in the mechanism, were introduced during the 18th century, and the first CHRONOMETER was also devised in this century. Electric clocks with synchronous motors are now commonly found in the home and office, while the ATOMIC CLOCK, which can be accurate to within one second in 3 million years, is of great importance in science.

CLOISONNÉ, decorative combination of metal and enamel. Metal strips are soldered edgewise to a metal surface forming compartments, or *cloisons*, that are filled with colored enamel paste. The enamel is fused to the surface by heating, and then highly polished to a smooth pattern. The technique, first known in MYCENAE, was developed by the Byzantines and then by the Chinese.

CLONE, a cell or organism that is genetically identical to the cell or organism from which it was derived. **Cloning,** the creation of clones, is asexual, so there is no mixing of parental GENES. Clones may be produced by such reproductive methods as cell division in BACTERIA, cell budding in yeasts, or vegetative duplication (plant cuttings). The experimental cloning of mice has been achieved by replacing the nucleus of a fertilized mouse egg cell with the nucleus of a cell from a mouse embryo. The egg cell then develops into a mouse that is genetically identical to the donor embryo.

CLOSED SHOP, an establishment where the employer accepts only members of a specified union as his employees, and continues to employ them only if they remain union members. The TAFT-HARTLEY ACT of 1947 forbids closed shops in industries involved in or affecting interstate commerce.

CLOTHING. See FASHION.

CLOTTING, the formation of semisolid deposits in a liquid by coagulation, often by the denaturing of previously soluble ALBUMEN. Thus clotted cream is made by slowly heating milk so that the thick cream rises; the curdling of skim milk to make CHEESE is also an example of clotting. Clotting of BLOOD is a complex process set in motion when it comes into contact with tissues outside its ruptured vessel. These contain a factor, **thromboplastin,** which activates a sequence of changes in the PLASMA clotting factors (12 enzymes). Alternatively, many surfaces, such as glass and fabrics, activate a similar sequence of changes. In either case, factor II (prothrombin, formed in the liver), with calcium ions and a platelet factor, is converted to **thrombin.** This converts factor I (fibrinogen) to **fibrin,** a tough, insoluble polymerized protein which forms a network of fibers around the platelets (see BLOOD) that have stuck to the edge of the wound and to each other. The network entangles the blood cells, and contracts, squeezing out the serum and leaving a solid clot. (See also ANTICOAGULANTS; EMBOLISM; HEMOPHILIA; HEMORRHAGE; THROMBOSIS.)

CLOTURE, (or closure) procedure for ending discussion and securing an immediate vote on an issue in a deliberative assembly. In the US Senate a motion to invoke cloture must be supported by a petition signed by 16 senators and passed by two-thirds of those present and voting. It is used against a delaying FILIBUSTER.

CLOUD CHAMBER, device, invented by C. T. R. WILSON (1911), used to observe the paths of subatomic particles. In simplest form, it comprises a chamber containing saturated VAPOR (see SATURATION) and some liquid, one wall of the chamber (the window) being transparent, another retractable. Sudden retraction of this wall lowers the temperature, and the gas becomes supersaturated (see SUPERSATURATION). Passage of SUBATOMIC PARTICLES through the gas leaves charged IONS that serve as seeds for CONDENSATION of the gas into droplets. These fog trails (condensation trails) may be photographed through the window. (See also BUBBLE CHAMBER.)

CLOUDS, visible collections of water droplets or ice particles suspended in the ATMOSPHERE. Clouds whose lower surfaces touch the ground are usually called FOG. The water droplets are very small, indeed of colloidal size (see COLLOID; AEROSOL); they must coagulate or grow before falling as rain or snow. This process may be assisted by **cloud seeding;** supercooled clouds are seeded with particles of (usually) dry ice (i.e., solid CARBON dioxide) to encourage CONDENSATION of the droplets, ideally causing RAIN or SNOW.

Types of Clouds. There are three main cloud types: **Cumulus** (heap) clouds, formed by convection, and often mountain- or cauliflower-shaped, are found from about 600m (2,000ft) up as far as the tropopause (see TROPOSPHERE), even temporarily into the stratosphere (see ATMOSPHERE). **Cirrus** (hair) clouds are composed almost entirely of icy crystals. They appear feathery, and are found at altitudes above about 6,000m (20,000ft). **Stratus** (layer) clouds are low-lying, found between ground level and about 1,500m (5,000ft). Other types of cloud include cirrostratus, cirrocumulus, altocumulus, altostratus, cumulonimbus, stratocumulus and nimbostratus.

CLOUET, Jean (c1485–1540), Flemish artist who was chief portrait painter at the court of Francis I of France. However, only one unsigned painting and about 130 drawings can be assigned to him.

CLOVIS I (c466–511 AD), Frankish king, founder of the Frankish monarchy. He amassed a huge kingdom from the Rhine R to the Mediterranean, defeating the Romans at Soissons (486) and the Visigoths under Alaric II of Spain at Vouillé (507). He became a Christian in c498. Clovis compiled the SALIC LAW, followed by his successors the MEROVINGIANS.

CLOWN, a comedy figure of the pantomime and circus. Modern clowns possibly derived from the vice figures of medieval miracle plays, but clowns were also known in ancient Greece and Rome, and as jesters or fools in medieval courts. They later figured as harlequins in the COMMEDIA DELL' ARTE; but their grotesque makeup, baggy clothes and slapstick and tumbling (see Joseph GRIMALDI) developed fully only in the 1800s. The best-known 20th-century circus clown was Emmett KELLY.

CLUBFOOT, deformity of the FOOT, with an abnormal relationship of the foot to the ankle; most commonly the foot is turned in and down. Abnormalities of fetal posture and ligamentous or muscle development, including CEREBRAL PALSY and SPINA BIFIDA, may be causative. Correction includes gentle manipulation, PHYSIOTHERAPY, plaster splints and sometimes SURGERY.

CLURMAN, Harold Edgar (1901–1980), US theatrical director and critic who in 1931 co-founded New York's Group Theater. He directed *Awake and Sing!* (1935), *Member of the Wedding* (1950) and *Tiger At The Gates* (1955) and wrote theatrical criticism for *The Nation* and *The New Republic*.

CLYDE, Scotland's most important river. It rises in N Dumfries and flows 106mi N then NW to the Firth of Clyde. From Hamilton on, the Clyde valley is occupied by heavy industry, notably shipbuilding and iron and coal mining. GLASGOW stands at the head of its navigable channel.

CLYTEMNESTRA, in Greek mythology, wife of AGAMEMNON and mother of ORESTES, ELECTRA and IPHIGENIA. Seduced by Aegisthus, her husband's cousin, she helped him to murder Agamemnon when he returned from Troy. In revenge Orestes killed both her and Aegisthus.

COAL, hard, black mineral burned as a FUEL. With its by-products COKE and COAL TAR it is vital to many modern industries.

Coal is the compressed remains of tropical and subtropical plants, especially those of the CARBONIFEROUS and PERMIAN periods. Changes in the world climatic pattern explain why coal occurs in all continents, even Antarctica. Coal formation began when plant debris accumulated in swamps, partially decomposing and forming PEAT layers. A rise in sea level or land subsidence buried these layers below marine sediments, whose weight compressed the peat, transforming it under high-temperature conditions to coal; the greater the pressure, the harder the coal.

Coals are analyzed in two main ways: the "ultimate analysis" determines the total percentages of the elements present (carbon, hydrogen, oxygen, sulfur and nitrogen); and the "proximate analysis" gives an empirical estimate of the amounts of moisture, ash, volatile materials and fixed carbon. Coals are classified, or ranked, according to their fixed-carbon content, which increases progressively as they are formed. In ascending rank, the main types are: **lignite**, or brown coal, which weathers quickly, may ignite spontaneously, and has a low calorific value (see FUEL), but is used in Germany and Australia; **subbituminous coal**, mainly used in generating stations; **bituminous coal**, the commonest type, used in generating stations and the home, and often converted into COKE; and **anthracite**, a lustrous coal which burns slowly and well, and is the preferred domestic fuel.

Coal was burned in Glamorgan, Wales, in the 2nd millennium BC, and was known in China and the Roman Empire around the time of Christ. Coal mining was practiced throughout Europe and known to the American Indians by the 13th century AD. The first commercial coal mine in the US was at Richmond, Va., (opened 1745) and anthracite was mined in Pa. by 1790. The

INDUSTRIAL REVOLUTION created a huge and increasing demand for coal. This slackened in the 20th century as coal faced competition from abundant oil and gas, but production is now again increasing. Annual world output is about 3 billion tons, 500 million tons from the US. World coal reserves are estimated conservatively at about 7 trillion tons, enough to meet demand for centuries at present consumption rates. (See also MINING.)

COAL GAS, a mixture of gases produced by the destructive distillation of COAL, consisting chiefly of hydrogen, methane and carbon monoxide. Other products are COKE and COAL TAR. Coal gas is used as a domestic fuel, but has been largely superseded by NATURAL GAS.

COAL TAR, a dense black viscous liquid produced by the destructive distillation of COAL; COKE and COAL GAS are other products. Fractional distillation of coal tar produces a wide variety of industrially important substances. These include ASPHALT (pitch) and CREOSOTE, a wood preservative; also various oils used as fuels, solvents, preservatives, lubricants and disinfectants. Specific chemicals that can be isolated include benzene, toluene, xylene, phenol, pyridine, naphthalene and anthracene—the main source for the pharmaceutical and other chemical industries.

COAST AND GEODETIC SURVEY, US. See NATIONAL OCEANIC AND ATMOSPHERIC ADMINISTRATION.

COAST GUARD, US, branch of the armed services supervised in peacetime by the Department of Transportation, in war by the navy. It helps to maintain law and safety wherever the US has jurisdiction on the high seas and navigable inland waters. Formed in 1915 by a union of the Life Saving Service and the Revenue Cutter Service, its duties are the following: search and rescue operations, maintaining weather ships and navigational aids, including the LORAN radio network, collecting meteorological and oceanographic data, ice-breaking in inland waters and patrolling the N Atlantic for icebergs, enforcing navigation and shipping laws and marine safety regulations for seamen and the construction and equipment of ships, and operating against smugglers. In wartime the coast guard assumes the regular duties of the navy.

COAST GUARD ACADEMY, US, an institution of higher education training career officers for the US COAST GUARD, located in New London, Conn. Students take a four-year course leading to a Bachelor of Science degree and an ensign's

commission in the US coast guard.

COAST RANGES, a series of mountain ranges along the Pacific coast of North America from Kodiak Island, S Alaska, to S Cal. The mountains are of widely varied geological composition. The highest peak in the entire series is Canada's Mt Logan (19,850ft).

COBALT (Co), silvery-white, hard, ferromagnetic (see MAGNETISM) metal in Group VIII of the PERIODIC TABLE; a TRANSITION ELEMENT. It occurs in nature largely as sulfides and arsenides, and in nickel and copper ores; major producers are Canada, Zaire and Zambia. An ALLOY of cobalt, aluminum, nickel and iron ("Alnico") is used for magnets; other cobalt alloys, being very hard, are used for cutting tools. Cobalt is used as the matrix for tungsten carbide in drill bits. Chemically it resembles IRON and NICKEL: its characteristic oxidation states are $+2$ and $+3$. Cobalt compounds are useful colorants (notably the artists' pigment cobalt blue). Cobalt CATALYSTS facilitate HYDROGENATION and other industrial processes. The RADIO-ISOTOPE cobalt-60 is used in RADIATION THERAPY. Cobalt is a constituent of the vital VITAMIN B12. AW 58.9, mp 1495°C, bp 2870°C, sg 8.9 (20°C).

COBB, Irvin S. (1876–1944), US writer, editor, lecturer and radio personality. He regularly contributed humorous essays and short stories to the *Saturday Evening Post* (1911–22) and *Cosmopolitan* (1922–32) and wrote the popular *Speaking of Operations* (1916).

COBB, Lee J. (1911–1976), US actor. A character actor in the 1930s and 1940s, he went on to star in *Death of a Salesman* (1949) and *King Lear* (1969), his first Shakespearian role. Among his more than 80 films were *On the Waterfront* (1954), *Exodus* (1960) and *The Exorcist* (1973).

COBB, Tyrus Raymond (1886–1961), the "Georgia Peach," one of baseball's greatest players. In 24 years with the Detroit Tigers and the old Philadelphia Athletics he appeared in more games, batted more times and made more hits than any other major leaguer; his lifetime average was a record .367.

COBBETT, William (1763–1835), British radical writer and reformer, best known for his *Rural Rides* (1830), which portrayed the misery of rural workers. His radical views forced him to live in the US 1793–1800 and 1817–19. His *Weekly Political Register* (founded 1802) was the major radical newspaper of its day. He was elected to parliament after the 1832 Reform Act.

COBDEN, Richard (1804–1865), British politician and reformer. A textile merchant, he was known as "the Apostle of Free Trade". He was a founder member of the Anti-Corn Law League 1838–39, and its chief spokesman in parliament 1841–46. In two pamphlets, *England, Ireland and America* (1835) and *Russia* (1836), he surveyed international relations and argued against British interventionist policies.

COBOL (Common Business-Oriented Language), COMPUTER language designed primarily for business use. It has the advantage that it can be easily learned and understood by people without technical backgrounds; and that a program designed for one computer may be run on another with minimal alteration.

COBRAS, poisonous snakes of the family Elapidae that spread the ribs of the neck to form a hood when alarmed. The king cobra, the longest poisonous snake, is about 5.5m (18ft) long. The Egyptian and Indian cobras are the traditional snake-charmer's snakes. They respond to movement, not to music, as they are deaf.

COCA, Imogene (1908–) US comedienne. Paired with Sid Caesar, she starred in one of television's earliest and most popular live comedy and variety programs, *Your Show of Shows* (1950–54). On stage, she appeared in *Prisoner of Second Avenue* (1973) and other plays.

COCAINE, an ALKALOID from the coca leaf, the first local anesthetic agent and model for those currently used; it is occasionally used for surface ANESTHESIA. It is a drug of abuse, taken for its euphoriant effect by chewing the leaf, as snuff or by intravenous INJECTION. Although physical dependence does not occur, its abuse may lead to acute psychosis. It also mimics the actions of the sympathetic NERVOUS SYSTEM.

COCHISE (c1815–1874), Chiricahua Apache chief. Wrongly antagonized by soldiers, he began a savage campaign against whites in Ariz. in 1861 and efffectively drove them from the area. In 1862 he was driven back by troops to the Dragon Mts., which he held until his capture by Gen. CROOK in 1871. He escaped, but gave himself up when the Chiricahua Reservation was formed in 1872.

COCHRAN, Jacqueline (1912?–1980), US pilot. She obtained her pilot's license in 1932, after only three weeks' flying. First woman to fly in a Bendix transcontinental race (1934), she won it in 1938. She organized and headed the Women's Airforce Service Pilots (WASP) in WWII, and was the first woman to fly faster than sound.

COCHRANE, Gordon Stanley "Mickey" (1903–1962), one of baseball's greatest catchers. He played for the old Philadelphia Athletics and was catcher-manager for the Detroit Tigers. His lifetime batting average was .320.

COCKER SPANIEL, smallest breed of hunting spaniel, named for the woodcocks it was bred to hunt. Standing 14–16in at the shoulder, it can weigh from 22 to 28lb. It has a soft coat, usually thick and curly.

COCKNEY, nickname for a Londoner, especially one born within the sound of the bells of St. Mary-le-Bow church. It derives from a derogatory term used c1500 of anyone city-bred.

COCONUT PALM, *Cocus nucifera,* an economically valuable tree found on many tropical coasts. It has a long trunk crowned by a cluster of large fronds. The fruits, coconuts, take one year to develop and a single palm normally produces up to 100 nuts in one year. Each nut is surrounded by a thick fibrous husk and contains a white kernel surrounding the "coconut milk." The kernel is dried to produce copra, which is the source of coconut oil, a vegetable oil much used in the US and Europe in detergents, edible oils, margarine, brake fluid etc. The fibers of the husk are used for mats and ropes.

COCOS ISLANDS (or Keeling Islands), two coral atolls in the E Indian Ocean, an Australian external territory. Declared a British possession in 1857, they were granted in perpetuity to the Clunies-Ross family, who had settled there in 1827. They passed to Australia in 1955 and in 1972 John Clunies-Ross surrendered authority to the Australian government. Most of the population are Malays employed on the coconut plantations.

COCTEAU, Jean (1889–1963), French author, artist and film director. He first rose to fame with poetry, ballets such as *Parade* (1917), and the novel *Thomas l'Imposteur* (1923). After overcoming opium addiction, he produced some of his most brilliant work, such as the play *Orphée* (1926) and the novels *Les Enfants Terribles* (1929) and *La Machine Infernale* (1934). A prolific writer in many fields, he also made several films, of which *Le Sang d'un Poète* (1932) is the most adventurous.

COD, members of the family Gadidae, important food fish of the N Atlantic and the Pacific, weighing up to 90kg (200lb). Cod form dense shoals, feeding on other fish and bottom-living animals. Females lay up to 6 million eggs at a time. The "cod banks" off New England and Newfoundland stimulated colonization of North America.

The cod were salted, their livers yielded vitamin-rich COD LIVER OIL and the swimbladder produced isinglass, a pure form of GELATIN.

CODE, systematic and usually comprehensive set of legal rules. Many early bodies of law, such as that of HAMMURABI (c1800 BC), took this form. Roman law was codified in the TWELVE TABLES and again by the Emperor JUSTINIAN in the 6th century AD. The law reform movement in modern CIVIL LAW countries chose the code as the most accessible form of law; first of these was the CODE NAPOLÉON of 1804–10. Britain, the US and other COMMON LAW countries have made only limited use of codes.

CODEINE, a mild NARCOTIC, ANALGESIC and COUGH suppressant related to MORPHINE. It reduces bowel activity causing CONSTIPATION and is used to cure DIARRHEA.

CODE NAPOLÉON, French legal CODE, officially the *Code Civil*. Napoleon I, as first consul, appointed a commission to devise a replacement for the confused and corrupt local systems formerly in force. The code, made up of 2,281 articles arranged in three books, was enacted in 1804 and, although much altered, is still in force today. Revision commissions were appointed in 1904 and 1945. The code has been the model for nearly all codes in CIVIL LAW countries. The La. civil code (1825) is closely based on it.

CODES AND CIPHERS, devices for conveying information secretly, mostly used in wartime and for espionage. In ciphers, individual letters or numerals that make up a message are transposed or replaced by other letters or numerals. But ciphers can often be "broken" because each letter of the alphabet tends to occur with a particular frequency.

Codes are based on units that may vary in length from letters to sentences. These units are given arbitrary code equivalents known to sender and receiver, who use identical code books listing code words and symbols. Machines have often been used to create complex codes and ciphers; today computers dominate the field. It is not clear how often cryptanalysts break cryptographers' ciphers and codes, since successes are seldom made public, but a dramatic example of the importance of cryptoanalysis in wartime was the solving of Germany's so-called unbreakable Enigma system in the early years of WWII by British mathematicians and cryptoanalysts. This allowed Allied leaders to know virtually all of Germany's intentions during the hostilities before they were carried out. US breaking of Japanese codes was another major contribution to Allied victory.

The US National Security Agency, NSA, is America's top cipher maker and breaker today. It is presently attempting to monitor breakthroughs in the commercial and academic sectors to prevent foreign governments from picking up information through scientific and trade journals.

A recent breakthrough in cryptography, public key cryptography, allows the key to the code to be transmitted in the clear since in this unique system the sender can encode but not decode a message and the receiver can decode but not encode it.

COE, Sebastian (1956–   ), British track star. In the space of 10 days in 1981 Coe and archrival Steve OVETT broke the mile record three times. Coe finally prevailed, in 3:47.33. He shattered the 800-meter, 1,500-meter and mile records within 41 days in 1979.

COELACANTHS, fish, common as 70-million-year-old fossils, thought to be extinct until rediscovered by scientists in 1938 off the E African coast, where fishermen knew one species, *Latimeria chalumnae*, well.

COFFEE, drink produced from the roasted fruit (beans) of the coffee plant. The coffee tree (or bush) belongs to the genus *Coffea*, the most extensively cultivated species being *Coffea arabica*. The coffee tree probably originated in Abyssinia. Its use as a drink rapidly spread through Arabia in the 13th century and it became popular in Europe during the 16th and 17th centuries. The US is now the largest market for coffee. Coffee is grown in many tropical countries. Brazil produces more coffee than any other country, but its share is becoming less. For many Latin American, African and Asian countries it is a very important export commodity. After picking, the ripe red berries are either naturally dried and the hulls, pulp and parchment removed (dry process), or are squeezed out of their skin and soaked when slight fermentation takes place, washed and then dried (wash process). The processed berries are roasted, which induces the coffee color and aroma, partly through the formation of CAFFEINE.

The coffee bush can also be grown as a house plant, requiring several hours sunlight in the winter, although young plants thrive under fluorescent light. Indoors, the temperature should not drop below 13°C (53°F) and the soil should be kept evenly moist. Propagation is by seeds and shoot tip cuttings.

COHAN, George Michael (1878–1942), US popular songwriter, actor, playwright and producer. A celebrated Broadway song and dance man, he is best remembered for composing such hits as 'Give My Regards to Broadway,' 'You're a Grand Old Flag,' 'Yankee Doodle Dandy' and the popular WWI song 'Over There,' for which Congress awarded him a special medal in 1940.

COHESION, the tendency of different parts of a substance to hold together. This is due to forces acting between its MOLECULES: a molecule will repel one close to it but attract one that is farther away; somewhere between these there is a position where WORK must be done to either separate the molecules or push them together. This situation results both in cohesion and in ADHESION. Cohesion is strongest in a SOLID, less strong in a LIQUID, and least strong in a GAS.

COIN, piece of stamped metal, of fixed value and weight, issued to serve as money. Coins were probably invented in Lydia, Asia Minor, in the 8th century BC. Their use spread through the civilized world, and coins remained the main medium of exchange until the introduction of bank notes. Coins are made in licensed government mints. They carry a design on both sides, traditionally including inscriptions giving their value and the name of the issuing ruler or state. Gold, silver and copper are the traditional metals, often alloyed with harder metals to reduce wear. Unscrupulous debt-laden rulers also practiced debasement—reducing a coin's precious metal content without changing its face value. The Massachusetts Bay Colony produced the first US coins in 1652. The first US mint was established in Philadelphia in 1792. (See also MONEY.)

COINTELPRO, the FBI's abbreviation for "Counterintelligence Program," in the course of which (1956–71) agents committed a wide variety of illegal and unsavory acts, including break-ins, mail openings, wiretapping and bugging. Their aim was to harass various organizations and individuals, ranging from the Communist and American Nazi parties to the Rev. Martin Luther King, Jr., and the actress Jean Seberg.

COKE, form of amorphous CARBON (also containing ash, volatile residues and sulfur) remaining when bituminous COAL is heated in special furnaces to distill off the volatile constituents. Before the exploitation of NATURAL GAS, much COAL GAS was thus produced. In the US 95% of coke is used in METALLURGY, mostly in BLAST FURNACES. Such coke must be strong (to support the weight of the charge), porous and relatively pure. Some coke is used as a smokeless fuel,

and to make WATER GAS.

COKE, Sir Edward (1552–1634), English lawyer and parliamentarian who defended the supremacy of the common law and the rights of parliament and the judiciary against the attempts of JAMES I and CHARLES I to govern by royal prerogative. He drafted the PETITION OF RIGHT in 1628 setting out the rights of a citizen. First lord chief justice of England, he is best known for his four Institutes (1628–44).

COLBERT, Jean Baptiste (1619–1683), French statesman, finance minister and comptroller general under LOUIS XIV. He transformed the finances of the state by reforming taxation, correcting abuses in the administration and encouraging industry and trade. He introduced protective tariffs, developed roads and canals, created the French navy and merchant marine, and was a patron of culture.

COLD, Common, or coryza, a mild illness of the NOSE and throat caused by various types of VIRUS. General malaise and RHINITIS, initially watery but later thick and tenacious, are characteristic; sneezing, COUGH, sore throat and headache are also common, but significant FEVER is unusual. Secondary bacterial infection of EARS, SINUSES, PHARYNX or LUNGS may occur, especially in predisposed people. Spread is from person to person. Mild symptomatic relief only is required.

COLDEN, Cadwallader (1688–1776), colonial American physician, administrator and naturalist. As lieutenant governor of N.Y. colony, he became unpopular for defending the British position during the STAMP ACT riots of 1765. He produced a botanical classification of American plants which was published by LINNEAUS in Sweden, and wrote a study of the IROQUOIS Indians, *History of the Five Indian Nations of Canada* (1727).

COLD SORE, vesicular SKIN lesion of lips or NOSE caused by *Herpes simplex* VIRUS. Often associated with periods of general ill-health or infections such as the COMMON COLD or PNEUMONIA. The virus, which is often picked up in early life, persists in the skin between attacks. Recurrences may be reduced by special antivirus drugs, applied during an attack.

COLD WAR, state of tension between countries, featuring mutually antagonistic policies but stopping short of actual fighting. The term is usually used to describe post-WWII relations between the Western powers led by the US and the communist bloc led by the USSR. Both sides built powerful alliances. The US established the NORTH ATLANTIC TREATY

ORGANIZATION and the USSR organized the WARSAW PACT. Meanwhile a nuclear arms race gained momentum. Famous incidents in the Cold War included the BERLIN AIRLIFT (1948–49), the Cuban missile crisis (1962), in which the US forced Russia to dismantle its missile bases in Cuba, and the Russian invasion of Hungary (1956). The rise of a communist, but independent China and a growing assertiveness by non-aligned nations tended to weaken the leadership of the superpowers by seeking détente and by negotiating arms-limitation treaties, the US and USSR sought to relax cold war tensions.

COLE, George Douglas Howard (1889–1959), British economist and labor historian, a leading advocate of guild socialism and chairman of the Fabian Society 1939–46. A teacher at Oxford U 1925–57, he wrote several important books, including *A Short History of the British Working Class Movement* (3 vol., 1927; rev. 1948) and *A History of Socialist Thought* (5 vol., 1953–60).

COLE, Nat "King" (1919–1965), US singer and jazz pianist. Born Nathaniel Adams Coles, he first became known as a pianist in the "Chicago Blues" manner, but his throaty individual singing brought him his greatest fame. In 1953, he became the first black entertainer with his own network TV show.

COLE, Thomas (1801–1848), British-born painter who founded the HUDSON RIVER SCHOOL. His best known works are views of the Catskills and the White Mountains. Cole's grandiose, Italianate paintings of the wilderness introduced landscape as a serious subject for US painting.

COLEMAN, James Samuel (1926–   ), US educator and professor of social relations at Johns Hopkins U. (1959–73). His controversial *Equality of Educational Opportunity* (1966), also known as the Coleman Report, influenced desegregation programs of the 1970s and was instrumental in effecting increased federal aid for schools.

COLEMAN, Ornette (1930–   ), US jazz musician, one of the most creative of the saxophonists. Playing in small groups, including his own trio, has developed an advanced, original style.

COLERIDGE, Samuel Taylor (1772–1834), leading English poet, essayist and critic. With WORDSWORTH he published *Lyrical Ballads* (1798), a landmark in early ROMANTICISM, in which Coleridge's major contribution was "The Rime of the Ancient Mariner," a tale in verse of the sea and fate. He is also remembered for an unfinished

dream poem, "Kubla Khan," published in 1816. He gave notable lectures on Shakespeare and his *Biographia Literaria* (1817) criticizes the philosophy of KANT, FICHTE and SCHELLING and the poetry of Wordsworth. Opium addiction blighted his early life.

COLES, Robert (1929–   ), US psychiatrist who studied migrant families, Southern black children involved in the civil rights struggle, and other people involved in the turmoil of social crisis. He is best known for *Children of Crisis* (5 vols., 1967–77) and *Women of Crisis* (2 vols. 1978–80).

COLETTE, Sidonie-Gabrielle (1873–1954), French writer and music-hall actress known for her sensuous and subtle characterizations of people, especially of slightly disreputable women in the demimonde which she knew so well. Her brilliant style was admired by PROUST. Her best-known heroine is Claudine, a thinly veiled self-portrayal.

COLITIS, INFLAMMATION of the colon (see GASTROINTESTINAL TRACT). Infection with VIRUSES, BACTERIA or PARASITES may cause it, often with ENTERITIS. Inflammatory colitis can occur without bacterial infection in the chronic diseases, ulcerative colitis and Crohn's disease. Impaired blood supply may also cause colitis. Symptoms include COLIC and DIARRHEA (with slime or blood). Severe colitis can cause serious dehydration or SHOCK. Treatments include ANTIBIOTICS, and, for inflammatory colitis, STEROIDS, ASPIRIN derivatives or occasionally SURGERY.

COLLAGE, modern art form in which various objects and materials are glued onto a canvas or board and sometimes painted. Pablo PICASSO and Georges BRAQUE extended it to CUBISM in 1912–13, and DADAISM developed it further. Collage gave rise to "assemblage," a modern art form using scrap-metal objects and wood.

COLLECTIVE BARGAINING, process by which labor unions and management arrange wages and conditions of work directly between themselves or their representatives without the involvement of an arbitrator or other third party. In the US the NATIONAL LABOR RELATIONS ACT (1935) actively encouraged collective bargaining.

COLLECTIVE FARM, state-organized farm, usually in communist countries, notably the USSR where there are thousands of collectives. Such farms were created to replace private farms and raise agricultural output on a communal basis. Though the land is worked collectively, members may retain small plots for their own use.

COLLECTIVE SECURITY, system whereby nations band together to guarantee each others' security against aggression. It was a basic principle of both the LEAGUE OF NATIONS and the UNITED NATIONS. However, it has not been successful in preventing aggression.

COLLECTIVE UNCONSCIOUS, term used, especially by JUNG, for the part of the UNCONSCIOUS that contains material derived from the experience of the human race, rather than individual experience.

COLLECTIVISM, political doctrine which places control of economic activity in the hands of the community or the government, as opposed to CAPITALISM, which emphasizes private ownership. Collectivists, beginning with ROUSSEAU, hold that it is only through submission to the community that the individual can fulfill himself and that economic power is too important to be left to the self-interest of individuals.

COLLIE, type of sheepdog originating in the UK. It is of medium size, with a long tapering head and bushy tail. Color is often black or brown and white. Both rough-and smooth-coated varieties are found.

COLLINS, Michael (1890–1922), Irish revolutionary leader. Imprisoned for opposing the British in the EASTER RISING of 1916, he later became a SINN FEIN leader and intelligence chief of the guerrilla IRISH REPUBLICAN ARMY. Collins helped to negotiate the treaty with Britain which set up the Irish Free State in 1921, and briefly headed the Irish army and finance ministry, but was ambushed and shot by Irish opponents.

COLLINS, (William) Wilkie (1824–1889), English novelist. A friend of DICKENS, he established his reputation in 1860 with the publication of *The Woman in White,* one of the first English detective stories.

COLOGNE (Köln), river port and leading industrial city in West Germany, on the Rhine R in the W of the country. Its products range from heavy machinery to toilet water (Eau de Cologne). Cologne's prosperity dates from its membership of the HANSEATIC LEAGUE. The cathedral of St. Peter (built 1248–1880) is its most renowned landmark. Pop 976,100.

COLOMBIA, republic in NW South America. It is the only South American country with both Pacific and Caribbean coastlines.

Land. Colombia has four major regions: the Andes; the Caribbean coastal lowlands; the Pacific coastal lowlands; and the E plains. Some 80% of the people live in the Andean region. Three *cordilleras* (mountain ranges) branch out northwards from the Pasto knot in the S, some peaks exceeding 16,000ft. The Caribbean lowlands are drained by sluggish rivers that frequently flood, but in the dry season big herds of cattle find good grazing there. The Pacific lowlands are wet and scantily populated. The N section of the E region forms part of the South American *llanos* or tropical grasslands; the S section is equatorial rain forest containing Leticia, Colombia's only port on the Amazon R. The country's climate varies from extreme cold to humid heat according to altitude and proximity to the coast.

People. More than half of Colombians are mestizos (of mixed European and Amerindian ancestry); there are about 20% whites and minorities of mulattoes, blacks and Indians. The literacy rate is about 80%.

Economy. Colombia is a major world coffee producer. It also grows cotton, bananas, sugar, tobacco, cocoa, rice, sorghum, corn, wheat and barley. Rich in minerals, the country has the largest coal reserves in Latin America and substantial reserves of uranium. Other resources include oil, gas and precious metals. Transportation is hindered by mountain ranges, but cities are joined by road, rail or river and an advanced air network. Tourism is becoming an important source of foreign exchange.

History. CHIBCHA INDIANS of the E Cordilleras had a highly developed culture before the Spanish arrived in the early 16th century. Spain ruled the area until independence, which followed Simón BOLÍVAR'S Boyacá victory over Spanish colonial forces (1819). At the end of the 19th century thousands died in fighting between Liberals and Conservatives—Colombia's two main political parties. Another civil war between Liberals and Conservatives, with about 200,000 casualties, lasted from 1948 until 1958 when a democratic government was reestablished. The late 1970s were marked by strikes, rioting and guerrilla activity.

Official Name: Republic of Colombia
Capital: Bogotá
Area: 439,737sq mi
Population: 25,867,500

Languages: Spanish
Religions: Roman Catholic
Monetary Unit(s): 1 Colombian peso=100 centavos

COLOMBO, capital and largest city of Sri Lanka (Ceylon). A port on the W coast of the island, it exports tea, rubber and coconut products and imports textiles and machinery. Founded in ancient times, the city is now the leading industrial center of Sri Lanka. Pop 624,000.

COLOMBO PLAN, cooperative program for economic development in S and SE Asia, inaugurated in 1951 at Colombo, Ceylon (now Sri Lanka). The first participants were members of the Commonwealth, who were joined by the US, Japan and some SE Asian countries. A consultative committee meets annually to discuss national accomplishments and plans. Capital aid consists of grants and loans from the industrial members to the developing countries.

COLOR, the way the brain interprets the wavelength distribution of the LIGHT entering the eye. The phenomenon of color has two aspects: the physical or optical—concerned with the nature of the light—and the physiological or visual—dealing with how the eye sees color.

The light entering the eye is either emitted by or reflected from the objects we see. Hot solid objects emit light with wavelengths occupying a broad continuous band of the electromagnetic SPECTRUM, the position of the most intense radiation depending on the temperature of the object—the hotter the object, the shorter the wavelengths emitted (see BLACKBODY RADIATION). We see the shortest visible wavelengths as blue, the longest as red. Hot or electrically excited gases, consisting of nearly isolated atoms, emit light only at specific wavelengths characteristic of the atoms (see SPECTROSCOPY).

The EYE can only see colors when the light is relatively bright; the rods used in poor light see only in black and white. The cones used in color VISION are of three kinds, responding to light from the red, green or blue portions of the visible spectrum. The brain adds together the responses of the different sets of cones and produces the sensation of color. The three colors to which the cones of the eye respond are known as the three primary colors of light. By mixing different proportions of these three colors, any other color can be simulated, equal intensities of all three producing white light. This is known as the production of color by addition, the effect being used in color TELEVISION tubes where PHOSPHORS glowing red, green and blue are employed. Color pigments, working by transmission or reflection, produce colors by subtraction, abstracting light from white and displaying only the remainder. Again a suitable combination of a set of three pigments—cyan (blue–green), magenta (blue–red) and yellow (the "complementary" colors of the three primaries)—can simulate most other colors, a dense mixture of all three producing black. This effect is used in color photography but in color printing an additional black pigment is commonly used.

Most colors are not found in the spectrum. These nonspectral colors can be regarded as intermediates between the spectral colors and black and white. Many schemes have been proposed for the classification and standardization of colors. The most widely used is that of Albert Henry Munsell which describes colors in terms of their hue (basic color); saturation (intensity or density), and lightness or brightness (the degree of whiteness or blackness).

Name of state: Colorado
Capital: Denver
Statehood: Aug. 1, 1876 (38th state)
Familiar name: Centennial State
Area: 104,247sq mi
Population: 2,888,834
Elevation: Highest—14,431ft, Mount Elbert, Lowest—3,350ft, Arkansas River
Motto: Nil Sine Numine (Nothing without Providence)
State flower: Rocky Mountain columbine
State bird: Lark bunting
State tree: Colorado blue spruce
State song: 'Where the Columbines Grow"

COLORADO, a W central state of the US bounded on the N by Wyo. and Neb., on the E by Kan., on the S by Okla. and N.M. and on the W by Ut. It is the highest state in the US.

Land. Colorado has three main areas. To the E, plateaus rise to meet the Rocky Mts. forming a narrow Piedmont (foothills) zone between the plateaus and the mountains. Ranges of the Rocky Mts crisscross central Colorado from N to S, and include the state's highest point, Mt Elbert (14,431ft). To the W, along the Ut. border, lies a region of lower mountains and plateaus crossed by rivers flowing in deep canyons. The Colorado, South Platte, Arkansas and upper Rio Grande are the state's main rivers. The climate is largely dry and sunny; average annual rainfall is only 17in and water is scarce, restricting agriculture. Three million acres are irrigated for the cultivation of sugar beet, vegetables and fruit; another 40,000 acres provide grazing for cattle and sheep and land for dry crops such as wheat and hay.

People. Colorado's population increased by nearly one-third 1970–80. Denver is the largest city, followed by Colorado Springs, Aurora, Lakewood and Pueblo--all five cities are located in the Piedmont zone.

Economy. Mining has always been important to Colorado's economy; discoveries of gold and silver were followed by zinc, oil, natural gas, molybdenum, vanadium and uranium. Manufacturing includes processed foods, metal goods, electronic equipment, machinery and aerospace products. Agriculture ranks after manufacturing in value of output. Tourism is also important, with spectacular mountain scenery and skiing the major attractions.

History. Traces of an ancient Indian culture in Colorado are evident in the MESA VERDE and other cliff dwellings. In the 1500s Spanish explorers entered the territory to be followed by the French. US trappers hunting beaver and buffalo came in the early 1800s and after the LOUISIANA PURCHASE (1803), explorers like Zebulon PIKE and traders like William BENT began to open up the territory. In the MEXICAN WAR (1848) the US conquered further Colorado territory and the discovery of gold near Denver in 1858–59 brought a rush of prospectors. In 1876 Colorado became the Union's 38th state.

Colorado was one of the early states to benefit from the shift of business and population to the Sun Belt, and has become one of the nation's most prosperous regions. Going into the 1980s, the state's economy continued strong, and it was predicted that by the turn of the century Colorado would be a world leader in oil shale development. Rapid growth, however, has been accompanied by the ills of air pollution, crime, and threatened water shortages, and many citizens have been calling for government controls on growth.

Colorado is still governed according to its original constitution. Governor and lieutenant governor are elected for a four-year term, and members of the Senate and House of Representatives serve four- and two-year terms respectively.

COLORADO RIVER, a major US river, rising in the Rocky Mts of N Col. and flowing 1,450mi SW to enter the Gulf of Cal. Features include the GRAND CANYON and the HOOVER DAM, one of a series of dams that provide irrigation for seven states.

COLOR BLINDNESS, inability to discriminate between certain COLORS, an inherited trait. It is a disorder of the RETINA cones in the EYE. The commonest form is red-green color blindness (Daltonism), usually found in men (about 8%), the other types being rare.

COLOR-FIELD PAINTING, contemporary school of painting that stresses the creation of large areas of color, often closely related in value or tone. Mark ROTHKO was a leading color-field painter. See MINIMALISM.

COLOSSEUM, huge oval amphitheater in Rome which held 45,000 spectators on several tiers of seats supported by arches. Built by the Flavian Emperor Vespasian and completed by his son, the emperor Titus, 80 AD, it was used for gladiatorial, wild beast and other displays up to the 5th century. It has been damaged by earthquakes and its marble was quarried as building stone in the Middle Ages.

COLOSSIANS, Epistle to the, book of the New Testament written by St. Paul to the Christians of Colossae in SW Asia Minor. It resembles EPHESIANS.

COLOSSUS OF RHODES, huge bronze statue of Helios, the sun god, and one of the SEVEN WONDERS OF THE WORLD. It was made c280 BC by the Greek sculptor Chares and stood over 100ft high at Rhodes harbor (not straddling the harbor entrance as a late account claimed). An earthquake toppled the statue c224 BC; the ruin was broken up only in 653 AD.

COLT, Samuel (1814–1862), US inventor and industrialist who devised the REVOLVER, a single barreled pistol with a revolving multiple breech (bullet chamber), in the early 1830s. His factories pioneered mass-production techniques and the use of interchangeable parts.

COLTRANE, John (1926–1967), leading US jazz tenor saxophonist. He worked with Dizzy GILLESPIE, Miles DAVIS and Thelonious MONK. In his last years he experimented in free forms.

COLUMBA, St. (c521–597 AD), Irish missionary to Scotland. After founding Irish monasteries at Derry and Kells, he made the island of IONA a base for the conversion of N Scotland.

COLUMBIA, District of. See WASHINGTON, D.C.

COLUMBIA, city in W central S.C.; capital and largest city of S.C. and seat of Richland Co. It produces or handles textiles, lumber and corn. It houses the U. of S.C. and five other institutions of higher education. Pop 99,296.

COLUMBIA RIVER, rises in the Rocky Mts of SE British Columbia, Canada. It flows 460mi to the US border and thence 745mi to the Pacific Ocean, forming the Wash.-Ore. border. The river's vast hydroelectric potential is partially harnessed by numerous dams, including GRAND COULEE DAM.

COLUMBIA UNIVERSITY, New York City, one of the nation's major private universities. Founded as King's College in 1754, it was renamed Columbia College in 1784 and became a university in 1896. Its schools and faculties include important research institutes for international relations and schools of journalism, business and social work. Its libraries hold valuable rare books and MS collections. It has some 20,000 students.

COLUMBUS, Christopher (1451–1506), Genoese explorer generally credited with the discovery of America. An experienced navigator, he hoped to sail W across the Atlantic to pioneer a new short route to the spice-rich East Indies (formerly reached by sailing E). Columbus failed to win Portuguese backing but Queen Isabella and King Ferdinand of Spain eventually agreed to finance the voyage.

On Aug. 3, 1492, Columbus, commanding the *Santa María* and accompanied by the *Niña* and *Pinta*, sailed from SW Spain for the Canary Islands. On Sept. 6 he set out due W and on Oct. 12 landed on Watling Island, in the Bahamas. After discovering Cuba and Hispaniola, he returned to Spain where he was created an admiral and governor of the new lands discovered and to be discovered.

Columbus made three further voyages to the New World. In Oct. 1493 he left Spain with 17 ships, planning to set up trading posts and colonies and carrying hundreds of colonists. He colonized Hispaniola, discovered Puerto Rico, Jamaica, the Virgin Islands and some of the Lesser Antilles and explored the S coast of Cuba. On his third voyage, 1498, he sighted South America and discovered Trinidad. But the Hispaniola colonists' discontent with living conditions threatened to break into revolt. Complaints against Columbus reached Spain, disorders continued, and Francisco de Bobadilla was sent out to replace him as governor. Columbus was sent back to Spain in disgrace. His fourth and last voyage

(1502–04) was again intended to find the elusive route to the East Indies. Instead he came upon the Central American coast at Honduras and followed it E and S to Panama. Columbus died two years after his last journey, poverty-stricken and almost forgotten.

COLUMN, in architecture, slim vertical structural support, usually cylindrical, consisting of a base, shaft and a capital. Columns support the ENTABLATURE on which the roof rests. A row of columns forms a colonnade. Widely used in early architecture, columns were characteristic of Egyptian temples and of classical Greek architecture. The three main Greek forms were the Doric, Ionic and Corinthian orders (see CLASSICAL ORDERS).

COMA, state of unconsciousness in which a person cannot be roused by sensory stimulation and is unaware of his surroundings. Body functions continue but may be impaired, depending on the cause. These include POISONING, head injury, DIABETES, and BRAIN diseases, including STROKES and CONVULSIONS. Severe malfunction of LUNGS, LIVER or KIDNEYS may lead to coma.

COMANCHE, North American Indians, closely related to the SHOSHONE INDIANS. Brilliant horsemen and fierce warriors, they were dominant among the S Great Plains peoples, warring as far afield as Mexico. They stubbornly defended the buffalo hunting grounds against white incursions until the 1870s. Some 3,000 Comanche still live in W Okla.

COMANECI, Nadia (1961–), Rumanian gymnast. She was the first gymnast in Olympic history to score a perfect 10 points, accomplishing the feat a phenomenal seven times as a 15-year-old at the 1976 games in Montreal. She also won two gold medals in the 1980 Olympics.

COMBUSTION, or burning, the rapid OXIDATION OF FUEL in which heat and usually light are produced. In slow combustion (e.g., a glowing charcoal fire) the reaction may be heterogeneous, the solid fuel reacting directly with gaseous oxygen; more commonly, the fuel is first volatilized, and combustion occurs in the gas phase (a flame is such a combustion zone, its luminance being due to excited particles, molecules and ions). In the 17th and 18th centuries combustion was explained by the PHLOGISTON theory, until LAVOISIER showed it to be due to combination with oxygen in the air. In fact the oxidizing agent need not be oxygen: it may be another oxidizing gas such as nitric oxide or fluorine, or oxygen-containing solids or liquids such as nitric acid (used in rocket fuels). If the fuel and oxidant are premixed, as in a BUNSEN BURNER, the combustion is more efficient, and little or no SOOT is produced. Very rapid combustion occurs in an explosion (see EXPLOSIVES), when more heat is liberated than can be dissipated, or when a branched chain reaction occurs (see FREE RADICALS). Each combustion reaction has its own ignition temperature below which it cannot take place, e.g. c400°C for coal. Spontaneous combustion occurs if slow oxidation in large piles of such materials as coal or oily rags raises the temperature to the ignition point. (See also INTERNAL-COMBUSTION ENGINE.)

COMEDY, literary work which aims primarily to amuse, often using ridicule, exaggeration or criticism of human nature and institutions, and usually ending happily. One of the two main traditional categories of drama (see also TRAGEDY), comedy also describes nondramatic art forms.

Comedy evolved in ancient Greece from the festivals of DIONYSUS and from the SATYR PLAYS, and developed in the satiric plays of ARISTOPHANES. It then became more consciously literary, employing stock characters and situations, as in the works of MENANDER, who was later imitated by the Roman poets PLAUTUS and TERENCE. Classical comedy elements survived the Middle Ages in folk plays and festivals. Roman comedies were revived in the Renaissance and influenced Italian COMMEDIA DELL'ARTE and the comedies of Spain's Lope de VEGA and the Elizabethans Ben JONSON and SHAKESPEARE. In 17th-century France MOLIÈRE wrote comic and satiric drama; the COMEDY OF MANNERS stemmed from his work and influenced CONGREVE and other writers of RESTORATION COMEDY. In the 18th century SHERIDAN and GOLDSMITH and Italy's Carlo GOLDONI wrote satiric, witty and more realistic comedies. From the 19th century onwards, outstanding writers of comedy included Oscar WILDE, who wrote English drawing-room comedies; G. B. SHAW, who wrote unique comedies of ideas; James BARRIE, who wrote romantic comedies; J. M. SYNGE and Sean O'CASEY, who wrote native Irish comedy; Noel COWARD, who wrote witty farces; and George S. KAUFMAN, Thornton WILDER, and Neil SIMON, in whose works humor is often mixed with serious social commentary. (See also BURLESQUE; FARCE; SATIRE.)

COMENIUS, (Jan Amos Komenský; 1592–1670), Czech educational reformer and theologian; last bishop of the old MORAVIAN CHURCH. He advocated universal education, teaching in the vernacular and Latin as a common language. His most famous books are *The Great Didactic* (1628–32) and *The Visible World* (1658–59).

COMET, a nebulous body which orbits the sun. In general, comets can be seen only when they are comparatively close to the sun, though the time between their first appearance and their final disappearance may be as much as years. As they approach the sun, a few comets develop tails (some comets develop more than one tail) of lengths of the order 1–100Gm, though at least one tail 300Gm in length—more than twice the distance from the earth to the sun—has been recorded. The tails of comets are always pointed away from the sun, so that, as the comet recedes into space, its tail precedes it. For this reason it is generally accepted that comets' tails are caused by the SOLAR WIND.

The head of the comet is known as the nucleus. Nuclei may be as little as 100m or as much as 100km in radius, and are thought to be composed primarily of frozen gases and ice mixed with smaller quantities of meteoritic material. Most of the mass of a comet is contained within the nucleus, though this may be less than 0.000,001 that of the earth. Surrounding the nucleus is the bright coma, possibly as much as 100Mm in radius, which is composed of gas and possibly small particles erupting from the nucleus.

Cometary orbits are usually very eccentric ellipses, with some perihelions (see ORBIT) closer to the sun than that of MERCURY, aphelions as much as 100,000 AU from the sun. The orbits of some comets take the form of hyperbolas, and it is thought that these have their origins altogether outside the SOLAR SYSTEM, that they are interstellar travelers.

In Greco-Roman times it was generally believed that comets were phenomena restricted to the upper atmosphere of the earth. In the late 15th and 16th centuries it was shown by M. Mästlin and BRAHE that comets were far more distant than the moon. NEWTON interpreted the orbits of the comets as parabolas, deducing that each comet was appearing for the first time. It was not until the late 17th century that HALLEY showed that at least some comets returned periodically.

COMICS, cartoon drawings in a STRIP of panels, panel or series of panels (strips), with consistent characters—involved in brief incidents or continuous stories. Captions or dialogue are often set in "balloons." The concept originated with satirical cartoons (18th–19th centuries), but developed in 20th-century America as a device to increase newspaper circulation. Early successes were *The Yellow Kid* (1895) and *The Katzenjammer Kids* (1897), while today's most popular comic strip is probably Charles Schulz's *Peanuts*. Comics range from humor or farce to adventure, crime and horror stories, science fiction, classics and satire and social criticism. See also CARICATURE AND CARTOON.

COMINFORM, Communist Information Bureau, an organization set up in 1947 to create unity among and assert Soviet influence over communist countries. Membership was limited to representatives of the communist parties of the USSR, its E European satellites, and France and Italy. Khrushchev disbanded the Cominform in 1956.

COMMAGER, Henry Steele (1902–   ), US historian who widely influenced the study of American history. His works include the standard textbook, *The Growth of the American Republic* (1930), with MORISON, *The American Mind* (1950), *Freedom, Loyalty, Dissent* (1954) and *The Search for a Usable Past.*

COMMANDO, military unit specializing in raids into enemy territory, and in hand-to-hand and night fighting. The British army took the name from Boer units in South Africa, and formed commando battalions which played an important role in liberating Europe in WWII. Commandos are now part of the British Royal Marines. US army RANGERS were modeled on British units.

COMMEDIA DELL'ARTE, form of Italian COMEDY which originated in the Middle Ages and flourished in the 16th–18th centuries. Traveling professional actors (often wearing masks) improvised action and dialogue around outline plots with stock characters. The *commedia* spread through Europe and had a lasting influence on the theater.

COMMERCE, Chambers of. See CHAMBERS OF COMMERCE.

COMMERCE, US Department of, the executive department of the government responsible for fostering and regulating domestic and foreign commerce. Its present name dates from 1913. The secretary of commerce, a member of the cabinet appointed by the president as chief adviser on federal policies affecting trade and industry, is aided by an under secretary and five assistant secretaries. The department operates the MARITIME ADMINISTRATION, Office of Business Economics, Economic Development Administration, BUREAU OF INTERNATIONAL COMMERCE, National Oceanic and Atmospheric Administration, Office of Telecommunications, BUREAU OF THE CENSUS, NATIONAL BUREAU OF STANDARDS, PATENT OFFICE, and Office of Equal Opportunity, among others.

COMMERCIAL ART, art which helps sell a product, service or point of view; also "advertising art." It involves design, drawing and type matter in advertisements and illustrations for books, magazines and newspapers, posters and packages, display and exhibition material, television and films. Commercial artists need a wide knowledge of art techniques and reproduction methods. (See also ADVERTISING; GRAPHIC ARTS.)

COMMERCIAL LAW, body of law governing commercial transactions and commercial organizations. Transactions are governed largely by the law of CONTRACTS dealing with the negotiation, breach and performance of legally enforceable business agreements. The laws governing commercial organizations lay down the legal forms in which business bodies may be constituted, such as the incorporation of companies. The law of AGENCY, making it possible for a person or corporation to transact business through employees, is important in this area.

Commercial law is as old as large-scale trade, but it expanded and consolidated after the Middle Ages. English mercantile law was gradually incorporated into the COMMON LAW and so inherited by the US, where it grew with the expansion of interstate trade in the 19th century, necessitating uniform legislation. Many states have adopted the Uniform Commercial Code of 1952 in an attempt to systematize national practice.

COMMITTEE OF PUBLIC SAFETY, committee elected by the Convention in April 1793 during the FRENCH REVOLUTION to enforce revolutionary law and govern the country. Under ROBESPIERRE'S leadership, the committee used its despotic power to crush "counter revolution" (see also REIGN OF TERROR).

COMMODITY MARKET, a formal market for dealings in raw materials and foods. Such exchanges trade simultaneously in present and future supplies, thus minimizing price variations caused by supply fluctuation and reducing the risks to traders. Coffee, tobacco, cotton, grain, livestock and metals are some of the commodities sold in this way. The largest commodity markets are in Chicago, New York City, and London. Their prices largely determine world prices. (See also FUTURES MARKET.)

COMMON CARRIER, an airline, railroad, bus company or shipping line in the business of carrying passengers or freight. The carrier is responsible for any loss or damage due to its negligence, but is not liable for losses caused by "acts of God" (floods, fires caused by lightning, tornadoes, blizzards) or by civil disturbances and strikes. The carrier can legally refuse to haul goods it believes to be perishable or dangerous, but otherwise it cannot legally refuse to transport the goods of anyone wanting to hire it.

COMMON CAUSE, a national nonpartisan citizens' lobby, organized in 1970 by John W. Gardner, former secretary of Health, Education, and Welfare. It has sought to reform campaign financing and end political corruption, to improve the internal workings of the federal and state governments and to protect the environment. With some 200,000 members, it monitors the work of Congress, recommends legislative reforms to its members, files lawsuits and engages in lobbying at the federal, state and local levels.

COMMONER, Barry (1917–), US biologist, ecologist and environmentalist who warned against the threats of technology and nuclear energy to the environment in such books as *The Closing Circle* (1971), *The Poverty of Power* (1976) and *The Politics of Energy* (1979). A democratic socialist, he has spoken out against the concentration of corporate power in the US and ran for the US presidency as a candidate of the Citizens' Party (1980).

COMMON LAW, body of law based upon custom and the established precedent of court decisions. Developed in England since early medieval times, it is the basis of the law of many other countries today, including the US. In late Anglo-Saxon and early Norman England, the growth of centralized government created a law common to all areas, administered by royal justices. Henry II and Edward I (12th–13th centuries) strengthened the law, laying the foundations of many modern practices and principles. Common law gradually absorbed much of English mercantile, sea and CANON LAW. By the 15th century, however, adherence to outdated, narrow and unsuitable legal formalities created many injustices. The lord chancellor, therefore, on behalf of the King, set up a court to "restore the equity" between parties involved in such situations. This created the modern body of EQUITY law, in which such concepts as TRUST and MORTGAGE are based.

At the same time, the custom of relying on precedents—preceding decisions—was becoming a firm principle, to be modified only by statute or a higher court. This contrasted with the CIVIL LAW system, derived from Roman law, which was popular in Europe. In this, the main legal rules are embodied in a central code such as the CODE NAPOLÉON, which courts theoretically apply without references to previous decisions. However, civil law often relies on precedent, just as many common law rules are codified by statute for convenience. Common law spread throughout the British colonies. It was generally adopted in the US, although La. state law is based upon the Code Napoléon and other states have partially codified systems.

COMMON MARKET, European, officially the European Economic Community (EEC), an economic union of W European nations. The Common Market grew out of the chaos created in Europe by WWII. W European nations sought new forms of cooperation in order to revive their war-damaged economies. The first step was the foundation of the EUROPEAN COAL AND STEEL COMMUNITY, set up in 1952 by the six future members of the EEC. The TREATY OF ROME creating the EEC was signed in 1957 by West Germany, France, Italy, Belgium, the Netherlands and Luxembourg. In 1973 "The Six" were joined by Great Britain, Ireland and Denmark.

The market's aims are to eliminate tariffs between member countries, to develop common policies for agriculture, free movement of labor, social welfare, transport and foreign trade, and to abolish trusts and cartels. The union is thus partly political, and many politicians see the Common Market developing into a United States of Europe, with economic and political power to rival that of the USSR or the US. The structure of the EEC includes an executive commission, the European Parliament and the Court of Justice. (See also EUROPEAN FREE TRADE ASSOCIATION.)

COMMONS, House of. See HOUSE OF COMMONS.

COMMON SENSE SCHOOL, in philosophy, a group of Scottish thinkers, including Thomas REID and Dugald STEWART, who, reacting against the idealism of BERKELEY and the skepticism of HUME, affirmed that the truths apparent to the common man—the existence of material objects, the reality of causality, and so on—were genuine, reliable and not to be questioned.

COMMONWEALTH, form of government based on the consent of the people ("common weal" means common well-being). In the US, the states of Mass., Pa., Va. and Ky. are known as commonwealths. Various nations are associated with Britain in the COMMONWEALTH OF NATIONS; and the federated states of Australia form the Commonwealth of Australia. In English history, the Commonwealth was a period of republican rule (1649–60).

COMMONWEALTH OF NATIONS, free association of Britain and over 40 former colonies, now independent states, and their dependencies. It is not governed by a constitution or specific treaty; member countries are linked by a common heritage and economic and cultural interests and recognize the British sovereign as symbolic head of the Commonwealth. Commonwealth prime ministers and other officials meet at periodic conferences and exchange views on international, economic and political affairs of mutual interest. Member nations range in size from Canada, Australia and India to tiny Tonga and Fiji. Membership tends to increase as more British colonies gain independence and opt to join. Burma chose to remain outside the Commonwealth; Ireland, South Africa and Pakistan have withdrawn.

COMMUNE, cooperative community formed for ideological, political or religious reasons. The self-governing towns of medieval Europe were known as communes; the term is also used of the period's religious communities, and of those in 17th-century America. In the 19th century, with the growth of Utopian socialism, a number of experimental communes were established, notably NEW HARMONY and BROOK FARM in the US. The farm collective of China is a form of commune, as is the Israeli KIBBUTZ.

COMMUNICATIONS SATELLITE, artificial earth-orbiting satellite used to relay radio signals between points on earth. The orbits of most such satellites are above the equator at a height of 22,300mi; at that altitude a satellite orbits the earth at the same rate as the earth turns and thus remains over a fixed point on the surface. The satellite carries a number of transponders that receive radio beams from earth and retransmit them back to earth. The power for the electronic equipment comes from SOLAR CELLS. Communications satellites carry television programs, telephone calls and a variety of business data. The great bulk of data communications between continents is carried by satellites and handled by COMPUTERS at each end. (See also COMSAT.)

COMMUNICATIONS SATELLITE CORPORATION. See COMSAT.

COMMUNION, Holy (Lord's Supper, Eucharist), a Christian SACRAMENT involving the consumption of the body and blood of Jesus Christ, which are received by eating and drinking consecrated bread and wine, as at the LAST SUPPER. Whether this receiving is actual or only symbolic has been much disputed (see TRANSUBSTANTIATION). Nonconformists, following ZWINGLI, see Holy Communion as merely a symbolic commemoration. The manner in which communion is a SACRIFICE, if at all, is equally controversial. In Holy Communion, the central act of all Christian worship, the Church celebrates the ATONEMENT made by Christ as the basis of its common life and faith. (See also CONFIRMATION; MASS.)

COMMUNISM, political doctrine based on the writings of Karl MARX and Friedrich ENGELS, developed along a number of different lines during the course of the 20th century by various communist states and parties throughout the world. The term communism was originally used of communities, generally small and short-lived, whose members enjoyed common ownership of all property and material provision for all according to need. All communist parties share the general belief that a state-run economy is superior to private enterprise and that land should be organized for communal cultivation.

Marx and Engels saw communism as an advanced stage of SOCIALISM and the term first acquired its modern associations with the appearance of their COMMUNIST MANIFESTO in 1848 (see MARXISM).

Communism differs from what in the West is generally called socialism in its adherence to the doctrine of revolution. The RUSSIAN REVOLUTION (1917) was the world's first successful communist revolution. It was led by LENIN, who had built upon 19th-century revolutionary POPULISM to create a disciplined Marxist movement (see BOLSHEVISM). Russia became the center of world communism.

The Comintern or Third INTERNATIONAL was founded in Moscow in 1919. It was to have been the spearhead of the world revolution which many saw as imminent. However, by March 1921 discontent at home and opposition to communism by European socialist parties forced Lenin to draw in his horns. He introduced the New Economic Policy, a compromise policy which meant a "temporary" abandoning of the world revolution and in time proved the seed of schism between right and left. On Lenin's death (1924), this schism broke out in the form of a power struggle between STALIN, whose priority was to strengthen socialism within Russia, and the internationalist TROTSKY. It was the first great rift in the world communist movement.

Stalin's repressive policies produced further rifts, such as that between Yugoslavia and the USSR (1948), throughout the European communist bloc as well as among communist parties in non-communist countries. The 1968 Soviet invasion of Czechoslovakia had much the same result.

The second great schism in world communism came after the success in 1949 of the Chinese Revolution, under the leadership of MAO TSE-TUNG. Within 15 years the reappearance of traditional tensions between the two giant neighbors, China and Russia, plus differences about the role each should play on the world stage, came to outweigh their nominal unity under the flag of Marxism-Leninism.

By the 1970s, there were communist movements in most countries throughout the world where not outlawed by the government. In Chile, under Salvador ALLENDE, the communists actually won power through free elections, but that regime was overthrown by a military coup. Attempts to build broad-based parties in the W, as in France and Italy, had mixed results. Widespread and outspoken hostility to the regime in POLAND, beginning in 1980, called attention to the failures of applied communist economic doctrine. At the same time, Soviet inability to put down resistance to the communist puppet regime in AFGHANISTAN underscored the limits to Soviet military power.

COMMUNIST PARTY, US, American political organization devoted to the ideals of COMMUNISM. Two parties, the Communist Labor Party and the Communist Party of America, emerged in 1919. They were united in 1921 and by 1925 were known as the Workers Party. In 1929 the party was renamed the Communist Party of the US, under the leadership of William Z. FOSTER. It became the leading revolutionary organization in the US, though post-depression economic recovery and the Nazi–Soviet pact of 1939 greatly reduced its appeal (see also Earl BROWDER). With the end of WWII and the onset of the COLD WAR, anti-communist legislation, for example the TAFT-HARTLEY ACT (1947), increased (see also MC CARTHYISM). The party was virtually outlawed in 1954 but in 1966 it resumed open activity.

COMMUNITY CHEST, organization coordinating fund-raising by different groups to help voluntary and welfare agencies. This method of financing charities originated in Liverpool, England, in 1873.

COMO, Lake, mountain lake in N Italy, N of Milan. It covers 56sq mi and has a maximum depth of 1,345ft. Many resorts border the lake, among them Bellagio and Varenna.

Official name: Federal and Islamic Republic of the Comoros
Capital: Moroni, on Grande-Comore
Area: 718sq mi
Population: 343,000
Languages: French, Comoran
Religions: Muslim and Christian
Monetary unit(s): 1 CFA franc = 100 centimes

COMOROS, independent nation occupying most of the Comoro Islands, an archipelago in the Indian Ocean, off the E coast of Mozambique.

Land. Comoros consist of several small islands and three main islands— Grande-Comore, Anjouan and Moheli. The island of Mahore, previously Mayotte, remains under French administration. Climate, rainfall and vegetation vary from island to island, but all are volcanic in origin.

People. The majority of the population have mixed Arab, Malagasy and African ancestry and are Muslims.

Economy. The islands are poor in resources, and rank among the world's lowest income countries. Most of the population is engaged in farming, but soils are poor and most food must be imported. Coconuts, cassava and bananas are produced for local consumption. Ylang-ylang, a stabilizer used in French perfumes, vanilla, sisal, copra and cloves are the main exports. France is the principal trade partner.

History. Arabs landed on the islands during the 1400s and ruled each island as a separate sultanate, until ceding them to the French in 1841. In 1975 the Comoros declared independence, with France retaining responsibility for the island of Mahore, where it has a naval base.

COMPASS, device for determining direction parallel to the earth's surface. Most compasses make use of the EARTH'S magnetic field (see GEOMAGNETISM); if a bar magnet (see MAGNETISM) is pivoted at its center so that it is free to rotate horizontally, it will seek to align itself with the horizontal component in its locality of the earth's magnetic field. A simple compass consists of a magnet so arranged and a compass card marked with the four cardinal points and graduated in degrees (see ANGLE). In ship compasses, to compensate for rolling, the card is attached to the magnet and floated or suspended in a liquid, usually alcohol. Aircraft compasses often incorporate a GYROSCOPE to keep the compass horizontal. The two main errors in all magnetic compasses are **variation** (the angle between lines of geographic longitude and the local horizontal component of the earth's magnetic field) and **deviation** (local, artificial magnetic effects, such as nearby electrical equipment). Both vary with the siting of the compass, and may be with more or less difficulty compensated for. (See also GYROCOMPASS; NAVIGATION.) A **radio compass**, used widely in aircraft, is an automatic radio DIRECTION FINDER, calibrated with respect to the station to which it is tuned.

COMPLEX, a nexus of often-repressed ideas and feelings from both the CONSCIOUS and UNCONSCIOUS which has an effect, favorable or adverse, on the actions or emotional state of the individual. ADLER used the term in connection with the superiority and INFERIORITY COMPLEXES, FREUD in connection with the CASTRATION COMPLEX and OEDIPUS COMPLEX.

COMPLEX NUMBERS, pairs of REAL NUMBERS that can be added, subtracted, multiplied and divided according to certain rules. The rule for addition is simply $(a, b) + (c, d) = (a+c, b+d)$, and similarly for subtraction. Complex numbers can be multiplied by writing them as $a+ib$ and using the rule $i^2 = -1$. Thus, $(a+ib)(c+id) = (ac-bd) + i(ad+bc)$. i is called the imaginary unit and numbers of the form $a+ib$ are called imaginary numbers (or pure imaginary numbers, the term imaginary number sometimes being applied to all complex numbers). This name arose because there is actually no number ("real" number) whose square root is -1. They were introduced into algebra so that every polynomial equation of degree n with real coefficients would have n roots (see ROOTS OF AN EQUATION). The equation $x^2 = -1$, for example, has no real roots; its roots are $+i$ and $-i$.

COMPOSITION, Chemical, the proportion by weight of each ELEMENT present in a chemical compound. The **law of definite proportions,** discovered by J. L. PROUST, states that pure compounds have a fixed and invariable composition. A few compounds, termed non-stoichiometric, disobey this law: they have latticed vacancies or extra atoms, and the composition varies within a certain range depending on the formation conditions. The **law of multiple proportions,** discovered by DALTON, states that, if two elements A and B form more than one compound, the various weights of B which combine with a given weight of A are in small whole-number ratios. (See also BOND, CHEMICAL; EQUIVALENT WEIGHT.)

COMPREHENSIVE TRAINING AND EMPLOYMENT ACT. See CETA.

COMPROMISE OF 1850, attempt by the US Congress to reconcile North and South in the pre–CIVIL WAR period on the question of extending slavery to new territories. Approved by Congress in Sept. 1850, Senator Henry CLAY'S compromise Omnibus Bill admitted Cal. as a free state; prohibited slave trade in the District of Columbia; proposed a stricter FUGITIVE SLAVE LAW; deferred a decision on slavery in Ut. and N.M. until they applied for statehood; and paid the slave state of Tex. $10 million to relinquish much of its western territory to the federal government. The Compromise temporarily saved the Union; the factions were too entrenched for it to do any more.

COMPTON, Arthur Holly (1892–1962), US physicist who discovered the Compton effect (1923), thus providing evidence that X RAYS could act as particles as predicted in QUANTUM THEORY. Compton found that when monochromatic X rays were scattered by light elements, some of the scattered radiation was of longer wavelength, i.e., of lower ENERGY than the incident. Compton showed that this could be explained in terms of the collision between an X-ray PHOTON and an ELECTRON in the target. For this work he shared the 1927 Nobel physics prize with C. T. R. WILSON.

COMPTON-BURNETT, Dame Ivy (1892–1969), English novelist who portrayed late-Victorian upper middle class life. Her novels dealt with familial corruption, property and greed and proceed almost entirely through mannered yet dramatically flexible dialogue. Among her best-known works are *Men and Wives* (1931) and *Mother and Son* (1955).

COMPTROLLER GENERAL OF THE UNITED STATES, head of the general accounting office, directly responsible to Congress for auditing all government spending. The comptroller is appointed by the president, with the advice and consent of the Senate, for one term of 15 years.

COMPULSION, an irresistible UNCONSCIOUS force that makes an individual perform conscious (see CONSCIOUSNESS) thoughts or actions which he would not normally perform, perhaps even against his will. The force may also come from outside, i.e., from someone whose character dominates the individual (see also BRAINWASHING; OBSESSIONAL NEUROSIS).

COMPUTER, any device which performs calculations. In this light, the ABACUS, CALCULATING MACHINE and SLIDE RULE may all be described as computers; however, the term is usually limited to those electronic devices that are given a program to follow, data to store or to calculate with, and means with which to present results or other (stored) information.

Programming. A computer program consists essentially of a set of instructions which tells the computer which operations to perform, in what order to perform them, and the order in which subsequent data will be presented to it; for ease of use, the computer may already have subprograms built into its memory, so that, on receiving an instruction such as LOG X, it will automatically go through the program necessary to find the LOGARITHM of that piece of data supplied to it as X. Every model of computer has a different machine language or code; that is, the way in which it should ideally be programmed; however, this language is usually difficult and cumbersome for an operator to use. Thus a special program known as a **compiler** is retained by the computer, enabling it to translate computer languages such as ALGOL, COBOL and FORTRAN, which are easily learned and used by operators and programmers, into its own machine code. Programmers also make extensive use of ALGORITHMS to save programming and operating time.

Input. Programs and data are fed into computers using either the medium of punched tape or, more commonly in recent years, that of punched cards. In both cases it is the positions of holes punched in the medium which carry the information. These are read by a card or tape reader which usually consists of a light shining through the holes and activating PHOTOELECTRIC CELLS on the far side. The computer "reads" the resulting electrical pulses.

Storage. Machine languages generally take the form of a binary code (see BINARY NUMBERS), so that the two characters 0 and 1 may be easily represented by + and −. Thus the ideal medium for data storage is magnetic, and may take the form of tapes, disks or drums. Magnetic tapes are used much as they are in a TAPE RECORDER; a magnetic head "writes" on the tape by creating a suitable magnetic flux, and can "read" the spots so created at a later date, retransmitting them in the form of electric pulses. Magnetic disks and drums work on a similar principle; the former are flat disks mounted in groups of up to twenty on a shared shaft, looking rather like a stack of phonograph records; drums are, as the name suggests, cylindrical, and are coated with a magnetic medium. Both drums and stacks of disks rotate constantly while the computer is in use, so that the maximum time taken for the read/write head to locate any specific area is that for one revolution. In all cases, each datum must be identified and given a specific "address" in the storage system, so that instructions for its retrieval may be given to the computer and so that the operator may take precautions against erasing it. (See INFORMATION RETRIEVAL.)

The computer's internal "memory" for programs and data that have been fed into it from these storage media usually consists of large-scale INTEGRATED CIRCUIT (LSI) chips that can store thousands of bits of information in a very small space.

Data processing. All the operations performed by the computer on the information it receives are collectively described as data processing. The main element of data processing is, of course, computation. This is almost exclusively done by addition, and performed using binary arithmetic (see BINARY NUMBERS). More complicated procedures, such as integration (see CALCULUS) or finding ROOTS, are performed algorithmically, suitable subprograms being built into the computer. Again the characters 0 and 1 are represented by + and −, where this may refer to a closed or open switch, a direction of magnetic flux (see MAGNETISM), etc. Moreover, the computer contains logic circuits so that it may evaluate information while performing a calculation. If, for example, it were performing an algorithm to find $\sqrt{2}$ to a specified number of decimal places (see APPROXIMATION), it has to have a system whereby it can check at the end of each cycle of the algorithm whether or not its result is correct to the accuracy required. These circuits are designed using an application of BOOLEAN ALGEBRA and are composed of simpler logic circuits that are electrical representations of the truth tables for the three operations *and*, *or* and *not* (see TRUTH TABLES). Combinations of these three operations are capable of handling any logical operation required.

Output. Before being fed out, the information must be converted from machine code back into the programmer's computer language, numerical data being translated from the binary into the DECIMAL SYSTEM. The information is then fed out in the form of paper tape, punched cards or, using an adapted teleprinter, as a printout.

Types of computer. We have been talking almost exclusively about the **digital computer**, since this is the most widely-encountered and certainly the most versatile type. As we have seen, it requires information to be fed into it in "bits." Contrarily, the other main type of computer, the **analog computer**, is designed to deal with continuously varying quantities, such as lengths or voltages; the most everyday example of an analog computer is the slide rule. Electronic analog computers are usually designed for a specific task; as their accuracy is not high, their greatest use is in providing models of situations as bases for experiment. (See also CYBERNETICS; DICTIONARY; SIMULATION, COMPUTER.).

COMPUTER CRIME. The increasing computerization of American society has opened new, lucrative avenues for crime. The average take in computer-related frauds and bank embezzlements is about $500,000, while thefts of over $1 million are not uncommon. Annual losses in the US from computer crime have been estimated to approach $300 million, but the figure may be higher, since it is also estimated that only 1% of such crimes are detected. When discovered, very few computer crimes result in convictions, primarily because most large companies are reluctant to press charges that would advertise the fact that they have been victimized. In Jan. 1980, California became the first state to pass a computer-fraud law, and 10 other states soon followed suit.

COMSAT (COMMUNICATIONS SATELLITE CORPORATION), a private corporation established by act of Congress on Aug. 31, 1962, to develop satellite systems for relaying telephone, telegraph and television transmissions. Comsat is the US member and general manager of the International Telecommunications Satellite Consortium (Intelsat), formed in 1964 under the auspices of the United Nations. Comsat's first satellite, Early Bird, also known as Intelsat I, was launched Apr. 6, 1965.

COMSTOCK, Anthony (1844–1915), US moral crusader and a founder of the New York Society for the Suppression of Vice (1873). He successfully campaigned for stricter legislation against gambling and prostitution in N.Y. and the mailing of obscene matter.

COMSTOCK LODE, rich vein of silver discovered in the 1850s in W Nev. and named for Henry T. P. Comstock, one of the lode's first claimants. For some 30 years after its discovery it produced about half the US's silver output.

COMTE, Auguste (1798–1857), French philosopher, the founder of POSITIVISM and a pioneer of scientific sociology. His thinking was essentially evolutionary; he recognized a progression in the development of the sciences: starting from mathematics and progressing through astronomy, physics, chemistry and biology towards the ultimate goal of sociology. He saw this progression reflected in man's mental development. This had proceeded from a theological stage to a metaphysical one. Comte then sought to help inaugurate the final scientific or positivistic era. His social thinking reflected that of Henri de Saint-Simon and in turn his own works, particularly the *Philosophie positive* (1830–42), became widely influential in both France and England.

CONANT, James Bryant (1893–1978), US educator and diplomat who was president of Harvard (1933–53) and US high commissioner (1953–55) for and ambassador (1955–57) to West Germany. He wrote several influential works on education, including *Modern Science and Modern Man* (1952) and *Slums and Suburbs* (1961).

CONCENTRATION CAMP, term now most commonly associated with the forced-labor and extermination camps of Nazi Germany and the USSR. Prisoners in a concentration camp usually belong to a particular category and are often rounded up and interred without a legal trial. The modern concentration camp dates from the Boer War (1899–1902), when the British interred families of guerrillas. In the US during WWII, more than 100,000 persons of Japanese ancestry were removed from the West Coast and placed in 10 relocation centers. Although the camps had basic amenities, even schools, and although the inmates were not abused, the camps were universally condemned in later years as a gross injustice.

In Russia, before and after the 1917 revolution, political prisoners were routinely sent to remote, cold areas for forced labor. In the 1930s this punishment was meted out to others, including peasants, residents of newly annexed areas regarded as untrustworthy and suspected collaborators with the Germans—as well as German prisoners.

In 1933 the new Nazi regime in Germany established camps. Camp populations remained small until WWII when millions, mostly Jews, were interred in Germany and in occupied countries. Many were worked to death in forced-labor camps, and others were sent to camps whose purpose was extermination, usually by gassing or shooting. Estimates of the number of victims begin at 4,000,000 and range upward. The infamous camp names include Auschwitz, Treblinka, Dachau and Buchenwald.

CONCEPTUAL ART, a modern movement that stresses the *idea* rather than the *object*. Conceptual "works" are often nonmaterial, consisting of performances, discussions, or actions of a symbolic nature.

CONCEPTUALISM, a modern term describing a position in scholastic philosophy with respect to the status of universals that was intermediate between the extremes of both NOMINALISM and REALISM. To a conceptualist, UNIVERSALS (general concepts such as chair-ness) indeed exist, but only as concepts common to all men's minds and not as things in the world of particular objects (such as chairs).

CONCERTINA, musical instrument patented in 1829 by Sir Charles WHEATSTONE. It consists of a hexagonal bellows stopped at each end by boards, in which are set a number of reeds. The concertina is played between the hands, by expanding and contracting the bellows and so forcing air through the reeds. A series of buttons on the end boards is used to select the required notes. (See also ACCORDION.)

CONCERTO, composition opposing unequal musical forces, usually one solo instrument against a large orchestra. The three-movement orchestral form was elaborated by J. S. Bach out of the *concerto da camera*, a type of CHAMBER MUSIC. Handel added the CADENZA as a regular feature. Mozart set the style for the modern concerto: the orchestra announces an opening subject with a *tutti*, a passage for full orchestra, then takes a subordinate position when the solo instrument enters, thus establishing the pattern of interchanges. Beethoven added many novel touches to Mozart's basic form; others, including Mendelssohn, Schumann, Chopin, Brahms and Elgar have developed the concerto, using a wide range of solo instruments. The form remains popular with more recent composers such as BARTOK, PROKOFIEV, STRAVINSKY and SHOSTAKOVITCH.

CONCERT OF EUROPE, philosophy of cooperation shared by the major 19th-century European powers, aimed at maintaining the balance of power and settling disputes through negotiation. It originated in the Treaty of Chaumont 1814 (see also QUADRUPLE ALLIANCE) and remained intact until the CRIMEAN WAR 1854–56. The spirit of the Concert of Europe, however, may be said to have lasted through to the outbreak of WWI.

CONCORD, Battle of, second engagement in the American Revolutionary War, after Lexington (see LEXINGTON, BATTLE OF). Both were fought on April 19, 1775. The British, 700 strong, marched on CONCORD, Mass. to destroy military stores. The Americans retreated, but returned on seeing smoke from burning supplies. Under Major John Buttrick, they met the British at North Bridge and routed them, raising American morale. Casualties for both battles totaled 273 British, 95 Americans.

CONCORD, residential town in NE Mass., on the CONCORD RIVER 19mi NW of Boston. Founded 1635, home of the MINUTEMEN and scene of a famous revolutionary skirmish (see CONCORD, BATTLE OF), it became the home of EMERSON, THOREAU and HAWTHORNE. WALDEN POND is nearby. Pop 16,293.

CONCORDAT, agreement between a pope and a secular government regulating religious affairs within that state, for instance the appointment of bishops and the status of church property. The first concordat was the Concordat of WORMS, in 1122. The LATERAN TREATY (1929) recognized Vatican City as a sovereign state and established Roman Catholicism as Italy's only state religion.

CONCORDE, supersonic commercial passenger plane, developed by France and Britain. It began operation on Jan. 21, 1976 from Paris and London to South America and the Middle East, and on Nov. 22, 1977, from those cities to New York.

CONCRETE, versatile structural building material, made by mixing CEMENT, AGGREGATE and water. Initially moldable, the cement hardens by hydration, forming a matrix which binds the aggregate. Various other ingredients—admixtures—may be added to improve the properties of the concrete; air-entraining agents increase durability. Since concrete is much more able to resist compressive than tensile STRESS, it is often reinforced with a steel bar embedded in it which is able to bear the tension. **Prestressed concrete** is reinforced concrete in which the steel is under tension and the concrete is compressed; it can withstand very much greater stresses. Concrete is used for all building elements and for bridges, dams, canals, highways etc., often as precast units.

CONCRETE MUSIC. See ELECTRONIC MUSIC.

CONCUSSION, a state of disturbed consciousness following head injury, characterized by AMNESIA for events preceding and following the trauma. Permanent BRAIN damage is only found in cases of repeated concussion, as in boxers who develop the punch-drunk syndrome.

CONDÉ, Louis II de Bourbon, Prince de (1621–1686), "the Great Condé," outstanding French general of the THIRTY YEARS' WAR, related to the royal family. He turned against MAZARIN, led troops in the FRONDE rebellion, and served with Spain; but was pardoned and fought for Louis XIV in the DUTCH WARS.

CONDENSATION, passage of substance from gaseous to liquid or solid state; CLOUDS are a result of condensation of water vapor in the ATMOSPHERE (see also RAIN). Warm air can hold more water vapor than cool air; if a body of air is cooled it will reach a temperature (the DEW POINT) where the water vapor it holds is at SATURATION level. Further decrease in temperature without change in pressure will initiate water condensation. Such condensation is greatly facilitated by the presence of condensation nuclei ('seeds'), small particles (e.g., of smoke) about which condensation may begin. **Condensation trails** behind high-flying jet aircraft result primarily from water vapor produced by the engines increasing the local concentration (see also CLOUD CHAMBER; GAS; VAPOR). Condensation is important in all processes using steam; and in DISTILLATION, where the liquid is collected, and condensed by removal of its LATENT HEAT of vaporization, in an apparatus called a **condenser**. In chemistry a **condensation reaction** is one in which two or more MOLECULES link together with elimination of a relatively small molecule, such as water.

CONDILLAC, Étienne Bonnot de (1715–1780), French philosopher, who broke with the teaching of LOCKE to found the doctrine of SENSATIONALISM, holding that all knowledge is derived from the senses.

CONDITIONING, term used to describe two quite different LEARNING processes. In the first, a human or animal response is generated by a stimulus which does not normally generate such a response (see conditioned REFLEX; PAVLOV). In the second, animals (and by extension humans) are trained to perform certain actions to gain rewards or escape punishment (see LEARNING).

CONDOMINIUM, in real estate, in-

dividual ownership in property, such as an apartment, which is part of a larger complex owned in common. In the 1960s and 1970s, a sharp increase in condominiums occurred in the US. In many cases landlords sought to convert existing rental properties into condominiums for economic reasons. A cooperative building differs from a condominium in that tenants do not actually own their apartments; they hold shares in a corporation entitling them to a long-term "proprietary" lease.

CONDORCET, Marie Jean Antoine Nicholas de Caritat, Marquis de (1743–1794), French philosopher, mathematician and revolutionary politician chiefly remembered for his theory that the human race, having risen from barbarism, would continue to progress toward moral, intellectual and physical perfection. His principal mathematical work was in the theory of probability. He played a prominent role in the Revolution, though his moderate opinions led to his outlawry and suicide.

CONDORS, two species of New World vultures, the California condor *Gymnogypes californianus* and the Andean condor *Vultur gryphus*. The California condor is extremely rare, there being only 40 extant individuals.

CONDOTTIERE, mercenary soldier of 14th- and 15th-century Italy. Powerful condottieri raised armies and sold their services to the highest bidder among warring states. Famous leaders were Francesco Sforza, Bartolomeo COLLEONI and an Englishman, Sir John Hawkwood.

CONDUCTING, the art of directing a group of musicians. Conducting evolved with the increasing complexity of music. Choirs had leaders by the 15th century, while by HANDEL'S day CONTINUO players guided orchestral works; but the idea of a conductor whose sole task was training and directing an orchestra emerged in the time of BEETHOVEN (who conducted his own works). Conducting became a virtuoso skill in the 19th century.

CONDUCTION, Heat, passage of heat through a body without large-scale movements of matter within the body (see CONVECTION). Mechanisms involved include the transfer of vibrational ENERGY from one MOLECULE to the next through the substance (dominant in poor conductors), and energy transfer by ELECTRONS (in good electrical conductors) and PHONONS (in crystalline solids). In general, solids, especially metals, are good conductors, liquids and gases poor. (See also RADIATION.)

CONDUCTIVITY, or specific conductance, the CONDUCTANCE of a 1-metre cube of a substance, measured between opposite faces. Measured in siemens per metre, conductivity is the RECIPROCAL of resistivity (see RESISTANCE), and expresses the substance's ability to conduct electricity.

CONDUCTORS, Electric, substances (usually metals) whose high CONDUCTIVITY makes them useful for carrying electric current (see ELECTRICITY). They are most often used in the form of WIRES or CABLES. The best conductor is SILVER, but, for reasons of economy, COPPER is most often used. (See also SEMICONDUCTORS; SUPERCONDUCTIVITY.)

CONE, a solid geometrical figure traced by the rotation of a straight line A (the generator) about a fixed straight line B which it intersects, such that each point on A traces out a closed CURVE. A cone has therefore two parts (nappes) which touch each other at the point of intersection, termed the vertex of the cone, of lines A and B; the two parts being skew-symmetrical (see SYMMETRY) about the vertex and of infinite extent. Usually one considers only one of these parts, limited by a PLANE which cuts it. The tracing of the closed curve of rotation on this plane is the directrix and the part of the plane bounded by the directrix is the base of the cone. The lines joining the vertex to each point of the directrix are the cone's elements. The PERPENDICULAR line from the vertex to this plane is the altitude or height of the cone; the line joining the vertex to the center of the base (if it has a center) is the axis, and in most cases coincides with line B. Should axis and altitude coincide, the cone is a right cone; otherwise it is oblique. A cone whose directrix is a circle is a circular cone, its volume being given by $\pi r^2 h/3$ where r is the radius of the directrix and h is the altitude. (See also CONIC SECTIONS.)

CONESTOGA WAGON, large covered wagon used by American pioneers. Originating about 1725 in the Conestoga region of Pennsylvania, it became the chief means of transporting settlers and freight across the Alleghenies until about 1850. It had big, broadrimmed wheels and a canvas roof supported by wooden hoops, and was pulled by four to six horses.

CONFEDERATE STATES OF AMERICA, government formed by the Southern states which seceded from the United States of America, Dec. 1860–May 1861. S.C. was the first state to leave the Union after the election of President LINCOLN and was followed by Miss., Fla., Ala., Ga., La., Tex., Va., Ark., Tenn. and N.C. Rebels from Mo. and Ky. (both of which remained in the

Union) set up their own governments-in-exile under the Southern banner and brought the number of Confederate states hypothetically to 13.

A constitutional convention was called for Feb. 4, 1861, in Montgomery, Ala., which became the Confederate capital. Jefferson DAVIS (Miss.) and Alexander STEPHENS (Ga.) were elected president and vice-president. A constitution much like that of the US—but with strong "states' rights" provisions—was produced on March 11.

War with the North began on April 13 with the bombardment of Union-held Fort Sumter. Davis was reelected in Nov. and inaugurated on Feb. 22, 1862, in the new capital, Richmond, Va. He led some 9,000,000 people—of whom about 3,500,000 were slaves—at war with the nearly 23,000,000 citizens of the Union. By April he had been forced to initiate the draft and his need for wide wartime powers brought clashes with his "states' rights" Congress.

As the war continued, the government's problems deepened. Reluctant to impose taxes, it issued vast amounts of currency and war bonds which caused ruinous inflation. The essentially agricultural South suffered an increasingly desperate shortage of munitions, heavy industrial goods, domestic supplies and even of food, worsened by a successful Union naval blockade which hampered export of cotton, the country's one major crop. The South's chief cotton consumer, Britain, sent ships and munitions but refused to enter the war.

Superb military leadership provided the South's early victories and kept the conflict alive into 1865. After several desperate peace initiatives, the Confederacy had to acknowledge total military surrender. By then much of its land was devastated and the economy was in ruins. (See also CIVIL WAR, AMERICAN.)

CONFESSION, admission of sin, an aspect of repentance and thus required for ABSOLUTION. General confession may be made in a congregation; private confession may be made to God, or also to a priest. The latter is a SACRAMENT of the Roman Catholic and Eastern churches, also observed in some Lutheran and Episcopalian churches.

CONFIRMATION, a rite of certain Christian churches, usually administered in adolescence. The candidates confirm the promises made at their BAPTISM and the bishop lays his hands on them, invoking the HOLY SPIRIT upon them. First COMMUNION generally follows. In the Roman Catholic and Eastern churches confirmation is a SACRAMENT.

CONFLICT OF INTEREST, usually refers to a situation in which a public official also has private interests which may conflict with the best interests of the state. The term may also apply to many private legal and business situations.

CONFUCIANISM, philosophical system based on the teachings of CONFUCIUS and practiced throughout China for nearly 2,000 years. Confucianism teaches a moral and social philosophy and code of behavior based on peace, order, humanity, wisdom, courage and fidelity. Confucius refused to consider the question of God but Confucianists hold there is a state of heavenly harmony which man can attain by cultivating virtues, especially knowledge, patience, sincerity, obedience and the fulfilment of obligations between children and parents, subjects and ruler. Confucianism's encouragement of the acceptance of the *status quo* is at odds with the ideology of continuing revolution of the Communist Chinese government.

CONFUCIUS (c551–479 BC), *K'ung Fu-tzu*, founder of the Chinese ethical and moral system CONFUCIANISM. Born in the feudal state of Lu, he was poor and self-educated but began teaching and gathering disciples when aged about 20. Distressed by political disunity and oppressive rule, over the next 30 years he evolved a system of "right living," a guide for wise government preserved by his disciples in a collection of his sayings, the Confucian *Analects*. Confucius became a magistrate of the city of Chang-tu but resigned from what proved to be a position of impotence. Little else is reliably known of his life.

Official name: People's Republic of the Congo
Capital: Brazzaville
Area: 132,046sq mi
Population: 1,600,000
Languages: French, Lingala, Kongo
Religions: Animist, Roman Catholic
Monetary Unit(s): 1 CFA franc=100 centimes

CONGO, a socialist republic in W central Africa, formerly part of French Equatorial Africa. It is about the size of Mont. and lies on the equator E of Gabon and the Atlantic and W of Zaire.

Land. A low, treeless plain along the coast gives way inland to the Myombé Escarpment, a mountainous rain forest. There is a savanna plateau in the N, and the Ubangi and Congo (Zaire) rivers and their hot, humid forests border the E and S.

People. Some 60% of the population is rural, but there has been a major drift to the towns, of which the largest are the capital Brazzaville and Pointe-Noire, the Atlantic port. Most people are Bantu speakers, notably the Bakongo whose roughly 15 tribes make up nearly half the population. Other main Bantu-speaking tribal groups are the Batcke and M'Bochi. French is the official language. The government has placed an emphasis on education, but the rate of illiteracy is still high. A national university catering to over 4,500 students was created in Brazzaville in 1972.

Economy. Although the Congo has rich oil resources, a varied manufacturing sector and ports providing it and its neighbors with vital outlets to the world market, it has had serious economic setbacks—due mainly to political instability and poor economic planning and management. The agricultural sector is undeveloped; the country has had to rely increasingly on food imports. Cocoa, coffee, sugar and palm oil are the main crops. Crude oil is the sole major cash earner, followed by timber and potash. The Congo R is a key waterway, and Brazzaville, the capital, is a major port city.

History. The Congo was originally part of the Kingdom of the Kongo, a region discovered by the Portuguese in the 15th century and later broken up into smaller states and exploited by European slave traders. It became a French colony in 1891, an overseas territory of France in 1946 and an independent republic in 1960. Periodic civil strife from 1963 onward led to an army takeover in 1968. Following a presidential assassination in 1977 and subsequent martial law, the Congolese Labor Party, the sole legal party since 1970, confirmed a military head of state in 1979.

CONGO (Kinshasha). See ZAIRE.

CONGO RIVER, also Zaire R, second-longest river in Africa. It exceeds 2,700mi from its source in the Chambezi R, Zambia, to the Atlantic Ocean in W Zaire. It drains 1,425,000sq mi, and in volume of water is second only to the Amazon. The Congo proper and its longest navigable portion

(1000mi) begins below Boyoma (Stanley) Falls near Kisangani (Stanleyville) and runs to Pool Malebo (Stanley Pool), linked by channels to BRAZZAVILLE and KINSHASHA. Below Livingstone Falls the Congo is navigable for 95mi from Matadi to the Atlantic. The river mouth was discovered by Diogo CAM in 1482, and David LIVINGSTONE explored its upper reaches in 1866–71. Henry Morton STANLEY first traced its course in 1874–77. It was renamed the Zaire by President Mobutu in 1971.

CONGREGATIONAL CHURCHES, Protestant churches which hold that each local church (congregation) should have complete autonomy, though they may form loose associations. In the 16th century Robert BROWNE first stated Congregational doctrine. In the 17th century Congregationalists established churches in the New England colonies and founded Harvard and Yale universities. Most US Congregationalists merged (1931) with the Christian Church (see DISCIPLES OF CHRIST) and then with the EVANGELICAL AND REFORMED CHURCH (1957) to form the UNITED CHURCH OF CHRIST. (See also MATHER; SEPARATISTS.)

CONGRESSIONAL COMMITTEES. See COMMITTEES, LEGISLATIVE.

CONGRESSIONAL RECORD, daily publication put out by the US GOVERNMENT PRINTING OFFICE since 1873. It contains the debates and proceedings of the US Congress and other material, such as presidential messages and speeches.

CONGRESS OF RACIAL EQUALITY (CORE), US interracial organization founded in 1942 by James FARMER to promote black CIVIL RIGHTS AND LIBERTIES through nonviolent direct action projects. Its voter registration drives and "freedom rides" in the South led to civil rights legislation in the 1960s. In the 1970s CORE became more militant (see also BLACK POWER).

CONGRESS OF THE UNITED STATES, legislative branch of the US federal government. It consists of two houses, the Senate and the House of Representatives. Under the UNITED STATES CONSTITUTION, the powers vested in Congress are to introduce legislation, to assess and collect taxes, to regulate interstate and foreign commerce, to coin money, to establish post offices, to maintain armed forces and to declare war. Congress convenes on Jan. 3 and is in session until adjournment, usually in the fall. A single Congress is two sessions; the first Congress met in 1789–90.

House of Representatives. Membership was 65 in 1789 and is now fixed at 435. Each

state has at least one representative; the total number per state is proportional to state population as determined by official census; state legislatures set the boundaries for congressional districts. A representative must be over 25, a US citizen for at least seven years and resident in the state (and usually the district) which elects him. Elections for representatives are held every two years on the Tuesday after the first Monday in Nov. The House has special powers to impeach federal officials (who are then tried by the Senate), originate revenue bills and elect the president if no candidate gains a majority in the ELECTORAL COLLEGE.

The Senate. There are 100 senators, two from each state. Direct popular elections were introduced in 1913. Until then senators had been elected by state legislatures. Senators serve overlapping six-year terms, one-third being elected every two years. They must be over 30, citizens for at least nine years and resident in the state which elects them. The Senate's special powers are to advise and consent on the appointments of important government officials, including ambassadors and federal judges, and to approve treaties. Through its foreign relations committee, the Senate wields large influence on the conduct of foreign affairs. Officially the vice-president presides over the Senate, but often delegates the task.

The Work of Congress. For a bill to become law it must be approved by both the House and Senate and signed by the president. If he vetoes the bill, Congress may pass it by a two-thirds majority in each house. When the House and Senate disagree on a bill, a joint committee may resolve the differences in a compromise bill, or the bill may die. Each house has committees for drafting and studying bills (see COMMITTEES, LEGISLATIVE). They are then debated by the house which originated them, and votes are taken to pass, reject or defer them. Debate is freer in the Senate than in the House because of the Senate's smaller numbers; a bill may be killed by FILIBUSTER unless a two-thirds majority can be reached to close the debate (see CLOTURE).

CONGRESS PARTY (Indian National Congress), Indian political party which came to power in 1947 with India's independence from Britain. The Indian National Congress was founded in 1885. It developed a wide national following under the leadership of Mahatma GANDHI and Jawaharlal NEHRU. The latter headed the Congress Party as India's prime minister 1947–64. His daughter, Indira GANDHI, has served twice as Congress Party leader and as prime minister (1966–77; 1980–   ).

CONGREVE, William (1670–1729), English Restoration dramatist, master of the COMEDY OF MANNERS. Among his comedies are *The Old Bachelor* (1693), *Love for Love* (1695) and his masterpiece *The Way of the World* (1700), which is often performed today.

CONIC SECTIONS, plane CURVES formed by the intersection of a PLANE with a right circular or right elliptical CONE: the three curves are the ellipse, the parabola and the hyperbola. An **ellipse** occurs when the ANGLE between the axis of the cone and the plane is greater than the angle between the axis and the generator (in special cases a CIRCLE may be produced). It may be defined as the locus of intersection of a PLANE with a right circular or about two fixed foci (singular, focus) F and F', such that $PF + PF = c$ where c is a constant greater than the distance FF'. The major axis of an ellipse is its axis of SYMMETRY concurrent with FF'; its minor axis is the axis of symmetry perpendicular to this, their point of intersection being defined as the center of the ellipse. If the length of the minor axis is 2b, b being a constant, then $c^2 = (FF')^2 + b^2$. The eccentricity of an ellipse is given by the distance FF' divided by the length of the major axis. A **parabola** occurs when the angle between the axis and the plane equals the angle between the axis and generator (in special cases a straight line may be produced). It may be defined as the locus of a point P such that its distance from a fixed focus F is constantly equal to its PERPENDICULAR distance from a fixed straight line XY. The curve, which has only one axis of symmetry, perpendicular to XY and passing through F, is of infinite extent. The **hyperbola** occurs when the angle between axis and plane is less than that between axis and generator (in special cases a pair of intersecting straight lines may be produced). It may be defined as the loci of two points, P' and P', about two foci, F and F, such that $PF' - PF = c = P'F - PF'$, where c is a constant less than the distance FF'. The curve, which is of infinite extent, has a real axis of symmetry passing through F and F', and an imaginary axis of symmetry passing perpendicularly through the midpoint of FF'. The hyperbola, though of infinite extent in the direction of its real axis, is bounded in the direction perpendicular to this (see ASYMPTOTE).

CONJUNCTIVITIS, INFLAMMATION of the conjunctiva, or fine skin covering the EYE and inner eyelids. It is a common but usually harmless condition caused by ALLERGY (as part of HAY FEVER), foreign bodies, or infection with VIRUSES or BACTERIA. It causes irritation, watering and sticky discharge, but does not affect VISION. Eye drops may help, as can ANTIBIOTICS if bacteria are present.

CONNALLY, Tom (Thomas Terry Connally; 1877–1963), US politician. He served five terms in the House from 1916 and was a senator from 1928 to 1953. Chairman of the Senate's foreign relations committee (1941–47; 1949–53), he helped secure ratification of the UN Charter, and was a US delegate to the UN General Assembly (1945–47).

Name of state: Connecticut
Capital: Hartford
Statehood: Jan. 9, 1788 (5th state)
Familiar names: Constitution State, Nutmeg State
Area: 5,009sq mi
Population: 3,107,576
Elevation: Highest—2,380ft, Mt. Frissell. Lowest—sea level, at Long Island Sound
Motto: Qui Transtulit Sustinet (He Who Transplanted Still Sustains
State flower: Mountain laurel
State bird: Robin
State tree: White oak
State song: "Yankee Doodle."

CONNECTICUT, state, NE US, bounded to the E by R.I., to the S by Long Island Sound (an arm of the Atlantic Ocean), to the W by N.Y., and to the N by Mass.; one of the original 13 states.

Land. Connecticut can be divided into three topographical areas: the Taconic Mts and Berkshires to the NW; a central lowland; and a hilly E upland. Major rivers include the Connecticut, Housatonic, and Thames. The climate is temperate and changeable.

People. Although about two-thirds of the state is forested, it is generally a highly urbanized area with many New York City commuter-residents.

Economy. Most of the state's prosperity comes from industry: Connecticut produces transportation equipment, fabricated metal goods and machine tools. Hartford, the state capital, is an important insurance center in the US. Yale, founded in 1701, was the nation's third university. Bridgeport and Hartford are the largest cities, followed by New Haven, Waterbury and Stamford.

History. The Connecticut R was first explored in 1614 by the Dutchman Adriaen BLOCK and in 1633 a Dutch fur-trading post was established at Hartford. In the 1630s, Puritans from Massachusetts Bay Colony settled Wethersfield, Hartford, Windsor and Saybrook, while Congregationalists from the Plymouth Bay Colony founded New Haven Colony, restricting voting rights there to members of the Congregational Church. In 1639, the river towns joined to form the Connecticut Colony to which New Haven also belonged after 1665. Colonial agriculture prospered in the Connecticut Valley and in the 18th century manufacturing developed with production of iron and tin products as well as textiles and clothing.

In 1788 Connecticut became the fifth state of the new union. It opposed Jefferson's EMBARGO ACT of 1807 and the WAR OF 1812. The HARTFORD CONVENTION, set up to protect New England interests during the War of 1812, was dissolved when the war ended and the new state constitution (1818) was introduced. In the Civil War, Connecticut supported the Union. The war increased industry, immigration and urbanization. WWI aided industrial expansion and WWII revived the economy after the depression of the 1930s. Connecticut thereafter maintained a steady growth in population and prosperity, with defense contracts remaining important. The increasing density of population brought problems of air and water pollution, but in the 1970's population growth tapered off to a low 2.5% while average per capita income remained high ($10,129).

Under the 1965 state constitution a governor and other officials are elected every four years. The General Assembly, consisting of 36 senators and 151 representatives, is elected biennially. Local government is conducted by townships and cities.

CONNECTICUT RIVER, longest river in New England. It rises in N.H., flows 407mi through Mass. and Conn. and empties into Long Island Sound. It was discovered in 1614 by Adriaen BLOCK.

CONNECTICUT WITS. See HARTFORD WITS.

CONNELLY, Marc (Marcus Cook Connelly; 1890–1980), US playwright, best known for his Pulitzer Prize-winning play, *The Green Pastures* (1930). He collaborated with George S. KAUFMAN on several plays, including *Beggar on Horseback* (1924).

CONNOLLY, Cyril (Vernon) (1903–1974), English literary critic and author, founder and editor (1939–50) of *Horizon*, a literary magazine. His collections of essays include *Enemies of Promise* (1938) which is semi-autobiographical, *The Condemned Playground* (1945) and *Previous Convictions* (1963).

CONNORS, Jimmy (1952–   ), US tennis player. He was the top-ranked player in the world through most of the 1970s, when he won the US Open (1974, 1976, 1978) and Wimbledon (1974). He popularized the left-handed, two-fisted backhand.

CONQUEST, (George) Robert (Acworth) (1917–   ), English poet, novelist and writer about E European affairs. His collections of poetry include *Poems* (1955), *Between Mars and Venus* (1962) and *Arias from a Love Opera* (1969). His political works include *Where Do Marxists Go from Here?* (1958) and *Russia After Khrushchev* (1965).

CONQUISTADORS, 16th-century military adventurers who founded Spain's empire in the Americas. Most famous among them were BALBOA, Hernán CORTÉS and Francisco PIZARRO.

CONRAD, Joseph (Jozef Teodor Konrad Korzeniowski; 1857–1924), Polish-born English novelist. He went to sea from 1874 to about 1894 and became a British citizen (1886). Conrad is best known for his studies of individuals and also of small groups or communities (such as those on board ship or in isolated jungle settlements) at moments of extreme moral crisis. His works include *The Nigger of the "Narcissus"* (1897), *Lord Jim* (1900), *Heart of Darkness* (1902), *Typhoon* (1903), *Nostromo* (1904) and *The Secret Agent* (1907).

CONRAIL, the official nickname for Consolidated Rail Corp., a quasi-governmental US organization created to take over seven bankrupt railroads in the NE and MW, including the Penn Central, Erie & Lackawanna, Lehigh Valley and Reading. Conrail began operations on Apr. 1, 1976. It carries c500,000 passengers daily and one-quarter of the nation's rail freight traffic.

CONSCIENCE WHIGS, members of the US WHIG party who joined the FREE SOIL PARTY (1847–54) which opposed the extension of slavery into new territories.

CONSCIENTIOUS OBJECTOR, person who refuses to bear arms and opposes military training or service. The position of objectors is based on conscience, according to their religious, political or philosophical beliefs. Groups refusing to bear arms have been persecuted at various periods in history. Most countries now have legal provisions for objectors, who are generally drafted into alternative noncombatant military duty or socially useful civilian work. (See also DRAFT, MILITARY; PACIFISM.)

CONSCIOUS, in psychoanalysis, the part of the mind in which rational, logical thought takes place. The EGO conducts conscious mental processes.

CONSERVATION, the preservation of the ENVIRONMENT, whether to ensure the long-term future availability of natural resources such as FUEL or to retain such intangibles as scenic beauty for future generations.

History. The conservation movement was born in the 19th century as a result of two developments: acceptance of the theory of EVOLUTION and the concept (later proved erroneous) of the BALANCE OF NATURE. It was estimated in that century that over 100 million acres of land in the US had been totally destroyed through EROSION OF SOIL caused by the reckless destruction of forests; Congress passed the Forest Reserve Act (1891) and the Carey Land Act (1894) but both were rendered ineffectual by commercial interests. The first genuinely conservationist president was Theodore ROOSEVELT, whose Newlands Reclamation Act of 1902 began the struggle for American conservation in earnest. More recently, where officialdom has been dilatory, conservation has been brought to the people by groups such as Friends of the Earth, earning through their efforts a powerful international membership.

The Part of Science. ECOLOGY, the study of the interrelationships of elements of an environment, has enabled many scientific disciplines to play a part in conservation. In AGRICULTURE, where protection of the soil from erosion is clearly of paramount importance, crop rotation, strip-cropping and other improvements in land use have been made. Important in all fields of human existence and endeavor is the conservation of WATER for IRRIGATION, industrial, drinking and other purposes. Careful use, plus the prevention or amelioration of POLLUTION, especially by industry, are essential. Conservation of raw materials is more complicated, since they cannot be replaced; however, much has been done in the way of good management, and science has developed new processes, artificial substitutes and techniques of RECYCLING. Conservation of wildlife, however, is probably the most dramatically successful of all conservation in this century. Many species, such as the koala and American bison, that were in danger of extinction are now reviving; and most governments are vigilant in areas such as hunting and industrial pollution. Important to all these efforts is the retention of the human population within reasonable limits. In this, CONTRACEPTION has a large part to play, and many governments are now active in their encouragement of it.

CONSERVATISM, term for social and political philosophies or attitudes, stressing traditional values and continuity of social institutions and rejecting sudden radical change, while at the same time maintaining ideals of progress. It was first used in the early 19th century of the policies of the British TORY party. Modern conservative political parties include the British Conservative and Unionist Party, the Canadian PROGRESSIVE-CONSERVATIVE PARTY and the American REPUBLICAN PARTY.

CONSIDÉRANT, Victor Prosper (1808–1893), French socialist. He promoted the doctrines of Charles FOURIER, edited *La Phalange*, the journal of Fourierism, and published *Destinée sociale* (1834–38) and *Principes du socialisme* (1847). He tried to establish a communistic community near Dallas, Tex. (1855–57).

CONSTABLE, John (1776–1837), English painter. He and J. M. W. TURNER were England's two greatest landscapists. Believing that painting should be pursued scientifically, he explored techniques of rendering landscape from direct observation of nature under different effects of light and weather. His naturalist approach had some influence on the French BARBIZON SCHOOL.

CONSTANTINE I (c280–337 AD), Roman emperor, known as the Great. He promoted and accepted Christianity, and transferred the empire's capital from Rome to Constantinople. He was proclaimed Caesar in the W by his father Constantius (306), who was Augustus in the W. After his father's death, he defeated one claimant for the throne, Maximilian (310), and then his son Maxentius at the battle of the Milvian Bridge (312), where he is said to have had a vision of a cross against the sun, which he adopted as his standard. In the *Edict of Milan*, Constantine, now Augustus in the W, and Licinius, Augustus in the E, agreed to tolerate Christianity in the empire. In 324 Constantine defeated Licinius and became sole emperor. His council at Arles (314) condemned DONATISM and the first general council of the Church at NICAEA (325) dealt with ARIANISM. He rebuilt Byzantium, inaugurating it as his eastern capital in 330 and renaming it Constantinople. He instituted a centralized bureaucracy, separated military from civil government and introduced many legal reforms.

CONSTANTINOPLE. See ISTANBUL.

CONSTANTINOPLE, Latin Empire of (1204–61), feudal empire set up by leaders of the Fourth Crusade, the Venetians and Latins. Throughout this disastrous period of Byzantine history, the city suffered massacres and pillages until its recapture by Greek Emperor Michael VIII. (See CRUSADES.)

CONSTIPATION, a decrease in the frequency of bowel actions from the norm for an individual; also increased hardness of stool. Often precipitated by inactivity, changed diet or environment, it is sometimes due to GASTROINTESTINAL TRACT disease. Increased dietary fiber, and taking of fecal softeners or intestinal irritants are usual remedies; enema may be required in severe cases.

CONSTITUTION, fundamental rules, written or unwritten, for the government of an organized body such as a nation. The US constitution defines the rights of citizens and of states, and the structure and powers of the federal government. It exists in documentary form, but those of many other nations do not. The British constitution is embodied in tradition and the law of the land. Some constitutions, such as that of the US, may only be altered by special procedures, while others, such as that of Britain, may be altered by a simple act of the legislature.

CONSTITUTION, USS, American frigate carrying 44 guns, known as "Old Ironsides." Launched in Boston in 1797, she served in the war with Tripoli and the War of 1812. In 1828 a plan to dismantle the warship provoked Oliver Wendell Holmes' poem "Old Ironsides." She was rebuilt, berthed in Boston, and opened to the public in 1934.

CONSTITUTIONAL LAW, US, body of law which interprets the US Constitution. The original constitution did not precisely define the roles or the limits of power of governmental institutions. Constitutional law studies their historical development in relation to contemporary issues. **Judicial review** deals with the power of the courts, ultimately the Supreme Court, to determine the constitutionality of laws or acts of government. Although the Constitution did not provide for this activity, the Supreme Court has claimed it since Chief Justice John MARSHALL's decision in MARBURY V MADISON (1803). He asserted that since the Constitution is the supreme law, and it is the courts' duty to uphold the law, the courts must invalidate any law or action they consider in conflict with the Constitution.

Separation of powers (formulated by MONTESQUIEU) combats despotism by dividing governmental power into branches which check and balance each other. Thus legislative power is granted to Congress, judicial power to the courts and executive power to the president. Each is supreme in its own sphere, but the 20th century has seen growth in executive power, which now initiates legislation.

The federal system divides governmental powers between the federal and state governments. The Constitution designated the federal government's powers and reserved all others to the states. Recently the use by Congress of its right to make all laws necessary and proper to carry out its constitutional function and to regulate interstate commerce has enormously increased federal power. The conflict between centralized and state power is reflected in US political parties: Democrats tend to favor centralized power and financial control, while Republicans favor STATES' RIGHTS and decentralized financial administration.

CONSTITUTIONAL UNION PARTY, US political party (the Do-Nothing Party), formed from remnants of the Whig and American (Know-Nothing) parties, active 1859–60. Its platform upheld the Constitution and the Union, while ignoring the slavery issue. As a result, the vote in 1860 was split and LINCOLN was elected by the ELECTORAL COLLEGE, the first president without a popular majority.

CONSTRUCTIVISM, artistic movement which was developed in Russia 1913–20 by TATLIN, LISSITZKY, PEVSNER and GABO. Partly influenced by CUBISM and FUTURISM, it was related to technology and industrial materials. The geometric abstract work of Russian constructivists was influential in Germany (in the BAUHAUS), France, England and the US.

CONSUBSTANTIATION, doctrine that in the Eucharist the blood and body of Christ coexist substantially with the bread and wine of the sacrament. This was introduced by LUTHER in opposition to belief in TRANSUBSTANTIATION, the changing of the wafer and wine into the body and blood of Christ.

CONSUL, Roman, the two chief magistrates of the Roman Republic, elected annually by the COMITIA centuriata. Consuls were the heads of state from the fall of the kings, c509 BC, until 27 BC; under the empire consulship became an honorary office.

CONSULATE, the French Republic's government from 1799–1804; in reality a military dictatorship under NAPOLEON, who became first consul and was then elected consul for life in 1802. The consulate ended when he became emperor.

CONSUMER AFFAIRS, Office of, agency established in 1970 under the executive branch of the US government. It coordinates consumer activity in government agencies and departments, advises on consumer policy and handles complaints.

CONSUMER PRICE INDEX (CPI), published monthly by the US Bureau of Labor Statistics, measures changes in the cost of goods and services, and thus charts rises and falls in the cost of living. The prices in a particular "market basket"—including housing, transportation, medical fees, etc.—are tracked and averaged. The total is compared with the average cost of the same items in 1967; the 1967 market basket is given the value of 100. In late 1981, the CPI stood at 270.2.

CONSUMER PRODUCTS SAFETY COMMISSION, a US government agency established in 1972. Its purposes are to protect the public against unreasonable risks of injury from consumer products, to help consumers evaluate the safety of products and to develop uniform safety standards.

CONSUMER PROTECTION, the body of laws and voluntary codes setting standards for goods and services sold and the agencies enforcing them, as well as the efforts of consumer groups. In recent years widespread recognition was given to the fact that the common law maxim "let the buyer beware" (*caveat emptor*) was no longer valid in superindustrial societies; today's buyer cannot necessarily protect his own best interests by judicious purchasing. The need for consumer protection arose because of the dangers of price-fixing by monopolies, of fraud and of the increasing difficulty in judging the quality or suitability of goods as technological production, packaging and sales techniques grow more sophisticated.

There are over 1000 consumer protection programs in the US under federal, state and local agencies. The federal government sets standards for weights and measures, product safety, packaging, food and drug composition and advertising descriptions. The FOOD AND DRUG ADMINISTRATION is the best known of the federal agencies. The departments of Justice, Transportation, Commerce, Housing and Urban Development, and the Federal Power Commission,

Trade Commission, Communications Commission and Interstate Commerce Commission are among those involved in consumer protection.

Consumer movements. The National Consumers' League was formed in 1899 to encourage purchase of articles made under good working conditions and of good standard. Its work inspired such books as *The Great American Fraud* by Samuel Hopkins ADAMS, which contributed to the passage of the Food and Drug Act in 1906 and the founding of the American Home Economics Association (1908). Upton SINCLAIR'S *The Jungle* (1906) exposed the unsafe and unsanitary conditions in the meat-packing industry. F. J. Schlink, coauthor with Stuart CHASE of *Your Money's Worth* (1924), helped to found a consumer's club that evolved into Consumer's Research Inc. (1929), which tested products and published its findings. An offshoot of this group formed the Consumers' Union in 1936 and began to publish *Consumer Reports,* which evaluates the cost and quality of products in an effort to protect consumers' interests. The Food, Drug and Cosmetic Act was passed in 1938.

Ralph NADER exposed defects in automobile design that affected motorists' safety in *Unsafe at Any Speed* (1965) and financed investigation of other products. With "Nader's Raiders," his volunteer assistants, he aroused consumer awareness, which was consolidated in boycotts and group lawsuits. Such action was at first bitterly opposed, but later won positive response from government, industry and the public. Congress approved the Auto Safety Act (1965), Consumer Protection Act (1969) and Consumer Products Safety Act (1972). Some companies have begun to manufacture products less harmful to consumers and the environment such as biodegradable detergents, lead-free gasoline, returnable bottles and foods free from chemical additives. The many governmental restrictions on production of consumer goods because of safety factors during the 1970s caused a backlash, however, and President Ronald Reagan's conservative administration began to relax stringent controls on production of consumer goods in the early 1980s.

CONTAINERIZATION, transport of cargo in unbroken unit loads, a growing trend from the 1960s. The cargo is packaged in containers which can be transferred from one mode of transport to another without unpacking. This has led to greater efficiency and speed in shipping, and railway and road transport.

CONTINENT, one of the seven major divisions of land on earth: Africa, Antarctica, Asia, Australia, Europe, North America, South America. These continents have evolved during the earth's history from a single landmass, PANGAEA (see also CONTINENTAL DRIFT; PLATE TECTONICS; GONDWANALAND; LAURASIA; CONTINENTAL SHELF).

CONTINENTAL ARMY, American force in the REVOLUTIONARY WAR, organized (1775) and commanded by George WASHINGTON. It consisted of about 5,000 volunteers, joined at irregular intervals by state militia, sometimes raising the number to around 20,000. It was financed by individual states and foreign loans, and was always short of money, food, clothing and ammunition.

CONTINENTAL CONGRESS (1774–89), body of delegates representing the colonies which was summoned before and during the American REVOLUTIONARY WAR. The First Continental Congress met in Philadelphia, Sept. 5, 1774, to seek relief from England's commercial and political oppression. There were 56 delegates, from all colonies except Georgia. The congress drafted a declaration of rights setting forth the colonists' demands as British subjects, formulated a "plan of association," denounced "taxation without representation" and agreed to boycott trade with England until their demands were met. When the Second Continental Congress met on May 10, 1775, battles had already been fought at Lexington and Concord, Mass. It appointed George Washington commander-in-chief of the army. It approved the Declaration of Independence on July 4, 1776, and drafted the ARTICLES OF CONFEDERATION, which served as a US constitution from 1781 until the present constitution was drawn up (1787). In the meantime, the Continental Congress acted as a federal government in maintaining an army, issuing currency and dealing with foreign policy.

CONTINENTAL DIVIDE, imaginary line which divides a continent at the point where its rivers start flowing in opposite directions and empty into different oceans. In North America it follows the Rocky Mts, in South America the Andes.

CONTINENTAL DRIFT, theory first rigorously formulated by WEGENER, later amplified by DUTOIT, to explain a number of geological and paleontological phenomena. It suggests that originally the land on earth composed a single, vast CONTINENT, PANGAEA, which broke up.

CONTINENTAL SHELF, the gently sloping portion of a continent that is submerged in the OCEAN to a depth of less than 200m (650ft), resulting in a rim of shallow water surrounding the landmass. The outer edge of the shelf slopes towards the ocean bottom, and is called the continental slope.

CONTINENTAL SYSTEM, attempted economic blockade of England initiated in 1806 by Napoleon. It was defeated by a counter-blockade by England's superior naval power. The British blockade interfered with American continental trade and was a major cause of the WAR OF 1812. (See also NAPOLEONIC WARS.)

CONTINUO, or thoroughbass, in 17th- and 18th-century European music, continuous accompaniment of a musical work, underlining its harmony and rhythm. Played on the harpsichord, double bass, cello, bassoon or other instruments, continuo involved a degree of improvisation, particularly in the harmonization.

CONTRACEPTION, the avoidance of conception, and thus of PREGNANCY. Many different methods exist, none of which are absolutely effective. In the **rhythm method,** sexual intercourse is restricted to the days immediately before and after MENSTRUATION, when fertilization is unlikely. **Withdrawal** (*coitus interruptus*) is removal of the PENIS prior to ejaculation, which reduces the number of sperm released into the vagina. The **condom** is a rubber sheath, fitting over the penis, into which ejaculation occurs; the diaphragm is a complementary device which is inserted into the vagina before intercourse. Both are more effective with **spermicide creams. Intrauterine devices** (IUDs) are plastic or copper devices which are inserted into the WOMB and interfere with IMPLANTATION. They are convenient but may lead to infection, or increased blood loss or pain at menstruation. **Oral contraceptives** ("the Pill") are sex HORMONES of the ESTROGEN and PROGESTERONE type which, if taken regularly through the menstrual cycle, inhibit the release of eggs from the ovary. While they are the most reliable form of contraception, they carry a small risk of venous THROMBOSIS, raised blood pressure and possibly other diseases. When the Pill is stopped, periods and ovulation may not return for some time, and this can cause difficulty in assessing fetal maturity if pregnancy follows without an intervening period. While the more effective forms of contraception carry a slightly greater risk, this must be set against the risks of pregnancy and induced ABORTION in the general context of FAMILY PLANNING. Indeed, many risky and costly abortions could be avoided, if only greater attention were given to contraception.

CONTRACTS, legally enforceable promises or agreements. Most are written, but verbal contracts may be equally binding in law. A contract is a bargain in which one party agrees to the terms offered by another party. To be binding there must be consideration: one party promises to do something in return for something of value promised by the other. Contracts are usually enforced under civil rather than criminal law. A party failing to fulfill a contracted promise is in breach of contract, and the court may award financial damages to the other party.

CONVECTION, passage of heat through a fluid by means of large-scale movements of material within the body of the fluid (see CONDUCTION). If, for example, a liquid is heated from below, parts close to the heat source expand and, because their DENSITY is thus reduced, rise through the liquid; near the top, they cool and begin to sink. This process continues until HEAT is uniformly distributed throughout the liquid. Convection in the ATMOSPHERE is responsible for many climatic effects (see METEOROLOGY; RADIATION.)

CONWAY CABAL, plot to oust George Washington as commander-in-chief of the Continental Army in 1777, during the American Revolution. Washington had lost at Brandywine and Germantown, but General Horatio Gates had won at Saratoga. Washington intercepted a letter from Gen. Thomas Conway to Gates criticizing Washington and revealing plans by an army and Congressional cabal to replace Washington by Gates. Washington published the letter and rallied Congressional support. Conway was forced to resign his command.

COOK, James (1728–1779), English navigator and explorer who led three celebrated expeditions to the Pacific Ocean (1768–71; 1772–75; 1776–80), during which he charted the coast of New Zealand (1770), showed that if there were a great southern continent it could not be so large as was commonly supposed, and discovered the Sandwich Islands (1778). He died in an attack by Hawaiian natives.

COOKE, Alistair (1908–   ), British-born US journalist and broadcaster. Educated at Cambridge U, he went to the US and broadcast a weekly BBC radio program, "Letter from America," from 1946. He is principally known as the host of such popular television series as the Emmy award-winning *Omnibus* (1952–61) and *Masterpiece Theater* on PBS. He wrote *Alistair Cooke's America* (1973).

COOKE, Jay (1821–1905), US financier who helped the federal government finance the Civil War. He formed the banking firm Jay Cooke & Co. in 1861, and sold over $1 billion in war bonds. His firm later underwrote the construction of the Northern Pacific Railway but failed in the financial crisis of 1873. Cooke made a second fortune in silver mining, 1878–79.

COOKERY. The transformation from raw to cooked food is based on several methods. **Boiling** involves cooking food in liquid at the boiling or bubbling point. The aim is either to retain the flavor of the meat or vegetable (and therefore the cook does not prolong the process) or to flavor the liquid (as in making soup). **Frying** means cooking in fat at high temperature; generally the food should be quite dry or coated in batter or crumbs. Deep-fat frying requires much fat; sautéing uses little fat, as does the Chinese technique of stir-frying. **Broiling** and **roasting** expose the food to direct, dry heat. The aim is to brown the food's surface but keep the inside juicy. **Steaming** is accomplished either by keeping food in a rack and tightly covered above boiling liquid or by using a little hot liquid or melted fat to steam the food gently. **Braising** and **stewing** impart tenderness to meat and a special flavor to all ingredients through a combination of methods: the food is first browned in fat, a small amount of liquid is added, and cooking proceeds at low temperature with the pot tightly covered.

Thickening and **sauce-mixing** can also be considered among basic cookery techniques. Thickening depends on using flour (or another starch) or egg yolk to thicken liquids. Other sauces (Hollandaise, mayonnaise, Béarnaise) are based on emulsions— combinations of egg yolks with butter or oil.

COOK ISLANDS, two groups of coral islands in the S Pacific, sighted 1773 by Capt. James Cook; a British protectorate (1888), then part of New Zealand (1901), and a self-governing dependency since 1965. The population is Polynesian. Exports include citrus fruit, copra and clothing.

COOLEY, Denton Arthur (1920–   ), US surgeon. Recognized as one of the world's most skillful heart surgeons, he was known to perform up to 12 operations a day and was the first to implant an artificial heart in a human being (1969).

COOLIDGE, (John) Calvin (1872–1933), 30th president of the US (1923–29), a moderately conservative Republican who continued Warren G. Harding's policies but replaced corruption with honesty. Born at Plymouth, Vt., he became a lawyer in Mass. and rose in local political office. He was mayor of Northampton 1910–11, state senator 1912–15, lieutenant governor of Mass. 1916–18 and governor 1919–20. His firm handling of the BOSTON POLICE STRIKE gave him national prominence, and in 1920 he was chosen US vice president, succeeding to the presidency on the death of Harding. He was elected president in 1924 over Democrat John W. Davis and Progressive Robert M. La Follette. His administration was characterized by caution, governmental efficiency and delegation of responsibility to such able men as Secretary of Commerce Herbert Hoover, Secretary of the Treasury Andrew Mellon, and Secretary of State Frank B. Kellogg.

Disapproving of government interference in economic affairs and believing in government frugality, Coolidge vetoed the McNary-Haugen Bill for relief to agriculture. He lowered taxes, reduced the national budget and the national debt and protected industry with high tariffs, creating a short-lived prosperity. He handled with restraint and integrity the oil-lease scandals of the Harding administration. In foreign affairs the country's policy was isolationist. The US kept out of the League of Nations but took part in League-sponsored conferences. Coolidge's wish for US participation in the World Court was blocked by Senate opposition. He sponsored the KELLOGG-BRIAND PACT (1927) outlawing war. His administration passed the DAWES PLAN to lend Germany money to rebuild its economy.

COOLIDGE, William David (1873–1975), US chemist who developed (1911) the pliable TUNGSTEN filaments used in lightbulbs and (1913) a high-vacuum X-RAY tube (the Coolidge tube) which was a major breakthrough in RADIOLOGY.

COOPER, Gary (1901–1961), US film actor who portrayed laconic, romantic heroes in such films as *A Farewell to Arms* (1933) and *For Whom the Bell Tolls* (1943). He won Academy Awards for roles in *Sergeant York* (1941) and *High Noon* (1952).

COOPER, James Fenimore (1789–1851), first major US novelist, best known for narratives about the American frontier. The series of *Leatherstocking Tales* (1823–41), with their hero, the scout Natty Bumppo, includes *The Pioneers, The Last of the Mohicans, The Prairie, The Pathfinder* and *The Deerslayer*. His attitude is romantic, his characterization shallow, his dialogue stilted; yet his work is readable. He also invented the sea romance and wrote works of social criticism.

COOPER, Peter (1791–1883), US indus-trial innovator and philanthropist. His Baltimore iron works built the first US steam locomotive, *Tom Thumb* (1830). He introduced structural iron beams and popularized the BESSEMER PROCESS. In 1854 he founded Cooper Union in New York City for free instruction in arts and sciences. In 1876 he was GREENBACK PARTY presidential candidate.

COOPERATIVE, in real estate, group ownership of a property, typically an apartment building. Individuals purchase shares in the corporation that owns the property and receive a "proprietary lease" to occupy a particular apartment and to use common areas controlled by the corporation.

COOPERATIVE, an association of producers or manufacturers and consumers to share profits which would otherwise go to middlemen. The pioneer Rochdale Society of Equitable Pioneers, founded in England 1844, set precedents of unrestricted membership, democratic organization, educational facilities and service at cost. That same year John Kaulbach, a Boston tailor, formed the first US consumers' cooperative among members of his trade union. The National Grange, founded in the US 1867, promoted Rochdale principles (see GRANGE, THE). Current US cooperative activity consists of farmers' purchasing and marketing, credit and banking, mutual insurance, wholesaling, group medical programs and consumer cooperatives. There are over 800,000 cooperative societies in the world.

COPENHAGEN (København), seaport capital of Denmark, on Sjaelland and Amager islands. It handles most of Denmark's trade, exporting ham, bacon, porcelain, silverware and furniture. Its main industries are shipping, shipbuilding, brewing and light manufacturing. The Royal Copenhagen porcelain factory and Georg Jensen handmade silverworks are famous. Landmarks include Christianborg Palace, Rosenborg Palace, Tivoli amusement park, the National Museum and several art museums. The university, founded 1478, is a major center for research in theoretical physics. A small fishing port until the 11th century, Copenhagen grew as a center on the Baltic trade route. In 1443 it became the royal residence and expanded under Christian IV (1577–1648). It was occupied by the Germans 1940–45. Pop 654,000; met pop 1,388,000.

COPERNICUS, Nicolaus, or Niklas Koppernigk (1473–1543), Polish astronomer who displaced the earth from the center of man's conceptual universe and made it orbit a stationary sun. Belonging to a wealthy German family, he spent several years in Italy mastering all that was known of mathematics, medicine, theology and astronomy before returning to Poland where he eventually settled into the life of lay canon at Frauenburg. His dissatisfaction with the earth-centered (geocentric) cosmology of PTOLEMY was made known to a few friends in the manuscript *Commentariolus* (1514), but it was only on the insistence of Pope Clement VII that he expanded this into the *De revolutionibus orbium coelestium* (*On the revolutions of the heavenly spheres*) which, when published in 1543, announced the sun-centered (heliocentric) theory to the world. Always the theoretician rather than a practical observer, Copernicus' main dissatisfaction with Ptolemy was philosophical. He sought to replace the equant, EPICYCLE and deferent of Ptolemaic theory with pure circular motions, but in adopting a moving-earth theory he was forced to reject the whole of the scholastic physics (without providing an alternative—this had to await the work of GALILEO) and postulate a much greater scale for the universe. Although the heliocentric hypothesis was not immediately accepted by the majority of scientists, its proposal did begin the period of scientific reawakening known as the Copernican Revolution.

COPLAND, Aaron (1900–), US composer using a distinctively American idiom. His lyrical and exuberant music incorporates jazz and folk tunes. His works include the ballet scores *Billy the Kid* (1938) and *Appalachian Spring* (1944), the song cycle *Twelve Poems of Emily Dickinson* (1950), the opera *The Tender Land* (1954), symphonies, piano and chamber works and film scores. His many awards include the 1945 Pulitzer price.

COPLEY, John Singleton (1738–1815), American portrait painter who brilliantly depicted colonial personalities. In 1774 he left America and settled in London. He became a member of the Royal Academy and painted large canvases with historical themes, including *The Death of Chatham* (1779–80).

COPPER (Cu), soft, red metal in Group IB of the PERIODIC TABLE; a TRANSITION ELEMENT. Copper has been used since c6500 BC (see BRONZE AGE). It occurs naturally as the metal in the US, especially Mich., and as the ores CUPRITE, CHALCOPYRITE, ANTLERITE, CHALCOCITE, BORNITE, AZURITE and MALACHITE in the US, Zambia, Zaire and Chile. The metal is produced by roasting the concentrated ores and

smelting, and is then refined by electrolysis. Copper is strong, tough, and highly malleable and ductile. It is an excellent conductor of heat and electricity, and most copper produced is used in the electrical industry. It is also a major component of many ALLOYS, including BRASS, BRONZE, GERMAN SILVER, cupronickel (see NICKEL) and beryllium copper (very strong and fatigue-resistant). Many copper alloys are called bronzes, though they need not contain tin: copper + tin + phosphorus is phosphor bronze, and copper + aluminum is aluminum bronze. Copper is a vital trace element: in man it catalyzes the formation of HEMOGLOBIN; in mollusks and crustaceans it is the basic constituent of HEMOCYANIN. Chemically, copper is unreactive, dissolving only in oxidizing acids. It forms cuprous compounds (oxidation state +1), and the more common cupric salts (oxidation state +2), used as fungicides and insecticides, in pigments, as mordants for dyeing, as catalysts, for copper plating, and in electric cells. **Copper (II) Sulfate** ($CuSO_4.5H_2O$), or **Blue Vitriol**, blue crystalline solid occurring naturally as chalcanthite; used as above. AW 63.5, mp 1083°C, bp 2567°C, sg 8.96 (20°C).

COPPERHEADS, Northern Democrats who opposed the Lincoln administration's Civil War policy and advocated peace with the Confederates. The term originated in a newspaper article depicting them as poisonous copperhead snakes. Most urged peace through negotiation, but some secret societies (KNIGHTS OF THE GOLDEN CIRCLE, Order of American Knights, SONS OF LIBERTY) harassed Northern sympathizers, helped deserters and sabotaged Union supplies.

COPPOLA, Francis Ford (1939–), US film director best known for his epics *The Godfather* (1972) and *The Godfather, Part II* (1975), both of which won Academy Awards, and *Apocalypse Now* (1979). He is also a producer and distributor.

COPRA. See COCONUT PALM.

COPTIC CHURCH, chief Christian Church in Egypt, led by a patriarch in Cairo and 12 diocesan bishops. Services are held in Greek, Arabic and the otherwise dead language Coptic, based on ancient Egyptian. The Copts broke from the Roman Church when the Council of Chalcedon in 451 rejected their doctrine of MONOPHYSITISM. After the 7th-century Arab conquest many Copts became Muslims. The Ethiopian Church derives from the Coptic.

COPYRIGHT, exclusive right of an author, artist or publisher to publish or sell a work. Anyone reproducing a copyrighted work without permission of the copyright holder is liable to be sued for damages and ordered to stop publication or distribution. Books, plays, musical compositions, periodicals, motion pictures, photographs, designs and other works of art, maps and charts, speeches and lectures may be copyrighted in the US. This involves publishing the work with the statutory copyright notice (usually followed by the year and copyright owner's name). Copies and a registration fee must be lodged with the US Copyright Office.

The first US Copyright Act of 1790 protected only books, maps and charts, but later legislation included other works. Current US copyright law grants exclusive rights for 28 years, renewable for another 28 years, after which the work becomes public domain. International agreements protect rights of authors in the markets of other countries. The Buenos Aires Convention protects copyright among 17 Western countries including the US. The Universal Copyright Convention covers over 50 nations including the US. (See also BERNE CONVENTION.)

CORALS, small marine invertebrates of the class Anthozoa (phylum CNIDARIA) whose limestone skeletons form coral reefs and islands in warm seas. Most corals join together in colonies and secrete external LIMESTONE skeletons. Branches and successive layers are formed by budding and by the addition of new members produced sexually which swim freely before attaching themselves and secreting their skeletons. Older members of the colony gradually die, leaving their skeletons behind. Vegetation, such as coraline algae, cements the discarded skeletons, forming coral reefs, of which there are three types: *fringing reefs* along the shore, *barrier reefs* offshore and *atolls,* circular reefs enclosing a lagoon.

CORAL SNAKES, poisonous SNAKES with black, yellow or white and red rings. They feed on small reptiles and insects. Two species inhabit the southern US (*Micrurus julvius* and *M. euryxanthus*).

CORBETT, James John (1866–1933), US world heavyweight boxing champion, known as "Gentleman Jim." In 1892 he knocked out John L. Sullivan, to become the first man to win the world heavyweight championship under Marquess of Queensberry Rules. He lost his title to Bob Fitzsimmons in 1897. Later he took up a stage and film career.

CORDAY, Charlotte (1768–1793), French assassin of the French revolutionary Jean Paul MARAT. Objecting to Marat's persecution of the GIRONDINS, she stabbed him to death in his bath on July 13, 1793.

She was guillotined by order of the revolutionary tribunal.

CORDELIERS, political club of the French Revolution, active 1790–94, led by DANTON and MARAT, and later by HEBERT. It espoused extremist policies, helping to overthrow the GIRONDINS in 1793 and disintegrating in 1794 after its leaders were executed for trying to seize power by force.

CORDOBA, city in SW Spain, capital of Córdob province, noted for its Moorish cathedral. It makes machinery, pottery, woolens, gold and silver filigree and leather work. Probably founded by Carthaginians, it was Rome's first Spanish colony. Under Muslim rule (711–1236) it became capital of Moorish Spain and W Europe's chief intellectual center. Pop 235,600.

CORDOBÉS, El (Manuel Benítez) (1937–), one of the flashiest, most courageous matadors of all time. He executed passes while on his knees in front of the bull, and while hopping onto the beast's back.

CORE. See CONGRESS OF RACIAL EQUALITY.

CORELLI, Arcangelo (1653–1713), Italian composer and violinist, pioneer of the concerto grosso form which led to the CONCERTO. He wrote largely for violin, viola and cello—instruments then replacing the older VIOL family.

CORFU (Kerkira), fertile Greek island (229sq mi) in the Ionian Sea off NW Greece and SW Albania. Settled by Corinthians c700 BC, it was occupied (as Corcyra) by Rome 229 BC, and later by Byzantines, Sicilians, Venetians and the British, being ceded to Greece in 1864. It produces olives, fruit and grain.

CORGI, Welsh dog used for cattle droving, now known in two distinct breeds: Cardiganshire and Pembrokeshire, named for the counties in which they were developed. Both are long bodied and short legged with rather foxy heads. The Cardiganshire is somewhat heavier (26lb), has a long tail like a fox's brush, stands 12in high and may be any color except white. Pembrokeshires may be red, sable, fawn or black and tan, sometimes with white markings on legs, neck and breast, and have a short, docked tail, slightly longer coat and weigh 24lb. The British Royal Family has greatly popularized this breed, which is intelligent and good with children.

CORINTH, ancient Greek city on the Isthmus of Corinth. Established under Dorian rule (9th century BC), it founded Syracuse and other colonies in the 7th century BC and was the chief Greek merchant city until outstripped by Athens. Destroyed by Rome in 146 BC, it was rebuilt by Julius Caesar in 44 BC. Modern Corinth (Kòrinthos) was founded in 1858 after an earthquake destroyed the old city. Pop 20,773.

CORINTHIANS, Epistles to the, two letters, the 7th and 8th books of the New Testament, written by St. Paul c52–55 AD to the Christian church of Corinth, Greece. The first discusses the discipline and organization of the divided church and ways of restoring unity. The second largely defends Paul's work and authority as an apostle.

CORIOLANUS, Gaius Marcius (5th century BC), legendary Roman patrician, hero of Shakespeare's *Coriolanus*. He was named for Corioli, a town he allegedly won for Rome from the Volscians in 493 BC. Exiled for his anti-plebeian attitude, he led a Volscian attack on Rome until his mother and wife persuaded him to relent.

CORIOLIS EFFECT, a FORCE which, like a centrifugal force (SEE CENTRIPETAL FORCE), apparently acts on moving objects when observed in a frame of reference which is itself rotating. Because of the rotation of the observer, a freely moving object does not appear to move steadily in a straight line as usual, but rather as if, besides an outward centrifugal force, a "Coriolis force" acts on it, perpendicular to its motion, with a strength proportional to its MASS, its VELOCITY and the rate of rotation of the frame of reference. The effect, first described in 1835 by **Gaspard de Coriolis** (1792–1843), accounts for the familiar circulation of air flow around CYCLONES, and numerous other phenomena in METEOROLOGY, oceanography and BALLISTICS.

CORK, protective, waterproof layer of dead cells that have thick walls impregnated with suberin, a waxy material. Cork is found as the outer layer of stems and roots of older woody plants. The cork oak (*Quercus suber*) of S Europe and North Africa produces a profuse amount of cork, which is harvested commercially every 3 to 4 years. (See also CAMBIUM; OAK.)

CORMORANTS, or shags, birds of the family Phalocrocoracidae related to PELICANS. Cormorants have long necks and bills, are usually black, and dive for fish food in coastal regions and in the larger lakes and rivers of the world.

CORN, or **maize,** *Zea mays,* a grain crop native to the New World, but now cultivated throughout the world and second among the world's crop plants to WHEAT in terms of acreage planted. The major area of cultivation is in the Midwest cornbelt of the US. Five main types of corn have been

developed. Most of the US yield is dent corn (so-called from the indentation in the crown of each kernel) used for animal feed. Flint corn grows in colder climates, such as Canada. It has a hard kernel and is used for animal feed. Sweet corn, containing sugar, is a familiar vegetable. Popcorn kernels have hard outer coatings to prevent moisture escape. When heated the internal steam pressure causes them to burst. Flour corn, grown in Peru, Bolivia and Ecuador, has soft kernels and is used for flour and corn meal. The plants grow 0.9–4.5m (3–15ft) high and require a frost-free growing season of at least 100 days. Each plant develops 1–3 ears. The male flowers are in tassels on top of the stem. The female inflorescences consist of a number of rows of ovaries; each ovary is crowned by a silk that projects from the top of the "cob." Pollination is by the wind, the pollen falling on the silks. Corn is subject to numerous diseases. Fungi attack young plants and improperly stored ears and bacterial leaf blights cause wilting. RUST, SMUT and VIRUS DISEASES also attack the crop. The CORN BORER is the worst insect pest. Corn is ground for feeding to animals and for human consumption. It is rolled and flattened for breakfast cereals. Cornbread, hominy, mash, griddle cakes and confections are made from corn. Industrially corn is processed to make alcohol, syrup and oil and is used in manufacturing plastics. The stalk is sometimes used in paper and wall board manufacture. The term "corn" is also used locally to indicate the CEREAL CROPS most important in the district, e.g., in England corn refers to wheat and in some parts of Scotland to OATS. (See also AGRICULTURE; PLANT DISEASES.)

CORNEA, the transparent part of the outer EYE, through which VISION occurs and the iris may be seen; it is responsible for much of the focusing power of the eye. Made of specialized cells and connective tissue, it may be replaced after trauma or infection by a graft from a cadaver.

CORNEILLE, Pierre (1606–1684), French dramatist, creator of French classical verse tragedy. His masterpiece, *Le Cid* (1637), though controversial in its time, was a great popular success. His many other plays included *Horace* (1640), *Cinna* (1641) and *Polyeucte* (1643). His popularity faded with the rise of his younger rival, RACINE.

CORNELL, Ezra (1807–1874), US businessman, a pioneer in telegraphy. He created America's first (Baltimore–Washington) telegraph line (1844) with Samuel MORSE, and was founder and director of the Western Union Telegraph

Company (1855). His gifts helped create Cornell U., Ithaca, N.Y. (1868).

CORNELL, Katharine (1898–1974), US actress, noted for her major roles in serious dramas, often directed by her husband Guthrie McClintic. Her most famous part was Elizabeth Barrett Browning in *The Barretts of Wimpole Street* (1931).

CORNET, valved brass wind instrument somewhat like a trumpet. It has a mellow tone controlled by lip vibration at the cupped mouthpiece, a two-and-a-half octave range and is usually tuned to B flat. Cornets have traditionally been used in brass bands but rarely in symphony orchestras. They have however, formed an important place in JAZZ.

CORNISH. See CELTIC LANGUAGES.

CORN LAWS, various laws regulating English import and export of grain from the 14th century to 1849. After the Napoleonic Wars the corn price was raised to offset agricultural depression. But protests from the poor and from manufacturers objecting to agricultural subsidy helped COBDEN and BRIGHT, leaders of the Anti-Corn Law League (1839–46), to persuade Prime Minister Sir Robert PEEL to repeal the Corn Laws (1846 and 1849).

CORNPLANTER (c1732–1836), Seneca Indian chief, son of a Dutch trader and a Seneca mother. He led Indian parties for the British in the Revolutionary War but in 1784 ceded Indian lands to the US. Pa. gave him a pension and a land grant on the upper Allegheny R.

CORNS AND CALLUSES, localized thickenings of the horny layer of the SKIN, produced by continual pressure or friction. Calluses project above the skin and are rarely troublesome; corns are smaller, and are forced into the deep, sensitive layers of skin, causing pain or discomfort.

CORNSTALK (c1720–1777), Shawnee Indian chief. He fought sporadically against Virginian settlers until 1763, and in 1774 led a major rising, but made peace after a defeat at Point Pleasant. Later held hostage there, he was killed in reprisal for an Indian ambush.

CORNWALLIS, Charles Cornwallis, 1st Marquis of (1738–1805), British general, whose surrender to Washington at Yorktown (Oct. 19, 1781) ended the Revolutionary War. Earlier, he had defeated Nathanael Greene in the Carolinas. He later gave important service as governor-general of India 1786–93 and 1805, and as viceroy of Ireland 1798–1801.

CORONADO, Francisco Vázquez de (1510–1554), Spanish explorer of SW North America. While governor of Nuevo Galicia (in Mexico) in 1540 he subdued the so-called Seven Cities of CIBOLA. Fruitlessly seeking gold, his expedition probed what is now N.M., Ariz., Tex. and Kan., and discovered the Grand Canyon.

CORONAGRAPH, instrument to study the SUN's outer atmosphere, or corona. The corona is normally visible only during a total solar eclipse, because of the brightness of the solar disk and the scattering of sunlight in the earth's atmosphere. The coronagraph uses a TELESCOPE to form an image of the sun that is intercepted by a so-called occulting disk to produce an artificial eclipse. A second lens, protected from stray light by a series of baffles, relays the image to an eyepiece or to a photographic plate.

CORONARY THROMBOSIS, myocardial infarction, or heart attack, one of the commonest causes of serious illness and death in Western countries. The coronary ARTERIES, which supply the HEART with OXYGEN and nutrients, may become diseased with ARTERIOSCLEROSIS which reduces BLOOD flow. Significant narrowing may lead to superimposed THROMBOSIS which causes sudden complete obstruction, and results in death or damage to a substantial area of heart tissue. This may cause sudden death, usually due to abnormal heart rhythm which prevents effective pumping. Severe persistent pain in the center of the CHEST is common, and it may lead to SHOCK or LUNG congestion. Characteristic changes may be seen in the ELECTROCARDIOGRAPH following myocardial damage, and ENZYMES appear in blood from the damaged heart muscle. Treatment consists of rest, ANALGESICS and drugs to correct disordered rhythm or inadequate pumping; certain cases must be carefully observed for development of rhythm disturbance. Recovery may be complete and normal activities resumed. Predisposing factors, including OBESITY, SMOKING, high blood pressure, excess blood FATS (including CHOLESTEROL) and DIABETES must be recognized and treated.

CORPORATE STATE (corporatism), theory which holds that a community consists of functional or economic groups rather than of individuals. It has been part of authoritarian governmental ideology in Fascist Italy, Nazi Germany, Spain and Portugal. In theory each group (labor unions, business firms, etc.) names representatives to a governing body which takes its views into account. In fact corporate ideology was usually a slogan giving dictatorship a veneer of respectability. Thus in Italy corporations were created under state direction.

CORPORATION, group of persons forming a legal entity independent of the individuals owning or managing it. As a legal "person" it may hold property, sue and be sued. Corporations may be public or private. Municipal corporations such as school districts and cities perform some governmental functions. National public corporations carry out large-scale enterprises. Private corporations carry on a vast range of business and other activities. Advantages of a corporation are that it can deal in its own name without risking the personal finances of its officers or stockholders; it has a permanence lacking in a partnership or individually owned business; and it may raise large amounts of capital by sale of stocks.

Corporations are chartered by state governments and usually managed by officers named by a board of directors elected by the votes of a stockholders' majority. Thus anyone owning 51% of the stock controls a corporation. Business corporations grew out of the great trading companies of 16th- and 17th-century England. In the US, N.Y. passed the first general corporation law in 1811. Today US corporations have assets valued at more than $1 trillion and employ over half the nation's work force.

CORREGGIO (real name: Antonio Allegri; c1494–1534), Italian Renaissance painter who influenced the BAROQUE style. His works (including most of his Parma frescoes) are primarily devotional, and are noted for softness and use of CHIAROSCURO.

CORREGIDOR, fortified rocky island (2sq mi) in the Philippines, at the entrance to Manila Bay. Under US control from 1898, it fell to the Japanese in May 1942 when Gen. Jonathan WAINWRIGHT surrendered after four months of fierce fighting. Recaptured in 1945, it is now a WWII memorial.

CORRELATION, statistical, the interdependent variation of two or more VARIABLES. Positive correlation between two variables occurs when increase in the value of one implies increase in the value of the other, decrease similarly implying decrease. Negative correlation occurs when increase in the value of one implies decrease in the value of the other. (See also STATISTICS.)

CORRIGAN, Douglas "Wrong-Way" (1907– , US pilot and mechanic. In 1938, after flying in a single-engine craft to New York from California, he took off for a return trip and "mistakenly" flew in the wrong direction, landing in Ireland. When he returned to the US, he was greeted with a hero's welcome.

CORRUPT PRACTICES ACTS, US federal and state legislation designed to stop unethical electioneering. The major act of 1925 regulated US Congressional elections. It limited campaign expenditure for would-be senators and representatives, forbade contributions from national banks and corporations and obliged treasurers of political committees and candidates for office to report contributions and expenditures. (See also HATCH ACTS.)

CORSAIRS, Muslim pirates from the BARBARY STATES who preyed on Mediterranean and Atlantic shipping, especially Christian vessels. Corsairs flourished in the 16th–19th centuries, after BARBAROSSA had used Turkish aid to make Algiers and Tunis strong pirate bases.

CORSICA, Mediterranean island and French department N of Sardinia, off W Italy, occupying 3,352sq mi. It is largely mountainous, with much Mediterranean scrub and forest. Its products include olive oil, wine and citrus fruits. The capital is Ajaccio. Its rulers have included Carthaginians, Romans, Vandals, Goths, Saracens and (1347–1768) the Genoese, who sold it to France. There is strong nationalist feeling on the island. Napoleon Bonaparte was born here.

CORSO, Gregory (1930–), US poet of the BEAT GENERATION. His books include *Gasoline* (1958), *The Happy Birthday of Death* (1960), *Long Live Man* (1962), and *Elegiac Feelings American* (1970).

CORTES (Spanish: courts), representative assembly of Spain. It originated in the medieval kingdoms' assemblies of nobles, clergy and burghers. The Cortes instituted in 1942 by General FRANCO had little power. Portugal under the monarchy had legislative bodies called cortes.

CORTÉS, Hernán (1485–1547), Spanish explorer, conqueror of Mexico. In 1504 he settled in Hispaniola (Santa Domingo) and in 1511 joined the conquest of Cuba, becoming mayor of Santiago. Sent to explore Yucatán, in 1519 he marched on the AZTECS' capital Tenochtitlán, where MONTEZUMA greeted him as the white god QUETZALCOATL. Cortés took Montezuma prisoner, but the latter was killed in an uprising against the Spaniards. Cortés retreated, but returned in 1521 and conquered the capital, ending the Aztec Empire. He later explored Honduras and Lower California.

CORTEX, in plant STEMS and ROOTS, the layer of mostly unspecialized packing cells between the EPIDERMIS and the PHLOEM. It is used to store food and other substances including resins, oils and tannins; in stems it may contain CHLOROPLASTS; in roots it transports water and ions inwards. The term is used for the outer layer of the BRAIN, KIDNEYS or ADRENAL GLANDS.

CORTOT, Alfred Denis (1877–1962), French pianist, conductor and teacher, a leading interpreter of Romantic piano works. With CASALS and Jacques THIBAUD, he formed a famous trio in 1905. In 1918 he founded the École Normale de Musique in Paris.

CORVETTE, escort warship smaller than a frigate. In sailing days corvettes were flush-deck vessels with one row of guns.

COSBY, Bill (1937–   ), US comedian and actor who became the first black to star in a dramatic television series, "I Spy" (1966–68). His numerous film roles and recordings have garnered several Emmy and Grammy awards.

COSGRAVE, Liam (1920–   ), Irish political leader, prime minister of the Republic of Ireland 1973–77. A member of the Dáil from 1943, he was minister for commerce and industry 1948–54, minister for external affairs 1954–57 and leader of the Fine Gael Party 1965–1977.

COSGRAVE, William Thomas (1880–1965), Irish statesman, president of the Irish Free State 1922–32. He was in the 1916 EASTER RISING, served in the first republican ministry 1919–21 and, as president, brought stability to the Irish nation.

COSMAS AND DAMIAN, Saints (4th century), patron saints of physicians. By tradition, the brothers were physicians of Asia Minor who refused payment for services, and were martyred under Diocletian. Roman Catholic feast day: Sept. 27.

COSMIC RAYS, ELECTRONS and the nuclei of HYDROGEN and other ATOMS which isotropically bombard the earth's upper ATMOSPHERE at VELOCITIES close to that of light. These primary cosmic rays interact with molecules of the upper atmosphere to produce what are termed secondary cosmic rays, which are considerably less energetic and extremely shortlived: they are SUBATOMIC PARTICLES that change rapidly into other types of particles. Initially, secondary cosmic rays, which pass frequently and harmlessly through our bodies, were detected by use of the GEIGER COUNTER, though now it is more common to employ a SPARK CHAMBER. It is thought that cosmic rays are produced by SUPERNOVAS, though some may be of extragalactic origin.

COSMOGONY, the science of the origins of the UNIVERSE or of the SOLAR SYSTEM. (See also COSMOLOGY.)

COSMOLOGY, study of the universe as an orderly system, the existence of which is held to demonstrate the existence of an intelligent Supreme Being who presumably made it according to a plan. The classic formulation of this argument is found in Rom 1:19-20: "For what can be known about God ... namely, his eternal power and destiny, has been clearly perceived in the things that have been made."

COSSACKS, Slavic warrior peasants living on the Ukrainian steppe and famed for horsemanship. Self-governing under leaders like CHMIELNICKI, they resisted outside authority, but served the tsars as irregular cavalry, pioneered in Siberia and fought the Bolsheviks 1918–21. Collectivization broke up their communities in the 1930s, but Cossack cavalry served in WWII.

COSTA BRAVA, the rugged coast of Catalonia in NE Spain, a popular tourist area. Inland lies a rich farming and cork-growing region.

COSTAIN, Thomas Bertram (1885–1965), Canadian-born US author of historical novels. His works include *The Black Rose* (1945), *The Silver Chalice* (1952), and *The Last Plantagenets* (1962).

Official name: Republic of Costa Rica
Capital: San José
Area: 19,153sq mi
Population: 2,125,600
Languages: Spanish
Religions: Roman Catholic
Monetary Unit(s): 1 Costa Rican colon = 100 céntimos

COSTA RICA, small republic in S Central America, bordered by Nicaragua on the N and Panama on the S.
Land. The country's topography varies from wet tropical plains on the coast to the temperate central plateau at about 3000ft, which is surrounded by two chains of volcanic mountains rising to over 12,000ft. A rainy season lasts from May to November.
People. The population is largely of Spanish descent; there are fewer mestizos in Costa

Rica than in other Latin American countries. A small minority of Negroes lives on the Caribbean coast. About 60% of the people live in rural areas, largely on small farms.

Economy. Coffee is Costa Rica's most important cash crop, monopolizing 95% of the arable land in the central plateau; bananas are grown in coastal areas. Agricultural exports bring in most of the country's foreign exchange. A lack of mineral resources has created an emphasis on light industry, producing for the home market, (food processing, textiles, fertilizers, plastic goods, chemicals, pharmaceuticals), but large sulfur deposits are now being exploited.

History. Columbus discovered Costa Rica in 1502, but because of its lack of resources the region escaped the ravages of the Conquistadors. Since few Indians survived, the white farmers worked their own land, establishing a significant middle class and avoiding the semifeudal peonage system so destructive in other South American countries. In 1821 Costa Rica declared independence from Spain, joining first the Mexican Empire and then the Central American Federation, which dissolved into anarchy in 1838. A power struggle followed, complicated by the invasion of the American adventurer William WALKER, defeated in 1857. Despite internal strife in 1919 and 1948, the country's history has been peaceful and its politics democratic. The welfare system, dating from 1924, is one of the most advanced in the hemisphere. The country has had traditionally good relations with the US.

COSTELLO, Frank (1891–1973), Italianborn US racketeer. A rumrunner during Prohibition, he became "prime minister" of the underworld during the 1930s. He was one of the principal targets of the US Senate's 1951 investigation of organized crime.

CÔTE D'AZUR, originally the French Mediterranean coast between Cannes and Menton, now loosely used for the French Riviera, especially the E end. An important tourist area, it is also a fruit-growing region and has a perfume industry.

COTONOU, chief port and largest business center of Benin. It became a French port in 1851. Pop 178,000.

COTOPAXI, the highest active volcano in the world, 19,347ft high. It is situated in the Andes in Ecuador, and last erupted in 1942.

COTSWOLDS, ridge of limestone hills in Gloucestershire, England, about 50mi long and rising to 1000ft. An important medieval wool-producing area, the hills are now a tourist attraction for their scenery and picturesque villages.

COTTON, a subtropical plant of the genus *Gossypium*, grown for the soft white fibers attached to its seed, which can be woven into cloth. The seeds are planted in the early spring and the plants bloom after four months. The white flowers redden and fall in a few days, leaving the seed pods, which are fully grown in another month or so. These pods then burst, showing the white lint, which is picked either by hand or mechanically. Each fiber is a single cell, with numerous twists along its length, which give it excellent spinning characteristics.

A number of species and their varieties are grown. Cultivated varieties of *Gossypium barbodense* produce fibers 36–64mm (1.4–2.5in) long, *G. hirsutum* (the American upland cotton) fibers 21–32mm (0.8–1.3in) and the Asiatic species *G. herbaceum* and *G. arboreum* fibers 9–19mm (0.4–0.8in). Cotton is produced in more than 60 countries; total world production exceeds 55 million bales annually, each bale weighing 222.6kg (490lb).

Cotton is prone to many pests and diseases, which cause enormous damage to the crop (averaging nearly 300 million dollars in the US every year). The main insect pests are the BOLL WEEVIL in the US and the PINK BOLL WORM in India and Egypt. Destructive fungus diseases that attack the plant include fusarium and verticillium wilt and Texas root rot. Boll rots can cause severe damage to the crop. Mechanization of the cotton processing industry was one of the first stages of the Industrial Revolution. It is still an important industry, although consumption of cotton has not risen since the development of man-made textiles. However, 80% of the yarn from spinning mills is still made into cloth, the remainder being used in industry. The seed is now used for oils and cattle food, while small fibers are made into cellulose. (See also COTTON GIN; PLANT DISEASES.)

COTTON, John (1584–1652), powerful Puritan minister of Boston, Mass., noted for his didactic writings. Born in England, Cotton fled to the colonies in 1632 to avoid religious persecution. He was later to become involved in the banishment of Ann HUTCHINSON and Roger WILLIAMS for their heretical views.

COTTON GIN, device for separating cotton fibers from the seeds, invented by Eli WHITNEY (1793), which revolutionized the cotton industry in the US South. Whitney's original gin comprised a rotating drum on which were mounted wire spikes that projected through narrow slits in a wire grid. The spikes drew the fibers through these slits, leaving behind the seeds, which are broader. A revolving brush removed the fibers from the drum. In 1794, Hodgen Holmes replaced the wire spikes by a circular SAW; and modern cotton gins still work on this principle.

COTTONMOUTH. See MOCCASIN.

COUGAR. See PUMA.

COUGH, sudden explosive release of air from the LUNGS, which clears respiratory passages of obstruction and excess MUCUS or PUS; it occurs both as a REFLEX and on volition. Air flow may reach high velocity and potentially infectious particles spread a great distance if the mouth is uncovered. Persistent cough always implies disease.

COUGHLIN, Charles Edward (1891–1979), Roman Catholic priest who became a national figure in the US in the 1930s with his radio broadcasts, attacking first the financial leaders he believed to be responsible for the Depression, and later F. D. ROOSEVELT. He formed the Union Party in 1936 in opposition to Roosevelt; its presidential candidate received 2% of the popular vote. In 1942 his activities were curbed by the Church, worried by his apparent Nazi sympathies.

COUNCIL OF ECONOMIC ADVISERS, three-member commission established in the US in 1946 to help prevent postwar depressions. It advises the president on economic and monetary problems.

COUNTERCULTURE, term that gained currency in the 1960s to refer to anti-establishment and antiwar movements and to those who were part of them. The counterculture disdained bourgeois, capitalist values, war (but not necessarily revolution), energy-wasteful technology and competitiveness. Participants favored "doing your own thing," civil disobedience in New Left causes, marijuana, rock music and natural foods and materials. The counterculture was celebrated in the best-selling *The Greening of America* (1970) by Charles Reich.

COUNTERFEITING, the forging of money in an attempt to pass it off as genuine. Since this threatens the monetary basis of any economy it is a serious offense, punishable by death in the USSR and China. As it requires a high degree of technical skill it is seldom successful as organized crime; successful counterfeiters are more often eccentric individuals rather than habitual criminals.

COUNTERPOINT, in music, a term for the art of combining two or more different melodic lines simultaneously in a composition. The term derives from latin *punctus contra punctum,* meaning "note against note." Originating in the *organum* style of the 10th century, it reached its zenith in BAROQUE music, especially that of J. S. BACH. It remains a widely used form; a mastery of counterpoint is considered essential for a composer.

COUNTER-REFORMATION, reform movement in the Roman Catholic Church during the 16th and 17th centuries, springing as much from internal demands for reform as from reaction to the Protestant REFORMATION. Many organizations, such as the Oratory of Divine Love, the CAPUCHINS and the URSULINES, were founded in an attempt to infuse more spiritual life into the Church. Most notable among these were the JESUITS, founded in 1534, whose emphasis on action and education did much to slow the spread of Protestantism. The reform movement within the Church culminated in the Council of TRENT, convened by Pope Paul III in 1545. Its reaffirmation of doctrine and its disciplinary reforms did much to improve the standing of the Church. The establishment of the congregation of the INQUISITION in Rome by Paul III helped check Protestant influence; there was also a revival of missionary work. A revival in the arts, which fostered BERNINI and PALESTRINA among others, accompanied the movement.

COUNTRY AND WESTERN MUSIC, a broad category of pop music that includes, at one end of its spectrum, country music derived from the traditional BLUEGRASS folk music of the SE US and, at the other, Western music (i.e., cowboy songs updated with swing and rock influences). The popularity of Country and Western rose rapidly in the 1960s and 1970s. Among its stars have been Loretta LYNN and Johnny CASH. The national center of Country and Western is the Grand Ole Opry theater in Nashville, Tenn.

COUPERIN, François (1668–1733), French composer, most celebrated member of an illustrious musical family. He wrote supremely for the harpsichord, which he taught to the French royal family. His authoritative treatise, *The Art of Harpsichord Playing* (1716), influenced J. S. BACH.

COURBET, Gustave (1819–1877), French painter noted for his development of the "Realist" style in paintings such as *The Burial at Ornans* (1849) and *The Studio* (1855). Influenced by the Dutch genre painters of the 17th century, he emphasized everyday life and landscape in his work, as a reaction to the Classical and Romantic schools.

COUREURS DE BOIS, illicit traders in 17th- and 18th-century French Canada, largely responsible for the corruption of the Indian population. In defiance of government regulations they ruthlessly exploited the fur trade, selling the Indians cheap alcohol at exorbitant rates.

COURRÈGES, André (1923–), French fashion designer. The miniskirt and the pastel, little-girl look he introduced in his 1964 collection created a major fashion trend. Annoyed with imitators of his work, he began to offer a ready-made line in 1967 along with his custom-made designs.

COURT-MARTIAL, tribunal for the trial of members of the armed forces for offenses under military (and in some cases civil) law. Under the US Uniform Code of Military Justice there are three types—*summary*, for minor offenses; *special*, for more serious offenses; and *general*, which may try any offense under the Uniform Code and may impose the maximum penalties prescribed, including death.

COURT OF CLAIMS, special federal court established in 1855 to hear all claims founded on any act of Congress, any regulation of any executive department, any contract with the US Government, and any torts or wrongs committed by an officer of the US.

COURTS, official assemblies for the administration of justice. A typical US court will consist of a judge, jury (when required), attorneys representing both parties to the dispute, a bailiff or marshal to carry out court orders and keep order, and a clerk to record the proceedings.

Though many nations have developed various types of judicial assembly, the court in Western countries is descended from the king's court, in which he dispensed justice. Since his justices were theoretically deputizing for him, their assemblies were still *curiae regis*—the king's courts. Unlike their European counterparts, the English courts did not base themselves upon Roman law but developed the system of legal interpretation known as the COMMON LAW, and this, with its accompanying judicial system, became one of Britain's most important and lasting exports to her colonies, including the US and Canada.

The US has two related court systems: federal and state. The federal court system covers cases involving the Constitution, the nation, foreign nationals, federal laws, interstate disputes and ships at sea. Federal courts comprise a SUPREME COURT, intermediate courts of appeals, and many district courts, as well as special courts such as the Tax Court, Court of Claims and the Court of Customs and Patent Appeals. In an individual state, the state court system deals with that state's affairs in both civil and criminal matters. Inferior (lower) state courts include magistrates' courts in urban areas, courts run by justices of the peace in rural areas, and juvenile and family courts, traffic courts, probate courts, rent courts and small-claims courts. Above these stand the county and municipal courts and other superior courts, and above these there are often appellate courts reviewing lower court decisions. The highest court in most states is called the state supreme court.

The US court system is a carefully designed judicial apparatus, but by the 1970s it was so overstrained that some defendants were waiting years for a trial. Expansion and procedural streamlining may improve the position.

Like the US, Canada has two related court systems: federal and provincial. The federal system features the Supreme Court (the highest court of appeal) and Exchequer Court (dealing largely with cases involving the national government). The provincial courts handle cases of federal and provincial law.

The INTERNATIONAL COURT OF JUSTICE meets at the Hague, in the Netherlands, to deal with cases under INTERNATIONAL LAW. Its 15 judges, each from a different country, are elected for nine-year terms by the UN Security Council.

COUSTEAU, Jacques-Yves (1910–), French naval officer and oceanologist who pioneered underwater exploration, coinventor of the aqualung and an underwater television system. His popular cinema and television films have made him world-famous.

COUSY, Bob (1928–), US basketball player, one of the greatest ball handlers in the game's history. He helped the Boston Celtics win six NBA titles between 1957 and his retirement in 1963. He used his small size to become a playmaker, and led the NBA in assists for eight seasons.

COVENANTERS, 16th- and 17th-century Scottish Presbyterians pledged by covenants to defend their religion against Anglican influences. They were suppressed, both by Cromwell and the Stuart kings. Their savage persecution after the Restoration was known as the "killing time".

COVERDALE, Miles (1488–1569), English Protestant reformer, royal chaplain to Edward VI and later bishop of Exeter. While studying in Europe, he produced in

1535 the first complete printed English translation of the Bible, revising large portions of it for inclusion in the Great Bible he prepared for Thomas Cromwell in 1539–40.

COWARD, Sir Noel (Pierce) (1899–1973), English actor, playwright and composer. He is famous for his witty comedies of manners, such as *Private Lives* (1930) and *Blithe Spirit* (1941), revues, musicals and serious plays such as *The Vortex* (1924). Their prevailing cynicism is offset by patriotic works such as the film *In Which We Serve* (1942).

COWBIRDS, birds of the family Icteridae, relatives of the grackles, so named because they follow cattle and feed on the insects they stir up. Two species live in the US but most are South American. Most lay eggs in the nests of other birds, which hatch and raise the cowbird young.

COWELL, Henry Dixon (1897–1965), US experimental composer. Like John CAGE, he sought to explore new sonorities in his music, as with "tone clusters," produced on the piano by striking groups of keys with the forearm.

COWLEY, Malcolm (1898–   ), US editor, poet, literary historian and critic, best known for *Exile's Return* (1934, 1951), a lively, partly autobiographical account of literary life in the 1920s. He wrote important critiques of the works of William FAULKNER, Ernest HEMINGWAY and F. Scott FITZGERALD.

COWPER, William (1731–1800), English poet. His work anticipates Romanticism in its lyrical delight in nature, expressed directly and simply. His best-known serious poem is *The Task* (1785). He also wrote many hymns, but is remembered for his comic ballad *John Gilpin* (1783).

COWPOX, a disease of cattle, caused by a virus related to the smallpox virus. It was by noting the IMMUNITY to SMALLPOX conferred on humans who contracted cowpox by milking infected cattle that JENNER popularized VACCINATION against smallpox.

COX, James Middleton (1870–1957), US politician and journalist who championed liberal reform. He became nationally known as a newspaper publisher, Democratic congressman (1909–13) and governor of Ohio (1913–15; 1917–21). In 1920 he ran for president on the Democratic ticket but lost heavily to Warren G. Harding.

COXEY, Jacob Sechler (1854–1951), US self-made businessman who, with revivalist Carl Browne, led a "living petition" of 500 unemployed to Washington from Massillon, Ohio, in 1894, in support of his plan for national reconstruction. The march of "Coxey's Army," or the "Commonweal of Christ," ended when Coxey was jailed for demonstrating on the Capitol lawn.

COYOTE, *Canis latrans,* a wild dog that looks like a small wolf and has a characteristic howl. It has spread from the plains of NW America to the Atlantic coast. Coyotes hunt small mammals or live as urban scavengers, some interbreeding with dogs.

COZZENS, James Gould (1903–1978), US novelist. His books, such as *By Love Possessed* (1957) and *Ask Me Tomorrow* (1940), deal with moral conflicts of the professional classes, seen by Cozzens as the custodians of social stability. *Guard of Honor* (1948) won him a Pulitzer Prize.

CRAB NEBULA (M1), a bright NEBULA in the constellation TAURUS, the remnants of the SUPERNOVA of 1054. It is 1,223pc from the earth and is associated with a PULSAR.

CRABS, crustaceans with 10 pairs of legs, the first pair usually modified as pincers. They are closely related to LOBSTERS and SHRIMPS and start life as small, swimming, lobster-like larvae that repeatedly molt before settling on the bottom and becoming adult crabs. The adults have rounded protective shells covering head and thorax, the abdomen curling under the body to form a series of plates. Most of the 4,500 species live in the sea or brackish water, eating small animals and carrion. They range in size from the tiny Pea crabs that live in oyster shells to the Giant crab of the Pacific, a Spider crab with a leg span of up to 3.8m (12.5ft).

CRAIG, Edward Gordon (1872–1966), English stage director and designer who helped to revolutionize theater production. He stressed the director's unifying role and abandoned realism in favor of a stark abstract style relying for its effects on lighting and mass.

CRAMP, the painful contraction of muscle—often in the legs. The cause is usually unknown. It may be brought on by exercise or lack of SALT; it also occurs in muscles with inadequate BLOOD supply. Relief is by forcibly stretching the muscle or by massage.

CRANACH, Lucas the Elder (1472–1553), major German Renaissance painter and engraver. His early paintings are mainly on biblical themes and set in romantic landscapes; later mythological treatments introduced his characteristic sinuous female nudes. A great portraitist, especially for the Saxon court, he produced many propagandist woodcuts for his friend Martin Luther. **Lucas Cranach the Younger** (1515–1586), who took over his father's workshop, also enjoyed great popularity.

CRANE, (Harold) Hart (1899–1932), a major US poet, influenced by Edgar Allen POE and Walt WHITMAN. His masterpiece was *The Bridge* (1930), an attempted epic of the modern American experience using the Brooklyn Bridge as its central image. Beset by personal problems, he drowned himself on a return voyage from Mexico.

CRANE, Stephen (1871–1900), US novelist, short story writer and poet, best known for *The Red Badge of Courage* (1895), a sensitive study of a young man's development towards manhood during the Civil War. *Maggie: A Girl of the Streets* (1893) frighteningly describes a girl's poverty, seduction and suicide in New York's slums. Crane died of tuberculosis at 28.

CRANES, large birds of the family Gruidae, with long necks and legs, both of which project in flight. Most are mainly white or gray and some have partly naked heads. Their coiled windpipe helps to produce a trumpeting call. Cranes eat small animals and grasses in marshes and on plains, and perform graceful leaping courtship dances. Most of the 14 species spread around the world are now rare. The sandhill crane and the nearly extinct whooping crane are found in North America.

CRANMER, Thomas (1489–1556), first Protestant archbishop of Canterbury and leader of the English Reformation. He favored the ascendancy of state over church and obtained royal favor by helping Henry VIII to divorce his second, third, fourth and fifth wives. As counselor to Edward VI, Cranmer compiled the first BOOK OF COMMON PRAYER (1549), his most enduring monument. Under the Roman Catholic regime of Mary Tudor he was stripped of office and burned at the stake as a heretic.

CRAPS, dice game invented by black Americans in New Orleans c1800. Almost exclusively a gambling game, the name comes from "crabs," the lowest scoring throw. Two dice are employed. The player "shooting" the dice usually determines the size of the bet. If he lands a total of 7 or 11 on his first throw, he wins all of the stakes; if he throws 2, 3, or 12, it is called a "crap," and he loses his money. Any other number thrown is called a point. The player continues shooting until he can duplicate this point. Should he succeed, he wins all the bets. If, however, he shoots 7 before he is able to do so, he loses, and the dice pass to another player.

CRASHAW, Richard (c1613–1649), Eng-

lish poet, whose poetry combined religious fervor with sensuous imagery. At first a High Church Anglican, he later became a Roman Catholic convert, and died as canon of Santa Casa Cathedral at Loreto. His *Carmen Deo Nostra* (1652) contains many of his best poems.

CRATER LAKE NATIONAL PARK, a 250sq mi area centered on Crater Lake in the Cascade Mts in SW Ore., established as a park in 1902. The crater, which is volcanic, measures 6mi across and the lake within it, noted for its vivid blue color, reaches a depth of 1,932ft.

CRAWFORD, Joan (1908–1977), US film actress noted for her roles as self-made, tough-minded women. Her best-known movies were *Rain* (1932), *The Women*, (1939), *A Woman's Face* (1941) and *Mildred Pierce* (1945), for which she won an Academy Award.

CRAWFORD, Thomas (1813–1857), US neoclassical sculptor who worked mainly in Rome. His monumental figure *Armed Freedom*, cast posthumously, surmounts the dome of the capitol in Washington, D.C.

CRAWFORD, William Harris (1772–1834), US lawyer and senator, one of four candidates in the indecisive 1824 presidential election after which the House of Representatives chose John Quincy Adams for the presidency. Crawford was secretary of war 1815–16 and secretary of the treasury 1816–25.

CRAZY HORSE (c1840–1877), chief of the Oglala Sioux Indians and the inspiration behind Indian resistance to the white man's invasion of the N Great Plains. He led the SIOUX and CHEYENNE victory over Gen. George CROOK at Rosebud R (June 17, 1876) and eight days later led the Sioux massacre of Gen. CUSTER's forces at Little Bighorn. Arrested on his surrender in 1877, he was killed some months later while attempting to escape.

CREATIONISM, theory held by fundamentalist Christians that the Earth and living beings were created as described in Genesis rather than through a process of evolution, such as is accepted in modern geology and biology. Creationists have survived numerous setbacks, including the Scopes trial in 1925, the push in the 1960s to improve science education, and a Supreme Court ruling in 1975 striking down a Tenn. law requiring discussion of Genesis in schools. Espousing supposedly nonreligious "scientific creationism," creationists of the 1970s won back lost ground, pressuring textbook publishers and science teachers nationwide into equivocating with regard to the validity of scientific knowledge. President Ronald Reagan himself supported the teaching of both creationism and evolutionary theory in public schools.

CREATION MYTHS, accounts of the creation of the earth, or of man's known world, and of man himself. They often form a basis for religious doctrine and as such have determined the structure of particular societies. Supreme deity myths are typified by the biblical account in GENESIS. Emergence myths, such as that of the Navajo Indians, are analogous to gestation and birth, seeing creation as a gradual unfolding of forces within the earth. Hindu and other Asian cultures represent the moment of creation in terms of the breaking of an egg. World-parent myths generally deal in personifications of the earth (mother) and the sky (father) and include the Babylonian *Enuma Elish* myth. Diving myths posit a watery chaos with mud as the stuff of creation. In accounts by the Crow Indians a duck dives for the mud; a Romanian version has the devil in the role of diver. Antagonism between newly-emergent life forms is a common mythological feature and serves to account for life's subsequent imperfections.

CRÉCY, Battle of (Aug. 26, 1346), battle in the HUNDRED YEARS' WAR near Crécy-en-Ponthieu in N France. Edward III of England's smaller army, with its high percentage of longbowmen, devastated Philip VI's French forces (mainly mounted knights) after some of them launched a premature attack.

CRÉDIT MOBILIER OF AMERICA, company involved in the construction of the Union Pacific railroad (1865–69). The subject of a financial scandal involving Congressman Oakes AMES, Crédit Mobilier came to symbolize corruption in US business during and after the RECONSTRUCTION period.

CREDIT UNION, a cooperative bank formed under government charter generally by groups of employees or members of a particular association or community. Members buy shares in the bank in return for which they can borrow at interest rates lower than those of commercial banks.

CREED, formal, authorized statement of religious belief, found in all major world religions, used in worship and to define and maintain doctrine. The Christian creeds grew out of early formulas of belief used in BAPTISM, and became standards of orthodoxy. The three "ecumenical creeds," accepted by virtually all WESTERN CHURCHES, the APOSTLES', NICENE and ATHANASIAN CREEDS, all express belief in God the Father, Son and Holy Spirit, the first two creeds having thus three sections. The Protestant Confessions of the 16th and 17th centuries, including the AUGSBURG CONFESSION, the THIRTY-NINE ARTICLES and the WESTMINSTER CONFESSION, are longer creeds defining controverted points, as is the Roman Catholic *Decrees and Canons* of the Council of TRENT.

CREE INDIANS, North American Indian tribe of the ALGONQUIAN group. Originally they were all woodland Indians, hunting and trapping in the forest of S Manitoba, Canada, but in time part of the tribe moved onto the plains of Alberta, Canada, and into the N US, where they hunted buffalo.

CREEK INDIANS, confederacy of North American Indian tribes of the MUSKOGEAN linguistic family. An agricultural people, they lived in the SE US, occupying a large area including most of present day Ala. and Ga. Under chief TECUMSEH they resisted white domination in the Creek War (1813–14), but were routed at the Battle of HORSESHOE BEND and as a result lost most of their lands. By 1840 they had been moved to the INDIAN TERRITORY as one of the FIVE CIVILIZED TRIBES.

CREOLE, term first used in the 16th century to describe people of Spanish parentage born in the West Indies. It is now far less specific, serving to describe the descendants of Spanish, Portuguese and French settlers in the West Indies, Latin America and parts of the US—where in La., for example, the term applies to French-speaking people of either French or Spanish descent. French- and Spanish-based patois are known as Creole languages. (See PIDGIN.)

CRESTON, Paul (1906–), US composer. Largely self-taught, he employed traditional techniques in most of his works, which include symphonies and compositions for orchestra and piano and for orchestra and chorus.

CRETE, mountainous but fertile Greek island in the E Mediterranean at the southern end of the Aegean. The largest of the Greek islands, it covers some 3,189sq mi. Agriculture is the mainstay, with grapes, oranges and olives the only significant cash crops. The island is of great historical interest, being the home of the ancient MINOAN CIVILIZATION, which had KNOSSOS, with its famous palace, as its leading city. The present-day capital is Canea.

CRETINISM, congenital disease caused by lack of THYROID HORMONE in late fetal life and early infancy, which interferes with normal development, including that of the

BRAIN. It may be due to congenital inability to secrete the hormone or, in certain areas of the world, to lack of dietary IODINE (which is needed for hormone formation). The typical appearance, with coarse SKIN, puffy face, large tongue and slow responses, usually enables early diagnosis. It is crucial that replacement therapy with thyroid hormone should be started as early as possible to minimize or prevent the mental retardation that occurs if diagnosis is delayed.

CRÈVECOEUR, Michel-Guillaume Jean de (1735–1813), French-born writer and settler in America—where he was known as J. Hector St. John. His popular *Letters from an American Farmer* (1782) is an important documentary source on the period. He was French consul in New York 1783–90.

CREW, in sports. See ROWING.

CRIBBAGE, card game essentially for two people, played with the standard deck and a special board with pegs for marking the score. Picture cards are valued at 10 points and all others at their face value. Each player discards two of his six cards, to create a spare hand, or crib, which goes to the dealer. The object is to make the pool of cards in play add up to no more than 31.

CRICHTON, (J.) Michael (1942–   ), US writer and physician best known for his popular "science-nonfiction" novel and film *The Andromeda Strain* (1969) about scientists struggling to destroy a virulent organism from outer space. Among his other works are *The Terminal Man* (1972) and *The Great Train Robbery* (1975).

CRICK, Francis Harry Compton (1916–   ), English biochemist who, with J. D. WATSON, proposed the double-helix model of DNA. For this, one of the most spectacular advances in 20th-century science, they shared the 1962 Nobel Prize for Physiology or Medicine with M. H. F. WILKINS, who had provided them with the X-ray data on which they had based their proposal. Crick's subsequent work has been concerned with deciphering the functions of the individual CODONS in the genetic code.

CRICKET, field game that originated in England before 1700 and is now most popular in Commonwealth countries. Basically it is played between two teams of eleven. A pair of batsmen from one side defend two wickets, one at each end of a 22yd pitch. The other team act as fielders. A hard ball is "bowled" (thrown overhand with a straight arm) at the defended wicket from the other; the batsman tries to hit out into the field to give himself time to score by running between wickets. If the ball strikes his wicket either directly or while he is running, or if it is caught off his bat, he is out. When all the batsmen are out the teams exchange functions and the "innings" ends; a game consists of not more than two innings per team. The side with most runs wins and the game is drawn if the innings cannot be completed.

CRICKETS, a large group of orthopterous INSECTS. Male ground-dwelling crickets make a chirping sound (stridulation) by rapidly rubbing together the front edge of their wing covers. Crickets have long antennae. Most species have wings, and most have hind legs developed for jumping. An exception is the mole cricket, whose hind legs are undeveloped, but whose fore legs are adapted for burrowing.

CRIME, a violation of criminal law. A distinction is made between *violent crimes*, which are directed against the person and comprise acts of murder, aggravated assault, forcible rape, and robbery; and *property crimes*, which encompass burglary, larceny-theft (including automobile theft), and arson. According to the Federal Bureau of Investigation's Uniform Crime Reports for 1980, the number of reported crimes in the US totaled 13,295,399 offenses. This represented an increase of 9% over 1979 and of 55% since 1971.

Because national statistics on crime have been kept only since 1930, it is not possible to assess to what degree the US has been a lawless society since the first days of western settlement. Outlaw bands such as that of Jesse JAMES proliferated after the Civil War. Organized crime is a legacy of the PROHIBITION era of the 1920s when Al CAPONE and other gangland bootleggers flourished. Bank robbers like John DILLINGER made headlines during the 1930s, but it was not until the post-WWII period that the MAFIA and other bastions of organized crime became deeply entrenched in American society. The steep rise in crime in recent years is commonly associated with high levels of unemployment and inflation and, especially in Europe, with political radicalism. It is the accelerating increase in violent crimes, particularly in large cities, that has most concerned criminologists and sociologists. Most violent crimes are committed in city slum and ghetto areas, where overcrowding, poor housing, a low level of education, and high unemployment breed both criminals and victims. During the 1970s, however, the US violent CRIME RATE increased substantially in the suburbs and rural areas as well. (See also CRIMINAL LAW; FEDERAL BUREAU OF INVESTIGATION; POLICE; PRISONS.)

CRIMEA, peninsula 10,425sq mi in area on

the N side of the Black Sea, an *oblast* (province) of the Ukrainian Republic, USSR; it is connected to the Ukrainian mainland by the Perekop Isthmus. Its population today is about 70% Russian and 20% Ukrainian, the indigenous Tatars having been absorbed or exiled.

Around 60% of the population lives in the major urban areas, which include the capital, Simferopol, Kerch, Sevastopol, Balaklava and Yalta. The Crimea is largely agricultural, but has important fisheries and mines, and the S is a popular resort area. The area belonged to the Ottoman Empire until 1783, when Catherine the Great annexed it to Russia. It was the scene of major battles in the CRIMEAN WAR, Russian Revolution and WWII.

CRIMEAN WAR (1853–56), war between Russia and an alliance of Britain, France, Turkey and later Sardinia. A chief cause was Russia's desire to expand to Constantinople and gain access to Mediterranean ports, justified by a claim to be protector of Christians in the Ottoman Empire. In July 1853, the Russians occupied the Turkish provinces of Moldavia and Walachia. In Oct., Turkey declared war on Russia. In March 1854, Britain and France allied with Turkey, out of concern at the general Russian threat to their interests elsewhere. On Oct. 17, the Allies began the siege and bombardment of Sevastopol. Major battles, chaotic and with heavy losses on both sides, followed at Balaklava (Oct. 25) and Inkerman (Nov. 5). The siege of Sevastopol ended in Sept. 1855 with Allied victory. After continued fighting, an armistice was concluded in Feb. 1856 and the Treaty of PARIS signed in March. It was the first conflict reported by war correspondents and photographers.

CRIMINAL LAW, defines those acts considered to be offenses against the state as distinct from civil wrongs committed against an individual. It also regulates legal procedures for the apprehension and trial of suspected offenders and limits the penalties of those convicted.

Modern US criminal law derives from the English common law system, with which it concurs on the broad definition of crime. An act cannot be a crime unless it contravenes a rule of law, customary or statutory, in two elements. The *actus reus* is the act (or failure to act) itself; it must be voluntary, but it is worth noting that self-induced incapacity (as through drugs or alcohol) is held to be reckless of consequences and is therefore voluntary. The *mens rea* requires intention to commit the act, rather than mere mistake. Recklessness

or carelessness is usually held to be sufficient *mens rea,* however.

The US system relies less on judicial precedent than its British ancestor. In several states, for example, no person may be tried for an offense not specified by statute in that state, although in other states offenses founded only on precedent, such as breach of the peace and conspiracy, still exist. In general, the flexible common law is not well adapted to the federal system of the US because it leads to inconsistencies between states. Since the 1800s La., Wis., Ill., Minn., N.M., N.Y. and Mich. have adopted penal codes on the lines of the CODE NAPOLÉON and other European codes, and many other states are studying them, especially the drafts produced by the American Law Institute in 1962 and the National Commission on Reform of Federal Criminal Laws in 1970.

CRITTENDEN COMPROMISE, measure sponsored by Senator John J. CRITTENDEN in Dec. 1860 in an attempt to avert the Civil War. It proposed the abolition of slavery N of 36°30′, and the protection of slavery S of that line. The domestic slave trade was to be free of all restriction; there was also to be a constitutional amendment preventing Congress from interfering with slave states. The compromise failed in committee and Crittenden won no support for a national referendum.

CRIVELLI, Carlo (c1430–1495), Italian painter. A Venetian, he worked in exile in the March of Ancona. In his intensely religious paintings, outlines are sharp and ornamentation rich and varied, though his figures are somewhat flat and stylized.

CROATIA, a constituent republic of Yugoslavia, 21,829sq mi in area. Long a province of Austria-Hungary, Croatia became part of Yugoslavia after WWI. Political and religious differences led to friction between the Croats and Serbs, and Croatia became autonomous as an Axis satellite during WWII. In 1946, when Yugoslavia adopted a federal constitution, Croatia became one of the constituent republics. Croatian agitation for greater autonomy led to political crises and terrorist activity in 1971–74.

CROCE, Benedetto (1866–1952), major Italian philosopher, historian and literary critic. Influenced by HEGEL and VICO, he was a leading exponent of Neo-Idealist philosophy and founder of the review *La Critica* in 1903. He was an active critic of fascism before and during WWII, and in 1943 refounded the Italian Liberal Party, becoming its president; he held various government posts after 1944.

CROCHET, method of making fabrics, garments, lace-like dress trimmings and rugs from yarn or, more rarely, straw, by a series of looped chain stitches made with a special hook. Silk, cotton, wool, or artificial-fiber yarn may be used. Many primitive cultures, including the American Indians, used some form of crochet work; it became popular in the modern US when reintroduced by Irish immigrants.

CROCKETT, Davy (David) (1786–1836), US frontiersman, politician and folk hero. A farmer and Tenn. politician, he was elected to Congress as a Democrat 1827–31, but in 1833 was returned as a Whig. The Whigs built him up as a "backwoods" alternative to Andrew Jackson, and he became famous for his shrewd and humorous speeches, and his memoirs of frontier life. He lost his seat in 1835, and led a Tenn. volunteer force to the ALAMO, where he was killed.

CROCODILE, a family (Crocodylidae) of aquatic reptiles closely related to the ALLIGATOR and GAVIAL. There are over a dozen species, which are distinguised from alligators by their narrower snout. True crocodiles are members of the genera *Crocodylus,* *Osteoblepharon* and *Osteolaemus.* They are found in the warmer areas of the world. Young crocodiles feed on small creatures such as frogs or insects, then graduate to fish and, finally, to mammals and birds. Large prey is knocked down and drowned; man-eating has been known to occur.

CROESUS, last king of Lydia c560–546 BC, and last of the Mermnad dynasty, proverbial for his wealth and generosity. At his height he ruled a large part of Asia Minor, but he was overthrown by Cyrus the Great c546 BC. He apparently became an honored courtier of Cyrus.

CROKER, Richard (1841–1922), US politician and TAMMANY HALL boss 1885–1901. In the late 1860s he was leader of New York's "Young Democracy" faction of Tammany Hall Democrats who opposed "Boss" Tweed. After Tweed's downfall he built a strong political machine, but the election of reformist mayor Seth Low (1901) ended Croker's career.

CROLY, Herbert David (1869–1930), US editor and political theorist. His attacks on political complacency and stagnation influenced presidents Theodore Roosevelt and Wilson. In 1914 he founded *The New Republic* magazine.

CRO-MAGNON MAN, a race of primitive Man named for Cro-Magnon, France, dating from the Upper Paleolithic (see STONE AGE) and usually regarded as AURIGNACIAN, though possibly more recent. Coming later than Neanderthal Man (see PREHISTORIC MAN), Cro-Magnon Man was dolichocephalic (see CEPHALIC INDEX) with a high forehead and a large brain capacity, his face rather short and wide. He was probably around 1.7m tall, powerfully muscled and robust.

CROME, John (1768–1821), English landscape painter, also called Old Crome, founder of the Norwich school. He was almost entirely self-taught. His best works, such as *Mousehold Heath* (1815) and *Poringland Oak* (1817–21), were done in later life. His main influences were HOBBEMA and other Dutch painters.

CROMER, Evelyn Baring, 1st Earl of (1841–1917), British colonial administrator, who ruled Egypt as consul general 1883–1907. His progressive policies brought the economic and social advances he believed were essential for political progress, but he was distrusted by nationalists. He retired in 1907, becoming leader of the free-trade group in the Unionist party.

CROMWELL, Oliver (1599–1658), Lord Protector of the Commonwealth of England, Scotland and Ireland 1653–58. A minor landowner, he became prominent in the early days of the English Civil War as a member of parliament and as commander of the "Ironsides" cavalry regiment he had created. Largely responsible for victory at Marston Moor (1644), he became lieutenant general of the New Model Army, leading his men to victory at Naseby and Langport in 1645. At first inclined to negotiate with Charles I, the king's untrustworthiness so infuriated him that he lent all his weight to the latter's trial and execution. As lord lieutenant of Ireland he led a campaign there (1649) marked by appalling massacres, and as captain general and commander-in-chief of the army defeated the Scots at Dunbar in 1650. He summarily dissolved the oligarchic and bigoted RUMP PARLIAMENT in 1653. Its beleaguered successor handed power over to him as Lord Protector; he refused the crown in 1657. Essentially a dictator, his wish to rule through parliament was continually thwarted by the intransigence of the Puritan politicians. His regime, though benevolent, suppressed rather than solved the nation's problems and they broke out anew at his death.

CROMWELL, Richard (1626–1712), son of Oliver Cromwell, on whose death he became Lord Protector of England (1658). He was deposed by military coup in 1659, and went into exile for 20 years.

CROMWELL, Thomas, Earl of Essex (c1485–1540), English statesman under Henry VIII. A ruthless administrator and the main agent for destroying papal power in England, he supervised the king's break with Rome under the Act of Supremacy (1534) and the dissolution of the monasteries (1536–39). He arranged the king's marriage with Anne of Cleves, and on its failure he was executed without trial on charges of heresy and treason trumped up by his many enemies.

CRONIN, A(rchibald) J(oseph) (1896–), Scottish doctor who devoted himself to writing after the success of his first novel, *Hatter's Castle* (1931). His other novels include *The Citadel* (1937) and *The Keys of the Kingdom* (1942).

CRONKITE, Walter Leland, Jr. (1916–), US broadcast journalist who joined CBS news in 1950, participated in the first televised national political convention (1952) and hosted the documentary series "You Are There." As anchorman for the CBS nightly evening television news (1962–81), he became the best-known and most influential newsman in the US.

CROOK, George (1829–1890), US cavalry officer. After service in the Civil War, he led campaigns against the Apache Indians in Ariz. (1871–74) and the Sioux and Cheyenne forces led by Sitting Bull and Crazy Horse (1875–77). From 1883 Crook led a temporarily successful campaign to subdue Geronimo.

CROOKES, Sir William (1832–1919), English physicist who discovered the element THALLIUM (1861), invented the RADIOMETER (1875) and pioneered the study of CATHODE RAYS. By 1876 he had devised the Crookes tube, a glass tube containing two ELECTRODES and pumped out to a very low gas PRESSURE. By applying a high voltage across the electrodes and varying the pressure, he was able to produce and study cathode rays and various glow discharges.

CROQUET, lawn game of French origin that became popular in 19th-century England. Competitors have to drive colored balls with a longhandled mallet in strict sequence against each other and through a series of iron hoops stuck into the ground.

CROSBY, Bing (Harry Lillis Crosby) (1904–1977), US popular singer and actor. He became known as a big-band singer with Paul Whiteman's "Rhythm Boys" and as a "crooner" and a witty, affable host on one of network radio's most durable variety programs (1931–49). His many films include the famous *Road* series with Bob Hope and Dorothy Lamour, and he won an Oscar for his performance in *Going My Way* (1943). His recording of "White Christmas" was one of the all-time bestsellers.

CROSSBOW, medieval weapon consisting of a small but very powerful box fixed transversely on a stock, grooved to take the missile. Its bowstring latched onto a trigger mechanism, often by a lever or winch. It fired a shaft called a bolt or quarrel, about 10in long; some varieties also fired stones. It had less range and accuracy than the LONGBOW and was slower to load.

CROSS-EYE. See STRABISMUS.

CROUP, a condition common in infancy due to VIRUS infection of LARYNX and TRACHEA and causing characteristic stridor, or spasm of larynx when the child breathes in. Often a mild and short illness, it occasionally causes so much difficulty in breathing that OXYGEN is needed.

CROW INDIANS, North American Indian tribe of the Siouan linguistic group, first encountered in Mont. and Wyo. A nomadic plains tribe living mainly by hunting bison and buffalo, they originally broke away from the Hidatsa tribe, and had two main divisions: the Mountain and River Crow. They now occupy a reservation in S Mont.

CROWS, a large group of black songbirds which are found worldwide. The true crows are members of the family Corvidae, related to ravens and jays. They are omniverous and are regarded as pests in agricultural areas. Crows are highly intelligent. They can imitate sounds and, with training, the human voice. The clough, jackdaw and rook are common forms of Eurasian crow.

CRUCIFIXION, execution by being nailed or tied to a cross by the limbs or, more specifically, the execution in this manner of Jesus Christ. Many countries of the ancient world used it as their most painful method of execution. The victim often suffered for days; death resulted from shock, exhaustion or exposure. The Romans inflicted crucifixion only on lower-class non-Roman criminals and on political agitators.

CRUIKSHANK, George (1792–1878), English artist and satirical caricaturist. He first won fame with his numerous political cartoons (1811–25), then turned to book illustration. His superb illustrations included those for Dickens' *Sketches by Boz* (1836–37) and *Oliver Twist* (1838).

CRUISE MISSILE, a long-range torpedo-like system that can be fired from air, land or sea. It can carry either nuclear or conventional warheads. The German V-1, one of the first of these weapons, was cumbersome, inaccurate and short-ranged.

Modern models, pilotless winged tubes, are powered by small jet engines. Their size (20 feet long) and ability to hug the terrain at levels as low as 200 feet, make them elusive to radar. The US currently envisions two types of cruise missile—the sea-launched cruise (SLCM) presently being developed under the name Tomahawk, and an air-launched model (ALCM) to be produced by Boeing aircraft. ALCMs with nuclear warheads, to be carried on B-52s and B-1s, would have ranges of 1,500 miles, weigh 3,000 lbs and attain speeds of 500 mph. Tomahawks carrying larger conventional bombs can fly up to 700 miles over land at speeds of 500 miles an hour. In a recent test a submarine-launched Tomahawk flew a 500-mile zigzag course, following the terrain, and struck a house-sized target 300 miles away. It can also fly over a target then parachute to earth. Cruise missiles operate through inertial guidance plus an internal system called Tercom which analyzes information received by the skimming missile's sensors and compares it to guide maps with which it has been programmed.

CRUISER, warship designed for speed and long-range attack, in size between the destroyer and aircraft carrier. Used as a small battleship in WWII, its function has been to maintain lines of sea communication and to defend carriers against air attack. The three traditional types of cruiser, heavy, light and antiaircraft, with 8in, 6in and 5in guns respectively, are being converted to or replaced by guided-missile cruisers, and the first such cruiser with nuclear power, USS *Long Beach*, was launched in 1959.

CRUMB, George Henry (1929–   ), US composer who used impressionistic effects, aleatory sections and silences in his music. His "Echoes of Time and the River" won the 1968 Pulitzer Prize.

CRUSADES, a series of religious wars from the end of the 11th to the 13th centuries, organized by European powers to recover Christian holy places in Palestine from the Muslims. Crusades arose from religious reform and revival, and because the SELJUKS of Asia Minor, who had taken Jerusalem (1071), were now threatening the Byzantine Empire, ruled by ALEXIUS I. There was an enthusiastic response to Pope URBAN II's appeal at the Council of CLERMONT to recover Jerusalem, but political and commercial interests on the part of European rulers confused the issues of religious zeal and wars of conquest.

The **First Crusade** (1095–99) was fought initially by French and German peasants,

but they were massacred in Asia Minor. A second force of four large European armies routed the Turks at Dorylaeum (1097) and, led by GODFREY OF BOUILLON, captured Jerusalem in 1099, slaughtering thousands of Muslims and Jews. The crusaders set up the Latin kingdom of Jerusalem, with fiefs at Tripoli, Antioch and EDESSA. The Turkish recapture of Edessa in 1144 caused the **Second Crusade** (1147–48), led by Louis VII of France and Conrad III of the Byzantine throne Germany. Their attack on Damascus failed because of mutual jealousy. The Muslims under SALADIN captured Jerusalem in 1187, thus provoking the **Third Crusade** (1189–92), led by the Holy Roman Emperor Frederick I, Philip II of France and RICHARD I of England. Disunited by rivalry, they were unable to take Jerusalem. However, Richard won Acre, gained a few coastal towns and made a truce with Saladin giving pilgrims access to Jerusalem.

The **Fourth Crusade** (1201–04) was diverted to Constantinople by Venetians and claimants to the Byzantine throne from Egypt. The Crusaders pillaged the city, and set up the Latin Empire of Constantinople (1204). The **Children's Crusade** (1212) was a fiasco: some children died on the way, others were sold into slavery. The **Fifth Crusade** (1218–21), against Egypt, the center of Muslim power, was the last launched by a papal legate. The invasion failed when the crusaders had to be evacuated from floodwaters near Cairo. On the peaceful **Sixth Crusade** (1228–29), the Holy Roman Emperor Frederick II claimed his title to Jerusalem and secured the city for the Christians; but it again fell to the Muslims in 1244. LOUIS IX, leading the **Seventh Crusade** (1248–54) to Egypt, was captured at Mansura; he undertook the **Eighth Crusade** in 1270 but died at Tunis. The last Christian city, Acre, fell to the Muslims in 1291 and there were no further large-scale Crusades. Although the Crusades were a military failure, Western Europe was profoundly affected by the prolonged contact with the East, which stimulated culture and trade. (See also KNIGHTS OF SAINT JOHN; KNIGHTS TEMPLAR; TEUTONIC KNIGHTS.)

CRUSTACEA, class of animals in the phylum ARTHROPODA, with jointed legs, including CRABS, SHRIMPS, WATERFLEAS, BARNACLES and WOODLICE. A few live on land or are parasitic, but most are aquatic, breathing by gills or through the skin and bearing paired series of antennae and limbs down the body. They are vital to the economy of the sea, forming the food of many marine animals.

CRYOGENICS (from Greek *kruos*, frost), the branch of physics dealing with the behavior of matter at very low temperatures, and with the production of those temperatures. Early cryogenics relied heavily on the Joule–Thomson effect (named for James JOULE and William Thomson, later Lord KELVIN) by which temperature falls when a gas is permitted to expand without an external energy source. Using this, James DEWAR liquefied HYDROGEN in 1895 (though not in quantity until 1898), and H. K. Onnes liquefied HELIUM in 1908 at 4.2K (see also ABSOLUTE ZERO). Several cooling processes are used today. Down to about 4K the substance is placed in contact with liquefied gases which are permitted to evaporate, so removing HEAT energy (see LATENT HEAT). The lowest temperature that can be reached thus is around 0.3K. Further temperature decrease may be obtained by para-magnetic cooling (adiabatic demagnetization). Here a paramagnetic material (see PARA-MAGNETISM) is placed in contact with the substance and with liquid helium, and subjected to a strong magnetic field (see MAGNETISM), the heat so generated being removed by the helium. Then, away from the helium, the magnetic field is reduced to zero. By this means temperatures of the order of 10^{-2}—10^{-3}K have been achieved (though, because of heat leak, such temperatures are always unstable). A more complicated process, nuclear adiabatic demagnetization, has been used to attain temperatures as low as 2×10^{-7}K.

Near absolute zero, substances can display strange properties. Liquid helium II has no VISCOSITY (see SUPERFLUIDITY) and can flow up the sides of its container. Some elements display SUPERCONDUCTIVITY: an electric current started in them will continue indefinitely. (See also CRYOTRON).

CRYPTOGRAPHY. See CODES AND CIPHERS.

CRYPTOZOIC, in GEOLOGY, the eon in which life first appeared (see EVOLUTION) and PRECAMBRIAN rocks were formed. The rocks do not contain FOSSILS that can be used for dating (see CAMBRIAN; CHRONOLOGY); hence the name Cryptozoic (hidden life). By contrast the eon of visible life, from the end of the Cryptozoic to the present, is called the PHANEROZOIC.

CRYSTAL PALACE, vast glass exhibition hall designed by Sir Joseph PAXTON for the Great London Exhibition of 1851. An innovative work, it was both the first cast-iron frame building and the first for which structural units were prefabricated

and then assembled on site. It was destroyed by fire in 1936.

CRYSTALS, homogeneous solid objects having naturally-formed plane faces. The order in their external appearance reflects the regularity of their internal structure—i.e., the arrangement of their atoms or molecules—this internal regularity being the keynote of the **crystalline state**. Although external regularity is most obvious in natural crystals and those grown in the laboratory, most other inorganic solid substances (with the notable exceptions of PLASTICS and GLASS) also exist in the crystalline state, although the crystals of which they are composed are often microscopic in size. True crystals must be distinguished from cut gemstones, which, although often internally crystalline, exhibit faces chosen according to the whim of the lapidary rather than developed in the course of any natural growth process. The study of crystals and the crystalline state is the province of **crystallography**. Crystals are classified according to the SYMMETRY that they display. This gives the 32 crystal classes, which can be grouped into the seven traditional crystal systems (six if trigonal and hexagonal are counted together). Crystals are allotted to their proper class by considering their external appearance, the symmetry of any etch marks made on their surfaces, and their optical and electrical properties. Although such observations enable the crystallographer to determine the type of "unit cell" which, when repeated in space, gives the overall LATTICE structure of a given crystal, they do not enable the actual dispositions of the constituent ATOMS or IONS to be determined. This can be done only by using X-RAY DIFFRACTION techniques. When a crystal is composed solely of particles of a single species and the attractive forces between molecules are not directionally localized, as in the crystals of many pure metals, the atoms tend to take up one of two structures that allow a maximum degree of close-packing. These are known as hexagonal close-packed (hcp) and face-centered cubic (fcc) and can both be looked upon as different ways of stacking planes of particles in which each is surrounded by six neighbors. Although much crystallography assumes that crystals perfectly exhibit their supposed structure, real crystals, of course, contain minor defects such as grain boundaries and dislocations. Many of the most important properties and uses of crystals depend on these defects.

CUBA, republic and largest island in the Caribbean Sea, at the entry to the Gulf of Mexico and 90mi S of Florida Keys.

Land. Cuba has three mountain ranges, the Sierra de los Organos in the W, the Sierra de Trinidad in the center and the Sierra Maestra in the SE—where Turquino, Cuba's highest peak, rises to 6,560ft. Only a few of the country's many rivers are major navigable waters. There are deep bays and natural harbors. The warm climate (temperatures between 72°F and 82°F), the usually plentiful rainfall, and the rich soil give Cuba a very wide variety of plant life (over 8,000 species) and great mountain forests. Hurricanes occur quite frequently.

People. The population is over 70% white, of Spanish origin, the rest are mulattoes and Negroes. More than half of all Cubans live in cities or towns. Most of the rural population lives near sugar factories. The literacy rate is over 90%.

Economy. Cuba is dependent upon one crop, sugar; tobacco is the second most important export. The agriculture has been further diversified by the production of coffee, citrus fruit and rice crops. The fisheries are a growing industry. The largest mineral resource is iron ore, and there are also deposits of nickel, cobalt, copper and manganese. Before 1959 industrialization was limited; after a period of rapid development (1959–63) it has progressed slowly. Neglected for almost 20 years, tourism began to grow in the late 1970s. All trade, commerce and industrial production is nationalized, and most of the cultivated land has been reorganized as state cooperatives. Cuba benefits from an extensive transport network.

History. COLUMBUS discovered Cuba in 1492 and it became important as the base for Spanish exploration of America and as a harbor for Spanish treasure ships. The native Indians, decimated by ill-treatment and disease, were replaced as a work force by West African Negro slaves, particularly in the 18th century when the sugar plantations developed rapidly. In the 19th century Spain's colonial policy led to a series of nationalist uprisings, and after the SPANISH–AMERICAN WAR (1898) Cuba became an independent republic, though it was under US military occupation 1899–1902 and 1906–09. In return for rights of intervention (see PLATT AMENDMENT), the US organized public services and invested heavily in Cuba's economy.

Between 1924 and 1959 Cuba was under virtually continuous dictatorship. Fulgencio BATISTA, who had come to power in 1940, was overthrown by Fidel CASTRO, aided by "Che" GUEVARA in 1959. Castro, as premier, established a socialist state and instituted sweeping land, industrial and educational reforms. After US firms had been nationalized, the US supported the abortive BAY OF PIGS invasion and enforced an economic blockade. Thereafter, the USSR and the communist bloc replaced US trade and provided great economic support. In 1962 Cuba accepted Russian nuclear missiles, which led to a major confrontation between US and USSR until the missiles were withdrawn. The ORGANIZATION OF AMERICAN STATES (OAS) expelled Cuba in 1962 but lifted its sanctions in 1975. Despite many setbacks the social policies have in general benefited the island. Fidel Castro became president in 1976. In the late 1970s a certain rapprochement between Cuba and the US took place and reestablishment of diplomatic ties seemed close. Cuban involvement in Africa, however, strained the relations. In 1980 Castro allowed free emigrations and within several months about 125,000 people went to the US.

Official name: Republic of Cuba
Capital: Havana
Area: 44,206sq mi
Population: 9,738,600
Languages: Spanish
Religions: Roman Catholic
Monetary unit(s): 1 Cuban peso=100 centavos

CUBAN BOAT LIFT, a flotilla of hundreds of private vessels that carried refugees from Mariel, Cuba, to Key West, Fla., in Apr.–May 1980. Some 90,000 refugees entered the US in this period (primarily by the boat lift), straining the capacity of Fla. and the nation generally to absorb them.

CUBAN MISSILE CRISIS, perhaps the world's closest approach to nuclear war. The crisis began officially on Oct. 16, 1962, when President John F. KENNEDY received photographs, taken by a U-2 reconnaissance plane, of launch sites being constructed for Soviet long-range missiles near San Cristóbal, Cuba. The president and his advisers leaned initially toward making a surprise air attack on the sites but decided instead on a naval blockade to prevent shipment of additional offensive weapons to Cuba. The idea was to apply sufficient pressure to force the Russians to remove their missiles but not so much pressure as to trigger an all-out nuclear war. Kennedy told the American nation about the missiles in Cuba and the imposition of the blockade in a televised address on Oct. 22. Emergency meetings of the ORGANIZATION OF AMERICAN STATES and the UN Security Council were called. Russian vessels en route to Cuba began turning back on Oct. 24, but work on the missile sites continued and contradictory messages were received from Soviet Chairman KHRUSHCHEV on Oct. 26. The first message offered to withdraw the missiles in return for assurances that the US would not invade Cuba while the second proposed a trade: The Russian missiles would be removed if American missiles were pulled out of Turkey. It was decided to ignore the second message and accept the terms of the first. The crisis was settled on this basis on Oct. 28, with Khrushchev's agreement to dismantle the launch sites and return the missiles to Russia.

CUBISM, influential modern art style created by PICASSO and BRAQUE in Paris between 1907 and 1914. Until 1912, in the "analytic" period, Cubist paintings represented subject matter in the pictorial form of an elaborately-faceted surface. After 1912, in the "synthetic" period, Cubists also stuck objects to their canvases, instead of representing them, and stressed color, texture and construction in COLLAGE. Cubism had a wide effect on all the arts. (See also ABSTRACT ART.)

CUCKOO, family of birds (Cuculidae), including the anis, coucals, guiras and roadrunners. The Common cuckoo of Europe, Asia and Africa lays its eggs in other species' nests where they are reared by their foster parents. The North American species raise their own broods.

CUKOR, George (1899–   ), US film director who was known for his polished social comedies and romances. His films featured many of Hollywood's leading actresses, including Katharine Hepburn (*Little Women*, 1933; *Philadelphia Story*, 1940), Greta Garbo (*Camille*, 1936), and Judy Garland (*A Star is Born*, 1954). He won an Academy Award for *My Fair Lady* (1964).

CULLEN, Countee (1903–1946), black US poet and member of the HARLEM RENAISSANCE. He wrote about the "New Negro" who has proud roots in an African past. Among his works are *Color* (1925) and a novel, *One Way to Heaven* (1932).

CULLODEN MOOR, site of the battle near Inverness, N Scotland, where CHARLES EDWARD STUART, the Young Pretender, and the JACOBITES were finally defeated in 1746 by the Duke of Cumberland. About 1,000 of the 5,000 Scots were slaughtered.

CULPEPER, Thomas Culpeper, 2nd Baron (1635–1689), English colonial governor of Virginia (1675–83), who ruled through deputies until compelled to go there after BACON'S REBELLION (1680). Uprisings because of the low tobacco prices led to a quarrel with the colonists, which resulted in his removal from office.

CULTURE, a controlled growth of living cells in an artificial medium, often in a PETRI DISH. The cells may be microorganisms isolated and studied in a pure culture, or made to compete with each other under various environmental and nutritional conditions (see MICROBIOLOGY); or they may be cells from animal or plant tissue cultivated for studies of heredity and function. The culture medium usually contains GELATIN or AGAR, salts and various nutrients.

CUMBERLAND GAP, a natural pass, 1,640ft high, through the Cumberland Mts near where Ky., Tenn. and Va. meet. Daniel Boone's WILDERNESS ROAD ran through the Gap, and it was one of the three early major routes to the West through the Appalachian Mts. In the Civil War it was a strategic point.

CUMMINGS, Edward Estlin (1894–1962), U.S. poet known as e. e. cummings, famous for his innovations in language, punctuation and typography. The content of his poems is often traditional and romantic, though colored by wit and satire. His best work is in the collection *Poems 1923–1954*.

CUNARD, Sir Samuel (1787–1865), Canadian ship-owner, founder of the Cunard line. He pioneered regular transatlantic steamship lines from 1840 after he had won a contract to carry British and North American mail.

CUNEIFORM (from Latin *cuneus*, wedge, and *forma*, shape), one of the earliest known fully developed writing systems. Each character is formed by a combination of wedge- or nail-shaped strokes. Invented probably by the Sumerians before 3,000 BC, it was soon adopted by the Akkadians and then by other peoples, such as the Hittites, and the Persians. The characters are stylizations of earlier pictographs, and were impressed in clay. Cuneiform was first deciphered in detail by RAWLINSON in 1846.

CUNNINGHAM, Merce (1919–   ), U.S. dancer and choreographer whose avant-garde style emphasizes experimental music and abstract movement. Much of his work is set to the music of John CAGE.

CUPID, or Amor, in Roman mythology, the god of love, identified with the Greek Eros and the son and companion of Venus. He is usually depicted as a small boy, winged, naked and armed with bow and arrow. Those wounded by him fall in love.

CURAÇAO, largest island (182sq mi) of the Netherlands Antilles, West Indies, 60mi N of NW Venezuela. It is flat and barren. The chief industries are oil-refining and phosphate mining. The liqueur *Curaçao* originated here. The capital is Willemstad.

CURARE, arrow-poison used by South American Indian hunters, extracted from various plants, chiefly of the genera *Strychnos* and *Chondodendron,* killing by respiratory paralysis. Curare is a mixture of ALKALOIDS, the chief being *d*-tubocurarine. By competing with ACETYLCHOLINE it blocks nerve impulse transmission to muscles, producing relaxation and paralysis. It has revolutionized modern surgery by producing complete relaxation without a dangerous degree of ANESTHESIA being required. (See also TETANUS.)

CURIA, properly Curia Romana, administrative and judicial organization that helps the pope govern the Roman Catholic Church. Directed by cardinals, it includes a secretariat of state, three tribunals, five sacred offices, various secretariats and 10 departments (sacred congregations). In ancient Rome a curia comprised several families within a tribe, and formed a political unit in the COMITIA Curiata. Curia eventually became synonymous with Senate.

CURIE, Marie (1867–1934), born Marja Sklodowska, Polish-born French physicist who, with her French-born husband **Pierre Curie** (1859–1906), was an early investigator of RADIOACTIVITY, discovering the radioactive elements POLONIUM and RADIUM in the mineral PITCHBLENDE (1898). For this the Curies shared the 1903 Nobel physics prize with A. H. BECQUEREL. After the death of Pierre, Marie went on to investigate the chemistry and medical applications of

radium and was awarded the 1911 Nobel Prize for Chemistry in recognition of her isolation of the pure metal. She died of LEUKEMIA, no doubt contracted in the course of her work with radioactive materials. Pierre Curie is also noted for the discovery, with his brother Jacques, of PIEZOELECTRICITY (1880) and for his investigation of the effect of TEMPERATURE on magnetic properties. In particular he discovered the Curie point, the temperature above which ferromagnetic materials display only PARAMAGNETISM (1895). The Curies' elder daughter, Irène JOLIOT-CURIE, was also a noted physicist.

CURLEY, James Michael (1874–1958), Democratic "boss" and mayor of Boston, Mass. for many years; also US congressman and governor of Mass. In 1947 he was convicted for fraudulent use of the mails, but his sentence was later commuted by President Truman. He was fully pardoned in 1950.

CURLING, game introduced from Scotland to North America over 100 years ago. Two teams of four players grasp handles attached to rounded 40lb stone *granites* and slide them down 138ft-long ice *rinks* at a *tee*—the marked center of a circle called the *house.* World championships date from 1959.

CURRIER AND IVES, firm of American lithographers which produced over 7,000 different prints showing lively scenes from 19th-century American life. Nathaniel Currier (1813–1888), became known in 1835 by producing a lithograph of a major New York City fire only four days after the event. James Merritt Ives (1824–1895), became Currier's bookkeeper in 1852, his partner in 1857.

CURTIS, Cyrus Hermann Kotzschmar (1850–1933), US founder of a publishing empire. From the age of 12, he started or bought magazines and newspapers including *The Saturday Evening Post, The Ladies' Home Journal* and the *New York Evening Post.*

CURTIZ, Michael (1888–1962), Hungarian-born US film director who was responsible for many of the most popular films of the 1930s and 40s, *Captain Blood* (1935), *Yankee Doodle Dandy* (1942) and *Mildred Pierce* (1945). He won an Academy Award for *Casablanca* (1943).

CURZON, George Nathaniel Curzon, 1st Marquess of Kedleston (1859–1925), British statesman, viceroy of India 1898–1905 and foreign secretary 1919–24. His reforms while viceroy included reorganizing government finance. (See also CURZON LINE.)

CUSA, Nicholas of. See NICHOLAS OF CUSA.

CUSH, Kingdom of, Egyptian-influenced Sudanese state flourishing c1000 BC–350 AD. Cushite kings, reigning from the capital, Napata, conquered Egypt, ruling as its 25th dynasty (8th–7th centuries BC). The later capital, MEROË, was Black Africa's first major iron-making center until its destruction in the 4th century AD.

CUSHING, Harvey Williams (1869–1939), US surgeon who pioneered many modern neurosurgical techniques and investigated the functions of the PITUITARY GLAND. In 1932 he described Cushing's Syndrome, a rare disease caused by STEROID imbalance and showing itself in obesity, high blood pressure and other symptoms.

CUSTER, George Armstrong (1839–1876), controversial American cavalry officer, killed in a famous battle with Indians. He proved himself an outstanding Union cavalry leader during the Civil War. Made a lieutenant colonel in 1866, he joined General Hancock's successful expedition against the Cheyenne Indians in Kan. and subsequently saw western patrol duty. In 1876 Custer and the 7th US Cavalry Regiment moved to herd Sioux Indians in Mont. into government reservations. Underestimating the size of an Indian village, Custer refused to await expected reinforcements and attacked, recklessly dividing his force into three columns. His own column was entirely wiped out. (See also CRAZY HORSE; LITTLE BIGHORN, BATTLE OF.)

CUVIER, Georges Léopold Chrétien Frédéric Dagobert, Baron (1769–1832), French comparative anatomist and the founder of PALEONTOLOGY. By applying his theory of the "correlation of parts" he was able to reconstruct the forms of many fossil creatures, explaining their creation and subsequent extinction according to the doctrine of CATASTROPHISM. A tireless laborer in the service of French Protestant education, Cuvier was perhaps the most renowned and respected French scientist in the early 19th century.

CUYP, Aelbert (1620–1691), outstanding member of a family of Dutch painters. His glowing river scenes with cattle are particularly fine, but he also painted portraits, still lifes and seascapes. He influenced later English landscape artists, and many of his best works are in Britain.

CUZCO, city of S Peru, capital of Cuzco department and former capital of the INCA Empire dating from c12th century. Located 11,024ft above sea level, it is an agricultural center with textiles, metalwork; and tourism based on Inca ruins and Spanish colonial architecture. Pop 120,881.

CYANIDES, compounds containing the CN group. Organic cyanides are called NITRILES. Inorganic cyanides are salts of hydrocyanic acid (HCN), a volatile weak ACID; both are highly toxic. Sodium cyanide is made by the Castner process: ammonia is passed through a mixture of carbon and fused sodium. The cyanide ion (CN^-) is a PSEUDOHALOGEN, and forms many complexes. Cyanides are used in the extraction of GOLD and SILVER, ELECTROPLATING and CASEHARDENING.

CYBELE, Great Mother of the Gods, supreme goddess of the Phrygians in Asia Minor. About 430 BC her orgiastic cult spread to the Greeks (who sometimes identified her with CRONUS's sister Rhea or with DEMETER). In 205 BC the cult reached Rome.

CYBERNETICS, a field of science which compares the communication and control systems built into mechanical and other man-made devices with those present in biological organisms. For example, fruitful comparisons may be made between DATA PROCESSING in COMPUTERS and various functions of the BRAIN; and the fundamental theories of cybernetics may be applied with equal validity to both.

CYCLADES, circular group of more than 200 mountainous islands in the S Aegean Sea. From the 5th century AD they were successively under Byzantines, Venetians and Turks, and have been part of Greece since 1829. The main islands include Andros, Delos, Naxos, Paros, Syres, Tenos and Thera.

CYCLONE, a low-pressure atmospheric disturbance (see ATMOSPHERE; METEOROLOGY) of a roughly circular form, a center towards which ground WINDS move, and at which there is an upward air movement, usually spiraling. Above the center, in the upper TROPOSPHERE, there is a general outward movement. The direction of spiraling is counterclockwise in the N Hemisphere, clockwise in the S Hemisphere, owing to the CORIOLIS EFFECT. Anticyclones, by contrast, are high-pressure atmospheric disturbances characterized by out-blowing winds and a clockwise circulation in the N Hemisphere (counterclockwise in the S Hemisphere). (See also HURRICANE; TORNADO.)

CYNICS, members of an ascetic Greek philosophical sect following DIOGENES (4th century BC), and influenced by SOCRATES. They ignored conventional standards, preached self-control, condemned immorality and renounced worldly comfort, living as simply as animals (hence, probably, their name: *kynikos* means "doglike"). Their movement influenced STOICISM but vanished in imperial Roman times.

CYPRIAN, Saint (Thascius Caecilianus Cyprianus; c200–258 AD), bishop of Carthage (248–258) and martyr, one of the CHURCH FATHERS. Converted to Christianity c246, Cyprian wrote and spoke influentially on order and conduct in the Church, stressing Church unity and episcopal authority. Feast day: Sept. 16.

Official name: The Republic of Cyprus
Capital: Nicosia
Area: 3,572sq mi
Population: 630,000
Languages: Greek, Turkish
Religions: Greek Orthodox, Turkish Muslim
Monetary Unit(s): 1 Cyprus pound = 1,000 mils

CYPRUS, island republic in the NE Mediterranean, about 40mi from the S Turkish coast. It is the third-largest island in the Mediterranean after Sicily and Sardinia. The island consists of fertile central lowlands with rugged mountains to the N and S. The N range comprises the Kyrenia and Karpas mountains (Akroman-dra, 3,357ft). In the SW, the Troodos massif has Mt Olympus (6,403ft), the island's highest peak. On the Mesaoria lowland between the mountain systems is Nicosia, the capital. The mountains are partly forested (pine, cypress, and juniper) and have much poor pasture. The climate is typically E Mediterranean.

People. The population is about 80% Greek and 20% Turkish. Both Greek and Turkish are official languages and English is widely spoken. In 1973 nearly 37% of the people lived in the six district capitals: Nicosia, Limassol, Famagusta, Larnaca, Paphos and Kyrenia, but recent events have changed the pattern.

The economy normally depends heavily upon irrigated agriculture (citrus fruits, vines, tobacco, cereals and vegetables). Mineral resources include cupreous and iron pyrites, asbestos, chromite and gypsum. Tourism was formerly important.

History. Ruled successively by the Ottoman Turks (1570–1878) and Great Britain, Cyprus became an independent republic, with Archbishop Makarios III as president, in 1960. But strife between Greek and Turkish Cypriots continued, and in 1974 a military coup organized by Greek army officers favoring *enosis* (union with Greece) ousted Makarios, whereupon Turkey invaded the island, setting up a "Turkish Federated State of Cyprus" under Turkish occupation in the NE third of the island.

CYRANO DE BERGERAC, Savinien de (1619–1655), French author. He gave up a military career to write plays and prose. A freethinker, influenced by GASSENDI, he satirized contemporary society in ingenious fantasies about voyages to the sun and moon. Edmond ROSTAND, in his play *Cyrano de Bergerac*, made him into a flamboyant Romantic hero, handicapped in love because of an unusually large nose.

CYRENAICS, members of a Greek school of philosophy centered in Cyrene in the 3rd and 4th centuries BC. Its founder, Aristippus (c435–356 BC), advocated seeking pleasure and avoiding pain. Pleasure was the only absolute good, but wisdom was a vital path to its attainment. Cyrenaic philosophy gave rise to EPICUREANISM.

CYRIL AND METHODIUS, Saints (c827–869 and c825–884), Greek missionaries, apostles to the Slavs, who deeply influenced Slavic culture. Invited to Moravia, from 863 the brothers rivaled Latin-speaking German missionaries in the Danube region, preaching in the local Slavic tongue, pioneering the Glagolitic script (precursor of Cyrillic) and translating biblical texts into Old Church Slavonic. Their feast day is July 7.

CYRUS, name of three rulers of ancient Persia. **Cyrus I** was king of Anshan in the late 7th century BC. **Cyrus II the Great** (c590/580–529 BC) was the son of Cambyses I and founder of the empire of the ACHAEMENIANS. Ruler of Anshan from c559 BC, he conquered Media, Lydia (c547 BC) and Babylonia (539 BC), building an empire from the Black and Caspian seas to the Arabian Desert and Persian Gulf (see also PERSIA, ANCIENT). He allowed the Jews to return to Palestine from their BABYLONIAN CAPTIVITY. **Cyrus the Younger** (d. 401 BC) was the second son of DARIUS II. Pardoned after unsuccessfully trying to oust his elder brother, ARTAXERXES II, he rebelled and was killed by Artaxerxes at the Battle of Cunaxa—which led to the famous retreat of 10,000 Greeks under XENOPHON.

CYST, a fluid-filled sac, lined by fibrous connective tissue or surface EPITHELIUM. It may form in an enlarged normal cavity (e.g., sebaceous cyst), it may arise in an embryonic remnant (e.g., branchial cyst), or it may occur as part of a disease process. They may be present as swellings or may cause pain (e.g., some ovarian cysts). Multiple cysts in KIDNEY and LIVER occur in inherited polycystic diseases; here kidney failure may develop.

CYSTIC FIBROSIS, an inherited disease presenting in infancy or childhood causing abnormal GLAND secretions; chronic LUNG disease with thick sputum and liability to infection is typical, as is malabsorption with pale bulky feces and MALNUTRITION. Sweat contains excessive salt (the basis for a diagnostic test) and heat exhaustion may result. Significant disease of LIVER, SINUSES and salivary glands occurs. Prompt treatment of chest infection with PHYSIOTHERAPY and appropriate ANTIBIOTICS is crucial to minimize lung damage; concentrated PANCREAS extract and special diets encourage normal digestion and growth, and extra salt should be given in hot weather. Although long-term outlook in this disease has recently improved, there is still a substantial mortality before adult life.

CYSTITIS, INFLAMMATION of the BLADDER, usually due to infection. A common condition in women, sometimes precipitated by intercourse. It occasionally leads to pyelonephritis, or upper urinary tract infection. Burning pain and increased frequency of urination are usual symptoms. ANTIBIOTICS are often needed. Recurrent cystitis may suggest an underlying disorder of bladder or its nervous control.

CYTOLOGY, the branch of BIOLOGY dealing with the study of CELLS, their structure, function, biochemistry, etc. Techniques used include tissue CULTURE and ELECTRON MICROSCOPY. (See also HISTOLOGY.)

CZÁRDÁS, a Hungarian dance, or its music. It is in two-four time, but it features violent changes of tempo. A slow movement (*lassu*) is usually followed by a quick one (*friss*).

CZECH, one of the two official languages of Czechoslovakia, spoken in Bohemia, Moravia and Silesia. It is a member of the Western branch of the SLAVONIC LANGUAGES.

CZECHOSLOVAKIA, central European communist republic between Poland on the N and Hungary and Austria on the S. The USSR lies to the E, West Germany to the W and East Germany to the NW.

Land. It comprises four distinct geogra-phical regions: Bohemia, Moravia, the Carpathians and Slovakia. Bohemia is the W plateau fringed by mountains—the Böhmer Wald (Bohemian Forest), Erz-gebirge (Ore Mountains), the Sudetic Mountains (Sněžka, 5,256ft) and the Bohemian–Moravian Heights. Cutting through the uplands in the S is the Vltava R, which flows through Prague, the Czech capital, on its way to the Elbe. Moravia, E of Bohemia, has rolling hills and fertile soils and is drained by the Morava R and its tributaries and, in the N, by the Oder R. The forested arc of the Carpathians dominates N Slovakia, its ridges separated by the Váh, Nitra and Hron rivers, all flowing to the Danube. In the High Tatra is Gerlachovka (8,711ft), the republic's highest peak. Slovakia's plains in the SW and SE are extensions of the Danube–Tisa (Pannonian) plain. The climate is central European, with hot, thundery summers and long, cold winters.

People. More than 60% of the population are Czech and about 30% Slovak, with Hungarians, Germans, Poles and Ukrain-ians accounting for the remainder. Prague is the only city with more than 1 million inhabitants. Other large cities are Brno, Bratislava, Ostrava, Plzeň and Košice.

Economy. Industry is the dominant sector of the economy. Heavy industry, especially engineering and chemicals, has been greatly expanded since WWII. Steel, armaments, machinery, precision instruments, electrical goods, glass, textiles and footwear are among Czechoslovakia's many products. Limited mineral resources (coal, oil, natural gas, iron ore, copper and lead-zinc ores) are supplemented by imports of bituminous coal, iron ore, oil and natural gas, mainly from the USSR. There are valuable forests

Official Name: The Czechoslovak Socialist Republic
Area: 49,365sq mi
Population: 14,500,000
Languages: Czech, Slovak
Religions: Roman Catholic, Protestant
Monetary Unit(s): 1 Koruna = 100 halérů
Capital: Prague

(mainly spruce and beech). Agriculture has been collectivized and provides cereals, sugar beets, potatoes, hops, grapes, fruit and beef and dairy cattle.

History. With the disintegration of Austria–Hungary at the end of WWI, the Czechs and Slovaks proclaimed the independent republic of Czechoslovakia (1918), which developed as a Western-style democracy. Seized by Nazi Germany (1938–39), Czechoslovakia came under Russian domination after WWII, and a communist regime took power. In 1968–69 an attempt by the Communist Party leader Alexander Dubček to liberalize the country was crushed by invading Russian and other Warsaw Pact troops. Dubček and other moderates were purged and the staunchly pro-Soviet Gustáv Husák put in control.

4th letter of the English alphabet, originally derived from the triangular Semitic symbol *daleth* (meaning door). The present form comes from the Latin alphabet. In chemistry D stands for DEUTERIUM; it is the second note of the musical scale of C, and the Roman numeral for 500.

DACCA, capital of Bangladesh, a port located on the Burhi Ganga R. The country's commercial and industrial center, it produces textiles, rubber goods and jewelry. It has been important since about 1600. Dacca came under British rule in 1765. It became capital of Bangladesh in 1971. Pop 1,679,522.

DACHAU, town in Bavaria, West Germany, 10mi NW of Munich. Many thousands were murdered at the Nazi concentration camp set up nearby in 1933, some in brutal medical experiments. Pop 32,713.

DACHSHUND, a dog originally bred in Germany to pursue small, burrowing animals. It has a long body, short legs, pointed nose, long ears and usually a reddish-brown or black-and-tan coat. It may be miniature (9lb) or standard size (12–28lb).

DADA, artistic movement which arose in Zurich and New York in 1915–16, spreading to Berlin and Paris. The name

was first used in Zurich by the poet Tristan TZARA, the artists Jean ARP and Marcel Janco, and the writers Hugo Ball and Richard Huelsenbeck. Dada was deliberately provocative, aiming at the destruction of aesthetic preconceptions. The Dadaists experimented with "ready-mades," phonetic or nonsense poetry, collage, anarchic typography and outrageous theater events. Dada was a prelude to SURREALISM and, though it effectively ended in 1923, it influenced many later artistic developments.

DAGUERRE, Louis Jacques Mandé (1789–1851), French theatrical designer and former partner of NIÉPCE who in the late 1830s developed the DAGUERREOTYPE process, the first practical means of producing a permanent photographic image.

DAGUERREOTYPE, the first practical photographic process, invented by DAGUERRE in 1837 and widely used in portraiture until the mid-1850s. A brass plate coated with silver was sensitized by exposure to iodine vapor and exposed to light in a CAMERA for several minutes. A weak positive image produced by mercury vapor was fixed with a solution of salt. Hypo soon replaced salt as the fixing agent and after 1840 gold (III) chloride was used to intensify the image. (See also PHOTOGRAPHY.)

DAHL, Roald (1916–   ), English writer famous for his macabre short stories. The collection *Over to You* (1946) contained stories based on his experiences as a pilot during WWII. Other collections include *Some Time Never* (1948), *Someone Like You* (1953) and *Kiss, Kiss* (1960). Dahl has also written novels and children's books.

DAIMLER, Gottlieb Wilhelm (1834–1900), German engineer who devised an INTERNAL-COMBUSTION ENGINE (1883) and used it in building one of the first AUTOMOBILES about 1886.

DAIREN. See PORT ARTHUR-DAIREN.

DAKAR, capital of Senegal and the largest port in W Africa, is located on Cape Verde Peninsula. Built as a fort by the French in 1857, Dakar is Africa's westernmost city and a major maritime and air center. It is also an important trading port for W African goods, and a leading medical and cultural center. Pop 800,000.

DALADIER, Edouard (1884–1970), French statesman and premier of France who, with Neville CHAMBERLAIN, signed the MUNICH AGREEMENT abandoning Czechoslovakia to Hitler. Premier in 1933, 1934 and 1938–40, he resigned in 1940 after failing to aid Finland against Russia. He was imprisoned by the Germans 1943–45, and later became leader of the Radical Party.

DALAI LAMA, title of the head of the dominant order of Tibetan Buddhists and, until 1959, Tibet's spiritual and temporal ruler. When a Dalai Lama dies, the next one is chosen from among young boys born within two years of his death. The 13th Dalai Lama (1875–1933) expelled occupying Chinese troops and declared Tibet independent in 1913. Independence was lost under the 14th Dalai Lama (1935–) when the Chinese communists invaded Tibet. The Dalai Lama went into exile in India in 1959.

D'ALEMBERT, Jean Le Rond. See ALEMBERT, JEAN LE ROND D'.

DALEY, Richard Joseph (1902–1976), US Democratic politician, mayor of Chicago from 1955 until his death. Born in Chicago, he was a state senator 1939–43, director of revenue 1948–50 and clerk of Cook Co. 1950–55. As mayor he improved Chicago in many ways, but was criticized for his failure to curb racial segregation and for his rough handling of demonstrators at the 1968 Democratic Convention. He was an adviser to presidents Kennedy and Johnson.

DALI, Salvador (1904–), Spanish surrealist painter whose works mix images as in dreams and hallucinations. Strongly influenced by Sigmund FREUD, Dali sought to portray the elements of the UNCONSCIOUS by using unusual methods and rich fantasy, combined with a refined draftsmanship.

DALLAPICCOLA, Luigi (1904–1975), Italian composer who adapted the 12-tone technique to his own emotionally expressive and melodic style. His works include vocal compositions and operas.

DALLAS, second-largest city in Tex., founded by John Neely Bryan in 1841 on the Trinity R and named for George Mifflin DALLAS. In the 1870s the railroads brought Dallas growth and lasting importance as a cotton processing and shipping center. When oil was discovered in E Tex. in the 1930s, Dallas became a major oil center. The banking and insurance capital for the Southwest, it also has many thriving industries (textiles, paper, machinery), and cultural and educational institutions. Pop 869,600.

DALMATIA, region in W Yugoslavia consisting of a mountainous strip bordering the Adriatic, and including about 300 islands. The area has been dominated by the Romans (1st century BC–5th century AD), Venetians (1420–1797), Austrians (1815–1918) and many other foreign powers. The present, largely Croatian population lives on tourism, fishing and farming. They produce wine, olive oil, cotton, ships, bauxite and limestone. Dalmatia acquired independence in 1918.

DALMATIAN, strong, muscular dog with a smooth white, black-spotted coat. Dalmatians weigh 50–55lb, and stand 20–23in in height. Often used as fire-station mascots, their supposed origin is Dalmatia, in modern Yugoslavia.

DALTON, John (1766–1844), English Quaker scientist renowned as the originator of the modern chemical atomic theory. First attracted to the problems of GAS chemistry through an interest in meteorology, Dalton discovered his **Law of Partial Pressures** in 1801. This states that the PRESSURE exerted by a mixture of gases equals the sum of the partial pressures of the components and holds only for ideal gases. (The partial pressure of a gas is the pressure it would exert if it alone filled the volume.) Dalton believed that the particles or ATOMS of different ELEMENTS were distinguished from one another by their weights, and, taking his cue from the laws of definite and multiple proportions (see COMPOSITION, CHEMICAL), he compiled and published in 1803 the first table of comparative ATOMIC WEIGHTS. This inaugurated the new quantitative atomic theory. Dalton also gave the first scientific description of COLOR BLINDNESS. The red-green type from which he suffered is still known as **Daltonism.**

DAM, a structure confining and checking the flow of a river, stream or estuary to divert its flow, improve navigation, store water for irrigation or city supplies or raise its level for use in power generation. Often a recreation area is made as a by-product. Dams are one of the earliest known man-made structures, records existing from c2900 BC of a 15m-high dam on the Nile. Construction methods were largely empirical until 1866, when the first scientifically designed dam was built in France. Dams are classified by profile and building material, these being determined by availability and site. They must be strong enough to hold back water; withstand ice, silt and uplift pressures, and stresses from temperature changes and EARTHQUAKES. The site must have stable earth or rock that will not unduly compress, squeeze out or let water seep under the dam. Borings, seismic tests, structural models and computer simulations are all design aids. **Masonry** or **concrete dams** are typically used for blocking streams in narrow gorges. The highest are around 300m high. A **gravity dam** holds back water by its own weight and may be solid, sloping downstream with a thick base, or buttressed, sloping upstream and strengthened by buttresses which transfer the dead weight sideways; these require less concrete. **Arch dams**, with one or more ARCHES pointing upstream, are often built across a canyon and transfer some water pressure to its walls. Hoover Dam, built in 1936, is a combination of arch and gravity types. **Embankment** or **earthfill dams** are large barriers of rock, sand, silt or clay for controlling broad streams. As in a gravity dam, their weight deflects the horizontal water thrust downward toward the broad base. The materials may be uniformly mixed or there may be zones of waterproof material such as CONCRETE either on the upstream face or inside the dam. During construction, temporary **cofferdams** are built to keep water away from the site. Automatic **spillways** for disposing of excess water from the dam, intakes, gates and bypasses for fish or ships are all important parts of a dam complex.

DAMASCENING, inlaid ornamentation of gold, silver or copper on the surface of metal objects; the process originated in Damascus, Syria before the 12th century. The surface is undercut with a chisel, and wires or chips of metal are hammered in. The term also applies to watered patterns on sword blades, etc., made from Damascus steel.

DAMASCUS, capital city of Syria, founded c2000 BC and reputed to be the oldest continuously inhabited city in the world. An oasis by the Anti-Lebanon Mts, it has been a halt for desert caravans since c1000 BC; it is still a market center, dealing in both produce and industrial products. The city's northern section is modern, the southern ancient, with the famous Great Mosque and a medieval citadel. The city has been controlled by Greeks, Macedonians, Romans, Arabs, Mongols, Turks, British and French until it became the capital of independent Syria in 1946. Pop 1,550,000.

D'AMBOISE, Jacques (1934–), American dancer and choreographer of the New York City Ballet. A pupil of George Balanchine, he danced many leading roles and choreographed several ballets. He appeared in the films *Seven Brides for Seven Brothers* (1954) and *Carousel* (1956).

DAMIEN, Father (Joseph de Veuster; 1840–1889), Belgian Roman Catholic missionary who spent his life in the leper colony of Molokai Island, Hawaii, which he turned from a mere refuge into a thriving community. He died of leprosy himself, having refused to be cured because he would have had to leave Molokai.

DAMOCLES, in Greek legend, a courtier of Dionysius the Elder of Syracuse. To illustrate the precariousness of power and position he made Damocles sit at a banquet on a throne over which a sword hung by a single thread. Hence the phrase "sword of Damocles."

DAMON AND PYTHIAS, in Greek legend the prototypes of true friendship. Damon surrendered himself to stand trial for Pythias, sentenced to death by Dionysius of Syracuse, while Pythias settled his affairs. Dionysius was so impressed when Pythias returned that he freed them both and sought their friendship.

DAMROSCH, Walter (1862–1950), German-born US conductor. As conductor at the Metropolitan Opera, he directed the first US performances of *Parsifal* and other Wagner operas; until 1927 he conducted the New York Symphony Orchestra. He also composed several operas.

DANA, Charles Anderson (1819–1897), American journalist who developed the "human interest" story. From 1841–46 he lived in the Utopian BROOK FARM; he then joined the *New York Tribune*, and in 1849 became its managing editor. From 1864–65 he was assistant to the secretary of war. As editor of the *New York Sun* in 1868, he became a national figure.

DANA, Richard Henry, Junior (1815–1882), American lawyer, social reformer and author of *Two Years Before the Mast* (1840), grandson of Francis DANA. Written after he had sailed to Cal. round Cape Horn, it exposed in realistic and readable detail the harsh treatment of sailors and started a reform campaign. He was a founder of the FREE SOIL PARTY.

DA NANG, one of the chief seaports and second largest city in South Vietnam. It was an important US naval base in the Vietnam war. Pop 437,668.

DANBURY HATTERS' CASE, a Supreme Court decision of 1908, that dealt labor unions a severe blow by upholding a suit by a non-union Danbury hat manufacturer against the hatters' union for boycotting his product. The court held that the boycott was in violation of the Sherman Anti-Trust Act (1890) outlawing "every combination in restraint of trade."

DANCE, the art of moving the body rhythmically, usually to music. The movements may be enjoyed for their own sake, they may express an idea or emotion or tell a story, or they may be employed to induce a frenzied or trancelike state in the dancer. These possibilities of dance have made it a central feature of the religious, social and artistic life of most cultures. From earliest times dance has played an important part in courtship rituals—the root of most popular dances in the West today—and in the celebration of notable public and private occasions. Among primitive peoples a belief in the magical potency of dance found expression in fertility and rain dances, in dances of exorcism and resurrection, and in dances preparatory to hunting or fighting. Religious dance, associated with paganism, has been played down by the Christian Church since the 12th century. In contrast, in the East traditional dancing is wholly religious in origin and there is little tradition of social dancing. Communal dance as a powerful symbol of group cooperation and mutual regard underlies enduring traditions in FOLK DANCING. Classical BALLET had its origins in the court dances in 15th and 16th-century Italy and France, which were increasingly elaborated into complete entertainments. The 19th century saw the development of the waltz, in which social dancing reached the height of popularity. 20th-century dance styles, promoted by the syncopated rhythms of popular music, have become increasingly free and uninhibited, often resembling primitive dances. One conspicuous innovation has been the conscious invention and commercial promotion of dance styles.

DANDOLO, Enrico (1108–1205), doge of Venice 1192–1205. He founded Venice's colonial empire and was active in the Fourth Crusade which led to the sack of Constantinople by the crusaders.

DANDRUFF, scaling of the SKIN of the scalp, part of the chronic skin condition of seborrheic DERMATITIS; scalp involvement is usually diffuse and itching may occur. The condition is lifelong but usually little more than an inconvenience. Numerous remedies are advertised but few are effective.

DANELAW, Anglo-Saxon name for areas of England colonized by Danish Viking forces in the 9th century, during the reign of Alfred the Great. The W Saxon king Edgar (959–975) granted autonomy to the Danelaw in return for fealty, and a Danish customary law developed in the area.

DANIEL, Book of, Old Testament book, placed among the Prophets in the Christian BIBLE; in the Hebrew Bible it is placed in the Writings. Parts of it are in Aramaic. It is the story of Daniel, thought to have been a Judaean noble brought to Nebuchadnezzar's court during the BABYLONIAN CAPTIVITY, and of his exploits and his apocalyptic visions.

DANIEL, Yuri (1926–   ), Soviet writer sentenced in 1966 with Andrei Sinyavsky to five years in a labor camp for publishing abroad (under the pen-names Arshak and Tertz) works allegedly slandering the Soviet Union.

DANIELS, Josephus (1862–1948), US public official and newspaperman. Editor of the Raleigh, N.C., *News and Observer*, he was active in the campaigns of William Jennings Bryan and Woodrow Wilson, who made him secretary of the navy, 1913–21. He was ambassador to Mexico, 1933–42.

DANILOVA, Alexandra (c1906–   ), Russian-born American ballerina, who studied at the Leningrad ballet schools. She rose to fame in Paris in Diaghilev's Ballet Russe, making her US debut in 1933. Her most famous role is Odette in *Swan Lake*.

DANISH. See SCANDINAVIAN LANGUAGES.

D'ANNUNZIO, Gabriele (1863–1938), Italian writer and adventurer. His poetry first made him famous, its sensuous imagery reflecting his life-style. His novel *The Flame of Life* (1900) is an account of his long liaison with Eleonora DUSE. As a politician he helped bring Italy into WWI on the Allies' side, himself serving in the air force, and in 1919 he occupied the Dalmatian port of Fiume, ruling it as dictator until 1920.

DANTE (Dante Alighieri; 1265–1321), Italy's greatest poet, author of the *Divine Comedy*. Scion of an old Florentine family, he mastered the art of lyric poetry at an early age. He probably attended Bologna University during 1287. His first major work is *The New Life* (c1292) which describes his early life and great love for Beatrice—probably Beatrice Portinari, whom he had known since he was nine; she died in 1290, but remained his lifelong inspiration. He married Gemma Donati c1285. Politically, he was active in Florentine affairs, and was exiled from Florence in 1302. He finally settled in Ravenna in 1318 and died there. *The Divine Comedy* (probably written between 1308 and 1320) is an account of the poet's travels through Hell and Purgatory, and his final glimpse of Heaven. A poetic masterpiece in itself, it is also a diatribe against the corruption Dante saw in the world around him.

DANTON, Georges Jacques (1759–1794), one of the leaders of the FRENCH REVOLUTION. A lawyer, a powerful orator and, in the end, a moderate, Danton strove to reconcile the GIRONDINS and JACOBINS. He dominated the first Committee of Public Safety, but by 1793 began to lose power to the militant Robespierre. Believing the revolution won, he was unable to stop the Reign of Terror, was accused of treason and executed by the Jacobins.

DANUBE RIVER, major European river,

1,776mi long, second only to the Volga in length. From its official source near Donaueschingen in West Germany, it flows through Austria, Czechoslovakia, Hungary, Yugoslavia, Romania, Bulgaria and along parts of the USSR border before emptying into the Black Sea. With over 300 tributaries, it drains almost one-tenth of Europe and provides a major transport system. It served as a major natural boundary for the Roman Empire and a useful highway for invaders from the east. The river becomes navigable at Ulm in Bavaria and flows through three capitals—Vienna, Budapest and Belgrade. Since 1856, international agreements have regulated its use, but seasonal obstructions and Europe's East–West political split have limited its traffic. In W Germany, the Main-Danube Canal links the Danube at Regensburg with the Main-Rhine river system at Bamberg, thus greatly stimulating development of a river formerly isolated from W Europe and exiting through Soviet-controlled E Europe.

DANZIG. See GDANSK.

DARDANELLES, narrow strait 44mi in length in NW Turkey, separating Asia Minor from Europe, formerly called the Hellespont; it is bordered on the W by the GALLIPOLI PENINSULA. It links the Sea of Marmora with the Aegean and is part of the waterway from the Black Sea to the Mediterranean. Together with the BOSPORUS, the Dardanelles are of great strategic importance for their control of access by Soviet vessels to the Mediterranean and the Suez Canal sea lanes.

DAR ES SALAAM, largest city and former capital of Tanzania (the new capital is Dodoma). A modern city, it is a commercial center with a fine harbor providing an outlet for exports of cotton, sisal, coffee, diamonds and gold. Pop 870,700.

DARIEN, Spanish settlement, also traditionally the E end of the Isthmus of Panama. From 1510–19 the colony was a base for exploration of the American mainland, notably by BALBOA. Santa Maria la Antigua del Darién, the original colony, soon declined, and some colonists moved to a site now called Porto Bello.

DARÍO, Rubén, pen name of Felix Rubén Garcí Sarmiento (1867–1916), Nicaraguan poet. He introduced the movement which revolutionized Spanish and Spanish–American literature *modernismo*. His best-known works are *Profane Hymns* (1896) and *Songs of Life and Hope* (1905).

DARIUS, three Persian kings of the Achaemenid dynasty. **Darius I, the Great,** reigned from 522–486 BC. An able ruler, he reorganized his empire into 20 satrapies under officials responsible to him who were supervised by ministers and secret police; he introduced efficient transport, a postal system, taxation, coinage and legal systems. He attacked the SCYTHIANS, overran Thrace and Macedonia, then attempted to subdue Greece but was finally defeated at MARATHON in 490. **Darius II** reigned from 423 BC until his death in 404 BC; his reign was corrupt, but he achieved much influence in Greece in an alliance with Sparta against Athens. **Darius III** (reigned 336-330 BC) was the last ruler of an independent Persia. Defeated by ALEXANDER THE GREAT, he was murdered by one of his own satraps.

DARK AGES, general term for the centuries of decline in Europe, c500–1000 AD, after the fall of the Roman Empire. Documentation for the period is sparse because, in the general instability, classical culture was stifled, though remnants of Greek and Roman tradition were preserved by Christian monks in Ireland, Italy, France and Britain. Charlemagne's rule (800–814) briefly reunited Europe but the true flowering of the MIDDLE AGES came after 1000.

DARLAN, Jean François (1881–1942), French admiral who held various cabinet posts in the Vichy government, becoming vice premier, foreign minister and heir-designate to Pétain in Feb 1941. In Nov 1942 he surrendered French North Africa to the Allies, but was soon afterward assassinated.

DARNLEY, Henry Stuart, Lord (1545–1567), second husband of MARY QUEEN OF SCOTS (1565); their son became James VI of Scotland and JAMES I of England. His intrigues for the Scottish crown led to his death by violence.

DARROW, Clarence Seward (1857–1938), US lawyer, a renowned defense attorney. After 20 years defending the interests of organized labor, he changed his practice to criminal cases. None of his clients on murder charges received the death penalty. His eloquence saved Leopold and Loeb in 1924 from the electric chair; and he won acclaim in 1925 for upholding the right of academic enquiry in his defense of John Scopes for teaching Darwin's theory of evolution.

DARTMOUTH COLLEGE CASE, US Supreme Court decision of 1819 which denied the N.H. legislature the right to revise Dartmouth's charter, originally granted during the reign of King George III. Such action was voided as impairing the the obligation of contracts, forbidden by the

US Constitution. The decision encouraged the growth of corporations, chartered by the states, since it gave them a measure of freedom from state interference.

DARTS, one of the most popular games in Britain, commonly played in pubs. In its British version, three darts are thrown by each player. The target board is a circular piece of cork divided into 20 radiating segments, each numbered with a scoring value, and further divided by a series of circles which the segments intersect. The innermost circle, or bull's-eye, has the highest value. The game originated in medieval England.

DARWIN, Charles Robert (1809–1882), English naturalist, who first formulated the theory of EVOLUTION by NATURAL SELECTION. Between 1831 and 1836 the young Darwin sailed round the world as the naturalist on board H.M.S. BEAGLE. In the course of this he made many geological observations favorable to LYELL's uniformitarian geology, devised a theory to account for the structure of coral islands and was impressed by the facts of the geographical distribution of plants and animals. He became convinced that species were not fixed categories as was commonly supposed but were capable of variation, though it was not until he read MALTHUS's *Essay on the Principle of Population* that he discovered a mechanism whereby ecologically favored varieties might form the basis for new distinct species. Darwin published nothing for 20 years until, on learning of A. R. WALLACE'S independent discovery of the same theory, he collaborated with the younger man in a short Linnean–Society paper. The next year (1859) the theory was set before a wider public in his *Origin of Species*. The rest of his life was spent in further research in defense of his theory, though he always avoided entering the popular controversies surrounding his work and left it to others to debate the supposed consequences of "Darwinism."

DASSIN, Jules (1911–   ), French film director and actor, born in the US. He is noted for *Rififi* (1954) and *Never on Sunday* (1960).

DATA PROCESSING. See COMPUTER.

DATE LINE, International, an imaginary line on the earth's surface, with local deviations, along longitude 180° from Greenwich. As the earth rotates, each day first begins and ends on the line. A traveler going east over the line sets his calendar back one day, and one going west adds one day.

DAUDET, Alphonse (1840–1897), French writer noted for his stories of his native Provence. He wrote with humor and compassion about the poor, and is best remembered for *Lettres de Mon Moulin* (1866) and *Tartarin de Tarascon* (1872).

DAUGHTERS OF THE AMERICAN REVOLUTION (DAR), US conservative women's organization aiming to foster education and patriotism, made up of direct descendants of patriots who "rendered aid" during the Revolutionary War. Founded 1890, its headquarters is in Washington D.C.

DAUMIER, Honoré (1808–1879), French caricaturist, painter and sculptor. In some 4,000 technically masterful lithographs, he satirized the bourgeoisie and contemporary politicians. In 1832, his cartoon of King Louis-Philippe earned him six months in jail. He was one of the first to paint scenes from modern life, and his acidly ironic vision has rarely been approached by others.

DAUPHIN, title given to the heir to the French throne after Philip VI purchased Dauphiné from the Count of Viennois in 1349. The title was renounced in 1830 following the abdication of Charles X.

DAUPHINE, historical region of SE France, now covering the departments of Drôme, Isére and Hautes Alpes. The Rhone valley is the main wine center; Grenoble the capital, manufacturing and cultural center.

DAVID, (d. c961 BC), King of Israel. A Judaean from Bethlehem, he became arms bearer to King Saul of Israel, and an intimate friend to Saul's son Jonathan. David killed the Philistine giant Goliath, and his subsequent popularity aroused Saul's envy and wrath. After years as an outlaw, he was chosen king of Judah on Saul's death, soon extending his authority over the northern tribes. David then seized Jerusalem, making it the religious and political capital of Israel and of a large empire. His highly prosperous reign lasted 40 years. David was the prototype of the MESSIAH through whom God mediated his blessing to Israel, and an ancestor of Jesus Christ. He is the reputed author of many of the psalms.

DAVID, Gerard (c1460–1523), last great master of the 15th-century Bruges school of painting. He is noted for his emotional power and depth, and accomplished technique, as in the altarpieces, *Rest on Flight into Egypt* and *Madonna with Angels and Saints*.

DAVID, Jacques Louis (1748–1825), French painter and leader of the French neoclassical movement. His style, which combines formal perfection with romantic feeling and didactic purpose, is exemplified in his *Oath of the Horatii* and *Death of Marat*. He appealed to the French Revolutionary spirit and was appointed painter to Napoleon. Exiled by Louis XVIII, he died in Brussels.

DAVID, Saint (d. c600), patron saint of Wales, who founded many monasteries of strict rule in the 6th century.

DAVIDSON, Bruce (1933–   ), US photographer who used a cumbersome studio camera in Spanish Harlem to create his candid study of the residents of *East 100th Street* (1970). His free-lance work appeared in *Life, Look, Réalités* and *Queen*. He joined the Magnum photo collective in 1959.

DAVIDSON, Jo (1883–1952), US sculptor, born N.Y. city, but lived in Paris. Among famous sitters for his portrait busts were Gertrude STEIN, Will ROGERS, Walt WHITMAN and Franklin ROOSEVELT.

DAVIES, Arthur Bowen (1862–1928), US painter in the romantic-idealist tradition. Davies was a leader of the American modern movement and a member of the ASHCAN SCHOOL as well as chief organizer of the 1913 ARMORY SHOW. Noted for the lyrical and abstract *Unicorns* and *Dreams* (1908).

DA VINCI, Leonardo. See LEONARDO DA VINCI.

DAVIS, Alexander Jackson (1803–1892), US architect and exponent of the Gothic Revival style. With his partner, Ithiel Town, he built the New York Customs House, and the capitols of Ill., Ind. and Ohio.

DAVIS, Benjamin Oliver (1877–1970), the first black general in the US Army (1940). Appointed brigadier-general, he supervised the desegregation of troops. His son, Benjamin Oliver, Jr., became the first black general in the US Air Force.

DAVIS, Bette (1908–   ), US movie actress. She won Academy Awards for *Dangerous* (1935) and *Jezebel* (1938), and in the 1960s won new fame in psychological thrillers. Her other films include *Dark Victory* (1939), *The Little Foxes* (1941) and *All About Eve* (1950).

DAVIS, Elmer (1890–1958), US writer and broadcaster. A political commentator for the *New York Times* (1914–24), he achieved fame as a CBS radio news analyst (1939–42) during the early years of WWII. He headed the Office of War Information (1942–45) before resuming his radio career with ABC. His bestselling *But We Were Born Free* (1954) was an attack on political witch-hunters.

DAVIS, Henry Winter (1817–1865), US Congressman and leader of the pre-Civil War Know Nothing party. A staunch Unionist who served in the House of Representatives from 1855–61 and 1863–65, he criticized Lincoln's lenient Reconstruction program for the South. With Benjamin Wade, he succeeded in getting his own Reconstruction bill through Congress, but Lincoln refused to sign it.

DAVIS, Jefferson (1808–1889), president of the Confederate States of America during the Civil War, born in Fairview, Ky. He represented Miss. in the US Senate (1847–51 and 1857–61) and was a leading defender of slavery and states' rights. He was a nationalist secretary of war, 1853–57, but when the Southern states began their secession Davis resigned from the Senate in Jan. 1861, when Miss. withdrew from the Union. His peace delegation to Lincoln was rebuffed and he ordered the attack on Fort Sumter, S.C., which opened the war. On Feb. 18, 1861 he became provisional president of the Confederacy and was elected for a six-year term. Although his leadership was criticized, he made the best of inferior numbers and poor industrial resources. In 1865 Davis was captured, and after two years in prison was released on bail.

DAVIS, Miles Dewey (1926–   ), US trumpeter and composer, associated with bebop jazz in the 1940s and cool jazz in the 1950s. He pioneered improvisations that were guided by scales rather than chords.

DAVIS, Ossie (1917–   ), US actor, director and writer who made his major breakthrough as the author and star of the Broadway hit *Purlie Victorious* (1961). With his wife, actress Ruby Dee, he was actively involved in the civil rights movement of the 1950s and 1960s.

DAVIS, Stuart (1894–1964), US abstract painter, illustrator and lithographer, studied in New York. A forerunner of the pop art movement, his style is characterized by brilliant colors, the use of printed words and interlocking shapes.

DAVIS CUP, silver bowl trophy for international tennis given by Dwight Filley Davis who organized the tournament in 1900. Eliminating rounds are played each year in various "zones" or areas of the world by national teams. Each meeting consists of four singles matches and one doubles match. The team surviving these eliminations meets the previous year's winner in the final or "challenge" round. Over the years, Davis Cup competition has been dominated mainly by US and Australian teams.

DAVITT, Michael (1846–1906), Irish nationalist, who in 1879 organized the Irish Land League, which sought to better the lot of the Irish tenant farmers. He was elected to parliament in 1892 and 1895 but resigned in 1899 over the South African War.

DAVY, Sir Humphry (1778–1829), English chemist who pioneered the study of ELECTROCHEMISTRY. Electrolytic methods yielded him the elements SODIUM, POTASSIUM, MAGNESIUM, CALCIUM, STRONTIUM and BARIUM (1807–08). He also recognized the elemental nature of and named CHLORINE (1810). His early work on nitrous oxide (see NITROGEN) was done at Bristol under T. Beddoes but most of the rest of his career centered on the ROYAL INSTITUTION where he was assisted by his protégé FARADAY, from 1813. A major practical achievement was the invention of a miner's SAFETY LAMP, known as the **Davy Lamp**, in 1815–16. From his Bristol days, Davy was a friend of S. T. Coleridge.

DAWES, Charles Gates (1865–1951), US statesman who shared the 1925 Nobel Peace Prize for his DAWES PLAN. Vice-president under Calvin Coolidge 1925–29, he was ambassador to Great Britain 1929–1932, when he became chairman of the Reconstruction Finance Corporation. He resigned the same year and returned to banking.

DAWES PLAN, plan developed by Charles Gates DAWES in 1924, to enable Germany to pay off WWI reparations by means of an international loan and mortgages on German industry and railways.

DAY, term referring either to a full period of 24 hours (the civil day) or to the (usually shorter and varying) period between sunrise and sunset when a given point on the earth's surface is bathed in light rather than darkness (the natural day). Astronomers distinguish the sidereal day from the solar day and the lunar day depending on whether the reference location on the earth's surface is taken to return to the same position relative to the stars, to the sun or to the moon respectively. The civil day is the mean solar day, some 168 seconds longer than the sidereal day. In most modern states the day is deemed to run from midnight to midnight, though in Jewish tradition the day is taken to begin at sunset.

DAY (or DAYE), Stephen (c1594–1668), American printer who set up in Cambridge, Mass., the first printing press in the American colonies. Forerunner of Harvard University Press, he printed the *Freeman's Oath* (1639) and the BAY PSALM BOOK (1640).

DAY, Clarence (Shepard) (1874–1935), US writer and humorist, best known for *This Simian World* (1920), *Life with Father* (1935) and *Life with Mother* (1936).

DAY, Doris (1924–   ), US singer and film star who was one of the most popular vocalists of the 1950s. Her typical film role was that of a high-spirited, innocent girl-next-door.

DAY, Dorothy (1897–1980), US social activist. A reporter for left-wing papers, she was active in the Socialist and Communist parties before joining the Roman Catholic Church (1927). Dorothy Day publicized the Catholic Church's social programs in the *Catholic Worker*, opened a house in New York for the hungry and homeless, and supported numerous liberal causes.

DAYAN, Moshe (1915–1981), Israeli military and political leader. Active in Israel's War of Independence (1948), he commanded the Israeli army in the 1956 Sinai Campaign. He was minister of defense during the Six-Day War of 1967 and from 1969 to 1974, when he resigned over the Yom Kippur War. He was foreign minister 1977–79.

DAY LEWIS, C. See LEWIS, CECIL DAY.

DAYLIGHT SAVING TIME, system that adjusts the clock to make maximum use of seasonal daylight; it was first adopted as a WWI fuel conservation measure.

DAYTIME SERIALS, continuing dramas in daily installments, originated on radio and now appearing on television. Also known as "soap operas," because of the prominence of toiletries distributors in early sponsorship, they started on evening radio in the 1920's, moving to the daytime hours when crowded out of the evening schedule by comedians and variety shows in the early 1930s. The comedy serial *Clara, Lu 'n' Em* was the first to make the move in 1932. The first dramatic daytime serial, *Betty and Bob* (1932), about an unstable marriage, was so popular with housewives that it set a permanent model for the subject matter. It was created by Frank and Anne Hummert, who subsequently introduced a myriad of additional radio "soaps," including some of the most popular, such as *The Romance of Helen Trent* (1933–1960) and *Our Gal Sunday* (1937–1959). Radio serials began to fade only after the appearance of the first televised daytime serials in 1950. TV started cautiously, but eventually grew somewhat bolder and less formula-bound. The most reknowned television serial writer and creator, Agnes Nixon, learned her craft from the radio writer, Irma Phillips. The longest-running television soaps are *Search For Tomorrow* (1951–   ) and *Love Of Life* (1951–   ), and the most popular daytime serials in 1981 were *General Hospital* (1963–   ) and *All My Children* (1970–   ).

D-DAY, in WWII, June 6, 1944, the day

fixed for the Allied landing in Normandy beginning the invasion of Europe, under the command of General EISENHOWER. Over 5,000 ships were used, from which 90,000 British, American and Canadian troops landed; around 20,000 more were delivered by parachute and glider. After some initial difficulties, the forces had linked up in a solid front by June 11. The invasion, code-named *Overlord*, was one of the most complex feats of organization and supply in history.

DDT, dichlorodiphenyltrichloroethane, a synthetic contact INSECTICIDE which kills a wide variety of insects, including mosquitoes, lice and flies, by interfering with their nervous systems. Its use, in quantities as great as 100,000 tons yearly, has almost eliminated many insect-borne diseases, including MALARIA, TYPHUS, YELLOW FEVER and PLAGUE. Being chemically stable and physically inert, it persists in the environment for many years. Its concentration in the course of natural food chains (see ECOLOGY) has led to the buildup of dangerous accumulations in some fish and birds. This prompted the US to restrict the use of DDT in 1972. In any case the development of insect strains resistant to DDT was already reducing its effectiveness as an insecticide. Although DDT was first made in 1874, its insecticidal properties were only discovered in 1939 (by P. H. MÜLLER).

DEACON, lowest rank in the threefold MINISTRY in episcopally-organized Christian churches, an elected lay official in some Protestant churches. Traditionally deacons have administered alms. Since the Second Vatican Council, a permanent office of deacon in the Roman Catholic Church has become open both to celibate and married men, where formerly it was a transitional rank as a step towards priesthood. In some Lutheran churches an assistant minister is called a deacon although fully ordained.

DEAD SEA, salt lake on the Israeli–Jordan border. It extends around 50mi S from the mouth of the Jordan R (its main affluent) and is up to 11mi wide. Much of it is more than 1000ft deep, and with a surface 1,302ft below sea level it is the lowest point on earth. Its biblical name of Salt Sea derives from its extremely high salt content (over 20%), resulting from the rapid evaporation in the area's hot climate. Some minerals are extracted from it commercially.

DEAD SEA SCROLLS, manuscripts on papyrus and leather (and even one on copper) discovered in five sites in what is now Israel and Israeli-occupied territory. The first discovery was made by shepherds at Khirbat Qumran on the NW shore of the Dead Sea. These scrolls were possibly part of the library of a Jewish sect, the Essenes, that flourished from c200 BC to 68 AD. The area's 11 caves contained hundreds of manuscripts, including large portions of the Hebrew Old Testament. This has proved that the modern Hebrew Bible has hardly changed in 2,000 years. Another site at Wadi al-Murabba'ah, a few miles away, contained both religious and secular documents dating from the anti-Roman rebellion led by Bar Cochba in 132–135 AD. They were probably left by fugitives from his army, as were those at a third site near Ein Gedi.

A cave near Jericho and an excavation at Masada produced further documents that, together with the other finds, clarify much of the complex history of the area and throw new light on the beginnings of Christianity. The manuscripts are not well preserved, and their transcription and interpretation is made more difficult by the necessity of carefully unrolling the ancient scrolls, and of salvaging and putting together pieces often smaller than postage stamps.

DEADWOOD, mining city and tourist center in S.D., seat of Lawrence Co. Originally a frontier boom town, it was the home of many legendary Western characters. Pop 2,409.

DEADWOOD DICK, "pulp" fiction hero of the 1880s. He was created by the popular novelist E. L. Wheeler, probably based on Dick Clark, an adventurer from Deadwood, S.D.

DEAF MUTE. See DUMBNESS.

DEAFNESS, or failure of hearing, may have many causes. Conductive deafness is due to disease of outer or middle EAR, while perceptive deafness is due to disease of inner ear or nerves of hearing. Common physical causes of **conductive deafness** are obstruction with wax or foreign bodies and injury to the tympanic membrane. Middle ear disease is an important cause: in *acute otitis*, common in children, the ears are painful, with deafness, FEVER and discharge; in *secretory otitis* or glue ear, also in children, deafness and discomfort result from poor Eustachian tube drainage; *chronic otitis*, in any age group, leads to a deaf discharging ear, with drum perforation. ANTIBIOTICS in adequate courses are crucial in acute otitis, while glue ear is relieved by tubes or "grommets" passed through the drum to drain the middle ear. In both, the ADENOIDS may need removal to relieve Eustachian obstruction. In chronic otitis, keeping the ears clean and dry is important, and antibiotics are used for secondary infection, while SURGERY, including reconstitution of the drum, may be needed to restore hearing. *Otosclerosis* is a common familial disease of middle age in which fusion of ANKYLOSIS of the small bones of the ear causes deafness. Early operation can prevent irreversible changes and improve hearing. **Perceptive deafness** may follow infections in PREGNANCY (e.g., GERMAN MEASLES) or be hereditary. Acute VIRUS infection and trauma to the inner ear (e.g., blast injuries or chronic occupational noise exposure) are important causes. Damage to the ear blood supply or the auditory nerves by drugs, TUMORS or MULTIPLE SCLEROSIS may lead to perceptive deafness, as may the later stages of MÉNIÈRE'S DISEASE. Deafness of old age, or *presbycusis*, is of gradual onset, mainly due to the loss of nerve cells. Early recognition of deafness in children is particularly important as it may otherwise impair learning and speech development. HEARING AIDS are valuable in most cases of conductive and some of perceptive deafness. Lip-reading, in which the deaf person understands speech by the interpretation of lip movements, and sign language are useful in severe cases.

DEÁK, Ferenc (1803–1876), Hungarian statesman who negotiated the 1867 Compromise with the Austrian emperor, giving Hungary internal autonomy within the dual monarchy of AUSTRIA–HUNGARY. A lawyer, he entered the Diet in 1833. In the 1848 revolution he became minister of justice, but resigned in disagreement with the revolutionary KOSSUTH the same year. He returned to the Diet in 1861, becoming the country's acknowledged leader.

DEAN, Dizzy (Jay Hanna Dean; 1911–1974), American baseball pitcher who played for the St. Louis Cardinals and Chicago Cubs 1932–41, winning 30 games in 1934, when the Cardinals won the World Series. He retired in 1941, and became a popular sports commentator.

DEAN, James (1931–1955), American actor, who became a cult hero after his death in a car crash. The films *East of Eden* (1955), *Rebel Without a Cause* (1955) and *Giant* (1956), characterized him as the symbol of rebellious youth.

DEANE, Silas (1737–1789), American diplomat, first envoy to Europe. Sent to France in 1776, he was successful in recruiting officers and obtaining arms. He was recalled on profiteering charges; these were never proved. Unpopular in America for urging reconciliation with England (1781), he went into exile in England.

DEATH, the complete and irreversible cessation of LIFE in an organism or part of an organism. Death is conventionally accepted as the time when the HEART ceases to beat, there is no breathing and when the BRAIN shows no evidence of function. Ophthalmoscopic examination of the EYE shows that columns of BLOOD in small vessels are interrupted and static. Since it is now possible to resuscitate and maintain heart function and to take over breathing mechanically, it is not uncommon for the brain to have suffered irreversible death but for "life" to be maintained artificially. The concept of "brain death" has been introduced, in which reversible causes have been eliminated, when no spontaneous breathing, no movement and no specific REFLEXES are seen on two occasions. When this state is reached, artificial life support systems can be reasonably discontinued as brain death has already occurred. The ELECTROENCEPHALOGRAPH has been used to diagnose brain death but is now considered unreliable.

After death, ENZYMES are released which begin the process of autolysis or decomposition, which later involves BACTERIA. In the hours following death, changes occur in muscle which cause rigidity or RIGOR MORTIS. Following death, anatomical examination of the body (AUTOPSY) may be performed. Burial, embalming or cremation are usual practices for disposal of the body in Western society.

Death of part of an organism, or *necrosis*, such as occurs following loss of blood supply, consists of loss of cell organization, autolysis and GANGRENE. The part may separate or be absorbed but if it becomes infected, this is liable to spread to living tissue. Cells may also die as part of the normal turnover of a structure (e.g., SKIN or blood cells), after POISONING or infection (e.g., in the LIVER), from compression (e.g., by TUMOR), or as part of a degenerative disease. They then undergo characteristic involutionary changes.

"DEATH OF GOD," Modern Protestant theological school fashionable in the late 1960s. It held that traditional concepts of God were meaningless to modern man for whom God was thus "dead." Its main tenets were explained in *The Gospel of Christian Atheism* (1966) by Thomas J.J. Altizer (b.1927).

DEATH PENALTY. See CAPITAL PUNISHMENT.

DEATH VALLEY, arid valley in Inyo Co., Cal. The highest recorded US temperature—134°F—was recorded here in 1913. Located near the Nevada border, it is 140mi long, and up to 15mi wide. The lowest point in the W Hemisphere, Badwater (282ft below sea level) is at the heart of the valley. Since rainfall is only 2in per year, it supports little vegetation. Large deposits of borax were discovered there in the late 19th century. In 1933 it was made part of the Death Valley National Monument.

DEBAKEY, Michael Ellis (1908–   ), US heart surgeon. He developed the pump for the heart-lung machine (1932), devised new surgical procedures and successfully implanted a mechanical device to help restore a diseased heart (1967).

DE BOW, James Dunwoody Brownson (1820–1867), US publisher and pioneering statistician, who founded the *Commercial Review of the South and Southwest* (also known as *De Bow's Review*) in New Orleans in 1846. He prepared the *Statistical View of the United States* (1854).

DEBRÉ, Michel Jean Pierre (1912–   ), French political leader. Active in the Resistance in WWII, he became an unswerving Gaullist and was De Gaulle's minister of justice in 1958. Principal author of the constitution of the 5th Republic, he became its first prime minister 1959–62, and later minister of economics and finance 1966–68, foreign minister May 1968 and defense minister 1969–73.

DE BROGLIE, Louis Victor Pierre Raymond, Prince (1892–   ), French physicist who was awarded the 1929 Nobel Prize in Physics for his suggestion that acknowledged particles should display wave properties under appropriate conditions in the same way that ELECTROMAGNETIC RADIATION sometimes behaved as if composed of particles.

DEBS, Eugene Victor (1855–1926), American labor organizer and socialist political leader. He was a national leader of the Brotherhood of Locomotive Firemen and in 1893 founded the American Railway Union. Debs was jailed in 1895 for defying a federal court injunction against strike action which interfered with the mails. Five times a socialist candidate for the presidency, he fought his last and most successful campaign in 1920 while still imprisoned under the WWI Espionage Act (1917) for his opposition to the war. He was released in 1921.

DEBUSSY, Claude (1862–1918), born Achille-Claude. French composer whose impact on the history of music was revolutionary. He involved music in the Impressionist movement (see IMPRESSIONISM) which was affecting painting and poetry at this time. His ideas on harmony and his innovations in orchestration and the

use of the piano were highly influential in the development of 20th-century music. His works include songs, some outstanding piano music, an opera, *Pelléas et Mélisande* (1902), and the orchestral pieces *Prélude à l'après-midi d'un faune* (1892–94) and *La Mer* (1905).

DEBYE, Peter Joseph Wilhelm (1884–1966), Dutch-born, German-US physical chemist chiefly remembered for the Debye-Hückel theory of ionic solution (1923). He was awarded the 1936 Nobel Prize for Chemistry.

DECAMERON, The, collection of 100 stories by the 14th-century Italian writer, Giovanni BOCCACCIO, one of the outstanding works in Italian literature. Amusing and often bawdy, the tales provide a shrewd commentary on 14th-century Italian life.

DECATHLON, ten-event contest in modern Olympic games. It consists of the 100-meter dash; the 400-meter and 1,500-meter flat races; the 110-meter hurdle race; pole vaulting; discus throwing; shot putting; javelin throwing; and the long and high jumps. Outstanding US Olympic decathlon champions have included Jim THORPE (1912), Bob MATHIAS (1948, 1952) and Bruce JENNER (1976).

DECATUR, Stephen (1779–1820), American naval hero. He was responsible for many victories in the BARBARY WARS, and later in the WAR OF 1812 until forced to surrender to the British in 1815. After the war he was sent to subdue Algiers, and then served as a US navy commissioner until his death in a duel. He is famous for his reply to a toast: "Our country, right or wrong."

DECCAN, name loosely applied to the entire peninsula of India, S of the Narmada R, more strictly the lava-covered plateau between the Narmada and Krishna rivers.

DECEMBER, 12th month of the year in the Gregorian calendar, taking its name from the 10th month in the Roman calendar. The winter solstice occurs about Dec. 21, and traditionally it is the month for celebrations, including CHRISTMAS.

DECEMBRIST REVOLT, unsuccessful uprising against the tsar of Russia (Dec. 1825). In the unrest following the French Revolution and the Napoleonic Wars, groups of officers and aristocrats formed secret revolutionary societies. On this occasion they attempted to take advantage of the confusion accompanying the accession of Nicholas I. They lacked effective organization and were quickly suppressed, but the uprising served as an inspiration to later Russian revolutionaries.

DECIMAL SYSTEM, a number system using the POWERS of ten; our everyday system of numeration. The digits used are 0, 1, 2, 3, 4, 5, 6, 7, 8, 9; the powers of 10 being written $10^0=1$, $10^1=10$, $10^2=100$, $10^3=1000$, etc. To each of these powers is assigned a place value in a particular number; thus $(4 \times 10^3) + (0 \times 10^2) + (9 \times 10^1) + (2 \times 10^0)$ is written 4092. Similarly, FRACTIONS may be expressed by setting their DENOMINATORS equal to powers of 10—

$$\frac{3}{4} = \frac{75}{100} = \frac{7}{10} + \frac{5}{100} = \frac{(7 \times 10^{-1}) +}{(5 \times 10^{-2}),}$$

which is written as 0.75. Not all numbers can be expressed in terms of the decimal system: one example is the fraction ⅓ which is written 0.333 3..., the row of dots indicating that the 3 is to be repeated an infinite number of times. Fractions like 0.333 3... are termed **repeating decimals**. APPROXIMATION is often useful when dealing with decimal fractions.

DECLARATION OF HUMAN RIGHTS, Universal, adopted by the UN General Assembly on Dec. 10, 1948. UN members pledged to guarantee not only civil rights such as life, liberty and freedom from arbitrary arrest, but also so-called social rights such as the rights to work and to education, on the principle that "all human beings are born free and equal in dignity and rights."

DECLARATION OF INDEPENDENCE, manifesto in which the representatives of the 13 American colonies asserted their independence and explained the reasons for their break with Britain. It was adopted on July 4, 1776, in what is now known as Independence Hall, in Philadelphia. The date has since been celebrated annually as Independence Day.

American discontent with British attempts at taxation began in the 1760s, but in these disputes colonists demanded only their "rights" as Englishmen. Even after the military confrontations at Lexington and Concord (1775), the Second Continental Congress convened at Philadelphia in May disavowed any desire for independence. However, after continued British provocations in 1775, opinion began to shift. Thomas Paine's pamphlet *Common Sense* (1776), which attacked the monarchy and called for independence, was extremely influential. During 1776 definite moves towards independence were taken.

On June 7 Richard Henry Lee of Virginia resolved before the Congress that "These United Colonies are, and of right ought to be, free and independent States." A committee consisting of Thomas Jefferson, Benjamin Franklin, John Adams, Robert Livingston and Roger Sherman was selected to draft a formal declaration of independence. The draft, almost wholly Jefferson's work, passed on July 2, with 12 colonies voting in favor and New York temporarily abstaining. The ensuing debate made the most significant changes in omitting the clauses condemning the British people as well as their government, and, in deference to the Southern delegates, an article denouncing the slave trade.

In Europe, including Britain, the Declaration was greeted as inaugurating a new age of freedom and self-government. As a manifesto for revolution it yielded to the French DECLARATION OF THE RIGHTS OF MAN AND THE CITIZEN, although its importance increased in the US. After the federal union was organized in 1789 it came to be considered as a statement of basic political principles, not just of independence.

The Declaration is on display for the public in the National Archives Building in Washington, D.C.

DECLARATION OF THE RIGHTS OF MAN AND THE CITIZEN, key philosophical document of the French Revolution, adopted by the National Assembly on Aug. 26, 1789. It reflects the French Enlightenment's rejection of the rule of absolute monarchy in favor of natural rights. These included fair taxation, self-determination in government and personal liberty under the rule of law. It was made the preamble to the 1791 Constitution.

DECLARATORY ACT, assertion by the British parliament (1766) of its authority to make laws binding on the American colonies. It was passed by the Marquess of Rockingham's government simultaneously with repeal of the Stamp Act to satisfy sections of British opinion which favored taxing the colonies.

DECLINATION, the angular distance of a celestial body from the celestial equator (see CELESTIAL SPHERE) along the MERIDIAN through the body. Bodies north of the equator have positive declinations, those south, negative. Together with right ascension, declination defines the position of a body in the sky.

DECOMPOSITION, Chemical, a reaction in which a chemical compound is split up into its elements or simpler compounds. Heat, or light of a suitable wavelength, will decompose many compounds, and some decompose spontaneously. Ionic compounds may be decomposed by ELECTROLYSIS. **Double decomposition** is a reaction of the type

$$AC + BD \rightarrow AD + BC$$

in which radicals are exchanged.

DECORATION DAY. See MEMORIAL DAY.

DECORATIONS AND MEDALS, awards for exceptional bravery in civil or military service. The highest US civil decoration is the Presidential Medal of Freedom; the Medal for Merit is also for outstanding services. The highest US military award, "for conspicuous gallantry at the risk of life" is the Congressional Medal of Honor. Soldiers wounded in action receive the Purple Heart. Important foreign decorations include the Victoria Cross and the George Cross (Britain and the Commonwealth), the Croix de Guerre and Legion of Honor (France), the Order of Merit for civilians (the German Federal Republic), the Order of Lenin (USSR), the Order of the Chrysanthemum (Japan) and the Order of the People's Liberation Army (China).

DÉCOUPAGE (from French *découper*, to cut out), a form of surface decoration. The craft originated as a form of furniture decoration in France during the 17th century. Engravings were cut out, colored, glued to the surface of pieces of furniture and then "sunk" under numerous coats of varnish or lacquer so that the final effect closely resembles that of fine inlay work.

DEDEKIND, Julius Wilhelm Richard (1831–1916), German mathematician who contributed to the theory of numbers. He proposed the method of "Dedekind cuts" for defining all the REAL NUMBERS in terms of RATIONAL NUMBERS.

DEDUCTION, method of reasoning from the general to the particular, from principle to practice or from law to a particular application of law; an inference or conclusion based on this method of reasoning, i.e. on certain underlying assumptions.

DEE, Ruby (Ruby Ann Wallace; 1924–), US actress who started her career with the American Negro Theater during WWII and went on to star in such plays as *Raisin in the Sun* (1959; film 1961), *Purlie Victorious* (1961), and *Boesman and Lena* (1970). She and her husband, actor-writer Ossie DAVIS, were active in the civil rights movement.

DEER, cloven-hoofed mammals of the family Cervidae, found in Europe, Asia and the Americas. The most remarkable characteristic of the deer family, which contains about 40 species, is the ANTLERS of the males. Only the Musk deer and the Chinese water deer lack antlers, while both sexes of the CARIBOU and the REINDEER are antlered. The smallest deer is the Chilean PUDU, 320mm (13in) at the shoulder, and the largest the North American MOOSE, up to 2.1m (7ft), and over 450kg (1000lb) in weight. Though many species are abundant, some, such as the Axis deer of India and Ceylon, are fast becoming rare and the Chinese Pere David's deer survives only in zoos.

DEERE, John (1804–1886), US inventor who developed and marketed the first steel plows.

DEFENSE, US Department of, executive department responsible for national security. It is the largest of the federal departments and receives the major part of the federal budget. It was created by the National Security Act of 1947 as a National Military Establishment, bringing together the three previously separate departments of the Army, Navy and Air Force. It was established in its present form in 1949 with the aim of achieving a more unified defense structure. It is headed by a civilian secretary of defense, appointed by the President, who is a member of his cabinet.

DEFOE, Daniel (1660–1731), English author, one of the founders of the English novel. Originally a merchant, he took to writing essays and pamphlets, including a satire against the Anglican High Church for which he was fined and pilloried. He was nearly 60 when he began writing the realistic novels for which he is best known, including *Robinson Crusoe* (1719), *Moll Flanders* (1722) and *A Journal of the Plague Year* (1722).

DEFOLIANTS, chemicals that cause plants to lose their leaves. They are used in agriculture to remove excess foliage and in war to deprive the enemy of the cover of vegetation (see AGENT ORANGE; VIETNAM WAR).

DE FOREST, Lee (1873–1961), US inventor of the TRIODE (1906), an electron tube with three ELECTRODES (CATHODE, ANODE and grid) which could operate as a signal AMPLIFIER as well as a RECTIFIER. The triode was crucial to the development of RADIO.

DEGAS (Hilaire-Germain Edgar de Gas, 1834–1917), French painter and sculptor associated with IMPRESSIONISM. The paintings of INGRES were the source of Degas' linear style, but his asymmetrical compositions were influenced by Japanese prints. His favorite subjects were ballet dancers, women dressing and horse racing. From the 1880s, Degas worked regularly in pastel, and produced small bronze sculptures of dancers and horses. Among his best-known paintings are *The Rehearsal* (1872) and *The Millinery Shop* (c1885).

DE GASPERI, Alcide (1881–1954), Italian

statesman, premier 1945–53. Active in political life from 1911, he was twice imprisoned for his opposition to the fascist regime. He clandestinely organized the Christian Democratic Party during WWII and as its leader became the first premier of the new Italian Republic in 1945.

DE GAULLE, Charles André Joseph Marie (1890–1970), French soldier and statesman, president 1945–46 and 1958–69, noted for his sense of personal destiny and unswerving devotion to France. De Gaulle was trained at Saint-Cyr military academy, and served under PÉTAIN as a captain in WWI. He then taught military history at Saint-Cyr, developing his advanced tactical theories. When France fell in 1940, he started the Free French movement in England. In 1944, his provisional government took over liberated France and did much to restore national morale. After resigning in 1946 he returned the following year with a new party, but met with little success and retired in 1953. On June 1, 1958, he was named premier at the height of the Algerian crisis; he assumed new and wider powers and passed many reforms which strengthened the economy. The Algerian crisis worsened, but De Gaulle was largely responsible for its resolution in 1962. He failed in his aim to make France the leader of a European political community, and during the 1960s pursued a policy of national independence. He resigned in 1969 on the defeat of a referendum designed to give him further powers for constitutional reforms.

DEIGHTON, Len (1929–   ), British author whose expert knowledge of secret service operations informs such espionage thrillers as *The Ipcress File* (1963) and *Blitzkrieg* (1980).

DEISM, religious system developed in the 17th and 18th centuries, expounded by VOLTAIRE and Jean Jacques ROUSSEAU. Deists believed in a Creator God, but rejected PROVIDENCE, REVELATION and the supernatural, holding that religious truth is known by reason and the light of nature. (See also THEISM).

DEKKER, Thomas (c1570–c1632), English dramatist and pamphleteer. On many plays he collaborated with Philip MASSINGER, Thomas MIDDLETON, John FORD and John WEBSTER. His best-known work is the comedy *The Shoemaker's Holiday* (1600). He was a vigorous pamphleteer and witty observer of London life.

DE KOONING, Willem (1904–   ), Dutch-born US painter, a founder of ABSTRACT EXPRESSIONISM. Influenced by GORKY, MIRO and PICASSO, he painted abstract and figurative pictures with thickly applied pigment. One famous work is *Woman I* (1952).

DE KOVEN, (Henry Louis) Reginald (1859–1920), US composer and music critic. His many successful operettas include *Robin Hood* (1890), which contains the song "O Promise Me," and *The Red Feather* (1903).

DELACROIX, Ferdinand-Victor-Eugène (1798–1863), French painter whose literary and historical themes are typical of ROMANTICISM. Such early works as *The Massacre of Chios* (1824) were influenced by GÉRICAULT, but his mastery of rich color schemes and handling of paint were largely learned from RUBENS, as shown by *Death of Sardanapalus* (1827), *The Justice of Trajan* (1840) and the many official decorative schemes he undertook. His frescoes for Saint-Sulpice, Paris, influenced IMPRESSIONISM.

DE LA MADRID MURTADO, Miguel (1935–   ), Mexican political leader. Budget minister (1976–82), he was designated (1981) by the country's ruling party, the Institutional Revolutionary Party, as its candidate for president for the term beginning in 1982.

DE LA MARE, Walter John (1873–1956), English poet and novelist. His work, much of which was intended for children, is characterized by its power to evoke the atmosphere of dreams and the supernatural. His best-known works are the novel *Memoirs of a Midget* (1921) and the childrens' poetry collection *Peacock Pie* (1913).

DELANEY, Shelagh (1939–   ), British playwright best known for *A Taste of Honey* (1958), about a daughter's alienation from her mother. Delaney's other works include *The Lion in Love* (1960) and a collection of stories, *Sweetly Sings the Donkey* (1963).

DELAUNAY, Robert (1885–1941), French abstract painter who with his wife Sonia founded the Orphist movement in 1910. His pictures comprise forms of brilliantly contrasting color.

Name of state: Delaware
Capital: Dover
Statehood: Dec. 7, 1787 (1st state)
Familiar name: First State; Diamond State
Area: 2,057sq mi
Population: 595,225
Elevation: Highest—442ft, New Castle County. Lowest—sea level, Atlantic coast
Motto: Liberty and Independence
State flower: Peach Blossom
State bird: Blue hen chicken
State tree: American holly
State song: "Our Delaware"

DELAWARE, state, in E US, bounded by the Atlantic Ocean and the Delaware R to the E, Md. to the S and W, and Pa. to the N; it was the first state to ratify the US Constitution.

Land. Most of the state is part of the Atlantic coastal plain, long and narrow in shape. The greater part consists of lowland, but the Piedmont area in the NW has rolling hills. The main river is the Delaware, running down the E boundary of the state. It has many other rivers and lakes. The climate is temperate but humid with quite mild winters and hot summers.

People. The state has become mainly urban. Its population, swelled by interstate migration, is chiefly concentrated in the Wilmington metropolitan area. The state legislature, the General Assembly, consists of a Senate of 21 members, elected for four-year terms, and a House of Representatives with 41 members who serve for two years.

Economy. Until 1920 the economy was mostly rural, but now agriculture (soybeans, vegetables, dairy products and chickens) accounts for only a fraction of the state's production, while the chemical industry is the state's largest producer of goods. The manufacture of processed foods, transportation equipment, clothing and metal goods is also important. Corporation taxes are unusually low, attracting many companies whose main business is often not in Del.

History. The English explorer Samuel ARGALL sailed into the Delaware R in 1610 and named it for Baron DE LA WARR, then governor of Virginia. The area was occupied by the Dutch and the Swedes until seized by the English in 1664; it was ruled as part of Pennsylvania until acquiring its own assembly in 1704. After the Revolution Delaware prospered; flour-milling was then the leading industry. Gunpowder mills were built by DU PONT in 1802, becoming the basis of the state's chemical industry. Quaker influence around Wilmington meant that many slaves were freed by 1860. From WWI on, the industrialization and urbanization of the N part of the state proceeded steadily, led by the Wilmington-based Du Pont company. Toward the end of the 1970s, the population distribution was marked by movement out of the cities into suburbs, and there was a rise in unemployment. The average per capita income, however, remained a respectable $9,327.

DELAWARE INDIANS, tribe of the ALGONQUIAN linguistic group who lived in the Delaware R basin area until driven out into Ohio in the 18th century by the incursions of colonists and the FRENCH AND INDIAN WARS. An agricultural tribe, they had a sophisticated culture and were respected by other tribes. Today their descendants are scattered through reservations in Okla. and Ontario, Canada.

DELAWARE RIVER, rises in the Catskill Mts of SE N.Y. and flows 300mi S into Delaware Bay. Forming the boundaries between Pa. and N.Y. and N.J., and between N.J. and Del., it is an important shipping channel for Philadelphia and the great industrial area of N.J. and is in its upper reaches a major water-supply source for the New York metropolitan region.

DE LA WARR, Thomas West, 12th Baron, (1577–1618), first governor of the Va. colony. Appointed for life in 1610, he revitalized the failing settlement despite a serious illness which forced his return to England in 1611. He continued to work for Va. and died while making a return voyage. The state of Delaware is named for him.

DELBRÜCK, Max (1906–1981), German-born US biologist whose discovery of a method for detecting and measuring the rate of mutations in BACTERIA opened up the study of bacterial GENETICS.

DE LEON, Daniel (1852–1914), US Marxist leader. An emigrant from Curaçao, he edited the Socialist Labor Party organ, *The People,* for some years. A cofounder of the INDUSTRIAL WORKERS OF THE WORLD in 1905, he was expelled from it in 1908, after which his influence declined.

DELFTWARE, earthenware covered with an opaque white glaze made from tin oxide. First produced in the Netherlands and particularly at Delft in the 16th century, it was designed to imitate Chinese porcelain. The style spread to England and remained popular until the 18th century, when porcelain was manufactured in the West.

DELHI, city in N India, its capital 1912–31. Adjacent to NEW DELHI, Delhi dates from the 17th century and has many historic buildings, such as the Red Fort, dating from that time. There are several light industries, and the city's craftwork in ivory, jewelry and pottery is famous. Most new building is now confined to New Delhi, and much of the old city, which has a much larger population, has become a slum. Pop 3,279,955.

DELIAN LEAGUE, confederacy of Greek states formed by Athens 478–477 BC to follow up the Hellenic League's victories against Persia. It was nominally governed by a council in which each member state had one vote, but was in fact entirely dominated by Athens. After considerable success against Persia, Athens began to turn the league into an empire, using its fleet to subjugate reluctant states such as Naxos. The so-called league endured until Athens was defeated by Sparta in the PELOPONNESIAN WAR. An attempt to revive it in 377 BC was crushed by Philip II of Macedon in 338 BC.

DELIBES, (Clément Philibert) Léo (1836–1891), French composer. Best known at first for his lighter works and operettas, some written in collaboration with OFFENBACH, he set a new high standard for ballet music with *Coppélia* (1870) and *Sylvia* (1876) and wrote the grand opera *Lakmé* (1883).

DELINQUENCY. See JUVENILE DELINQUENCY.

DELIRIUM, altered state of consciousness in which a person is restless, excitable, hallucinating and is only partly aware of his surroundings. It is seen in high FEVER, POISONING, drug withdrawal, disorders of METABOLISM and organ failure. SEDATIVES and reassurance are basic measures.

DELIRIUM TREMENS, specific delirium due to acute alcohol withdrawal in ALCOHOLISM. It occurs within days of abstinence and is often precipitated by injury, surgery or imprisonment. The sufferer becomes restless, disorientated, extremely anxious and tremulous; FEVER and profuse sweating are usual. Characteristically, hallucinations of insects or animals cause abject terror. Constant reassurance, SEDATIVES, well-lit and quiet surroundings

are appropriate measures until the episode is over. Treatment of dehydration and reduction of high fever may be necessary, though fatalities do occur.

DELIUS, Frederick (1862–1934), English composer. An orange-grower in Fla. 1884–86, he studied in Leipzig, where he met and was influenced by Edward GRIEG. He is best known for orchestral pieces such as *Florida* (1886–87) and *Brigg Fair* (1907), and for tone poems such as *Summer Night on the River* (1911) and *Sea Drift* (1903). His best-known opera is *A Village Romeo and Juliet* (1900–01). In old age he became blind and paralysed, but continued to compose by dictation.

DELLA FRANCESCA, Piero. See PIERO DELLA FRANCESCA.

DELLA ROBBIA. See ROBBIA, DELLA.

DELLO JOIO, Norman (1913–   ), US composer whose style blends neoclassicism and late romanticism. His orchestral work *Meditations on Ecclesiastes* (1956) won a 1957 Pulitzer Prize. He has composed operas such as *Blood Moon* (1961), choral works, ballet scores and much chamber music, as well as television scores.

DELOS, small Greek island of the Cyclades group in the S Aegean Sea. In Greek mythology Delos was said to be the birthplace of ARTEMIS and APOLLO. After the wars against Persia, it was the headquarters of the DELIAN LEAGUE from 478 to 404 BC. In Roman times Delos became an important port and center of the slave trade.

DELPHI, Classical Greek site located on the lower slopes of Mt PARNASSUS. Delphi was considered by the Greeks to be the center of the world, and was the seat of the most important ORACLE in ancient Greece. The oracular messages often had a strong influence on state policy. Excavations begun in 1892 revealed the magnificent temple of Apollo, now partially reconstructed, treasuries, a theater and a stadium.

DEL SARTO, Andrea. See ANDREA DEL SARTO.

DEL TREDICI, David (Walter) (1937–   ), US composer and pianist. Roger SESSIONS and Darius MILHAUD were among his teachers, the latter urging him to compose. His works include *Scene and Arias from Alice in Wonderland* (1969) and *In Memory of a Summer Day*, which won a 1980 Pulitzer prize.

DELVAUX, Paul (1897–   ), Belgian painter who often evoked a surrealistic atmosphere by creating disquieting images, such as those in which nude women and clothed men were posed together on otherwise deserted city streets. His paintings were influenced by DALI and

MAGRITTE.

DEMAND. See SUPPLY AND DEMAND.

DEMENTIA, loss or serious reduction of mental faculties (such as loss of memory), usually because of organic brain disease. (See KORSAKOV'S PSYCHOSIS.) *Dementia praecox* is an obsolete term roughly corresponding to SCHIZOPHRENIA.

DEMETER, in Greek mythology, the goddess of agriculture, identified with the Roman CERES. Demeter was sister of ZEUS and mother of PERSEPHONE and the presiding deity of the ELEUSINIAN MYSTERIES.

DE MILLE, Agnes George (1909–   ), US dancer and choreographer. She pioneered the combination of ballet and American folk music. Her ballets include *Rodeo* (1942) and *Fall River Legend* (1948). Her choreography for the Rodgers and Hammerstein musical *Oklahoma!* (1943) revolutionized dance in musical comedy by using ballet as an integral part of the plot acting.

DE MILLE, Cecil Blount (1881–1959), US motion picture producer and director, noted for his use of spectacle. He directed such epics as *The Ten Commandments* (1923 and 1956), *The Sign of the Cross* (1932), *Samson and Delilah* (1949) and *The Greatest Show on Earth* (1952).

DEMOCRACY, system of government which recognizes the right of all members of society to influence political decisions, either directly or indirectly. Direct democracy, in which political decisions are made by the whole citizen body meeting together, is only possible where the population is small. (See GREECE, ANCIENT.) The direct democracy of some ancient Greek city-states has had little influence on the development of modern representative democracies, in which political decisions are made by elected representatives responsible to their electors.

Representative democracy began to evolve during the 18th and 19th centuries, in Britain, Europe and the US. Its central institution is the representative parliament, in which decisions are effected by majority vote. Institutions intrinsic to representative democracy are: regular elections with a free choice of candidates, universal adult suffrage, freedom to organize rival political parties and independence of the judiciary. Freedom of speech and the press, and the preservation of civil liberties and minority rights are also implicit in the idea of liberal representative democracy. The American and French revolutions, and the growth of the classes following the INDUSTRIAL REVOLUTION, were important influences in the formation of modern democracies. The concepts of natural rights and political equality expressed by such philosophers as John LOCKE in the 17th century, VOLTAIRE and Jean Jacques ROUSSEAU in the 18th century, and BENTHAM and J. S. MILL in the 19th century, are vital to the theory of representative democracy. (See also CONSTITUTION; PARLIAMENT; REPUBLIC; TOTALITARIANISM; UNITED STATES CONSTITUTION.)

DEMOCRATIC PARTY, one of the two major political parties in the US. Democrats trace their history back to the Democratic Republican Party (1792) of Thomas JEFFERSON, who favored popular control of the government. Following the inauguration of Andrew JACKSON in 1828, the party's base was broadened, with representation from the new West as well as the East. Jackson was a man of the people, and his administration marked the beginning of a period of dominance for the Democrats that only ended with the election in 1860 of Abraham Lincoln, the first successful candidate of the new REPUBLICAN PARTY. The slavery controversy and the Civil War split the party into northern and southern sections and, apart from the success of Woodrow WILSON just before WWI, it was not until the election of Franklin D. ROOSEVELT in 1932 that the party reemerged with its old vigor. Roosevelt's NEW DEAL transformed the party's traditional policies, introducing broad governmental intervention in the economy and social welfare. This approach was continued on Roosevelt's death in 1945 by Harry S. TRUMAN, whose FAIR DEAL measures were, however, largely thwarted by a coalition of Republicans and Southern Democrats. In the 1950s, under Eisenhower's Republican administration, the party was led by Adlai E. STEVENSON. It controlled both houses of Congress from 1954, but the solidity of the South's adherence to the party began to fracture with the drive for black civil rights. The election of John F. KENNEDY in 1960 led to important legislation in this sphere, but also contributed further to the breakup of the traditional alliance between the urbanized North, with its many ethnic minorities, and the rural, disadvantaged South which had benefited from New Deal policies. On Kennedy's assassination in 1963, Vice-president Lyndon B. JOHNSON came to power. By 1968 the party was riven by dissent, particularly over policy in Vietnam. In 1968 Hubert H. HUMPHREY lost the presidential election to Richard M. NIXON, and in 1972 he was replaced as leader of the party by George S. MCGOVERN. The

Democrats retained control of Congress. In 1976 Jimmy CARTER became party leader, but he lost his bid for a second term to Ronald Reagan in 1980.

DEMOCRITUS OF ABDERA (c460–370 BC), Greek materialist philosopher. One of the earliest exponents of ATOMISM, he maintained that all phenomena were explicable in terms of the nomic motion of atoms in the void.

DEMOGRAPHY, a branch of sociology, the study of the distribution, composition and internal structure of human populations. It draws on many disciplines (e.g., genetics, psychology, economics, geography), its tools being essentially those of STATISTICS: the sample and the CENSUS whose results are statistically analyzed. Its prime concerns are birth rate, emigration and immigration. (See also POPULATION.)

DEMOLAY, Order of, international organization sponsored by Masonic orders to promote high ideals and character among boys from 14 to 21 years of age. It was founded in 1919 at Kansas City, Mo.

DEMOSTHENES (384–322 BC), famous Athenian orator and statesman. Demosthenes was the author of the *Philippics* (351–341 BC) and the *Olynthiacs* (349–348 BC)—speeches designed to awaken the Athenians to the danger of conquest by Philip II of Macedon. Demosthenes' most famous speech was *On the Crown* (330 BC), in which he vindicated himself against charges brought by AESCHINES of financial corruption, cowardice in battle and indecisiveness in policy.

DEMPSEY, Jack (1895–   ), US boxer, one of the great heavyweights. He won the world championship from Jess WILLARD in 1919 at Toledo, Ohio, and held the title until defeated by Gene TUNNEY in 1926. Again defeated by Tunney in 1927, he retired from the ring in 1928.

DEMUTH, Charles (1883–1935), US watercolorist, painter and illustrator. Demuth, who was influenced by both CUBISM and EXPRESSIONISM and worked in a number of styles, is best known for his precise and delicate studies of flowers. He liked to paint the stark, simple shapes generated by the machine age and is also noted for his illustrations of works by Poe, Zola and Henry James.

DENDROCHRONOLOGY, the dating of past events by the study of tree-rings. A hollow tube is inserted into the tree trunk and a core from bark to center removed. The ANNUAL RINGS are counted, examined and compared with rings from dead trees so that the chronology may be extended further back in time. Through such studies

important corrections have been made to the system of RADIOCARBON DATING.

DENGUE FEVER, or breakbone fever, a VIRUS infection carried by mosquitoes, with FEVER, headache, malaise, prostration and characteristically severe muscle and joint pains. There is also a variable skin rash through the roughly week-long illness. It is a disease of warm climates, and may occur in EPIDEMICS. Symptomatic treatment only is required.

DENIKIN, Anton Ivanovich (1872–1947), Russian leader of the anti-Bolshevik "White" forces in the civil war following the RUSSIAN REVOLUTION of 1917. In 1918 he succeeded KORNILOV as commander of the Whites in S Russia, but was convincingly defeated at Orel, 250mi from Moscow, in 1919. Denikin resigned his command the following year and fled to France. He emigrated to the US in 1945.

DENIS, Saint, patron saint of France and martyr. He is thought to have lived in the 3rd century and to have been the first bishop of Paris. His feast day is Oct. 9.

Official Name: The Kingdom of Denmark
Capital: Copenhagen
Area: 16,629sq mi
Population: 15,120,000
Languages: Danish
Religions: Lutheran
Monetary Unit(s): 1.Krone=100 øre

DENMARK, constitutional monarchy consisting of the Jutland peninsula, between the North and Baltic seas in NW Europe, and 482 islands off the peninsula, the two largest of which are Zealand (where Copenhagen is situated) and Fyn, and also the FAEROE ISLANDS and GREENLAND. Denmark's 42mi S land boundary is with West Germany. Her E and N neighbors are respectively Sweden and Norway. Denmark is the smallest of the Scandinavian countries.

Land.   The W half of the country, is fairly flat, consists of coastal dunes and lagoons and relatively infertile plains with sandy soil and peat bogs. The E has hilly moraines, cut by deep inlets and valleys, a pattern continued in the islands. The soils in this region are loamy and fertile. Climate is moist, with cool summers and, for the latitude, relatively warm winters.

The People. Denmark's population is almost entirely Scandinavian. A German minority of about 30,000 lives in SW Jutland, while some 40,000 Danes live in German Schleswig. The majority of people live in the towns, with Greater Copenhagen the most densely populated district. Hinterlands are restricted and the Danes have become increasingly aware of the extent to which fertile farmland is being swallowed up by urban development. Denmark has a highly developed state education system and advanced social security schemes.

The Economy. Agriculture was the chief support of the economy until recently, and although some 60% of the country is given over to intensive farming, manufacturing now supplies more than 60% of Denmark's total exports. About 30% of the Gross National Product is provided by industry, 7% by agriculture and 16% by commerce. Industry employs about 30% of the work force, agriculture about 9%.

Among the major products are foodstuffs (particularly dairy products), furniture, glass, silverware, leather goods and clothing. There are important shipbuilding and agricultural engineering industries, while fishing and tourism also make an important contribution to the economy. Denmark depends heavily on imported raw materials, particularly iron, coal and oil. From 1958–72 it was a member of the EUROPEAN FREE TRADE ASSOCIATION; in 1973 it joined the COMMON MARKET.

History. Denmark has a rich early history as the center of VIKING expansion. She maintained her influence through to the 16th century, as a dominant partner in the KALMAR UNION. From about 1600 Danish power waned under Swedish pressure. Norway remained under Danish rule until it was taken by Sweden in 1814. Prussia and Austria wrested Schleswig-Holstein from the Danes (1864), who eventually recovered N Schleswig after a plebiscite (1920). During WWII Denmark was occupied by Germany (1940–45).

DENSITY, the ratio of MASS to volume for a given material or object. Substances that are light for their size have a low density. Objects whose density is less than that of water will float in water, while a hot air BALLOON will rise when its average density becomes less than that of air. The term is also applied to properties other than mass: e.g., **charge density** refers to the ratio of electric charge (see ELECTRICITY) to volume.

DENTISTRY, the branch of MEDICINE concerned with the care of TEETH and related structures. Dental CARIES is responsible for most dental discomfort. Here the bacterial dissolution of dentine and enamel leads to cavities, especially in molars and premolars, and these allow accumulation of debris which encourages further bacterial growth; destruction of the tooth will gradually ensue unless treatment restores a protective surface. Each tooth contains sensitive nerve fibers extending into the dentine; exposure of these causes toothache, but the fibers then retract so that the pain often recedes despite continuing caries. The dentist removes all unhealthy tissue under ANESTHESIA and fills the cavity with metal AMALGAM which hardens and protects the tooth, although a severely damaged tooth may require extraction. Traumatic injury to teeth is repaired by a similar process. In some instances a tooth may be reconstructed on a "peg" of the original by using an artificial "crown." Maldeveloped or displaced teeth may need extraction or, during childhood, braces or plates to encourage realignment with growth. Wisdom teeth (rearmost molars), in particular, may need extraction if they erupt out of alignment or if they interfere with the normal bite. Infection of tooth pulp with ABSCESS formation destroys the tooth; PUS can only be drained by extraction. False teeth or dentures, either fitted individually or as a group on a denture plate that sits on the gums, are made to replace lost teeth, to allow effective bite and for cosmetic purposes. Dentistry is also concerned with the prevention of carious decay and periodontal disease by encouragement of oral hygiene, including regular adequate brushing of teeth. Fluoride and protective films are important recent developments in preventive dentistry.

DENVER, state capital and largest city in Col., seat of Denver Co. It is located to the east of the foothills of the Rocky Mts, a mile above sea level. Settled in 1858, Denver is known today as the commercial center of the Rocky Mountain region, with large sheep and cattle markets and modern industries, including aerospace, mining machinery and printing. It is also the site of numerous federal agencies and educational establishments, including the U. of Denver. The fine dry climate and opportunities for skiing make it a popular tourist resort. Pop 491,396.

DENVER, John (1943–), US singer and songwriter whose optimistic, gentle songs celebrated life's more wholesome pleasures. Among his biggest hits were "Rocky Mountain High" and "Annie's

Song." He also starred in the film *Oh God!* (1979).

DEOXYRIBONUCLEIC ACID (DNA). See NUCLEIC ACIDS.

DEPRESSION, a common psychiatric condition marked by severe dejection, pathologically depressed mood, and characteristic somatic and sleep disturbance. Many authorities divide depressions into those due to external factors, and those where depression arises without obvious cause, including manic-depressive illness. SHOCK THERAPY, ANTIDEPRESSANTS and psychotherapy are the major methods of treatment.

DEPRESSION, in economics, a major decline in business activity, involving sharp reductions in industrial production, bankruptcies, massive unemployment and a general loss of business confidence. Although minor recessions occur regularly in industrial nations, the most serious and widespread depression was the GREAT DEPRESSION commencing in 1929 and lasting worldwide through most of the 1930s.

DE QUINCEY, Thomas (1785–1859), English essayist and critic, author of *Confessions of an English Opium Eater* (1821), in which he recounted his experiences under opium. His output, affected by lifelong opium addiction, was erratic, but included some penetrating essays and powerful descriptions of drug-inspired dreams.

DERAIN, André (1880–1954), French painter, one of the original fauves (see FAUVISM). He was also attracted for a time to CUBISM. Later, rejecting nonrepresentational extremes, he returned to a more traditional style.

DERBY, Edward (George Geoffrey Smith) Stanley, 14th Earl of (1799–1869), British statesman and Conservative prime minister 1852, 1858 and 1866–68. His third and last administration saw the passing of the REFORM BILL of 1867, which increased the franchise.

DERBY, classic annual horse race at Epsom, England, instituted in 1780 by the 12th Earl of Derby. (See also KENTUCKY DERBY.)

DEREN, Maya (1908–1961), Russian-born US avant-garde film director, called "the mother of underground film." She pioneered the presentation of experimental films and founded the Creative Film Foundation to help finance them. Her movies included *Meshes of the Afternoon* (1943) and *The Very Eye of the Night* (1959).

DERMATITIS, SKIN conditions in which INFLAMMATION occurs. These include ECZEMA, contact dermatitis (see ALLERGY) and seborrheic dermatitis (see DANDRUFF). Acute dermatitis leads to redness, swelling, blistering and crusting, while chronic forms usually show scaling or thickening of skin. Cool lotions and dressings, and ointments are used in acute cases, whereas tars are often useful in more chronic conditions. Avoidance of allergens in contact or allergic dermatitis is essential.

DERMATOLOGY, subspeciality of MEDICINE concerned with the diagnosis and treatment of SKIN DISEASES: a largely visual speciality, but aided by skin BIOPSY in certain instances. Judicious use of lotions, ointments, creams (including STEROID creams) and tars is the essence of treatment, while the recognition of ALLERGY, infection and skin manifestations of systemic disease are tasks for the dermatologist.

DERRINGER, short-barreled pocket pistol of large caliber. It was designed by Henry Derringer, Jr. (1786–1868), a Philadelphia gunsmith.

DERVISH, a Muslim mystic, member of one of the Sufi brotherhoods that emerged in about the 12th century. Members served a period of initiation under a teacher and each order had its own ritual for inducing a mystic state which stressed their dependence on the unseen world. The best known are the "whirling" and "howling" dervishes, who used forms of dancing and singing. (See also SUFISM.)

DESAI, Moraji (1896–   ), Indian political leader. A disciple of Mahatma Gandhi and a devout Hindu, he held cabinet posts under Nehru and was deputy prime minister for Indira Gandhi (1967–69) before breaking with her. She imprisoned him 18 months during a "state of emergency" but following her defeat he served as prime minister (1977–79).

DESALINATION, or **desalting,** the conversion of salt or brackish water into usable fresh water. DISTILLATION is the most common commercial method; heat from the sun or conventional fuels vaporizes BRINE, the vapor condensing into fresh water on cooling. Reverse OSMOSIS and electrodialysis (see DIALYSIS) both remove salt from water by the use of semipermeable membranes; these processes are more suitable for brackish water. Pure water crystals may also be separated from brine by freezing. The biggest problem holding back the wider adoption of desalination techniques is that of how to meet the high ENERGY costs of all such processes. Only where energy is relatively cheap and water particularly scarce is desalination economic, and even then complex energy conservation procedures must be built into the plant.

DESCARTES, René, or **Renatus Cartesius** (1596–1650), mathematician, physicist and the foremost of French philosophers, who founded a rationalist, à priorist school of philosophy known as **Cartesianism**. After being educated in his native France and spending time in military service (1618–19) and traveling, Descartes spent most of his creative life in Holland (1625–49) before entering the service of Queen Christiana of Sweden shortly before his death. In mathematics Descartes founded the study of ANALYTIC GEOMETRY, introducing the use of CARTESIAN COORDINATES. He found in the deductive logic of mathematical reasoning a paradigm for a new methodology of science, first publishing his conclusions in his *Discourse on Method* (1637). The occult qualities of late scholastic science were to be done away with; only ideas which were clear and distinct were to be employed. To discover what ideas could be used to form a certain basis for a unified A PRIORI science, he introduced the method of universal doubt; he questioned everything. The first certitude he discovered was his famous *cogito ergo sum* (I think, therefore I am) and on the basis of this, the existence of other bodies, and of God, he worked out his philosophy. In science, Descartes, denying the possibility of a VACUUM, explained everything in terms of motion in a plenum of particles whose sole property was extension. This yielded his celebrated but ultimately unsuccessful VORTEX theory of the solar system and statements of the principle of INERTIA and the laws of ordinary REFRACTION. In psychology Descartes upheld a strict DUALISM: there were no causal relationships between physical and mental substances; in biology, his views were mechanistic; he regarded animals as but complex machines.

DESERTS, areas where life has extreme difficulty in surviving. Deserts cover about one third of the earth's land area. There are two types.

Cold Deserts. In cold deserts, water is unavailable during most of the year as it is trapped in the form of ice. Cold deserts include the Antarctic polar icecap, the barren wastes of Greenland, and much of the TUNDRA. (See also GLACIER.) Eskimos, Lapps and Samoyeds are among the ethnic groups inhabiting such areas in the N Hemisphere. Their animal neighbors include seals and the polar bear.

Hot Deserts These typically lie between latitudes 20° and 30° N and S, though they exist also farther from the equator in the centers of continental landmasses. They can be described as areas where water precipitation from the ATMOSPHERE is greatly exceeded by surface EVAPORATION and plant TRANSPIRATION. The best known, and largest, is the Sahara. GROUNDWATER exists but is normally far below the surface; here and there it is accessible as SPRINGS or WELLS (see ARTESIAN WELL). In recent years, IRRIGATION has enabled reclamation of much desert land. Landscapes generally result from the surface's extreme vulnerability to EROSION. Features include arroyos, BUTTES, DUNES, MESAS and WADIS. The influence of man may assist peripheral areas to become susceptible to erosion, and thus temporarily advance the desert's boundaries. (See also DUST BOWL.)

Plants may survive by being able to store water, like the cactus; by having tiny leaves to reduce evaporation loss, like the paloverde; or by having extensive ROOT systems to capture maximum moisture, like the mesquite. (See also DRY FARMING.) Animals may be nomadic, or spend the daylight hours underground. Best adapted of all is the camel.

DE SEVERSKY, Alexander Procofieff (1894–   ), Russian-born US aviator and aeronautical engineer. He founded the Seversky Aero Corporation in 1922, and has served as an adviser to the US Government.

DE SICA, Vittorio (1901–1974), Italian film director. His earlier films, such as *The Bicycle Thief* (1948), are outstanding for their compassionate treatment of social problems in the Neorealist style. The later films are not thought to be of the same standard, though many, like the *Garden of the Finzi Continis* (1971), have won international acclaim.

DES MOINES, capital and largest city of Ia., seat of Polk Co. Founded in 1843, it is now an important commercial, educational, governmental and communications center. Industries include plastics, chemicals, printing and agricultural implements. Pop 191,003.

DESMOULINS, Camille (1760–1794), journalist and leader in the FRENCH REVOLUTION. His oratory helped incite the mob to storm the BASTILLE in 1789, and his writings helped to radicalize public opinion. He and DANTON led the moderate faction in 1793–94, and were eventually arrested by Robespierre and guillotined.

DE SOTO, Hernando (1500–1542), Spanish explorer, discoverer of the Mississippi R. He served as second in command in PIZARRO's conquests in Peru (1531–35), and supported the Inca emperor ATAHUALPA. He returned to Spain with a fortune and set out again to explore the Florida region. He landed in 1539 at Charlotte Harbor and spent two years exploring what is now the SE US. He reached the Mississippi R in May 1541. Turning back in 1542, he died and his body was sunk in the Mississippi.

DESSALINES, Jean-Jacques (1758–1806), first black emperor of Haiti. Brought to Haiti as a slave, he took part in the rebellion against the French in the 1790s. After the final expulsion of the French in 1803 he became governor-general. In 1804 he proclaimed an independent country and took the title of Emperor Jacques I. His rule, characterized by extreme hostility to whites, ended when he was killed in a mulatto revolt.

DE STIJL, modern art movement in the Netherlands taking its name from the magazine *De Stijl* (*The Style*). Founded in 1917 by a group of artists including MONDRIAN and Van DOESBURG, it stressed purity of line and the use of primary colors. Its theories were also applied to interior decoration, furniture and architecture, of which the Schröder House in Utrecht (1924) is a good example.

DESTROYER, small, fast naval vessel which evolved in the 1890s out of earlier torpedo boats. In the two world wars destroyers were used principally as escorts for convoys and for attacking submarines. Some of the modern destroyers are nuclear-powered and many carry guided missiles. Some embark one or two helicopters. A new class of destroyer, the *Spruance* class, displacing 7,800 tons, is replacing some of the WWII destroyers still in service with the US Navy.

DÉTENTE (French for "relaxation"), the name given to the policy of easing tensions between the US and USSR that occurred in the late 1960s and 1970s. It was particularly associated with President NIXON (and his adviser Henry KISSINGER) during whose presidency the first SALT (Strategic Arms Limitation Treaty) agreement was signed (1972). It was continued by President FORD, who signed the HELSINKI ACCORDS in 1975. In the last years of the 1970s, however, tensions between the US and USSR rose again, and détente was finally eclipsed by the Russian invasion of Afghanistan in 1980.

DETERMINISM, the philosophical theory that all events are determined (inescapably caused) by preexisting events which, when considered in the context of inviolable physical laws, completely account for the subsequent events. The case for determinism has been variously argued from the inviolability of the laws of nature and from the omniscience and omnipotence of God.

Determinism is often taken to be opposed to the principles of FREE WILL and indeterminacy.

DETROIT, city in SE Mich., situated on the W bank of the Detroit R, directly opposite the city of Windsor, Canada. The sixth-largest city in the US and one of the world's largest automobile manufacturing centers: over a quarter of all American-made cars are built there. It is also a major Great Lakes port and shipping center. A major steel center, Detroit produces a wide variety of metal goods and machine tools; pharmaceuticals, paints and chemicals are other important industries. One of the largest salt mines in the US lies beneath the city. Detroit is also a prominent educational and cultural center: Wayne State U. and the U. of Detroit, the city's symphony orchestra and the Detroit Institute of Arts are nationally known.

The city's history began in 1701 with the founding by Antoine CADILLAC, at "la place détroit," of a French trading post. It rapidly gained in importance and was a British possession 1706–96. Rebuilt after a fire in 1805, it was capital of Mich. until 1847; it achieved city status in 1815. Auto building had already begun by 1896, and within 10 years such famous firms as Cadillac, Ford, Oldsmobile and Packard were well established. Pop 1,203,339.

DEUTERIUM (D or $_1H^2$, or "heavy hydrogen," an ISOTOPE of HYDROGEN discovered in 1931, whose nucleus (the deuteron) has one PROTON and one NEUTRON (see also TRITIUM). It forms 0.014% of the hydrogen in naturally occurring hydrogen compounds, such as water, and is chemically very like ordinary hydrogen, except that it reacts more slowly. It is obtained as HEAVY WATER by the fractional electrolysis of water. Deuterium is the major fuel for nuclear FUSION (see HYDROGEN BOMB) and is used in tracer studies. (See also NUCLEAR REACTORS.)

DEUTERONOMY, fifth book of the Old Testament and last book of the PENTATEUCH. Supposedly a testament left by Moses to the Israelites about to enter Canaan, it is primarily a recapitulation of moral laws and laws relating to the settlement of Canaan. Much of it was written long after Moses, parts being added during the reforms under King JOSIAH (621 BC). It may have been the "Book of the Law" discovered by Hilkiah in the Temple at that time.

DEUTSCH, Babette (1895–   ), US poet, writer of juvenile books and translator of Russian and German poetry. Her *Collected Poems, 1919–1962* was published in 1963. She has also written several novels

and an award-winning biography of Walt
Whitman for children.

DEVALERA, Eamon (1882–1975), Irish
statesman, prime minister 1937–48;
1951–54; 1957–59; and president of Ireland
1959–73. Born in New York City, he was
raised in Ireland, and became an ardent
republican. Only his US citizenship saved
him from execution after the 1916 EASTER
RISING. He was imprisoned by the IRISH FREE
STATE for refusing to recognize the
Anglo-Irish treaty of 1922; in 1924 he
organized the FIANNA FÁIL party which won
power in 1932. In 1937 he declared Ireland
independent of Britain, and during WWII
preserved Irish neutrality.

DE VALOIS, Dame Ninette (Edris
Stannus; 1898–   ), Irish dancer and
choreographer, founder of the company at
Sadler's Wells which, in 1956, became the
Royal Ballet. She directed the company
1931–63.

DEVIL (from Greek *diabolos*, slanderer or
accuser), in Western religions and sects, the
chief spirit of evil and commander of lesser
evil spirits or DEMONS. Dualistic systems
(see DUALISM)—notably ZOROASTRIANISM,
GNOSTICISM and MANICHAEISM—have
regarded the devil as the uncreated equal of
God, engaged in an eternal war for evil
against good. Such beliefs, often leading to
devil worship, have appeared sporadically in
connection with the OCCULT. In Judaism,
Christianity and Islam, the devil, SATAN, is a
fallen angel, powerful but subordinate to
God, who opposes God and tempts
mankind, but is to be utterly defeated and
bound at the LAST JUDGMENT. (See also
EXORCISM; MAGIC.)

DEVIL'S ISLAND, small island off the
coast of French Guiana. Formerly the site of
a notorious French penal colony for political
prisoners, among whom was Alfred
DREYFUS. The penal colony was abolished in
1938.

DEVOLUTION, War of (1667–68),
conflict between Spain and France over the
right of succession to the Spanish
Netherlands. LOUIS XIV claimed that by an
old law of devolution the territory should
have reverted to his wife MARIE THÉRÈSE
upon the death of her father, Philip IV.
Although his military campaign was
successful, Louis was forced to withdraw in
the face of the Triple Alliance of England,
the United Provinces and Sweden; and the
matter was settled in 1668 (see
AIX-LA-CHAPELLE, TREATIES OF). Spain
ceding to France 12 small fortified towns
along the French border.

DEVONIAN, the fourth period of the
PALEOZOIC, which lasted from about 400 to
345 million years ago. (See GEOLOGY.)

DE VOTO, Bernard Augustine
(1897–1955), US journalist and author. He
won national fame as a contributor to
Harper's Magazine. His books include
Mark Twain's America (1932), the Pulitzer
prizewinning *Across the Wide Missouri*
(1947) and the novel *The Crooked Mile*
(1924).

DE VRIES, Peter (1910–   ), US
novelist noted for his witty and irreverent
comic novels such as *The Tunnel of Love*
(1954), *The Blood of the Lamb* (1962) and
The Glory of the Hummingbird (1974).

DEWEY, George (1837–1917), US naval
hero promoted admiral of the navy—the
highest possible rank—for his victory at the
Battle of Manila Bay and the capture of the
Philippines from Spain. On May 1, 1898,
during the SPANISH-AMERICAN WAR, Dewey
led the Asiatic squadron into Manila Bay
and, without losing a man, destroyed the
Spanish eastern fleet. In August, aided by
Filipino rebels and US army forces, he
received the surrender of Manila; the
Philippines then fell to the US. Dewey later
served as president of the general board of
the Navy Department.

DEWEY, John (1859–1952), US philosopher and educator, the founder of the
philosophical school known as INSTRU-
MENTALISM (or experimentalism) and the
leading promoter of educational reform in
the early years of the 20th century.
Profoundly influenced by the PRAGMATISM
of William JAMES, Dewey developed a
philosophy in which ideas and concepts
were validated by their practicality. He
taught that "learning by doing" should
form the basis of educational practice,
though in later life he came to criticize the
"progressive" movement in education,
which, in abandoning formal tuition
altogether, he felt had misused his
educational theory.

DEWEY, Thomas Edmund (1902–1971),
US lawyer and Republican presidential
candidate defeated in 1944 by Franklin D.
Roosevelt and in 1948 by Harry S. Truman,
although his election had been thought a
foregone conclusion. In the 1930s, as US
attorney for the southern district of N.Y.
state and then as special prosecutor in New
York City, Dewey gained a national
reputation for successful campaigning
against organized crime. He was governor
of N.Y. 1943–55. He declined the post of
chief justice under Richard M. Nixon
(1968).

DEWEY DECIMAL SYSTEM, a system
devised by Melvil DEWEY (1851–1931) for
use in the classification of books in libraries,

and based on the DECIMAL SYSTEM of numbers. Dewey divided knowledge into ten main areas, each of these into ten subdivisions, and so on. Thus a book could fall into one of a thousand categories, from 000 to 999. Extensions of this system added further classificatory numbers after the decimal point.

DEWHURST, Colleen (1926–), Canadian-born US stage and film actress. She first appeared on Broadway in Eugene O'Neill's *Desire Under the Elms* (1952), and won critical acclaim for her performance in O'Neill's *A Moon for the Misbegotten* (1973). She performed in the works of Shakespeare, Jean-Paul Sartre, Arthur Miller and Edward Albee.

DE WITT, Jan (1625–1672), Dutch statesman, grand pensionary (ruler) of Holland 1653–72, and republican opponent of the House of Orange. In 1667 he made peace with England (see BREDA, DECLARATION OF) and, in 1668, negotiated the Triple Alliance with England and Sweden against Louis XIV, to end the War of DEVOLUTION. When Louis XIV invaded Holland and the Dutch people called William III to power, he and his brother **Cornelius De Witt** (1623–1672) were brutally murdered by a mob.

DEW LINE (*Distant Early Warning* Line), joint United States–Canadian defense chain of about 30 radar posts, mainly along or near the 70th parallel, some on land, some on ships or planes. Completed in 1958, it was designed to give up to two hours' advance warning of the approach of hostile aircraft and 15–30 minutes' warning of an intercontinental ballistic-missile attack. Radars located in the Arctic waste are being replaced by automated stations.

DHARMA, important concept in HINDUISM, BUDDHISM and JAINISM. To Hindus, it denotes the universal law ordaining religious and social institutions, the rights and duties of individuals or, simply, virtuous conduct. Buddhists consider it the universal truth proclaimed to all men by Buddha. In Jainism, it also represents an eternal substance.

DIABETES, a common systemic disease, affecting between 0.5 and 1% of the population, and characterized by the absence or inadequate secretion of INSULIN, the principal hormone controlling BLOOD sugar. There are many causes, including heredity, VIRUS infection, primary disease of the PANCREAS and OBESITY. Though it may start at any time, two main groups are recognized: juvenile (beginning in childhood, adolescence or early adult life)—due to inability to secrete insulin; and late onset

(late middle life or old age)—associated with obesity and with a relative lack of insulin. High blood sugar may lead to coma, often with keto-ACIDOSIS, excessive thirst and high urine output, weight loss, ill-health and liability to infections. The disease may be detected by urine or blood tests and confirmed by a glucose tolerance test. It causes disease of small blood vessels, as well as premature ARTERIOSCLEROSIS, RETINA disease, CATARACTS, KIDNEY disease and NEURITIS. Poor blood supply, neuritis and infection may lead to chronic leg ULCERS. Once recognized, diabetes needs treatment to stabilize the blood sugar level and keep it within strict limits. Regular medical surveillance and education is essential to minimize complications. Dietary carbohydrate must be controlled and for late onset cases this may be all that is needed; in this group, drugs that increase the body's insulin production are valuable. In juvenile and some late onset cases, insulin itself is needed, given by subcutaneous injection by the patient. Regular dosage, adjusted to usual diet and activity, is used, but surgery, PREGNANCY and infection increase insulin requirement. Control can be assessed by a simple urine test. Insulin overdose can occur, with sweating, confusion and COMA, and prompt treatment with sugar is crucial. EYE complications should be recognized early, especially in juvenile onset cases, as early intervention may prevent or delay BLINDNESS.

DIAGHILEV, Sergei Pavlovich (1872–1929), Russian impresario and founder (Paris, 1909) of the Ballets Russes which inaugurated modern BALLET. His magazine *World of Art* (1899–1904) led a movement for Russian involvement in Western European arts. He moved to Paris in 1906. The Ballets Russes broke with the formalism of classical choreography and aimed to unify music, dance and stage design. Its productions included the dancers and choreographers FOKINE, PAVLOVA, NIJINSKY and MASSINE, the composers STRAVINSKY and PROKOFIEV and the designers BENOIS and BAKST. MATISSE, PICASSO, DEBUSSY, RAVEL and many others also worked for Diaghilev.

DIALECTIC, in philosophy, variously: a method of forcing a respondent to alter his opinion by leading him into self-contradiction (SOCRATES); the process of getting to know the world of ideal forms (PLATO); sound reasoning from generally accepted opinions rather than from self-evident truths (ARISTOTLE); argument exposing the folly of reasoning that employs the categories of understanding outside the world of experience (KANT), or a dynamic logic, common to true philosophy and the historical process, in which apparent contradictories—theses and antitheses—are reconciled in syntheses (HEGEL).

DIALYSIS, process of selective DIFFUSION of ions and molecules through a semipermeable membrane which retains COLLOID particles and macromolecules. It is accelerated by applying an electric field (see ELECTROPHORESIS). Dialysis is used for DESALINATION and in artificial kidneys (see ARTIFICIAL ORGANS). (See also OSMOSIS.)

DIAMOND, allotrope of CARBON (see ALLOTROPY), forming colorless cubic crystals. Diamond is the hardest known substance, with a Mohs hardness of 10, which varies slightly with the orientation of the crystal. Thus diamonds can be cut only by other diamonds. They do not conduct electricity, but conduct heat extremely well. Diamond burns when heated in air to 900°C; in an inert atmosphere it reverts to GRAPHITE slowly at 1000°C, rapidly at 1700°C. Diamonds occur naturally in dikes and pipes of KIMBERLITE, notably in South Africa (Orange Free State and Transvaal), Tanzania, and in the US at Murfreesboro, Ark. They are also mined from secondary (alluvial) deposits, especially in Brazil, Zaire, Sierra Leone and India. The diamonds are separated by mechanical panning, and those of GEM quality are cleaved (or sawn), cut and polished. Inferior, or industrial, diamonds are used for cutting, drilling and grinding. Synthetic industrial diamonds are made by subjecting graphite to very high temperatures and pressures, sometimes with fused metals as solvent. sg 3.51.

DIAMOND HEAD, extinct volcano forming a 761ft high promontory on the SE shore of Oahu, Hawaii. An ancient burial ground, it is now the site of US Fort Ruger.

DIARRHEA, loose and/or frequent bowel motions. A common effect of FOOD POISONING, GASTROINTESTINAL TRACT infection (e.g., DYSENTERY, CHOLERA) or INFLAMMATION (e.g., COLITIS, ENTERITIS, ABSCESS), drugs and systemic diseases. Benign or malignant TUMORS of the colon and rectum may also cause diarrhea. Slime or blood indicate severe inflammation or tumor.

DIAS (or Diaz), Bartholomeu (d. 1500), Portuguese navigator and explorer who, in 1488, discovered the sea route around Africa past the Cape of Good Hope to India. He explored much of the W coast of Africa. In 1500 he took part in Pedro CABRAL'S expedition, which discovered Brazil.

DIAZ, Porfirio (1830–1915), Mexican general and president. Renowned for his part in the war against the French (1861–67), he came to oppose Benito JUÁREZ and gained power in 1877. President until 1880 and again from 1884, he was politically ruthless. However, his policies and foreign investment brought stability and prosperity, although peasant conditions were wretched. He was overthrown in 1911 and died in exile in Paris.

DICE, two six-sided cubes with sides numbered from one to six. They are used in gambling games and in many board games. Dice in games of chance go back at least 5,000 years, the earliest such cubes having been found in the Sumerian royal tombs of Ur, dating to the third millennium BC. See also CRAPS.

DICKENS, Charles John Huffam (1812–1870), one of the great English novelists. His brief childhood experience of a debtor's prison and work in a blacking factory shaped his future imagery and sympathies. Trained as a stenographer and lawyer's clerk, he began his literary career in London as a magazine contributor, under the pseudonym "Boz," publishing *Sketches by "Boz"* in 1836. His comic work *The Pickwick Papers* (1837) made him famous. Most of his novels were published first in monthly installments, for popular consumption, and this affected their structure and style. His chief concern was the effect of moral evil, crime and corruption on society. He created some memorable comic characters, as in *David Copperfield* (1850), which was based on his own experiences. His works include *Oliver Twist* (1838), *Bleak House* (1853), *Little Dorrit* (1857), *Great Expectations* (1861) and *Our Mutual Friend* (1865). Dicken's novels were dramatized, and he made successful reading tours of England and the US. His works influenced the Russian writer DOSTOYEVSKY.

DICKEY, James (Lafayette) (1923–   ), US poet, novelist and critic, best known for his novel *Deliverance* (1970), which was made into a movie in 1972. His collection of poems *Buckdancer's Choice* (1965), which like his novel explores themes of violence, won a National Book Award in 1966.

DICKINSON, Emily Elizabeth (1830–1886), important American poet. She spent most of her life secluded in her father's home in Amherst, Mass. Her concise lyrics, witty and aphoristic in style, simple, even sentimental, in expression and remarkable for metrical variations, are chiefly concerned with immortality and nature. Of 1,775 poems, only seven were published during her lifetime.

DICKINSON, John (1732–1808), American colonial statesman and political writer, who opposed British colonial policy but was against separation from Britain. He wrote *Letters from a Farmer in Pennsylvania* (1767 and 1768) and, while a member of the CONTINENTAL CONGRESS 1774–76, probably drew up the *Declaration of the Causes of taking up Arms*. He also wrote the first draft of the ARTICLES OF CONFEDERATION, in 1776. Dickinson refused to sign the DECLARATION OF INDEPENDENCE but supported the Constitution.

DICTATORSHIP, form of government in which one person holds absolute power and is not subject to the consent of the governed. The term derives from the Roman *dictator* who was a magistrate appointed to govern for a six-month period, following a state emergency. Both SULLA and Julius CAESAR, however, abolished the constitutional limits to their dictatorial power. In the 20th century, HITLER and STALIN assumed dictatorial powers and committed hideous atrocities; there have also been dictatorships in Portugal, Spain and Greece and in many South American and African countries. (See also DESPOTISM; TOTALITARIANISM.)

DICTIONARY, alphabetically arranged book giving the orthography, syllabication, pronunciation, meanings and uses, and etymology of words. Until the 18th century, dictionaries amounted to little more than lists, furnishing simple glossaries. The first large-scale compilation was *A New English Dictionary* (1702), containing 38,000 entries. Nathan Bailey's *Universal Etymological English Dictionary* (1721), besides containing etymologies, marked word stress and syllabication and established a methodology of word collection. In 1755 Samuel JOHNSON published the famous *Dictionary of the English Language*, in two volumes, the first English language dictionary to give literary examples of usage. Johnson's work was expanded by Noah WEBSTER in the US, who produced *An American Dictionary of the English Language* (1828). In 1857 Richard Chenevix Trench proposed *A New English Dictionary on Historical Principles* known, since 1894, as the *Oxford English Dictionary*. Its 12 volumes were published between 1884 and 1928, with supplements appearing in 1933 and 1973. Bilingual and special subject dictionaries are also made.

DIDEROT, Denis (1713–1784), French encyclopedist, philosopher and man of letters. His versatility as a novelist, playwright and art critic made him prominent in the ENLIGHTENMENT. His fame rests on the *Encyclopédie*, which he edited

with d'ALEMBERT and published between 1751 and 1771. The *Encyclopédie*, comprising 17 volumes of text and 11 of engravings, contained essays on the sciences, arts and crafts by such eminent contributors as BUFFON, CONDORCET, Jean Jacques ROUSSEAU and VOLTAIRE, as well as by d'Alembert and Diderot themselves. It presented the scientific discoveries and more advanced thought of the time. As a result the French government tried to suppress it in 1759. Diderot's works included the play *Le père de famille* (1761) and the novel *jacques le fataliste* (1796).

DIDION, Joan (1934–   ), US essayist and novelist concerned with the "atomization" of post-WWII society. Her works include the collections of essays *Slouching Towards Bethlehem* (1968) and *The White Album* (1979) and the novels *Play It As It Lays* (1970) and *A Book of Common Prayer* (1977).

DIEFENBAKER, John George (1895–1979), Canadian prime minister 1957–63. After repeated attempts he succeeded in being elected to parliament from Saskatchewan, in 1940. Becoming leader of the PROGRESSIVE CONSERVATIVE PARTY in 1956, he headed a minority government in 1957, after 22 years of Liberal rule. The 1958 election produced a record government majority. He instituted agricultural reforms but the economic recession, the Cuban missile crisis, and the nuclear arms debate, which aggravated relations with the US under Kennedy, brought on his defeat in 1963 by Lester PEARSON and the Liberals. He served in the Commons until his death.

DIEGO GARCIA, the largest of five coral atolls in the Chagos Archipelago in the Indian Ocean. During World War II it was a British air base and in 1965 it became a part of the newly constituted British Indian Ocean Territory, intended to serve as a British-US defense facility. In the mid-1970s the US began expanding a naval base on the atoll.

DIEM, Ngo Dinh (1901–1963), American-backed president of the South Vietnam republic 1954–63. His Roman Catholic regime's harsh oppression of the Buddhist majority (leading to cases of self-immolation), his corrupt politics and failure to effect land reform, led to a withdrawal of US support. He was assassinated in a coup led by his own generals.

DIEN BIEN PHU, military outpost, in North Vietnam, where in 1954 France was finally defeated in the Indochina war. During a 55-day siege, the French army lost 15,000 men in their bid to resist the onslaught of Gen. Vo Nguyen Giap's

Vietminh forces. France formally withdrew from Indochina at the GENEVA CONFERENCE (1954).

DIEPPE, historic French port on the English Channel. Its castle (begun 1435) contains a museum with ivories and paintings. In 1942 during WWII, Allied troops made a tragic and unsuccessful attempt to capture the city from the Germans.

DIESEL ENGINE, oil-burning INTERNAL-COMBUSTION ENGINE patented by **Rudolf Diesel** (1858–1913), a German engineer, in 1892 after several years of development work. Air enters a cylinder and is compressed by a piston to a high enough TEMPERATURE and PRESSURE for spontaneous combustion to occur when fuel is sprayed in. This method of operation differs from that of a gasoline engine in which air and fuel are mixed before entering the cylinder, there is less compression and a spark is needed to initiate combustion. In the first (intake) stroke of the cycle of a 4-stroke diesel engine, the piston moves down, drawing in air through a valve. In the second (compression) stroke, the piston returns up, compressing the air and heating it to over 300°C. (The exact value depends on the COMPRESSION RATIO, which may be between 12:1 and 22:1.) Near the end of the stroke, fuel is sprayed into the cylinder at high pressure through a nozzle and ignites in the hot air. In the third (power) stroke, the burning fuel–air mixture increases the pressure in the cylinder, pushing the piston down and driving the crankshaft. Then, in the fourth (exhaust) stroke, the piston moves up again and drives the burnt gases out of the cylinder. There are also 2-stroke diesel engines. These have only compression and power strokes, the exhaust gases being scavenged and new air introduced by a blower while the piston is at the bottom of its stroke. Diesel engines are less smooth-running, heavier and initially more expensive than gasoline engines but make more efficient use of cheaper fuel. They are widely used in ships, heavy vehicles and power installations, and increasingly in passenger cars.

DIETRICH, Marlene (1904–   ), German-born US film actress and cabaret artist. Her classic role was that of the "femme fatale" nightclub singer in the German film *The Blue Angel* (1930). She became famous for her sultry glamor and sophistication.

DIFFERENTIAL EQUATIONS, EQUATIONS involving derivatives (see CALCULUS).

DIFFERENTIAL GEOMETRY, the branch of GEOMETRY dealing with the basic properties of curves and surfaces, using the techniques of CALCULUS and ANALYTIC GEOMETRY.

DIFFERENTIATION. See CALCULUS.

DIFFRACTION, the property by which a WAVE MOTION (such as ELECTROMAGNETIC RADIATION, SOUND or water waves) deviates from the straight line expected geometrically and thus gives rise to INTERFERENCE effects at the edges of the shadows cast by opaque objects, where the wave-trains that have reached each point by different routes interfere with each other. Opaque objects thus never cast completely sharp shadows, though such effects only become apparent when the dimensions of the obstruction are of the same order as the wavelength of the wave motion concerned. It is diffraction effects which place the ultimate limit on the resolving power of optical instruments, RADIO TELESCOPES and the like. Diffraction is set to work in the diffraction grating. Here, light passed through a series of very accurately ruled slits or reflected from a series of narrow parallel mirrors produces a series of spectrums by the interference of the light from the different slits or mirrors. Gratings are ruled with from 70 lines/mm (for infrared work) to 1,800 lines/mm (for ultraviolet work).

DIFFUSION, the gradual mixing of different substances placed in mutual contact due to the random thermal motion of their constituent particles. Most rapid with gases and liquids, it also occurs with solids. Diffusion rates increase with increasing TEMPERATURE; the rates at which gases diffuse through a porous membrane vary as the inverse of the square root of their MOLECULAR WEIGHT. Gaseous diffusion is used to separate fissile URANIUM-235 from nonfissile uranium-238, the gas used being uranium hexafluoride (UF_6).

DIGESTIVE SYSTEM, the mechanism for breaking down or modifying dietary intake into a form that is absorbable and usable by an organism. In unicellular organisms this is by phagocytosis and enzyme breakdown of large molecules; in larger animals it occurs outside cells after liberation of ENZYMES. In higher animals, the digestive system consists structurally of the GASTRO-INTESTINAL TRACT, the principal absorbing surface which also secretes enzymes, and the related organs: the LIVER and PANCREAS, which secrete into the tract via ducts. Different enzymes act best at different pH, and **gastric juice** and BILE respectively regulate the acidity of the STOMACH and alkalinity of the small intestine. PROTEINS are broken down by pepsin in the stomach and by trypsin, chymotrypsin and peptidases in the small intestine. CARBOHYDRATES are broken down by specialized enzymes, mainly in the small intestine. FATS are physically broken down by stomach movement, enzymatically by lipases and emulsified by bile salts. Food is mixed and propelled by PERISTALSIS, while nerves and locally regulated HORMONES, including gastrin and secretin, control both secretion and motility. Absorption of most substances occurs in the small intestine through a specialized, high-surface area mucous membrane; some molecules pass through unchanged but most in altered form. Absorption may be either by an active transport system involving chemical or physical interaction in the gut wall, or simply by a passive DIFFUSION process. Some VITAMINS and trace metals have specialized transport systems. Most absorbed food passes via the portal system to the liver, where much of it is metabolized and toxic substances removed. Some absorbed fat is passed into the LYMPH. BACTERIA colonize most of the small intestine and are important in certain digestive processes. **Malabsorption** occurs when any part of the digestive system becomes defective. Pancreas and liver disease, obstruction to bile ducts, alteration of bacteria and inflammatory disease of the small intestine are common causes.

DIGGERS, or True Levellers, 17th-century English radical cooperative movement, followers of Gerrard WINSTANLEY. In April 1649, following the execution of King Charles I after the Civil War, they occupied the common land on St. George's Hill, Surrey, and began to cultivate it. They claimed land should be given to the poor and held in common. They were dispersed in 1650.

DIGITALIS, drug derived from the FOXGLOVE and acting on the muscle and systems of the HEART. WITHERING in 1785 described its efficacy in heart failure or dropsy; it increases the force of cardiac contraction. It is also valuable in treatment of some abnormal rhythms; however, overdosage may itself cause abnormal rhythm, nausea or vomiting.

DILLINGER, John (1903–1934), notorious US gangster, who terrorized the Midwest in 1933 after escaping from jail. He was responsible for 16 killings and was shot in Chicago in 1934.

DILLON, Clarence Douglas (1909–), US financier and public official. He headed the Wall Street firm of Dillon Reed & Co. Inc. (1946–53) before entering government service as ambassador to France (1953–57) and undersecretary of state (1958–61).

Although a Republican, he was President John F. Kennedy's secretary of the treasury (1961–65).

DILTHEY, Wilhelm (1833–1911), German philosopher who sought to achieve for "historical reason" in the human sciences (law; religion; history; psychology and the arts), what KANT had achieved for the natural sciences in the *Critique of Pure Reason.*

DIMAGGIO, Joseph Paul (1914–), US baseball outfielder. He played for the New York Yankees from 1936 until his retirement in 1951, set a new record with consistent safe-hitting in 56 consecutive games (1941), hit 361 home runs and had a career batting average of .325. He entered the Baseball Hall of Fame in 1955.

DIME NOVEL, fast-moving melodramatic tale of adventure. Dime novels were first popular from the 1860s to the 1890s. Selling for 10 cents, they usually told stories about the American Revolution, the frontier period or the Civil War. They became popular again from the 1920s to the 1940s, when they sold for 10 or 15 cents and were printed on pulp stock with soft covers. Their subjects, typically, were romance, horror, crime or science fiction.

DINARIC ALPS, mountain range in S Europe, part of the E Alpine system. Its rocky and largely barren limestone ridges run 400mi down the E coast of the Adriatic Sea, from NW Yugoslavia into Albania. The highest peak is Mt Durmitor (8,274ft).

D'INDY, (Paul Marie Théodore) Vincent (1851–1931), French composer and teacher, a pupil of César FRANCK and cofounder of the Schola Cantorum academy, Paris (1894). He thought French 19th-century music superficial, admiring the German classics and Renaissance polyphony. He urged a renovated French style derived from folk idioms. His works include *Symphony on a French Mountain Air* (1886).

DINE, Jim (1935–) US artist. His work made use of "found" objects, such as old shoes or tools, which he often attached to his canvases to create a vivid imagery.

DINESEN, Isak, pseudonym of Karen Christence Dinesen, Baroness Blixen-Finecke (1885–1962), Danish author of romantic tales of mystery, such as *Seven Gothic Tales* (1934). The autobiographical *Out of Africa* (1937) was based on her 20 years in E Africa as a planter.

DINGO, Australian wild dog, probably introduced by the aborigines. The size of a small wolf, dingos commonly attack livestock but, unlike wolves, they rarely hunt in packs.

DINOSAUR NATIONAL MONUMENT, an area of national parkland in NE Ut. and NW Col., covering some 200,000 acres. The monument was established in 1915 and is of vast scientific interest, being rich in quarries of well-preserved fossils.

DINOSAURS, extinct REPTILES that flourished for 125 million years from the TRIASSIC to the CRETACEOUS periods. They ranged in size from small forms no larger than a domestic chicken to giants such as *Diplodocus* which was 27m (90ft) long and weighed about 30 tons. Early in their history two distinct dinosaur groups evolved: the Saurischia and the Ornithischia.

The **Saurischians** (or lizard-hipped dinosaurs) had pelvic girdles typical of lizards, with three prongs to each side. They included the two-legged carnivorous theropods, such as *Tyrannosaurus* and *Allosaurus*, with enormous skulls and large teeth; and the four-legged herbivorous sauropods, such as *Brontosaurus* and *Diplodocus*, with very small heads and long necks and tails.

The **Ornithischians** (or bird-hipped dinosaurs) had bird-like pelvic girdles, with four prongs to each side. All were herbivorous. Four-legged types include the stegosaurs, with triangular bony plates along the back, and the armadillo-like ankylosaurs. The two-legged duck-billed dinosaurs were well equipped for swimming.

At the end of the Cretaceous period, about 65 million years ago, dinosaurs disappeared. The reasons for this sudden extinction are not known and are the subject of much debate and controversy among paleontologists.

DIOCLETIAN (Gaius Aurelius Valerius Diocletianus; c245–316), Roman emperor from 284 to 305, when he abdicated. He reformed the army and administration, dividing the empire into four regions (293), ruled by two emperors and two caesars. Much of his great palace at Split, Yugoslavia, survives. In 303 he initiated the last universal persecution of the Christians.

DIOGENES (c412–323 BC), Greek philosopher, living in Athens. He rejected tradition and social conventions. Contemptuous of his contemporaries and their values, he was nicknamed "the Dog" and his followers the CYNICS (*kynikos*, "doglike"). He abandoned all his possessions, begged his living and reputedly lived in a barrel. Supposedly, when Alexander the Great asked what he could do for him, Diogenes answered, "Just step out of my light."

DIONYSIUS THE AREOPAGITE, Saint (1st century AD), converted by St. Paul and traditionally the first bishop of Athens. In the 6th century certain Greek philosophical treatises were wrongly attributed to him. These books by the **Pseudo-Dionysius** introduced important themes of neo-Platonism into Western Scholastic philosophy.

DIONYSUS, Greek god of wine and fertility, also called BACCHUS, a son of Zeus. He founded the art of vine culture. In early times his devotees, notably the MAENADS, practiced an orgiastic cult of divine possession.

DIOR, Christian (1905–1957), French fashion designer, whose "New Look" of 1947 helped to reestablish Paris as the leader of fashion after WWII. His salon opened in 1946 and Dior rapidly became the undisputed leader of world fashion.

DIPHTHERIA, BACTERIAL DISEASE, now uncommon, causing FEVER, malaise and sore throat, with a characteristic "pseudomembrane" on throat or PHARYNX; also, the LYMPH nodes may enlarge. The LARYNX, if involved, leads to a hoarse voice, breathlessness and stridor; this may progress to respiratory obstruction requiring tracheotomy. The bacteria produce TOXINS which can damage nerves and HEART muscle; cardiac failure and abnormal rhythm, or PARALYSIS of palate, eye movement and peripheral NEURITIS may follow. Early treatment with ANTITOXIN and use of ANTIBIOTICS are important. Protection is given by VACCINATION.

DIPLOMACY, conduct of negotiations and maintenance of relations in time of peace between sovereign states. A diplomatic mission is generally headed by an ambassador, supported by attachés, chargés d'affaires and other officials specializing in economic, political, cultural, administrative and military matters. An embassy building is considered to have "extraterritoriality," that is, to be outside the jurisdiction of the receiving state. Accredited diplomats are immune from prosecution and customs regulations. Abuse of this privileged diplomatic immunity can lead to a diplomat being asked to quit the host country as *persona non grata*. The most common abuse is espionage. The whole body of diplomats in a capital is known as the diplomatic corps and its spokesman is the longest serving ambassador.

International contacts have been handled by diplomats since ancient times. In medieval Europe they were generally appointed for the duration of specific missions. The first permanent residential missions were established by the Italian city states c1400. Diplomatic protocol and the forms of accreditation owed much to the practice of papal missions from the Vatican. Latin was the official language of diplomacy until the 17th century, when it was superseded by French, later joined by English. The Congress of Vienna (1815) further clarified diplomatic procedure. The traditional formulas of diplomatic exchange allow sharp expressions of protest without ruptures in international dealing. Improved communications have strengthened direct links between governments and diplomacy is now often conducted at "summit conferences" between heads of state. (See also INTERNATIONAL RELATIONS.)

DIRAC, Paul Adrien Maurice (1902–), English theoretical physicist who shared the 1933 Nobel physics prize with E. SCHRÖDINGER for their contributions to WAVE MECHANICS. Dirac's theory (1928) took account of RELATIVITY and implied the existence of the positive ELECTRON or positron, later discovered by C. D. ANDERSON. Dirac was also the codiscoverer of fermi-dirac statistics.

DIRECTION FINDER, device used to locate the direction of an incoming RADIO signal. Usually a loop ANTENNA is rotated until maximum reception strength is achieved, giving the line of the transmission. If this is repeated from a different position, the transmitting station may be located. The **radiocompass** used in air and sea NAVIGATION is a direction finder: position is determined by finding the directions of two or more transmitters.

DIRECTOIRE, French decorative style of the DIRECTORY period (1795–99). It was a transitional phase between the heavy and ornate style of Louis XVI and the Neoclassical style of the Empire, and stressed simple designs with accents on straight lines and minimal ornament.

DIRECTORY, name given to the government of Revolutionary France 1795–99. It consisted of five directors appointed by the bicameral legislature. Military failures, international disorders and growing inter-

nal corruption made it unpopular, enabling Napoleon to seize power with the assistance of the director Sieyès.

DIRIGIBLE. See AIRSHIP.

DISARMAMENT, the abolition, reduction or limitation of military forces and weapons. The aim of disarmament provisions may be to reduce the likelihood of war by reducing the military capabilities of contracting parties, to prevent a defeated aggressor from again disturbing the peace, or to ban the use of some weapon considered especially inhumane. Probably the first instance of this was a papal promulgation of 1139 against the use of the crossbow in war between Christians. More recently, the 1925 Geneva Protocol, ratified by over 40 nations, prohibited the use of chemical and biological weapons; and the 1972 Convention on Prohibition and Destruction of Bacteriological Weapons came into force in 1975.

Attempts to restrain aggressors have rarely been successful. After WWI the victors imposed crippling arms limitations on Germany, but inadequate inspection procedures, a recurrent problem in disarmament agreements, and considerable ingenuity in design enabled the German arms industry to circumvent them. After WWII, a ban was imposed on the arms industries of defeated Japan. General disarmament agreements have had little effect. The HAGUE PEACE CONFERENCES (1899 and 1907) failed to restrain the arms race in Europe. At the WASHINGTON CONFERENCE (1921–22), the US, Britain, Japan, France and Italy agreed to naval limitations for a 15-year period. After WWII, East–West confrontation led to a renewed arms buildup, reaching a climax of tension in the 1962 Cuban Missile Crisis. In 1963 the US, Britain and the USSR signed a Nuclear Test Ban Treaty, banning atomic tests in the atmosphere, underwater and in space. The UN Disarmament Committee drafted the Nuclear Non-Proliferation Treaty in 1968; by 1975 it had been ratified by 94 countries, including the US and the USSR. Development of new weapons systems that threatened to upset the balance of power between the US and the USSR, and the Strategic Arms Limitation Talks (SALT) in Helsinki and Vienna began in 1969. In May 1972 President Nixon signed two agreements in Moscow, limiting each nation to two antiballistic missile sites and prohibiting any increase in the development of long-range offensive missiles. An agreement in 1975 placed limitations on future additions to the already massive arsenals of the superpowers.

DISCIPLES OF CHRIST, now the International Convention of Christian Churches, US religious body founded (1832) by followers of Alexander CAMPBELL. It has no formal ministry or creed, teaching simple, personal faith in the Bible and the primitive gospel of Christ. This, it holds, should be the basis for union of Christian churches. It has missions all over the world. Its membership in North America is about 1,600,000.

DISCUS, wooden disk used in the sport of discus throwing. It has a smooth metal rim and brass plates set in its sides; the men's discus weighs not less than 4lb 6.5oz and the women's 2lb 3.25oz. The sport dates from Classical times, and is now an Olympic Games track-and-field event.

DISEASE, disturbance of normal bodily function in an organism. MEDICINE and SURGERY are concerned with the recognition or diagnosis of disease and the institution of treatment aimed at its cure. Disease is usually brought to attention by symptoms, in which a person becomes aware of some abnormality of, or change in, bodily function. Pain, HEADACHE, FEVER, COUGH, shortness of breath, DYSPEPSIA, CONSTIPATION, DIARRHEA, loss of BLOOD, lumps, PARALYSIS, numbness and loss of consciousness are common examples. **Diagnosis** is made on the basis of symptoms, signs on physical examination and laboratory and X-RAY investigations; the functional disorder is analyzed and possible causes are examined. Causes of physical disease in man are legion, but certain categories are recognized: trauma, congenital, infectious, inflammatory, vascular, tumor, degenerative, deficiency, poison, metabolic, occupational and iatrogenic diseases.

Trauma to body may cause SKIN lacerations and BONE FRACTURES as well as disorders specific to the organ involved (e.g., CONCUSSION). **Congenital diseases** include hereditary conditions (i.e., those passed on genetically) and diseases beginning in the FETUS, such as those due to drugs or maternal infection in PREGNANCY. **Infectious diseases** include VIRAL DISEASE, BACTERIAL DISEASE and PARASITIC DISEASE, which may be acute or chronic and are usually communicable. Insects, animals and human carriers may be important in their spread and EPIDEMICS may occur. INFLAMMATION is often the result of infection, but **inflammatory disease** can also result from disordered IMMUNITY and other causes. In **vascular diseases**, organs become diseased secondary to disease in their blood supply, such as ARTERIOSCLEROSIS, ANEURYSM,

THROMBOSIS and EMBOLISM.

Tumors, including benign growths, CANCER and LYMPHOMA are diseases in which abnormal growth of a structure occurs and leads to a lump, pressure on or spread to other organs and distant effects such as emaciation, HORMONE production and NEURITIS. In **degenerative disease**, DEATH or premature aging in parts of an organ or system lead to a gradual impairment of function. **Deficiency diseases** result from inadequate intake of nutrients, VITAMINS, minerals, calcium, iron and trace substances; disorders of their fine control and that of hormones leads to **metabolic disease**. **Poisoning** is the toxic action of chemicals on body systems, some of which may be particularly sensitive to a given poison. An increasingly recognized side-effect of industrialization is the occurrence of **occupational diseases**, in which chemicals, dusts or molds encountered at work cause disease—especially PNEUMOCONIOSIS and other LUNG disease, and certain cancers. **Iatrogenic disease** is disease produced by the intervention of doctors, in an attempt to treat or prevent some other disease. The altered ANATOMY of diseased structures is described as **pathological**. **Psychiatric disease**, including psychoses (schizophrenia and depression) and neuroses, are functional disturbances of the BRAIN, in which structural abnormalities are not recognizable; they may represent subtle disturbances of brain metabolism. **Treatment** of disease by SURGERY or DRUGS is usual, but success is variable; a number of conditions are so benign that symptoms may be suppressed until they have run their natural course.

DISINFECTANTS. See ANTISEPTICS.

DISMAL SWAMP, coastal region of some 750sq mi in SE Va. and NE N.C. It has a rich and varied tree cover, though most of the swamp is now drained and used for lumbering and agriculture. In the center of the swamp is Lake Drummond.

DISNEY, Walt (Walter Elias Disney; 1901–1966), US pioneer of animated film cartoons. Starting in the 1920s, the Disney studios in Hollywood created the famous cartoon characters Mickey Mouse, Pluto, Donald Duck and Goofy. Disney's first full-length cartoon feature, *Snow White and the Seven Dwarfs* (1938), was followed by *Pinocchio* (1940), *Fantasia* (1940) and *Bambi* (1942) among others. He also produced many popular nature and live-action films.

DISNEYLAND, amusement center at Anaheim, Cal., built by Walt DISNEY. The park was opened in 1955 and now includes

160 acres of amusements and recreations based on Disney films and cartoon characters. A larger counterpart, **Disney World**, was subsequently constructed in Orlando, Fla.

DISRAELI, Benjamin, 1st Earl of Beaconsfield (1804–1881), British Conservative statesman of Jewish descent, prime minister 1868 and 1874–80. A member of Parliament from 1837, he was chancellor of the exchequer 1852, 1858–59 and 1866–68. His influence was crucial in the passing of the 1867 Reform Bill, which enfranchised some 2 million working-class voters. His brief first ministry ended when the Liberals under GLADSTONE won the 1868 elections. His second period of office included domestic reforms: slum clearance, public-health reform and improvement of working conditions. Abroad, Disraeli fought imperial wars, bought control of the Suez Canal (1875), had Queen Victoria proclaimed Empress of India (1876) and annexed the Transvaal (1877). In the confrontation between Russia and Turkey (1877–78), he forced concessions on Russia (see BERLIN, CONGRESS OF). A prolific writer, he published many books, notably the novels *Coningsby* (1844) and *Sybil* (1845)— both on social and political themes.

DISSENTERS. See NONCONFORMISTS.

DISSOCIATION, in chemistry, the reversible decomposition of a compound, often effected by heat. **Ionic dissociation** is the dissociation of a covalent compound—a weak electrolyte (see ELECTROLYSIS)— into IONS when dissolved in water or other ionizing SOLVENTS. It accounts in part for the phenomena of electrolytic CONDUCTIVITY.

DISTEMPER, term applied to several animal diseases, but particularly referring to a specific VIRAL DISEASE of dogs. It commonly occurs in puppies, with FEVER, poor appetite and discharge from mucous membranes; bronchopneumonia and ENCEPHALITIS may be complications. VACCINATION is protective.

DISTILLATION, process in which substances are vaporized and then condensed by cooling, probably first invented by the ALEXANDRIAN SCHOOL and used in ALCHEMY, the still and the ALEMBIC being employed. It may be used to separate a volatile liquid from nonvolatile solids, as in the production of pure WATER from seawater, or from less volatile liquids, as in the distillation of liquid air to give oxygen, nitrogen and the noble gases. If the boiling points of the components differ greatly, **simple distillation** can be used: on gentle heating, the components distill over in order (the most volatile first) and the pure fractions are collected in different flasks. Mixtures of liquids of similar boiling points require **fractionation** for efficient separation. This technique employs multiple still heads and fractionating columns in which some of the vapor is condensed and returned to the still, equilibrating as it does so with the rising vapor. In effect, the mixture is redistilled several times; the number of theoretical simple distillations, or theoretical plates, represents the separating efficiency of the column. The theory of distillation is an aspect of PHASE EQUILIBRIA studies. For ideal solutions, obeying RAOULT'S law, the vapor always contains a higher proportion than the liquid of the more volatile component; if this is not the case, an AZEOTROPIC MIXTURE may be formed. When two immiscible liquids are distilled, they come over in the proportion of their VAPOR PRESSURES at a temperature below the boiling point of either. This is utilized in **steam distillation**, in which superheated steam is passed into the still and comes over together with the volatile liquid. It is useful when normal distillation would require a temperature high enough to cause decomposition, as in **vacuum distillation**, in which the pressure reduction lowers the boiling points. A further refinement is **molecular distillation**, in which unstable molecules travel directly in high vacuum to the condenser.

DISTRICT OF COLUMBIA. See WASHINGTON, D.C.

DITTERSDORF, Karl Ditters von (1739–1799), Austrian composer and violinist. He composed light operas, establishing the SINGSPIEL form, and various other works. Among his works are the operas *Doctor und Apotheker* (1786), *Hieronymus Knicker* (1789) and *Das Rote Kappchen* (1790).

DIURETICS, drugs that increase urine production by the KIDNEY. Alcohol and CAFFEINE are mild diuretics. Thiazides and other diuretics are commonly used in treatment of HEART failure, EDEMA, high blood pressure, LIVER and KIDNEY disease.

DIVINATION, the term applied to various methods of foretelling the future, by means of oracles, omens or signs. These methods include dream interpretation, astrology, investigation of parts of the body, (e.g., palmistry, phrenology), the study of animal entrails, and the interpretation of the cries of birds and animals (augury). Divination is one of the most ancient of practices, and has been found in almost all societies. (See ASTROLOGY; FORTUNE-TELLING; ZODIAC.)

DIVINE, Father. See FATHER DIVINE.

DIVINE COMEDY. See DANTE.

DIVING. See SWIMMING AND DIVING.

DIVING, Deep Sea, the descent by divers to the sea bed, usually for protracted periods, for purposes of exploration, salvage, etc. SKIN DIVING is almost as old as man and the Romans had primitive diving suits connected by an air pipe to the surface. This principle was also known in the early 16th century. A breakthrough came when John Lethbridge devised the forerunner of the armored suits used today in deepest waters (1715): it looked much like a barrel with sleeves and a viewport, and was useless for depths of more than a few meters. In 1802 William Forder devised a suit where air was pumped to the diver by bellows. And in 1837 (improving his earlier design of 1819) Augustus Siebe (1788–1872) invented the modern diving suit, a continuous airtight suit to which air is supplied by a pump. The diving suit today has a metal or fiberglass helmet with viewports and inhalation and exhalation valves, joined by an airtight seal to a metal chestpiece, itself joined to a flexible watertight covering of rubber and canvas; and weights, especially weighted boots, for stability and to prevent the diver shooting toward the surface. Air or, more often, an oxygen/helium mixture is conveyed to him via a thick rubber tube. In addition, he has either a telephone wire, or simply a cord which he can tug, for communication with the surface. Nowadays SCUBA diving, where the diver has no suit but carries gas cylinders and an AQUALUNG, is preferred in most cases since it permits greater mobility. In all diving great care must be taken to avoid the bends through too-rapid ascent to the surface. (See also BATHYSCAPHE; BATHYSPHERE.)

DIX, Dorothea Lynde (1802–1887), US social reformer and crusader for the humane and scientific treatment of mental illness. In 1841 she was shocked to see mentally sick people in jail and launched a successful campaign to establish mental hospitals.

DIX, Otto (1891–1969), German painter and leader of the "new objectivity" school of social realism. His most famous work is the cycle of 50 etchings entitled *Der Krieg* (The War; 1924) depicting WWI horrors. He was jailed (1939–45) by the Nazi government. In later years he turned to a form of religious mysticism in his work.

DIXIECRATS, Southern faction of the US Democratic Party which opposed the 1948 party platform on civil rights. They ran their own candidates, Governor Strom Thurmond of S.C. for president and Governor Fielding Wright of Miss. for vice-president, against the incumbent President Truman, and received 1,169,000 national and 39 electoral votes.

DIXIELAND, name given to one of the earliest jazz styles. It originated in New Orleans as an attempt by white musicians to copy early Negro jazzmen. It has since come to be applied to a strictly standardized brand of jazz that stresses improvisation and is somewhat smoother and more sophisticated than early New Orleans jazz.

DJAKARTA. See JAKARTA.

Official name: Republic of Djibouti
Capital: Djibouti
Area: 8,800sq mi
Population: 325,000
Languages: Arabic, French
Religion: Muslim
Monetary unit (s): 1 Djibouti Franc = 100 centimes

DJIBOUTI, a republic in NE Africa, situated where the coast of Africa approaches the Arabian peninsula, bounded by Ethiopia and Somalia.

Land and Economy. Most of the country is stoney desert. The climate is hot. Rainfall is usually scant, but in some years torrential rainfall causes flooding. Because of the character of the terrain, agricultural activity is limited. There are no known mineral resources, and industry is negligible. Livestock are important; hides and skins and live animals are the main exports.

People. The population is almost evenly divided into two main ethnic groups: the Afars (from Ethiopia) and the Issas (from Somalia), the latter having a slight predominance. Both groups are traditionally nomadic and depend on livestock; however, the Issas are more urbanized than the Afars. The nation's government is carefully balanced between the two groups, but historical rivalries persist. The capital, also called Djibouti, is the economic and political hub of the country, with a port and a railway terminus.

History. In 1896 France signed treaties with Britain, Italy and Ethiopia to define the boundaries of French Somaliland. In 1967 the colony voted to remain a French possession and became the French Territory of the Afars and the Issas. It became independent in 1977. Djibouti has remained neutral during strife between its neighbors, Somalia and Ethiopia, despite close ethnic ties. Thousands of refugees have streamed into Djibouti, creating serious economic problems. France maintains a military presence in the country.

DJILAS, Milovan (1911–), Yugoslav communist leader and writer. He was a leading WWII partisan alongside TITO, and became a vice-president after the war. But because of his outspoken criticisms of the regime and his general indictment of communism as a form of government he was imprisoned 1956–66. Among his works are *The New Class* (1957) and *Conversations with Stalin* (1962).

DNA, deoxyribonucleic acid, a NUCLEIC ACID comprising two strands of NUCLEOTIDE wound around each other in a double helix, found in all living things and VIRUSES.

DNIEPER RIVER, second-longest river in the European USSR, about 1,400mi long. Rising in the Valdai Hills, it flows SW to empty into the Black Sea E of Odessa. Leading tributaries are the Desna, Pripyat, Berezina and Sozh. It is a major water transport route, and also has many hydroelectric plants.

DNIESTER RIVER, river in the USSR, about 877mi long. It rises in the Carpathian Mts in the Ukraine and empties into the Black Sea W of Odessa. It carries timber and grain and has hydroelectric potential.

DOBERMAN PINSCHER, a German breed of dog much used by police forces. Its hard, smooth coat is black and brown in coloring. In the US, it has clipped ears and tail, and a strong square build. Its height is about 25in and its weight is about 60–65lb.

DOBSON, William (1610–1646), English portrait painter, one of the first significant English painters. He was much influenced by Venetian works, and worked for King Charles I at Oxford 1642–46.

DOBZHANSKY, Theodosius (1900–), Russian-born US biologist, famed for his study of the fruit fly, *Drosophila*, which demonstrated that a wide genetic range could exist in even a comparatively well-defined species. Indeed the greater the "genetic load" of unusual genes in a species, the better equipped it is to survive in changed circumstances. (See EVOLUTION; HEREDITY.)

DOCTOROW, E(dgar) L(aurence) (1931–), US novelist. His critically acclaimed books include *The Book of Daniel* (1971), an historical novel about Julius and Ethel Rosenberg and their children; *Ragtime* (1975), which inter-

weaves fictional portraits of Freud, Jung, Harry Houdini, and Henry Ford, among others; and *Loon Lake* (1980), a complex and haunting novel set during the Great Depression.

DODECANESE, group of Greek islands in the SE Aegean Sea off Turkey. There are 12 main islands, and, except for Rhodes and Cos, they are largely rocky and infertile. Italy seized the group in 1912 from the Turks, but after WWII they were ceded to Greece.

DODECAPHONIC MUSIC. See TWELVE-TONE MUSIC.

DODGE, Mary Elizabeth Mapes (1831–1905), US children's author, who founded and edited the magazine *St. Nicholas* (1873). She is best known for her book *Hans Brinker, or The Silver Skates* (1865), a classic of children's literature.

DODGE CITY, city in SW Kan. on the Arkansas R, seat of Ford Co. In the late 1800s it was a cattle center on the Sante Fe Trail, at the head of the Santa Fe Railroad, and it became notorious for its wild frontier life. It now has railroad shops and makes agricultural implements. Pop 18,001.

DODGSON, Charles Lutwidge. See CARROLL, LEWIS.

DODO, *Raphus cucullatus,* an extinct bird that was native to Mauritius. The dodo was about the size of a turkey, had a bulky body, short legs and feet and reduced wings. The head was most unusual, being large and carrying a heavy, strongly hooked, dark colored bill. The dodo was first discovered in 1507 but, mainly due to the effects of man and the animals he introduced, it was extinct by 1681.

DODOMA, rapidly expanding new capital of Tanzania scheduled for completion in 1983. Some of the nation's administrative functions were relocated here from Dar-es-Salaam, the former capital, in 1975 when the decision to move the capital inland was first announced.

DOENITZ, Karl (1891–1980), German admiral, head of the WWII U-boat service and later commander in chief of the German navy (1943–45). On Hitler's death in 1945 he became head-of-state, and subsequently surrendered to the Allies. He was tried for war crimes at Nuremberg and served 10 years in prison.

DOESBURG, Theo van (1883–1931), Dutch painter and author, a leader of the DE STIJL group. He turned to abstract art in 1916, influenced at first by MONDRIAN, and taught at the BAUHAUS 1921–23.

DOG, carnivorous mammal of the family Canidae, usually with long legs, long muzzle and bushy tail that lives by chasing its prey. Many live in packs. Wild dogs include the Raccoon dog of Asia and several South American forms like the Bush dog and the Maned wolf. Domestic dogs are members of the species *Canis Familiaris*.

DOGE, title of the heads of the republics of Venice (from the early 8th century) and Genoa (from 1339). The Venetian doge ruled for life; his dictatorial powers were increasingly restricted from the establishment of the Council of Ten in 1310. In Genoa, Andrea DORIA in 1528 reduced the doge's term of office to two years. Both offices were abolished by Napoleon when he overthrew the republics (1797).

DOGGER BANK, large shoal in the North Sea about 60mi off the NE coast of England. It is some 60mi long and 65mi wide, and is 50ft below sea level at its highest point. Cod, haddock and herring have been fished here since the Middle Ages.

DOG-SLED, type of dog-drawn vehicle, used in Arctic regions since ancient times. Huskies, samoyeds, Eskimo dogs or Alaskan malamutes are used, harnessed either in line or in a "fan," with a separate lead for each dog. Dog sled racing is popular in Norway, Canada, Alaska and North America.

DOHNÁNYI, Ernst von (1877–1960), Hungarian composer and pianist, conductor of the Budapest Philharmonic Orchestra (1919–44). His music, influenced by Brahms, includes the light-hearted *Variations on a Nursery Song* (1913) and *Ruralia Hungarica* (1924), both for piano and orchestra.

DOLCI, Danilo (1924–   ), Italian writer and social reformer. Since 1952 he has worked to improve the lot of the Sicilians, despite opposition from both the authorities and the Mafia. He won the 1957 Lenin Peace Prize. His books include *To Feed the Hungry* (1959) and *"Where There's Smoke"* (1971).

DOLE, Sanford Ballard (1844–1926), US judge and leader of the Republic of Hawaii. In 1893, he led the movement which overthrew Queen Liliuokalani and resulted in the establishment of the Hawaiian republic, of which Dole was proclaimed president (1894–1900). After US annexation in 1898, he served as territorial governor 1900–03.

DOLIN, Anton (born Patrick Healey-Kay; 1904–   ), English dancer and choreographer. He made his debut in DIAGHILEV'S *The Sleeping Princess* (1921). In 1931 he began his renowned partnership with Alicia MARKOVA. Dolin worked with the Ballet Theater, New York, 1940–46, and in 1949,

with Markova, founded the London Festival Ballet, where he danced until 1961.

DOLLAR, name for the monetary units of the US, Canada, Australia and many other countries. The word is said to derive from the German *taler*, meaning silver coin. Since WWII the US dollar has been the world's principal RESERVE CURRENCY and medium of international trade. (See also GOLD STANDARD.)

DOLLFUSS, Englebert (1892–1934), Austrian chancellor and fascist dictator (1933–34). He allied with Mussolini to keep Austria independent of Hitler and banned the Austrian Nazi party. In Feb. 1934, his Fatherland Party decimated the Social Democrats in street fighting. Dollfuss was assassinated in an unsuccessful Nazi *putsch* the following July.

DOLOMITES, Alpine mountain range in NE Italy mainly composed of vividly-colored dolomitic limestone. The highest peak is Marmolada (10,965ft). A popular tourist and climbing resort, its main center is Cortina d'Ampezzo.

DOLPHINS, a group of aquatic mammals. Dolphins are small toothed WHALES living in schools and feeding mainly on fish. The largest, the KILLER WHALE, also feeds on seals and the largest whales. The Pilot whale is another large dolphin, but the most well-known member of the family (Delphinidae) is the Bottlenosed dolphin, a highly intelligent mammal with an amazingly developed system of echolocation (see ECHO) for finding food and avoiding obstacles. A second family of dolphins (Platanistidae) lives in fresh water, and includes the Chinese Lake dolphin and the Blind susu or Ganges dolphin. (See also PORPOISE.) The Pacific spout fish of the family Corphaenidae is also known as the dolphin. It has a blunt head and forked tail, and can swim at great speed. It is a popular Hawaiian food fish.

DOME, in architecture, an oval or hemispherical vault, used to roof a large space without interior supports. The first domes were built around 1000 BC by the Persians and Assyrians but these were small and the dome did not become architecturally significant until Roman times. The PANTHEON, in which the dome rests on a drum-shaped building, is an outstanding example of the large-scale dome. The Byzantine architects of HAGIA SOPHIA in Constantinople evolved the PENDENTIVE, a device enabling the construction of a great dome over a square central area. Brunelleschi's dome on the cathedral in Florence has an inner and an outer shell; Sir Christopher Wren's dome for St. Paul's

London, has three shells. Modern techniques and lightweight materials permit the spanning of vast areas, as at the Houston Astrodome.

DOMENICHINO (born Domenico Zampieri; 1581–1641), Italian Baroque painter from Bologna, noted for the landscape settings of his pictures. Trained by the CARRACCI brothers, he painted large fresco schemes, notably *The Life of St. Cecilia* (1613–14), in palaces and churches in Rome.

DOMESDAY BOOK, a survey of most of England compiled for William I the Conqueror in 1085–86. It describes "ploughland and habitations...men.... both bond and free," housing conditions, services and rents owned by gentry and peasants, land values and every detail of rural economy in the years 1066–1085. It was compiled largely by itinerant commissioners with the aid of juries of inquiry. A statistical record unique in medieval Europe, it is an invaluable source for English national and local history.

DOMINGO, Placido (1941–), Spanish-born Mexican tenor. In 1961 he made his debut in Mexico as Alfredo in LA TRAVIATA and his US debut with the Dallas Civic Opera. He sang in Israel (1963–65), with the NY City Opera (1965–67) and joined the Metropolitan Opera in 1968.

DOMINGUEZ, Luis Miguel (1926–), Spanish bullfighter. He was the most knowledgeable matador of his generation, but his serene, almost aloof style made him less than the most popular.

DOMINIC, Saint (c1170–1221), Spanish churchman, founder of the DOMINICAN ORDER. From 1207 he was leader of a mission to the ALBIGENSIAN heretics of S France. In 1216 the pope approved Dominic's plans for a new preaching order based on ideals of poverty and scholarship. The order grew rapidly and Dominic spent the rest of his life supervising it. He was canonized in 1234. His feast day is Aug. 4.

DOMINICA, an indepenent state, is the largest island in the Windward Islands of the Lesser Antilles group, between Guadeloupe and Martinique.

Land. Dominica is crossed from N to S by a mountain range, which contains Morne Diablotin (4,747ft), the highest point in the Lesser Antilles. The climate is tropical, without great seasonal variations. Average temperature reaches 80°F and rainfall is heavy.

People and economy. Most people are Negroes or mulattoes. The rich volcanic soil produces bananas, coconuts, citrus fruits and cinnamon. Dominica also exports

pumice. Tourism is not yet fully developed, but is actively encouraged by the government. Dominica's economy was badly hurt in 1979 when hurricane David destroyed almost all banana and citrus plantations.

History. Discovered by COLUMBUS in 1493 and colonized by France in the early 17th century, Dominica was acquired by Britain in 1805 and became internally self-governing in 1967. In 1978 the island achieved full independence.

Official name: Commonwealth of Dominica
Capital: Roseau
Area: 290sq mi
Population: 81,000
Languages: English, French patois
Religions: Roman Catholic
Monetary unit(s): 1 East Caribbean dollar = 100 cents

DOMINICAN ORDER, officially the Order of Preachers (O.P.), Roman Catholic order of FRIARS. It was founded (1216) by St. DOMINIC, with approval from Pope Honorius III, as a band of highly trained priests, pledged to poverty, study and itinerant preaching. The first friaries were intended as hostels, not permanent residences. The "Black Friars," as they were popularly named for the black cloak they wore over their white habit while preaching, played a major role in the medieval INQUISITION and produced many great missionaries and theologians, notably AQUINAS. There were associated orders of nuns (see CATHERINE OF SIENA) and of lay men and women. The religious reformer SAVONAROLA was a Dominican.

DOMINICAN REPUBLIC, state in the eastern two-thirds of the island Hispaniola, which it shares with Haiti.

Land. Parallel mountain chains run from NW to SE. The biggest of these, the Cordillera Central, contains Pico Duarte, which at 10,490ft is the highest point in the West Indies. The main rivers (Yaque del Norte, Yaque del Sur and Yuna) rise there. To the N of the range lie the Cibao and Vega Real lowlands, the main agricultural area. The climate is subtropical, with an annual rainfall averaging 50in. Hurricanes tend to occur between Aug. and Nov. In 1979 hurricane David devastated the island.

People. About 65% of Dominicans are mulattoes, 20% are Negroes and 15% are Caucasians. More than half of the people live in rural areas. About 30% of the population is illiterate.

Economy. Sugar, coffee, cocoa, tobacco and bananas are the principal crops. 75% of exports are agricultural. Industry is concentrated around the capital, and apart from agricultural processing includes cement, textile and plastic manufacture. There is also some mining of bauxite and nickel, and tourism is increasingly important.

History. Hispaniola was discovered by COLUMBUS in 1492. The E part remained Spanish, while the W part was ceded to France in 1697. After centuries of turmoil the independent Dominican republic emerged in 1844, but continued to be torn by internal troubles under a succession of dictators and revolutions. It was occupied by the US Marines (1916–1924). In 1930 an army revolt put General TRUJILLO in power. His dictatorship ended with his assassination in 1961. Free elections followed, but the new left wing government of JUAN BOSCH was overthrown by a military coup in 1963. An attempt to reinstate Bosch prompted US intervention in the form of armed occupation of Santo Domingo (1965). In 1966 Dr. Joaquín Balaguer became president. He was reelected in 1970 and 1974.

Official name: Dominican Republic
Capital: Santo Domingo
Area: 18,700sq mi
Population: 5,275,000
Languages: Spanish
Religions: Roman Catholic
Monetary unit(s): 1 D.R. peso=100 centavos

DOMINION DAY, July 1, Canadian national holiday commemorating the creation of the independent Dominion of Canada under the BRITISH NORTH AMERICA ACT (1867).

DOMINO, Fats (Antoine D., Jr., 1928–), best-selling rhythm-and-blues pianist and singer, whose first hit songs ("Ain't That a Shame," 1955, and "Blueberry Hill," 1956) were followed by dozens of others in the next decade. Sales of his records are outnumbered only by those of Bing Crosby and Elvis Presley among solo singers.

DOMINOES, a game for two or more people played with flat rectangular blocks whose faces are divided into two sections and marked with dots in every possible combination from 0–0 to 6–6. In the best-known version of the game, players try to match a block or "domino" in their hand with one of the two exposed ends on the table. The first to dispose of his hand wins the game.

DOMITIAN (51–96 AD), Roman emperor, 81–96, son of VESPASIAN and brother of TITUS, whom he succeeded. He governed efficiently but harshly, his last years amounting to a reign of terror. He was assassinated at the instigation of his wife.

DONATELLO (c1386–1466), Florentine sculptor, a major figure of the Italian Renaissance. He trained as a metal worker with GHIBERTI, and as a marble sculptor. His many commissions for the Duomo of Florence include the famous *putti* for the singing gallery. Other major works are *St. George Slaying the Dragon* (1415–17), the graceful bronze *David* (c1432) in the Bargello, Florence, and the equestrian statue known as the Gattamelata Monument (1447–53), in Padua.

DONATION OF CONSTANTINE, document purporting to be addressed to Pope Sylvester I by Emperor Constantine I (d. 337), but forged, probably in the 8th century. According to it, Constantine, the first Christian emperor, renounced imperial political authority over Italy and spiritual authority over the Church in favor of the pope. The forgery was exposed by Lorenzo VALLA c1440, though the document's authenticity was contested on into the 18th century.

DONETS BASIN, or Donbass, region along the Donets and lower Dnieper rivers in the USSR. It has the USSR's richest coalfield, covering nearly 9,000sq mi and supplying about 35% of the country's coal. It also produces more iron and steel than any other region in the USSR.

DONIZETTI, Gaetano (1797–1848), Italian opera composer. Influenced by ROSSINI, he developed the traditions of serious and comic opera. His operas include *L'Elisir d'Amore* (1832) *Lucia di*

Lammermoor (1835) and *Don Pasquale* (1843). He influenced VERDI.

DON JUAN, legendary libertine, often the subject of dramatic works in which, after a dissolute life, he was led off to hell. The earliest-known dramatization is TIRSO DE MOLINA'S *The Rake of Seville* (1630). Other versions are by MOLIÈRE, MOZART (*Don Giovanni*), BYRON and G. B. SHAW (*Man and Superman*).

DONKEY, the domesticated form of the wild ass, it is descended from the African wild ass of Ethiopia. The donkey is related to the horse, but has long ears, a large head and a short mane, a tuft of hair on the end of the tail and no callosities on the hind legs. A dark band usually runs along the back and another over the shoulders. Crossbreeding with the horse produces the MULE or the HINNY, which is sterile. It is surefooted and intelligent and much used as a pack animal.

DONLEAVY, J(ames) P(atrick) (1926–   ), US novelist and playwright known for his blackly humorous vision of life in such works as *The Ginger Man* (1955), *A Singular Man* (1963), and *Shultz* (1979).

DONNE, John (1572–1631), English METAPHYSICAL POET and divine. His love poems and religious verse and prose are characterized by sophisticated argument, complex metaphors and a passionate and direct tone. His imagery relies upon both Scholastic philosophy and 17th-century scientific thought. After a long period of exclusion from court life he took orders in 1615 and became dean of St. Paul's, London, where he gave many fine sermons. His most famous writings are the love-lyrics *Songs and Sonnets*, and the religious works *Holy Sonnets, Sermons* and *Devotions*.

DONNELLY, Ignatius (1831–1901), US politician and writer. A Republican Congressman for Minn. 1863–69, he later led the GREENBACK PARTY and in the 1890s the Populist Party. He wrote the party platform and was the Populist nominee for vice-president in 1900. He wrote several speculative works, including the Utopian novel *Caesar's Column* (1891).

DONNER PARTY, group of 87 settlers from Ill., led by George Donner, who were trapped by snow in the Sierra Nevada, N Cal., in the winter of 1846–47. When food ran out, the surviving members resorted to cannibalism. Only about half the group were rescued.

DONOVAN, William Joseph (1881–1959), US soldier, attorney and government official. Nicknamed "Wild Bill," he won a Congressional Medal of Honor for his service in WWI. During WWII he created and headed the Office of Strategic Services (OSS), which was the forerunner of the CENTRAL INTELLIGENCE AGENCY.

DON QUIXOTE. See CERVANTES SAAVEDRA, MIGUEL DE.

DON RIVER, river in the USSR, about 1,224mi long. Rising SE of Tula (about 100mi S of Moscow) it flows SE to within 48mi of the VOLGA, to which it is linked by the VOLGA-DON CANAL, and then SW to the Sea of Azov. It is mostly navigable and carries coal, timber and grain. The Don is rich in fish and has many fishing villages on its banks.

DOOLEY, Mr. See DUNNE, FINLEY PETER.

DOOLEY, Thomas Anthony (1927–1961), US physician, author and a founder of MEDICO, an international medical aid organization for underdeveloped countries. In *Deliver Us from Evil* (1956) he tells how he supervised care for 600,000 Vietnamese refugees in Haiphong in 1954–55.

DOOLITTLE, Hilda (1886–1961), US poet, known as **H.D.** She lived in Europe after 1911. H.D. was one of the first IMAGISTS in America, and she continued to develop the Imagist style in her later poetry. Her works include *Sea Garden* (1916), *The Walls Do Not Fall* (1944) and the novel *Bid Me To Live* (1960).

DOOLITTLE, James Harold (1896–   ), US pilot and WWII air hero. Famous as a racing pilot in the 1920s and early 1930s, he led the first air raid on Tokyo on April 18, 1942, thereby slowing the Japanese offensive. After the war he was an executive in the aerospace industry.

DOPPLER EFFECT, the change observed in the wavelength of a sonic, electromagnetic or other wave (see WAVE MOTION) because of relative motion between the wave source and an observer. As a wave source approaches an observer, each pulse of the wave is closer behind the previous one than it would be were the source at rest relative to the observer. This is perceived as an increase in frequency, the pitch of a sound source seeming higher, the color of a light source bluer. When a sound source achieves the speed of sound, a SONIC BOOM results. As a wave source recedes from an observer, each pulse is emitted farther away from him than it would otherwise be. There is hence a drop in pitch or a reddening in COLOR (see LIGHT; SPECTRUM). The Doppler Effect, named for **Christian Johann Doppler** (1803–1853) who first described it in 1842, is of paramount importance in astronomy. Observations of stellar spectra can determine the rates at which stars are moving towards or away from us, while observed red shifts in the spectra of distant galaxies are generally interpreted as an indication that the universe as a whole is expanding.

DORATI, Antal (1906–), Hungarian-born US conductor. He became musical director of the Washington National Symphony Orchestra (1969–77) and of the Royal Philharmonic Orchestra, London, in 1975. He has recorded all Haydn's symphonies.

DORÉ, Gustave (1832–1883), French engraver, illustrator and painter. He created dreamlike, grandiose scenes in a fantastic, bizarre style and is known especially for line engravings of unusual power provided for editions of Balzac's *Contes Drolatiques* (1855), Dante's *Inferno* (1861), Cervantes' *Don Quixote* (1863) and the Bible (1866).

DORIANS, people of ancient Greece. Originating from the lower Balkans, they probably defeated the ACHAEANS and conquered the Peloponnese between 1100 and 950 BC, subsequently extending their influence to the Aegean Islands, Crete, Sicily and parts of Asia Minor, Africa and Italy.

DORR, Thomas Wilson (1805–1854), US constitutional reformer and leader of Dorr's Rebellion. Elected to the R.I. state legislature in 1834, he became head of a popular party agitating for the extension of voting rights. In 1842 the R.I. state legislature and Dorr's party formed separate administrations, but Dorr's administration collapsed after an armed confrontation. He was jailed for treason 1844–45.

DORT, Synod of (1618–19), assembly of the DUTCH REFORMED CHURCH, held at Dordrecht (Dort), which rejected the ARMINIANS' doctrines. It affirmed unconditional election, limited atonement, man's total depravity, God's irresistible grace, and the impossibility of falling from grace.

DOS PASSOS, John (Roderigo) (1896–1970), US novelist and writer of American social history. His trilogy, *U.S.A.* (1937), depicts 20th-century American life up to 1929, making use of innovative, collage-like reportage techniques. Other works are *Manhattan Transfer* (1925), *District of Columbia* (a trilogy; 1952) and *Midcentury* (1961).

DOSTOYEVSKY, Fyodor Mikhailovich (1821–1881), major Russian novelist. He spent several years in the army but resigned his commission in 1844 to devote himself to writing. Arrested in 1849 as a member of a socialist circle, Dostoyevsky was condemned to be shot; however, the sentence was commuted in the execution yard to four years' hard labor in Siberia. During the 1860s he founded two journals and traveled in Europe after his consumptive wife and his brother had died, and after he had incurred large gambling debts. He did not finally return to Russia until 1871. In 1876 he edited his own monthly *The Writer's Diary*. Suffering from epilepsy for most of his life, he died after an epileptic attack. Dostoyevsky's major novels, *Crime and Punishment* (1866), *The Idiot* (1868), *The Devils* (1871–72) and *The Brothers Karamazov* (1879–80), reveal his deep understanding of the complex psychology of human character and the problems of sin and suffering.

DOU, Gerard (1613–1675), Dutch painter. His father, a glass painter, first apprenticed him to an engraver, and he later (1628–1631) became a pupil of REMBRANDT. Dou developed the tradition of small, minutely finished pictures, with enamel-like surfaces, painting GENRE scenes, portraits, still lifes and landscapes. He influenced METSU.

DOUAY BIBLE, first official Roman Catholic English version of the Bible. It was translated from St. JEROME'S Latin VULGATE Bible by English Catholics exiled in Douai. The New Testament was published in 1582, the Old Testament in 1609–10. The translation was revised by Bishop Challoner 1749–72.

DOUBLE-BASS, stringed musical instrument, contrabass of the violin family. About 6ft high, it has four strings tuned in fourths; a fifth string or an extension at the neck is sometimes added. The double-bass is usually bowed, but jazz basses are plucked.

DOUBLEDAY, Abner (1819–1893), US Union general, credited with the invention of baseball in 1839 at Cooperstown, N.Y. He fired the first Union gun in defense of Fort Sumter and was a hero of the Battle of Gettysburg.

DOUBLE JEOPARDY, principle embodied in the 5th Amendment of the US Constitution, protecting a person against being tried twice on the same charge. The US Supreme Court, in *Benton v. Maryland* (1969), held that this principle was applicable to the states through the "due process" clause of the 14th Amendment. Neither federal nor state officers can appeal a verdict of acquittal, but the accused may appeal a verdict of guilty.

DOUBLE STAR or **binary star**, a pair of stars revolving around a common center of gravity. Less frequently the term "double star" is applied to two stars that merely appear close together in the sky though in reality at quite different distances from the earth (optical pairs) or to two stars whose motions are linked but which do not orbit each other (physical pair). About 50% of all stars are members of either binary or multiple star systems, in which there are more than two components. It is thought that the components of binary and multiple star systems are formed simultaneously. **Visual binaries** are those which can be seen telescopically to be double. There are comparatively few visual binaries, since the distances between components are small relative to interstellar distances, but examples are CAPELLA, PROCYON, SIRIUS and ALPHA CENTAURI. **Spectroscopic binaries**, while unable to be seen telescopically as doubles, can be detected by RED SHIFTS in their spectra, their orbit making each component alternately approach and recede from us. **Eclipsing binaries** are those whose components, due to the orientation of their orbit, periodically mutually eclipse each other as seen from the earth.

DOUGHTY, Charles Montagu (1843–1926), English writer, traveler and poet. *Travels in Arabia Deserta* (1888), written in Elizabethan style, describes his experiences living and traveling in Arabia in the mid-1870s.

DOUGHTY, Thomas (1793–1856), US landscape painter, a founder of the HUDSON RIVER SCHOOL. His pictures of woodlands, river valleys and lakes have a silvery light. Among his works are *On the Hudson* and *A River Glimpse*.

DOUGLAS, Stephen Arnold (1813–1861), US politician, affectionately known as the "Little Giant." He is remembered for his debates with Abraham Lincoln (see FREEPORT DOCTRINE) in the Ill. Senate elections (1858) which brought Lincoln to national attention. He was a Democratic congressman from Ill. 1843–47, and senator 1847–61. Involved in the issue of slavery in the new states, he helped draft the COMPROMISE OF 1850, based on SQUATTER SOVEREIGNTY, and the KANSAS-NEBRASKA LAW (1854). In 1860 he was the unsuccessful Democratic presidential candidate, but later supported Lincoln and the Union.

DOUGLAS, William Orville (1898–1980), justice of the US Supreme Court 1939–1975, longer than any other justice. An expert on business law, he had been chairman of the SECURITIES AND EXCHANGE COMMISSION. As a justice, he favored a broad exercise of court powers and was an ardent defender of civil rights and free speech. He wrote some 30 books, many defending nature and wilderness.

DOUGLAS-HOME, Alec (1903–), British Conservative prime minister 1963–64. After being foreign secretary 1960–63, he renounced six peerages in order to sit in the House of Commons while serving as prime minister. He followed a moderate anticommunist policy and achieved some compromise on Commonwealth racial issues. After serving again as foreign secretary 1970–74 he received a life peerage.

DOUGLASS, Frederick (1817–1895), US escaped slave (born Frederick Augustus Washington Bailey) who became a leading abolitionist and orator. He lectured for an antislavery society in Mass. and published *The Narrative of the Life of Frederick Douglass* (1845). He campaigned in England, purchased his freedom and returned to establish his own newspaper, *North Star*, in Rochester, N.Y. In the Civil War he recruited Negroes for the North, and during Reconstruction pressed for Negro civil rights. He held various federal posts and was US minister to Haiti 1889–91.

DOUKHOBORS, Russian pacifist religious sect, now settled in Canada. Founded in the 18th century, the sect rejected all forms of religious, ecclesiastical and secular authority in favor of individual direct revelation. The Doukhobors were often exiled and persecuted by the tsars. In 1898, assisted by their leader Peter Verigin and by Leo TOLSTOY, over 7,000 emigrated to Saskatchewan, some moving later to British Columbia. Their communities have developed economically, but there has been continuous trouble with the Canadian government, particularly from the extremist splinter group, Sons of Freedom, over issues of technology and compulsory education.

DOVER, borough and seaport in Kent, England, on the English Channel. Settled by the Romans, as Dubris, it was used by the Saxons and later the Normans. Dover is the major UK port for cross-channel ferries. Pop 98,700.

DOVER, Strait of, narrow passage separating SE England from N France, connecting the English Channel with the North Sea. It is around 19mi across at its narrowest point. The chief ports are Dover, Folkestone, Calais and Boulogne. Of great strategic importance, the strait was the scene of the first repulse of the Spanish ARMADA (1588), the Dover (antisubmarine) Patrol of WWI and the evacuation from DUNKERQUE (1940). The strait is frequently crossed by long-distance swimmers.

DOVER, city in Del., state capital and seat of Kent Co., on the St. Jones R, 40mi S of Wilmington. It is a major industrial and commercial center and is the site of the

Dover Air Force Base. Manufactures include chemicals and spacesuit equipment. Pop 23,512.

DOVZHENKO, Alexander (1894–1956), Ukrainian motion-picture director. With such films as *Arsenal* (1929), *Ivan* (1932) and *Frontier* (1935), he earned international recognition for the Soviet cinema. He won two Stalin prizes.

DOW JONES INDUSTRIAL AVERAGE, the most frequently cited gauge of US stock market performance. Compiled since 1884, the Dow Jones Industrial Average is a composite of the prices of 30 leading industrial stocks. In addition, Dow Jones compiles a Transportation Average (20 stocks), a Utility Average (15 stocks) and a Combined Average (all 65). Other key market indicators are Standard and Poor's Stock Prices (500 issues) and the New York Stock Exchange Price Index (all stocks traded on the exchange).

DOWNING, Sir George (1623–1684), English diplomat for whom London's Downing Street is named. He was educated in America at Harvard College. Charles II appointed him envoy to Holland where his aggressive behavior contributed to the outbreak of the Second DUTCH WAR. As secretary to the treasury (1667), he introduced important reforms.

DOYLE, Sir Arthur Conan (1859–1930), British writer, creator of the detective Sherlock Holmes, in many short stories and four novels. A doctor, soldier and campaigner for law reform, he also wrote historical novels such as *Micah Clarke* (1889) and science fiction, as in *The Lost World* (1912). In later life he became an adherent of spiritualism.

D'OYLY CARTE, Richard (1844–1901), English impresario who produced GILBERT AND SULLIVAN's first operetta *Trial by Jury*, in 1875. In 1878 he founded the D'Oyly Carte Opera Company, and in 1881 built the Savoy Theatre, London, as a stage for works by Gilbert and Sullivan.

DRACO (7th century BC), lawgiver in Athens. His code (c621 BC) made both serious and trivial crimes punishable by death—hence the term "Draconian" to describe any harsh legal measure. SOLON later repealed all the laws except those dealing with homicide.

DRACULA, in the book of that name by Bram STOKER, a Transylvanian VAMPIRE count, subject of many horror films. The name, meaning "demon," was applied to Vlad IV the Impaler, a 15th-century Walachian prince upon whom Stoker based the character.

DRAFT, Military, or conscription, system of raising armed forces by compulsory recruitment. The modern practice is more aptly described as selective service. Obligatory military service dates back to ancient times but conscription as we know it began to evolve only in the late 18th century when, in France, Napoleon I imposed universal conscription of able-bodied males. Conscription in Prussia 1807–13 was used to build up large reserves of trained men. Peacetime conscription became standard practice in the 19th century, except in Britain where it was not imposed until prior to WWII (wartime conscription was practiced in both Britain and the US during WWI). During the American Civil War both North and South used conscription, but mainly to encourage volunteering. In the US peacetime conscription was first introduced in 1940 and, though dropped briefly in 1947, continued through to 1973 to meet the demands of the Korean and then the Vietnamese commitment. Conscription has frequently given rise to civil protest (see NEW YORK DRAFT RIOTS). During Johnson's presidency (1963–69), anti-draft demonstrations, with mass burning of draft cards, became a popular form of protest against involvement in Vietnam. In June 1980, President Carter reinstated the Selective Service System, which had been in a "standby" position since the start of the All Volunteer Force in 1973. U.S. males born in 1960 or later and at least 18, including citizens, resident aliens and conditional entrants to the US, were required to register with the Service through the post office. (See also CONSCIENTIOUS OBJECTOR; IMPRESSMENT.)

DRAKE, Sir Francis (c1543–1596), English admiral and explorer, the first Englishman to sail around the world (1577–80). During his circumnavigation aboard the *Golden Hind*, Drake seized a fortune in booty from Spanish settlements along the South American Pacific coast. He was knighted on his return by Queen Elizabeth I. In 1587 he destroyed a large part of the Spanish fleet at anchor in Cadiz harbor. The following year he was joint commander of the English fleet which, with the help of a storm, dispersed and destroyed the Spanish ARMADA.

DRAMA. See THEATER.

DRAUGHTS. See CHECKERS.

DRAVIDIANS, subgroup of the Hindu race, some 100,000,000 people of (mainly) S India. They are fairly dark-skinned, stocky, have rather more NEGROID features than other Indics, and are commonly dolichocephalic (see CEPHALIC INDEX). (See also RACE.) The **Dravidian languages** are a family of some 22 languages, perhaps the most important from a philological point of view being Tamil, texts in which date back to at least the 1st century BC (see also PHILOLOGY).

DRAWING, the art of delineating figures, objects or patterns on a surface, usually paper. Two general types of medium are used: dry mediums such as graphite, metalpoint, charcoal, chalks and crayons, and wet mediums, inks and washes, applied by pen or brush. Drawings have traditionally served as preparatory studies for paintings, sculptures or works of architecture. Artists like the 13th-century architect Villiard d'Honnecourt or the Renaissance painter PISANELLO drew and collected together many detailed studies for use in other works. LEONARDO DA VINCI drew to create and elaborate his artistic ideas, and like RAPHAEL, DÜRER, MICHELANGELO and REMBRANDT made drawing an art form in its own right. During the 17th century, drawing evolved into an important artistic discipline. In the 19th century, INGRES was a major exponent of this discipline. Modern masters of drawing include PICASSO, KLEE and MATISSE.

DREADNOUGHT, British battleship (1906) of revolutionary design. Weighing 18,000 tons and capable of traveling at 21 knots, the *Dreadnought* carried ten 12in guns. At the time of her completion there was nothing afloat to match her for speed and firepower. By the outbreak of WWI nine *Dreadnought* class ships and 12 other big-gun battleships were in service in the British navy.

DREAMS, fantasies, usually visual, experienced during sleep and in certain other situations. About 25% of an adult's sleeping time is characterized by rapid eye movements (REM) and brain waves that, registered on the ELECTROENCEPHALOGRAPH, resemble those of a person awake (EEG). This REM-EEG state occurs in a number of short periods during sleep, each lasting a number of minutes, the first coming some 90min after sleep starts and the remainder occurring at intervals of roughly 90min. It would appear that it is during these periods that dreams take place, since people woken during a REM-EEG period will report and recall visual dreams in some 80% of cases; people woken at other times report dreams only about 40% of the time, and of far less visual vividness. Observation of similar states in animals suggests that at least all mammals experience dreams. Dreams can also occur, though in a limited way, while falling asleep; the origin and nature of these is not known. **Dream interpretation** seems as old as recorded history. Until the mid-19th century dreams were regarded as supernatural, often prophetic; their possible prophetic nature has been examined in this century by, among others, J. W. Dunne. According to FREUD, dreams have a *latent content* (the fulfilment of an individual's particular UNCONSCIOUS wish) which is converted by *dreamwork* into *manifest content* (the dream as experienced). In these terms, interpretation reverses the dreamwork process.

DRED SCOTT CASE, suit brought by Scott, a slave from Mo., on the grounds that temporary residence in a territory in which slavery was banned under the MISSOURI COMPROMISE had made him free. The majority opinion of the US Supreme Court, read by Chief Justice TANEY, held that Scott, as an African Negro, could never be a citizen of any state, and therefore could not sue his owner in federal court. Taney should have ended his opinion here but, instead, plunged on to declare that even if Scott could sue, his sojurn in free territory did not make him free because Congress' ban on slavery in the Missouri Compromise was unconstitutional; furthermore, said Taney, Congress had no power to keep slavery out of any US territory. This decision inflamed and divided the nation, making the Civil War all but inevitable.

DREISER, Theodore (1871–1945), US novelist whose naturalistic fiction, concerned with the dispossessed and criminal, dealt with the grimmer realities of American life. Dreiser's work, often artistically raw, has at its best a massive energy and power. His novels include *Sister Carrie* (1900) and *An American Tragedy* (1925).

DRESDEN, city in East Germany, capital of Dresden district, on the Elbe R. Until WWI it was the capital of the Kingdom of Saxony. Today Dresden is a communications and cultural center containing world-famous art museums, and many historic buildings, extensively restored since WWII. It produces optical and electrical equipment and has food processing industries. The famous DRESDEN CHINA is manufactured nearby. Pop 515,400.

DRESDEN CHINA, also known as Meissen ware, after the town near Dresden where china has been made since 1710. Europe's first true porcelain, the process of its manufacture was discovered by Johann Friedrich Böttger c1707. (See POTTERY AND PORCELAIN.)

DRESS. See FASHION.

DRESSLER, Marie (1869–1934), Canadian-born US actress who began her career as a vaudeville comic and singer. She appeared in *Tillie's Punctured Romance* with Charlie Chaplin (1914), and was later typecast as an alcoholic in 1930s films such as *Dinner at Eight* (1933). She won an Academy Award for her role in *Min and Bill* (1931).

DREW, Charles Richard (1904–1950), black US physician, surgeon and medical researcher who founded the American Red Cross blood bank.

DREW, Daniel (1797–1879), US financier, notorious for his speculative dealing in connection with the Erie railroad, of which he became a director (1857). With Jay GOULD and James FISK, Drew conspired to thwart the ambitions of Cornelius VANDERBILT.

DREYER, Carl (1889–1968), Danish film director whose films subordinated narrative to the exploration of emotion. Well known works are *The Passion of Joan of Arc* (1928), *Day of Wrath* (1943) and *Gertrud* (1964).

DREYFUS AFFAIR, notorious French political scandal of the Third Republic. In 1894, Alfred Dreyfus (1859–1935), a Jewish army captain, was convicted of betraying French secrets to the Germans. Further evidence pointed to a Major ESTERHAZY as the traitor; but when tried (Jan. 1898), he was acquitted on further secret, and forged, evidence. Dreyfus' conviction had aroused ANTI-SEMITISM; and although evidence against him had been forged, the army was reluctant to admit error. As public interest in the case was aroused, it became known that the Roman Catholic Church supported the conviction. After Esterhazy's acquittal, Émile ZOLA published an attack on the army's integrity, *J'accuse*, which roused intellectual and liberal opinion to a furor. With the suicide of an army officer who acknowledged the forgeries and Esterhazy's flight from France, a new trial began, but Dreyfus was found "guilty with extenuating circumstances" (Aug. 1899). Public opinion was outraged, and in Sept. the government gave him a pardon. He served in WWI and retired a lieutenant-colonel. The scandal had thrown the government, army and Church into disrepute. Legislation followed which led to separation of Church and State (1905). The original verdict against Dreyfus was quashed in 1906.

DRILLS, tools for cutting or enlarging holes in hard materials. There are two classes: those that have a rotary action, with a cutting edge or edges at the point and, usually, helical fluting along the shank; and those that work by percussive action, where

repeated blows drive the drill into the material. Rotary drills are commonly used in the home for wood, plastic, masonry and sometimes metal. They are usually hand-turned, though electric motors are increasingly used to power drills in home workshops. In metallurgy the mechanical drilling machine or *drill press* is one of the most important MACHINE TOOLS, operating one or several drills at a time. As great heat is generated, LUBRICATION is very important. Most metallurgical drills are of high-speed STEEL. Dentists' drills rotate at extremely high speeds, their tips (of TUNGSTEN carbide or DIAMOND) being water-cooled: they are powered by an electric motor or by compressed air. Rotary drills are used for deeper oil-well drilling: a cutting bit is rotated at the end of a long, hollow drill pipe, new sections of pipe being added as drilling proceeds. **Percussive drills** are used for rock-boring, for concrete and masonry, and for shallower oil-well drilling. Rock drills are generally powered by compressed air, the tool rotating after each blow to increase cutting speed. The pneumatic drill familiar in city streets is also operated by compressed air. *Ultrasonic drills* are used for brittle materials; a rod, attached to a TRANSDUCER, is placed against the surface, and to it are fed ABRASIVE particles suspended in a cooling fluid. It is these particles that actually perform the cutting. (See also ULTRASONICS.)

DROMEDARY. See CAMEL.

DROPSY. See EDEMA.

DRUG ADDICTION, an uncontrollable craving for a particular DRUG, usually a NARCOTIC, which develops into a physiological or sometimes merely psychological dependence on it. Generally the individual acquires greater tolerance for the drug, and therefore requires larger and larger doses, to the point where he may take doses that would be fatal to the nonaddict. Should his supply be cut off he will suffer **withdrawal symptoms** ("cold turkey") which are psychologically gruelling and often physically debilitating to the point where death may result. Many drugs, such as ALCOHOL and TOBACCO, are not addictive in the strictest sense but more correctly HABIT forming (but see ALCOHOLISM). Others, such as the OPIUM derivatives, particularly HEROIN and MORPHINE, are extremely addictive. With others, such as LSD (and most other HALLUCINOGENIC DRUGS), COCAINE, HEMP and the AMPHETAMINES, the situation is unclear: dependence may be purely psychological, but it may be that these drugs interfere with the chemistry of the

BRAIN; for example, the hallucinogen MESCALINE is closely related to ADRENALINE. The situation is even less clear with such drugs as MARIJUANA which appear to be neither addictive nor habit forming. An inability to abstain from regular self-dosage with a drug is described as a **drug habit.**

DRUGS, chemical agents that affect biological systems. In general they are taken to treat or prevent disease, but certain drugs, such as the OPIUM NARCOTICS, AMPHETAMINES, BARBITURATES and cannabis, are taken for their psychological effects and are drugs of addiction or abuse (see DRUG ADDICTION). Many drugs are the same as or similar to chemicals occurring naturally in the body and are used either to replace the natural substance (e.g., THYROID HORMONE) when deficient, or to induce effects that occur with abnormal concentrations as with STEROIDS or oral CONTRACEPTIVES. Other agents are known to interfere with a specific mechanism or antagonize a normal process (e.g., ATROPINE, CURARE). Many other drugs are obtained from other biological systems; FUNGI or BACTERIA (ANTIBIOTICS) or plants (DIGITALIS), and several others are chemical modifications of natural products. In addition, there are a number of entirely synthetic drugs (e.g., barbiturates), some of which are based on active parts of naturally occurring drugs (as with some antimalarials based on QUININE).

In devising drugs for treating common conditions, an especially desirable factor is that the drug should be capable of being taken by mouth; that is, that it should be able to pass into the body unchanged in spite of being exposed to STOMACH acidity and the ENZYMES of the DIGESTIVE SYSTEM. In many cases this is possible but there are some important exceptions, as with INSULIN which has to be given by INJECTION. This method may also be necessary if VOMITING or GASTROINTESTINAL-TRACT disease prevent normal absorption. In most cases, the level of the drug in the BLOOD or tissues determines its effectiveness. Factors affecting this include: the route of administration; the rate of distribution in the body; the degree of binding to PLASMA PROTEINS or FAT; the rates of breakdown (e.g., by the LIVER) and excretion (e.g., by the KIDNEYS); the effect of disease on the organs concerned with excretion, and interactions with other drugs taken at the same time. There is also an individual variation in drug responsiveness which is also apparent with undesired **side-effects.** These arise because drugs acting on one system commonly act on others. Side effects may be nonspecific (nausea, DIARRHEA, malaise or SKIN rashes);

allergic (HIVES, ANAPHYLAXIS), or specific to a drug (abnormal HEART rhythm with digitalis). Mild side effects may be suppressed but others must be watched for and the drug stopped at the first sign of any adverse effect. Drugs may cross the PLACENTA to reach the FETUS during PREGNANCY, interfering with its development and perhaps causing deformity as happens with THALIDOMIDE.

Drugs may be used for symptomatic relief (ANALGESICS, antiemetics) or to control a disease. This can be accomplished by killing the infecting agents; by preventing specific infections; by restoring normal control over MUSCLE (anti-Parkinsonian agents) or mind (ANTIDEPRESSANTS); by replacing a lost function or supplying a deficiency (e.g., VITAMIN B_{12} in pernicious ANEMIA); by suppressing inflammatory responses (steroids, ASPIRIN); by improving the functioning of an organ (digitalis); by protecting a diseased organ by altering the function of a normal one (e.g., DIURETICS for heart failure), or by toxic actions on CANCER cells (cancer CHEMOTHERAPY). The scientific study of drugs is the province of PHARMACOLOGY.

DRUIDS, ancient Celtic priestly order in Gaul (France), Britain and Ireland, respected for their learning in astronomy, law and medicine, for their gift of prophecy and as lawgivers and leaders. Little is known of their religious rites, though human sacrifice may have been involved. Because of their power, they were banned by the Romans.

DRUM, musical instrument of the percussion family, common to most cultures. It consists of a shell, usually cylindrical, with a membrane, or skin, stretched over one or both ends. The skin is struck with the hand or with sticks. The principal drum in the symphony orchestra is the kettledrum, or tympanum (see TIMPANI). Other types include the tenor, snare and bass drums. The last two also figure in jazz, where they are important in the rhythm section.

DRUNKENNESS. See INTOXICATION.

DRURY LANE THEATER, famous theater in Covent Garden, London, first opened in 1663 as the Theatre Royal and rebuilt three times. The second theater was built by WREN in 1674; the present building dates from 1812. GARRICK and SHERIDAN were among its many famous actors and managers.

DRUZES, Islamic sect of about 300,000 living in Lebanon, Syria, Israel and the US. They form a closed community, and most of their doctrines are jealously guarded secrets. They have their own scriptures, and profess MONOTHEISM and the divinity of al-Hakim, 6th caliph (996–1021) of the Egyptian FATIMID dynasty.

DRYDEN, John (1631–1700), English poet and dramatist, also considered the father of English literary criticism. Dryden's career began around the time of the RESTORATION (1660). He became Poet Laureate in 1668 and Historiographer Royal in 1670. One of his best-known plays is *All for Love* (1677); his famous critical *Essay of Dramatick Poesie* appeared in 1668. *Absalom and Achitophel* (1681) and *Mac Flecknoe* (1682) are brilliant satirical poems. After the accession of William of Orange, Dryden worked largely on translations, notably of Virgil (1697).

DRY TORTUGAS, coral island group, part of Monroe Co., Fla., 50mi SW of the mainland at the entrance to the Gulf of Mexico. Named by the Spanish for their abundant tortoise populatin and lack of fresh water.

DUALISM, any religious or philosophical system characterized by a fundamental opposition of two independent or complementary principles. Among religious dualisms are the unending conflict of good and evil spirits envisaged in ZOROASTRIANISM and the opposition of light and darkness in Jewish apocalyptic, GNOSTICISM and MANICHAEISM. The Chinese complementary principles of *yin* and *yang* exemplify a cosmological dualism while the mind–body dualism of DESCARTES is the best-known philosophical type. Dualism is often opposed to MONISM and pluralism.

DUBAI, one of the sheikhdoms of the UNITED ARAB EMIRATES which extends about 45mi along the Persian Gulf, bordered on the S and W by Abu Dhabi. Over 90% of the population live in the capital, Dubai, a port with an international airport a commercial center. Oil, shipbuilding, and aluminum production are mainstays of the economy. Pop 206,861.

DU BARRY, Marie Jeanne Bécu, Countess (1743–1793), the last mistress of LOUIS XV of France. Her years as mistress (1769–74) were marked by her generosity and good nature but little political influence. She was executed in Paris for coming out of retirement to aid royalist émigrés during the French Revolution.

DUBCEK, Alexander (1921–   ), Czechoslovak statesman. As first secretary of the Communist Party in 1968, he led popular measures to liberalize and "de-Stalinize" communism in Czechoslovakia. But USSR and Warsaw Pact forces invaded and put an end to hopes for "socialism with a human face." In 1975 Dubček was expelled from the Communist Party.

DUBINSKY, David (1892–   ), Russian-born US labor leader; president of the International Ladies Garment Workers Union (1932–66). Known for combating Communist and underworld infiltration of the union, he negotiated increased benefits for its members. He was also a founder of New York's Liberal Party (1944) and a vice-president of the AFL-CIO (1955–66).

DUBLIN (Baile Atha Cliath), capital of the Irish Republic (Eire) and of County Dublin. Located at the mouth of the Liffey R and Dublin Bay on the Irish Sea, Dublin is the political and cultural center of Ireland. Its fine buildings include the Four Courts, the Custom House, Trinity College, the National Library, Museum and Gallery and the Royal Irish Academy, in addition to many Georgian streets and squares. There is also a famous medical center and zoological gardens dating from 1830, as well as the Abbey Theatre and University College. English rule, which severely restricted Dublin's commercial development, was finally removed after the EASTER RISING (1916) and the establishment of the Irish Free State (1921). Dublin is an industrial seaport and the city manufactures stout, whiskey and textiles. There is a direct rail and steamer link to London. Pop 566,000.

DU BOIS, William Edward Burghardt (1868–1963), US black educator and author, who helped transform the Negro view of the black man's role in America. Professor of economics and history at Atlanta U., 1897–1910, and head of its sociology department, 1934–44, he wrote *The Philadelphia Negro* (1899), *The Souls of Black Folk* (1903) and *Black Reconstruction* (1935). A hero of black intellectuals, he became increasingly alienated from the US and died in Ghana in self-imposed exile.

DUBOS, René Jules (1901–   ), French-born US microbiologist who discovered tyrothricin (1939), the first ANTIBIOTIC to be used clinically. He wrote more than 30 books, including *So Human An Animal* (Pulitzer Prize; 1969), and founded the René bos Center for Human Environments.

DUBROVNIK, Dalmatian seaport in SW Yugoslavia, in the republic of Croatia. The old city wall and streets and a promontory setting make it a picturesque tourist resort. It was a flourishing medieval trading port and Slav cultural center, and an independent republic until 1808, becoming part of Yugoslavia after WWI. Pop 31,106.

DUBUFFET, Jean (1901–), French artist influenced by spontaneous, primitive amateur art, known as *art brut* ("raw art"). He uses gravel, tar etc. to produce fantastic impasto paintings that constitute fierce protests against conventional esthetic criteria.

DUCCIO DI BUONINSEGNA (c1255–c1319), Italian painter, first great master of the Sienese school. Combining Byzantine austerity with French Gothic grace, Duccio's work strongly influenced the development of Renaissance painting. The altarpiece *Maestà* is regarded as his masterpiece.

DUCHAMP, Marcel (1887–1968), French artist, a pioneer of DADA, CUBISM and FUTURISM, initially influenced by CÉZANNE. His *Nude Descending a Staircase* shocked the American public in 1913. Having settled in New York in 1915, he abandoned art for chess in 1923 and became an American citizen in 1955.

DUCHAMP-VILLON, Raymond (1876–1918), French sculptor whose concern with the fluidity of motion and the dissection of dynamic figure into its component parts can be seen in his bust of Baudelaire and his studies of human and animal forms. His work influenced the later cubist sculptors.

DUCKS, aquatic birds comprising most of the smaller members of the family Anatidae which also contains the GEESE and SWANS. The word "duck" also is used to describe the females of many members of the Anatidae, the males being called drakes. Ducks are, broadly, of two types: surface-feeding or dabbling, and diving ducks. The most familiar ducks are dabblers and include the MALLARD which is found throughout the N Hemisphere and is the ancestor of the domestic duck. Many ducks are killed for sport and food. Their down, particularly that of the EIDER, is of commercial importance.

DUE PROCESS, constitutional guarantee of fairness in the administration of justice. This concept can be traced back to MAGNA CARTA, and is embodied in the 5th Amendment to the US Constitution: "No person shall be ... deprived of life, liberty or property without due process of law." The 14th Amendment extended this limitation on the federal government to include the states. Due process has two aspects. *Procedural* due process guarantees fair trial in the courts, and *substantive* due process places limitations on the content of law. It is under this latter heading that the Supreme Court has struck down many state laws restricting civil liberties as infringements of the Bill of Rights. (See also CIVIL RIGHTS AND LIBERTIES; UNITED STATES CONSTITUTION.)

DUFAY, Guillaume (c1400–1474), Flemish composer, the greatest of his period. Attached to Cambrai Cathedral from 1445, he wrote church music and songs, developing the mass in a graceful, expressive style, much influenced by John DUNSTABLE.

DUFY, Raoul (1877–1953), French painter influenced by FAUVISM, CUBISM and the works of CÉZANNE. He is best known for gay sporting scenes in brilliant colors executed with great dash.

DUHAMEL, Georges (1884–1966), French writer who stressed human values and distrusted material progress. Works include war stories and two cycles of novels: *Salavin* (1920–32) and *The Pasquier Chronicle* (1933–45).

DUKAS, Paul Abraham (1865–1935), French composer of the colorful orchestral piece, *The Sorcerer's Apprentice.* He also wrote a symphony, a ballet, an opera and piano works.

DUKE, James Buchanan (1856–1925), US industrialist and philanthropist, member of a family with expanding tobacco interests. In 1890 he became president of the powerful merger-built American Tobacco Company. He helped found Duke U. in N.C. and endowed colleges, churches and hospitals.

DUKE, Vernon (real name Vladimir Dukelsky, 1903–1969), Russian-US composer. He left the USSR in 1920 and during the 1920s composed ballets in France for DIAGHILEV. After settling in the US in 1929 he wrote for the stage and motion pictures, producing scores for *Cabin in the Sky* (1940) and other films, and continued to compose classical works, such as his 1942 violin concerto.

DULCIMER, musical instrument with a set of strings stretched across a thin, flat soundbox and struck with mallets. Of ancient origin, it is still used in the folk music of Central Europe, where it is called the cimbalom.The Kentucky dulcimer, a US folk instrument, is plucked.

DULLES, name of two prominent American brothers. **John Foster Dulles** (1888–1959), lawyer, US secretary of state under Eisenhower (1953–59), employed a strong foreign policy to block communist "cold war" expansion. He was legal counsel at the WWI peace conference, worked on the UN charter during WWII and negotiated the Japanese peace treaty, 1951. **Allen Welsh Dulles** (1893–1969), American lawyer and intelligence official, negotiated the Nazi surrender in Italy in WWII. He directed the CENTRAL INTELLIGENCE AGENCY 1953-61, considerably influencing foreign policy, as in the American-backed BAY OF PIGS invasion of Cuba.

DUMA, elected assembly in tsarist Russia, instituted by Nicholas II in 1906. The first two dumas were radical, and were swiftly dissolved. The third and fourth (1907-12 and 1912-17), though restricted, introduced some reforms. Revolution in 1917 did away with the institution.

DUMAS, name of two 19th-century French authors, a father and his illegitimate son. **Alexandre Dumas** (1802-1870), "Dumas père,' wrote the famous historical novels *The Three Musketeers* (1844) and *The Count of Monte Cristo* (1845). Historically inaccurate and lacking in depth, these adventures nevertheless remain popular. **Alexandre Dumas** (1824-1895), "Dumas fils," won fame with his tragic play *La Dame aux Camélias* (known in English as *Camille*, 1852) which formed the basis of Verdi's opera *La Traviata*. He also wrote moralizing plays aimed at the reform of such social evils as prostitution and illegitimacy.

DU MAURIER, name of' two English novelists. **George Louis Palmella Busson du Maurier** (1834-1896), caricaturist, illustrator and novelist, best known for *Peter Ibbetson* (1891) and *Trilby* (1894). **Daphne du Maurier** (1907-), George's granddaughter, has written romantic novels. Her most famous work is *Rebecca* (1938).

DUMBARTON OAKS CONFERENCE, meeting of diplomats of the "Big Four" (China, the US, USSR and UK), held Aug. 24-Oct. 7, 1944, at the Dumbarton Oaks estate in Washington, D.C. Its discussions were the first major step towards establishing a postwar international security system (see UNITED NATIONS).

DUMBNESS, inability to speak. Failure of speech development, usually associated with congenital DEAFNESS (deaf-mute) is the most common cause in childhood. APHASIA and hysterical mutism are the usual adult causes. If comprehension is intact, writing and sign language are alternative forms of communication, but in aphasia language is usually globally impaired. (See SPEECH AND SPEECH DISORDERS.)

DUNANT, Jean Henri (1828-1910), Swiss philanthropist, founder of the RED CROSS. Horrified by unrelieved suffering at the Battle of SOLFERINO (1859) he publicized the need for effective aid for injured in war and peace. His efforts led to the Geneva Convention of 1864 (see GENEVA CONVENTIONS) and to the formation of the Red Cross. He shared in the first Nobel Peace Prize in 1901.

DUNAWAY, Faye (1941-), US actress specializing in the portrayal of cold, beautiful and sometimes dangerous women. Major films include *Bonnie and Clyde* (1967), *Network* (1976) and *Mommie Dearest* (1981), in which she played Joan CRAWFORD.

DUNBAR, Paul Laurence (1872-1906), black US poet and novelist. His poems about black rural life were influenced by the sentimental dialect poems of James Whitcomb RILEY. His works include *Lyrics of Lowly Life* (1896) and the novel *The Sport of the Gods* (1902).

DUNBAR, William (c1460-1520), greatest of the old Scottish poets. He became a priest, employed by James IV on court business. His mainly short poems show great satiric power, originality, versatility and wit.

DUNCAN, David Douglas (1916-), US photographer who covered WWII as a Marine photographer and the Palestine conflict and the Korean War for *Life* magazine. His publications include *This is War* (1951) on Korea, and two books on Picasso (1958, 1961).

DUNCAN, Isadora (1878-1927), US dancer, a pioneer of modern dance, encouraging a spontaneous personal style. She danced in a loose tunic, barefoot, to symphonic music. After European concert successes, she founded schools of dancing in Germany, the USSR and the US. She was strangled by a scarf caught in a car wheel.

DUNGEONS & DRAGONS, a fantasy, role-playing game of recent vintage for any number of players. The game is currently gaining popularity among adolescents and young adults in the US. Through story-telling techniques players try to build up the character and strength of their roles as they are beset by various dangers and threatening situations, such as attacks by monsters or dragons, during their travels through an imaginary dungeon. A dungeon-master directs the players along their imaginary paths. Many books describing rules and possible tactics are available.

DUNKERQUE (Dunkirk), seaport in N France, on the English Channel, 10mi from Belgium. A shipbuilding, oil-refining and food processing center, and railway terminus. In WWII (May 27-June 4, 1940) some 1,000 vessels evacuated 337,000 trapped British and Allied troops from here. Pop 27,504.

DUNKERS (Dunkards), any of several bodies of Brethren, or German Baptists. They are theologically rooted in 17th-century Lutheran PIETISM and named for their practice of triple baptismal immersion. The movement began in 18th-century Germany but most members went to America where they now number over 230,000, most in the Church of the Brethren.

DUNMORE, John Murray, 4th Earl of (1732–1809), English governor of New York (1770–71), Virginia (1771–75) and the Bahamas (1787–96). He launched "Lord Dunmore's War" (1774) against the Indians. Opposing the rebels, he three times dissolved the Virginia assembly (1772–74) but in 1776 an uprising forced him out of Virginia.

DUNNE, Finley Peter (1867–1936), US journalist and humorist. He created "Mr. Dooley," an Irish-American saloonkeeper, whose amusing and satirical comments on current events Dunne first published in the press, then in books such as *Mr. Dooley in Peace and War* (1898).

DUNNE, Irene (1904–   ), US singer and film actress who distinguished herself in sentimental dramas, musicals and light comedies. She starred in *Back Street* (1932), *Show Boat* (1936), *The Awful Truth* (1937) and *I Remember Mama* (1948).

DUNS SCOTUS, John (c1265–1308), Scottish philosopher and theologian. He joined the Franciscans (1280), was ordained in 1291 and taught at Cambridge, Oxford, Paris and Cologne. His system of thought embodied chiefly in his commentary on LOMBARD'S *Sentences*, was adopted by the Franciscans and was highly influential. Typical of SCHOLASTICISM, it differs from AQUINAS in asserting the primacy of love and the will over reason. He was the first in the West to defend the IMMACULATE CONCEPTION.

DUNSTABLE, John (c1385–1453), English composer whose flowing, harmonious works influenced European music. He wrote some 60 works, including motets and secular part-songs.

DUODECIMAL SYSTEM, a number system using the POWERS of twelve, which are allotted place values as in the DECIMAL SYSTEM. The number written in decimals 4092 can be expressed as $(2 \times 12^3) + (4 \times 12^2) + (5 \times 12^1) + (0 \times 12^0)$ or, in duodecimals, 2450. Fractions are expressed similarly. Two extra symbols are needed for this system to represent the numbers 10 and 11; these are generally accepted as X (dek) and Σ (el) respectively. The advantage of this system can be realized by consideration of the integral (see INTEGERS) FACTORS of 10 and 12: 10 has two (2,5) while 12 has four

(2,3,4,6). The most common examples of everyday use of this system are the setting of 12 inches to the foot. 12 months to the year.

DUODENUM, the first part of the small intestine, leading from the STOMACH to the jejunum (see GASTROINTESTINAL TRACT). The BILE and pancreatic ducts end in it and its injury may result in a FISTULA. Peptic ULCERS are common in the duodenum.

DUPLEIX, Joseph François (1696–1763), governor-general of French possessions in India, 1742–54. He tried to extend French influence in central and S India by supporting Indian rulers against their British-backed rivals. Defeated by CLIVE, Dupleix was discredited and returned to France to die in poverty.

DU PONT, US industrial family of French origin. **Pierre Samuel du Pont de Nemours** (1739–1817), French economist and statesman, publicized the PHYSIOCRATS' doctrines. He was a reformist member of the Estates General (1789) and secretary general of the provisional government (1814). He fled to the US in 1799 and, having returned in 1802, fled again in 1815. His son **Éleuthère Irénée du Pont** (1771–1834) established a gunpowder factory near Wilmington, Del., in 1802. The company expanded enormously during the Mexican, Crimean and Civil wars under Éleuthère's son **Henry du Pont** (1812–1889), who in 1872 organized the "Gunpowder Trust" which soon controlled 90% of explosives output. **Alfred Irénée du Pont** (1864–1935), **Thomas Coleman du Pont** (1863–1930) and **Pierre Samuel du Pont** (1870–1954) reorganized the firm in 1902, and after WWI it exploited the valuable dye-trust patents confiscated from Germany. Under Pierre's brothers **Irénée du Pont** (1876–1963) and **Lammont du Pont** (1880–1952) the firm built up an immensely powerful synthetic chemicals industry, developing rayon, cellophane, neoprene, nylon and other materials.

DUPRÉ, Marcel (1886–1971), French organist and composer, director of the Paris Conservatoire 1954–56. His compositions include symphonies and many organ works.

DURAND, Asher Brown (1796–1886), US painter and engraver, a founder of the HUDSON RIVER SCHOOL. He made his name by engraving John Trumbull's painting *The Signing of the Declaration of Independence* (1820). He painted realistic landscapes and portraits, and also designed banknotes.

DURANT, Thomas Clark (1820–1885), US railroad pioneer, chief founder of the Union Pacific Railroad (1862). Founder president of the CRÉDIT MOBILIER OF AMERICA (1863–67), he was ousted by rivals, but remained a Union Pacific director till 1869.

DURANT, William Crapo (1861–1947), US automobile executive who founded the General Motors Corporation in 1916 with the aid of Louis Chevrolet (1879–1941). He lost control in 1920.

DURANT, Will(iam James) (1885–1981), US educator and popular historian. He wrote the stylishly lively bestseller *The Story of Philosophy* (1926) and, with his wife, **Ariel** (1898–1981), the 11-volume *The Story of Civilization* (1935–75).

DURANTE, Jimmy (1893–1980), US entertainer, born James Francis Durante, famous for his outsized nose. He began in show business in 1910 and appeared in many films and musicals.

DURAS, Marguerite (1914–   ), French novelist, playwright and scriptwriter, associated with the New Wave French writers of the 1950s and 1960s. Her works include the novels *The Sea Wall* (1950) and *Moderato Cantabile* (1958) and the film script *Hiroshima, Mon Amour* (1960).

DÜRER, Albrecht (1471–1528), German artist who introduced Italian Renaissance outlook and style to Germany, though tempered by Gothic tradition. Bellini, Mantegna and Leonardo da Vinci all influenced Dürer after his visits to Venice (1494–95 and 1505–07). He became court painter to the emperors Maximilian (1512) and Charles V (1520), and produced a huge output of masterly, vividly detailed drawings, engravings, woodcuts and paintings. His themes included religious subjects, plant and animal studies and evocative landscapes in watercolor.

DURHAM, John George Lambton, 1st Earl of (1792–1840), English statesman, author of DURHAM'S REPORT. A radical Whig, he was lord privy seal 1830–33 and helped draft the Reform Bill of 1832. Governor general of Canada 1838, he was criticized for his leniency towards rebels, and resigned.

DURHAM'S REPORT, report by Lord Durham which laid down the basic principles of British colonial administration. *The Report on the Affairs of British North America* (1839) urged the union of Canada and the granting of internal self government.

DURKHEIM, Émile (1858–1917), pioneer French sociologist who advocated the synthesis of empirical research and abstract theory in the social sciences and developed the concepts of "collective consciousness" and the "division of labor."

DUROCHER, Leo Ernest "Lippy" (1906–   ), US baseball player and manager. Beginning in 1925, he played shortstop for major league teams, then managed the Brooklyn Dodgers (world champions 1941), New York Giants (world champions 1951 and 1954) and Chicago Cubs.

DURRELL, Lawrence (George) (1912–   ), English novelist and poet, known for the sensuous lyricism and rhythmic vitality of his style. His works include *The Alexandria Quartet*, four novels—*Justine* (1957), *Balthazar* (1958), *Mountolive* (1958) and *Cleo* (1960)— exploring one story from different viewpoints; and several volumes of poetry and travel literature.

DÜRRENMATT, Friedrich (1921–   ), Swiss playwright and novelist. His often bizarre tragicomedies employ biting satire, and include *The Visit* (1956) and *The Physicists* (1962). He has also written crime novels.

DURYEA, Charles Edgar (1861–1938), US inventor and manufacturer who, with **J. Frank** (1870–1967), built what was probably the first commercially viable gasoline-powered automobile in the US (1893). They manufactured cars independently from 1898 to 1914.

DUSE, Eleonora (1859–1924), Italian dramatic actress, rivaling Sarah Bernhardt as the greatest actress of her period, notably in plays by Ibsen and by Duse's lover Gabriele D'Annunzio.

DUST BOWL, area of some 400,000km² in the S Great Plains region of the US which, during the 1930s, the Depression years, suffered violent dust storms owing to accelerated SOIL EROSION. Grassland was plowed up in the 1920s and 1930s to plant wheat; a severe drought bared the fields, and high winds blew the topsoil into huge dunes. Despite rehabilitation programs, farmers plowed up grassland again in the 1940s and 1950s, and a repetition of the tragedy was averted only by the action of Congress.

DUTCH, West Germanic language spoken in the Netherlands and (as FLEMISH) in N Belgium, also in Surinam and the Dutch Antilles. AFRIKAANS, spoken in South Africa, is derived from Dutch. Dutch evolved largely from the speech of the Franks, who settled in the Low Countries in the 4th–5th centuries. About 20 million people speak Dutch.

DUTCH EAST INDIES, former Dutch overseas territory, now INDONESIA. Colonized by the Dutch East India Company in the 17th century, the area came under Dutch government in 1798, was occupied by Japan in WWII and gained independence in 1949 after a nationalist struggle.

DUTCH GUIANA. See SURINAME.

DUTCH REFORMED CHURCH, largest and oldest Protestant church of the Netherlands and dominant church in South Africa. It was the first reformed church from mainland Europe to be established in North America.

DUTCH WARS, three 17th-century wars fought by the Dutch and English for maritime supremacy. The *First Dutch War* (1652–54) began after England's First Navigation Act (1651) excluded the Dutch from trade with English possessions. The English temporarily lost control of the English channel and failed to sustain a blockade. War ended with the Treaty of Westminster (1654). British attacks on Dutch colonies provoked the *Second Dutch War* (1665–67), in which the French aided the Dutch. Impoverished by plague and the Great Fire of London, England signed the Treaty of Breda (1667). This gave the Dutch Surinam and relaxed the navigation laws, but gave England New Netherland (New York). In the *Third Dutch War* (1672–74), the English and French attacked the Dutch but failed to subdue the Dutch fleet. France invaded the Dutch Republic until halted by deliberate flooding and a powerful alliance including Austria, Spain and Brandenburg. Disheartened by lack of success, England made peace with the Dutch in 1674. But Franco–Dutch fighting continued until 1678.

DUTCH WEST INDIA COMPANY, association of Dutch merchants incorporated in 1621 to monopolize Dutch trade with Africa and the Americas and to found colonies there. It colonized Caribbean islands (1634–48) and Surinam (1667). Harassed by Spain, Portugal and England, it lost other New World possessions and was dissolved in 1674. Reorganized in 1675, it was absorbed by the Dutch state in 1791 and finally dissolved in 1794.

DUTCH WEST INDIES. See NETHERLANDS ANTILLES.

DUVALIER, François "Papa Doc" (1907–1971), autocratic president of Haiti 1957–71. A physician turned politician, he was elected to power as a reformer but ruled as dictator, helped by a political police force, the Tonton Macoutes. He made himself president for life in 1964.

DUVEEN OF MILLBANK, Joseph Duveen 1st Baron (1869–1939), English art dealer who advised wealthy American collectors such as MELLON and John D. ROCKEFELLER. He largely created and satisfied the American taste for fine old masters, now represented in many American art museums.

DVORAK, Antonín (1841–1904), major Czech composer, who developed the national style founded by SMETANA. A viola player, his richly lyrical music began to win him acclaim in the 1870s. He spent 1892–95 in the US, as director of the National Conservatory of Music, New York City. His works include 9 symphonies, 10 operas, concertos, the Slavonic dances and other orchestral compositions, choral works and chamber music.

DWARFISM, or small stature. This may be a family characteristic or associated with congenital disease of CARTILAGE or BONE development (e.g., achondroplasia). Failure of growth-HORMONE (see PITUITARY GLAND) or THYROID-hormone production during growth, and excess STEROID, ANDROGEN or ESTROGEN can cause small stature by altering control of bone development. The condition can also arise from spine or limb deformity (e.g., SCOLIOSIS), MALNUTRITION, RICKETS, chronic infection or visceral disease.

DWARF TREE. See BONSAI.

DWIGGINS, William Addison (1880–1956), US designer and calligrapher whose new typefaces and layouts revolutionized book and magazine design. He created Alfred A. Knopf's house style and wrote the influential *Layout in Advertising* (1928) and *MSS by WAD* (1949).

DWIGHT, Theodore (1764–1846), American author, one of the HARTFORD WITS. He served in Congress 1806–07 and was secretary of the HARTFORD CONVENTION (1814–15). His journal on the convention was published in 1833.

DYAK. See DAYAK.

DYER, Mary (d. 1660), Quaker martyr in Massachusetts. A supporter of Anne HUTCHINSON, she visited imprisoned Quakers and preached in Boston, despite orders banishing her from the settlement. She was reprieved in 1659, but was rearrested the following year and sentenced to be hanged.

DYER-BENNET, Richard (1913–   ), British singer, guitarist, lutenist and composer. His repertoire of Elizabethan, classic, and folk songs, which he presented annually in New York (from 1944), helped reawaken public interest in the art of minstrelsy.

DYES AND DYEING. Dyes are colored substances which impart their color to textiles to which they are applied and for which they have a chemical affinity. They differ from PIGMENTS in being used in solution in an aqueous medium. Dyeing was practiced in the FERTILE CRESCENT and China by 3000 BC, using natural dyes obtained from plants and shellfish. These were virtually superseded by synthetic dyes—more varied in color and applicability—after the accidental synthesis of mauve by PERKIN (1856). The raw materials are AROMATIC hydrocarbons obtained from COAL TAR and PETROLEUM. These are modified by introducing chemical groups called chromophores which cause absorption of visible LIGHT (see also COLOR). Other groups, auxochromes, such as amino or hydroxyl, are necessary for substantivity—i.e., affinity for the material to be dyed. This fixing to the fabric fibers is by HYDROGEN BONDING, ADSORPTION, ionic bonding or covalent bonding in the case of "reactive dyes" (see BOND, CHEMICAL). If there is no natural affinity, the dye may be fixed by using a MORDANT before or with dyeing. Vat dyes are made soluble by reduction in the presence of alkali, and after dyeing the original color is re-formed by acidification and oxidation; INDIGO and ANTHRAQUINONE dyes are examples. Dyes are also used as biological stains (see MICROSCOPE), INDICATORS and in PHOTOGRAPHY.

DYLAN, Bob (born Robert Zimmerman; 1941–   ) US folk-singer and composer. His distinctive blues style had a strong influence on popular music in the 1960s. He later turned to country and ballad music.

DYNAMITE, high EXPLOSIVE invented by Alfred NOBEL, consisting of NITROGLYCERIN absorbed in an inert material such as KIESELGUHR or wood pulp. Unlike nitroglycerin itself, it can be handled safely, not exploding without a DETONATOR. In modern dynamite SODIUM nitrate replaces about half the nitroglycerin. Gelatin dynamite, or **gelignite,** contains also some NITROCELLULOSE.

DYSENTERY, a BACTERIAL or PARASITIC DISEASE causing abdominal pain, DIARRHEA and FEVER. In children, **bacillary dysentery** due to *Shigella* species is a common endemic or EPIDEMIC disease, and is associated with poor hygiene. It is a short-lived illness but may cause dehydration in severe cases. The organism may be carried in feces in the absence of symptoms. ANTIBIOTICS may be used to shorten the attack and reduce carrier rates. **Amebic dysentery** is a chronic disease, usually seen in warm climates, with episodes of diarrhea and CONSTIPATION, accompanied by MUCUS and occasionally BLOOD; constitutional symptoms occur and the disease may resemble noninfective COLITIS. Treatment with emetine, while effective, is accompanied by a high risk of toxicity; metronidazole is a less toxic antiamebic agent introduced recently.

DYSLEXIA, difficulty with reading, often a developmental problem possibly associated with suppressed left-HANDEDNESS, and spatial difficulty; it requires special training. It may be acquired by BIRTH injury, failure of learning, visual disorders or as part of APHASIA.

DYSPEPSIA, or indigestion, a vague term usually describing abnormal visceral sensation in upper ABDOMEN or lower CHEST, often of a burning quality. Relationship to meals and posture is important in defining its origin; relief by ANTACIDS or milk is usual. HEARTBURN from esophagitis and pain of peptic (gastric or duodenal) ULCERS are usual causes.

DYSPHASIA. See APHASIA; SPEECH AND SPEECH DISORDERS.

DZERZHINSKI, Felix Edmundovich (1877–1926), Polish-born revolutionary, one of the founders of the USSR. From 1917 until his death he organized and headed the CHEKA, the Soviet secret police, known after 1922 as the OGPU. He also became commissar of transport 1921 and was head of the supreme economic council 1924.

E, 5th letter of the English alphabet, derived from an ancient Semitic letter and the Greek *epsilon*. It is a vowel and can be long as in *feet*, or short as in *met*, or it can lengthen the preceding vowel as in *bite*. In music, *E* is the note *mi* in the scale of *C*.

e, the base of the natural LOGARITHMS, known also as EULER's number and always symbolized by the letter *e*. It is defined as the REAL NUMBER such that

$$\int e^{x^{-1}} dx = 1, \text{ and is an}$$

IRRATIONAL NUMBER whose value to six decimal places is 2.718284. (See also EXPONENT.)

EAGLES, powerful BIRDS OF PREY found in many highland regions such as North America, Scotland and Asia. Their nests (eyries) are found between 275 and 600m (900–2,000ft). The eagles comprise four groups: Sea and Fish eagles; Snake eagles; Crested eagles; and "true" or Aquiline eagles. All have characteristic soaring flights made possible by broad wings with spans of up to 2m (6.5ft). Being carnivores, eagles have hooked beaks and clawed feet. They are diurnal. Eagles have frequently figured in mythology, especially of North American Indians.

EAKINS, Thomas (1844–1916), important US realist painter, considered a major American portraitist. Among his most famous paintings is *The Gross Clinic* (1875). His insistence on paintings from nature—and especially from the nude—was controversial in his time, but his work became a powerful influence on younger US artists. Eakins was also an early action photographer.

EAMES, Charles (1907–1978), US designer, who influenced contemporary furniture design. He created plywood and fiberglass form-fitting chairs, and the upholstered "Eames chair."

EAR, a special sense organ in higher animals, concerned with hearing and balance. It may be divided into the outer ear, extending from the tympanic membrane or ear drum to the pinna, the inner ear embedded in the SKULL bones, consisting of cochlea and labyrinth, and between them the middle ear, containing small bones or ossicles. The cartilaginous pinna varies greatly in shape and mobility in different animals; a canal lined by skin leads from it and ends with the thin tympanic membrane stretched across it. The middle ear is an air-filled space which communicates with the PHARYNX via the Eustachian tube. This allows the middle ear to be at the same pressure as the outer and also secretions to drain away. The middle ear is also connected with the MASTOID antrum. Three ossicles (malleus, incus, stapes) form a bony chain articulating between the ear drum and part of the cochlea; tiny muscles are attached to the drum and ossicles and can affect the intensity of SOUND transmission. The inner ear contains both the cochlea, a spiral structure containing fluid and specialized membranes on which hearing receptors are situated, and the labyrinth which consists of three semicircular canals, the utricle and the saccule, all of which contain fluid and receptor cells. Nerve fibers pass from the cochlea and labyrinth to form the eighth cranial nerve.

In hearing, sound waves travel into the outer ear, funneled by the pinna, and cause vibration of the ear drum. The drum and ossicular chain, which transmits vibration to the cochlea, effect some amplification. The vibration set up in the cochlear fluid is differentially distributed along the central membrane according to pitch. By a complex mechanism, this membrane movement causes certain groups of receptor cells to be preferentially stimulated, giving rise to auditory nerve impulses, which are conducted via several coding sites to higher centers for perception. These centers can in turn affect the sensitivity of receptors by means of centrifugal fibers. In balance, rotation of the head in any of three perpendicular planes causes stimulation of specialized cells in the semicircular canals as fluid moves past them. The utricle and saccule contain small stones which respond to gravitational changes and affect receptor cells in their walls. All these balance receptor cells cause impulses in the vestibular nerve, and this connects to higher centers.

Disease of the ear usually causes DEAFNESS or ringing in the ears. Peripheral disorders of balance include VERTIGO and ATAXIA, which may be accompanied by NAUSEA or VOMITING. MÉNIÈRE'S DISEASE is an episodic disease affecting both systems.

EARHART, Amelia (1898–1937), US pioneer aviator. She was the first transatlantic woman passenger (1928), first solo transatlantic woman pilot (1932) and made the first ever solo flight from Hawaii to the US mainland (1935). She disappeared over the Pacific Ocean on an attempted around-the-world flight in 1937.

EARLE, Ralph (1751–1801), American portrait painter. His distinctively rugged portraits were influenced by John Singleton COPLEY. He is noted for his Revolutionary War battle scenes.

EARP, Wyatt Berry Stapp (1848–1929), US frontier lawman and folk hero. He was deputy sheriff and US marshal in several Kan. and Ariz. "cow towns." He is most famous for the gunfight at O.K. Corral in Tombstone, Ariz. (1881).

EARTH, the largest of the inner planets of the solar system, the third planet from the sun and, so far as is known, the sole home of life in the solar system. To an astronomer on Mars, several things would be striking about our planet. Most of all, he would notice the relative size of our MOON: there are larger moons in the SOLAR SYSTEM, but none so large compared with its planet—indeed, some astronomers regard the earth as one component of a "double planet," the other being the moon. Our Martian astronomer would also notice that the earth shows phases, just as the moon and Venus do when viewed from earth. And, if he were a radio astronomer, he would detect a barrage of radio "noise" from our planet—clear evidence of the presence of intelligent life.

The earth is rather larger than VENUS. It is

slightly oblate (flattened at the poles), the equatorial diameter being about 12,756.4km, the polar diameter about 12,713.6km. It rotates on its axis in 23h 56min 4.09s (one **sidereal day**), though this is increasing by roughly 0.00001s annually due to tidal effects (see TIDES); and revolves about the sun in 365d 6h 9min 9.5s (one **sidereal year**: see SIDEREAL TIME). Two other types of year are defined: the **tropical year**, the interval between alternate EQUINOXES (365d 5h 48min 46s); and the **anomalistic year**, the interval between moments of perihelion (see ORBIT), 365d 6h 13min 53s. The earth's equator is angled about 23.5° to the ECLIPTIC, the plane of its orbit. The direction of the earth's axis is slowly changing owing to PRECESSION. The planet has a mass of about 5.98×10^{21} tons, a volume of about 1.08×10^{21} m³, and a mean DENSITY of about 5.52 tons/m³.

Like other planetary bodies, the earth has a magnetic field (see MAGNETISM). The magnetic poles do not coincide with the axial poles (see NORTH POLE; SOUTH POLE), and moreover they "wander." At or near the earth's surface, **magnetic declination** (or **variation**) is the angle between true N and compass N (lines joining points of equal variation are **isogonic lines**); and **magnetic dip** (or **inclination**) the vertical angle between the MAGNETIC FIELD and the horizontal at a particular point.

Isomagnetic lines can be drawn between points of equal intensity of the field. There is also evidence to suggest that the direction of the field reverses from time to time. These changes are of primary interest to the paleomagnetist (see PALEOMAGNETISM). The earth is surrounded by radiation belts, probably the result of charged particles from the sun being trapped by the earth's magnetic field (see VAN ALLEN RADIATION BELTS; AURORA).

There are three main zones of the earth: the ATMOSPHERE; the HYDROSPHERE (the world's waters); and the LITHOSPHERE, the solid body of the world. The atmosphere shields us from much of the harmful radiation of the SUN, and protects us from excesses of heat and cold. Water covers much of the earth's surface (over 70%) in both liquid and solid (ice) forms (see GLACIER; OCEANS). There are permanent polar icecaps. The earth's solid body can be divided into three regions: The **core** (diameter about 7,000km), at a temperature of about 3,000K, is at least partly liquid, though the central region (the inner core) is probably solid. Probably mainly of NICKEL and IRON, the core's density ranges between about 9.5 and perhaps over 15

tons/m³. The **mantle** (outer diameter about 12,686km), probably mainly of OLIVINE, has a density around 5.7 tons/m³ toward the core, 3.3 tons/m³ toward the **crust**, the outermost layer of the earth and the one to which all human activity is confined. The crust is some 35km thick (much less beneath the oceans) and composed of three classes of ROCKS: IGNEOUS ROCKS, SEDIMENTARY ROCKS and METAMORPHIC ROCKS. FOSSILS in the strata of sedimentary rocks give us a geological time scale (see GEOLOGY). The earth formed about 4.5 billion years ago; life appeared probably about 3.2 billion years ago, and man around 4 million years ago. Man has thus been present for about 0.1% of the earth's history, and civilization for less than 0.0001%.

It is now known that the earth's configuration of continents and oceans has changed radically through geological time—as it were, the map has changed. Originally, this was attributed to continents drifting, and the process was called CONTINENTAL DRIFT (see also Alfred WEGENER). However, although this term is still used descriptively, the changes are now realized to be a manifestation of the theory of PLATE TECTONICS, and so a result of the processes responsible also for EARTHQUAKES, MOUNTAIN building and many other phenomena.

EARTHQUAKE, a fracture or implosion beneath the surface of the earth, and the shock waves that travel away from the point where the fracture has occurred. The immediate area where the fracture takes place is the **focus** or **hypocenter**, the point immediately above it on the earth's surface is the **epicenter**, and the shock waves emanating from the fracture are called seismic waves.

Earthquakes occur to relieve a stress that has built up within the crust or mantle of the EARTH; fracture results when the stress exceeds the strength of the rock. The reasons for the stress build-up are to be found in the theory of PLATE TECTONICS. If a map is drawn of the world's earthquake activity, it can be immediately seen that earthquakes are confined to discrete belts. These belts signify the borders of contiguous plates; shallow earthquakes being generally associated with MID-OCEAN RIDGES where creation of new material occurs, deep ones with regions where one plate is being forced under another (see BENIOFF ZONE).

Seismic waves are of two main types. Body waves travel from the hypocenter, and again are of two types: P (compressional) waves, where the motion of particles of the earth is in the direction of propagation of the wave; and S (shear) waves, where the particle motion is at right angles to this direction. Surface waves travel from the epicenter, and are largely confined to the earth's surface; Love waves are at right angles to the direction of propagation; Rayleigh waves having a more complicated, backward elliptical movement in the direction of propagation.

The experienced intensity of an earthquake depends mainly on the distance from the source. Local intensities are gauged in terms of the Mercalli Intensity Scale, which runs from I (detectable only by SEISMOGRAPH) through to XII ("Catastrophic"). Comparison of intensities in different areas enables the source of an earthquake to be located. The actual magnitude of the event is gauged according to the RICHTER SCALE.

The study of seismic phenomena is known as **seismology**. (See also FAULT; TSUNAMI.)

EASTER, chief festival of the Christian CHURCH YEAR, celebrating the RESURRECTION of Jesus Christ, and subsuming the Jewish PASSOVER. Easter has been observed by the Western Church since the Council of NICAEA, on the Sunday after the first full moon following the vernal EQUINOX. It traditionally included a night vigil and the BAPTISM of catechumens. Easter is celebrated at a later date by the Eastern churches.

EASTER ISLAND, easternmost island of Polynesia in the S Pacific Ocean about 2,000mi W of Chile, which annexed the island in 1888. This small, grassy, volcanic island features hundreds of colossal stone statues up to 40ft high, carved and raised on burial platforms by a pre-Columbian culture, which have been the subject of much speculation by Thor Heyerdahl and others. Easter Island was discovered on Easter Sunday, 1722, by the Dutch admiral Jakob Roggeveen.

EASTER LILY, *Lilium longiflorum*, a tall LILY with fragrant white trumpet-shaped flowers. Hothouse plants bloom before Easter. Family: Liliaceae.

EASTERN CHURCH, one of the two great branches of the Christian Church. From the apostolic age itself a natural distinction arose between the Greek-speaking church of the eastern Roman empire and the Latin-speaking church of the west. The Eastern Church developed its own liturgical traditions, patriarchal government, outlook and ethos, and resisted the increasing claims of the papacy. It became a family of ORTHODOX CHURCHES, finally breaking with

Rome in the Great Schism of 1054. The non-orthodox Monophysite Churches separated in the 5th and 6th centuries but share the common eastern tradition. (See also CHRISTIANITY.)

EASTERN QUESTION, the international political problems raised in the 19th century by the decline of the OTTOMAN EMPIRE. The rival ambitions of Russia, Austria-Hungary, Britain and France in the E Mediterranean led to the CRIMEAN WAR (1854–56) and BALKAN WARS (1912–13) and were partly responsible for the outbreak of WWI.

EASTERN STAR, Order of (General Grand Chapter), US fraternal organization dedicated to service to the needy, community improvement and social enjoyment, founded 1876. The order consists of Freemasons and their immediate female relatives, and totals 3 million members.

EASTER RISING, Irish rebellion against British rule, begun on Easter Monday, 1916. Although itself abortive, it proved a turning point in the Irish struggle for Home Rule. Sir Roger CASEMENT tried in vain to obtain arms from Germany, but the rising went ahead at the insistence of CONNOLLY and PEARSE and some 1,500 volunteers seized public buildings, notably the Post Office, in Dublin. The British suppressed the rebellion after fierce street fighting and executed its leaders, an act which further fueled the nationalist cause.

EAST INDIA COMPANY, name of several private trading companies chartered by 17th-century European governments to develop trade in the E Hemisphere, after the discovery of a sea route to India. They competed for commercial supremacy and eventually aided European colonial expansion. **The Dutch East India Company** (1602–1798) dominated trade with the East Indies but failed to survive the French invasion of Holland in 1795. **The British East India Company** (1600–1858) monopolized trade with India and, in the 18th century, gained administrative control of most of India. Its power was curbed by William PITT in 1784 and successive British governments took complete control of the Company and made India an imperial possession.

EAST INDIES, the former Dutch East Indies, now Indonesia. Modern usage confines the term to the Malay Archipelago. It is the largest island group in the world.

EASTMAN, George (1854–1932), US inventor and manufacturer who invented the Kodak CAMERA, first marketed in 1888. Earlier he perfected processes for manufacturing dry photographic plates (1880) and flexible, transparent film (1884). He took his own life in 1932. (See also PHOTOGRAPHY.)

EASTMAN, Max (1883–1969), US author and editor. He edited two influential socialist magazines and was a Communist Party member until 1923. He became a critic of Stalinism in such works as *Marxism, Is It Science?* (1940) and *Stalin's Russia* (1940). He was also a literary critic (*Enjoyment of Poetry*, 1913) and poet (*Poems of Five Decades*, 1954).

EAST PRUSSIA, historic region of Europe, bounded, (between WWI and WWII), by the Baltic Sea, Poland, Lithuania and Danzig. It was a stronghold of the Teutonic Knights in the Middle Ages, and later belonged variously to Poland, Prussia and Germany. East Prussia was separated from the rest of Germany from 1918 to 1939 by the "Polish Corridor," and after WWII it was partitioned between the USSR and Poland.

EASTWOOD, Clint (1930–   ), US actor. The star of television's "Rawhide," he became an enormously popular film star in the Italian-made western *Fist Full of Dollars* (1964). His films include *Coogan's Bluff* (1969) and *Play Misty For Me* (1971), which he also directed.

EATON, Cyrus Stephen (1883–1979), Canadian-born US industrialist who was a founder of the Republic Steel Corporation 1930 and director of many large corporations. In his later years he advocated nuclear disarmament and improved US-Soviet relations, and was awarded the Lenin Peace Prize (1970) by the Soviet government.

EBAN, Abba Solomon (1915–   ), Israeli political leader and diplomat. Born in South Africa and educated in England, he became Israel's first UN delegate (1949–59) and ambassador to the US (1950–59). He was then minister of education 1960, deputy prime minister 1963–65 and foreign minister 1966–74.

EBBINGHAUS, Hermann (1850–1909), German psychologist who developed experimental techniques for the study of rote LEARNING and memory. In later life he devised means of intelligence testing and researched into color VISION.

EBERT, Friedrich (1871–1925), first president (1919–25) of the German WEIMAR REPUBLIC. A lifelong Social Democrat and moderate Marxist, he initiated many social reforms and helped to reconstruct Germany after WWI.

EBRO RIVER, second-largest river of Spain, 565mi long. It rises in the Cantabrian Mts and flows ESE through Santander, Navarre, Saragossa and Tarragona provinces to the Mediterranean Sea. The site of an imperial canal system begun in the 16th century, it is partly navigable, but is mainly important as a source of irrigation. The upper part of its basin, the Rioja Alta, is noted for the production of Rioja wine.

ECCLESIASTES, Old Testament "wisdom" book, pessimistic and skeptical in tone. It was traditionally attributed to King Solomon, but modern experts favor a much later author, possibly of the 3rd century BC.

ECCLESIASTICUS, Old Testament book included in the APOCRYPHA by Jews and Protestants. It was written c180 BC by Jesus son of Sirach, and is a collection of instructive observations, influenced by the Book of PROVERBS.

ECHEVERRIA, Luís (1922–   ), Mexican political leader. After holding several political and academic posts, he was president of Mexico 1970–76. Rapid population growth, especially in cities, inflation and unemployment burdened his administration.

ECHO, a wave signal reflected back to its point of origin from a distant object, or, in the case of RADIO signals, a signal coming to a receiver from the transmitter by an indirect route. Echoes of the first type can be used to detect and find the position of reflecting objects (echolocation). High-frequency SOUND echolocation is used both by boats for navigation and to detect prey and by man in marine SONAR. RADAR, too, is similar in principle, though this uses UHF radio and MICROWAVE radiation rather than sound energy. The range of a reflecting object can easily be estimated for ordinary sound echoes: since sound travels about 340m/s through the air at sea level, an object will be distant about 170m for each second that passes before an echo returns from it.

ECK, Johann (1486–1543), German scholar and theologian. Though advocating church reform, he was a bitter opponent of LUTHER and the REFORMATION. He influenced the 1520 papal bull against Luther, and presented the Roman Catholic case at the Diet of Augsburg (1530).

ECKENER, Hugo (1868–1954), German aeronautical engineer and pioneer airship pilot who commanded the *Graf Zeppelin* on its historic 12-day round-the-world flight (1929). He later piloted the *Hindenburg*.

ECKERMANN, Johann Peter (1792–1854), German writer and literary assistant of GOETHE, notable for his *Conversations* *with Goethe* (3 volumes, 1836–48).

ECKHART, Johann (c1260–1327), also called Meister Eckhart, German Dominican theologian, regarded as the founder of German mysticism. He was influenced by neoplatonism and by the works of Saint AUGUSTINE and Thomas AQUINAS.

ECLIPSE, the partial or total obscurement of one celestial body by another; also the passage of the moon through the earth's shadow. The components of a binary star (see DOUBLE STAR) may eclipse each other as seen from the earth, in which case the star is termed an eclipsing binary. The moon frequently eclipses stars or planets, and this is known as OCCULTATION.

A **lunar eclipse** occurs when the moon passes through the umbra of the earth's SHADOW. This happens usually not more than twice a year, since the moon's orbit around the earth is tilted with respect to the ECLIPTIC. The eclipsed moon is blood-red in color due to some of the sun's light being refracted by the earth's atmosphere into the umbra. A partial lunar eclipse occurs when only part of the umbra falls on the moon.

In a **solar eclipse**, the moon passes between the sun and the earth. A total eclipse occurs when the observer is within the umbra of the moon's shadow: the disk of the sun is covered by that of the moon, and the solar corona (see SUN) becomes clearly visible. Total eclipses are particularly important since only during them can astronomers study the solar corona and prominences. The maximum possible duration of a total eclipse is about 7½min. Should the observer be outside the umbra but within the penumbra, or should the earth pass through only the penumbra, a partial eclipse will occur.

An **annular eclipse** is seen when the moon is at its farthest from the earth, its disk being not large enough to totally obscure that of the sun. The moon's disk is seen surrounded by a brilliant ring of light.

ECOLOGY, the study of plants and animals in relation to their ENVIRONMENT. The whole earth can be considered as a large ecological unit: the term BIOSPHERE is used to describe the atmosphere, earth's surface, oceans and ocean floors within which living organisms exist. However, it is usual to divide the biosphere into a large number of ecological sub-units or **ecosystems**, within each of which the organisms making up the living community are in balance with the environment. Typical examples of ecosystems are a pond, a deciduous forest or a desert. The overall climate and topography within an area are major factors determining the type of ecosystem that

develops, but within any ecosystem minor variations give rise to smaller communities within which animals and plants occupy their own particular niches. Within any ecosystem each organism, however large or small, plays a vital role in maintaining the stability of the community.

The most important factor for any organism is its source of energy or food. Thus, within any ecosystem, complex patterns of feeding relationships or **food chains** are built up. Plants are the primary source of food and energy; they derive it through PHOTOSYNTHESIS, utilizing environmental factors such as light, water, carbon dioxide and minerals. Herbivores then obtain their food by eating plants. In their turn, herbivores are preyed upon by carnivores, who may also be the source of food for other carnivores. Animal and plant waste is decomposed by microorganisms (BACTERIA, FUNGI) within the habitat and this returns the raw materials to the environment. The number of links within a food chain are normally three or four, with five, six and seven less frequently. The main reason for the limited length of food chains is that the major part of the energy stored within a plant or animal is wasted at each stage in the chain. Thus if it were possible for a carnivore to occupy, say, position 20 within a food chain, the area of vegetation required to supply the energy needed for the complete chain would be the size of a continent.

The plants within an ecosystem, as well as the major environmental features, help create habitats suitable for other organisms. Thus, in a forest ecosystem, the humid, dimly illuminated environment covered by a thick canopy is suitable for mosses, lichens and ferns and their associated fauna. Within any ecosystem the raw materials nitrogen, carbon, oxygen and hydrogen (in water) are continually being recycled via a number of processes including the NITROGEN CYCLE, CARBON CYCLE and photosynthesis.

Most natural ecosystems are in a state of equilibrium or balance so that few changes occur in the natural flora and fauna. However, when changes occur in the environment, either major climatic changes or minor alterations in the inhabitants, an imbalance results and the ecosystem changes to adapt to the new situation. The sequence of change that leads to a new period of equilibrium is called a succession and may take any length of time from a few years, for the establishment of a new species, to several centuries, for the change from grassland to forest.

Over millions of years, nature has moved

toward the overall creation of stable ecosystems. Natural changes, such as adaptations to the slow change of climate, tend to be gradual. However, man often causes much more sudden changes—the introduction of a disease to a hitherto uninfected area, the cutting down of a forest or the polluting of a river. The effects of this type of change upon an ecosystem can be rapid and irreversible. Up to now these changes have not been too serious on a worldwide scale but there is an increasing awareness of what could happen if a worldwide disturbance in the biosphere occurred. The forms of life as they are known today depend entirely upon the sensitive balance within the environment and any change with worldwide effects could have devastating consequences for man and life in general.

ECONOMIC ADVISERS, Council of. See COUNCIL OF ECONOMIC ADVISERS.

ECONOMICS is basically concerned with the most efficient use of scarce resources (factors of production such as land, labor, capital) in producing various types of goods and services to satisfy numerous different and competing demands. The American economist Paul SAMUELSON has called economics the study of how, what and for whom to produce. The difficulty of defining economics precisely stems from the various concerns that have characterized the evolution of economic thought. Analytical economics began with XENOPHON who coined the word *oikonomikos*, a combination of two Greek words, one meaning home or household, and the other to manage or rule. While theologians in the Middle Ages wrote about economic matters, serious and organized economic studies date only from the 17th century. Since then there have been seven major schools of economic thought: Mercantilists (17th and 18th centuries); PHYSIOCRATS (mid-18th century); Classicists (18th and 19th centuries); Marxists (19th and 20th centuries); Neoclassicists (19th and 20th centuries); Keynesians, and Post-Keynesians (both of them 20th century).

Mercantilists were concerned with trade, especially foreign trade, and argued for a surplus of exports over imports. They also advocated development of local industries protected by tariffs from foreign competition as a means of reducing unemployment and minimizing the reliance on imports in times of national emergency. In contrast, the Physiocratic school is best known for the *Tableau économique*, a work by its founder François QUESNAY. In this school the economy is visualized in terms of circular flows of outputs and income among its members, thus displaying the general interdependence of industries in the economy. The Physiocrats were eventually eclipsed by the work of the three most eminent Classicists: Adam SMITH, who favored free trade and competition (LAISSEZ-FAIRE); Thomas MALTHUS and David RICARDO, whose treatises on rent and the labor theory of value have influenced all subsequent discussions on problems of distribution and value.

A separate school of thought, MARXISM, developed during this period. However, the work of its two founders, Karl MARX and Friedrich ENGELS, was preoccupied with describing and analyzing how the capitalist economy behaves. They used philosophical and sociological principles to postulate "inexorable laws of development," and concluded that capitalism was doomed and that socialism was inevitable.

The Neoclassicists, of which the most famous were William Stanley JEVONS in England, Karl Menger in Austria and Léon Walras in Switzerland, were concerned with diverse theoretical aspects of the problems of value and distribution, and for the first time applied mathematics to the study of economics in systematic fashion. In the 20th century, two new schools of thought came into being. The Keynesians applied basic principles of supply and demand to analyze problems of national income, unemployment and inflation. The Post-Keynesians concern themselves with issues of post-WWII economic development. Among these are growth economics (at what rate should the economy grow and what is the rate of investment needed?); economic planning (guidance and control of the economy to achieve certain objectives); and development economics (how best can developing countries industrialize?).

Under the influence of KEYNESIAN ECONOMICS, US government policies from the 1950s emphasized increasing demand by both manipulating tax rates and increasing the money supply. However, starting in the 1970s, inflation and a stagnating or decreasing gross national product brought these fiscal policies under question, strengthening the influence of non-Keynesian economists. The SUPPLY-SIDE ECONOMICS favored by President Reagan's administration advocates increasing the growth of input (capital, raw materials) by government policies that are intended to encourage investment, such as tax incentives to invest in new plants and machinery, increased depreciation write-offs and lowered tax rates on capital gains and high incomes. Monetarists (see MONETARISM) view inflation as today's prime economic problem and urge the FEDERAL RESERVE SYSTEM to keep a tight rein on the money supply, which by increasing lifts the rate of inflation.

Official name: Republic of Ecuador
Capital: Quito
Area: 109,484sq mi
Population: 8,078,000
Languages: Spanish
Religions: Roman Catholic
Monetary unit(s): 1 Sucre = 100 centavos

ECUADOR, republic in NW South America, lying S of Colombia and N and W of Peru, on the Pacific coast. Its territory includes the GALAPAGOS ISLANDS in the Pacific.

Land. Ecuador is divided by two Andes ranges running N to S, between which lie about 10 plateaus around 8,000ft high. This is the most densely populated region of the country, and the capital, Quito, is situated in its N part. Between the Andes and the Pacific lie the coastal lowlands, also well populated, while to the E of the Andes there are almost uninhabited equatorial forests. The central Andean area has a mild climate all the year around, but the lowlands are hot and wet.

People. Of the population, roughly 10% are white, 10% Negro, 40% Indian and 40% mestizo—people of mixed Indian and white ancestry. The official language is Spanish but Quechua is widely spoken. Most Ecuadorians live near subsistence level either by working their own small landholdings or more commonly as laborers on large estates and plantations. The educational system is poor—the illiteracy rate being about 25%.

Economy. Although only 5% of the land is cultivated, agriculture was the basis of Ecuador's economy until 1972, when exploitation of petroleum began. Ecuador is now a leading producer of oil in Latin America (after Venezuela). Oil revenues contributed to a rapid economic growth in the 1970s but the country remains underdeveloped. Exports also include bananas, coffee, cocoa, and fish products. Many foodstuffs, transportation equipment, chemicals and consumer goods must be imported. Manufacturing (textiles, food processing, cement and pharmaceuticals) grew substantially in the 1970s.

History. Following the conquest of the Incas by PIZARRO in 1533, Ecuador became part of the Spanish Empire. It has been an independent republic since 1830, but has always suffered from political instability, marked by conflict between the landed bourgeoisie of the Andean region, the mercantile interests centered in the leading port of Guayaquil and, more recently, the urban working classes. Military coups have been common—the most recent successful one in January 1976. A civilian government was installed in 1979.

ECUMENICAL MOVEMENT, modern movement among the Christian churches to encourage greater cooperation and eventual unity. Various organizations such as the International Missionary Council, and the Life and Work and the Faith and Order conferences (after WWI) studied the churches' doctrinal differences. But substantial progress was not made until 1948, when representatives of 147 world churches agreed to form the WORLD COUNCIL OF CHURCHES. Most Protestant and Orthodox churches have since joined the council, and the Roman Catholic Church, though not a member, participates in some joint studies.

ECZEMA, form of DERMATITIS, usually with redness and scaling. It is often familial, being worst in childhood, and is associated with HAY FEVER and ASTHMA.

EDDA, name of two works of Old Icelandic literature known as the *Prose (Younger) Edda* and the *Poetic (Elder) Edda.* The *Prose Edda* was written c1200 by SNORRI STURLUSON for aspiring court poets as a guide to the subject matter and techniques of SKALDIC POETRY. The *Poetic Edda*, compiled later in the 13th century, contains 34 mainly alliterative poems written between c800 and 1200. It represents the finest extant body of ICELANDIC literature.

EDDINGTON, Sir Arthur Stanley (1882–1944), English astronomer and astrophysicist who pioneered the theoretical study of the interior of STARS and who, through his *Mathematical Theory of Relativity* (1923), did much to introduce the English-speaking world to the theories of EINSTEIN.

EDDY, Mary Baker (1821–1910), US founder of CHRISTIAN SCIENCE. After a period of study under Phineas QUIMBY she began to formulate her own ideas on spiritual healing and published these in

Science and Health (1875). She founded the *Christian Science Monitor* newspaper in 1908.

EDEMA, the accumulation of excessive watery fluid outside the cells of the body, causing swelling of a part. Some edema is seen locally in INFLAMMATION. The commonest type is gravitational edema (**dropsy**), where fluid swelling is in the most dependent parts, typically the feet. HEART or LIVER failure, MALNUTRITION and nephrotic syndrome of the KIDNEY are common causes, while disease of VEINS or LYMPH vessels in the legs also leads to edema. Serious edema may form in the LUNGS in heart failure and in the BRAIN in some disorders of METABOLISM, trauma, TUMORS and infections. DIURETICS may be needed in treatment.

EDEN, Garden of, in biblical tradition, the garden paradise created by God for ADAM and EVE. In the Old Testament book of Genesis it is described as being watered by four streams, including the Tigris and the Euphrates, which suggests that it was set somewhere in ancient Mesopotamia.

EDEN, Robert Anthony, Earl of Avon (1897–1977), British diplomat and prime minister (1955–57), famous for his antiappeasement stand in the 1930s and for his part in the SUEZ CANAL crisis of 1956. Eden became foreign secretary in 1935 but resigned in 1938 in protest against Chamberlain's negotiations with Hitler and Mussolini. He served again at the foreign office 1940–45 and 1951–55. As prime minister he promoted an ill-advised invasion of Egypt (1956) to restore Anglo-French control of the Suez Canal after the Egyptians had nationalized it. He resigned the next year because of ill health.

EDERLE, Gertrude Caroline (1906–   ), US swimmer, the first woman to swim the English Channel. She broke all previous records, crossing the 35mi from France to England on Aug. 6, 1926, in 14hr 31min.

EDGEWORTH, Maria (1767–1849), Anglo-Irish novelist. Her gifts for social observation and colorful, realistic portrayal of Irish domestic life and young people influenced many later novelists including Sir Walter SCOTT. Among her works are *Tales of Fashionable Life* (1809–12).

EDINBURGH, capital of Scotland, the seat of Midlothian Co., and the second largest Scottish city, located on the S shore of the Firth of Forth. The Old Town, dominated by Edinburgh Castle, dates from the 11th century, but has remains of fortifications from c617. The city became Scotland's capital in 1437. It has always been Scotland's cultural center. HOLYROOD HOUSE is situated here; Edinburgh U. was founded in 1583. The city has many public and private buildings which are beautiful examples of Neoclassical architecture. Since 1947 Edinburgh has been world-famous for its annual summer arts festival. Today the city is a thriving commercial center for banking, insurance and finance; its industries include brewing, distilling, engineering, printing and publishing. Pop 453,000.

EDISON, Thomas Alva (1847–1931), US inventor, probably the greatest of all time with over 1,000 patents issued to his name. His first successful invention, an improved stock-ticker (1869), earned him the capital to set up as a manufacturer of telegraphic apparatus. He then devised the diplex method of TELEGRAPHY which allowed one wire to carry four messages at once. Moving to a new "invention factory" (the first large-scale industrial-research laboratory) at Menlo Park, N.J., in 1876, he devised the carbon transmitter and a new receiver which made A. G. BELL's TELEPHONE commercially practical. His tin-foil PHONOGRAPH followed in 1877 and in the next year he started to work toward devising a practical incandescent lightbulb. By 1879 he had produced the carbon-filament bulb and electric LIGHTING became a reality, though it was not until 1882 that his first public generating station was supplying power to 85 customers in New York.

Moving his laboratories to West Orange, N.J., in 1887 he set about devising a motion-picture system (ready by 1889) though he failed to exploit its entertainment potential. In all his career he made only one important scientific discovery, the **Edison effect**—the ability of ELECTRICITY to flow from a hot filament in a vacuum lamp to another enclosed wire but not the reverse (1883)—and, because he saw no use for it, he failed to pursue the matter. His success was probably more due to perseverance than any special insight; as he himself said: "Genius is one percent inspiration and ninety-nine percent perspiration."

EDMONTON, capital of Alberta, Canada,

on the N Saskatchewan R. The city developed from a trading post founded in 1795 by the HUDSON'S BAY COMPANY and prospered after the railroad arrived in 1891. Today it is a transportation and agricultural marketing center; its main industries include oil refining and the production of petrochemicals and plastics. The U. of Alberta is located at Edmonton. Pop 438,215.

EDUCATION, US DEPARTMENT OF, established as a cabinet-level department Sept. 27, 1979, as part of President Jimmy Carter's plan to reorganize the federal government. With an initial budget of $14.1 billion and some 17,400 employees, the new department was split out of the Department of Health, Education, and Welfare, whose name was changed as a result to the Department of HEALTH AND HUMAN SERVICES. Within a year of its creation, however, President Ronald Reagan promised while campaigning for the presidency to abolish the new department. After taking office in 1981, he began to phase it out.

EDWARD, eight kings of England. (See also EDWARD THE CONFESSOR.) **Edward I** (1239–1307), reigned 1272–1307. He subjugated Wales and, inconclusively, Scotland, centralized the national administration and reduced baronial and clerical power. He summoned the Model Parliament (1295). **Edward II** (Edward of Caernarvon, 1284–1327), first heir apparent to be created Prince of Wales (1301), reigned 1307–27. He spent his reign trying to resist the barons. His poorly directed Scottish campaigns were highlighted by his defeat at Bannockburn (1314) by Robert Bruce. In 1326 he was unseated in a revolt led by his wife, Queen Isabella, and her paramour Roger de Mortimer. Edward was imprisoned, and forced to abdicate in favor of his son, and was probably murdered. **Edward III** (1312–1377), reigned 1327–77. Edward's claim to part of Guienne in France was one of the causes of the HUNDRED YEARS WAR. Despite decisive victories at Crécy (1346) and Poitiers (1356), he had lost most French territory by the end of his reign. In 1348–49, the BLACK DEATH decimated the population, resulting in major economic and social upheavals. **Edward IV** (1442–1483), reigned 1461–70 and 1471–83, during the Wars of the ROSES. A Yorkist, Edward deposed the Lancastrian Henry VI in 1461 and again in 1471 after the latter had been restored in 1470 by the Earl of WARWICK. Edward reestablished the power of the monarchy, improved administration and law enforcement and increased

England's trade and prosperity. **Edward V** (1470–1483?), reigned April–June, 1483, one of the "princes in the tower." He is believed to have been murdered at the order of his uncle and protector, Richard Duke of Gloucester, who became Richard III. Edward acceded to the throne as a minor and was immediately a victim of a ruthless power struggle between his uncles Gloucester and Earl Rivers. **Edward VI** (1537–1553), Henry VIII's only son, reigned 1547–53. A sickly child who was to die of consumption, he succeeded to the throne as a minor. Struggles over the succession, and between Protestants and Roman Catholics soon engulfed him. His reign saw the introduction, under Archbishop CRANMER, of the first *Book of Common Prayer* (1549). **Edward VII** (1841–1910), king of Great Britain and Ireland, 1901–10. A popular king, with a reputation as a *bon vivant*, he was particularly concerned with Britain's role in Europe and he helped to promote ENTENTES with France and Russia and to defuse the rivalry with Germany. **Edward VIII** (1894–1972), king of Great Britain and Ireland, Jan. 20–Dec. 11, 1936. Edward enjoyed great popularity as Prince of Wales and heir, but his association with the American divorcée, Mrs. Wallis Warfield Simpson, was treated as a scandal by the press and met stern opposition from government and Church. Edward acceded to the throne but to avoid a constitutional crisis abdicated, becoming Duke of Windsor. He married Mrs. Simpson in 1937 and thereafter lived mainly in France.

EDWARD, the Black Prince (1330–1376), Prince of Wales, son and heir of Edward III. His nickname may derive from the color of his armor; he is remembered mainly as a brilliant soldier. Given his first independent command in France in 1355, he won the battle of POITIERS in 1356, capturing the French king. Made Prince of Aquitaine in 1362, he alienated his subjects, who revolted. Mortally ill, he returned to England in 1371 and died there a year before his father.

EDWARDS, Blake (1922–   ), US film director and writer with a special flair for comedy. His films include *Breakfast at Tiffany's* (1961), *The Pink Panther* (1963), *10* (1979) and *S.O.B.* (1981).

EDWARDS, Jonathan (1703–58), American theologian, and philosopher of wide-ranging interests (see also ENLIGHTENMENT). A Calvinist in the Puritan tradition, he furthered the GREAT AWAKENING by his preaching, but was dismissed by his church in 1749 for his opposition to the HALF-WAY COVENANT. In 1757 he became president of the College of New Jersey (Princeton U.). Influenced by LOCKE, he wrote many works of philosophical theology, most notably *The Freedom of the Will* (1754) and *Religious Affections* (1746).

EDWARD THE CONFESSOR, Saint (c1003–1066), king of England from 1042. Brought up in Normandy, he was respected for his piety but was dominated throughout his reign by the powerful Earl GODWIN. Edward alienated the country by attempting to exile Godwin and introduce Normans into the government. He had named William of Normandy as his heir, but on his deathbed chose HAROLD, Godwin's son, precipitating the NORMAN CONQUEST.

EELS, long slender fish of the order Anguilliformes, without pelvic fins and with dorsal and ventral fins joining the tail fin. They include the CONGER, moray, snake, snipe and freshwater eel families. Some eels are covered in slime, and some have tiny scales on the skin. Moray eels live in warm water and are a danger to divers. American and European freshwater eels spawn in the Sargasso Sea. The leaf-like larvae cross the ocean, and enter rivers as young eels or elvers. When adult they swim back to the Sargasso Sea to spawn and die.

EFFICIENCY, in THERMODYNAMICS and the theory of MACHINES, the ratio of the useful WORK derived from a machine to the ENERGY put into it. The mechanical efficiency of a machine is always less than 100%, some energy being lost as HEAT in FRICTION. When the machine is a heat engine, its theoretical thermal efficiency can be found from the second law of thermodynamics but actual values are often rather lower. A typical gasoline engine may have a thermal efficiency of only 25%, a STEAM ENGINE 10%.

EGALITARIANISM, the doctrine that all men, in spite of differences of character or intelligence, are of equal dignity and worth, and therefore are entitled to equal rights and privileges in society. Interpretation of this doctrine has varied from the notion of equal access to opportunity to that of equal satisfaction of basic needs or to the leveling of social, political and economic inequalities. Thus it has been claimed as a guiding principle by such diverse political philosophies as democratic capitalism, socialism and communism.

EGLEVSKY, André (1917–1977), Russian-born US virtuoso ballet dancer and teacher. A member of the Ballet Russe de Monte Carlo 1939–42 and the New York City Ballet 1951–58, he appeared with many of the world's greatest companies.

EGO, the structured part of the individual's psychic makeup, developing, according to FREUD, from the ID through experience and closely related in concept to the CONSCIOUS. (See also SUPEREGO.)

Official name: Arab Republic of Egypt
Capital: Cairo
Area: 385,201sq mi
Population: 41,000,000
Languages: Arabic, French, English, Berber
Religions: Muslim, Coptic Christian
Monetary unit(s): 1 Egyptian pound = 100 piastres

EGYPT, Arab republic in NE Africa, bordered on the N by the Mediterranean, on the NE by Israel and the Red Sea, on the S by the Sudan and on the W by Libya. The Suez Canal and Gulf of Suez separate the Sinai Peninsula from the rest of Egypt.

Land is 96% desert, only some 13,800sq mi being habitable. The chief physical feature, the fertile Nile R valley, runs narrowly for about 930mi from the Sudanese frontier to the Mediterranean, developing, N of Cairo, into a large alluvial delta where most of the population lives. The Nile separates the Western Desert (260,000sq mi) from the Eastern Desert where the Red Sea Mts (Gebel Sha'ib, 7,175ft) parallel the coast. Egypt's highest peak, Gebel Katherina (8,652ft), is in the thinly populated Sinai Peninsula. The climate everywhere is arid and hot. Rainfall is low, being 3in annually or even less in most of the S.

People are mainly of Hamitic origin. There are small Greek and Armenian communities. The largest cities are Cairo, the capital, and Alexandria. Other important towns are Giza, Port Said, Suez and Ismailia. Arabic is the official language, but most educated Egyptians also speak French or English. Almost 50% of the adult population is literate. Most Egyptians are Sunni Muslims, but Coptic Christians are numerous.

Economy. Agriculture (especially cotton, wheat, corn, millet and rice) depends mostly on irrigation from the Nile and provides about 30% of the GNP. Mineral resources include iron ore, salt, natural gas and petroleum, and phosphates. The production of textiles and processed foods dominate the industrial sector, although there is some oil refining, and manufacturing of iron and steel, cement, and rubber products. Tourism is highly developed. The ARAB-ISRAELI WARS severely strained the economy. Following the reopening of the Suez Canal (1975), Egypt sought foreign investment to redevelop the canal area.

History (see also EGYPT, ANCIENT). After the Arab invasion (641 AD), Egypt had a variety of rulers including the Mamluks and Ottomans. Financially insolvent after the opening of the Suez Canal (1869), Egypt was a British protectorate 1914–36. From 1948 it played a major role in the Arab-Israeli conflict. In 1952 an army coup deposed King Farouk and the republic was proclaimed in 1953, Col. Gamal Abdel NASSAR becoming president in 1956. He used aid from the USSR to modernize the army and to a lesser extent industry, building the Aswan High Dam. Much Egyptian territory was lost in the Six-Day War. On Nasser's death (1970) Anwar al-SADAT became president; he regained much lost territory in the Yom Kippur War of 1973 and through a 1975 pact with Israel. He expelled the Russians from Egypt and sought closer links with the US. In 1978 Sadat and Israeli Prime Minister Menachim Begin signed a peace accord and Israel began a phased withdrawal from the Sinai in 1979. After Sadat's "separate peace" with Israel, Egypt was severely isolated by the other Arab countries, leaving the country heavily dependent on the US for both economic and military aid. In 1981 Sadat was assassinated by Muslim fundamentalists; he was succeeded by Vice-President Lt. Gen. Muhammed Hosni Mubarak.

EGYPT, Ancient, one of the cradles of world civilization. Egyptian civilization began more than 5,000 years ago in the fertile Nile Valley. Actual dates are much disputed, but Upper and Lower Egypt seem to have been united c3110 BC under MENES, a southern ruler; he made his capital at Memphis, on the boundary between the two. In this period HIEROGLYPHICS developed.

The Old Kingdom (3rd–6th dynasties). The 4th dynasty of pharaohs developed the PYRAMID as a royal tomb. Under them Egypt became a massive and powerful state. Official worship centered on the sun god RA. The 94-year reign of Pepi II seems to have led to civil war, foreign infiltration and the breakup of the kingdom. After a century of anarchy a stable kingdom was set up in Middle Egypt.

The Middle Kingdom (11th–13th dynasties). The restoration of stability was completed by the 11th dynasty. Under the 12th dynasty the country flourished. Irrigation became more systematic, resulting in increased food production and raised standards of living. Trade extended to Crete and cultural activity reached a new peak. But the 13th dynasty evidently lost power to foreign nomadic rulers, the HYKSOS, who were overthrown by the 17th and 18th dynasties.

The New Kingdom (18th–21st dynasties). The 18th dynasty completed the reconquest, and under THUTMOSE III Egypt ruled from the Sudan to the Euphrates. AKHENATON, rejecting traditional polytheism, introduced the sun worship of ATON and founded a new capital at Akhetaton (now TELL EL AMARNA). Traditional religion revived under his son-in-law TUTANKHAMEN. Incursions by Hittites, Libyans and other foreign tribes were now weakening Egypt, despite revivals under RAMSES II and III.

The Late Period (21st dynasty–641 AD). Egypt now came increasingly under foreign control, divided between Libyan rulers and CUSH. Invaded by Assyria (668 BC), Egypt was later annexed by Persia (525 BC), then taken by Alexander the Great (332 BC). Alexander founded Alexandria and made his general PTOLEMY governor of Egypt. He fathered the Ptolemaic dynasty of Macedonian rulers which persisted until the death of Cleopatra in 30 BC. Egypt then became a Roman province. In the 4th century AD the country became Christian and c395 it passed under the control of the Byzantine Empire. Byzantine misrule made Arab conquest easy in 641. Egypt became a province of the Arab empire, from which it takes its present character. (For recent history see EGYPT.)

EHRENBURG, Ilya Grigoryevich (1891–1967), Russian author. He emigrated to Paris in 1911 and did not return to Russia until 1924; he then lived in Europe as a journalist until 1941. He received the Stalin Prize for the panoramic novel *The Fall of Paris* (1942). The novel *The Thaw* (1954) was a major work of the post-Stalin liberalization.

EHRLICH, Paul (1854–1915), German bacteriologist and immunologist, the founder of CHEMOTHERAPY and an early pioneer of HEMATOLOGY. His discoveries include: a method of staining (1882), and hence identifying, the TUBERCULOSIS bacillus (see also Robert KOCH); the reasons for immunity in terms of the chemistry of

ANTIBODIES AND ANTIGENS, for which he was awarded (with METCHNIKOFF) the 1908 Nobel Prize for Physiology or Medicine; and the use of the drug SALVARSAN to cure syphilis (see VENEREAL DISEASES), the first DRUG to be used in treating the root cause of a disease (1911).

EICHMANN, Adolf (1906–1962), lieutenant–colonel in the GESTAPO, head of the Jewish Division from 1939. He was responsible for the deportation, maltreatment and murder of European Jews in WWII. He escaped to Argentina, but was abducted, tried and executed in Israel.

EIFFEL, Alexandre Gustave (1832–1923), French engineer best known for his design and construction of the Eiffel Tower, Paris (1887–89), from which he carried out experiments in AERODYNAMICS. In 1912 he founded the first aerodynamics laboratory.

EIGHT, The. See ASHCAN SCHOOL.

EINSTEIN, Albert (1879–1955), German-born Swiss-American theoretical physicist, the author of the theory of RELATIVITY. In 1905 Einstein published several papers of major significance. In one he applied PLANCK'S QUANTUM THEORY to the explanation of photoelectric emission. For this he was awarded the 1921 Nobel Prize for Physics. In a second he demonstrated that it was indeed molecular action which was responsible for BROWNIAN MOTION. In a third he published the special theory of relativity with its postulate of a constant VELOCITY for LIGHT (c) and its consequence, the equivalence of MASS (m) and ENERGY (E), summed up in the famous equation $E=mc^2$. In 1915 he went on to publish the general theory of relativity. This came with various testable predictions, all of which were spectacularly confirmed within a few years. Einstein was on a visit to the US when Hitler came to power in Germany and, being a Jew, decided not to return to his native land. The rest of his life was spent in a fruitless search for a "unified field theory" which could combine ELECTROMAGNETISM with GRAVITATION theory. After 1945 he also worked hard against the proliferation of nuclear weapons, although he had himself,

in 1939, signed a letter to President F. D. Roosevelt alerting him to the danger that Germany might develop an ATOMIC BOMB, and had thus perhaps contributed to the setting up of the Manhattan Project.

EIRE. See IRELAND, REPUBLIC OF.

EISENHOWER, Dwight David (1890–1969), "Ike," 34th president of the United States (1953–1961) and supreme commander of Allied troops in Europe during WWII.

Born in Denison, Tex., the third of seven sons, he spent most of his childhood in Abilene, Kan. He left Abilene in 1909 to attend West Point. The year after his graduation he married Mary (Mamie) Geneva Doud, by whom he had two sons, Doud David (1917–1921) and John Sheldon Doud (1922–   ). In 1926 he graduated first out of 275 from the Fort Leavenworth Staff School. By 1941 he had become a brigadier-general, and in the summer of 1943 he was sent to London as commanding general of US forces in the European theater of operations. He directed victorious Allied operations in North Africa and Sicily. As supreme commander of the Allied Expeditionary Force he directed the D-Day assault in 1944 and the campaign which led to the German surrender at Rheims in 1945. He headed the occupation force until 1948, when he became president of Columbia University, taking leave of absence to serve as supreme commander of NATO in 1950.

He became the Republican presidential candidate in 1952, was elected by a large majority, and reelected in 1956. Domestically he sought "moderation," appealing, often fruitlessly, for bipartisan support from a Democratic Congress which consistently rejected such Republican programs as the repeal of the TAFT-HARTLEY ACT and a reduction in tariffs.

The CIVIL RIGHTS legislation of 1957 and 1960 was among the most significant measures of his presidency. Although he sent troops to Little Rock, Ark., to enforce an antisegregation court order, he personally doubted the ability of such legislation to effect social change. One of his first foreign-policy moves was to arrange a truce in the KOREAN WAR. He supported the COLD WAR strategy of his secretary of state, John Foster DULLES. which resulted in some of the highest peacetime military budgets ever proposed. Eisenhower himself warned of the massive potential for "misplaced power" such military expenditures entailed, in his famous "military-industrial complex" speech, given when he retired at the age of 70—the oldest president to complete his term in office.

EISENSTAEDT, Alfred (1898–   ), pioneering American photojournalist who worked for *Life* magazine for over 30 years. From the early 1930s he helped to develop news and candid photography from mere reportage into an art form.

EISENSTEIN, Sergei Mikhailovich (1898–1948), Soviet film director who was a major influence on the development of the cinema. He extended editing techniques, especially the use of montage. His films, notably *The Battleship Potemkin* (1925), *Ten Days that Shook the World* (1927), *Alexander Nevsky* (1938) and *Ivan the Terrible* (1944–46), are undisputed classics.

EISTEDDFOD, ancient Welsh poetry festival which died out after the 16th century, though enough of the "bardic" tradition survived to revive it in the 19th century; it is now a festival of all the arts. A National Eisteddfod is held each summer in N or S Wales alternately.

EL-ALAMEIN, Battle of, decisive British victory in the N African campaign in WWII. The 8th Army under General MONTGOMERY forced the Axis troops under Field-Marshal ROMMEL to withdraw from Egypt and Libya into E Tunisia, thus paving the way for their total defeat soon after.

ELASTICITY, the ability of a body to resist tension, torsion, shearing or compression and to recover its original shape and size when the stress is removed. All substances are elastic to some extent, but if the stress exceeds a certain value (the elastic limit), which is soon reached for brittle and plastic materials, permanent deformation occurs. Below the elastic limit, bodies obey Hooke's Law (see MATERIALS, STRENGTH OF).

ELATH, also Eilat, port city and beach resort at Israel's southern extremity, on the Gulf of Aqaba. Israel's only direct access to E Africa and the Far East, it has often been blockaded by Egypt. Pop 18,900.

ELBA, Italian island in the Mediterranean, 6mi SW of Tuscany, famous as the place to which NAPOLEON I was exiled. The island is about 20mi long and less than 10mi wide,

and is very mountainous. Industries include iron mining, marble quarrying, fishing and agriculture.

ELBE RIVER, major river in central Europe. It rises in the Riesengebirge in NW Czechoslovakia and flows 725mi N through East and West Germany into the North Sea beyond Hamburg. The river is navigable for some 525mi and is connected by a canal system to the Oder. Important cities on the Elbe include Hamburg, Dresden and Magdeburg.

ELBURZ MOUNTAINS, range in N Iran between the S shore of the Caspian and the central plateau. Mt Demavend (18,934ft) is the highest peak.

EL DORADO (Spanish: the gilded one), South American Indian chief who was reputed to cover himself with gold dust at festivals and then, as a sacrifice, wash it off in a lake into which his subjects also threw gold. Much of the Spanish exploration and conquest of South America was fired by the quest for the legendary city of El Dorado.

ELEANOR OF AQUITAINE (c1122–1204), daughter and heiress of William, Duke of Aquitaine; queen consort first to Louis VII of France (marriage annulled 1152) and then to Henry II of England. Her marriage to Henry in 1152 brought almost all of W France under English domination. In 1173 she supported her sons (later kings Richard I and John) in rebellion against their father and was afterwards kept in captivity until Henry's death in 1185. She was subsequently active in politics in support of her sons.

ELEATICS, pre-Socratic school of Greek philosophy mentioned by PLATO and ARISTOTLE. Founded by PARMENIDES, it also included ZENO OF ELEA and Melissus, taking its name from Elea, their native city. The central Eleatic doctrine, in contrast to the theory of HERACLITUS. is that the world is one uniform whole, an abstract "being" remaining unchangeable and absolute, and change is a mere illusion of the senses. Because the Eleatics were the first to develop purely formal arguments they are often regarded as the founders of LOGIC.

ELECTION, method of choice by poll, often used by democratic bodies, including states, to select officeholders. Some public officials in ancient Greece and Rome were elected, but the modern system of government by elected representatives derives largely from the British parliamentary system and the American system based on it.

When the American states adapted the British system, however, they wished to avoid having a hereditary head of state and upper house, but did not wish to "degrade" these offices by putting them up for straightforward competitive election. President and Senate were therefore to be chosen by indirect election. The Senate is no longer elected by the state legislatures, but the president is technically still elected by the ELECTORAL COLLEGE.

PRIMARY ELECTIONS, a reform adopted by a number of states in the late 19th century, might also be considered a form of indirect election, since voters actually elect a delegate of a particular party, who is usually then pledged to vote in convention for those voters' candidate for the party's nomination. The general tendency in American government has been to extend the franchise, by giving all citizens, regardless of color, sex, etc., the right to vote, and individual representation has been channeled to the various people for whom each citizen votes—local officials, county officials, some judges, state governors and legislators, US Representatives and Senators and so on.

A system of proportional representation, as opposed to the plurality system, operates by awarding parties seats in a national legislature, for example, on the basis of the proportion of the total popular vote each party has received. Although operated widely in Europe, proportional representation has only been used experimentally in the US, except in the special case of some primary elections.

ELECTORAL COLLEGE, body created to elect the president and vice president of the US. The college was conceived as a compromise between direct popular elections for the nation's highest office and rule by appointment or inheritance. It was originally intended in the Constitution that the electors would be chosen by the state legislatures. But this has been modified so that the electors are chosen by the voters of each state—often without their names appearing on the ballot—by the indirect method of allowing voters to indicate their choice for president and vice president and then allowing the winning party's electors to cast the states' votes for the candidates chosen. Each state has as many votes in the college as the total number of its senators and representatives. If no candidate receives a majority of electoral votes, the House of Representatives elects the president from among the top three candidates. This happened twice in the 19th century—in 1800, when Thomas Jefferson was chosen by the House, and in 1824, when John Quincy Adams was chosen. Since the winning candidate in each state receives all that state's electoral votes, it is mathe-

tically possible for the losing presidential candidate to receive more popular votes than the man elected by the college. This happened in 1824 with Jackson and Adams, in 1876 (see ELECTORAL COMMISSION 1877) with Tilden and Hayes and in 1888 when Benjamin Harrison defeated Grover Cleveland. There has been constant dissatisfaction with the electoral college, but the institution still survives. (See also UNITED STATES CONSTITUTION.)

ELECTRIC CAR, an automobile driven by electric MOTORS and (usually) using storage BATTERIES as the ENERGY source. Although an electrically-powered carriage was built as long ago as 1837, it was only in the 1890s that electric cars became common. After WWI they lost ground to AUTOMOBILES with INTERNAL-COMBUSTION ENGINES although, particularly in Europe, electric traction has remained popular for urban delivery vehicles. With increasing concern being felt at the energy- and pollution-costs of the gasoline automobile, renewed interest is being shown in the electric car in spite of its relatively short range between charges. It is pollution-free, robust and simple to drive and maintain. The only difficulty is its low power-to-weight ratio, largely due to the weight of the lead-acid storage batteries commonly used. Much research is being put into finding alternative, lighter battery systems or powerful-enough FUEL CELLS to make electric cars once again an attractive proposition for urban transportation.

ELECTRICITY, the phenomenon of charged particles at rest or in motion. Electricity provides a highly versatile form of ENERGY, electrical devices being used in heating, LIGHTING, machinery, telephony, and ELECTRONICS. **Electric charge** is an inherent property of matter; ELECTRONS carry a negative charge of 1.602×10^{-19} coulomb each, and atomic nuclei normally carry a similar positive charge for each electron in the ATOM. When this balance is disturbed, a net charge is left on an object; the study of such isolated charges is called **electrostatics.** Like charges repel and unlike charges attract each other with a FORCE proportional to the two charges and inversely proportional to the square of the distance between them (the inverse-square law). This force is normally interpreted in terms of an ELECTRIC FIELD produced by one charge, with which the other interacts. A field is represented graphically by field lines beginning at the positive and ending at the negative charge. The lines show by their direction that of the field, and by their density its strength. Pairs of equal but opposite charges separated by a small distance are called dipoles, the product of charge and separation being called the DIPOLE MOMENT. Dipoles experience a TORQUE in an electric field that tends to align them with the field, but they experience no net force unless the field is nonuniform. The amount of work done in moving a unit charge from one point to another against the electric field is called the electric **potential difference**, or voltage, between the points; it is measured in VOLTS (V = joules/coulomb). The ratio of a charge added to a body to the voltage produced is called the CAPACITANCE of the body.

Materials known as electric CONDUCTORS contain charges that are free to move about—for example, VALENCE electrons in metals, and IONS in salt solutions. The presence of an electric field in conductors produces a steady flow of charge in the direction of the field; such a flow constitutes an **electric current**, measured in AMPERES (A = coulombs/second). The field implies a voltage between the ends of the conductor, which is normally proportional to the current (OHM'S LAW). This ratio, called the RESISTANCE of the conductor, is measured in ohms (ohms [Ω] = volts/amps); it normally rises with temperature. Materials with high resistance to currents are classed as insulators. (See also SEMICONDUCTOR; DIELECTRIC.) The energy acquired by the charges in falling through the field is dissipated as HEAT—and LIGHT, if a sufficient temperature is reached—the total POWER output being the product of current and voltage. Thus, for example, a 1-kW heater supplied at 110 V draws a current of about 9 A, and the hot element has a resistance of about 12Ω.

Electric sources such as BATTERIES or GENERATORS convert chemical, mechanical, or other energy into electrical energy (see ELECTROMOTIVE FORCE), and will pump charge through conductors much as a water pump circulates water in a radiator heating system. Batteries create a constant voltage, producing a steady, or **direct current** (DC); many generators, on the other hand, provide a voltage that changes in sign many times a second, and so produce an **alternating current** (AC), in which the charges move to and fro instead of continuously in one direction. This system has advantages in generation, transmission, and application and is now used almost universally for domestic and industrial purposes.

An electric current is found to produce a MAGNETIC FIELD circulating around it, to experience a force in an externally generated magnetic field, and to be itself generated by a changing magnetic field. For more details of these properties, on which most electrical machinery depends, see ELECTROMAGNETISM.

Static electricity was known to the ancient Greeks; the inverse square law was hinted at by J. PRIESTLEY in 1767 and later confirmed by H. CAVENDISH and C. A. COULOMB. G. S. OHM formulated his law of conduction in 1826, although its essentials were known before then. The common nature of all the "types" of electricity then known was demonstrated in 1826 by M. FARADAY, who also originated the concept of electric field lines.

ELECTRIC MOTOR. See MOTOR, ELECTRIC.

ELECTROCARDIOGRAPH, instrument for recording the electrical activity of the HEART, producing its results in the form of multiple tracing called an electrocardiogram (ECG). These are conventionally recorded with twelve combinations of ELECTRODES on the limbs and CHEST wall. The electrical impulses in the conducting tissue and muscle of the heart pass through the body fluids, while the position of the electrodes determines the way in which the heart is "looked at" in electrical terms. ECGs allow CORONARY THROMBOSIS, abnormal heart rhythm, disorders of the heart muscle and PERICARDIUM to be detected, as well as diseases of the METABOLISM that affect the heart.

ELECTROCHEMISTRY, branch of PHYSICAL CHEMISTRY dealing with the interconversion of electrical and chemical energy. Many chemical species are electrically-charged IONS (see BOND, CHEMICAL), and a large class of reactions—OXIDATION AND REDUCTION—consists of electron-transfer reactions between ions and other species. If the two half-reactions (oxidation, reduction) are made to occur at different ELECTRODES, the electron-transfer occurs by the passing of a current through an external circuit between them (see BATTERY; FUEL CELL). The ELECTROMOTIVE FORCE driving the current is the sum of the electrode potentials (in volts) of the half-reactions, which represents the free energy (see THERMODYNAMICS) produced by them. Conversely, if an emf is applied across the electrodes of a cell, it causes a chemical reaction if it is greater than the sum of the potentials of the half-reactions (see ELECTROLYSIS). Such potentials depend both on the nature of the reaction and on the concentrations of the reactants. Cells arising through concentration differences are one cause of CORROSION.

ELECTROENCEPHALOGRAPH, instrument for recording the BRAIN's electrical activity using several small electrodes on the scalp. Its results are produced in the form of a multiple tracing called an electroencephalogram (EEG). The "brain waves" recorded have certain normal patterns in the alert and sleeping individual. Localized brain diseases and metabolic disturbances cause abnormal wave forms either in particular areas or as a generalized disturbance. The abnormal brain activity in EPILEPSY, both during CONVULSIONS and when the patient appears normal, usually allows diagnosis. The interpretation of EEGs requires skill and experience.

ELECTROLYSIS, production of a chemical reaction by passing a direct current through an electrolyte— i.e., a compound which contains IONS when molten or in solution. (See ELECTROCHEMISTRY.) The CATIONS move toward the CATHODE and the ANIONS toward the ANODE, thus carrying the current. At each electrode the ions are discharged according to FARADAY's laws: (1) the quantity of a substance produced is proportional to the amount of electricity passed; (2) the relative quantities of different substances produced are proportional to their EQUIVALENT WEIGHTS. Hence one gram-equivalent of any substance is produced by the same amount of electricity, known as a **faraday** (96,500 coulombs). Electrolysis is used to extract electropositive metals from their ores (see ELECTROCHEMICAL SERIES), and to refine less electropositive metals; to produce SODIUM hydroxide, CHLORINE, HYDROGEN, OXYGEN and many other substances; and in ELECTROMETALLURGY.

ELECTROMAGNET, a magnet produced (and thus easily controlled) by the electric current in a coil of wire which is usually wound on a frame of highly permeable (see PERMEABILITY) material so as to reinforce and direct the MAGNETIC FIELD appropriately.

ELECTROMAGNETIC RADIATION, or radiant energy, the form in which ENERGY is transmitted through space or matter using a varying ELECTROMAGNETIC FIELD. Classically, radiant energy is regarded as a WAVE MOTION. In the mid-19th century MAXWELL showed that an oscillating (vibrating) electric charge would be surrounded by varying electric and magnetic fields. Energy would be lost from the oscillating charge in the form of transverse waves in these fields, the waves in the electric field being at right-angles both to those in the magnetic field and to the direction in which the waves are traveling (propagated). Moreover, the VELOCITY of the waves would depend only on

the properties of the medium through which they passed; for propagation in a vacuum its value is a fundamental constant of physics—the **electromagnetic constant,** $c = 299,792.5$km/s. At the beginning of the 20th century PLANCK proposed that certain properties of radiant energy were best explained by regarding it as being emitted in discrete amounts called quanta. Einstein later proposed that the quanta should be regarded as particles, called PHOTONS, and that the energy travels through space in that form. The energy of each photon is proportional to the frequency of the associated radiation (see QUANTUM THEORY).

The different kinds of electromagnetic radiation are classified according to the energy of the photons involved, the range of energies being known as the electromagnetic SPECTRUM. (Equivalently, this spectrum arranges the radiations according to wavelength or frequency.) In order of decreasing energy the principal kinds are GAMMA RAYS, X-RAYS, ULTRAVIOLET RADIATION, LIGHT, INFRARED RADIATION, MICROWAVES and RADIO waves. In general, the higher the energies involved, the better the properties of the radiation are described in terms of particles (photons) rather than waves. Radiant energy is emitted from objects when they are heated (see BLACKBODY RADIATION) or otherwise energetically excited (see LUMINESCENCE; SPECTROSCOPY); man uses it to channel and distribute both energy and information (see INFORMATION THEORY).

ELECTROMAGNETISM, the study of ELECTRIC and MAGNETIC FIELDS, and their interaction with electric charges and currents. The two fields are in fact different manifestations of the same physical field, the electromagnetic field, and are interconverted according to the speed of the observer. Apart from the effects noted under ELECTRICITY and MAGNETISM, the following are found:

1. Moving charges (and hence currents) in magnetic fields experience a FORCE, perpendicular to the field and the current, and proportional to their product. This is the basis of all electric MOTORS, and was first applied for the purpose by M. FARADAY in 1821.

2. A change in the number of magnetic field lines passing through a circuit "induces" an electric field in the circuit, proportional to the rate of the change. This is the basis of most GENERATORS, and was also established by M. Faraday, in 1831.

3. An effect analogous to the above, but with magnetic and electric fields interchanged, and usually much smaller. This

was hypothesized by J. C. MAXWELL, who in 1862 deduced from it the possibility of self-sustaining electromagnetic waves traveling at a speed which coincided with that of LIGHT, thereby identifying the nature of visible light, and predicting other waves such as the RADIO waves found experimentally by H. HERTZ shortly afterwards.

ELECTROMOTIVE FORCE (emf), loosely, the voltage produced by a BATTERY, GENERATOR or other source of ELECTRICITY, but more precisely, the product of the current it produces in a circuit and the total circuit RESISTANCE, including that of the source itself. The actual voltage across the source is usually somewhat lower.

ELECTRON, a stable SUBATOMIC PARTICLE, with rest MASS $9.109 \, 1 \times 10^{-31}$kg (roughly 1/183,6 the mass of a HYDROGEN atom) and a negative charge of 1.6021×10^{-19}C, the charges of other particles being positive or negative integral multiples of this. Electrons are one of the basic constituents of ordinary MATTER, commonly occupying the ORBITALS surrounding positively charged atomic nuclei. The chemical properties of ATOMS and MOLECULES are largely determined by the behavior of the electrons in their highest-energy orbitals. Both CATHODE RAYS and BETA RAYS are streams of free electrons passing through a gas or vacuum. The unidirectional motion of electrons in a solid conductor constitutes an electric current. Solid conductors differ from nonconductors in that in the former some electrons are free to move about while in the latter all are permanently associated with particular nuclei. Free electrons in a gas or vacuum can usually be treated as classical particles, though their wave properties become important when they interact with or are associated with atomic nuclei. The anti-electron, with identical mass but an equivalent positive charge, is known as a positron (see ANTIMATTER).

ELECTRONIC GAMES, a variety of computerized, electrically operated games which began to gain enormous popularity in the 1970s, almost as fast as they were developed. More than 300 million were sold in the US from 1977–80. The basis of the engineering of all these games, which range from hand-held, battery-operated units to large, enormously complex machines, is the MICROPROCESSOR. Video games, usually available in the form of cartridges that can be set into a master computer unit, with a home-TV picture tube functioning as the display screen, were registering rapid increases in sales in 1981.

ELECTRONIC MUSIC, compositions in which musicians use sounds created solely on electronic equipment. **Concrete Music** uses recordings of natural sounds as the basis for composition; and works mixing both approaches are called "tape music." Experiments with electronic composition began as early as the 1890s but widespread production began only after WWII, as universities and broadcasting authorities in many countries began setting up studios to encourage this use of modern technology. John CAGE, Karlheinz STOCKHAUSEN and Edgar VARÈSE have produced important works in this field.

ELECTRONICS, an applied science dealing with the development and behavior of ELECTRON TUBES, SEMICONDUCTORS and other devices in which the motion of electrons is controlled; it covers the behavior of electrons in gases, vacuums, conductors and semiconductors. Its theoretical basis lies in the principles of ELECTROMAGNETISM and solid-state physics discovered in the late 19th and early 20th centuries. Electronics began to grow in the 1920s with the development of RADIO. During WWII, the US and UK concentrated resources on the invention of RADAR and pulse transmission methods and by 1945 they had enormous industrial capacity for producing electronic equipment. The invention of the TRANSISTOR in 1948 as a small, cheap replacement for vacuum tubes led to the rapid development of COMPUTERS, transistor radios, etc. Now, with the widespread use of integrated circuits, electronics plays a vital role in communications (TELEPHONE networks, information storage, etc.) and industry. All electronic circuits contain both active and passive components and transducers (e.g., MICROPHONES) which change ENERGY from one form to another. Sensors of light, temperature, etc., may also be present. **Passive components** are normally conductors and are characterized by their properties of RESISTANCE (R), CAPACITANCE (C) and INDUCTANCE (L). One of these usually predominates, depending on the function required. **Active components** are electron tubes or semiconductors; they contain a source of power and control electron flow. The former may be general-purpose tubes (diodes, triodes, etc., the name depending on the number of ELECTRODES) which rectify, amplify or switch electric signals. Image tubes (in TELEVISION receivers) convert an electric input into a light signal; photoelectric tubes (in television cameras) do the reverse. Semiconductor diodes and transistors, which are basically sandwiches made of two different types of semiconductor, now usually perform the general functions once done by tubes, being smaller, more robust and generating less heat. These few basic components can build up an enormous range of circuits with different functions. Common types include: power supply (converting AC to pulsing DC and then smoothing out the pulsations); switching and timing (the logic circuits in computers are in this category); AMPLIFIERS, which increase the amplitude or power of a signal, and oscillators, used in radio and television transmitters and which generate AC signals. Demands for increased cheapness and reliability of circuits have led to the development of microelectronics. In **printed circuits**, printed connections replace individual wiring on a flat board to which about two components per cm³ are soldered. INTEGRATED CIRCUITS assemble tens of thousands of components in a single structure, formed directly by evaporation or other techniques as films about 0.03mm thick on a substrate. In monolithic circuits, components are produced in a tiny chip of semiconductor by selective diffusion.

ELECTRON MICROSCOPE, a microscope using a beam of ELECTRONS rather than light to study objects too small for conventional MICROSCOPES. First constructed by Max Knoll and Ernst Ruska around 1930, the instrument now consists typically of an evacuated column of magnetic lenses with a 50-1500 kV electron gun at the top and a fluorescent screen or photographic plate at the bottom. The various lenses allow the operator to see details almost at the atomic level (0.1 nm) at up to a million times magnification, although many specimens deteriorate under the electron bombardment at these limits. The greater magnification results from the shorter wavelengths of electrons compared to the light waves of optical microscopes.

Standard instruments are called *transmission* electron microscopes because the beam is transmitted through the thin-sliced specimen. In the *scanning* electron microscope, which resembles a TELEVISION system, a beam of 1-20 kV intensity is instead focused to a point and scanned over the specimen area. A synchronized television screen displays the intensity of the secondary electrons reflected back, or scattered, from the surface. Resolution is limited to about 3 nm, but the surface topography is seen as an image. Scanning electron microscopes can also be used in a *transmission* mode.

In the *field emission* electron microscope, invented by Erwin Müller in 1936, the object itself—the sharp tip of a metal or semiconductor specimen—is the source of

the electrons, when it is subjected to a strong ELECTRIC FIELD. An image of the tip's surface appears on a fluorescent screen without the use of a focusing system. Very high resolutions can be obtained by using charged atoms instead of electrons; images of individual atoms in the tip have been obtained in this way.

Electron microscopes are used for structural, defect and composition studies in a wide range of biological and inorganic materials.

ELEGY, in classical poetry, refers to a lyric poem of alternate two-line stanzas written in a distinctive meter on a variety of themes. However, the term has been used since the Renaissance to describe any poem expressing sorrow, particularly about death, such as Milton's *Lycidas* (1637) or Thomas Gray's *Elegy Written in a Country Churchyard* (1750).

ELEMENT, Chemical, simple substance composed of ATOMS of the same atomic number, and so incapable of chemical degradation or resolution. They are generally mixtures of different ISOTOPES. Of the 106 known elements, 88 occur in nature, and the rest have been synthesized (see TRANSURANIUM ELEMENTS). The elements are classified by physical properties as METALS, METALLOIDS and NONMETALS, and by chemical properties and atomic structure according to the PERIODIC TABLE. Most elements exhibit ALLOTROPY, and many are molecular (e.g., oxygen, O_2). The elements have all been built up in STARS from HYDROGEN by complex sequences of nuclear reactions, e.g., the CARBON CYCLE.

ELEMENTARY PARTICLES. See SUBATOMIC PARTICLES.

ELEPHANTIASIS, disease in which there is massive swelling and hypertrophy of the SKIN and subcutaneous tissue of the legs or scrotum, due to the obstructed flow of LYMPH. This may be a congenital DISEASE, due to trauma, CANCER, or infection with FILARIASIS, TUBERCULOSIS and some VENEREAL DISEASES. Recurrent secondary bacterial infections are common and chronic skin ULCERS may form. Elevation, elastic stockings, DIURETICS and treatment of infection are basic to relief, while some cases are helped by SURGERY.

ELEPHANTS, the largest living land mammals, comprising two species, the African *Loxodonta africana* and the Indian *Elephas maximus*. The African elephant is up to 3.3m (11ft) tall and may weigh 6.6 tons; the Indian species is slightly smaller. Both species are characterized by their trunks, elongated extensions of the nose and upper lip, and by huge incisor teeth in the males prized as the source of ivory. The African elephant has large ears that distinguish it from the Indian species. Both live in herds feeding on grass and foliage. In spite of, and because of, its size the Indian elephant has long been tamed as a beast of burden.

ELEUSINIAN MYSTERIES, secret religious rites of the seasons in ancient Greece. They were originally performed in honor of DEMETER at Eleusis near Athens and dramatized the descent of PERSEPHONE into the underworld. Later the rites were performed in Athens.

ELGAR, Sir Edward William (1857–1934), English composer. In general Elgar followed the German orchestral and choral traditions of the 19th century, but his *Enigma Variations* (1899) and *Pomp and Circumstance* reflected a style which was clearly English in character. His other works include the oratorio *The Dream of Gerontius* (1900); two symphonies, violin and cello concertos, and the concert overture *Cockaigne (1901).*

ELGIN MARBLES, ancient sculptures (mostly from the Athenian ACROPOLIS) brought to Britain by Thomas Bruce, 7th Earl of Elgin and British envoy at Constantinople (1799–1802). Now in the British Museum, they include a frieze from the Parthenon and parts of the Erechtheum temple.

EL GRECO. See GRECO, EL.

ELIJAH, Hebrew prophet of the late 9th century BC, mentioned in the Koran and the Old Testament Book of Kings. He fought against the worship of BAAL introduced from Phoenicia during the reign of King Ahab of Israel by his Queen, JEZEBEL. In the New Testament Elijah appears with Christ at the TRANSFIGURATION.

ELIJAH MUHAMMAD. See MUHAMMAD, ELIJAH.

ELIOT, Charles William (1834–1926), US educator, President of Harvard University from 1869–1909 and editor of the original *Harvard Classics* series. Eliot had a profound influence on American education.

ELIOT, George (1819–1880), pseudonym of the famous English novelist, Mary Ann Evans. Her work, notably *Adam Bede* (1859), *The Mill on the Floss* (1860), *Silas Marner* (1861), *Middlemarch* (1871–72) and *Daniel Deronda* (1876) brought a new breadth of intellect, technical sophistication and moral scope to the English novel and greatly influenced later novelists. Her creative work was encouraged by writer and editor George Henry Lewes, with whom she lived for 24 years, defying convention. She was a friend of Herbert SPENCER, was subeditor of the *Westminster Review* (1851–53) and a notable translator of German works.

ELIOT, Sir John (1592–1632), An eloquent Parliamentary critic of royal policies, his advocacy of such reforms as the PETITION OF RIGHT (1628) angered CHARLES I who ordered Eliot's imprisonment in the Tower of London, where he died.

ELIOT, Thomas Stearns (1888–1965), major 20th-century poet and critic. Born in St. Louis, Mo., he settled permanently in England. He was a leading modernist who found his own poetic voice as early as *Prufrock and Other Observations* (1917). His most famous poem, *The Waste Land*, appeared in 1922, and was noted for its portrayal of the chaos and squalor of modern life. His criticism (*The Sacred Wood*, 1920) expressed belief in tradition and the life of the spirit, however. Increasingly meditative and philosophical poetry followed (e.g. *Ash Wednesday*, 1930, and his masterpiece, the *Four Quartets*, 1944). He wrote successful poetic dramas such as *Murder in the Cathedral* (1935) and *The Cocktail Party* (1950). He was awarded the Nobel Prize for Literature in 1948.

ELISHA, Hebrew prophet, a disciple of and successor to ELIJAH. Greatly gifted as a soothsayer and healer, he was successful in driving out BAAL worship from the northern state of Israel.

ELISOFON, Eliot (1911–1973), US photographer who specialized in photographs of art, architecture and exotic scenery in the style of Gauguin. He was a color consultant on films such as *Moulin Rouge* (1953).

ELIZABETH (1709–1762), Empress of Russia from 1741, daughter of PETER the Great. In 1741 she staged a coup against her cousin, the regent and reasserted her father's principle of government. She rid the court of German influence, founded Moscow University, and pursued the SEVEN YEARS WAR against Prussia.

ELIZABETH I (1533–1603), Queen of

England and Ireland 1558–1603, and the last TUDOR monarch. A daughter of HENRY VIII, who had broken with the Catholic Church to marry ANNE BOLEYN, her mother, her initial task as queen was to reestablish her supremacy over the English Church after the reign of her Catholic sister, MARY I. The defeat by her navy of the Spanish ARMADA (1588) established England as a major European power. At home, industry, agriculture and the arts (especially literature) throve under conditions of relative peace and financial stability, while colonization of the New World was encouraged. The settlement of the Protestant succession became the *bête noire* of the reign as Elizabeth was unmarried and childless. After the execution of her Catholic cousin, MARY QUEEN OF SCOTS, a possible heir, Elizabeth finally acknowledged the succession of JAMES VI of Scotland, Mary's son, thus securing the peaceful Union of England and Scotland.

ELIZABETH II (1926–   ), Queen of the United Kingdom of Great Britain and Northern Ireland (from 1952) and head of the COMMONWEALTH OF NATIONS. One of the world's few remaining monarchs, she is extremely popular at home and abroad and has traveled extensively as her country's representative. She is married to Philip Mountbatten, Duke of Edinburgh, and has four children.

ELK, large member of the DEER family Cervidae. It inhabits some of the forest areas of N Europe and Asia and is closely related to the larger American MOOSE. The American elk is also called the WAPITI.

ELK HILLS, US oil reserve of 46,000 acres in California, now leased to the navy. Dubious lease arrangements for the reserve, and that at TEAPOT DOME, became the subject of Senate investigations in 1923 and led to one of the great political scandals in US history. In 1976, in a response to the energy crisis, the US Congress passed a bill providing for commercial production of oil from Elk Hills, which was known to have reserves of more than one billion barrels.

ELKS, American fraternal and charitable organization, formally titled Benevolent and Protective Order of Elks, founded in New York (1868) and now Chicago-based. The Elks National Foundation was set up to direct benevolent works, including college scholarships and aid to war veterans.

ELLINGTON, Edward Kennedy "Duke" (1899–1974), US composer, pianist and orchestra leader, one of the giants of JAZZ music. After a formal musical education, Ellington formed his first band in 1918 and by the 1930s enjoyed an international

following. His superbly disciplined orchestra remained the envy of the jazz world for several decades, playing music composed by its leader for its well-known instrumental soloists. Ellington wrote such hit songs as "Mood Indigo," "Sophisticated Lady" and "Satin Doll," suites such as *Black, Brown and Beige* (1943) and, late in life, considerable sacred music. He was awarded the Presidential Medal of Freedom in 1969.

ELLIS, Henry Havelock (1859–1939), British writer chiefly remembered for his studies of human sexual behavior and psychology. His major work was *Studies in the Psychology of Sex* (1897–1928).

ELLIS ISLAND, island of about 27 acres in upper New York Bay, within the boundaries of New York City. Bought by the government in 1808, it was the site of a fort and later an arsenal. From 1891 to 1954, it was an immigration station through which some 20 million immigrants entered the US.

ELLISON, Ralph Waldo (1914–   ), black US writer. He is best known for his novel *Invisible Man* (1952), a story of black alienation in a hostile white society, which won a National Book Award.

ELLSWORTH, Lincoln (1880–1951), US polar explorer and the first man to cross both the Arctic and Antarctic by air. He flew from Spitsbergen to Alaska with AMUNDSEN and NOBILE, in the dirigible *Norge* (1926), and in 1935 he made a 2,300mi flight over the Antarctic in a single-engine airplane.

ELLSWORTH, Oliver (1745–1807), American statesman and jurist reputedly responsible for the use of the term "United States" in the American Constitution. He represented Conn. at the Constitutional Convention (1787), where he helped promote the "Connecticut compromise," providing equal state representation in the Senate. He was Senator from Conn. 1789–96, and chief justice of the US 1796–1800.

ELMAN, Mischa (1891–1967), Russian-born US violinist. He made his international debut in Berlin (1904), and first performed in the US in 1908. He became an American citizen in 1923.

EL MISTI, a dormant volcano 19,031ft in S Peru, NE of Arequipa. It was held sacred by the Incas.

EL PASO, industrial city in Tex., seat of El Paso Co. It is a port of entry on the Rio Grande on the Mexican border. Industries include oil and copper refining, smelting and food processing. Fort Bliss is nearby. Pop 322,261.

EL SALVADOR, the smallest Central

American republic, bordered by Guatemala and Honduras, and having a Pacific coastline.

Land. Two parallel volcanic mountain ranges cross the country from SE to NW enclosing high fertile plateaus and valleys irrigated in the W by the Lempa R. To the E of the narrow coastal plain the Gulf of Fonseca forms a natural harbor for the chief port, La Unión.

People. About 89% of the population are mestizos, 10% Indians and 1% white. Some Indians still speak Nahuatl. The country has one of the highest illiteracy rates in Latin America (almost 40%).

Economy. El Salvador depends on agriculture, which supports most of its population at subsistence level. Corn, rice, sugar, cotton and beans are grown, and coffee, from the rich volcanic areas of the highlands, is the chief export. The developing industries include food processing and the production of textiles, cement and asbestos. The country trades mainly with the US, importing machinery, foodstuffs and chemical products, and since 1961 has been a member of the Central American Common Market.

History. El Salvador was discovered in 1524 by a Spanish expedition led by ALVARADO. Unrest during the early 19th century led to independence from Spain in 1821. After brief involvement in the Mexican Empire, El Salvador joined the first Central American Federation 1823–38. It became an established independent republic in 1841. From the beginning the nation was beset by ideological disputes, political rivalries and military coups. A long-standing hostility between El Salvador and Honduras erupted into an armed conflict in 1969. The 1970s were marked by violence, guerrilla activities and kidnappings.

Official name: Republic of El Salvador
Capital: San Salvador
Area: 8,260sq mi
Population: 4,353,758
Languages: Spanish
Monetary unit(s): 1 Salvadoran colón = 100 centavos

Religions: Roman Catholic

ELY, Richard Theodore (1854–1943), US political economist. He advanced the study of economics and helped found the American Economic Association (1885). As a leader of the Society of Christian Socialists, he supported the growth of the labor unions.

ELYSÉE PALACE, official residence in Paris of the president of France. It was built in 1718 for Henri La Tour d'Auvergne and was once the home of Madame de Pompadour.

EMANCIPATION PROCLAMATION, decree issued by Abraham Lincoln on Jan. 1, 1863, during the Civil War. It abolished slavery in the rebel states, although Lincoln was not an Abolitionist and pledged in 1860 not to interfere with slavery. It was a shrewd military and political maneuver designed to deprive the Confederacy of its economic base, namely slavery. Nevertheless, the proclamation boosted the Abolitionist cause and three years later the 13th Amendment brought all slavery in America to an end. (See also CIVIL WAR, AMERICAN.)

EMBOLISM, the presence of substances other than liquid BLOOD in the BLOOD CIRCULATION, causing obstruction to ARTERIES or interfering with the pumping of the HEART. The commonest embolism is from atheromatous plaques (see ARTERIOSCLEROSIS) or THROMBOSIS on a blood vessel or the HEART walls. FAT globules may form emboli from bone MARROW after major bone FRACTURES, and amniotic fluid may cause embolism during childbirth. Stroke or transient cerebral episodes, pulmonary embolism, CORONARY THROMBOSIS and obstruction of limb or organ blood supply with consequent cell DEATH are common results, some of them fatal. Some may be removed surgically, but prevention is preferable.

EMBROIDERY. See NEEDLEWORK.

EMBRYO, the earliest stage of the life of a FETUS, the development from a fertilized EGG through the differentiation of the major organs. In man, the fertilized egg divides repeatedly, forming a small ball of cells which fixes by IMPLANTATION to the wall of the WOMB; differentiation into PLACENTA and three primitive layers (endoderm, mesoderm and ectoderm) follows. These layers then undergo further division into distinct organ precursors and each of these develops by a process of migration, differentiation and differential growth. The processes roughly correspond to the phylogeny or evolutionary sequence leading to the species. Much of development depends on formation of cavities, either by splitting of layers or by enfolding. The HEART develops early at the front, probably splitting into a simple tube, before being divided into separate chambers; the gut is folded into the body, although for a long time the bulk of it remains outside. The NERVOUS SYSTEM develops as an infolding of ectoderm, which then becomes separated from the surface. Facial development consists of mesodermal migration and modification of the bronchial arches, remnants of the GILLS in phylogeny; primitive limb buds grow out of the developing trunk. The overall control of these processes is not yet understood; however, infection (especially GERMAN MEASLES) in the mother, or the taking of certain DRUGS (e.g., THALIDOMIDE) during PREGNANCY may lead to abnormal development and so to congenital defects, including heart defects (e.g., BLUE BABY), limb deformity, HARELIP and CLEFT PALATE and SPINA BIFIDA. By convention, the embryo becomes a fetus at three months' gestation.

EMBRYOLOGY, the study of the development of EMBRYOS of animals and humans, based on anatomical specimens of embryos at different periods of gestation, obtained from animals or from human ABORTION. The development of organ systems may be deduced and the origins of congenital defects recognized, so that events liable to interfere with development may be avoided. It may reveal the basis for the separate development of identical cells and for control of growth. The ANATOMY of an organism may be better understood and learnt by study of embryology. The principal embryologists of past ages have included ARISTOTLE; William HARVEY and Marcello MALPIGHI in the 17th century, and Karl Ernst VON BAER in the 19th century.

EMERALD, valuable green GEMSTONE, a variety of BERYL. The best emeralds are mined in Colombia, Brazil and the USSR. Since 1935 it has been possible to make synthetic emeralds.

EMERSON, Ralph Waldo (1803–1882), US philosophical essayist, poet and lecturer. He resigned a Unitarian pastorate (1831) and, after traveling in Europe, settled in Concord, Mass. His *Nature* (1836) was the strongest motivating statement of American TRANSCENDENTALISM. After 1837 he became renowned as a public speaker and after 1842 as editor of the Transcendentalist journal, *The Dial*. He later adjusted his idealistic view of the individual to accommodate the American experience of man's historical and political limitations, especially over the issue of slavery.

EMILIA-ROMAGNA, fertile, low-lying historic region in N Italy, bounded by the Po R, the Adriatic and the Apennines. Named for the ancient Roman road, the Via Aemilia, whose route is now followed by a railroad, it was once part of the Papal States, and contains the noted art centers of Bologna, Ferrara, Ravenna and Parma.

EMMET, Robert (1778–1803), Irish patriot. After a poorly planned uprising against the British in 1803, Emmet was tried and hanged for treason, which assured his fame as a martyr and romantic hero.

EMOTION, in psychology, a term that is only loosely defined. Generally, an emotion is a sensation which causes physiological changes (as in pulse rate, breathing) as well as psychological changes (as disturbance) which result in attempts at adaptations in the individual's behavior. Some psychologists differentiate types of emotion: one such classification is into primary (e.g., fear), complex (e.g., envy) and sentiment (e.g., love, hate); but such schemata are controversial. The causes of emotion are not fully understood, but they may be associated with biochemical changes in various parts of the body. (See also IDEA; INSTINCT.) Modern psychoanalysts generally prefer the term affect for emotion.

EMPEDOCLES (c490–430 BC), Sicilian Pythagorean philosopher who developed the notion that there were four fundamental elements in matter—earth, air, fire and water. In medicine he taught that blood ebbed and flowed from the heart and that health consisted in a balance of the four HUMORS in the body.

EMPHYSEMA, condition in which the air spaces of the LUNGS become enlarged, due to destruction of their walls. Often associated with chronic BRONCHITIS, it is usually a result of SMOKING but may be a congenital or occupational disease. Subcutaneous emphysema refers to air in the subcutaneous tissues.

EMPIRE STYLE, Neoclassical style in architecture, interior decoration and furniture design which reached its peak during the Napoleonic empire (1804–14). In architecture, Roman grandeur was imitated; mahogany and gilt were favored materials for furniture; and costume design was inspired by Classical drapery. The style evolved into the German BIEDERMEIER and the English REGENCY styles. (See also NEOCLASSICISM.)

EMPIRICISM, in philosophy, the view that knowledge can be derived only from sense experience. Modern empiricism, fundamentally opposed to the RATIONALISM that derives knowledge by deduction from principles known À PRIORI, was developed in the philosophies of LOCKE, BERKELEY and HUME. Other thinkers in the "British empiricist tradition" include J. S. MILL and the Americans J. DEWEY and W. JAMES.

ENAMEL, vitreous glaze (see CERAMICS; GLASS) fused on metal for decoration and protection. Silica, potassium carbonate, borax and trilead tetroxide (see LEAD) are fused to form a glass (called flux) which is colored by metal oxides; tin (IV) oxide makes it opaque. The enamel is powdered and spread over the cleaned metal object, which is then fired in a furnace until the enamel melts.

ENCEPHALITIS, infection affecting the substance of the BRAIN, usually caused by a VIRUS. It is a rare complication of certain common diseases (e.g., mumps, herpes simplex) and a specific manifestation of less common viruses, often carried by insects. Typically an acute illness with HEADACHE and FEVER, it may lead to evidence of patchy INFLAMMATION of brain tissue, such as personality change, EPILEPSY, localized weakness or rigidity. It may progress to impairment of consciousness and COMA. A particular type, *Encephalitis lethargica*, occurred as an EPIDEMIC early this century leading to a chronic disease resembling PARKINSON'S DISEASE but often with permanent mental changes.

ENCLOSURE, in Britain especially, the practice of fencing off land formerly open to common grazing or cultivation. It began in the 12th century and increased from the 15th century onwards as land values rose, often causing social dislocation and hardship in the countryside.

ENCOMIENDA, system of tributary labor imposed by the Spanish in South America in the 16th century. Spanish settlers, *encomenderos*, were assigned groups of Indians, from whom they exacted tribute and labor. The Spaniards were ostensibly supposed to pay the Indians, protect them and Christianize them. The system died out in the 18th century.

ENCOUNTER GROUPS, unorthodox offshoot of traditional group therapy, a technique characterized by marathon group sessions (sometimes led by people with little or no professional training), physical contact among members and frank confrontations. Encounter groups became extremely popular in the 1960s, often promising profound results after a few or even only one session; some companies set up encounter groups to help employees improve their interpersonal relations. The outcome was generally disappointing, however, and the fad had faded by the 1980s.

ENCYCLOPEDIA, reference work comprising alphabetically or thematically arranged articles selectively covering the whole range or a part of human knowledge. The earliest extant encyclopedia is the *Natural History* of PLINY the Elder (1st century AD) in 37 volumes. The most famous medieval encyclopedia was the *Speculum Majus* of Vincent de Beauvais (13th century), and in 1481 William CAXTON issued one of the earliest encyclopedias in English, the *Mirror of the World*. Ephraim Chambers' *Cyclopaedia* (1728) used specialist writers and formed the basis of the most ambitious and influential work of its kind, the French *Encyclopédie* (1751-72; see DIDEROT, DENIS). The *Encyclopaedia Britannica*, which first appeared 1768-71, and the *Great Soviet Encyclopedia*, whose production began in the 1920s, are the most compendious of the world's general encyclopedias.

ENDOCRINE GLANDS, ductless glands in the body which secrete HORMONES directly into the BLOOD stream. They include the PITUITARY GLAND, THYROID and PARATHYROID GLANDS, ADRENAL GLANDS and part of the PANCREAS, TESTES and OVARIES. Each secretes a number of hormones which affect body function, development, mineral balance and METABOLISM. They are under complex control mechanisms including FEEDBACK from their metabolic function and from other hormones. The pituitary gland, which is itself regulated by the HYPOTHALAMUS, has a regulator effect on the thyroid, adrenals and gonads.

ENDORPHINS, substances produced in the brain that inhibit certain brain cells from transmitting impulses and thereby block or reduce the sensation of pain. Morphine and similar drugs are thought to owe their effectiveness to their chemical similarity to endorphins. Synthetic endorphins may prove to be effective and non-addictive painkillers.

ENERGY, to the economist, a synonym for fuel; to the scientist, one of the fundamental modes of existence, equivalent to and interconvertible with MATTER. The MASS-energy equivalence is expressed in the Einstein equation, $E = mc^2$, where E is the energy equivalent to the mass m, c being the speed of LIGHT. Since c is so large, a tiny mass is equivalent to a vast amount of energy. However, this energy can only be realized in nuclear reactions and so, although the conversion of mass may provide energy for the STARS, this process does not figure much in physical processes on earth (except in nuclear power installations). The law of the conservation of mass-energy states that the total amount of mass-energy in the UNIVERSE or in an isolated system forming part of the universe cannot change. In an isolated system in which there are no nuclear reactions, this means that the total quantities both of mass and of energy are constant. Energy then is generally conserved.

Energy exists in a number of equivalent forms. The commonest of these is HEAT—the motion of the MOLECULES of matter. Ultimately all other forms of energy tend to convert into thermal motion. Another form of energy is the motion of ELECTRONS, ELECTRICITY. Moving electrons give rise to electromagnetic fields and these too contain energy. A pure form of electromagnetic energy is ELECTROMAGNETIC RADIATION (**radiant energy**) such as light. According to the QUANTUM THEORY, the energy of electromagnetic radiation is "quantized," referable to discrete units called PHOTONS, the energy E carried by a quantum of radiation of FREQUENCY v being given by $E = hv$, where h is the PLANCK CONSTANT. When macroscopic bodies move, they too have energy in virtue of their motion; this is their **kinetic energy** and is given by $\frac{1}{2}mv^2$ where m is the mass and v the velocity of motion. To change the velocity of a moving body, or to set it in motion, a FORCE must be applied to it and work must be done. This work is equivalent to the change in the kinetic energy of the body and gave physicists one of their earliest definitions of energy: the ability to do work. When work is done against a restraining force, **potential energy** is stored in the system, ready to be released again. The restraining force may be electromagnetic, torsional, electrostatic, tensional or of any other type. On earth when an object of mass m is raised up to height h, its gravitational potential energy is given by mgh, where g is the acceleration due to gravity. If the object is let go, it falls and it will strike the ground with a velocity v, its potential energy having been converted into kinetic energy $\frac{1}{2}mv^2$. SOUND energy is kinetic energy of the vibration of air. Chemical energy is the energy released from a chemical system in the course of a reaction. Although all forms of energy are equivalent, not all interconversion processes go with 100% EFFICIENCY (the energy deficit always appears as heat—see THERMODYNAMICS). The SI UNIT of energy is the joule.

ENERGY, US DEPARTMENT OF, created Aug. 4, 1977, to centralize national energy planning at the cabinet level. The new department consolidated activities previously conducted within the Department of the Interior and by the Energy Research and Development Administration, the Federal Energy Administration, and the Federal Power Commission. Ronald Reagan promised during his campaign for the presidency to disband the Department of Energy, which was slated for extinction after he took office in 1981.

ENESCO (Enescu), Georges (1881–1955), Romanian composer and violinist. Strongly influenced by folk music, he is best known for his two Romanian Rhapsodies.

ENEWETAK, Pacific atoll at the NW end of the Ralik Chain of the NW Marshall Islands. It served as a US test site for atomic weapons in the 1940s and 1950s and was declared (1978) uninhabitable for at least 30-50 more years because of radiation levels.

ENGELS, Friedrich (1820–1895), German socialist, philosopher and close associate of Karl MARX. Born into a wealthy German family, he went to England in 1842 as the manager of a family factory and there became interested in SOCIALISM. In 1844 he met Marx, whom he supported both financially and politically. Four years later he and Marx published the influential COMMUNIST MANIFESTO. Engels edited the 2nd and 3rd volumes of Marx's *Capital*, and among other works wrote *Anti-Duehring: Socialism, Utopian and Scientific* (1878) and *The Origin of the Family, Private Property and the State* (1884).

ENGINE, a device for converting stored ENERGY into useful WORK. Most engines in use today are heat engines which convert HEAT into work, though the EFFICIENCY of this process, being governed according to the second law of THERMODYNAMICS, is often very low. Heat engines are commonly classified according to the fuel they use (as in gasoline engine); by whether they burn their fuel internally or externally (see INTERNAL-COMBUSTION ENGINE), or by their mode of action (whether they are reciprocating, rotary or reactive). (See DIESEL ENGINE; GAS TURBINE; JET PROPULSION; STEAM ENGINE; STIRLING ENGINE; TURBINE.)

ENGINEERS, Army Corps of, technical and combatant corps of the US army. It performs civil as well as military construction and maintenance operations on projects such as harbors, waterways, airfields and missile bases. In war it provides combat and supply support.

ENGLAND, largest and most populous part of the UK, covers 50,333sq mi and has a multiracial population of over 46 million. It is bounded on the S by the English Channel, on the N by Scotland, on the W by the

Atlantic Ocean, Wales and the Irish Sea, and on the E by the North Sea. It includes the Isle of Wight and the Scilly Isles, and its coast is much indented. Physical features include the Pennine Chain (Cross Fell 2,930ft) running N from Derbyshire; the Cumbrian Mts containing the country's highest point (Scafell Pike 3,210ft); and numerous lowlands and low hills such as the London basin between the Chiltern Hills and North Downs, the Fens bordering on the Wash and, in the SW, the Cotswold Hills, Exmoor, Dartmoor and Bodmin Moor. Among the largest cities are London, capital of both England and the UK, Birmingham, Manchester, Liverpool, Newcastle, Sheffield, Leeds and Bradford, all centers of industry. Leading industries, some now state-controlled or nationalized, include mining (especially coal), iron and steel, chemicals, and manufacturing of all kinds (including automobiles, ships and aircraft). Agriculture is important, and much food—and industrial raw materials, too—has to be imported. See also GREAT BRITAIN.

ENGLISH, language native to the British Isles, spoken there and in North America and Australasia, also in parts of Africa, in India and throughout many other former British colonies. English is taught as the first foreign language in numerous countries over six continents. It is the foremost international language. Several centuries of British colonial expansion facilitated its dispersal while, given the stability this expansion ultimately afforded, the language's qualities of relative simplicity and flexibility enhanced its chances of taking root and surviving in foreign lands.

English is of the INDO-EUROPEAN LANGUAGE family, its parent tongue being referred to as Proto-Indo-European, and it evolved from West Germanic (as did Dutch, Flemish and Frisian). The first steps in its development may be traced back to the Jute, Saxon and Angle settlement in Britain during the 5th and 6th centuries, a settlement gradually given cohesion by the spread of Christianity, and hence of Latinate influences, which followed St. Augustine's landing in Kent in 597. The language that evolved from this settlement is known as Anglo-Saxon or Old English, of which there were four dialects: Northumbrian, Mercian, West Saxon and Kentish. Of these, West Saxon, the dialect of Wessex in which the period's literature has survived, is referred to as standard Old English. It is the language of such works as BEOWULF and the ANGLO-SAXON CHRONICLE. Incursions by VIKING invaders in the 9th century left their mark on the language in the form of numerous Scandinavian loan words.

The Middle English period begins with the Norman Conquest of 1066 and extends to the 15th century, the death of CHAUCER in 1400 being chosen as a convenient closing point. The language absorbed many French (and thereby also many Latin) influences during the period. Two factors are of key importance: the requirement through the Statute of Pleading (1362) that all court proceedings should be in English, and the fact that Chaucer chose to write his major works not in Latin or French, nor even Italian, but in the East Midlands English dialect then spoken in London.

After 1400, there followed a century of transition in which London speech became established, the language undergoing a process of standardization which was to be aided by the introduction of printing by CAXTON in 1476.

With the RENAISSANCE, a host of Greek and Latinate words were introduced and, amid considerable controversy, the English vocabulary expanded. By Shakespeare's time the language was only a little more inflected than it is today. The King James Bible appeared in 1611 and just under a century and a half later Dr. Johnson's *Dictionary* (1755) was published. (See also DICTIONARY.)

American English dates from the 17th century. It diverges to a degree in spelling, being often more accurate phonetically, and is also idiomatically different. Its influence on the language has been considerable, especially in the sphere of new coinages, among which scientific words predominate.

ENGLISH CHANNEL, an arm of the Atlantic Ocean separating England and France, called *La Manche* by the French. About 300mi long, it varies in width from about 112mi to about 21mi at the Strait of Dover. Plans to construct a tunnel under the channel (proposed in 1874) began in 1974 but were later abandoned. There are frequent crossings by ferries and Hovercraft.

ENGLISH HORN, an alto oboe, somewhat larger than a standard oboe. Its "bell" is a pear-shaped bulb that helps to give the instrument a dark, melancholy tone.

ENGLISH LITERATURE. Early English literature divides into two periods. ANGLO-SAXON literature ends roughly with the Norman Conquest (1066). Poems which survive, such as the epic BEOWULF (8th century), the religious and quasi-mystical *Dream of the Rood*, and the historical narrative *The Battle of Maldon*, remind us both of the rich culture that produced them and of the pre-literary oral traditions that influenced them. The prose ANGLO-SAXON CHRONICLE is a major chronicle of the age of King Alfred. After the Conquest, as the language developed, the literature widened in range and subject manner. *Sir Gawain and the Green Knight* is perhaps the finest Arthurian poem in the 14th century and such poets as GOWER and LANGLAND were notable, but Geoffrey CHAUCER (c1340–1400) is the indisputable genius of the era. He is accessible to modern readers because he wrote in the Midlands dialect upon which modern English is based (see ENGLISH) and because his style and temperament have the timeless quality of all great writers. Modern literature can be said to begin with his work which was the first in English to synthesize successfully a number of widespread European influences. The Middle English period ends by 1476 when CAXTON's press became a decisive factor in completing the standardization of the language. Poetry in the 15th century is dominated by the name of John SKELTON (c1460–1529) although there was a steady production of anonymous lyrics and ballads. Memorable prose of this period includes MALLORY's *Morte d'Arthur* (c1470) and the Paston letters; while the MYSTERY and MORALITY PLAYS presaged the drama.

The continuing political stability after the WARS OF THE ROSES permitted a belated appearance of RENAISSANCE humanism under the TUDORS. In this period PROTESTANTISM was established; the language, like the country, grew prosperous, confident and eclectic; in every genre a rich flair for linguistic experimentation and development of new forms reflected the spirit of adventure of a country that was exploring the globe. Sir Thomas WYATT (1503–1542) and Henry Howard, Earl of Surrey (c1517–1547) introduced Italian literary influences into England, particularly adapting the SONNET, and Surrey's early experiments with blank verse were of major importance to dramatists. As important to the linguistic termperament of the era were Sir Philip SIDNEY's *Arcadia* (1590) and *Defence of Poesie* (1595), both widely known in manuscript before publication. The quintessential Renaissance allegory, uniting moral vision with aesthetic virtues, is Edmund SPENSER's *The Faerie Queene* (1590–96). The specific voice of Puritanism appeared, among other places, in ASCHAM's *The Schoolmaster* (1570). Prose works like LYLY's *Euphues* (1578–80) and Robert Greene's fiction seemed to presage development of the novel, but it was in the

field of drama that the glory of the age was expressed. to entertain and stir an insatiable audience. In one to entertain and stir an insatiable audience. In one generation the theater progressed from tentative efforts such as Sackville and Norton's blank verse tragedy *Gorboduc* (1562) and the anonymous farce *Gammer Gurton's Needle* (1575) to the plays of KYD, MARLOWE, DEKKER, Ben JONSON, MARSTON, and, of course, the consummate artistry of SHAKESPEARE. The impetus given to drama after the building of theaters in the 1570s carried through to the Civil War and the closing of the theaters in 1642, adding such names as BEAUMONT AND FLETCHER, WEBSTER, MIDDLETON, MASSINGER and FORD to the list of major dramatists. It was also the period of such offshoots of theater as the MASQUE. A flowering of Elizabethan and Jacobean prose was reached within the Authorized Version of the BIBLE (1611), but the English genius for discursive prose continued to develop in Robert BURTON's *Anatomy of Melancholy* (1621), the work of Sir Thomas BROWNE (1605–1682), and Thomas HOBBES's *Leviathan* (1651).

The dual trauma of the English Civil War and the Puritan Commonwealth produced a profound shift in sensibility. The diaries of Samuel PEPYS (1644–1703) reflect the social flavor of the Restoration period. In the theater a brief flourish of sophisticated, artificial RESTORATION COMEDY gave way by c1800 to a taste for sentiment and prudery that constrained the English drama until the 20th century, except for the brief resurgence of wit in the plays of SHERIDAN and GOLDSMITH in the late 18th century. The great poet of the Puritan movement was John MILTON (1608–1674), who, in retirement after the Restoration, wrote the incomparable Christian epic *Paradise Lost* (1667), a study of the origin of evil which is Homeric in scope. John DRYDEN (1631–1700) was another pivotal writer of the times. Inheritor and supreme exponent of the ideals of the Renaissance, he produced prose, poetry and drama which looked forward to the tone and ambitions of the succeeding era of Neoclassicism. BUNYAN's *The Pilgrim's Progress* (1678), is perhaps the major achievement of Puritan prose literature.

The first years of the prosperous 18th century were the years of ADDISON and STEELE's suave prose and fashionable periodicals. Alexander POPE (1688–1744) was the most famous and admired poet of his era, subtle in his experimentation, wide-ranging in his wit, irony and compassion, while his friend Jonathan SWIFT

(1667–1745), also a considerable poet, was a master prose-satirist. His *Gulliver's Travels* (1726) can be seen along with fictitious narratives by Daniel DEFOE (1660–1731)—such as *Robinson Crusoe* (1719) and *Moll Flanders* (1722)—as prime simulators of the growth of the novel. Coincidental with the increase in economic and political dominance of the middle classes, the new genre was established with the epistolary novels of RICHARDSON (*Pamela*, 1740) and the satirical novels of FIELDING (*Joseph Andrews*, 1742). Tobias SMOLLETT (1721–1771) and Laurence STERNE (1713–1768) were also among the first professional novelists. Increasingly in the 18th century, prose literature in all forms dominated the taste and outlook of the age, the labors and personality of Samuel JOHNSON (1709–1784) being of major importance along with BOSWELL's *Life of Dr. Johnson* (1791–99), and GIBBON's monumental *History of the Decline and Fall of the Roman Empire* (1776–88). Following upon the Gothic mysteries of Horace WALPOLE (1717–1797) and Mrs. RADCLIFFE (1764–1823), precursors of ROMANTICISM. The novels of Jane AUSTEN (1775–1817) are rooted in the 18th-century standards of moderation and elegance, while they established new complexities of irony, psychology and social observation. Later novelists were to develop the territory which she mapped out and to take as models her achievement in formal and technical skills.

The 19th century began with the impact of the Romantic era in poetry: WORDSWORTH, COLERIDGE, BYRON, SHELLEY and KEATS reflected both German literary and French Revolutionary movements. The novels of Sir Walter SCOTT (1771–1826) are as much in keeping with Romantic restlessness, gusto and individuality of utterance as are the criticism of HAZLITT, LAMB and COLERIDGE and the confessional writings of Thomas DE QUINCEY (1785–1859). The Victorian Age which followed, seemingly more staid, was troubled by the early results of the industrial revolution and the political consequences of expanding imperialism in the post-Napoleonic era. Despite adherence to certain conventions, the mid-century poetry of TENNYSON, BROWNING and ARNOLD is innovative in content as well as style. Thomas MACAULAY and Thomas CARLYLE (1795–1881) satisfied the Victorian taste for heavy and moralizing non-fiction. The controversies instigated by Cardinal John Henry NEWMAN (1801–1890) and Charles DARWIN (1809–1882) raged with much

publicity and rebuttal and reached wide audiences. It was also an age of popular and literary magazines, in which many of the most famous novels first appeared as serials. The great novels of DICKENS, THACKERAY, Emily and Charlotte BRONTË and George ELIOT dominated the period 1830–75 and reflected the major social, political, psychological and historical debates of the country.

Transitional novels by TROLLOPE (1815–1882), MEREDITH (1828–1909) and GISSING (1857–1903) lead to the novels of Thomas HARDY (1840–1928) and American-born Henry JAMES (1843–1916) who in their different ways usher in the modern era. Joseph CONRAD (1857–1924), a Pole who chose to write in English, and E. M. FORSTER (1879–1970) were among those who even before WWI introduced foreign influences into English literature. It was about this time, however, that a split began to occur between "serious" and "popular" literature: the more journalistic fiction of Arnold BENNETT (1867–1931), John GALSWORTHY (1867–1933) and H. G. WELLS (1866–1946), along with imperialistic and conservative prose and poetry by Rudyard KIPLING (1865–1936), Hilaire BELLOC (1870–1953) and G. K. CHESTERTON (1874–1936), were also more widely read. This division has been exacerbated since WWI by the increasing complexity of various schools of "modernism." Symbolism, Expressionism and Vorticism were but three experiments in literature (and the visual arts) of the first decades of the 20th century. James JOYCE (1882–1941), Virginia WOOLF (1882–1941) and D. H. LAWRENCE (1885–1930) came to dominate fiction in the interwar period (1918–1939) while YEATS (1918–1939) and T S. ELIOT (1888–1965) established the new voice of modern poetry. For the first time in 200 years there was a major revival in drama (coinciding with the European revival led by IBSEN, STRINDBERG and CHEKOV), headed by the Irishmen Oscar WILDE (1854–1900) and George Bernard SHAW (1856–1950) in London and J. M. SYNGE (1871–1909), Sean O'CASEY (1884–1964), and Yeats in association with the ABBEY THEATRE in Dublin.

By WWII a new generation of writers had begun to appear. Concern about the tortured politics of Europe was reflected by poets such as W. H. AUDEN (1907–1973) and C. Day LEWIS (1904–1972) and the journalist-novelists Arthur KOESTLER (b. 1905) and George ORWELL (1903–1950). Graham GREENE (b. 1904), Christopher ISHERWOOD (b. 1904) and Evelyn WAUGH

(1903–1966) were among the most interesting novelists of the same generation.

Since the war, the most consistently lively activity in England has been in the theater: John OSBORNE (b. 1929), Harold PINTER (b. 1930), Athol FUGARD (b. 1932) and Tom STOPPARD (b. 1937) have produced striking work. Individual works in other genres have attracted attention. William GOLDING (b. 1911) and Doris Lessing (b. 1919) among novelists, and Philip Larkin (b. 1922) and Seamus Heaney (b. 1937) among poets have been of particular interest. It has also become evident that the critical writings of T. S. ELIOT, William Empson (b. 1906) and F. R. LEAVIS (b. 1895) among others, have established a new age of the prose essay in English literature.

For the literature of the US, see AMERICAN LITERATURE.

ENGLISH SETTER, long-legged sporting dog standing up to 27in high, weighing 56–66lb. Its long, silky coat may be white with black, lemon or liver, or black, white and tan. One of the oldest bird dog breeds, it crouches on the ground when it scents game and creeps up on the birds. Affectionate, it makes a good pet but needs plenty of exercise.

ENGRAVING, various craft and technological techniques for producing blocks or plates from which to print illustrations, banknotes etc.; also, an individual print made by one of these processes. Line engraving refers to preparing a plate by scratching its smooth surface with a highly-tempered steel tool called a burin or graver. If the desired design is left standing high as is common with woodcuts and linocuts, this is known as a relief process. If the ink is transferred to the paper from lines incised into the plate, the surface of the inked plate having been wiped clean, this is known as intaglio. Drypoint and mezzotint are mechanical engraving processes developed from line engraving; other techniques, including AQUATINT, involve chemical ETCHING processes. (See also LITHOGRAPHY.)

ENIWETOK. See ENEWETAK.

ENLIGHTENMENT, The, also known as The Age of Reason or *Aufklärung,* a term applied to the period of European intellectual history centering on the mid-18th century. The empiricist philosophy of LOCKE and scientific optimism following the success of NEWTON'S *Principia* provided men with the confidence to deem reason supreme in all the departments of intellectual enquiry.

ENNIUS, Quintus (239–169 BC), classical Roman poet. His most important work was the *Annales,* a history of Rome beginning with the fall of Troy and ending with his own times, of which only about 600 lines have survived. It was the national poem of Rome until the *Aeneid* of VIRGIL.

ENOCH, Books of, three books describing experiences and visions of the Old Testament patriarch Enoch. The first, complete only in an Ethiopic version, is one of the Jewish PSEUDEPIGRAPHA. It is an important aid to New Testament study. The second is written in Slavonic and the third, which is sometimes anti-Christian in tone, is in Hebrew.

ENSOR, James Sydney, Baron (1860–1949), Belgian painter whose bizarre, sometimes macabre canvases were influenced by BOSCH and BRUEGEL and anticipated SURREALISM. Among his best-known works are *Entry of Christ into Brussels* and *The Temptation of St. Anthony,* both painted in the late 1880s.

ENTENTE (French: understanding), political term for a friendly relation between countries, based on diplomatic agreement rather than formal treaty. The term originated in the 17th century, and has been applied particularly to the relationship between Britain and France, the Entente Cordiale (1904) which in 1907, when it included Russia, became the TRIPLE ENTENTE.

ENTERITIS, INFLAMMATION of the small intestine (see GASTROINTESTINAL TRACT) causing abdominal COLIC and DIARRHEA. It may result from VIRUS infection, certain BACTERIAL DISEASES or FOOD POISONING, which are in general self-limited and mild. The noninfective inflammatory condition known as **Crohn's disease** causes a chronic relapsing regional enteritis, which may result in weight loss, ANEMIA, abdominal mass or VITAMIN deficiency, as well as colic and diarrhea. In bacterial enteritis, ANTIBIOTICS may help, while Crohn's disease is sometimes helped by anti-inflammatory drugs or STEROIDS; SURGERY may also be required, but is often hazardous and may lead to FISTULA formation.

ENTERPRISE, the first nuclear-powered aircraft carrier, commissioned by the US Navy in 1961. Displacing over 75,000 tons, it was the largest warship ever built at the time. Armed with Sea Sparrow missiles, it carries approximately 84 aircraft.

ENTOMOLOGY, the study of INSECTS. In a broader sense the term is sometimes erroneously used to describe studies on other arthropod groups. Entomology is important, not only as an academic discipline, but because insects are among the most important pests and transmitters of disease.

ENTROPY, the name of a quantity in STATISTICAL MECHANICS, THERMODYNAMICS, and INFORMATION THEORY representing, respectively, the degree of disorder in a physical system, the extent to which the ENERGY in a system is available for doing WORK, the distribution of the energy of a system between different modes, or the uncertainty in a given item of knowledge. In thermodynamics the infinitesimal entropy change δQ when a quantity of HEAT δQ is transferred at absolute TEMPERATURE T defined as $\delta S = \delta Q/T$. One way of stating the second law of thermodynamics is to say that in any change in an isolated system, the entropy (S) increases: $\triangle S \geq 0$. This increase in entropy represents the energy that is no longer available for doing work in that system.

ENVER PASHA (1881–1922), also known as Enver Bey, Ottoman leader who organized the Young Turk revolution of 1908 and one of the triumvirate that ruled Turkey from 1913–18. As minister of war he took Turkey into WWI on Germany's side (1914). Edged from power by Mustafa Kemal (see ATATURK), he died leading Turkish Uzbek factions against Russia.

ENVIRONMENT, the surroundings in which animals and plants live. The study of organisms in relation to their environment is called ECOLOGY. Organisms are affected by many different physical factors in their environment, such as temperature, water, gases, light, pressure and also biotic factors such as food resources, competition with other species, predators and disease.

ENVIRONMENTAL PROTECTION AGENCY, US agency established in 1970 to coordinate government action on environmental issues. It absorbed several existing agencies and as well as serving as the public's advocate in pollution cases also coordinates research by state, local government and other groups. Some of the agency's stringent controls on pollution were relaxed by the Reagan administration in 1981.

ENZYMES, PROTEINS that act as catalysts (see CATALYSIS) for the chemical reactions upon which LIFE depends. They are generally specific for either one or a group of related reactions. Enzymes are responsible for the production of all the organic materials present in living CELLS, for providing the mechanisms for energy production and utilization in MUSCLES and in the NERVOUS SYSTEM, and for maintaining the intracellular environment within fine limits. They are frequently organized into subcellular particles which catalyze a whole sequence of chemical events in a manner analogous to a production line. Enzymes are themselves synthesized by other enzymes on templates derived from NUCLEIC ACIDS. An average cell contains about 3,000 different enzymes. In order to function correctly, many enzymes require the assistance of metal IONS or accessory substances known as **coenzymes** which are produced from VITAMINS in the diet. The action of vitamins as coenzymes explains some of the harmful effects of a lack of vitamins in the diet. A majority of enzymes function in a neutral aqueous environment although some require different conditions. For instance, those which digest food in the stomach require an ACID environment. Cells also contain special activators and inhibitors which switch particular enzymes on and off as required. In some cases a substance closely related to the substrate (the substance on which the enzyme acts) will compete for the enzyme and prevent the normal action on the substrate; this is termed **competitive inhibition.** Again, the product of a reaction may inhibit the action of the enzyme so that no more product is produced until its level has dropped to a particular threshold, this being known as FEEDBACK control. Enzymes either synthesize or break down chemical compounds or transform them from one type to another. These differing actions form the basis of the classification of enzymes into oxidoreductases, transferases, hydrolases, lyases, isomerases and synthetases. Enzymes normally work inside living cells but some (e.g., digestive enzymes) are capable of working outside the cell. Enzymes are becoming important items of commerce and are used in "biological" washing powders, food processing and brewing.

EOCENE, the second epoch of the TERTIARY period, lasting from about 55 million to about 37–38 million years ago. (See also GEOLOGY.)

EPÉE, Chales Michel, Abbè de l' (1712–1789), French pioneer in the teaching of mutes and inventor of a sign language enabling them to communicate and receive instruction.

EPHESIANS, Epistle to the, New Testament book attributed to the apostle Paul, closely resembling COLOSSIANS. Probably written during Paul's first imprisonment in Rome c60 AD, its main theme is the universality and unity of the church, Jewish and Gentile Christians alike being saved in Christ.

EPIC, long narrative poem concerned with heroism, either of individuals or of a people. GILGAMESH, the earliest known epic, dates from c2000 BC, but epics were considered the highest literary form until at least the 14th century. Many, such as the ODYSSEY and ILIAD, and BEOWULF, must have existed as oral tradition before being written down; the KALEVALA was only collated in the 19th century. Others, such as VIRGIL's *Aeneid*, SPENSER's *Faerie Queene* and MILTON's *Paradise Lost*, draw on traditional material but are very much individual works. Many epics, such as the NIBELUNGENLIED, are nationalistic in flavor, blending actual history with myth and fable. (See also, for example, ARTHURIAN LEGENDS; CHANSON DE GESTE; CHANSON DE ROLAND; SAGA.)

EPICTETUS (c55–135 AD), Greek Stoic philosopher. An educated Roman slave, after he was freed he taught philosophy, but was expelled with other philosophers by Emperor Domitian in 90 AD, moving to Nicopolis in Greece. His teachings, recorded by his pupil ARRIAN, indicate that the key to conduct is self-control and acceptance of the natural order—itself the will of God. (See also STOICISM.)

EPIC THEATER, form of theater developed in the 1920s and 1930s by PISCATOR and BRECHT, emphasizing the narrative and political aspect of staged events. Brecht's theories stressed the arousal of a critical response by alienating the spectator from the staged action.

EPICUREANISM, philosophy propounded by EPICURUS in the 4th century BC. It regarded the purpose of human life as the attainment of pleasure, by which was meant contentment and peace of mind in a frugal life. The school was viciously attacked, particularly by Christians; and this has debased the name into merely signifying sensual hedonism.

EPICURUS (c341–270 BC), Athenian philosopher, the author of Epicureanism. Reviving the ATOMISM of DEMOCRITUS, he preached a materialist, sensationalist philosophy which emphasized the positive things in life and remained popular for more than 600 years.

EPIDEMIC, the occurrence of a disease in a geographically localized population over a limited period of time; it usually refers to INFECTIOUS DISEASE which spreads from case to case or by carriers. Epidemics arise from importation of infection, after environmental changes favoring infectious organisms or due to altered host susceptibility. A **pandemic** is an epidemic of very large or world-wide proportions. Infectious disease is said to be **endemic** in an area if cases are continually occurring there. Travel through endemic areas may lead to epidemics in nonendemic areas.

EPIDEMIOLOGY, the study of the factors contributing to the occurrence and distribution of a disease, injury or other physiologic debilitation prevalent within a human population. Epidemiology uses statistical and other methods to discover causative agents, determine the elements affecting rate of incidence and degree of severity, and establish the means of control.

EPIGRAM, terse and pointed saying in either prose or verse, often in couplet form. It is named for Greek monumental inscriptions, but the modern form was established by the Romans, particularly CATULLUS and MARTIAL. COLERIDGE defined it thus:

What is an epigram? A dwarfish whole.
Its body brevity, and wit its soul.

EPILEPSY, the "sacred disease" of HIPPOCRATES, a chronic disease of the BRAIN, characterized by susceptibility to CONVULSIONS or other transient disorders of NERVOUS-SYSTEM function and due to abnormal electrical activity within the cerebral cortex. There are many types, of which four are common. **Grand mal** convulsions involve rhythmic jerking and rigidity of the limbs, associated with loss of consciousness, urinary incontinence, transient cessation of breathing and sometimes CYANOSIS, foaming at the mouth and tongue biting. **Petit mal** is largely a disorder of children in which very brief episodes of absence or vacancy occur, when the child is unaware of the surroundings, and is associated with a characteristic ELECTROENCEPHALOGRAPH disturbance. In **focal or Jacksonian epilepsy**, rhythmic movements start in one limb, progress to involve others and may lead to a grand mal convulsion. **Temporal lobe or psychomotor epilepsy** is often characterized by abnormal visceral sensations, unusual smells, visual distortion or memory disorder, and may or may not be followed by unconsciousness. **Status epilepticus** is when attacks of any sort occur repetitively without consciousness being regained in between; it requires emergency treatment.

Epilepsy may be either primary due to an inborn tendency, often appearing in early life, or it may be symptomatic of brain disorders such as those following trauma or brain SURGERY, ENCEPHALITIS, cerebral ABSCESS, TUMOR, or vascular disease. The ELECTROENCEPHALOGRAPH is the cornerstone of diagnosis in epilepsy, helping to confirm its presence and localize its origin, and suggesting whether there is a structural cause. If epilepsy is secondary, the cause may respond to treatment such as surgery, but all cases require anticonvulsant

EQUATION 431

medication in the long term. Phenytoin (Dilantin), Phenobarbitone (see BARBITURATES), ethosuccimide, carbamazepine, diazepam and related compounds are important anticonvulsants, suitable for different types. DIETARY FOOD (ketogenic diet) may be effective in some cases.

EPIPHANY (from Greek *epiphania*, manifestation), feast of the CHURCH YEAR held on Jan. 6. Originating in the 3rd century in the Eastern Church, where it commemorates Christ's baptism, it came into the Western Church in the 4th century and there celebrates the manifestation of Christ to the gentiles, represented by the MAGI.

EPIPHYTE, or **airplant**, a plant that grows on another but which obtains no nourishment from it. Various LICHENS, MOSSES, FERNS and ORCHIDS are epiphytes, particularly on trees. Epiphytes thrive in warm, wet climates.

EPISCOPAL CHURCH, Protestant, US denomination that formed itself from the remnants of the Church of England in the colonies after the Revolutionary War, and was finally given a constitution at a convention in Philadelphia in 1789. It now has 100 dioceses and a membership of around 3,500,000. Its administrative body is the Executive Council in New York, and it is governed by the triennial General Convention, composed of a House of Bishops and a House of Clerical and Lay Deputies. It is part of the Anglican Communion, and in recent years has been prominent in the ecumenical movement and in social action among minority groups.

EPISTEMOLOGY, from the Greek *episteme* (knowledge), the branch of philosophy that inquires about the sources of human knowledge, its possible limits, and to what extent it can be certain or only probable. Epistemology is connected with other branches of philosophy, such as psychology and logic.

EPITHELIUM, surface tissue covering an organ or structure. Examples include skin and the mucous membranes of the LUNGS, gut and urinary tract. A protective layer specialized for water resistance or absorption, depending on site, it usually shows a high cell-turnover rate.

E PLURIBUS UNUM ("out of many, one"), Latin motto referring to the unification of the original 13 American colonies. Chosen for the Continental Congress by John Adams, Franklin and Jefferson, it is now inscribed on the great seal of the US and on many US coins.

EPSTEIN, Sir Jacob (1880–1959),

American-born sculptor, living in London, whose work often caused controversy. His early sculptures were influenced by African sculpture, Constantin BRANCUSI and VORTICISM, but after 1915 he turned, in more conventional style, to religious subjects and portraiture. His works include *Rock Drill* (1913) and *Ecce Homo* (1935).

EQUAL EMPLOYMENT OPPORTUNITY COMMISSION. See FAIR EMPLOYMENT PRACTICES.

EQUALITY, in mathematics, the relation between two or more expressions which represent the same thing, represented by the symbol "=". Thus $3 + 4 = 7$ is an equality. The expressions need not represent numbers but may denote SETS (see SETS, THEORY OF), GROUPS or any other kind of mathematical object.

EQUAL RIGHTS AMENDMENT (ERA), a proposed Constitutional amendment prohibiting the denial or abridgment of a person's Constitutional rights because of sex. First introduced in Congress in 1923, it finally passed in 1972. Ratification by the states proceeded expeditiously at first but then faltered; the deadline for ratification was extended in 1978 to 1982. By fall 1981, 35 states out of the necessary 38 had ratified the amendment. (See also WOMEN'S RIGHTS.)

EQUATION, a statement of equality. Should this statement involve a VARIABLE it will, unless it is an invalid equation, be true for one or more values of that variable, though those values need not be expressible in terms of REAL NUMBERS: $x^2 + 2 = 0$ has two imaginary (see IMAGINARY NUMBERS) roots, $+ \sqrt{-2}$ and $- \sqrt{-2}$.

Linear equations are those in which no variable term is raised to a POWER higher than 1. Solution of linear equations in one variable is simple. Consider the equation $x + 3 = 7$. The equation will still be true if we add or subtract equal numbers from each side:

$$x + 3 = 7,$$
$$x + 3 - 3 = 7 - 3$$
$$\text{and } x = 4.$$

Linear equations are so called because, if considered as the equation of a curve (see ANALYTIC GEOMETRY), they can be plotted as a straight line (see also FUNCTION).

Quadratic equations are those in a single variable which appears to the power 2, but not higher. A quadratic equation always has two roots (see ROOTS OF AN EQUATION) though these roots may be equal.

Cubic equations are those in a single variable which appears to the power 3, but not higher. Cubic equations always have three roots, though two or all three of these may be equal.

Degree of an equation. Linear, quadratic and cubic equations are said to be of the 1st, 2nd and 3rd degrees respectively. More generally, the degree of an equation is defined as the SUM of the EXPONENTS of the variables in the highest-power term of the equation. In $ax^5 + bx^3y^3 + cx^2y^5 = 0$, the sums of the exponents of each term are, respectively, 5, 6 and 7; hence cx^2y^5 is the highest-power term, and the equation is of the 7th degree.

Radical equations are those in which ROOTS of the variables appear: e.g., a $\sqrt[p]{x}$ + b $\sqrt[p]{x}$ + c= 0. Radical equations can always be simply converted into equations of the nth order, where $n = 1,2,3 \ldots$, by raising both sides of the equation to a power, repeating the process where necessary.

Simultaneous equations. A single equation in two or more variables is generally insoluble. However, if there are as many equations as there are variables, it is possible to solve for each variable. Consider

$$2x + xy + 3 = 0 \qquad (1)$$

and
$$x + 2xy = 0. \qquad (2)$$

Multiplying equation 1 by 2 we have
$$4x + 2xy + 6 = 0 \qquad (3)$$
and, subtracting equation 2 from this,

$$3x + 6 = 0.$$

Hence
$$x = -2.$$

Substituting this value into equation (1) we find the value $y = -\frac{1}{2}$. More complicated simultaneous equations can be solved in the same way.

EQUATOR, an imaginary line equal to the circumference of the earth drawn about the earth such that all points on it are equidistant from the N and S poles (see NORTH POLE; SOUTH POLE). All points on it have a latitude of 0° and it is the longest of the parallels of latitude. (See also CELESTIAL SPHERE; LATTITUDE and LONGITUDE.)

Official name: Republic of Equatorial Guinea
Capital Malabo, on Bioko
Area: 10,830sq mi

Population: c340,000
Languages: Spanish, African languages
Religions: Roman Catholicism, Animism
Monetary unit(s): 1 Ekuele = 100 centimos

EQUATORIAL GUINEA, the least populated and only Spanish-speaking black African country, is a tiny republic on the W coast of Africa. It consists of two provinces: the mainland territory of Rio Muni (bordered by Cameroon and Gabon and the Gulf of Guinea); and the island of BIOKO, which lies in the Gulf of Guinea about 100mi from Rio Muni.

People. Main ethnic groups are the Fang, in Rio Muni, and the Bubi, in Bioko. Spanish is the official language, but tribal languages and a form of pidgin English are widely spoken.

Economy. Agriculture, including forestry, is the mainstay of the economy, engaging most of the labor force. Cocoa is the main export, followed by coffee, wood, and bananas. Despite the richness of its soil and its potential natural resources, the country is exceedingly poor.

History. In 1778 Portugal gave Spain the island now called Bioko. In 1885 Spain formally obtained Rio Muni. Independence was granted in 1968; Macías Nguema (president 1968–79) proclaimed himself life president in 1975. His erratic leadership and internal unrest brought the country close to economic ruin. In 1979 the military seized power and Macías Nguema was subsequently executed.

EQUINOXES, (1) The two times each year when day and night are of equal length. The spring or **vernal equinox** occurs in March, the **autumnal equinox** in September. (2) The two intersections of the ECLIPCTIC and equator (see CELESTIAL SPHERE). The vernal equinox is in PISCES (see also First Point of ARIES), the autumnal between VIRGO and LEO.

EQUITY, legal term for the application of certain principles by the judiciary to prevent injustice that would result from strict application of the law. In fact, however, in English and US COMMON LAW these principles have hardened into rules of law and have been incorporated into the system. They originated in the judicial remedies of the English Court of CHANCERY, which introduced and shaped such essential legal forms as the TRUST, EASEMENT and MORTGAGE.

ERA. See EQUAL RIGHTS AMENDMENT.

ERA OF GOOD FEELING, a newspaper's term for the two administrations of President James Monroe, 1817–25. Coined after Monroe's friendly reception by Boston Federalists and the virtual disappearance of the Federalist party nationally, it was belied by the ill feeling and discord in the Republican administration among Monroe's potential successors.

ERASISTRATUS (3rd century BC), Greek physician of the ALEXANDRIAN SCHOOL who is credited with the foundation of PHYSIOLOGY as a separate discipline.

ERASMUS, Desiderius (c1466–1536), Dutch Roman Catholic humanist and advocate of church and social reform. The illegitimate son of a priest, he was forced by his guardians to enter a monastery and was ordained in 1492. Studies in Paris imbued him with a deep dislike of Scholastic theology, and on a visit to England in 1499 he met and was influenced by the humanists John COLET and Thomas MORE. He published *The Christian Soldier's Handbook* (1503), with an emphasis on spiritual simplicity. *In Praise of Folly* (1509) is a light, witty satire on Church corruptions, paving the way for the REFORMATION. The foremost scholar of his time, Erasmus produced the first critical edition of the Greek New Testament (1516) and edited the works of the Fathers. Although a moderate reformer, he called for religious peace, and opposed LUTHER in his *Diatribe on Free Will* (1524), which drew a crushing reply from Luther. Erasmus died embittered by the Reformation controversies, accepted by neither side.

ERASTIANISM, doctrine that the state should have complete control over the affairs of the Church. It is named for ERASTUS who, in fact, believed that only a Christian state could administer church discipline.

ERASTUS, Thomas (1524–1583), Swiss physician for whom ERASTIANISM was named, although he never subscribed to it. An adherent of ZWINGLI, he clashed with the Calvinists, particularly over the practice of excommunication, which he opposed in his *Explicatio gravissimae quaestionis* (1589).

EREBUS, Mount, active volcano on James Ross Island in Antarctica, around 12,450ft high. It has three cones, only one of which is active.

ERGOT, disease of GRASSES and SEDGES caused by fungal species of the genus *Claviceps*. Also, the masses of dormant mycelia (sclerotia) formed in the flower heads of the host plant. Ergots contain toxic ALKALOIDS which if eaten by animals or man, can cause serious poisoning (ergotism or St. Anthony's fire).

ERHARD, Ludwig (1897–1977), West German economist and political leader. Forced out of academic life by the Nazis in 1942, he was appointed to various posts by the occupying powers in 1945–49. In 1949 he became economics minister under Konrad ADENAUER, and in this post he was the prime architect of West Germany's post-WWII revival. He succeeded Adenauer as chancellor in 1963, but was removed from the chancellorship and party leadership in 1966 after the economy began to decline.

ERICSON, Leif (flourished 999–1002 AD), Norse explorer, son of ERIC THE RED. On a voyage from Greenland in 1000 AD, he discovered some part of the North American coast (called VINLAND in old Norse sagas). Modern scholars do not agree on the location of Vinland, but excavation at a Norse site in Newfoundland in the 1960s lends credence to the story.

ERIC THE RED (10th century AD), Norse chieftain and discoverer of Greenland. He settled in Iceland with his exiled father, but was banished for manslaughter about 980. Eric sailed W and discovered Greenland, then returned to Iceland where he organized a voyage about 985 to colonize Greenland. He founded settlements near present-day Julianehaab and Osterbygd, which may have survived for as long as 500 years.

ERIE, Battle of Lake, major naval engagement in the WAR OF 1812. The US forces, led by Commodore Oliver Hazard PERRY, defeated the British at Put-in-Bay, Ohio, Sept. 10, 1813. The victory gave the US control of Lake Erie and the NE.

ERIE, Lake, one of the five GREAT LAKES of North America, bordered by N.Y., Pa., Ohio, Mich. and Ontario, Canada. Named for the ERIE INDIANS, it is the shallowest and fourth-largest (9,910sq mi) of the Great Lakes. Erie is icebound much of the year and is heavily polluted by waste from industry and large cities. Some of its chief ports are Buffalo, N.Y., Erie, Pa., Cleveland and Toledo, Ohio. The US–Canadian boundary passes through the center of the lake. (See also ST. LAWRENCE SEAWAY.)

ERIE CANAL, historic artificial waterway in the US, which once connected Buffalo, N.Y., on Lake Erie with Albany, N.Y., on the Hudson R. The NEW YORK STATE BARGE CANAL now follows part of the old Erie Canal route, which was completed in 1825 as a result of the political support of N.Y. Governor DeWitt CLINTON. The canal, originally 365mi long, stimulated the growth and financial development of New York and many Midwestern cities.

ERIGENA, John Scotus (c810–877), Irish theologian and philosopher, who taught at Paris, probably the most advanced thinker of his time. He attempted to combine

Christian theology and NEOPLATONISM.

ERIKSON, Eric Homburger (1902–   ),
German-born US psychoanalyst who
defined eight stages, each characterized by
a specific psychological conflict, in the
development of the EGO from infancy to old
age. He studied also the IDENTITY,
introducing the concept of the identity
crisis.

ERITREA, province of N Ethiopia, on the
W coast of the Red Sea. Eritrea is populated
by many ethnic groups, with diverse
socio-cultural systems. Less than 5% of this
hot, dry, mountainous region is cultivated.
The capital, Asmara, produces some food
products, textiles and hide. Roads, a
railroad and air service link the province
with the Sudan and the rest of Ethiopia.
Eritrea became an Italian colony in 1890
and an Ethiopian province in 1962. Since
then sporadic warfare has been carried on
by rebels to gain independence from
Ethiopia.

ERIVAN. See YEREVAN.

ERMINE, term for any WEASEL which turns
white in winter. In the Middle Ages ermine
fur was used only by royalty; it was later
associated with high-court judges. Ermine
fur is obtained from the Russian STOAT and
several species of North American weasel.

ERNST, Max (1891–1976), German-born
artist, leader of the DADA and SURREALISM
movements in Paris. Foremost among the
expressive techniques that Ernst developed
were COLLAGE and *frottage* (rubbing on
paper placed over textured surfaces). He
also painted in oil and produced graphics
and sculpture, revealing in all genres an
exceptionally adventurous imagination.

EROS, an ASTEROID measuring roughly
$35 \times 16 \times 8$km discovered in 1898 by G.
Witt. Eros' eccentric orbit brings it close to
earth every seven years, sometimes within
22 million km. Its orbital period is 643 days.

EROSION, the wearing away of the earth's
surface by natural agents. Running water
constitutes the most effective eroding agent,
the process being accelerated by the
transportation of particles eroded or
weathered farther upstream: it is these that
are primarily responsible for further
erosion. GROUNDWATER may cause erosion
by dissolving certain minerals in the rock
(see also KARST). OCEAN WAVES and
especially the debris that they carry may
substantially erode coastlines. GLACIERS are
extremely important eroding agents, eroded
material becoming embedded in the ice and
acting as further abrasives (see ABRASION).
Many common landscape features are the
results of glacial erosion (e.g., DRUMLINS,
FJORDS). Rocks exposed to the atmosphere

undergo **weathering**: mechanical weathering usually results from temperature
changes (e.g., in **exfoliation**, the cracking
off of thin sheets of rock due to effects of
"unloading"; chemical weathering results
from chemical changes brought about by,
for example, substances dissolved in RAIN
water. Wind erosion may be important in
dry, sandy areas. (See also SOIL EROSION.)

ERTEGUN, Ahmet (1923–   ), Turkish-
born US music producer who founded
Atlantic Records (1947), which pioneered
in the recording of black popular music for
the mass market. He signed such stars as
Ray CHARLES, Aretha FRANKLIN, the BEE
GEES and the ROLLING STONES before merging
his company with Warner Brothers (1967).

ERVIN, Samuel James, Jr. (1896–   ),
US lawyer and public official. After serving
in the US House and on the superior and
supreme courts of North Carolina, Ervin
was a US Senator 1954–75. The Senate's
leading authority on the Constitution, he
headed the committee investigating the
Watergate Affair. He fought President
Nixon's use of executive privilege to
withhold evidence and testimony, and
enlivened the hearings with humor and
quotations from the Bible.

ERVING, Julius "Dr J" (1950–   ), US
basketball player. He revolutionized the
slamming, dunking style with his springing,
twisting drives. He gave the fledgling ABA
credibility when he signed with the Virginia
Squires and subsequently played with the
New York Nets and the Philadelphia 76'ers
in the NBA.

ERYSIPELAS, or St. Anthony's fire, a SKIN
infection, usually affecting the face, caused
by certain types of STREPTOCOCCUS. It is
common in infancy and middle age.
ERYTHEMA and swelling spread with a clear
margin and cause blistering. It is a short
illness with FEVER; if it affects the trunk it
may however cause prostration and can
prove fatal. PENICILLIN is the ANTIBIOTIC of
choice.

ESCHATOLOGY, the study of the "last
things." A universal theme in religion,
especially Christianity and Judaism,
eschatology deals with the meaning of
history and the final destiny of the world,
mankind and the individual. Old Testament
eschatology centers on the expected
MESSIAH. Christian eschatology includes the
doctrines of death, RESURRECTION, HEAVEN,
HELL, the SECOND COMING of Christ and the
LAST JUDGMENT (see also MILLENNIUM). The
benefits of the "age to come" are in part
realized now in the Church (see KINGDOM OF
GOD).

ESCOFFIER, Georges-Auguste (1846–

1935), world-famous French chef, director of the Carlton and Savoy Hotel kitchens (London), and author of many cookbooks, including *Ma Cuisine* (1924). He was awarded the *Légion d'Honneur* (1920) for his culinary achievements.

ESCORIAL, monastery and palace in central Spain, 26mi NW of Madrid. One of the most magnificent buildings in Europe, it was built (1563–84) by PHILIP II and houses a church, palace, college, library and a mausoleum in which many Spanish kings are buried. Its famous art collection contains works by VELÁSQUEZ, EL GRECO and TINTORETTO, among others.

ESCU, Nicolae (1918–   ), president of Romania from 1967. First elected a full member of the Romanian Communist Party central committee in 1948, he became head of the committee in 1965. As president, he instigated a policy of independence within the Soviet bloc.

ESDRAS, the Latin form of EZRA, a Jewish priest often called the "second Moses." Esdras is the name given to four Old Testament books, two in the Jewish canon (Ezra and Nehemiah) and two in the Protestant APOCRYPHA (1 and 2 Esdras, called 3 and 4 Esdras in the Vulgate). (See also PSEUDEPIGRAPHA.)

ESENIN, Sergei (1895–1925), Russian poet. Born to a peasant family, he celebrated village life in lyric verse infused with religious and folk themes. He welcomed the Russian revolution, but became disillusioned and went abroad. Married briefly to Isadora DUNCAN, he committed suicide in 1925.

ESHKOL, Levi (1895–1969), Israeli political leader and prime minister, 1963–69. He emigrated from Russia to Palestine (1914), helped found one of the first *kibbutzim* (1920) and *Histadrut* (the labor federation). He succeeded BEN-GURION as prime minister, unified the labor parties in Israel to gain a majority in the KNESSET and led the country in the SIX-DAY WAR (1967).

ESKIMO, a Mongoloid race native to the Arctic coasts of Greenland, North America and NE Asia, believed to have crossed the Bering Strait from Asia in about 2000 BC. Considering their widespread distribution, the Eskimos, who speak dialects of the Eskimo-ALEUT language family and today number some 70,000, have preserved their cultural identity to a remarkable degree. Although the white man's influence has been important in education and medical welfare and in the establishment of cooperatives, the Eskimos have only intermarried with white settlers, to any

significant extent, on Greenland. Many still live by hunting and fishing, using traditional skills to exploit the unyielding Arctic environment. Seals, fish, walrus and whales are hunted for food, fuel and clothing. Travel on land is by DOG-SLED and on the water by KAYAK or *umiak*, a skin boat. During hunting expeditions, temporary IGLOO shelters are sometimes built, but the basic home, in which the Eskimos live in small communal groups, is made of sod, driftwood and stone. Tents of hide or sealskin are used in the summer. The traditional Eskimo religion draws heavily on a rich folklore. On Greenland, many Eskimos are Christian. SHAMANISM is also practiced.

ESOPHAGUS, the thin tube leading from the PHARYNX to the STOMACH. Food passes down it as a bolus by gravity and PERISTALSIS. Its diseases include reflux esophagitis (HEARTBURN), ULCER, stricture and CANCER.

ESP, or **Extrasensory Perception,** perception other than by the recognized SENSES of an event or object; and, by extension, those powers of the mind (such as **telekinesis,** the moving of distant objects by the exercise of willpower) that cannot be scientifically evaluated. The best known and most researched area of ESP is **telepathy,** the ability of two or more individuals to communicate without sensory contact: though laboratory tests (see PARAPSYCHOLOGY) have been inconclusive, it seems probable that telepathic communication between individuals can exist. Another important area of ESP is **precognition,** the prior knowledge of an event: again, despite a mass of circumstantial evidence, laboratory tests have been inconclusive. The term **clairvoyance** is sometimes used for ESP.

ESPERANTO, artificial language created by Dr. L. L. ZAMENHOF of Poland to enable people of different linguistic backgrounds to communicate more easily and with less misunderstanding. Consisting of "root words" derived from Latin, Greek and the Romance and Germanic languages, Esperanto is easy to learn and has enjoyed more popularity since its introduction in 1887 than other artificial "universal" languages such as Volpük and Interlingua. Probably around 8 million people speak Esperanto. (See also BASIC ENGLISH.)

ESPIONAGE, clandestine attempt to gather confidential information, usually of a political, military or industrial nature. Espionage is an ancient practice; it is mentioned in the Bible and in the *Iliad*. Espionage activities are primarily carried on by individual nations to gain data on other nations, although industrial espionage is becoming widespread. Undercover espionage may be severely penalized; although espionage is not illegal under international law, every country has laws against it. (See also CENTRAL INTELLIGENCE AGENCY; INTELLIGENCE SERVICE; NATIONAL SECURITY COUNCIL; OFFICE OF STRATEGIC SERVICES.)

ESSEN, city in West Germany, North Rhine-Westphalia state. Originally the site of a convent, Essen was the home of German industrialist Friedrich KRUPP and is now the largest industrial center in the RUHR coal field, producing iron, steel, chemicals and glass. Pop 652,500.

ESSENCE, in philosophy, a term referring to the permanent actuality of a thing, the that-by-which it can be recognized, whatever its outward appearance. Different philosophers have used the term with various detailed significations; LOCKE, for instance, distinguished a thing's real essence, the what-it-is-in-itself, from its nominal essence, the what-it-appears-to-be, the name men give it.

ESSENES, ascetic sect which flourished in Palestine from about 200 BC to about 100 AD. Gathered in small monastic communities, the Essenes held property in common and observed the law of Moses strictly. The DEAD SEA SCROLLS may have been written by a community of Essenes.

ESSEX, Robert Devereux, 2nd Earl of (1567–1601), a favorite of Queen ELIZABETH I. He acquired some fame in European military campaigns and was knighted in 1589 and made lord lieutenant of Ireland in 1599, a post he lost by failing to crush the Earl of Tyrone's rebellion. Unfailingly ambitious for power, he later attempted a coup to establish his own party at court, was defeated and then executed.

ESSEX JUNTO, name of a group of US New England Federalist property owners who supported Alexander HAMILTON and earlier had opposed Mass. radicals in the American Revolution. They were regarded as traitors by many Americans.

EST, self-improvement system developed by Werner Erhard in 1971 and promulgated in Erhard Seminars Training (whence the acronym "est"). In the lengthy training sessions (often lasting 18 hours), some 200 persons subject themselves to the authority of a "trainer," who attempts to modify their thinking patterns. Although est has been enormously popular (and lucrative), outsiders are critical of its semimystical jargon and demeaning techniques.

ESTAING, Jean Baptiste Charles Henri Hector, Compte d' (1729–1794), French admiral, commander of a French fleet which assisted the Americans in the REVOLUTIONARY WAR. In 1779 he took part with General Benjamin LINCOLN in the abortive attack on Savannah.

ESTERS, organic compounds formed by CONDENSATION, of an ACID (organic or inorganic) with an ALCOHOL, water being eliminated. This reaction esterification, is the reverse of HYDROLYSIS. Many esters occur naturally: those of low molecular weight have fruity odors and are used in flavorings, perfumes and as solvents; those of higher molecular weight are FATS and WAXES.

ESTHER, Old Testament book. It tells of Esther, formerly named Hadassah, a Jewess, queen of the Persian King Ahasuerus (probably XERXES I) who prevented the king's favorite, Haman, from massacring all Persian Jews. Instead the Jews' enemies were slain. The story is the origin of the feast of PURIM.

ESTONIA, or Estonian Soviet Socialist Republic, constituent republic of the USSR, S of the Gulf of Finland and E of the Baltic Sea. The largest cities are Tallin, the capital, Tartu and Pärnu. A third of the land, which consists of plains and low plateaus, is forested. The climate is temperate. Estonians are ethnically and linguistically related to the Finns. More than half the population is urban, although agriculture, especially dairy farming, is the chief industry. Other important industries are shipbuilding, electrical engineering, cement, fertilizers and textiles. Ruled at various times by the Danes, the TEUTONIC KNIGHTS, the Swedes and the Russians, Estonia became independent in 1918. Its annexation by the USSR in 1940 along with that of LATVIA and LITHUANIA, is not recognized by the US. (See USSR.)

ESTROGENS, female sex HORMONES concerned with the development of secondary sexual characteristics and maturation of reproductive organs. They are under the control of pituitary-gland GONADOTROPHINS and their amount varies before and after MENSTRUATION and in PREGNANCY. After the menopause, their production decreases. Many pills used for CONTRACEPTION contain estrogen, as do some preparations given to menopausal women. Their administration may lead to venous THROMBOSIS, and some other diseases.

ETCHING, an ENGRAVING technique in which acid is used to "bite" lines into a metal plate which is then printed, usually intaglio. The plate, usually copper or zinc, is first coated with a resin "ground" through which the design is drawn with a needle. Only the exposed metal is etched away. Different line thicknesses can be obtained by selective stopping out and repeated exposure to the acid. (See also AQUATINT.)

ETHANOL, (C_2H_5OH), or ethyl alcohol, also known as grain alcohol; the best-known ALCOHOL; a colorless, inflammable, volatile, toxic liquid, the active constituent of ALCOHOLIC BEVERAGES. Of immense industrial importance, ethanol is used as a solvent, in ANTIFREEZE, as an ANTISEPTIC and in much chemical synthesis. Its production is controlled by law, and it is heavily taxed unless made unfit for drinking by adulteration (denatured alcohol); see METHANOL. Most industrial ethanol is the azeotropic mixture containing 5% water. It is made by FERMENTATION of sugars or by catalytic hydration of ETHYLENE. MW 46.1 mp –112°C, bp 78°C. (See also DISTILLED LIQUOR.)

ETHELRED THE UNREADY (968?–1016), king of England, 978–1016. His name refers to his lack of sound counsel. He succeeded his brother EDWARD THE MARTYR, whom he possibly murdered. Danish power spread in England during his reign and he paid DANEGELD to the Danes. Ethelred fled when the Danes ruled England, 1013–14, and then negotiated his restoration in a pact with his subjects.

ETHER, a hypothetical medium postulated by late 19th-century physicists in order to explain how LIGHT could be propagated as a wave motion through otherwise empty space. Light was thus thought of as a mechanical WAVE MOTION in the ether. The whole theory was discredited following the failure of the MICHELSON-MORLEY EXPERIMENT to detect any motion of the earth relative to the supposed stationary ether.

ETHEREGE, Sir George (1634?–1691), English dramatist, an important writer of RESTORATION COMEDY, who influenced both CONGREVE and WYCHERLEY. His three plays are *The Comical Revenge* (1664), *She Wou'd if She Cou'd* (1668) and *The Man of Mode* (1676).

ETHICAL CULTURE, movement based on the belief that ethical tenets are not necessarily dependent on philosophical or religious dogma. Ethical Culture has undertaken programs of social welfare, education and race relations. The movement was founded by Felix ADLER in 1876 in New York City and has now spread throughout the world.

ETHICS, principles or moral values of a person or a group of people which guide their actions and behavior. The term comes from the Greek word *ethos* which in the plural means character.

Ethical actions may be approved of in that they are "good," "desirable," "right" or "obligatory," or disapproved of because they are "bad," "wrong," "undesirable" or "evil." In philosophy ethics is the study of moral principles. A traditional philosophical question is whether right and wrong are inherent in the nature of things and therefore "absolute," or mere conventions and thus "relative" to time and place. Some recent thinkers claim that an ethical judgment, such as "Lying is bad," can be neither true nor false but only an expression of the speaker's feelings. See PLATO. ARISTOTLE; SPINOZA; KANT; MILL; MOORE. and other main philosophers, and doctrines such as UTILITARIANISM.

Official name: Ethiopia
Capital: Addis Ababa
Area: 471,799sq mi
Population: c32,574,000
Language: Amharic, many tribal languages and dialects
Religions: Christian (Ethiopian Orthodox Church), Muslim
Monetary unit(s): 1 Birr = 100 cents

ETHIOPIA, East African state lying between Sudan and the Red Sea, with Kenya and Somalia to the S and E, formerly known as Abyssinia. It consists basically of mountainous W and E highlands divided by the GREAT RIFT VALLEY. In the center of the W highlands, or Abyssian Plateau, is the capital Addis Ababa, 8,000ft above sea level. Spectacular river gorges including that of the Abbai R (or Blue Nile) which runs from Lake Tana, cut through the Plateau. Ras Dashan in the N is Ethiopia's highest peak (15,158ft). In the SE is the great plain of the Ogaden and the Haud. Average highland rainfall is 40in, but overall rainfall varies from 80in in the S and W to 4in on the Red Sea Coast. The lowlands are tropical.

People. The Ethiopians comprise many linguistic, cultural and racial groups. The Galla are the largest single group (33% of the population) but the Amhara and the Tigre (together 37%) have been historically and politically the most important peoples. Other significant groups are the Walamo, the Somali and the Gurage. Although education is expanding, only a small minority is literate. The majority of the population is concentrated in the fertile high-rainfall area of the highlands. About a tenth of the population is town-dwelling and the chief towns are Addis Ababa, Asmara, Dire Dawa and Harar.

Economy. In the late 1970s renewed drought severely affected the Ethiopian economy, which is largely dependent on agriculture and livestock. Coffee is the most important export, followed by skins and hides. Imports exceed exports, and manufacturing activity is limited. A deposit of natural gas has been found, but a general lack of natural resources has hampered industrialization. There is some gold and platinum, and iron, potash and copper, but large mineral deposits have not been discovered. All agricultural land was nationalized in 1975. Smallholdings by individuals are allowed, and state farms are being encouraged.

History. Ethiopia is one of the most ancient kingdoms of the world. Former kings claimed descent from the son of King Solomon and the Queen of Sheba. The kingdom of Aksum, prominent from the 1st to the 8th century, was converted to Coptic Christianity in the 4th century. In medieval times Ethiopia was isolated and was thought to be the realm of PRESTER JOHN. Frequent Muslim invasions and internal feuds for long undermined Ethiopian power but MENELIK II reconsolidated the empire and defeated the Italians in 1896 at ADOWA. The Italians remained in ERITREA and in 1935–36 invaded Ethiopia, which was liberated in 1941 when Emperor HAILE SELASSIE ·was restored to the throne. Ethiopia made considerable economic and technical advances, but after unrest the army mutinied in 1974 and Haile Selassie was deposed. In 1975 a socialist one-party state replaced the military government. Unrest has continued in Eritrea where there is a strong movement for secession, and in the Ogaden, where Somalia and Ethiopia are engaged in a territorial dispute.

ETHNIC GROUP, individuals united by ties of culture and/or heredity who are conscious of forming a subgroup within society. RACIAL MINORITIES may constitute ethnic groups, but this is not always the case. Major US ethnic groups include Irish, Italian, Polish, Jewish, Chinese, Japanese and Hispanic Americans. At times they have clashed with each other or with blacks. Similar tensions due to a diversity of ethnic groups also mark British and Canadian society.

ETHNOLOGY, the science dealing with the differing races of man, where they originated, their distribution about the world, their characteristics and the relationships between them. More generally, the term is used to mean cultural ANTHROPOLOGY.

ETNA, frequently active volcano in NE Sicily, highest volcano in the Mediterranean region. Its height (about 10,900ft) varies with eruptions. The peak is snow-covered through much of the year. The fertile lower slopes are intensely cultivated.

ETON, town in Berkshire, England, on the Thames R, near Windsor, most famous for Eton College. Founded in 1440–41 by Henry VI, the college is possibly the most prestigious private school for boys in Britain. Pop 3,954.

ETRUSCANS, ancient race of Etruria, located in what is now modern Tuscany, Italy. Their civilization lasted from the 8th to the 1st century BC but had begun to decline from the beginning of the 5th century BC. It is generally accepted that the Etruscans migrated from the Aegeo-Asian region to Italy in the 8th century BC, although some may have settled there as early as the 13th century BC. The Etruscans called themselves the "Rasenna" but the Romans named them the "Tusci" or "Etrusci."

No Etruscan literary works are extant and, even though some documents and funerary inscriptions remain, so far it has only been possible to understand a few words. Etruria comprised 12 "populi" or city-states, including Arretium, Caere, Perusia, Tarquinii, Veii, Volci, Volsinii and Volterrae. The cities were associated in a league but each was politically independent. The early governments were monarchical and changed subsequently to republican states which were controlled by oligarchies. The Etruscans were extremely powerful. They enjoyed extensive maritime trade with the Greeks and Phoenicians, and had colonies in Sicily, Corsica, Sardinia, the Balearic Islands and Spain. Another source of wealth were the rich mineral deposits, especially those of copper, lead and iron. The Etruscans are famous for their gold and bronze craftsmanship and for their black *bucchero* ceramic ware. They decorated their tombs with large mural paintings. After the 5th century BC the Etruscan cities were absorbed by the expanding Roman state.

ETYMOLOGY (from Greek *etymos*, true

meaning, and *logos*, word), the history of a word or other linguistic element; and the science, born in the 19th century, concerned with tracing that history, by examining the word's development since its earliest appearance in the language; by locating its transmission into the language from elsewhere; by identifying its cognates in other languages; and by tracing it and its cognates back to a (often hypothetical) common ancestor. **Cognates** (from Latin *co*, together, and *nasci*, to be born) of English words appear in many languages: our "father" is cognate with the German "*Vater*" and French "*père*" all three deriving from the Latin "*pater*." An **etymon** is the earliest known form of a word, though the term is sometimes applied to any early form. (See also LINGUISTICS; PHILOLOGY.)

EUBOEA, second largest island in the Greek archipelago. In the Aegean Sea close to the E coast of Greece, it is dominated by three mountain ranges with fertile and well-wooded valleys and plains. Its ancient cities of Chalcis and Eretria led the Greek colonization of southern Italy, and the fine white marble of Euboea was used in the building of imperial Rome.

EUCHARIST. See COMMUNION, HOLY.

EUCLID (c300 BC), Alexandrian mathematician whose major work, the *Elements*, is still the basis of much of geometry (see EUCLIDEAN GEOMETRY): its fifth postulate (the Euclidean axiom) cannot be proved, and this lack of proof gave rise to the NON-EUCLIDEAN GEOMETRIES. Other ascribed works include *Phaenomena*, on SPHERICAL GEOMETRY, and *Optics*, treating vision and PERSPECTIVE.

EUCLIDEAN GEOMETRY, the branch of GEOMETRY dealing with the properties of three-dimensional space. It is commonly split up into plane geometry, which is concerned with figures and constructions in two or less dimensions, and solid or three-dimensional geometry, which deals with three-dimensional figures and the relative spatial positions of figures of three dimensions or less. It takes its name from EUCLID, whose *Elements*, written c300 BC, summarized all the mathematical knowledge of contemporary ancient Greece into 13 books; those on geometry were taken as the final, authoritative word on the subject for well over a millennium and still form the basis for many school geometry textbooks. (SECTION; PLANE; PYRAMID; PYTHAGORAS' THEOREM; TRIANGLE; VOLUME.)

EUDOXUS OF CNIDUS (c400–c350 BC), Greek mathematician and astronomer who proposed a system of homocentric crystal spheres to explain planetary motions; this system was adopted in ARISTOTLE'S cosmology (see ASTRONOMY). He was probably responsible for much of the content of Book V of EUCLID's *Elements*.

EUGENE OF SAVOY, Prince (1663–1736), Austrian general, one of Europe's greatest commanders. He served the emperors Leopold I, Joseph I and Charles VI, and won many victories, most notably over the Turks at Zenta (1697), Peterwardein (1716) and Belgrade (1717). He was also a patron of the arts.

EUGENICS, the study and application of scientifically directed selection in order to improve the genetic endowment of human populations. Eugenic control was first suggested by Sir Francis GALTON in the 1880s. People supporting eugenics suggest that those with "good" traits should be encouraged to have children while those with "bad" traits should be discouraged or forbidden from having families. But who is to decide which traits are "good?"

EUGÉNIE (1826–1920), Empress of the French 1853–70 as wife of NAPOLEON III. The daughter of a Spanish noble, she was a major influence on her husband and was three times regent in his absence. After his downfall she escaped to England.

EUKARYOTE; eukaryotic cell. See CELL.

EULENSPIEGEL, Till, trickster hero of a group of German tales originally published c1515. The historic Till may have been a 14th-century Brunswick peasant. His pranks demonstrated peasant cunning triumphing over establishment figures of his day. He was the subject of the Richard STRAUSS tone poem that bears his name.

EULER, Leonhard (1707–1783), Swiss-born mathematician and physicist, the father of modern ANALYTIC GEOMETRY and important in almost every area of mathematics. He introduced the use of analysis (especially CALCULUS, a field which he also profoundly affected) into the study of MECHANICS; and made major contributions to modern ALGEBRA. **Euler's Relation** links the logarithmic and trigonometric functions: $e^{ix} = \cos x + i \sin x$ (see COMPLEX NUMBERS; TRIGONOMETRY). He worked also on a theory to explain the motions of the MOON and pioneered the science of HYDRODYNAMICS.

EUMENIDES. See FURIES.

EUPHRATES RIVER, 2,235mi long, is the major river in SW Asia. It rises in NE Turkey and crosses the plains of Iraq where it finally joins the TIGRIS R to form the SHATT-AL-ARAB. It fostered the great civilizations of MESOPOTAMIA.

EURASIA, landmass composed of Asia and Europe, politically and culturally separate continents. In fact there is hardly any physical division, although the Ural and Caucasus Mts may be taken as a border.

EURATOM (European Atomic Energy Community), organization formed by France, Belgium, Luxembourg, The Netherlands, Italy and West Germany in 1958 to develop the peaceful uses of nuclear energy and establish a nuclear industry on a European scale, supervising and coordinating trade, research and development. Military applications are outside its scope.

EURIPIDES (c480 BC–406 BC), one of the greatest Greek playwrights. He appears to have been unpopular in Athens in his lifetime, possibly because of his agnostic and cynical views. He is thought to have written 92 plays, of which 19 have survived. The best-known are *Medea, The Trojan Women, Electra, Orestes* and *The Bacchae.*

EURODOLLARS, foreign deposits of dollars with US banks, payable only in dollars but redeposited in foreign banks, chiefly in Europe. The foreign banks may lend these dollar deposits at interest to commercial borrowers or other banks, thus providing an international money market in Eurodollars that has become increasingly important in world trade.

EUROPE, the world's second smallest continent after Australia, is bounded on the N by the Arctic Ocean, on the W by the Atlantic and on the S by the Caucasus Mts and Black and Mediterranean seas. Because its E boundary, conventionally the Ural Mts and Ural R, is not generally agreed, and because Europe has thousands of offshore islands (including the British Isles and Iceland), estimates of its area range from 3,800,000sq mi to over 4,000,000sq mi. With Asia it forms a vast, single landmass (Eurasia).

The Land is dominated by great mountain systems including the Kjølen Mts and other peaks in Scandinavia, and the Hercynian system—the mosaic of plateaus, uplands and mountains extending E from Brittany and the Iberian peninsula and embracing the Central Massif of France, the Bohemian plateau and the Urals. Alpine Europe, including the Pyrenees, Alps, Carpathians and Caucasus, has many high peaks such as Mont Blanc (15,777ft) in the Alps and Elbrus (18,481ft) in the Caucasus, Europe's highest peak. Peninsular Italy has the Apennines, and the Dinaric fold mountains swing through Yugoslavia and into Greece. Volcanoes occur in Iceland and in Mediterranean Europe (especially Italy), and earthquakes and tremors are common

in the Balkans. The most prominent lowland is the North European Plain, which broadens eastward from Belgium and The Netherlands reaching across N Poland and into Russia. Other lowlands are associated with major rivers like the Rhine and Danube. Europe's longest river is the Volga. Other important rivers include the Rhône, Elbe, Oder, Vistula and Don.

Climate and Vegetation. Most of Europe has a relatively mild climate, though winters in the N and E are long and severe. Rainfall is mostly plentiful. Mediterranean lands are known for their hot, dry summers and mild, wet winters. Vegetation ranges from the tundra plants and coniferous forests of the N to the alpine plants and varied forests of the high mountains, and the olives, cypress and scrub of the Mediterranean lands. The W has much natural grassland.

The People. Some 659,000,000 people, about 17% of the world's population, live in Europe. It is the most densely-populated continent. Its peoples are of many different ethnic and linguistic groups. It has 34 countries and more than 60 languages. Some areas, due to their harsh environments, are thinly populated. Rural densities of population are highest in the lowlands, while the highest concentrations are centered on coal fields and industrial centers. In most areas people are tending to move from the countryside and into the towns. The pattern has also been changed by the influx of millions of migrant workers from the Mediterranean lands into highly-industrialized W countries like France and West Germany. Though it has more than 4,000,000 Jews and about 13,000,000 Muslims, Europe is mainly a Christian continent, Roman Catholics being by far the most numerous.

EUROPE, Council of, organization of Western European nations, founded in 1949 to discuss items of mutual interest and promote European unity, protection of human rights, and social and economic progress. By 1978, the original membership of 10 had grown to 21.

EUROPEAN COAL AND STEEL COMMUNITY (ECSC), international agency established in 1952 to integrate the coal and steel industries of France, West Germany, Italy, The Netherlands, Belgium and Luxembourg. In 1967 its executive body was merged with those of the European COMMON MARKET and EURATOM.

EUROPEAN CURRENCY UNIT (ECU). A monetary system adopted by the countries of Western Europe with the exception of Great Britain in 1979, as part of the effort to promote economic integration. It established ECUs as a measure for translating other currencies and facilitating central banking exchanges between countries. Each country placed 20% of its gold or dollars into a fund and in turn received a supply of ECUs for use in making transactions.

EUROPEAN FREE TRADE ASSOCIATION (EFTA), customs union and trading group formed in 1960 by Austria, Britain, Denmark, Norway, Portugal, Sweden and Switzerland to promote free trade between members. Finland became an associate member in 1961, and Iceland joined in 1970. Denmark and Britain seceded by joining the COMMON MARKET in 1973, but the Market as a unit maintains agreement with individual EFTA countries.

EUROPOORT, large-scale port complex begun opposite the Hoek van Holland, on the SW coast of the Netherlands, in 1958. Part of the port of Rotterdam, Europoort primarily handles petroleum shipping. Several large oil refineries are in operation.

EURYDICE. See ORPHEUS.

EURYTHMICS, art of expressing musical rhythms through body movement. It was developed by the Swiss professor of music Emile Jaques-Dalcroze in an attempt to increase his students' awareness of rhythm, and has been a major influence on modern dance and, most recently, physical fitness programs.

EUSEBIUS OF CAESAREA, bishop, 4th-century scholar, remembered for his *Ecclesiastical History*, a primary source for the early history of the Church. Originally an Arian sympathizer, he was exonerated of heresy by the Council of NICAEA (325).

EUTHANASIA, the practice of hastening or causing the DEATH of a person suffering from incurable DISEASE. While frequently advocated by various groups, its practical and legal implications are so controversial that it remains illegal in most countries. (See QUINLAN CASE).

EUTROPHICATION, the increasing concentration of plant nutrients and FERTILIZERS in lakes and estuaries, partly by natural drainage and partly by POLLUTION. It leads to excessive growth of algae and aquatic plants, with oxygen depletion of the deep water, causing various undesirable effects.

EVANGELICAL AND REFORMED CHURCH, Protestant church formed by the union of the Reformed Church of America and the Evangelical Synod of North America (1934); since 1957 part of the UNITED CHURCH OF CHRIST.

EVANGELICALISM, meaning "pertaining to the Gospel," the name of a theological movement, found in most Protestant denominations, that emphasizes the primary authority of the Bible. It stresses Christ's atoning death, human sinfulness, JUSTIFICATION BY FAITH, the necessity of personal conversion and expository preaching, and opposes Roman and Anglo-Catholicism.

EVANGELICAL UNITED BRETHREN (EUB), Protestant church, essentially Methodist, formed by the merger (1946) of the Evangelical Church and the Church of the United Brethren in Christ. In 1968 they became part of the UNITED METHODIST CHURCH.

EVANS, Sir Arthur John (1851–1941), English archaeologist famous for his discovery of the MINOAN CIVILIZATION from excavations at KNOSSOS in Crete. He was curator of the Ashmolean Museum, Oxford 1884–1908 and professor of prehistoric archaeology at Oxford from 1909.

EVANS, Bergen (Baldwin) (1904–1978), US educator and author best known as the master of ceremonies on such television shows as *Down You Go* (1951–56) and *The Last Word* (1957–59). He was also the author of *A Dictionary of Contemporary American Usage* (1957) and *Dictionary of Quotations* (1968).

EVANS, Bill (1929–1981), avant-garde jazz pianist and composer with Miles Davis (esp. "So What," 1959), and with his own group. His 1963 "Conversations with Myself" was one of the first uses of recorded overdubbing. An influential piano stylist, he has won five Grammy awards.

EVANS, Dame Edith (1888–1976), British actress famous for her work in classical and contemporary theater and in films, of which the best-known are *The Importance of Being Earnest* (1953) and *The Whisperers* (1967). Her first stage appearance was in 1912.

EVANS, Gil (1912–), Canadian jazz arranger whose work with Miles Davis and a large jazz orchestra (1949–50, 1957–60) used instruments rarely heard in jazz before and produced music on a new level of lyricism. Evans formed his own orchestra in 1969.

EVANS, Mary Ann. See ELIOT, GEORGE.

EVANS, Maurice (1901–), Welsh-American actor famous for his performances of Shakespeare and Shaw, and in many films and television plays.

EVANS, Walker (1903–1975), US photographer who documented the Depression in the southern US. He published his work in *Let Us Now Praise Famous Men* (1941) and in *Fortune Magazine*, of which he was an editor.

EVAPORATION, the escape of molecules from the surface of a liquid into the vapor state. Only those molecules with sufficient kinetic ENERGY are able to overcome the cohesive forces holding the liquid together and escape from the surface. This leaves the remaining molecules with a lower average kinetic energy, and hence a lower TEMPERATURE. In an enclosed space, the pressure of the vapor above the surface eventually reaches a maximum, the saturated vapor pressure (SVP). This varies according to the substance concerned and, together with the rate of evaporation, increases with temperature, equalling atmospheric pressure at the liquid's BOILING POINT.

EVE, the first woman, according to the Bible, wife of ADAM, from whose rib God created her. She is the subject of Jewish, Christian and Muslim legend.

EVELYN, John (1620–1706), English writer and humanist whose *Diary*, published in 1818, is one of the most important sources for English life in the 17th century.

EVEREST, Mount, highest mountain in the world (29,028ft), situated in the Himalayas on the Nepalese-Tibetan border. It is named for Sir George Everest, British surveyor general of India 1830–43. After several unsuccessful attempts, it was first climbed on May 29, 1953 by Edmund HILLARY and Tenzing Norkay.

EVERETT, Edward (1794–1865), US statesman and orator. A Unitarian clergyman, he received from the University of Göttingen the first Ph.D. given to an American (1817). He became professor of Greek at Harvard in 1815, was a congressman 1825–35, governor of Mass. 1836–39, minister to England 1841–45, president of Harvard 1846–49, secretary of state 1852–53 and in 1860 the Constitutional Union Party's vice-presidential candidate.

EVERGLADES, swampy region in S Fla. Covering an area of about 5,000sq mi, the Everglades extend from Lake Okeechobee in the N to the S end of the Florida peninsula. The flooded sawgrass swamps support abundant wild animals and plants, many peculiar to the area. Indians inhabited the Everglades before the 1500s. In the 1830s the US tried to drive the SEMINOLE Indians out. Part of the Everglades was drained in the late 19th century, producing rich agricultural land, but drainage now conflicts with conservation plans. In 1947 the Everglades National Park was established in the S.

EVERGOOD, Philip (Philip Blashki; 1901–73), US artist. An advocate of social realism, he was best known for murals painted while he was participating in the Federal Works Project during the 1930s. His later work emphasized biblical and mythological symbolism.

EVERS, name of two US black civil rights leaders, **(James) Charles Evers** (1922–), was the first black mayor of Fayette, Miss. in 1969, and in 1971 ran for governor of Miss. **Medgar Wiley Evers** (1925–1963), his brother, was the state's first black field secretary of the National Association for the Advancement of Colored People, and organized the registration of black voters. He was assassinated by a sniper.

EVERT LLOYD, Chris (1954–), US tennis player. From 1975–78 she set a record by winning four consecutive US Opens, then won again in 1980. She has also captured two Wimbledon titles, and many other major championships.

EVERYMAN, late 15th-century morality play about a man (Everyman) who, when summoned by Death, finds that of all his friends only Good Deeds aided by Knowledge accompanies him. The allegory has been often used by dramatists.

EVIDENCE, in law, that which is advanced by parties to a legal dispute as proving, or contributing to the proof, of their case. To be admissible in court evidence must conform to various rules in order to ensure a clear and fair presentation of it to the trier of fact, a jury or a judge. Such evidence may consist of the oral testimony of witnesses summoned by either side, of documentary evidence of physical objects, as for example an alleged murder weapon. The evidence may be direct, supporting the facts of the case, or it may be circumstantial, evidence from which those facts may reasonably be deduced. An eyewitness account of an auto accident is direct evidence; unaccountable damage to the defendant's auto may be circumstantial evidence. Evidence may be excluded for three main reasons—if it is not sufficiently relevant, if it arises out of privileged circumstances, and if it is hearsay—"second-hand" evidence arising out of a statement made outside court by a person not called as a witness, who cannot therefore be cross-examined. In a 1970 case the US Supreme Court held that a state's rules on hearsay evidence do not necessarily have to be as strict as those in federal courts. Business and public records likely to be accurate are exempted from the hearsay rule, as in some circumstances is a statement made by a dying person. Privileges protect certain interests, such as the right not to incriminate oneself, and certain relationships considered essential to society, such as that between a husband and wife, who are therefore not required to give evidence against each other.

EVOLUTION, the process by which living organisms have changed since the origin of life. The formulation of the theory of evolution by NATURAL SELECTION is credited to Charles DARWIN, whose observations while sailing around the world on HMS BEAGLE, when taken together with elements from MALTHUS' population theory and viewed in the context of LYELL's doctrine of UNIFORMITARIANISM, led him to the concept of natural selection, but the theory also later occurred independently to A. R. WALLACE. Other theories of evolution by the inheritance of ACQUIRED CHARACTERISTICS had earlier been proposed by E. DARWIN and LAMARCK. Darwin defended the mechanism of natural selection on the basis of three observations: that animals and plants produced far more offspring than were required to maintain the size of their population; that the size of any natural population remained more or less stable over long periods, and that the members of any one generation exhibited variation. From the first two he argued that in any generation there was a high mortality rate, and from the third that, under certain circumstances, some of the variants had a greater chance of survival than did others. The surviving variants were, by definition, those most suited to the prevailing environmental conditions. Any change in the environment led to adjustment in the population such that certain new variants were favored and gradually became predominant.

The missing link in Darwin's theory was the mechanism by which heritable variation occurs. Unknown to him, a contemporary, G. MENDEL, had demonstrated the principle of GENETICS and had deduced that the heritable characters were controlled by discrete particles. We now know these particles to be GENES which are carried on the CHROMOSOMES. Mendel's variants were caused by RECOMBINATION and MUTATION of the genes. Natural selection acts to eradicate unfit variants either by mortality of the individual or by ensuring that such individuals do not breed. How then can natural selection lead to the evolution of a new character? The key is that a character that is advantageous to an individual in the normal environment may become disadvantageous if the environment changes. This means that individuals that happen through variation to be well adapted to the new set of circumstances will tend to survive and thus

become the norm.

An example of natural selection at work is provided by studies carried out recently on North American sparrows. Large numbers of sparrows were trapped and their various characteristics recorded. In this way the "normal" sparrow was identified. A further collection was made of dead sparrows which had succumbed to the adverse conditions of a particularly severe winter. It was found that the individuals in the second sample were all different in some important respect from the "normal" sparrow. Natural selection could thus be seen to be maintaining a population that was ideally suited to the North American environment.

Today, the evidence for evolution is overwhelming and comes from many branches of biology. For instance, the comparative anatomy of the arm of a man, the foreleg of a horse, the wing of a bat and the flipper of a seal reveals that these superficially different organs have a very similar internal structure, this being taken to indicate a common ancestor. Then, the study of the embryos of mammals and birds reveals that at some stages they are virtually indistinguishable and thus have common ancestors. Again, vestigial organs such as the appendix of man and the wing of the ostrich have no use to these mammals, but in related species such as herbivores and flying birds they clearly are of vital importance. Evidently these individuals have progressively evolved in different ways from a common ancestor. The hierarchical classification of plants and animals into species, genus, family etc. (see TAXONOMY) is a direct reflection of the natural pattern that would be expected if evolution from common ancestors occurred. Again, the geographical distribution of animals and plants presents many facts of evolutionary significance. For example, the tapir is today centered in two widely separated areas, the E Indies and South America. However, it probably evolved in a single center, migrated across the world and then became extinct in many areas as habitats changed. Indeed FOSSILS of tapirs have been found in Asia, Europe and North America. Fossils in general provide convincing evidence of evolution. Thus, the theory of the evolution of birds indicates descent from now extinct reptiles. The fossil ARCHAEOPTERYX, a flying reptile with some bird-like features, was belived to represent the missing link in this development.

LIFE probably first evolved from the primeval soup some 3000-4000 million years ago when the first organic chemicals were synthesized due to the effects of lightning. Primitive ALGAE capable of synthesizing their own food material have been found in geological formations some 2,000 million years old. Simple forms of animals and fungi then evolved. From that time there has been a slow evolution of multicellular organisms.

EVTUSHENKO, Evgeny See YEVTU-SHENKO, Yevgeny.

EWELL, Richard Stoddert (1817–1872), US Confederate general who served with distinction throughout the Civil War. he fought in "Stonewall" JACKSON's Shenandoah Valley Campaign. After losing a leg he led the second corps in the battle of GETTYSBURG and the battle of the WILDERNESS.

EXCLUSIONARY RULE, law derived from the Supreme Court ruling in Mapp vs. Ohio (1961), which held that in a criminal case, evidence seized illegally cannot be used in a trial of the case, this law had already been established by federal courts and some state courts. The High Court pointed out that blanket exclusion appears to be the only way to prevent police abuses, but the rule has never been popular with law-enforcement officers. In 1981 the Court delivered rulings which peripherally weakened the rule.

EXCLUSION PRINCIPLE, a law, proposed by W. PAULI, accounting for the different chemical properties of the ELEMENTS and numerous other phenomena. Applying to those particles called fermions, particularly ELECTRONS. it is a consequence of the fact that particles of the same kind are indistinguishable, and states that only one such particle can occupy a given quantum state (see QUANTUM MECHANICS) at a time. In atoms, the energy levels fill up as the number of electrons increases; it is the electrons in the outer unfilled "shells" that are responsible for the chemical properties of an atom.

EXCRETION, the removal of the waste products of METABOLISM either by storing them in insoluble forms or by removing them from the body. Excretory organs are also responsible for maintaining the correct balance of body fluids. In VERTEBRATES the excretory organs are the KIDNEYS: blood flows through these and water and waste products are removed as URINE. Other forms of excretory organs include the Malpighian tubes of insects, arachnids and myriapods, the contractile vacuoles of Protozoa and the nephridia of annelids. In plants, excretion usually takes the form of producing insoluble salts of waste products within the cells.

EXECUTIVE, that part of government which carries out the business of governing. In the US it shares power with the LEGISLATURE and the JUDICIARY. Under the Constitution it is charged with taking care "that the laws be faithfully executed." It is headed by the president, who appoints all executive officers, usually subject to Senate approval. His cabinet, federal departments such as the defense department, foreign ambassadors and hundreds of boards and commissions come under the jurisdiction of the executive. The term is also used of that part of a private organization or company that manages and controls its business. (See also SEPARATION OF POWERS.)

EXERCISE, or physical exertion, the active use of skeletal muscle in recreation or under environmental stress. In exercise, MUSCLES contract actively, consuming OXYGEN at a high rate, and so require increased BLOOD CIRCULATION; this is effected by increasing the HEART output by raising the PULSE and increasing the blood expelled with each beat. Meanwhile, the CAPILLARIES in active muscles dilate. The raised demand for oxygen and, more especially, the increased production of carbon dioxide in the muscles increase the rate of RESPIRATION. Some energy requirements can be supplied rapidly without oxygen but, if so, the "oxygen debt" must be made good afterward. GASTROINTESTINAL TRACT activity is reduced during exercise. Changes in the autonomic and central NERVOUS SYSTEMS. HORMONES and local regulators are responsible for adaptive changes in exercise. In athletes, exercise increases muscle efficiency and cardiac compensation.

EXILE, The. See BABYLONIAN CAPTIVITY.

EXISTENTIALISM, twentieth-century branch of philosophy which stresses that since "existence precedes essence," man is what he makes himself and is also responsible for what he makes of himself. It is a rejection of traditional metaphysical thought, which views truth as timeless and unchanging and sees man as subject to external verities termed "essences." The important precursor of Existentialism was Søren KIERKEGAARD, who held that man's sense of dread and despair arose from his responsibility for his own decisions and for his relationship with God. Theologians influenced by Kierkegaard are Karl BARTH. Martin BUBER. Karl JASPERS, Gabriel MARCEL, Reinhold NIEBUHR and Paul TILLICH. Edmund HUSSERL's philosophy of PHENOMENOLOGY influenced his two students Martin HEIDEGGER and Jean-Paul SARTRE to consider the nature of human experience and of responsibility and freedom. Sartre, who eventually became a Marxist, influenced Albert CAMUS and Simone de BEAUVOIR.

EXOBIOLOGY, or xenobiology, the study of life beyond the earth's atmosphere. Drawing on many other sciences (e.g., biochemistry, physics), it is for obvious reasons a discipline dealing primarily in hypotheses (though FOSSIL organic matter has been found in certain meteorites (see METEOR). An important branch deals with the effects on man of nonterrestrial environments.

EXODUS, second book of the Old Testament, and of the TORAH. The book describes the escape of the Israelites from slavery in Egypt, the covenant made at Mt Sinai between Moses and Yahweh and includes the Ten Commandments.

EXOGAMY. See ENDOGAMY AND EXOGAMY.

EXORCISM, the expulsion of DEMONS from places or persons, common in pagan religions, and found also in Judaism and Christianity. In the New Testament, Jesus cast out demons from the possessed by a word, and the apostles did likewise in his name. In the early Church anyone so gifted could exorcise; in the 3rd century exorcism was restricted to ordained clergy, in particular a minor order called **exorcists,** finally suppressed in 1972. Now somewhat controversial, exorcism is practiced as a last resort and with medical advice. Regulated by canon law and requiring episcopal permission, it is a ceremonial rite with set prayers. An exorcism to ward off evil (not presupposing possession) forms part of the Roman Catholic service of baptism.

EXOSKELETON, any skeletal material that lies on the surface of the animal's body. In this position it not only performs the mechanical functions common to any other SKELETON but, in addition, affords protection. Exoskeletons are particularly well developed in arthropods such as crabs, lobsters and insects.

EX PARTE MILLIGAN. See MILLIGAN, EX PARTE.

EXPLOSIVES, substances capable of very rapid COMBUSTION (or other exothermic reaction—see THERMOCHEMISTRY) to produce hot gases whose rapid expansion is accompanied by a high-velocity shock wave, shattering nearby objects. The detonation travels 1000 times faster than a flame. The earliest known explosive was GUNPOWDER, invented in China in the 10th century AD, and in the West by Roger BACON (1242). Explosives are classified as **primary explosives,** which explode at once on ignition, and are used as DETONATORS; and **high explosives,** which if ignited at first merely burn, but explode if detonated by a primary explosion. The division is not rigid. Military high explosives are usually mixtures of organic nitrates, TNT, RDX, PICRIC ACID and PETN, which are self-oxidizing. Commercial blasting explosives are less-powerful mixtures of combustible and explosive substances; they include DYNAMITE (containing NITROGLYCERIN, ammonium nitrate and sometimes NITROCELLULOSE), ammonals (ammonium nitrate + aluminum and Sprengel explosives (an oxidizing agent mixed with a liquid fuel such as nitrobenzene just before use). Obsolete explosives include the dangerous chlorates and perchlorates, and the uneconomical liquid oxygen explosives (LOX). Explosives which do not ignite firedamp (see DAMP) are termed "permissible," and may be used in coal mines. Propellants for guns and rockets are like explosives, but burn fast rather than detonating.

EXPONENT, a number such as x in the expression a^x, a being a number to be used as a FACTOR x times: e.g., $a \cdot a \cdot a$. In the expression, a is termed the base. (See also POWER.)

EXPORT-IMPORT BANK OF THE UNITED STATES (Eximbank), US government agency set up in 1934 to assist foreign exports. It makes loans to foreign borrowers who wish to buy US goods and services. After developing world trade and particularly that of Latin America and the Allied countries after WWII, Eximbank now supports US exports especially to developing countries.

EXPOSITIONS. See FAIRS AND EXPOSITIONS.

EX POST FACTO LAW, law acting retrospectively, most commonly to make illegal actions which were legal when committed. The US Constitution prohibits *ex post facto* criminal laws; in English law they are permitted but are rare. The NUREMBURG TRIALS were based on *ex post facto* legislation.

EXPRESSIONISM, early 20th-century movement in art and literature which held that art should be the expression of subjective feelings and emotions. Expressionist painters preferred intense coloring and primitive simplified forms, in that these seemed to convey emotions directly. VAN GOGH, ENSOR and MUNCH influenced the movement which developed in both France and Germany after 1905. In France the style was represented by the Fauvists (see FAUVISM), MATISSE and ROUAULT, and in Germany by Die Brücke and the BLAUE REITER artists like KANDINSKY, KIRCHNER,

KOKOSCHKA, NOLDE, GROSZ, and MARC. Expressionist writers include STRINDBERG, WEDEKIND and KAFKA.

EXTERNAL-COMBUSTION ENGINE, an engine that burns its fuel in a separate container outside the engine itself, as in the STEAM ENGINE, steam or gas TURBINE or STIRLING ENGINE. Unlike an INTERNAL-COMBUSTION ENGINE (gasoline or DIESEL ENGINE), an external-combustion engine requires only a source of heat and thus is not dependent on refined petroleum fuels designed to burn inside its cylinders.

EXTORTION, seeking to obtain money from a person by non-physical intimidation, often by the threat of a criminal charge or the exposure of some secret. Physical intimidation is usually considered ROBBERY. Some specific kinds of extortion are usually known as blackmail.

EXTRASENSORY PERCEPTION. See ESP.

EXTRATERRITORIALITY, privilege granted by a country to resident foreign nationals, allowing them to remain under the jurisdiction of the laws of their own country only. Generally extended only to diplomatic agents.

EXTRAVERSION. See INTROVERSION AND EXTRAVERSION.

EXTREMELY LOW FREQUENCY (ELF), a system aimed at improved linkage of submarines to communication networks. Water being notoriously opaque to electromagnetic signals, submarines have been forced to rise to the surface to receive or send signals on conventional radio frequencies. ELF radiowaves, however, have good penetrating power. For over a decade the US Navy has been trying to develop an ELF radio wave system using a giant broadcast antenna. The first plan, involving the sinking of 5,000 miles of antenna wire through Wisconsin and Michigan was stalled by environmentalists and others fearing possible low radiation effects. In late 1981, President Reagan gave the go ahead for a Michigan and Wisconsin-based system using a total 84 miles of cable. By 1985, 20 US submarines are scheduled to be fitted with receivers and the ELF system is slated to become operational.

EXTREME UNCTION, or Anointing of the Sick, a SACRAMENT of the Roman Catholic and Eastern Orthodox churches; a rite including anointing with oil, laying on of hands and prayer for healing. From the Middle Ages until recently in the Roman Catholic Church it was administered chiefly to the dying as preparation for death, but its healing use is now emphasized. It is practiced in some other churches.

EYE, the specialized sense organ concerned with VISION. In all species it consists of a lens system linked to a LIGHT receptor system connected to the central NERVOUS SYSTEM. In man and mammals, the eye is roughly spherical in shape, has a tough fibrous capsule with the transparent CORNEA in front, and is moved by specialized eye muscles. The exposed surface is kept moist with tears from lacrymal glands. Most of the eye contains VITREOUS HUMOR—a substance with the consistency of jelly—which fills the space between the lens and the retina, while in front of the lens there is watery or AQUEOUS HUMOR. The colored iris or aperture surrounds a hole known as the pupil. The focal length of the lens can be varied by specialized ciliary muscles. The RETINA is a layer containing the nerve cells (rods and cones) which receive light, together with the next two sets of cells in the relay pathway for vision. The optic nerve leads back from the retina to the BRAIN. Rods and cones receive light reflected from a pigment layer and contain pigments (e.g., RHODOPSIN) which are bleached by light and thus set off the nerve-cell reaction.

EYE BANK, a department in a hospital or some other organization where eyes or corneas are stored (for up to three weeks) for use in corneal grafts by ophthalmic surgeons. Sometimes removed in a necessary operation on someone living, the eyes usually come from the dead (within 10 hours of decease) by permission either of a will or of surviving relatives.

EYRE, Lake, largest salt lake in Australia, in NW South Australia. About 3,600sq mi in area, its occasionally flooded basin lies about 40ft below sea level. Its specialized ecology is of great scientific interest.

EZEKIEL, early 6th-century BC Hebrew priest and prophet. He lived in Jerusalem but in 597 BC was taken by Babylon. The Old Testament book which bears his name foretells the destruction of Jerusalem, pronounces judgment on foreign nations and predicts the restoration of Israel.

EZRA, 5th-century BC Babylonian Jewish priest and religious leader, whose teachings are recorded in the Old Testament Book of Ezra. He advocated an exclusive and legalistic doctrine, prohibiting marriages between Jews and gentiles.

If you would like more copies of the Concord Desk
Encyclopedia, the publisher's edition is available
directly to you.

Extra copies ideal for
- gifts
- office
- students

Fill in, clip and mail handy coupon.

☐ Please send me _____ additional copies of the Concord
Desk Encyclopedia at $8.85 plus $2.00 for postage and
handling (total $10.85).

Name _____

Address _____

City _____ State _____ Zip _____

Mail Payment to:

Concord Reference Books
135 W. 50th St.
New York, New York 10020

Offer expires 12/31/82.